THE DICTIONARY
OF HOMOPHOBIA

ARSENAL PULP PRESS
Vancouver · *arsenalpulp.com*

THE DICTIONARY OF
HOMOPHOBIA

A GLOBAL HISTORY OF GAY & LESBIAN EXPERIENCE

Edited by LOUIS-GEORGES TIN

Translated by Marek Redburn

with Alice Michaud and Kyle Mathers

THE DICTIONARY OF HOMOPHOBIA
Translation copyright © 2008 by the translators
Original edition © 2003 by Presses universitaires de France

ARSENAL PULP PRESS
Suite 200, 341 Water Street
Vancouver, BC
Canada V6B 1B8
arsenalpulp.com

This book was published with the support of the French Ministry of Culture—National Book Center. Ouvrage publié avec le concours du Ministère français chargé de la culture—Centre national du livre.

The publisher gratefully acknowledges the support of the Government of Canada through the Book Publishing Industry Development Program and the Government of British Columbia through the Book Publishing Tax Credit Program for its publishing activities.

Efforts have been made to locate copyright holders of source material wherever possible. The publisher welcomes hearing from any copyright holders of material used in this book who have not been contacted.

Book design by Shyla Seller
Editing by Brian Lam, Robert Ballantyne, and Bethanne Grabham. Editorial assistance by Suzanne Hawkins, Shirarose Wilensky, Jon Fleming, and Richard Swain

Printed and bound in Canada

Library and Archives Canada Cataloguing in Publication:

    The dictionary of homophobia : a global history of gay & lesbian experience / edited by Louis-Georges Tin, editor ; translated by Marek Redburn.

Translation of: Dictionnaire de l'homophobie.
Includes bibliographical references and index.
ISBN 978-1-55152-229-6

    1. Homophobia—Dictionaries. 2. Homosexuality—Dictionaries.
I. Tin, Louis-Georges II. Redburn, Marek, 1968-

HQ76.4.D5313 2007   306.76'603   C2007-906136-2

CONTENTS

PUBLISHER'S NOTE

When *Dictionnaire de l'homophobie* was first published by Presses universitaires de France in 2003, it was hailed as a groundbreaking achievement: the work of seventy-six esteemed researchers in fifteen countries, the goal of which was to document the social, political, medical, legal, and criminal treatment of homosexuals throughout history to present-day. Arsenal Pulp Press is very pleased to bring the English translation of this important book, *The Dictionary of Homophobia*, to a global English-speaking audience.

In the time since the *Dictionnaire* was originally published, history has moved along. So while we wished to maintain the integrity of the original text, we have updated certain entries where new information became available, and where circumstances had changed, particularly with regard to legal and criminal codes in various countries. The status of the LGBT community within mainstream society is changing on a daily basis, for the most part (but not always) in positive ways; in short, the *Dictionary* will never be absolutely up-to-date.

It should also be noted that because the book was originally written for a French audience, some essays focus on events, personalities, and circumstances in France. We have kept this in mind while editing this translation and, where useful, added material which speaks to homophobic experience elsewhere in the world; the essays in which this new material appears are noted as such. At the same time, the essays on France offer illuminating evidence of one particular country's experience with the phenomenon of homophobia which informs our own response to it no matter where we live.

Also, a few words of explanation: quotations that appear in this book are mainly direct translations of the text that appears in the original *Dictionnaire*; if an English edition of the book or other source material being quoted from is available, the quotations may appear slightly different. Further, the bibliographies list the sources as they appear in the original *Dictionnaire*; as much as possible, we included an English translation for readers' reference. Finally, we embellished the "Further Reading" lists where it was felt there were not enough English-language translations in the bibliography.

A last word: we would like to note the remarkable efforts of Louis-Georges Tin, editor of the original *Dictionnaire*, in founding the annual International Day Against Homophobia, and hope that it will take hold as a beacon of courage and global change for all members of the LGBT community, as well as those who support it, in all parts of the world.

—*Robert Ballantyne, Associate Publisher;*
Brian Lam, Publisher
Arsenal Pulp Press

PREFACE TO THE ORIGINAL EDITION

Everyday, France's Republican tradition is assaulted by racist, sexist, and homophobic discrimination; each of these are an insult to democracy. At the dawn of the twenty-first century, how can we tolerate someone being "assaulted"—whether verbally or physically—simply due to their real or perceived identity?

In terms of the specific issue of homophobia, this complex book has the immense merit of clarifying the debate and opening opportunities for advancement, by simply revealing the stakes at issue. Linguistic representations, be they the usual insults or the usual jokes, can be traumatic, especially given the lack of response or solidarity demonstrated by those in authority.

Certainly, homosexuality is more socially acceptable and less of a taboo than it once was. But how can we deny the fact that a demonstration by tens of thousands of people can still be used as a platform for abject slogans that convey utter hatred ("Burn the fags")?

Each act of discrimination is an act of violence: real violence, when we are denied a place to live or a job because of our identity; and symbolic violence, when homophobia is integrated into behavior and becomes a reflex, a gratuitous and cruel game, a part of everyday language that is equally present in certain media. This violence also takes the form of personal tragedies—educational, professional, or family rejection; emotional wounds and feelings of despair—that still continue to destroy lives.

That is why every tangible act of progress is a reason for hope, as the establishment of the French law Pacte civil de solidarité (PaCS; Civil solidarity pact) in 1999 clearly illustrates. It is important to thank the French government under Lionel Jospin for having put an end to old injustices, for having advanced the equality of individual rights, and for having contributed to an evolution of thinking on this issue. For the first time, thanks to these reforms, France has recognized the existence and the legitimacy of both heterosexual and homosexual couples outside of marriage.

Nonetheless, the fight is far from over. It must be noted, for example, that French law still sanctions homophobia, however tacitly. The challenge is not only legal and political, but also cultural, pedagogical, and even philosophical.

How do we change our perception of the Other and make real the values of respect, generosity, and brotherhood? How do we deconstruct the social, psychological, and political mechanisms of rejection and intolerance? This book also has the merit of answering these very key questions. In order to go forward, it is first necessary to understand.

Undoubtedly, it is up to governments to act with determination, and in consultation with communities, to help to affect all future change.

We need to hammer home the idea that diversity is an inexhaustible source of collective wealth; and that our differences, be they cultural, generational, or identity-based, are an asset to our society. We need to assert that our everyday lives must be founded on respect for each and every person's dignity.

With this approach, we can look to the remarkable work done, for example, by the government of South Africa in the elaboration of its new constitution, and also to the European Union Charter of Fundamental Rights, or even the addendum to the European Convention for the Protection of Human Rights and Fundamental Freedoms. All of these texts strive explicitly to prevent any stigmatization based on choices related to personal and intimate life.

—*Bertrand Delanoë*
Mayor of Paris
2003

EDITOR'S PREFACE TO THE ENGLISH-LANGUAGE EDITION

When *The Dictionary of Homophobia* first appeared in France in May of 2003, it was unanimously well-received; it was praised as a work without precedence, scientifically rigorous and politically sound. It was featured on the front page of *Le Monde*'s book review section, and, even though it was written in French, received positive reviews in Japan, Italy, Brazil, the United States, and beyond. However, as the book's editor, my own career did not enjoy a similar fate. In the past, I had enjoyed great success in the academic milieu, but following the publication of the *Dictionary*, I discovered to my dismay that doors that had previously been open were now closed to me. The contract I had with the University of Paris, which was to be renewed, was abruptly terminated. The department chair and vice-chair confirmed that the scientific council's decision was linked to the publication of the *Dictionary*. They sincerely regretted the decision, but admitted (without formal proof or written statements) that there was nothing that could be done. In short, the wide acclaim for the book would seem to suggest that homophobia is now generally condemned by French society, perhaps a thing of the past. However, my personal experience shows that the reality is slightly more complex.

This particular circumstance sheds light on the paradox that has characterized homophobia in the world since 2003, when the *Dictionary* was first published. The social, political, and cultural advances for LGBT people have been numerous, but there have been many setbacks as well. In the United States, for example, there have been several positive instances which gave many a sense of optimism. On June 26, 2003, in an historical decision, the federal supreme court struck down state sodomy laws that were still in existence: in *Lawrence v. Texas*, the court found in favor of two men who had been arrested after Houston police entered a man's apartment and witnessed him and another adult man engaging in a private, consensual sexual act; the decision rendered the sodomy laws that still existed in twelve other US states null and void. Another encouraging sign occurred on May 17, 2004, when marriage between same-sex partners became legal in the state of Massachusetts (only the sixth jurisdiction in the world to do so, after the Netherlands, Belgium, and the Canadian provinces of Ontario, Quebec, and British Columbia). As a result of these breakthroughs,

it was rightly believed that the status of LGBT people in North America was moving forward. In fact, a little over a year after the decision by the Supreme Court of Massachusetts, Canada's House of Commons approved same-sex marriage for the entire country.

However, in November 2004, when Americans were asked to choose their new president, thirteen states also held referendums in which voters defined marriage as being limited to a union between a man and a woman, thus preventing the possibility of same-sex marriage. After the great strides made in the area of gay and lesbian rights, the referendum decisions were a crushing blow, and an enormous victory for the far right, demonstrating once again that progress for gays and lesbians was anything but linear.

In Europe, the situation since 2003 has also been mixed. There has been remarkable progress in the recognition of same-sex couples in the Netherlands, Denmark, Sweden, France, Belgium, Spain, Switzerland, Hungary, and Great Britain. Even where same-sex marriage is not yet legal, there are civil union contracts that grant same-sex couples certain rights, such as spousal benefits and (to varying degrees) the right to adopt children. Moreover, in 2004, the Buttiglione incident was proof that European authorities take the question of homophobia seriously. José Manuel Barroso, president of the European Commission, had nominated Rocco Buttiglione for the position of the European Union's commissioner for Justice, Freedom, and Security. During a three-hour hearing to confirm his position, he declared quite matter-of-factly that "homosexuality is a sin" and that "the family exists in order to allow women to have children and have the protection of a male who takes care of them." These excessive comments led parliamentarians not only to refuse to approve him for the sensitive position, but also to refuse to reappoint him to another post within the commission. Until then, it was taken for granted that homophobia was the problem of a minority, and that, consequently, it was a minor problem. The European Parliament demonstrated that, as far as it was concerned, it is a question the affects the majority and, consequently, is a major issue.

However, many facts suggest that homophobic resistance remains extremely strong in Europe, particularly in Eastern Europe. Lech Kaczyński, who was elected president of Poland in 2005, has made some extremely offensive comments about homosexuals, including suggesting that the human race "would disappear if homosexuality was freely promoted"; he also banned Gay Pride parades in 2004 and 2005, stating that they would promote "the homosexual lifestyle." Other Pride marches have been regularly attacked in many large cities, such as Krakow, Poland; Riga, Latvia; Moscow, Russia; and Vilnius, Lithuania. In Belgrade, Serbia in 2001, gay and lesbian demonstrators were attacked and beaten not only by skinheads and religious fundamentalists, but also by passersby who decided to join in, trampling the activists who were already lying in the street.

In Africa as well, the situation is extremely ambivalent. The recently launched Coalition of African Lesbians, which includes activists from fourteen countries, constitutes a very positive sign, and LGBT associations are popping up everywhere. However, homophobic beatings, arrests, and condemnations continue, and in some areas are on the rise. The majority of the continent's countries condemn same-sex relations, and even though these laws are not regularly enforced, they help to maintain a climate of fear and concealment, to the social and political detriment of LGBT individuals and associations.

With regard to transnational relations, political recognition of LGBT people is, and remains, rare. Refugees who are threatened in their homeland because of their sexual orientation or gender identity and who wish to find sanctuary elsewhere are, more often than not, rejected by their prospective new country. Immigration agents often do not consider the laws that condemn LGBT people in their country of origin as sufficient argument for political asylum, even when such laws call for the death penalty. With their requests denied, and knowing the fate that awaits them at home, certain asylum seekers see no way out: In September 2003, after his refugee request was rejected by British authorities, Israfil Shiri walked into the offices of Refugee Action in Manchester, doused himself in gasoline, and burned himself alive rather than be deported back to Iran. In 2004, a transsexual who had been whipped in Iran because of her sexuality, and whose request for asylum had been rejected by Sweden, committed suicide in Stralsund, near Stockholm. In 2005, an Iranian man being held at Schiphol Airport in Amsterdam was on the verge of being returned to his homeland. A few years earlier, he had been arrested in Iran; he managed to escape, but his partner was hanged. Recent death sentences carried out against homosexuals in Iran finally convinced

Dutch authorities to stop the expulsion order.

Finally, at the international level, the situation is just as worrisome. In recent years, the Vatican has been working in concert not only with other Catholic nations but also with the United States and Protestant, Orthodox, and Muslim countries in order to promote its conservative, reactionary agenda that includes largely homophobic and sexist positions. Pope John Paul II understood that it was possible, and useful, to overcome theological differences with other nations and churches in order to affirm the moral affinities that they share. Using his charisma, he fostered agreements and alliances that were once unthinkable. This surprising coalition has already achieved some success, such as in 2003, when it effectively opposed a Brazilian resolution at the United Nations that aimed to prohibit discrimination based on sexual orientation. Moreover, Cardinal Ratzinger, who succeeded John Paul II as pope in 2005, and who had co-signed many Vatican documents opposing gay and lesbian rights, immediately made his position clear by forbidding gay men from becoming priests.

Following the publication of the original Dictionary of Homophobia, I launched and coordinated the first International Day Against Homophobia (IDAHO). In my mind, it was an obvious extension of what I had hoped the Dictionary would achieve. At a time when the globalization of the world's economy is on every national agenda, it is vital that we remain conscious of its political, ethical, and philosophical ramifications, which include equal rights for all. The first IDAHO was celebrated for the first time on May 17, 2005, fifteen years to the day after the World Health Organization decided to remove homosexuality from the list of mental illnesses; it was launched simultaneously in over forty countries, from Brazil to Russia, by way of Kenya, Canada, Portugal, and Lebanon. It was an impetus for lively debates, film screenings, radio and television broadcasts, concerts, street festivals, and school events. As a result, China hosted public LGBT marches for the first time in its entire history. The day was officially recognized by European Parliament, by Belgium, the United Kingdom, Mexico, Costa Rica, France, and several regions or provinces in Canada, Spain, Brazil, Italy, and other countries. In 2006, the IDAHO committee launched a petition addressed to the United Nations "for a universal decriminalization of homosexuality." We were fortunate enough to be supported by several Nobel Prize laureates (Dario Fo, Elfriede Jelinek, José

Saramago, Amartya Sen, Desmond Tutu), many famous artists (Victoria Abril, David Bowie, Elton John, Tony Kushner, Cyndi Lauper, Meryl Streep), distinguished intellectuals (Judith Butler, Noam Chomsky, Taslima Nasrin, Salman Rushdie, Cornel West), political leaders (Jacques Delors, former president of the European Commission; Michel Rocard and Laurent Fabius, two former French prime ministers; Thomas Hammerberg, commissioner for human rights, Council of Europe; Bertrand Delanoë, mayor of Paris). On May 17, 2008, the French government responded favorably to the IDAHO committee: the secretary of state for human hights, Rama Yade, announced that May 17 would then become an official national day, and that France would support a UN declaration for a universal decriminalization of homosexuality. Of course, it is only the beginning of a long-term process, but I believe there is cause for hope.

—*Louis-Georges Tin*
2008

INTRODUCTION

The problem is not so much homosexual desire as the fear of homosexuality: why does the mere mention of the word trigger off reactions of hate? We must therefore question how the heterosexual world conceives and fantasizes about "homosexuality."
—Guy Hocquenghem, *Homosexual Desire*, 1972

According to widespread opinion, homosexuality is more liberated today than it has ever been: it is present and visible everywhere, in the streets, in the newspapers, on televisions, in the movies. It is even completely accepted, as witnessed by recent legislative advances in North America and Europe regarding the recognition of same-sex couples (Vermont, Quebec, the Netherlands, Denmark, Belgium, France, Sweden, Germany, Finland, Switzerland, England, etc.). Certainly, further adjustments remain necessary in order to eradicate sexuality-based discrimination, once and for all, but it would be nothing more than a simple question of time: time to bring to its conclusion a grassroots movement launched many decades ago.

But then again, perhaps not. Truth be told, the twentieth century was, without a doubt, the most violently homophobic period in history: deportations to concentration camps under the Nazi regime, gulags in the Soviet Union, and blackmail and persecution in the United States during the Joseph McCarthy anticommunist era. For some, particularly in the western world, much of this seems very much part of the past. But quite often, living conditions for gays, lesbians, and transgenders in today's world remain very difficult. Homosexuality seems to be discriminated against everywhere: in at least seventy nations, homosexual acts are still illegal (e.g., Algeria, Cameroon, Ethiopia, Kuwait, Lebanon, and Senegal) and in a good many of these, punishment can last more than ten years (India, Jamaica, Libya, Malaysia, Nigeria, and Syria). Sometimes the law dictates life imprisonment (Guyana and Uganda), and, in a dozen or so nations, the death penalty may be applied (Iran, Mauritania, Saudi Arabia, and Sudan). In Africa, many nations' leaders have brutally reaffirmed their will to personally fight against the "scourge," which is, according to them, "anti-African." Even in countries where homosexuality is not illegal, or explicitly named in the penal code, persecution is on the rise. In Brazil, for example, death squads and skinheads spread terror: 1,900 homophobic murders have been officially reported during the last twenty years, without having prompted any real action from either police or legal authorities. In such conditions, it is difficult to imagine that the world's "tolerance" of gays, lesbians, and transgenders has gained much ground, if at all. On the contrary, in the majority of these nations, homophobia appears to be more violent than ever.

This brief overview of the situation seems even more sinister as it belies the naïve impression of those who would believe that the overall acceptance of gays and lesbians in society is growing. But in reality, pessimism and blind optimism constitute two symmetric pitfalls for both thought and action, inasmuch as both of these attitudes rest upon completely illusory presuppositions: one, that homophobia has and always will exist, and is a constant in human society; the other, that homophobia is generally a thing of the past. In reality, homophobia as it exists today is neither a transhistorical inevitability, impossible to fight, nor an historical residue destined to disappear by itself over time. It constitutes a problem of humanity, serious and complex and with many ramifications.

But what exactly is homophobia? Apparently, the term was first used in the 1960s, but it is credited to Kenneth Smith, author of a 1971 article entitled "Homophobia: A Tentative Personality Profile." Although the word appeared later in other languages—particularly in French through the writing of Claude Courouve in the 1970s—it did not appear in dictionaries until 1994. It is, therefore, a recent term with a relatively rich history.

Over time, the word's semantic spectrum has consistently broadened. In 1972, psychotherapist George Weinberg defined homophobia as "the fear of being in a closed space with a homosexual." This very narrow definition quickly overflowed into common usage, as witnessed by the standard definition found in the *Concise Oxford Dictionary*: "An extreme and irrational aversion to homosexuality and homosexuals." Didier Eribon proposed to extend the notion by introducing the idea of a homophobic continuum "which goes from those words shouted on the street, which every gay or lesbian has heard, 'fuckin' fag' or 'fucking dyke,' to those words that are implicitly written on the archway of the city hall wedding hall: *Homosexuals Not Admitted*." From this perspective, the notion fully integrated into everyday homophobia the theoretic dialogue of judicial, psychoanalytical, or anthropological allegiance, thereby seeking to confirm or justify the established inequality between homosexuals and heterosexuals.

Pushing the limits of analysis, Daniel Welzer-Lang suggested a new definition. For him, homophobia "is, in a greater sense, the disparagement of those said feminine qualities in men and, to a certain extent, those said masculine qualities in women." As such, he sought to link "specific homophobia, which is practiced against gays and lesbians, and generalized homophobia, which takes root in the construction of the hierarchical organization of gender." The phenomenon can affect any individual, which explains why the insult "fag" can be applied to those who are clearly heterosexual, in the sense that, beyond sexual orientation, it condemns a deficiency in the "perfect" virility that society expects and demands in men.

Evidently, the notion of homophobia has progressively broadened as research has allowed us to understand that acts, words, and attitudes that are clearly perceived as homophobic are nothing more than the by-product of a more general cultural construction representative of violence throughout society as a whole. As a result, the semantic extension of the word has obeyed a metonymic logic that has permitted the linking of the act of homophobia to its ideological and institutional foundations, which are also denounced under this term.

However, parallel to this semantic broadening, there has been an inverse movement of lexical differentiation operating at the heart of the concept of homophobia. Because of the specificity of attitudes towards lesbianism, the term "lesbophobia" has been introduced into theoretic discourses, a term which brings to light particular mechanisms that the generic concept of homophobia tends to overshadow. With one stroke, this distinction justifies the term "gayphobia," since much homophobic discourse, in reality, pertains only to male homosexuality. Similarly, the concept of "biphobia" has also been proposed in order to highlight the singular situation of bisexuals, often stigmatized by both heterosexual and homosexual communities. Moreover, we need to take into consideration the very different issues linked to transsexual, transvestite, and transgendered persons, which brings to mind the notion of "transphobia."

Another distinction has been proposed in order to clarify the political uses of the notion of homophobia. According to sociologist Eric Fassin,

The actual use hesitates between two very different definitions. The first emphasizes the phobia in homophobia: it is the rejection of homosexuals and of homosexuality. We are at the level of an individual psychology. The second sees a certain heterosexism in homophobia. It is the inequality between sexualities. The hierarchy between heterosexuality and homosexuality returns us to the collective level of ideology.

To this, he adds, "perhaps in this case, using the distinction between misogyny and sexism as an example, it would be clearer to distinguish between 'homophobia' and 'heterosexism' in order to avoid the confusion between the psychological and ideological meanings. That, for my part, is what I propose and practice." In these terms, regarding subjects such as same-sex marriage or adoption rights, those who do not believe themselves to be the slightest bit homophobic, while refusing equal rights to others in the name of some religious, moral, anthropological, or psychoanalytical privilege reserved for heterosexuals, will have to at least recognize that this is, technically speaking, a heterosexist attitude; such a recognition could constitute a first step.

That being the case, these semantic evolutions, extensions, or distinctions enrich, albeit considerably complicate, the debate. And the political stakes are quite real, since more and more citizens, associations, and politicians have become conscious, notably in France during the battle for PaCS (Pacte civil de solidarité; Civil solidarity pact), of the necessity to resist and even penalize homophobia in the same manner as racism or anti-Semitism. In effect, after the passing of homosexuality from the criminal law code to the civil law code, homophobia could, contrarily, pass from civil society, where is still remains, to criminal law, where it is not yet contained. Shifting the focus from homosexuality to homophobia constitutes, as correctly noted by Daniel Borrillo, "a change that is not only epistemological, but political as well." But for the time being, in the fight against homophobia much remains to be done.

In order to fight homophobia, it is necessary to determine its real causes. Homophobia's deep origin is, without a doubt, to be found in heterosexism, that compulsory rule of heterosexuality that feminist writer and poet Adrienne Rich criticized. This regime tends to construe heterosexuality as the only legitimate sexual experience possible, or even thinkable, which explains why so many people go through life without ever having considered the homosexual reality. Better than a norm—which would require explication—heterosexuality becomes, for those it has conditioned, the *non thought* of their particular psychic makeup and the apriorism of all human sexuality in general. Far from being self-evident, this transparency of self, which is a forced exclusion of the other, constitutes one of the fundamentals of social learning. In its rigidity, it ends up as, and not only for heterosexuals, a model by which to perceive the world, individuals, and gender. In these conditions, it becomes difficult to imagine not only homosexuality, whose simple existence risks shaking the foundations of universal beliefs, and consequently values, but also heterosexuality, which, being the usual point of view on the world, is nonetheless that point of view's blind spot.

In fact, by not evaluating all the horror that homosexuality can represent, we expose ourselves to not understanding homophobia—as much as we *can* understand it—in its more radical form. The general and convulsive feeling of hatred that Copernicus aroused when he dared knock the Earth off its epistemological pedestal might give us an approximate idea. The concept of heterocentrism, fashioned after geocentrism, may be described as a world view circling a self-proclaimed center of reference, in this case heterosexuality. From this perspective, other sexualities may not be anything other than strange galaxies, obscure nebulae, or, at the very least, extraterrestrial life forms. Whether the earth was, or was not, at the center of the universe changed very little in everyday life; however, the necessity to objectively rethink God's order, which was in fact Man's order, aroused a veritable subjective fury whose reasoning went beyond strict religious belief, which was fundamentally never put into question by the theories of either Copernicus or Galileo.

Thus, for those individuals who are strongly conditioned by heterosexism, the simple existence of homosexuals—who, objectively speaking, pose no threat—subjectively constitutes a threat against a valued psychological construct built on exclusion. This allows us to understand how fear—and even more the resulting hate—can lead to the most brutal violence. Clearly, this fear could never constitute mitigating circumstances, even less justification, for homophobic murders. And when claims are made in American courts, sometimes successfully, by individuals who go to cruising areas,

baseball bats in hand to "bash some queers," the notion of *sex panic* appears to be the height of dishonesty and cynical cruelty. Nonetheless, it is the deep origin of extreme reactions, linked to heterosexist conditioning, that dictates the male identity as based on the more or less "gentle" control of women and the more or less harsh repression of homosexuality.

For theories—be they theological, moral, legal, medical, biological, psychoanalytical, anthropological, et cetera—are never more than concocted reasons to justify, after the fact, obviously unjustifiable personal convictions aligned with the status quo. Thus, during the fight for PaCS, arguments based on theology and religious morality were not well received, so the Catholic Church did not hesitate to resort to more fashionable psychoanalysis, whose theories the Church had not so long ago condemned as being obscene and permissive. Similarly, it is generally useless to explain to those who see homosexuality as a type of defect or pathology that their beliefs have long been invalidated by medical science itself. Far from being the cause of their homophobia, the obsolete medical argument is nothing more than the occasional manifestation of homophobia and, at most, its confirmation. Thus, belief can both precede and obstinately survive the theories upon which it is seemingly based, theories that were, in fact, nothing more than a contextual formulation and justification.

Truth be told, the theories themselves matter very little; they are often interchangeable. The divine, natural, moral, public, symbolic, or anthropological orders are nothing but the decline of the one and the same concept, though diversely constructed, invoked to legitimize a condition that is profoundly inegalitarian. We must use all means necessary to change this. From all evidence, the theories or arguments set forth are nothing more than a conjectural means set in motion by generic homophobia, whose conscious origin must be sought deep within this thought, or rather this heterosexist non thought, which contains the stigmatization of all homosexuals. However, this respectable heterosexism does not always lead, thankfully, to murderous violence. Therefore, it remains to be understood why homophobia arises or resurfaces more violently during certain periods, areas, and conditions.

Beyond everyday manifestations, it seems that large waves of homophobia generally obey opportunist motivations and history is rife with lessons. In the first years of the communist revolution, homosexuality was relatively "tolerated." In the Soviet Union, after the abolition of the penal code of 1832, the crime of sodomy was not reintroduced in the codes of 1922 or 1926. And in its first edition in 1930, the *Great Soviet Encyclopedia* asserted quite clearly that homosexuality was neither a crime nor a sickness. Likewise, in Cuba, at the beginning of the New Revolution, homosexuals enjoyed a short-lived yet real liberty, as witnessed by writer Reinaldo Arenas, however, the instant political difficulties appeared, they were systematically hunted and locked away in camps. Similarly in the USSR, the difficulties in the regime and the ascension of Stalin contributed to a hardening of living conditions. Homosexuality was once again penalized in 1933, soon became a crime against the state, a sign of bourgeois decadence, and, even worse, a fascist perversion to be harshly condemned. But, as Daniel Borrillo notes, "by a sad irony of history, at the same time, Nazi Germany put into place a plan to persecute and exterminate homosexuals by putting them in the same category as communists."

These examples clearly show that heterosexism's latent and inherent homophobia can suddenly be re-awakened by a serious crisis that justifies the search for a scapegoat. Accused of all evils, homosexuality can become sufficient reason for purges perceived as necessary. That is why, depending on the historical moment considered, it is adjusted to each particular situation and projected upon an adversary who is to be stigmatized or eliminated. Thus, likened to Bulgarian heresy during the Middle Ages, sodomy was regularly used as the main charge in the fight against religious "deviancy," such as the charge against the Knights Templar. Similarly, during the French Religious Wars, homosexuality became a Catholic vice according to the Huguenots, and a Huguenot vice according to the Catholics. During the same period, it was ascribed to Italian morals, in the sense that the French Court seemed to be submerged by Italian culture; then to English morals, when the British Empire was at its pinnacle; to German morals, at the time when the Franco-German rivalry was at its peak; to Jewish cosmopolitanism, whose alleged aims were so worrisome to the nation; to American communitarianism, whose principles threatened, we are told, the French Republic. While a bourgeois vice to the proletariat of the nineteenth century, it was considered by the bourgeois to be a phenomenon of the immoral working classes, or of the necessarily decadent aristocracy. In

the Near East, India, China, or Japan, it is perceived as a Western practice; in Black Africa, it is, of course, a white phenomenon.

In short, homosexuality constitutes a symbolic protean component, typically characteristic of an adversary or enemy, be it a rival nation, a particular social group, or an individual on the street. It is the simplest and most certain means to disqualify another, and it is why it finds such a favorable ground in areas where social, religious, racist, xenophobic, or anti-Semitic hate is already deeply rooted. It is the strange common denominator of various resentments that rally around the same cause. That is, in a heterosexist culture, crises and difficult circumstances favor the formation of homophobic sentiments and practices, which offer an opportunity for any "charismatic" leader in search of popular support. Under such conditions, it is not surprising that homosexuality is so often the designated target for regimes who, at least in appearance, are not only dissimilar, but in polar opposition. As soon as any cloud darkens the sky, the mobilization of homophobic discourse is a useful method to divert attention from real problems, while guaranteeing support of the moralists. And often, that which was nothing more than an opportunistic pretext becomes an end in itself, justified by sentiments most acceptable to the public. It is the end making a virtue out of necessity.

However, it remains necessary to examine the numerous methods used by homophobia. It is not so much a question of putting together a *catalogue raisonné*—a grim and fastidious task—as it is of analyzing its complex workings. Methods are often ambiguous and it is difficult to classify these diverse forms of violence, be they formal, i.e. practiced under government authority (death penalty, forced labor, whipping, chemical or physical castration, clitoridectomy, incarceration, internment), or informal (terrorism, assassination, punitive rape, beating, physical or verbal assault, harassment). Moreover, this distinction itself is subject to caution in the sense that, in certain countries, informal violence benefits largely from the approval—if not the outright complicity—of authorities who are supposed to condemn it. And even where homosexual practices are not penalized, legal detours may be used in order to incriminate these practices with other charges, as fantastic as they may appear to be: unlawful meeting, conspiracy, blasphemy, mutual assault and battery, even if it occurs in a private home. Since the roles played by authorities are rather ambiguous, the line between formal and informal violence is often difficult to trace.

Beyond this more or less state-sanctioned homophobia, the more widespread social homophobia is practiced everywhere: in families, school, army, workplace, politics, media, sport, prison, et cetera. These types of physical violence or moral coercion are often less understood, and those who suffer from them—sometimes simultaneously—often refuse to denounce them. The fear of having their homosexuality revealed and the fear of reprisals—especially when these acts are committed within a group setting, barracks, or team—compels to silence those victims who are the most vulnerable.

But it is in the symbolic order that everyday homophobia is best practiced. Beyond even the acts, attitudes, and discourses that are clearly homophobic, society's framework constitutes a structure in which daily violence is, doubtless, difficult to imagine for those whose experience is organized in accordance with that framework. As Eribon notes, no matter how racist the area in which he is born, a black child has every chance to grow up in a family that will allow him to construct his identity with a sense of relative legitimacy. However, in heterosexual families in which the majority of gay youth grow up, the developing consciousness of their desire constitutes, generally, a trial that is even more difficult in the fact that it must remain secret. The shame, the solitude, the despair of never being loved, the pure panic of one day being discovered locks away the spirit in a sort of interior prison that pushes the individual to sometimes overestimate the negative attitudes expressed by his or her social circle. Thus, we see tearful parents who are incapable of comprehending their gay child's suicide; of course they would have accepted his or her difference; moreover, they had never said anything against homosexuality. The problem is that they had never said anything in its favor, either. They cannot understand, but the general silence surrounding this taboo subject, the absence of images and dialogue were, for their son, for their daughter, the strongest condemnation.

It is in these extreme cases, more numerous than we would want to believe, that homophobia's symbolic violence is best measured; it does not need to be expressed to be committed. Silence is its home. Cursing and condemnations are often useless. Parents, friends, neighbors, television shows, films, children's books, and magazines, all repeatedly celebrate the heterosexual couple. As they grow up all children understand, said or unsaid, consciously or unconsciously, that the alternative is impossible—homosexuality is outside of language, if it isn't against the law. It remains only in the basest of insults, "fag," "cocksucker," and other charming words, whose homophobic charge isn't even understood by those who use them, thereby relegating male homosexuality to the level of ignominy and female homosexuality to being beyond thought.

Consequently, even in silence, this symbolic violence imposes itself upon the minds of its victims. Far from arousing their revolt, it often succeeds in ensuring their collaboration in exchange for some eventual tolerance. As Erving Goffman so rightly explained, "We ask, therefore, the stigmatized to show some manners and not take too much advantage of their luck. It is unacceptable for them to test the limits of the acceptance they've been given, nor that they take advantage of it for new demands. Tolerance is almost always part of the bargain." Thus, the more a homosexual gives proof of proper conduct, the more a homosexual believes that he or she will receive acceptance by others. This type of condescending homophobia with its liberal, tolerant façade encourages gays and lesbians to multiply the pretences and honorable lies that, even when they deceive no one, appear to be the prerequisites for an always precarious recognition, whose limitations always surprise those who so naively believed in a definitive "integration."

This logic of social acceptance at any cost drives those who submit to it to adopt, in their position of being dominated, the dominant point of view, which is a source of immeasurable heartbreak and psychological disorder. It creates within them a sense of internalized homophobia, a veritable self-loathing, which may be the cause of the greatest violence. The necessity to prove their perfect "normalcy" pushes certain individuals to assault or persecute those whom they perceive as homosexuals. Of this, contemporary history has offered a blatant example. It is unknown to many that the American "witch hunts" were largely aimed at homosexuals. But it is also believed that one of the primary players, J. Edgar Hoover, director of the FBI, was gay or bisexual and the purpose of his homophobic, patriotic, and strong-armed internal policies was to prove, especially to himself, his infallible virility. This mental disposition—a profound split between a desire for the other and the denial of self—may also lead to rape. Frequently in non-mixed environments, such as prisons, barracks, or boarding schools, where masculinity is exacerbated, the practice of rape—to the degree that it teaches a lesson to a victim who is perceived as less "virile"—offers a double advantage of satisfying a secretly homosexual libido while proving to others an incontestable sexual power that is, in this paradoxical logic, completely heterosexual.

Nonetheless, this internalized homophobia, whose violence is vented against other homosexuals or, more often, against the subject himself, is without a doubt one of the most appalling aspects of the symbolic order, since it acts without having been seen to do so. The shame that it arouses and fuels exempts it from visibility—so much so that many reasonable people do not believe that homophobia actually exists and suspect, rather, that those who complain about it suffer from some form of paranoia. By refusing to see precisely this characteristic of symbolic violence—that it can be committed without any apparent constraints—they become the allies of a system which they refuse to recognize. In this way, the relentless machine that is homophobia of the symbolic order, anonymous and collective, seems particularly formidable: those who submit to it, by internalizing its principles, contribute implicitly to its legitimization; those who denounce it, by questioning its violence, discredit themselves, especially since they appear, like Don Quixote, to be tilting at windmills.

That being the case, the fight against homophobia, whose causes are profound and whose methods so effective, appears to be a difficult venture. Inasmuch as laws that condemn or discriminate against homosexuality are the effect rather than the cause of rampant homophobia, the simple act of abolishing them appears to be a necessary, if not sufficient, measure. It would be necessary to go further in order to create the conditions that would permit a true evolution of thought. However, minds cannot be so easily changed, and the necessary work requires time, energy, and clear-headedness.

To contribute to this long-term project, it is useful to compile a summary as overview of the problematics associated with homophobia. In order to do that, it seems appropriate to revive the tradition of critical dictionaries of the Age of Enlightenment: long ago, philosophers Bayle, Diderot, d'Alembert, and Voltaire resorted to this format in order to fight prejudice and other forms of intolerance.

The dictionary format offers entries on every aspect of the subject matter. They are independent, detachable, reusable elements able to feed new development.

Clearly displaying both a scientific and political vocation, this dictionary of homophobia is, as a result, a work of knowledge and of battle.

The articles here, presented in the alphabetical order expected of any dictionary, can nonetheless be divided into five categories whose titles made up the generative principles for the definition of the various entries. Firstly, consideration was given to the theories that may have been used to justify homophobic acts, attitudes, or discourses—from theology to psychoanalysis by way of medicine, biology, or anthropology. Historical agents of homophobia, such as Joseph McCarthy and Anita Bryant, for example, were also included, as were the historical victims of homophobia, such as Radclyffe Hall or Oscar Wilde. Next, many articles focus on different countries (France, Germany, India, China, etc.) or regions (Maghreb or Central and Eastern Africa, the Middle East, Southeast Asia, Latin America, etc.) creating a panorama which, without being exhaustive, allows us to think about homophobia geographically and historically. Another group of articles concerns environments and institutions, such as family, school, the armed forces, or workplace, where social homophobia engenders very specific practices and thought that are of interest to study. And finally, the everyday themes of homophobic rhetoric—such as debauchery, sterility, proselytism, and AIDS—have also justified a group of articles.

In total, more than seventy people from over fifteen countries have worked on this book. It has many voices, not only for the sake of plurality, but also, and fundamentally, because homophobia is a collective violence. When it targets one individual, it always targets him as a supposed element of a group that it seeks to stigmatize. Consequently, faced with this collective violence, it is necessary to respond collectively. For all that, gathering these articles in one book does not suppose a unified thought; but if there is a lesson to be had, it can be none other than the need to fight against homophobia is essential.

Beyond this, the subject's complexity and diversity do not permit us to draw any general conclusions. Furthermore, homophobia does not always present the same face. Indeed, it may seem problematic to use the term for cultures in which the concept of homosexuality does not exist *per se*. But in truth, it is not necessary to conceive of the existence of a social and sexual system, such as ours, in order to use the notion of homophobia. Whether homosexuality exists or not as a category in different societies, homophobia may be thought of as a tool for analysis and can be defined as the totality of physical, mental, or symbolic violence targeting sexual relations between persons of the same gender, regardless of the significance given to these relations. Each entry is composed by authors who, conscious of the term's limits, attempt to highlight different details, while avoiding the dangers of anachronism or ethnocentrism.

However, though the authors worked alone, it is clear that the various articles blend with, complete, and respond to one other, inviting the reader to explore according to his or her whim. And in order to simplify the book's use, keywords have been listed at the end of each article. Furthermore, the bolded words indicate words that have their own specific entry. These comments are sufficient operating instructions for any book whose goal is to clarify, in the general sense, an issue whose topicality reveals its crucial importance. Also, this dictionary should be considered a synthesis rather than a whole. It will seem incomplete to those who wish to go further into one aspect or another. For them, the bibliographical entries will suggest some additional avenues to explore. For all others, it will without a doubt constitute a true basis of reflection and, possibly, action.

—*Louis-Georges Tin*
2003

Borrillo, Daniel, and Pierre Lascoumes, eds. *L'Homophobie: comment la définir, comment la combattre*. Paris: Ed. Prochoix, 1999.

Eribon, Didier. "Ce que l'injure me dit. Quelques remarques sur le racisme et la discrimination." In *L'Homophobie, comment la définir, comment la combattre*. Paris: Editions ProChoix, 1999.

Fassin, Eric. "Le Outing de l'homophobie est-il de bonne politique?." In *L'Homophobie, comment la définir, comment la combattre*. Paris: Editions ProChoix, 1999.

Goffman, Erving. *Stigma*. New York: Simon & Schuster, 1998.

Rich, Adrienne. "La Contrainte à l'hétérosexualité et l'existence lesbienne." *Nouvelles questions féministes*, no. 1 (1981). [Published in the US as "Compulsory Heterosexuality and Lesbian Experience," *Signs* 5, no. 4 (Summer 1980).]

Smith, Kenneth. "Homophobia: A Tentative Personality Profile," *Psychological Report*, no. 29 (1971).

Weinberg, George. *Society and the Healthy Homosexual*. New York: St Martin's Press, 1972.

Welzer-Lang, Daniel. "La Face cachée du masculin." In *La Peur de l'autre en soi*. Edited by Michel Dorais, Pierre Dutcy, and Welzer-Lang. Montreal: VLB, 1994.

THE ANTI-ANTHOLOGY

An anthology? Not really. The term "anthology," from the root word "antho," which means flower, usually defines a collection of writing chosen for its beauty and grace. But here, we deal with homophobic discourse, which is ugly and spiteful. So it is perhaps more appropriate to call this book an "anti-anthology." The objective of this selection, however, is not merely to produce a formal catalog of hatred, but rather to give voice to opinions and protests, as an illustration of homophobia, before proceeding with analysis, which is the core of this book. Here you will find people as sinister as Himmler and as honorable as Saint Paul. The inclusion of such different individuals is not to suggest that they are in any way equal, in a sort of shared and dark ignominy, but rather to show that homophobic discourses can be found in extremely varied contexts, crossing the ages and divides, each time taking on very different meanings that the dictionary entries examine.

However, this selection cannot hope to be a representative sample, for beyond open and public statements, homophobia is also expressed through silence: by night, in unreported physical aggression or police brutality; by day, in curt words and unspoken thoughts. And in most countries in the world, acts of physical, moral, or symbolic violence are the most prevalent expressions of homophobia, ones that words do not reveal…

If a man lies with a male as with a woman, both of them have committed an abomination; they shall surely be put to death; their blood is upon them.
—Lv 20:13

Do not be deceived: neither the sexually immoral, nor idolaters, nor adulterers, nor men who practice homosexuality; nor thieves, nor the greedy, nor drunkards, nor revilers, nor swindlers will inherit the kingdom of God.
—St **Paul**, I Cor 6:9–10

Truly, there is no way to compare this **vice** to any other vice, because it surpasses the scope of all vices. In effect, this vice means the death of the body, and the destruction of the soul. It pollutes the flesh; it extinguishes the light of the spirit, it opens the door to Hell, and closes the gates of Heaven…. This vice can tumble men from the heart of the ecclesiastical community, and forces them to pray alongside the possessed and those who work for the Devil.
—St Peter Damian, *Liber Gomorrhianus* (*Book of Gomorrah*), c. 1050

He who is a proven sodomite, must lose his balls, and if he does it a second time, he must lose his member; and if he does it a third time, he must be burned"; "The woman who does it must each time lose a member, and the third time must be burned. And all their belongings belong to the king.
—*Justice et Plet*, ancient customs of Orléans, c. 1260

Who errs against faith, as like heathenism, from which he does not want to come to the voice of truth, or if he commits sodomy, he must be burned.
—Philippe de Beaumanoir, *Les Coutumes de Beauvaisis* (*The Costumes de Beauvaisis*), c. 1285

In each temple or important place of worship, they have one or two men, if not more, dressed as women since childhood, and who speak like them and imitate their habits, their dress and all. The men—and the chiefs in particular—have immoral carnal relations with them on feast or holy days, as if it were a rite or a ceremony. I know because I punished two of them.
—Pedro Cieza de Léon, *Crónica del Peru*, 1533

During the time I was among these people [Native Americans in what is now Florida], I saw a diabolical thing: a man married to another man.
—Alvar Nunez Cabeza de Vaca, *La Relacion o naufragios*, 1542

If a man consents to being sodomized, the guilty will be condemned to wearing the cang for a month and to 100 strikes of the stick.
—Code of the Qing Dynasty (Da Qing Mi), 1734

The pederast contravenes to hygiene, to cleanliness and he is ignorant of the lustration that purifies. The state of the backside, the weakness of the sphincter, the funnel-shaped anus or the shape and dimension of the penis show the membership in this new race. Monster in the new gallery of monsters, the pederast is in part linked to the animal; in his coitus, he invokes the dog. His nature associates him to excrement.
—Ambroise Tardieu, *Etude médico-légales sur les attentats aux mœurs* (Medical-legal studies of assaults against decency), 1857

Without going all the way to death, I regret that this

infamy that has begun to propagate itself amongst us, be treated with so much indulgence. I would like it to be, in all cases, associated to rape, and punished by twenty years of reclusion.
—Pierre-Joseph Proudhon, *Amour et marriage* (Love and marriage), 1858

Homosexuality is a functional stigmatism of **degeneracy** and a nervous psychopathological defect.
—Richard von Krafft-Ebing, *Psychopathia Sexualis*, 1886

Homosexuality is the negation of human will in one of its weakest points, for human will has in it the living ideal of perpetuation. This simple fact suffices to impose heterosexuality as the standard and to place all perversions, including masturbation, at the level of crime, aberrations or sin.
—Dr Alfred Adler, "Le Problème de l'homosexualité" (published in English as "On Homosexuality," 1917)

Imagine exactly what sexual practices between men are, and try not to vomit.
—Camille Mauclair, *Les Marges*, March 1926

I believe that this perversion of natural instinct, like many other perversions, is an indicator of the profound social and moral **decadence** of a certain part of current society.
—Henri Barbusse, *Les Marges*, March 1926

Homosexuality foils all productivity…. We must understand that if this vice continues to spread throughout Germany without our being able to fight it, it will be the end of **Germany**, the end of the Germanic world.
—Heinrich Himmler, speech of February 18, 1937

In Soviet society, homosexuality is repressed as a sexual depravation and punished by law, with the exception of mental disorders…. In the bourgeois countries, homosexuality, sign of the moral decomposition of the ruling classes, is an impossible fact to punish.
—"Homosexuality," in the *Great Soviet Encyclopedia*, vol. 12, 1952

In thirty-eight years, the school has produced no homosexuals. The reason is that freedom results in healthy children.
—Dr Alexander-Sutherland Neill, *Libres enfants de*

Summerhill (*Summerhill: A Radical Approach to Child Rearing*), 1960

Don't come and tell us, under the pretense that it is an accepted—celebrated even—perversion, that it is not a perversion. Homosexuality remains what it is: a perversion.
—Jacques Lacan, "Le Transfert," in *Séminaire* (*Seminar of Jacques Lacan*), vol. 8, 1960–6

The pure homosexual, unscathed of all neurotic potentiality, seems to me an exception; we do not see any in our offices.
—Dr Marcel Eck, "Sodome," 1966

Homosexuality remains the dead-end of non-fraternity and of non-life.
—Dr Eliane Amado Lévy-Valensi, *Le Grand désarroi*, 1973

I respect homosexuals just as I respect the infirm. But if they wish to transform their infirmity into health, I must say that I do not agree.
—Monsignor Elchinger, bishop of Strasbourg, 1982

It is necessary to sanction homosexual **proselytism**. In fact, the greatest danger that threatens the world is the decrease in the birthrate in the West and the increase in the birthrate in the Third World. For this reason, I consider that it will lead, if it continues, to the end of the World.
—Jean-Marie Le Pen, president of the National Front Party of France, 1984

Unless we get medically lucky, in three or four years, one of the options discussed will be the extermination of homosexuals.
—Dr Paul Cameron, Conservative Political Action Conference, 1985

Heterosexuality is best.
—Edith Cresson, French prime minister, 1991

This virus [HIV] has had the genius to attack those who have transformed the physiology of reproduction into adulterated pleasure…. In these times when everything that is immoral, even unnatural, is admired, this virus knew where to strike.
—P. German, president of France's Académie nationale de pharmacie, 1991

There are areas in which it is not unjust discrimination to take sexual orientation into account, for example, in the placement of children for adoption or foster care, in employment of teachers or athletic coaches, and in military recruitment.
—Cardinal Ratzinger, Pope Benedict XVI, "Some Considerations Concerning the Response to Legislative Proposals on Non-Discrimination of Homosexual Persons," 1992

Homosexuals are worse than pigs and dogs.
—Robert Mugabe, president of Zimbabwe, 1995

For those who have the responsibility to speak of and name regulations or the establishment of norms in a context of education, teaching, and support, it seems to me to be intellectually and morally honest to dare to insist on the non equivalence between homosexual and heterosexual forms of affection. Differently from other qualifications evoked above, expressions such as 'abnormal form of sexuality' or 'objectively deficient conducts' do not seem to me to be either insulting or humiliating. Who does not have deficiencies in certain aspects of their character, in their sexuality in particular? Sexuality is not only the area of our capacities and performances, it is also that of our vulnerabilities and weaknesses.
—Xavier Lacroix, *L'Amour du semblable, questions sur l'homosexualité* (Love of the same: questions on homosexuality), 1995

I admit that there must be some homosexuals in the National Front, but there are no queens. They are invited to go elsewhere.
—Jean-Marie Le Pen, National Front Party, 1995

Basing itself on Sacred Scripture, which presents homosexual acts as acts of grave depravity, tradition has always declared that 'homosexual acts are intrinsically disordered.' They are contrary to the natural law. They close the sexual act to the gift of life. They do not proceed from a genuine affective and sexual complementarity. Under no circumstances can they be approved.
—"The Vocation to Chastity: Chastity and Homosexuality," *Catechism of the Catholic Church*, 2357–59, 1997

Some people are going to scream, but I am willing to say that you cannot be gay and happy.

—Sébastien, *Ne deviens pas gay tu finiras triste*, 1998

For homosexuals, Islam has prescribed the most severe punishments. After guilt has been established according to the dictates of *sharia*, the individual must be seized, be kept standing, and divided in two with a sword and either cut off his head, or split him completely in two. He (or she) will fall.… After his death, a pyre must be made, the body placed on it, fire set to it and burn it, or brought to the top of a mountain and thrown from a cliff. Then, the body parts must be assembled and burned. Or a hole must be dug, a fire started in it and he must be thrown in alive. We have no such punishments for other crimes.
—Ayatollah Musava Ardelsili, Tehran, 1998

Homosexuality is part of the first stages of human sexuality; it does not represent the final stage of sexuality, which, in the best of cases, progresses towards heterosexuality. Homosexuality is in no way a choice of one object among others, but a complex which indicates the failure of the internalization of the other.
—Tony Anatrella, priest and psychoanalyst, *Le Monde*, October 10, 1998

If you ask me if an avowed homosexual teacher can teach, my answer is no. It would be morally wrong that an avowed homosexual person or someone who, when all is said and done, considers pedophilia to be a form of love be allowed to teach. They should be excluded from public service.
—Gianfranco Fini, leader of Italy's National Alliance political movement, 1998

I cannot be favorable to those that I call the gravediggers of humanity, those who do not guarantee the future, homosexuals.
—François Abadie, senator, France's Radical Left Party, *Nouvel observateur*, June 2000

It is not good that a man goes with another man, or that a woman goes with another woman. It goes against African tradition and the teachings of the Bible.
—Daniel arap Moi, president of Kenya, 2000

My words are like a dagger with a jagged edge /
That'll stab you in the head / Whether you're a fag or
a lez / Or the homosex, hermaph, or a trans-a-vest /
Pants or dress—hate fags? The answer's yes.

—Eminem, "Criminal," *The Marshall Mathers LP*, 2000

Lesbians use the orifice of life in their lovemaking. However, homosexuals use the orifice of excrement.
—Didier Ratsiraka, president of Madagascar, *La Tribune de Madagascar*, March 27, 2001

The youth must fight against the temptation of violence, immorality, sins against nature, alcoholism and the hell of drugs. The fact that evil risks invading our world and that the abnormal tends to be considered normal must worry us all.
—Monsignor Teoctist, patriarch of the Romanian Orthodox Church, 2001

On the battle in France over **PaCS** *(the legislative proposal to legalize civil unions, including between same-sex couples):*

The reason for which homosexual couples do not have access to marriage is that it is the institution that etches gender differences into the **symbolic order**, by linking couple and descent.
—Irène Théry, *Notes de la Fondation Saint-Simon and Esprit*, October 1997

Where will we set the boundary, for an adopted child, between homosexuality and pedophilia?
—Christine **Boutin**, Union for French Democracy member of parliament, member of the Pontifical Council for the Family, *Le "Mariage" des homosexuels?* ("Marriage" between homosexuals?), 1998.

It is the foundations of civilization and democracy that would be put into question.
—Boutin, *Le "Mariage,"* 1998.

Homosexuals, I piss in their asses.
—Michel Meylan, France's Liberal Democracy Party member of parliament, 1998

It is homosexuality and every perversion that invades **literature**, **cinema**, **theater**, and the **media**, and which assails the very young who have no appropriate defenses.
—Avenir de la culture (Future of the Culture) handout, 1998

Unsuitable to ensure the renewal of the members that make it up [society], homosexuality is, by nature, a

behavior that is deadly to society. This is not a moral or subjective appreciation, but an elementary biological statement of fact.
—Judge Jean-Luc Auber, note in the decision of the Court of Cassation, 1998

Every sociological study has proven that, in general, homosexual couples have higher incomes than heterosexual couples, and for obvious reasons. It is thus unreasonable to offer to everyone the same advantages when the justifications for such advantages are lacking.
—Bernard Beignier, columnist, 1997

To accept that couples can be constituted otherwise than in the conjugal relation of a man and a woman is to go against the natural balance established by God. Under the guise of democracy, our society tends to legislate according to the evolution of mores.... When man assaults nature, he assaults God and himself.
—Joseph Sitruk, chief rabbi of France, 1996

Sterilize them!
—Pierre Lellouche, Rally for the Republic member of parliament, 1998

To entrust children to male homosexual couples (as will happen one day or another by logical evolution if PaCS is adopted) will only increase the risks of pedophilia, which are already constantly growing.
—Emmanuel Le Roy Ladurie, *Le Figaro*, October 19, 1998

This project arouses a deep repulsion, including amongst socialist voters. It is legislation of decadent times, worse than that at the end of the Roman Empire.
—Jean Foyer, French secretary of state, 1998

The PaCS revolution is a return to barbarism.
—Philippe de Villiers, member of the European parliament, 1998)

No nephews for the aunties; The homosexuals of today are the pedophiles of tomorrow; Fags to the pyre!
—Slogans from an anti-PaCS demonstration, January 31, 1999

TABLE OF ENTRIES

CONTRIBUTORS

Abega, Séverin Cécile: anthropologist, specialist in African societies.

Albertini, Pierre: former student at the Ecole normale supérieure (ENS), historian.

André-Simonet, Mathieu: lawyer with the Barreau de Paris.

Avezou, Laurent: former student at the Ecole des chartes, historian, specialist on modern France.

Boehringer, Sandra: resident of the Fondation Thiers, historian, specialist in gender issues in antiquity.

Borrillo, Daniel: jurist, researcher associated with the Centre nationale de la recherche scientifique (CNRS), assistant professor at the Université de Paris X-Nanterre, specialist in issues of discrimination related to sexual orientation.

Brisson, Luc: CNRS researcher, specialist on Plato.

Broqua, Christophe: anthropologist, specialist in gender issues.

Busscher, Pierre-Olivier de: historian, sociologist, specialist in the history of medicine, assistant to the director of Sida Info Service.

Cardon, Patrick: festival director and publisher at Editions Questions de genre/GayKitschCamp.

Cascais, Fernando: philosopher, professor at the faculty of social sciences at the Universidade Nova de Lisboa.

Celse, Michel: former student at the ENS, German scholar, ACT UP-Paris activist.

Chauvin, Sébastien: student at the ENS, sociologist.

Chevaux, Hervé: historian, specialist in contemporary history.

Colomb, Philippe: philosopher, specialist in moral philosophy and politics.

Deschamps, Catherine: sociologist, specialist in gender issues.

D'Penha, Mario: historian, specialist on India.

Eloi, Thierry: former student at the ENS, assistant professor in language and Latin literature at the Université de Perpignan.

Fassin, Eric: sociologist, instructor at the ENS.

Faure, Michael: sociologist, specialist on prison issues.

Fernandez, André: Spanish scholar, assistant professor at the Université Marc Bloch, Strasbourg, specialist on the history of sexuality in Spain.

Finnegan, Brian: founder and chief editor of the Irish magazine *GI*.

Firdion, Jean-Marie: Institut national d'études démographiques sociologist.

Formond, Thomas: jurist, specialist in issues of discrimination related to sexual orientation.

Fourest, Caroline, chief editor of *ProChoix* magazine.

Frioux, Dalibor: former student at the ENS, philosopher.

Gaspard, Françoise: sociologist at the Ecole des hautes études en sciences sociales.

Gérard, Raymonde: head of the Coordination lesbienne nationale's Lesbophobia Commission.

Gillis, Joseph Roy: professor of psychology at the University of Toronto.

Godbout, Louis: secretary of the Archives gaies du Québec.

Gross, Martine: co-president of the French Association des parents et futurs parents gays et lesbiens.

Hamel, Christelle: anthropologist, specialist on the Maghreb.

Huyez, Guillaume: sociologist, member of the editorial committee of *ProChoix*.

Jeannelle, Jean-Louis: former student at the ENS, graduate assistant in French language and literature at the Université de Paris IV-Sorbonne.

Kandel, Liliane: former co-head of Cedref at the Université Paris VII-Denis-Diderot, member of the editorial committee of *Temps modernes* magazine.

Krikorian, Gaëlle: sociologist, specialist in transgender issues.

Le Bitoux, Jean: founder and director of the Centre d'archives et de documentations homosexuelles de Paris.

Le Doaré, Christine: president of SOS homophobie.

Legrand, Raphaëlle: professor of musicology at the Université de Paris IV-Sorbonne.

Leroy-Forgeot, Flora: jurist, instructor at Paris XIII and at Reims, specialist in the legal history of homosexuality.

Lesselier, Claudie: historian, feminist activist.

Lestrade, Didier: journalist, cofounder of ACT UP-Paris and *Têtu* magazine.

Liotard, Philippe: sociologist, assistant professor at the Université Lyon I, illustrator at *Quasimodo* magazine.

Long, Laurent: specialist in Chinese affairs and gender issues.

Mangeot, Philippe: former student at the ENS, former president of ACT UP-Paris, director of *Vacarme* magazine.

Masanet, Philippe: former student at the ENS, historian.

Mendès-Leite, Rommel: ethno-sociologist, instructor at EHESS, specialist on AIDS and gender issues.

Mott, Luiz: professor of anthropology at the Federal University of Bahia, specialist in gender issues, founder and president of Grupo Gay da Bahia and the Bahia Anti-AIDS Center.

Ouardi, Samira: PhD student in information and communication sciences at CELSA, Université Paris-Sorbonne.

Pénet, Martin: journalist, PhD student, specialist in the history of song.

Plagne, Nicolas: former student at the ENS, historian, specialist on Russia.

Plummer, David: professor at the University of New England, Australia, specialist in gender issues.

Queiroz, Jean-Manuel de: professor of sociology at the Université Rennes II.

Raemdonck, Dan van: linguist, professor at the Université Libre de Bruxelles, president of the European Association for the Defense of Human Rights.

Rebreyend, Anne-Claire: research and teaching assistant in contemporary history at the Université Marc Bloch, Strasbourg.

Ressouni-Demigneux, Karim: art historian, specialist in the Middle Ages and the Italian Renaissance.

Revol, Thierry: assistant professor at the Université Marc Bloch, Strasbourg, specialist on the Middle Ages.

Riethauser, Stéphane: journalist, founder and coordinator of the Swiss Commission jeunesse et école de l'antenne gaie suisse Pink Cross.

Rommeluère, Eric: vice-president of the Université Bouddhique Européenne.

Rousseau, Jean-Marie: union official, former editor of the monthly magazine *Homophonies*.

Row Kavi, Ashok: journalist, founder of the Indian gay newspaper, *Bombay Dost*, founder of The Humsafar Trust.

Sibalis, Michael: professor at Wilfrid Laurier University, Canada, specialist in the history of homosexuality in France.

Sidéris, Georges: historian, specialist on Byzantine history.

Simonetti, Gian-Luigi: former student at the Scuola normale superiore in Pisa, Italy, specialist in Italian literature.

Siouffi, Gilles: former student at the ENS, linguist, assistant professor at the Université Montpellier III.

Tamagne, Florence: historian, assistant professor at the Université Charles de Gaulle-Lille III, specialist on the history of homosexuality.

Tassin, Claude: biblical exegete, historian of Judaism, professor of theology and religious studies at the Institut catholique de Paris.

Teboul, Roger: hospital psychiatrist, ethnologist.

Tin, Louis-Georges: former student at the ENS, specialist on Renaissance literature, specialist in gender issues.

Vale, Alexandra Fleming Câmara: anthropologist, professor at the Universidade Estadual do Vale do Acaraú, Brazil, specialist in gender issues.

Venner, Fiammetta: publication director of *ProChoix*.

Waipang, Au: pioneer of gay activism in Singapore, leader of People Like Us.

Weishut, Daniel: psychologist, member of Amnesty International's LGBT Commission.

Weiss, Adam: student at Harvard University, specialist in gender issues during the Middle Ages.

Yi Huso: researcher, co-director of the Korean Sexual-Minority Culture and Rights Center.

Zaoui, Pierre: former student at the ENS, former member of ACT UP-Paris, specialist on ethical and political philosophy.

A

ABNORMAL

Anthropologist Mary Douglas contends that "it is not possible to define deviance until the extent of normalcy has been defined." Applied to the consolidation of sexual categories, Douglas's proposition can be inverted without questioning the ontological links between what is normal and what is excluded, or abnormal. Thus, speaking of heterosexuality does not absolutely imply a necessarily orthodox sexuality, as assumed by normative morality requirements. Douglas's proposition, therefore, carries with it a germ of criticism of nineteenth-century categorization, a method which simultaneously confirms one of its unspoken objectives: to normalize differently, but always normalizing. Obviously, the application of objective justification tests to subjective representations immediately results in a typological control and prioritization. Even without initial mention of negative or positive value, either implied or under the alibi of scientific character, perceptions inevitably establish morals, set limits, and reveal the forbidden or the wrongly authorized. Contemporary interpretation leaves little doubt about this and, as Mary McIntosh in "The Homosexual Role" contends: "the practice of social labeling of certain individuals as being deviants demonstrates a double mechanism of social control." The word "homosexuality" ("*homosexualität*") publicly appeared in print for the first time in 1869, in Prussia, in two pamphlets distributed by Karl Maria Kertbeny (alias Karoly Maria Benkert) in reaction to a Prussian bill intending to penalize sodomy. From that date forward, the word "homosexuality" has retained much of its essential meaning, always referring to the sexuality between persons of the same gender. It is very probable that the word "heterosexuality" ("*normalsexualität*") appeared around the same time or shortly thereafter. However, unlike the term "homosexual," whose definition has changed little since the nineteenth century, the meaning attributed to "heterosexual" has varied consistently over the years. Jonathan Katz, in his evocatively titled book, *The Invention of Heterosexuality*, notes that the word "heterosexual," introduced for the first time in the United States in 1892 in a Chicago medical journal, referred to a **perversion**, a "morbid sexual passion for a member of the opposite sex." The author of the article, Dr James G. Kiernan, claimed to refer to the definition proposed by Richard von Krafft-Ebing, whose *Psychopathia Sexualis* was not translated into English until 1893. But Kiernan in fact had mistranslated the German text, a mistranslation that persisted for quite some time; as late as the 1920s, for example, a prominent American dictionary continued to associate heterosexuality with a perversion. The confusion surrounding the definition of "heterosexual" may be further attributed to the fact that prior to current categorization, the sexual norm would have been linked to procreative sexuality, and not necessarily heterosexuality, as the terms are not interchangeable.

The denotative rigidity of the term "homosexual," while perhaps initially established to garner social scorn and therefore validate the normalcy of its binary opponent, "heterosexual," nonetheless attests to its originating and constant status. Following this logic, we could go so far as to assert that heterosexuality was born of homosexuality—the normal born of the abnormal.

The initial confusion between heterosexuality and "perversion" is possibly the effect of this mechanism; that the assumptions upon which the nineteenth-century authors had relied were the "anomalies." Then, in a process of contagion, everything that had been cited or mapped, whether positive or negative, became confused in a climate of "monstrosity." One only need look, even today, at the reactions of certain heterosexual people who are not inclined to question or even name their heterosexuality. They are so unused to defining and naming their practices, that when others qualify them, they perceive it as an insult.

The abnormal, therefore, is that to which we continually assign an identifying label, or word. Depending on the historical period, the abnormal person was an introvert, a Jew, a fag, a dyke, etc., who, once identified, was beaten, locked-up, disqualified, or mocked. While particulars vary, the abnormal person is always the one singled out. Disqualification, exclusion, and homophobia are all predicated upon the identification and articulation of the abnormal. Ironically, it is also through this identification that resistance is established: for the abnormal individual strikes back, forming alternative sub-cultures and political ideologies. However, it is important to keep in mind that abnormal persons, or minorities, also create, name, and reject representations of the abnormal within their own communities. Queen, fag, butch are labels that speak of internalized homophobia.

—*Catherine Deschamps*

Douglas, Mary. *Ainsi pensent les institutions*. Paris: Usher, 1989. [Published in the US as *How Institutions Think*. 1st ed. Syracuse, NY: Syracuse Univ. Press, 1986.]

Dynes, Wayne, ed. *Encyclopedia of Homosexuality*. New York: Garland Publishing Inc, 1990.

Foucault, Michel. *Les Anormaux, cours au Collège de France*. Paris: Gallimard/Le Seuil, 1999. [Published in the US as *Abnormal: Lectures at the Collège de France, 1974–1975*. New York: Picador, 2003.]

Goffman, Erving. *Stigmates*. Paris: Minuit, 1963. [Published in the US as *Stigma: Notes on the Management of Spoiled Identity*. New York: Prentice-Hall, 1963.]

Katz, Jonathan. *L'Invention de l'hétérosexualité*. Paris: EPEL, 2002. [Published in the US as *The Invention of Heterosexuality*. New York: Dutton, 1995.]

McIntosh, Mary. "The Homosexual Role." In *Queer Theology/Sociology*. Cambridge, Oxford: Blackwell Publishers, 1966.

Plummer, Kenneth. *Sexual Stigma: An Interactionist Account*. London: Routledge & Kegan Paul, 1975.

Rosario, Vernon, ed. *Science and Homosexualities*. New York, London: Routledge, 1997.

—*Heterosexism; Medicine; Otherness; Perversions; Psychiatry; Rhetoric; Shame; Theology.*

ADOPTION

With regard to adoption rights in France, the homosexuality of the adopting parents is considered prejudicial to the child's interest. Although the French Civil Code stipulates that "all persons aged twenty-eight years or older" have the right to adopt, in reality, candidates are often denied at the mere mention of their homosexuality. The procedure for adoption in France is made up of an administrative phase during which applicants must first be approved by social services; this is followed by a judicial phase during which the adoption is confirmed. In 1993, a single man mentioned his homosexuality during the social services interview and was immediately denied approval; the reasons given for the refusal were the "absence of a constant maternal reference" as well as his "lifestyle choice." At first overruled during the judicial phase, the rejection was finally validated by the Council of State in 1996, thus creating a legal precedence on the subject: the homosexuality of the adoptive parent or parents was enough justification to automatically refuse approval.

Initially, this **jurisprudence** could be considered in tandem with previous legal decisions in France with regard to single heterosexuals who wished to adopt. In one such case, the judge affirmed that the justification of the denial was not so much the single person's refusal to lead a "married" lifestyle, but rather the presumed "absence of the image of the other sex" in the life of the adopted child. However, when the adoptive parent is homosexual, it is a further complication: homosexuality itself implies the "absence of the image of the other sex." In this light, and contrary to what is officially provided for in the law, a homosexual in France can never hope to be allowed to adopt.

This jurisprudence is not unanimous in all jurisdictions of France, however. Regularly in fact, administrative courts annul refusals of acceptance based on the candidate's homosexuality. In their judgments, these courts consider that "this aspect of the [petitioner's] personality cannot justify a refusal of acceptance, unless it is accompanied by behavior that is prejudicial to the child's education." However, the Council of State inevitably **censures** these decisions.

Moreover, in February 2002, the European Court of Human Rights rendered a judgment, which is open to criticism, stating that refusal of acceptance by reason of homosexuality is not discriminatory, given the "divisions" among specialists with regard to the child's best interests, the "profound divergences" of national and international public opinion on the subject, as well as the small number of children available to be adopted in France.

As for same-sex couples, their legal inability to adopt lies in the fact that the Civil Code only allows adoption by married couples (that is to say, given the current status regarding gay marriage, heterosexual married couples). This legal language is nothing short of **discrimination** specifically targeted against gays and lesbians. Nevertheless, there is also an official will to explicitly maintain this form of discrimination. For example, in France in 1996, to guard against the possibility of allowing homosexuals to adopt, adoption rights were also refused to common-law couples. Moreover, during the 1999 debates on PaCS (Pacte civil de solidarité [Civil solidarity pact]), which would recognize civil unions between couples, whether gay or straight), the Minister of Justice repeatedly said: "The government will not propose to modify the legislation to allow two individuals of the same sex to jointly adopt a child." Further, she claimed that children need a "mental, social, and relational identity," which was only possible when the child had, "during his childhood and adolescence, a father and a mother." Previously invoked by psychoanalysts, anthropologists, and sociologists, the argument of the necessity of a masculine/feminine dynamic in children's lives was now being taken up by jurists.

Fundamentally, this definition of what makes a good parent puts into question the legitimacy of single-parent families, who are nevertheless protected by French law in the same manner as other families. Further, the definition contradicts the evolution of family law in France since the end of the 1960s, which has been characterized by a decreased importance placed on masculine or feminine parental roles. The view may be changing, however; in 2006, the Court of Cassation (the court of last resort) ruled that parental rights over one partner's biological child can be granted to partners in a same-sex relationship. In Denmark, Germany, Israel, and Norway, same-sex partners also may adopt their partner's child. Elsewhere, as of 2007, Andorra, Belgium, Guam, Iceland, the Netherlands, South Africa, Spain, Sweden, and the United Kingdom permit same-sex couples to adopt children. On the other side of the Atlantic, numerous states in the US also recognize this right of same-sex partners to adopt the other partner's child, whether biological or adopted; and some states

also recognize the right of joint adoption by homosexuals. As for Canada, eight of ten provinces now allow adoption by same-sex couples. Despite these recent strides, however, many countries still do not allow gays and lesbians to adopt at all.

—*Daniel Borrillo and Thomas Formond*

Association des parents gays et lesbians. *Petit guide biblio-graphique à l'usage des familles homoparentales et des autres.* Paris: APGL, 1997.

Borrillo, Daniel. "La protection juridique des nouvelles formes familiales; le cas des familles homoparentales" *Mouvements*, no. 8 (March–April 2000).

———, and Thierry Pitois. "Adoption et homosexualité; analyse critique de l'arrêt du Conseil d'Etat du 9 octobre 1996." In *Homosexualités et droit*. Paris: Presses universitaires de France, 1999.

Borrillo, Daniel, Eric Fassin, and Marcela Iacub, eds. *Au-delà du PaCS*. Paris: Presses universitaires de France, 1999.

Formond, Thomas. "Les Discriminations fondées sur l'orientation sexuelle en droit privé." Doctoral thesis on privacy rights. Université de Paris X–Nanterre (September 2002).

Gross, Martine, ed. *Homoparentalités, Etat des lieux*. Paris: ESF, 2000.

Leroy-Forgeot, Flora. *Les Enfants du PACS, réalités de l'homoparentalité*. Paris: L'Atelier de l'Archer, 1999.

Nadaud, Stéphane. *Homoparentalité, une nouvelle chance pour la famille?* Paris: Fayard, 2002.

—*Discrimination; European Law; Family; Jurisprudence; Marriage; Parenting.*

AFRICA. See *Africa, Central & Eastern; Africa, Southern; Africa, Western*

AFRICA, CENTRAL & EASTERN

Because they were colonized by a variety of nations, the countries that make up Central and East Africa do not all have homophobic legislation. It is significant to note that, as a remnant of France's influence, many former French colonies do not have sodomy laws; homophobia may be quite strong in these countries, but it is social rather than legal. Such is the case in the Central African Republic, the Gabonese Republic, the Republic of Chad, and the Democratic Republic of the Congo (DRC) (but even though homosexual relations are not illegal in the DRC, its diplomats continue to profess that "the practice of homosexuality does not exist" in their country). Elsewhere in the region, the law criminalizes homosexuality, with varying degrees of severity.

As is common in the rest of the continent, homophobia in Central Africa is often linked to the idea that homosexuality is not part of the history of its societies. More recently, the taboo has been lifted, and ethnologists have remarked that while homosexuality as a permanent way of life was very rare in African societies—as a result of the condemnation of a sexual practice which does not lead to reproduction—instances of homosexual activity among young people were by contrast relatively frequent; for example, among the Tutsi and Hutu populations and notably in the royal court, where women were excluded. The Azande, who live primarily in the DRC but also make up about forty-five percent of the Central African Republic's population, even had forms of homosexual marriage among warriors. Among the Lango of Uganda, there was a small class of men known as *jo apele* ("the impotents") who could marry men, dress as women, and simulate female menstruation. It was believed that men who behaved in this manner were inhabited by the spirits of the ancients, and in this respect, they were considered useful to the community. More markedly, the issue of the Uganda Martyrs (a group of Ugandan Christians murdered by Mwanga II, the king between 1885 and 1887 of what was then Buganda) provides insight into the breadth of homosexuality in certain precolonial African courts and the acute crisis engendered by the homophobia of British missionaries: Mwanga II, who passionately loved young men, slept with his pages, but was outraged and had them massacred when they vehemently refused his advances after they converted to Christianity.

Laws are more homophobic in East Africa. As can be seen by looking at the map drawn by afrol News, the African news agency, homosexuality is currently illegal in almost every state of the region (Ethiopia, Djibouti, Kenya, Somalia, Sudan, and Tanzania). It would seem that Christian (Ethiopia and Kenya) and Muslim influences account for part of the reason for this (Islamist thought is increasing throughout the region, as proven by Sudan and Somalia's recent history). The question of the degree to which **Islam** influences African homophobia is unclear: for one thing, it appears that

Muslims in Zanzibar—the principal leaders of East Africa's economy prior to European colonization during the nineteenth century (they were particularly formidable slave traders)—actually contributed to the spreading of homosexual activity between older men and adolescents. With regard to the rest of the region, there is a linguistic term for the male couple in Swahili, the region's dominant language: *basha/msenge* (erastes/eromenos). It is even said that in present-day Tanzania, coastal Muslim populations are more tolerant of homosexuality than Christians or Animists in the interior. That being said, in Africa as elsewhere, homosexuality remains a taboo according to Islam. It may be easy enough to engage in homosexual relations, but it is understood that one does not discuss them, let alone make them the subject of demands; and the taboo is even greater with regard to lesbianism.

Sudan

Even though the various peoples of Sudan (notably the Nubas and the Azandes) have rich homosexual traditions, including forms of marriage between males, the country is one of the world's most homophobic states, as exemplified by the particulars of its penal code and the actions of its representatives on international matters.

Subject to radical Islamism since a coup in 1989 brought the National Islamic Front to power, and long exhausted by the effects of a protracted civil war that preceded it (between the Islamist authorities in the north and the rebel forces of the Sudan People's Liberation Army in the south), Sudan does not meet the legal standards of a democratic state, as revealed by its harsh penal code. Article 316 of the 1983 code that was based on *sharia* (the body of Islamic religious law) provides for the death penalty for married men who commit any act of sodomy (and 100 lashes for those who are unmarried). Even though it appears that the death penalty is actually not carried out for this crime, Sudanese homosexuals are nonetheless condemned to the spiral of silence (the fact that asserts that a person is less likely to be vocal on a subject for fear of reprisal or isolation from the majority) that often prevails in Islamic countries. Further, in Sudan, the most obscurantist homophobia is accompanied by other dubious practices, such as a rather widespread **tolerance** of pedophilic violence, an active slave trade, and the ongoing sexual mutilation of young girls through female circumcision.

On the international front, in 2006, Sudan, as a member of the United Nations Economic and Social Council, voted to deny UN consultative status to two gay rights organizations, the International Lesbian and Gay Association (ILGA), based in Brussels, and the Danish National Association for Gays and Lesbians of Denmark. Joining Sudan in voting "no" were such countries as Iran and the United States (Sudan voted the same way when the ILGA applied four years earlier, in 2002).

Ethiopia

Ethiopia is doubly unique: it is both a very old Christian state (with a Muslim minority) and a region that was only belatedly and to a small degree colonized (by Fascist Italy). It was its indigenous Christian influence that resulted in Article 629 of the Ethiopian penal code that prohibits homosexual acts, male or female. Such acts are punishable by up to ten years in prison, particularly if the victim was subjected to acts of cruelty or was under the age of fifteen.

Ethiopia, like Sudan, also voted against granting the ILGA consultative status on the UN Economic and Social Council in 2002.

Somalia

In Somalia, where the majority of the population is Muslim, Article 409 of the penal code of 1973 makes all homosexual relations punishable by three months' to three years' imprisonment. Additionally, Article 410 provides for, among other things, "security measures" (i.e. police surveillance) against those who have been convicted for the crime of homosexuality "to ensure that [they do] not engage in these activities again."

Somalia's political instability over the past twenty years, instigated by the start of the Somali Civil War beginning in 1986, has worsened the situation for homosexuals. In February 2001, the press in Somalia's capital Mogadishu reported that an Islamist tribunal in Bosaso (in the autonomous northeast region of Puntland) had condemned a lesbian couple to death by stoning. Under strong international pressure, Puntland authorities claimed that the media had fabricated the entire story in order to discredit the newly autonomous region. It is difficult to ascertain the exact fate of homosexuals in the various parts of the country, but every indication leads one to believe that it is far from favorable.

Kenya

In Kenya, homosexuality is criminalized according to Sections 162 to 165 of the penal code, and punishable by five to fourteen years' imprisonment. Homophobia is strong, reinforced by politicians (notably Daniel Arap Moi, Kenya's president from 1978 to 2002) and the churches (which have often conveyed the **heterosexism** and the taboos of Kenya's former colonizer, Britain). Homosexuals are commonly ridiculed, harassed, and beaten; violence against them is high in the capital Nairobi and slightly rarer on the Mombasa coast. It must be noted, however, that Kenya's indigenous homosexual tradition is relatively rich, in part due to the Arab-Muslim influence, as suggested in the book on the history of homosexuality in Africa, *Boy-Wives and Female Husbands* (edited by Will Roscoe and Stephen O. Murray).

In the twentieth century, Kenya played an important role in the construction of a homophobic African identity: As early as 1938, Jomo Kenyatta, the future first president of an independent Kenya, affirmed in his book *Facing Mount Kenya* (the first ethnographic work written by an African, with a preface by anthropologist Bronislaw Malinowski) that homosexuality was unknown among the Kikuyu, Kenya's most populous ethnic group. He based this theory on the (erroneous) belief that there was no word for homosexuality in any African language. Further, the practice of mutual masturbation between men was common in precolonial African societies, a fact which Kenyatta went to great lengths to disassociate from homosexuality. The acclaim accorded to Kenyatta's book contributed to the establishment of postcolonial stereotypes, presently embraced by a number of Africans and African-Americans, which associate black cultures with a certain sexual purity, manifested by their "exclusive" heterosexuality untainted by the perversions of European cultures.

Uganda

In Uganda, any person who has "carnal knowledge of any person against the order of nature" is a criminal under Articles 140, 141, and 143 of the penal code. The maximum penalty is life imprisonment for an "active" homosexual, but only seven years' imprisonment for a "passive" homosexual. Also, homosexual fondling (considered a gross indecency) can be punished by up to five years in prison.

Public opinion in Uganda is very hostile toward gays

and lesbians: those who are known to be homosexual are driven away by their families and lose their friends, jobs, homes, and right to an education (in 1999, twenty-five students were expelled from a high school in Ntare for being gay; later that same year, four students were expelled from a university for the same reason). According to some, Ugandans are generally in favor of punishing homosexuals by stoning.

Yoweri Museveni, the president of Uganda since 1986, is very homophobic: on September 27, 1999, he declared that homosexuality is foreign to Ugandan culture and threatened the gay population with widespread arrest, imprisonment, and fines (and he asked the Ugandan Secret Service to be prepared to make such arrests). President Museveni's homophobic declaration aroused a strong international reaction: a month later, the US State Department issued a statement to the Ugandan government expressing "deep concern and consternation" over his anti-gay stance. But a wave of repression still followed Museveni's provocative statement: at the end of the same year, five gay and lesbian activists who were members of the newly formed homosexual group Right Companion were arrested, beaten, and subject to extortion. In 2000, a gay activist from another group, Lesgabix, was assassinated in Kampala.

On the religious front, homosexuality has also caused rifts among various Christian factions in the country. In May 2001, Christopher Ssenyonjo, a former bishop of the Anglican Church of Uganda, took up the defense of homosexuals (he is also active with the gay Anglican organization Integrity Uganda). His former colleagues, choked with indignation, accused him of "betraying his faith for thirty pieces of silver" and serving the interest and neocolonialist culture of gay America. (In 2006, Ssenyonjo, excommunicated from the Anglican Church of Uganda, formed the new Charismatic Church of Uganda.) Also, the Catholic Church, through Cardinal Emmanuel Wamala, condemns homosexuality at the same level as corruption, abortion, and "all forms of behavior that are contrary to the laws of God and our own culture."

Tanzania

Male homosexuality has been illegal in Tanzania since colonial times (Tanzania was a German colony from 1884 until World War I, then a British colony until independence was declared in 1961). Articles 154 to 157 of Tanzania's penal code render all homosexual relations between men punishable by fourteen years' imprisonment (there is no mention of women).

Having said this, the law does not seem to be regularly applied, or if so, only erratically. In 1998, a British citizen was expelled from Tanzania for homosexuality; however, it appears that the fact he was a successful businessman in the country was the bigger offense. And there is a burgeoning gay movement in the country; Community Peer Support Services (CPSS), an association for the defense of gays and lesbians, has been in existence since 1997 and currently has 334 members whom it trains to become activists. According to CPSS, the situation of gays and lesbians is better in Tanzania than in all its neighboring countries.

Democratic Republic of the Congo (formerly Zaire, Congo-Kinshasa, Belgian Congo)

It is believed that male homosexuality in the Democratic Republic of the Congo (DRC) (a separate country than its neighbor to the west, the Republic of the Congo) is punishable by up to five years' imprisonment, but in fact, the legal status of homosexuals in the DRC is unclear: Articles 168, 169, and 172 of the penal code make sexual assault a crime, not sexual relations between consenting adults. The same vague legislation can be found in neighboring Rwanda.

Nonetheless, hostility toward homosexuals in this former Belgian colony is strong, marked by the proselytism of Christian missionaries in the nineteenth and twentieth centuries (the population is seventy-five percent Catholic, twenty percent Protestant). In 1992, the most virulent anti-gay delegate at the General Conference of the United Methodist Church was Reverend Kasongo Muza from the DRC, who declared: "We do not want our culture to be contaminated by a disease." But homosexuality was not imported into Congolese culture; there is evidence that it is indigenous. In certain Mbo tribes, for example, it is traditional for a homosexual to play a part in the initiation rites of boys.

Cameroon

According to Article 347 of Cameroon's penal code, homosexuality is illegal and punishable by six months' to five years' imprisonment, and the punishment is doubled if one of the participants is under the age of twenty-one. It is often said in Cameroon, as in much of the rest of Africa, that homosexuality was imported from elsewhere, in this case introduced by German, then French colonizers; this is not true, however. As early as 1914, German ethnographer Günther Tessman discovered evidence of sodomy as a tradition among the Fang culture; these relations were supposed to bring material benefits to the dominant participant.

The reality of life for Cameroon's homosexuals is poorly documented, but the evidence that exists suggests that it is very bad. Cameroon is in fact one of the countries where legal and judicial corruption is the most common; and of the hundreds of individuals each year who are arrested, tortured, and even executed without a fair trial by paramilitary units, it is highly likely that a disproportionate number are homosexual. However, despite these odds, a handful of courageous gay activists from Cameroon participated in the ILGA's 1999 world conference.

—*Pierre Albertini*

Bleys, Rudi C. *The Geography of Perversion: Male to Male Sexual Behaviour Outside the West and the Ethnographic Imagination, 1750–1918*. London: Cassell, 1996.

Delaney, Joyce, and Catherine McKinley, eds. *Afrekete: An Anthology of Black Lesbian Writing*. New York: Anchor Books, 1995.

Epprecht, Marc. "Africa: Procolonial Sub-Saharan Africa." In *Gay Histories and Cultures*. Edited by George E. Haggerty. New York/London: Garland, 2000.

Hyam, Ronald. *Empire and Sexuality: The British Experience*. Manchester, UK: Manchester Univ. Press. 1990.

Kenyatta, Jomo. *Facing Mount Kenya: The Tribal Life of the Gikuyu*. London: Secker & Warburg, 1938.

Murray, Stephen O. "Gender-Defined Homosexual Roles in Sub-Saharan African Islamic Cultures" and "The Will Not To Know: Islamic Accommodation of Male Homosexuality." In *Islamic Homosexualities: Culture, History & Literature*. Edited by Stephen O. Murray and Will Roscoe. New York: New York Univ. Press, 1997.

———, and Will Roscoe. *Islamic Homosexualities: Culture, History & Literature*. New York: New York Univ. Press, 1997.

———, eds. *Boy-Wives and Female Husbands: Studies of African Homosexualities*. London: Macmillan, 1998 [notably the English language translation of the article by Gunther Tessmann, "Homosexualities among the Negroes of Cameroon and a Pangwe Tale" [public domain in German], 1921.

Towles, Joseph. *Nkumbi Initiation: Ritual & Structure Among the Mbo of Zaire*. Tervuren, Belgium: Musée royal de l'Afrique centrale, 1993.

—*Africa, Southern; Africa, Western; Anthropology; Islam; Maghreb.*

AFRICA, SOUTHERN

While individuals who were exclusively homosexual were rare in precolonial times, it appears that homosexual practices have existed in the region of Southern Africa since ancient times. Ethnologists have determined that "homosexual marriage" existed among Zulu warriors (which was supposed to give them a sense of solidarity with one another) as well as in societies where the male-to-female ratio was unbalanced (in particular as a result of polygamy among the elite), as was the case with the Kololo-Lozi of western Zambia. Moreover, in Angola, transvestite "sodomites" were endowed with positive magical powers by neighboring societies. Starting in the fifteenth century, such behavior was considered scandalous by the region's European colonizers, be they Portuguese, Dutch, or British. It was also discovered that some slaves from the region maintained these behaviors when they were transported overseas; they were among those condemned to be burned at the stake during the Spanish and Portuguese **Inquisitions** in Latin America. In the nineteenth century, the reinforcement of colonization in Southern Africa, as well as the prevalence of missionary activities in the area, underlined the colonizers' homophobia and their consideration of homosexuality as taboo, at the price of often-noted paradoxes: firstly, many colonizers (among them Cecil Rhodes) were themselves homosexual; and secondly, the mining industry developed by British colonizers in the region resulted in large concentrations of male workers, thereby fostering homosexual practices among the black populations.

This period of the homosexual taboo in Southern Africa has only recently ended. It was during the mid-1990s that the homosexual question became a very important political theme, due to the policy of recognizing gay and lesbian rights adopted by the country of South Africa at the end of the apartheid era. South Africa's progressive advances at this time created tension among neighboring states, as well as outbursts of sometimes extremely violent homophobia. But these advances also launched a continent-wide debate on homosexuality and homophobia, and its commensurate relationship to democracy (or lack thereof). These discussions initiated a new way of thinking on the subject as a result. Sheila Lapinsky, a well-known lesbian activist and African National Congress (ANC) member in South Africa, was the first to demand the acknowledgment that the homophobia of the Rwandan bishops not be separated from their terrible compromise during the genocide.

South Africa

Apartheid provided a great example of the ties that exist between homophobia and racism. If Afrikaners in South Africa were generally more racist than the British (who abolished slavery between 1833 and 1834), both shared the same good old homophobic sensibilities that were Protestant in origin. Afrikaner legislation condemned male homosexuality in the seventeenth and eighteenth centuries, followed by British legislation in the nineteenth century. It is known that the British victory in the Boer War (1899–1902) led, paradoxically, to further empowering the Afrikaners, who during the twentieth century dominated the Union of South Africa since its creation in 1910. South Africa officially adopted the apartheid system in 1948 when it enacted a number of harsh segregationist laws (including making interracial marriage illegal); in 1957, it adopted homophobic legislation in the form of the Sexual Offences Act, forbidding sodomy, homosexual intercrural coitus, mutual masturbation, and all homosexual acts in public places or "private areas where there are more than two people." Until the 1980s, South African police often raided reputedly "gay" private parties in order to uphold the Act; in 1966, one party in particular with some 350 guests received a great deal of media coverage. In 1967, and again in 1985, there were movements to criminalize all forms of homosexuality, private or otherwise, including lesbianism (which was never illegal, even if it was often clandestine). Regardless, the legislation of 1957 was rigorously applied well into the final years of apartheid. The apogee of legal proceedings against male homosexuals occurred in 1991, when 476 proceedings resulted in 324 convictions. As for the South African **army**, it subjected soldiers accused of homosexuality to various types of aversion therapy, which could include electrical shocks and chemical castration, until the 1980s.

Afrikaner homophobia had very deep religious roots: for the Boers, apartheid was founded on the Biblical "Curse of Ham," in which blacks are "cursed" to be servants; similarly, the forbidding of homosexuality was based on an ancient source, specifically the Biblical condemnation of **Sodom** as well as the writings of St **Paul**. It was also linked to the Boer population's Anglophobia, as Britain was viewed as a country of decadent morals. It also shared some similarities with homophobia as it was expressed by the Nazis: for example, both considered homosexuality not only a sign of biological **degeneracy** (a serious pathology that compromised the survival of a threatened, dominant race), but also a gravely asocial attitude in that it had little regard for the barriers and separations erected by the state; the fact that certain white homosexuals were more apt to associate with non-whites made them even more **criminal**. In order to staunch any political or legal progress either by homosexuals or non-Afrikaners, the platform of the National Party, which dominated the political scene in South Africa at the time, was based on Afrikaner populism, which was hostile to the mixing of social classes, urban culture, and intellectuals, and played up the confusion between homosexuality and **pedophilia**. It also encouraged political splits within the newly forming gay community. For example, the Gay Association of South Africa, the first South African gay association founded in 1982, was almost exclusively composed of whites and claimed to be "apolitical," meaning it refused to condemn apartheid. It was not until 1988 that an anti-apartheid homosexual association formed: the Gay and Lesbian Organisation of the Witwatersrand (GLOW), a multiracial and political association hostile to all forms of **discrimination**.

From that moment, a radically new political context emerged in South Africa, marked by the liberation of Nelson Mandela from prison in 1990, the abolition of apartheid laws in 1991, and finally the election of Mandela to the Presidency of the Republic in 1994. Concurrent to these political strides, progress was also made by the country's gay and lesbian community. The first ever Gay Pride in South Africa, and in fact on the whole African continent, was organized by GLOW in 1990. Gay and lesbian visibility increased, as did the number of areas where they could congregate; suddenly it was possible for groups like LILACS (Lesbians in Love and Compromising Situations) to flourish. The gay community, more and more conscious of itself, began to demand equal rights, based on the model that black ANC militants had honed over the decades. It is thus that the 1996 South African Constitution affirmed (the first in the world to do so) the equality of all of its citizens, "regardless of their race, sexual identity, gender, **family** situation, social or ethnic origins, skin color, sexual orientation, age, eventual handicaps, religion, beliefs, culture, language and birth" (Constitution of the Republic of South Africa, Bill of Rights, Law Number 108 of 1996). This document is of capital importance because it takes precedence over all other laws as a last resort: for example, the National Coalition for Gay and Lesbian Equality refers to it when lobbying for the repeal of older laws. The Constitution is also invoked in order to obtain certain other legal advances for gays and lesbians, notably relating to non-discrimination, **employment** law, and matrimonial law. In 2006, same-sex **marriage** became legal in South Africa when the Civil Unions Bill was enacted, becoming the first country in Africa to do so. Due to progressive legislation such as this, morale among gays and lesbians in South Africa is high, as a black participant of Pride of Johannesburg noted in 1994: "I'm nothing more than a little drag queen; but you know what? Since I've heard speak of this constitution, I feel free inside."

Such constitutional protection does not, however, signify the end of homophobia in South Africa; it survives among white conservatives and Christian and Muslim lobbyists who did everything possible to prevent the introduction of the equality clause in the 1996 Constitution. Homophobia can also be found among certain black South Africans sensitive to the "pseudo-ethnic" idea that homosexuality is an element of "non-African" culture imported by colonizers. This is what friends and defenders of Winnie Mandela affirmed in 1991, when she was tried for having kidnapped and murdered a fourteen-year-old adolescent whom she claimed she was "saving" from the homosexual advances of a white clergyman: outside her trial, a banner read "Homosex is not in black culture." And when Barney Pityana, Chair of the South African Human Rights Commission, was confronted by the idea that "the freedom of sexual orientation is not African," he responded: "If you are correct, then the repression of minorities, corruption, and the violation of human rights are fundamentally African." Finally, despite legal advances, gays and lesbians are not immune to the high level of violence that continues to plague South African society. (customs not being as advanced as the law).

Zimbabwe
As is often the case, one of the effects of colonization

in what was Rhodesia (a British colony from 1895 to 1920), along with widespread Christian **proselytism**, was the consideration of conjugal, monogamous heterosexuality as the only legitimate means of sexual relations. The territory endured the harshness of homophobic Anglo-Saxon laws even beyond its independence in 1965 and its later decolonization when it was renamed Zimbabwe in 1980. It should be noted, however, that British colonization itself, through its development of a mining industry populated almost exclusively by male workers, created conditions ripe for homosexual behavior, in which "marriages" took place between older workers and younger ones who were referred to as "the wife"; the same appears to have existed among the women left in the villages, in "mother-baby" partnerships. (The same phenomenon occurred in South Africa.)

Since its independence, Zimbabwe has not changed its harsh laws regarding homosexuality, a crime which can result in prison sentences of up to ten years. In 1989, a gay and lesbian group called Gays and Lesbians of Zimbabwe (GALZ) was established, composed of both whites and blacks, and it was not long before it clashed with Zimbabwe's President Robert Mugabe, who, during the 1990s, revealed himself to be one of the most homophobic heads of state in the world. His anti-gay stance has many origins: Christian catechism learned from missionaries as a youth; the influence of Kenyan leader and ethnologist Jomo Kenyatta who, as early as 1938, affirmed that homosexuality was completely unknown to African populations; and an open hostility towards South Africa's recent political and social evolution and, more precisely, Nelson Mandela who, at Mugabe's expense, became the biggest political personality in the region of Southern Africa as a result of the end of apartheid. In 1995, not satisfied with refusing GALZ to have a booth at the Zimbabwe International Book Fair in Harare, Mugabe felt it appropriate to explain his position in the following way: "Lesbians and gays are inferior to dogs and pigs; they deserve no rights. They represent a form of Western **decadence** that has no real ties to authentic Zimbabwean culture." This statement, which aroused considerable emotion around the world, expresses rather well the mental state in which homophobes find themselves, in this case confusing the natural with the historical and native traditions with missionary practices. While Cecil Rhodes' sexual orientation is of no doubt, we know today that homosexual-like

relations existed in the Shoa and Ndebele populations before the arrival of colonizers. Historian Marc
Epprecht uncovered evidence that, since the beginning
of Rhodesian colonization, simple villagers who had
never had contact with Westerners were condemned
for homosexuality; and research by psychologist Marc
Carlson revealed that homosexuality as a tradition is
present in 122 tribes in Zimbabwe.

In 1996, GALZ challenged Mugabe's Harare Book
Fair refusal before Zimbabwe's High Court, which sided with the association. However, this only served to
increase the level of intimidation by homophobic students, religious leaders, and Mugabe's henchmen, and, at
the last moment, the country's Minister of the Interior
published a decree once again prohibiting GALZ from
participating in the book fair in order "to take care of
the Zimbabwean people's culture's health." Ever since,
gays and lesbians in Zimbabwe serve regularly as scapegoats for the nation's myriad frustrations created by its
catastrophic economic situation. Police harassment is
incessant, taking the form of arbitrary arrests, beatings,
and even assassinations. But GALZ's role was revolutionary, as noted by South African researcher Peter Vale:
never before had a minority rights group in the region
dared to defy the authority of a national leader. Thus,
GALZ cleared the way for other groups demanding
progressive change, including unions, churches, and
human rights organizations. Meanwhile, the protests
against Mugabe have become international in scope:
one example is British gay activist Peter Tatchell who,
inspired by Chilean dictator Augusto Pinochet's arrest
when he landed on British soil, requested the same
of the Zimbabwean president while on British soil in
October 1999, to no avail; he did the same in 2001
when Mugabe arrived in Brussels, where Tatchell was
violently attacked by the president's bodyguards as a
result. Mugabe himself, who is also quite anglophobic,
once criticized Tony Blair's government as being made
up, according to him, of "gay gangsters."

In a twist of fate, Robert Mugabe's presidential predecessor, Methodist pastor Canaan Banana, was himself
caught up in a sensitive morality scandal, accused of
having committed, during his presidency (1980–87),
numerous homosexual rapes of his collaborators and
bodyguards. Banana fled to Botswana, and then to South
Africa. Despite Mugabe's attempts to silence the scandal, Banana was condemned in absentia to one year in
prison in 1998; he returned to his country to serve his
sentence and was released in 2001. He died in 2003.

Zambia

Conditions for homosexuals are very poor in Zambia
(formerly Northern Rhodesia), where the nation's
sodomy law calls for sentences of up to fourteen years
in prison. Zambian President Frederick J. T. Chiluba
(from 1991 to 2002) was only slightly less homophobic than Zimbabwe's Robert Mugabe. His Minister
of Justice, Vincent Malambo, once publicly stated that
"homosexuality is an abomination as much for Africans
as it is for Christians."

Under the progressive influence of South Africa,
however, things started to change in Zambia at the
end of the 1990s. In July 1998, a young homosexual named Francis Chisambisha came out in an article published in *The Post*, Zambia's leading newspaper. He stated that his sexual identity in no way
betrayed his African heritage. A few weeks later, in
September 1998, at the instigation of Zambian gay
activist Gershom Musonda, the country's first gay
organization, LEGATRA (Lesbians, Gays, Bisexuals
& Transgender Persons Association), was formed,
with the goal of supplying members with psychological support, legal advice, and health information.
LEGATRA works closely with Amnesty International,
the Zimbabwean association GALZ, and the Zambian
rights organization Zambia Independent Monitoring
Team (ZIMT), which specializes in monitoring the
nation's elections, and whose courageous president,
Alfred Zulu, affirmed that the simple application of
Zambia's existing Constitution could be enough to
ensure protection of the gay community. LEGATRA
has sought to obtain official recognition from the government, but this has been in vain given that the nation's anti-sodomy laws are still in effect; according to
the government, such recognition would "encourage
the crime." Unfortunately, without this recognition
(which would permit legal lobbying), it is unforeseeable that the sodomy law will be repealed.

In 2001, the debates still raged in Zambia between
liberals in favor of decriminalizing homosexuality and
conservatives who consider that any reform would
be damaging to African culture and Christian morality. It should be noted that gay and lesbian activists in
Zambia are in a constant state of danger: the president
of LEGATRA has been assaulted twice, resulting in
permanent damage, at any moment, a homosexual can
be arrested for disobeying the law or for conspiring
against it. In December 2006, the Zambian government said it will never pass a law to allow gay mar-

riages. Minister of Home Affairs, Ronnie Shikapwasha, indicated that the country must maintain its Christian status and will not allow sinful practices, as homosexual marriages are a sin in the eyes of God.

Namibia

The nation of Namibia, formerly known as South West Africa, was colonized first by the Germans, then placed under British mandate after World War I, but in effect governed by South Africa; it has only known independence since 1990. The country's new Constitution was liberal and egalitarian, and did not outlaw homosexuality. That being said, many of its leaders have been clearly homophobic, not only referencing Biblical interdicts, but also taking up the notion that homosexuality was imported to the region by colonizers, and is foreign to African tradition. (It is interesting to note that such politicians also stigmatize foreigners present upon Namibian soil.) Around 1995, many of the nation's cabinet ministers denounced homosexuality as a "non-African scourge on society" and a "mental illness" treatable by hormone therapy. Beginning in 1996, Sam Nujoma, President of Namibia between 1990 and 2005, formally condemned homosexuality on many occasions, accusing gays and lesbians of being agents of European imperialism and of destroying local culture by virtue of their "gayism." In October 2000, he asked gays and lesbians to leave the country; around the same time, Nujoma's Minister of the Interior Jerry Ekandjo commissioned a 700-man police unit aimed at "the elimination of gays and lesbians from the surface of Namibia." Ekandjo also remarked that the Namibian Constitution does not guarantee any rights to homosexuals.

In spite of these very difficult conditions, or because of them, a gay and lesbian movement surfaced in Namibia in 1989, when a group of lesbians founded the Sister Namibia Collective; later, they associated themselves with other gay activists to launch the Rainbow Project in 1997, composed of over 1,000 members. The Rainbow Project was the third gay and lesbian movement in Africa, in addition to those in South Africa and Zimbabwe; in addition, the first Gay Pride celebration in Namibia took place in the capital city of Windhoek in 2000.

Botswana

In Botswana, a state surrounded by South Africa, Namibia, and Zimbabwe, male homosexuality has been outlawed since colonial times; deemed "carnal relations against nature," such crimes are punishable by up to two years of imprisonment. Homophobia among the political establishment is also rampant, as evidenced by the criminalization of lesbianism in a broadening of sodomy laws in June of 1998.

In January of 1999, the Botswana Christian Council called for the repeal of laws on homosexuality. Reverend Rupert Hambira based the decision on evangelical charity ("We must not judge others; we must leave judgment to God") and noted that homophobic laws cannot be based on the Bible, as it is "full of human errors and subjective opinions" and was used by the Boers to justify apartheid. Hambira was supported by the head of the University of Botswana's sociology department, Dr Mulingi, who, while personally disapproving of homosexuality, refuted the homophobic argument pertaining to its non-African character: on the contrary, he argued, homosexual relations were common in Central Africa before colonization. These affirmations provoked violently hostile reactions from University of Botswana students, whose leader, Biti Butale, decried: "We are horrified by homosexuality and other fads of Western philanthropists."

A gay and lesbian movement, LeGaBiBo (Lesbians, Gays, and Bisexuals of Botswana), appeared at the end of the 1990s, developed under the protection of a very active human rights organization named Ditshwanelo, which in 2000 received the Felipa de Souza Award for its actions in support of homosexuals. In 1996 and in 2001, encouraged by South Africa's progressive achievements, a gay activist named Utjijwa Kanani, with the support of renowned British human rights lawyer Peter Duffy, contested the homophobic articles of the Botswanan penal code before the High Court, believing that they contradicted the fundamental values of the nation's Constitution.

Mozambique

Like Angola, another former Portuguese colony, Mozambique considers homosexuality to be a behavior prejudicial to public morality. Articles 70 and 71 of the Mozambiquan penal code criminalize male homosexuality; they stipulate that homosexual acts are punishable by three years of imprisonment in a re-education center, where inmates are subject to forced labor. However, there is reason for optimism; as of November 2007, a new gay rights movement has begun in the form of a gay organization (albeit unregistered), and politicians have not ruled out pro-gay legal reforms in the future.

—*Pierre Albertini*

Clark, Bev. "Zimbabwe." In *Lesbian Histories & Cultures.* New York/London: Garland, 2000.

Delaney, Joyce, and Catherine McKinley, eds. *Afrekete: An Anthology of Black Lesbian Writing.* New York: Anchor Books, 1995.

De Vos, Pierre. "Une nation aux couleurs de l'arc-en-ciel? Egalité et préférences: la Constitution de l'Afrique du Sud." In *Homosexualités et droit.* By Daniel Borrillo. Paris: Presses universitaires de France, 1998.

Dunton, Chris. *Human Rights and Homosexuality in Southern Africa.* Uppsala, Sweden: Nordiska Afrikainstitutet, 1996.

Epprecht, Marc. "Good God Almighty, What's This!: Homosexual 'Crime' in Early Colonial Zimbabwe." In *Boy-Wives and Female Husbands: Studies of African Homosexualities.* Edited by Steven O. Murray and Will Roscoe. London: Macmillan Press, 1998.

Gevisser, Mark, and Edwin Cameron, eds. *Defiant Desire: Gay & Lesbian Lives in South Africa.* Johannesburg: Ravan, 1994.

Hyam, Ronald. *Empire and Sexuality: The British Experience.* Manchester: Manchester Univ. Press, 1990.

Isaacs, Gordon, and Brian McKendrick. *Male Homosexuality in South Africa: Identity Formation, Culture and Crisis.* Cape Town: Oxford Univ. Press, 1992.

Murray Steven O., and Will Roscoe, eds. *Boy-Wives and Female Husbands: Studies of African Homosexualities.* London: Macmillan Press, 1998.

Zwicker, Heather. "Zimbabwe." In *Gay Histories & Cultures.* Edited by George E. Haggerty. New York/London: Garland, 2000.

—*Africa, Central & Eastern; Africa, Western; Anthropology; Rhetoric; Violence.*

AFRICA, WESTERN

The region commonly referred to as West Africa comprises numerous countries: Benin, Burkina Faso, Cape Verde, the Ivory Coast, Gambia, Ghana, Guinea, Guinea-Bissau, Liberia, Mali, Mauritania, Niger, Nigeria, Senegal, Sierra Leone, and Togo; Cameroon might also be added to this list, given its history and diverse ethnic groups (Fulani, Hausa, etc.) are largely tied to this region.

Currently, each country in this region has tended toward political pluralism, which has allowed a certain degree of democratic functioning. In Ghana, Mali, and Senegal, the changeover of political power between parties has been relatively satisfactory; however, other countries such as the Ivory Coast, Liberia, Niger, and Nigeria have experienced political instability in this regard. Generally, citizens in these countries have demanded constitutional reforms that would allow for greater democracy; however, the revision of legal texts and political policy necessary for such change are not to be found on many ruling governments' agendas. In such unfavorable conditions, debate on individual liberties, let alone the **decriminalization** and recognition of homosexuality, is not possible.

Thus, in Ghana, as in Nigeria, Togo, and Mali, homosexuality is illegal. In Cameroon, Article 347 of its penal code condemns all "acts that are immodest or **against nature** with an individual of one's gender"; those convicted of the crime face six months to five years' imprisonment and a fine ranging from the equivalent of $40 to $400 US (if the person involved is between 16 and 21 years old, the penalties doubles). In Senegal, the penal code is as severe; Article 319 prescribes from one to five years' imprisonment and a fine between the equivalent of $200 and $300 US. In Burkina Faso, where homosexuality is also punishable, the legal system takes advantage of the vague definition of "public indecency" to prosecute homosexuals, a phenomenon which also occurs in Senegal and Cameroon. While all countries in West Africa recognize the right of individuals to a "satisfying sexuality," few could have foreseen its consequences with regard to homosexuals.

In West Africa, religion constitutes an important point of reference with regard to identity. Certain countries still strongly abide by old traditional religions, almost all of which are organized around the worship of ancestors, such as the Ivory Coast (65% Animist, 12% Christian, 23% Muslim), Benin (70% Animist, 15% Christian, 15% Muslim), and Guinea-Bissau (56% Animist, 5% Christian, 30% Muslim). Others are more apt to follow **Islam**, such as Mali (90% Muslim), Guinea (85% Muslim), and Niger (90% Muslim). Ghana, on the other hand, is mainly Christian (63%, with 21% Animist and 16% Muslim). In general, religious cohabitation is harmonious. In West Africa, **Christianity** arrived with colonization, whereas Islam, present in the region longer, arrived not by way of conquest, but rather more diffusely through intertribal exchange, a fact which has not led to the phenomenon of Arabization. This cohabitation has incited very little religious proselytism in the region, except in Nigeria (10% Animist, 40% Christian, and 50% Muslim), where proselytism is an ancient tradition and which, in the nineteenth century, inspired a call to jihad which led to the formation of the Fulani Empire of Sokoto (which encompassed the territories situated today in Cameroon, Nigeria, and Niger). More recently, the establishment of *sharia* (Islamic religious law) in certain states in Nigeria has brought about a cycle of violence between Christians and Muslims, and has resulted in death penalties imposed upon women accused of adultery.

Just as it is difficult to adequately summarize the vastness and diversity of West Africa as a geographic region, it is equally difficult to summarize the various forms of homophobia found there, which differs from country to country. However, it can be examined in relation to the region's history and traditions, and how well countries have adapted to the changing mores and sexual practices of contemporary society.

The History of the Region
The history of West Africa includes powerful pre-colonial states such as the Ghanaian Empire (starting in the 4th century), the Yoruba States in Benin and Hausa (10th century), the Malian Empire (11th century), the Sosso Empire (12th century), the Ashanti kingdoms (13th century), the Songhai Empire (14th century), and the Sokoto Empire (19th century). These states that emerged, but in the Niger region and on the Atlantic coast or by Lake Chad, were halted in their succession and destroyed by colonization in the nineteenth century. What followed was a process of re-tribalization which, by administrative will, divided populations into ethnic groups. This explains the broad definition of what, in this region, is considered a tribe or ethnic group. For example, the Fulani are present in nine countries, including Cameroon and Chad; the Mandinka are found not only in Mali, but also in Guinea, Niger, Senegal, and Sierra Leone; the Hausa are in Libya, Chad, Niger, Cameroon and Nigeria; and the Yoruba are in Benin and Nigeria. Members of these ethnic groups number in the millions; they are further made up of subgroups, whose origins are composites of ancient alliances, pacts, or blood relations. Ethnicity in this region is thus often a construct whose origins are

difficult to explain, and becomes a sort of convenient catch-all phrase used to justify historical precedence for particular beliefs or behaviors, all the while playing an important role in the construction of identity.

Historically, the creation of great empires in West Africa had the effect of mobilizing great armies, each exclusively male, with the exception of the Kingdom of Dahomey (now Benin) from the fifteenth to nineteenth centuries, where one found the famous Dahomey Amazons, an all-female military regiment. For the most part, these empires projected the image of a strong and dominant masculinity, which resulted in an important social stratification that first appeared among the Mandinka in the Empire of Mali in the form of castes, organized according to myths by the empire's founder himself, Soundiata Keita. Accordingly, in the great chieftainships, certain powerful men could live with another man, who assumed the status of spouse or wife. To this day, in Yaoundé, Cameroon, there is evidence of homosexual relationships between man-wives and their customary husbands.

In fact, while homosexual relations are generally condemned, old traditions have sometimes created social conditions in which these relations can take place, as in Gagnoa in the Ivory Coast, where one finds the concept of male couple known as *woobi/yossi* (female/male). Ferdinand is a young man, a *woobi* who performs the role of the wife in his relationship with a *yossi*. He states: "In my family, my homosexuality has never been a problem. My grandmother raised me as a little girl. It was no surprise to anyone that I was feminine. At the age of ten, I knew I was a *woobi*." Moreover, he explains: "On the other side of the country, in the East, there is another tradition, the day of the Abissa. On that day, girls dress as boys and boys dress as girls. But most of all, each has the right to reveal his or her life to their family, who must accept it without reproach. It is the day when young *woobis* talk to their parents." However, if local traditions allow a certain amount of flexibility in gender and sexuality, on the whole, stigmatization remains the general rule.

Animist Traditions
In West Africa, while religions of Semitic origin value masculinity above all, ancient myths represent divinities who are often twins (male and female) or hermaphrodites; and in agrarian societies, a good number of divinities are female, which makes it easy to find female priests, seers, healers, initiates, and members

of secret sects. Traditions inherited from ancestors often include initiation rituals celebrating masculinity or femininity that conform to social group models, which include the act of male circumcision, a procedure which almost every man in the region has undergone to this day, and female circumcision, still present in countries such as Burkina Faso, Mali, Niger, Nigeria, and Senegal. In these ways, sexuality remains highly controlled by the social group, especially as pro-birth attitudes in the region are quite present, given the fact that child mortality remains high and life expectancy is between forty-seven and fifty-four years of age (and decreasing further since the beginning of the AIDS pandemic). In this context, any dialogue pertaining to sexuality is restricted to the issue of procreation; as a result, the discussion of homosexuality is silenced from the start.

In these ancient cultures, homosexual relationships find their structure, logic, and significance in the idea of duality, which permits the understanding of numerous aspects of sexuality of certain ethnic groups, including their life experience, made easier by the fact that they largely congregate in urban areas such as Yaoundé, Cameroon, or Lagos, Nigeria. The concept of duality also allows us to understand homosexuality on one side, and the stigmatization it causes on the other. It gives it a mythological coherence. Anthropological literature on witchcraft suggests the plurality of the human individual, in which all of us possess a double who is invisible and immaterial. It is this double who participates in encounters between sorcerers, and it is through the double that occult cannibalism occurs (the sorcerers' doubles eat their victims' doubles, and then continue to live). As well, what happens to one's double has repercussions on the person's material half. Among the Fulani, as in a number of other African ethnic groups, sleep is the moment when the soul, the immaterial double, leaves the body, escaping the laws of space and time. It is at that moment that sorcerers can attack and annihilate it.

This fundamental concept is important when studying the entire field of sexuality in West Africa, even among those many who insist they no longer believe in it. It allows us to understand local representations of sexuality, including homosexuality, erotic dreams and fantasies, and also allows a deeper understanding of the dual notions of sex and gender, and masculinity and femininity. According to this concept, human beings possess two sexes, one that is apparent and another invisible, that falls within the realm of the double; they can be similar to one another, or different; they can be equal in size, or not. One can have power over one's double and act through it, or not; according to tradition, this is what distinguishes sorcerers from others. When one has this power, one can act against others through their double: they can be attacked, take away someone's strength, strike someone with illness, or devour someone; they can even force someone into a sexual act. Given that sleep is when one's double is most vulnerable, these acts occur during a person's dream state. Sorcery or witchcraft is thus a universe of doubles, where certain individuals are conscious, can see, and have power over others, who have no consciousness and are blind and inert.

Men usually have a masculine double, but it may also be the case that their double is feminine. Moreover, there are women whose double is masculine. This fact is important in determining one's sexual orientation. According to legend, it is the work of sorcerers who can control one's double, often taking on the appearance of an individual in order to mislead those who could discover their activities. It is also thought that sorcerers seize the penis of a sleeping man and use it as a whistle or horn in order to send messages to other sorcerers. In the same manner, some women whose double is feminine can take the genital organs of a man in their circle and use them during relations with other women without the man, the husband for example, ever knowing. This form of castration manifests itself in the visible world by the man's timorous character, especially his timidity before the castrator (the woman). Thus, neither masculinity nor femininity are stable constructs; a woman can hide an invisible male sexual organ or transform her feminine double into a masculine one in a form of fantastical transsexuality.

Under these conditions, the idea of responsibility is, of course, unfounded. On one hand, the double can act while one sleeps. On another, a stranger or spirit can take over another body. This leads to a notion of transferal of responsibility, which can offer an explanation for illness or failure. We may not succeed because of the will of another who has a hold over us. With regard to sexuality, this idea is also used to explained infertility, particularly given a culture that holds both procreation and the worship of its ancestors in such high regard. How can one become an ancestor oneself if one does not procreate? Sterility is considered a woman's greatest failure: in such cases, the husband is permitted to take another wife, maintain concubines, or even renounce the woman who does not bear him any children. Infertility can also be attributed to erotic dreams with a homosexual theme.

Moreover, according to these beliefs, certain individuals know how to manipulate this energy to their own advantage. Thus, it is believed that homosexual men seeking sexual services characteristically have a certain portliness about them, apparently due to the semen absorbed from their partners. Alternatively, a heterosexual man who engages in sexual relations with a homosexual runs the risk of losing weight, his energy being sucked out by his partners. Homosexuality is thus an activity by which men's doubles (whether masculine or feminine) attack others' doubles in order to feed off their vital energy.

This helps us to understand why homosexuality is so feared in these cultures. Going against the norm, the homosexual is therefore stigmatized. It is linked to the world of sorcery or witchcraft, that is to say, violence. In this world, the homosexual possesses a feminine double; he is a woman in one dimension and a man in the other. This is why he manifests a sexual attraction to a gender that is identical to his own in the visible world. Homosexuality is thus "rationalized" as being a heterosexuality of doubles. It is said that during intimacy, homosexuals assume their feminine form and have normal relations. This so-called "rationalization" reveals how difficult it is in this culture to understand how someone can be attracted to one's own gender. According to this interpretation, there can only be sexual relations between opposite genders. Because of homosexuality's historical link to sorcery, it is considered an aberration and thus a crime.

In this light, homosexuality is automatically condemned without consideration of other views. Associated with witchcraft, it is considered a great sexual perversion, an act against nature. To this day, many young people in West Africa insist that they are incapable of submitting to such perversions, even for large sums of money.

Islam and Christianity

Islam and Christianity are not truly opposed to traditional cults, from which they borrow and recycle back to them. In West Africa, the invocation of the precepts of Islam or Christianity to denounce homosexuality is constant. According to Christianity, homosexual relations constitute a sin and even an abomination, and ac-

cording to Islam, in those areas where *sharia* is applied, sodomy can be punishable by death.

Even though it is often fused with animist beliefs, the view expressed by Christians in the region is meant to be highly orthodox; they refer to the church's most absolute homophobic tradition. In this sense, African Christianity is often harsher, more dogmatic, and more violent than the views ordinarily expressed in, say, Western Europe, where many Christians long ago learned to temper their words and adjust their rhetoric in societies that are not disposed to having a fundamentalist diktat imposed upon them. By comparison, in West Africa, religious views generally resonate better with the populace. Consequently, West African Christians do not hesitate to express more radical views with regard to morality, in general, and homosexuality, in particular. As an example, Father Jean Ndjewel, Catholic priest of St Stephen's Congregation in Yaoundé, published an online document in which he affirms:

> Homosexuality is sodomy, an abomination, an active manifestation of Satan.… The works of Satan are the opposite of all that which is of divine creation. They are tainted with irregularity, cheating, and abomination. The Church in its sanctifying function must, by way of its sacraments, bring perpetual salvation to those lamentable individuals, that is to say the infirm, the sick, and those assaulted by the devil.… The exorcisms that are the powerful prayers of the Church and are appropriate to root out impure spirits from the bodies of human beings are, therefore, fitting solutions for the eradication of the homosexual phenomenon.

As far as Islam is concerned, *imams* (spiritual leaders) sometimes advocate the death penalty for homosexuals, in accordance with *sharia*. The power and influence these leaders hold over the faithful embolden these views. However, while homosexuality is widely condemned, Islamic tradition also demands the separation of the sexes, which leads to the formation of same-sex groups who are always together and who have little access to those of the opposite sex. Paradoxically, homosexual relationships tend to develop under such conditions, even if they remain discreet, including in such deeply Islamic cities as Bamako (Mali), Conakry (Guinea), Freetown (Liberia), and Niamey (Niger).

New Contours of Homophobia Today

Today, homosexuality remains highly stigmatized in all countries of West Africa. The existence of a dual judicial system that in one area is based on tribal custom and in another on law makes legal recourse random at best. In November 2002, the Archbishop of Freetown publicly accused the government of being responsible for the murder of five nuns during the turmoil that swept the country. Reacting angrily to this accusation, the Prime Minister accused the prelate of homosexuality, which according to this logic, was considered a worse crime than the murder of five people. For his part, Mathias Ble, a teacher in the Ivory Coast, suggested in a 2001 document that his country's government should open "social and moral rehabilitation establishments, [in order] to reform our brothers and sisters ... versed or advanced on this road of savage, sexual violence."

On the whole, homosexuality is described and discussed in West Africa with violent language, revealing the poor regard in which homosexuals are held. As in other regions of Africa, terms such as "ancestral tradition" (which was and must remain heterosexual) and "our negritude" (which makes each African a defender of that which has been agreed to be called "black," "negro-African," or "African" values) are uniformly invoked in such discussions. It is surprising to note that stasis is considered the norm, and that cultural uniformity appears as a fact, whereas historical and ethnographical research clearly refutes the idea of the universal heterosexuality of African traditions. The differences among African societies are numerous, and the history of the peoples of Africa is neither singular nor stationary. The abundance of cultures and their various mutations and subsections are so numerous that neither negritude, nor negro-African or African values, have ever really meant anything.

It is, however, curious to note the paradox that surrounds Western culture's contribution to the construction of the sexual identity of the people of Africa today. It is the West that introduced Christian dogma (largely homophobic) to the region, as well as colonial laws that were often very strict with regard to homosexual relations; but presently, the West is often perceived in Africa as a poor model because of its general **tolerance** toward homosexuality. If homosexuality is considered a foreign **vice** in the region, then contemporary homophobia should also be considered an import. At the March 1997 Cotonou Conference, which dealt with the elimination of legal barriers to sexual and reproduc-

tive health in French-speaking Africa, many important observations were made: for one, contemporary laws of African states are based on colonial laws, but they have not evolved; this leads to the fact that the national laws are often incompatible with large, international apparatus and the resolutions from international conferences. As for the states that have emerged from French colonization, the situation is somewhat confusing: the Napoleonic Code, upon which they more or less base themselves, does not criminalize homosexuality, but the articles regarding the affront to public decency allow for its repression. With regard to states that were once controlled by Great Britain, the situation is much clearer: since the sixteenth century, English law punished homosexuality, and the Labouchère Amendment of 1885 allowed this law to be extended to the various colonies. Today, all countries in West Africa remain on the same page with regard to homosexuality: it remains a criminal offence, and not only is decriminalization not on the agenda, but the official homophobic position has been reinforced again and again.

However, in the last few decades, conditions have changed that improve the lives of homosexuals in the region. Increasing urbanization is a determining factor. The average rate of urbanization is currently between 30 and 48%. Certain countries remain very rural, with very low urbanization levels, such as Burkina Faso (18%), Niger (20%), or Mali (29%), whereas others are much more urbanized, such as Senegal (46%), the Ivory Coast (46%), or Liberia (47%). Strikingly, countries that do not have access to the sea are the least urbanized. Linked to the history of colonization, larger cities in the region, such as Lagos, Abidjan, Dakar and Accra, are found on the Atlantic coast, former commercial ports that sprang up with "triangular commerce" (between Africa, Europe, and America) and later became the capitals of the countries that emerged from colonization. Their political-economic role, which attracted a large workforce from the rural interior and from neighboring countries, explains their rapid growth into melting-pots with populations of diverse origins. The city is, therefore, a meeting place, a place for mixing and sharing ideas, for being aware of social change; it is also a place that allows for anonymity and individual autonomy, away from the stifling pressures of community, **family**, and "traditions." These conditions create a greater opportunity for homosexual relations, even if they remain strongly condemned. Thus, the city, a place where new ideas are disseminated, becomes a privileged space where homosexuals can engage one another.

This urbanization is an essential factor in understanding homosexuality's place in the region today. The idea that homosexuality is a minority activity controlled by taboos and witchcraft is slowly changing, thanks to urbanization. In the large cities, there are nightclubs frequented by homosexuals, and homosexuality is often perceived as a phenomenon of certain social strata, notably the affluent, who are then likely to purchase the services of same-sex partners. Sometimes female prostitutes serve as fronts and intermediaries for their male counterparts who dare not openly offer their services for hire. Some women complain about this competition that not only reduces the number of customers, but is also more lucrative. In recent years, Europeans have been accused of maintaining a huge homosexual "network" in the region, but this accusation falls in the line with the idea that homosexuality is imported; thus, AIDS is a "white illness" (in the same way that it is a "black illness" according to some outside of Africa). In rural areas, it is also believed that sexually transmitted diseases are exclusive to the city. In this way, the context of what is believed to constitute urban life largely colors the populace's views concerning sexuality.

In Cameroon, homosexuals have for a long time been called freemasons, as they are believed to belong to the esoteric world of mystic brotherhoods who practice this form of sexuality in order to acquire supernatural powers. It is thought that some do it in order to become wealthy, and others to increase the strength of their double. This concept is also linked to political power. In modern political mythology from Congo to Cameroon that is more current in the cities than in rural areas, there is mention of politicians who request that those who come to see them wishing to be hired for a particular job or contract are to be accompanied by their wives. In such a scenario, the wife enters the politician's office alone while the husband waits outside; how the wife "performs" has a direct consequence on her husband's career. In a variation of this tale, however, the wife is nowhere to be found, and it is the husband who must undress before his potential boss. This particular idea seems to be inspired by the beliefs that tie homosexuality to witchcraft and the manifestation of the double, but it is important to distinguish it in a homophobic light—given that this link is only made because it has to do with homosexuality. In the version where the wife is involved, it is

construed not as an invocation of witchcraft but as an abuse of authority.

The homophobic **discourse** in West Africa is thus based on old traditions and beliefs that have been adapted to the ideas of the contemporary world. These representations remain vivid in the heart of the public, and if they are not often talked about, it is due to a common fear of being stigmatized as being an irrational, superstitious fetishist. However, other components, such as the law, negritude, and the religions of Semitic origin, offer rhetoric that is just as homophobic, and, if not more so, encouraging a negative view of homosexuality. But just as the threat of stigmatization does not prevent people from having these traditional beliefs, neither does it prevent homosexuality from being more present and more visible in the cities.

—*Séverin Cécile Abega*

Abega, Séverin Cécile. "La Maîtresse du temps," *Annales de la FLSH: série sciences humaines* 2, no. 2 (1986).

———. *Contes d'initiation sexuelle*. Yaoundé, Cameroon: Clé, 1995.

———. *Les Choses de la forêt*. Yaoundé, Cameroon: Presses de l'UCAC, 2000.

Alès, Catherine, and Cécile Barraud. *Sexe relatif ou sexe absolut?* Paris: Maison des Sciences de l'Homme, 2001.

Amnesty International. *Briser le silence: Violations des droits de l'homme liés à l'orientation sexuelle, homosexualités et droits de l'homme*. Amnesty International, France, 2002.

Anonymous, *Encyclopédie Microsoft Encarta 1993–2001*. Microsoft Corporation, 2002.

Ba, Amadou Hampaté. *L'Eclat de la grande étoile*. Paris: Armand Colin, 1974.

Bamony, Pierre. "Science et anthropologie. De la notion de l'âme en général et de sa conception singulière chez les Lyéla du Burkina Faso," *Anthropos* 95, 2000/2, (2000).

Bastide, Roger. "Le Principe d'individuation." In *La Notion de personne en Afrique noire*. Paris: Centre national de la recherche scientifique, 1971.

Bonnet, Doris. *Corps biologique, corps social*. Paris: ORSTOM, 1988.

Douglas, Mary. *Purity and Danger*. London: Penguin, 1966.

Dupré, Georges. "Sorcellerie et salariat. Njobi et la Mère, deux cultes anti-sorciers," *Les Temps modernes* 3, (1977).

Evans-Pritchard, Edward. *Sorcellerie, oracle et magie chez les Azande*. Paris: Gallimard, 1972. [Published in the US as *Witchcraft, Oracles and Magic among the Azande*. New York: Oxford, 1976.]

Gray, Robert. "Structural Aspects of Mbugwe Witchcrafts."

In *Witchcraft and Sorcery in East Africa*. Edited by John Middleton and E. H. Winter. London: Routledge & Kegan, 1963.

Held, Suzette. "Witches and Thieves: Deviant Motivations in Gisu Society." *Alan* 21 (1986). Helman, Cecil. *Culture, Health and Illness*. Oxford/Boston: Heinemann, 1994.

Laburthe-Tolra, Philippe. *Minlaaba*. Lille II, Atelier de l'Université, thèse de doctorat d'État soutenue à la Sorbonne, 1977.

Lallemand, Suzanne. *L'Apprentissage de la sexualité dans les contes de l'Afrique de l'Ouest*. Paris: L'Harmattan, 1985.

——. *La Mangeuse d'âmes*. Paris: L'Harmattan, 1988.

Lavignotte, Henri. "L'Evur, croyance des Pahouins du Gabon." In *Cahier missionnaire*, no. 20. Paris: Société des Missions évangéliques, 1936.

Lepape, Marc, and Claudine Vidal. "Libéralisme et vécus sexuels à Abidjan," *Cahiers internationaux de sociologie* 1976 (1984).

Mallart-Guimera, Louis. *Ni dos ni ventre*. Paris: Société d'ethnographie, 1981.

Marwick, Max, ed. *Witchcraft and Sorcery*. London: Penguin Modern Sociology Readings, 1970.

Murray, Steven O., and Will Roscoe, eds. *Boy-Wives and Female Husbands, Studies of African Homosexualities*. London: Macmillan Press, 1998.

Nadel, Siegfried Frederick. "Witchcraft in Four African Societies," *American Anthropologist* 54, (1952).

Ombolo, Jean-Pierre. *Sexe et société en Afrique noire*. Paris: L'Harmattan, 1990.

Pradelles de Latour, Charles Henri. *Ethnopsychanalyse en pays bamiléké*. Paris: EPEL, 1991.

Thomas, Louis Vincent, and René Luneau. *La Terre africaine et ses religions*. Paris: Larousse, 1975.

Vignal, Daniel. "L'Homophilie dans le roman négro-africain d'expression anglaise et française." In *Un sujet inclassable? Approches sociologiques, littéraires et juridiques des homosexualités*. Edited by Rommel Mendès-Leite. Lille: Cahiers GayKitschCamp. 1995.

Vincent, Jeanne-Françoise. *Entreliens avec les femmes beti du Sud-Cameroun*. Paris: Orstom/Berger Levraut, 1976.

Further Reading

Amnesty International. *Breaking the Silence: Human Rights Violations Based on Sexual Orientation*. Amnesty International USA, 1994.

—*Africa, Central & Eastern; Africa, South; AIDS; Anthropology; Family; Islam; Rhetoric; Sterility.*

AGAINST NATURE

The expression "against nature" is not specifically Christian. Though it can be found in the writings of St Paul (Rom 1:26), it originally stems from pagan philosophy, and in a more general sense, from a certain Greek and Roman interpretation of sexual morals. In fact, nothing is more cultural than this concept of nature. Traditionally, neither the Greeks nor the Romans were, properly speaking, homo- or heterosexual, but rather their sexuality was based on roles accorded to them by their social status: the dominant role (i.e. penetrating the other) was played by free male citizens, while the passive role (i.e. being penetrated by the other) was played by everyone else, that is, women, slaves, and adolescents. This was the practice of pederasty in its original pedagogical sense. In this context, someone who is, or acts, "against nature" (*para phusin*) does not respect this simple social norm; the word "nature" in this sense has almost the same meaning as "society."

Things began to change with the introduction of the popular form of Stoicism, which promotes an ethic of "living according to nature." Here, the word "nature" takes on a very different meaning (further yet from its contemporary sense), referring to the "divine order of things." Thus, following nature did not mean conforming to some sort of instinct (as is the current meaning), but rather to reason, as defined by one's biological function. This meant following physical laws, especially, of course, that of procreation. The goal was to seek out *ataraxia* (serene calmness) through the struggle against pleasures, desires, emotion, etc. The body was devalued as being the source of irrational passions, a contingent part of man.

This philosophical and existential system had a strong influence on the Church Fathers, who took up the body/soul dualism (a dualism missing from the **Bible**, even in the writings of St Paul), as well as the disdain for sexuality (which was contrary to the Biblical concept of Creation), reducing it to its "rational" end, meaning **marriage** and reproduction. Under these conditions, homosexuality certainly does appear to be "against nature" and relations between members of the same sex (sodomy in particular) were considered an insult to nature. In this context, homophobia is represented by the fear of the body, sexuality, and pleasure, and by the reduction of sexuality to its reproductive ends. Yet, the extreme example of **sterility** is, on its own, not enough to annul a religious marriage; it is not

enough even to justify a sort of chastity. But pleasure is free, in that it does not always need to have procreation as its goal. What is considered against nature in one case is not in another, and it is the very definition of nature that wavers: a pseudo-concept that is only ever invoked in a partial manner when condemning homosexual relations and those who practice them.
—*Thierry Revol*

Boswell, John. *Christianisme, tolérance sociale et homosexualité.* Paris: Gallimard, 1985. [Published in the US as *Christianity, Social Tolerance, and Homosexuality: Gay People in Western Europe from the Beginning of the Christian Era to the Fourteenth Century.* Chicago: Univ. of Chicago Press, 1980.]

Damien, Peter. *Liber Gomorrhianus, Patrologia, Series Latina* [ed. Migne]. Paris: Garnier Frères, 1844. Translated by Pierre J. Payer in *Book of Gomorrah.* Waterloo, ON: Wilfrid Laurier Univ. Press, 1982.

Jordan, Mark. *The Invention of Sodomy in Christian Theology.* Chicago: Univ. of Chicago Press, 1997.

Halperin, David. *Cent ans d'homosexualité (et autres essais sur l'amour grec).* Paris: EPEL, 2000. [Published in the US as *One Hundred Years of Homosexuality: And Other Essays on Greek Love.* New York: Routledge, 1990.]

Lacoste, Jean-Yves, ed. *Dictionnaire critique de théologie.* Paris: Presses universitaires de France, 1998. [Published in the US as *Encyclopedia of Christian Theology.* New York: Routledge, 2005.]

Leroy-Forgeot, Flora. "Nature et contre nature en matière d'homoparentalité." In *Homoparentalité, états des lieux.* APGL symposium. Paris: ESF, 2000.

McNeill, John. *L'Eglise et l'homosexuel, un plaidoyer.* Geneva: Labor & Fides, 1982. [Published in the US as *The Church and the Homosexual.* Kansas City: Sheed Andrews and McMeel, 1976. Fourth edition: Boston: Beacon Press, 1993.]

Thévenot, Xavier. *Homosexualités masculines et morale chrétienne.* Paris: Le Cerf, 1985.

—*Bible, the; Biology; Damien, Peter; Debauchery; Decadence; Degeneracy; Heresy; Judaism; Medicine; Paul; Sterility; Theology; Vice.*

ANCIENT GREECE. *See Greece, Ancient*

AIDS

It has become commonly accepted that sympathy for the gay community as a result of the AIDS epidemic contributed to a decline in homophobia and to greater social acceptance of homosexuality, at least in Western culture. The introduction of the **PaCS** (Pacte civil de solidarité; Civil solidarity pact) domestic partnership proposal in France was in part inspired by a desire to address the problems encountered by homosexuals when confronted with the death of their partner. With the epidemic and the tragedy it engendered, the world of fiction began introducing characters who were portrayed as being less stereotypical. The crisis mobilized the gay community that had been struck head on by the epidemic, resulting in the establishment of numerous and important AIDS organizations, which helped to forge an image of gay solidarity as well as pave the way for gays and lesbians to enter the political arena. In this sense, the battle against AIDS led in some respects to the institutionalization of homosexuality.

We would be well advised not to deny facts, but at the same time we must not forget each setback. While the adoption of PaCS in France—following vitriolic debate in which homophobes in France had their say—was justified based on an acknowledgment of French law to protect the rights of gay and lesbian couples, the arguments of those in favor of it were almost exclusively framed in the tragic context of HIV and AIDS; in this way, the debate moved from the political (regarding the equality of domestic partners, whether gay or straight) to the personal (by invoking compassion for those suffering under the inefficiencies of the health system). If it is true that the AIDS crisis created opportunities for a new representation of gays and lesbians, it must also be noted that this image of homosexuals was more "marketable" because it was sympathetic and indeed tragic. In the end, some wish that discussions of the "exemplary" character of the gay community, underlined again and again by political figures and those in the **media**, would have been an occasion for an analysis of the political context in which gays and lesbians were forced to be "exemplary": the widespread indifference of governments, the media, and the general public toward the suffering and deaths of thousands of homosexuals during the early years of the epidemic. The gay community acted as it did in the mid-1980s simply because it was forced to; it could not count on others to help. In short, one cannot deny that the tragedy of AIDS contributed to pushing "the homosexual issue" forward and that the two decades since the crisis started were also years in which the gay community made huge strides toward full "liberation." But at the same time, the price of this "liberation" was dear, and improvements in how mainstream society treats gays and lesbians might best be described in the context of a repentant homophobia.

In industrialized nations, AIDS did not strike randomly, but rather in socially defined categories, starting with male homosexuals. For gay men, the impact of AIDS was intensified by a culture that encouraged multiple partners and sexual experimentation. AIDS itself, however, was not directly related to multiple partners, or to homosexuality itself; HIV is transmitted by specific practices, and therein was the process by which to stop it. In this context, the epidemic's impact on the gay community was exacerbated by the slowness in setting up public prevention policies around the world.

In France, as well as in most wealthy countries, it was not until the mid-nineties that gay men no longer made up the majority of new AIDS cases. This was due, in part, to the spreading of AIDS to other communities, to the point where those now most affected by it (at least in industrialized cultures) live in socially precarious situations (such as intravenous drug users). Nevertheless, more than half of the 40,000 people who have died in France due to complications from AIDS were homosexual. The epidemic hit the gay community during a time when there was little or no medical response available; and the impact was long-lasting: today there are few gay men of a certain generation who, having lived through the 1980s and 90s, were not tragically affected by AIDS through the loss of friends or lovers.

But the story does not end there; while the gay community was being decimated by AIDS, it also constantly crossed paths with homophobia. Without subscribing to a naïve, unambiguous causality, it can be stated that the AIDS crisis set the stage for a revival of homophobic **rhetoric**, and in turn the homophobic rhetoric exacerbated the AIDS crisis.

It is necessary to note that at the height of the epidemic, there were huge difficulties and delays in disseminating correct preventative information and establishing proper policies. What France went through might shed light on similar experiences elsewhere in the Western world: it was apparent that as long as the epidemic seemed restricted to homosexuals and drug users, governments were reluctant to get involved. A prevention campaign might have been helpful for "queers" and "druggies," but it would be at the risk of compromising one's political reputation by being seen as encouraging practices that were questionable at best. It is thus that in France, the government constantly delayed the implementation of a minor legal mechanism that would have at least allowed the advertisement of condoms, prohibited in the country since the 1920s by a law from another age designed to fight a national decline in the birthrate. The 1967 Neuwirth law, which made contraception legal, did not have much impact: the promotion of contraceptive practices remained forbidden, and, consequently, so did the promotion of condoms. It was not until 1986 that it became legal to advertise condoms in France; the very first public prevention campaigns did not appear until a year later in 1987, but it was not until the late 1990s that such campaigns aimed at the general public included characters who could be identified as gay. Until then, government authorities, who had been reluctant to launch any kind of prevention campaign, refused to include the representation of homosexuals in television commercials, posters, or newspaper ads; they claimed these decisions were made to avoid "stigmatizing" the gay community by directly linking homosexuals to the epidemic. In the end, the main consequence of this was to perpetuate the invisibility of homosexuals in the public discourse.

Meanwhile, organizations aimed at fighting AIDS were being established; one of their main goals was to bridge the political gap between public health policy and AIDS. Though the majority of their members were gay, they held different views on the homosexual dimension of the epidemic: on one hand, groups such as AIDES (Association de lutte contre le VIH/Sida et les hepatitis; Association for the Fight Against HIV/AIDS and Hepatitis), which had established the most important network of gay solidarity in France, preferred not to emphasize the link between homosexuality and AIDS in order to avoid its categorization as the "gay disease" at a time when mainstream society might think that the death of "a few queers" might not seem so bad. On the other hand, groups such as ACT UP underscored the relationship between AIDS and the queer community in order to highlight the government's inaction on the crisis, and to counter the vicious circle of **shame** in which AIDS sufferers were trapped. The different strategies may have been in conflict with one another, but the groups had common goals: responding to the effects of homophobia on the spread of the epidemic, and finding ways, both politically and physically, in which to treat the afflicted. They also agreed that AIDS revealed the fragility of society, spreading to groups in direct proportion to the level of **discrimination** they had already suffered; and the devastating emotional and social impact of AIDS further worsened that fragility. It became necessary to think about the political and social conditions that allowed AIDS to spread, including the idea that it took root in communities that were unable to resist it, that is to say, wherever the social component was weak or nonexistent. However, this also meant understanding that AIDS was not only symptomatic of a rupture in a community's well-being, but that it worsened it as well.

"AIDS Cures Fags": Preparations for an anti-gay demonstration.

In this context, it was unthinkable to fight AIDS without fighting the homophobic rhetoric that arose and developed along with it during its early years. The ravages of AIDS on the gay community not only failed to silence many homophobes, but gave them a new reason to revive the anti-gay rhetoric that had weakened over time. We can identify some of their motives for this, from the most brutal to the most subtle.

"At-Risk Groups"
On one hand, there is the obvious: HIV is transmitted by high-risk activities, and halting these activities

can prevent its spread. On the other hand, there is a persistent myth purporting that HIV is solely an issue for "at-risk groups." It is well-known that AIDS was first absurdly referred to by the media as "the gay cancer." Since then, this logic has been repeated elsewhere: AIDS is regularly categorized as the illness of "others," from whom it is important to protect oneself. It is the "4-H disease": homosexuals, heroin addicts, Haitians, and hemophiliacs. In this sense, many homophobic views concerning AIDS belong to the more general category of exclusion, which purports to adhere to a policy of AIDS prevention, or imaginary methods of protection, based on the identification and isolation of entire portions of the general population. The French **far right** has thus designated homosexuals and immigrants as the troublemakers; in Japan or in China, AIDS is a Western disease, and in black Africa, a white disease. Each time, the effect of this type of representation has been (and still is in many countries) two-pronged: a denial of the realities of the epidemic on one hand, which legitimizes the absence of a coherent government policy that includes prevention, care, and treatment; and the proliferation of catastrophic discourses on the other, from which exclusionary, discriminatory laws and policies are developed. The anti-AIDS arguments of ultra-orthodox Catholics in France, to cite one example, are symptomatic of this dual dimension: they insist that the epidemic is "marginal" and that it "only kills a very small portion of the population," ("La marée rose," *Permanences* [monthly magazine of civic and cultural action, according to Christian and Natural Law], no. 340 [March-April 1997]) thus contesting any attempt at mobilization against it; at the same time, they warn against homosexuality becoming "commonplace," and advocate discriminatory measures against it. This view is influenced by pseudo-medical, homophobic literature whose main objective is to deconstruct the "myth of heterosexual AIDS." Such advocates made some inroads politically: in 1991, while France's penal code was being revised, Senators Sourdille and Jolibois convinced the French senate to adopt two amendments which they claimed were justified by the urgent nature of the AIDS epidemic. The first allowed homosexuality to be named as an aggravating circumstance in crimes and misdemeanors; the second had the effect of recriminalizing homosexuality by reinstituting a different age of consent for gays and lesbians than for heterosexuals. These amendments were later rejected by the National Assembly.

In many countries, in order to contain "at-risk groups," conservative political leaders, including those on the far right, recommended homophobic public health policies such as the compulsory testing of homosexuals. In France, National Front leader Jean-Marie Le Pen suggested the establishment of "aidsatoriums," where those afflicted with HIV or AIDS would be isolated from the greater population. In the United States, Louisiana gubernatorial candidate David Duke made another suggestion: "I believe in the idea of an unerasable tattoo, with AIDS written on it. It would be placed in an intimate area, maybe even in red and black letters. This tattoo would save lives…."

Natural/*Against Nature*

The day after Michel Foucault's death in 1984, the French daily *Libération,* usually less homophobic than the majority of newspapers of the time, printed a strongly worded response to statements made by "insolents" who had "sullied [Foucault's] memory" by suggesting that he had died of AIDS (which was true). If we are to believe the obituaries written in the years that followed, many young men were dying as a result of "violent leukemia" or sudden cancer: it was in fact impossible for people to publicly confront the stigma of AIDS and the suspicion of homosexuality that accompanied it. AIDS not only was construed as the symptom of a depraved life, but also as a verdict, the price to be paid for having strayed from the sexual order as deigned by God or his non-religious aspect, "nature."

The idea of "divine punishment" was popular among religious groups and puritans of all sorts. We must remember Pat **Buchanan**'s remark, "Those poor homosexuals, they declared war on nature, and now, it is nature that has struck them with a frightening retribution," or those of designer Paco Rabanne, in an attempt to revive in France the ghost of apocalyptic "divine punishment." The test was the proof: it was said that the sick were dying as a consequence of their lifestyles. In 1991, Albert German, president of the National Academy of Pharmacology in France, addressed an unflinching assembly: "The AIDS virus had the genius to attack those who turned reproductive physiology into degenerate pleasure." And in 2002, Hani Ramadan, director of the Geneva Islamic Center, wrote an article in *Le Monde* (the subject of which was to justify the stoning of adulterous women) that the AIDS virus "did not appear out of nowhere" and that "only those with deviant behavior expose themselves to it."

The Flaw of **Otherness**

The obviously archaic idea that AIDS was divine punishment or nature's revenge upon a disruptive homosexuality required refinement in order to become credible outside of ultra-orthodox circles. In 1991, the Conference of French Bishops released *Catéchisme pour adultes* (Catechism for adults), which included references to AIDS that were greatly inspired by ideas developed by priest-psychoanalyst Tony Anatrella. The *Catechism* demonstrated how the Catholic Church had reinvented its theoretical well-being by cloaking its pronouncements in **psychoanalysis** gone astray. In it, the prevalence of AIDS among the gay male population was directly linked to a definition of homosexuality, presented as a "refusal"—or according to the texts, an "incapacity"—to confront **gender differences**. The result, under these conditions, was an example of "bad faith" exclusive to a "homosexual psychology" that "favors a tendency to cheat in relationships" (Anatrella, *Non à la société dépressive*, 1993). When one is incapable of understanding the other, then one is also incapable of the respect the other is due, and one becomes less scrupulous about possibly contaminating him. These ideas around AIDS were directly related to homophobic thinking: AIDS functions as the new indicator of otherness consistent with homosexuality; conversely, the denial of otherness that characterizes homosexuality is the touchstone of this AIDS theory. In addition, if it is agreed that AIDS is not exclusive to homosexuals, then these thoughts are welcome by the homophobic writers: they permit the transformation of those newly diagnosed with HIV into metaphorical homosexuals. For Anatrella, the homosexual's denial of otherness is a symptom of a depressed contemporary society.

On the surface there is a great distance between the moralizing homilies of Anatrella and the apocalyptic sociology of Jean Baudrillard, but a close reading reveals a strange resonance between their texts. AIDS is the central theme of Baudrillard's *La Transparence du mal* (1990) (in English, *The Transparency of Evil* [1993]), just as it is in Anatrella's *Non à la société dépressive*. Both describe it as the signal for a general denial of otherness by those afflicted, the majority of whom are homosexual. Baudrillard's reasoning is based on analogy: according to him, the AIDS virus is to the modern body what the AIDS epidemic is to the gay community. After so much time spent preventing diseases and ridding itself of germs with artificial means, the modern body can no longer react to unforeseen adversity: its system of defense has the same flaws as artificial intelligence. The modern body can thus be characterized by a tendency to reject otherness, which Baudrillard also observes in homosexual groups, identifiable by the "compulsion of resemblance" and by their "closed-circuit habits." Having "expelled their negative elements," the modern body is "on the verge of complete *positivization*" and could be more vulnerable to HIV: "the absence of otherness creates this other elusive otherness, this absolute otherness that is the virus." By refusing to be confronted by the other (in this case, gender), homosexuals may make themselves vulnerable to a more radical otherness: death.

Guilty Patients & Innocent Victims

It eventually became apparent that homosexuals and drug users were not—and would not be—the only ones infected, and because shame continued to be associated with the illness, it was necessary to distinguish among the infected, to classify and sort them according to group. On one side were those who "deserved" their fate as a result of their behavior (homosexuals and drug users); on the other were the "innocent" victims who were unjustly infected, such as those contaminated through blood transfusions (like hemophiliacs) or men and women "deceived" by their HIV-positive sexual partners. For the first group, AIDS was a verdict on their behavior, and for the second, it was a great injustice. It appeared that there was a gulf between "kinds" of AIDS, depending on the type of transmission, but from the point of view of an infected person, there is no difference. Still, it was apparent that the major discussions on AIDS did not center on the affliction itself but rather on its origins. Behind the categories, too, were the accusations: if homosexuals were considered responsible for their illness, they were also often considered responsible for others who had it but did not deserve it. At various AIDS conferences, renowned cancer specialist Henri Joyeux calmly spelled out HIV: "In the school of Life and Love, H stands for Homosexuality, I for Innocence, and V for Violence." That's all it took to turn AIDS into a fable of innocence destroyed by violence and homosexuality. Albert German, previously cited, named homosexuals as "responsible for the death of hemophiliacs and transfusion patients, and the millions who will die";

and Tony Anatrella underlined the "bad faith" of bisexuals, because they transmitted the virus from the homosexual population to members of society who did not deserve it.

Revisionism

There was heated debate following the release of Frédéric Martel's *Le Rose et le noir* (1996) (in English, *The Pink and the Black* [1999]), his book on the contemporary history of homosexuals in France, about his insinuation that the French "gay movement" did not do enough during the early years of the AIDS crisis. Even if there is little doubt today that the community's early response to the epidemic was difficult, some comments surrounding Martel's work demonstrated unabashed homophobia. Those who had not bothered to worry about the threat of AIDS during a time when it could still be contained or criticize government inaction, now held homosexuals and their representatives as irrefutably responsible for its spread. Such accusations ignored the difficulty in accurately defining the threat designated as the "gay cancer." Hervé Guibert wrote that Foucault would have laughed the first time he heard about AIDS: "A gay cancer that only affects homosexuals, it would be too good to believe, it's so funny you could die." The anecdote is more ironic than precise, but it recalls a time when the media connected AIDS to collective punishment: between the AIDS threat and the Puritan threat, the second was preferable, as it was better known.

Proselytism

In France until the mid-1990s, AIDS organizations were largely founded and directed by homosexuals, from the most explicitly gay community-based (such as ACT UP) to those that were less so, such as SolEnSi (Solidarité Enfants Sida), whose objective was to organize a solidarity network for children with AIDS and their families. The occasion was too perfect: gay activists were held responsible for the most patent failures of the fight against AIDS. This is exactly what Annie Birraux, director of the Department of Research on Adolescence at the Université Paris VII-Denis-Diderot and consultant with the French government's AIDS agency, until its closure in 1994, did; in a 1992 essay entitled "Perversion or Proselytism," Birraux explained how AIDS, beginning in its early years, had been a godsend for homosexuals by allowing them to finally attain political power: by assuming the monopoly of prevention, the "gay **lobby**" had usurped the "representations of AIDS" and contained the risks "in a collection of minority behaviors. Even worse (according to Birraux), prevention policies would have only resulted in "homosexual proselytism" aimed at adolescents. Thus, gays "contributed to the extension of the AIDS epidemic" because they made AIDS their "baby."

This type of reasoning had promise: American sociologist Albert O. Hirschmann noted well how the argument of the perverse effect (*perversity*) constitutes one of the recurring themes of "reactionary rhetoric." It can be seen—once again—in the ideas of Anatrella, who sees every AIDS prevention campaign, no matter how careful it is to skip over homosexuals in the field of representation, as surreptitiously promoting the "homosexual model." This is the same logic upon which the views of the Catholic Church are based, from Pope John Paul II to the Conference of French Bishops; they see a further danger in the promotion and distribution of condoms, the risk of the disillusion of "love for sale," and the pitfall of the "banalization of sexual union," which they believe contribute "paradoxically" to the extension of the epidemic.
—*Philippe Mangeot*

ACT UP-Paris. "Le Sida, combien de divisions." Paris: Dagorno, 1994.

"Aides," *Remaide* magazine (n.d.)

Anatrella, Tony. *Non à la société dépressive*. Paris: Flammarion, 1993.

Baudrillard, Jean. *La Transparence du mal, essai sur les phéno-mènes extrêmes*. Paris: Galilée, "L'Espace critique" collection, 1990. [Published in the US as *The Transparency of Evil: Essays on Extreme Phenomena*. New York/London: Verso, 1993.]

Edelmann, Frédéric, ed. *Dix clefs pour comprendre l'épidémie, dix années de lutte contre le Sida*. Paris: Le Monde Editions, 1996.

Fee, Elizabeth, and Daniel M. Fox, eds. *AIDS: The Burden of History*. Berkeley: Univ. of California Press, 1988.

Guibert, Hervé. *A l'ami qui ne m'a pas sauvé la vie*. Paris: Gallimard, 1990.

Gross, Larry. *Contested Closets: The Politics and Ethics of Outing*. Minneapolis/London: Minnesota Univ. Press, 1993.

Kramer, Larry. *Report from the Holocaust: The Making of an Activist*. New York: St Martin's Press, 1989.

Martel, Frédéric. *Le Rose et le noir, les homosexuels en France depuis 1968*. Paris: Seuil, 1996. [Published in the US as

The Pink and The Black: Homosexuals in France since 1968. Stanford, CA: Stanford Univ. Press, 1999.]

Mendès-Leite, Rommel. *Chroniques socioanthropologiques au temps du Sida, trois essais sur les (homo)sexualités masculines*. Paris: L'Harmattan, 2000.

Pinell, Patrice, ed. *Une Epidémie politique, la lutte contre le Sida en France, 1981–1996*. Paris: Presses universitaires de France, "Science, Histoire et Société" collection, 2002.

Pollak, Michael. *Les Homosexuels et le sida. Sociologie d'une épidémie*. Paris: A. M. Métailié, 1988.

———, and Marie-Ange Schiltz. *Les Homo- et bisexuels masculins face au Sida, six années d'enquête*. Paris: GSPM, 1991.

Watney, Simon. *Policing the Desire: Aids, Pornography, and the Media*. Minneapolis: Univ. of Minnesota Press, 1989.

—*Against Nature; Communitarianism; Contagion; Medicine; Otherness; Peril; Proselytism; Rhetoric; Shame.*

ANTHROPOLOGY

It may seem difficult for some to imagine that this discipline, for which **otherness** is a constituent part of the social and cultural world that it seeks to understand, could be associated with homophobia. But if anthropology, despite its pretensions, can be criticized because of its link to colonialism, it can also possibly be associated with homophobia. However, it is necessary to begin a critique of the underlying prejudices within anthropology with a historical situating of the knowledge and evaluation of its own theoretical and methodological suppositions in order to take inventory of the elements that interpret a normative—if not heterosexist—vision of the socio-cultural world.

In academia, researchers who study sexuality are often confronted with the prejudices of their colleagues, as sexuality is usually perceived as belonging to the private sphere and thus excluded from the traditional hierarchy of scientific interests. Despite the development over the last twenty years of research on the social relations of sex as well as feminist criticism of androcentrism, the stigma against the study of sexuality persists; some of these themes are considered "minor," and their anthropology "unhealthy," "sordid," "strange," or "exotic." Under these conditions, it is no surprise that a British study by Edward Evans-Pritchard (1970), describing institutionalized homosexual relationships among the Azande people of north-central Africa, was published in the United States, rather than **England**, just three years before the author's death, and thirty years after being written. One of the reasons behind this attitude doubtlessly resides in the fact that since its origin, anthropology has privileged categories that highlight order (social organization, structures, and models) to the detriment of the individual, of subjectivity, and of history.

Certainly, anthropology has not always excluded these realities, but it has locked them into an idea of social order that remains quite inferior to the observable facts within contemporary society, especially with regard to the analysis of sexuality. As underlined by Laurent Bazin, Rommel Mendès-Leite, and Catherine Quiminal, "If anthropology has always considered immediate and extended family as its preferred theme, the construction of an issue around sexuality, which is effectively situated at its epicenter without being locked in, runs up against a definite skepticism despite precedents of great notoriety, such as the works of Malinkowski, Mead, Godelier or even Herdt."

Thus, evoking a "political economy of sexuality," Bazin et al emphasize that it "is always and everywhere conceived as a central issue within the most diverse interactions that occur on the micro and macro-social scales." Thus, the study of sexuality, when it does not remain locked away by the constraints of prevention (specifically, **AIDS** prevention) or activism (notably that which has developed within AIDS prevention groups), is a favored subject for the understanding of political expressions of socio-sexual differences. As Mendès-Leite has stated, it is not a question of underestimating the interest of the work conducted for useful purposes, nor the work conducted from a militant perspective, but to preserve the vast horizon of possibilities that sexuality can offer as a complete subject of inquiry, and by that fact, the qualitative research on sexuality has been quickly confronted by the necessity to elaborate upon often bold field methodologies that ask essential questions.

From a strictly etymological point of view, anthropology is the discipline that studies man within society. Though man has never stopped questioning himself about himself, the composition of scientific knowledge which studies humanity appears quite late on the social-philosophical scene. Thus, anthropological thought is contemporary to the expansion of commercial capitalism and the exploitation of the New World. Its first confrontation with otherness, even if it refers to cultural difference, cannot be understood outside the context of this colonial exploration. If the Renaissance sought to know the definition of man through the diversity of human societies, this Other is often nothing more than an object/pretext. Blinded by their need to civilize, to catechize, and to acquire riches, the Conquistadors often asked themselves, "Do Indians have a soul?" and "What should be done about these sodomite practices?"

It is in this context, and in particular with the tales of travel to America, that anthropological science took its first steps; as a result, new and unnerving figures of otherness, such as sodomites, Amazonians, and hermaphrodites, began to populate the pages of travel stories. Today, according to Guy Poirier, these tales can be read as revealers of image hang-ups, insofar as they offer "the keystone to European anxiety-provoking networks." In their casting of otherness, these texts represent a key moment in the history, or pre-history, of anthropology. Certain travelers, such as Jean de Léry (considered by Lévi-Strauss to be the first ethnologist), briefly mention this "abominable sin," while others, like the Spaniard Nuñez Cabeza de Vaca who, after his exploration of Florida, are more specific: "During the time I was among these people, I saw a diabolical thing: a man married to another man." Similarly, in his 1533 *Chronicles of Peru*, Cieza de Léon wrote: "In each temple or important place of worship, they have one or two men, if not more, dressed as women since childhood, and who speak like them and imitate their habits, their dress and all. The men—and the chiefs in particular—have immoral carnal relations with them on feast or holy days, as if it were a rite or a ceremony. I know because I punished two of them." In Mexico, all the elements of future tragedies were already in place: In his July 10, 1519 letter to Charles Quint, Cortez said that the Indians "are sodomites and practice the abominable sin." In this regard, in their writings, the great travelers express their fascination for this New World as well as their horror for the crime of sodomy, which appears to be widespread on the continent. In this context, nascent anthropology is largely supportive of colonialist aims, religious proselytism, and homophobic thought.

However, this argument against sodomy goes well beyond the Amerindian context. The descriptions of Eastern morals gave place to incredibly homophobic descriptions and fantasies. Thus, as far as Christianity was concerned, Muslims were the enemy *par excellence* of the time. Travelers never ceased to be scandalized by the unnatural morals, the harems, and the universal lustfulness of the region. *The Travels of Seigneur de Villamont*, first published in 1595, expresses the author's dismay regarding adolescents whom the sultans "guard more jealously that their own wives." The reality of the practices described is not necessarily false, but the moral judgment of them is often reproachful. From that time, the medieval confusion by which sodomy became a form of **heresy**, a heresy in love, is revived within this Muslim context. Sixteenth-century French geographer Nicolas de Nicolay insists that after the capture of Constantinople, religious buildings were transformed into "stables and bordellos for bardascia (effeminate young males) and whores," demonstrating the link between religious profanation and sexual profanation. As for Bartholomeus Georgiewitz, who was enslaved by the Turks, he conjures up a terrifying image of the fate awaited by victims: "All night long you will hear the wails and the screams of the youth of all ages, whom they abuse. Not even a child of six or seven will the miserable sodomites spare of their villainy, and they will carry out their abominable and unnatural intentions."

In all, whether the Americas, the Orient, Africa, or Oceania, every group has been perceived, with reason or not, as a center of unnatural relations. These observations, or fantasies, have often been determining factors at the center of social imagination where xenophobic impulses, religious fanaticism, and economic lust have contributed to the elaboration of a long-lived homophobic doxa: homosexuality is a foreign **vice**. Obviously, this argument does not constitute real anthropological knowledge, but represents a form of prehistory of anthropology whose characteristics weigh heavily on the history of the discipline, which sometimes has great difficulty freeing itself from its old demons.

Thus, this idea of foreign vice, conveyed by a rather primitive anthropology, was taken up and reflected by a more knowledgeable, though no less homophobic, anthropology, as demonstrated by the works of anthropologist Jomo Kenyatta. In 1938, Kenyatta, who later became the first president of an independent Kenya, published a book prefaced by famed Polish anthropologist Bronislaw Malinowski, titled *Facing Mount Kenya*, in which he strived to prove that homosexual relationships were foreign to the Kenyan Gikuyu culture and, more generally, to African culture. Since then, this idea, which, as can be imagined, has been well received in **Africa**, has given rise to many other works and arguments that claim homosexuality to be a European vice, a White vice, in short … a foreign vice. Today, these themes are propagated across Africa and are used to justify homophobic violence, as ancestral black cultures are, "naturally," exempt of this decadent perversion.

In short, the role of anthropology in the establishment of homophobic **rhetoric** is not new. But what does twentieth-century social and cultural anthropology (from the travel story to formal research) finally teach us about homosexuality and homophobia? Firstly, that most non-Western societies have types of "homosexuality," but they do not correspond to the definition we give homosexuality in the West. Most often, the category of "homosexual" does not exist. And it is rare to find sexual relations (or unions) between persons of the same social gender or even of the same generation, as is presently most often the case in the West. By simplifying, we can say that these societies have two large forms of homosexual practices. The first is based on a gender differentiation (i.e. one partner has a social gender that is different from his biological gender), and the second is based on generational differentiation; sometimes both forms are combined (Dynes and Donaldson, 1992). Thus, far from being repressed, the forms of homosexuality that we encounter in many non-Western societies often have a limited, but accepted place in those societies. For example, it is not rare for these individuals to be in charge of religious or spiritual matters, or that **marriages** between same-sex couples or their adoption of children to be accepted. What anthropology finally teaches us is that many societies function by dispensing with homophobia; that it is not a social inevitability. However, until the recent appearance of gay and lesbian studies, anthropology has never bothered to really develop an in-depth, methodical knowledge of the way certain societies ignore homophobia. This is why anthropologist Walter L. Williams, who has focused on the study of homosexual subcultures, was in favor of a commitment by researchers to the study of "non-homophobic" societies (i.e. societies that reserve an equal place to homosexuals), "before they disappear."

If we take into consideration what anthropology teaches with regard to the social recognition of homosexuality in various cultures or societies, we would find it paradoxical that the inegalitarian social and legal treatment of homosexuals in France was justified by certain "experts" who opposed equal rights in the name of "**symbolic order**" and "laws" allegedly based on anthropological constants. These arguments were used by sociologist Irène Théry, and repeated by many others after her, in her endless fight against complete legal recognition of same-sex couples. On the other hand, many researchers, such as Eric Fassin, Jeanne Favret-Saada, and Marie-Elisabeth Handman, have demonstrated the partial and instrumental logic of such arguments, by reaffirming the high malleability of cultural, social, or symbolic limits that those resistant to legal advances insist are immutable. But, in conforming with anthropology's long silence on homosexuality, the great majority of anthropologists has remained silent, such as Claude Lévi-Strauss (Fassin, 1999), or Françoise Héritier, who categorically refuses to integrate the homosexual question into her texts, even when it would seem inevitable (Héritier, 2002).[1]

Thus, no situation seems more favorable to the evaluation of contemporary anthropology's normative dimension than the debate surrounding same-sex unions and gay families. In fact, generally speaking, anthropology in France and elsewhere has assumed a normative role in response to a political demand. It has been recuperated and exploited by researchers who have succumbed to the "charm of *a priori* expertise," forgetting, as sociologist Eric Fassin said, that "politicians look to the experts in order to justify their refusals." Fassin also underlines that in this democratic debate, there is no use in saying that sexual differences are the "impassible impediments of thought" or in setting limits to what is considered in the "neutrality of knowledge." If it is not conceived through the process of acknowledging the context of the production and reception of its knowledge of the social world it will always be restricted to the normative dimension.

In this sense, setting up themes within taboos reinforces its normative dimension, prevents the expression of the critical dimension that should be its own, and betrays the homophobia that Anthropology disclaims.

Consequently, anthropology would benefit from reexamining the works of Michel Foucault which, as much by his criticism of **essentialism** and of the reifying character of social sciences as by his proposal of a "history of problematics," would no doubt pave the way for the development of scientific knowledge that is neither condemning nor totalitarian.

—*Christophe Broqua and Alexandra Fleming Câmara Vale*

Blackwood, Evelyn, ed. *Anthropology and Homosexual Behavior.* New York: The Haworth Press, 1986.

Bleys, Rudi C. *The Geography of Perversion: Male-to-Male Sexual Behavior Outside the West and the Ethnographic Imagination, 1750–1918.* New York: New York Univ. Press, 1995.

Borrillo, Daniel, Eric Fassin, and Marcela Iacub, eds. *Au-delà du PACS: l'expertise familiale à l'épreuve de l'homosexualité.* Paris: Presses universitaires de France, 1999.

Dynes, Wayne R., and Stephen Donaldson, eds. *Ethnographic Studies of Homosexuality.* New York: Garland, 1992.

Eliacheff, Caroline, Antoine Garapon, Nathalie Heinich, Françoise Héritier, Aldo Naouri, Paul Veyne, and Heinz Wismann. "Ne laissons pas la critique du PaCS à la droite!" *Le Monde,* (January 27, 1999).

Evans-Pritchard, Edward. "Sexual Inversion among the Azande," *American Anthropologist,* no. 72 (1970).

Fassin, Eric. "L'Illusion anthropologique: homosexualité et filiation," *Témoin,* no. 12 (May–June 1998).

———. "Le Savant, l'expert et le politique," *Genèses,* no. 32 (1998).

———. "Usages de la science et science des usages: à propos des familles homoparentales," *L'Homme,* no. 154–155 (2000).

Favret-Saada, Jeanne. "La-Pensée-Lévi-Strauss," *Journal des anthropologies,* no. 82–83 (2000).

Godard, Didier. *L'Autre Faust: l'homosexualité masculine pendant la Renaissance.* Montblanc: H & O Editions, 2001.

Goldberg, Jonathan. "Sodomy in the New World: Anthropologies Old and New," *Social Text,* no. 9 (1991).

Handman, Marie-Elisabeth. "Sexualité et famille: approche anthropologique." In *Au-delà du PACS: l'expertise familiale à l'épreuve de l'homosexualité.* Paris: Presses universitaires de France, 1999.

Héritier, Françoise. *Masculin/Féminin 2: Dissoudre la hiérarchie.* Paris: Odile Jacob, 2002.

Kenyatta, Jomo. *Facing Mount Kenya: The Tribal Life of the Gikuyu.* London: Secker & Warburg, 1938.

Mauss, Marcel. *Sociologie et anthropologie (1950).* Paris: Presses universitaires de France, 2001.

---

1 All the while Héritier was taking an **anti-PaCS** stand by co-signing an article that appeared in *Le Monde,* titled "Ne laissons pas la critique du PaCS à la droite!" (Let's not leave the criticism of PaCS to the right!), written by sociologist Nathalie Heinich and published a few days before the famous demonstration organized by Christine Boutin.

Mendès-Leite, Rommel. *Le Sens de l'altérité: penser les (homo-sexualités)*. Paris: L'Harmattan, 2000.

Poirier, Guy. *L'Homosexualité dans l'imaginaire de la Renaissance*. Paris: Honoré Champion, 1996.

Théry, Irène. "Différence des sexes et différences des généra-tions: l'institution familiale en déshérence," *Esprit*, no. 12 (1996).

———. "Le Contrat d'union sociale en question." *Esprit*, no. 10 (1997). Also published as no. 91 of *Notes de la Fondation Saint-Simon*.

———. "PaCS, sexualité et différence des sexes." *Esprit*, no. 257 (1999).

Williams, Walter L. "Being Gay and Doing Fieldwork." In *Out in the Field: Reflections of Lesbian and Gay Anthropologists*. Urbana-Chicago: Univ. of Illinois Press, 1996.

—Africa, Central & Eastern; Africa, Southern; Africa, Western; Essentialism/Constructionism; Heresy; History; Latin America; Marriage; Oceania; Parenting; Southeast Asia; Rhetoric; Sociology; Symbolic Order.

ANTI-PaCS

The Pacte civil de solidarité (Civil solidarity pact), better known as PaCS, was proposed by the French government of Prime Minister Lionel Jospin in 1998 (after being initially drafted a year earlier) and ap-proved by the French Parliament in November 1999, but not without controversy. PaCS is a form of legal partnership between two adults (whether same-sex or opposite-sex) with some, but not all, of the rights and responsibilities of traditional marriage. When it was first introduced, there was vocal opposition, some of which came from those on the political left. However, the expression "anti-PaCS" specifically applies to the opposition expressed by right-wing groups and indi-viduals (including politicians) who rallied against the adoption of a bill that would extend rights to same-sex couples. The name echoes "anti-IVG" (*interrup-tion volontaire de grossesse*; elective abortion), a pro-life movement whose members also became involved in the fight against PaCS; Génération anti-PaCS, the col-lective that spearheaded protests against the proposal, represented the convergence of militants from family (i.e. pro-life) associations with those from two political parties, the right-wing RPR (Rassemblement pour la Republique; Rally for the Republic) and the centrist

UDF (Union pour la democratie Française; Union for French Democracy). While demonstrations against the proposal were highly visible during the final months of parliamentary debate, these protests were the result of years of campaigning led by extreme right-wing organizations. The idea of a law recognizing same-sex couples mobilized the ultra-conservative group Associations familiales catholiques (AFC; Catholic Family Associations) as early as 1997. Of all the family associations, this group was ideologically the closest to the right-wing National Front party, which explains why the National Front was only marginally visible as a separate entity in the anti-PaCS campaign. This battle was considered so important by the AFC that it pre-ferred to delay its annual pilgrimage to the sacred site of Lourdes, France, in order to "allow families to mo-bilize against PaCS." Its campaign launched in January 1998 with the distribution of a four-page document describing the then-named CUCS (Contrat d'union civile et sociale; Civil and social union contract) as a "discount **marriage**" "with all the rights (advantages)" of a marriage, "without its duties (inconveniences)," and claiming that it originated as a result of the "pow-erful homosexual **lobby**." At the same time, the AFC stated that, if passed, the law would cause a number of things to happen: destabilize society, disintegrate the nation's social fabric, threaten traditional common-law marriage, act against the best interests of children, eventually lead to the legal recognition of polygamy, and even give rise to "the emergence of a multicultural society that will result in the formation of **ghettos** and increase exclusion." In all, 100,000 copies were distrib-uted, mostly during World Youth Day events. The idea of lobbying followed; the most successful operation was one organized by the Collectif des maires pour le mar-iage républicain (Collective of mayors for republican marriage), known as the "Anti-CUS Mayors" ("CUS" being the appended form of CUCS) campaign, which was officially supported by a UDF mayor but can be traced back to the AFC.

The "Anti-CUS Mayors" Campaign

The anti-CUS mayors' campaign began with an April 15, 1998 article published in the French newspaper *Le Monde* with the headline "12,000 Mayors Opposed to Social Union Contract." At the time, the CUS pro-posal was still being formulated and had not yet been debated in Parliament, so the news of a revolt by a collective of 12,000 mayors, all of whom were signatories to a petition opposing "gay marriage," made a lot of noise. But how were the document's signatures collected, and who financed it? Information supplied from organizers revealed the rudimentary details of a mail campaign that took place over a three-month period. All that is known is that a first letter, accompanied by a declaration of intent to be returned to the organizers, was sent to the 36,700 mayors of France on March 2. In an alarmist tone, the letter asked them to "defend republican marriage" by opposing the CUS, which it claimed would allow "real homosexual marriage." To this end, the recipients needed only to sign a form letter, by which they would declare themselves to be "concerned with the preservation of the family as a natural and fundamental element of any society" and opposed "to the establishment of a union contract for same-sex couples ... and the implication of the mayor, as a civil officer, in officiating over such a contract." The result: 12,000 signatures collected in a few weeks. In a press release proudly announcing the operation, the Collectif proclaimed the 12,000 French mayors to "safeguard republican marriage," and that many mayors would resign should the CUS be adopted. Buoyed by this success, Michel Pinton, spokesperson for the Collectif, even circulated a repulsively homophobic "Call to Mayors for a Real Debate": "In our unhealthy French society, two healthy components—the family and the municipality, both vitally important for our democracy—are threatened by catastrophic deterioration" by the "poison" of the CUS. But soon thereafter, doubts began to surface.

Three weeks after the announcement of the petition, neither Pinton nor Vianney Mallein, the chief of the communication agency responsible for the file, were willing to publish the list of petitioners, despite repeated calls from journalists. However, when the list was finally obtained, it was primarily composed of mostly rural mayors of tiny municipalities and with no political affiliation. Still, another association was active in the campaign against the CUS: the Avenir de la culture (Future of the Culture), whose campaign against the proposal resulted in a huge number of protest postcards sent to the Prime Minister's Matignon office (and official residence).

The Campaigns of Avenir de la Culture

In the summer of 1998, five months after the anti-CUS petition, the Avenir de la culture set up an operation aimed at flooding the Matignon office with pre-

addressed postcards against the "homosexual marriage" bill, which it considered "loathsome" and "repugnant." It featured an image of a traditional family pierced by lightning, over a background image of a torn map of France; the other side of the card contained a hate-filled message:

> Mister Prime Minister, your project to recognize homosexual 'marriage' and the equality between cohabitation and marriage is unacceptable.... It is the choice of a decadent society, which sets us back two thousand years. Tomorrow, in France, sexual deviation will become the norm and marriage outdated!... Mister Prime Minister, I enjoin you to renounce this loathsome bill that will destroy the remains of civilization that still separate us from barbarism.

In all, Matignon received between 70,000 and 100,000 cards between July and August 1998. Though the government mail service may have shredded the cards immediately, the sheer number and the media coverage were enough to guarantee the desired affect.

So who is Avenir de la culture? Founded in 1986 and under the direction of Luc Berrou, the association appears to be linked to a Brazilian sect known as TFP (Tradition, Family, Property). Launched in 1960 by Plinio Corrêa de Oliveira, TFP became known in France in the mid-1980s by participating in large protests against the controversial films *Je vous salue, Marie* (*Hail Mary*) by Jean-Luc Godard and *The Last Temptation of Christ* by Martin Scorsese. It also intervened in South Africa and in Namibia alongside extreme right-wing and pro-apartheid groups. In the United States, its representative was none other than Paul Weyrich, the conservative activist and a founding member of the religious right who pioneered the direct-mail technique of political lobbying that was hugely successful, paving the way for the campaign conducted by Avenir de la culture against the CUS. However, doubtless because of its extremism, Avenir de la culture was superseded in its opposition to PaCS by the more presentable, and thus more efficient, Générations anti-PaCS collective.

Anti-PaCS Demonstrations

Générations anti-PaCS was built up over the course of numerous demonstrations through alliances formed by a growing number of large conservative associations opposed to the bill. Initially led by the AFC, the anti-PaCS offensive resonated with the UNAF (Union nationale des associations familiales [National Union of Family Associations]), which was mostly made up of conservative Catholic groups. The AFC confederation organized what it called a "marriage operation" with three other pro-family groups which would become part of the pro-marriage, anti-PaCS collective: the Familles de France, Associations familiales protestantes (Associations of Protestant Families), and Union des familles musulmanes (Union of Muslim Families). Together, but mainly under the influence of the AFC, these associations invited their sympathizers to go to their city halls and sign a symbolic registry in which they would declare "their attachment to the commitments made during marriage" and "demand that government not extend the specific rights of marriage to other forms of cohabitation." The AFC confederation behind this "marriage operation" soon claimed to have collected tens of thousands of signatures; it owed this success in part to the Alliance pour les droits de la vie (Alliance for the Rights of Life), the umbrella organization for conservative, religious-right politician's Christine **Boutin**'s para-parliamentary pro-life activities since 1995. Meanwhile, the number of anti-PaCS demonstrations increased through to October 9, 1998, the date of the first debates on the proposal in the National Assembly; however, most of these met with little success. The first demonstrations to have had some effect occurred on October 3. Following a call to arms by the four main family associations who had coordinated the "marriage operation," protests were simultaneously organized in fifty cities. It was the first official action taken by the Collectif pour le mariage et contre le PaCS (Collective for Marriage and Against PaCS), or CMCP. In some cities, the demonstrations encountered opposition from antifascist activists from Ras l'front (Enough of the Front), CNT union anarchists (Confédération nationale de travail; [National Work Confederation]) and gay and lesbian associations. In the town of Ille-et-Vilaine, thirty demonstrators came to blows. But everything changed as the parliamentary debates began and other groups opposed to PaCS came onto the scene, inclined to engage in less militant forms of protest.

The opening debates on October 9 marked a turning point in the methods used to mobilize anti-PaCS protests. While the debates were stopped for a breakfast break, several hundred PaCS opponents loudly demonstrated outside the Palais Bourbon. Surprisingly, with the exception of a few Members of Parliament who joined them, the demonstrators were mostly youths, dancing to the rhythm of techno beats, all wearing green and orange T-shirts; unusual for a demonstration with such reactionary objectives. However, their appearance was only skin-deep: backed by rather aggressive security, the protest organizers only allowed those people who appealed to them to join the demonstration. Nonetheless, amid the protesters, the chorus of the song "I Will Survive" could be heard. Certainly, the 1970s disco hit is often used as the theme song of the LGBT Pride movement, but very few people know that it was also the theme of a new, self-proclaimed youth movement called Survivants, made up of youths born after the passing of the 1975 "Veil Bill" (which allowed for access to abortion), and who considered themselves "abortion survivors." Despite this group's sad motivation, its appearance at the October 9 demonstration revealed the inventiveness that the anti-PaCS initiative felt was needed to reinvigorate its course of action. From that moment on, every pro-family association mobilized in preparation for the next major protest on November 7.

On that day, while debates in the French National Assembly continued, thousands of anti-PaCS militants demonstrated outside. Their ranks had grown with the addition of other associations that had joined the CMCP, such as the Rassemblement pour les mères au foyer (Gathering for Mothers of the Hearth), the Comité évangélique protestant pour la dignité humaine (Evangelical Protestant Committee for Human Dignity), the Coordination étudiante contre le PaCS (Organization of Students Against PaCS), Enfance et sécurité (Childhood and Security), Collectif des maires de France pour le mariage républicain (Collective of French Mayors for Republican Marriage), and the Mouvement mondial des mères (World Movement of Mothers). The number of protesters was estimated at between 40,000 and 50,000. Like the October 9 protest, the march was colorful and lively; demonstrators at times danced to amusing beats (like the Macarena), at other times to old standards. The protest also had inspired elements meant to prove the "modernism" and imagination of the new moral order; at the head of the parade was a fluorescent-colored float carrying a couple dressed as newlyweds. And the slogans on the placards were just as gaudy: "PaCS Out," "2 Daddies, 2 Mommies, What a Mess," "PaCS in November,

Adoption in December," "6 Billion for PaCS: Who Will Foot the Bill?," "PaCS and BUST," "Oh PaCS, Oh Despair, Oh Misguided Youth," even "PS = PD" (Parti socialiste = Fags). When interviewed, a female protester stated, "Whether my hairdresser is gay or not is none of my business; it needs to remain a private affair." And asked about the fate of children raised by homosexuals, a demonstrator opined that "these children will have a lot of problems" and that "they will need to see a **psychiatrist** as soon as possible." Another stated: "Sometimes, in gay couples, it's possible for one of them to be very effeminate—possibly due to a **genetic** disorder—so that he could play the role of the mother. It's better than nothing...." Among other comments recorded by media: "Put the fags in **prison**!" "Would you like to be raised by a couple **against nature**?" and "Fags are [the work of] Satan! They're evil! They need to be fought!" The march ended up at Place Vauban, where protesters called out to every parliamentary opposition member in attendance, including future French president Nicolas Sarkozy, as well as their biggest political ally, Christine Boutin, for whom they shouted, "Chris-tine! Chris-tine!" The press was surprised by the moral order's new look. Quoted in *Libération*, a passerby admits that he was confused; "I thought they were demonstrating in favor of PaCS." For its part, the commentary in *Le Figaro* was ecstatic: "Young, in vogue: the anti-PaCS demonstration surprised adversaries and partisans alike." Nevertheless, another national demonstration was in the works.

The most famous anti-PaCS protest, and the most violent, remains the one that took place on January 31, 1999, launched by Boutin herself and involving the members of pro-family and religious organizations as well as a good number from France's far right. It was for this demonstration that the CMCP, in an effort to promote its new youthful image, transformed itself into Générations anti-PaCS, which was imprinted on thousands of stickers with the slogan, "For Social Cohesion." The demonstration was expected to rival one that had taken place in support of private schooling, which had united nearly 1 million people in the streets of Paris. In all, organizers expected 400 buses from ninety-one regions of France. Fearing that the police would downplay the number of demonstrators, for the first time, organizers used an electronic system in order to count protesters.

Meanwhile, gays and lesbians were mobilizing in anticipation of the march. On the morning of January 31, activist members of ACT UP-Paris arrived at the home of Boutin armed with fog horns and shouting, "Boutin, wake up! The queers are below!" Earlier, a group of gay activists took advantage of the early morning light to tear up anti-PaCS placards, or plaster them with home-made stickers that read "Hetero-terrorist" and "You're ridiculous in your t-shirts." The first groups of anti-PaCS demonstrators arrived around nine a.m., transforming the 7th arrondissement into a sea of uniformed youths dressed in long, dark blue capes; revealing glimpses of shaved heads beneath their caps, there was little doubt that the far right's muscle had been requisitioned. The march got underway at three p.m. to the strains of "Here Comes the Bride" and "I Will Survive." Marchers were applauded as they passed by, while a group of well-dressed men with brush-cuts and berets sang, to the beat of a drum, the catchphrase "PaCS won't go through!" to the tune of a well-known French monarchist song. The blatant homophobia apparent in the marchers, not to mention their racism and sexism, shocked those not opposed to PaCS who had the courage to approach the procession. Among the slogans on the 18,000 placards brandished by protesters: "Love doesn't work with PaCS," "The homosexuals of today are the **pedophiles** of tomorrow!" and "Burn the queers!"

Although they had been discreet in the past, right-wing politicians proudly marched alongside the demonstrators, banners aflutter. Members of the National Front demonstrated while surrounded by fundamentalist flags with fleurs de lys and eighteenth-century counter-revolutionary symbols, their arms linked as they marched.

The "Perverse" Effect of Homophobic Violence

The large anti-PaCS demonstrations did not have the hoped-for effect, however; in fact, it was quite the opposite. The day following the January 31 protest, observers noted the relatively low turnout: 98,271, a far cry from the 1 million predicted by organizers. However, the greatest misdeed was the homophobic violence that organizers failed to contain. The worst occurred at the Trocadéro Theater; in guise of a "welcoming committee," members of ACT UP-Paris working with the Observatoire du PaCS, arranged to unveil a large banner reading "Homophobes," and signed by "les folles de Chaillot" ("the queens of Chaillot"; the Trocadéro was housed on the site of the former Palais de Chaillot). As soon as they saw the banner, anti-PaCS militants exploded in fury and with iron bars in hand, they pounced on the ACT UP members, shouting "Fucking fags!" "Burn in hell!" and "Piss off with your AIDS!"; they were cheered on by other demonstrators. In the days that followed, the Catholic newspaper *La Croix* was assailed by letters from upset Catholics, many of whom declared that they did not recognize themselves in this demonstration of intolerance. Looking back, some gay and lesbian activists agree that this homophobic violence served to shock public opinion which until then had been indifferent. However, much more energy, talent, communication, and strategy was required to turn this change in opinion into real sympathy that was beneficial to PaCS and gay and lesbian couples throughout France.

—*Caroline Fourest*

Borrillo, Daniel, Eric Fassin, and Marcela Iacub, eds. *Au-delà du PACS. L'expertise familiale à l'épreuve de l'homosexualité*. Paris: Presses universitaires de France, 1999.

Boutin, Christine. *Le "Mariage" des homosexuels? CUCS, PIC, PACS et autres projets législatifs*. Paris: Critérion, 1998.

Brunnquell, Frédéric. *Associations familiales, combien de divisions?* Paris: Ed. Dagorno, 1994.

Camus, Jean-Yves, and René Monzat. *Les Droites nationales et radicales en France*. Lyon, France: Presses universitaires de Lyon, 1992.

Fourest, Caroline. "Ces Symboles qui tiennent le PaCS à distance de l'égalité," *ProChoix*, no. 7 (1998).

———. "Quand les manifestations anti-PaCS singent la gay pride," *ProChoix*, no. 8 (1998).

———, and Fiammetta Venner. *Les Anti-PaCS*. Paris: Ed. Prochoix, 1999.

Monroe, Laurence. "Des familles se fâchent contre le PaCS," *La Croix* (October 3, 1999).

—*Adoption; Boutin, Christine; Catholic Church, the; Family; Far Right; Marriage; Parenting; Rhetoric; Violence.*

ARENAS, Reinaldo

Cuban writer and novelist Reinaldo Arenas was born on July 16, 1943. After being abandoned by his father, he and his mother went to live with his grandfather on his farm in Holguín, in the Cuban *provincia* of Oriente. There, Reinaldo grew up surrounded by his aunts and his mother, a tender woman who not only taught him how to read and write, but also filled his childhood

with a magical appreciation of the stars and other mysteries of the night.

In 1958, at the age of fifteen, Arenas sought to join the Castroist guerrillas who had risen against General Rubén Fulgencio Batista. Though he did not participate in any military combat, he witnessed the summary executions decreed by the revolutionary tribunals which took place inside La Pantoja which, under Batista, served as a military school in the city of Holguín. After its post-revolution "rehabilitation" to become the School of Planification, Arenas, then sixteen, enrolled to begin his studies to become an agronomist. It was during this time that his first experiences of the new communist regime's homophobia took place, as those who praised the revolution simultaneously condemned homosexuality. Those students caught engaging in homosexual acts were brought before the headmaster to be expelled, then marched past other students to be beaten and stoned. In the 1960s, Castroist homophobia was expressed in the form of boisterous and reproachful demonstrations that denounced homosexual intellectuals.

In his autobiography, *Antes que anochezca* (*Before Night Falls*), Arenas contrasts two opposing forces in the lives of homosexuals in Cuba. On one hand, he describes a powerful and erotic homosexual underground, which, come nightfall, pervades the streets of Havana, its parks, and along the waterfront (El Malecón), where gay men go to satisfy their urgent impulses. (Arenas admits to his own participation, and describes his impressive record: hundreds of encounters in town, on trains, in the darkness of theaters.) On the other hand, he recounts legislation that, since 1963, allowed for the severe repression of homosexuals in Cuba. A culture of hypermorality which praised **work** and glorified the homeland and its heroes led to a campaign of persecution, in which homosexuals were subject to denunciation, arrest, and imprisonment, or sent to the specially created UMAP (Military Units for Aide in Production) work camps. However, this legislated repression, as imposed by the regime, generated a defiant response from homosexuals.

Meanwhile, at the age of twenty, Arenas applied to the prestigious Biblioteca Nacional José Martí for the position of storyteller. As part of his application, he wrote a story, then recited it by heart before the jury and the library director who were so impressed that he got the position. His new duties allowed him to come in contact with great writers, which proved to be a significant step in his literary education. His first novel (and the only one ever published in Cuba), *Celestino antes del alba* (*Singing from the Well*), published in 1967, received the first Honorable Mention prize awarded by the UNEAC (National Union of Cuban Writers and Artists). From 1969 onward, however, Arenas fell under the surveillance of the state police who sought to identify his relationships with foreigners and to stop the export of his manuscripts to writers and other allies outside of the country.

In his autobiography, Arenas revealed the circumstances by which his writings, despite these obstacles, were sent abroad. On one occasion, he was aided by Cuban expatriate painter Jorge Camacho, who resided in Paris with his wife Margarita, and with whom Arenas enjoyed a lifelong friendship. He managed to pass along to them his novel *El mundo alucinante* (*Hallucinations*), which was translated by Didier Coste and published in France. Arenas edited *Hallucinations* with the help of Cuban novelist and poet Virgilio Piñera (1912–1979), a gay atheist and anti-communist who eventually became his literary mentor. Subsequent manuscripts, however, such as *Otra vez el mar* (*Farewell to the Sea*), ended up hidden in order to escape the notice of the state police. A friend, Aurelio Cortés, was entrusted with the original copy of *Farewell to the Sea*, who later passed it on to nuns for safekeeping. When the novel's existence became known, however, it provoked a **scandal** and the novel was destroyed. Two years later, Arenas wrote a new version, though this too he kept hidden under the rooftop tiles where he lived. Police surveillance was becoming more and more intense, as Arenas's room was regularly inspected and his mail intercepted. In 1970, he was sent to "voluntarily" work in the sugar cane fields, which for him was a hellish experience. That same year, the first Educational and Cultural Congress in Cuba adopted a series of discriminatory measures aimed specifically at gay artists and writers. A system was put into place in which individuals were excluded from certain rights and subsequently forced into work camps because of their sexuality; these individuals were duly informed of the political and moral motives justifying this treatment. In what was more or less a witch-hunt, some writers became informants.

In the summer of 1973, Arenas was arrested in Guanabo after being accused by the police of being a counterrevolutionary; he was freed on bail. After a second arrest, however, he was imprisoned, but succeeded in escaping and headed toward Guantanamo, where he hoped to cross the border into the American military base there. This attempt resulted in failure. Upon covertly returning to Havana, he took refuge in Lenin Park and began writing *Before Night Falls*, which he hurriedly finished in the event he was caught. He was arrested again in December of 1973, convicted of gross indecency, and imprisoned at the notorious El Morro Castle alongside murderers and rapists. He remained behind bars for over two years, interrupted by a three-month stay at state police headquarters, then transferred to the Reparte Flores prison; he was finally released in 1976.

On May 4, 1980, as part of the massive Port of Mariel exodus which aimed to rid Cuba of unwanted elements such as murderers, prostitutes, and homosexuals, Arenas thought he could finally leave the country, but he discovered that because his banned work was such a vivid representation of the country's problems, the government would not allow him to leave. However, he eluded authorities by changing his name to "Arinas" on his passport, and escaped to the United States, first to Florida, then New York. In 1983, along with other Cuban refugees, he founded the literary magazine *Mariel*, whose first issue was dedicated to the late gay Cuban writer José Lezama Lima. Arenas enjoyed his newfound freedom, often traveling to universities in America and Europe to read from his work. In 1987, however, Arenas was diagnosed with **AIDS**. Three years later in 1990, after battling his illness, Arenas took a fatal overdose of drugs and alcohol in New York. But his legacy continues through his writing, including many works translated into English: *The Palace of the White Skunks*, *Farewell to the Sea*, *Graveyard of the Angels*, *Hallucinations*, *Singing from the Well*, *The Color of Summer*, *The Assault*, *The Doorman*, *Before Night Falls*, *Old Rosa*, and *Mona and Other Tales*. Arenas also collaborated with numerous directors in the production of various films, such as Jorge Ulla's *En sus propias palabras*, Carlos Franqui's *La otra Cuba*, Nestor Almendros and Orlando Jiménez Leal's *Conducta impropia* (1984), and Jana Bokova's *Havana* (1990). In 2001, New York painter and sculptor Julian Schnabel directed the film adaptation of Arenas' autobiography *Before Night Falls*, starring Academy Award nominee Javier Bardem as Arenas.

—*André Fernandez*

Arenas, Reinaldo. *Antes que anochezca*. Barcelona: Tusquets
    Editores, SA, 2001. [Published in the US as *Before Night*

Falls. Translated by Dolores M. Koch. New York: Penguin, 1994.]

Montaner, Carlos Alberto. *Viaje al corazón de Cuba.* Barcelona: Plaza & Janés Editores, SA, 1999. [Published in the US as *Journey to the Heart of Cuba: Life as Fidel Castro.* New York: Algora, 2001.]

Verdes-Leroux, Jeannine. *La Lune et le Caudillo, le rêve des intellectuels et le régime cubain (1959–1971)*. Paris: Gallimard, 1989.

—*Armed Forces; Censorship; Communism; Gulag; Latin America; Literature; Police; Violence.*

ARMED FORCES

In the Western world to this day, the armed forces remain highly homophobic. It is first a homophobia of proximity. Until recently, the army was an exclusively male domain, and historically has been a place where homoeroticism could easily flourish, as proven by the sacred battalion of Thebes, the armies of Louis XIV, the Prussian regiments under Frederic II, and British colonial troops. Evidence of homophobia in the military is thus linked to the real or imagined perception of a homosexual "threat," and recruiting officers, perhaps under the impression that the army is an attractive place to many homosexuals, are driven by the fear that the army might become a "lair," a twisted logic that associates "entryism" with "**contagion**."

In authoritarian or totalitarian societies, the issue of prestige is important to the army, which must serve as both a school and a model. For example, we can note that evidence of Heinrich **Himmler**'s extremely violent homophobia in Nazi Germany was linked to his concern that the army's morals would rub off on German society in the case of a general mobilization, to the (paradoxical) discovery that the warrior society of the Third Reich risked separating the sexes, defeminizing women, and, in short, forgetting "Nature." In all, between 1939 and 1944, roughly 7,000 Wehrmacht combatants were imprisoned for the crime of homosexuality.

Generally speaking, in Western military circles, the homosexual threat was more often related to the theme of **treason**, as demonstrated by the Redl Affair in 1913 Austria, or the Kiessling-NATO Affair of 1983–84. Whether homosexuality was considered an element of the perverse **psychology** of impulsive and spineless men, as it was seventy years ago, or if it made men thus afflicted vulnerable to blackmail, the end result has been the persistent belief that homosexuals are unsuited for fighting (although André **Gide**, in his book *Corydon*, fought for opposite argument).

Military homophobia is also sociological in origin. In most countries, officers are mainly recruited from the population's most traditionalist (i.e. reactionary) sectors, notably the Catholic right (such as in France, Spain, Portugal, and Latin America), and the more conservative Protestant milieu (as in the United Kingdom and the United States). Such recruits are not in the habit of questioning social conventions, sexual roles, or the Christian **symbolic order**, and it is quite significant that the great Western homophobes of the twentieth century include such notables as Marshal **Pétain**, General Franco (who was obsessed by the danger of homosexuality among young officers), General Pinochet, General Eisenhower, and Field Marshal Montgomery (who incidentally has been outed in recent accounts about him).

Further, in nations where a draft for required military service is in place, the military aims to construct a perfectly virile, heterosexual identity for itself among the conscripts called up for national service. In France, a speech by World War II officer Marcel Bigeard that referred to the "little boys" who, thanks to him, became real men (i.e. "not queers") is significant. And as sociologist Henning Bech notes, the harshest insults in the homophobic arsenal "are necessary ingredients in the relation between the instructor and the recruit, like that between the torturer and the victim." Since the end of the nineteenth century, the work of turning military recruits into homophobic "real men" (based in part on a general contempt for all forms of male delicateness) has traditionally been passed along to junior officers. For recruits, it is difficult to resist such indoctrination, as one's refusal is immediately seen as suspicious. The offensive label "fag," which has become commonplace, owes much to the barracks during the two World Wars. And the leap from verbal to physical **violence** against homosexuals in the military is a short one; those in the military have traditionally been encouraged to exact violence against those caught cruising, or worse. Such homophobia relies on the stereotype of the effeminate homosexual who is the perceived opposite of the military man, and vice versa. In this sense, the "virilization" of the gay male image since the 1970s has been extraordinarily destabilizing for the homophobes in uniform, who are thus deprived of their stereotypical points of reference: as a result, hyper-masculinity, long considered as belonging to the arena of the military as a heterosexual trait, instead becomes a perceived threat.

Homophobia has a long-standing tradition in the army. It appears first in a number of military regulations in numerous countries, which in turn have served as models for more general anti-homosexual restrictions (this was the case in Russia: homosexuality was first forbidden for servicemen at the beginning of the eighteenth century, and then later or the general male population in 1832). That being said, in the Ancien Régime in France, punishment was relatively "benign": the 1689 edict on the navy stipulated that "indecent actions will be punished with six lashes of the winch rope, performed by the provost marshal; doubled in case of repeat infringement," which was not too severe in comparison to other contemporary regulations. The most famous examples of military homophobia can be found in the regulations of English-speaking countries, however. In the United States, an anti-homosexual clause was put into place between 1918 and 1943 (as early as 1919, the US Navy set traps for its personnel in order to weed out homosexuals). What followed was a veritable witch-hunt against homosexuals in the military, notably at the end of the 1940s and the beginning of the 1950s, when the Pentagon charged psychiatrists with the task of "locating homosexuals, first by their airs or their effeminateness, and second by watching their reactions when homosexual jargon is pronounced in their presence." Expulsions from the military reached a height of 3,000 people a year in the early 1960s before slowing down to an average of 1,500 expulsions per year during the 1980s (51% of whom were from the Navy), and then to 1,000 expulsions per year during the 1990s. In 1982, an official Pentagon document reminded personnel that "homosexuality is incompatible with active service," insisting that it affects "discipline," "order," "morale," "mutual confidence," "rank hierarchy," "operational efficiency," "recruitment," "the public image," and "security." In this, we can see that the supporters of the prohibition of homosexuality essentially have three major fears: (1) that the showers and barracks will become area of promiscuity; (2) that relationships will develop between servicemen of different ranks, resulting in **scandal** and demonstrating a lack of discipline; and (3) that breaches of security will be created due to

all manner of blackmail. The anti-homosexual rule was also applied to women when they became eligible to sign up, which had a notable effect on them, in particular those who entered into undesired heterosexual relationships in order to protect themselves from being labeled lesbian (women, who made up 11% of US soldiers, constituted 22% of the cases of expulsion for homosexuality).

Though presidential candidate Bill Clinton had stated during his 1992 election campaign that he would completely remove the ban on homosexuals in the army, he later backed down when confronted by the powerful military lobby, which was in a favorable position following the revelation of Clinton's refusal to serve in Vietnam. As President, Clinton settled on the now-infamous policy of Don't Ask, Don't Tell, Don't Pursue. The Clinton doctrine, which had been established in 1993, revealed itself to be unsatisfying in its applications: those in command were no longer to look for gays and lesbians in the military, but neither were they to recognize their existence. In short, this policy conferred no dignity upon homosexuals equal to that of heterosexuals, and it prohibited any effective fight against the still-prevalent homophobic atmosphere in the military (in 1999 alone, 968 anti-gay incidents in the US Army were reported, including one murder). Gay and lesbian service personnel were still to be dismissed if, in one way or another, they divulged their homosexuality (the National Gay and Lesbian Task Force affirms that, in 1999, the Pentagon carried out three dismissals per day on such grounds).

A similar ban in the British armed forces was lifted in 2000. But for over thirty years, the 1967 decriminalization of homosexuality did not apply to those serving in the military because British authorities, just like the Pentagon and for the same reasons, considered that the open presence of homosexuals in the armed forces would create an untenable situation for heterosexual personnel. From 1967 to 1999, British military police, based on the even the smallest suspicion (such as a tip from a blackmailer or a young woman whose advances had been rejected), carried out inquiries, interrogations, and searches of those personnel suspected of being homosexual. Even if the officers in charge of such investigations were not homophobic themselves (in fact some, as would be later discovered, were closeted gays placed in situations where conscience and duty conflicted), British respect for the law eliminated any room for compromise: dismissals from the British military averaged sixty per year and, as it became more gender-inclusive, women were targeted as often as men. Over the years, however, protests multiplied and those dismissed formed an association, Rank Outsiders. In 1999, the European Court of Human Rights, having taken up the case of four former army personnel (Jeannette Smith, Duncan Lustig-Prean, Graeme Grady, and John Beckett), found the British government guilty of violating Articles 8 and 14 of the Charter of Fundamental Rights of the European Union and, by this decision, obliged Britain to lift the ban on homosexuals in the military. Certain high-ranking opponents expressed themselves through the British media, recanting the arguments of 1967, but the opinions published in the November 1999 issue of the British magazine *Gay Times* clearly showed that the ban was not supported by a majority of army and navy personnel. After his dismissal for being homosexual, despite a shining service record and a brilliant future in the British Royal Navy, Lieutenant Commander Duncan Lustig-Prean was flooded with expressions of sympathy from his superiors, his colleagues, and the men under his command, many of whom admitted they had long guessed his sexual orientation and that they could not have cared any less about it. For the rest, there was no mistake: the lifting of the ban did not signify that homosexual relationships were now authorized among those serving in the British armed forces (the same applied to heterosexual relationships); it only meant that one could now be openly gay and a member of the military. However, this trend among English-speaking countries does not eclipse the fact that, as recently as in 2001, many countries that had decriminalized homosexuality, such as Greece, Portugal, and Russia, still did not allow homosexuals to serve in the military.

Military homophobia, however, is not only manifested through law. The French armed forces offer many examples of homophobic practices in a country where, for the last two centuries, homosexuality has been neither a crime nor an offence—at least in theory. But the French military has had a checkered past regarding its homosexual members, as demonstrated by certain notorious court cases implicating military personnel (the most recent, and also one of the worst, being the Chanal Affair, in which French army veteran Pierre Chanal killed himself shortly after his trial began for the sexually motivated murders of three men in the 1980s). In the nineteenth century, most of these scandals dealt with prostitution involving soldiers or navy person-

nel; authorities were worried about the corruption that "anti-physiques" (those "against nature," according to eighteenth-century discourse) would introduce in the elite forces, threatening their health and morale, and they sought to reintroduce a *de facto* ban by way of police surveillance and ridicule in the media. For example, soldiers who attacked two Chartres homosexuals in 1805 were vigorously supported (the issue reaching all the way to the Emperor); the 1824 beating of the Marquis de **Custine** on the road to St-Denis by a group of soldiers, with one of whom Custine allegedly had attempted to have a sexual encounter, was applauded; Captain Voyer was caught "red-handed," fondling an artilleryman in the woods near Vincennes on June 18, 1880, and was then arrested and tried for public indecency; and during the years between the World Wars, the streets and squares of Toulon were combed in order to find sailors out for a good time and prostituting themselves (the guilty were subject to disciplinary sanctions and some were dismissed). It is quite clear that military authorities used these events to affirm the dishonorable character of homosexuality.

Military authorities also received the backing of the French medical establishment who denounced homosexuality as a menace that threatened the nation's colonial troops (in 1907, according to Dr René Jude, first-class medical officer in the hospitals of Tunisia, two-thirds of the soldiers in the "battalions of Africa" were pederasts). It also received the support of civilian authorities who associated homosexuality in the military with every form of subversion that threatened the nation's power (including opium addiction, antimilitarism, anarchism, and **communism**). And when the "guilty" was an officer, *esprit de corps* demanded his resignation (as was the case for a lieutenant commander from Lorient, at the end of the 1920s) drove him to **suicide** (such as that of General MacDonald by the British in 1903, after he was caught masturbating in a train car with Singhalese soldiers) or forced him into situations that would cause his death (in 1824, Custine was advised that he be killed with weapons in hand, or enter *La Trappe* [a Cistercian monastery]; in 1915, French military officer Maxime Weygand sent Robert d'Humières, a liaison officer to the British army, to his death because he had had a weakness for a Hindu soldier). Also, for homosexuals in the French military, social threats replaced legal ones: even General Hubert Lyautey, whose homosexuality was widely discussed and who had a great number of friends in high places, was forced to marry at the age of fifty-five in order to quell all rumors. This social pressure was alleviated somewhat, but not entirely, due to the political and ideological specifics of the military, the recent affair surrounding Christophe Carrion being a good example. In 1998, this gendarme stationed at the French embassy in Addis-Ababa fell in love with a young Ethiopian, set him up in his home, and divorced his wife; as a result, he was repatriated to France eight months before the end of his mission. It is important to note the strong, heterosexual social model that the military expected its personnel to follow, manifested in trips to the brothels while young and, later, marriage. It is understandable that, in France, many gay servicemen were compelled to extreme **discretion** or to lead a double life. Perhaps things are changing, however. At least, that was the impression that General Alain Raevel hoped to give by granting a rather benevolent interview to the French gay monthly *Têtu* in 2000.

But the taboo against homosexuality remains particularly ingrained in the French Foreign Legion where, since its creation in 1831, rumors suggest not only that homosexual acts among personnel took place, but also that homosexual relationships between Legionnaires existed. These relationships appear to have been numerous at the beginning of the twentieth century, in the garrisons of southern Oran (Algeria), where younger Legionnaires or *girons* submitted to their elders. Numerous elements contributed to this fact: the uprooting and imposed celibacy of new recruits, the continuous physical training and the cult of the virile male, the harsh discipline, the importance of non-verbal communication between men who do not share a common language, and even a marching song that could be considered a confession: "And what do I care of all those girls that I never loved, yes, never knew how to love." It is known that in the first decade of the twentieth century, large numbers of homosexuals ("musicians") joined the French Foreign Legion, and that between the wars, it attracted a certain type of gay male: young, virile, and at odds with society (Jean Genet joined at the age of nineteen, though he deserted quickly enough). That being said, Legion authorities disapproved of homosexual relations between their men (which they saw as leading to poor attitudes, jealousy, and suicide) and they forbade personnel from publicly disclosing their homosexuality: any Legionnaire accused of "**proselytism**" of this sort was expelled (as was the case with Jean-Claude Poulet-

Dachary, who later became a cabinet director for the mayor of Toulon and was assassinated in 1995). When filmmaker Claire Denis announced she would direct a movie about relationships between Legionnaires (*Beau Travail*, 1999), she came up against hostility from military authorities and Legionnaires themselves, who refused to be compromised in a "film about queers." As far as Denis was concerned, those responsible clearly acted as if "homosexuality was the most important danger faced by Legionnaires." This was not a new phenomenon, as in the nineteenth century, the growing of a beard was required by the Legion in order to prevent the development of "unnatural morals" (which were believed to develop as a result of confusion between the feminine and masculine physique). Tolerance toward the acquisition of *congaï* (girlfriends) in Indochina and, in the years between wars, to the introduction of MCBs (military-controlled bordellos) in Algeria followed the same type of logic. It is known that military authorities knowingly constructed a myth exalting the absolute heterosexuality of the Legionnaire (to which Edith Piaf even paid tribute in one of her famous songs of the 1930s). Nonetheless, this construct can be taken down in an instant, as demonstrated in 1987 when French singer Serge Gainsbourg humorously reinterpreted Piaf's song without changing a single word.

In the homosexualized environment of the military, homophobia is expressed in its most perverted and violent form in what may be called "gay rape" (almost always committed in "self-denial" mode by the aggressor, especially when part of a group). French security forces have dealt with many incidents of this kind, which have more or less been officially covered up, but which, in cases where suicide results, have come to the attention of the public and the media. However, it is in the former USSR that the phenomenon took on importance from 1967 to 1991. When young Soviet conscripts first arrived at the barracks, older conscripts would await them, and in a manner resembling the hierarchy in British private schools, the young "fags" were forced to serve the *stariki* or *ded* ("grandfathers"): they had to obey them, becoming their personal slaves, wash their clothes, wax their boots, allow themselves to be insulted, beaten with belts and, in many cases, raped. This extremely violent form of hazing (called *dedovchtchina*) was a major contributing factor to the demoralization of the Soviet army in the 1980s. It was in fact the reason for the creation of an independent association made up of the mothers of Soviet military personnel, which testified to the widespread social violence linked to Stalinism and the **gulags**.

—*Pierre Albertini*

Bech, Henning. *When Men Meet: Homosexuality and Modernity*. Cambridge, UK: Polity Press, 1997.

Bérubé, Allan. *Coming Out Under Fire: Lesbian and Gay Americans and the Military During World War II*. New York: The Free Press, 1989.

———. "Marching to a Different Drummer: Lesbian and Gay GIs in World War II." In *Hidden from History: Reclaiming the Gay and Lesbian Past*. Edited by George Chauncey, Martin Duberman, and Martha Vicinus. New York: New American Library, 1989.

Dover, Kenneth. *Homosexualité grecque*. Paris: La Pensée Sauvage, 1982. [Published in the US as *Greek Homosexuality*. New edition. Cambridge, MA: Harvard Univ. Press, 1989.]

Fromaget, Georges. *Les Mesures de protection à l'égard des pervers qui s'engagent dans l'armée*. Lyon: Bosc Frères, 1935.

Grau, Günther: *Hidden Holocaust? Gay and Lesbian Persecution in Germany, 1933–1945*. London: Cassell & Cie, 1995.

Gury, Christian. *L'Honneur perdu d'un capitaine homosexuel en 1880*. Paris: Kimé, 1999.

Halley, Janet E. *Don't: A Reader's Guide to the Military's Anti-Gay Policy*. Durham, NC: Duke Univ. Press, 1999.

Hyam, Ronald. *Empire and Sexuality: The British Experience*. Manchester: Manchester Univ. Press, 1990.

Odom, William E. *The Corpse of the Soviet Military*. New Haven, CT/London: Yale Univ. Press, 1998.

Porch, Douglas. *La Légion étrangère 1831–1962*. Paris: Fayard, 1994. [Published in the US as *The French Foreign Legion*. New York: HarperCollins, 1991.]

Roynette, Odile. *"Bons pour le service," l'expérience de la caserne en France à la fin du XIXe siècle*. Paris: Belin, 2000.

Williams, Colin and Martin Weinberg. *Homosexuals and the Military: A Study of Less than Honorable Discharge*. New York: Harper & Row, 1971.

—*Contagion; Custine, Astolphe de; Fascism; Heterosexism; Himmler, Heinrich; Pétain, Philippe; Police; Symbolic Order; Treason; Violence.*

ARMY. *See* Armed Forces

ART

This entry does not claim to be exhaustive and covers only certain periods in Western art, seeking to offer a number of ideas by way of a few examples. In fact, it is notable that homophobia as such has never been an artistic issue. Unlike Nazi or colonial art, there has never been a homophobic art form whose formal expression coincided with the will to propagate a certain ideology. At most, we find, throughout history, particular homophobic works or, for more recent periods, works that touch on the issue of homophobia. Of course, we could make a list. Although, the work involved would be considerable; it would eventually identify a permanence in homophobic impulses and perhaps establish a timeline of homophobia that would confirm, or shed light on, the nuances of the historical moments (underlined by recent gay and lesbian studies) when **tolerance** of homosexuals permitted the birth of homophile art. Nonetheless, apart from the contemporary period, this list would still come up against a major obstacle: because of existing sources and the inherently mutable nature of **insults** and of mockery, it is often difficult to ascertain the real homophobic character of the works in question. A few examples allow us to illustrate this fact.

The first concerns the representation of male couples in certain Christian paintings of the Renaissance. In an article that appeared in 1989, historian Joseph Manca cited many examples, among them the famous *Miracles of Saint Vincent Ferrier*, painted around 1470 by Ercole de Roberti, and now in the Vatican Museum. These same-sex couples would have been painted in order to symbolize the perversity of the pagan world, before the coming of Christ. If this is a plausible explanation of homophobia, it is also important to note certain sacred images that, during the same period, represent similar pagans, such as Michelangelo's *Tondo Doni* in which two beautiful, naked young men appear behind the Holy Family, and upon whom the artist does not seem to have heaped opprobrium.

The second example also refers to the Italian Renaissance. Images and texts appear to mock Borso d'Esté, the Duke of Ferrara, representing him as unmasculine and preferring the company of young, pretty male prostitutes who took themselves for the Three Graces. In a well documented article, Werner Gundersheimer demonstrates that this effeminacy is not homophobic, for it served the interests of Borso d'Esté, who sought to differentiate himself from his brutal predecessor in the Ferrara court.

Thus, the search for specific, presupposed homophobic works is even more problematic because the conditions under which they were produced and received often remain hermetic. For example, a drawing by Italian painter Marco Zoppo, dating from 1460 and preserved at the British Museum in London, shows numerous traits that converge to define it as homophobic: in the background, two men embrace, the older of the two firmly holding the pommel of his sword, a phallic symbol at the time; in the foreground, cherubs are at play, one shoving a bellows into the other's posterior. Nevertheless, the drawing's obvious private character and our inability to reproduce the artist's motivations and the objective he intended for his work make it impossible to determine the piece's homophobic character; it may simply reveal a secret, a preference for young men that Marco Zoppo and his eventual patron may have shared. This is also the case with certain paintings, and certain satirical sonnets mocking homosexuality by Bronzino. These works can hardly be defined as homophobic as everything leads us to believe that Bronzino as well as the intended audience for his sonnets were gay.

Although it is often difficult to confirm the eventual homophobic character of works of art, or even **caricatures**, homophobia can be more easily found in the arguments of art historians and in institutionalized **censorship**, as well as in public opprobrium. Statements by historian Louis Réau are symptomatic of a certain homophobia that has long prevailed in this field. Expressing himself in a reference manual on the iconography of St Sebastian, Réau notes that "all that remains (for St Sebastian) is the compromising and shameful patronage of sodomites or homosexuals, seduced by his beautiful apollonian nudity, glorified by the Sodoma." This argument reveals a common theory that postulates that art—as an inspiration to beauty, to the sublime, to transcendence—cannot be suspected of **vice**, and that all perversity exists only in the eyes of the ill-intentioned spectator. It is not the painting representing St Sebastian that is erogenous, it is the troubled look from the homosexual that is at fault.

This approach prevailed as early as the sixteenth century, when art history, as a discipline, was born. For a long time, it forbade the use of homosexuality as one of the parameters that governed the creation of artworks and their posterity, even though heterosexual desire largely served as an explanatory undercurrent. This attitude is particularly sensitive in the historiographical posterity of the three geniuses of the Renaissance: Raphael, Michelangelo, and Leonardo da Vinci. Raphael's heterosexuality allowed for his sensitivities to be largely taken into consideration when analyzing his works. In contrast, no effort was spared to deny or hide the assumed homosexuality of Michelangelo or da Vinci in order to defend their works from any and all "dishonor." Thus, Michelangelo's first critics protested his innocence and, in 1623, editing the artist's sonnets and madrigals for the first time, his great-great-nephew modified them in order to give the impression that they were addressed to a woman and not, as was the case for most of them, to his lover Tommaso Cavalieri (this edition was considered the philological standard until 1897, when Karl Frey, referring to the manuscripts, reestablished the original texts). Finally, in order to account for Michelangelo's glorification of the male body, Florentine Neo-Platonism had always been privileged, which had long allowed the question of homosexuality—viewed as trivial—to be avoided. The fate reserved for Leonardo da Vinci was different. Nineteenth-century historiography constructed around him, the myth of the melancholic, sexless artist whose proclaimed love for young men was purely intellectual. This myth has been demolished by recent research which restored Leonardo's hedonistic character and thus permitted the reevaluation of the sensuality of his work.

Finally, it must be noted that the greatest mark of homophobia on the arts lies with the general intolerance in which these artists worked and lived. Certainly, the prevailing talent and marginality of the artistic life being expected, gay artists, under the pretext of their penchants, were rarely prevented from practicing their art. For example, neither Perugino, Botticelli, nor Leonardo da Vinci, each one accused of sodomy in the opinion of a particular jurisdiction, were stopped from working for the greatest patrons of their time. Even during the first years of photography, there was a public that both purchased and encouraged the works of Baron Wilhelm von Gloeden or Fred Holland Day. However, these artists were also frustrated by their inability to express their love for men in their work. In fact, censorship and opprobrium, which were for so long the iron fist of homophobia, created an atmosphere in which artists were forced to be either self-censoring—the love of men being misrepresented or suppressed—or clandestine—Baron von Gloeden's photos were only in circulation in underground networks and have only been passed down in posterity by way of collectors who purchased them in secret (the original plates having been destroyed by Italy's Fascist regime). The refusal of self-censorship or clandestineness implied risk, a risk that was taken by American painter Thomas Eakins (1844–1916). Although Eakin's work was widely recognized and held an eminent academic position, he was undermined from the moment he set out to exhibit a certain part of his work that was openly homophile. As a result, his teaching, based on the study of the nude, and in particular the male nude, criticized and suspected of being nothing more than an intellectual cover for his excesses, he was forced to resign.

At the end of the nineteenth century, when more and more artists refused to be put in the **closet**, censorship sought mostly to control the public exposition of homophile art.

For years, American museums that preserved John Sargent's homoerotic watercolors refused to show them. In this same country, at the end of the twentieth century, works sanctioned by both critics and the market, such as those by Robert Mapplethorpe, were shown with great difficulty. In the end, it is rather symbolic that French photographers Pierre and Gilles were forced to remove certain photos judged to be pornographic in order for a retrospective of their work to be shown in the United States.

—*Karim Ressouni-Demigneux*

Grand-Carteret, John. *Derrière "Lui": L'homosexualité en Allemagne*. Followed by *Iconographie d'un scandale, les caricatures politiques et l'affaire Eulenburg*. By James Steakley. Lille: Cahiers GayKitschCamp, 1992.

Gundersheimer, Werner. "Clarity and Ambiguity in Renaissance Gesture: the Case of Borso d'Este," *The Journal of Medieval and Renaissance Studies* 23, no.1 (1993).

Manca, Jospeh. "Sacred vs. Profane: Images of Sexual Vice in Renaissance Art," *Studies in Iconography* 13 (1989).

Meyer, Richard. *Outlaw Representation: Censorship and Homosexuality in Twentieth-Century American Art*. Oxford: Oxford Univ. Press, 2002.

Réau, Louis. *Iconographie de l'art Chrétien*. Vol 3. Paris: Presses universitaires de France 1955-1959.

The San Francisco Lesbian and Gay History Project. "'She Even Chewed Tobacco': A Pictorial Narrative of Passing Women in America." In *Hidden from History: Reclaiming the Gay and Lesbian Past*. By George Chauncey, Martin Duberman, Martha Vicinus. New York: Meridian, 1989.

Saslow, James. *Ganymede in the Renaissance: Homosexuality in Art and Society*. New Haven: Yale Univ. Press, 1986.

Tamagne, Florence. *Mauvais Genre?* Paris: La Martinière, 2001.

Further Reading:

Merrick, Jeffery, and Bryant T. Ragan, Jr, eds. *Homosexuality in Modern France*. New York: Oxford University Press, 1996.

Steakley, James, Gert Hekma, and Harry Dosterhuis, *Gay Men and the Sexual History of the Political Left*. New York: Haworth Press, 1995.

Schiller, Gertrud. *Iconography of Christian Art*. Vol 1 & 2. Second edition. Greenwich, CT: New York Graphic Society, 1971–72.

Steakley, James. "Iconography of Scandal: Political Cartoons and the Eulenberg Affair," *Studies in Visual Communication* 9, no. 2 (Spring 1983).

Tamagne, Florence. *A History of Homosexuality in Europe*, New York: Algora 2004.

—*Caricature; Censorship; Cinema; Comic Books; Dance; Literature; Media; Music; Publicity; Song.*

ASHAMED. *See* Shame

ASSOCIATIONS

The first true association for gay rights that was not simply a cultural circle or meeting place was organized by German doctor Magnus **Hirschfeld**. Born in the city of Kolberg in 1868, Hirschfeld specialized in nervous and psychiatric disorders after his studies in medicine. He became involved in the fight against anti-homosexual legislation (the Prussian penal code, then Paragraph 175 in Germany) by dealing with the question from a medical perspective: if the homosexual falls under the jurisdiction of medicine and psychiatry, he cannot be "responsible" before the law, and therefore he is not a **criminal**. Oscar **Wilde**'s sensational trial in Britain in 1895 served to highlight this question with more acuity. Shortly thereafter, in 1897, Hirschfeld founded the Scientific-Humanitarian Committee, the WhK (Wissenschaftlich-humanitäre Komitee), an association which aimed to undertake research to defend the rights of homosexuals in light of Paragraph 175. The committee's actions were sufficient to initiate parliamentary debate in Germany over the legislation. However, the rise of the Nazi party brutally ended the WhK's activities, and Magnus Hirschfeld fled to France, living out his days in Nice.

France prior to World War II had an important gay "scene," but its expression was mostly cultural: everyone read Proust and **Gide**, but there were no organized demonstrations or demands for the recognition of homosexuals. One short-lived publication, however, sought to oppose homophobia: *Inversions* (which later became *L'Amitié*), established in November 1924, sought to "tell inverts that they are normal and healthy beings." In March of 1927, however, its publishers were sentenced to three months' imprisonment for the "affront to public decency."

During this period, the ability and willingness among gays and lesbians to discreetly organize themselves came about mainly in European countries and in the United States. In the years between wars, American gays and lesbians organized dances and "salons." In particular, a spirit of freedom blew through New York City, where Greenwich Village became a much frequented neighborhood for homosexuals. Between 1950 and 1960, many gay bars opened in the city, and in 1967, activist Craig Rodwell opened the world's first gay bookstore, the Oscar Wilde Memorial Bookshop, which served as a center for gay discussions and initiatives. After the historic **Stonewall** riots of June 1969, a good number of gay rights associations were formed, in particular the National Gay and Lesbian Task Force (NGLTF), which is still active to this day. As a result, the gay movement in the US entered a phase of politics and protest.

After World War II, gay associations in France were limited to a discreet group named Arcadie, united around the monthly periodical created by André Baudry in 1954. Arcadie allowed many gays to congregate, but their discussions were confined within an association that was moralizing and overly cautious. The association's official name was Clespala (Club littéraire et scientifique de pays latins, Literary and Scientific Club of Latin Countries). It was not until after the social upheaval of May 1968 that more proactive gay associations appeared in France. In 1971, on the heels of the growing **feminist** movement, the Front homosexuel d'action révolutionnaire (FHAR; Homosexual Revolutionary Action Front) saw the light of day; despite its fleeting existence, it had a long-lasting effect on the French gay movement. Unlike Arcadie, FHAR was not simply a social club, nor was it clandestine; its members were openly gay and lesbian, and its goals were explicitly political.

Following in the footsteps of FHAR, gay groups began to expand in the main cities of France under the banner of Groupes de libération homosexuelle (GLH; Groups for Homosexual Liberation). Despite this commonality, each group was very diverse, politicized, and more focused on how the oppression of gays and lesbians had been characterized by society rather than on the fight against oppression itself. If the development of a "gay argument" was desirable and necessary, it nonetheless masked the inability of these associations to actively oppose homophobic repression and to work toward the decriminalization of homosexuality. Also, apart from ideological quarrels, the essential differences between gay associations and their lesbian counterparts slowed down organized efforts to fight homophobia. GLH were mostly male, whereas lesbians tended to organize themselves in associations representing multiple ideals (e.g., feminism).

This acknowledgment of impotence pushed some gay militants to create organizations that allowed each interest group to retain its ideological specificity, while working toward collective action. The task was an arduous one given the divisions and the general wariness among groups. Eventually, the Parisian GLH split up into three distinct groups: Politique et Quotidien, Groupe de base, and 14 décembre (the date of the split). Arcadie, in a slow state of collapse, refused to get mixed up in "this agitation," which it feared. The task was not made any easier by the anti-homosexual hostility, whether implied or outright, expressed by various political parties, unions, associations, or cities. Abroad, however, there was a will among gays to organize themselves. In England in 1978, the International Gay Association (IGA) was founded (later known as ILGA, with the addition of lesbians). This first international initiative for gay "liberation" had ramifications for the French gay movement.

The Marseille GLH, one of the few groups having registered for association status under the 1901 law in France (under the humorous name CORPS [body], Centre ouvert de recherché populaire sur la sexualité, the Open Centre for Popular Research on Sexuality), took the initiative to organize the Université d'été homosexuelle (UEH; Homosexual Summer School) in 1979. Some 400 gay and lesbian activists took part;

Marseille, where the "school" took place, was relatively welcoming toward one of "the city's numerous communities," as stated by the mayor at the time. It was during this first Marseille UEH that the idea of a mixed association structure centered on the fight against the **discrimination** of homosexuals was launched, and groups that were formerly at odds with one another were invited to join. The initiative, supported by influential figures such as Jacques Fortin, Hervé Liffran, Mélanie Badaire, and Geneviève Pastre, was named the Comité d'urgence anti-répression homosexuelle (CUARH; Homosexual Anti-Repression Emergency Committee). A letter dated July 28, 1979, addressed to various gay and lesbian groups in France, stated the following: "The CUARH is a structure for the coordination of homosexual groups who wish to join it in order to launch campaigns and take initiatives with regard to significant cases. The CUARH will also work toward democratic rights and freedoms for homosexuals (campaign against homophobia, suppression of files, suppression of Article 16 from the civil service, reformation of the penal code, etc.). The CUARH will need to develop ties in order to lead eventual common campaigns with anti-oppression groups, and political, union, and democratic organizations."

At the same time in France, gay media specializing in analysis and commentary started to appear: *Gai-Pied*, *Masques*, *Vlasta*, and *Lesbian Magazine* served to publicize the fights taken up by the gay rights groups. Initially known as a group that coordinated activities among others, CUARH progressively became active on its own by way of its magazine *Homophonies,* launched in November 1980 and sold on newsstands from 1982 until its final issue in February of 1987. The magazine's editorial board became somewhat of a pseudo-autonomous militant group, and its particular place within CUARH made it the driving force behind various mobilization campaigns.

The changing vocabulary, iconography, and media bear witness to the changes and difficulties faced by the gay rights movement in the 1980s. It is important to note that the new term "homophobia" began cropping up more and more, on one hand as a means to avoid the wordiness of the expression "anti-gay racism," and on another to avoid debate raised by the characterization of the oppression of gays and lesbians as "racist."

From its foundation, CUARH led a determined fight for the repeal of discriminatory aspects of the penal code in France. This battle was aimed at specific homophobic articles which, among other issues, established a difference in the "age of consent": while heterosexual relations were legal at the age of fifteen, gay relations remained illegal below the age of eighteen (and prior to that, twenty-one, before President Valéry Giscard d'Estaing lowered it). These articles had been originally introduced by the Vichy government in 1942 and reaffirmed in 1945 after liberation. In 1960, a parliamentary amendment by Member of Parliament Paul **Mirguet** added homosexuality to a list of "social scourges" along with alcoholism and prostitution (in 1968, a short-lived gay publication entitled *Scourge of Society* started). According to the French Minister of Justice, 6,487 individuals were prosecuted between 1958 and 1975 as a result of parliamentary law. In June of 1978, Senator Henri Caillavet proposed the repeal of anti-homosexual articles to the Senate, who accepted it, but the National Assembly, under the leadership of MP Jean Foyer, rejected the proposal in April 1980. In protest, on June 21, 1980 CUARH organized a demonstration of nearly 1,000 supporters who marched to the National Assembly.

The approaching presidential elections in 1981 gave CUARH the opportunity to launch a pro-gay rights media campaign, which included a national petition against the discriminatory laws. Not only did the petition gather signatures from many artists including Dalida, Yves Montand, Costa-Gavras, and François Truffaut, but it was also signed by politicians such as Robert Badinter, Huguette Bouchardeau, Raymond Forni, Gisèle Halimi, and Brice Lalonde. The mobilization campaign allowed CUARH to compel various organizations to publicly state their position on the issue, the most important of which was the Socialist Party, whose candidate François Mitterrand, declared: "Homosexuality must not be a basis for any form of inequality or discrimination."

As a finale to its campaign, after having gathered over 6,000 signatures on its petition, CUARH organized a national march in Paris on April 4, 1981, in which 10,000 people participated. It was the largest autonomous gay demonstration of the time, to which previous demonstrations could not compare. Its success led CUARH to organize a yearly national march in June; on Saturday, June 19, 1982, the first "real" French Gay Pride demonstration, the Marche nationale homosexuelle et lesbienne (National Gay and Lesbian March), took place. The term "Gay Pride" would only come into regular use in France a few years later (at the first Parisian demonstration commemorating Stonewall in June 1977). The change in political power brought about by François Mitterrand's election paved the way for Minister of Justice Robert Badinter to prepare the amendment of the penal code. As a result, the discriminatory subsection of Article 331 was abrogated by the law of August 4, 1982—the age of consent for homosexuals was lowered to be the same as for heterosexuals.

CUARH also mobilized responses to cases in which individuals had lost their jobs because of their homosexuality, such as Jacques Odon, who was fired from his job at Rouen's City Hall, and Jean Rossignol, a dormitory monitor from Marseille who was fired by the Ministry of National Education in 1978. However, the most prominent cases were those where homosexuality was both the only and official reason for firing; CUARH invoked the German term of *Berufsverbot* (prohibition to practice on the grounds of a criminal record or membership in a particular group). Such was the case of Eliane Morissens, a Belgian teacher who had participated on a television show where she stated she was a lesbian; her employer's response, the Province of Hainaut, was swift: she was automatically "retired."

CUARH ceased all activities in 1987. Around the same time, the gay association milieu in France became more diversified, including the establishment of various social interest groups (e.g., **sports**, **music**, dating). Additionally, the fight against homophobia was no longer exclusive to gay and lesbian associations, as political parties, unions, and humanitarian associations also took up the fight. A number of activists from the gay groups of the 1970s and 1980s had worked in these large organizations and were a driving force behind their consideration of the homosexual issue. Ad hoc commissions around gay rights were sometimes created within political parties (the Green Party), union confederations, and associations (Amnesty International), sometimes serving more as a means of "internal education" rather than an external role. Politicians led Gay and Lesbian Pride marches, and union leaders actively participated. Progressively, as the fight against homophobia passed from simple statements of intent to action, it ceased to be waged solely by gay and lesbian associations and became a general political issue.

Moreover, the international gay association landscape was profoundly transformed at the end of the twentieth century. If the older gay associations in Europe survived the passage of time and were able to preserve their solid foundations (e.g., NVIH-COC in the Netherlands, RFSL in Sweden, SETA in Finland, ARCIGAY in Italy, and HOSI in Austria), other European gay groups were wracked by internal fragmentation (LBL in Denmark, FAGL and FWH in Belgium). On the other hand, gay associations in Eastern Bloc countries before the fall of Communism remained under the will of the Iron Curtain, all pro-gay initiatives were quickly quashed. In 1984, an attempt to form a gay group in Leningrad in the former Soviet Union was put down by the KGB. It would be necessary to wait until the arrival of Mikhail Gorbachev and the spirit of *perestroika* (economic restructuring) for the Moscow gay and lesbian alliance to see the light of day in 1989, and for a Russian gay newspaper, *Tema*, to be officially registered.

However, a new revolution, this one technological, turned the landscape of gay rights groups of the 1990s upside down. The distribution and accessibility of electronic communication brought about a remarkable change in the sociology of the gay community. The Internet increased the visibility of groups who had previously very little access to traditional media (such as in Turkey and **Eastern Europe**). Most of all, however, the Internet permitted the creation of websites that supplemented or replaced the need for formal gay associations in countries where such associations had been difficult, if not illegal, to create. It is thus that a gay information network was established in all parts of the world. It is also thanks to the Internet that public opinion was quickly informed of homophobic episodes in other countries, such as the anti-gay trials in Egypt in 2001. Thus, the new "Information Society" as described by the United Nations (for the World Summit on the Information Society that occurred in Geneva in 2003, and in Tunisia in 2005) did not only describe a technological revolution, but also a revolution in the associations and networks of gays and lesbians.

—*Jean-Michel Rousseau*

Adam, Barry D., Jan Willem Duyvendak, and André Krouwel, eds. *The Global Emergence of Gay and Lesbian Politics: National Imprints of a Worldwide Movement.* Philadelphia: Temple Univ. Press, 1999.

Duyvendak, Jan Willem. *Le Poids du politique. Nouveaux mouvements sociaux en France.* Paris: L'Harmattan. 1994. [Published in the US as *The Power of Politics: New Social*

Movements in France. Boulder, CO: Westview Press, 1995.]

Front homosexual d'action révolutionnaire. *Rapport contre la normalité*. Paris: Ed. Champ-Libre, 1971.

Gonnard, Catherine, and Jean-Michel Rousseau. "Homophonies: une sonorité différente." In *Actes du colloque international homosexualité et lesbianisme, mythes, mémoire et historiographie*. Lille: Cahiers GayKitschCamp, 1990.

Tamagne, Florence. *Histoire de l'homosexualité en Europe, Berlin, Londres, Paris, 1919–1939*. Paris: Le Seuil, 2000. [Published in the US as *A History of Homosexuality in Europe: Berlin, London, Paris, 1919–1939*. New York: Algora, 2004]

Thompson, Mark, ed. *The Long Road to Freedom: The Advocate History of the Gay and Lesbian Movement*. New York: St Martin's Press. 1994.

Working for Lesbian and Gay Members. Public Services International and Education International: Brussels, 1999.

—*Criminalization; Decriminalization; Hirschfeld, Magnus; Mirguet, Paul; Politics; SOS homophobie; Stonewall.*

B

BALKANS, the

The relative visibility of homosexuality in the Balkans is a recent development, closely tied to increased attention to events in the rest of the world which have resulted in, among other things, the adoption of radical new trends from gay and lesbian movements in the West. This new situation in many Balkan countries, however, is accompanied by extreme homophobic **violence**, which can only be understood through an analysis of the homosexual and homophobic characteristics in traditional Balkan society.

Albania, Greece, Romania, and the former Yugoslavia—all very heterogeneous in both people and language—have long been defined by rural patriarchies. This fact can be linked to the relative absence of democracy in these countries during the nineteenth and twentieth centuries (democracy was not restored in Greece until 1974 with the collapse of the military government; other countries were not democratic until after the fall of the Berlin Wall in 1989) and to the kind of regime that allowed its society's dominant values to perpetuate. These two political characteristics explain the homophobic violence, legal or otherwise, that has accompanied the opening of these countries to Western concepts.

Granted, the vast heterogeneousness of information sources, as well as the lack of substantial studies on the experiences of homosexuals in the region (especially in the nineteenth century), demands that care be taken when examining this issue. In addition, as is often the case, the relative lack of information on lesbianism and **lesbophobia** precludes a proper analysis here. However, certain basic phenomena can still be identified.

Homosexuality & Homophobia in Traditional Balkan Society

The first serious anthropological texts concerning Balkan societies are Westerners' records of travel, beginning in the eighteenth century and continuing through the nineteenth, but whose style could hardly be deemed scientific. These should be read with caution, as they tend to imprecisely define the Balkans as the meeting-point between the Occident and Orient. Two characteristic traits were identified by American historian Larry Wolff, beginning with accounts of eighteenth-century life (as revealed in his 1994 book *Inventing Eastern Europe*), as well as in texts from the nineteenth century: the control of wives and their fidelity through a strong patriarchal authority, and the encouragement of male violence, individual or collective, especially with regard to the use of weapons. For instance, about twenty percent of the legal code established by the Prince of Montenegro for his people in 1850 was devoted to the subject of the patriarchal control of women, and another fifty percent to the use of weapons.

The control of women and the fraternity of men were no small part of the traditional customs. Take, for example, the tradition of sworn brotherhood in Montenegro in the late nineteenth century: two young men present themselves in church, armed, and swear to live and die for one another, then swap weapons. Homosexual or otherwise, this symbolized a passionate love made legitimate by its masculinity and the exclusion not only of women, but also femininity.

At the other extreme, the tendency to patriarchal power often led to other traditions, such as the "sworn virgins" of northern Albania (a phenomenon that continued into the twentieth century). In the absence of a male heir to a family, a young girl would be raised as though she were a boy, and in adulthood would take on both the clothing and demeanor of a man; she would also be referred to by others as a man. This allowed the woman to be the "patriarch" of a family that would otherwise not be able to remain autonomous. These women were normally celibate, although there is evidence of a few unions between "sworn virgins" and other women. In this example, what was worrisome was not the potential for homosexuality, but rather the risk of gender confusion or anything else that might contest the perceived virility of society's traditional masculine relationships.

The same elements can be found in remnants of traditional Greek culture, still present in modern times. The physical, as well as emotional, separation of men and women arguably encouraged passionate bonds between adolescent boys as well as between adult men, as revealed in several works (such as Marie-Christine Anest's studies on Greek children and adolescents during the campaigns against Cypress and Corfu in the 1970s, and those by sociologist Kostas Yannakopoulous on adults in Pyraeus and Athens between 1990 and 1992). Although such relationships were criticized for their overly sentimental nature, the potential for them to become sexual usually went unremarked.

In this way, denial played an important role. The phallocentric ideology of people in this region, combined with the physical and emotional separation of the sexes, did not allow for the recognition of overt homosexuality. All those who dared to declare themselves homosexual—or in the words of their detractors, "pederasts" or "fags" (*poustides* in Greek, for example)—were subject to utter contempt and even violence. In her book *Black Lamb and the Grey Falcon* (1941), Rebecca West, while describing a lengthy voyage in Yugoslavia, echoes this denial by declaring that there are no homosexuals in Serbia (unlike her home country of Britain, she laments). An understanding of this denial is essential, as it explains how any concepts of male homosexuality are treated in the region as completely alien.

New Visibility of Homosexuality & Hard-Line Homophobia

It is then easy to understand that the arrival of the Western model of gay and lesbian liberation since the 1970s and especially the 90s was not well-received by traditional Balkan society (as demonstrated by the homophobic campaigns launched by the various national Orthodox churches in the region. However, progress

made on the various legal and political fronts, connected to a new willingness to open up to the West, allowed the new gay ideal to be tolerated. But as revealed by Yannakopoulos, who has written on same-sex relations in Greece, a paradoxical, internalized kind of homophobia can be observed in the tension between male homosexuals who still live according to the old traditions and those who embrace the new "queer" identity. Individually, many gay men possess a "mish mash" of the two identities, in which internalized homophobia and true liberation are made to coexist.

It is primarily in the former **communist** states where homophobic violence in the region is most visible today. The 1990s drastically changed the landscape for gays and lesbians; a number of issues, such as vehicles for public debate on the subject, the persistence of extremist anti-gay violence, the slow pace of legal change, and pressure from the West, all contributed to turning these countries into veritable laboratories for nascent gay and lesbian rights as they made the sometimes awkward transition to full democracy.

Prior to the end of communism, homosexuality was a punishable crime in all communist countries in the region with the exception of the former Yugoslav states Croatia (which decriminalized homosexuality in 1977) and Slovenia (decriminalized in 1976), as well as Bulgaria (decriminalized in 1968). In the countries where homosexuality was illegal, their patriarchal values meshed well with those instilled by the Soviet Union (where homosexuality had been illegal since the 1930s). As an example of the harsh laws, homosexual acts and even tendencies were punishable in Albania by up to ten years in prison (before it was decriminalized in 1995). With the fall of communism at the end of the 1980s, one of the central issues became that of minorities. In the midst of a serious identity crisis, the new voices demanding rights for gays and lesbians were all that more shocking.

As an example, Serbia's treatment of homosexuals since 1990 was defined by two major events. On June 27, 1991, Arkadija, the country's sole gay and lesbian association, held its first convention whose theme was "The Right to be Different." The same day, the Yugoslav government of Slobodan Milošević attacked Slovenia, who had just declared its independence, sparking a ten-year civil war against Croatia, Bosnia, and Albanians in Kosovo, which included a hunt for homosexuals in the region. Then on June 30, 2001, two days after Milošević was taken into United Nations custody, the very first Gay Pride parade took place in Belgrade. But the **police**, despite having been alerted, did nothing to defend parade-goers from being violently beaten by homophobes who included neofascist football supporters, young orthodox Christians, and followers of **far right** nationalist leader Vojislav Šešelj.

Herein lies one of the key characteristics of the region: the strong links among nationalism, institutional violence, and homophobic violence, which have slowed the pace of progress for gays and lesbians. The principal characteristic of homophobia in the region over the last fifteen years has been the use of insults, stereotypes, and insinuations, the most extreme of which is the accusation of **treason**: in 1994, the members of the only gay **association** in Albania were arrested, beaten, and accused of espionage, and a 1998 study on homophobia conducted by the Romanian homosexual association ACCEPT revealed that the most frequent accusation against gays and lesbians is that they wanted to forcibly "Europeanize" the country. And in 2001, during hostile protests against the new democratic government in Serbia, pro-Milošević supporters accused Prime Minister Zoran Djindjic of being "a pederast, a Jew, and an agent of NATO" (Djindjic was assassinated in 2003).

Using this concept, along with the impression of being supported by society as well as by the government, police justify carrying out acts of violence and torture against gays and lesbians. Many examples of this have been documented, such as in Albania (1994) and Bulgaria (1996), but we need look no further than the cases of Mariana Cetiner and Boris Aleskov. Cetiner was arrested in the summer of 1995 by Romanian police for "attempting to seduce another woman"; beaten, humiliated, and insulted, she was "made to stand for eleven hours in a position like Jesus Christ" (Amnesty International report, 1998). In July 2001, Aleskov, a gay Serbian, was taken into police custody by members of the state security, who attempted to force him to confess to connections with illegal organizations by beating him and threatening him with rape. Both Cetiner and Aleskov were forced into exile after being freed.

The experience of Mariana Cetiner reveals the important role that Christianity plays in the motivation and justification of homophobic acts, as well as the form it takes. But traditional Christian values, as homophobic in the Orthodox Church as they are in the Catholic Church, are not the only motivation at work here. In effect, the churches in orthodox Balkan countries (Bulgaria, Greece, Macedonia, Montenegro, Romania, and Serbia) are organized on a national level and play a fundamental role not only in the formation of the ethnic majority's identity but also in the rejection of minorities, even when the majority of the population are not practitioners (as is the case in Serbia). Consider the rabid fight headed by Teoctist Arăpaşu, Patriarch of the Romanian Orthodox Church, against the **decriminalization** of homosexuality, all in the name of preserving Romanian values. Again, the crux of the problem lies in a nationalism that excludes all minorities (including sexual ones, but also chiefly ethnic minorities: e.g., Hungarians in Romania; Albanians and Muslims in Serbia; Turks in Bulgaria and Greece; and Roms, or Gypsies, in all parts of the region) and is closely tied to concepts of patriarchal power. In this way, feminist organizations are also subject to persecution.

Today, thanks to the efforts of local gay and lesbian organizations as well as external pressure from Western Europe, homosexuality has been decriminalized in every Balkan state. Of course, one cannot assume, however, that homophobia no longer exists, since the current situation regarding gay and lesbian rights in the region is complex and full of contrasts.

The Struggle Against Homophobia in Formerly Communist States

The Balkan countries can be organized into three distinct groups, according to their political situations. The first category is made up of Slovenia and Croatia. The case of Slovenia is the most remarkable; it was the first country to have a gay organization (in 1984), the first to guarantee true equality for homosexuals, and during its transition to independence in 1991, all democratic parties supported gay and lesbian rights. Since then, there has been a visible gay scene which includes cultural events, magazines, and even a radio show, and in 2001 Slovenia had its first Gay Pride parade. The only debates on homosexuality in Slovenia these days concerns gay **marriage**, which is also the case in Croatia. In fact, despite the lack of progress during the years of Franco Tudjman's nationalist government (from 1990 until his death in 1999), Croatia is making strides regarding gay rights and on the same path as its neighbor to the north.

The second group includes those countries where pro-gay legislation was passed but where gay associations have a troubled existence and homophobic protests are still numerous. Albania decriminalized homosexuality in 1995, but only reluctantly, and its only gay rights organization is fragile at best. Bulgaria passed decriminalization laws before 1991, but the first gay organization was not formed until that year, and it has only been since the late 1990s that such organizations have made strides. The Federation of Bosnia and Herzegovina decriminalized homosexuality in 1998, but that same year the first attempt to create a gay and lesbian organization did not succeed (there are now two). Nonetheless, despite having no fixed or identifiable gay areas in the country, there is a small gay community, reinforced by the strong Western presence in the federation's capital, Sarajevo. This city, which continues to attract gay Bosnians from the Serbian Republic of Bosnia (Republika Srpska), is also one of the few places in the country where multiculturalism flourishes.

The third group is comprised of Romania and Serbia, where frequent instances of homophobic violence have occurred over the past fifteen years. In 1993, the Council of Europe obtained a promise by the Romanian government to repeal its homophobic laws (specifically Article 200 of the penal code, which criminalized homosexual relationships) as part of its acceptance into the European Union, sparking a veritable battle in the country; in 1994, the Romanian parliament refused outright to consider the request. Finally, in 1996, Article 200 was amended, but only to decriminalize homosexual sex in private between consenting adults, leaving same-sex relations "taking place in public or resulting in public **scandal**" still a crime; this left the door open to interpretation, as the latter concept was not defined by Romanian law. Moreover, it specified that "inciting or encouraging a person to the practice of same-sex relations, as well as to propaganda, association, or other act of proselytizing within the same scope" was punishable by one to five years in prison. The application of this law made any open expression of a gay lifestyle dangerous. However, despite this precarious position, Romania's gay organizations found strength in international support as well as in drawing attention to the country's application to the European Union, given that in 2000, the European Convention on Human Rights expressly included the rejection of all **discrimination** based on sexual orientation. In 2001, Romania's Parliament at last completely repealed Article 200. However, violently ho-

mophobic rhetoric remains a key part of the strategy of the country's powerful far right.

Serbia is a very different case, being a country long ruled by a nationalistic government during its post-communist years, as well as devastated by war (1991–2001). Despite this, the capital of Belgrade can still claim to be a relatively open-minded city, at least compared to the rest of the country. While an openly gay lifestyle has been possible since the 1980s, it became more difficult under the post-communist regime, as gay rights were contradictory to the chauvinistic, warrior ideals of nationalist president Slobodan Miloševi´c (1989–2000). Boris Davidovich's shocking book, published in English under the title *Serbian Diaries,* is a chronicle of the political and sexual life of a clandestine homosexual in Belgrade during the civil war years. It describes how the Serbian regime made frequent homophobic insults, aimed not only at its political opponents but also the Yugoslavian ethnic minority. The regime, which relied on the army as well as militia to carry out its campaign of ethnic purification in the rebel states of Croatia and Bosnia, had much to gain from encouraging homophobic violence within its own borders, just as it encouraged the rape of Bosnian women by the Serbian military and paramilitary.

This is why gay activists in Serbia were often part of feminist and pacifist groups extolling not only peace, but also the struggle against any form of domination or male violence (for instance, the efforts of the gay organization Marble Ass against the war in Bosnia). The remarkable Serbian chapter of the international organization Women In Black has nonviolently fought for over fifteen years against "militarism, war, sexism, [and] nationalism" and against discrimination of women based on national differences as well as ethnic, religious, sexual, cultural, and ideological differences (according to its website). Serbian society remains divided, but its conservative elements are quite active. As elsewhere, recent efforts at democratization can be judged as much by the effectiveness of the struggle against homophobia as by any other measure.

Present & Future
Through these examples, it is clear how homophobia and the struggles to abolish it are fundamental measures of a country's democracy, along with issues such as ethnic diversity and women's rights. **Heterosexism** and male violence, traditional forms of power in

Balkan societies, were concepts reinforced under communist regimes. The end of communism led to a new openness to Western ideas, but this has often unfortunately taken place in a context of war and/or grave economic crisis. The West's demand for the equal treatment of minorities (including gays and lesbians) coincided with the establishment of the region's first gay and lesbian organizations, but at the same time has also incited a homophobic backlash. The requirements of the Council of Europe and others, however, have nonetheless played an essential role, not only by inspiring and educating gay activists, but also by serving as a reminder to Western Europe of its commitment to set an example, through organizations such as the Dutch association Cultuur en Ontspannings-Centrum (COC; Centre for Culture and Leisure), the International Lesbian and Gay Association, and even Amnesty International. Opportunity for gays and lesbians in the Balkans today comes from the timid but committed growth of gay organizations at the local level (at least in the large cities), which recognize that the ideology of Western Europe cannot be simply imported wholesale, but rather incorporated in such a way that is sensitive to the particulars of the region.

—*Philippe Masanet*

Adam, Barry D., Jan Willem Duyvendak, and André Krouwel, eds. *The Global Emergence of Gay and Lesbian Politics: National Imprints of a Worldwide Movement.* Philadelphia: Temple Univ. Press, 1999.

Anest, Marie-Christine. *Zoophilie, homosexualité, rite du passage et initiation masculine dans la Grèce contemporaine.* Paris: L'Harmattan, 1994.

Davidovich, Boris. *Serbian Diaries.* London: The Gay Man's Press, 1996.

Durandin, Catherine. *Roumanie, un piège?* St-Claude-de-Diray: Ed. Hesse, 2000.

Human Rights Watch and the International Gay and Lesbian Human Rights Commission. *Public Scandals: Sexual Orientation and Criminal Law in Romania.* New York: Human Rights Watch, 1998.

Krekic, Barisa. "Abominandum Crimen: Punishment of Homosexuals in Renaissance Dubrovnik," *Viator,* no. 18 (1987).

Wolff, Larry. *Inventing Eastern Europe.* Stanford, CA: Stanford Univ. Press, 1994.

Women In Black. Serbia chapter. http://www.zeneucrnom .org/index.php?lang=en (accessed January 29, 2008).

Yannakopoulos, Kostas. "Amis ou amants? Amours entre homes et identities sexuelles au Pirée et à Athènes," *Terrain,* no. 27 (1996).

—*Communism; Europe, Central & Eastern; Greece, Ancient; Orthodoxy; Police; Russia; Treason.*

BIBLE, the

As a "religion of the Book," Christianity forms the core of its dogma and beliefs from the teachings of the Bible. Despite being presented as a single volume, the Bible is actually made up of several books, divided between the Old Testament and New Testament. The New Testament relates the coming of Jesus, who is considered the Son of God sent to Earth to save humanity from sin, a decisive part of the Divine revelation. This essential event notwithstanding, the Old Testament is still quite valid: in fact, the arrival of the Son of God is the crowning moment up to which the Old Testament builds. Thus, the Old Testament is used by both Christianity and **Judaism** (which recognizes neither the New Testament nor Jesus as the prophesied Savior, and therefore refers to the Old Testament as part of its Hebrew Bible). All of the various denominations of Christian churches rely heavily on the Bible, considered to be the word of God, to justify their faith and doctrines.

Old Testament

Homosexuality is very clearly condemned in many of the books of the Old Testament. The churches extrapolate norms for modern society (really, for any society, no matter where it is situated in time and place) from these texts, despite the fact that they are historically and culturally tied to very specific temporal and geographic points: the **Middle East** mainly, and more specifically within the various Jewish locales of that region, set among a people the Bible calls Israel. The period of time covered by these texts is extremely long, stretching over a millennium, from the eleventh to second centuries BCE. No single unifying style can be identified (it includes collections of laws as well as narratives, prophecies, and even poetry), nor a single language (Hebrew being the most common, but Aramaic and Greek can also be found). There are some close relationships between characters of the same sex which may evoke suspicion despite never being presented in a negative way (the powerful love between David and

Jonathan, for example), but, otherwise, homosexual practices are condemned on many occasions

The first of these condemnations is also the most well-known. It is found in the book of Genesis (the opening book and the oldest part of the Bible) and tells the tale of **Sodom and Gomorrah**. In several verses (Gn 19:1–29), the Old Testament describes how two angels (who are also referred to as two men) come to Sodom to visit Lot and his family. Residents of the city appear because, as the Old Testament describes, they desire to "know" the two visitors; Lot is required to protect his guests. The next day, God rains down "brimstone and fire" (Gn 19:24) upon Sodom, as well as upon the city of Gomorrah. The term "sodomite" originates from this story—literally meaning "citizen of Sodom." This little word incurs a heavy religious, moral, and social reprobation; so heavy, in fact, that anyone to whom the word applies is theoretically doomed to be burned at the stake. The punishment by fire, threatened and imposed over the ages, takes its justification directly from this divine punishment as set out in the Old Testament; fire being symbolic of purification. Brimstone, too, is a disinfectant, but it also represents sterility (see Jb 18:15), which is also a common homophobic argument to justify labeling homosexual unions as a **perversion**. Fire and brimstone together are of course associated with hell, which evokes imagery of flames and the smell of noxious fumes. It should also be noted that this episode from Genesis describes homosexual relations only metaphorically, through the verb "to know." This metaphor is common in the Bible, used most often to describe heterosexual relations (see Gn 4:1). Thus, the term itself is neutral and only takes on a negative connotation when describing relations between members of the same sex. More specifically, here it refers to relations between men; the city of Gomorrah is described several times in close connection to Sodom, but relations between women are never mentioned. Today, and since the nineteenth century, the word "gomorrahan" is used as a sort of female equivalent to sodomite, meaning lesbian. The Old Testament never specifies what perversion reigned in Gomorrah, and there is never any mention of relations between women. It seems that the modern meaning of the word gomorrahan was deduced simply through the close proximity of the two biblical cities, by way of symmetry. Despite being a more literary word, the term gomorrahan nonetheless has taken on all the negative connotations associated with sodomite. The two words can be included in any homophobic reprobation invoking the book of Genesis and this specific biblical story.

While the first biblical mention of sexual relations between men required the guise of a metaphor, those that follow (from the book of Leviticus) are much more explicit and literal, and much more violently homophobic. This difference in how the same subject is treated is not due to a difference in stance (male homosexuality is condemned in both cases), but a difference between the books themselves. Genesis tells a story, literary trappings and all, while Leviticus takes a more direct approach by clearly laying out what is permitted and what is not. As such, the book of Leviticus is really a collection of biblical laws and cultural mores (the Levites are the members of the tribe of Levi, charged with ministering to the priests responsible for keeping the temple). The book itself was composed relatively recently (between the fifth and fourth centuries BCE) and, logically, the ritual law set out therein is seldom cited in the rest of the Bible or in church tradition. Nonetheless, its moral laws of holiness, of purification, and of sacrifice serve as background for many passages in the New Testament and have influenced the image the church has built up for itself. (An introduction to Leviticus from a 1980 publication of the Old Testament by Le Cerf states that holiness is one of the principal concepts of that book, and of all the Old Testament; it is closely related to the concept of purity.) This holiness implies a moral obligation for the faithful, because one's personal holiness reflects that of God. It is in this context that the laws of holiness condemn, twice, homosexual relations as being impure: "Thou shalt not lie with mankind, as with womankind: it is abomination" (Lv 18:22), and "If a man also lie with mankind, as he lieth with a woman, both of them have committed an abomination: they shall surely be put to death; their blood shall be upon them" (Lv 20:13). The style of each verse identifies the nature of the text: the use of the singular second person "thou" clearly identifies the first verse as legislative; the second extract proposes a punishment for the crime. Note here not only the explicit condemnation of homosexual acts, but also more seriously, the condemnation of those who practice these acts. The fact that these verses are part of a code of holiness for Jewish people (and more specifically, those who have dealings with pagans) does nothing to diminish the violence of a death sentence. This homophobic call to violence is even more noteworthy given that it was also taken up by the Catholic Church and enforced for many centuries; trial by fire for homosexuals is simply another facet of this violence invoked under Biblical decree.

New Testament

The New Testament is the part of the Bible written after the coming of Jesus. It describes the life of Christ (in the Gospels), the first acts of the disciples, and the early church (in the Acts of the Apostles). It also establishes the fundamentals of the new Christian theology (see the Book of Revelations and the Epistles, particularly those of St **Paul**). The Christian church acknowledges the Jewish writings of the Old Testament, but logically, the New Testament is referred to far more frequently, given that it was composed after the coming of Christ. The church relies heavily on this word of God for its legitimacy and a large part of its doctrine. Before examining homophobia in the New Testament, it is important to point out that the Gospels contain no explicit condemnation or even negative mention of homosexual acts or those who practice them. Other than a few tenuous hints from which one might extrapolate (Jesus, unmarried, lived with a group of men, apparently also unmarried; the Gospel of John (13:23) mentions a disciple "whom Jesus loved"), there is never any question of homosexuality in the Gospels. Therefore, the church does not derive its homophobia from the Gospels or even from the teachings of Jesus. In fact, it should be noted that Jesus was particularly **tolerant** toward those of a marginal or often-denounced sexuality (he was friendly with prostitutes as well as an eunuch). But the church can easily find condemnation in other writings of the New Testament, in particular the Epistles of Paul.

These writings show that one of Paul's central preoccupations was purity, necessary to one's conversion to the law of Christ. In this context, homosexuality is impure because it represents the persistence of pagan laws. Those who practice it will never attain the kingdom of God; they are spiritually dead. In this light, it is easily understandable how Western history is rife with evidence of capital punishment for this type of crime; Paul, an essential reference within church theology, had declared that those who practice the **vice** of homosexuality had already lost their (true) life. The First Epistle to the Corinthians explains that "neither fornicators, nor idolaters, nor adulterers, nor effeminates, nor abusers of themselves with mankind, nor

thieves, nor covetous, nor drunkards, nor revilers, nor extortioners, shall inherit the kingdom of God" (1 Cor 6:9-10). It should be noted that the expression "effeminate and abusers of themselves with mankind" (King James Version) is a little more euphemistic than the original Greek, in which a more literal translation would be "effeminates and pederasts." For "pederast," the Vulgate's Latin uses a less restrictive and less culturally specific expression, *masculorum concubitores*, which means literally, "men who sleep with men." A brief look at the original text shows that, even today, expressions for homosexuality are euphemized by translators, indicating a puritanical tendency in work that should be completely scientific.

Coming back to Paul's proposed list of vices, the apostle confuses and assimilates homosexuality with more consequential disturbances, such as instances of theft or lying. It follows that, within the doctrine of the church, homosexuals were confused with common **criminals** and sentenced to **prison** or death. In another Epistle, addressed to one if his disciples (First Letter to Timothy), Paul justifies the strictness of the law by the vices of the "lawless and disobedient." Here again, the *masculorum concubitores* find themselves mixed in with all sorts of criminals, among "murderers of fathers and murderers of mothers, manslayers, whoremongers" and "menstealers, liars, perjured persons" (1 Tim 1:9-10). History shows that sodomites were indeed punished along with other criminals, based on this treatment of homosexuality as a crime.

One more passage from an Epistle of Paul deserves to be cited and analyzed in detail, not only because it condemns homosexuals without equating them with common criminals, but also because it mentions female homosexuality. It is found in the Letter to the Romans:

> God gave them up unto vile affections: for even
> their women did change the natural use into that
> which is against nature. And likewise also the men,
> leaving the natural use of the woman, burned in
> their lust one toward another; men with men working that which is unseemly, and receiving in themselves that recompense of their error which was
> met. (Rom 1:26-27)

In this passage, homosexuality is still considered a sign of impurity in those who reject the word of God. It is also a mark of divine and just punishment, according to the formula "that recompense of their error which was met." Homosexuality should then be understood as a chastisement deserved by those who do not know God; referring, again, to the practice of ancient paganism. Greek mores and beliefs had already been stigmatized in the two previous Letters. Here, anyone who refuses the word of God is targeted by this reprisal. Considering homosexuality as a heavy punishment for the rejection of God shows just how much the subject troubled Paul; his denunciation was no less strong.

In general, the church and Christian society have always justified homophobic violence by citing these texts. They have been taken literally, and certain passages are still regularly invoked today. The expression "vile affection" is doubly pejorative: not only is the adjective strongly negative, but the term "affection" is as well, given that the "affection" refers to the affections of those who choose to be ruled by love of their bodies and not of God. Men and women alike are capable of this depravity—this being the only instance where female homosexual love gained sufficient importance to be mentioned explicitly. Finally, the expression "**against nature**" should also be noted, as it has been used repeatedly as justification for all sorts of homophobic persecution.

—*Thierry Revol*

Ancien Testament. Paris: Le Cerf/Les Bergers et les Mages, 1980.

Boswell, John. *Christianisme, tolérance sociale et homosexualité*. Paris: Gallimard, 1985. [Published in the US as *Homosexuality, Intolerance, and Christianity*. New York: Scholarship Committee, Gay Academic Union, 1981.]

Cazelles, Henri, ed. *Introduction à la Bible* (8 volumes): *Introduction critique à l'Ancien Testament*. Vol 2. 1973 and *Introduction critique au Nouveau Testament*. Volume 3. Paris: Desclée, 1976–89.

Gilbert, Maurice. "La Bible et l'homosexualité," *Nouvelle Theologie*, no. 109 (1987).

Kader, Samuel. *Openly Gay, Openly Christian: How the Bible Really is Gay Friendly*. San Francisco: Layland Publications, 1999.

Léon-Dufour, Xavier. *Dictionnaire du Nouveau Testament*. Paris: Le Seuil, 1975. [Published in the US as *Dictionary of the New Testament*. New York: Harper & Row, c. 1980.]

Lohse, Eduard. *Théologie du Nouveau Testament (Grundriss der neutestamentlichen Theologie)*. Geneva: Labor & Fides, 1987.

McNeill, John. *L'Eglise et l'homosexuel, un plaidoyer*. Geneva: Labor & Fides, 1982.

Nouveau Testament. Paris: Le Cerf/Les Bergers et les Mages, 1983. [Published in the UK as *The Church and the Homosexual*. London: Darton, Longman and Todd, 1977.]

Paul, André, ed. *Petite Bibliothèque des sciences bibliques*. Paris: Desclée, 1981–85.

Scrogg, Robin. *The New Testament and Homosexuality: Contexual Background for Contemporary Debate*. Philadelphia: Fortress Press: 1983.

Thévenot, Xavier. *Homosexualités masculines et morale chrétienne*. Paris: Le Cerf, 1985.

Zimmerli, Walter Christophe. *Esquisse d'une théologie de l'Ancien Testament*. Paris: Le Cerf, 1990.

—*Against Nature; Catholic Church, the; Debauchery; Heresy; Judaism; Orthodoxy; Paul (of Tarsus); Protestantism; Sodom and Gomorrah; Sterility; Theology; Vice.*

BIOLOGY

Just as is the case with **medicine**, a biological approach to homosexuality only further demonstrates the ambivalence of using scientific arguments in homophobic discourse, given that how they are used can often lead to diametrically opposed conclusions.

The history of homosexual "biology"—outside of zoological, anthropological (in the sense of physical anthropology), and genetic facts—is really a philosophical treatise on mankind and Nature. In this sense, if biology's contribution to a scientific discussion of homosexuality seems marginal, or for that matter if it has even ever had any influence over the fate of homosexuals, it has nonetheless played a central part in the constitution of traditional sexual morality; the constancy of the biological debate over the years only proves this. Thus, for a very long period of time, the same basic question is continually asked: is homosexuality "natural"?

This question has its origins in scientific inquiries during the period of Classical Antiquity, specifically the anatomy and behavior of animals. Three species in particular were studied—the rabbit, hyena, and weasel—and it was upon these three animals that much of the theological reasoning of the late Antiquity and early Middle Ages relating to the question of sexual relations between humans was based. Since the time of the Greek scientific revolution in the fifth century BCE, many philosophers and naturalists have collected facts and anecdotes about the animal kingdom. A mix of empirical observations and traditional legends, these treatises by authors such as Aristotle, Aristophanes of Byzantium, and Anaxagoras assign (although not without contradictions among them) various (and imaginative) characteristics to these same three animals; characteristics which during the time of Christianity became known as sexual "curiosities." Thus, the rabbit, who (according to Aristotle) urinates backwards, became known as an animal that loses its anus once a year; the hyena was thought to change its sex every year, taking on the role of male or female as necessary; and the weasel was supposed to have sexual intercourse through its mouth.

Thus it was during the time of Christianity that many theologians began to associate the sexual "nonconformism" of these animals with the various interdictions set out in the book of Leviticus. It was in this way that the Epistle of Barnabas (today considered apocryphal) describes Hebrew alimentary prohibitions as being based on the supposed mores of these animals: the ban against rabbit meat was linked to the risk of developing an attraction to boys; the ban against the meat of the hyena, to the risk of adultery or seduction; and the rejection of the meat of the weasel was linked to the rejection of oral sex. These were all very free interpretations of the writings, considering that nothing of the sort was ever specifically mentioned in the texts, and in Leviticus, the hyena was not even mentioned at all. However, this union between zoological "knowledge" and the theological carried on through time, after being taken up by Clement of Alexandria in the third century CE, a founding father of the Church of Alexandria, whose work played a central role in the constitution of the Church's sexual morals.

However, around the same time (and partly by the same Christian authors), biology was again invoked in the condemnation of homosexuality, but in a way that was diametrically opposite. Through the idea of Nature (a concept conveniently borrowed from the Stoic school of thought that was so popular during the apogee of the Roman empire, which did, in truth, share certain similarities with the Christian faith), over a period of time stretching all the way to the eighteenth century, a paradigm was established regarding the perception of relations between members of the same sex. Even if Clement of Alexandria could maintain that sexual relations without procreation as its goal "outraged nature" while describing (without any worry of contradiction) how hyenas did exactly that, it

was not until later, during the High Middle Ages, that the concept of "**against nature**" began to take on its full meaning.

The argument was not without its failings. It implies that the natural order reflects the will of God, and that reproduction, as the "natural" conclusion of sexuality, represents the way set out by God. Of course, it did not escape the attention of many that animal customs, where instances of multiple partners or incest occur frequently, are not exactly compatible with Christian morals. But most of all, the chief concern of this age, marked by the belief in an imminent final judgment, was chastity. To St Augustine (or *a fortiori*, St Jerome), sexuality, even within marriage, was highly suspect.

It would not be until the twelfth and thirteenth centuries that, as part of an enormous effort by the church to codify sexual, matrimonial, and conjugal practices, the argument refuting homosexuality as a "crime against nature" would be fully exploited, thereby becoming widespread. To Albert the Great, homosexuality represented the gravest sexual sin that could be committed, by offending "grace, reason, and nature" (whereas adultery only managed to offend grace and reason); to Thomas Aquinas, it was a **sin** because it prevented the reproduction of the human species. St Thomas's beliefs were unique because he grouped homosexuality together with other "unnatural **vices**" such as masturbation, bestiality, and even heterosexual acts where the man was **sterile**. In a sense, the positioning of homosexuality and other acts as being "against nature" is more important than the nature of the sexual practice itself, which makes interpretation of the word "sodomite" more difficult in Middle Age and Classical texts.

It was only after an essential change in the very concept of sexuality during the second half of the eighteenth century and into the nineteenth century that this approach to homosexuality began to change. During this time, scientific discourse became secular, detaching itself from theological discourse and casting aside the legends and traditions of the medieval bestiaries. Progressively, as the question of homosexuality was appropriated by the realm of medicine, it began to become part of the "natural" world through its new definition as a pathological entity. The change was gradual, though, and the terms "unnatural" and "antiphysical" would continue to be applied by medical law in the nineteenth century to those very elements it was in the process of naturalizing. And despite psychiatrist Richard von Krafft-Ebing's belief that the "**perversion**" of homosexuality constituted a mental illness, **psychiatry** itself was evolving in such a way that by the end of the nineteenth century, a biological undercurrent had been added to the question of homosexuality. From then on, the issue centered around two points. The first was the question of heredity. This understanding of homosexuality as a pathology was developing at a time when all mental illness was considered as a sort of **degeneracy**. The theory proposed by the French psychiatrist Bénédict Morel around 1850 described all forms of insanity as "morbid deviations from the human norm," transmitted through heredity. Even if Morel's theory has since fallen out of favor, the idea of homosexuality being due to an innate and hereditary characteristic has persisted throughout the twentieth century. The second point was the idea of etiology: that homosexuality must have a strictly biological cause. From the first publication of works labeling homosexuality as a mental illness, new research focused on finding an organic alteration within the brain as the cause. The introduction of endocrinology as a branch of medicine added the study of hormones to this line of research, which in turn complemented the **genetic** theories.

This "return" of homosexuality to the "natural" order was generally regarded as a sign of progress.

Indeed, the first German homosexual movement, built around the emblematic figure of the doctor Magnus **Hirschfeld**, embraced his theories, going so far as to talk of "**inversion**" as being nothing more than a "diversion in evolution." Compared to the concept of homosexuality as an "unnatural" crime, its identification as a sickness probably appeared to be the lesser evil; not only because of the legal consequences, but because it allowed those "afflicted" people to make sense of their difference. Nonetheless, studies in animal behavior during this period reinforced the need to find structure in biological order, enabling a rejection of the pathological approach to homosexuality, after the fashion of André **Gide**'s *Corydon*.

Strangely, these same theories originating from the medical field—used to justify the horrible torture of homosexuals (especially in **Germany** under the Third Reich)—form the basis of contemporary genetic and neuroanatomical work being carried out by gay or "pro-gay" researchers, especially in a **North American** context where the argument of "natural" exempts the individual from any charge of fault or sin.

Likewise, based on the works of American biologist Edward O. Wilson, sociobiology attempts to integrate the question of homosexuality into a Darwinian theory of evolution. In defining homosexuality as healthy and natural (which appeals to the altruistic compulsions of humanity), sociobiology synthesizes all previous work on the etiology of homosexuality. However, even that which appears to be a form of evolutionist teleology is unable to completely extricate itself from the same perspective shared by those late Antiquity, fathers of the church, as it seeks to measure the moral value of human behavior against a presumed "yardstick" of natural origin. Especially within the American context, this research could prove to be beneficial for the homosexual cause. However, historical precedent has clearly shown the repressive, homophobic potential of this type of work.

—*Pierre-Olivier de Busscher*

Bagemihl, Bruce. *Biological Exuberance: Animal Homosexuality and Natural Diversity*. New York: St Martin's Press, 1999.

Boswell, John. *Christianisme, tolérance sociale et homosexualité*. Paris: Gallimard, 1985. [Published in the US as *Homosexuality, Intolerance, and Christianity*. New York: Scholarship Committee, Gay Academic Union, 1981.]

Burr, Chandler. *A Separate Creation: The Search for Biological Origins of Sexual Orientation*. New York: Hyperion, 1996.

De Cecco, John and David Allen Parker. *Sex, Cells and Same-Sex Desire: The Biology of Sexual Preference*. New York: Haworth Press, 1995.

Dorais, Michel. "La Recherche des causes de l'homosexualité: une science-fiction?" In *La Peur de l'autre en soi, du sexisme à l'homophobie*. Edited by Michel Dorais, Pierre Dutey, and Daniel Welzer-Lang. Montreal: VLB Editeurs, 1994.

Dynes, Wayne, and Stephen Donaldson, eds. *Homosexuality and Medicine: Health and Science*. New York: Garland, 1992.

LeVay, Simon. "A Difference in Hypothalamic Structure Between Heterosexual and Homosexual Men," *Science*, no. 253 (1991).

———. *Queer Science*. Cambridge: MIT Press, 1996.

Schuklenk, Udo. "Is Research Into the Cause(s) of Homosexuality Bad for Gay People?" *Christopher Street*, no. 208 (1993).

———. "Scientific Approaches to Homosexuality." In *Gay Histories and Cultures: An Encyclopedia*. Edited by George E. Haggerty. Florida Citrus Commission. Vol 2. New York: Garland, 2000.

Tarczylo, Théodore. *Sexe et liberté au siècle des Lumières*. Paris: Presses de la Renaissance, 1983.

—*Against Nature; Degeneracy; Endocrinology; Genetics; Medicine; Medicine, Legal; Rhetoric; Sterility; Theology; Treatment.*

BIPHOBIA

The need to differentiate biphobia from homophobia is based on different dynamics of rejection. Phobias themselves, when they discriminate against others, are based on the construction of the purity and superiority of an individual or collective over an individual or collective which is perceived and represented as not only different, but inferior. Veiled or otherwise, they are often expressed by stereotyping individuals who are identified as "other" in order to increase one's self-worth; in this way, phobias are related to a fear of not measuring up to a social ideal. They often go beyond this, however, as is often the case with homophobia or biphobia, which can be said to be based on a fear of disrupting the unconscious social order. It is, therefore, not enough to show the falsehoods inherent in statements of discriminatory stereotypes. It is also important, if we hope to call into question the basis of all phobias, to reveal the cross-social ideologies which give them life and the constraints they imply, including those expressed and imposed by those who practice exclusion.

If biphobia can be explained by a foundation which is common to homophobia and the hierarchical organization of the sexes and genders, it should also be understood by the forms of rejection which are peculiar to it. One characteristic of biphobia is that it is expressed not only by heterosexual women and men who make up the normative majority, but also by gay men and lesbians, representatives of a sexual minority. Initially, it could be suggested that bisexuality's apparent "in between" position, combined with its nascent and still largely invisible history, is sufficient to explain the **discrimination** to which bisexual women and men are subjected. In this case, the rejection of bisexuality would be comparable to the exclusion of all intermediary groups who have neither political nor cultural history. Yet if certain elements confirm the relevance of this comparison, they are not sufficient to understand the depths of biphobia. As an example, biphobia often

takes the form of the staunchly expressed affirmation that "bisexuality does not exist"; therefore, bisexuals do not exist, are not legitimate because they have no physical reality, and are a false pretense of the mind, an abstraction. However, to use a comparison with other intermediate groups, no one would deny the existence of biracial individuals. Admittedly, skin color is a physical manifestation; it can be seen whereas bisexuality seems to leave no imprint on external appearance. But this absence of physical marking denoting difference is a characteristic of homosexuality as well. Yet we would not deny a lesbian who has not had a lover in the last ten years the right to call herself a lesbian; the same goes for a gay man, and for heterosexuals as well. Therefore, there is something specific that comes into play when bisexuality is rejected based on the idea that it does not exist.

Bisexuals might try to respond by using a tactic of their detractors and affirming their existence openly and publicly. Inspired by J. L. Austin, Judith Butler has demonstrated well the idea of repetition, which can be used to establish phobic standards while at the same time becoming a performative strategy to undermine them. By repeating something which is not perceived to exist, one calls into question the construction of the dominant social order. In this context, the repeated affirmation of bisexuality's existence can be a tool with which to respond to biphobic statements, and thus chip away at the principles of hierarchical organization and exclusion which make up these statements.

There are numerous fears that bisexuality seems to instill among its detractors; among them is the fear of infidelity. This brings up a principal paradox regarding bisexuals in response to biphobia: in proving their existence to detractors, bisexuals multiply their male and female sexual partners for doubters to see, which in turn intensifies criticism of them because of their perceived unfaithfulness. Thus, the proof of bisexuality's existence is that which is so disagreeable to its detractors: multiple partners. But how can we interpret the stigmatization of people by reason that they are sexually non-exclusive? This picture of biphobia based on a disapproval of bisexuals' infidelity is underlined by a belief common to all sexual orientations: that exclusive love remains possible. In this way, it is difficult to forgive bisexuals, as they are represented, for casting doubt on the fantasy of fidelity.

People's desire to always be seen in the best possible light, which is learned from being excluded by others because of some difference, explains in part biphobia's rejection of bisexuality: bisexuals are different from the norm because they appear to collude with heterosexuals and take advantage of the privileges heterosexuality offers (unlike homosexuals); at the same time, they refuse to name themselves, whether through the **media** or their political actions. Consequently, it can be stated by bisexuality's opponents that their biphobia can be blamed on bisexuals themselves; in this way, they can avoid asking questions about themselves in the false belief that all their fears have been banished.

—*Catherine Deschamps*

Butler, Judith. *Gender Trouble: Feminism and the Subversion of Identity*. New York: Routledge, 1990.

Deschamps, Catherine. Le *Miroir bisexuel. Socio-anthropologie de l'invisible*. Paris: Ed. Balland, 2002.

———, Rommel Mendès-Leité, and Bruno Proth. *Bisexualiy: le dernier tabou*. Paris: Calmann-Lévy, 1996.

Hall, Donald E., and Maria Pramaggiore, eds. *RePresenting Bisexualiy: Subjects and Cultures of Fluid Desire*. New York/London: New York Univ. Press, 1996.

Pontalis, Jean-Baptiste, ed. *Bisexualité et différence des sexes*. Paris: Gallimard, 1973.

Tucker, Naomi, ed. *Bisexual Politics: Theories, Queries, and Visions*. New York: Haworth Press, 1995.

—*Debauchery; Gayphobia; Heterophobia; Heterosexism; Lesbophobia; Psychoanalysis; Transphobia.*

BOUTIN, Christine

Christine Boutin, a conservative, devout Catholic politician in France, is best known for her vehement 1998 opposition to the **PaCS** (Pacte civil de solidarité; Civil solidarity pact) proposal, which was to recognize domestic same-sex partnerships in France (short of same-sex marriage). Many remember the moment when Boutin, who was a member of the party, Union pour la democratie française (UDF), spoke for five hours straight in the French National Assembly during debates over PaCS, which she believed would encourage homosexuality in the country; during her speech, she often brandished a copy of the **Bible**. According to her, "What is homosexuality if not the impossibility of reaching another being through their sexual difference? And what is the inability of accepting this difference, if not an expression of exclusion?" She also

claimed that "all civilizations that recognized and justified homosexuality as a normal lifestyle fell into **decadence**." By the time Boutin's marathon session ended, it earned her the reputation of a fanatic. From the start of her political career, her faith was central to her work, much to the joy of fundamentalist Christian associations, which finally had a significant ally in the French parliament. Having a similar political background as right-wing fundamentalists in the US Congress, Boutin quickly realized that it was in her interest to use her political power to serve a cause shared by interest groups within her own constituency of Yvelines (outside Paris). And though her involvement in debates around issues such as legalized abortion, gender parity, and most of all PaCS revealed a profoundly reactionary personality, she more recently tried to make-over her image by opposing other right-wing opinions on the subject of prisons, where it was widely agreed that she showed great compassion. Not long after, though, her old habits returned, and she has since led a new crusade against pornography.

Born February 6, 1944, Christine Boutin lost her mother at the age of five. An only child for some time, she became a member of, in her words, "one of those damned" blended families after her father remarried. Following studies in law at Assas (in the University of Paris) and her marriage in 1967, she became a press attaché at the Centre nationale de la recherche scientifique (a government-funded research organization), then a journalist. As a member of the UDF, she ran for office in Yvelines with the support of former Prime Minister Raymond Barre, whom she met through UDF president Charles Millon. Rare as it was, she flirted with several conservative political groups (including the National Front) and, despite not being nominated by her party, she did not hesitate to run for president of France in 2002. Her political colleagues are regularly shocked by the outrageousness of her statements; however, Boutin seems to have a certain support that the right wing would not want to lose.

With the 1995 publication of the encyclical *Evangelium vitae*, Pope **John Paul II** named her as "consultant to the Pontifical Council for the **Family**," the nerve center for the international "pro-life" activities of the Holy See. Thus, she enjoys a status nearly identical to that of a Vatican diplomat, which would normally seem awkward for a deputy of the French people. As a result, there are very few pro-life organizations in France that do not have a connection to

Boutin. It should be noted that she is also a patron of the very sectarian and very homophobic Cercle de la cité vivante, a "Christian place for the defense against the inducement of the **perversion** of mores." However, since 1994, the bulk of her non-legislative activities have been with an organization more directly under her thumb: the Alliance pour les droits de la vie (Alliance for the Right to Life). The Alliance mostly plays a coordinating role in petition campaigns against issues or subjects such as pornography in the **media**, gay **marriage**, and even publishers of children's books (such as Ecole des loisirs), whom they accuse of trying to pervert children with books about homosexuality or **suicide**. Recently, the Alliance added lobbying to its arsenal. And who were those many senior citizens in attendance during the National Assembly's PaCS debates, with whom Boutin was always exchanging knowing looks? The answer was found once more within the Alliance, when its secretary explained that its president, Boutin, had been for years inviting her faithful friends to a chapel to pray for the souls of the French politicians, "so that they could save and protect life and family." This ritual took place every Wednesday evening—right next door to the Assembly!

Boutin also played a major part in the fight against legalized abortion in France. From 1986 to 1998, as head of an interparliamentary organization called le Groupe parlementaire pour favoriser l'accueil de la vie (the Parliamentary Group in Favor of Welcoming Life), she firmly entrenched opposition to legalized abortion within parliament, thanks to the support of the National Front. She then encouraged leaders of the right to consider granting amnesty to those convicted as anti-abortion activists. As a result, in May 1995, Minister of Justice Jacques Toubon and a long-time opponent of the 1967 Neuwirth law which made the sale of contraceptives legal in France, drafted a bill for amnesty and presidential pardon for such activists, explaining that he was trying to create "an equilibrium between those who fight for and those who fight against abortion." When it was debated in the Assembly on June 21, it was severely criticized by numerous opponents; as a result, the government conceded and proposed revisiting the text, but affirming the need to return to the strict application of the law with regard to the condemnation of those who either encourage abortion, or fail to discourage women from it.

But Boutin's greatest notoriety resulted from her hardline stance on PaCS. She did not hesitate to take the lead in the fight against the recognition of homosexual couples. Her speeches, along with her book *Le "Mariage" des homosexuels?* (Homosexual "marriage"?), constitute in and of themselves a veritable anthology of contemporary homophobia in France. According to her, homosexual movements seek to "undermine the fundamentals of our society," and that if PaCS were passed, "not only the coherence of the law, but also the financial equilibrium of the State would be compromised." Her statements regularly make use of **rhetoric** that is at once both banal and sinister, employing amalgamations of the most odious type: "Where is the line drawn, for an adopted child, between homosexuality and **pedophilia**?" She also attempts to play on the fears of the public, making homosexuality out to be the **peril** of perils: "the very fundamentals of civilization and of democracy are being questioned," and thus, "entire parts of society could be swallowed up, without rhyme or reason, in this bottomless pit" that is the recognition of homosexual couples. In short, she believes, "we are back in barbaric times."

Yet, Boutin does not believe that she is homophobic. After all, "homophobia exists often only within their [homosexuals'] own hearts," she writes in her book, and that "it would be difficult to foster the perpetration of **violence** against homosexuals if informed by objective information." In her infinite charity, she goes even further: she claims to understand "the reality of the suffering of homosexuals," and declares her "love" for them after all, affirming in all modesty that "to each their own truth, no matter how monstrous or contradictory to human beings."

(In 2007, Christine Boutin was named Minister of Housing and the City, under the newly-elected government of President Nicolas Sarkozy.)
—*Fiametta Venner*

Boutin, Christine. *Le "Mariage" des homosexuals? CUCS, PIC, PACS et autres projets législatifs.* Paris: Critérion, 1998.
Desfossé, Bertrand, Henri Dhellemmes, Christèle Fraïsse, and Adeline Raymond. *Pour en finir avec Christine Boutin.* Paris: H & O Editions, 1999.

—*Anti-PaCS; Catholic Church, the; Decadence; Far Right; France; Marriage; Mirguet, Paul; Peril; Politics; Rhetoric; Theology; Tolerance.*

BRYANT, Anita

In the latter half of the 1970s, Anita Bryant, who was once a popular American singer, a former Miss Oklahoma, and the star of orange juice commercials, became a well-known spokesperson for the religious right in America in the battle against homosexual rights. Specifically, she campaigned extensively to repeal a local ordinance in Miami, Florida, where she lived, which prohibited the discrimination on the basis of sexual orientation; her campaign was named "Save Our Children." As such, she came to represent the homophobic views of fundamentalist and born-again Christians, the latter comprised of the newly converted who had rediscovered the Bible after a long period of distance from or indifference to religion. Curiously, Bryant's crusade against homosexuality was launched in reaction to actions set in motion by another born-again Christian (but this one a moderate), President Jimmy Carter. Following his election in 1976, Carter instituted a policy that supported the rights of gays and lesbians, encouraging the repealing of laws against sodomy in many states, and pushing local governments to pass bylaws that would protect homosexual rights. The city of Miami's vote on its anti-discrimination ordinance became the founding act of Anita Bryant's new career as an anti-gay lobbyist, and in the end, she was successful in having the ordinance overturned.

The intense media coverage sparked the largest national "anti-gay" campaign ever, the likes of which the country had not seen since the days of **McCarthyism**. Anti-gay lobbying groups were created in cities and counties that had either adopted anti-discrimination legislation or were about to, particularly in the Great Plains and Rockies states that were known for their strong, puritanical, Protestant tendencies; this led to the repeal of the legislation in cities such as St Paul, Minnesota; Wichita, Kansas; and Eugene, Oregon. Also, the state of Oklahoma approved a law allowing the dismissal of any teacher who "practiced" homosexuality, and California senator John Briggs attempted to launch a state referendum ("Proposition 6") that would ban the hiring of openly gay teachers (an initiative that was rejected with help from both Republican and Democratic anti-Briggs forces such as Ronald Reagan, Gerald Ford, and President Carter). This legislative turmoil and anti-gay lobbying was matched by an increase in instances of homophobic **violence** throughout the US, including the murder of a San Francisco gardener,

whose mother declared: "His blood is on the hands of Anita Bryant."

Ironically, Anita Bryant's actions had the additional effect of provoking the largest mobilization of gays and lesbians since **Stonewall**, inspiring protests in major cities as well as a boycott of Florida Citrus Commission products (for which Bryant was spokesperson). And it could be said that despite her success in repealing the Miami ordinance, Bryant's career was never the same again, as she would always be linked to her anti-gay campaign.

—*Pierre-Olivier Busscher*

Bryant, Anita. *The Anita Bryant Story: The Survival of Our Nation's Families and the Threat of Militant Homosexuality.* Old Tappan, NJ: Fleming H. Revell, 1977.

Shilts, Randy. *The Mayor of Castro Street.* New York: St Martin's Press, 1983.

—*Buchanan, Pat; McCarthy, Joseph; Music; North America.*

BUCHANAN, Pat

Pat Buchanan—American politician, editorialist, Republican presidential candidate in 1992 and 1996, Reform Party presidential candidate in 2000 (the party created in 1995 by Texas billionaire Ross Perot)—is a symbol of American anti-gay activism fueled by evangelistic renewal and Republican Party-style conservatism. A staunch Catholic, Buchanan belongs to a generation of Americans who choose to overlook religious differences of the church to establish in the US a "Christian coalition" (including even orthodox Jews) united around common moral struggles, foremost among them being the fights against abortion rights and against gay and lesbian rights. An old supporter of Nixon and Reagan, Pat Buchanan is one of the main architects behind the "infiltration" of the Republican Party by the religious right, forcing even moderate party members to stand up for "the reestablishment of family values" (that is, against abortion and against homosexuality). A constant champion of Anita **Bryant's** anti-homosexual campaign in the 1970s, the emergence of **AIDS** in the early 1980s gave Buchanan an opportunity to properly express his hatred toward gays, such as in a 1983 editorial when he explained that AIDS was nature's revenge against those who had defied its order: "The poor homosexuals—they have declared war upon nature, and now nature is extracting an awful retribution."

However, Pat Buchanan's isolationist views on economics and international policy, as well as regular evidence of his anti-Semitism, slowly caused him to become marginalized and then ostracized by the Republican Party, leading to his exit just prior to the presidential campaign of 2000. His short-lived investiture in the Reform Party, despite opposition from founder Ross Perot and Jim Mangia, its national secretary (who himself was homosexual), lends hope for his continued political marginalization in a system of American politics in which most attempts at a "third path" between Republicans and Democrats end in failure.
—*Pierre-Olivier de Busscher*

Adams, Barry, Jan Willem Duyvendak, and Andre Krouwell. *The Global Emergence of Gay and Lesbian Politics: National Imprints of a Worldwide Movement.* Philadelphia: Temple, 1999.

Miller, Neil. *Out of the Past: Gay and Lesbian History from 1869 to the Present.* New York: Vintage, 1995.

—*Boutin, Christine; Bryant, Anita; Hoover, J. Edgar; McCarthy, Joseph; North America.*

BUDDHISM

During the middle of the fourteenth century, when St Francis Xavier and the early Christian missionaries discovered Japan, they were horrified by the "sodomite" environment that seemed to abound in the Buddhist monasteries they visited. Even if the Jesuits' descriptions were probably quite exaggerated, homosexuality (or more specifically, pederasty) has always been associated with Buddhism in this country. From the late Middle Ages to early modern times, romantic relationships between monks and young male initiates seem to have been a common occurrence in monasteries. These initiates, usually adolescents, often wore facial powder and makeup, and were occasionally the object of internal struggles among the monks. Some texts trace this tradition all the way back to Kukai (774–835 CE), one of the great Japanese Buddhist saints, founder of the esoteric school of Shingon. Monks usually came from the nobility or the warrior class, where pederastic relationships, considered a cultural sophistication, were

held in high regard while relations between men and women were held in a lower esteem. This type of love was considered under the benediction of Manjushri, the bodhisattva of wisdom, a mythical being who usually took on the form of a young man, and whose Japanese title, Monjushiri, even evoked the buttocks (*shiri*) of the ephebes....

However, these homosexual relationships involving Japanese monks were quite marginal, all the more so because monks of all schools of Buddhism were required to be chaste, and heterosexual relations forbidden. Paradoxically, these pederastic mores had a certain legitimacy, given the near absence of any reference in Buddhist writings to homosexual relations. This granted the relationships a tacit permission: "Homosexuality as such was never really discussed," wrote Bernard Faure, a professor of Japanese religion. The early disciplinary texts went into great detail listing all the types of sexual relations forbidden to monks, including some rather improbable items (in the mouth of a frog, in the trunk of an elephant, etc.). Yet while heterosexual relations, onanism, and many forms of bestiality are laid out in meticulous detail, the interdiction of homosexual relations is hardly mentioned, and only in a roundabout way. For the devoted layman, Buddha proposes five moral precepts based on the principle of "Do not do unto others that which you would not have done to you": do not kill, do not steal, etc. The third precept forbids "sexual misconduct," a term so ambiguous that a famous Indian Buddhist commentary, the *Abhidharma-kosa*, defines it in detail by dividing it into four interdictions: sexual misconduct being the occurrence of sexual relations with a forbidden woman (e.g., a young girl, a married woman), in a forbidden way (e.g., fellatio, sodomy), in forbidden places (e.g., a temple), and during a forbidden time (e.g., menstruation). Technically, the forbidden ways never make direct reference to homosexual relations that are, as such, unknown.

Much attention has been paid to the term *pandaka*, given in the Buddhist canon to those individuals who are not permitted to become monks. Its ambiguous definition has been variously translated as eunuch, hermaphrodite, and even homosexual by certain Western translators. This exegesis merely demonstrates that it refers to a vague category of individuals whose psycho-physical sexual identity is unclear. Buddhagosa, a great Buddhist commentator of the fifth century, even categorized the impotent as *pandaka*. However, the

rejection of this type of postulant does not necessarily imply a condemnation of homosexual relations as
such, since the early Buddhist texts have strangely very
little to say on the subject. Notwithstanding, throughout the long development of Buddhism over the years,
a few negative scriptural references toward homosexuality can be found. A Buddhist text from the beginning
of the Christian era describes a type of hell where homosexuals are inexorably drawn toward beings of fire,
and are burned in mid-embrace. The *Samantapâsâdika*,
a later text attributed to Buddhagosa (after centuries of
uncertainty), states that monks are not to have relations
with women, nor men, nor asexual beings (meaning
the *pandaka*). In his Path of the Great Perfection, Patrul
Rinpoche (1808–87), a great Tibetan erudite of the
nineteenth century, describes sexual misconduct for
the continuity of Indian texts: "Masturbation, having
sexual relations with someone who is married or engaged, with an unattached person in the open, with
someone observing the ritual fast of a day, with someone who is sick, with a woman who is pregnant or in
pain, during menstruation, immediately after birth, in
the presence of the three jewels [Buddha, his teachings,
and his community], with one's parents or family, with
a prepubescent girl, and finally by way of mouth, of the
anus, etc." Here again, even if homosexuality as such
is not mentioned, sexual relations between people of
the same sex seem to be nevertheless implicitly condemned. This was the interpretation made by the current Dalai Lama, when asked about the subject during
the first years of his exile.

However, the change in the Dalai Lama's position was
exemplary. After representatives of the gay community
in the US declared themselves hurt by his opinion, he
publicly apologized, and declared that only mutual respect and devotion should govern a couple's relationship, be it heterosexual or homosexual. Consequently,
in the United States many Buddhist communities were
created based on homosexual identity, and it is not uncommon to see the term gay or lesbian associated with
a Buddhist center. The gay Buddhist community in
the US even has its own icons, such as Tommy (Issan)
Dorsey, a one-time drag queen and junkie turned Zen
master, who established a hospice in the gay quarter
of San Francisco, "for all my boys," as he often said; he
died of **AIDS** in 1989. The hospice is still open today.
—*Eric Rommeluère*

Robinson, B. A. "Buddhism and Homosexuality." Religious
    Tolerance.Org. http://www.religioustolerance.org/hom_
    budd.htm (accessed October 11, 2007).
Connor, Randy, David Hatfield, and Mariya Sparks. *Cassell's
    Encyclopedia of Queer Myth, Symbol and Spirit*. New York/
    London: Cassell: 1997.
Faure, Bernard. *Sexualités bouddhiques: entre désirs et réalités*.
    Aix-en-Provence: Le Mail, 1994.
———. *The Red Thread: Buddhist Approaches to Sexuality*.
    Princeton: Princeton Univ. Press, 1998.
Patrul, Rinpoche. *Le Chemin de la grande perfection*. St-Léon-
    sur-Vézère, France: Ed. Padmakara, 1997.
Thompson, Mark. *Gay Soul: Finding the Hearth of Gay Spirit
    and Nature*. San Francisco: Harper, 1995.

—*China; Hinduism; India; Japan; Korea; Southeast Asia.*

C

CAMPS. *See* Deportation; Gulag

CARICATURE

From the Latin *caricatura*, to load. "To caricature" is to exaggerate a characteristic; in the case of minorities, this characteristic can be highly discriminatory, especially when it takes on a nationalist or racist dimension (the Jewish **peril**, the yellow peril). As such, the history of caricature is often neglected, especially when the subject matter (homosexuality, in particular) remains sensitive. There is also the issue of relevance: the frame of reference has either been lost or is no longer current. In principle, caricatures should identify flaws in society and thereby aspire to correct them; in reality, however, caricatures have tended to encourage discrimination, not discourage it. The history of the portrayal of homosexuals in caricature has yet to be written. The homophobic elements are not always obvious; it depends not only on how homosexuals are represented, but also on how one perceives them to be, and whether or not such portrayals are derogatory—a drawing of an effeminate boy, for example, is not necessarily homophobic. Moreover, many homosexual men and women have no fear of being mistaken for a caricature; they embrace the role, mocking both how others perceive them as well as the stereotypical image being forced upon them.

The history of the homosexual caricature is thus also a history of its reception. The ease of identifications and interpretation of homosexual elements varies widely. They are more obvious when the caricature depicts sexual acts between men, but more difficult when there is a representation of masculine or feminine characteristics, whether in dress or in attitude. Take, for example, an "effeminate" drawing of **Henri III** adorning Pierre de L'Estoile's *Registre-journal de Henri IV*—what

was once considered effeminate and exaggerated is no longer so by today's standards. Additionally, exaggeration of the male member was more often considered a homage to male virility, rather than the pleasure it could offer. While the image of Priapus weighing his phallus in the *Casa dei Vettii* of Pompeii clearly represents exaggeration, it is not a caricature. More ambiguous perhaps are the sexual acts between men depicted in the grotesques of Renaissance Italian villas, or the woodcarving illustration of three men from Sebastian Munster's *Cosmographia universalis* of 1544, wherein one man is ostensibly touching the codpiece of another.

Regardless of its origins, the evolution of caricature is closely linked to that of the press, which expanded along with civil liberties during the late eighteenth century. Caricatures often accompanied hand-written pamphlets, portraying Queen Marie-Antoinette or Mademoiselle Raucourt as lesbians, for example, or the Marquis de Villette as a sodomite. But it was mostly during the nineteenth and early twentieth centuries—the golden age of the industrial press—that caricature enjoyed its largest popularity. In France, six magazines in particular featured numerous illustrations of effeminate characters: *Le Canard sauvage, L'Assiette au beurre* (March 1902–October 1912), *Le Rire* (which also published as *Fantasio), La Charrette charrie,* and *Le Sourire.*

Political Affairs

The international political affairs of the early twentieth century inspired a great number of homophobic caricatures, especially the events concerning Emperor William II of Prussia. In France, the desire for revenge (after Prussia's annexation of Alsace and Lorraine during the Franco-Prussian War) appears to demasculinize the enemy, while at the same time Prussia's imperial behaviour was denounced throughout France and Europe. The intention of critics was to mock the scientific militancy of Magnus **Hirschfeld**'s German

L'Assiette au beurre, (December 2, 1911):
"What's up with the Emperor's advisors? They're not doing anything."
"They're sitting on the points of their helmets."

homosexual movement, as well as a German **army** which had been shaken by sensational trials. As early as 1907, French writer and journalist John Grand-Carteret assembled more than 150 such caricatures in a single collection, published by E. Bernard in Paris.

The magazine *L'Assiette au beurre* dedicated no less than two issues to these same subjects, whose content linked Prussia to acts of sodomy and prostitution. Paradoxically, in these caricatures, homosexuality is depicted to suggest not only the officer's abuse of authority over his soldiers, but his to pacifism and anti-militarism (i.e. his weakness) as well.

The cover illustration by Jean Villemot, of the November 16, 1907, issue of *L'Assiette au beurre*, made reference to a man's ancestral fear of submissive sodomy … but not just any man! Depicted was none other than Emperor William II seated on his throne, thinking to himself: "*My word! I can barely bring myself to stand up!*" Many other caricatures conjure up the image of the German nation completely overtaken by this **contagion**, from the Emperor to his ministers and high-ranking officers all the way down to soldiers. *L'Assiette* approached the subject again in the June 20,

1908, issue, entitled *Harden-Party*, chronicling the ups and downs of the military trials in Germany regarding accusations of homosexual conduct by prominent members of William II's cabinet. The distinctive shape of German helmets took on a particular meaning, as illustrated by *L'Assiette* on December 2, 1911: "*What's up with the Emperor's advisors? They're not doing anything. They are sitting on the points of their helmets.*" During World War I, the magazine *Fantasio* did not hesitate to keep up the tradition of depicting homosexuality, instead publishing a drawing by A. Guillaume, *Le Jugement de Paris (version boche)* (Judgment of Paris [Kraut version]), wherein a young, not-so-masculine soldier, accompanied by two junior officers, reports to a superior proffering an apple.

Fantasia: "The Judgment of Paris (Kraut version)"

In France, the suggestion of homosexuality was never used as an attack against the government; homosexuality was considered a private affair, reserved for black masses or the "*ballets bleus.*" At the same time, the emasculation of politicians was regularly depicted, usually by way of cross-dressing: Joseph Reinach, best known as a champion of Alfred Dreyfus, was drawn wearing a wedding gown held by two clergymen in the May 28, 1898 issue of *Le Rire*, 1898; Leon Blum was often portrayed dressed in women's clothes; a photographic montage depicted Jean Jaurès in women's shoes holding in his hands the head of Aristide Briand (June 1, 1907, issue of *Fantasio*) and the War Minister, General Picquart, was also shown dressed in women's clothes, all the while being severely reprimanded as he tightens his corset (drawing by A. Barrère, November 15, 1906, issue of *Fantasio*).

L'Assiette au beurre: "Mesdam' messieurs"

Civil Affairs

In France, caricatures typically targeted the supposed **decadence** of the subjects they depicted. This decadence was largely considered to be the province of those born of affluence (Adelswärd-Fersen), or a luxury enjoyed by the "fine-mannered" bourgeoisie. The clash of the sexes and genders combined with the battle of the classes in these sometimes stinging, sometimes simply amusing drawings. The decadence of the *Belle Epoque* ("Beautiful Era," pre-World War I) was often tied to the image of the effeminate boy or with infantilism, while the sporty fashion of the waif of the *Années folles* ("Mad Years," post-World War I) played on the masculinization of women. Many different expressions became popular to describe homosexual men and women: *ces messieurs-dames* ("these gentlemen-ladies"), *les p'tits jeun'hommes* ("young l'il boys"), and *mesdames-messieurs* ("lady gentlemen"). "The third sex" or "third gender" were also common phrases, along with various

epithets (terrible, queer, …); all were expressions that permitted many effective plays on words in French.

Dedicated entirely to the *p'tits jeun'hommes*, issue 422 of *L'Assiette au beurre* (1909) is an extraordinary volume. In only a few pages, it references a good number of turn-of-the-century negative archetypes; throughout, the image of the *p'tit jeun'homme* is mocked for his outrageous makeup and flamboyant style of dress. The cover illustration depicts a young boy with blond hair, holding a finger to his brightly painted red lips. With a large flower in his lapel, rings on his fingers, a cravat, and a rakish stance, he is out to seduce by any means possible—he make his historical references (*"Plato was one … Socrates too"*), and is shown to be in direct competition with women, in whom he does not see any erotic use (*"Wouldn't you say that the greatest achievement of our time will be that women will be no longer necessary for love?"*). On the other hand, a certain complicity is implied between these depictions—after all, what does one's sex matter if the "gender" is the same? In this vein, the July 15, 1924, issue of *Fantasio* was presented under the title of "Daily Affairs," *l'éphèbe et la garçonne (presque une fable)*—"the ephebe and the waif (practically a fairy tale)"—featuring an illustration of a young man and a young woman seated together at the same table, practically the mirror image of the each other.

Les gâcheuses (The wastefuls) was the subject and the title of a special August 1923 issue of the magazine *La Charrette "Charrie"* (issue 21). "*Les gâcheuses*" was a rarely-used expression, containing two reproaches against the choice of a homosexual lifestyle—physiological **sterility**, and the waste of both bodily fluids and affection, implying that both stem from a lack of judgment. The concept of the "loss of seed," as Emile Zola called it in his preface to Dr Laupts' *Invertis et homosexuals*, is clearly illustrated in a symbol-laden drawing entitled *Tendresse ancillaire* (Ancillary affection)—"You must pay more attention, my love! You have once again let the milk burn," declares a gentleman in a pink jacket with a flower on the lapel to his "butler." **Perversion** creates confusion when categorizing places of leisure; for example, the cover illustration shows a short-haired woman dressed in a smoking jacket and tie, looking perplexed as she stands in front of the "Men's" sign outside the toilets. This confusion leads to waste: affection becomes the sentimentality of effeminate males and transvestites striving toward hyperbole in order to cover up their miserable and ridiculous condition. A dispute becomes a *Drame passionnel* (Drama of passion);

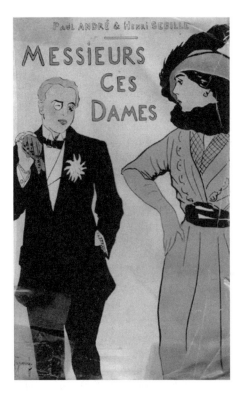

L'Assiette au beurre: *"Messieurs Ces Dames"*

to Chantecleer, a successful work of his father's), and depicted in *Le Sourire du jeudi* of May 25, 1933, as a naked woman, with the caption *Soyez les bien vu nus* ("good to see you naked"; "*bien vu nu*" is a phonetic pun on the word for welcome, "*bienvenue*"). In a April 25, 1903, special edition of *L'Assiette au beurre* dedicated to the "Esthetics," Paul Iribe confirmed dandyesque poet Robert de Montesquiou's reputation on the cover page, with the following page of writer Pierre Loti (who had recently published *Mon frère Yves*)—in which a woman berates a distinguished-looking man holding a book entitled *Mon frère IV*, by Pierlo To, saying, "Come now, my dear—you don't have the excuse of being a sailor!" Also in the same issue: "You're coming to supper, right? We're having Pierre Loti and his new brother Yves…," implying homosexual activity.

Women, too, were not safe from these illustrators (all men), although they benefited from a different sort of treatment. While the feminization of a man was considered an insult, the masculinization of a woman was a badge of honor, especially during a time of growing

the "women" take up sewing or needlepoint to forget about the problems at home, or become wallflowers at balls because they're too old or too ugly. Separation becomes a fetishist drama in *Lorsque tout est fini* (After it's all over). And in *Relique d'amour* (Relic of love), an old man sitting on a bench stares nostalgically at the picture on the wall of a boy in suspenders.

The French literary world, too, was not safe from accusations of promoting **inversion**, as shown by its many representations of male homosexuality in educated circles (a French trait, it would seem). The illustrator Camara mocked writer Jean Lorrain's academic aspirations with a ring-bedecked appearance on the March 7, 1903, cover of *L'Assiette au beurre*. Baron Adelswärd-Fersen, whose trial for offenses of indecency was constantly in the news, found himself the subject of a July 26/August 1, 1903, special edition of *Canard sauvage*, entitled "Black masses." The emphasis in this instance was placed on the "abominable" habits of an aristocracy, who considered heterosexuality the province of a rabble who just did not understand poetry. The writer Maurice Rostand, too, was persecuted throughout the length of his career: sketched in the February 15, 1922, issue of *Fantasio* as "Chanteclarinet" (an allusion

L'Assiette au beurre: *"P'tits jeun'hommes"*

feminism. More so than the effeminate male, it seems the lesbian was the paragon of female independence.

At the end of the nineteenth century, women were muscling their way in, earning their turn: the illustrator Steinlen drew these women as "rivals" to heterosexual men in the February 22, 1896, issue of *Le Rire*; wherein they were portrayed as originating from a homeland to which they would sometimes return, alone (caption to Pourriol's drawing *Cruise through the Archipelago*: "Lesbos? Don't bother, Captain. We're better off visiting that island on our own!"). In France in 1902, the lesbian was quite fashionable and featured in the February 1902 issue of *Les Articles de Paris*: two pairs of women dancing together, as drawn by Minartz in *L'Assiette au beurre*, proclaim, "*Dire que les gommeux / S'imaginent, les malheureux / Qu'on ne peut pas se passer d'eux!*" ("Just think that those dandies / Believe, the poor souls / That we can't live without them!").

This same publication devoted its entire March 2, 1912, issue to artist Jils Garrine depicting these "*mesdam'messieurs*," at the same time as the *P'tits Jeun'hommes* issue. From the first page, these women are portrayed as being nothing more than a harmless distraction. In a drawing entitled "Honor Intact!," an elderly woman says to a man in a smoking jacket: "And you allow your wife … with her friend …," to which he responds, "Bah! It's just how I keep from being cuckolded."

But after World War I, boyish women became rivals, at least according to the caricatures. In the February 1, 1927, issue of *Fantasio*, "A New Time, Another Danger," such women play up the confusion between the sexes to escape their conjugal duties. In the May 7th, 1931, issue of *Le Sourire du jeudi*, under the brush of J. Leclerc, a woman talks on the telephone while sitting next to a boyish girl: "Alas, my dear, I can't today, I'm seeing my aunt…." However, a May 21, 1932, issue of *Le Rire* devoted exclusively to *Dames seules* (Solitary ladies), written by Maryse Ghoisy (who would often dress as a man while reporting) and drawn by Vertès, portrays lesbians as well-adjusted people. Astonishingly, the issue begins and concludes with examples of what would today be called gay **parenting**. On the front cover, a childless couple has reached their quarter century together in "Silver anniversary": "To think that we would have a twenty-five-year-old son by now." And on the back cover, while sitting together, a woman breaks into tears upon discovering the pregnancy of her friend, who replies: "Now my dear, please don't cry; the child is yours."

This type of drawing in France was not restricted to humor magazines; it could also be found on the covers and in the illustrations of popular novels with extravagant storylines: *Amour inverti* (Inverted love), by Dr J.

Le Rire: "*Voilà un garçon qui a bien mauvais genre.*"
"*C'est vrai : il a le genre féminin!*"
("There goes a boy who looks like trouble."
"Yes, trouble with her gender.")

de Cherveix, 1907; *Féminisé* (Feminized), by Jacques de Bandol, 1922; *Léon dit Léonie* (Léon, a.k.a Léonie), by Charles-Etienne, 1922; *Messieurs ces dames* (Ladies these gentlemen), by Paul André et Henri Sébille; *Billy*, by Jean d'Essac, 1937; *Frédi s'amuse* (Fredi at play), *Frédi en ménage* (Fredi at home); and *Frédi à l'école* (Fredi at school), by Max des Vignons, 1929. Postcards also provided a venue for this type of caricature.

After the end of the golden age of caricature in France (and particularly homophobic caricature), the genre began to fade away, replaced by a preference for simple humorous drawings in publications like *Le Canard enchaîné, Libération,* or *Le Monde* (though the valiant satirical weekly *Charlie Hebdo* is still publishing, despite years of interruption).

Contemporary caricature is rare, but is nonetheless important. Edith Cresson, who became France's first female prime minister in 1991, once rather tempestuously declared that one in four Britons were homosexual. The cartoonist from *Canard enchaîné* responded by illustrating, in the issue of June 19, 1991, three kilted Britons in a row, followed by a fourth in nylons, garters, and feathers ("Great Britain According to Cresson"). A Wiaz caricature in the *Nouvel observateur* (August 8–14,

1991) shows a gay man in a baseball cap and muscle shirt, ultra virile and tough, complete with a tattoo of a heart dedicated to his mother on his left arm. More in tune with the gay world, the artist Cunéo depicted the prime minister as "Edith the Terrible," armed with a whip and dressed in leather, catching a colleague's son naked with another man. The two are terrified; two condoms and a bottle of petroleum jelly lay next to the mattress on the floor.

Be that as it may, the days of exclusively portraying gays and lesbians as a systematic inversion of the heterosexual world have passed. Gay and lesbian culture is capable of representing itself (with artists such as Ralf König in Germany, or Copi and Cunéo in France) complete with its own brand of gender inversion, free from any heterosexism. While efforts to force the mainstream press to acknowledge its homophobia have not yet fully succeeded, the pressure has resulted in fewer instances of homophobic caricature, even if jests like those of Philippe Bouvard still echo the homophobic past.

—*Patrick Cardon*

Baecque, Antoine de. *La Caricature révolutionnaire.* Paris: Presses du CNRS, 1988.

Cameron, Vivian. "Political Exposures: Sexuality and Caricature in the French Revolution." In *Eroticism and the Body Politic.* Baltimore: John Hopkins Univ. Press, 1991.

Collwill, Elizabeth. "Les Crimes de Marie-Antoinette: images d'une femme mutine dans le discours révolutionnaire." In *Les Femmes et la Révolution.* Edited by Marie-France Brive. Toulouse: Presses Universitaires du Mirail, 1990.

Choisy, Maryse. *Dames seules.* Illustrations by Vertès and preface by Nicole Alber. New edition. Lille: Question de Genre/GayKitschCamp, 1995.

Grand-Carteret, John. *Derrière "Lui": L'homosexualité en Allemagne.* 1906. Followed by *Iconographie d'un scandale, les caricatures politiques et l'affaire Eulenburg.* By James Steakley. Lille: Cahiers GayKitschCamp, 1992.

Hirschfeld, Magnus. *Les Homosexuels de Berlin.* Lille: Cahiers GayKitschCamp, 1992.

Roellig, Ruth Margarete. *Les Lesbiennes de Berlin, 1928.* New edition. Lille: Question de genre/GayKitschCamp, 2000.

—*Art; Comic Books; Decadence; France; Germany; Humor; Literature; Publicity; Rhetoric; Song.*

CATHOLIC CHURCH, the

The position of the Catholic Church with regard to morality hasn't changed much since it became the official religion of the Roman Empire in the fourth century, or even before that, since the **Bible**, as reflected in the writings of **Paul** in particular. Over the centuries, and despite being increasingly confronted by the contemporary world, the moral imperative of the ecclesiastic hierarchy has remained steadfast and absolute, and the theologians who dared to offer different interpretations of holy texts (or an *aggiornamento,* a theological "updating" in the spirit of change, open-mindedness, and modernity, a term used during the second Vatican Council) were summarily punished and thus silenced. On "moral" issues such as abortion, sex, the role of women, and the **family**, not to mention homosexuality, the Church's position never varied—not that this institution could be expected to demonstrate any propensity to change or reform itself. The election of Pope John Paul II in 1978 did, however, bring about some significant changes in the Church's administration (the Curia, the State of the Vatican) as well as in pastoral life (such as the Pope's highly visible and frequent travels abroad); as well, exegetical reflection and theological research were taking place in all reaches of the world. At the same time, however, the Catholic Church remained unrelentingly conservative and repressive in its attitudes and positions on moral issues both old and new. Further, the Vatican did not hesitate to interfere politically, in **Italy** and elsewhere, when it felt that its views and its leadership were being contested.

In this context, the Church's frequent references to a so-called gay **lobby**, whose sole aim apparently was to persecute the Church and the "traditional family," are evidence of the paranoid mentality of the Church, as well as that of its official representatives, toward its "opponents." Recent events reveal the scope of this paranoia: for one, the legislated approval of same-sex unions and gay rights in general in numerous countries provoked outrageous and violently homophobic statements by Vatican representatives and Pope John Paul II himself. For example, in the weeks preceding the World Pride 2000 gay rights march in Rome, the bishop of Genoa condemned rights given to homosexuals; Georges Cottier, one of the Pope's advisors, shared this view, referring to the "problems and human dramas" that homosexuality engendered. Despite scientific views to the contrary, the Church's highest hierarchy still considers homosexuality to be a sort of debilitative illness. The latest version of Roman Catholic Catechism formalizes its position: "Basing itself on the Holy Scriptures …, the Tradition has always declared that 'homosexual acts are intrinsically reckless,' they go against natural order; they close off the sexual act from the gift of life; they do not stem from a true affective and sexual complementarity; under no circumstances would they be approved." On the opposite side, more liberal Catholic figures, such as French Bishop Jacques Gaillot, were firmly asked by the Vatican to remain silent on the issue. Even the usually pro-Catholic Italian press expressed its misgivings with regard to these demonstrations of intolerance (notably *Repubblica* and *Corriere della sera*).

By 1992, John Paul II had condemned homosexuals on numerous occasions, even justifying **discrimination** against them in areas such as employment and housing. He also did not hesitate to publish, along with Cardinal Josef Alois Ratzinger (who later succeeded John Paul II as Pope Benedict XVI in 2005), a paper entitled "Some Considerations on the Response to Private Bills on the Non-Discrimination of the Homosexual People," in which he asserted, without flinching, "In certain areas, taking sexual orientation into account is not unjust discrimination, for example in the adoption of children or placing in foster care, in the hiring of teachers and sports coaches and in military recruiting." Going even further, John Paul II was staunchly against the decriminalization of homosexuality in his homeland of Poland, his home country, and in Eastern European countries in general, without ever giving consideration to the physical, moral, and symbolic homophobic **violence** that could be legally inflicted if **criminalization** were maintained in these countries.

Most recently, however, it is the institutionalization of same-sex civil unions, in Europe and elsewhere, that has provoked the Catholic hierarchy's most virulent homophobia. On November 21, 2000, the Vatican demanded that such unions not be officially recognized, as they would have grave consequences on the family and on the common good of society in general. In Madrid that same year, the Socialist opposition (unsuccessfully) presented a "bill on civil unions" that the Spanish episcopate's spokesperson condemned as "an assault against the family and **marriage**" (*El Pais,* September 20, 2000). He did note that homosexuals must be treated with **tolerance**, but asserted that the

Church and notions of the family must be preserved. In Quebec, Canada, the Catholic Church led a crusade against the provincial law that would recognize same-sex unions and give gay couples the right to **adopt**. These efforts, however, did not stop the bill from being unanimously approved by Quebec's parliament. As stated by Paul Bégin, Quebec's Minister of Justice: "What was at the center of the debate was love, and the priests never spoke of love." In France, the Conference of Bishops regarded the **PaCS** law (Pacte civil de solidarité; Civil Solidarity Pact), as being "useless and dangerous." Without any originality, the bishops cited the Church's homophobic **theology** and concluded that a law such as PaCS was prejudicial against the Church and to families, who were severely threatened as a result. They also used a hitherto unheard-of financial argument: how much will it cost society? In these and other ways, the Catholic Church hierarchy continues to reinforce the most homophobic positions of its historic past.

—*Thierry Revol*

Congrégation pour la doctrine de la foi. "Persona humana. Déclaration sur quelques questions d'éthique sexuelle." *La Documentation catholique* (1976). [Published in English as "Persona Humana: Declaration on Certain Questions Concerning Sexual Ethics." By The Congregation for the Doctrine of the Faith, The Roman Curia (1975).]

———. "Au sujet des propositions de loi sur la non-discrimination des personnes homosexuelles." *La Documentation catholique,* no. 2056 (1992). [Published in English as "Some Considerations Concerning the Response to Legislative Proposals on Non-Discrimination of Homosexual Persons." By The Congregation for the Doctrine of the Faith, The Roman Curia (July 23, 1992).]

Furey, Pat, and Jeanine Grammick, eds. *The Vatican and Homosexuality.* New York: Crossroad, 1988.

Marinelli, Luigi. *Le Vatican mis à nu.* Paris: Robert Laffont, 2000.

Melton, Gordon. *The Churches Speak on Homosexuality.* Detroit: Gale Research, 1991. *Osservatore romano,* Official Vatican newspaper.

Sarfati, Georges-Elia. *Le Vatican et la Shoah ou comment l'Eglise s'absout de son passé.* Paris: Berg International, 2000.

Weigel, Georges. *Jean-Paul II, témoin de l'espérance.* Paris: Jean-Claude Lattes, 1999.

—*Abnormal; Against Nature; Damien, Peter; Family; Heresy;*

Inquisition; Marriage; Paul (of Tarsus); Sodom and Gomorrah; Theology.

CENSORSHIP

In his preface to Bernard Sergent's book, *Homosexuality in Greek Myth*, Georges Dumézil reminisces about his studies as a young Hellenic scholar:

> It was 1916, at the Sorbonne, and the illustri-
> ous scholar Emile Bourguet, renowned expert
> on ancient and modern Greece, was explaining
> *Symposium* to his students. Upon reaching the sec-
> tion which Victor Cousin had nobly titled "Socrates
> declines Alcibiades' gifts," he warned us all to "not
> go imagining anything." To which Dumézil ex-
> claimed, "Imagine? One has only to read!"

This quote illustrates the fact that, on the subject of homosexuality, censorship has long been a tradition among learned scholars, who expand upon its usual definition, i.e. the control exerted by a government over the press and the public. Three types of homophobic censorship can be identified: intellectual, institutional, and self-censorship.

Intellectual censorship applies to all sorts of alterations made to texts by translators, commentators, and others. Historically, this was the first type of censorship, and appears to have been perpetrated most often by medieval Christian authors working on the *corpus* of Greek and Latin works. They employed three methods of censorship: travesty, reinterpretation, or omission. Travesty was both the simplest and the most common method—when confronted with a text describing a relationship between two men, one of the names was changed to a feminine one. Take, as an example, the couple of Socrates and Alcibiades, the latter of whom was often presented as the female companion of Socrates. In Rémi d'Auxelle's commentary on Boethius's *Consolation of Philosophy*, Alcibiades is presented as "a woman famed for her beauty, said to be the mother of Hercules." And in the sixteenth century, Michelangelo's masculine sonnets were modified by his great-nephew. Or more recently, in his 1955 screen adaptation of the novel *Les Diaboliques*, Henri-Georges Clouzot turns the lesbian couple into the wife and mistress of the same man, of whom they are both victims and murderers.

The reinterpretative method of censorship is just as intellectually dishonest, whereby the original homosexual meaning of a text is warped to make it heterosexual. For example, in one of the books making up Ovid's *The Art of Love*, a phrase correctly translated as "That is why boys please me but little" was amended by some moralist to become "That is why boys do not attract me at all," and even included a footnote informing the reader: "You can see that Ovid was not a sodomite" (cf. Domenico Camparetti, *Virgilio nel Medio Evo* [Livourne: 1872], p. 115). This preoccupation with reinterpreting or disguising text pertaining to homosexuality sometimes led translators to introduce concepts that did not exist at all. For example, Robert Graves once "translated" a phrase by Suetonius that was not present in the original text which suggested the existence of a law prohibiting homosexual practices.

Straightforward omission is the most radical of these methods of intellectual censorship, in which, during the translation or transmission of a text, homosexual characteristics are removed outright. This can range from the omission of a single word (which identified a character's gender, for example) to the removal of an entire volume of work (such as Pseudo-Lucian's *Amores* [*Affairs of the Heart*], which Thomas Francklin deliberately left out of his 1781 edition of *The Works of Lucian* because it debated the issue of which gender is better for a man to love). He unabashedly explained his decision: "[A]s this is a point which, at least in this nation, has been long since determined in favor of the ladies, it stands in need of no further discussion: the Dialogue is therefore, for this, as well as some other still more material reasons, which will occur to those who are acquainted with the original, entirely omitted." This brand of intellectual censorship remained in vogue for a long time; for example, it was not until 1993, the centennial anniversary of French poet Paul Verlaine's death, that his homosexual-themed poetry from the 1891 collection *Hombres* (Men) was finally published in his *Complete Works* by the Bibliothèque de la Pléiade.

Institutional censorship, a recent phenomenon, is more powerful than intellectual censorship; it requires an authority that possesses both the will and the power to exert control over the expression of ideas. The Christian church long filled this role in the western world, but its censorship of homosexuality has been far from constant or virulent (as indicated by John Boswell in his 1980 book *Christianity, Social Tolerance, and Homosexuality*). In the chapter entitled "The Triumph of Ganymede: Gay Literature of the High Middle Ages," he even identified signs of what he called a "gay subculture" appearing between 1050 and 1150 in the writings of high-ranking clergymen Anselm of Canterbury and Baudri of Bourgeuil. Despite the fact that Boswell's analyses have been challenged since first being published (most notably in France by Jean-François Cottier), it can be concluded at least that between the eleventh and twelfth centuries, the church did not practice homophobic censorship. This was not only because the church had other priorities at the time (such as converting the last western pagans, Christianizing **marriage** and asserting its spiritual authority over laymen), but also because it did not yet have the means to exact this kind of censorship. Boswell also pointed out that if there appeared to be a turning point in Christian intolerance toward homosexuals after the Third Council of the Lateran in 1179, it was because homosexuals were lumped together with heretics. It is striking to note that, in all the great accusations of **heresy** that occurred at the end of the Middle Ages, from the Cathars to the Hussites, and including the trial of the Knights Templar in France, concurrent accusations of sodomy were made time and again. Now enacted regularly by secular authorities, religious censorship of the *bougres* was in full swing, involving coercion, torture, burning at the stake, and the like.

Challenged by Protestantism during the sixteenth century, the Catholic Church found renewed moral vigor, and it is interesting to note that it is within this climate of anti-Reformation that homophobic censorship developed in reaction to libertine poets. The chief characteristic of libertine philosophy is to be as heterodox in habit as in religion. Herein lies the collusion between homosexuality and heresy that was assumed during the Middle Ages, notably in the libertine theory that Jesus Christ and St John the Baptist were lovers. This statement figured among the charges laid against libertine Francesco Calcagno in 1550, and again in 1593, among charges brought against Christopher Marlowe, who was accused of stating that "St John the Evangelist was bedfellow to Christ and leaned always in his bosom, and that he used him as the sinners of **Sodom**."

In 1623, French poet Théophile de Viau was the subject of homophobic censorship. **Viau** was known for his impious subject matter, as well as his masculine loves, notably with poet Jacques Valée des Barreaux. *Le Parnasse satyrique* was published in 1622, a work in which he lambasted the censors and the devout of his era, who promptly went on the attack. The Jesuit Father Garasse published *La Doctrine curieuse* in 1623 (a book which earned the subtitle of "anti-Théophile"), in which he called into question the poet's Catholic devotion, given that Viau was a recent convert who had renounced **Protestantism**, and in the process, accused him of homosexuality. The *procureur général* of the Parliament of Paris, Mathieu Molé (a supporter of the Jesuits), led the campaign against Viau beginning in April 1623 by gathering up copies of *Le Parnasse satyrique*, then ordering the poet's arrest in July. Taken in for questioning near St-Quentin in September, Viau was incarcerated in Paris's *Conciergerie* (in the same cell as Henri IV's murderer François Ravaillac), where he waited two years for his trial. While imprisoned, he wrote, attempting to clear himself of the accusations made against him, most notably producing *L'Apologie de Théophile*, in which he responded to Father Garasse concerning the "sodomite sonnets" he had composed:

> For one who is vowed to chastity and having taken on the sacred title of Jesuit, you have without a doubt gone against the nature of your profession in the great care taken to fabricate these verses of sodomy, and also publicly teaching this enormous **vice** under the guise of denouncing it.... Composing verses of sodomy does not make a man guilty of the act: poet and pederast are two different qualities.

In September 1625, Viau was banished from France by an act of Parliament and died a year later at the age of thirty-six. His case is a textbook example of modern homophobic censorship, as it involved a contentious work that was seized, and included the intervention of the state (in this case, the Parliament of Paris).

In the modern era, the growth of civil institutions (at the expense of religious ones) has meant that they are now the most likely to resort to censorship to maintain order. Examples of homophobic censorship at its peak can be found in totalitarian regimes, such as the Nazis in Germany, who in 1933, destroyed German physician Magnus Hirschfeld's Institute for Sexual Research and burned all its contents; or in **communist** regimes, where homosexuality was frequently equated with a bourgeois **vice**, thus leading to the radical censorship of all forms of its expression.

Even in those democracies where freedom of expression is considered a fundamental right, forms of homophobic censorship can still be found. In France, the case of homosexual media is a good example. In the early decades of the twentieth century, attempts to publish homosexual magazines were thwarted based on grounds of their being "an offense against good values" as written in the penal code (for example, the magazine *Inversions* in 1924); and as of 1949, the law pertaining to publications aimed at youth, which banned the display of "offensive" magazines as a result, forced many gay publications out of business (with the exception of *Arcadie*, which managed to survive solely through subscriptions from 1955–75). Publications which fell victim to this law included *Futur* and *Juventus* in the 1950s and 60s, and those published by FHAR (Front homosexuel d'action révolutionnaire) and other gay liberation groups in the 70s; they were regularly prosecuted, including Pierre Guénin, a pioneer in gay men's publications in France.

Even the well-known magazine *Gai-Pied* had its share of confrontations with French authorities over censorship. Miraculously escaping the censors during its first years of existence (mostly thanks to the support of the intelligentsia, which was earned through publishing articles and interviews with the likes of Michel Foucault and Jean-Paul Sartre), the magazine was targeted for banning in March 1987 by the Minister of the Interior, Charles Pasqua. In response, *Gai-Pied* received as much support from journalists (seeing the threat as an attack on freedom of the press), as from politicians; with regard to the latter, sympathizers not only came from the left (such as Jack Lang of the Socialist Party, who was seen at the Paris Book Fair with a copy of *Gai-Pied* under his arm) but also from the right, such as Minister of Culture François Léotard (who by doing so provided another example of the great **tolerance** of the "liberal" right, which had the effect of rupturing government solidarity). What is interesting about the *Gai-Pied* affair is the anachronistic nature of its proposed censorship. Only a dozen years earlier, a similar ban would have been met with a quasi-general indifference; now, it was widely considered inappropriate, and a thing of the past, clearly demonstrating that censorship requires the cooperation of both state and society. If the latter applies sufficient pressure, the former has no choice but to concede.

Self-censorship is by its nature more subtle than intellectual or institutional censorship. Carried out by

homosexual authors, this type of censorship comes from internal, not external, pressures, and can be the result of numerous circumstances: for example, the inner turmoil of one who is uncomfortable with his or her homosexuality, or the internalization of dominant social norms. Self-censorship could also be a preventative or precautionary mechanism to shield one from criticism, or even a strategy aimed at deceiving external censors. It has been said that Nobel Prize-winning author Roger Martin du Gard would not let his novel *Le Lieutenant-colonel de Maumort* be published until after his death (it was finally published in 1983, twenty-five years after he died), which some have construed as an example of self-censorship. But what can be said about André **Gide** (who was Gard's longtime friend) and his long hesitations before finally publishing *Corydon*, against the advice of others, which resulted in a veritable **scandal** over its content? Further, there has been little that has not been said about Marcel Proust and the meanderings in his work on the subject of homosexuality. Who really is Albertine of *La Recherche du temps perdu* (*In Search of Lost Time*), an obvious object of Proust's desire, and whose point of view is Proust's, that of the narrator, or the character of Charlus? And what is one to take from the terrible passages devoted to "women-men" at the beginning of *Sodome et Gomorrhe* (*Cities of Pain / Sodom and Gomorrah*) (Vol. 2), the indulgent account of the sexual encounter between Jupien and Charlus in *Le Côté de Guermantes* (*The Guermantes Way*) or the bordello for men in *Temps retrouvé* (*The Past Recaptured / Time Regained*)?

Proust clearly represents a borderline case of self-censorship, but one which is fundamental and to which most homosexual authors can relate. It is thus quite significant to see writer Jean-Louis Bory quote Proust as part of an article entitled "Le Refus du masque" (Refusing the mask), in which he recalls his own self-censorship:

> From my very first piece, I knew that one day or another I would get around to writing plainly about this subject [of homosexuality]. For far too long I would avoid it, I would procrastinate, I would … in the end … cheat, in the same way that Proust cheated. It was in one of my first novels (entitled *Usé par la mer* [Worn by the Sea]) where I finally dealt with the subject frankly (yet still hypocritically), by telling the story of the love of a man named Félicien with a certain … Georgette, who (extraordinarily) was

in the military. It is possible; there are some in the AFAT (Army Women's Auxiliary). The feminization, the Albertine side to my Georgette, was so awkward it was transparent—Georgette even had tattoos! And naturally, no one was really fooled. But I still wasn't proud of it; it was still evading the subject. And yet in the same book, I described a passionate relationship between Mr Bonaventure, a film presenter, and Mr Suzanne, a hairdresser. Again, I made a little progress, but it was simply a nod. And the subject is really too serious for a simple nod. Then, in a later book, *Un Noël à la tyrolienne* [A Tyrolean Christmas], I described, much more precisely, the love between a man named Aloys and a man named Pierre. But even then I was already thinking of the next book, to be entitled *La Peau des zèbres* [The skin of zebras]. I burned my bridges. We can see that Aloys is really named François-Charles, and he was in love with Pierre. Here we find again Félicien from *Usé par la mer*, and become aware of the true nature of the relationships. The mask was terribly transparent now, but it was still a mask, in so far as the "I" that I used was the "I" of a novel. You knew that it was François-Charles or Félicien who was doing the talking. You could say to yourself: "Okay, here it's François-Charles, and here it's Félicien … but where is the author in all of this?"

—*Hervé Chevaux*

Bier, Christophe. *Censure-moi, histoire du classement X en France*. Paris: L'Esprit frappeur, 2000.

Bory, Jean-Louis. "Le Refus du masque," *Arcadie* ("L'Homophilie à visage découvert," November 1973).

Boswell, John. *Christianity, Social Tolerance, and Homosexuality: Gay People in Western Europe from the Beginning of the Christian Era to the Fourteenth Century*. Chicago: Univ. of Chicago Press, 1980.

Courcelle, Pierre. *La Consolation de philosophie dans la tradition littéraire*. Paris: Editions augustiniennes, 1967.

Dollimore, Jonathan. *Sex, Literature and Censorship*. Cambridge, UK: Polity Press, 2001.

Douin, Jean-Luc. *Dictionnaire de la censure au cinéma*. Paris: Presses universitaires de France, 1998.

Francklin, Thomas. *The Works of Lucian*. London: T. Cadell, 1781.

Meyer, Richard. *Outlaw Representation: Censorship and Homosexuality in Twentieth Century American Art*. New York/Oxford: Oxford Univ. Press, 2002.

Ory, Pascal, ed. *La Censure en France à l'ère démocratique (1848-)*. Brussels: Ed. Complexe, 1997.

Russo Vito. *The Celluloid Closet: Homosexuality in the Movies*. New York: Harper & Row, 1987.

Sergent, Bernard. *L'Homosexualité dans la mythologie grecque*. Paris: Payot, 1984. New edition in *Homosexualité et initiation chez les peuples indo-européens*. Paris: Payot, 1996. [Published in the US as *Homosexuality in Greek Myth*. Boston: Beacon Press, 1986.]

Viau, Théophile de. *Théophile en prison et autres pamphlets*. Utrecht: Jean Jacques Pauvert, 1967.

—*Communism; Fascism; Gide, André; Heterosexism; Hirschfeld, Magnus; History; Literature; Media; Police; Scandal; School; Viau, Théophile; Villon, François.*

CENTRAL EUROPE. *See* Europe, Central & Eastern

CHINA

To the Chinese, sexuality is something natural, and to indulge in it on a moderate basis is considered a key to one's health and longevity. Thus, erotic practices for their own sake were not to be condemned nor legislated against; in addition, the Chinese did not believe that one's personality was centered around one's sexual orientation. However, a careful study of historical Chinese literature identifies some reticence against homosexuals, beginning in particular during the Ming (1368–1644) and Qing (1644–1912) dynasties. It was not until the twentieth century, with the intrusion of Western ideologies and Western medical and psychiatric theories, that this reticence was transformed into a radical and systemic homophobia, manifested mostly in ostracizing "deviants," including loved ones.

Marriage was considered vital by most families in order to ensure descendants, but even so, it was not necessarily an obstacle to masculine or sapphic love. Once the familial relationship is duly met, nothing forbade a spouse (at least, not the man) from loving someone else or seeing a young man on the side (all it took was finding an accommodating wife). On the other hand, it was inconceivable and antisocial for one to refuse to marry; only Buddhist clergy were permitted to avoid this obligation (not that this granted the celibate any greater legitimacy).

Perdition's Favorite

Many works written by ancient China's moralists and chroniclers speak out against debauchery, but it is the excesses of passion and the abuse of wine and women (or young men) that they condemned, and not the act itself. The philosophers warned against the deleterious influence of royal favorites, catamites, or eunuchs on those managing the affairs of the empire. Historians made examples of fallen kingdoms and imperial houses ruined by men who fell victim to their passions. The fate of the state or even a family was too important to subject to irrational ardor, and chroniclers castigated the useless sycophants who lured the rulers into trouble.

Buddhism *Against the Sins of the Flesh*

Buddhism, which first appeared in China around the first century CE and exerted a profound influence on the religions of the Middle Kingdom between the sixth and ninth centuries, introduced the concept of the sins of the flesh. Sexuality in general was considered an obstacle to spiritual life. It was mostly the female temptress that one must resist (Buddhist texts were written by men for men, after all); there was a recognition of homosexuality as well, which was usually condemned, but only slightly more than heterosexual acts. In **India**, a system of rules for both laymen and men of religion was developed which was far more detailed than China's interdictions against crimes such as rape and adultery. All Buddhists were required to abstain from lustful acts, including those with men. The *Vinaya*, the curriculum of rules and procedures for Buddhist monks, which describes all variants of sexual acts, was more precise. Penetration with ejaculation, regardless of the orifice or the partner, would mean exclusion from the community. Mutual masturbation among monks would incur a slight penance, and nuns would not incur any. Sins committed with a *pandaka* (definitions vary, but usually a transvestite or a eunuch) were punished less severely than if they were committed with a woman, but more so than if they were committed with a virile man. There were also rules set out so monks might avoid temptation, such as governing their quarters, baths, and latrines. Nonetheless, these rules did not prevent monks or nuns from having relationships, whether they be masculine or sapphic, and pederast traditions, such as that of monks and their catamite *chigo* in Japan.

Toward a Moral Order

During the Song dynasty (960–1279), a kind of Puritanism arose that was inspired by neo-Confucianism and influenced by Buddhism which insisted on abstinence and mastery over desire. This tendency became government orthodoxy by the beginning of the Ming dynasty. Certain members of the elite viewed the increasingly urbanized societies of the sixteenth and seventeenth centuries as hedonistic and the empire as incompetent while outside threats loomed (such as the Japanese and the Manchurians); as a result, they reacted negatively against what they perceived as dilettantism and the corruption of traditions which threatened their security. The Qing Empire, taking care to get scholars on their side, carried out a campaign of moral renewal, which included confining sexuality to heterosexual marriage.

Shanshu, or morality books, which began to appear during the Song dynasty alongside treatises on public morals, as well as *gongguoge*, or "ledgers of merit and demerit" (which rated acts as either good or bad deeds), had a strong influence during the sixteenth and seventeenth centuries. Based on the Buddhist idea of retribution but representing a syncretism of popular Confucianism, Buddhism, and Taoism, these texts promoted an ethic that was zealously strict. Hostile to the concepts of adultery and debauchery, at least two texts from the seventeenth century criticized same-sex male love affairs, in which concubines and male prostitutes were denounced, as well as pederasty and the frequenting of brothels.

The law began to address sodomy (but not lesbianism) around the middle of the Ming dynasty. Previously, two literary sources (though not legal texts) of the Song dynasty made mention of a Zhenghe era law which allowed for the arrest and beating of the capital's prostitutes for indecent offenses. Anal penetration (though not necessarily with a man) was criminally unclean, likened to introducing refuse into the mouth, as noted by a Jiajing era (1522–67) amendment to the legal code established during the Ming dynasty which made it punishable by 100 strokes of a cane. The code of the Qing dynasty adopted the same laws, but grouped them under a coherent category, "Fornication." These laws were designed to address not only the kidnapping and rape of male youths (which may or may not cause their death), but also consensual sodomy (*jijian*). Those convicted of these crimes were punished by 100 strokes of a cane and were forced to wear a cangue (a

device used for public humiliation and corporal punishment, similar to the stocks but instead of being fixed
in place, the board had to be carried by the prisoner)
for a month. The seduction of a boy younger than
twelve was also considered rape Essentially, the same
scale of punishments was used for all sexual crimes.
The application of this legislation against kidnapping,
rape, and murder is well-documented by the archives
of the Minister of Justice and the royal courts. It is
more difficult, however, to find evidence of actions
taken against consensual sodomy, which did not require the approval of the central authorities.

The end of the Ming dynasty and the beginning of
the Qing saw the arrival of a homophobia that was
more asserted by certain authors. In a culture where
social norms were considered more important than
laws with regard to governing the populace, sexual passivity was seen as subverting the hierarchy of the sexes
as well as social status. It was associated with servility
and prostitution (both particularly visible under these
two dynasties), and brought with it a fear of dishonor,
gossip, and sometimes even blackmail. The fickleness
of male prostitutes (whose chief preoccupations were
money and privilege) only fueled more distaste. The
first homophobic **insults** that began to appear mostly
referred to the "feminine role," but more generally,
love between men was judged to be absurd (without
any real explanation why) and a pitiful substitution
for heterosexuality (when it occurred in **prison** or
in the **army**, for example). The union of the *yin* and
yang was considered the ultimate design of heaven and
earth, and the love of a woman was part of the order of
things. The love of boys was thus a curiosity, made unclean because of anal penetration (which in turn made
its pleasure incomprehensible and "**against nature**");
and when combined with a refusal to marry, it was
evidence of a supreme immorality.

Medical Discourse & the Bourgeois "Morals"
This new intolerance, however, did not obstruct those
with a taste for cross-dressers, nor did it dampen same-
sex affairs between students or scholars. But the intrusion of the West in the twentieth century intensified
the spread of homophobia, condemning homosexuality to silence. Traumatized by the humiliations inflicted by both Westerners and the Japanese during the
Opium Wars, the intelligentsia of the early twentieth
century called for a complete intellectual, cultural, and
political "modernization" of the country, based on for-

eign examples. The fall of the empire in 1911 and the
May Fourth Movement of 1919 opened the floodgates
to a disjointed sort of Westernization which identified tradition and Confucianism as the source of all
troubles. Democracy and science (viewed as social and
moral virtues) became the new idols. But intellectuals
and students, in their desire to shake off the chains of
ancient standards, did not realize that they were en-
dorsing a narrow and petit-bourgeois mentality, not to
mention blind scientism, all of which had an impact on
the course of homophobic attitudes.

Medical and psychiatric discourse on sexuality and
the concept itself first appeared in China via translations
(works by Havelock Ellis, the British sexual psychologist, were published there in 1926 and 1947), and was
crystallized as a result of essays by Chinese **medical**
doctors and **psychologists** during the 1920s and 30s,
which incorporated Western ideas. The term "homosexuality" (*tongxinglian*) along with its crazy trappings
appeared in the 1920s and displaced all of the ancient
theoretical concepts on the subject. The new Chinese
discourse incorporated all of the associated ways of
thinking: homosexuality was an "anomaly" (i.e. transi-
tory and curable), an "**inversion**," and was now under
the jurisdiction of medicine and **psychiatry**. Medical
literature on the art of lovemaking and on how to
create beautiful children lent credence to the idea
that medicine dictated matters of sexuality. The ancient preoccupation with social and moral correctness
produced a sexology that was more normative than
the previous one, which was analytical and focused on
the individual's search for pleasure. Concerned for the
"quality" of the population, theorists began to steer
the subject toward eugenics, whereby all examples of
non-procreative sexuality (e.g., prostitution, masturbation, sodomy) were considered either sicknesses to
be stamped out (by any means, including electroshock
therapy) in the name of the **family** and the state, or a
"social scar" that was condemned to absolute silence.
The subject became taboo: China produced *nothing*
on the subject of homosexuality between 1940 and
1980; even Taiwan and Hong Kong had nothing to
say on the subject until the 1970s. There were not
even any public, inflammatory diatribes (à la Heinrich
Himmler) to be found in literature published by the
Chinese government, whether nationalist or communist. Between 1950 and 1970, one could almost
seriously deny that gays and lesbians even existed in
China, or claim that homosexuality had somehow

been "eradicated" (in the same way as venereal diseases). Embraced by the totalitarian regimes and popularized by the **communists**, this was the general opinion in mainland China until the 90s (and in Taiwan until the 80s), isolated as it was from Western ideas on the subject. In fact, it was not until 2001 that the Chinese Society of Psychiatry took homosexuality off its list of mental illnesses.

Christianity and its accompanying homophobic arguments had little influence, except in Hong Kong. Psychiatric discussions aside, Westernization translated into a realignment of mores with the "civilized" habits of the Victorian nineteenth century, as well as a desire to "eliminate the barbaric elements of the past" and a leap to follow the latest foreign fashions. Thus, the only permissible relationship was a strictly monogamous, heterosexual one, resulting in marriage. The traditional marital obligation, now reinforced, took on a homophobic pallor; young boy lovers were no longer silently tolerated, nor were same-sex games between boys and between girls. One was only to court (or be courted by) a member of the opposite sex. Moral conventions dictated that the unmarried and the homosexual, because they contradicted the procreative, patriarchal norms, were pushed to the outermost fringes of society; in this way, homophobia was expressed more through ostracism than laws. Constrained to marriages of convenience, Chinese homosexuals lived in fear of being discovered, which would result in a loss of face as well as employment. The impossibility of privacy in a society that focused on the family, not to mention cramped lodgings within plain view of anyone, did not help matters. However, there were almost never any violent public reactions against homosexuals, no "gay bashings." Even certain examples of homoeroticism were tolerated, provided they did not advocate a different way of life, nor use the word "homosexual" (considered barbaric and taboo).

Repression

If social norms were the greatest enemy of Chinese homosexuals, the courts were not far behind. From 1865, then again in 1901, the English introduced their own legislation in the colony of Hong Kong, condemning those convicted of sodomy to life in prison, of crimes of indecency between men to two years' isolation, and of attempted sodomy or indecency to a maximum sentence of ten years. Most of these laws were finally abolished in 1991 (however, men younger

than twenty-one who engage in sodomy can still be jailed for life), bringing local laws in line with legislation in Britain passed in 1967, but not before drawing fierce opposition from the colony's Chinese elite.

The modern Republican civil code established in 1929–30 (still in use in Taiwan), based on the European continental model, removed sodomy as a crime. However, this legislation was not always recognized (even in recent years in Taiwan), nor did it stop police harassment in gay and lesbian locales.

Referencing the Soviet model, the communist People's Republic of China after 1949 took its own repressive approach to homosexuality. The communists' preoccupations were often the same as those of the Qing lawmakers, but imprisonment did not play as large a role as in other totalitarian systems. No article of law expressly forbade homosexuality, contrary to what could be found in the Soviet Union's laws. This did not prevent homosexuality from being repressed in China (as was any expression of sexuality outside of wedlock), but the absence of a strict legal qualification confused the issue somewhat. In a country where communities handled their social problems without need for regular recourse to a judicial system, the "work units" (*danwei*), the name given to places of employment in communist China which also held sway over individuals' entire way of life, had access to an efficient arsenal of control over its subjects: the maintenance of personal files, warnings, exclusion from the Party, demotion, and exile. In this system entirely run by the state, these chastisements which targeted an individual's (and his or her family's) reputation and means of existence were formidable. Most moral offenses were (and still are) handled in these ways. Keeping in mind the general arbitrariness of the regime, as well as its periods of anarchy, an entire range of legal punishments were applied to "bad elements" and other "counter-revolutionaries." It was in this way that transvestite performers popular before the communists took power were deported and many homosexuals were executed (under aggravating circumstances, it seems, the latest being in 1977) and sentenced to prison or internments of variable length at camps for "re-education through labor" (*laogai*). Evidence of homosexual behavior was enough to justify extending a convict's prison sentence, on the basis of political crimes. Article 160 of the 1979 penal code "clarified" the issue somewhat, establishing the crime of "hooliganism," a catch-all phrase to describe brawls, mob violence, the undermining of public order, violence against women (from indecent behavior to conducting orgies), and other acts. It was under this article that the legal repression of homosexuality continued, resulting in lengthy prison or internment sentences until the 80s. The criminal code reform of 1997 abolished the crime of "hooliganism" but at the same time criminalized "gatherings resulting in **debauchery**." As a result, there were widespread police crackdowns on homosexual gathering places, resulting in fines, detention, and even blackmail. Further, the suspicions of those in power regarding any citizens' initiative not under their control essentially doomed any attempt to form gay associations.

Opening Up to Change (and its Limits)

China's much-vaunted openness since 1978, two years after the death of Mao Zedong, has been rather selective. Foreign motion pictures, television programs, and the latest trends were all making their way into China with increasing ease, with the exception of the gay liberation movement. The popular image of Americans as perpetuated by the **media** was that of the well-groomed, "normal" heterosexual couple which included a blond-haired, heartthrob male hero; China's view of popular culture was (and is) seen through rose-colored glasses, and as a result was blind to anything that swayed from the heterosexual norm. Cultural standards have already changed, though. Fifteen years ago, two men or two women holding hands in the street would not have shocked anyone; it was simply an expression of friendship. A man and a woman holding hands, however, was shocking, given the Chinese abhorrence for public displays of sexuality. Now, the opposite is true; the former is now viewed as evidence of homosexuality.

In Hong Kong and Taiwan, homosexuality was condemned to absolute silence by the press until the 1980s. In the People's Republic, the silence was lifted only partway, enough to popularize the word and the concept. In commercial businesses, homosexuality became acceptable because it helped to drive voyeuristic and sensationally-inspired media, which increased sales. But at the same time, homophobia thrived, given that homosexuality was linked to a wide range of criminal behaviors and social ills: murder, rape, prostitution, **suicide**, and **AIDS**. News on gay rights demonstrations and the gay movement in the West simply served to illustrate how commonplace foreign **vice** was; the image of the gay community was summed up in the image

of the drag queen. Vigorous action on the part of the *tongzhi* ("queer") movement, which started in Taiwan and Hong Kong in the 1990s, obliged journalists to exercise more objectivity, though not consistently.

The universal decline of classical schooling, combined with a general lack of education, has cut the Chinese, gays and lesbians included, off from their roots, and the silent **tolerance** of homosexuality in the past has fallen to the wayside without need for **censorship**. It would seem that ancient texts remain available, but the most erotic passages (heterosexual as well as homosexual) are banned or excised. This, coupled with the complicity of scholars, has led to distorted heterosexual interpretations of the known texts and anecdotes. In this way, what is nothing more than imported puritanism takes on the guise of custom or Confucianism. Many Chinese leaders have preached with sanctimonious and ethnocentric zeal on how homosexuality "violates Chinese tradition, and the natural way of things," and in doing so (since the 1970s) cast it as a foreign vice from a decadent West. Accordingly, gay or lesbian activists are portrayed as being uniquely Western or Japanese.

Despite having been inspired by concepts both foreign and traditional, homophobic discourse in China, supported by the regime, seems to be firmly established and resistant to change (no matter how highly praised in the Western world).

—*Laurent Long*

Domenach, Jean-Luc. *Chine: l'archipel oublié.* Paris: Fayard, 1992.

Insch, Bret. *Passions of the Cut Sleeve: The Male Homosexual Tradition in China.* Berkeley/Los Angeles/Cambridge: Univ. of California Press, 1990.

Chou, Wah-shan. *Tongzhi: Politics of Same-Sex Eroticism in Chinese Societies.* Binghamton: Harrington Park Press, 2000.

Dikötter, Frank. *Sex, Culture and Modernity in China: Medical Science and the Construction of Sexual Identities in The Early Republican Period.* London: Hurst & Company, 1995.

Long, Laurent. "Manches coupées" et "Repas en tête-à-tête," *La Revue h,* no.4 (1997).

Matignon, Jean-Jacques. "Deux Mots sur la pédérastie." In *La Chine hermétique; superstition, crime et misère.* Paris: Paul Geuthner, 1936.

Ng, Vivien W. "Homosexuality and the State in Late Imperial China." In *Hidden from History: Reclaiming the Gay and Lesbian Past.* Edited by George Chauncey,

Martin Duberman, and Martha Vicinus. New York: Penguin, 1990.

Pasqualini, Jean. *Prisonnier de Mao, sept ans de camp de travail en Chine*. Paris: Gallimard, 1975.

Sommer, Matthew H. "Qing Sodomy Legislation." In *Sex, Law and Society in Late Imperial China*. Stanford, CA: Stanford Univ. Press, 2000.

Wu, Chunsheng. "La Vie gaie et lesbienne en Chine," *La Revue h*, no. 4 (1997).

Zhou, Huashan. *Histoires de 'Camarades'; les homosexuels en Chine*. Paris: Paris-Méditerranée, 1997.

—*Buddhism; Communism; Heterosexism; Japan; Korea; Medicine; Russia; Southeast Asia.*

CHRISTIANITY. *See* Bible, the; Catholic Church, the; Orthodoxy; Protestantism; Theology

CINEMA

Artistic creation is always a concern of the state. All the arts are eventually confronted by this reality, whether it be in the form of **censorship** or taxation measures. As a means of self-protection, some artists engage in a form of self-censorship, even during more favorable periods by force of habit or out of caution. Cinema is no exception to this rule. From the beginning, films which openly depicted sexuality were censored, although this did not keep some amateur cinematographers from privately circulating pornographic films, in which it was not rare at all to find homosexual scenes—and not just of lesbians, as one might expect.

It was after the industrialization of cinema and its eventual mass production and distribution, however, that the state would seriously get involved. Censorship was particularly concerned with artistic productions containing sex scenes, sometimes with surprising effects, such as in theater, where for a long time the profession of actress was highly stigmatized, leaving the female roles to be played by men in drag. This subterfuge, guaranteed to be comical, sometimes allowed a paradoxical freedom, especially with regard to feminist questions (demonstrating what might happen if you, the male audience member, were a woman). In film, transvestite characters were originally men as women (e.g., 1915's *A Woman/Mademoiselle Charlot* by Charlie Chaplin and 1933's *Twice Two* with Laurel and

Hardy), but could also be women as men (e.g., 1919's *Ich möchte kein Mann sein* (I Don't Want to Be a Man) by Ernst Lubitsch and Reinhold Schünzel's *Viktor und Viktoria* in 1933, which was remade the same year in France [*Georges et Georgette*], then in England in 1935 [*First a Girl*], and by Blake Edwards in the US in 1982 [*Victor/Victoria*]); cinema found a creative gold mine in the innuendo of gender switching between masculine and feminine. American feminism provided examples which would allow transvestites to be unmasked without ruining their roles, which was the triumph of "camp" movies: a means to depict homosexuality while maintaining the appearance of heterosexuality. The culture of excess was also represented, where primarily women (but also occasionally men) portrayed caricatures of their traditionally-assigned roles to the point of the absurd (e.g., Marlene Dietrich in 1930's *The Blue Angel*, Mae West in 1933's *I'm No Angel*, and the numerous films of Bette Davis).

Given the rarity of motion pictures about them, gays and lesbians had to be content with cryptic depictions and sly nods, such as the dialogue between John Ireland and Montgomery Clift in Howard Hawks' *Red River* (1948), where the two men compare the calibers of their respective revolvers; the ambiguous rapport between Charlton Heston and Stephen Boyd in William Wyler's *Ben-Hur* (1959); the effeminate Fatty Arbuckle, in the comedy *Good Night, Nurse!* (1918); the "close friendship" of Laurel and Hardy in *Their First Mistake* (1932); and Cary Grant's declaration in Howard Hawks' *Bringing Up Baby* (1938): "I just went gay all of a sudden."

In the United States, from 1930 to 1966, censorship guidelines regarding motion pictures were determined by the industry's production code (also known as the Hays Code), which directors had to sign; the code outlined "general principles" that had to be followed, including: "No picture shall be produced that will lower the moral standards of those who see it. Hence the sympathy of the audience should never be thrown to the side of crime, wrongdoing, evil, or sin." It wasn't until 1952 that the US Congress decided that motion pictures could benefit from the freedom of expression granted by the First and Fourth Amendments. In 1965, the bare breast made its first appearance in mainstream American cinema (in Sidney Lumet's *The Pawnbroker*); the following year, a woman's pubes showed up in Michelangelo Antonioni's *Blowup* (1966), as straight critics and commentators tell us. But when would the time come when cinema would begin depicting homosexual encounters, whether male or female? But homosexuality was doubly "pornographic," first as sexuality, then again as homosexuality. This has been evident in various uproars over cinematic homosexual depictions over the years, such as in 1987, when there were attempts to ban Pedro Almodóvar's film *Law of Desire*, which showed two men together in bed. In an attempt to better address the new sexual frankness in films without resorting to censorship, in 1968 the Motion Picture Association of America replaced the production code with a film rating system that included "R" and "X." In France, the "X" rating was established in 1975, whereby such films were obliged to be shown in specialized theaters which then had to pay a surtax of half the ticket price for the privilege. Many directors had their films threatened with "the X," such as Philippe Vallois' 1976 *Johan, carnet intime d'un homosexuel* (Johan, the Intimate Journal of a Homosexual); it was defended by Jean-Louis Bory and Yves Navarre. And the folks from the Société des réalisateurs de films (the French Association of Film Directors) decided to show it as part of the category "Perspectives du cinéma" at Cannes. Finally, it was only restricted from those under eighteen years of age. *Race d'Ep* (1979), by Lionel Soukaz and Guy Hocquenghem, suffered the same fate (see also *Bout tabou* [2000], a short piece that has been censored and rated X). It should be noted that it always seems to take pressure from an illuminated intelligentsia, or by screening it at a festival, for censorship to be lifted from a film (in part or in full).

In the US, the 1995 documentary film *The Celluloid Closet* by Rob Epstein and Jeffrey Friedman, about the history of homosexuality in motion pictures (based on the nonfiction book by Vito Russo), is an impressive retrospective on **heterosexist** modifications that were regularly imposed on screenwriters and their scripts. A few examples: in Robert Mulligan's *Inside Daisy Clover* (1965), with a screenplay by Englishman Gavin Lambert based on his novel, the main character was homosexual. However, after pressure from the actor playing the role, Robert Redford, as well as by the producer, Lambert made the character bisexual. In the 1947 film *Crossfire*, based on Richard Brooks' novel *The Brick Foxhole*, the subject matter was supposed to be about homophobia in the **army**, but in the end it was made to be about anti-Semitism. Scenes that were deemed too suggestive of homosexuality were cut from three adaptations of plays by Tennessee Williams:

Joseph Mankiewicz's *Suddenly, Last Summer* (1959), Elia Kazan's *A Streetcar Named Desire* (1951, though a restored version is now available), and Richard Brooks' *Cat on a Hot Tin Roof* (1958). And in a scene cut from Stanley Kubrick's 1960 film *Spartacus*, Laurence Olivier (Crassus) approaches Tony Curtis (Antoninus) in a bath to confide that he likes snails just as much as oysters (the scene was restored in a 1992 video release).

Production Obstacles, Cabals, Bans, Destructions
The first film about homosexuality in the history of cinema to be banned was Richard Oswald's *Anders als die Andern* (1919) (*Different from the Others*), about a violin virtuoso and an aspiring violinist, both of whom are gay. The German censorship authorities stated on August 18, 1920, that the film could not be exhibited "except to certain categories of people, such as doctors and medical personnel in educational establishments and institutes of research." It was thus possible to see it at the Institute for Sexual Research in Berlin, established by Magnus **Hirschfeld** (1868–1935), the physician and ardent gay activist in the Weimar Republic.

Despite its censorship, parts of this film are still around thanks to a documentary filmed in 1927 by Hirschfeld entitled *Gesetze der Liebe* (*The Laws of Love*), which included an abridged version of *Anders als die Andern*. This film was itself banned, but was miraculously saved thanks to a copy that was supposed to have been shipped to the Ukraine; it was discovered in East Berlin in 1976.

In France in 1964, Jean Delannoy filmed *Les Amitiés particulières* (*This Special Friendship*) at the Royaumont Abbey in Val-d'Oise, based on the eponymous novel by Roger Peyrefitte about a relationship between a twelve-year-old boy and an upperclassman. The film drew the ire of French writer François Mauriac who, in the *Le Figaro*, exclaimed: "I cannot believe that a film could cause me such sadness, such disgust, almost to the point of despair. How, I ask myself, could parents consent to this, could a director debase himself in this way?" Two years later, Jacques Rivette directed *Suzanne Simonin, la Religieuse de Diderot* (released as *The Nun* in English), about a young girl forced against her will to take vows as a nun. During production, French Minister of Justice Jean Foyer forbade Rivette from filming in the abbey at Fontevrault due to its subject matter. The resulting film was banned despite multiple protests and against the recommendation of the French film review board, Commission de contrôle cinématographique; in 1966, the ban was overturned through a decision of the administrative tribunal of Paris, and the censorship board subsequently approved its showing to viewers eighteen years and older.

Meanwhile, gay filmmakers around the world were subject to violent homophobic acts. In the Soviet Union, seminal Russian director Sergei Eisenstein was a regular victim of extortion, and in 1974, filmmaker Sergei Parajanov was convicted of homosexuality (specifically, "the rape of a Communist Party member") and sentenced to a **gulag**. The next year, Italian director Pier Paolo **Pasolini** was brutally murdered at the beach of Ostia by a teenaged hustler (although he later retracted his confession, the exact circumstances of Pasolini's death remain a mystery).

Meanwhile, Western cinema was being liberated: in Bernardo Bertolucci's *Last Tango in Paris* (1973), Marlon Brando offers his anus to the skilled fingers of Maria Schneider. Homosexuality was also considered a worthy subject: *The Boys in the Band* (1970), *Death in Venice* (1971, based on the Thomas Mann novel), the French films *La Meilleure façon de marcher* (*The Best Way to Walk*) (1976) and *La Cage aux folles* (1978), and *Making Love* (1982). Pasolini's 1975 film *Salo, or The 120 Days of Sodom* set the tone for a sadomasochistic esthetic (as an allegory for fascism), while Jean Genet's 1950 film *Un Chant d'amour* (*A Song of Love*), banned in France for twenty-five years, was finally rediscovered in 1975 thanks to the Collectif jeune cinéma (Youth Cinema Collective), which organized a public viewing at the American Cultural Centre on Boulevard Raspail in Paris. Not long after, the ban was lifted. In 1980, the sexually explicit film *Caligula*, directed by Tinto Brass, produced by *Penthouse* publisher Bob Guccione, and written by Gore Vidal (who later disavowed it), was first refused a rating classification in the US, but later received an R-18 rating (meaning viewers eighteen years and older could see it) but only after twenty minutes from the film were cut.

The influx of positive cinematic portrayals of homosexuality in the 1990s was often met by violent homophobic reactions. In 1995, the release of the British film *Priest,* directed by Antonia Bird, in the week before Easter was denounced as a provocation by the Catholic Church. This film about a homosexual priest living in a poor Liverpool neighborhood also shocked Catholics in Poland, who immediately called for a boycott and threatened to burn down any theater where it was shown and even sued the filmmakers for the

"propagation of pornography." Catholic organizations in Britain also demanded it be pulled from theaters, while in the United States, the fundamentalist faithful of the **far right** picketed cinemas in protest, and religious conservatives called for a boycott of Disney, which distributed the film. In 1998, screenings of the Canadian film *Fire*, directed by Deepa Mehta (a love story between two openly lesbian women), in New Delhi and Mumbai were interrupted by radical Hindus, who took offense at the subject. However, the Indian government reacted in favor of the film's distribution, citing that "the obligation of the state is to protect the lives, the liberty, and the goods of its citizens."

Filmmakers and governments are nonetheless susceptible to homophobic influences. In 1996, the widow of Japanese writer Yukio Mishima, who had refused to allow her husband's name to be associated with works of a homosexual nature, obtained an agreement from the producers of the 1968 Japanese film *Black Lizard* (directed by Kinji Fukasaku), which featured a screenplay by Mishima, that all existing copies would be destroyed; the lead role had been played by Akihiro Maruyama, Japan's most famous female impersonator. And in 2001, the French government, after pressure from Vice-Minister of **Family** and Childhood Ségolène Royal, decided against broadcasting a television public service announcement on **AIDS** prevention that featured snippets of homoerotic scenes from films.

Resistance

It has been noted that international film festivals like Cannes are influential when it comes to responding to the issue of homophobic censorship, but mention should also be made of the role played by special-interest festivals (i.e. gay and lesbian), which are not always taken into account in the historiography of homosexual movements. These festivals were started in response to the difficulties encountered in screening films that featured openly gay subject matter. In France in April 1977, the Groupe de libération homosexuelle politique et quotidien (GLHPQ; Group for Political and Everyday Homosexual Liberation) instigated a week of gay-themed films at the Olympic Theatre in Paris; the seven-day festival was declared a huge success by the newspaper *Libération*. Two months later in July, the La Rochelle film festival took place; however, the original theme of "Ciné, pédé, gouine, et les autres" (Films, Fags, Lesbos, and More) was rejected by the municipality. In September 1977, the Hyères and Belfort festivals took their turn welcoming young gay directors, but this trend was struck a blow with the brutal police crackdown at La Quinzaine du cinéma homosexuel (The Fifteenth Annual Festival of Homosexual Cinema) put on by the GLHPQ in January 1978 in Paris; Michel d'Ornano, then Minister of Culture, banned some seventeen films from being screened at the festival.

The first lesbian film festival in France appeared in 1992: Quand les lesbiennes se font du cinéma (When Lesbians Make Movies), launched by the organization Cineffable. The same year saw the debut of the Question de genre festival in Lille; in association with this, Paris's own version was launched in 1994. Since then, gay and lesbian film festivals have blossomed all over the world; many take into account the increasing visibility of the bisexual, the transgender, and the queer. The website *planetout.com* lists no fewer than 140; notable among these are the Gay and Lesbian Film Festival of Brussels, Berlin's Teddy Awards (part of the Berlin International Film Festival, which awards to the best queer films of the year), Montreal's image + nation festival, and Amsterdam's Roze Film Dagen festival. The pioneer of gay and lesbian film festivals, Frameline in San Francisco, celebrated its thirty-second anniversary in 2008. And in a promising development for both gay rights and progressive cinema, the very first gay film festival in India occurred in 2003, in a college auditorium on the outskirts of Mumbai.

—*Patrick Cardon*

Anger, Kenneth. *Hollywood Babylon*. New York: Dell, 1975.

Bakshi, Sandeep. "Soupçon d'un espace alternatif: étude de deux films du cinéma parallèle en Inde," *Inverses,* no.2.

Bourne, Stephen. *Brief Encounters: Lesbians and Gays in British Cinema, 1930–1971*. London: Cassel, 1996.

Boze, Hadleigh. *Hollywood Lesbians*. New York: Barricade Books, 1996.

Douin, Jean-Luc. *Dictionnaire de la censure au cinéma*. Paris: Presses universitaires de France, 1998.

———. *Films à scandales*. Paris: Chêne, 2001.

———. *Les Ecrans du désir*. Paris: Chêne, 2000.

Durgnat, Raymond. *Sexual Alienation in the Cinema: The Dynamics of Sexual Freedom*. London: Studio Vista, 1972.

Dyer, Richard. *Now You See It: Studies in Lesbian and Gay Film*. New York: Routledge, 1990.

Ehreinstein, David. *Open Secret: Gay Hollywood, 1928–1998*. New York: William Morrow & Co., 1998.

Garsi, Jean-François. "Cinémas homosexuels," *Cinémaction*, no. 15, Papyrus. 1981.

Grossman, Andrew. *Queer Asian Cinema: Shadows in the Shade*. Binghamton: Harrington Park Press, 2000.

Jablonski, Olivier. "De l'ouverture du ghetto à la dépolitisation. Les festivals de films gais et lesbiens en France en questions," *La Revue h*, no. 5–6 (1997).

Kirkham Pat, and Janet Thumim. *You Tarzan: Masculinity, Movies and Men*. London: Lawrence & Wishart, 1993.

———. *Me Jane: Masculinity, Movies and Women*. London: Lawrence & Wishart, 1995.

Lauretis, Teresa de. *Technologies of Gender: Essays in Theory, Film, and Fiction*. Bloomington: Indiana Univ. Press, 1987.

Lenne, Gérard. *Le Sexe à l'écran*. Paris: Artefact, 1978. [Published in the US as *Sex on the Screen: Eroticism in Film*. New York: St Martin's, 1985.]

Leraton, René-Paul. *Gay Porn. Le film porno gay: histoire, représentations et construction d'une sexualité*. Montblanc: H & O Editions, 2002.

Menicucci, Garay. "Unlocking the Arab Celluloid Closet, Homosexuality in Egyptian Film," http://www.merip .org/mer/mer206/egyfilm.htm (accessed May 8, 2008).

Murray, Raymond. *Images in the Dark: An Encyclopedia of Gay and Lesbian Film and Video*. Philadelphia: TLA Publications, 1995.

Olson, Jenni. *The Ultimate Guide to Lesbian & Gay Film and Video*. New York/London: Serpent's Tail, 1996.

Philbert, Bertrand. *L'Homosexualité à l'écran*. Paris: Charles Veyrier, 1984.

Roen, Paul. *A Gay Guide to Camp and Cult Films*. Two volumes. San Francisco: Leyland Publications, 1994–97.

Russo, Vito. *The Celluloid Closet: Homosexuality in the Movies*. Revised edition. New York: Harper & Row, 1987.

Straayer, Chris. *Deviant Eyes, Deviant Bodies: Sexual Re-Orientation in Film and Video*. New York: Columbia Univ. Press, 1996.

Suarez, Juan A. *Bike Boys, Drag Queens and Superstars: Avant-Garde, Mass Culture, and Gay Identities in the 1960s Underground Cinema*. Bloomington/Indianapolis: Indiana Univ. Press, 1996.

Tasker, Yvonne. *Spectacular Bodies: Gender, Genre and the Action Cinema*. New York: Routledge, 1993.

Tyler, Parker. *Screening the Sexes: Homosexuality in the Movies*. New York: Anchor Books. 1973.

UC Berkeley Library. Gays, Lesbian & Transgendered People in Motion Pictures: A Bibliography of Materials in the UC Berkely Library. Media Resources Center, Moffit Library. *http://www.lib.berkeley.edu/MRC/GayBib.html* (accessed January 28, 2008).

Waugh, Thomas. *The Fruit Machine: Twenty Years of Writings on Queer Cinema*. Durham, NC/London: Duke Univ. Press, 2000.

—Art; Censorship; Comic Books; Dance; Heterosexism; Literature; Music; Pasolini, Pier Paolo; Song.

CLASS

Is homophobia a matter of class? Sociologists are paid to think so, but lacking proper research, what do we really know? One cannot help but be aware of homosexuality's unequal social distribution: among gays, the wealthier classes are twice as numerous, and there are twice as many university graduates. Further, it is no surprise that homosexuality is much more widespread in large urban centers. These tendencies are not dependent on nationality; studies confirm them in such countries as France, Great Britain, and the United States.

Can we then also deduce the unequal social distribution of homophobia? The reasoning is obvious: naturally, gays and lesbians tend to gather and thus thrive in environments that are less hostile to them, thus the overrepresentation of homosexuals among the economic and cultural elite. Though the difference can be explained to a certain degree by assuming a bias among survey respondents, it is difficult to deny that the higher amount of reticence among the lower socioeconomic classes is inversely indicative of a much stronger hostility toward homosexuality in those classes. In other words, going against the homophobic argument that the prevalence of homosexuality in the social elite is a symptom of their **decadence**, could it be said that it is instead a sign of a much more liberal level of **tolerance**?

The underlying ideology behind this sociological hypothesis is familiar: it is based on the **philosophy** of the eighteenth-century Enlightenment and inspired by its criticism of prejudice. The defense of Reason is effectively embodied by a representation of society: the enlightened elite lead the way, ahead of the common people. The same perspective is applied not only to homophobia; racism and sexism have also been denounced in the name of the Enlightenment. Thus, to cast off these types of prejudice is to resolutely declare one's modernity, differentiating oneself by one's liberalism from the common classes, which are presumably more conservative in spirit.

It is tempting to turn this hypothesis upside-down by proposing a different, albeit more political, sociological model. For example, it could be said that recent debates on homosexuality are based on a resistance to the advancement of rights (such as **marriage** or parenting), a resistance that is in fact stronger among the elite than among the common classes. Doubtless, it is difficult to quantify this kind of hypothesis. Nonetheless, small clues abound: in France between 1997 and 1999, progressive news items that were favorable toward the PaCS (Pacte civil de solidarité; Civil solidarity pact) domestic partnership pact (and by extension, gay marriage and **parenting**) first appeared in mass **media** outlets rather than in the media of the elite. One can only assume that mass media, being more "of the people," were naturally more sensitive to a change in public opinion, while the "elitist" media (whose self-declared role is to enlighten the people) took much longer to come to this conclusion. In more general terms, it can be assumed that the dominant ideology is protected by those who dominate, who are also resistant to change; they are better armed, culturally-speaking, to fight the evolution of their belief system. This overturns the first sociological hypothesis: far from holding a privileged place among the common people, homophobia instead would seem to be far more firmly anchored among the elite.

Should preference be given to one or the other of these hypotheses: the first, which is based on the logic of liberal modernization, or the second, which takes up a radical criticism of the elite? The first case assumes a common people plunged into the obscurity of their prejudices, while the second imagines an elite ensconced within the arrogance of its ideology. Rather than pit upper and lower classes against each other, let us instead form a hypothesis separate from those already mentioned, which sets aside the inherent difficulty of the definition. Homophobia may be the name given to the entirety of discussions and practices that contribute to the exclusion or belittlement of homosexuals, but there is nothing that says homophobia must be uniform, nor that it cannot be measured by degrees as it appears in various social milieus.

On the contrary, if one can accept the idea of a heterogeneous homophobia that changes according to time and place, then it becomes possible to establish a correlation between homophobia and social classes not in terms of degrees, but nature. Between variable historical configurations (that is, different social and political contexts), one never encounters the same type of homophobia. Its protean nature stems from the fact it never expresses a consistent ideology. In reality, homophobia is nothing more than a collection of strategies opposed to the legitimization of homosexuality (that is to say, anything that calls heterosexual norms into question).

Following this hypothesis, one must surrender trying to quantify homophobia as it moves up or down along the socioeconomic ladder. If sociology were to provide the questionnaire for a survey on homophobia, one should not expect to find a unique scale that can be used as a point of comparison between hierarchical groups ("Are you more or less homophobic?"). Rather, in the absence of being able to identify the strong and weak points, the research could establish the form homophobia takes based on the particular milieu—in other words, the diverse strategies employed in the service of **heteronormativity**.

—*Eric Fassin*

Borrillo, Daniel, and Pierre Lascoumes, eds. *L'Homophobie, comment la définir, comment la combattre.* Paris: Ed. Prochoix, 1999.

Bourdieu, Pierre. *La Distinction.* Paris: Minuit, 1970.

Chauncey, George. *Gay New York: Gender, Urban Culture and the Making of the Gay Male World, 1890–1940.* New York: Basic Books, 1994.

D'Emilio, John. "Capitalism and Gay Identity." In *The Lesbian and Gay Reader.* Edited by Henri Abelove, Michèle Aina Barale, and David Halperin. New York: Routledge, 1993.

Fassin, Eric. "Sexe, mensonge et veto." Discussion with Jean-Marie Durand and Joseph Ghosn. *Les Inrockuptibles,* no. 247 (June 2000).

Grignon, Claude, and Jean-Claude Passeron. *Le Savant et le populaire. Misérabilisme et populisme en sociologie et en littérature.* Paris: Gallimard, Le Seuil, "Hautes Etudes," 1989.

Hoggart, Richard. *La Culture du pauvre.* Paris: Minuit, 1970.

Pollak, Michael. "L'Homosexualité masculine, ou: le bonheur dans le ghetto?" *Communication,* no. 35 (1982).

Raffo, Susan, ed. *Queerly Classed: Gay Men and Lesbians Write About Class.* Boston: South End Press, 1997.

—*Heterosexism; Parenting; Philosophy; Rhetoric; Sociology; Symbolic Order.*

CLOSET, the

In an interview with the French publication *Journal du sida* (Journal on **AIDS**) in April 1995, essayist Alain Finkielkraut reminisced about the "art of homosexual living," characterized by "discretion, ambiguity, indetermination, and reserve," and regretted its disappearance. Had he simply been describing a general concept of good manners, his comments would have been relegated to the ranks of trivial banter. But Finkielkraut managed to transform it into a set of morals specific to homosexuals, modes of behavior set out by gays and lesbians as a means of survival—in a context where the simple act of living out one's sexuality in the same way as any heterosexual placed gays and lesbians in danger, and turned parents, neighbors, or workplace colleagues into implacable adversaries. Finkielkraut seemed to forget (or refused to see) that homosexual discretion has a history that is both individual and collective, irreducibly linked to **insult** and **discrimination**; he was also unaware (or preferred not to know) that the "art of homosexual living," whose return he was naïvely advocating, was in actual fact linked to another, more significant metaphor for gay and lesbian experience: the closet.

"Closet" is a gem of a word whose effectiveness can be measured by its translinguistic reach (it translates well into French as *placard* and into Spanish as *armario*). The term is used to describe the social and psychological space in which gays and lesbians lock themselves up to hide their homosexuality. For all the time that it has been in use since the **Stonewall** riots, the metaphor has not lost any of its descriptive power; the "closet" speaks of both the ridicule and the discomfort: in bourgeois theater, illegitimate loves are always hidden away in the closet, as precarious a hideout as it is. In this sense, usage of the word "closet" also refers to a declaration—it is primarily used by those who have lived through the same experience and moved on; those who have come out of the closet. This is why the term "closet" is often used in contrast with gay "pride," a term in which those upholders of "discretion" tend to see only shamelessness and **exhibitionism**.

The concept of the "closet" can be seen in two ways: on one hand, it is individual and biographical, and on the other, collective and historical. Given the usual assumption of a heterosexual preference, the experience of the closet is the original condition of every homosexual. But it must not be forgotten that the term is historically situated: it was born during those years of homosexual liberation as a generation attempted to free itself from a past of invisibility—with this perspective, we can see that modern research in gay and lesbian historiography tends to nuance the linearity of a history that only ever seems to be presented as an imperious march toward emancipation.

At the beginning, there is the presumption of heterosexuality: a heterosexual is never faced with the question of knowing whether or not he should say what he is; his sexuality is an assumed part of the playing field for all his social relations. Under these conditions, the discovery of a homosexual preference is immediately linked with the delicate experience of the closet. Every homosexual, man or woman, can attest to this: at one moment or another in their lives, they experienced a painful disassociation between that which they are, and that which others perceive them to be, or tacitly oblige them to be. If there is a homosexual culture, its roots spring from that one intimate moment, shared by all: the closet is the original experience, the site of a continuous effort that demanded an unfailing vigilance to social situations, which sometimes required a secret or double life, ambiguity or self-affirmation.

This common experience launched a vast range of unique situations: one person might carefully keep his sexual preferences from his **family**, but has no problem affirming them in the **workplace**; another might take careful measures to ensure that his colleagues never suspect his homosexuality, yet sees no harm in telling his parents. Despite being shared, the experience of the closet is nonetheless very fluid: one is in or out of the closet depending on the time and place, dictated by a particular situation's degree of acceptance (or not) of homosexuality. In this way, a type of social intelligence is amassed, halfway between intuition and specific experience, which is common to all minority populations and whose functioning Erving Goffman described in *Stigma: Notes on the Management of Spoiled Identity* (1963).

But the experience of the closet can also lead those who stay in it, or return to it occasionally, into a Catch-22 situation. Without a doubt, maintaining secrecy about one's homosexuality allows one to elude the many manifestations of homophobia, from the seemingly harmless to the explicitly violent. But this veil of secrecy is a form of self-loathing, which only serves to exacerbate homophobic attitudes because the closeted person appears to agree that homosexuality is shameful and unmentionable. Further, the effort required to keep the closet door tightly shut may lead one to stubbornly insist on maintaining a heterosexual façade and thus adopt behaviors that are openly hostile to gays and lesbians. In these ways, the effects of homophobic oppression can be much harder on those who hide than it is on those who affirm their homosexuality. The closet, then, is a fictional means of protection that renders one even more vulnerable to blackmail and **violence**; it is difficult to report a crime having been the target of an aggression without also exposing the reason. As a result, coming out of the closet, despite its risks, can also be considered the most certain way of breaking a vicious circle.

However, in her remarkable book *Epistemology of the Closet*, Eve Kosofsky Sedgwick tempers this kind of optimism. She reminds us that the supposed protection of the closet is never really certain, because one is never completely inside: even a homosexual's silence can confer an extraordinary privilege on a friend or family member of a homosexual who knows without the homosexual knowing that he or she knows. This person refrains from initiating a discussion that would break the spell, leaving the homosexual with the impossible task of making an admission whose false air of confession inevitably makes his homosexuality seem like a fault or a **sin**. But Sedgwick also shows that one can never completely leave the closet either, because the revelation of a person's homosexuality forcibly assigns him or her a new identity through which, from this point forward, everything will be interpreted; gays and lesbians know all too well that there is always someone ready to draw a connection between their homosexuality and the slightest defect or mediocrity. Sedgwick also reminds us that no matter what, a person's coming out of the closet will always be both too early ("Was it really necessary to push this on us right now?") and too late, thereby risking ridicule ("Everyone has known for a long time already") or suspicion ("Why did you have to wait so long before talking about it?").

In other words, far from putting an end to homophobia, coming out of the closet seems only to force it to manifest on a different level, leading to a vague renewal of categories of identity and to the legitimization of a sexual hierarchy of which heterosexuals are the symbolic and practical masters. Compared to all the illusions of coming out of the closet—which only really changes the type of captivity without completely removing it—it seems that one has to prefer the "queer" route, in which one deconstructs labels and norms by affirming identities so numerous and unforeseeable that they become unassignable.

The reclamation of the expression "queer" is priceless for many reasons, including the fact that it does not qualify its critique of coming out of the closet with any calls for discretion (just the opposite, in fact). However, the term is perhaps not sufficiently expressive of the urgency and necessity called for by collective mobilizations, such as the war against AIDS, for example, when it became apparent that the disease was ravaging the homosexual population. In fact, the epidemic made it apparent that the praising of those who escape or adopt multiple sexual identities was in vain, given that the method of infection resulted from specific sexual practices; at the same time, a general indifference to the fate of homosexuals explained the absence of a coherent policy to fight the epidemic. Because of this, the closet encouraged both the extension of the AIDS epidemic as well as the suffering encountered by certain people who contracted the disease—because it is understood and has been demonstrated many times over that secrecy about one's sexuality (and often accompanied by **shame**) does not mesh well with the self-respect required to adopt preventative measures (i.e. safe sex), nor with the vigilance necessary for rapid testing and appropriate care (how may gays shun testing out of fear of encountering homophobic reactions?). Further, many sufferers often refrain from telling family members about their illness, which would risk having to reveal their sexual preferences. In light of this experience, the act of coming out of the closet, though sometimes limited in its effects, becomes a more urgent matter, both individually and collectively.

Historically, the concept of the closet crystallized the moment when a new generation of gays and lesbians realized the political necessity of coming out. This is why the concept was unthinkable until the gay liberation movement in the United States during the 1960s, although traits characteristic of the closet existed well before then: the need for discretion, the leading of double lives, the self-hatred and ensuing internalized homophobia. Within gay activist organizations such as France's FHAR (Front homosexuel d'action révolutionnaire), the militant argument was constructed mostly against the notion of a homosexuality that was both secretive and respectable, developed by the ranks of the group Arcadie, led by André

Baudry, an example of the closet's aporia.

The development of a history of homosexuality, particularly in English-speaking countries, is nuanced by a rigorously binary concept based largely on the militant mythology. This brings to mind, among others, the works of social history by American George Chauncey, who sought to reposition the closet in history by situating its peak (at least in the United States) during the 1940s. In his book *Gay New York: Gender, Urban Culture, and the Making of the Gay Male World, 1890–1940*, Chauncey shows that during the early decades of the twentieth century, a unique male homosexual culture and community existed, integrated into public space and urban life according to details which, despite bearing little resemblance to the gay liberation years of the 1970s, did not fit the concept of the closet. Rather, they were made up of a series of complex social negotiations which blended together the art of evasion, subtext, and the provocative irony of the camp esthetic. The homosexual culture that was forged during the 70s was refined compared to the historical experience of the closet, which was born in the 1920s thanks to the promulgation of repressive laws aimed at diminishing the growing visibility of homosexuals, the subsequent toughening of these laws in the 1930s, and their consolidation during the Cold War.

The example from Chauncey's works permits a reconsideration of the modern perception of the closet years that has been largely built up by a progressive mythology born of militant heroism. Doubtless, the sociability created within gay and lesbian activist organizations allowed for a new means of freedom and self-invention for some, that is, the creation of a homosexual culture largely unconnected to earlier gay communities. This is also what Chauncey's more recent research reveals about the closet years, during which the phrase "coming out" was coined to describe the frequenting of homosexual venues, clandestine or otherwise. These efforts at rehistoricization, flying in the face of a "progressive" or whiggish history, leads one to describe the history of homosexuality less as the implacable march toward emancipation from the closet and more as a series of fluctuations between secrecy and visibility.

In any event, the gay liberation movement established "coming out of the closet" as part of the collective vocabulary. "Coming out" was thought of as both a survival technique as well as a way to define heterosexuality, if not as a problem per se, then at least as something that should not be assumed. In a certain sense, coming out of the closet inaugurated what would become an integral element of minority politics in the 1990s: the necessity of initiating a first-person discourse that serves the purpose of both calling current norms into question, and undermining the privilege of those experts who so easily pronounce their opinion on—and against—minority issues (e.g., doctors, psychiatrists, psychoanalysts, and the like).

It did not take much for new demands for discretion to be heard, aimed at thwarting the effects of coming out of the closet, in response to visible manifestations of homosexuality, under the pretext that one's sexuality was nothing to be proud of; "Live your sexuality any way you like," opponents said, "so long as we don't have to see or hear anything about it." The naysayers' claims that sexuality was a private matter was aimed at pushing homosexuality back behind closed doors, while at the same time turning a blind eye to myriad public manifestations of heterosexuality in everything from literature to television to ads in magazines. In every case, the idea of homosexual discretion implied conformity with the heterosexual norm in which the only thing lacking was a companion of the opposite sex. Of course, this level of discretion, which essentially is invisibility, would never be required of a heterosexual.

In conclusion, it should be noted that the demand for a return to the closet is accompanied by a demand to return to the way things were prior to gay liberation. Indeed, the call for discretion and the yearning for the era of when homosexuality was illegal are simply two sides of the same phenomenon. The distance from the old closet to a new one, however golden, is short indeed.

—*Philippe Mangeot*

Berube, Allan. *Coming out Under Fire: The History of Gay Men and Women in World War Two*. New York: Plume Penguin, 1990.

Chauncey, George. *Gay New York: Gender, Urban Culture and the Making of the Gay Male World, 1890–1940*. New York: Basic Books, 1994.

Fassin, Eric. "'Out,' la métaphore paradoxale." In *Homosexualités: expression/répression*. Edited by Louis-Georges Tin. Paris: Stock, 2000.

Finkielkraut, Alain. "Il faut résister au discours de la dénonciation," *Journal du sida*, no.72 (1995).

Gross, Larry. *Contested Closets: The Politics and Ethics of Outing*. Minneapolis/London: Minnesota Univ. Press, 1993.

Guillemaut, Françoise. "Images invisibles: les lesbiennes." In *La Peur de l'autre en soi, du sexisme à l'homophobie*. Edited by Michel Dorais, Pierre Dutey, and Daniel Welzer-Lang. Montreal: VLB Editeur, 1994.

Herdt, Gilbert, and Andrew Boxer. *Children of Horizons: How Gay and Lesbian Teens are Leading a New Way Out of the Closet*. Boston: Beacon Press, 1993.

Kosofsky Sedgwick, Eve. *Epistemology of the Closet*. Berkeley, CA: Univ. of California Press, 1990.

Russo, Vito. *The Celluloid Closet: Homosexuality in the Movies*. New York: Harper & Row, 1987.

—*Discrimination; Exhibitionism; Heterosexism; Outing; Privacy; Proselytism; Rhetoric; Stonewall; Shame; Tolerance; Violence.*

COMIC BOOKS

A successor to the legacy of **caricature** and illustrated novels and, depending on who is asked, a literary genre as well as a "ninth art," the comic book made its first appearance at the end of the nineteenth century. It was quickly adopted as a narrative vehicle aimed at children and adolescents, and as such, the comic book abstained from addressing the issue of homosexuality in its early years. More precisely, until the 1970s the vast majority of comic book heroes evolved in a primarily asexual universe, populated more often than not by anthropomorphic creatures; any romantic relationships between characters were strictly heterosexual, even in the most realistically depicted settings. The one exception to this rule was the clandestine pornographic comic book publications such as the Tijuana Bibles, which flourished in America during the 1920s.

Paradoxically, the asexual aspect of the comic book opened the door to all sorts of *a posteriori* interpretations concerning the relationships between characters. Outside of short, purely comical narratives (usually four panels long, produced mainly for newspapers), the largest international body of works were stories of adventure. In this context, the heroes were joined by one or more secondary, same-sex characters with whom they maintained friendly relationships, relationships which seemed to subscribe to a "pedagogical" need to extol the virtues of male camaraderie to the young audience. This only begs the (rather contemporary) reinterpretation of a latent homosexuality in these characters. The list of duos to whom this description can be applied is long: Tintin and Captain Haddock, Tintin and Chang (*The Blue Lotus*), Bob Morane and Bill Ballantine, etc. However, aside from the very particular case of Alix (where author Jacques Martin's discreet commitment on the subject left little doubt as to the nature of the relationship between its two protagonists), it is difficult to readily accept this kind of reinterpretation for most European comic books.

The situation in America was much more complex. The dominant type of American comic book since 1938, the superhero genre, also saw the creation of the sidekick character: a young male adolescent who fights alongside the heroic main character, possessing the same powers or skills, and to whom the adult serves as mentor or father figure (Green Arrow and Speedy, Flash and Kid Flash, Aquaman and Aqualad, Captain America and Bucky, and of course, Batman and Robin). This tradition has its roots in another familiar figure of American culture, the hobo. Typically an itinerant worker accompanied in his travels by a younger sort who is learning the trade, the hobo shares with the superhero the same image of virility and sense of adventure. However, it was also suggested that the nature of this hyper-masculine scenario dictated that the younger hobo provide sexual favors in return for his apprenticeship. It was probably the similarity between these two types of relationships that engendered the reinterpretation of the nature of the bond between superhero and sidekick, such as that between the famous duo of Batman and Robin. The case of Batman is even more striking in that his principal rival (created in 1940) was the Joker, the lanky and sinister clown who dressed in purple and green and wore face powder and makeup, not unlike that used by the flamboyant gays of New York during the 1930s.

In the Batman comics, it is not possible to conclude that Batman is truly portrayed as a manly homosexual, wiith his young friend Robin, fighting against a highly effeminate Joker. Nonetheless, this interpretation first opened the door to criticism, accusing the comic book of homosexual **proselytism**. Indeed, it was during **McCarthyism** in the US during the 1950s that the first edition of the book *Seduction of the Innocent* was published, in which psychiatrist Fredric Wertham denounced the corruption of American youths as promoted through the medium of the comic book. From then on, comics were blamed for all sorts of youth-

ful trouble, from delinquency to suicide. According to critics, comics warped young minds doubly through violence (especially in the horror publications of EC Comics, such as *Tales from the Crypt*) and sex. From the promotion of homosexuality by Batman and Robin; of lesbianism by Wonder Woman, the "Amazon princess"; of sadomasochism through the countless girls appearing bound and tied at the hands of a super-villain: the writing was on the wall. In an America preoccupied with chasing internal enemies, comic books were identified as willing accomplices of the growing red menace.

The success of this hypothesis was such that the large comic book publishers (with the exception of EC Comics, which went out of business as a result of these criticisms) were forced to create an agency of self-censorship and "good behavior": the Comics Code Authority, an organization whose purpose was to approve all comics before they could be published. The American industry would have to wear this millstone around its neck until the 1980s—thus in comic books at least, sex, and in particular, homosexuality, did not exist.

France did not experience the same type of psychosis as its neighbor across the Atlantic, but the French law of 1948 regarding the protection of children had a similar effect on comic books that did not end until the 1980s. In the 60s, however, some young French authors (e.g., Marcel Gotlib, Nikita Mandryka, and Claire Brétécher), mostly published by Pilote, began to abandon the idea that comics were only for children. Alongside the post-1968 counterculture, titles such as *L'Echo des savanes*, *Charlie*, and *Fluide glacial* began appearing: new French comics conceived for adults, where sexuality finally could be depicted. However, other than a few drawings by Jean-Marc Reiser or Philippe Vuillemin, it was not until the publication of the gay magazine *Gai-Pied* that the theme of homosexuality would really find its place in comics, which were starting to become increasingly political (e.g., the works of "Copi" and José Cunéo). Even then, it was not until the early 1990s that a "mainstream" publisher, Glénat, dared to publish an openly gay comic book, the translation of German cartoonist Ralf König's work, *La Capote qui tue (The Killer Condom)*. Thereafter, a dichotomy began to appear in comics, between the type of comic book "series" targeted primarily at children and adolescents, and adult-oriented, "artistic" comic books (considered more in the same vein of literature); the latter allowed a place for the expression of homosexual themes, albeit limited to "strictly gay" comic books (as was the case for gay **film** and gay **literature**). Any sort of homophobic outrage was avoided, however, given that these comics were directed at gay audiences.

The situation that developed in American comics was quite the opposite. During the revolution of the "silver age" of superheroes in the 1960s, ushered in by the hegemony of Marvel Comics (e.g., *Spider-Man* and the *Fantastic Four*), a wholesale change in the demographics of comic book readership took place. The superheroes were now appealing less to younger readers and more to adolescents and young adults, specifically the fifteen-to-thirty-year-old market. From this began a trend in the 1970s and 80s toward greater realism in comics, wherein the principal approach was to have the superheroes encounter characters and situations which echoed current American social issues. Thanks to this trend, the Comics Code Authority (CCA), little by little, fell by the wayside. The first salvo was fired by Marvel Comics at the end of the 1960s, when an issue of *Spider-Man* was published without CCA approval because it depicted the use of drugs. By the end of the 70s, the issue of homosexuality began to be addressed. However, in an industry where characters were largely owned by the publisher (and mostly by the two principal companies, Marvel and DC) yet produced by a steady stream of different writers and artists, the conditions were such that the stance on homosexuality became a defining point between those writers and artists who were gay-positive (some of whom had come out themselves during the 1980s and 90s) and those who were not. The opportunity was also ripe for homophobic subtext—indeed, one of the first clear allusions to homosexuality can be found in *Hulk Magazine* at the end of the 70s, a black-and-white comic targeted at an "adult" audience. A secondary male character, upon discovering Dr Robert Bruce Banner half naked and dressed in rags, states very clearly his intention to take advantage of the doctor, with or without his consent.

Nonetheless, the relative liberalism that existed in the world of comic book creators led to a trend that started with the introduction of secondary gay and lesbian characters, such as Arnold Roth in *Captain America*, and Maggie Sawyer in *Superman*, leading further to the creation of gay and lesbian superheroes within existing groups (e.g., Extraño in *The New Guardians*, Hector of the Pantheon in *The Incredible Hulk*), and finally the coming out of already-existing superheroes (e.g., Northstar in *Alpha Flight*, and Shrinking Violet,

Lightning Lass, and Element Lad in the *Legion of Super-Heroes*). On the other hand, efforts to create an original gay superhero were practically nonexistent. The one rare attempt was *Enigma*, which, confined to a limited edition miniseries of a DC Comics collection aimed at a mature audience, had more in common with the Franco-Belgian art-house comics than with traditional comic books.

However, this tentative embrace of homosexual themes was fragile and limited. Extraño is a good example of this. First appearing in *Millennium* at the end of the 1980s, the character became caught up in a controversy between several gay-positive comic book artists making accusations of homophobia given Extraño's flamboyantly gay South American characteristics. The debate over the legitimacy of this effeminate representation of homosexuality was quickly cut short by the new editor who was tasked with launching The New Guardians team (including Extraño) into its own series, and who declared that there was no question about Extraño's sexuality, but upon joining the ranks of The New Guardians he was "cured." Likewise, the lesbian couple of Shrinking Violet and Lightning Lass, along with their male counterpart Element Lad, in the *Legion of Super-Heroes* (who had become veritable icons for gay and lesbian comic book fans in the US), were heterosexualized by DC Comics in the mid-1990s in a revisionist scheme to rewrite the world of superheroes and remodel main characters with an updated image. Even though this kind of ploy is common in the world of comics, it nonetheless enabled DC to erase the progressions of the previous decade.

Today, the new direction in comic books comes from Japan, where manga has been around for several decades but is only now starting to flood the Western market. In manga, homosexuality is comfortably accepted, and even has its own special genre: *shōnen-ai*, where masculine love is expressed through tender romance. The more sexually-explicit version of this genre is known as *yaoi*. As difficult as it might be for a Westerner to believe, this genre is usually written by women, with an audience of young girls who appreciate this new expression of a complex masculinity that is both familiar and strange, romantic yet strong. In this sense, these works could potentially contribute to the valorization of male homosexuality and help fight homophobia in Japan. However, the real social and cultural impact, if any, remains to be seen. At the same time, the production of *hentai* enjoys a similar popularity, in which romantic and sexual relationships between women take center stage. However, this genre of comic book, produced by men for men, presents an objectified, reified, and stereotypical image of lesbians that surely cannot go far to improve the social acceptance of female homosexuality in Japan.

—*Pierre-Olivier de Busscher*

Busscher, Pierre-Olivier de. "Paroles et silence. Les representations du sida et des sexualités dans un media grand public: l'example de la bande dessinée américaine," *Sociétés. Revue des sciences humaines et socials*, no. 39 (1993).

Leyland, Winston, and Jerry Mills, eds. *Meatmen: An Anthology of Gay Male Comics*. San Francisco: GS Press, 1986.

HentaiSeeker.com: http://www.hentaiseeker.com (accessed January 5, 2008).

MAG: Mouvement d'affirmation des jeunes gais et lesbiennes: http://www.mag-paris.org/magazette/33/mangas.php (site now discontinued).

Mangels, Andy. "Out of the Closet and into the Comics." *Amazing Heroes*, no. 143–44 (1988).

Suvilay, Bounthavy. "Le Héros était une femme: le travestissement dans le manga." *ProChoix*, no. 23 (2002).

—*Art; Caricature; Cinema; Literature; Media; Publicity.*

COMING OUT. *See* Closet, the; Exhibitionism; Outing; Shame

COMMUNISM

On the whole, the history of international communism is one of the saddest chapters in the history of homophobia during the nineteenth and twentieth centuries. It was bad from the start, given that Friedrich Engels, the cofounder of Marxism, was fiercely homophobic. In a letter to Karl Marx in 1869, in which he violently attacked the German sexologist Karl Ulrichs, Engels wrote: "Henceforth the slogan shall be '*Guerre aux cons, paix aux trous-du-cul*' ['War for the cunts, peace for the assholes']. It is fortunate that we, personally, shall be too old to have to fear that, when the party wins, we shall be required to pay physical tribute to the victors." And in his work *The Origin of the Family, Private Property, and the State* (1884), he denounced "the repugnant practice of Greek pederasty,"

which he saw as the result of the decline of morals. Of course, this position was not unique to Marxists; for many nineteenth-century progressives, homosexuality was a vice of the elite, the result of a moral breakdown unavoidably brought on by aristocratic luxury and the capitalist system, having abandoned all that is healthy and natural. This theme appears in the work of French historian Jules Michelet, who contrasted the homosexuality of the gloomy seventeenth century with the heterosexuality of the glorious eighteenth century. It can also be found in the work of socialist philosopher Pierre-Joseph Proudhon, who was furious that fellow philosopher Charles Fourier, in his defense of homosexuals, had "sanctified unisexual unions"; and in the literature of Emile Zola, most notably at the end of his 1871–72 novel *La Curée* (*The Kill*). That said, certain social democratic leaders of the German Empire (i.e. Karl Kautsky and August Bebel) were in favor of abrogating Paragraph 175, and the famous socialist theoretician Eduard Bernstein, in defending Oscar **Wilde** in 1895, refuted the idea that homosexuality was an **unnatural** act and a sign of **decadence**.

While Russia's Bolshevik Revolution of 1917 began by emancipating homosexuals and abolishing the criminal code of 1832 (then excluding sodomy as a crime in the codes of 1922 and 1926), the Bolsheviks themselves had little patience for homosexuals—in fact, the great leaders had no appetite for sexuality in general ("the disorder of one's sexual life is bourgeois, and a manifestation of decadence," Lenin declared in 1922). They did not consider homosexuality to be a crime, but rather it had all the signs of a sickness. Above all, it was considered a **vice** of aristocrats (i.e. Tchaikovsky and Sergei Diaghilev)—not a good thing in a country seeking to break with its Tsarist past. Starting in 1924, there were massive arrests of homosexuals who were "of poor origin," as attested to in the correspondence of writer Mikhail Kuzmin. However, it was Joseph Stalin who instigated the most radical homophobic acts in Russia to date: on December 17, 1933, male homosexuality (*muzhelozhstvo*) was recriminalized according to Russia's criminal code, and Article 154 (which later became Article 121), introduced in April 1934, made all homosexual acts punishable by three to five years' incarceration. Soon thereafter, numerous arrests of homosexuals took place in Moscow, Leningrad, Kharkiv, and Odessa, notably in the realms of theater, **music**, and the **arts**. After Kuzmin's death in 1936, his lover, Yury Yurkun, and most of his friends were arrested and shot. The same year, Commissar of Justice Nikolai Krylenko declared homosexuality to be a crime against the Soviet state and the proletariat.

To Stalinists, homosexuality was not simply a deplorable legacy of the old regime; it was also intrinsically linked to **fascism**, as author Maxim Gorky implored in the May 23, 1934 issue of *Pravda* (not long before the infamous Night of the Long Knives purge in Nazi Germany): "Remove homosexuality, and fascism will disappear." (There is an unverified rumor that the recriminalization of homosexuality was in fact the result of a personal request to Stalin made by Gorky, whose adopted son had been seduced by a homosexual.) This theory of fascist **perversion** (the "habits of the Nazi SA") gave the Soviet public a reason to oppose homosexuality (socialism was aligned with nature, health, and virtue, and Nazism with all that was unnatural, **degenerate**, and unvirtuous), all the while ignoring the reality of Nazi homophobic violence. This theory also had the advantage of combining popular Russian prejudices with orthodox ones (the end of the 1930s in the Soviet Union was marked by the triumph of a pro-Russian reactionary populism): it is thus that homosexuality's recriminalization in 1933–34 took place in the context of what an American historian once called "the great Stalinist regression." Abortion was recriminalized, divorce became more difficult to obtain, and the contributions of women were no longer acknowledged—in short, the revolutionary advances that had begun to take hold between the 1900s and 1920s were stopped cold. In this way, the regime renewed the homophobic image of a sort of mystical heterodoxy from the turn of the century, typified by Vasily Rozanov, author of "The Family Problem in Russia" (1903) [not published in English], who saw in the questioning of sexual roles and in Russian patriarchal holism (*sobornost*) a victory for the "sodomites" and the "third sex." On closer inspection, it is easy to see how Stalinist society allowed no room for homosexuality: after all, to Stalin, people were nothing more than nuts and bolts in service to the socialist state, and sexual pleasure not aimed at reproduction was considered a waste of energy not permissible by socialist society. As stated during the same era by proponents of Lysenkoism (the repressive political and social campaigns undertaken in science and agriculture, spearheaded by Trofim Denisovich Lysenko, Stalinist director of the Soviet Institute of Genetics), the external environment will always modify behavioral characteristics; it followed,

then, that banning homosexuality would make it disappear completely.

The fallout from this discourse would be felt for more than fifty years: film director Sergei Eisenstein was the victim of extortion from 1938 until his death in 1948; filmmaker Sergei Parajanov was jailed twice for homosexuality, once in 1952, and again in 1974; and dancer Rudolf Nureyev, unable to tolerate the blackmail to which he was subjected, defected in 1961. Certainly the reforms undertaken by Nikita Khrushchev did nothing for homosexuals: Khrushchev, leader of the Soviet Union from 1953 to 1964, was very homophobic, and frequently made connections (no doubt thanks to his rural origins) between homosexuality and the intelligentsia. In December 1962 while visiting an art exhibit, he used the word "queers" to describe the painters of pieces too modern for his tastes. The years under the leadership of Leonid Brezhnev (1964–82) did not improve matters either: during the 1970s and 80s, the arm of the militia responsible for dealing with homosexuals frequently blackmailed those identified as such (some were even forced to perform sexual acts) and the KGB arrested an average of over 1,000 homosexuals a year. The accusation of homosexuality, reinforced by the claim of mental illness, was often used against political dissidents, such as mathematician Leonid Plyushch or archeologist Lev Klein; and a clandestine gay organization known as the "Gay Laboratory" set up in Leningrad in 1984 was quickly dismantled by the KGB shortly after it made contact with homosexuals in Finland. Lesbians were always at risk of psychiatric confinement, with effects felt for years afterward. And homosexuals were the lowest ranking prisoners in the **gulags**, and were subjected to rape (sometimes even gang rape) and sexual servitude.

The terror produced by such a system explains why it was not until the final years of the Soviet Union (that is, 1989–90) that an authentic Soviet gay movement finally appeared: the Moscow Association of Sexual Minorities was established near the end of 1989, and later became the Gay and Lesbian Alliance of Moscow. Then in 1990, in Tallinn (in what would soon become the independent nation of Estonia), an international conference was held on "the status of sexual minorities and the changing attitude towards homosexuality in Europe in the twentieth century." But while strides were being made, there was still more evidence of Soviet homophobia: in 1989, at the same time a non-Soviet television station broadcast an unprecedented debate on homosexuality, a group of medical students issued a series of ultra-violent messages stating that the "pederasts" did not deserve to be called human and that they should be sent away to special camps. And in 1994, eighteen percent of Russians still believed that homosexuals should be "liquidated" and another twenty-three percent thought they should be "isolated" from mainstream society.

Stalin was not the only communist leader with a violently homophobic streak: the same could also be said of Mao Zedong and Fidel Castro. The Maoist revolution of 1949 was very difficult on homosexuals in China, who were accused of "decadent and Western" behavior (in spite of a rich, indigenous tradition of homosexuality) and were often sent to labor camps for re-education (this included many male opera singers who performed the roles of women). As well, many homosexuals were arrested, subjected to "criticism," and incarcerated during both the Cultural Revolution (1966–76) and as a result of the Tiananmen Square protests in Beijing (June 1989). In China, as elsewhere, homophobia and anti-intellectualism went hand-in-hand. Tens of thousands of homosexuals were sent to the Chinese gulag, the *laogai*, although often under the guise of other accusations, usually **treasonous**, (such as foreigners, half-breeds, Catholics, Westernized intellectuals), where they were always harshly treated. In *Prisoner of Mao* (1973), Jean Pasqualini (a.k.a. Bao Ruo-Wang) describes the execution of a homosexual repeat offender around 1960: the man had been condemned to the gulag for seven years for his homosexuality, and his sentence was subsequently doubled when he was convicted of theft; when he was later accused of having seduced a fellow prisoner, he was sentenced to death and immediately executed in front of other prisoners. Pasqualini pointed out the impossibility of homosexuality being acted out in the gulags: prisoners risked being summarily shot if they were caught, and besides, most of them were in such a state of malnutrition that they had practically no libido. In this way, Chinese authorities were able to boast that they had successfully eradicated all "unnatural behavior" from China, but of course this was a false claim; in fact, Western psychologists noted with amusement the large numbers of "impotent" citizens appearing in official Chinese statistics. For years, through to the end of the 1980s, the taboo of homosexuality in China remained more or less intact, the result of the regime's systemic homophobia combined with popular sentiment (in Confucianism, the worst thing a man can do is not produce a son to carry on the family name).

By the beginning of the 1990s, things slowly began to change, though the trail is far from clear given that the evolution has been anything but linear. Gay groups started to form and meeting places were established (notably in Shanghai and Guangzhou); then in 2001, Chinese authorities removed homosexuality from its list of mental illnesses. That said, even though Chinese law no longer recognizes homosexuality as a crime, the gay movement in China has had limited success in promoting itself or having much visibility. As recently as 1996, the Minister of Propaganda announced that homosexual themes were to be banned from all publications, literary or journalistic, although major **media** could now address the issue of homosexuality without being subject to hysteria. And China's weak judicial culture continues to make life difficult for homosexuals: the **police** still harass them and find pretexts for their arrest, and even illegally extort money from them.

Cuba is another example of communist homophobia: although most homosexuals there supported the revolution in 1959, Fidel Castro soon instituted virulent anti-gay policies, the result of his considering homosexuality to be (like prostitution) a bourgeois and Western perversion. (Efforts to associate vice with the Western world even went so far as declaring that The Beatles were gay.) Homosexuality was declared illegal and punishable by four years' imprisonment, and parents were expected to turn in their homosexual children to authorities. By the mid-60s, Cuba's homosexuals—isolated by family and coworkers, branded as *escorias* ("eaters of dead flesh"), and subjected to intense harassment by the Committees for the Defense of the Revolution—were interned in camps until Castro sent them on a mass exodus by boat to the United States in 1980; among those sent away was the celebrated writer Reinaldo **Arenas**, who wrote about his time in a sugar cane plantation camp in *El Central* (1981; *El Central: A Cuban Sugarmill*) and *Antes que anochezca* (1992; *Before Night Falls*). The harsh treatment of homosexuals in Cuba began to relax somewhat in the 80s, under the external influence of protests by humanitarian associations and internal influence by East German advisors; finally, in 1992, Castro officially recognized that "homosexuality is a natural tendency that must be respected." Nonetheless, the status of Cuban homosexuals remains quite ambiguous: homosexual behavior that "incites public **scandal**" is punishable by twelve months in **prison**; homosexuals are not considered worthy of admission into the Communist Party; and there are no authorized homosexual publications or organizations: the Cuban Association of Gays and Lesbians, created in 1994, was banned in 1997 and its members arrested.

With regard to the Parti communiste française (PCF; French Communist Party): in 1934, under the influence of Stalinism, the PCF became more family-centric and homophobic. Until 1970, its leaders had in common with communists elsewhere in the world the belief that homosexuality was a bourgeois vice, "a tradition foreign to the working class" (to use a phrase of the French General Confederation of Labor), and an unnatural pathology, as suggested by French communist politician Jacques Duclos' violent outburst in 1971 against members of the gay group Front homosexual d'action révolutionnaire: "Go get treatment, you pederasts; the PCF is healthy!" Within the PCF, homosexuals needed to be extremely discreet: such was the case with writer and Communist Party member Louis Aragon, whom party officials knew only as an author, not the bisexual he was.

In this way, the PCF began to seem increasingly out of step with the rest of society: its ongoing discomfort with the issue of homosexuality was exemplified in a 1976 editorial by Guy Poussy, member of the party's central committee:

> Perversions exist, but this is not a matter for politics nor for the **police**, but rather a matter of medical science…. "'Unfettered pleasure" is not part of the revolutionary vocabulary. The majority of French people do not experience a feeling of liberation, but rather one of disgust in the face of perversion and immorality. And with good reason…. Revolution may not be found in barracks, but neither is it found in a brothel.

It has only been through pressure from young members that the Party's stance on the issue has evolved (essentially between 1985 and 1995), and the current PCF leadership could never be called homophobic, having proven themselves by their call to the fight against **AIDS** and in the debates on the **PaCS** (Pacte civil de solidarité; Civil solidarity pact) domestic partnership proposal.

In these matters, the PCF has a rarely mentioned precursor: the Kommunistiche Partei Deautschlands

(KPD; Communist Party of Germany) from 1918 to 1933. During this period, while the gay scene in Germany was flourishing despite the ongoing existence of legal interdiction (the infamous Paragraph 175), the KPD was putting together a combined front of both homosexuals and proletarians who were united against their common persecutors, the members of the ruling class supported by the churches. On numerous occasions (in 1924, 1927, 1929, and 1932), the KPD demanded that the law consider homosexuality and heterosexuality in the same way, and that Paragraph 175 be abrogated (this was one of the reasons why the radical psychoanalyst Wilhelm Reich belonged to the Party in 1930). The German communist discourse grew ambiguous by the end of the Weimar Republic once it became clear that a number of homosexuals could be found in the ranks of the Nazis, especially within the SA. But the party line did not officially change until after the advent of Adolf Hitler: it was only in 1934 that the clandestine KPD, under the influence of Moscow, would define homosexuality as a "fascist perversion."

—*Pierre Albertini*

Arenas, Reinaldo. *Avant la nuit*. Paris: Julliard, 1992. [Published in the US as *Before Night* Falls. New York: Viking, 1993.]

Arguelles, Lourdes, and Ruby Rich. "Homosexuality, Homophobia, and Revolution: Notes Towards an Understanding of the Cuban Lesbian and Gay Male Experience," *Signs* (1984). Reprinted in *Hidden from History: Reclaiming the Gay and Lesbian Past*. Edited by George Chauncey, Martin Duberman, and Martha Vicinus. New York: Meridian, 1990.

Delpla, François. "Les Communistes français et la sexualité (1932–1938)," *Le Mouvement social* 91 (1975).

Fourier, Charles. *Vers la liberté en amour*. Texts selected and presented by Daniel Guérin. Paris: Gallimard, "Folio," 1975.

Karlinsky, Simon. "Russia's Gay Literature and Culture: The Impact of the October Revolution." In *Hidden from History: Reclaiming the Gay and Lesbian Past*. Edited by George Chauncey, Martin Duberman, and Martha Vicinus. New York: Meridian, 1990.

Kon, Igor. *The Sexual Revolution in Russia: From the Age of the Tsars to Today*. New York: The Free Press, 1995.

Pasqualini, Jean. *Prisonnier de Mao, sept ans de camp de travail en Chine*. Paris: Gallimard, 1975.

Vichnevski, Anatoli. *La Faucille et le rouble, la modernisation conservatrice en URSS.* Paris: Gallimard, 2000.

—*Arenas, Reinaldo; China; Far Right; Fascism; France; Germany; Gulag; Latin America; Russia.*

COMMUNITARIANISM

Communitarianism is not a political philosophy but rather a polemical motif which, in France, is used to emphasize, *a contrario*, the reformulation of a culture that is republican, secular, and national, supposedly threatened by anyone questioning its blind spots. "Communitarianism" aims to discredit the politicization of minority issues. It must be pointed out that the history of gay mobilization is not the same as that of "communitarianist reasoning." The question of communitarianism goes far beyond gays and lesbians, encompassing the struggles of all minorities. One must not jump to the conclusion that all anti-communitarian discussion is necessarily homophobic; this can only be determined on a case by case basis. Besides, anti-communitarianist rhetoric, at least in France, cannot be properly understood without bringing it to the more general level of what French sociologist Eric Fassin has called the "**rhetoric** of America"; the development of the notion of communitarianism in France is more related to the promotion of America as a scarecrow (i.e., something which is supposed to be frightening, but which, in fact, is not at all)—the counter-model for the French Republic—than to the fear of minority issues.

As Fassin has also noted, the concept of the communitarianist **peril** arose in France around 1989. The fall of the Berlin Wall was celebrated by those whose energies had been focused on fighting totalitarianism; at the same time, they suddenly found themselves deprived of their biggest opponent. The same year, there was a virulent debate in France over three female Islamic students who were suspended for not removing their head scarves; for those who agreed with the decision, a new adversary was created that was no longer Soviet totalitarianism: it was American-style multiculturalism and political correctness. Previously admired as a model of liberalism, America became the example pitted against the virtues of secularity and the "French model of republican integration." Within American university departments, political correctness became the target of a conservative offensive against the power held by minorities suspected of subscribing to the dangerous

"French way of thinking" (Derrida, Foucault, etc.). In the French context, the opposition to political correctness paved the way for attacks on minority advocacy groups, which were themselves accused of fomenting social war—between ethnicities, between genders, and between sexualities, all of which, it was said, was evidenced in an America torn apart by ghettoized communities. The accusation of communitarianism was first leveled at ethnic minorities, then was used against feminists, and finally against any gay or lesbian expression of community. On the other hand, the traditional communities—**family**, **class**, nation—were all spared.

The distinction between the public and the private is pivotal to this discussion. There was no question that all people have identities; one can be Basque or Muslim, Jewish or gay. However, those differences were believed to fall within the sphere of private matters. On the contrary, the public sphere, which includes citizenship, is characterized by its indifference to whether or not one is part of this or that group. The anti-communitarianist argument thus makes its claim to be part of the heritage of the Enlightenment and the French Revolution (contrary to the "organic" values of the Ancien Régime whereby the individual did not exist as such and owed his or her rights and obligations solely to being part of a hierarchy of communities). This argument affirms three rules: a universalist norm that postulates that minority rights should be limited to their equality to others; an integrationist principle that regards assimilation and emancipation as one and the same; and a vision of democracy that demands that communication between a nation and its citizens should not be hindered by any other mediation or minority interference. Mobilizations by minority communities thus contradict these rules, and do nothing but stir up trouble between individuals, groups, and cultures; in the specific case of gays and lesbians, anti-communitarians believed they had even less reason to mobilize, since the offense of homosexuality was abolished in 1982 (when the age of consent for homosexuals and heterosexuals was equalized; thus, gays and lesbians had all the rights they needed).

Discussion on the subject in France changed in 1998 and 1999 with the debates on PaCS (the Pacte civil de solidarité; Civil solidarity pact), which deigned to legally recognize domestic partnerships. Though it originated from minority demands, PaCS was designed for all types of couples, regardless of sexuality. Yet at the same time, the gay and lesbian demand for the right to marry and adopt children is based on the universalist principle of republican equality. Under such conditions, the validity of an anti-communitarianist notion—whose very touchstone is the denunciation of a political system dominated by lobbyists representing special interest groups—begins to fall apart. In fact, the specter of American communitarianism began to fade, only to be replaced by a new rhetoric which henceforth would be used to oppose gay and lesbian demands—that of a **symbolic order** guaranteed by a single difference, itself different from all the others: that of **gender**.

Nevertheless, anti-communitarianist sentiment in France enjoyed a resurgence, buoyed this time by the fledgling Fondation du 2 mars (March 2nd Foundation), a French think-tank. One of the foundation's members, *Le Figaro* editorialist Joseph Macé-Scaron, produced the most complete reformulation of this new wave of anti-communitarianism in a book succinctly entitled *La Tentation communautaire* (The communitarian temptation), its title modeled on a book by Jean-François Revel, *The Totalitarian Temptation*. Here again, communitarianism is cast as the main enemy, its gay and lesbian component being but one of its avatars. As before, the **universalist** and republican argument is invoked; however, it is developed around several themes, following a bombastic rhetoric whose polemical efficiency is such that it defies all attempts to find concrete answers to the questions it asks, at the risk of confusing the universal with the majority.

On *Ghettos*

A priori, the mere existence of a gay community, and its gathering places, will not bring society to ruin. Nonetheless, the development of such places and their concentration in certain neighborhoods tends to be the focus of criticism by anti-communitarianists: they consider such neighborhoods to signal the fragmentation of public spaces, usurped by special interest groups; the term "ghetto" when describing the gay community seems to be proof enough, a term used even by gays and lesbians themselves. The term is apt, though, provided one perceives the irony: it is a reminder that not all neighborhoods are safe for homosexuals who would prefer that a simple kiss on the month not become an unwitting act of heroism. Anti-.communitarians should have been comforted by the development of gay neighborhoods. After having long been banished to meeting places hidden from plain sight, the establishment of gay neighborhoods meant that homosexuals could finally be out in the open and interacting in public space. Those who claim to be offended by these neighborhoods are in fact merely frustrated at not being the sole owners of public places which, until then, seemed to be exclusively their own.

On Gay & Lesbian Studies

The same hostility manifested itself around the development of gay and lesbian studies. One is reminded of the sarcasms of Alain Finkielkraut and Frédéric Martel, when in June 1997, a conference on gay and lesbian culture was held at the Centre Pompidou in Paris, organized by Didier Eribon. As many American intellectuals participated, the specter of "minority studies" loomed over the French research. However, one has only to compare the amplitude of the American bibliography to the dearth of French works to get an inkling that something is not quite right. To work on gay and lesbian culture requires a methodology of specific questions based on (among others) historiographic study of subordinate classes or **privacy** issues, though it cannot be simplified to only these two subjects. It is arguable that Frédéric Martel's book *Le Rose et le noir* (*The Pink and the Black*), on the history of homosexuals in France since 1968, could have been more rigorous had the author availed himself of some of the methodological instruments used in America, found in books such as those by Lillian Faderman, John D'Emilio, Esther Newton, and George Chauncey. Anti-communitarianists prefer to shift the debate in a different direction, proposing that gay and lesbian studies are designed only for gays and lesbians, and that they present a risk that homosexuals will want to rewrite history filtered only through the lens of homosexuality. One hesitates even to respond to such absurd objections. Anti-communitarianists pretend to be surprised that gay and lesbian matters, for the most part, are brought up by gays and lesbians, as though the issues could be separated from the lifestyle. This shows a disquieting intellectual intolerance; gay and lesbian studies, like all minority studies, tackle norms and the notion of what is universal from their fringes. This should come as no surprise to those who believe that knowledge never comes without a shift in viewpoint; by those who believe that truth comes from the diverse objects of study; and by those who think that, above all, the purpose of science is not so much to reassure us of what we already know, but rather to shake up our complacent certainties.

On the Public & the Private

As has been noted elsewhere, anti-communitarianist discourse came to prominence in France during the height of the **AIDS** crisis. Logically, the recognition of the epidemic should have weakened certain principles on which anti-communitarianist rhetoric depended: the separation of the private from the public and the distinction between what is social and what is political. It is the nature of all matters of public health to tie together the experiences of the individual (the body, suffering, and death) with the concerns of the collective (prevention, research, and care). This was all the more clear in the case of AIDS: handling epidemics is the most directly political aspect of public health. Yet HIV is, for the most part, transmitted in the most private of ways: sexual intercourse. Within the context of AIDS, anti-communitarianism appears to be a denial of reality and its associated urgencies. The epidemic demanded that questions concerning sexuality, including homosexuality, be treated as political ones. Yet it was also necessary that communities and their networks serve as channels of communication between the state and individuals, a fact that required their institutionalization within the political realm. It is pointless to reiterate the details of the failures of the struggle against AIDS in France; the responsibility of the struggle fell almost solely on the homosexual community, which was long used to being failed by public authorities. Suffice it to say that for the most part the struggle against an epidemic hinges on cooperation between public institutions and the communities affected by it. It is telling that those parts of the population affected the most by AIDS are those whose community networks are the most fragile.

On the Specific & the Universal

However, there is more: the routes taken by the gay and lesbian community in the struggle against AIDS refute anti-communitarianists who might claim that such communities are structured to obtain special rights. Practically all of the associations formed to fight AIDS originated in the homosexual community. And all these organizations immediately opened their doors to put their knowledge and considerable efforts into the service of all populations affected by the epidemic—in other words, in service of the "common good." Thus, the struggle against AIDS was a reminder that it is not

necessary, in order to be a good citizen, to abandon one's own needs, and that in fact to fight for oneself is a struggle which is larger than any one individual. It shows how a community can take the understanding of its particular sufferings (such as AIDS, and the experience of being excluded) and elevate it from the level of an individual to the collective. In the end, the teaching of one community's struggles can help draw different aspects of the larger social realm together, and establish a political position that neither compartmentalizes individual identities, nor forces recognition of a single abstract citizenship. In short, it negates the need for having to choose between private identity and universal citizenship.

Indeed, it could even be said that political minorities are more republican than the republicans. The French republican ideal, in all its grandeur, consists of not recognizing differences in practices, beliefs, gender, skin color, or origin; this leads to **discrimination**. Thus, it is by virtue of this ideal and the most precious of its principles—equality—that a minority policy, careful to avoid discrimination, has been able to flourish: in law, because the Republic of France did not always recognize the equality of genders or sexual orientations; in practice, because the principle of republican universalism, in its abstraction, frequently permits discrimination (against gender, sexual preference, skin color, etc.) to quietly pass unnoticed. "We are the universalists," one could say, because we do not mistake the normal majority for the universal.

On *Lobbying*

Even though both the republican criticism of gay and lesbian lobbying and the fallacy of homosexual lobbying as imagined by the **far right** deal with very ambiguous concepts, it is prudent to distinguish between them. The latter refers to the belief that such lobbying consists of bed-hopping arrangements, favors, and assorted conspiracies. The former sees the issue as a matter of disturbing the workings of democracy, where minority mobilization disrupts the political balance by lobbying, to the detriment of the legitimate majority. Communitarianism then inevitably leads to a perversion of a system held hostage between various zones of influence.

However, such criticism of lobbying reveals an inability to envision political jockeying as anything other than as an unfair means of increasing representation or as a greedy quest for power. Minority movements never claim to try to become the majority, no more than they wish to seize power (which distinguishes them from the traditional idea of revolutionary movements); they are defined by their members whom they represent. It is this fact that Martel had a difficult time understanding when he claimed to have discovered a communitarian aporia in the description of the annual Lesbian and Gay Pride parade in Paris, when its organizers stated that it was their hope that "all gays and lesbians will trust them to collectively negotiate their recognition by the authorities." But the organizers were not usurping representation; they received their authorization from those who marched with them. And there was no real negotiation, because their goal was essentially to make political parties and those in power aware of issues that were critical to the gay and lesbian community. In this way, the organizers occupied a position unique to minority movements: neither internal, nor integrated into social democracy; nor external, nor utopist. Nor even a perversion of democracy, but rather an augmentation of its power.

On Victims

If its detractors can be believed, communitarianism assumes the political persona of the victim (i.e. weak), to the detriment of the persona of the citizen (i.e. strong), which, taken to its extreme, would lead to the stripping of all rights of citizens except for those who claim to be victims of the system or its driving principles. This type of argument is not always exempt, in its rhetoric or its examples, from sexist or homophobic slips, especially when it uses gender metaphors to explain itself: such as French essayist Philippe Muray, who often portrayed Gay Pride as the fable of an emasculated political system; or psychoanalyst Michel Schneider, in whose book *Big Mother: psychopathologie de la vie politique*, he observed the "maternal drift" of a state that has renounced its "masculine functions" in order to smother with love citizens shorn of their responsibilities.

It is true that minority movements often originate from external violence inflicted upon those individuals who make up the community: the politicization of minorities is the politics of adversity. That alone should be enough for its defense: there is no reason that a community should remain silent when it comes to the misfortune of its members. But it does not stop there. Pride (to use the most visible example) is nothing less than the protest of victims; a community's street festival is a political moment in spite of itself. Thus, commu-

nities are spaces of subjectification where those who cannot find a place for themselves within the normal majority can learn the practical application of democracy. With regard to the assimilationist rhetoric of the republicans, who cannot conceive of minorities as anything other than objects to emancipate, such individuals respond by posing as subjects for their emancipation.

On Identity

According to Macé-Scaron, the last word of the "communitarianist temptation" resides in the normative definition of minority identity: the idea that communities impose acceptable ways of living and existing on their members, and that they exert a paranoid level of control on how they are portrayed. Such analyses are often only partial, and one could just as easily speak of normative definitions of the extreme of heterosexual identities, too. However, with regard to the gay and lesbian community, the contrary should be noted in how it reacts and objects to clichés, stereotypes, and all manner of normalization; a critical task whose main goal is to initiate a debate on the power of the dominant culture and on the specter of available representation. Nonetheless, one would be hard-pressed to find a community that is capable of unanimously describing itself in a way that is both correct and fair. Instead of worrying about the norms that communities, supposedly, try to impose on their members, one should first recognize their diversity, starting with the depiction of gays and lesbians in the media, literature, and entertainment, which is crucial to community empowerment. In Hollywood **films** today, for example, there are no fewer backstabbing fags, foppish antiquarians, venomous lesbians, or good ol' trucker girls (to name just a few of the cinematic clichés from the last century) than there were in the past. At the same time, however, there has been an increase in other portrayals of homosexuals which, if not necessarily "positive," have at least gained in complexity.

In this context, the community does not impose a single way of being and identity so much as it offers a multiplicity of possible strategies. To someone used to being referred to as a "queer" or as a "lesbo," the options are no longer restricted to the invisibility of the **closet** or conformity to a socially accepted homosexual persona simply because it has been identified and represented (e.g., the village dandy, the sensitive hairstylist, the effeminate boy). It is within the parameters

of the community and the freedom of space it allows that members can learn to play among the identities available to him or her: the ability to play a role, drop it, and even make up new ones. It is significant that the concept of "queer," having taken on the challenge of the dismantling of established identities through their very dissemination, was not able to develop except within the confines of an established community. The anti-communitarianists are short-sighted: far from being the last word in minority policy, the community is first and foremost the necessary condition through which the freedom of minorities becomes possible.
—*Philippe Mangeot*

ACT UP-Paris. *Le Sida*. Paris: Ed. Dagorno, "Combien de divisions," 1994.

Chauncey, George. *Gay New York: Gender, Urban Culture and the Making of a Gay Male World, 1890–1940*. New York: Basic Books, 1994.

D'Emilio, John. *Sexual Politics, Sexual Communities: The Making of a Homosexual Minority in the United States, 1940–1970*. Chicago: Univ. of Chicago Press, 1983.

Delphy, Christine. "L'Humanitarisme républicain contre les mouvements homos," *Politique: La revue*, no.5 (1997).

Eribon, Didier. *Réflexions sur la question gay*. Paris: Fayard, "Histoire de la pensée," 1999. [Published in the US as *Insult and the Making of the Gay Self*. Durham, NC: Duke University Press, 2004.]

———. *Papiers d'identité: Interventions sur la question gay*. Paris: Fayard, 2000.

Fassin, Eric. "Notre oncle d'Amérique," *Vacarme*, no.12 (2000).

———. "L'Epouvantail américain: penser la discrimination française," *Vacarme*, nos. 4–5 (1997).

Finkielkraut, Alain. "Chroniques hebdomadaires," *France Culture*.

Levine Martin P. "Gay Ghetto," *Journal of Homosexuality*, no.4 (1979).

Julliard, Jacques. "Chroniques hebdomadaires," *Le Nouvel Observateur*.

Lévy, Elisabeth. *Les Maîtres censeurs*. Paris: Jean-Claude Lattès, 2002.

Macé-Scaron, Joseph. *La Tentation communautaire*. Paris: Plon, 2001.

Mangeot, Philippe. "Bonnes Conduites? Petite histoire du 'politiquement correct'," *Vacarme*, nos. 1–2 (1997).

Martel, Frédéric. *Le Rose et le noir. Les homosexuels en France depuis 1968*. Paris: Le Seuil, 1996. [Published in the US as *The Pink and The Black: Homosexuals in France since 1968*.

Stanford, CA: Stanford Univ. Press, 1999.]

Muray Philippe. *Chers Djihadistes*. Paris: Mille et une Nuits, "Fondation du 2 mars," 2002.

———. *On ferme*. Paris: Les Belles Lettres, 1997.

Newton, Esther. *Cherry Grove, Fire Island: Sixty Years in America's First Gay and Lesbian Town*. Boston: Beacon Press, 1993.

Pollak, Michael. "L'Homosexualité masculine, ou: le bonheur dans le ghetto?" *Communications*, no. 35 (1982). New edition in *Sexualités occidentales*. Edited by Philippe Ariès and André Béjin. Paris: Le Seuil, 1984. [Published in the US as *Western Sexuality: Practice and Precept in Past and Present Times*. New York: Blackwell, 1985.]

———. "Homosexualité et le sida." In *Une identité blessée*. Paris: Ed. Métailié, 1993.

Schneider, Michel. *Big Mother: psychopathologie de la vie politique*. Paris: Odile Jacob, 2002.

Taguieff, Pierre-André. *Résister au bougisme. Démocratie forte contre mondialisation techno-marchande*. Paris: Mille et une Nuits, "Fondation du 2 mars," 2002.

—*AIDS; Associations; Gender Differences; Ghetto; Heterophobia; Lobby; North America; Peril; Privacy; Rhetoric; Symbolic Order; Universalism/Differentialism.*

CONSTRUCTIONISM. *See* Essentialism

CONTAGION

The concept of homosexuality as a contagion, one of many strains of homophobia derived from **medicine**, is nonetheless deeply rooted in the religious concept of evil. At its origin is the notion that Satan tries to lead men into **sin** with fairly successful results (e.g., sins of the flesh, the forbidden fruit). Evil is thus something that is not innate but rather imposed on the subject, who is an unwitting victim. In the same cultural context, homosexuality becomes a sort of contagious moral disease; such was the point of view of theologian Albert the Great in the thirteenth century: "It is a contagious disease that spreads from one person to another," to which the wealthy are most at risk. No doubt this was also the thinking of King Louis XIV of France when he expelled a number of notorious sodomites from the court, whose influence on one of his sons (the Count of Vermandois) he had begun to fear.

The medical community returned to the theme

of contagion in the nineteenth century. In his *Etude médico-légale sur les attentats aux mœurs* (Medical-legal studies of assaults against decency), published in 1857, Auguste Ambroise Tardieu, president of the French Academy of Medicine, dusts off some old metaphysical prejudices against homosexuals and couches them in pseudoscientific positivist terms, claiming that the true pederasts (the inverted) are few in number, but go about "recruiting" "aunties" (the perverted). Most doctors and psychiatrists lapped up this theory, and by the end of the nineteenth century a clear concept of the homosexual predator who pounces on his unsuspecting prey had developed. This was clearly the perspective of those who prosecuted Oscar **Wilde** on charges of gross indecency in 1895: one accused the writer of "being the center of a circle that systematically corrupted young men," and the Crown prosecutor spoke of "a moral infection threatening society … that would not fail, given enough time, to corrupt and affect it in its entirety." Here, it could be seen that the theme had evolved to take into consideration Louis Pasteur's recent advances in science: the homosexual was now a microbe seeking to undermine and corrupt healthy organisms. In short, what was once a minority sexual taste became a mental illness, then a social pathology capable of transforming itself into a pandemic. For this reason, up until the 1960s, sexologists and educators were obsessed with the danger of homosexual contagion. In 1895, Dr Garnier wrote in *Epuisement nerveux et génital* (Nervous and genital exhaustion): "An important point that must be kept in mind with regard to sexual psychopaths is that they should never be permitted to visit well-frequented social locations where they risk encountering those intent on finding recruits." The German educator Heinrich Többen, in his *Die Jugendverwahrlosung und ihre Bekämpfung* (The depravities of youth and how to combat them), published in 1922, stressed that the fashionable doctrines "carry with them the danger of homosexual poisoning, that is, the premeditated perversion of our youth." In 1930, the French moralist Théodore de Félice wrote, in *Le Protestantisme et la question sexuelle* (Protestantism and the sexual question): "The aversion of homosexuals to members of the opposite sex classifies them neatly among the sick, and among the dangerous sick, as they are always on the hunt for new partners to render abnormal in turn."

For this reason, as permitted by law, judges were particularly severe in cases involving the "corruption of a minor," such as when the accused was a boy's first sexual partner, even when the latter is consenting. In France, the hardening of anti-homosexual laws from 1942 to 1960 was based on the notion that homosexuals were sick individuals contaminating youth (in particular, according to Quentin Crisp, homosexuality was "thought to be of Greek origin, less widespread than socialism, but more dangerous, especially for children"). And while Sigmund Freud put an end to the opposition between the inverted and the perverted, he maintained that there were differing gradations of inverts, defining three: "absolute invert," "contingent invert," and "amphigenetic invert," or bisexual. As for later, a certain number of psychoanalysts, especially American ones, maintained the vocabulary of **perversion** and contamination well after homosexuality was officially struck from the list of metal illnesses in 1973.

The myth of "recruitment" or "conversion" supposedly carried out by the inverted has proven persistent. Behind this myth is a popular fantastical rationalization: unable to reproduce, homosexuals must seduce and thus convert innocent victims in a perverted attempt at propagation. This dramatic interpretation of sexual identity is at the heart of persistent suspicions of homosexual teachers (the idea of recruitment, especially). Homophobia evident in youth movements (in 1990, the Boy Scouts of America no longer allowed open homosexuals to be troop leaders) and the military (until recently, admitting gays into the **army** was likened to leaving the door open to general contamination) can be explained in the same way. It also explains the frenzy of right-wing organizations such as France's Avenir de la culture (Future of the Culture) against the increased visibility of gays and lesbians in the media: according to the homophobic Christian right, the more attention homosexuals receive, the more they are able to recruit others to their "lifestyle." Even **AIDS** (which many homophobes originally saw as a blessing) has begun to appall them, in that it is now viewed as making homosexuality appear commonplace in the media.

But where one sees contamination, one also sees the possibility of a cure. For years, many doctors and psychiatrists have claimed that it is possible to bring those who "stray" back to the straight path, and all sorts of remedies to this effect have been proposed (behavioral, psychological, and biomedical) to counter the effect of "perverse" habits. This illusion is perpetuated by militant members of far right groups such as the Moral Majority Coalition and the Christian Coalition in the

United States, which strive to fight against "gay pro-paganda" (or "gay ideology," as pronounced by Pope John Paul II). There are many examples of campaigns of reparative therapy, in which homosexuals can be "cured," launched during the 1990s within prayer groups known as **ex-gay** ministries. But this therapy has had limited success, as noted by one "ex-ex-gay" humorously: "You pick a prayer partner the first evening, you pray with him the second evening, and on the third evening, your prayers are answered."

This leads us back to dealing with the contagion and the drive to isolate and neutralize the contaminating agents, the origin of the sickness. First of all, there is the need to identify the various absolute inverts, pederasts, and predators; hence the extreme efforts made to apply an external characterology to homosexuals. The effeminate homosexual is the most reassuring, being easily identifiable. However, homosexuals who are indistinguishable from heterosexuals—the Cary Grants, Jean Marais, Dirk Bogardes, or Rock Hudsons—have always posed a far more troubling problem to doctors. Once identified, the converted pederast can be set apart. It was in the Nazi concentration camps where the fallacy of quarantine was promoted the furthest. The Nazis were obsessed with the danger posed by absolute inverts to the German population: their perverted actions were believed to contaminate adolescents, especially the most handsome (that is to say, the superior racial stock that was most vital for future supermen). Thus, the Nazis made a distinction between "genetic homosexuals" (who were deported and sentenced to hard labor, sometimes forced to undergo medical experiments and castration, and often murdered), and "situational homosexuals," who were treated with more indulgence, in hopes of setting them back onto the right path.

—*Pierre Albertini*

Bayer, Ronald. *Homosexuality and American Psychiatry: The Politics of Diagnosis.* Princeton: Princeton Univ. Press, 1987.

Foucault, Michel. *Les Anormaux, cours au Collège de France.* Paris: Gallimard, Le Seuil, 1999. [Published in the US as *Abnormal: Lectures at the Collège de France, 1974–1975.* New York: Picador, 2003.]

Grau, Günther. *Hidden Holocaust: Gay and Lesbian Persecution in Germany, 1933–1945.* London: Cassell, 1995.

Herman, Didi. *The Antigay Agenda.* Chicago/London: Univ. of Chicago Press, 1997.

Himmler, Heinrich. *Discours secrets.* Paris: Gallimard, 1978.

Krinsky, Charles. "Recruitment Myth." In *Gay Histories and Cultures.* Edited by George E. Haggerty. New York/London: Garland, 2000.

—*Armed Forces; Debauchery; Decadence; Degeneracy; Ex-Gay; Medicine; Peril; Proselytism; School; Sterility; Theology; Treatment.*

CRIMINAL

In the past, homosexuals almost everywhere were considered criminals, in the real sense of the word; in many countries, they still are. Even though France decriminalized homosexual acts between consenting adults in 1791, and though their example was followed by many nations (such as the Netherlands, who brought their criminal code into alignment with that of the French in 1810), homosexuals in other European or Commonwealth countries had to wait for over a century for **decriminalization** (Poland in 1932, England in 1967, Canada in 1969, etc.). Today, many countries across the world still have laws condemning sodomy and homosexuality.

Nevertheless, even in those places where homosexuals were not criminals in the eyes of the law, homosexuality was often perceived as a defect and a social transgression. Consequently, the confusion between criminal and homosexual was commonplace, as both defied the norms of good behavior, rubbing elbows together during their nightly adventures (if the homophobic talk was to be believed), and thus were perceived as a threat to the establishment. As French policeman François Carlier noted in 1887, "[Homosexual] passion leads to, in the social sense, the most monstrous of partnerships. The master with his servant, the thief with the man with no criminal record, the cad in rags with the dandy—all accept the other as though they were part of the same class of society." In this same vein, writer Ali Coffignon wrote in 1890: "The millionaire and the tramp fraternize; the official and the ex-convict exchange their ignoble caresses."

The first French "experts" to write about homosexuality in the nineteenth century—at that time, one would call it "pederasty"—were most often medical examiners (Auguste Ambroise Tardieu, for example, author of *Etudes medico-légale sur les attentats aux mœurs* [Medical-legal studies of assaults against decency],

1857) or policemen (such as François Carlier, author of *Les Deux prostitutions* [The two prostitutions], 1887). They tended to link crime to homosexuality, even holding the victim of a crime (theft, murder, blackmail) as being responsible for his situation by simple fact of his homosexuality. To this effect, Tardieu quoted a magistrate who in 1845 stated during the trial of twenty people accused of blackmailing Parisian homosexuals (known as the Rue de Rampart affair): "It can be said that in Paris, pederasty is the school in which the most capable and most audacious criminals are educated." Without showing any sympathy for gay victims of crime, Tardieu went on to explain that "these shameful habits [homosexuality] have become a means and a particular technique of theft, for the purpose of which guilty associations have been formed," and that "under graver circumstances, pederasty has served as the pretext, and in some ways the catalyst, for murder." As for Carlier, he stated that "Pederasty is peculiar in that it excites the appetites of all wrongdoers. You could say that it is a provocation for crime." He followed this with: "The ease with which pederasts spill blood is truly frightening; these people who are so timid, so pusillanimous, so soft in ordinary life, can all of a sudden take on a cruelty to rival that of the most hardened wrongdoers."

Italian Cesare Lombroso (1835–1909), one of the founders of scientific criminology and author of *Criminal Man* (1876; English translation published 1911) and *Crime, Its Causes and Remedies* (1899; English translation published 1911), believed that crime was for the most part hereditary, and that the **psychology** and even the physical appearance (e.g., the shape of the head) of born criminals differed from that of others. Lombroso further suggested that criminals are subject to primitive and "atavistic" passions and to an "abnormal sexual appetite" (i.e. homosexual desire). Lombroso's ideas were very influential. Their echoes can be heard in a French psychologist known simply as Dr Bérillon, who declared in the journal *L'Eclair* in 1908, concerning a homosexual charged with murder, that "a man with errant tastes is more inclined toward crime than another." Further, he added: "There are individuals who only have the appearance of being men. You have everything to fear from them."

Bérillon was speaking here of hotel manager Pierre Renard, a homosexual accused of having murdered his employer in June 1908 in his hotel on Rue de la Pépinière in Paris. During the trial, the prosecutor asked the jury, "There is no … material proof against Renard, but is it even necessary?" In effect, Renard's homosexuality was the more serious charge laid against him during the trial, and it was enough to sentence him, in February 1909, to a life sentence of forced labor. According to the newspaper *Le Matin*, inclined to believe that Renard was innocent, "the prosecution's argument, in short, went like this: it started with homosexuality, and finished with the crime." The newspaper article was a succinct summary of the homophobic attitudes of the era, which too often confused homosexuality with crime, and which André **Gide** would denounce, thinking specifically of Renard, in his book *Corydon*.

This sort of homophobia would persist for decades in France within the **police** force and the justice system. This was why, in 1958, the director of criminal investigation for the Paris police gave a speech in which he described the homosexual milieu as "an environment that favored delinquency," and as "a breeding ground where criminal viruses are spawned"; he also warned the public against taking part in "those dangers that could lead to activities that promote homosexuality" (e.g., theft, prostitution, murder). The sensational French press, too, did their part to maintain these homophobic sentiments. Here are two examples out of many: on January 10, 1935, *Détective* magazine published an article on the death of a young pastry cook, found strangled in his apartment on Rue Tournefort in Paris, in which the police inspector sighed, "Another story of 'aunties'." The magazine also explained to its readers the difficulties of a police investigation in such an environment: "Crimes of loners, and of homosexuals, are the very soul of the secret crime." And, after the murder of an antiquarian in Cannes by an old lover in 1947, *Police-Hebdo* on October 21, 1947, published his photograph on the cover with the eye-catching caption: "This man was killed by his own habits."

This homophobic attitude can also be found in popular culture, especially cinema and literature. In 1981, Vito Russo published *The Celluloid Closet*, a study of homophobia in Hollywood films, in which he identified two contrasting stereotypes of homosexuals: the sissy (the effeminate and ridiculous dandy) and the criminal (the devious and dangerous pederast, or the murderous lesbian). Alfred Hitchcock's films are particularly good examples, such as *Rebecca* (1940), in which the sinister Mrs Danvers, who was fiercely in love with her employer's first wife, threatens the happiness (and life?)

of the second; or *Rope* (1948), in which two young lovers kill a college classmate for the simple pleasure of killing, but also to prove their intellectual superiority over normal people. The controversy brought about by William Friedkin's controversial film *Cruising* (1980) should also be mentioned, given that it mobilized the gay community in the United States: a police officer investigating a series of murders in a gay neighborhood ends up falling victim himself to homosexual and murderous impulses, as if homosexuality and criminality were contagious and somehow connected.

On the other hand, literary representations of what French writer and queer theorist Guy Hocquenghem called *homosexualité noire*, or "dark homosexuality"—because it was nocturnal, dangerous, sometimes violent, and even criminal—were often written by homosexuals themselves, who sometimes basked in a state of marginality and lawlessness. Jean Genet is perhaps the best example of this, although as French philosopher Didier Eribon has shown, "the great theme of similarity between homosexuals and criminals" can be found in many other homosexual writers, such as Oscar **Wilde**, Marcel Proust, Marcel Jouhandeau, and Julien Green.

Thanks to the social evolution of the gay and lesbian lifestyle since the 1960s (which put an end to secrecy and initiated the phenomenon of "coming out"), as well as the development of a militant activist movement and in particular the slow but steady improvement in public attitudes toward homosexuals over the past two or three decades (at least in the West), the perception of homosexuals as criminals has finally started to disappear. That said, less than ten years ago, a police commissioner from the 3rd arrondissement in Paris actually told the author of this essay: "You have to admit that there are still a lot of criminals in the homo environment."

—*Michael Sibalis*

Amnesty International. *Breaking the Silence: Human Rights Violations Based on Sexual Orientation*. London: Amnesty, 1997.

Buhrke, Robin A. *Matter of Justice: Lesbian and Gay Men in Law Enforcement*. New York/London: Routledge, 1996.

Carlier, François. *Etudes de pathologie sociale: Les Deux prostitutions*. Paris: E. Dentu, 1887.

Eribon, Didier. *Une morale du minoritaire: Variations sur un thème de Jean Genet*. Paris: Fayard, 2001.

Fernet, Max. "L'Homosexualité et son influence sur la délinquance," *Revue internationale de police criminelle* (1959).

Guérin, Daniel. *Shakespeare et Gide en correctionnelle*. Paris: Edition du Scorpion, 1959.

Gury, Christian. *L'Honneur perdu d'un politicien homosexuel en 1876*. Paris: Kimé 1999.

———. *L'Honneur perdu d'un capitaine homosexuel en 1880*. Paris: Kimé, 1999.

Hahn, Pierre. *Nos ancêtres les pervers*. Paris: Olivier Urban, 1979.

Peniston, William A. "Love and Death in Gay Paris: Homosexuality and Criminality in the 1870s." In *Homosexuality in Modem France*. Edited by Jeffrey Merrick and Bryant T. Ragan Jr. Oxford: Oxford Univ. Press, 1996.

Rey, Michel. "Police et sodomie à Paris au XVIIIe siècle," *Revue d'histoire moderne contemporaine*. (1982).

Russo, Vito. *The Celluloid Closet: Homosexuality in the Movies*. New York: Harper & Row, 1981.

—*Cinema; Criminalization; Decriminalization; Deportation; Devlin, Patrick; European Law; Gulag; Jurisprudence; Literature; McCarthy, Joseph; Media; Medicine, Legal; Peril; Police; Prison; Proselytism; Scandal; Treason; Vice.*

CRIMINALIZATION

In 1994, the United Nations Human Rights Committee declared that outlawing sexual relations between people of the same sex was an infringement on the right to **privacy**. Nevertheless, still today, many countries around the world actively repress homosexuality; in 2007, according to the International Gay and Lesbian Human Rights Commission, there were eighty-five countries that have laws that discriminate against homosexuals, with penalties ranging from, in the best of cases, the age of consent being set later than for heterosexual relations, to, in the worst of cases, long **prison** sentences, torture, physical punishment, and even execution.

At the time of this writing, nine states (Afghanistan, Chechnya, Iran, Mauritania, Pakistan, Saudi Arabia, Sudan, the United Arab Emirates, and Yemen; as well as some parts of Nigeria and Somalia) punish "homosexual acts" by death. In other countries, the threat of arbitrary arrest, police brutality, expedited trials, and imprisonment are a daily reality for many gays and lesbians, especially those who are active in fighting for their rights as homosexuals. Moreover, in certain countries where the law does not specifically name homosexuality as a crime, other, more generalized infractions (indecency, sexual molestation, public **scandal**, crimes against the **family**, **unnatural** acts, etc.) are invoked in order to take legal action. For example, in Egypt in 2001, fifty-two men were arrested and tried for an "offense to morality and to public sensitivity" when in fact they were being reproached for being homosexual.

The penalty inflicted can be particularly violent: in **India**, for example, homosexual crimes are considered "carnal intercourse against the order of nature" and sexual relations between men can be punishable by ten years to life imprisonment. In Iran and Chechnya, convicted gay men or lesbians are whipped and stoned; in Pakistan, the law allows for life imprisonment and a punishment of 100 lashes of the whip. Elsewhere, gays and lesbians can be sentenced to prison for anywhere from one month to twenty-five years.

The criminalization of homosexuality today is mostly limited to countries in the **Middle East** or Africa. There is a general tendency in the West toward the elimination of discrimination against homosexuality or differences with regard to the age of consent. Membership in the European Union requires the repeal of anti-homosexuality legislation. Therefore, no European countries have laws against homosexuality, except the Turkish Republic of Northern Cyprus, a de facto independent republic that has received diplomatic recognition only from Turkey. However, there are still a few European states that maintain a higher age of consent for homosexuals (Gilbraltor, Greece, and the Bailiwick of Guernsey, including Alderney, Herm, and Sark).

The persistence of homosexual repression in certain countries, however, appears to correlate to their autocratic and/or religious tendencies. The most explicit and harshest sentences for the crime of homosexuality are imposed by Muslim countries that invoke *sharia* (Muslim law) (such as Afghanistan, Iran, Kuwait, Mauritania, Qatar, Saudi Arabia, Sudan, and Yemen). Additionally, until such state laws were overturned by the US Supreme Court in 2003, fully one-third of the states in the US condemned the act of sodomy on the same terms as in Leviticus in the Bible, i.e. as an "act against nature"; under the uniform code of military justice, sodomy is illegal for members of the United States Armed Forces. However, given that the United States is fully democratic, this long-lived legal stigmatization can only be explained by these states' reliance on an outdated moral code based on a strong religious tradition.

In 2006, the IDAHO Committee (the NGO coordinating the International Day Against Homophobia) launched a petition calling for the universal decriminalization of homosexuality, which was supported by many significant persons, including several Nobel Prize winners, prominent intellectuals, artists, and entertainers, and political leaders. On May 17, 2008, as requested by Louis-Georges Tin, the founder of IDAHO, French Secretary of State for Human Rights Rama Yade announced that France would bring forth a declaration to the United Nations for the universal decriminalization of homosexuality.

—*Arsenal Pulp Press*
[Based on the original essay by Daniel Borrillo and Thomas Formond.]

Amnesty International. "Breaking the Silence: Human Rights Violation Based on Sexual Orientation." Report. Amnesty International, 1998.

———. "Identité sexuelle et persecutions." Les Editions francophones d'Amnesty International, 2001.

Assemblée parlementaire du Conseil de l'Europe. "Situation des lesbiennes et des gays dans les Etats membres du Conseil de l'Europe." Report (document 8755) http:// stars.coe.fr/doc/doc00/fdoc8755.htm (accessed June 6, 2000).

Buhrke, Robin A. *Matter of Justice: Lesbian and Gay Men in Law Enforcement.* New York/London: Routledge, 1996.

International Gay and Lesbian Human Rights Commission: http://www.iglhrc.org (accessed January 4, 2008).

International Lesbian and Gay Association: http://www.ilga .org (accessed January 4, 2008).

—*Decriminalization; Discrimination; Devlin, Patrick; European Law; Jurisprudence; Privacy; Utilitarianism; Violence.*

CUSTINE, Astolphe de

Astolphe, Marquis de Custine (1790–1857), was at the origin of a great homosexual **scandal** that took place in France in the nineteenth century. Born into the French nobility, his family's privileges ended when both his father and grandfather were guillotined for sympathizing with the monarchy during the French Revolution. Raised by his mother Delphine (who was the writer Chateaubriand's mistress), Custine knew from a very early age that he was attracted to boys. In order to ensure her son's financial independence, Mme de Custine embarked on a plan to get him married, and found a girl for him named Claire de Duras. Astolphe asked for Claire's hand in marriage but the engagement broke up in 1818, stirring up the first wave of nasty rumors (it was claimed that the German naturalist Alexander de Humboldt had proven to the girl that Custine had the handwriting of an invert). This did not prevent him from marrying a wealthy orphan of the upper class, Léontine de St-Simon Courtemer, in 1821; a year later, she gave birth to his son. The same year, 1822, he traveled without his wife to England and Scotland, after having met Edward St-Barbe (a gentleman who would change his name to Edouard de Ste-Barbe), who became Custine's "close friend" (he later lived with the Marquis and stayed faithful to him until his death). Their meeting and the premature death of Léontine in 1823 had the effect of intensifying the sexual needs of Custine, who started chasing after handsome soldiers.

The scandal in question broke out on October 28, 1824. On his way to a rendezvous at St-Denis with a young gunner, Custine was ambushed. In the stables of an inn, he was attacked by three of the gunner's comrades-in-arms, who decided to teach him a lesson: they stripped off his clothes, beat him to a pulp, and left him bleeding and naked on the side of the road. Custine's friends tried to make it out as a vicious, unprovoked attack, but the truth spread quickly. The new king, pious Charles X, had no pity for Custine. The minister of the **police** informed Custine that he could not file charges against his attackers. The following day, he was refused entry into the society clubs of St-Germain: he was now nothing more than a fallen nobleman, whose reputation would remain scandalous until the day he died.

In 1824, Anne-Sophie ("Madame") Swetchine wrote: "Never have I seen such a widespread outburst, an indignation more lively and venomous; all of society is enraged, as though it were a personal betrayal. He has to account mostly for the esteem in which he used to be held." According to another, "Custine has fallen right to the bottom, from where he will never be able to lift himself up." Custine spent the next years writing poetry and novels, and eventually became enamored with travel writing. But twenty years later, a witness to all that had transpired remarked: "Everyone read him, savored him, but no one held him in any esteem." And in 1848, the publisher of the *Revue des Deux Mondes* received many letters demanding that the magazine be closed to "the friends of M. de Custine." Those rare few who remained in touch with him shied away from shaking his hand, as though even his body were sullied. Even the most benevolent of people, such as Philarète Chasles, the French man of letters, saw his habits as a sign of biological extenuation, a symptom of the end of the human race. As for Ste-Barbe, in his obituary, a magistrate described him as a paragon of all **vices**: "He had, beneath his handsome appearance, something even more monstrous than his infamous habits: he reeked of murder."

The Custine affair clearly illustrates the magnitude of aristocratic homophobia in nineteenth-century France, and represented the culmination of several lines of thought. First, it marked a return to Christian tradition, as the nobility turned again to Catholicism after the French Revolution and wished to cut itself away from the libertinism of the previous centuries. Add to this the mystique of family lineage and the desire to be part of an unbroken chain, for which heterosexuality and **marriage** are prerequisites. Finally, there is the code of honor that attributes a large importance to virility, associated in a quasi-etymological way to the virtues of the group, the nobility standing as a confirmation of natural character and the stark opposition of sexual roles. As such, the "inverted" were constantly sneered at in society clubs (Custine, who was not particularly effeminate, was still often referred to as "Madame, the Marquise de Custine"). The Custine affair also serves to show how the disgrace of such a scandal was shared by the entire family: in the weeks that followed, fingers were pointed at Custine's relatives as well.

Following the scandal, Custine retired to his estate. The social death to which he was condemned was also a sort of liberation: he no longer had to wear a mask. After losing his son and his mother, he traveled with Ste-Barbe (to Italy, England, Switzerland, Germany, and Spain), and began his writing career (in addition to poetry and novels, he also wrote a play, *Beatrix Cenci,* which was performed without success in 1832). A novel, *Aloys,* was published anonymously in 1829; strongly autobiographical, it tells the story of a young man (who confides, "No matter the condition under which Heaven had called me, I was certain to ruin it") and his failed attempt to marry: after his betrothal to the daughter of his lover, he is revealed to be an invert through his handwriting and ends up joining the clergy. Returning to Paris in the early 1830s, Custine and Ste-Barbe, still frozen out of aristocratic society, befriended many writers who possessed a more open spirit (such as Hugo, Balzac, Nodier, and Stendhal), and whom the Marquis was able to charm with his art for conversation and sumptuous dinners. In 1835, however, Custine fell in love with a dashing young Polish man, Ignatius Gurowski, who moved in with the Marquis and Ste-Barbe. But when Russia demanded Gurowski's return to Poland, Custine traveled for two months to St Petersburg and Moscow in order to obtain a pardon from Tsar Nicholas I. He failed to get the pardon, but he did accumulate enough material to write his most famous work, *La Russie en 1839* (Russia in 1839), published in 1843.

In 1841, the bored Gurowski left to secretly marry a young Spanish girl, which finally earned him expulsion from France. Gurowski's departure was a terrible shock for Custine, and marked the beginning of his old age. He traveled some more, yet was bored, despite the relative fame afforded to him by his book on Russia. He died in 1857, whereupon the faithful Ste-Barbe inherited most of his considerable fortune. Custine's cousins launched an appeal, requesting that the civil court nullify the inheritance on account of coercion "achieved through perseverance and by the most damnable means." The request was rejected in July 1858, then again on appeal, in December of the same year. The French judicial system of the nineteenth century may have certainly been homophobic, but there was nothing it could do about a properly prepared will and testament.

—*Pierre Albertini*

Luppe, Marquis de. *Astolphe de Custine*. Monaco: Le Rocher, 1957.

Muhlstein, Anka. *Astolphe de Custine, le dernier marquis*. Paris: Grasset, 1996.

—*France; Police; Scandal; Violence.*

D

DAMIEN, Peter

Born in 1007 in Italy, Peter Damien was one of the most influential figures of the Catholic Church during the eleventh century, especially during the reign of Pope Leo IX. Damien was a monk, cleric, bishop, and cardinal who played an important role in the reform of the Church during the second half of the eleventh century. He is perhaps best known for his role in the Investiture Controversy, a significant crisis of power between the papacy and the Empire, in which Damien had defended the right of secular officials to choose and consecrate bishops.

But Damien was also the author of a little book written in Latin, entitled *Liber Gomorrhianus* (*Book of Gomorrah*). Written between 1048 and 1054, it was addressed directly to Pope Leo IX, but also to those he accused of sin. He began his argument by identifying the four categories of sexual sins that were "**against nature**": those who sin alone, those who practice mutual masturbation, those who practice copulation between the thighs, and those who "commit the complete act against nature," that is, anal penetration. According to Damien, these are the "four practices that stem from … a sodomite impurity, like a poisoned root."

Damien goes on to explain that those who are guilty of these acts should not be welcomed into the clergy, and those already in the clergy who are guilty of these acts should be removed from office. He was particularly concerned about men who confess to those clergy with whom they had committed these sins, such that "those at fault become the judges." And while Damien would state elsewhere that a bishop guilty of simony (the crime of paying for ecclesiastical positions, a significant problem between the tenth and fifteenth centuries) should nonetheless retain his title, he affirmed that a man of the Church who practiced sodomy was

sinning against nature and as a result, was unable to fulfill his ecclesiastical function: "No sacred offertory that has been sullied by crimes of impurity may be received by God."

The language Damien used was particularly severe: "Truly, there is no way to compare this **vice** to any other vice, because it surpasses the scope of all vices. In effect, this vice means the death of the body, and the destruction of the soul. It pollutes the flesh; it extinguishes the light of the spirit, it opens the door to Hell, and closes the gates of Heaven…. This vice can tumble men from the heart of the ecclesiastical community, and forces them to pray alongside the possessed and those who work for the Devil." Further, after examining the penitentials written by his predecessors, Damien condemned them for being too lenient on homosexual practices. To Damien, the only way to fight this form of hedonism was to meditate upon the reward brought about by chastity, i.e. Heaven.

At first glance, Damien's treatise seems to be quite conventional. The ideas that it conveys are familiar enough: the description of homosexuality as an act against nature, its connection with the Biblical events of **Sodom and Gomorrah**, and the fear of sexual relations between clergy and those whom they guide. However, the ideology as presented in this opuscule was something that was completely new. Naturally, there were interdictions against homosexual practices during the first millennium of the Christian era, but these were not very rigorous, and in most parts of Europe homosexual acts were in fact tolerated, permitted, and sometimes even acceptable. Prior to this treatise, there was no clear definition of "sodomy," and this work is one of the earliest in which sodomy was so clearly associated with (or rather against) nature.

Under these conditions, Peter Damien's ideas were

considered particularly radical at the time they were published, and as historian John Boswell has indicated, "Peter did not succeed in convincing anyone that the problem of homosexuality required such severe attention." In a letter to Damien, the Pope thanked him for having written the treatise, but informed him that it would not be possible to remove clergy from office except for those who had been committing these acts for a long period (or alternatively, with many men for a shorter period), or those who had "sunk to the level of engaging in anal practices." The Pope recognized that these acts constituted a sin, but he did not treat them as severely as Damien had demanded.

Nevertheless, the *Liber Gomorrhianus* found its audience during the next century. Damien's extraordinarily severe **rhetoric** concerning sodomy was codified by the for the first time in 1179, during the Third Lateran Council, in the following way: "Let all who are found guilty of that unnatural vice for which the wrath of God came down upon the sons of disobedience and destroyed the five cities with fire; if they are clerics, they are to be expelled from the clergy or confined in monasteries to do penance; if they are laymen, they are to incur excommunication and be completely separated from the society of the faithful." The religious sensitivity of the era, having already introduced many oppressive measures against other groups (such as Jews, heretics, and lepers), used the ideology developed by Damien a century before to justify its own attitude toward homosexuality, an attitude whose effects are still felt today.

—*Adam Weiss*

Liber Gommorhianus, Patrologia, Series Latina [ed. Migne]. Paris: Garnier Frères, 1844. [Published in Canada as *Book of Gomorrah: An Eleventh Century Treatise Against Clerical Homosexual Practices.* Translation with an introduction and notes by Pierre J. Payer. Waterloo, ON: Wilfrid Laurier Univ. Press, 1982.]

Boswell, John. *Christianisme, tolérance sociale et homosexualité.* Paris: Gallimard, 1985. [Published in the US as *Christianity, Social Tolerance, and Homosexuality: Gay People in Western Europe from the Beginning of the Christian Era to the Fourteenth Century.* Chicago: Univ. of Chicago Press, 1980.]

Jordan, Mark. *The Invention of Sodomy in Christian Theology.* Chicago: Univ. of Chicago Press, 1997.

Leclerq, Jean. *Saint Pierre Damien, ermite et homme de l'Eglise.* Rome: Edizioni di storia e letteratura, 1960.

Tierney, Brian. *The Crisis of Church and State.* Toronto: Univ. of Toronto Press, 1988.

—*Against Nature; Bible, the; Catholic Church, the; Heresy; Inquisition; Paul (of Tarsus); Sodom and Gomorrah; Theology; Vice.*

DANCE

In a scene from the 2000 British film *Billy Elliot*, the young twelve-year-old protagonist, an aspiring dancer, argues with his father, who had caught the boy taking a classical dance lesson instead of the boxing lessons in which he had been enrolled:

> What's wrong with ballet?
> What's "wrong" with ballet?
> It's perfectly normal.
> "Perfectly normal"?
> I used to go to ballet.
> See? Aye, for your nanna. For girls, not for lads, Billy. Lads do football, or … boxing, or … wrestling. Not frigging ballet.

Among homosexual stereotypes in the public imagination, the dancer has a prime spot alongside the hairdresser, antiquarian, and decorator. The reaction by Billy's father to his son's proclivity is emblematic of strict, old-fashioned beliefs in the gender divide (boys should play team **sports** such as soccer or baseball, or violent ones like boxing, while girls should engage in activities that are more feminine such as sewing or dancing), which includes the assumption that males who engage in classical dance are homosexual. It is not so much the idea in itself that his son wants "to be a dancer" that repulses Billy's father, it is the image of seeing him become a ballet dancer.

This homophobic image of the male ballet dancer seems to be linked to the history of classical dance in the West, more specifically in France, where it was born and developed. From the beginning, however, classical dance was a heterosexual matter: Louis XIV, the "dancer king" who founded the Académie royale de danse near the beginning of his personal reign in 1661, was also a notorious skirt-chaser. It is an irony of history that the king, who was not terribly valiant when it came to war, had a younger brother (**Monsieur**, Philippe d'Orléans), who took strongly both to warfare as well as to men. There was no perceived relation between dance and homosexuality at the end of the seventeenth century, and consequently, no homophobic portrayal of male dancers.

But by the nineteenth century, the perception of classical dance began to change. With the advent of pointes and tutus, the romantic idea of ballet found its place, based around the image of the prima ballerina; from Carlotta Grisi to Marie Taglioni, the vocabulary of classical dance revolved around the women who dance. In this new choreographic trend, the male dancer (*danseur*) was nothing more than a foil, a secondary role to better bring out his partner's femininity and grace. These women dancers attracted attention from the great nineteenth-century writers: from Théophile Gautier, a great lover of ballet who most notably composed the libretto for *Giselle*, to Paul Valéry, author of *L'Ame et la danse* (*Dance and the Soul*), as well as Stéphane Mallarmé, author of *Hérodiade*, women were the primary subject matter in writings about dance. The *danseur*, on the other hand, was the subject of disdain: Gautier, in his *Ecrits sur la danse* (Writings on dance; published in English as *Gautier on Dance*) evoked with repugnance the "muscled body of the *danseur*, drenched in sweat." In fact, men no longer had a respected place in classical dance, henceforth considered as a privilege of women, and an art without virility; the *danseur* was considered neither man nor woman, eliciting only disgust.

It is in Anatole France's nineteenth-century novel *Thaïs* that one can perhaps find the most apt description of this new image of the *danseur*:

> This decrepit freak, of no age and no sex, treated the child badly, on whom he vented the hate he had for all womankind. A rival of ballerinas whose grace he was nonetheless affected by, he taught Thaïs the art of pantomime, and how to mimic, by expression, gesture, and attitude, all human passions, and more especially the passions of love. He was a clever master, though he disliked his work; but he was jealous of his pupil, and as soon as he discovered that she was born to give men pleasure, he scratched her cheeks, pinched her arms, or pricked her legs, as a spiteful girl would have done.

Moreover, those few authors who did take an interest in the *danseur* were often themselves homosexual, which could not help but add to the growing association between male dance and homosexuality. It is thus that Pierre Loti, with a certain indulgence, wrote in his 1886 novel *Pêcheur d'Islande* (*An Iceland Fisherman*):

> He was a charming dancer
> Straight as a forest oak
> He turned with a grace at once light and noble
> His head thrown back

Thus, dance became associated with sensuality, femininity, effeminacy, and, of course, male homosexuality. But it also evoked lesbianism: specifically, feminine eroticism, which was decried by moralists. At the beginning of the twentieth century in England, Member of Parliament Noel Pemberton Billing headed a homophobic crusade which, among other things, denounced the "cult of the clitoris" by accusing dancer Maud Allan of lesbian **proselytism** after her performance of *Vision of Salomé* (based on Oscar **Wilde**'s work). It is true that certain contemporary ballets seemed to cultivate a kind of Sapphic eroticism, as illustrated by *Les Biches* (The Hinds), a show created by the Ballets Russes in 1924, based on an idea by Jean Cocteau and choreographed by Bronislava Nijinska, in which young women meet and touch each other in a rather erotically charged atmosphere. Francis Poulenc, the show's composer, explained: "*Les Biches* is not about love … [I]n this ballet, one does not love in order to live, one lays." More scandalous yet, the famed French writer Colette, who had relationships with both men and women, had no qualms about dancing nude at the literary salon of her lesbian friend Natalie Barney, in the role of Mata Hari. There, at least, the show was private, but she would perform again in 1907, this time publicly at the Moulin Rouge, where she danced in a very sensual way and kissed her lover, known simply as Missy, onstage. This performance provoked a riot, resulting in the **police** raiding the premises; the press denounced it as the **scandal** and the show was banned. The commotion only served to reinforce the connection between dance, **debauchery**, and lesbianism.

Since then, dance performances have been associated as much with female homosexuality as with male homosexuality. As for male classical dance, despite attempts at rehabilitating the image of the *danseur* in the twentieth century by the likes of Nijinsky and Maurice Béjart, it proved impossible to overcome the negative legacy of male dancers established in the nineteenth century. The homophobic portrayal of the *danseur*, feeding on the appearance of overtly homosexual performers such as Jacques Chazot, was deeply engrained in the public subconscious. The image of the *danseur* had been stigmatized: he was homosexual, effeminate, and lacking in intelligence. Indeed, even recently, and in openly gay or gay-friendly works, this same negative image can be found. For example, in Christopher Ashley's 1995 film *Jeffrey,* the eponymous hero finds himself being advised by his friend Micha to move in with another man. But when Micha holds up the example of his relationship with his boyfriend Darius, Jeffrey retorts:

> But Darius is a dancer … a dancer in *Cats.*
> So what? I said that you need a man, not a brain.

In many respects, from the homophobic viewpoint, male dancers have rather a two-sided status: they are often stigmatized, and, given the public nature of their profession, more prone to homophobic attacks. Rudolf Nureyev was subjected to numerous pressures of this kind in the Soviet Union, which was the main reason he defected to the West in 1961. However, the prestige associated with their art also gives homosexual dancers a certain degree of freedom: for example, the recent coming out of Spanish dancer and choreographer Nacho Duato was largely well-received. And sometimes, in certain societies of the Middle East and India, dancers (as well as actors) can safely take on a specific feminine role for which they are already personally known, although if any other male dancer or actor attempted the role, it would be widely condemned. Nevertheless, this **tolerance**, like all others, is very often precarious: such was the case in **China**, where male dancers and opera singers, who had enjoyed public favor despite their feminine attributes, were quickly arrested by the police at the beginning of the Maoist Revolution in 1949 (as depicted in the 1993 film *Farewell, My Concubine*), and sometimes even sent to "re-education" camps, where they were subjected to particularly cruel **treatment**.

Over and above professional dancing, dancing for recreation and pleasure (such as ballroom dancing) should also be considered, as it has also been the object of homophobic tension. In France, for the entire duration of the Fourth Republic (1946–58), a police ordinance forbade male couples from dancing together in public places. The same rule prevailed in the United States during the same era, and the **Stonewall** Inn was originally famous for being the only bar in New

La Faune des dancings, 1925 (Dancehall Wildlife): "These little gentlemen" who gather to dance (here, rue de Lappe), appear to simultaneously arouse amusement and disgust in caricaturist Jean Auscher.

York where men could dance together without being troubled. Even today, all over the world, gay and lesbian nightclubs often find themselves the target of police surveillance and repression. Incidentally, the dangers of men dancing together goes far to explain the part of the success of disco dancing in gay culture: in effect, this new type of music enabled one to dance solo, as opposed to the music of previous generations (from the waltz to rock and roll), which obliged homosexual males to engage in heterosexual flirting despite themselves if they wanted to dance. Females who dance together are, generally, more accepted, and their heterosexuality is not usually called into question. However, if they persist, they risk arousing suspicion, being perceived (whether true or not) as lesbians, and being stigmatized as such.

Dance occupies an important place in the social organization of sexual conventions. Balls, sock-hops, parties, and other social events where people dance are often also where adolescents experience their first erotic interactions. In this way, learning to dance constitutes a sort of initiation to heterosexuality, despite the fact that it often starts solo (with a broom, for instance) or part of a same-sex pair (two friends together, alone in a room). Technical mastery of dancing is thus a crucial symbolic issue: after all, if the adolescent does not know how or does not want to dance, he risks being exposed to ridicule or suspicion. He must prove his power and his ability to "lead" a girl, even if only on the dance floor, to avoid having his masculinity called into question. Conversely, he may be suspect if he enjoys dance too much, or engages in the activity with a little too much enthusiasm. The 1997 film *In & Out* makes a good example of this when the hero, a repressed homosexual, buys an instructional cassette to help him explore his masculinity. He is unable to resist dancing to the music accompanying the tape, whereupon the audio recording warns him to calm down, and that a "real man" would be able to resist! Arnold Schwarzenegger would never dance like this; he is so muscular, he can hardly walk. In short, these contradictory injunctions portray the homosexual as someone who dances too much, or too little, while once again, the heterosexual man is the one who remains moderate in all things.

—*Hervé Chevaux and Louis-Georges Tin*

Ashley, Christopher, and Paul Rudnick. *Jeffrey, Sex or not Sex?* Film. Orion Classics, 1995.

Daldry, Stephen. *Billy Elliot.* Film. Universal Pictures, 2000.

Desmond, Jane, ed. *Dancing Desires: Choreographing Sexualities On and Off the Stage.* Madison, WI: Univ. of Wisconsin Press, 2001.

Fédorovski, Vladimir. *Histoire secrète des ballets russes: de Diaghilev à Picasso, de Cocteau à Stravinski et Noureev.* Monaco: Le Rocher, 2002.

Gautier, Théophile. *Ecrits sur la danse.* Arles, France: Actes Sud, 1995.

France, Anatole. *Thaïs.* Lausanne, Switzerland: Editions du Livre Monte-Carlo, 1948.

Kristeva, Julia. *Le Génie féminin III, Colette.* Paris: Fayard, 2002.

McNair, Brian. *Striptease Culture.* New York: Routledge, 2002.

Oz, Frank, and Paul Rudnick. *In & Out.* Film. Paramount, 1997.

Schouvaloff, Alexander. *The Art of Ballets Russes.* New Haven: Yale Univ. Press, 1998.

Thomas, Anthony. "The Gay Black Imprint on American Dance Music," *Out/Look* (Summer 1989).

—*Art; Debauchery; Heterosexism; Literature; Music; Songs (France); Sports.*

DEBAUCHERY

The word *debauchery* is usually defined as "excessive or unmoderated use of all the pleasures of the senses, especially sex or food." In the moral vocabulary of the sixteenth, seventeenth, and eighteenth centuries, the term was mostly used to describe a morally reprehensible excess, an infringement of the bourgeois principles of economy, but also suggested the stigma of giving in to one's senses, to the detriment of reason. Any discourse on debauchery is rooted in a line of thought that started in Ancient Greece and Rome, as well as Biblical precepts. In a recurring and sometimes obsessive manner (though not explicitly), debauchery was referred to in a particular definition of masculinity, part of a code of conduct specific to men; that is, activities which expended one's energies, both moral and sexual. Consequently, it comes as no surprise that from very early on, debauchery was associated with male homosexuality (much more than lesbianism). In one of his epistles, St **Paul** the Apostle drew a connection between a person who had lain with a prostitute, "whose body becomes one with her," and men of despicable morals: "Neither the immoral, nor idolaters, nor adulterers, nor homosexuals … will inherit the kingdom of God" (1 Cor 6:9–10). In the definition of the true role of Biblical law, found at the beginning of the First Epistle to Timothy (from the New Testament, in which St Paul counseled his younger colleague about his ministry), "immoral persons" and "sodomites" (this last term as used by the Revised Standard Version translation of the **Bible**) appear side by side in a list of those whom Biblical law primarily addresses.

A term often used in Christian condemnation of debauchery was "fornication." To Thomas Aquinas, the thirteenth-century Italian priest considered by many Catholics to be the Church's greatest theologian, fornication was first and foremost adultery, but it could also be considered anything that "offends nature," according to the concept of "natural law" specific to this philosophy. It is interesting to inquire as to how the connection that was said to exist between a definition of debauchery that was essentially heterosexual, and male homosexuality, came to be; it was believed that there was a continuum between the two. "The effeminates throughout the realm ruled supreme, and carried on their debauchery without restraint," the monk and historian Orderic Vitalis wrote in the twelfth century. Debauchery was thus characterized as a way of life particular to homosexuals (such as **Henri III**'s court **favorites**), or that which implicated the heterosexual world itself.

At the beginning of the seventeenth century, two phenomena brought a new tone to the association between debauchery and homosexuality. For one, around 1600, "libertinism" first appeared, a trend in which the old Epicureanism (which had originated around 300 BCE) was reborn in an environment that was as free from religious beliefs as it was from traditional decrees. While libertinism was purely philosophical in origin, its definition evolved over time to the point that it became a synonym for debauchery. And since certain famous homosexuals of the period were associated with libertinism (such as the French writer Théophile de **Viau**), this gave rise to accusations that linked libertinism with sodomy. As a result, terms like "debauchee" and "sodomite" became increasingly interchangeable. This convergence remained in place during the period of the Ancien Régime in France (i.e. until the end of the eighteenth century), where the term "sodomy" had not yet taken on the meaning it has today, but rather suggested an image of debauchery as something essentially strange, if not monstrous, and at any rate at odds with normal conduct.

Seventeenth-century France—and England—were notable for a common practice among the aristocracy: a form of male companionship, often against the law and occasionally homosexual, which was specifically defined as "debauchery." The French writer Roger de Bussy-Rabutin, in his *L'Histoire amoureuse des Gaules* (*The Amorous History of the Gauls*), claimed that these relationships resulted from a belief that the women of the Court had become too "easy." Between the years 1680 and 1682, there were numerous controversial affairs, one implicating the son of Jean-Baptiste Colbert, a minister in the French government, and another involving the son of Louis XIV himself, the Count of Vermandois, who had joined an openly homosexual brotherhood, which resulted in his public flogging (in the presence of his father) and subsequent exile. Also associated with this phenomenon was the overindulgence in food and drink, as well as the frequenting of brothels, both female and male.

In the eighteenth century, it became commonplace to believe that a person was "not born debauched," but instead became so by way of a bad influence. Thus, according to writer Maurice Lever, when **police** arrested a young male prostitute, one of their first questions

they asked was, "Who debauched you the first time?" In Abbé Prévost's novel *Manon Lescaut*, there is an ambiguous passage where the protagonist Des Grieux describes "an abbot who patted me on the cheek, saying that I was a handsome boy, but that I should be on my guard in Paris, where young men were easily debauched." Debauchery then necessarily took on a homosexual connotation, such as in the case of an old rake trying to snare a young man. Conversely, it would seem that homosexuality could only lead to debauchery. To the Baron D'Holbach, "these friendships … are founded in nothing but **vice** and debauchery" (*La Morale universelle*, 1776, 5, 5). Both Rousseau and Voltaire had roughly the same opinion, expressing incomprehension and repugnance for a moral world that they perceived as habitually stepping beyond what they referred to as "nature." Philosopher Denis Diderot had a different opinion; he believed that a "debauchery of wine" from time to time never did any harm, and in his book *Entretiens sur le fils naturel* (*Conversations on the Natural Son*), he did not include homosexuality in his list of humanity's most pernicious behaviors. Regardless, the general discourse on debauchery expanded considerably in the eighteenth century. The word appeared many times in the works of Pierre de Marivaux, Rétif de la Bretonne, the Baron de Montesquieu, and the Marquis de Sade, among others. So strongly was the notion integrated into common usage that almost all mention of homosexuality on its own completely vanished, relegated to anecdotes of debauchery. The obsession with debauchery—like that of **perversion**—was part of a profound questioning of the values of civilization, such as the role of luxury in society, the importance of public action, and the respective responsibilities of men and women.

What was profoundly troubling about debauchery, however, was that it was not usually a solitary activity. One way or another, it implied an intimate relationship with another that was outside the parameters of conjugal faith as sanctioned by religion and society. Like modern "swinging," debauchery removed the barriers between the sexes, or to be exact, the barriers between the roles that each sex must play in a well-adjusted society. Given this, it is easy to understand its association with homosexuality. Debauchery as described could thus be an affair between men, a different kind of sociality. And while women could be accused of debauchery (as they had been since Biblical times), in the collective understanding debauchery was always perceived as an essentially male impulse; under these conditions, the debauched woman was imagined to be strong, masculine, and potentially lesbian. Consequently, in descriptions of debauchery, the homosexual always played a part, as did the Jew (in César de St-Réal's *Dom Carlos*, for example, or Lesage's *Gil Blas*). In this way, debauchery was distanced from society, situated as a place of fundamental otherness. But this characterization might have been the result of envy as much as it was a condemnation. In those who stigmatized homosexuals, one might find an element of jealousy which vacillated between real homosexual desire and a simple longing for male companionship beyond the social norm. In the same way as for the Jew, it is easy to attribute to the homosexual that which one does not have: in this case, the possibility of "having access to numerous partners without being obliged to resort to the path of sentiment," to use philosopher Elisabeth Badinter's phrasing from her 1992 book *XY, de l'identité masculine* (*XY: On Masculine Identity*). Like homosexuality, debauchery was a breach of the male condition. The obsessive dread of debauchery, which Madame de Sévigné, the seventeenth-century French woman of letters, curiously said caused "more harm to men than to women," was closely linked to the obsessive dread of male homosexuality, bound together by a fear of **sterility** (both physical and social), and an inanity vis-à-vis God. To this effect, the Comte de Mirabeau once said (not without double meaning), that "debauchery does not children make."

If, during the eighteenth century, there was a strong link between homosexuality and debauchery, this was much less the case in the nineteenth century when, in the new medical discourse, homosexuals were now considered ill, and not simply a debauched person who chose his lifestyle. It should also be noted that there was a distinction made between inversion, which was considered to be a pathological condition (be it psychological, anatomical, or endocrinological in origin, depending on the various competing theories) and "perversion," which was seen as an acquired or voluntary behavior. Around the latter concept, some of the obsessive fears characteristic of debauchery recurred, such as the potential **contagion** of homosexual practices. These fears inspired many awareness campaigns designed to warn youths of the risks inherent in perversion, which also advised them to be on guard against certain categories of people, such as military conscripts or vagabonds.

Furthermore, the nineteenth century was still sensitive to the social disturbance caused by homosexual companionship, insofar as it was connected to the suspicion of collusion between decadent noblemen and penniless knaves. Like sycophancy, homosexuality was seen as a shady way to undertake certain social maneuverings, or a means to attain a social freedom that was both enviable and morally reprehensible. In the works of Proust, it can be seen clearly how certain characters (such as the couple of Charlus and Jupien, and also Odette or Albertine) evolve within worlds that are opaque, parallel, and impenetrable to the common mortal, representing for the narrator both a mystery and a profound destabilization of the social, psychological, and affective laws he attempts to establish. These worlds are summed up by the narrator in a single word: vice. The manner in which he describes them—as an intrigued voyeur, constantly at the edge but never fully involved—shows just how ambiguous the status of debauchery was in modern society.

At first glance, it would seem that the degrading association of homosexuality with debauchery is no longer as common, especially in light of the gay liberation movements of the 1970s. However, two recent events demonstrate the persistence of this link. First, the **AIDS** epidemic; in many countries, including the United States, religious fundamentalists presented the disease as God's chastisement of homosexual debauchery. For them, this so-called "gay cancer" seemed to be fate's response to the uncomfortable demands made by gay activist movements. This position was accompanied by their claim that there was a distinction between victims: the "innocent" (such as blood transfusion recipients) and the "guilty" (such as homosexuals and intravenous drug users). Second, the issue of gay parenthood; various debates on the subject led gay rights opponents to return to the notion that children and the gay "lifestyle" are incompatible. Looming large over this belief is the fear that children adopted by gays and lesbians will become homosexual themselves, as well as the fear that they may end up in the hands of pedophiles. It would seem that even while homosexuals make their claim for social integration, they must continue to pay for the outdated attitudes toward debauchery that societies have maintained for centuries.
—*Gilles Siouffi*

Aron, Jean-Paul, and Roger Kempf. *Le Pénis et la démoralisation de l'Occident*. Paris: Grasset, 1978. New edition: Le

Livre de Poche, 1999.

Boswell, John. *Christianisme, tolérance sociale et homosexu-
alité*. Paris: Gallimard, 1985. [Published in the US as
Christianity, Social Tolerance, and Homosexuality. Chicago:
Univ. of Chicago Press, 1980.]

Coffignon, Ali. *La Corruption à Paris*. Paris: Librairie illustrée,
1888.

Godard, Didier. *L'Autre Faust. L'Homosexualité masculine
pendant la Renaissance*. Montblanc: H & O Editions, 2001.

———. *Le Goût de Monsieur, l'homosexualité masculine au
XVIIe siècle*. Montblanc: H & O Editions, 2002.

Hahn, Pierre. *Nos Ancêtres les pervers. La vie des homosexuels
sous le Second Empire*. Paris: O. Orban, 1979.

Kimmel, Michael, and Michael Messner, eds. *Men's lives*.
Fifth edition. Boston: Allyn & Bacon, 2001.

Lever, Maurice. *Les Bûchers de Sodome*. Paris: Fayard, 1985.

Raynaud, Ernest. *La Police des mœurs*. Paris: Malfère, 1934.

Servez, Pierre. *Le Mal du siècle*. Givors: André Martel, 1955.

Spencer, Colin. *Histoire de l'homosexualité de l'Antiquité à nos
jours*. Paris: Le Pré aux Clercs, 1998. [Published in the US
as *Homosexuality in History*. New York: Harcourt Brace,
1995.]

—*AIDS; Against Nature; Contagion; Damien, Peter;
Decadence; Degeneracy; Favorites; Henri III; Literature;
Medicine; Paul; Philosophy; Sodom and Gomorrah; Sterility;
Theology; Viau, Théophile de; Vice.*

DECADENCE

The association between decadence and homosexuality (by which evidence of the latter presumes the former) constitutes a narrative construction whose objective is either to discredit homosexuality by showing
that it corrupts society, or to discredit another society
by showing that it has a homosexual component. This
narrative can either be constative, with the intention
of reassuring a culture of the positive aspects of its homophobic values, or normative, where decadence is
interpreted as the result of a transgression of prescribed
norms, and calls for a reform of the society in which
"dangerous" homosexuals lurk.

Part of the approach used by homophobes to characterize homosexuality as decadent is to emphasize its
fecundity by, on one hand, associating homosexuality
with a weakening of the people and, on the other, with
a negative secondary stage of life.

Concerning the weakening of the people, from a

qualitative viewpoint, those who link homosexuality to
decadence often refer to evidence from Antiquity. This
is the classic explanation for the fall of Rome, throughout the accounts and interpretations of Christian authors who, more or less consciously, condemned the
regime because of its persecution of **Christianity**.
Nevertheless, this interpretation is still open to debate. For instance, eighteenth-century Italian philosopher Cesare, Marquis of Beccaria, in his chapter
"Of Crimes of Difficult Proof" from his treatise *On
Crimes and Punishments*—where he discusses adultery,
sodomy, and infanticide—he states that "[t]he gener-
ality of men want that vigor of mind and resolution
which are as necessary for great crimes as for great virtues, [and] that great crimes do not always produce the
destruction of a nation." Eighteenth-century English
philosopher Jeremy Bentham also refers to Antiquity
when he argues that, if homosexuality causes weakening, then the only victim should be the homosexual.
However, there is no physiological proof that this is
indeed the case, and on the contrary, the soldiers of
ancient Greece and Rome, who were practitioners of
homosexuality, had an incontestable vigor that undermines this hypothesis.

From a quantitative viewpoint, a commonly accepted belief that emerged around the same time as the
modern state is that decreases in population are linked
to increases in decadence, and conversely, increases
in population are linked to increases in the well-being and strength of the populace (Thomas Hobbes,
Montesquieu). This "proof" of decadence thus became
an integral element of nationalist and pro-birth agendas, encouraging the **criminalization** of homosexuality. But Bentham contested this idea, arguing that the
threat posed to population increases by relationships
between men was baseless.

In addition, homosexuality has frequently been considered a (decadent) secondary stage of life (for the individual as well as for the collective), following a first
stage that is neutral or positive. The dichotomy between
innate and acquired, as well as primary and secondary,
is underlined by the cultural reference to original **sin**:
good is primary and evil is secondary. Opposed to this
interpretation, German sexologist Magnus **Hirschfeld**
participated as an expert witness in many criminal trials involving homosexuals in **Germany** at the beginning of the twentieth century, and was one of the first
to support the idea of homosexuality as innate. In most
of the trials, he was beneficial in getting defendants

acquitted by invoking the homosexual's lack of responsibility, but after a series of high-profile cases involving prominent statesmen, his influence waned and his theories became less accepted (or even outright rejected) in the face of arguments that homosexuality is acquired and thus a product of decadence, correlative to the **degeneracy** of power.

Further, the approach that understands decadence to be the result of the transgression of norms is not simply about reinforcing the validity of a homophobic society, but rather reforming a society that is not sufficiently homophobic, thus closing a fissure between the present and the future.

This type of allegation began near the end of the Middle Ages, developed under the influence of **Protestantism**, and then was reintroduced by the thinkers of the seventeenth and eighteenth centuries. Those using this argument challenged the inner workings of political and Catholic religious structures as well as the validity of the reigning monarchy, alleging a social and political sterility that needed to be replaced by a new type of society.

As a result, religious organizations, monasteries, and convents in particular, found themselves targeted. Martin Luther criticized the Catholic Church by alluding to the homosexuality of the clergy and monks, and frequently drew the association between Rome and **Sodom**. This controversy became a central point of debate between Catholics and Protestants; the argument found strength in the words of authors of the Enlightenment (Voltaire, Gervaise de Latouche, Diderot), who condemned homosexuality as the behavior of a certain caste of French nobles and men of the cloth who were cloistered away from society, thus contributing to the myth of the homosexual in court and convent.

The hypothesis of a homosexual elite within the clergy and the nobility implied that its members were concerned with simply serving their own interests instead of those of society. The principal goal of this hypothesis was to destabilize their political legitimacy based on the idea that their sexual practices were selfish and thus corrupt, evidence of their own decadence as well as that of society. At the heart of this theory was the perceived failure of the elite's collective responsibilities which needed to be countered in order for society to achieve moral rectification; such means ranged from criminal laws targeting homosexuals to attempts at destroying the elite by way of extraordinary penal measures or even revolution.
—*Flora Leroy-Forgeot*

Albert, Nicole. *Saphisme et décadence dans l'art et la littérature en Europe à la fin du XIXe siècle.* Thesis under the supervision of Jean Palacio. Paris: Sorbonne-Paris IV, 1998. New edition: Martinière, 2005.

Aron, Jean-Paul, and Roger Kempf. *Le Pénis et la démoralisation de l'Occident.* Paris: Grasset, 1978. New edition: Le Livre de Poche, 1999.

Boswell, John. *Christianisme, tolérance sociale et homosexualité.* Paris: Gallimard, 1985. [Published in the US as *Christianity, Social Tolerance, and Homosexuality: Gay People in Western Europe from the Beginning of the Christian Era to the Fourteenth Century.* Chicago: Univ. of Chicago Press, 1980.]

Laurent, Emile. *La Poésie décadente devant la science psychiatrique.* Paris: Maloine, 1897.

Leroy-Forgeot, Flora. *Histoire juridique de l'homosexualité en Europe.* Paris: Presses universitaires de France, 1997.

Lever, Maurice. *Les Bûchers de Sodome, histoire des "infâmes."* Paris: Fayard, 1985.

Tamagne, Florence. *Histoire de l'homosexualité en Europe, Berlin, Londres, Paris, 1919–1939.* Paris: Le Seuil, 2000. [Published in the US as *A History of Homosexuality in Europe: Berlin, London, Paris, 1919–1939.* New York: Algora, 2004.]

Servez, Pierre. *Le Mal du siècle.* Givors: André Martel, 1955.

—*Against Nature; Contagion; Debauchery; Degeneracy; Gide, André; Literature; Perversion; Philosophy; Rhetoric; Sodom and Gomorrah; Sterility; Theology.*

DECRIMINALIZATION (France)

France was the first country to abolish sodomy as a crime. In effect, those responsible for both the Revolutionary Code of 1791 and the Penal Code of 1810 determined that it was no longer expedient to maintain the criminalization of homosexuality as had been the case under the Ancien Régime. The justifications for this change of heart were varied; these included the push for secularization of the **law**, the liberal **philosophy** of the Enlightenment, and the incrimination only of those behaviors that were deemed a threat to the **family**. But while French law since that time has never criminalized relations between consenting adults of the same sex, criminal judges since the middle of the nineteenth century nonetheless encouraged the stigmatization of homosexuality, which was entrenched in legislation by the Vichy regime in 1942; it would not be until the early 1980s that the last of these discriminatory measures disappeared.

Around 1850, criminal jurisdictions began to re-interpret the Code, finding ways around those areas of law where the text was vague (indecent assault, enticement of minor to **debauchery**) in an attempt to legally isolate what could be called "homosexual **perversion**" and thus specifically condemn it. This **jurisprudence**, supported by the Court of Cassation (the main court of last resort in France) until the 1930s, was assigned the mission—even at the risk of abusing the legal principles behind the specific crimes and punishments—of filling in the "blanks" of a legal system that, it claimed, did not sufficiently protect minors from "perverts" (as homosexuals were designated according to medical standards).

During the latter half of the twentieth century, homophobic politicians took over from judges in presiding over this trend, continuing efforts to repress homosexuality wherever it could. While they determined that French law would still not incriminate relations between adults of the same sex, they were also confident that the same law would concern itself with moralistic jurisprudence, confirming the "abnormality" of homosexuality that was dangerous to society. A law was passed by the Vichy regime on August 6, 1942 under the guise of protecting society against prostitution, but the underlying intent was to repress homosexual acts. Henceforth, anyone who "committed one or more immoral or unnatural acts with a minor under the age of twenty-one, in order to satisfy one's own passions" would be punished with a jail sentence of six months to three years.

The post-war years in France did not put an end to this legislative trend; quite the contrary, in fact. During the Liberation, relations between an adult and a minor of the same sex were reevaluated by the government, and punishments for the crime were increased. At the same time, the age of sexual consent for heterosexual relations was set at fifteen years of age, but twenty-one for homosexual relations (decreased to eighteen years of age in 1974). On July 30, 1960, the National Assembly passed a law that added homosexuality to a list of *fleaux sociaux* ("social plagues")—which also included alcoholism, prostitution, and diseases such as tuberculosis—that the government was charged to

combat. Later that same year in November, another law was passed that expanded the scope of sexual offenses and established as extenuating (and as a result, doubling the punishment) those circumstances where the offense was the result of "acts **against nature** committed with a person of the same sex."

It would not be until the beginning of the 1980s that a shift began to take place. During the debates on modifications to the laws criminalizing rape and indecent assault, the National Assembly agreed to abrogate the increased penalty for sexual offenses when it involved homosexuals; during the debates, those in favor of this move argued that it was time, given the evolution of social mores. But the difference between the ages of sexual consent would remain in place, despite heated debates that took place between 1978 and 1980 in the National Assembly; the argument for the necessity of protecting youth in particular from these "acts against nature" won out.

France's presidential elections of May 1981, in which the left assumed power under presidential candidate François Mitterand, gave hope to gays and lesbians given Mitterand's campaign promises to abolish all measures that discriminated against homosexuals. At the end of 1981, parliamentary debates over the difference between the ages of sexual consent were once again intense; they revealed that the issue was not so much potential relations between adults and minors as it was homosexuality itself, specifically the fear and hatred it evoked in the imaginations of certain individuals. To them, maintaining these interdictions in the law was a means of permanent and symbolic social reprobation designed to "discourage" a sexuality they considered abnormal.

The law of August 4, 1982 finally reestablished equality in the criminal code by no longer categorizing any relations between an adult and a minor under the age of fifteen as homosexual or heterosexual. After the removal of sodomy as a crime in 1791, the elimination of the last legal text stigmatizing relations between individuals of the same sex signaled the complete decriminalization of homosexuality in France. In addition, this achievement, which established an official respect for fundamental rights concerning sexual orientation, completed the transition of homosexuality's place in French society from marginalization to one in which true sexual liberty was recognized.

This process of decriminalization has led to a progressive **criminalization** of homophobia, specifically the introduction to the penal code of "behaviors" deemed discriminatory as a result of drawing distinctions between individuals: from this point on, any refusal to furnish a good or a service, any refusal to hire, or any layoff motivated by homosexuality would be punishable by fines or even prison terms. But the shift from the incrimination of homosexuality to that of homophobia is far from complete. On one hand, the prosecution of cases involving homophobic **discrimination** are problematic given the victim's difficulty proving the accused's intent to discriminate; further, there are far more insidious discriminatory practices against homosexuals that not covered by the criminal code. More recently, a law was passed that served to reduce the burden of proof and introduce the concept of "indirect discrimination," but this applies only to cases involving employment. However, another victory occurred in 2004, when the National Assembly adopted legislation making the **insult** of homosexuals illegal, potentially resulting in year-long prison terms for anyone found guilty of the crime.

Moreover, on May 17, 2008, as requested by Louis-Georges Tin, the founder of the International Day Against Homophobia, the French government decided to bring forth a declaration to the UN General Assembly for the universal decriminalization of homosexuality.

—*Daniel Borrillo and Thomas Formond*

Borrillo, Daniel, and Pierre Lascoumes, eds. *L'Homophobie: comment la définir, comment la combattre.* Paris: Ed. Prochoix, 1999.

Danet, Jean. "Le Statut de l'homosexualité dans la doctrine et la jurisprudence française." In *Homosexualités et droit.* Edited by Daniel Borrillo. Paris: Presses universitaires de France, 1997.

Leroy-Forgeot, Flora. *Histoire juridique de l'homosexualité.* Paris: Presses universitaires de France, 1997.

Mossuz-Lavau, Janine. *Les Lois de l'amour (les politiques de la sexualité en France 1950–1990).* Paris: Payot, 1991.

—*Against Nature; Criminalization; Discrimination; Insult; Jurisprudence; Medicine, Legal; Mirguet, Paul; Philosophy; Symbolic Order.*

DEGENERACY

The theory of degeneracy (or degeneration) was for-mulated by the French psychiatrist Bénédict-Auguste Morel across several works during the mid-nineteenth century. It was based on an etiological hypothesis surrounding the gamut of mental illnesses (in the broadest sense of the word, covering all diseases described during that era as "nervous," which included epilepsy as well as myopathy), and extending to other pathologies, such as pulmonary tuberculosis and syphilis. The theory's main posit was the existence of a morbid heredity that is manifested in the form of a sickness or a kind of behavioral aberration, becoming increasingly frequent as it descends the genealogical tree, leading to the "degeneration" of the family line.

Ignoring Mendelian theories on **genetics**, the theory of degeneration postulates that a grandfather's alcoholism, a maternal aunt's hysteria, a cousin's myopathy, or an individual's homosexuality could all be related as part of a "heredity of defects." The theory was influential far beyond the medical field; the literary works of Emile Zola attest to its importance in the attitudes at the end of the nineteenth century. Though a little lax in its scientific formulation, this theory was easily integrated into the new data on human genetics, after the fashion of Darwinism or the "rediscovery" of Mendel's laws.

It was Richard von Krafft-Ebing, the Austro-German psychiatrist and the author of *Psychopathia Sexualis,* who was the first to formally link "sexual **perversions**," specifically homosexuality, with the concept of degeneration. This seminal act (despite the fact that Krafft-Ebing did not devote much space to the question in his work) instilled the notion that homosexuality is hereditary, a subject of discussion for genetic researchers to this day. It is due to this theory that homosexuals are often portrayed as the "end of the family line" and homosexuality is portrayed as a symptom of the decline of Western civilization—a perception that borrows from the notion of **decadence** (often as a reference to the history of the Roman Empire).

—*Pierre-Olivier de Busscher*

Albert, Nicole. *Saphisme et décadence dans l'art et la littérature en Europe à la fin du XIXe siècle.* Thesis under the direction of Jean Palacio. Paris: Sorbonne-Paris IV, 1998. New edition: Martinière, 2005.

Aron, Jean-Paul, and Roger Kempf. *Le Pénis et la démoralisation de l'Occident.* Paris: Grasset, 1978. New edition: Le Livre de Poche, 1999.

Lantéri-Laura, Georges. *Psychiatrie et Connaissance.* Paris: Ed.

Sciences en Situation, 1991.

—*Biology; Decadence; Endocrinology; Ex-Gay; Fascism; Genetics; Himmler, Heinrich; Hirschfeld, Magnus; Inversion; Medicine, Legal; Perversions; Psychiatry; Psychoanalysis; Treatment.*

DEPORTATION

The deportation of homosexuals, along with the torture and psychological abuse that often accompany it, is found in some of the most tragic chapters in the history of homophobia. In the twentieth century, the phenomenon affected the lives of many, who were variously banished to unsanitary islands during the reign of Benito Mussolini, dispatched to work camps during the Stalinist era, or sent away to concentration camps between 1933 and 1944; it is specifically the deportations that were ordered by the Nazis in Germany that is of primary interest here.

On the night of February 27, 1933, a few weeks after Adolf Hitler was appointed Chancellor by President Paul von Hindenburg, the Reichstag, home to the German government, was destroyed by fire. The alleged arsonist, Marinus van der Lubbe, in addition to having Communist sympathies, was accused of being a homosexual. The press insisted on the matter of his homosexuality: "Lubbe is essentially a homosexual. Numerous witnesses confirm it, his manners are feminine, he is reserved and timid in the presence of women, and his taste for male companionship is notorious." After a sham trial, Lubbe was executed by guillotine (but was posthumously pardoned by Germany in 2008). The Reichstag fire allowed Hitler to suspend all public liberties, including unions and other political parties. It also ushered in a climate of terror for homosexuals; nightspots became the targets of raids and brutality, most notably on the part of the SA and the SS. The Institut für Sexualwissenschaft (Institute for Sexual Research), which had been established in 1919, was sacked on May 6, 1933; its entire contents were publicly burned. The next day, the Nazi newspaper *Der Angriff* noted: "This institute, under a veneer of science, was revealed by the raid to be nothing more than a sanctum for scum and garbage." Dr Magnus **Hirschfeld**, the Jewish doctor who founded the institute, was despised by the Nazis. For years, his public appearances gave rise to trouble and **violence** of all

kinds, orchestrated by Nazi sympathizers; nine years earlier in 1921, he had been shot and wounded, and in 1923 in Dresden, he was beaten and left for dead with a cracked skull. The local press commented,

> Weeds simply will not die. The famous Dr Magnus Hirschfeld had been so seriously injured as to be on death's doorstep. Today, we have learned that he is recovering from his wounds. We will waste no time in saying that it is unfortunate that this terrible and shameless poisoner of our people did not find the end he deserved.

In 1934, he was stripped of his German citizenship, and ultimately died of a heart attack in Nice in 1935. Hitler described him as "the personification of all that is most ignoble of the Jewish spirit."

If the issue of homosexuality seemed to be a particular focus of the Nazis, it was in part because of their policy to protect and perpetuate the "Aryan race." They had no interest in the homosexuality of any of the other European people; on the contrary, they were content to let it contribute to the **decadence** and birth rate decrease of these other populations. Heinrich **Himmler**, commander of the SS, himself initiated the pro-birth, anti-homosexual argument. His speech in front of SS dignitaries on February 18, 1937, made it abundantly clear: "After we took power, we uncovered many homosexual **associations**. Together, they totaled more than two million members…. If the situation does not change, it means that our people will be destroyed by this contagious disease. No people can resist such a disturbance to their lives and to their sexual equilibrium over the long term."

Between 100,000 and 150,000 homosexuals were rounded up by the Nazis; 60,000 of them ended up in **prison**, and 10,000 to 15,000 in concentration camps. (Although homosexual women did not fall under the jurisdiction of Paragraph 175, which targeted only men, certain lesbians were branded as "asocial" and deported wearing the black triangle.) The actions taken against homosexuals were ostensibly for their refusal to take part in the Third Reich's pro-birth campaign. The men were mostly marked by the pink triangle, but being of various ages, social **classes**, and walks of life, they could not express solidarity as a group (unlike political prisoners). The deportation proved to be particularly horrible, as 60% of homosexuals would die in the camps, compared to 41% of political prisoners.

In addition to Nazi persecution, they also were subjected to the homophobia of the *kapos* (that is, of their co-detainees), as witnessed by Heinz Heger, a prisoner first at Sachsenhausen, then at Flossenburg: "Up until 1942, in an effort to reduce the number of prisoners, it was usual for each camp, from time to time, to send a contingent of 100 or more deportees to the extermination camps where they would killed by gas or injection. The choice of who to liquidate fell to the camp's secretariat of prisoners, led by the dean. Whenever this dean was a political deportee himself, we always noticed that the largest number, by far, of those sent for extermination was made up of deportees wearing the pink triangle." Under these conditions, most homosexuals sent to the concentration camps died within their first year of imprisonment.

The deportees wearing the pink triangle shared a fate similar to that of the Gypsies: they were assigned the most vile and demanding tasks or subjected to hormonal experiments or castration, and were usually housed in designated huts which no one was allowed to approach. The historian Gerard Koskovitch explained: "Male homosexuals were assigned in much greater proportions to the most painful and dangerous commando jobs, including the gravel quarry and compression roller at Dachau, the Sachsenhausen clay quarry, the tunnel excavations at Mittelbau-Dora, the stone quarry at Buchenwald, or the squads sent out to collect live bombs after Allied air raids on Hamburg. The men assigned to these tasks and commando units had a much lower life expectancy than that of the other deportees." As for the rest, the tragic reality was described by Rudolf Höss himself, commandant of Auschwitz, who wrote in his memoirs: "The homosexuals were made to work day and night. Rare were those who got out of it…. Nor was it difficult to foresee a fatal outcome whenever sickness or death took one of these men from his friend. Many killed themselves. In a number of cases, we would see two friends kill themselves together."

The homosexuals of Germany were not the only ones subjected to Nazi hatred. There were also those countries and regions annexed by the Third Reich, such as Austria, or Alsace and the Moselle; it is from these places that the testimonies of homosexual prisoners such as Austrian Heinz Heger or Alsatian Pierre Seel originate.

These kinds of testimonies appeared very late, having only been published in the late 1970s and early 80s, and at first usually anonymously or under a pseudonym. The end of World War II certainly did not automatically grant survivors a platform for their stories. As far as homosexuality was concerned, the post-war years did not change attitudes at all, and the Allies all maintained their homophobic articles in their respective criminal codes. Even after Liberation, Paragraph 175 was not abrogated in Germany, and certain homosexual deportees left the camps only to finish serving their sentence in prison—and in some cases, the sentence was not even reduced by their years spent in the camp! It would not be until after the emergence of homosexual movements in these countries that the full scope of this tragedy would finally emerge, by which time the surviving victims were already in their old age. For decades, historians such as the various federations of French deportees did nothing to acknowledge the experiences of the pink triangles (for example, Alsatian Pierre Seel was not granted official acknowledgment as a victim of the Holocaust until 2003).

For the past thirty years, on the national Holocaust Remembrance Day in Paris and other major cities in France, the French gay movement has placed a spray of flowers in the memory of those homosexuals deported by the Nazis, to the chagrin of other groups who were persecuted. In 1976, the flowers were trampled underfoot because it "sullied the memory of the millions of martyrs of Nazism"; in 1985, people shouted, "Queers to the ovens!" and "We should re-open the camps to lock up the queers"; and in 1994, a group of fellow deportees wrote to the Memorial to the Homosexual Deportation (an association working to memorialize homosexual prisoners of the Holocaust):

> There is no reason whatsoever to accord homosexuals a place in the deportation. The recognition you seek will not be achieved by a travesty of historical fact. This is why we will not tolerate any demonstration by you or your adherents at our patriotic demonstrations. Our security will use all means possible to oppose any intrusion by you. We have also informed the Minister of our ward as well as the **police** authorities providing security.

However, this denial of **history** was finally eroded by the historical reality that was difficult to deny. Recently, homosexual delegations have begun to receive official invitations to take part in Holocaust Remembrance Day services. The reality of the persecution of homosexuals has begun to appear in official statements. Also, many elected officials have been persuaded to acknowledge the spray of flowers dedicated to the homosexuals persecuted and deported under Nazism. On April 26, 2001, to the consternation of many federations of deportees, French Prime Minister Lionel Jospin declared, "No one should be left behind by the workings of memory. It is important that our country fully recognize the persecutions perpetrated during the Occupation against certain minorities: Spanish refugees, Gypsies, and homosexuals." Moreover, a historical commission has been established under the aegis of the Fondation pour la Mémoire de la Déportation (Foundation for the Memory of the Deportation), which has been officially entrusted with learning more about the fate and the numbers of homosexuals of Alsace and the Moselle who were victims of deportation. The commission was tasked with estimating the human cost of Article 331 of the French criminal code, the homophobic article of law put in place in 1942 by Marshal **Pétain** and not abrogated until 1982.

—*Jean Le Bitoux*

Boisson, Jean. *Le Triangle rose*. Paris: Fayard, 1988.

Celse, Michel, and Pierre Zaoui. "Négation, dénégation: la question des 'triangles roses'." In *Conscience de la Shoah, critique des discours et des représentations*. Edited by Philippe Mesnard. Paris: Kimé, 2000.

Crompton, Louis. "Gay Genocide from Leviticus to Hitler." In *The Gay Academic*. Edited by Louie Crew. Palm Springs: ETC Publications, 1978.

Daumet, Charles-Henri. *Le Jour des roses rouges*. Radio drama inspired by the testimony of Pierre Seel. France Culture, April 19, 1997.

Epstein, Rob, and Jeffrey Friedman. *Paragraph 175*. Documentary film on the last witnesses of the deportation and persecution of homosexuals. ASC distribution, 1999.

Grau, Günther. *Hidden Holocaust: Gay and Lesbian Persecution in Germany, 1933–1945*. London: Cassell, 1995.

Haeberle, Erwin. "Swastika, Pink Triangle, and Yellow Star: The Destruction of Sexology and the Persecution of Homosexuals in Nazi Germany." In *Hidden from History: Reclaiming the Gay and Lesbian Past*. Edited by George Chauncey, Martin Duberman, and Martha Vicinus. New York: Penguin Books, 1990.

Heger, Heinz. *Les Hommes au triangle rose*. Paris: Persona, 1980.

Le Bitoux, Jean. *Les Oubliés de la mémoire*. Paris: Hachette, 2002.

Mathias, Sean. *Bent*. Film adaptation of the play by Martin Sherman, with Lothaire Bluteau and Mick Jagger. Channel Four Films, 1996.

Mercier, Claude. "Rapport gouvernemental français de la Fondation pour la Mémoire de la Déportation sur la déportation de Français pour homosexualité," (2001).

———. "Rapport international de la Pink Triangle Coalition à l'adresse de la Cour fédérale américaine," (2002).

Sarcq, André. *La Guenille*. Poem inspired by the testimony of Pierre Seel. Arles: Actes-Sud, 1995.

Seel, Pierre. *Moi Pierre Seel, déporté homosexuel*. Paris: Calmann-Lévy, 1994. [Published in the US as *I, Pierre Seel, Deported Homosexual: A Memoir of Nazi Terror*. New York: Basic Books, 1995.

———. "Là bas si j'y suis." Interview with Daniel Mermet in *France Inter* (April 14, 1993).

Sherman, Martin. *Bent*. Play inspired by the testimony of Heinz Hagger. Martel: Ed. du Laquet, 1996. [Published in the US as *Bent*. New York: Avon Books, 1979.]

Tamagne, Florence. *Histoire de l'homosexualité en Europe, Berlin, Londres, Paris, 1919–1939*. Paris: Le Seuil, 2000. [Published in the US as *A History of Homosexuality in Europe: Berlin, London, Paris, 1919–1939*. New York: Algora, 2004.]

Triangle Roses website. http://www.triangles-roses.org (accessed February 11, 2008).

Van Dijk, Lutz. *La Déportation des homosexuels*. Paris: H & O Editions, 2001.

—*Communism; Contagion; Decadence; Far Right; Fascism; Germany; Gulag; Himmler, Heinrich; Hirschfeld, Magnus; History; Scandal; Violence.*

DEVLIN, Patrick

On August 24, 1954, after a series of scandalous trials that indicted homosexuals, the British Parliament created a committee "to consider … the law and practice relating to homosexual offences and the treatment of persons convicted of such offences by the courts." The committee's findings were collected in the Wolfenden report (named for the committee's chairman, Lord Wolfenden), published on September 3, 1957, which recommended, among other things, that homosexual acts taking place in private between consulting adults should be decriminalized. This and other recommendations, if approved, would have constituted a break with tradition going back all the way to the Henry VIII's Statute 25 of 1533, also known as "the Buggery Act."

In the aftermath of the report, an ideological clash took place between legal professor and philosopher H. L. A. Hart, who was in favor of the recommendations, and Patrick Devlin, a British lawyer and judge who was staunchly against it. Hart developed a utilitarian argument based on the view that the law had no right to intervene in private acts that did no harm to anyone, while Devlin invoked traditional Judeo-Christian morality in arguing for the continued **criminalization** of homosexual acts.

Devlin's conceptions seemed to reflect a desire to reinstate the sexual morals of medieval Christianity (or at least of the Reformation), likening them to the loyalty owed by a citizen to the modern state. Hart responded to this by stating that only this sort of ancient society would "support Devlin's denial that such a thing as a private immorality can exist, as well as his comparison of sexual immorality, even when it takes place 'in private,' to **treason**."

One major point of discussion consisted of establishing the definition and statute of morality. According to Devlin, every society needs a moral code that is shared and dominant and which is entrenched in the law. He maintained that a society which fails to oversee the morality of its individuals is condemned to fail, and even advanced the opinion (then current, but rejected today) that historically there was evidence of the connection between the loss of moral bonds and a society's disintegration. Hart agreed that a certain amount of common morality was essential to the existence of any society, but argued that it was unacceptable that any change to a society's moral code would bring about its destruction.

Devlin also stated that "English law has its own basis of reference—the reasonable man, the right-minded man, the man on the Clapham bus [a middle-class neighborhood in South London]—who should not have to defend his belief that a behavior he instinctively views as abominable is abominable." In this way, Devlin contradicted himself, the implication being that his previous arguments premised on historical precedents were in fact moot; here, he seemed to say that if the general public wanted to maintain homosexuality's criminalization, then that should be the case.

Devlin's vigorous opposition to the Wolfenden report ultimately failed, however. Ten years after it was published, the recommendations led to the passage of the Sexual Offences Act 1967, which replaced previous anti-homosexual laws that had existed since 1861. The Act served to partially decriminalize private homosexual acts between two men over the age of twenty-one, paving the way for its full **decriminalization** later on.

—*Flora Leroy-Forgeot*

Devlin, Patrick. *The Enforcement of Morals*. Oxford: Oxford Univ. Press, 1965.

Hart, H. L. A. *Law, Liberty and Morality*. Oxford: Oxford Univ. Press, "The Harry Camp Lectures," 1963.

Leroy-Forgeot, Flora. *Histoire juridique de l'homosexualité en Europe*. Paris, Presses universitaires de France, 1997.

———. "Expression, répression et démocratie: le débat Hart-Devlin et la dépénalisation de l'homosexualité en Angleterre." In *Homosexualités, expression/répression*. Edited by Louis-Georges Tin. Paris: Stock, 2000.

Wolfenden, Sir John, et al. "Report of the Committee on Homosexual Offenses and Prostitution." London: H. M. Stationary Office, 1957, GMD 247.

—*Criminalization; Decriminalization (France); Discrimination; England; European Law; Tolerance; Utilitarianism.*

DIFFERENCE. *See* Gender Differences

DISCOURSE. *See* Rhetoric

DISCRIMINATION

For a long time, homosexuality has been perceived in a negative light, even though today, this tends to happen less and less, at least in the Western world. Paradoxically, the evolution of this tolerance coincides with the appearance of the fight against homophobia. Tolerance does appear to diminish homophobia. On the one hand, some complain about modern homophobia, which they see as being strong; on the other hand, others challenge the validity of these complaints, believing that homophobia is not an issue. These diverging views are closely linked to the evolution of the concept of "discrimination," of which homosexuals have been victims (and still are, in some ways).

In the beginning, homosexuality was closely identified with "evil" and was suppressed, an act which was not perceived as discriminatory because it was legitimate in the eyes of the majority. Those few who contested this legitimacy did not raise the flag of "discrimination" or "homophobia"; the fight against the repression of homosexuality was simply a fight against intolerance. It was not a question of equality, but rather about the right to not be killed or imprisoned because of one's homosexuality.

Little by little, homosexuality was decriminalized in many countries. Simply put, its status changed from a crime to an illness. In this context, the fight against homosexual discrimination slowly became possible. In theory, because gays and lesbians were no longer considered responsible for their sexuality, they should be treated as equals to heterosexuals, barring certain "legitimate" exceptions. It was in this way that France removed certain discriminatory laws against homosexuals, but all the while maintaining certain other inequalities that were considered justified, such as the lack of any official recognition of same-sex couples.

Today, as the fight against homosexual discrimination (at least in the Western world) becomes increasingly successful, it is apparent that it is transforming itself into a fight against homophobia. There has not been any extreme division between the two struggles; rather, there was a crucial change of perspective when it was recognized that the problem was no longer homosexuality, but homophobia. Since then, any inequality between homosexuals and heterosexuals (including those related to **marriage** and to **adoption**) is now considered a form of homophobia that must be tackled.

It is this change of perspective that explains the paradox identified above: the intensity of discrimination against homosexuals is weakening (at least, again, in the Western world); however, in light of this new fight against homophobia, such discrimination is becoming less tolerated. Thus, the fight against homophobia is a renewal of the fight against homosexual discrimination: identifying the limitations of the law (homophobia is a sociological reality capable of remaining discreet, which can make it difficult to fight homosexual discrimination). In addition, it breathes new life into the struggle: in fact, the fight against homosexual discrimination has transformed into a matter of political choice (to refuse any inequality, even with regard to marriage and adoption), rather than a subject for judicial reasoning.

Homophobia & Discretion

Today in many countries, certain acts of discrimination against homosexuals are forbidden. For example, according to French **workplace** law, it is theoretically forbidden to fire a person due to his or her "manners" (or "customs"); that is, especially by reason of his or her homosexuality. In practice, though, it is difficult to prevent homophobic infractions because it is difficult, if not impossible, to learn the real reason behind certain behaviors. As a result, homophobia, being a sociological issue, cannot be eradicated by law alone. Even if it is obviously progressive to have laws in place which protect against homosexual discrimination, it is no less true that the new "evil" (homophobia) will not disappear unless such laws are accompanied by a corresponding sociological evolution. The discretion of homophobia is thus an obstacle in the struggle against homosexual discrimination. This discretion can manifest itself not only as part of daily life, but also in a "learned" way in the discourse of certain magistrates.

To understand the mechanism of this "learned homophobia," it is useful to remember that there are two major aspects to law: one corresponds to a complex, logical machine in which there is no room for subjective opinions. This "objectivity" is to ensure what is known as "legal certainty." A case brought before the courts is not subject to the goodwill of the judge; it is submitted to the objective machine that is the law. The other aspect of law determines that the legal system is a machine of such complexity that the path leading from legal problem to legal solution is not always the same. There are many possible "legal constructions," and it is from these that a judge must choose the one that seems the most appropriate. In this context, a desire for one solution over another is not exactly neutral. As such, homophobia can influence the reasoning of certain magistrates, without this influence ever being visible. The debates surrounding the establishment of the legal definition of "cohabitation" should leave no doubt about this fact.

Cohabitation (*concubinage*, in France) is a de facto situation characterized by a life shared by two people who are not married. In the beginning, it was considered to be a shameful situation, with no laws to protect it, but over time those who "lived together" outside of marriage became commonplace and, according to many, entitled to certain rights. It was in this context that lawmakers began to debate the definition of "cohabitation." Did the term assume that it was necessarily between a man and a woman? An answer of "no" would have been correct from a linguistic and historical point of view. However, for many important magistrates (including the Court of Cassation, the court of last resort in France), the answer was yes. This decision, when taken out of context, would be relatively harmless. In practice, though, it had the consequence of excluding same-sex couples from a number of rights (most notably, that of a surviving partner to retain his deceased partner's lease). The result was a type of discreet homophobia: homophobic in that it originated in the desire to keep certain rights from same-sex couples, and discreet in that it concealed what was really an ideological debate (whether or not to grant these rights to gays and lesbians) with a technical debate that was seemingly neutral, ideologically (the definition of the word "cohabitation").

To fight discrimination against homosexual cohabitants, it was first necessary to contest the linguistic pertinence on which the discrimination was based. In recent years, French law took a stand and stated that cohabitation is defined as two people living together, regardless of their gender. Learned homophobia has not been eradicated, though: it holds sway in other levels of the law and requires those working in the legal system to be particularly vigilant against the phenomenon.

Faced with the discretion of homophobia, it becomes apparent that the law must be both modest and rigorous in fighting discrimination. Modest because, regardless of what the law states, the difficulty in obtaining proof often prevents the law from accomplishing its mission; rigorous, because the fight against discrimination takes place less often at the ideological level (lawyers will seldom claim to be racist or homophobic) than the technical (it is usually by way of a judicial construction that homophobia can, quite alarmingly, find a foothold and lend a façade of legitimacy to discrimination).

Homophobia & Political Choice

The legal fight against discrimination is based on the insistence that two parties (such as homosexuals and heterosexuals) be treated in an equal manner, unless there are "legitimate" reasons otherwise. In the case of extending adoption rights to same-sex couples, many opponents claim that there are indeed legitimate reasons to refrain from doing so.

Those who consider this denial of rights to be legitimate most often invoke the necessity of putting the interests of the child first, the implication being that allowing homosexuals to be adoptive parents would be against the child's best interests. Those who, on the contrary, fight for the right of gays and lesbians to adopt refer to studies that contradict such claims.

This debate, as interesting as it is, clouds the fact that debates over some of the most pertinent social issues cannot be properly resolved by science; at a certain level of reasoning, a "political" is required. No one can know with absolute certainty whether or not it is detrimental for children to be raised by homosexual partners; by the same token, it is impossible to know whether or not it is detrimental for children to be raised by divorced heterosexual parents. With regard to these questions, a political choice (between the avoidance of discrimination or the avoidance of risk) must be made.

This is why the issue of the right to marry or to adopt does not necessarily elicit the same response, depending on whether one's rationale is "non-risk" or "non-homophobia." In the first, one debates the legitimacy of a discrimination based on an instinctual risk, such as that of a child's best interests. In the second, such an instinctual risk is a symptom of homophobia and, as a consequence, is suspect. This kind of discrimination could only ever be tolerated if it were justified to some extent, and if this justification were proven. In short, doubt should benefit those who are being discriminated against.

In conclusion, it appears that the relatively recent introduction of the concept of homophobia into judicial analysis has permitted new light to be shed on debates related to homosexual discrimination. This clarity would appear to be useful; however, it should not be forgotten that homophobia remains unfortunately quite common in a heterocentric society, and that, confronted with this apparently ancient phobia, it is important not only to remain vigilant, but also to instruct, be tolerant, and have patience.

—*Mathieu André-Simonet*

Borrillo, Daniel. *Homosexualités et droit*. Paris: Presses universitaires de France, 1998.

———. "L'Orientation sexuelle en Europe: esquisse d'une politique publique antidiscriminatoire," *Les Temps modernes*, no. 609 (2000).

———, and Pierre Lascoumes, eds. *L'Homophobie: comment la définir, comment la combattre*. Paris: Ed. Prochoix, 1999.

Congrégation pour la doctrine de la foi. "Au sujet des propositions de loi sur la non-discrimination des personnes homosexuelles." La Documentation catholique, no. 2056 (1992). [Published in English as "Some Considerations Concerning the Response to Legislative Proposals on Non-Discrimination of Homosexual Persons." By The Congregation for the Doctrine of the Faith, The Roman Curia (July 23, 1992).]

Dawidoff, Robert, and Michael Nava. *Created Equal: Why Gay Rights Matter to America*. New York: St Martin's Press, "Stonewall Inn Editions," 1994.

Delor, François. *Homosexualité, ordre symbolique, injure et discrimination: Impasses et destins des expériences érotiques minoritaires dans l'espace social et politique*. Brussels: Labor, 2003.

Duberman, Martin, and Ruthann Robson, eds. *Gay Men, Lesbians and the Law (Issues in Gay and Lesbian Life)*. New York: Chelsea Publishing, 1996.

Eribon, Didier. "Ce que l'injure me dit. Quelques remarques sur le racisme et la discrimination." In *Papiers d'identité, Interventions sur la question gay*. Paris: Fayard, 2000.

Fassin, Eric. "L'Epouvantail américain: penser la discrimination française," *Vacarme*, no. 4–5 (1997).

Formond, Thomas. *Les Discriminations fondées sur l'orientation sexuelle en droit privé*. Doctoral thesis on private law. Université de Paris X–Nanterre, 2002.

Herman, Didi. *Rights of Passage: Struggles for Lesbian and Gay Legal Equality*. Toronto: Univ. of Toronto Press, 1994.

Leroy-Forgeot, Flora, and Caroline Mécary. *Le PaCS*. Paris: Presses universitaires de France, 2000.

Mécary, Caroline, and Géraud de La Pradelle. *Les Droits des homosexuels*. Paris: Presses universitaires de France, 1998.

Gross, Martine, ed. *Homoparentalités, état des lieux, parentés et différence des sexes*. Paris: ESF, 2000.

Newton, David. *Gay and Lesbian Rights: A Reference Handbook (Contemporary World Issues)*. Santa Barbara: ABC-Clio, 1994.

Tin, Louis-Georges, ed. *Homosexualités, expression/répression*. Paris: Stock, 2000.

Watts, Tim. *Gay Couples and the Law: A Bibliography*. Public Administrations Series P-2810. Monticello, IL: Vance, 1990.

—*Adoption; Closet, the; Criminalization; Decriminalization (France); European Law; Insult; Jurisprudence; Marriage; Parenting; Privacy; Tolerance; Workplace.*

DISCRIMINATORY LAW. *See* Discrimination

DISEASE. *See* Medicine

DURAS, Marguerite

Writer Marguerite Duras (1914–96) was born in French Indochina (now Vietnam), where her parents had moved in response to a French government campaign encouraging citizens to work in the colony. In 1932 at the age of eighteen, she went to France, where she began to study mathematics, but then switched to political science, and finally to law. After finishing her studies, she joined the Communist Party of France, and got involved in the French resistance during World War II. In the 1950s, she became the darling of literary Paris, accumulating one success after another—*Un barrage contre le Pacifique* (published in English as *The Sea Wall*), *Moderato Cantabile* (same title in English), *Le Ravissement de Lol. V. Stein* (*The Ravishing of Lol Stein*), *Le Vice-Consul* (*The Vice Consul*), and *L'Amant* (*The Lover*), the last for which she received the prestigious Prix Goncourt in 1984. The opacity of life, the difficulty of existence, the torpor of desire never realized—these sum up the recurring themes in her diverse *oeuvre*.

At the same time, Duras constituted an interesting case of homophobia, for two reasons. First of all, she displayed a type of feminine (but not feminist) homophobia, based on a concept of woman that is both exalted and restrictive. In her view, a woman was only able to connect with her true nature through a relationship with a man and a bond with a child; it was only in this manner that she could achieve the glorious joy of being. "I do not see passion as anything but heterosexual, thunderous and brief," she once declared, and as her biographer Laure Adler noted, "in [Duras'] opinion, childless women were not real women," a narrowly **heterosexist** point of view that correlated to a hostility toward homosexuals in general. Duras' close friends were often struck by the virulence with which she regularly attacked those "*sales pédés*" ("dirty queers"), justifying her **insults** with paradoxical allegations: "I see in the seeming softness of homosexuality the provocation of violence."

The irony of fate would be that in 1980, Marguerite Duras fell in love with Yann Andréa Steiner, despite (or perhaps because of) the fact that he was gay. This final passion of her life, and its accompanying contradictions, provided the subject matter for several of her books.

Notably, 1982's *La Maladie de la mort* (*The Malady of Death*) included the strange scene of a man who was trying for the first time to make love to a woman, who cruelly observes: "You don't love anything or anyone; you don't even love the difference you think you embody. The only grace you know is from the bodies of the dead, of those just like you."

Beginning with its title, *The Malady of Death* combines two themes common to homophobic rhetoric: to the individual, homosexuality is an illness, and to society, it represents the **peril** of death. Through the gauze of the novel's beautiful language, Duras, by her own admission, tried to impose her negative views of homosexuality on readers. For those (and they were many) who had missed the lessons contained in the novel, she set out a laborious explanation in another book, 1987's *La Vie matérielle* (published in English as *Practicalities*). Describing, as it were, the advent of homosexuality, she stated: "It will be the greatest catastrophe of all time," and that it would lead to population decreases until no one is left: "We will be asleep....The death of the last man will pass unnoticed."

Homosexuality became an object of both fascination and hatred in her work as well as in her life, and this helps to explain some of her public positions in favor of homosexuality as well as many of her statements that were hostile to gay men. Frustrated by her relationship with Steiner, she tormented him as much as she saw in him a desirable monster:

> In the morning, when I hear you come downstairs,
> always late, always light and charming, words of
> vomit fill my head: "fag," "queer," "auntie." That's it,
> that's him. But it seems as though you are a charm-
> ing young man, about whom I ask myself why he is
> with me. However, you are the only person in the
> world who I could stand in spite of the abjection
> you represent to me.

Nonetheless, in 1986's *Les Yeux bleus cheveux noirs* (*Blue Eyes, Black Hair*), Duras makes an attempt at a reconciliation. Employing the same kind of sparse narrative, this time she comes to a sort of resignation: "The way you detest me, it isn't about me. It comes from God, it has to be accepted like that, respected like nature, or the sea." Yet in the book homosexuality was no less of a theme of suffering, tears, and hatred. She tried to give shape to this painful experience for a third time with a work tentatively entitled "Le Sommeil" (Sleep), but she abandoned the project, exhausted.

Certainly, Marguerite Duras was not the most homophobic literary figure of the century; far from it. But it was her opinionated will, however desperate, to struggle, fight, and comprehend homosexuality through her writing that constitutes (with regard to homophobia) the other interesting aspect of the Duras example. Further, while her homophobia was tied to her experiences as a woman whose vocations as lover and mother were both denied by homosexuality, it was also a source of literary influence, albeit profoundly ambiguous. In public, her crude **heterosexism** led her to make declarations that were quite violent, and at times, quite stupid. (For example, she refused to acknowledge Roland Barthes as a master of thinking for the simple reason of his homosexuality.) In her work, on the other hand, her homophobia is evidenced (and thus distanced) in a way that was poetic and contained, and thus embraced by many fans, including homosexuals.

—*Louis-Georges Tin*

Adler, Laure. *Marguerite Duras*. Paris: Gallimard, 1998.
  [Published in the US as *Maguerite Duras: A Life*. Chicago:
  Univ. of Chicago Press, 2000.]
Duras, Marguerite. *La Maladie de la mort*. Paris: Minuit, 1982.
  [Published in the US as *The Malady of Death*. New York:
  Grove Press, 1986.]
———. *Les Yeux bleus cheveux noirs*. Paris: Minuit, 1986.
  [Published in the US as *Blue Eyes, Black Hair*. New York:
  Pantheon Books, 1987.]
———. *La Vie matérielle*. Paris: POL, 1987. [Published in
  the US as *Practicalities: Marguerite Duras Speaks to Jérôme
  Beaujour*. New York: Grove Weidenfeld, 1990.]
———. *Yann Andréa Steiner*. Paris: POL, 1992. [Published
  in the US as *Yann Andréa Steiner*. Brooklyn: Archipelago
  Books, 2006.]
Eribon, Didier. *Papiers d'identité*. Paris: Fayard, 2000.

—*Feminism (France); Gender Differences; Heterosexism;
Literature; Rhetoric.*

E

EASTERN EUROPE. *See* Europe, Eastern &
Central

EMPLOYMENT. *See* Workplace

ENDOCRINOLOGY

In 1912, while looking for incontestable scientific proof
for his theory of the third sex, Magnus **Hirschfeld**
claimed the existence of "gandrin" and "gynecin," hormones behind the principles of male and female. This
hypothesis was formulated in the context of new scientific knowledge that led to the creation of the field
of endocrinology, which deals with disorders of the en-
docrine system and its secretions known as hormones.
Much of this knowledge was originated by physiolo-
gist Charles-Edouard Brown-Séquard, who was one of
the first to identify the existence of hormones, which
led to the therapeutic use of organ extracts to treat disorders. Supported by the scientific autonomy earned
by physiologists during the early nineteenth century,
interest in this new field turned almost immediately
to the sexual glands. In an 1893 report to the French
Academy of Sciences, Brown-Séquard made claims of
the physiological and therapeutic attributes of a liquid
extracted from the testicles which had a positive effect
on an impressive list of pathologies, ranging from in-
fluenza to cancer, and from gangrene to hysteria.

And so began the quest for the sexual hormones,
which was finally accomplished between 1923 and
1934 with the discovery of estrogen, progesterone,
and testosterone. However, in 1929, a relatively unexpected discovery was also made at the same time by
Ernst Laqueuer at the University of Amsterdam, who
identified the presence of female sexual hormones in
the urine of "normal, healthy" men. This fact, confirmed in 1934 by an article in *Nature* magazine that
revealed evidence of a significant amount of estrogen
in the urine of a stallion, naturally lent credibility to
the idea of an intermediary gender, and to the concept that homosexuality was the result of an imbalance
between male and female hormones. The theory enjoyed immediate success. On one hand, it fit perfectly
into previously established knowledge, confirming the
theories of **inversion** and precisely locating the female
factor in men and the male factor in women. On the
other hand, hormonal theory (finally) paved the way
for new therapies that were far less nebulous than those
attempted by psychotherapy.

Clinical trials on homosexuals based on the new
principle of hormonal rebalancing sometimes led to
rather comical situations, such as the essay published
by Doctors J. C. Glass and W. Johnson in the *Journal of
Clinical Endocrinology* in 1944, which concluded that
the treatment had not only failed in eight cases (being
successful in only three), but that all eight ended up
with increased homosexual impulses! But this amusing
anecdote should not conceal the fact that many homosexuals became guinea pigs for endocrinologists during
this period. Testing the new theories under the guise
of therapy sometimes led to grave consequences, not
to mention that the purity of many of the hormonal
extracts with which subjects were injected, at least at
first, were not exactly "ideal." More dramatically, it was
in the framework of this therapeutic research that the
Danish endocrinologist Carl Vaernet, encouraged by
Nazi SS leader Heinrich **Himmler**, tested the implan-
tation of an "artificial male gland," which administered
testosterone into the bloodstream over a prolonged period of time. In fact, endocrinology was the basis for
numerous serious attempts at "curing" homosexuality,
including ones that were carried out in the United

States as recently as the 1960s. Nonetheless, the endocrinologists' lack of their success meant that they failed to prove their hypothese, and therefore they have never really threatened the hegemony held by **psychiatry** on the subject.

—*Pierre-Olivier de Busscher*

Borell, Merriley. "Organotherapy and Reproductive Endocrinology," *Journal of History of Biology* 18, no. 1. Dordrecht: Reidel Publishing Company, 1985.

Oudshoorn, Nelly. "Endocrinologists and the Conceptualization of Sex, 1920–1940," *Journal of History of Biology* 23, no. 2 (1990).

———. "The Making of Sex Hormones," *Social Studies of Science* 20, no.1. London: Sage, 1990.

—*Biology; Degeneracy; Fascism; Ex-Gay; Genetics; Himmler, Heinrich; Hirschfeld, Magnus; Inversion; Medicine; Medicine, Legal; Perversions; Psychiatry; Psychoanalysis; Treatment; Turing, Alan.*

ENGLAND

Twelfth to Nineteenth Century

In England during the Middle Ages, the "crime of sodomy" fell under the jurisdiction of the clergy; ecclesiastical law provided for the imposition of the death penalty. The number of homosexuals condemned of this crime remains unclear, given that sodomy was also the name assigned to other crimes such as bestiality and heresy. Around 1090, under the reign of William II (Rufus), the chronicler Orderic Vital criticized the morals of Norman youth who grew their hair long, adopted effeminate characteristics, and practiced sodomy. Thus, when the ship carrying two such youths—the sons of Henry I, William and Richard—sunk in 1120, chroniclers such as Henry of Huntingdon and William of Nangis deemed the wreck a just punishment for their vice.

Around 1290, under the reign of Edward I, sodomy was punishable first by drowning, then by burning at the stake. One of the more famous victims of this law was Edward II, immortalized in a play by Christopher Marlowe which demonstrated how homosexuality is transgressive and can disrupt the strict hierarchical social order. According to his accusers, Edward II, under the influence of his constant companion Piers Gaveston, imperiled the kingdom by neglecting the legitimate nobility in favor of his favorite, thus placing personal matters ahead of the kingdom; and the criticism of his weakness (in which the reproach of his effeminacy is very present) laid the groundwork for a potential civil war. Political treachery combined with moral condemnation culminated in Edward II's "exemplary" murder, by which a white-hot stake was driven up his anus. These dramatic machinations that were later depicted in Marlowe's play proved eerily similar to the playwright's own fate: Marlowe himself was accused of **treason** and **heresy** (he ascertained that Christ had a homosexual love for his disciple John) and was assassinated.

In 1533, a turning point in British homophobia occurred: in a conflict between Henry VIII and the papacy, Parliament decreed that sodomy (buggery) "with another human being or an animal" would fall under royal jurisdiction to be recognized as a felony. As a result, the "sodomite" was no longer only a sinner and debauched individual, but also a man without honor and an enemy of the state. This law, aimed at a precise sexual act and not a category of person, sought to protect the reproduction of the species by preventing the wrongful dispersion of the male seed; the law was again promulgated under Elizabeth I. Those accused of sodomy were judged by the tribunals and ran the risk of being hanged. However, by the time Elizabeth became queen in 1558, not only was the number of executions limited, so were the number of accused: in the counties of Essex, Hertfordshire, Kent, and Sussex, only four reported cases of sodomy were brought before the judges. By comparison, between 1558 and 1603, the county of Essex alone saw 15,000 people called before the court for sexual misconduct. Under the weight of biblical condemnation, the crime of sodomy was often considered unthinkable and thus not used to describe homosexual practices alone. Instead, the accusation of sodomy was more often used to discredit political or religious adversaries, such as during conflicts between Protestants and "papists." Satire and ridicule seemed to be the preferred means by which to denounce the homosexual sympathies of the powerful: the posthumous printings of the 1684 play entitled *Sodom, or the Quintessence of Debauchery* by John Wilmot, Earl of Rochester (himself a bisexual), was a critique of the morals of the court of Charles II. The most famous sodomy **scandal** implicated Mervyn Touchet, Lord Audley, Earl of Castlehaven in 1631: in addition to multiple acts of sodomy with his servants, he was accused of abetting the rape of his wife and offering his twelve-year-old stepdaughter to his favorite servant in order to make him his heir; to the "**unnatural**" crime was added a crime against family honor. In 1640, the Bishop of Waterford was the last English man hanged for sodomy in the seventeenth century. During all this time, lesbianism remained outside of the law and seems to have attracted less interest than male homosexuality. It must be noted, however, the Sapphic friendships of Queen Anne were the object of caustic allusion on the part of satirists.

At the beginning of the eighteenth century, harsher repressive measures resulted in a change in representations of homosexuality. The figure of the libertine bisexual, which had dominated the preceding centuries, was progressively pushed aside by the moral bourgeoisie who advocated monogamy and the protection of the family, leading to homosexuality becoming an increasingly exclusive practice. As a result, a specific homosexual culture began to form around molly houses, places where gay men could rendezvous, which were centered in the Holborn quarter of London and around St James's Park. In these clubs, shows were staged that parodied men getting married or even giving birth. Around 1690, Puritan associations, the Societies for the Reformation of Manners, had already begun to organize their surveillance of suspected homosexuals, and would soon orchestrate raids that would terrorize the homosexual population from 1710 to 1720, resulting in many homosexual men committing **suicide**. Hundreds were arrested and many of those convicted were hanged; still others were sent to the stocks, a humiliating and frightening experience that often ended in serious wounds or death. The general populace, including women, took advantage of such occasions to unleash its wrath, heaping garbage, rocks, and dead cats upon the unfortunate prisoner. In addition, abusive lampoons, often enhanced with woodcuts, were distributed to fuel the hatred, bearing titles such as *The Women's Complaint to Venus* or *The Women Hater's Lamentation*. The popular **literature** of the time, often expressing itself also through satire, was also susceptible to instances of homophobia: in Tobias Smollett's *The Adventures of Roderick Random*, the eponymous hero must suffer the advances of Captain Whiffle and the Earl of Strutwell.

The eventual disappearance of the Puritan societies, discredited by their methods, did not signify the end of the persecution of homosexuals, however. Vengeful

pamphlets such as *Satan Harvest Home* (1749) and *The Phoenix of Sodom* (1813) continued to be published in order to alert the public to the extent of homosexual networks. The 1810 scandal involving the Vere Street Coterie, a group of gay men arrested at a molly house called the White Swan, also contributed to the public's homophobic prejudice. Meanwhile, the ongoing Napoleonic Wars reinforced a sense of insecurity among the English: the advance of homosexuality was attributed to the French, while the British Navy hardened its policy with regard to sodomy. For many homosexuals living in England, exile appeared to be the only solution, even more so as many European nations, following the French example, were **decriminalizing** sodomy. In order to escape rumors of their sexuality, both William Beckford, the richest man in England, and Lord Byron chose to live abroad, in Italy, Greece, and Portugal.

Stratford, 1763: *Man in the stocks put to death by the people:* "Take this Buggume pear! —Flog him! —Here's a fair mark! —Cut it off! —Shave him close!" The sodomite appears to have learned his lesson: "Now I'm in the hole. Indeed, come all in my friends."

Although lesbianism per se was not condemned, transvestism among women sometimes incurred the wrath of the law; while women who dressed as men in order to join their husbands on the field of battle were rarely pursued, those who used their disguise to affirm their autonomy or to engage in sexual relations with other women ran the risk of serious punishment. Mary Hamilton, whose case was invoked in Henry Fielding's novel *The Female Husband* (1746), was publicly flogged for having illegally practiced medicine while disguised as a man. Generally speaking, lesbianism enjoyed a greater degree of **tolerance** because judges and public opinion were repelled at the very idea of the existence of female homosexuality. In 1811, Marianne Woods and Jane Pirie, teachers at the upper-class boarding school for girls in Drumsheugh, Scotland, were accused by Dame Helen Cumming Gordon of being lesbians; they sued for defamation and won because the presiding judge Lord Gillies refused to believe in the existence of the "presumed crime."

Nineteenth Century to 1967

In the late nineteenth century, while certain English philosophers such as Jeremy Bentham were in favor of the decriminalization of homosexuality, the United Kingdom did not go in this direction. Certainly, in 1861, the penalty for a sodomy conviction was reduced from possible death to a prison sentence ranging from ten years to life. This punishment was again reduced in 1885 with the adoption of the Labouchere Amendment to the Criminal Law Amendment Act (which followed a number of scandals including the notorious 1871 trial of Boulton and Park, two transvestites), intended to change the laws concerning juvenile prostitution. Thereafter, "all acts of gross indecency" between two men were punishable by imprisonment for up to two years of hard labor. Although the amendment considerably reduced the potential duration the sentence, it broadened the scope of the law to specifically include all forms of sexual conduct between two men; as a consequence, it placed homosexuals at the mercy of blackmailers. Further, whereas the sodomy law of 1861 had been rarely enforced, the revised Criminal Law Amendment Act resulted in a considerable increase in the numbers of those accused and convicted. Homosexuals were again targeted in 1898, when the Vagrancy Act was extended to make homosexual solicitation illegal.

In the twentieth century, homosexuals were also the target of a smear campaign during World War I. Stigmatized as the "German vice" since the **Eulenburg affair**, homosexuality was seen as nothing else but the mark of traitors in power. While journalist Arnold White asserted that Germany intended to "abolish civilization as we know it, substitute **Sodom and Gomorrah** for New Jerusalem, and infect the healthy nations with Hunnish erotomania," Member of Parliament Noel Pemberton Billing took up an anti-homosexual crusade, contending that German

Secret Services had in their possession a black book containing the names of 47,000 high-ranking homosexuals, whom the Germans were blackmailing. Also, in an article entitled "The Cult of the Clitoris," he attacked actress Maud Allan, then appearing in a production of Oscar **Wilde**'s *Salomé,* accusing her of pro-lesbian propaganda.

During the period between the two world wars, there was an average of 702 arrests annually in the United Kingdom for homosexual crimes and misdemeanors, which were classified as "unnatural offences," "acts of indecency," or "attempt(s) to commit unnatural offences." The number of arrests continuously increased during this period on a yearly basis. These figures reflected the concerns of the British judiciary, police, and military forces who gathered at a May 7, 1931 conference on homosexual crimes, which sought to put an end to the sexual activities of soldiers of the Guard in the parks of the capital, among other matters.

Police harassment sometimes resulted in raids on London's gay bars, but it most often consisted of surveillance of urinals by plainclothes policemen, in keeping with the ongoing fear of "**contagion**." Generally speaking, the homosexual criminal was viewed with contempt by those in law enforcement who made every effort to publicize the outward "signs" of his "perversion": powder compact, makeup, and petroleum jelly. However, these police actions themselves did not increase the number of arrests or convictions due to the difficulty in catching the guilty in the act as well as the reluctance of witnesses to testify. But the objective was less a desire to make arrests than it was to maintain pressure on regulars who frequented the bars and urinals. In this sense, homosexuals who cruised public areas, be it by preference or by need for lack of companionship, were the most at risk. The working classes were thus overrepresented in the statistics of those arrested. In addition, in an effort to shield the privileged, the British government attempted to silence any case implicating known figures, a tradition going back decades to the Cleveland Street scandal (1889–90), in which a number of aristocrats, such as Prince Albert Victor, son of the Prince of Wales, had been involved. However, while the trials of Oscar Wilde, which saw the writer cast out from British society, contributed to bringing homosexuality into the British public eye, they also reinforced the prejudices of public opinion that associated homosexuality with high society, debauchery, and effeminacy. At this point, homophobia attained its apex in the United Kingdom, resulting in many homosexuals choosing to immigrate to France rather than run the risk of dishonor. The very name of Oscar Wilde became synonymous with vice and corruption for years to come.

During the inter-war period, the suspicion of treason continued to be periodically evoked notably against homosexual intellectuals close to the Communist Party, such as W. H. Auden, Stephen Spender, and Christopher Isherwood, who were nicknamed "Homintern" (short for "Homosexual International," which is a play on "Comintern," which is short for "Communist International"). The increased visibility of homosexuals among the British elite, particularly writers, fueled the angst of public opinion. Oxford University, where the "cult of homosexuality" was said to rule over certain groups, became the target of vengeful articles denouncing it as a "lair of debauchery and effeminacy." The 1920s also saw the development of a veritable dread of lesbianism. Whereas homosexual women had not until then been a preoccupying subject, feminist agitation, combined with the affirmation of the New Woman in the form of the independent-minded "flapper," led some to believe in a lesbian "contagion." In the context of this fear, also fed by the weakened male-to-female ratio as a result of World War I, a legal amendment aiming to outlaw lesbianism, modeled on the homosexual male model, was proposed by three Conservative members of parliament in 1921. Among the arguments they invoked were a decreased birthrate, the idea that young women who were seduced by other women would be pushed to depression or insanity, and the risk of national **decadence**. Adopted by the House of Commons on August 4, 1921, the House of Lords ultimately rejected the amendment, which was considered not only useless, but would also expose ignorant women to the existence of such vices and thus expose them to blackmail. However, the failure to criminalize lesbianism cannot be interpreted as a triumph of British tolerance, for in the media and in literature, the face of the lesbian **criminal** and psychopath was quite in vogue. The 1928 publication of **Radclyffe Hall**'s novel, *The Well of Loneliness*, intended to portray lesbian love in a sympathetic light, instead generated a scandal. A venomous media campaign, coupled with a legal trial for indecent offense, led to the book being banned and the writer forced into exile. That same year, a good many satires of Hall's novel, such as Beresford Egan's *The Sink of Solitude* and

Compton Mackenzie's *Extraordinary Women*, took great pleasure in being ironical about the "masculine" look of certain famous lesbians, and ridiculed their intellectual pretensions.

After World War II, anti-homosexual paranoia attained its apex. In 1951, the "Spies of Cambridge," homosexual diplomats Guy Burgess and Donald Maclean, defected to the East. Under the influence of the United States, then suffering from the weight of full-on **McCarthyism**, the British initiated a campaign aimed at identifying homosexuals present in different governmental services. Similar measures were taken by the Admiralty and the Ministry of War, and a director of Scotland Yard was sent to study investigative methods used by the FBI in this situation. The accused, under the cover of immunity, were pressured to denounce their sexual partners, resulting in mass arrests, including key figures such as actor John Gielgud and mathematician and World War II hero Alan **Turing**, who later committed suicide in 1954. In 1955 alone, over 2,500 men were arrested. The widespread presence of homosexuals reinforced an ongoing sense of insecurity in England, which was already distraught over problems in its various colonies as well as its overall loss of international influence. Newspapers and magazines devoted many pages to articles on homosexuality, asserting that this practice was particularly rampant among intellectuals. *The Practitioner*, a medical journal of the time, proposed the idea of exiling homosexuals to St Kilda in the Hebrides, where they could benefit from the "natural and invigorating" climate. In 1954, the sensational trial of Lord Montagu, his cousin Michael Pitt-Rivers, and *Daily Mail* journalist Peter Wildeblood, all accused of indecent conduct, was a turning point that revealed the abuses perpetrated by police in their pursuit of homosexuals. Under the pressure of certain politicians as well as the church, Minister of the Interior Sir David Maxwell Fyfe, who considered homosexuals to be "exhibitionists and proselytizers," accepted the creation of a commission of inquiry into the treatment of homosexuals, under the direction of Sir John Wolfenden. In its 1957 report, the Wolfenden Committee advocated the decriminalization of private homosexual relations, but insisted on the necessity of severely punishing acts committed in public, prostitution in particular, and requested that the legal age of consent be raised to twenty-one, versus sixteen for heterosexual and lesbian relations. While the **censorship** of literature and films progressively vanished, it was not until 1967 that the recommendations of the Wolfenden Committee were accepted into law.

1967 to Present

The Sexual Offences Act of 1967 incorporated the conclusions of the Wolfenden report, but it did not apply to those serving in the **Army** or the Marines, and its scope was limited to England and Wales. In fact, the reforms could not be interpreted as a definitive victory over homophobia, as the number of homosexuals being arrested actually increased in the years following the law's adoption. It would be necessary to wait until 1980 for the reforms to be applied in Scotland, and 1982 in Northern Ireland, where gays were the target of harassment by the Royal Ulster Constabulary and Ian Paisley, a Protestant leader, who launched a petition titled "Save Ulster from Sodomy," which gathered 70,000 names. In Britain, the legal age of consent was reduced to eighteen in 1994 and then to sixteen in 2000, two years after an attempt to lower it had failed due to opposition by the House of Lords, who were backed by the Primate of the Church of England.

In the last twenty years, certain groups such as the police and the army, long reputed for their homophobia, are now very open to gays and lesbians. In 1990, the Gay Police Association (GPA) was formed, uniting gay and lesbian police officers from Scotland Yard; at the same time, the police started taking greater action against homophobic **violence**. With regard to the armed forces, homosexuality among those in service was legalized in 1994. Nevertheless, the Ministry of Defence maintained that "homosexuality is incompatible with military service," and gays and lesbians ran the risk of an "administrative discharge" if their homosexuality were to be discovered. In September 1999, the European Court of Human Rights condemned the United Kingdom for discharging from the armed forces three men and one woman convicted of homosexual practices. But as of January 2000, discrimination against gays and lesbians in the armed forces became illegal in Britain.

The progressive decriminalization of homosexuality has not, however, signified the end of homophobic attitudes and habits. A 1983 survey on British social attitudes indicated that for 65% of respondents, homosexual relations are considered "always" or "often" wrong. In fact, during the 1980s, in the context of the **AIDS** epidemic and the rise to power of Margaret Thatcher and the Conservative Party, homosexuals became a popular target. More so than in other countries, the media, in particular the tabloids, associated AIDS with the gay community, generating panic and hysteria in public opinion. The accusation of homosexuality was also used to political ends: the Conservatives attempted to discredit the rival Labour Party by highlighting its sympathy for the gay cause, focusing particular attention on Ken Livingstone, leader of the Greater London Council (1981–84), known for his encouragement in favor of gay and lesbian cultural projects. It was in this context, in 1988, that Clause 28 (a.k.a. Section 28) was passed, forbidding local governments from "promoting" homosexuality. (This amendment is still in place today, despite attempts by groups such as ACT UP, OutRage!, and Stonewall to have it struck down.) Homophobic remarks continue to be published regularly in tabloids such as *The Sun*, which ran a headline in November 1998 on the "Pink Mafia" that supposedly ran the country. In fact, the most common form of homophobia to which gays and lesbians are subjected is **insults**, be it in **schools**, the **workplace**, public areas, or even at home from family members. According to a 1995 survey of gays and lesbians conducted by Stonewall, 73% of respondents had been the victim of insults regarding their sexual orientation during the previous five years; further, 34% of men and 24% of women had suffered different forms of physical violence, including being queer-bashed. Certain legal issues still remain in limbo, such as those pertaining to same-sex partnership or adoption. In 2001, Mayor of London Ken Livingstone (re-elected in 2000 as London's first mayor under the new Greater London Authority) established the United Kingdom's first register for both same-sex and heterosexuals, the London Partnership Register, which, while not granting the same legal rights as official marriage, was seen as a crucial first step toward same-sex marriage rights in the country.

—*Florence Tamange*

Bray, Alan. *Homosexuality in Renaissance England*. London: GMP, 1988.

Bredbeck, Gregory W. *Sodomy and Interpretation: Marlowe to Milton*. Ithaca, NY: Cornell Univ. Press, 1991.

Crompton, Louis. *Byron and Greek Love: Homophobia in 19th-Century England*. Berkeley: Univ. of California Press, 1985.

Davenport-Hines, Richard. *Sex, Death and Punishment: Attitudes to Sex and Sexuality in Britain since the Renaissance*. London: Fontana Press, 1991.

Gilbert, Arthur N. "Buggery and the British Navy 1700–

1861." *Journal of Social History* 10 (Autumn 1976).

Jeffery-Poulter, Stephen. *Peers, Queers and Commons: The Struggle for Gay Law Reform from 1950 to the Present.* New York/London: Routledge, 1991.

Jeffreys, Sheila. *The Spinster and Her Enemies: Feminism and Sexuality, 1830–1930.* London: Pandora, 1985.

Miller, Neil. *Out of the Past: Gay and Lesbian History from 1869 to the Present.* London: Vintage, 1995.

Norton, Rictor. *Mother Clap's Molly House: The Gay Sub-culture in England 1700–1830.* London: GMP, 1992.

Rousseau, George Sebastian. *Perilous Enlightenment: Pre- and Post-modern Discourses, Sexual, Historical.* Manchester: Manchester Univ. Press, 1991. [Published in the US by St Martin's Press, 1991.]

Sinfield, Alan. *The Wilde Century: Effeminacy, Oscar Wilde, and the Queer Moment.* London: Cassell, 1994. [Published in the US by Columbia Univ. Press, 1994.]

Tamagne, Florence. *Histoire de l'homosexualité en Europe: Berlin, Londres, Paris, 1919–1939.* Paris: Le Seuil, 2000. [Published in the US as *A History of Homosexuality in Europe: Berlin, London, Paris, 1919–1939.* New York: Algora, 2004.]

Weeks, Jeffrey. *Coming Out: Homosexual Politics in Britain from the Nineteenth Century to the Present.* New York/London: Quartet Books, 1990.

—*Armed Forces; Debauchery; Devlin, Patrick; McCarthy, Joseph; North America; Police; Radclyffe Hall, Marguerite; Turing, Alan; Utilitarianism; Vice; Violence; Wilde, Oscar.*

ESSENTIALISM/CONSTRUCTIONISM

The debate between essentialists and construction-ists is linked to a number of philosophical and epis-temological disputes that have occurred throughout the intellectual history of the Western world. From a chronological point of view, the debate goes all the way back to the divergence between the followers of Platonic theory and those of the Aristotelian approach. This kind of epistemological opposition permeates the history of how we think, and exists (explicitly, or oth-erwise) in many scientific fields.

In **anthropology**, **sociology**, and **history**, the de-bate is very apparent where the study of sexuality is in-volved. In this context, and in a rather simplistic way, it can be said that essentialists analyze sexuality in terms of historical and cultural continuity, while on the other hand, constructionists do so in terms of discontinuity.

To essentialists, there is a base homosexual identity (masculine and feminine) that is both ahistorical and acultural: homosexuals and lesbians have always existed everywhere. Alternatively, from the constructionist point of view, the concept of "sexuality" (and conse-quently that of heterosexuality and homosexuality) is a category which exists in practically all cultures, but which can acquire meanings and symbolic values that are often quite different, even opposed. For example, speaking of homosexuality among the Ancient Greeks would be an anachronism, and using the same name for sexual contact between two New Guinea aborigi-nals would be ethnocentrism, although neither of these statements denies the existence of sexual attraction be-tween people of the same sex in other time periods or in different cultural circles from our own.

Until the latter half of the twentieth century, a ma-jority of authors writing on sexuality approached it from the essentialist point of view. It was not until the anthropological studies of the early 1960s—a period when the cultural diversity of mores and sexual prac-tices became a subject of interest—that the construc-tionist approach to sexuality began to emerge. Shortly thereafter, the works of Michel Foucault in France and Jeffrey Weeks in the United Kingdom established a theoretical and empirical basis for social construction-ism.

These two paradigms coexist in various studies and scientific analyses, but they also appear in other forms of learning, most notably in common knowledge. As such, anthropologist Carole Vance points out, we all have an essentialist perception of sexuality: the essen-tialist idea that human behavior is natural and predeter-mined by immutable genetic, biological, or physiologi-cal mechanisms, a notion that can be found practically everywhere and within everyone. The same is true for the tendency to categorize in a homogeneous manner those people who in our eyes engage in similar behav-ior: i.e. that all homosexuals must be the same, as well as bisexuals, and even heterosexuals. However, upon refinement of this analysis, one can see that sexual ori-entation does not make all individuals the same. Yet it cannot be denied that it is easier for the human mind to view these categories as being stable, rather than to have to consider more flexible concepts.

As much from a scientific point of view as political, both the essentialist and constructivist approaches can be used in very different ways. It would be too simplis-tic to classify essentialists as conservative and all constructionists as progressive. It would be equally false to claim that both schools of thought are homogeneous and diametrically opposed. What is true is that certain approaches to sexuality, like those inspired by the sexological or biomedical disciplines, tend to be mostly essentialist—perhaps because the analysis is conducted in terms of normality and deviance. A discipline which favors research into the etiology of homosexuality (such as **endocrinology**, **genetics**, **psychiatry**, **psychology**, etc.) neglects the "causes" of heterosexuality, which is assumed to be "normal." Other forms of essentialism can also be found in the humanities: some historians examine the existence of "gays" in the Middle Ages, for example, while anthropologists talk about "homosexuality" in Native Americans, and zoologists record species of animals in which "homosexual" behavior can be observed.

In political terms, the use of both approaches is not necessarily univocal. The goal behind the creation of the term "homosexual" in the mid-nineteenth century by militant Hungarian scholar Karl-Maria Kertbeny was to demonstrate the existence of a homosexual "true nature," in order to keep gays and lesbians from being persecuted under Paragraph 175 of the German penal code. A large number of gay and lesbian militants during the latter half of the nineteenth century (including the famous sexologist Magnus **Hirschfeld**) adopted similar stances.

In the twentieth century, this kind of argument was also used, especially in research on the supposed biological origins of homosexuality—such as that conducted by neuroscientist Simon LeVay, who claimed there was a difference in the average size of the hypothalamus between heterosexual and homosexual men. According to the openly gay scientist, the size of the hypothalamus in a homosexual man is closer to that of a woman's (though there is no mention of the woman's sexual orientation). Note that this biological view has a difficult time accounting for additional variables, such as bisexuality (just how big would a bisexual hypothalamus be?), not to mention that it also poses certain ethical problems, as indicated by bioethicist Udo Schuklenk.

For some champions of contemporary gay and lesbian activism, establishing a scientific truth confirming the existence of a cause for homosexuality based in nature would be a way to "legitimize" their plight. The argument of a natural cause that would in effect "normalize" homosexuality would then serve to counteract all types of homophobic prejudices and social sanctions. This hearkens back to the same arguments used since the nineteenth century by other homosexual activists such as Germany's Karl Heinrich Ulrichs. This reasoning, such as that behind the theory of the "third sex," shows that the very concept of "nature" is adaptable to whatever use is required. Thus, the theories of a biological origin for homosexuality can also be applied to dangerous derivations that also claim scientific legitimacy, such as a supposed "cure" for homosexuality, or even medical intervention to "prevent" it from occurring.

The "scientific" quest for the origins of the social in the biological is an old demon that has, in the past, led to ideological manipulations that offer a pseudo-legitimacy to deterministic methods, of which eugenics, so dear to Nazi scientists and ideologists, is one of the darkest examples.

—*Rommel Mendès-Leite*

Boswell, John. "Revolutions, Universals, and Sexual Categories." In *Hidden from History: Reclaiming the Gay and Lesbian Past*. Edited by George Chauncey, Martin Duberman, and Martha Vicinus. New York: Penguin Books, 1990.

De Cecco, John. "If You Seduce a Straight Person, Can You Make Them Gay? Biological Essentialism versus Social Constructionism." In *Lesbian and Gay Identities*. Edited by John De Cecco and John Elia. New York: Harrington Press, 1993.

Foucault, Michel. *Histoire de la sexualité.* Vol. I : "La volonté de savoir." Paris: Gallimard, 1976. [Published in the US as *The History of Sexuality*. New York: Pantheon Books, 1978.]

LeVay, Simon. "A Difference in Hypothalamic Structure Between Heterosexual and Homosexual Men." *Science*, no. 253 (1991).

MacIntosh, Mary. "The Homosexual Role." *Social Problems* 4 (1968).

Schuklenk, Udo. "Is Research Into The Cause(s) of Homosexuality Bad for Gay People?" *Christopher Street*, no. 208 (1993).

———. "Scientific Approaches to Homosexuality." In *Gay Histories and Cultures: An Encyclopedia.* Vol. II. Edited by George E. Haggerty. New York/London: Garland, 2000.

Stein, Edward, ed. *Forms of Desire: Sexual Orientation and the Social Constructionist Controversy*. New York: Routledge, 1992.

Vance Carole. "Social Construction Theory: Problems

in the History of Sexuality." In *Homosexuality, Which Homosexuality?* Edited by Dennis Altman, Carole Vance, Martha Vicinus, and Jeffrey Weeks. Amsterdam/London: Uigeverij An Dekker-Schorer and GMP Publishers, 1989.

Weeks, Jeffrey. *Coming Out: Homosexual Politics in Britain from the Nineteenth Century to the Present.* London: Quartet Books, 1977.

—*Anthropology; Biology; Gender Differences; History; Medicine; Philosophy; Psychology; Psychoanalysis; Sociology; Theology; Universalism/Differentialism.*

EULENBURG AFFAIR, the

The scandal known as the Eulenburg affair (also referred to as the Harden-Eulenburg affair) was a series of court-martials and regular trials in Germany resulting from accusations of homosexual conduct among members of Kaiser Wilhelm II's cabinet and entourage between 1907 and 1909. The episode upset German political life and sparked a wave of homophobia among the general public.

In 1886, Prince Philipp of Eulenburg-Hertefeld, a diplomat and aristocrat known for his artistic talents, struck up a close friendship with Kaiser Wilhelm II, to whom he became an advisor. Named ambassador to Austria-Hungary, his anti-imperialist stance and his readiness to reconnect politically with **France** earned him the resentment of the disciples of Chancellor Otto von Bismarck. Despite the fact that he got married in 1875, it was a well-known secret that Eulenburg (as Prince Philipp was known) regularly engaged in homosexual acts. Beginning in 1893, he became the target of a press campaign initiated by journalist Maxmilian Harden, editor of the newspaper *Die Zukunft*, who threatened to reveal his personal life and forced him, in 1902, to resign.

In 1906, as Eulenburg began to renew his political career, the Algeciras Conference took place to resolve the crisis over the colonial status of Morocco between France and Germany; the conference favored France, which had the support of Great Britain and the US, a serious setback for German foreign affairs. In the wake of this, Harden relaunched his accusations against Eulenburg, publishing various parodies which contained allusions to both him (referring to him as "the Harpist") and to the Count Kuno von Moltke, military commander of Berlin (known as "Sweetie")

as homosexuals, perhaps under pressure from military circles which had been rocked by a series of homosexual **scandals** (between 1906 and 1907, six military officers committed suicide after being blackmailed for their homosexuality; previous to this, some twenty other officers were convicted by court-martials for being homosexual). Harden seemed to believe that his revelations would lead to a beneficial change in the **army** and the aristocracy, and would put an end to the spread of homosexuality, which was perceived as a sign of **decadence**. However, the campaign also had political motivations: both Eulenburg and Moltke were also suspected of having given privy information to the first secretary of the French embassy in Berlin, Raymond Lecomte (also gay), who was then purported to have revealed to the French Ministry of Foreign Affairs that Germany had been bluffing during the Algeciras Conference of January–April 1906.

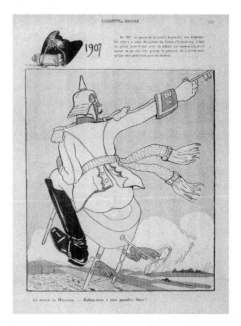

Image published in *L'Assiette au beurre*, 1907. Its caption explains: "In 1907, a prince of the Imperial family, von Hohenau, was involved in the pastoral frolics of the Prince of Eulenburg. He was a good and just prince to soldiers (the *cuirassiers*); though this love could not quite be qualified as paternal, rather, more like that of an auntie for her nephews." The artist also illustrated the prince speaking the famous words of Henri IV: "Rally round my white pants!"

The ultimate goal of Harden's tactics was to weaken Wilhelm II by discrediting his entourage. Yet despite being in possession of compromising documents about the Kaiser's sexuality, Harden refused to make use of them. On April 27, 1907, Harden officially outed both Eulenburg and Moltke, confirming their identities in his previously published parodies. In face of the scandal's growing scope, Wilhelm II demanded Moltke's resignation, and Eulenburg was obliged to quit the diplomatic service and give up his decorations. However, the affair was far from over; just as in Great Britain with regard to Oscar **Wilde**, the scandal led to the courtroom. Moltke began by launching a criminal libel suit against Harden. The trial opened on October 23, 1907, and quickly became sensational. The crowd pressed in to hear the revelations of Lili von Elbe, Moltke's estranged wife, who testified that she had only had sexual relations with her husband on two occasions, and that he would place a pot full of water in the bed in order to discourage her advances. A soldier known as Bollhardt, who had participated in homosexual orgies organized by many renowned aristocrats, described to the court the attraction of the uniform worn by *cuirassiers* (mounted cavalry soldiers), and stated that homosexual relations were quite widespread within the army. Finally, Magnus **Hirschfeld**, the German sexologist and leader of the WHK (Wissenschaftlich-Humanitäres Komitee, or Scientific Humanitarian Committee, a gay movement fighting to abolish the homophobic Paragraph 175) testified as an "expert" and confirmed that Moltke's "unconscious orientation" could be described as homosexual, after having witnessed his "feminine" sensibilities. The goal of Hirschfeld's testimony was to denounce the hypocrisy of the German government, which ignored the homosexuality of those who were highly placed, while condemning anyone else. The tactic did not go as planned: on October 29, Harden was acquitted, although the trial was voided on the grounds of procedural defects. At the same time, another trial began: this one pitted Adolf Brand, publisher of the world's first gay periodical *Der Eigene* (The special), against the chancellor of the German Empire from 1900 to 1909, Prince Bernhard von Bülow, who was suing him for libel. Brand, one of the originators of the "**outing**" phenomenon, had written a pamphlet describing how Bülow had been blackmailed for alleged homosexuality. Brand was sentenced to eighteen months in prison. In December, during the new trial of *Harden v. Moltke*, medical experts diagnosed Moltke's wife as having hysteria, and Hirschfeld re-

tracted his testimony. Harden was sentenced to four months in prison. The trial against Eulenburg was never completed, as the prince fell gravely ill; he died in 1921 without being acquitted, unlike Moltke.

The Eulenburg affair fomented a deep public prejudice toward the homosexual "cause." Homophobic demonstrations abounded, often combined with anti-Semitic, anti-feminist, and anti-modernist movements, while arrests in the name of Paragraph 175 sharply increased. In the press, **caricatures** depicting homosexuals as effeminate or bestial (sometimes in the form of dogs or pigs) found a resurgence, just as the association of homosexuality with treason became more common: the testimony of Hirschfeld (who was Jewish and homosexual) during the trial led to whispers of a conspiracy between those two groups to bring about the downfall of the Empire. What is certain is that Hirschfeld had made a tactical error in testifying; as a result, financial support for his organization fell by two-thirds, a sign of the disaffection of the well-heeled homosexuals who had until then provided funding but who now feared being exposed. The ramifications of the affair were extreme and were felt beyond the borders of Germany, even if historians have long resisted recognizing this fact. In France, homosexuality began to be known as the "German **vice**," Berlin was renamed "**Sodom-**sur-Sprée" (Sodom on the Spree, a reference to the river that runs through the city), and Germans themselves were referred to as "Eulenbougre" (*bougre* meaning a "bugger"). Even in French urinals, invitations to homosexual activity took on a new form: "Do you speak German?"

More generally, the Eulenberg affair marked a turning point in the representation of homosexuality: it saw the popularization of the term "homosexual," which had previously been restricted to the medical domain but was now defined using psychological criteria such as effeminacy, passivity, or an artistic temperament. It would also open the door in Germany to the use of homosexuality for political ends, which would reach an apex during the 1930s.

—*Florence Tamagne*

Hull, Isabel V. *The Entourage of Kaiser Wilhelm II, 1888–1918*. Cambridge: Cambridge Univ. Press, 1982.

Steakley, James D. "Iconography of a Scandal: Political Cartoons and the Eulenburg Affair in Wilhelmin Germany." In *Hidden from History: Reclaiming the Gay and Lesbian Past*. Edited by George Chauncey, Martin

Duberman, and Martha Vicinus. New York: Penguin
Books, 1990.

—Armed Forces; Caricature; Decadence; Hirschfeld, Magnus;
Germany; Media; Scandal; Treason.

EUROPE, EASTERN & CENTRAL

The history of eastern and central Europe is particularly complex. The countries that make up this area today were essentially established in the wake of the large
empires that fell apart at the end of World War I. The
history of the region prior to 1918 will only be summarized here, as it largely pertains to the three dominant powers of Austria-Hungary, Russia, and Germany,
each of which operated separate spheres of influence
which were often contested. For the period following
1918, countries in the region are discussed individually
here, because each has had a different history when it
comes to the penal repression of homosexuality.

Before 1918: The Foundation of a Repressive Tradition
In eastern and central Europe, laws against sodomy,
which were largely religious, originated in the Middle
Ages and remained in effect up until the mid-nineteenth century. The formulation and application of
these laws varied with the time and place, but each,
in a generalized way, targeted all sexual practices that
were unrelated to procreation. The definition of sodomy at the time was fairly broad, and included relations between people of the same sex (women as well
as men) as well as bestiality. This definition prevailed
throughout the Austro-Hungarian Empire and part
of the German Empire; moving east to **Russia**, the
concept of sodomy was narrower. There it was defined
explicitly by anal penetration, and in fact excluded relations between women.

In the mid-nineteenth century, contrary to much
of western and southern Europe—which had radically abolished the old sodomy laws under the influence of the French Revolution and the Napoleonic
Code—the nations of central and eastern Europe
established modern criminal codes based on their
respective heritages. The concept of sodomy gave
way to "unnatural" **debauchery**. The regional characteristics of the ancient sodomy laws could still be
observed: male homosexuality remained criminalized in Russia and the German state of Prussia, and

in 1871 throughout the entire German Empire. The
Austro-Hungarian Empire's new penal code, adopted
in 1852, punished both male and female homosexuality with harsh prison sentences. The only country to
differ from this logic was Romania which, at the end
of the nineteenth century, established a penal code inspired by the Napoleonic Code. Homosexuality was
not distinguished from heterosexuality and thus was
legal, as far as the law was concerned. This particular
situation, however, would only last until 1936, when it
was criminalized.

The Baltic States
The Baltic states of Estonia, Latvia, and Lithuania,
whose history has been dominated by Swedish, Polish,
German, and Russian interests, achieved a short-lived
independence in 1920–21. During their brief existence
between the two world wars, the three new nations did
not institute any legislation specific to homosexuality.
This absence of formal criminalization was not a sign
of **tolerance**, though. The few large cities and ports
doubtless had areas conducive to homosexual encounters; however, these were never intended nor advertised
as such: there were no identifiable gathering places for
homosexuals, nor any organized community. The political climate was not favorable to the freedom of mores. The three nations, though originally democratic,
quickly drifted toward authoritarianism, which in the
1930s developed into ultra nationalistic dictatorships;
Latvia was even openly Fascist.

The 1940 annexation of the three Baltic states by
the USSR meant that the Soviet Union's anti-homosexual legislation of 1934 (Article 121 of the penal
code) was now also applicable to the Baltic region.
Male homosexuality was punishable by heavy **prison**
sentences throughout the entire period of annexation.
The collapse of the Soviet Union and the subsequent
independence of the three countries in 1991 changed
nothing at first: in all three republics, politicians across
the board, largely reflecting popular sentiment, were
resolutely against the abrogation of the Soviet Article
121. However, the three Baltic governments had to
come to terms with this issue eventually in order to
satisfy the demands of the Council of Europe, which
they wished to join. Anti-homosexual laws were abrogated in Estonia and Latvia in 1992, and in Lithuania
in 1993, which in turn sparked new discriminatory
measures with regard to age of consent. These measures were removed in Latvia in 1998 (becoming six-

teen years for all), and in Estonia in 2001 and Lithuania in 2004 (becoming fourteen years). Yet these changes were nothing more than concessions to pressures exerted by European gay and lesbian organizations such as the International Lesbian and Gay Association (ILGA). At the same time, Baltic gay and lesbian **associations** had difficulty obtaining legal recognition. Moreover, they were never consulted during the debates over the abrogation.

Meanwhile, many politicians, particularly those with highly nationalistic tendencies, and the various churches continued to spread violently homophobic messages. Despite this, there was noticeable improvement in the tolerance of homosexuals by Baltic society throughout the 1990s. Homosexuality became a common subject of debate in the **media**, which no longer uniformly cast it in a negative light. There are now active gay and lesbian associations in each of the Baltic states whose members have become highly visible, such as the five Lithuanian activists who came out in one of the largest daily newspapers in the country. The number of gay and lesbian establishments remains quite modest, however. Vilnius, the capital of Lithuania, can claim only one discotheque; Tallinn, the capital of Estonia, has a few bars and saunas; and Riga, the capital of Latvia, has a large discotheque called Purvs, which was the target of a bombing in 1998. A few weeks earlier, a **far right** political party had led an intense anti-homosexual campaign, during which it designated the nightclub as a "den of degeneracy."

Poland

Between the two world wars, the criminal code in Poland was quite unique. The Polish state, newly reconstructed after World War I, was composed of territories that had previously been German, Austro-Hungarian, and Russian. Until the adoption of a proper penal code in 1932, each region provisionally maintained criminal laws that had been in effect prior to independence. Thus, male homosexuality was criminalized throughout Poland, and female homosexuality only in those regions where the Austrian penal code of 1852 was enforced. The Polish penal code of 1932, based on that of France, made no distinction between homosexuality and heterosexuality, which included setting a single age of consent of fifteen years for all.

The **German** invasion of Poland in 1939 was accompanied by the annexation of the eastern regions by the USSR, to which Soviet laws were immediately ap-

plied, including Article 121. In the territories annexed or occupied by Germany, the anti-homosexual policy of the Nazis theoretically only applied to Germans, and not the Polish "sub-humans." Nonetheless, the repression would still affect Polish homosexuals in cases of relations with Germans. Just like their German partners, they risked being sent to prison or concentration **camps**.

With the exception of the period of German and Soviet annexation from 1939 to 1945, it is interesting to note that the complete **decriminalization** of male and female homosexuality introduced by the adoption of the 1932 penal code has never been questioned. In this way, Poland is an exception compared to the rest of central and eastern Europe, as much during the 1930s as during the communist years after World War II. Nonetheless, the liberalism of the law was not enough to create a climate that was truly more favorable to homosexuals than elsewhere. In reality, the liberal influence of the Enlightenment and the French penal code did not affect more than a fraction of Poland's intellectual elite. Other, more striking, influences combined to create a social climate that was noticeably hostile to homosexuals: the ultra nationalistic and reactionary trend that occurred between the wars; the post-war communist dictatorship that tightly controlled social mores right up through the 1980s; and the considerable influence of the Catholic Church.

The formation of activist gay and lesbian groups began with the transition toward democracy: ETAP in Wroclaw, FILO in Gdansk, and the WGA in Warsaw all appeared between 1986 and 1987. Throughout the 1990s, the presence of gay and lesbian associations in Poland (the Lambda network in particular since 1997) has increased; as a result, gays and lesbians have begun to visibly assert themselves, as attested to by the existence of Rainbow in Warsaw, a gay and lesbian informational center that is unique among eastern European countries. However, this progress seems to be limited to the major cities. An ILGA study in 2001 suggests that the general public's attitude remained deeply homophobic: eighty-eight percent believe that homosexuality is "**against nature**." Roughly half of Poles think it should be tolerated nonetheless, while the other half consider it unacceptable. The study also revealed that gays and lesbians are still frequently exposed to verbal and physical **violence**, particularly from their circles of family, friends, or colleagues following the disclosure or discovery of their homosexuality.

Austria, Hungary, Czech Republic & Slovakia
After 1918, the countries which were formed following the end of the Austro-Hungarian Empire maintained the tradition of repression, in which male and female homosexuality was illegal, socially unacceptable, and obliged to remain hidden. Yet the political, economical, social, and moral chaos engendered by World War I and the crumbling of the old order encouraged a kind of liberalization of social mores in the 1920s, although this was really only evident in the big cities of Vienna, Prague, and Budapest, which already enjoyed a certain degree of freedom since the time of the Austro-Hungarian monarchy.

Hungary, and Budapest in particular, underwent an evolution reminiscent of Berlin's during the same period, though less glamorous. The contradictions there were doubtless even sharper. The effervescent nightlife, unbridled pleasures, and rowdy luxury were essentially the privilege of a small minority of wealthy tourists. Sexual contact was largely the result of prostitution, during this period of extreme economic difficulty. Gay male prostitutes were common, but they were usually dabblers, not full-time professionals. The city's famous baths, though, played a role in developing a kind of homoerotic culture; the baths themselves were not the site of sexual activity, but they were places where it became easy for homosexuals to establish contact, directly and explicitly. A few gay bars and clubs opened up, but in contrast to Berlin, homosexual life in Budapest was very discreet. In addition, there was no accompanying protest movement. This climate—liberal yet ambiguous, and limited to Budapest—did not survive the dictatorial and ultra nationalistic changes to the Hungarian regime in the 1930s and during World War II.

In the 1950s, a strict Stalinist moral order was the rule of the day. However, in 1961, homosexuality between consenting adults was decriminalized, although there was a higher age of consent for homosexuals: twenty, compared to fourteen for heterosexuals. During this time, Hungarian authorities opted for a slightly more flexible control of social life and individual liberties than that of the other countries in the Eastern Bloc. This "Hungarian exception" benefited homosexuals: while official statements and prevailing attitudes were still largely homophobic, certain homosexual gathering places were quietly tolerated. During the mid-1960s, a café called Egypt in the heart of Budapest transformed at night into a gay bar, and was

semi-officially tolerated as such. This venue, which for a long time was the only one of its kind in the Eastern Bloc, combined with the baths made Budapest an El Dorado of sorts for homosexuals from the other eastern European nations.

The evolution of gay rights in Hungary since the fall of communism has been full of striking contrasts. Not counting the large number of bars and clubs (often with a "backroom"), gay life in Budapest is marked by a veritable culture of outdoor pick-up spots, such as at various squares or the on banks of the Danube. These places are numerous, well-frequented even during the day, and with little or no effort being made to disguise them from the heterosexual public, they stand in contrast to homosexuals who continue to avoid coming out of the closet. Openly declaring a gay or lesbian identity is still extremely difficult, as evidenced by the weakness of those organizations that have appeared since 1989. Politicians and their respective parties rarely take a positive stance on homosexuality; many, the government included, openly declare their desire to fight against this "deviance" that they see as dangerous to society and the **family**. Modern Hungary is a paradox: among the post-communist nations, it is one of the most homophobic in its discourse and representation, yet also one of the few where gay establishments (at least in Budapest) are the most abundant and festive.

In the former Czechoslovakia between the world wars, despite the fledgling nation's commitment to democracy, which in principle provided a more favorable environment than the dictatorial regimes of its neighbors, the situation for homosexuals did not evolve accordingly. The nationalistic and political rifts throughout the nation historically tended to favor the reversion to a more traditional moral order. After Germany dismantled the country from 1938 to 1945, the Nazis' systematic repression of homosexuals (prison, concentration camps) was instituted "by law" in the Sudetenland, annexed by the Third Reich in 1938, and "by fact" of all populations (of German extract or otherwise) in Bohemia and Moravia; the region of Slovakia, which had become a pseudo-independent state, managed to escape these provisions.

After World War II, as in Hungary, the installation of Stalinist **communism** in Czechoslovakia maintained the criminal, social, and moral repression of homosexuality. In 1962, the law prohibiting homosexual acts between consenting adults was abrogated, though accompanied by discriminatory legislation on the age of consent. However, contrary to Hungary, it would not be until the 1980s that the first explicitly gay establishments appeared in Prague.

Since 1990, the situation has evolved quite favorably in the Czech Republic, although less so in Slovakia, independent of each other since 1993. The separate age of consent for homosexuals was abrogated in 1990, to the effect that according to the law, both nations currently make no distinction between homosexuality and heterosexuality.

Today Prague, along with a few other smaller Czech cities, has numerous gay and lesbian establishments as well as active organizations. Many political groups, including the large Social Democratic Party, as well as high-level politicians, such as former president Vaclav Havel, support gays and lesbians in the form of equal rights and anti-discriminatory measures. In 2001, the Czech parliament adopted a new article in the labor code explicitly prohibiting discrimination "by reason of a person's sexual orientation." As far as prevailing attitudes are concerned, a 2006 Angus Reid poll found that approximately 52% of the Czech Republic's population favored same-sex marriage, above the European average.

The evolution of gay rights in Slovakia has been more mixed. There have been many attempts to lay the groundwork for a gay and lesbian community, and while there are over ten gay and lesbian establishments in the capital of Bratislava, politicians are on the whole apathetic if not explicitly opposed to the advancement of gay rights. The Christian Democratic Movement is the most virulently homophobic political party, asserting the will of the Catholic Church, which retains a strong influence over the whole of Slovakian society.

In Austria, section 129 of the 1852 penal code prohibiting male and female homosexuality between consenting adults was not challenged in the period between the two world wars, and there were numerous convictions. The punishment, as in Germany prior to the Nazis, was relatively moderate—a prison sentence of one to five years. However, with Germany's annexation of Austria in 1938 (becoming the Anschluss), the Nazi policy dedicated to the "eradication of homosexuality" that had been in effect in Germany since 1933 was extended to Austria. Raids increased, and punishments were brought in line with those of the Reich. From 1938 to 1945, the fate of Austrian homosexuals in prisons and in concentration camps mirrored that of German homosexuals.

As in Germany, the end of World War II resulted in only semi-liberation for homosexuals in Austria. The mortal peril of the camps had disappeared, but not section 129, nor the legacy of Nazi ideology. In fact, Austrian society, its police, and its judges equated homosexuals with **criminals** more than ever. Anti-gay laws were enforced with more zeal than at the turn of the century or during the 1920s. Further, homosexual survivors of the camps, in Austria as in Germany, were not viewed as victims of Nazism, and thus were excluded from reparations or pensions.

Among Europe's democratic countries, Austria was one of the last to decriminalize homosexuality, in 1971. But in return for their compliance, the Catholic Church and the country's conservative parties were appeased by the introduction of many new discriminatory laws: the criminalization of male homosexual prostitution (Paragraph 210, removed in 1989); of all forms of enticement to debauchery with a person of the same sex (Paragraphs 220 and 221, removed in 1996), and last but not least, the establishment of a separate age of consent for homosexuals (eighteen, compared to fourteen for heterosexuals) (Paragraph 209).

Paragraph 209 remained in effect until 2002, despite contradicting many Austrian legal and constitutional acts, as well as resolutions of the European Parliament and the Council of Europe. Both of these institutions have called upon Austria on many occasions, but always in vain, to align its **laws** with the rest of Europe, but any attempts at abrogation have always been obstructed by opponents on the far right. This intransigence is not just symbolic: the number of convictions, which had fallen to less than fifteen per year during the early 1990s, rose to an annual average of thirty-five by the end of the decade. More than a third of those charged were between eighteen and twenty years of age, and three-quarters were under forty. The removal of Paragraph 209 in 2002 was not the result of an act of parliament, but rather through an invalidation by the Constitutional Court of Austria, which determined that the law violated the principle of equal treatment of citizens.

A major difference between Austria and countries in the Eastern Bloc can be seen in its freedom of expression and association that has permitted a highly organized and very active gay and lesbian movement since the 1970s. Homosexual activists have forced many politicians to become more progressive, and today they can count on the support of the Green Party and the Social Democrats. Austrian society has also changed considerably. The traditional homophobia, fed by remnants of Nazi ideology and the strong influence of the Catholic Church, has lessened considerably, particularly in the younger generation. But a portion of the population continues to maintain a violently homophobic stance, which in turn is exacerbated by politicians of the populist right and far right. In a 1991 poll, 27% of Austrians declared themselves in favor of the strict pre-1971 laws against homosexuality.

Romania

In Romania, homosexuality was not specifically criminalized until 1936, under the influence of the Fascist Iron Guard, whose goal was to restore moral discipline over the populace. Strictly speaking, the law did not forbid homosexual acts, but rather the "public indecency" resulting from them. As defined, only a handful of people needed to be aware of a homosexual act in order for it to constitute an offense.

The fall of Romanian Fascism did not bring about any softening of the law. On the contrary, a law prohibiting homosexual relations (both male and female) was adopted in 1948. Unlike other communist countries such as Hungary, Czechoslovakia, or East Germany— which abolished this kind of wholesale interdiction in the 1960s and tolerated (especially in the 1980s) a discreet gay social life in its major cities—the Romanian regime under autocratic leader Nicolae Ceaucescu carried out a systematic repression of homosexuals until it dissolved in 1989. This tactic became part of the general evolution of the Romanian dictatorship, which did not soften at all during the 1970s.

Post-communist Romania is by far the most homophobic country in eastern Europe. Homosexuality was not decriminalized until 1996, in favor of a return to the more general legislation of offenses against public decency from the period of 1936–48. Article 200 of the Romanian penal code, which was not repealed until June 2001, provided for the punishment of any act between persons of the same sex if it was "committed in public or caused a public scandal." With regard to what constitutes "public," **jurisprudence** is particularly severe: for acts taking place in private, the offense occurs as soon as more than two people have knowledge of the act (neighbors, for example). Article 200 also penalized any inducement of homosexual relations, including any "propaganda, association, and

proselytism." This constituted a real obstacle to the dissemination of information on homosexuality, and severely limited the freedom of gay and lesbian associations, who were forced to dance around the law in order to simply exist.

The complete decriminalization of homosexuality, fiercely fought by many politicians and by the Orthodox Church, was, as in the Baltic countries, merely a concession to European demands. Pressure from the Council of Europe, the European Parliament, human rights associations, and the ILGA helped to bring about the abrogation of Article 200 and all other discriminatory measures against homosexuals.

Homosexuality is becoming ever more visible in Romania, and is gradually incurring some measures of political support. There are now several gay clubs in Bucharest, as well as other cities. As well, Bucharest celebrated its first Gay Pride day, or GayFest, in 2004, with financial support from some sections of government. And while civil partnerships or same-sex marriages are not permitted in Romania, the debate surrounding these issues is becoming more open.

—*Michel Celse*

ACCEPT Romania. http://www.accept-romania.ro (accessed March 3, 2008).

Adam, Barry D., Jan Willem Duyvendak, and André Krouwel, eds. *The Global Emergence of Gay and Lesbian Politics: National Imprints of a Worldwide Movement.* Philadelphia: Temple Univ. Press, 1999.

Bucharest Acceptance Group (ACCEPT). *Sexual Orientation Discrimination in Romania: A Survey of Violence, Harassment and Discrimination against Romania's Lesbian, Gay, Bisexual and Transgender Community.* Bucharest, 2001.

Clapham, Andrew, and Kees Waaldijk, eds. *Homosexuality: A European Community Issue. Essays on Lesbian and Gays Rights in European Law and Policy.* Dordrecht/Boston/London: Martinus Nijhoff Publishers, 1993.

Durandin, Catherine. *Roumanie, un piège ?* St-Claude-de-Diray, France: Ed. Hesse, 2000.

Grau, Günter, ed. *Homosexualität in der NS-Zeit.* Frankfurt am Main, Germany: Fischer, 1993. [Published in the US as *Hidden Holocaust?: Gay and Lesbian Persecution in Germany, 1933–45.* Chicago: Fitzroy Dearborn, 1995.]

Gay.lt. Lithuania. http://www.gay.lt (accessed March 3, 2008).

Graupner, Helmut. *Homosexualität und Strafrecht in Österreich: eine Übersicht.* Vienna: Rechtskomitee Lambda, 2001.

Háttér Society for Gays and Lesbians in Hungary, Labrisz

Lesbian Association. *Report on the Discrimination of Lesbians, Gay Men and Bisexuals in Hungary.* Budapest, 2001.

Homosexuelle Initiative (HOSI) Wien. *Rosa Liebe unterm roten Stern.* Kiel, Germany: Frühlings Erwachen, 1984.

————.Vienna, Austria. http://www.hosiwien.at (accessed March 3, 2008).

International Lesbian and Gay Association-Europe. http://www.ilga-europe.org (accessed March 3, 2008).

http://lambdawa.gejowo.pl/pozostale/english.html [Poland] (site now discontinued).

Human Rights Watch and the International Gay and Lesbian Human Rights Commission. *Public Scandals: Sexual Orientation and Criminal Law in Romania.* New York: Human Rights Watch, 1998.

ILGA-Europe. *L'après Amsterdam: l'Union européenne et l'orientation sexuelle.* Brussels, 1999.

Lambda Warszawa Association. *Report on discrimination on grounds of sexual orientation in Poland.* Warsaw, 2001.

Levin, Eve. *Sex and Society in the World of the Orthodox Slavs 900–1700.* Ithaca, New York: Cornell Univ. Press, 1989.

Rechtskomitee LAMBDA (RKL). Austria. http://www.rklambda.at (accessed March 3, 2008).

Steakley, James. "Sodomy in Enlightenment Prussia: From Execution to Suicide." In *The Pursuit of Sodomy: Male Homosexuality in Renaissance and Enlightment Europe.* Edited by Gerard Kent and Hekma Gert. New York: Harrington Park Press, 1989.

Wolff, Larry. *Inventing Eastern Europe.* Standford, CA: Standford Univ. Press, 1994.

—Balkans, the; Communism; Europe, Northern; European Law; Fascism; Germany; Russia.

EUROPE, NORTHERN

With good reason, the countries of northern Europe today have a reputation for **tolerance** of gays and lesbians, and some (Denmark and the Netherlands, in particular) have even been pioneers in gay rights issues, such as protection from **discrimination**, the legal recognition of same-sex couples, and the right to **adopt**. Of course, this does not mean that discrimination and other forms of hostile behavior against homosexuals have disappeared entirely from northern Europe. However, the adoption of laws upholding the rights of gays and lesbians in northern Europe reflects an evolution in social attitudes the region, demonstrating that the majority of the population has accepted the idea

that homosexuality is a "normal" variant of sexuality, and that it deserves to be legally recognized as such. As well, these laws serve to help fight against prejudice and homophobic attitudes by insisting on respect for sexual orientation as a social norm.

Historically, this evolution represents a reversal of values over the course of the last thirty years. Previously, it was certainly true that northern European countries had a much less severe tradition of repression, particularly in Scandinavia, and even a liberal tradition in the Benelux (the economic union representing Belgium, the Netherlands, and Luxembourg); however, there were never any positive views of homosexuality or of the idea that homosexuals should be accepted into mainstream society. As in all Western countries in general, the turning point took place during what is known as the "sexual liberation" of the 1960s and 70s, marked by the development of a strong homosexual movement whose visibility and activism played a major role in helping to change society's attitudes as well as instigate new legislation.

The Long Process of Decriminalizing Homosexuality

The penal codes of the Benelux nations had long differed from those in the Nordic countries, the direct result of the French Revolution's influence. In 1792–95, occupation of territories that today correspond to Belgium, the Netherlands, and Luxembourg by French revolutionary armies led to the straightforward abrogation, as in France, of the medieval and religious sodomy laws. The concept of sodomy covered not only the practice of anal penetration but more generally any non-procreative sexual practice; laws forbidding it punished any relations between individuals of the same sex, male or female. The Napoleonic rule that followed the revolutionary period saw the decriminalization of homosexuality written into law, with the adoption of a penal code that made no distinction between homosexuality and heterosexuality.

Since then, this freedom of homosexual relations between consenting adults has never been challenged in these three countries. However, with regard to matters of age of consent, certain discriminatory acts appeared during the twentieth century, although these have since been repealed.

In Belgium in 1846, the minimum age of consent was set for the first time to fourteen years of age for everyone, then raised to sixteen years in 1912. It was not until 1965, for reasons comparable to those that instigated the **Mirguet** amendment in France in 1960 (which added homosexuality to a list of "social scourges," along with alcoholism and prostitution), that Belgium increased the minimum age to eighteen years for homosexual relations, male or female. This law was repealed in 1985 to make the age of consent sixteen years for both homosexuals and heterosexuals.

Similarly to Belgium, Luxembourg had no regulations for age of consent until 1854, when it set the minimum age for all sexual relations at fourteen years. This law remained in place until 1971 when it established a separate age of consent for homosexuals, the same discriminatory measure that Belgium had instituted in 1965. It would not be until 1992 that the age of consent became the same for everyone, at sixteen years.

In the Netherlands, the age of consent for all relations was set at sixteen years in 1886. In 1911, the age was raised to twenty-one years for gays and lesbians, which remained in the Dutch penal code until 1971, when the minimum age for everyone was set at sixteen years.

The same decriminalization of homosexuality did not occur in Nordic countries at the end of the eighteenth century—the penal codes of the nineteenth century regularly punished gay male relations without exception. Lesbianism, too, was criminalized in Sweden and in Finland, but not in Norway or in Denmark.

The Nordic region's decriminalization process began in 1930 in Denmark and in 1944 in Sweden when homosexuality between consenting adults was legalized. However, both countries introduced discriminatory laws with regard to separate ages of consent, set at eighteen years for homosexual relations, and fifteen for heterosexual relations. As well, these new laws included female homosexuality, which previously had not been mentioned. The laws were removed in 1976 in Denmark and in 1978 in Sweden, replaced by an age of consent of fifteen years for everyone. Other discriminatory measures in Danish criminal law, such as the "incitement" of homosexual relations, prostitution, and various sexual crimes and offenses, were progressively repealed between 1967 and 1981. Iceland, an autonomous Danish territory prior to becoming a republic in 1944, adopted the Danish legislation of 1930. Abrogation of its discriminatory aspects would have to wait until 1992, including the setting of a single age of consent for everyone at fourteen years.

Decriminalization took longer in Norway and Finland. In Norway, the prohibition of sexual acts between men (but not women) was repealed in 1972; the age of consent was subsequently set at sixteen years for both homosexual as well as heterosexual relations. In Finland, homosexuality was decriminalized in 1971, but "promotion" of it remained illegal. Three laws continued to differentiate between homosexuals and heterosexuals: the age of consent (eighteen years versus sixteen years); the law prohibiting a person in a position of authority from abusing a minor, identified as someone between sixteen and twenty-one for homosexuals, compared to sixteen to eighteen years old for heterosexuals; and the specific offense of "enticement to homosexual relations." These laws were finally repealed in 1999, thus completing the process of decriminalization in the northern European nations.

The 1960s–70s: A Social Turning Point

In order to measure the evolution of social attitudes in northern European countries toward homosexuals, it is important to refrain from interpreting too positively the absence of criminalization of adult homosexuality in the Benelux countries, or the decriminalization that took place in Denmark and Sweden. In the latter two countries, decriminalization did not mean that society and government suddenly considered homosexuality to be a "normal" or acceptable orientation, but rather as a pathology that was better handled by **medicine** or **psychiatry** than the penal system. The idea grew that society must intervene when it came to protecting its youth; in this way, the goal of legal reform was less an issue of decriminalization than the "modernization" of law in order to more efficiently protect minors against the "derailment" of their "normal" sexual development. The same tendency can be more clearly observed in countries like Belgium and Luxembourg, whose separate age of consent legislation flew in the face of more than 500 years without any legal restriction of homosexuality.

These initiatives in Belgium and Luxembourg appear to be a conservative reaction that seems anachronistic compared to the evolution of social attitudes in western European cities beginning in the mid-1960s. Cities such as Amsterdam or Copenhagen were emblematic of the new counterculture where political debate, **feminism**, sexual liberation, and alternative lifestyles came together. Over and above the radical proclamations of sexual liberation, the evolution of social and moral norms with regard to sexuality was tangible in every country, within the space of only a few years. Homosexuals everywhere came together, asserted themselves, and achieved an unprecedented visibility, decisively benefiting from this new progressive climate and actively taking part in it.

Soon, homosexuality was no longer spoken of in terms of a sexual pathology and came to be seen more as a variant of sexuality. The legal reforms of the 1970s (including those which abolished separate ages of consent for homosexuals) were the result of legislators becoming sensitive to the new sexual revolution. The speed with which laws protecting the rights of homosexuals followed decriminalization simply confirms the radical transformation of the perception of homosexuality in the region. The respect of one's sexuality had become a fundamental human right, and it fell on legislators to act in cases where an individual's sexuality made him subject to discrimination.

This evolution has also taken place as a result of the active role played by gay and lesbian organizations in each country. In the Netherlands and the Nordic countries, an important characteristic of the gay and lesbian movement is its unity through the existence of a large national gay and lesbian **association**. Most of these organizations were created quite early on, between 1945 and 1950, but their audience and their influence remained modest until the early 1970s, when their ranks swelled with new activists who toughened their stance and put public visibility at the heart of their every action. This unity, despite internal debates that were often quite intense, allowed them to establish themselves as legitimate institutions representing the gay and lesbian community to the public authorities and political parties, which looked to these organizations when establishing the new legislative frameworks for gay and lesbian rights.

Laws to Protect Gay & Lesbian Rights
Since the early 1980s, all of the countries in northern Europe (with the exception of Belgium) progressively introduced explicit legislative measures intended to protect gays and lesbians from discrimination based on their sexual orientation: Norway in 1981, Denmark and Sweden in 1987, the Netherlands in 1993, Finland in 1995, and finally Iceland and Luxembourg in 1996–97. Generally, these measures modified existing anti-discriminatory laws designed to protect individuals or groups based on their ethnicity, race, or religion; "sexual orientation" was then added to this list. The discrimi-

natory acts prohibited by this type of law vary slightly from one country to another, but two are consistently mentioned: acts that provoke or incite discrimination, hostility, hatred, or **violence** toward an individual or a group of people, and a refusal to provide a good or a service.

Most of the countries have also adopted (sometimes simultaneously, sometimes at a later date) legal measures protecting gays and lesbians from discrimination in the **workplace**. The Netherlands was first in 1994, followed by Finland (1995), Denmark (1996), Luxembourg (1997), Norway (1998), and finally Sweden (1999); these laws not only protect employees from being fired because of their sexual orientation, but also from being unfairly treated with regard to salary, promotion, responsibilities, or workplace conditions.

"New Laws": The Recognition of Same-Sex Couples
In 1989, Denmark created a sensation by being the first country in the world to legally recognize same-sex couples. The Danish civil union, contrary to PaCS adopted in France ten years later, is an institution reserved specifically for same-sex couples, thus clearly intended to support "gay **marriage**." Symbolically—though use of the word "marriage" is avoided—the civil union ceremonies held at city hall do not differ significantly from heterosexual civil marriages. The Danish civil union allows for the same rights and responsibilities as a civil marriage, with two exceptions: adoption by same-sex couples is restricted to stepchildren, and (as of a 1997 law) they do not have the right to medically assisted procreation. The Faeroe Islands, which belong to Denmark but enjoy a certain amount of legislative autonomy, have not adopted the civil union.

Many other northern European countries instituted a type of civil same-sex union inspired by the Danish model: Norway in 1993, Sweden in 1995, Iceland in 1996, the Netherlands in 2001, and Finland in 2001. In the case of the Netherlands, the union is also available to heterosexual couples. These various legislations all offer a legal framework very similar to that of civil marriage, but with the consistent exception of the rights to parenthood and adoption.

Finally, in Belgium, a proposal to allow same-sex unions (albeit with the same restrictions against parenthood and adoption) was approved by the Council of Ministers in 2001, voted in by the Senate in November 2002, and adopted by the Chamber in 2003. Further, in 2000 Belgium adopted a law on "legal cohabitation" whose focus was quite different: it did not recognize same-sex couples per se but rather was a contract of communal living between two people regardless of their sexual orientation and the nature of their relationship. Thus, it is as much available to same-sex couples as it is to a brother and sister or two friends. Essentially, it establishes financial solidarity between the parties involved, and dictates how goods acquired during cohabitation are handled in case of separation. In 2006 the Belgian senate passed legislation recognizing the rights of same-sex couples to be parents and to adopt.

In the span of just ten years, across almost all of northern Europe, a sort of legal standard has been achieved which grants same-sex couples essentially the same rights as heterosexuals in terms of lodgings, taxation, legacy, or civil unions, with the exception of issues regarding parenthood (be it shared parental authority over the child of one of the partners, access to medically assisted procreation for lesbians, or simply the adoption of a child by a same-sex couple). Legislation of civil unions has the merit of recognizing the right for gays and lesbians to officially unite, but paradoxically introduces a new source of discrimination by creating a status more or less specific to same-sex couples, while refusing full access to the right to marry. Concerning these distortions, Denmark in 1999 took an additional step forward by granting each partner the right to adopt the other's children from a previous relationship.

The Netherlands was the first country to make a radical break with that logic of selective rights; since April 2001, two people of the same sex are authorized to enter into a civil marriage that is in every way the same as a marriage between heterosexuals, including the right to parenthood and adoption. In 2005, the Dutch cabinet passed a law relaxing rules prohibiting same-sex couples from adopting children from abroad. The Dutch civil union, legalized in 1998 and also open to heterosexual couples, continues to exist independent of marriage. By 2002, other northern European countries were engaged in a similar evolution, particularly Sweden, which in June of that year approved a law allowing same-sex couples to adopt children (including those from foreign countries), under the same conditions as heterosexual couples. Moreover, in 2005, Belgium became the first country in the world to officially recognize the International Day Against Homophobia (May 17).

—*Michel Celse*

Boone, Marc. "State Power and Illicit Sexuality: The Persecution of Sodomy in Late Medieval Bruges," *Journal of Medieval History*, no. 22 (1996).

Cultuur en Ontspannings-Centrum (COC—Centre for Culture and Leisure)—Netherlands. http://www.coc.nl (accessed February 18, 2008).

Danish National Association of Gays & Lesbians, the (LBL). http://www.lbl.dk (accessed February 18, 2008).

Graham, Mark. "Identity, Place, and Erotic Community within Gay Leather Culture in Stockholm," *Journal of Homosexuality* 35, no. 3–4 (1998).

Hansen, Bent. *Nordisk bibliografi: Homoseksualiteit.* Copenhagen: Pan, 1984.

Hekma, Gert. "Homosexuality and the Left in the Netherlands: 1890–1911," *Journal of Homosexuality* 29, no. 2–3 (1995).

Homosexuelle Initiative (HOSI) Vienna. *Rosa Liebe unterm roten Stem.* Kiel, Germany: Frühlings Erwachen, 1984.

International Lesbian and Gay Association-Europe. http://www.ilga-europe.org (accessed February 18, 2008).

———. "L'après Amsterdam: l'Union européenne et l'orientation sexuelle," Brussels (1999).

International Homo/Lesbian Information Center and Archives (IHLIA)—Netherlands. http://www.homodok.nl (accessed February 18, 2008).

Landsforeningen for lesbisk og homofil frigjøring (Gay and lesbian rights organization, Norway). http://www.llh.no (accessed February 18, 2008).

Liliequist, Jonas. "State Policy, Popular Discourse, and the Silence on Homosexual Acts in Early Modern Sweden," *Journal of Homosexuality* 35, no. 3–4 (1998).

Naerssen, Ax van, ed. *Interdisciplinary Research on Homosexuality in the Netherlands.* New York: Haworth Press, 1987.

Nilsson, Arne. "Creating Their Own Private and Public: The Male Homosexual Life Space in a Nordic City During High Modernity," *Journal of Homosexuality* 35, no. 3–4 (1998).

Noordam, Dirk Jaap. "Sodomy in the Dutch Republic, 1600–1725." In *The Pursuit of Sodomy: Male Homosexuality in Renaissance and Enlightment Europe.* Edited by Gert Hekma and Gerard Kent. New York: Harrington Park Press, 1989.

Oresko, Robert. "France, Germany, and Scandinavia: Homosexuality and the Court Elites of Early Modern France: Some Problems, Some Suggestions, and an Example," *Journal of Homosexuality* 16, no. 1–2 (1988).

Riksförbundet för homosexuellas, bisexuellas och transpersoners rättigheter (RFSL—The Swedish Federation for

Lesbian, Gay, Bisexual and Transgender Rights) http://
www.rfsl.se (accessed February 18, 2008).

Rosen, Wilhelm von. "Sodomy in Early Modern Denmark:
A Crime without Victims," *Journal of Homosexuality* 16,
no. 1–2 (1988).

Van Der Meer, Theo. "Tribades on Trial: Female Same-Sex
Offenders in Late Eighteenth-Century Amsterdam,"
Journal of Homosexuality 1, no. 3 (1991).

———. "The Persecutions of Sodomites in Eighteenth-
Century Amsterdam: Changing Perceptions of Sodomy,"
Journal of Homosexuality 16, no. 1–2 (1988).

*—Adoption; Discrimination; European Law; Europe, Eastern &
Central; Marriage; Parenting.*

EUROPEAN LAW

For the last twenty years, Europe has been the site of
some of the most important and unprecedented legal battles involving the rights of gays and lesbians.
Today in many European countries, many legislated
anti-discriminatory policies have been implemented,
based in part on the recommendations of the Council
of Europe (forty-seven countries signed the European
Convention for the Protection of Human Rights) and
resolutions passed by the European Union, as well as
judgments passed down from the European Court of
Human Rights. Calling for the respect and equality of
gay and lesbian rights in various realms of the law, the
European judicial order undeniably constitutes one of
the most important engines in the fight for gay and
lesbian equality and against homophobia.

Passed in 1981, the European Court of Human
Rights' judgment on the case *Dudgeon v. United
Kingdom* constituted the first instance of a state found
guilty of discriminating against a citizen by reason
of his homosexuality. In this particular case, Jeffrey
Dudgeon, a shipping clerk and gay activist in Belfast,
Northern Ireland, was interrogated by the police about
his sexual activities, resulting in Dudgeon filing a complaint with the European Commission of Human
Rights. In its judgment, the Court deemed Northern
Ireland's current legislation, in which homosexual acts
committed between consenting adults were still illegal,
to be a violation of the right of **privacy** as protected
by the European Convention. This decision establishing **jurisprudence** on the subject led those European
nations with laws at odds with the Convention to be-

gin the process of modifying legislation to be more favorable toward gay and lesbian rights. Since then, both
the European Union and the Council of Europe have
insisted that countries requesting admittance must
abolish any existing discriminatory laws against homosexuals. Further, those states that were already members of the European Union but had retained anti-gay
measures were regularly denounced by the European
Parliament.

Since the beginning of the 1980s, the influence of
European law has extended beyond that of penal law;
it also influences both the social perception of homosexuality and the daily lives of gays and lesbians. In
this way, a 1979 recommendation was adopted by the
Parliamentary Assembly of the Council of Europe, asking the Committee of Ministers from various countries to "[sensitize] public opinion on the problems
facing the moral and legal protection of homosexuals,"
as well as work toward eliminating work-related "and
other" discrimination, and institute new measures to
ensure the security of gays and lesbians, including "the
enjoyment of the same rights and facilities granted
to all citizens." In 1981, the Assembly adopted a text
recommending not only the cessation of all activities
or research "designed to alter the sexual orientation
of adults," but also to ensure, "no more no less," the
equality of gays and lesbians with regard to issues such
as employment, custody, visiting rights, and housing. In
1984, the Parliament of the European Union adopted
a resolution on sexual discrimination in the workplace
and, in 1986, it asked all member states to apply the
principle of non-discrimination based on sexual preference to their respective constitutions.

An important step was taken in 1994 when
the European Parliament adopted a resolution on
equal rights for gays and lesbians in the European
Community. The resolution requested member states
to put an end to the criminal punishments as well as to
discrimination; it also urged them to fight against homophobic violence and to organize campaigns against
all forms of social discrimination aimed at homosexuals. Also, for the first time, an appeal was launched in
favor of recognizing the rights of same-sex couples
"so that an end can be brought to the interdiction
preventing them from marrying or benefiting from
equivalent rights," as well as "the right for gays and
lesbians to be parents, to adopt, and to raise children." Further, in 1999 as part of a judgment criticizing Portugal, the European Court of Human Rights

affirmed that the refusal to grant visitation rights to a parent by reason of his or her homosexuality constituted an unjustifiable discrimination with regard to the Convention. Some time later, the same Court criticized the United Kingdom for its policy of excluding homosexuals from the **army**.

European law further entrenched its commitment against discrimination based on of sexual orientation in 1997 with the Amsterdam Treaty, which amended the original agreement establishing the European Union; overall, it provided for a greater emphasis on citizenship and the rights of individuals aiming at more democracy overall within the Union, and was the first international document that explicitly prohibited this kind of discrimination. This step forward was significantly reinforced by the Charter of Fundamental Rights of the European Union, adopted in December of 2000, whose Article stipulates against "discrimination based on any ground such as … sexual orientation." Since then, the Council of the European Union adopted a resolution obliging member states to scrupulously ensure equal treatment of gays and lesbians in matters of work and employment.

There have recently been some advances in the European Court of Human Rights when it comes to recognizing the right to marry and the right of same-sex couples to have families. In 2003, the European Parliament recommended that homosexuals be allowed to legally marry and adopt children. It urged the European Union to abolish all forms of discrimination against homosexuals, both legislative and de facto. The Parliament recommended that member states recognize both heterosexual and homosexual non-marital relationships, adopt a broader definition of the family, and confer the same rights on partners in such relationships as to those who are married. However, legislation recognizing and providing equal rights to same-sex couples has reached different stages in EU member states. There have been several cases in which the European Court of Human Rights has ruled in favor of these advancements. For example, in 2003 in Karner v. Austria, the Court ruled that a homosexual who lost his tenancy when his partner died was a victim of unlawful discrimination, and in 2008 in E.B. v. France, the Court ruled that exclusion of individuals from adopting children based on sexual orientation was discriminatory and in breach of the European Convention. Furthermore, between 2006 and 2007 the European Parliament passed three resolutions addressing the in-

crease of homophobia in Europe, which would see sentences handed down for homophobic offences, and at the same time officially recognizing the International Day Against Homophobia (May 17) in Europe.
—*Daniel Borrillo and Thomas Formond*
[Original essay updated by Arsenal Pulp Press.]

Assemblée parlementaire du Conseil de l'Europe. "Situation des lesbiennes et des gays dans les Etats membres du Conseil de l'Europe." Report, document 8755 (June 6, 2000). http://assembly.coe.int/Mainf.asp?link=/Documents/WorkingDocs/Doc00/FDOC8755.htm (accessed February 11, 2008). [In English as "Situation of Gays and Lesbians and Their Partners in Respect of Asylum and Immigration in the Member States of the Council of Europe." By the Parliamentary Assembly of the Council of Europe. Recommendation 1470, document 8654 (2000). http://assembly.coe.int/Documents/AdoptedText/ta00/EREC1470.htm (accessed February 11, 2008).]

Borrillo Daniel. *L'Homophobie*. Paris: Presses universitaires de France, 2000.

———. "L'Orientation sexuelle en Europe: esquisse d'une politique publique anti-discriminatoire." *Les Temps modernes*, no. 609 (2000).

Clapham, Andrew, and Kees Waaldijk, eds. *Homosexuality: A European Community Issue, Essays on Lesbian and Gay Rights in European Law and Policy*. Dordrecht/Boston/London: Martinus Nijhoff Publishers, 1993.

Meyer, Catherine-Anne. "L'Homosexualité dans la jurisprudence de la Cour et de la Commission européenne des droits de l'homme." In *Homosexualités et droit*. Edited by Daniel Borrillo. Paris: Presses universitaires de France, 1999.

Newton, David. *Gay and Lesbian Rights: A Reference Handbook (Contemporary World Issues)*. Santa Barbara, CA: ABC-Clio, 1994.

Wintemute, Robert. "Libertés et droits fondamentaux des personnes gays, lesbiennes et bisexuelles en Europe." In *Homosexualités et droit*. Edited by Daniel Borrillo. Paris: Presses universitaires de France, 1999.

———. "Strasbourg to the Rescue? Same-Sex Partners and Parents Under the European Convention." In *Legal Recognition of Same-Sex Partnerships*. Edited by Mads Andenaes and Robert Wintemute. Oxford: Hart Publishing, 2001.

—*Criminalization; Decriminalization; Discrimination; Jurisprudence; Parenting; Privacy.*

EX-GAY

The "ex-gay" movement first appeared in the United States during the 1970s, composed of men and women whose homosexuality had been supposedly "cured" and who encouraged other gays and lesbians to follow them on this course. Strongly influenced by religion, in particular the "born again" Christian movement (Christians who have rediscovered the "truth" of the Gospels after a period of atheism or religious indifference), the growth of the ex-gay phenomenon is directly linked to the removal of homosexuality from the American Psychiatric Association's list of mental illnesses in the early 1970s. While this victory for gays and lesbians did put an end (at least symbolically) to a century of social control at the hands of psychiatrists, it also had the undesirable consequence of abandoning a large number of people who wanted to be "cured" of their attraction to people of the same sex. Among them, those who could not reconcile their religious faith with their sexual orientation subsequently organized themselves, sometimes in alliance with their churches, into self-help groups to mutually assist one another in their quest to become heterosexual. Many ex-gay organizations were created in this way, commonly aligned with fundamentalist church communities. Beginning in 1976, most of these organizations came together as part of a larger association known as Exodus (now Exodus International), which provides services for those who seek "freedom from homosexuality."

The primary activity of ex-gay organizations centers on the concept of "reparative therapy," which combines religious exercises with psychotherapy. In most cases, the therapeutic practice takes the form of group prayer, **Bible** study, sessions with a "Christian" psychologist, and group discussions. Some groups take their inspiration directly from established techniques used to fight addictions; one obvious example is Homosexuals Anonymous, modeled after the twelve-step program used by groups like Alcoholics Anonymous and Narcotics Anonymous. Another common method of treatment reinforces the traditional negative perception of homosexuality as a type of gender **inversion**, in which groups help lesbians become more feminine, and gay men more masculine, through workshops on such subjects as makeup application, automobile mechanics, and basketball. Finally, the most radical groups have been to known to practice exorcisms or electroshock aversion therapy.

Up until the late 1990s, these groups received rather timid and discreet support from the religious right in America, despite having much in common. This was in part because, although they had "repented" and were trying to become "cured," the gays and lesbians making up these groups often continued to have relationships with and desire for people of the same sex. Further, it was not long before many "ex-ex-gays" began to speak out, citing not only the failure of such therapy to work, resulting in depression and suicidal feelings and attempts, but also the fact that they had finally come to terms with their sexual orientation and did not need to be "cured." Indeed, the two male cofounders of Exodus finally abandoned their movement to live together as a couple, subsequently becoming two of the main figures in the fight against ex-gay movements. In this context, it becomes obvious why these groups appear to be rather untrustworthy "allies" in the eyes of the conservative religious movement.

In recent years, however, the situation has changed. The legislative progress achieved in certain cities and counties by new anti-discriminatory laws during the Clinton administration, combined with the appearance of a gay conservative faction within the Republican Party with strong lobbying pull, brought the ex-gay movement closer to forces from the religious right. Together, they put forth the argument that anti-discriminatory laws protecting homosexuals were irrelevant because gays and lesbians could in fact change their sexual orientation. In 1998, this alliance resulted in a national advertising campaign entitled "Truth in Love," the cost of which ($500,000) was borne by eighteen groups from the religious right; as part of the campaign, full-page advertisements promoting the ex-gay movement appeared in some of the most widely read newspapers in the US, such as *USA Today*, the *Wall Street Journal*, and the *Washington Post*. The first one appeared in the *New York Times* featuring Anne Paulk, a "wife, mother, and former lesbian" who declared, "I am living proof that the Truth can set you free." Since then, many more campaigns targeted at the general public have appeared, showing that the ex-gay movement has become an integral part of the religious right's strategy against gays and lesbians.

The ex-gays constitute what is probably one of the most pathetic chapters in the history of homophobia in North America. The stories told by "ex-ex-gays" attest to how destructive this self-hatred can be when it is experienced collectively. The best defense against these practices can be found in the work of some gay **associations** and churches that aim to reconcile religious faith with homosexuality. And despite Exodus having established chapters in many countries, it remains for the time being a North American phenomenon. However, the growth of evangelical sects in **Latin America**, **Africa**, **Eastern Europe**, and **Southeast Asia** raises the uncomfortable possibility that the ex-gay movement may be able to extend its influence worldwide.

—*Pierre-Olivier de Busscher*

Cameron, Paul. *What Causes Homosexual Desire and Can It Be Changed?* Washington, DC: Family Research Institute, 1992.

Human Rights Campaign website. "Finally Free: How Love and Acceptance Saved Us From the Ex-Gay Ministries" PDF. HRC (2000) http://www.hrc.org/publications (accessed February 12, 2008.)

———. "Mission Impossible: Why Reparative Therapy and Ex-Gay Ministries Fail." PDF. HRC (1998) http://www.hrc.org/publications (accessed February 12, 2008.)

http://www.truluck.com/html/sexual_orientation_and_the ex.html (site now discontinued).

Murphy, Timothy. "Redirecting Sexual Orientation Techniques and Justifications," *The Journal of Sex Research* 29. no. 4 (1992).

Pennington, Sylvia. *Ex-Gays? There Are None.* Hawthorne: Lambda Christina Fellowship, 1989.

Sébastien. *Ne deviens pas gay, tu finiras triste.* Paris: Ed. François-Xavier de Guibert, 1998.

—*Heterosexism; Medicine; North America; Protestantism; Psychiatry; Theology; Treatment.*

EXHIBITIONISM

In French society, which distinguishes itself by its Republican attitude (and which even looks down on the concept of "community"), it is sometimes difficult to reveal one's true colors. In this way, the history of gays and lesbians does not differ greatly from that of feminist movements, or the struggles against racism and **AIDS**. A crucial question has long been at the heart of the gay and lesbian community's struggle to assert its identity: just how much should be revealed in order to change society's prevailing attitude toward

it? For many, attesting to one's homosexuality is itself a form of exhibitionism: "*on s'affiche*," to use the French term. The dictionary's definition of the exhibitionism denotes a lapse in morals: "The act of publicly displaying one's feelings, one's **private** life, *that which should remain hidden* [author's emphasis]." On closer inspection, however, the rules that govern the separation of the public and the private do not seem to work equally for everyone. Heterosexuals enjoy the social privilege of being permitted to display all the outward signs of their heterosexuality (from wedding rings to open displays of affection) without ever being accused of exhibitionism. Conversely, the mention or manifestation of homosexuality, whether individual or collective, is often seen as inappropriate; it is sometimes perceived as being in poor taste ("Why are you divulging this information?"), and also suggests some kind of moral fault. Any homosexual discourse is considered excessive if it goes beyond the limits of the **discretion** that society demands of it. In short, for many, exhibitionism begins where the **closet** ends.

Homosexual exhibitionism, at least as it appears in homophobic **rhetoric**, has a long history. Truth be told, in the beginning, the very idea of homosexual exhibitionism would have been completely improbable. During the Ancien Régime, the social perception of "sodomites" was so extreme as to link them with occult sects, secret societies, and invisible networks—a virtual underworld of **vice**, the shadowy depths of which Marcel Proust would still hint at even as late as the early twentieth century. In these conditions, far from being incorrigible exhibitionists, sodomites were seen instead as masters of dissimulation. Naturally, there were some sodomites who were notoriously open, but in general, homosexuality was shrouded in silence (or at least whispers) which corresponded to a sort of tacit agreement that was in the mutual public interest. To avoid prosecution by the law, "sexual deviants" kept themselves hidden from view wherever possible. The authorities preferred to look the other way; they tried to keep prosecutors from drawing too much public attention to affairs that might compromise certain highly-placed individuals, and to prevent the corruption of young innocents by ensuring that they remained unaware of such practices. Whether it came to the moralists or the debauchees, everyone preferred to stay quiet for fear of saying too much.

By the end of the nineteenth century, however, homosexual exhibitionism had become a common topic of discussion. But this did not mean there was a sudden change in attitude. This new theme did not replace the old; rather, it was superimposed over the old in a paradoxical way, like an indissoluble photographic negative, depicting the homosexual as an exhibitionist who liked to hide, or perhaps a secretive person who liked to expose himself. So did this new portrayal translate into a rising tide of visible homosexuality in Europe? While not impossible, it has yet to be proven. Regardless, it became common for people to pine for the good old days, when at least the vice was kept hidden from public view.

In the 1926 issue of *Les Marges*, dedicated to the literary preoccupation with homosexuality, François Mauriac, writing on the influence of André **Gide** and Marcel Proust, commented on the matter in the same way; that henceforth, "*many who were hidden would stop keeping themselves hidden*" (Mauriac's emphasis). In the same issue, the French author Rachilde (Marguerite Vallette-Eymery) states, "Almost all homosexuals are exhibitionists, and when they are artists or writers, they feel the need to tell their story." The words used here are important. At the time, the descriptive noun "exhibitionist" was a recent lexicological creation, dating back to 1880, and belonged to the vocabulary of medical science, more precisely, **psychiatry**. In the works of Richard von Krafft-Ebing, Jean-Martin Charcot, or Valentin Magnan, the word designates a pathology similar to homosexuality. Both are often associated together, given that homosexuality is frequently associated with all sorts of **perversions**. The concept of homosexual exhibitionism is then part of a pseudo-scientific vernacular, which reveals how the old, immoral image of the "sodomite" was systematically medicalized. In this sense, the simple transition from a moral vocabulary to a medical one becomes clear—previously, where one would speak of homosexuality in terms of vice, now it was in the context of pathological exhibitionism. This new formulation gave this concept of homosexuality a kind of incontestable scientific legitimacy, as suggested by the quasi-apodictic character of Rachilde's comments. This psychiatric vernacular would appear again in the commentary of French writer Thomas Raucat, to whom the new homosexual fashion in literature was tied to a Freudian-inspired exhibitionistic and narcissistic ecstasy: "Ever since an eminent Austrian psychiatrist made the discovery that the human soul is really a cesspool, these gentlemen writers seem to have gotten together to organize, just as they do in Bois de Boulogne [a park in Paris] on summer nights, pleasure parties lit by dark lanterns." In short, it seems clear: by adding one perversion to another, all homosexuals must be exhibitionists (the worst of these being writers, of course).

Today, the idea of homosexuality as a sickness is less popular, though it was very much in vogue only thirty or forty years ago. Under these conditions, it is easy to imagine that the idea of homosexual exhibitionism should have fallen apart on its own, given the link to this medical and psychiatric concept. In reality, though, it endured, and in fact shifted to the realm of the political. Today, several decades after what was considered the beginning of the real struggle for gay and lesbian rights, the concept is still around. For homophobes, the increased visibility of homosexuals—be it sexual, social, political, or health-related—is perceived as if it were an intolerable breach of some invisible boundary. Further, the word "exhibitionism" is associated with the concepts of pleasure, pride, and ego; in this sense, if gays and lesbians express themselves with a sense of joy and identity, it is somehow perceived as "exhibitionist" by homophobes and thus unacceptable. Lesbian and gay "pride" is thus often associated with exhibitionism: according to this view, all those naked homosexuals, all those drag queens, paint a bad picture of homosexuality (despite the fact that no one ever talks about a poor image of heterosexuality as a result of the Carnival in Rio de Janeiro); even the simple act of homosexuals walking in the street is considered exhibitionism. This fear, it seems, dates back to the earliest gay and lesbian **associations**. Historians have shown that during the 1950s, gays and lesbians who tried to respond to the **discrimination** expressed against them encountered not only opposition from homophobes, but also the incomprehension of their peers. For some homosexuals, when faced with the dangerous prospect of **scandal** if exposed, it was preferable to stay hidden. To come out of hiding—to assert oneself as human—was to risk a backlash, even exclusion, from mainstream society, their unnamable identity plunging them into infamy. Homophobia is thus the keystone to this issue: external homophobia from society, and internalized homophobia from other gays and lesbians.

Many gay and lesbian writers still refuse to allude to their homosexuality, even though it is often at the heart of their creative process. This refusal of exhibitionism is fed by a feeling of fear, which may or may not be acknowledged but is common all the same, even in members of the intelligentsia. The desired goal of gays and lesbians who feel this way is to obtain the best of what society has to offer (legal recognition and rights, marriage, **parenting**, etc.) without ever having to reveal oneself for who one really is. The reticence of many homosexuals to come out, to the point of contorting the truth about themselves on a daily basis, is a form of perpetual shame. Therein lies the problem—it is obvious that any real improvement to the lives of gays and lesbians comes through the direct promotion of their culture, which requires a certain degree of courage that, according to some, is really just a form of exhibitionism. Gay-positive actions such as directing a film about homosexuality, opening a gay or lesbian bar, or even identifying oneself in the street by way of certain social signals or attire, can only be accomplished through the affirmation not only of oneself, but also of others. It is true that many "natural" heterosexual social habits—such as holding hands in public, or talking about one's partner with colleagues—are considered exhibitionist when undertaken by gays and lesbians. But if homosexuality is to be truly legitimate, as many recognize it to be (at least officially), then this exhibitionism must be viewed as an exercise, pure and simple, of the same freedom of expression enjoyed by heterosexuals.

—*Didier Lestrade*

Adam, Barry D., Jan Willem Duyvendak, and André Krouwel, eds. *The Global Emergence of Gay and Lesbian Politics: National Imprints of a Worldwide Movement*. Philadelphia: Temple Univ. Press, 1999.

Guillemaut, Françoise. "Images invisibles: les lesbiennes." In *La Peur de l'autre en soi, du sexisme à l'homophobie*. Edited by Michel Dorais, Pierre Dutey, and Daniel Welzer-Lang. Montreal: VLB Editeur, 1994.

Krafft-Ebing, Richard von. *Psychopathia sexualis*. Paris: G. Carré, 1895. [Published in English as *Psychopathia Sexualis*.]

Lever, Maurice. *Les Bûchers de Sodome*. Paris: Fayard, 1985.

Les Marges 35, no. 141 (March 1926). New edition by Patrick Cardon, Cahiers GaiKitschCamp, no. 19. Lille, France: 1993.

Tamagne, Florence. *Histoire de l'homosexualité en Europe, Berlin, Londres, Paris, 1919–1939*. Paris: Le Seuil, 2000. [Published in the US as *A History of Homosexuality in Europe: Berlin, London, Paris, 1919–1939*. New York: Algora, 2004.]

Thompson, Mark, ed. *The Long Road to Freedom: The Advocate History of the Gay and Lesbian Movement*. New York: St Martin's Press, 1994.

—*Associations; Communitarianism; Closet, the; Gide, André; Heterosexism; Literature; Outing; Politics; Rhetoric; Scandal; Shame; Wilde, Oscar.*

F

FAMILY

For many homosexuals, the family is the first source of what may be referred to as the "homophobic experience." Familial homophobia is so common and destructive, in fact, that many homosexuals would rather fight for better social and political rights for themselves and others than deal with the very personal issue of family. Like the state, **school**, and the church, the family is a key institution in the fabric of society, but compared to other institutions, it has a more profound and damaging impact on gays and lesbians when it comes to instance of homophobia.

Over the last thirty years, the political struggle for gay and lesbian rights has advanced in many domains, such as spousal rights, gay **marriage**, and gay **parenting**. In the effort to combat familial homophobia, however, two aspects of the subject must be identified: homophobia within the family, and the homophobic usage of the idea of the family.

Homophobia Within Family

The impact of familial homophobia is based on the role the family, as an institution, plays in society and the lives of gay and lesbian children. Children are taught from the outset that the family is the only place where one can develop an acceptable and healthy identity. As French sociologist Pierre Bourdieu has written, the family is "dedicated to offering a model for all social bodies," and it is "the place for the naturalization of the social arbitrariness." As it stands, even society and the state recognize the family's great power over its members. Starting very early in life, children take in messages about what is proper behavior for girls and boys. These messages may be direct or indirect. A boy who is not masculine enough or a girl who is too masculine is quickly brought under control. The message, how-

ever, is just as strong when a child witnesses members of his or her own family issue homophobic **insults** or perform acts of homophobic **violence** against others. These insults, this violence, immediately establish a standard of acceptable behavior within the family.

For the gay or lesbian child coming out to his or her own family, this standard can have dramatic consequences, including verbal and physical violence or psychological blackmail. Such tactics are used by parents in the name of love, yet negative words and acts can be devastating and irreparable. Furthermore, gays and lesbians, particularly youths, find it extremely difficult to talk openly about homophobic violence in the family more so than other types of family violence. We know it is one of the critical causes of the high rate of **suicide** among homosexual teenagers (eight times more than heterosexuals, according to an American study).

Even in the absence of physical violence or outright rejection, it often takes a great amount of time for families to accept that one of their members is homosexual. There is symbolic violence: first denial, the idea that "it's going to go away"; then the refusal to talk about it, sometimes accompanied by the request to keep quiet: "Don't tell your father," etc. The list of typical family responses is long and well known to gays and lesbians. Changes in social attitudes toward gays and lesbians may have improved relations between many homosexuals and their families in ways that would have been unthinkable in the past, although heterosexism persists. To understand the complexity of the situation, one must consider the diversity of familial models and familial homophobias as inherent products of Western history.

The most ancient model of family still holds strong for many of us: the clan-family, or the traditional family, made up of multiple generations, is still typical in the majority of Western societies since before the nineteenth century. Take modern-day Latin America, for example. Here, the family typically controls its members from birth until death; deeply patriarchal, it mandates and controls the **marriages** of its children. The head of the family is granted full authority to maintain family order at any cost, thus justifying homophobic violence when members "betray" the family by becoming gay or lesbian. The **Catholic Church** still largely refers to this family model, explicitly in developing countries and implicitly in Western ones. By advocating the control of its members all their lives, this family model strongly discourages any activity that undermines the family order. Thus, the only homosexuals who are slightly visible under this control are social outcasts, victims of violence, and young men who have not married. Homosexuals must live in secret and **shame**.

But this traditional model evolved as a result of the industrial revolution and the environment of the twentieth century. The new traditional family was smaller, centered on the married couple with fewer children, with the ideal of the stay-at-home wife. The parents' control over their children remained absolute, based on a desire that the children learned to "conform" to a society and its standardized values. The pressure to get married was stronger than ever. Within the family, homophobia as a means to control behavior was ferocious, but outside, the state now played a much larger role.

This family model took its final shape in the 1950s, corresponding to the height of legal homophobia in the United States and France. This model remains in place today in Europe and more so in the US, and is the basis for a large number of homophobic practices and discourses, mostly in the purported name of "best interest of the child." Despite this (or perhaps because of this), these same families produced the first lesbian and gay militants (the word was coined then) in the 1970s. The development of capitalist, industrial societies in the twentieth century caused a social revolution by breaking the power of the extended family; it also allowed for greater socialization outside the family, promoting the will of the individual that ultimately led, among other things, to the birth of gay and lesbian culture in the West.

In fact, the 1970s saw the end of the traditional family as it had been known, and multiple variations on the idea of family became common. There started a strong dissociation between couples and marriage, between marriage and children, and a de-legitimization of the separation of sexual roles; there was also a drastic decrease in parental authority, and an explosion in the divorce rate. All of this led to new forms of familial relations that would open the debate on what now must be acknowledged by law.

Thus we can understand how homophobia within families can also change and evolve. Parents and children are now witness to the new visibility of homosexuals within society, and homophobia finally has a name. Although it still has potentially damaging ramifications, it now becomes possible to identify oneself as homosexual or lesbian within the family; to identify oneself as a parent, brother, or sister of a homosexual; and to call oneself a gay parent. At the same time, expressions of homophobia within families are now challenged. This evolution in the family model has created an ideological battle on the very idea of family, a battle that is also played out in the media and the political arena.

Family as an Argument in the Homophobic Discourse
Traditionally, homophobic comments about family have been unapologetic. A recent example can be found in *Vivre ensemble en famille* (Living together as a family), a book for six- to eight-year-olds, published in 1998 in France by Bayard, a Catholic publisher, where the existence of gays and lesbians in families is not mentioned, and where we find written that "families have always existed because men and women have always had children," and that "[the family] is a set of people that are linked together by marriage, birth or **adoption.**" Nothing more is said on what constitutes a family. Thus, this book dismisses all alternative models, including gay parenting.

But times are changing. Homophobic people who speak in the public domain are, for the first time, put on the defensive. They are forced to address a wide range of controversial subjects including adoption by gay couples, the status of homosexual partners, and medically assisted procreation. This is the reason we have seen of late the emergence of a whole set of somewhat dispersed homophobic discourses that purport to protect and defend the family. To understand them, one has to see what they have in common and what differentiates them.

Almost all homophobic discourses on the family borrow heavily on the theme of moral **decadence**, a common feature of reactionary thinking. They are based on the same assumptions: the family is undergoing a serious crisis that threatens to bring down the whole social system with it, and it is urgent that we protect and strengthen it. That leads to the second common feature of such discourses, the call to political action, often in response to gay activism. Indeed, at stake is the refusal of social advances for gays and lesbians, such as the French Civil Solidarity Pact called **PaCS** (Pacte civil de solidarité), but also the will to reestablish the central place of marriage in society. "Marriage and family are at the heart of the State's duty" because "family is the basic model that allows society to establish itself and last," reactionary French politician Christine **Boutin** wrote in *Le "mariage" des homosexuels?* in 1997. Indeed, to quote a recent book expressing similar concerns, *La famille à venir* (The family to come): "[family is] an absolute necessity in the context of unprecedented crisis of society and economy." In this view, homosexual demands threaten the family; the state must oppose it, and even react to it.

Recent Attempts to Establish a Homophobic Theory of Family

As we have seen, the old argument of nature and natural law to justify homophobia is, by itself, no longer convincing. Those in France arguing against PaCS thus used several different tactics, supposedly scientific, to justify the exclusion of spousal and family rights from homosexuals. To use the words of psychoanalyst Michel Tort, homophobia theory is today "a symbolic estuary where Levi-Strauss, Lacan and the traditional family right flow together."

Let us first consider **psychoanalysis** as an argument to justify homophobia. Without going into too much detail, let us note the use of a Lacanian vulgate that makes gender **difference** the basis for all adult sexuality and a structural component from the parental point of view, of all future personality of the child. Its commonality with Christian thinking on the subject is apparent, and we are not surprised when priest-psychoanalyst Tony Anatrella writes: "There is only love between a man and a woman because love implies a fundamental otherness." He also contends that "parental love exists only through the mediation of conjugal love," which lets us better understand Christine Boutin's assertions when she says that PaCS would "put the child and *human love* in danger" (which is the title of a chapter of her book, cited earlier). Boutin can thus negate even the remote possibility that a gay couple could be equal

in dignity and nature to a married couple, homosexuality being an "ephemeral and **sterile** project"; in this way, she attempts to give legal credence to the idea that the homosexuality and the gay couple threatens society as we know it.

In a less hateful and apparently more acceptable manner, we can consider that gay couples, due to their unsettled sexuality, are, in a futile way, imitating heterosexuals. This is Sylviane Agacinski's thesis in her book *Politique des sexes,* published in 1998. In this sense, the gay couple is "slightly fabricated," and remains separate from society (their desire not being "universal"), and therefore they should not pretend that they are a family. We can see how Agacinski's condemned gay couple and Boutin's beloved heterosexual family flow together in a closed homophobic loop. But, stiff opposition from psychoanalytic communities on this use of Lacan, and particularly the heinous character of Tony Anatrella's comments which very nearly justify homophobic violence, prove the academic and practical limits of the psychoanalytical approach to this subject.

Anthropology offers another justification for homophobia. Granted, sociologist Irène Théry, family specialist, does not offer heinous comments like Anatrella. She clearly acknowledges gay couples, but at the same time aims to deny them the right of adoption. Théry claims that healthy child development is predicated on two parents of opposite sexes. Her stance against gay adoption is thus not based on political rhetoric, but on "scientific," anthropological "evidence." In so doing, she legitimizes homophobic comments about gay parents, including scandalous pedophilic connotations in which such parents pose a "danger to children."

Past & Present Strategies for Non-Homophobic Families

At the end of this analysis, we can better understand the evolution of gay strategies toward the family institution and define its key moments. For gays and lesbians in traditional families, escape was often the only solution; in the twentieth-century family model, the struggle of gays and lesbians was still difficult, consisting of maintaining a space of **tolerance** beside the family institution. In *Corydon,* published in 1922, André **Gide** demonstrates that the notion of homosexuality which he defends could not hurt families, but on the contrary, make them stronger. In 1999, writer Dominique Fernandez subscribed to this same logic when he affirmed in his essay, "Le Loup et le chien" (The wolf and the dog), that "family concerns the majority of French citizens; PaCS, the minority that is situated outside the family. PaCS has nothing to do with family and consequently does not threaten it in any way." During the 1970s and 1980s, attitudes relaxed somewhat although social hostility toward issues involving gays and the family remained strong. Today we see many gays and lesbians reinvest in the idea of the family by defining family for themselves, outside of the traditional model, to include friends and lovers. Armistead Maupin's books (such as *Tales of the City*) are symbolic of this. The road traveled permits hope for new ideas of family, whether gay or heterosexual, where full equality can be guaranteed and defended for both children and adults.

—*Philippe Masanet*

Agacinski, Sylviane. *Politique des sexes*. Paris: Le Seuil, 1998. [Published in the US as *Parity of the Sexes*. Translated by Lisa Walsh. New York: Columbia Univ. Press, 2001.]

Anatrella, Tony. Preface to *L'Amour en morceaux*. By Gérard Leclerc. Paris: Presses de la Renaissance, 2000.

Bernstein, Robert. *Straight Parent/Gay Children: Keeping Families Together*. New York: Thunder's Mouth Press, 1995.

Borrillo, Daniel, Eric Fassin, and Marcela Iacub, eds. *Au-delà du PaCS, l'expertise familiale à l'épreuve de l'homosexualité*. Paris: Presses universitaires de France, 1998.

Boutin, Christine. *Le "Mariage" des homosexuels? CUCS, PIC, PACS et autres projets législatifs*. Paris: Critérion, 1998.

Bozett, Frederick W. and Marvin B. Sussman, eds. *Homosexuality and Family Relationships*. New York: Harrington Park Press, 1996.

Carrington, Christopher. "No Place like Home: Relationships and Family Life Among Lesbians and Gay Men." *Journal of Homosexuality* 42 no. 2.

Clauzard, Philippe. *Conversations sur l'homophobie. L'Education comme rempart contre l'exclusion*, Paris: L'Harmattan, 2002.

Desfossé, Bertrand, Henri Dhelhemmes, Christèle Fraïssé, and Adeline Raymond. *Pour en finir avec Christine Boutin, aspects moraux, juridiques et psychologiques du rejet des homosexuals*. Paris: H & O Editions, 1999.

Fernandez, Dominique. *Le Loup et le chien, un nouveau contrat social*. Paris: Pygmalion, 1999.

Lensel, Denis and Jacques Lafond. *La Famille à venir, une réalité, menacée mais nécessaire*. Paris: Economica, 2000.

Leroy-Forgeot, Flora. "Nature et contre nature en matière d'homoparentalité." In *Homoparentalité, Etats des lieux*. Association des Parents Gays et Lesbiens symposium. Paris: ESF, 2000.

Nadaud, Stéphane. *L'Homoparentalité, une chance pour la famille?* Paris: Fayard, 2002.

Ryan, Bill and Jean-Yves Frappier. "Quand l'autre en soi grandit: les difficultés à vivre l'homosexualité à l'adolescence." In *La Peur de l'autre en soi. Du sexisme à l'homophobie*. Edited by Michel Dorais, Pierre Dutey, Daniel Welzer-Lang. Montreal: VLB, 1994.

Tort, Michel. "Homophobies psychanalytiques," *Le Monde* (October 15, 1999).

Weston, Kath. *Families Who Choose: Lesbians, Gays, and Kinship*. New York: Columbia Univ. Press, 1991.

—*Adoption; Anthropology; Decadence; European Law; Gender Differences; Heterosexism; Jurisprudence; Marriage; Otherness; Parenting; Psychoanalysis; Rhetoric; Shame; Sterility; Suicide.*

FAR RIGHT, the

The formation of what can be referred to as right-wing politics was based on the reaction of the traditional elite to the French Revolution, more specifically to those ideas that the Revolution embodied (that is, the philosophical theories of the Enlightenment). Since its inception, the right has tended to reject the new, progressive principles of equality between men (over and above differences of class and race), democratic politics (which can be limited, in practice), religious **tolerance**, the secular role of the state, and the universal right to education, among other things. Throughout the nineteenth century, the right as a whole seemed to turn and began to integrate these principles, although some steadfastly refused to compromise over these progressive ideas. It was in this way that around the beginning of the twentieth century, a new faction began to take shape: the far (or extreme) right. More combustive and less elitist than what is usually understood as the right, the far right seeks to secure the support of the masses for its reactionary agenda.

As French political professor Ariane Chebel d'Apollonia, who has authored books on the far right, explains it, "the mentality of the far right is based on the affirmation of specific values. Despite the heterogeneity of its ideas, certain common themes can be identified." These values include a strong and authoritarian government, the rejection of liberal individualism and capitalism, anti-intellectualism, new spirituality (whether it is based on fundamentalist **Christianity** or even neo-paganism), nationalism, militarism, anti-feminism (and the belief that the "natural" function of women is procreation), racism, xenophobia, and anti-Semitism. While **Fascism**—as demonstrated by the Italian Fascist party and the German Nazi party between the years 1920 and 1940—is probably the most well-known example, since the beginning of the twentieth century and right up to the present day, political parties can be found in all parts of the world which embrace these core ideas that can be seen as characteristic of the far right.

Even if homosexuality had never been one of its main concerns, the far right has nevertheless consistently shown itself to be strongly homophobic. Desiring to defend the patriarchal order and obsessed with moral **decadence**, the far right is deeply conservative with regard to any issue related to mores and sexuality. This explains its fierce opposition not only to abortion (which it likens to the murder of innocent children and associates with the trend toward birthrate decreases in Western nations) and pornography (which it claims corrupts youth), but also sexual freedom in all its forms. Considered by the far right to be decadent and **against nature**, homosexuality according to this view is far more than a simple individual **vice** or personal defect; it threatens to bring entire nations to ruin by sapping the virility out of citizens.

Nonetheless, there is a certain ambiguity in the relationship between homosexuality and the far right. This was well-illustrated by the Fascists of the 1920s to 1940s, whose cult of virility, strength, and youth (plus, one might even say, a generalized ambience of homosociality and homoeroticism) was a source of fascination and attraction for certain homosexuals, although they never made up much more than a small minority among partisans of the far right. Ernst Röhm, friend and right arm of Adolf Hitler before the Führer ordered his assassination in 1934, is one of the most famous examples of extreme right-wing homosexuals, but he is far from the only one. In France, a handful of them, such as Abel Bonnard (Minister of Education from 1942 to 1944), nicknamed "Gaystapo" ("*Gestapette*") by Marshal **Pétain**, served the Vichy government and collaborated actively with the German occupiers. These sentiments were also shared by a few lesbians who lived in Paris, for example, the American Natalie Barney, who was an anti-Semite, detested the common masses, and declared that the Fascists and the Nazis had "a superior cause" to that of the Allies. It is noteworthy that the left was often as homophobic as the right during this era, and

did not hesitate to accuse the Fascists of a predilection for homosexuality. There are more recent examples of homosexuals among the far right: the magazine *Gaie France*, published by Michel Caignet starting in 1986, was both fascistic and openly gay; and the heretofore hidden homosexuality of certain neo-Nazi leaders was uncovered by the press in both Great Britain (Martin Webster) and Germany (Michael Kühnen and Bernd E. Althans). Also worthy of mention is Pim Fortuyn, an openly homosexual Dutch political leader, who was assassinated on May 6, 2002. He was often portrayed outside of the Netherlands as being a member of the far right, even though his ideas were most often closer to those of populist or republican parties.

Given these numerous examples, it is clear that the link between homosexuality and Fascism has been regularly referenced throughout the twentieth century, leading homosexual writer and anti-Fascist Klaus Mann to observe in 1934: "Homosexuality and Fascism are very close to being considered the same thing.... Homosexuals are being made out to be the Jews of the anti-Fascists. It's abominable." In addition, Luchino Visconti's 1969 film *The Damned* portrayed the Nazis as a band of homosexuals, decadent, degenerate, and effete. More recently, a sensationalistic 2001 book by German historian Lothar Machtan, *Hitler's Geheimnis* (published in English as *The Hidden Hitler*) claimed to have proof of Hitler's homosexuality, an issue that was already an old chestnut of Nazi historiography: as early as the 1930s, Hitler was sometimes portrayed as a "hopeless queer" in **caricatures**. Independent of their truthfulness (which has never been established), these kinds of allegations were often created by Fascism's opponents to draw connections between the far right and homosexuality, despite the fact that the vast majority of far right militants and leaders are proudly heterosexual and resolutely homophobic.

Right-wing homophobia appeared in Europe during the eighteenth century, when partisans of the established order accused certain philosophers of being sodomites, and dubbed sodomy as the "philosophical **sin**." They used the same argument against many well-known revolutionaries during the 1790s (no doubt for controversial ends, and without really believing it), including the prudish Maximilien Robespierre. In return, the philosophers and revolutionaries made the same accusations against their opponents, denouncing the clergy and the aristocracy as effeminates and pederasts. Soon after it became entrenched as a political force, the far right took up this tradition. For example, in the 1890s during the French political scandal known as the Dreyfus Affair, the nationalistic and anti-Semitic far right depicted the Dreyfusards (supporters of Dreyfus) as intellectuals and esthetes lacking in virility, and taunted Colonel George Picquart, who also defended Dreyfus, by calling him "Georgette" and caricaturing him as a coward and a queer.

During the 1930s, the Nazis instituted a homophobic policy in Germany, and 10,000 to 15,000 homosexuals perished during the **deportations** and in concentration camps. To the Nazis, homosexuality was a sign of a lack of virility (a characteristic essential to a warrior society) and moral decadence, equal in offense to racial corruption (i.e. the Jews). Thus, according to the official Nazi party line,

> It is necessary that the German people live. This can never come about unless its virility is maintained. And it cannot maintain its virility without proving its discipline … and deviance conflicts with discipline. Consequently, we must reject all forms of lechery, homosexuality in particular, because it robs us of our last chance to free our people from the oppression under which we struggle today.

As well, "Sexual relations with animals, with one's brothers or sisters, with people of the same sex: all these aberrations which were born of the Jewish soul and offend the very idea of divine creation, will find the chastisement they so deserve: the rope or expulsion."

Victory over the Nazis in 1945 did not destroy the far right nor did it discredit its homophobic ideals. Today, the same mix of homophobia, xenophobia, and intolerance can be found in many contemporary "thinkers." For example, in a 2000 book by Guillaume Faye, one of the major theorists of the French New Right, *La Colonisation de l'Europe, discours vrai sur l'immigration et l'Islam* (*The Colonization of Europe: The Truth about Immigration and Islam*), he complains about the "demasculinization" of the Western world, because "the virility of a people is the condition by which they keep their place in history." According to the author, some of the traits of this demasculinization are "modern homophilia, like the wave of feminism … the numerous ideological rejections of the **family** … decreases in the birth rate, the spectacular valorization of Blacks and Arabs, the constant defense of cross-breeds, [and] the refusal to recognize the worth of the warrior." Faye

and his editor were both convicted by a Paris court for inciting racial hatred—though, of course, not for inciting homophobia.

Jean-Marie Le Pen, the controversial leader of France's far right party, the National Front, has often spoken out against homosexuals in rude and offensive ways. In 1987, he described people with **AIDS** as akin to "a kind of leper"; in 1984, he stated that "homosexuality is not a crime, but … a biological and social anomaly." To this, he added: "Homosexual activism poses a mortal peril to our civilization" through social disintegration and the decreases in birth rates in the Western world; based on this, he concluded that "homosexual **proselytism** must be outlawed." Since then, he modified his extreme stance somewhat; in 1995, he stated that it was likely there were homosexuals in his party (which he tempered by further saying, "[But] there are no queers"), and that "homosexuality is part of everyone's individual freedom; it's only militant homosexuality that is reprehensible." These statements notwithstanding, his homophobia, and that of his party, leaves little doubt. As for Bruno Mégret, Le Pen's former lieutenant and now leader of his own far-right party, the Mouvement National Républicain (National Republican Movement), he has spoken out against the **media** in terms that could not be more racist and homophobic, especially in his essay "Pour remettre de l'ordre en France" (To Return order to France). According to him,

> The only thing worthy in [the media's] eyes is that which is deviant, marginal, and subversive. In order to be seen and applauded … you had better not be French and especially not right-wing. It is better to not be a father and the head of a family, and not express your religious faith, unless it is Islam or **Buddhism**. If you're a militant homosexual, even better; if you're doping up and everyone knows it, it's an asset. And moreover, if you're Arab or Black, that's perfect! The only thing left is to start vilifying all that is moral, traditional, familial, and national.

This type of opinion, of course, is not limited to the French far right. In 1997, a campaign manifesto issued by the far right British National Party stated: "We promise … laws prohibiting homosexual acts so that these revolting practices can be pushed back into the **closet** where they belong." In Italy, the Lega Nord (Northern League) declared that "society is crumbling little by little and has permitted the development of the pathological behaviors of homosexuality, juvenile delinquency, and drugs," while a far-right politician stated that "gay meeting places should be shut down, the same way we would shut down meeting places for bank robbers if they existed; gays, like thieves, harm society."

In the United States, dozens of small far-right extremist groups are flagrantly racist, anti-Semitic, and homophobic, not to mention prone to violence; some of them even maintain their own armed secret militia. The Ku Klux Klan is perhaps the most notorious of these groups. Often, the ideologies of such groups are largely based on a **Protestant** fundamentalism which distorts the message of the Gospel. In this way of thinking, at least according to the Reverend Peter J. Peters, pastor of a small parish in Colorado, northern Europeans are the "chosen people" spoken of in the **Bible**, while blacks are inferior to whites, Jews are a menace to the Western world, and all homosexuals should be executed. Even if the potential impact of such an extreme fanatic is small, it is all too true that in the United States, the far right in general is greatly influenced by backward, fundamentalist religious beliefs. The Christian Coalition boasts that it has over 1 million members, and almost 10% of the American population identifies with the "Christian right," which works to impose its so-called family and Christian values on elected officials and the general public, and which openly declares that "God hates fags!" According to a 1995 survey in *Newsweek* magazine, 21% of Americans and 43% of Evangelical Christians (that is, fundamentalist) believe that the gay movement is "Satan incarnate."

In many **Latin American** nations, far-right homophobia is not limited to hate speech, as homophobic individuals (often police officers or soldiers) or death squads do not hesitate to assassinate homosexuals (just as they murder Marxists, militant unionists, the homeless, and street kids) in order to "cleanse" the country. In Colombia, a country torn apart by violence and political murder, death squads have declared that "the homosexuals … are a plague that needs to be wiped out." In Peru, members of a small far-right group known as Mata Cabros (that is, "Kill the Queers") assassinated forty transvestites in Lima between 1990 and 1991. But it is Brazil that, despite its reputation as a gay paradise, has been declared "the world leader in homophobia" by human rights associations. According to 1998 sta-

tistics, which underestimate the reality, at least 1,900 homosexuals were killed in Brazil by the far right over the preceding twenty years, usually after being brutally tortured; during the 1980s, there was an average of eighty per year, and during the 1990s, an average of 120 per year (meaning one homophobic murder every three days). In 1996 alone, the Brazilian far right was deemed responsible for the deaths of 116 homosexuals: seventy-three gay men, seven lesbians, and thirty-six transvestites or transsexuals, the latter being particularly detested by partisans of the "moral order."

All of this evidence reveals that the far right has no use for trying to understand homosexuality other than to use it for its own ends, and sometimes seeks to destroy it. Homosexuality provokes an immediate reaction in those on the far right in large part because of what it represents: the rejection of the traditional, familial, national, and collectivistic values that they take great pains to maintain in a world of change and progress.

—*Michael Sibalis*

Algazy, Jean. *L'Extrême droite en France de 1965 à 1984.* Paris: L'Harmattan, 1989.

Aron, Jean-Paul, and Roger Kempf. *Le Pénis et la démoralisation de l'Occident.* Paris: Grasset, 1978. New edition: Le Livre de Poche, 1999.

Chebel D'Appollonia, Ariane. *L'Extrême droite en France de Maurras à Le Pen.* Brussels: Complexe, 1996.

Fourest, Caroline. *Foi contre Choix. La droite religieuse et le mouvement "prolife" aux Etats-Unis.* Paris: Ed. Golias, 2001.

Hewitt, Andrew. *Political Inversions: Homosexuality, Fascism, and the Modernist Imaginary.* Stanford, CA: Stanford Univ. Press, 1996.

Le Bitoux, Jean. *Les Oubliés de la mémoire.* Paris: Hachette, 2002.

Petitfils, Jean-Christian. *L'Extrême droite en France.* Third edition. Paris: Presses universitaires de France, "Que sais-je?," 1995.

Ras l'Front website for network against fascism. http://www.raslfront.org/index.php (accessed February 11, 2008).

—Anti-PaCS; Bible, the; Caricature; Communism; Contagion; Decadence; Deportation; Fascism; France; Germany; Himmler, Heinrich; Italy; McCarthy, Joseph; North America; Peril; Pétain, Philippe; Proselytism; Rhetoric; Scandal; Spain; Sterility; Theology; Violence.

FASCISM

The term "Fascism" has its origin in the Latin fasces (a bundle of elm or birch rods); this name and symbol became the foundation of Benito Mussolini's political party in Italy in 1919. By extension, the designation "fascist" was applied to other movements and parties that developed in Europe between 1919 and 1945 that shared certain characteristics such as nationalism, militarism, single-party dictatorship or corporatism, and, the "Cult of the Leader." The German national-socialism (i.e. Nazism) was a form of Fascism, but with essential differences; the most important being its emphasis on racial theory, which justified eugenistic actions and the conquest of a "vital space" necessary for the domination of the "master race."

During this period, fascist regimes did not grant equal importance to the question of homosexuality. Only Nazi **Germany** put in place a thorough system of surveillance and repression of homosexuals. However, these conclusions must be addressed with prudence, due to the lack of extensive research on the subject. Only the fate of gays under Nazism is well documented today.

In analyzing the turbulent relationship between Fascism and homosexuality, one must start with its legal and historical framework. In the Mediterranean countries in the late nineteenth century, masculine and feminine homosexuality enjoyed relative **tolerance**, fostered by the strict separation of men and women in their daily lives. Certainly, the **Catholic** tradition condemned sodomy, and the passive and effeminate "pervert" was the object of ridicule and slight because he challenged gender-based hierarchies. Gay practices, however, were not generally seen as constitutive of a specific identity; and bisexuality was relatively popular: in this way, soldiers and sailors that prostituted themselves did not consider themselves to be gay. The absence of anti-homosexual legislation explains how these countries, particularly **Italy**, attracted numerous gay foreigners wishing to escape the monitoring in place in their own countries. After Oscar **Wilde**'s trial, in 1895, the Italian island of Capri became a particularly appreciated resort: Baron Adelswärd-Fersen, Somerset Maugham, E. F. Benson, Norman Douglas, Natalie Barney, and Romaine Brooks met there. The situation was very different in Germany where, since the Unification of 1871, Article 175 punished male homosexuality with imprisonment. Although 1920s Berlin attracted many gay foreigners, due to its bohemian culture, tolerance of homosexuals was merely superficial, and homophobic prejudices, exacerbated by churches, conservative political parties and the press, were still deeply ingrained in German public opinion.

Nazi homophobia thus found a relatively favorable breeding ground in which to foment its own argument: homosexuality became a "crime against race," a sign of **degeneracy** that threatened the vitality of the German nation. Heinrich **Himmler**, second in command to Hitler, engaged in popularizing this interpretation in his speeches, and organized the national repression of "**vice against nature**." Popularized when the Nazis took power in 1933, it was reinforced starting in 1935, following the infamous "Night of the Long Knives" when Hitler ordered the purge of his rivals and opponents (including SA leader Ernst Röhm, who was a known homosexual). The idea of "curing" homosexuality, however, was no stranger to Nazi thinking, because it allowed for the reintegration of "seduced" men in the national body, particularly in the **army**. Nonetheless, the shipment of homosexuals to concentration **camps**, thought of in terms of "rehabilitation," included hazardous "medical" experiments and **treatments** that went as far as castration. The accusation of homosexuality was also not devoid of political motives; it was used many times against the Nazi regime's enemies.

In Italy, the ascension to power by the Fascists, in 1922, did not result in any immediate changes to the fate of gays. In 1930, during a discussion on the new Italian penal code, Mussolini even opposed the introduction of homophobic legislation, under the pretense that Italians were too virile to be gay. Besides, it seemed that economic interests overrode moral interpretations: gay tourism, a source of foreign currency, was not to be upset. Finally, militant movements such as those known in Germany were not found in Italy, and any danger posed by an organized gay community seemed non-existent. Gays in Italy were nonetheless the object of new **discriminations**: a number of bars were raided and certain homosexuals judged too public were exiled. Starting in 1938 however, likely the result of the Nazi regime's influence, new legal edicts were approved, aimed this time directly at gays. As revealed in Ettore Scola's 1977 film, *Una Giornata particolare* (*A Special Day*), gays were now considered "political" **criminals** and risked **prison** and exile. Homosexual members of the Fascist party were forced to resign, while in Germany, SS members known for being gay were condemned to death. However, while life for many homosexuals in fascist states meant fear, suffering, and humiliation, others survived this period unscathed.

Similarly in **Spain** during this time, it appears that the repression of homosexuality was never contemplated on a general scale. Certainly, homophobic violence increased, as evidenced by the execution, in 1936, of gay republican poet Federico García Lorca. However, Spain's fascist dictator Francisco Franco did not give in to Hitlerian pressures on this subject, and in the last years of the regime, he permitted the rebirth of a gay subculture.

At the same time, even if fascist regimes did not necessarily develop common arguments and practices, they were nonetheless hostile to homosexuality. And so the Russian Communist Party's 1934 assertion that homosexuality was a "fascist perversion," for instance, is unfounded. Although it is possible to see a strong homoerotic component in certain Nazi groups, such as Ernst Röhm's SA (the storm-trooper division) and although certain gay personalities may have been sensitive to the fascist ideology (as well as the many heterosexual personalities), this does not detract from the persecutions and discriminations suffered by tens of thousands of gays under different fascist regimes.

—*Florence Tamagne*

Haeberle, Erwin J. "Swastika, Pink Triangle, and Yellow Star: The Destruction of Sexology and the Persecution of Homosexuals in Nazi Germany." In *Hidden from History: Reclaiming the Gay and Lesbian Past*. New York: Penguin, 1990.

Hewitt, Andrew. *Political Inversions: Homosexuality, Fascism, and the Modernist Imaginary*. Stanford, CA: Stanford Univ. Press, 1996.

Le Bitoux, Jean. *Les Oubliés de la mémoire*. Paris: Hachette, 2002.

Leroy-Forgeot, Flora. *Histoire juridique de l'homosexualité en Europe*. Paris: Presses universitaires de France, 1999.

Tamagne, Florence. *Histoire de l'homosexualité en Europe, Berlin, Londres, Paris, 1919–1939*. Paris: Le Seuil, 2000. [Published in the US as *A History of Homosexuality in Europe: Berlin, London, Paris, 1919–1939*. New York: Algora, 2004.]

—Armed Forces; Communism; Decadence; Deportation; Far Right, the; Germany; Gulag; Himmler, Heinrich; Hirschfeld, Magnus; Italy; Pétain, Philippe; Police; Treatment; Violence.

FAVORITES

The French public referred to the entourage of **Henri III** (who reigned over France from 1574 to 1589) as the "favorites" or "dainties," with their extravagant attire, trivial occupations, and unbalanced behavior; one might add "sodomites." Thomas Artus, Sieur d'Embry (Lord of Embry), in his 1605 political satire *L'Isle des hermaphrodites*, tried to caricature the sophistication of members of the last Valois court, whose suspected sexual deviance was sufficient to discredit them and judge them as unworthy and degenerate. Thomas Artus also reported on accusations made in the 1580s by René de Lucinge, Savoy's ambassador to France who denounced the king's cabinet as "a true harem of lustfulness and bawdiness, a school of sodomy."

Who were these dainties so vilified by the nation? The term itself did not have the current connotation that is often associated with it, but was commonly used as a synonym of "favorite." Henri IV, strong heterosexual that he was, had his dainties, so named, without being suspected of sodomy, while Henri III's favorites were unique compared to both their predecessors and successors in that the king transformed them into a political weapon. Coming from the middle nobility, the favorites were positioned to counterbalance the influence of those more powerful (and thus threatening) and, as well, to act as a screen between them and their sovereign. Dainties did not often possess the physical features of what one might consider an effeminate man. If there was "daintiness" in their behavior, it was found in their readiness to draw swords for the most laughable of reasons, exemplified by the famous duel of dainties on April 27, 1578, which left four of the six antagonists dead in the field. Moreover, it was often the disputed favors of a woman that was at the origin of these bloody quarrels. There is almost no trace of homosexual behavior among Henri III's favorites, even if the poet Marc de Papillon de Lasphrise identified Louis de Maugiron, a favorite and a victim of the 1578 duel, as one of his sexual partners in a work published in 1597; however, it must be noted that this was an era of intolerance toward homosexuals, whereby those caught were subject to being burned at the stake. Only Hercule François, also known as the Duke of Alençon or simply as **Monsieur**, protected by his stature as brother to the king, was able to show himself in public with his male lover d'Avrilly without being vilified in the publications of the time, unlike his older brother, the supposed "bugger" king. In such criticisms, homophobia appears as a form of political disparagement aimed at a king intent on changing the rules of government by surrounding himself with a group of young men who were elegant and well built (conforming to a Platonic ideal of beauty and good) but above all devoted, to the great dismay of nobility and religious factions. The nobility's disdain toward the dainties on moral grounds was a means to bring about their political marginalization.

—*Laurent Avezou*

Boucher, Jacqueline. *La Cour de Henri III*. Rennes: Ouest-France, 1986.

Le Roux, Nicolas. *La Faveur du roi. Mignons et courtisans au temps des derniers Valois (vers 1547–vers 1589)*. Seyssel: Champs Vallon, 2001.

—*Decadence; France; Henri III; Monsieur; Rhetoric.*

FEMINISM (France)

"There is no lesbian problem, there is only a heterosexual problem": this could have been the slogan summing up the position of Mouvement de liberation des femmes (MLF; Women's Liberation Movement, a collective of varied groups who rejected the oppression of women) during debates in **France** on homosexuality, at the beginning of the 1970s. Such was, in 1971, the *raison d'être* for the collective's movement, and the explosive exit of a large number of lesbian militants (and a few others) from a meeting that was focused in particular on the "problems of gay women," organized by those who would become the group known as "Psychanalyse et politique" (Psychoanalysis and Politic). This was also the reason for the disruption of Ménie Grégoire's radio broadcast "*l'homosexualité, ce douloureux problème*," by the MLF and FHAR (Front homosexuel d'action révolutionnaire) on March 10, 1971. And the reason for the creation, as early as spring of 1971, of the group provocatively named "Gouines rouges" (Red Dykes).

This radical or "revolutionary" position was common to many social movements of the time. The feminists' objective was not so much to improve the situation

of women in existing society—even less to "reform" it—but to analyze, expose, subvert, and, in time, destroy the constraints, domination, and power structures that existed between sexes: specifically the "patriarchy," and notably, sexual domination. One has to remember that while the focus of the feminist movement (in relation to those that preceded it) was really to emphasize questions about the body and sexuality, these questions were never separated from the analysis of all other places and modalities of oppression. This is why feminists were at the same time contesting in-vogue ideologies of "sexual liberation."

It was thus neither the defense of homosexuality nor the support of its greater visibility that the feminist militants first focused on, but really the identification of a problem and the virulent critique from the heterosexual patriarchy. It is this work, and its multiple facets, that first had to be done. And this happened in many different ways, directly or indirectly, through spontaneous or theorized actions, slogans or songs, demonstrations or articles.

We know that the movement's founding act was the segregation decision: the political break from male and mixed movements. We also know that this homosociality, decided upon for mainly strategic reasons, was interpreted from the start by the movement's adversaries as sexual, as a result this branch of the women's movement was immediately reviled and stigmatized as a bunch of "dykes and unloved women." At the same time, many (heretofore heterosexual) women joined the feminist movement which opened them up to the possibility of relations between women.

To this trend were added numerous feminist texts, petitions, and campaigns against the **heterosexist** discourse, which Monique Wittig later called "the Straight Mind." As an example, the first publication of the French journal *Partisans* (1970) contained texts on the "myth of vaginal orgasm," the "myth of feminine frigidity," rape, and even abortion and unwanted pregnancies. Others texts would follow, on family abuse, sexual violence against women, and later, the "coercion to heterosexuality" according to Adrienne Rich's formula. All discourses concerning the "evident," "natural," and essential character of heterosexual relations thus became problematic, and were analyzed and disassembled, and in the end, made laughable and unacceptable.

It was this long and aggressive work of fighting against patriarchal institutions and myths (in particular those of "feminine sexuality")—of shredding the patriarchy's best claimed "evidences"—that resulted in the rhetorical and political claim of lesbian visibility being heard outside the movement and, also, inside it.

This transformation, however, was not without intense and painful controversies. Starting at the end of the 1970s, a set of lesbian critiques of the feminist movement developed, charging it with not having named and challenged heterosexuality, thus in effect denying the presence of its feminist lesbian members. This is why during the meetings of the Coordination des groups femmes (1977–78), and in one of the first gay newspapers *Quand les femmes s'aiment* (1978–80), gay women stated that they were being negated and made invisible, while at the same time exposing diverse forms of oppression within the movement; specifically, the fact that an emancipation movement can reproduce within itself the oppression of minority groups. In particular, they emphasized the constraints of silence in the name of the movement's alleged priorities (i.e. "not to scare off the majority of women") and the marginalization of the discussion on homosexuality (and heterosexuality) "when it should be an integral part of the struggle against the sexual norm for women's rights to dispose of their body and their sexuality" ("Was the Women's Movement an answer for lesbians?," *Rouge,* April 1977).

Certainly, homosexuality is "accepted" in the context of the class struggle, but as a "special feature," and this **"tolerance"** makes lesbians all the more self-conscious of their role as "outsiders": "We feel negated by this pseudo-acceptance" (Stage femmes d'Orsay, "Texte des lesbiennes," 1977). What these women were saying was that homosexuality remains scary. They particularly stressed the fact that few heterosexual women acknowledge gay women, or their questions, even though lesbians are very active in all women's struggles, such as the right to abortion. In other areas, the issues become more complex, particularly differences between "new" and "old" gay women. Gay-identified women sometimes voluntarily held themselves outside lesbian groups, fearing the return to the **"ghetto"** from which they had already freed themselves by joining the feminist movement. Inversely, women who became gay after joining the movement could hardly understand the uneasiness and specific oppression of "old lesbians" who suffered and sometimes internalized repression.

For their part, "radical lesbians" called to fight against "heteropower" (heterosexuality as a patriarchal strategy) and also criticized feminism, or as they called it, "heterofeminism," as a form of "collaboration" (texts from the lesbian meeting of June 1980, reported in *Nouvelles questions féministes,* no. 1). Their ambition was to build a gay political force on the basis of the analysis of lesbianism as a political choice and a privileged form of resistance to the appropriation of women by men. It must be noted that any divergences from these points, within the lesbian movement have almost always divided lesbians among themselves. They also ended in the violent and painful rupture of the collective Questions feminists, paralyzing all public debate on these questions for a long period.

During the 1980s and 90s, there was an increase in the number of lesbian initiatives (including archives, cafés, festivals, groups, national meetings, and publications), but the rest of the militant or academic feminist movement continued to fail to address lesbian claims. The more institutional feminist groups in particular, wanting to be recognized by public powers, be it in academia or in conventional political life, largely ignored lesbians and their claims of the most serious problems with the heterosexual system. As well, the majority of studies on women, or feminist studies, remain heterocentered. At the National Conference for Women's Rights in France in 1997, lesbians were once again sidestepped, as lesbianism was depicted as a peculiarity, a simple sexual choice. In fact, the problem became more general; in any movement it is difficult to construct a broad, non-fragmented vision while at the same time include different perspectives on different oppressions and resistances within that same movement.

The contestation that occurred during these conferences, and the organization of the Coordination lesbienne nationale, has changed the situation in France; lesbians have managed to achieve more representation in the national Collectif droits des femmes (Women's Rights Collective, composed of **associations**, parties, and unions). At the international level, however, the same conflict arose during the organization of the World March of Women in the summer of 2000; the majority of women groups from countries represented refused to have the struggle for lesbian rights, or even the freedom of "sexual orientation," included in a world-wide platform. In France, certainly, there is an agreement to include lesbophobic **discrimination** when describing the struggles of feminists, but this only happens if lesbians themselves push for it.

Fear still persists: feminist movements dread that

lesbian visibility will "discredit" or endanger the movement. In fact, refusing to face **lesbophobia**, or thinking that it is a problem faced by lesbians only, means that we are leaving intact one of the major weapons of sexism; making lesbians and lesbianism invisible is one of the means for patriarchal power to deny the affirmation of independence and strength by women, by controlling and dividing them, as emphasized by Suzanne Pharr.

Certain young lesbian militants today believe that they have no link to the feminist movement, and some consider feminism, by not giving a real place to lesbian claims, to be truly "homophobic." However, the issue is infinitely more complex. The question of the place of the lesbian questioning within feminist theorization is always present. But—and this independently of life choices made by lesbians and heterosexual women—there was a real divergence between the two main theoretical options present from the beginning of the movement.

On one hand, revolutionary and radical feminists maintained that said notions of "woman" and "man" had been completely constructed historically, socially, and politically, and that they only made sense within a specific discourse, such as patriarchal domination. As early as 1970, Christine Delphy described this relationship as one of class. For her, as for Colette Guillaumin or Monique Wittig, just as the disappearance of capitalist exploitation would mean the end to antagonist categories of "worker" and "boss," the disappearance of "patriarchal" would automatically result in the disappearance of the two categories "man" and "woman": women would thus lose all at once their necessity in the social game, as well as their pertinence in sexual relations. These positions, similar in principle to Simone de Beauvoir's thesis in her 1949 book *Le Deuxième Sexe* (*The Second Sex*), were clearly anti-naturalist, anti-essentialist, and pro-equality and **universalism**. Inversely, for other militants and theorists, the "**gender difference**" is an inevitable component of the human species ("there are two genders"), and the feminine, as an objective of the movement, up until then oppressed and repressed by male power, was to be exposed, developed, and even glorified. A real mysticism of the "gender difference," and often of motherhood, was created at the same time in the movement, particularly by the Psychanalyse et politique group led by Antoinette Fouque, and in numerous circles of female thinkers and artists, including Luce Irigaray, Hélène

Cixous, Annie Leclerc, and Chantal Chawaf. One must stress that the idea of valorization, which could lead to the essential rending of "differences," was common to many movements of this period (particularly anti-racist movements), the differential MLF were the only ones to justify them through arguments that were openly or implicitly naturalistic and biological ("The shop belongs to the worker, the uterus belongs to women, production of living things belongs to us," wrote Psy and Po). It should be noted that it is this line of thinking that is, curiously, read and thought of in the US as being solely representative of French feminism.

That said, these themes have since been taken up by intellectual women and a few men—such as Sylviane Agacinski, Julia Kristeva, and Pierre Legendre—as part of the debate on gender parity. In numerous countries, this feminism of maternity, often linked to the defense of **family**, has more than once been highlighted with homophobic pronouncements. In the same way, feminist movements in India, the first country in the world to vote for man/woman parity in Parliament, bitterly criticized Deepa Mehta's 1996 film *Fire*. This film, which was the first in India to depict a lesbian relationship, was accused of presenting a poor image of women. In so doing, these Indian feminists were in tacit agreement with right-wing Hindu religious groups which vandalized movie theaters where the film was shown. Incidentally, this overriding value granted to gender difference is also found in numerous associations of women, feminists, or more often anti-feminists, particularly in the US, where they are generally aligned with pro-family, pro-life religious groups. This is exemplified by Wilma Leftwich's declaration in 1998 at the annual convention of the Concerned Women for America association that suggested the existence of a world conspiracy aiming at "reducing the American population by generalizing abortion, sterilizing mothers of large families, and promoting homosexuality."

Was this emphasis placed on "gender difference," or even the cult of this "difference," compatible with the idea of equality of gay and lesbian sexualities and struggles? The question was posed right at the beginning of the movement by radical feminists, for whom "gender difference" was only another ruse of the patriarchy in order to resign women to the boundaries of their gender and their oppression. This was clearly set forth beginning at the end of the 1970s, particularly by Wittig, who maintained that "lesbians are not women" because "lesbianism is above gender categories."

It was not until the end of the 1990s, and the debates that accompanied homosexual union, that "gender difference" became the ultimate weapon brandished by the adversaries of **PaCS**, gay **marriage**, and gay **parenting**. Supporters were thus accused of attacking "**symbolic order**" (a notion inappropriately borrowed from Claude Lévi-Strauss), as demonstrated by enthologist Jeanne Favret-Saada, and thereby undermining the entire basis of Western civilization, or worse, the possibility of all rational thinking. For anthropologist Françoise Héritier, gender difference is the essential condition of all thought, its "ultimate doorstop." Legendre also uses this "hard core of reason that is gender difference" and the "universal principle of non-contradiction: a man is not a woman, a woman is not a man," to conclude that in the PaCS episode, "the State is divesting itself of its functions of guarantor of reason [to] leave the space to a hedonist logic inherited from Nazism."

Curiously, speakers on behalf of the feminist movement—those who had fought differential and identity discourses of "feminineness"—as well as their advocates have been dramatically absent from the debate. However, the reservations expressed by some women toward the institution of family and the legitimization of the couple (even gay couples), was probably not absent, nor was the fear that these happen to weaken fundamental feminist claims for the acknowledgment of everyone—"man" or "woman," "homo" or "hetero," "trans" or "bisexual" (even "asexual")—as persons in their own right.

—*Liliane Kandel and Claudie Lesselier*

Anne. "La Difficile frontière entre homosexualité et hétérosexualité." In *Les Femmes s'entêtent, 1973.* CLEF (Centre lyonnais d'études féministes). *Chronique d'une passion. Le mouvement de libération des femmes à Lyon.* Paris: L'Harmattan, 1989.

Delphy, Christine. "L'Ennemi principal," *Partisans,* no. 54–55 (1970).

Favret-Saada, Jeanne. "La Pensée-Lévi-Strauss," *Prochoix,* no. 13 (2000).

———. "Les Femmes s'entêtent," *Les Temps modernes,* no. 333–34 (1974). New edition: Gallimard, "Idées," 1975.

Fourest, Caroline. *Foi contre Choix, la droite religieuse et le mouvement "prolife" aux Etats-Unis.* Lyon: Golias, 2001.

Franklin, Sarah, and Jackie Stacey. "Le Point de vue lesbien dans les études feminists," *Nouvelles questions féministes* 16–18 (1991).

Guillaumin, Colette. *Sexe, Race et Pratique du pouvoir. L'idée de nature.* Paris: Côté-femmes, 1992. [Published in the UK and US as *Racism, Sexism, Power, and Ideology.* London/New York: Routledge, 1995.]

Héritier, Françoise. "Hétérosexualité et lesbianisme," *La Revue d'en face* 9–10 (1981).

———. *Masculin/féminin. La pensée de la différence.* Paris: Odile Jacob, 1996.

Jackson, Stevi. "Récents débats sur l'hétérosexualité: une approche féministe matérialiste," *Nouvelles questions féministes* 17, no. 3 (1996).

Kandel, Liliane. "Sur la différence des sexes, et celle des feminisms," *Les Temps modernes,* no. 609 (2000).

Legendre, Pierre. "Nous assistons à une escalade de l'obscurantisme," *Le Monde* 23 (October 2001).

Lesselier, Claudie. "Féminisme, lesbianisme, hétérosexualité," *Politique La Revue,* "Homos en mouvements" (1997).

———. "Les Regroupements de lesbiennes dans le mouvement féministe parisien: positions et problèmes 1970–1982." In GEF, *Crises de la société, féminisme et changement,* Paris: Ed. Tierce, 1991.

———. "Libération des femmes année zero," *Partisans,* no. 54–55 (1970).

MacNair, Rachel. *Prolife Feminism: Yesterday and Today.* New York: Sulzburger & Graham, 1995.

Mathieu, Nicole-Claude. *L'Anatomie politique. Catégorisations et idéologies de sexe.* Paris: Côté-Femmes, 1991.

———. *Nouvelles questions féministes,* no. 1, "Editorial" (1981) (Christine Delphy) and "Documents: Quel féminisme ?".

———. *Nouvelles questions féministes* 17, no. 1, "France-Amérique: regards croisés sur le féminisme" (1996).

Onlywomen Press, eds. *Love Your Enemy: The Debate Between Heterosexual Feminism and Political Lesbianism.* London: Onlywomen Press, 1981.

Pharr, Suzanne. *Homophobia: A Weapon of Sexism.* Inverness: Chardon Press, 1988.

Picq, Françoise. *Libération des femmes: Les années mouvement.* Paris: Le Seuil, 1993.

Pisier, Evelyne. "Sexes et sexualités: bonnes et mauvaises differences," *Les Temps modernes,* no. 609 (2000).

Rich, Adrienne. "La Contrainte à l'hétérosexualité et l'existence lesbienne." *Nouvelles questions féministes,* no. 1 (1981). [Published in the US as "Compulsory Heterosexuality and Lesbian Experience," *Signs* 5, no. 4 (Summer 1980).]

———. "Le Sexisme ordinaire," *Les Temps modernes,* 1973–83 and Le Seuil, 1979.

Tort, Michel. "Sur la différence psychanalytique des sexes,"

Les Temps modernes, no. 609 (2000).

———. "Variations sur des thèmes communs," *Questions féministes,* no. 1 (1977)

———. "Votre Libération sexuelle n'est pas la nôtre," *Tout!,* no. 15 (1971).

Wittig, Monique. *La Pensée straight.* Paris: Balland, 2000. [Published in the US as *The Straight Mind and Other Essays.* Boston: Beacon Press, 1992.]

—*Essentialism/Constructionism; Family; Gender Differences; Heterosexism; Lesbophobia; Marriage; Parenting; Symbolic Order; Tolerance; Universalism/Differentialism.*

FILM. *See* Cinema

FRANCE

For a long time, France has had an ambiguous attitude toward homosexuality: as a revolutionary power, France was the first country to decriminalize it (in 1791), but at the same time, due to its **Catholic** and Latin influences, it has also tended to associate homosexuality with **sin** and disgrace. France's liberal morality, long associated with the national identity, has thus remained strictly heterosexual and may in fact be tacitly homophobic (the idea of homosexuality being "**against nature**" was well received in France). The history of the emancipation of France's homosexuals is not linear: while the visibility of gays and lesbians increased during World War I and the 1920s (at least in the large cities and according to literary works of the time), the period starting with the Vichy years to the beginning of the 1970s was clearly a setback: this was the era of homosexuality as a "social scourge."

The Middle Age & the Modern Era
The popular prejudice toward homosexuality goes back to ancient times, which relates it in particular to sexual passivity and a lack of physical **virility**. The attitude of those in power has had a more complex evolution. While the eleventh and twelfth centuries saw homosexuality among monks become commonplace—as well as the development of a gay subculture, according to gay historian John Boswell—the second half of the thirteenth century established the theological and canonical stigmatization of homosexuals; a consequence of the Third Lateran Council of 1179, the first ecumenical council to condemn homosexuality. *The Complaint of Nature* by French theologian Alain de Lille articulated the awakening moral fury behind this phenomenon that affected the whole of the Christian West; between 1250 and 1300, homosexual acts, until then largely ignored by European law, became a crime punishable by death.

During this time, homosexuals were the victims of many phenomena that in some ways were interconnected. There was a growing fascination with the figure of the goddess of nature as an arbiter of moral **theology**; according to Boswell, it was ironic that a mythological figure who came unmistakably from paganism now had influence over dogmatic theology. Other phenomena of the time which had an impact on the attitude toward homosexuals included the growing hatred toward minorities, the anti-Islamic xenophobia linked to the Crusades, and the connections made (particularly by the Catholic Church) between sodomy and **heresy**; it is significant that in the twelfth century, the homosexual was often called a *hérite*, based on the word "heretic." (It seems apparent that the Church—which had a difficult time ensuring the celibacy of priests—took this position in part to refute accusations of homosexuality lodged against it during this time.) In the end, Parisian theology of the thirteenth century firmly condemned homosexuality; for St Albert the Great, it was the most severe type of sexual sin because it simultaneously offended "grace, reason and nature." For St Thomas Aquinas, the sexuality of men had to be heterosexual and monogamous, "like that of birds" (in this analogy he repeated a common popular myth that homosexuality did not exist among animals). He also stressed that **vices** that were "against nature"—such as masturbation, bestiality, and homosexuality, as well as heterosexuality that did not have procreation as its goal—were the most contemptible forms of sexuality; he compared homosexuality to violent or revolting acts of the worst sort, such as cannibalism, bestiality, and even the ingestion of feces. As such, Thomas Aquinas gave credence to popular prejudices of the time; following him, no Catholic theologian dared to defend homosexuality.

Having obtained the support of theologians, homophobic legislation in France first appeared between 1246 and 1300. The *coutume* (law) of Touraine-Anjou in 1246 set out, in Paragraph 78, for sodomites to be burned at the stake, a sentence that also appeared in the *coutume* of Paris in 1270. *Le Livre de jostice et de plet*, compiled by the legal school of Orléans in 1260, made a distinction between buggery (heresy) and sodomy (homosexuality), and further stated: "He who is proven a sodomite must lose his balls; … a woman who does it must each time lose a limb, and the third time, be *burned*." Under Philip the Fair (1285–1314), the illegal status of homosexuals was set in place, which would remain that way until the French Revolution. Between 1317 and 1789, the kingdom of France recorded at least thirty-eight executions for the crime of sodomy; the number is relatively low, presumably because authorities refused to apply the sentence to all cases of homosexuality that were made known to them, fearing that it would publicize the crime that was to be punished. The imperative for discretion can be further explained by the fact that documents relating to the cases of sodomy were burned along with the condemned, "so that there was no remnant of this abomination"; the unmentionable character of the crime was also referred to as the "mute sin." As late as 1750, it was emphasized that one must use the pyre "due to the indecency of these sorts of examples that teaches youth what it does not know" and, at the end of the Ancien Régime, Louis-Sébastien Mercier wrote that "the punishment of this vileness is a public **scandal** … a shameful show that must be covered by the thickest veil." On the other hand, religious authorities were rather indulgent when culprits were teenagers (prescribing rather soft sentences for them) and monastic homosexuality, particularly in liberal orders (Clunisiens, Carmelites) had continued to be relatively common.

The Templars' affair (1307–14) was the first case of wide magnitude in France that focused on homosexuals or men reputed to be such (the reality of gay practices within the Templar order continues to divide historians). Templars belonged to an order that was both religious and military, charged with ensuring the protection of the Holy Land. While the order had lost some of its military usefulness with the fall of the last piece of the Latin state in Palestine in 1291, it still had very rich possessions in the West. But the Templars were refusing to accept the fusion of the three great military orders, the Templars, Hospitallers and Teutonic Knights, that was proposed by Philip the Fair. Following a denunciation made around 1305–06 by a certain Esquieu de Floyran, the king of France charged the Templars with heresy and sodomy (it was thought that the initiation of Templars included kisses on the mouth, navel, anus,

and penis; it was also thought that the order encouraged its members to make love to each other rather than at the brothel with prostitutes; in short, they were suspected of being, with respect to sex, under "Muslim influence"). The Templars, so accused were victims of a carefully laid trap (approximately 2,000 arrests in the whole kingdom of France), tortured with severe **violence** that induced confessions, then judged outside all respect of procedures (a theologian of Paris University contended that "the proof of facts makes the crime of public record"), and for a number of them, condemnation to the pyre: fifty-four were burned in Paris in May 1310 and Grand Master of the Order Jacques de Molay, in March 1314; there were other pyres in the towns of Senlis and Carcassonne. Philip the Fair's personal motives were not clear: did he really believe the Templars were homosexual? Did he only want to accelerate the fusion of orders or lay his hands on the Templars' wealth? It is, however, interesting to note that the same Philip the Fair had a few years earlier, in 1303, brought the same accusation against his mortal enemy, Pope Boniface VIII, at the height of the fight over clerical taxation and theological-political supremacy between the pope and the king. It is clear that the accusation of homosexuality was extremely serious, and used as a last resort.

Two centuries later, homophobia, becoming also a form of xenophobia (it was called the "Italian **vice**"), reinforced the religious cleaving and blossomed in political satire. Renaissance **Italy** knew a higher gay visibility under the effect of growing urbane neo-Platonism and the cult of physical beauty displayed by painters and sculptors. Italians who came to France in the sixteenth and seventeenth centuries were frequently accused of introducing a condemnable sexuality to the Kingdom of the Lilies. Through Italians, male homosexuality is now associated with luxury and excessive preoccupation with physical appearances, more suited to the domain of women than of men.

The theme of effeminacy of elites, which first appeared in the fourteenth century at the time of great defeats by the English, was revived under **Henri III** (1574–89): The king's dainties (see **favorites)** were said to be his lovers and, moreover, men at court were dressing up as women, which was particularly scandalous, as is recalled by Sylvie Steinberg: "men that wear women's clothing breach the known ideal set for their gender." In the context of religious wars, all this fed Protestantism, in particular Huguenotism, which was expressed by Théodore Agrippa D'Aubigné in *Les Tragiques*. According to D'Aubigné, Henri III's Court of Valois represented the world turned upside down:

> Those that really reign, those are real kings, / That establish laws over their passions, / That reign over themselves, of a constant mind / Break fickle and powerless ambition; / Not bisexual, effeminate monsters, / corrupted, bourdeliers and higher born / more servants of prostitutes than Lords over men. ("Princes," c. 663–69).

The exact nature of the relation between Henri III and the dainties is not very clear (they all seem to have had feminine relations); what is important here is that the court and the people saw something sexual in it, as well as monetary reward. Even Ronsard wrote a stanza that describes the king's companions as exchanging sexual favors for money:

> The King as is said lays beside, kisses and licks / Of his darling fresh-faced dolls, night and day. / They for money, lend him one after the other / Their curvaceous backsides and endure the breach. / These asses turned cunts swallow up more goods / Than the Gulf of Scylla hated by the Ancients.

Accusations of sodomy and tyranny were combined in satirical **literature**: dainties' avarice ruined the state, and consequently depleted the country, as Edward II's lovers were supposed to have depleted England at the beginning of the fourteenth century. During the time of the Fronde civil war (1648–53), we find the same accusations against Cardinal Mazarin: numerous pamphlets and libels accused him of being a "*bougre bougrant*" ("sodomizing sodomite") and a "*bougre bougré*" ("sodomized sodomite"), for having tried to infect the young King Louis XIV and having succeeded in contaminating his younger brother, **Monsieur**, and of having converted the Queen herself, Anne of Austria, "to the Italian vice"). Here, one can note the importance of the theme of foreign homosexuality: homosexuality was so vile that it couldn't be French; and sodomites were foreign bodies doggedly ruining the country.

It is also in the Renaissance that a discourse took place that was hostile to love between women. Christian doctrine on female homosexuality was, up to then, very scarce. It was the discovery of antique works, and particularly **Sappho**'s, re-edited by Henri

Estienne, that brought the threat of lesbianism into view. At the same time that it was realized that two women could have amorous feeling for one another (once again, "this manner was imported from Italy," according to the French historian Brantôme), it was immediately stigmatized. Estienne invented the then pejorative word "*tribade*," which was very widely used up to the Revolution. For a woman, the *tribade* ("fricative," "rubbing") was associated with forgery, fake, and imitation, as she could not penetrate her companion. In short, sexuality without a virile member was a scandal ("a woman needs a husband or a fence" went a then popular saying) and a lesbian was a liar: women who dressed as men were brought before the courts. While for theologians, cross-dressing was deeply idolatrous and thus negated the divine will, for civil authorities, it was mostly a "crime of falsehood."

Homophobia acquired other motifs in the seventeenth century. The main ones were "libertinage" (in the sense of irreligion), the confusion of rank, and **debauchery**. In a massively Christian society, homosexuals were frequently accused of ungodliness: this was the case with poet Théophile de **Viau** in the 1620s and within the Grand Condé a generation later. They were also accused of disrupting the natural harmony of social ranks: sodomy was a vice of aristocrats who slept with their menservants; the threat of subversion was doubled in the case of the Marshal Vendôme who, not only made love to commoners, footmen, grooms, and chair bearers, but was also content to play a strictly passive role with them. Sodomites were more and more often accused of depravity or "wickedness," which were recurrent themes of mundane preaching of the Great Century: rich people's luxury caused them to fall into a spiral of greater and greater sins (they tried to awaken their "dulled senses" by "extravagances"), the unsurpassable summit of the horror being "*crimen nefandum inter cristianos*." Concerned with order and good taste and furious about the spectacle of his brother, Louis XIV did not like sodomites and took measures against them. Roused by his confessors and preachers against "these monsters that Scripture prevent from naming but that His Majesty knows and hates," he dealt harshly against the "brotherhood," a secret society of ultramontanes created at court around 1678 that endangered the integrity of the Count of Vermandois, son of the king and Louise de la Vallière. Then at fourteen years of age, in June 1682, Vermandois, pressured by questions, denounced the other followers. He was reprimanded and whipped, and the rest of the brotherhood was driven out of court. This being said, the arsenal of measures against gays of high rank (very numerous in Versailles under Louis XIV, at least if we believe La Palatine and St-Simon) were rather limited: they were reprimanded, threatened or temporarily exiled, in certain cases, if they were young, they were whipped or forced to marry. Trials and especially pyres were reserved exclusively for commoners: the Lament of Chausson and Fabbri, executed for sodomy in 1661, denounced these "double standards": "If we burned all those that act like them, in a very short time, I'm afraid several Lords of France, and important prelates, would be deceased." For their part, gay Parisians dealt mainly with the general guard of **police** in Paris, created in 1667. Its director, the lieutenant general of police, was all powerful; he had a network of spies and informers, the "flies," which let him see all and hear all so he could blackmail homosexuals. He had the power to punish and send people to jail. At the beginning of Louis XV's reign, two men were burned at the stake for sodomy, out of an estimated 20,000 persons that were arrested for "soliciting" sex with other men. Those arrested were met with various penalties; according to their social condition, they were simply admonished, sent to the Bastille (the elitist jail), sent to the prison of the bishop, or to the small Châtelet prison, or to the Bicêtre prison-hospital (for those suffering from venereal disease), and very seldom tried (there were seven executions for homosexuality between 1715–83, and in five cases out of seven, the accused were charged with more serious crimes). High-ranking lesbians were equally subjected to surveillance and their names were proposed to the king for internal exile measures (this was the case for Madame de Murat).

The eighteenth century saw the transformation (but not the disappearance) of homophobia under the effect of Enlightenment thought that gradually drifted from sin to social pathology. Now, for enlightened minds, homosexuality was less a sin against divine law than a vice against nature (sodomites were more often called "antiphysics") and it is interesting to note that lesbianism was more and more often reported as clitoromegaly (a medical condition of abnormally enlarged clitoris). Most philosophers did not see homosexuality favorably: for Montesquieu (who nevertheless requested the end of pyres), it was the result of special conditions (Ancient Greek influences, nudity, grouping of teenagers in colleges)—conditions that a civilized society

had to abolish ("that we do not encourage this crime, that it be proscribed as all morality violations, and we will suddenly see nature either defend its rights or take them back"). For Voltaire, homosexuality was typical of Jesuits, and on these grounds, deeply ridiculous. Incidentally, even if it shouldn't have been subject to a legal penalty, homosexuality seemed to Voltaire to be an "error" that social morality had to continue to censor. As for Rousseau, he felt a physical repulsion for the "Chevaliers de la manchette," and believed very much in natural "complementarity" of sexes. Only a few discordant voices were heard: some refused the very idea of "against nature." "All that is cannot be either against or outside nature" stated Diderot who, nonetheless, in *La Religieuse*, considered monastic Sapphism as a particularly negative effect of the cloister: "the depraved retreat." Others maintained the right to freedom of reasonable sexual pleasure. For example, philosopher Marquis de Condorcet stated, "sodomy, when there is no violence, cannot fall under criminal laws. It does not violate the rights of any man." That being said, for most, homosexuality was always part of depravity, as proven by the very aggressive use of the lesbian-themed accusations against Marie-Antoinette in the last years of the Ancien Régime and until her trial by the Revolutionary Tribunal, in October 1793.

From 1791 to 1942: Decriminalization Without Acceptance

As proposed by the Marquis de Condorcet, the French Revolution secularized public order and relegated sodomy, along with blasphemy and witchcraft, to the rank of "imaginary crimes." This **decriminalization** was maintained, thanks to Jean-Jacques-Régis de Cambacérès, in the 1810 Napoleonic Code which did not show sodomy as a crime. In French law, nothing was prohibited anymore for two consenting adults of the same sex in sexual relations. However, this silence of the law did not in the least mean that social **tolerance** was widespread, or even greater than it had been in the preceding century. In a country anguished by the infinite potential of revolutionary challenges, homosexuality, as **feminism**, fell victim to a myth of Nature, which imposed impassable limits to the legislator's boldness. Besides, we find in nineteenth-century France, the idea that the silence of the law was the most appropriate social response to this "horror of such monstrosity" that was sometimes defended by magistrates, and it was clear that judiciary power had only applied the law grudgingly: homosexuality was automatically seen in justice as an aggravating circumstance. Furthermore, administrative arbitrariness is not negligible: in 1800, a Paris police prefecture ordinance prohibited women from "dressing up as men"; in 1804, public authorities intervened outside all legal guidelines against a couple of gay male servants who had been condemned by a simple police decision to be kept inside in separate locations. In society as a whole, the taboo was very strong, as historian Anne-Marie Sohn reminds us: the subject was very rarely mentioned in everyday conversation, and until the 1950s, homosexuality cases give rise to a kind of disbelief (this taboo no doubt motivates the development of gay prostitution in big cities, between 1870 and 1900). All this explains why as recently as the middle of the 1970s, a very large number of French people believed that homosexual relations between consenting adults were still illegal.

While the 1830s and 40s had been marked, at least in literary works, by a certain fluidity in relation to sexual roles, we note a hardening and reinforcement of boundaries and identities by the middle of nineteenth century. The Second Empire, born out of social fear from June 1848 to December 1851, associated homosexuality more and more with delinquency and crime. This negative stereotype is shown quite clearly in the increasing number of novels with gay characters: Joseph Méry's *Monsieur Auguste* in 1859, Théodore de Banville's *Les Parisiennes de Paris* in 1866, Ernest Feydeau's, *La Comtesse de Chalis ou les mœurs du jour* in 1868, and Adolphe Belot's *Mademoiselle Giraud, ma femme* in 1870. At the same time, certain magistrates did their best to use Article 334 of the penal code, from punishing for the incitation of minors to debauchery to creating asymmetry between heterosexual acts and homosexual acts (judgment of the Angers Court of Appeal, September 1, 1851), before the Court of Cassation imposed the return to the letter of the penal code. Other magistrates, fighting pornography in literature, saw the lesbian themes in Baudelaire's poetry *Les Fleurs du mal*, published in 1857 ("Lesbos," "damned women") as an "offence to morality" that deserved condemnation.

The Second Empire was a time when police action started up again. This action developed in a non-legal area (only the struggle against **pedophilia** was based on consistent legislation, 1832 provisions related to "indecent assault without violence" on eleven-year-old minors; the age was raised to thirteen in 1863). In keeping with the tradition of the Ancien Régime, morality squads patrolled areas of prostitution and made arrests. Files were kept on gay prostitutes and occasionally made them "abetting agents." The Second Empire also heralded the strengthening of medical stigmatization. The most important name here is that of the medical examiner Auguste Ambroise Tardieu, who in 1857 published the first edition of his famous *Etude médico-légale sur les attentats aux mœurs* (Medical-legal studies of assaults against decency). Throughout this book, he consistently based homophobia in positivism and biological determinism, comparing the homosexual to both woman and to animals. Also, he claimed the homosexual had psychic characteristics said to be feminine: chit-chat, fickleness, and duplicity) and animal (the pederast, in his coitus and his organs, recalls the dog; and sodomy associates him to excrement). Tardieu set the anatomical and physiological characteristics of the male homosexual population for generations of medical students: "The excessive development of buttocks, the anus funnelform, sphincter relaxation, effacing of folds, ridges and caruncles of the anus periphery, extreme dilatation of anal orifice, matter incontinence, ulcerations, rhagades, hemorrhoids, fistulas, and rectal gonorrhea," without forgetting the penis was formed like a canine's. He created a caricatured typology, which was destined to last: "queer" for occasional homosexual, "true pederast" for born gay, and "active" pederast as well as "passive" pederast. He claimed that there was a socially subversive effect that homosexuality caused that linked together French and foreigners (speaking of the "cosmopolitism of these degrading passions"). Tardieu was enormously interested in gay prostitution and its menace to public order, by blackmail and crime (a series of recent killings had "clearly revealed the cruel end that may be the fate of those that can only find in the foam of the world the most vile of these unconfessed liaisons in which they demand satisfaction of their monstrous desires"). One will note that contradictions abound in his writing; the concerns of clinical science is accompanied on each page by the **rhetoric** of depravity; the thesis of innate pederasty goes hand in hand with that of vice, or immoral choice.

Around 1880, in a context of national doubt and anxiety over declining French power and fearing **decadence**, homosexuality gained the status of mental disease. Jean-Martin Charcot, a professor of neurology and anatomical pathology, described the first French case of "genital sense **inversion**" in 1882, and Ladame endeavored to treat homosexual patients through hypnosis as early as the end of the 1880s. It has been said that Charcot pathologically psychologized homosexuality in France and thus helped further diminish its social acceptance. It was he who, in 1882, created the expression that would have a prosperous future, "sexual **perversion**," where medical, social, and moral preoccupations are linked. *Les Archives d'anthropologie criminelle, de criminologie et de psychologie normale et pathologique* (Archives of criminal anthropology, criminology and normal psychology), founded in 1885 by Alexandre Lacassagne and Gabriel Tarde, clearly affirmed the overrepresentation of sexual perverts in prison population. At the same time, under the influence of social Darwinism, homosexuality became a sign of hereditary **degeneracy**. Psychiatrist Henri Legrand du Saulle, in 1876 in *Société médico-psychologique*, affirmed that a lot of "reproductive perversions" were due to hysterical heredity; and it is for this reason that Dr Charles Féré, in *L'instinct sexuel, évolution et dissolution* (*The Evolution and Dissolution of the Sexual Instinct*) in 1899, invites his colleagues not to pressure homosexuals into **marriage**. All this bears the legacy of Tardieu: to French medicine, for more than a century, homosexuality was never normal but always a sickness; and as Daniel Borrillo says, "in trying to explain how one becomes gay, all medical theories take for granted that one should not become one." Finally, discordant voices were not heard: Dr Thoinot, in *Attentats aux mœurs et perversion du sens génital* (Attacks on public morals, and perversion of the genitals), stressed, against Tardieu, the invisibility of homosexuals; and when Marc-André Raffalovitch affirmed in *Uranisme et uni-sexualité* (1896) that a large number of gays were very virile and not at all degenerate, he was met with ridicule and personal insults from the medical establishment. The growing medicalization of homosexuality did not prevent the parallel progression of police intervention, and this notwithstanding liberal principles of the Third Republic. At the end of the nineteenth century, morality squad raids multiplied around urinals and in the better known soliciting places, as in certain public cafés and dance halls patronized by gays. Service men were watched. The recording of information, already very important in Pierre Carlier's time, was strengthened by the creation in 1894 of the "*brigade mondaine*," a social brigade that was responsible for writing up "morals files" on the who's who in Paris.

The end of the nineteenth century also saw the beginning of the development of **lesbophobia**. Paradoxically, it seemed to diminish among the *bambocheurs* (party crowd); the spread of recreational heterosexuality promoted the **Sapphic** theme in literature, as witnessed by Pierre Louys' *Chansons de Bilitis,* in 1894, but also in pornography and high-level prostitution, which feeds polygamous fantasies of dejected males. This empowerment of lesbianism in the homophobic unconscious left traces up to today: it is still an excellent criterion of "*beaufisme*" ("between men, it disgusts me, but between women, I do not refuse," explained sport journalist Thierry Roland. The end of the nineteenth century, however, also saw the emergence of the lesbian threat theme, global society being threatened by perversion. Warnings multiplied, as in Julien Chevalier's medical 1885 textbook, *De l'inversion de l'instinct sexuel* (On the inversion of the sexual instinct), or with the vaguely sociological pretension of Ali Coffignon's *Paris vivant: la corruption à Paris* (1889) and Léo Taxil's *La corruption fin de siècle* (1891; The Corruption at the end of the century). In the same era, certain medical doctors pretended to "cure" lesbianism by clitoris ablation.

The first utterance of homosexual expression at the beginning of the twentieth century, then from the First World War, with growing visibility of gays, challenging sexual roles, and de-naturalizing sexual identities, resulted in an upsurge of homophobia. From its origin, the Olympic movement produced homophobic residue: according to Pierre de Coubertin in his *Essais de psychologie sportive,* 1913 (Essays on sports psychology), "psychoneuroses are characterized by a kind of disappearance of the virile sensibility and only **sport** can restore and affirm it." Literature for the general public associated homosexuality with decadence (Gustave Binet-Valmer: *Lucien,* 1909, *Sur le sable couchées,* 1929; Willy et Menalkas: *L'Ersatz d'amour,* 1923; Charles-Etienne: *Notre-Dame-de-Lesbos* and *Les Désexués,* 1924; Victor Margueritte: *La Garçonne,* 1922; Charles-Noël Renard: *Les Androphobes,* 1930). The conservative literary critics of the interwar years regularly admonished the invasion of the homosexual theme in literature (in *Le Temps,* October 23, 1931, André Thérive talked about "baneful propagandism") and the satirical magazine *Fantasio,* which published between 1906 and the middle of the 1930s a large number of gay **caricatures**, affirming that it was defending heterosexual bawdiness, a healthy element of an endangered national heritage. The right wing of the 1920s and 30s saw homosexuality as an important factor in depopulation: for it, gays, women who work, and abortionists were the main people responsible for the weakening of the country. As for lesbianism, it was often assimilated into **feminism** by its detractors, as proven by rumors circulated about the radical feminist Madeleine Pelletier or the media treatment of the accused in the Marthe Hanau affair in 1928–32.

Homosexuality brought up for many an image of foreign behavior: in the Belle Epoque, Dr Laupts (Georges St-Paul's alias, friend of Emile Zola) maintained against Raffalovitch that it was very rare in France, that "inversion is unknown in most regions, and the large majority of French people ignore the existence of this tendency; French people who heard of it expressed an extreme repulsion toward it"; and Dr Riolan, in *Pédérastie et homosexualité* (1909), contended with a straight face that Greeks were gay because their wives were ugly, but because French women were very beautiful, homosexuality could not develop in their country. In the nineteenth century, it was often called "Arabic behavior." Around 1910, the many works on homosexuality and the unveiling of the **Eulenburg affair** in Germany brought forth the adoption of the expression "German vice," that held until World War II (this premise explains why French newspapers covered the homophobic policies of Nazism so badly, repeating until 1940 refrains from the Weimar Republic on "Berlin, the New **Sodom**"). England was not spared by this savage ethno-sexology: *Fantasio* maintained in 1927 that one quarter of English men were gay, the same fantasist proportion was taken up by French Prime Minister Edith Cresson sixty years later.

In the 1920s and 30s, the name that focuses the most animosity and the homophobic hate of do-gooders in France is André **Gide**. Anti-Gidism became a durable ingredient of French homophobia, having crystallized in the enormous scandal produced by *Corydon* in 1924–25. In this essay, Gide had taken the other side of the numerous prejudgments: he affirmed that gays were not necessarily effeminate and could make excellent soldiers, that pederasty (love of teenagers and very young people; the age of majority was then thirteen) offered an excellent solution to protect young girls from prostitution and venereal diseases and that its emotional richness made it a real preparation to responsibilities of marriage and **family**. In short, pederasty was not a calamity but a benefit to French society. The reaction of physicians and psychologists was

immediate and violent: Dr François Nazier published *L'Anti-Corydon* as early as 1924 (with the epigraph, "Nature holds Gide in horror"); Angelo Hesnard did the same in *Psychologie homosexuelle* (1929). These authors refused to admit that homosexuality could be healthy or honorable. For them, gays were immature beings, particularly when they refused to admit that they are sick, and Gide was a very dangerous misleader of youth. Beyond the medical world, the Catholic Right unleashed itself against Gide in the name of family rights and the future of France. The poet and dramatist diplomat Paul Claudel, particularly horrified, wrote to him: "If you are not a pederast, why is this strange predilection for this type of subjects? And if you are one, unfortunate being, heal yourself and do not spread these abominations." In 1931, Claudel launched a homophobic boycott, ending his collaboration with renowned actor Louis Jouvet when Jouvet took it upon himself to direct *Un Taciturne* (A silent man), a play by Martin du Gard featuring some representations of homosexuality. General de Castelnau and Member of Parliament Henri Roulleaux-Dugage took advantage of the *Corydon* scandal to re-apply for the "family vote," to denounce the egotism of unmarried people that did not prepare the future (a future so much darker since World War I left such an imbalanced sex ratio), and to implore women to come back to their natural role and to eternal femininity (for certain authors of this era, male homosexuality was caused by the multitude of domineering mothers under the influence of feminism). Those more moderate, like François Porche in *L'Amour qui n'ose pas dire son nom* (1927; The Love that dare not speak its name), maintained that homosexuality was a vice that could not coexist with love; they accused Gide of not respecting the boundaries of private life, of wanting to engage in **proselytism** and of "planting a flag" for homosexuality. For a while, there were reproaches to Gide coming from everywhere, as described by Didier Eribon, for "wanting to bring to life a gay speech on homosexuality." This anti-Gidism was a very influential phenomenon. It painted the homosexual into a sort of monster, doggedly trying to ruin the family, in a phantasmagoria that lasted until the **PaCS** debate; it very clearly inspired the Vichy government's 1942 law criminalizing homosexual relations with a twenty-one-year-old minor; it consistently saturated the core of the French elite and a significant part of the teaching body; and it offered common ground to the journalistic right for a long time. While Gide's attitude was very peculiar and most gays lived hidden, it was written that pederasts were practicing **exhibitionism** and proselytism; and, on a model of imputation already used against Jewish people, it was affirmed that cultural circles were infested by this mob and that one had to be "one of them" to make it there.

Homophobia, however, did not only involve the elite of the Catholic Church or medical establishments during the interwar period. In France of the early twentieth century, there was an avant-garde of homophobia. We find it among feminists: Christine Bard demonstrated that most of them were afraid to be associated with lesbians and described them as the very enemy of woman. It is significant that the heart of Parisian lesbian life was mostly constituted of Anglo-Saxon women. Homophobia was rampant among the surrealists. (André Breton: "I accuse pederasts of bringing to human tolerance a mental and moral deficit that tends to erect itself into a system and to paralyze all enterprises that I respect." Albert Valentin: "Pederasts disgust me more than anything in the world." Paul Eluard: "I have the most heinous feelings for the lesbian males.") It finally developed in the **Communists** after 1934: under Stalin's influence, the Party resumed the refrain of "German vice" and continued to associate homosexuality with **Fascism** and the decadence of bourgeois society.

From 1942 to 1971: Homosexuality as a "Social Plague"
The Vichy Government's family policies, hostile to republican individualism, were fundamentally homophobic: under influence of Catholicism and the **far right** Action française, Vichy developed a critique of the moral liberalism and hedonist individualism which was derived from the French Revolution, declining birth rates, and declining principles. The law adopted August 6, 1942, for the first time since 1791, specifically criminalized homosexual relations: it created a new section of the penal code, Section 334, which mandated **prison** sentences for "immodest acts or acts against nature" with a minor of less than twenty-one being of the same sex as the agent. This law was clearly aimed at much loathed Gidism, but it also propped up Republican familialism of the end of the 1930s; we find here the "Republican origins of Vichy," studied by Gérard Noiriel. The Code of the Family of 1939 and the law of January 1940 sanctioning anti-natalist propaganda had contributed to the diffusion to

the public, before Vichy, of the belief in a weakening of France due to loose living. For many people, according to René Gillouin (Petain's speech writer) France was "devastated by alcoholism, rotten from eroticism, undermined by low birth rates." The regime meant to rectify this trend: women's eternal femininity would anchor sexual roles, as would patriarchal structures. It was the time of the *Le Voile bleu* (*The Blue Veil*), a film released in 1942 about a woman who devotes her life to caring for children, projecting for the feminization of feminine education, and efforts for the virilization of elites.

This being said, Vichy did not send gays to death as was rumored (in France, the only deported gays were from Alsace-Moselle, a territory directly under the rule of Paragraph 175 of the German penal code between 1940 and 1944).

Vichy's homophobia became a key element of postwar familialism consensus: the content of the 1942 law ended up in the 1945 ordinance. At Liberation, policymakers moved to institutionalize heterosexual familialism, which was maintained until the 1990s: defense of family was written in the 1946 constitution, the Union nationale des associations familiales became continuous influence on public authority, and other essential agencies aimed to defend family structure (Union nationale des caisses d'allocations familiales, Haut conseil de la population et de la famille, and Ministère de la population et de la famille). There was from then on an important family lobby, much more powerful than before the war. This lobby summarized the Church family doctrine (founded on an esoteric concept of family and very hostile to the individual) and state familialism (more pragmatic, aiming to fight lower birth rates and help large families). In 1946, Emmanuel Mounier, a leader of the Catholic intelligentsia, published the homophobic doctrine in his *Traité du caractère*.

In the political sphere, Christian democrats, Communists, and Gaullists shared the same conception of family, kinship, and good morals, and an unquestioned homophobia. The unprecedented power of the French Communist Party inside of the left, the fact that Centrism was from then on a lot more Christian democrat than radical (while the Popular Republican Movement often played the role of "Pétainist's recycling machine"), the moral caution that Gaullism gave to the least appealing ideas of the hardest right, all combined to bring about particularly devastating effects. The years 1945–68 were thus the "era of combat" in the law. The 1945 Ordinance, making Section 334 of Vichy, Sections 331–32 of the new penal code, penalized "immodest acts against nature with a minor"; the law of July 16, 1949 on publications aimed at youth limited the distribution of gay literary works and publications; the 1960 Ordinance, creating Sections 330–32, factored in an aggravated punishment in cases of public homosexual immodest offences; and finally in 1968, France officially adopted the World Health Organization classification that made homosexuality a mental disease. Gays thus became second-class citizens, at best tolerated and without any possibility of protestation or free expression, which was clearly expressed by **Mirguet**'s 1960 amendment. Everywhere, enactments reminded homosexuals that the social order is heterosexual and that they must live hidden. Until 1982, the Tenancies Act stipulated that tenants had to occupy their housing units as "good patresfamilias"; until 1983, public servants had to be of "good behavior and good morality"; and from the end of the 1940s to the end of the 60s, police ordinances prohibited gender impersonators and dancing of two same-sex individuals in public places.

This legal battery is accompanied by a reinforcing of public fears: Alfred Kinsey's *Sexual Behavior in the Human Male,* published in the United States in 1948, was immediately translated into French and led to the perception that gays were much more numerous than previously thought. Chiefly under the effect of the circulation of the Freudian thesis of "infantile blockage" (promulgated by most women's magazines, many popularizing medicine books and the increasing numbers of childhood development professionals), homosexuality was more and more perceived as the result of an error of education. The feelings of parental responsibilities then became enormous, to the extent that it was social catastrophe to have a gay child. In the middle and upper classes, parents felt obliged to watch more closely over children's play, discourage cross-dressing, offer toy weapons to boys and dolls to girls, and refrain from having too strong a relationship develop between sons and mothers.

In short, families had never felt with as much acuteness as in those postwar decades the duty to make their progeny heterosexual. The neurotic character of this obsession was reinforced in the middle class by the presence of a relatively strong Puritanism. Homophobia was so fertile, it bloomed in the most unexpected places. For example, Simone de Beauvoir's

courageous campaign against sexist prejudices did not preclude her from writing in 1949 in *Le Deuxième sexe* (*The Second Sex*) on lesbians: "Nothing gives a worse impression of parochial approach and mutilation than those (lesbians) clans of liberated women."

In 1960, a political apogee was reached with the Mirguet amendment that made homosexuality a "social scourge" which public authority must control. In a surprise vote in a night session, Gaullist member Paul Mirguet (who pretended to want to save civilization and in a context of postcolonial doubt, resumed the anti-Gide theme of the protection of children) included homosexuality with prostitution and alcoholism. Through the Mirguet amendment, homophobia was from now on offensive: the act went beyond the repressive framework intended to organize prophylaxis; by any means, public authority had to prevent the development of sexuality, considered as scourge, but even more, to keep it invisible. The symbolic violence of the Mirguet amendment was so strong that according to Frédéric Martel, many French gays were thinking of leaving the country. The 60s were years of generalized homophobia in France: do-gooder homophobia was perfectly embodied by the presidential couple (the very prudish Yvonne de Gaulle was said to be particularly hostile to "special behavior"); and popular homophobia like songwriter George Brassens ("Les Copains d'abord," 1964). The era also saw an intensification of homophobic **insults**: queer, poof, fag, bugger, sod, fairy, and nancy-boy, were heard all day long in the streets, school yards, cafés, stadiums, barrack rooms, and commissaries; in variety theater television, like the kind found in Pigalle's cabarets of "cross dressers"; in Roger Pierre and Jean-Marc Thibault's sketches; and in the never-ending jokes in works Jean Cocteau, Jean Marais, Jean-Louis Bory, and Jacques Chazot. France's accelerated urbanization of the time increased the visibility of homophobia: if gays were mostly an urbanite population, homophobia also grew mainly in the city, on the street, and in public places, providing infinite occasions for verbal aggression. Homophobic themes also fed generational conflict, very acute in the second part of the 60s (the fathers' generation, who had known the war, confronted the sons' generation born in the baby boom era): the elders found that the youth did not know hardships, lacked virility, and believed in collective depravation by overconsumption and democratization of Hedonism, and saw in hippie singer Antoine's long hair and the high-pitched voices of yé-

yé singers the signs of sexual confusion.

But protesters themselves were not protected from prejudice. There was an extreme left-wing homophobia: in May 1968, in the occupied Sorbonne, eight posters were taken down that had been put up by the mysterious Comité d'action pédérastique révolutionnaire (Committee of Revolutionary Pederastic Action) that was denouncing social and police repression that gays were suffering; and there was the homophobia of the psychoanalytic avant-garde: Jacques Lacan, very well known in Paris intelligentsia, exclaimed, "Do not tell us that under the pretext that it was a received, approved, even celebrated perversion, that it was not a perversion; homosexuality remains nevertheless what it is: a perversion." It is not surprising under these conditions, that the first surveys on the subject in 1968 show a massive hostile opinion: homosexuality was perceived as "either a disease to cure, or a perversion to fight," as Christine Bard said.

There remained self hatred: the embryo of the gay movement that was known in France in the 50s and 60s was the one that was constituted around the magazine *Arcadie*, created in 1954 by André Baudry, which had thousands of subscribers. *Arcadie* had almost no proper distribution, as proven by barriers put up by public authority to selling of the magazine; from which was born a strategy for respectability that led Baudry to continually sit in judgment of other "homophiles" and to have, in his own way, a homophobic discourse (particularly on cruising for prostitutes, in the name of love), transforming *Arcadie* meetings into slightly ridiculous preaching. This strategy was completely empty: it had no effect on public opinion, did not neutralize any prejudice, and even contributed to the reinforcement of the negative gay self image.

Since 1971: Resistances to Emancipation
Well behind the Anglo-Saxon countries, the gay and lesbian revolution established itself in France in 1971. Gay visibility increased and homosexuals started to make demands. Chiefly, they took advantage of the new vision of the global society on sexuality and pleasure. On all fronts, homophobia was losing ground. It crystallized itself, however, around four themes that also corresponded to three moments: the refusal of decriminalization, the fears rising around **AIDS**, and the hostility to gay marriage and gay **parenting**.

The desire to maintain the legal stigmatization of homosexuality was first and foremost the domain of the **Catholic Church** (and particularly of Pope John Paul II, elected in 1978 and one of the most violently homophobic voices of his time): for the Roman master, homosexuality remained a depravity. In April 1982 Léon-Arthur Elchinger, Bishop of Strasbourg, shockingly declared: "I respect homosexuals as I respect disabled people. But if they want to convert their infirmity in health, I must say that I do not agree." And the last version of the Roman catechism prescribed: "Based on the Holy Scriptures … tradition has always proclaimed that 'homosexual acts are intrinsically disordered'; they are contrary to natural law; they close the sexual act to the gift of life; they do not proceed from a real sexual and affective complementarity; they can't in any case receive approbation." The pope himself approved in 1992 certain specific discriminations on homosexual hiring, lodging, and social protection, going as far as limiting AIDS sufferers' rights (*Osservatore Romano,* August 4, 1992); he tried by all means to stop decriminalization of homosexuality in Eastern European countries; finally, he condemned the "judicial approbation" of homosexuality by European Parliament (1994).

For the right and far right, of which a part is sensitive to the Vatican discourse, gays were always sick people (lesbians are often perceived, at least in private, as "missed loved"). The 1970s sexual revolution, the growing visibility of gays, the high level of sexual consumption by certain gays, the arrival of backrooms in gay bars*,* the leather look, and S/M trends were perceived as a threat to civilization, the sign of a real decadence; thus causing the refusal of decriminalization, specifically the repealing of Sections 331-32. Between 1980 and 1982, the business of the day was the question of whether the legal age for gay sex (eighteen years old since 1974) should be aligned with the heterosexual legal age of fifteen years old. For the members of parliament of the right wing of 1981, homosexuality remained a social scourge and a danger to the family: it was against nature, it should not be trivialized; a normally constituted head of a family would not support the idea of a lecherous old man sodomizing his fifteen-year-old son (to which Minister of Justice Robert Badinter responded very to the point: "But sir, what head of the family could support the same vision of a lecherous old man sodomizing a fifteen-year-old girl?").

We clearly see here the two concepts of liberty that so often oppose themselves in French political life:

one extensive concept, rather left wing (liberty must encompass the most possible differences), and one normative concept, rather right wing (liberty must be inscribed in a frame of social interdictions). Once homosexuality was decriminalized, the right wing didn't hesitate to make use of bad faith arguments, often maintaining confusion between homosexuality and pedophilia, which helped to infuriate public opinion. In March 1987, Charles Pasqua tried (in vain) to use the act of 1949 on publications aimed at youth to eradicate France's most prominent gay magazine of the time, *Gai-Pied*. It is clear that, for the far right of the era, gays, being not numerous and voting mostly for the left, seemed to be an ideal scapegoat: the rub is that many heterosexuals now feel a lot more supportive of gays than of moral order promoters, and that these anti-gay operations were completely counterproductive to gaining votes from the center.

If homophobia was most often found in the right wing, it also concerned a part of the left, particularly in the 1970s. The Communists, very family-oriented since the influence of Stalin, were often hostile to the first aspirations of the gay movement. Communist Party leader Jacques Duclos insulted Front homosexual d'action (FHAR; Homosexual Revolutionary Action Front) militants in 1971, remarking, "A bunch of pederasts, go get yourselves treated!"; in 1972, Roland Leroy called the movement "the decay of capitalism in its decline"; and highly homophobic texts appeared in the French communist daily newspaper *L'Humanité*, 1975–76. A part of the extreme left was not much more favorable to gays; the splinter group Vive la révolution, where Guy Hocquenghem was a member, self-destructed in the spring of 1971 on the gay question and its pro-worker elements split off. During the same period, the French Communist Union, or Lutte ouvrière (Worker's struggle), critiqued the petit-bourgeois individualism of gays, saying that the content of the special gay edition of the Maoist newspaper *Tout!* "is at the level of street urinal graffiti." As for the Revolutionary Communist League, it only agreed to create a Gay National Commission in 1977. There are finally isolated cases of homophobia among the moderate left: the populist homophobia of Prime Minister Edith Cresson, said in 1987 that homosexuality was a "sort of disease," and talked about Anglo-Saxon countries where, according to her, one-quarter of men are homosexual, and again in 1991, claimed that "heterosexuality is better." The pathological homophobia of

François Abadie, the Left Radical Party senator for the Pyrenees region, declared to the *Observateur*, in June 2000: "I cannot be in favor of those that I call the gravediggers of humanity, those that do not assure the future, homosexuals." He was later excluded from his own Party after having made incredible insults against Sébastien Chenu, National Counselor of the Liberal Democracy.

French mainstream **media**, with the exception of leftist newspaper *Libération*, were in the 1970s very timid toward the demands of the growing gay movement. The most notable example is Menie Grégoire's radio program on RTL, March 10, 1971, "Homosexuality, this painful problem," on which the host stated: "It is a fact that it is not good to be gay!" Further, between 1973 and 1975, the television network ORTF refused to deal with the issue of homosexuality on its news program *Dossiers de l'écran*. As for the first gay or gay-friendly media, they were charged in 1971 for "offence against good morals" and "pornography" by Raymond Marcellin, the unremitting Minister of the Interior: luckily, Jean-Paul Sartre, editor of *Tout!* protested and justice gave him reason (a judgment of the Constitutional Council, dated July 16, 1971, declared the infringements on free expression and association were unconstitutional). Finally, even if gay visibility had made progress in French **cinema** in the 70s, it is most revealing that films for the general public of the same period still offered unbelievable examples of caricatures, like Jean Yanne's film *Moi y'en a vouloir des sous* (1973) and Edouard Molinaro's *La Cage aux folles* series (1978–85).

The AIDS crises revived, in certain parts of the culture, some forms of homophobia during the 1980s. Because in France, as elsewhere, "the degree of social acceptance of homosexuality is very important to understand the fear of AIDS" (Michael Pollak). One part of the right wing thought that it finally held a key to the end of the gay movement. As early as February 15, 1982, a member of parliament for Rally for the Republic (RPR) from Aveyron, Jacques Godfrain, drew the attention of the Health Minister on the rapidly increasing number of Kaposi's Sarcoma cases and suggested a campaign of information aimed at youth on "the dangers of homosexuality" (this was at the origin of more euphemistic notions of "risk groups" or "high risk sexuality"). At the beginning of the epidemic, the windfall seemed real: the disease affected particularly those whose sexuality challenged the familial Catholic conservative norms; even if the theme of AIDS as God's punishment did not have much success in France, it showed up here and there, even among certain doctors. While the moderate right held its tongue somewhat, the far right tried, albeit without much success, to bring back the fear of the plague: in early 1987, National Front leader Jean-Marie Le Pen announced that the situation was extremely serious and that France had to create "AIDS centers" in order to quarantine "AIDS victims." This **rhetoric**, however, did not take root, even in the National Front, as homophobia was much less prevalent in the 80s than xenophobia or racism. This being said, one noted that the Association des polytransfusés (Association of Multiple Blood Transfusion Recipients) believed in 1995 that it had to denounce "the freedom of the gay way of life which by spreading AIDS caused the death of so many hemophiliacs and recipients of transfusions," thus underlining and constructing a model of opposition between "innocent" victims and "guilty" patients. Nevertheless, at the end of the 90s, the conservatives were foiled: the epidemic greatly increased the integration of gays into French society, allowing middle-class France to discover that gay love could have the strength of heterosexual love and that parental homophobia, even inherited from a Christian prejudice, was sometimes monstrous.

Even if it escaped the conservatives' delusions about a plague, the left-wing government was not always comfortable in managing its public handling of AIDS. Certainly, at the beginning of the epidemic, it did not see it as a strictly homosexual disease, but when in 1985 the all new association Aides (Association for the Fight Against HIV, AIDS, and Hepatitis) requested funds from public authorities, Matignon (the prime minister's official residence) refused, in order to, according to a counselor, "not give the impression that we are helping the fags." The same uneasiness explained why the same Fabius government decided not to authorize publicity on condoms in 1985–86. As for Pierre Bérégovoy, (prime minister under President Mitterand) easily intimidated by the Catholic family lobby, he prohibited on his sole authority a televised campaign of the French Association against AIDS in May 1992.

The most recent major flare-up of homophobia in France had at stake the PaCS act, the acknowledgment of gay couples, between fall 1998 and summer 1999. The parliamentary left was nevertheless extremely prudent in this case, even timid: it refused to associate the debate on PaCS to a debate on gay parenting (PaCS does not concern filiations); and it did not make PaCS an equivalent to marriage (it accepts the dictate of the right that prohibited the PaCS from being signed at City Hall).

Without surprise, the Catholic Church plays a major role in the crusade against the legal acknowledgement of gay couples. This acknowledgment was, in fact, for the Holy See a symbolic catastrophe, as it marginalized even more the Catholic discourse on family and sexuality, more and more disconnected from law and fact. In the Pope's eyes, the Christian **symbolic order** is based on the refusal of homosexuality, and the consideration of it by objective law, even by lay people, cannot but result in a non-Christian order, a return to Paganism and barbarity. In order not to appear to question secularism, France's Church took care to avoid the use of Biblical laws and carefully window-dressed its catechism with **anthropology** and **psychoanalysis**: its major expert on the matter, Father Tony Anatrella, appeared in the media with alleged scientific considerations (stating that homosexuality is a primitive sexuality; the will to acknowledge gay couples makes us slide toward jeopardizing or putting in **peril** the symbolic and anthropological order, and toward individual and social unreason; gay militants are this way portrayed as the gravediggers of civilization). But the main voice of the Catholic lobby in the battle with the Union pour la démocratie Française (UDF; Union for French Democracy) was Member of Parliament for Yvelines, Christine **Boutin**, consultant for the Pontifical Council for the Family: completely sold on the Vatican rhetoric, she saw in homosexuality "the tragedy of refusal of **otherness**" (note the sophism that demands that the other is inevitably of the other sex) and for this reason, refused to accept that one can talk of gay "couple." She was supported in her efforts by various Catholic networks: Avenir de la culture (an association linked to a far-right Brazilian sect, practicing intimidation of public officials and companies determined to be gay-friendly), Catholic Family Associations, Cercle de la cité vivante (whose bible is *La Marée noire de la pornographie* [The black tide of pornography]), and the Alliance pour les droits de la vie (Alliance for the Right to Life). The originality of this Catholic mobilization was that it tried to solicit the support of the other main religions represented in France—Protestant family associations, Jewish and Muslim authorities—collecting all monotheists in a kind of homophobic ecumenism.

It was, however, the homophobia of the political class that was most visible in 1998–99. The Gaullist right, Christians, and Liberals each felt they had gone to the end of their capacity for tolerance in accepting decriminalization. They did not want to hear about legal recognition (homosexuality was to remain in the private domain, ideally discreet, invisible), let alone gay parenting. Because French conservatives did not really accept the family revolution of the 1980s and 90s (fewer marriages, more divorces, more "blended" families, more single-parent families), inasmuch as this silent revolution destroys the myth of the natural, simple, and universal family, specifically the pro-family credo in place since Vichy and the Liberation. For the right wing, the law had to fight against the fact, to bring forward a "norm," to maintain a "symbolic civilizing Order," to save "Nature" (note the "fondness for capitals," nicely pointed out by Sabine Prokhoris); it is particularly suitable to recall the symbolic inequality of sexualities by affirming that only heterosexuality is worthy of being public, published, taught, and celebrated. The right wing then cried conspiracy: as early as 1993, Ernest Chénière, RPR member of parliament for Oise, denounced "a minority of remarkably organized gay and addicted dropouts," who "launched a powerful campaign to ensure the passage in law, under pressure, of the objective legalization of their perversions and of their deviances." Regularly, the right wing alleged to be the mouthpiece of "good Republican sense": Michel Pinton, UDF mayor of Felletin, called upon the mayors of rural towns and in spring 1998, circulated a petition among them against "the establishment of a union contract for same-sex persons and the implication of the mayors as State officials in celebrating such a contract," gathering 12,000 signatures, which was well publicized (one-third of France's mayors signed, but it should be stressed that their constituents only constituted 10% of the French population). Conservative members of society felt legitimized by this call to resistance that came from the depths of the country, which probably explained the surge of conjectural homophobic writings, proven by the letters to the editor of *Figaro* or extremely aggressive, sometimes hateful letters addressed to the very courageous Roselyne Bachelot, the main personality of the parliamentary right to defend the PaCS.

The majority of conservative politicians purported, for their part, that they were defending civilization and the future: at the parliamentary debate, young UDF Member of Parliament Renaud Dutreil, claimed to have anthropological knowledge acquired at the Ecole Normale Supérieure that permitted him to assert that the PaCS was "a sort of transgenic corn in the matter of human relations." In response, Philippe de Villiers, leader of the Movement for France, exclaimed: "Your innovation of the PaCS is quite simply a return to barbarism; you are walking in the steps of those who in order to undermine society started by undermining family; one day victims will rise and turn to you to tell you a terrible expression: 'You are the destructive socialism.'" The far right was quite clearly supported in this combat by President Chirac, at least as long as public opinion had not pronounced itself in favor of the project, since Chirac's francocentric populism included homophobia. As mayor of Paris, he was behind the negative **jurisprudence** of the Council of State, and as president on June 6, 1998, he declared that "one must not risk altering the nature of **marriage** nor trivialize it by putting it at the same level of other human realities of our times, that lead very far from fundamental family values."

But the proponents of homophobia did not find the popular support they counted on. Several anti-PaCS demonstrations followed one another, whose organizers secretly hoped that they would be comparable to the giant gatherings of 1984 in favor of Catholic teaching. The November 7, 1998 demonstration was attended by 40,000 to 50,000 people brandishing new slogans like "2 Daddies, 2 Mommies; Welcome to the Mess." The largest one was on January 31, 1999, attended by 98,000 people: several of its slogans sunk to new lows—"Today's Gays are Tomorrow's Pedophiles" and "Fags to the Pyre,"—the moderate right wing giving the impression of having been hijacked by the far right. The results of all this agitation were negative for the parliamentary right, whose efforts were defeated (PaCS was enacted on November 15, 1999). This did not prevent, one year later, the RPR Renaud Muselier from starting a petition for stopping gay couples from adopting, arguing that gay parenting would expose children to danger (this petition was signed by 168 members of parliament).

Debates on PaCS also underlined the high level of resistance among the left-wing intelligentsia with regard to gay parenting, including Guy Coq, sociologist Irène Théry, the magazine *Esprit*, or feminist writer and teacher Sylviane Agacinski. Some members of the left believed that they were authorized with the mission of saving the "symbolic order" and "Nature" from the increasingly unreasonable demands of "extremists." If Coq made himself ridiculous with his anger and intolerance, Théry, the leading expert on the blended family and official representative in Martine Aubry's cabinet, lost some of her intellectual credibility in view of Eric Fassin's flawless rationality. The reserved *Esprit*, which had nevertheless known a period of openness at the beginning of the 1990s, now manifested the inevitable decline of the Catholic intelligentsia. Doubtless thinking to legitimize her husband's prudishness (Lionel Jospin, who was then prime minister), Agacinski, in her *Politique des sexes* (1998), thought she could affirm the natural heterosexuality of humanity and relegate homosexuality to the romanticism of transgression unworthy of equality. Certain left-wing essayists, among them Frédéric Martel, also denounced, the **communitarianism** of French homosexuals derived from an American model that would be dangerous to French republican political values. In the university milieu, a similar argument was used to impede the introduction of gay and lesbian studies, whose intellectual legitimacy is disputed by people who ignore almost all Anglo-Saxon or French research on the subject.

It would be tempting to conclude by stressing the decline of homophobia in society. Certainly, homosexuality in France still provokes insults, aggression, dismissals, and intimidation of all sorts, identified in reports issued by **SOS homophobie** in 1994, and it is interesting to note that certain successful published works are still clearly homo- or lesbophobic. It becomes apparent that homophobia does not have the same weight everywhere: the South of France (macho France, France with "honor" societies) remains generally more hostile to gays than in the North; elites (political and economical), country people, and suburbanites (the middle and working classes), are more homophobic than the urban middle class or the intelligentsia (even if, as we saw, this group is less gay friendly than we often think); people sixty years of age or older have more prejudices than those under thirty; and "practicing believers" (whatever their religion) are infinitely more homophobic than those who are not.

Nevertheless, opinions are changing and surveys are proving it: from 1985–87, homosexuality was "a way among others to live one's sexuality" for a majority of French. Besides, the same surveys showed a generational disagreement that was extremely promising for the future: in 1993, for 76% of teenagers interviewed, homosexuality was not objectionable; and at the end of the 90s, a large majority of people under the age of thirty were not only favorable to PaCS but also to gay marriage. This diminution of homophobia has several origins. The essential explanation is due to the unprecedented decline of the moral and cultural influence of France's Catholic Church. A great majority of French think that an adult's sexuality should not be controlled by any other authority than the individual conscience, and what is condemned by the Church is not necessarily condemned by the general public. To this, AIDS has tragically sanctified a social category that before was often jeered or scorned: the gay person is not automatically ridiculed anymore. Certain media have accentuated the phenomenon by reporting truthfully and responsibly on gay issues (one can underline the highly pedagogical action of Jean-Luc Delarue's television program *Ça se discute*, and the significant evolution of *Le Monde* newspaper).

Communalization equally played a role in improving the visibility and image of homosexuals: participation in Paris Lesbian and Gay Pride has become massive since the 1990s (Gay Pride 1988: 1,000 participants; 1992: 10,000; 1995: 60,000; 2001: 250,000); and since 1997–98, there has been an increase in the number of gay and lesbian associations in post-secondary institutions, universities, and companies.

All this paradoxically paved the way for the **criminalization** of homophobia; the slogan of Lesbian and Gay Pride 2000 significantly played on the infamous Mirguet amendment: in future, it is not homosexuality anymore, but it is homophobia that is a "social scourge."

In 2004, the National Assembly approved legislation that made homophobic and sexist comments illegal. As of 2001, 55% of French people considered homosexuality "an acceptable lifestyle," and a 2006 survey showed that 62% supported same-sex marriage and 44% believed same-sex couples should have the right to adopt. However, although a parliamentary report on family and the rights of children in 2006 recommended increasing some rights given in PaCS, it recommended increasing prohibitions against same-sex marriage, adoption, and access to medically-assisted reproduction. Such legislation, and events like the attempted murder of the gay mayor of Paris, Bertrand Delanöe, show that even in France, intolerance is always a threat for homosexuals.

However, in 2005, on May 17 (fifteen years to the day after the World Health Organization decided to remove homosexuality from their list of mental disorders), the French intellectual Louis-Georges Tin launched the first International Day Against Homophobia, known in fifty countries worldwide as IDAHO. More than 100 events were organized on this occasion, including public demonstrations, debates, exhibitions, film screenings, and street campaigns. The initiative was widely supported by left-wing parties, but in 2008, in order to show that homophobia was also a concern for the right-wing parties, the conservative government (which nonetheless included the anti-PaCS Christine Boutin) decided to give the day official recognition. Moreover, at the urging of the IDAHO committee, French Secretary of State Rama Yade decided to bring forth a declaration to the UN General Assembly for the universal decriminalization of homosexuality.
—*Pierre Albertini*
[Original essay updated by Arsenal Pulp Press.]

Agacinski, Sylviane. *Politique des sexes*. Paris: Le Seuil, 1998. [Published in the US as *Parity of the Sexes*. New York: Columbia Univ. Press, 2001.]

Ahlstedt, Eva. *André Gide et le débat sur l'homosexualité; de L'Immoraliste (1902) à Si le grain ne meurt (1926)*. Gothenburg, Sweden: Acta Universitatis Gothoburgensis, 1994.

Anatrella, Tony. *La Différence interdite*. Paris: Flammarion. 1998.

Bachelot, Roselyne. *Le Pacs, entre haine et amour*. Paris: Pion, 2000.

Bard, Christine. *Les Femmes dans la société française au XX siècle*. Paris: Armand Colin, 2001.

———, ed. *Un siècle d'antiféminisme*. Paris: Fayard, 1999.

Bluche, François. "Vice ultramontain (Relativité du)." In *Dictionnaire du Grand Siècle*. Paris: Fayard, 1990.

Bonnet, Marie-Jo. *Les Relations amoureuses entre les femmes du XVT au XXe siècle*. Pans: Odile Jacob, 1995.

Borrillo Daniel. *Homosexualités et droit*. Paris: Presses universitaires de France, 1998.

———. *L'Homophobie*. Paris: Presses universitaires de France, 2000.

———, Eric Fassin, and Marcela Iacub, eds. *Au-delà du PaCS, L'expertise familiale à l'épreuve de l'homosexualité*. Paris: Presses universitaires de France, 1999.

Boswell, John. *Christianisme, tolérance sociale et homosexualité*. Paris: Gallimard, 1985. [Published in the US as *Christianity, Social Tolerance, and Homosexuality: Gay People*

in Western Europe from the Beginning of the Christian Era to the Fourteenth Century. Chicago: Univ. of Chicago Press, 1980.]

Bourdieu, Pierre. *La Domination masculine*. Paris: Le Seuil, 1998. [Published in the US as *Masculine Domination*. Stanford: Stanford Univ. Press, 2001.]

Boutin, Christine. *Le "Mariage" des homosexuels? CUCS, PIC, PaCS et autres projets législatifs*. Paris: Critérion, 1998.

Camus, Renaud. *Journal d'un voyage en France*. Paris: Hachette-POL, 1981.

Carlier, François. *Etudes de pathologie sociale, Les deux prostitutions*. Paris: E. Dcntu, 1887.

Charcot, Jean-Martin, and Victor Magnan. "Inversion du sens génital et autres perversions sexuelles," *Archives de neurologie*, nos. 7 and 12 (1882).

Corbin, Alain. "Amour et sexualité." In *Histoire de vie privée*. Vol. 4: "De la Révolution à la Grande Guerre." Edited by Georges Duby and Philippe Ariès. Paris: Le Seuil, 1988. [Published in the US as *A History of Private Life*. Cambridge, MA: Belknap Press of Harvard Univ. Press, 1987–91.]

———. *Les Filles de noce, misère sexuelle et prostitution (XIX siècle)*. Paris: Aubier Montaigne, 1978.

Dejean, Joan. *Sappho. Les fictions du Désir: 1546–1937*. Paris: Hachette, 1994.

Delphy, Christine. "L'Humanitarisme républicain contre les mouvements homos," *Politique: La revue*, no. 5 (1997).

Dubost, Jean-François. *La France italienne, XVIe-XVIIe s.* Paris: Aubier, 1997.

Eribon, Didier. *Réflexions sur la question gay*. Paris: Fayard, 1999. [Published in the US as *Insult and the Making of the Gay Self*. Durham, NC: Duke University Press, 2004.]

Fassin, Eric. "Homosexualité, mariage, famille," *Le Monde* (November 5, 1997).

———. "L'Intellectuel spécifique" et le PaCS: politique des saviors," Mouvements, no. 7 (2000).

———. "Le Savant, l'expert et le politique. La famille des sociologues," *Genèses*, no. 32 (1998).

Flandrin, Jean-Louis. "Contraception, mariage et relations amoureuses dans l'Occident Chrétien," *Annales ESC* (November–December 1972).

Fourest, Caroline, and Fiammetta Venner. *Les Anti-Pacs ou la dernière croisade homophobe*. Paris: Pro Choix, 1999.

Fraisse, Geneviève. *Muse de la raison, la démocratie exclusive et la différence des sexes*. Paris: Alinéa, 1989.

Girard, Jacques. *Le Mouvement homosexuel en France (1945-1980)*. Paris: Syros, 1981.

Graille, Patrick. *Les Hermaphrodites aux XVII et XVIII siècles*. Paris: Les Belles Lettres, 2001.

Hernandez, Louis. *Les Procès de sodomie aux XVI, XVII, XVIII siècles.* Paris: Bibliothèque des curieux, 1920.

Hervé, Frédéric, *La Censure du cinéma en France à la Libération.* Paris: ADHE, 2001.

Leroy-Forgeot, Flora and Caroline Mécary. *Le PaCS*, Paris: Presses universitaires de France, 2001.

Lever, Maurice. *Les Bûchers de Sodome.* Paris: Fayard, 1985.

Martel, Frédéric. *Le Rose et le noir. Les homosexuels en France depuis 1968.* Paris: Le Seuil, 1996. [Published in the US as *The Pink and The Black: Homosexuals in France since 1968.* Stanford, CA: Stanford Univ. Press, 1999.]

———. "Les Risques supposés du communautarisme gay," *Le Figaro* (January 24, 2001).

Merrick, Jeffrey, and Bryant T. Ragan, Jr., eds. *Homosexuality in Modern France.* Oxford: Oxford Univ. Press, 1996.

Merrick, Jeffrey., and Michael Sibalis, eds. *Homosexuality in French History and Culture.* New York: Harrington Park Press, 2001.

Meynard, Philippe. *Le Prix de la différence.* Paris: Michel Lafon, 2000.

Mossuz-Lavau, Janine. *Les Lois de l'amour: les politiques de la sexualité en France (1950–1990).* Paris: Payot, 1991.

Mounier, Emmanuel. *Traité du caractère.* Paris: Le Seuil, 1946.

Pellegrin, Nicole. "L'Androgyne au XVIe siècle, pour une relecture des saviors." In *Femmes et pouvoirs sous l'Ancien Régime.* Edited by Danielle Haase-Dubosc and Eliane Viennot. Paris: Rivages/Histoire, 1991.

Poirier, Guy. *L'Homosexualité dans l'imaginaire de la Renaissance.* Paris: Champion, 1996.

Rey, Michel. "Police et sodomie à Paris au XVIII siècle," *Revue d'histoire moderne et contemporaine* (1982).

Robinson, Christopher. *Scandal in the Ink, Male & Female Homosexuality in Twentieth Century French Literature.* London: Cassell, 1995.

Sibalis, Michael David. "The Regulation of Male Homosexuality in Revolutionary and Napoleonic France, 1789–1815." In *Homosexuality in Modern France.* Edited by Jeffrey Merrick and Bryant T. Ragan, Jr., eds. Oxford: Oxford Univ. Press, 1996.

Sohn, Anne-Marie. *Du premier baiser à l'alcôve, la sexualité des Français au quotidien (1850–1950).* Paris: Aubier, 1996.

SOS homophobie. *Rapport 2001 sur l'homophobie.* Paris: SOS homophobie, 2001.

Steinberg, Sylvie. *La Confusion des sexes, Le travestissement de la Renaissance à la Révolution.* Paris: Fayard, 2001.

Tamagne, Florence. *Histoire de l'homosexualité en Europe, Berlin, Londres, Paris, 1919–1939.* Paris: Le Seuil, 2000. [Published in the US as *A History of Homosexuality in Europe: Berlin, London, Paris, 1919–1939.* New York: Algora, 2004.]

Tardieu, Ambroise. *Etude médico-légale sur les attentats aux mœurs.* Paris: J-B. Baillière, 1857.

Théry, Irène. *Couple, filiation et parenté aujourd'hui, le droit face aux mutations de la famille et de la vie privée.* Paris: Odile Jacob, "La Documentation française," 1998.

Thévenot, Xavier. *Homosexualités masculines et morale chrétienne.* Paris: Le Cerf, 1992.

Tin, Louis-Georges, ed. *Homosexualités, expression/répression.* Paris: Stock, 2000.

Tissot, S. *L'Onanisme dissertation sur les maladies produites par la masturbation.* Lausanne: Chapuis, 1760.

—Adoption; Against Nature; Anti-PaCS; Boutin, Christine; Caricature; Cinema; Communism; Custine, Astolphe de; Far Right, the; Favorites; Gide, André; Henri III; Heresy; Heterosexism; Literature; Marriage; Medicine; Media; Mirguet, Paul; Monsieur; Parenting; Pétain, Philippe; Police; School; Theology; Viau, Théophile de; Villon, François.

G

GAY PARENTHOOD. *See* Parenting

GAYPHOBIA

The idea that "gayphobia" (where "gay" is defined as gay men) and "homophobia" are one and the same has the effect of rendering lesbians invisible, which is one of the essential tenets of **lesbophobia**. Nevertheless, there are specific forms of homophobia that only or principally concern gay men.

One such example is the idea that all homosexuals are pedophiles, a belief that is without a doubt enhanced by the linguistic proximity between the term "**pedophilia**," referring to a sexual attraction to children, and the word "pederasty," which has long been a synonym of homosexuality. Apart from any historical references, the contemporary link between homosexuality and pedophilia functions on two levels: the first is a moral one, which tends to ascribe morality to sexual practices; the second is a political one, in which conservatives with an anti-homosexual agenda encourage the belief that gay men are pedophiles. One example of the latter in France was a drawing which appeared on the front page of the right-wing newspaper *Présent* depicting a male couple promising a small boy that they would receive him with "open bed sheets"; the publication of this image resulted in a lawsuit brought by the Gay and Lesbian Center and Pro Choice FLH (Fonds de lutte contre l'homophobie, a legal organization) against the newspaper. Similarly, in *Le Figaro* in 1998, historian Emmanuel Le Roy-Ladurie contended: "The fact of entrusting children to gay male couples (as will happen some day by logical evolution if PaCS [Pacte civil de solidarité; Civil solidarity pact] is adopted) will contribute to increasing the risk of pedophilia which is already high"; his reference to "gay

male couples" reveals its gayphobia, as it is masculine homosexuality that is clearly the target.

Another example of gayphobia based on the perceived link between male homosexuality and pedophilia is the ongoing fight against sexual awareness and education programs in schools, based on the belief that students need to be "protected." Suspicion of pedophilia is thus a form of anti-gay **rhetoric** which does not apply to lesbians (although in a definition that appeared in the 1999 edition of the *Larousse Dictionary* in France, the entry for "pedophile" included a reference to "pedophile lesbians"). Further, the website Media G (*media-g.net*) identified specific examples of the link between homosexuality and pedophilia, particularly when there were criminal trials involving the "pedophilia network," or **scandals** like the one that befell the Catholic Church in the United States in 2002.

Gayphobia has also appeared in the rhetoric of certain heterosexual or lesbian feminists, such as with regard to the issue of gay **parenting**. While the approval of gay men and lesbians raising children is far from unanimous, it is generally presumed that lesbian parents are less suspect than gay male parents at raising children. In the same manner, sociologist Irène Théry believes that children can be educated by lesbians, but not by gay men. In this prejudicial belief that is shared by some of the most progressive feminists, one can see a type of residual sexist ideology which proposes that maternity represents the essence of femininity.

More damaging is the fact that some feminists accuse gay men of being as much society's oppressors as heterosexual men. At Paris's Lesbian and Gay Pride Parade in 2001, the Groupe du 6 novembre (November 6 Group), which defines itself as a network of "lesbians whose history is linked to proslavery, colonization, imperialism, and forced migrations," distributed stickers that read: "Slaves have their master, prisoners have their screw, women have their rapist, lesbians have their gay," an analogy that puts gay men at the same level as rapists and slavekeepers.

This form of gayphobia, which can also extend to male transsexuals, reproaches gay men for their masculinity—the flip side to the gayphobia expressed by heterosexual men who consider that homosexuals are not "true men." This latter logic was expressed by Jean Genet in *Notre-Dame-des-Fleurs:* "A male that screws another one is a double male"; in essence, the male homosexual is always the "buggered," never the "buggerer." This form of sexual **insult**, which is not without links to misogyny, is less aimed at the sexual practice itself (even if the moral dimension is not absent) than at the loss of social status as determined by one's passive (i.e. feminine) position. This form of gayphobia is also evident in some gay men themselves, whose internalized gayphobia is manifested by presenting themselves as hyper-masculine in order to counter any accusations of passivity or the symbolic submission to domination.

Another form of gayphobia refers to the paradoxical perception that gay men are overprivileged: the idea that they make up the majority of DINKs ("Dual Income, No Kids"), enjoying socio-economic success which is somehow undeserved. Lesbians are not often included in this description, given the belief that on average women earn less than the norm in society.

This perception that homosexuals are generally well off, and hence do not need or even deserve legislative protection, was evident the day after legislative elections in France in June 1997, when an article in the newsweekly *Marianne* stated that the task of the new government was to deal with unemployment, not homosexuals. It echoes French politician Henri Emmanuelli's famous retort to homosexuals: "You are a pain in the neck with your fag problems, as they do not interest the people." In fact, the 1998 debates in France over PaCS, the proposed civil union pact, was an occasion for new expressions of gayphobia, in that there were no similar discourses aimed specifically at lesbians. However, it is important to note that few French feminists publicly supported the idea that the government should acknowledge gay couples. Their stunning silence might be explained by the fact that, initially, PaCS appeared to be a Band-Aid legal solution for gay male survivors of partners who had died of **AIDS**, who found themselves with no spousal rights; perhaps the reticence of feminists was due to their disparaging opinions about **marriage**, an institution they often criticize.

At any rate, in French conservative circles, the approval of PaCS was less a question of whether it would reduce discrimination aimed at homosexuals, but whether it could be justified based on the "differential" contribution of homosexuals and heterosexuals to the public good. In November 1998, Member of Parliament Jacques Myard, who once equated homosexuality with zoophilia, warned that "the real goal of PaCS is to recognize gay couples and to grant them rights without asking for anything in return." In the same way, in an April 1997 article published in *Droit de la famille* (Right of the family), Bernard Beignier wrote: "Sociological studies have demonstrated that a gay couple generally earns an income superior to that of a heterosexual couple, for evident reasons. It is thus unreasonable to offer the same benefits when justifications of these benefits are lacking." It would be interesting to find out which "sociological studies" the author was referring to, not to mention which "evident reasons." In any event, the implication is that gay men are not charitable, an idea which Pierre Lellouche, a Paris member of French president Jacques Chirac's party, used to describe PaCS as "tragic for the equilibrium of our society." The fiscal argument, traditional in Neo-Poujadist trends, was also made during the anti-PaCS debates; it was advised that the real "costs" of PaCS should be weighed against the contributions, financial and otherwise, of homosexuals.

Finally, among specifically gayphobic discourses, we must also mention the issue of AIDS. Significantly, soon after AIDS became known in the early 1980s, it was referred to as the "gay cancer," as if it were a punishment designed specifically for Sodom (but which spared Gomorrah, apparently). Odious beliefs became widespread: some thought that gay men, as a "group at risk," should be subject to mandatory screening or tattooing, or quarantined in "AIDS-a-toriums." Gay men were being punished for their sins; the **debauchery** of the gay male lifestyle was finally getting its just reward. Further, in addition to being responsible for their misfortune, gays were also guilty for the misfortune of other "innocent victims" of AIDS: hemophiliacs, patients receiving transfusions, and heterosexuals. When it became clear that more and more heterosexuals were contracting the disease, the gayphobic arguments lost some of their rhetorical relevance, and thus their effectiveness. And AIDS, which seemed like a "windfall" for hard-core homophobes, ended up para-doxically providing a more socially sympathetic image of gays due to their suffering and pain.

Overall, gayphobia is manifested in two areas of perceived privilege for gay men: their sexuality and their power (be it social, economic, or political). Lesbians are exempt from these, given that they are perceived to have neither a self-determined sexuality nor significant socioeconomic power. On the other hand, this notion of gayphobia allows a better understanding of the differential treatment accorded to gay men and lesbians in most societies. It is arguable that homophobia is most often directed at gay men rather than lesbians, as exemplified by the frequent use of gayphobic insults that are also used to insult heterosexual men ("queer," "poof," "fag," etc.); lesbophobic insults are less common. The difference between gayphobia and lesbophobia is directly connected to differences in social constructs as they relate to **gender**.

In heterosexist culture, sexual relations between women are often perceived as either benign or unthinkable; they are hardly considered a threat to heterosexual men, and may in fact be a source of sexual excitement—after all, if they fail to fall into line, such women can always be controlled by forced marriage or punitive rape. On the other hand, sexual relations between men are perceived as the **peril** of perils, a direct threat to masculinity and thus to public, natural, and divine order. These differences seem to correspond to the differences inherent in the two phobias: lesbophobia generally involves a forced reclusion of the nearly powerless—women who fail to adopt society's social arrangements disappear from view, while gayphobia more often resorts to forced exclusion, a visible and spectacular exclusion from the social field.

—*Guillaume Huyez*

Bourdieu, Pierre. *La Domination masculine*. Paris: Le Seuil, 1998.

Capitan, Colette, and Colette Guillaumin. "L'Ordre et le sexe: discours de gauche, discours de droite." *ProChoix*, no. 20 (2002).

Fourest, Caroline, and Fiammetta Venner. *Les Anti-pacs ou la dernière croisade homophobe*. Paris: Prochoix, 1999.

Huyez, Guillaume. "Dix Ans de ghetto: le quartier gay dans les hebdomadaires français," *ProChoix*, no. 22 (2002).

Rubin, Gayle S. "Penser le sexe," (1984). In *Marché au sexe*. By Gayle Rubin and Judith Butler. Paris: EPEL, 2001. [Published in English as "Thinking Sex: Notes for a Radical Theory of the Politics of Sexuality."]

—*Anti-PaCS; Discrimination; Gender Differences; Feminism (France); Heterophobia; Lesbophobia; Marriage; Pedophilia; Rhetoric; Transphobia.*

GENDER. *See* Gender Differences

GENDER DIFFERENCES

In the humanities and social sciences, it may be possible to suggest a connection between gender differences and homophobia. But the answer is not so simple.

Gender Differences & Relationships
The difficulty lies in that the field of gender studies is dominated by the issue of gender inequality. This issue is certainly legitimate, but causes us to forget that the study of the relationships between genders relegates gender difference to the rank of an intangible that is based on unquestionable evidence: that two human genders exist, male and female; no more and no less. It is precisely because there are two genders that it is necessary for the two to relate to each other, and that this relationship be studied in its various forms. In other words, gender relationships and gender differences are nothing more than two aspects of the same issue. But the unequal treatment of men and women has largely eclipsed the presupposition edifying male domination: to dominate the other, the first and most fundamental condition is that one must establish one's otherness.

To be able to establish a possible connection between a homophobic position and the very idea of gender differences, one must reconstruct an intermediary bridge between the two, and ask how sexual differences come into play around the question of gender relationships. Thus, through infinite variations in doctrine, the answer is structured around two positions that appear to have little in common: either the justification (or lack thereof) for the oppression of women, or the fight against it. Both subscribe to a theorization of sexual differences, but it is only after having examined them that one can tell for certain whether or not there is an implication of homophobia.

Woman-Nature, Man-Culture
For a long time, and including today, androcratic ide-

ologies have haunted scholarly rhetoric. The example of one of the great founders of sociology, Emile Durkheim (1858–1917), is typical of this situation. Durkheim, sensitive to problematic new developments within "the social division of labor," attempted to preserve a "sexual division" that is particularly and clearly conservative, full of the inequality and oppression which we are more conscious of today. Perhaps one day, he conceded, women in society could occupy certain jobs that were traditionally reserved for men, but under the condition that they stay confined to domains to which they were already strongly predisposed, such as education.

It is not hard to feel the reticence in Durkheim's concession to a regrettable yet inevitable evolution. Even more interesting than this is the argument that serves as the basis for his statement: the nature of sexual difference. In truth, it is a strange sort of argument, but one that merits being uncovered: the real difference between the genders is not simply biological or functional, of a nature that is "natural," but is much more deeply rooted in the opposing ways in which each gender relates to its "nature." The nature of men predisposes them to a greater socialization, the "civilization" of his instincts, a superior mastery of his emotions, and a greater receptiveness to reason. The nature of women, on the other hand, is the inverse of men's: resisting the push toward rationalization that is part of a man's nature. A woman's nature is more closely tied to impulse and sentiment. By way of example, in his study on the subject of **suicide**, Durkheim noted: "The needs specific to the female gender are of a less mental character, because, in general, her mental life is less developed…. Because woman is a more instinctual being than man, in order to find peace and calm, she has only to follow her instincts." At the very least, credit has to be given to this argument for being clear: the differences between the genders, which justify woman's subordinate place in social life, are based on the existence of two opposing "psychological types."

In androcratic thinking, of course, there are other ways to establish an irreducible specificity of male and female natures, which most of the time are treated as fact. However, no matter how far back one goes in the exploration of the various relationships between men and women, and no matter how shocking the interpretations, one always seems to come to the same conclusion: man somehow finds the legitimacy necessary to establish and maintain his superiority.

Is this thesis a sign of collusion with a heteronormative point of view? It is easy to see that following this line of thinking, the concept of homosexuality is inconceivable. Indeed, in this perspective, the homosexual is more than just a moral monstrosity (the point of view as taken by religion and psychiatry: the pervert); he is a monstrosity of logic. If the masculine is defined by its greater socialization in comparison to the feminine (i.e. more "civilized," less "emotional," and more "rational"), then what to make of a man who possesses a feminine side?

Based on this, we can come to a first conclusion: the masculinist tradition permeating the history of the humanities and social sciences, the wide existence of androcratic structures and representations (or phallocratic, another word meaning male domination), correlate (be it indirectly or implicitly) to the existence of homophobic mental structures. In other words, to perceive the relationship between genders as, in essence, unequal supposes a naturalizing perception of the difference between genders that, in turn, implies a heteronormativity. Male dominance and homophobia both belong to the same kind of discourse, to the same "ideology," so much so that the identification of the inferiorization or deprecation of women can always be considered symptomatic of a negative perception of homosexuality: the two go hand in hand.

Symbolic Law & Homophobia
Is it then possible to turn this proposition on its head and find an intrinsic, inverse link between **feminism** and the struggle against homophobic prejudice? The contemporary history of feminist and homosexual struggles reveals specific convergences: oppressed women and homosexuals discern that they have common adversaries. It is all the more interesting to consider this in the context of gender difference within the confines of **anthropology** and **philosophy**. The **symbolic order** in its entirety, and for that matter the very possibility of thought, is supposedly founded upon this difference that is primordial, irreducible, and even precious. As French anthropologist Françoise Héritier claimed in her opposition to the recognition of homosexual couples: "It is the observation of the difference between genders that is at the basis of all thought, traditional as well as scientific…. It is the ultimate endpoint of thought, on which a fundamental conceptual opposition is based, that which contrasts the identical with the different."

Thus, Lacan's theory of sexuation is intertwined with a sexual order, where the difference between genders plays the crucial role. It is important to properly understand the scope of this leap in logic. Certainly, humanity is divided according to the sexes, but this fact does not explain its pertinence nor what value should be conferred, except to immediately recognize within it a "symbolic law" that defines what is human, a sort of figurative "naturalization" that closes the gap between a fact (the sexual being) and the meaning assigned to it.

Starting from the same sacred premise of sexual difference, French psychoanalyst Pierre Legendre's emphasis is on parentage, a fundamental expression of the difference between man and woman. From this perspective, the idea of a homosexual union constitutes, in the strictest sense, not only an absurdity, but the very soul of a crime of *lese humanity*. Herein lies homophobia's claim to legitimacy.

A further example is interesting, insofar as it is deployed in a feminist and "left wing" space. One quickly grasps how an essentialist perception of the gender difference can lead unmistakably, despite an obvious prudence of form, to a philosophy that is unimaginatively conservative and homophobic. "What to think of the difference between genders," French philosopher Sylviane Agacinski wrote, "when they cease to depend on one another, when they separate, and instead of the desire for the opposite sex, the desire for the same is encountered, which today is called homosexuality?"

A striking point emerges from this. There are two important threads: whether it is linked to a psychological nature, in the inegalitarian and phallocratic sense (the Durkheim case), or to the "nature" of a symbolic law in the egalitarian and feminist sense (the Héritier case), the difference between the sexes can be used (implicitly in the first sense, and explicitly in the second) by a blind adherence to heteronormativity, that is to say, homophobia.

The avenues shared by those who reinforce or struggle against male domination—by those who, in order to analyze socio-sexual relationships, invoke either a "nature" or a "symbolism" of the difference between the sexes—are also not shared by homophobes and non-homophobes alike. To put it differently, simply criticizing male domination or the inequalities between men and women is not enough to evade homophobia. The way in which the relationships between the sexes are analyzed reveals that this is a concept underlying

gender difference: this is the base on which there is a certain hostility toward relationships that can develop between the same kind of human beings. It is only by uprooting this base that we can hope for a culture in which there is no need to struggle against homophobia, as it will have simply disappeared.

Deconstructing "Gender Differences"

In closing, we ask the question then of how to identify any clues that foreshadow such a culture to come. Let us propose the identification of a few such clues, though their interpretation is obviously subjective.

In the purely philosophical realm, any criticism of the concept of identity stems from this kind of movement. But it is the work of Gilles Deleuze that constitutes the most energetic undertaking of the destruction of essentialist ontological categories and the identities they assign. Sexuation, too, is not left out of this insidious process of undermining. Like any other form of dual opposition setting the intangible limits of identity, the way in which every individual is trapped by the choice between "male" or "female" is broken up in favor of the concept of "becoming a minority," which implies not only two but multiple genders. This reformulation must first employ a new concept of unconscious, an anti-Oedipal unconscious that disassociates sexuality from the family, placing the libido in relation to an "outside" and "showing how our loves are derived from universal history, and not from Mommy and Daddy."

This critical version of **psychoanalysis** was championed vigorously in the work of Sabine Prokhoris, which, inspired by the genealogical perspectives of Neitzsche and Foucault, updated the historicity of the "norms of existence." In them, the fundamental hold enjoyed by the heteronormative imposition of the "difference between the sexes" in the life of humans is meticulously dismantled. To this effect (to use Lacan's formulation), "man, woman, and child are nothing more than signifiers," and one can begin to explore the explosive consequences, starting with this: it becomes impossible to base these signifiers on a "symbolic order" constituting humanity's ultimate nature, and impossible to found a "normal and realized" sexuality based solely on the anatomical differences between men and women.

Finally, the American theoretical and political movement that has developed around queer theory, as illustrated by Eve Kosofsky Sedgwick's famous work

Epistemology of the Closet, has also contributed to the deconstruction of the evidence of the sexual division. One could even speak of a paradigm of transvestism to designate the multitude of invented conducts and strategies—notably sexual—that invalidate the pertinence of identity based on the difference between men and women. The transvestite then does not embody a confusion of genders, but rather serves to help understand that the status of sex as incarnated into a role is simply that: a role, one interpretation among many. This deconstruction of the difference between the sexes is a small part of the much greater movement refusing dualistic classifications, which includes the homo- and heterosexual opposition—even though "circumstances" have allowed gays to mount a struggle for acceptance, by taking part in the "politics of identity," they are still playing by the rules of their adversaries. The realm of the minority is more creative, and much more suited to the dissolution of inherited identity barriers. Herein can be found one of Foucault's grand themes which attempts to disentangle the (political) knots between sexuality and identity. It is well known that this same Foucauldian perspective on the subject of **perversion** was developed in *The History of Sexuality.* But Foucault extended it to gender differences in a book he edited in 1979 entitled *Memoirs of a Nineteenth-Century French Hermaphrodite* which highlights how the uncertainty of gender is so unbearable to those in power, despite the fact that even "nature" herself has provided anatomical proof of this indiscernibility.

—*Jean-Manuel de Queiroz*

Agacinski, Sylviane. *Politique des sexes.* Paris: Le Seuil, 1998.

Bersani, Leo. *Homos.* Paris: Odile Jacob, 1998.

Borrillo, Daniel, Eric Fassin, and Marcela Iacub, eds. *Au-delà du PaCS, l'expertise familiale à l'épreuve de l'homosexualité.* Paris: Presses universitaires de France, 1999.

Butler, Judith. *Gender Trouble: Feminism and the Subversion of Identity.* New York: Routledge, 1990.

Deleuze, Gilles. *L'Ile déserte et autres textes.* Paris: Minuit, 2002.

———, and Félix Guattari. *Mille plateaux.* Paris: Minuit, 1992. [Published in the UK as *A Thousand Plateaus.* London: Athlone Press, 1987.]

Eribon, Didier. *Papiers d'identité. Interventions sur la question gay.* Paris: Fayard, 2000.

Foucault, Michel, ed. *Herculine Barbin, dite Alexina B…* Paris: Gallimard, "Les Vies parallèles," 1978.

———. *Histoire de la sexualité.* Vol. I : "La volonté de savoir."

Paris: Gallimard, 1976. [Published in the US as *The History of Sexuality.* New York: Pantheon Books, 1978.]

Héritier, Françoise. *Masculin, féminin.* Paris: Odile Jacob, 1996.

Kosofsky, Sedgwick Eve. *Epistemology of the Closet.* Los Angeles: Univ. of California Press, 1990.

Laplantine, François. *Je, nous et les autres.* Paris: Ed. du Pommier, 1999.

Prokhoris, Sabine. *Le Sexe prescrit, la différence sexuelle en question.* Paris: Champs Flammarion, 2000.

Weston, Kalh. *Families We Choose: Lesbians, Gays, Kinship.* New York: Columbia Univ. Press, 1991.

—*Anthropology; Essentialism/Constructionism; Feminism (France); Heterosexism; History; Marriage; Otherness; Parenting; Philosophy; Psychoanalysis; Psychology; Sociology; Symbolic Order; Transphobia; Universalism/ Differentialism.*

GENETICS

The historical links between homosexuality and genetics can be divided into three phases. The first, before 1940, was generally based on the formulation of a formal genetic hypothesis on homosexuality. Certainly, the existence of morbid hereditary aspects of homosexuality had been accepted since the days of Richard von Krafft-Ebing, the nineteenth-century German psychiatrist who wrote *Psychopathia Sexualis,* his famous study on sexual perversity; however, this idea did not pervade French, English, or American discussions on eugenics. Next, this situation changed after 1940 in the United States, when studies of homozygote and heterozygote twin siblings led to a consideration of the idea that homosexuality could be transmitted from generation to generation, raising the alarming possibility—in pre-**Stonewall**, pre-gay rights American society—of the forced sterilization of homosexuality. And the third phase occurred after the 1970s, the link between homosexuality and genetics was raised again, but this time by gays themselves (at least in the United States), as an attempt—in the heady days of gay liberation, and in response to the politically conservative forces who opposed them—to prove the genetic "naturalness" of homosexuality. In this sense, genetic research is prone to paradox, in that the same scientific claims regarding homosexuality can be used on one hand to eradicate or "prevent" it and on the other to emancipate or legitimize it.

The idea of "homosexual" heredity is founded in the **degeneracy** theory, which describes the hereditary transmission of mental diseases, leading to the progressive degeneracy of a lineage. It is within this concept, in fact, that Krafft-Ebing released *Psychopathia Sexualis*. From then on, homosexuality was widely thought to contribute to the weakening of the "race," on the same level as alcoholism or nervous disorders. As a consequence, as early as 1904, Swiss psychiatrist Ernst Rüdin—who in 1933, joined the Nazi committee on heredity as overseen by Heinrich **Himmler**, and who ultimately became director of the foremost eugenics research in Nazi Germany—recommended the sterilization of homosexuals as a means to protect the race. Outside the Nazi context, however, the question of the link between homosexuality and genetics remained largely unexplored by eugenists in other countries during this time.

A few years later in the US, it was a student of Rüdin's, Franz Kallmann, who made significant claims based on his research into genetic causes of homosexuality. Rather ironically, Kallmann, a militant eugenist who was evidently sympathetic to Hitler's regime, was forced to flee Germany in 1936 due to his partial Jewish lineage. Kallmann was one of the first to study the potential genetic basis of psychiatric disorders. In the 1940s, he began a series of studies on sets of twins; the number of matches in sexual orientation between twins led him to the conclusion that homosexuality was genetically determined. Without explaining the long-term objective of his research (which was probably mass sterilization of those with "disorders" such as homosexuality), this study led Kallmann to demand world-wide public health measures designed to "protect" future generations.

Paradoxically, Kallmann's work, from a methodological point of view, directly influenced studies conducted since the late 1980s by a number of geneticists (e.g., the team of J. Michael Bailey and Richard Pillard; and Dean Hamer) supporting the idea of genetic causes for homosexuality that were, in fact, supported by gays and lesbians. Hamer's 1993 study, which caused a great deal of controversy, identified the existing of a "gay gene," leading some to conclude that homosexuality was predetermined and thus inevitable in some. In spite of numerous critics who denounced these findings, the fact remained that for many, the genetic determinism of homosexuality was now "proven," which, on one hand,

provided justification for wider acceptance of homosexuals, but on the other, suggested the potential for new, homophobic forms of eugenics in which homosexuality may be identified through prenatal diagnosis.
—*Pierre-Olivier de Busscher*

Allen, Garland. "The Double Edged Sword of Genetic Determinism: Social and Political Agendas in Genetic Studios of Homosexuality, 1940–1994." In *Science and Homosexualities*. Edited by Vernon Rosario. New York/London: Routledge, 1997.

Dorais, Michel. "La Recherche des causes de l'homosexualité: une science-fiction?" In *La Peur de l'autre en soi, du sexisme à l'homophobie*. Edited by Michel Dorais, Pierre Dutey, and Daniel Welzer-Lang. Montreal: VLB Editeurs, 1994.

LeVay, Simon. *Queer Science*. Cambridge, MA: MIT Press, 1996.

Schuklenk, Udo. "Is Research Into the Cause(s) of Homosexuality Bad for Gay People?" *Christopher Street*, no. 208 (1993).

———. "Scientific Approaches to Homosexuality." In *Gay Histories and Cultures: An Encyclopedia*. Edited by George E. Haggerty. Vol. 2. New York/London: Garland Publishing Inc., 2000.

—*Biology; Degeneracy; Endocrinology; Fascism; Medicine; Medicine, Legal; Psychiatry; Sterility; Treatment.*

GERMANY

From its Origins to 1871: Sodomy, from the "Crime Against God" to "Crime Against Nature"

The repression of homosexuality among the ancient Germanics is not well documented. The majority of the known laws do not mention it, even if Tacitus (56–117 CE) of the Roman Empire, which at the time included Germania, affirmed that the "loathsome ones" were drowned in the marshes. It would appear, in fact, that this type of punishment only applied to "passive" or "effeminate" men who did not conform to the duties of warriors. Homosexual relations, when they did not threaten the hierarchies related to sexual roles, were not punished by law and were only subject to the judgment of families. Lesbianism was never mentioned.

Starting in the fifth century, following the fall of the Western Roman Empire, the first Germanic kingdoms were established. The Germanic codes, written in Medieval Latin between the fifth and ninth centuries, applied to the territories that stretched from present-day **Portugal** to Germany. Inspired by the Roman model, Germanic law was progressively influenced by Christian morality, which considered sodomy to be both a sin and a crime. Starting from the sixth century, a series of laws were drafted, such as those of King Kindasvith (650) and King Receswinthe (654) in Spain, which called for sodomites to be punished by castration. In Portugal, the Code of Alaric II (506) added public ostracism, head shaving, lashing, and the death penalty to the list of punishments. The Sixteenth Council of Toledo (693), under the influence of King Egica, provided for the defrocking of bishops, priests, and deacons guilty of sodomy. In the Visigothic kingdoms, however, the repression of homosexuality remained limited until the sixteenth century, even if there were examples of men condemned for "sodomy" in the Germanic states of the German and Italian territories. Such men were hanged in Souabe in 1328, while in 1409 in Augsburg, at the instigation of Bishop Eberhard, a tanner and a clergyman were burned alive. Two other men convicted of sodomy, Ulrich Frey and Jakob Kiess, were suspended from a tower, their hands and feet bound; they remained there without food for six days before being hanged. The exact definition of the word "sodomy" during this time is, however, difficult to determine, as it could as easily refer to homosexual relations as to heterosexual relations, bestiality, or **heresy**. Starting in the sixteenth century, homosexuality as a "crime **against nature**" is mentioned in the *Constitutio Criminalis Bambergersis* of 1507 and again in the *Constitutio Criminalis Carolina* of 1532. Enforced in the empire of Charles Quint, which spread over Germany, the Netherlands, and Spain, the *Carolina* called for death by fire for the crime of sodomy. Thus, it was in 1731 that the King of Prussia, Frederick William I, condemned a sodomite by the name of Lepsch to burning.

While executions remained rather infrequent, demonstrations of homophobia took on other forms. For example, the accusation of sodomy was often used to discredit a religious or political adversary. In the thirteenth century, Emperor Frederick II was the object of such attacks, incited by the popes who were hostile toward him, while in the sixteenth century, Luther alluded to numerous instances of homosexuality among the Catholic clergy. Even though lesbian-

ism did not fall under the province of the law, some women were, in very rare cases, tried for "sodomy," including Catharina Margaretha Linck and Catharina Margaretha Mühlhahn in Halberstadt, Prussia in 1721. Linck, disguised as a man, had joined several army divisions before marrying an unsuspecting Mühlhahn in 1717; Linck used a leather penis to make her partner believe she was a man. Linck was condemned to death, whereas Mühlhahn was condemned to three years' imprisonment and banished, given that she continued to have sexual relations with her "husband," even after having discovered the truth.

Under the influence of the Enlightenment (Aufklärung), legislators in the eighteenth and nineteenth centuries sought to establish a "natural law," more respectful of human nature; as a result, the death penalty was progressively abandoned. In 1794, Prussian law began to punish "sodomy and other crimes against nature, which cannot be named here because of their abominable nature," with a penalty of forced labor accompanied by beating. It was, however, the adoption of the Napoleonic Code, at the beginning of the nineteenth century, which proved to be decisive. As a result, many German states began to revise their penal codes along the lines of the French model that, since the revolutionary laws of 1791, did not provide for the criminalization of sodomy. Bavaria, which in 1751 still punished sodomy by condemnation to the stake after beheading, abolished the laws that condemned homosexual acts between consenting adults in 1813; Württemberg followed suit in 1839, and Brunswick and Hanover in 1840. In the Baden region, only those acts committed in public were punished, and in Saxony, Oldenburg, and Thüringen, the maximum punishment was one year in prison. This evolution remained intact until the much more restrictive Prussian Criminal Code of 1851 came into play, which would serve as the basis for the German Criminal Code. Applied initially to Hanover, annexed in 1867, then to the Confederation of Northern Germany in 1869, it was imposed over the entire Empire in 1871.

1871–1933: Homosexuality & Politics Under the Wilhelm Germany and the Weimar Republic
According to Section 175 of the Criminal Code of the German Empire (1871), "sexual acts against nature (*widernatürliche Unzucht*) that are perpetrated, whether between persons of male gender or between men and animals, are punishable by imprisonment. There may

also be a pronouncement of loss of civic rights." Even though the formulation of the paragraph remained vague, **jurisprudence** chose to restrict its interpretation to apply only to "acts resembling coitus" (*beischlafähnliche Handlungen*). Consequently, the police discovered relatively few homosexuals, and if they were, it was either because they were exposed, or because their habits (for example, cruising the urinals) exposed them. The working class was thus overrepresented among those charged. However, it is important not to underestimate the reach of the law: between 1902 and 1918, the average number of arrests per year was 380, and 704 between 1919 and 1934. Punishment, which varied notably with regard to the "gravity" of the act perpetrated and the age of the protagonists, was, in the majority of cases, less than three months of **imprisonment**, but the intensity of the repression was not the same depending on the region. The capital of Berlin, in particular, enjoyed a reputation for **tolerance**, as police repression was rarely practiced in areas where homosexuals congregated, which allowed for the blossoming of a real homosexual subculture. It appears, nonetheless, that the **police** maintained lists of homosexuals (*Rosa Listen*), which were then used by the Nazis to follow through with their destructive projects. On the other hand, the threat of the law always placed homosexuals at the mercy of blackmailers, and sometimes led them to commit **suicide**. As for Section 175, despite militant action by several homosexual groups such as Magnus **Hirschfeld**'s Wissenschaftlich-humanitäres Komitee (Humanitarian Scientific Committee), and the tabling of several bills at the Reichstag seeking to revise it, it was never abolished. A 1929 bill which did provide for Section 175's abolishment, and which was supported by leftist parties such as the Sozialdemokratische Partei Deutschlands (SPD; Social Democratic Party of Germany) and the Kommunistische Partei Deutschlands (KPD; Communist Party of Germany), was finally abandoned following a change in the majority.

Meanwhile, homophobic public opinion was constantly fed by various **scandals** and media campaigns. In 1902, industry magnate Alfred Krupp was challenged by the socialist newspaper *Vorwärts*, which accused him of entertaining young men in his villa on the island of Capri, pushing him to suicide. It was, however, the **Eulenburg affair** (1907–09), concerning accusations of homosexual conduct among members of Kaiser Wilhelm II's cabinet and entourage that

resulted in court-martials and trials, that made a lasting mark on the public imagination. First uncovered by journalist Maximilian Harden, and following a series of military scandals, it brought to issue associates of Wilhelm II; Prince Philipp of Eulenburg, one of his councilors and friends; and Count Kuno von Moltke, the military commander of Berlin. The political implications were not absent, for Eulenburg, who favored a reconciliation with France, had, during the Moroccan Crisis (between Germany and France over the colony of Morocco), drawn upon himself the resentment of the military. The trials that followed, which were highly sensational, were widely covered by the press and contributed to encouraging homophobic and anti-Semitic prejudices among the public (Magnus Hirschfeld, who was called to witness, was Jewish). The accusation of **treason** against homosexuals, often leveled in the past, became popular again, and elsewhere on the continent, homosexuality was often described as the "German **vice**." Concern was such that a 1909 bill sought not only to make Section 175 stronger, but also have it apply to lesbians (it was not approved). However, lesbians, if they remained discreet, did not worry, even if the image of the single and independent woman was often denounced as a danger to the **family** and to public morals. In the 1920s, feminists were often designated as lesbians. In fact, after World War I, the greater visibility of homosexuals led people to believe in a "**contagion**" of sorts. Certain religious groups (such as the committee of the German Evangelical Church, led by Reinhard Mumm) as well as some political parties (such as the Deutschnationale Volkspartei [German National People's Party], which grouped conservative and extreme right-wing forces) led an active campaign "against trash and smut" (*gegen Schund und Schmutz*) in order to protect the young from "modern" dangers, such as homosexuality. A certain number of gay and lesbian publications paid the price. Richard Oswald and Hirschfeld's film, *Anders als die Andern* (1919) (Different from the others), fell under the hammer of **censorship** after riots broke out in cities, including Munich, following screenings.

At the end of the 1920s, homophobic arguments in Germany were increasingly used for political ends. The SPD and the KPD, which had until then supported the gay cause, did not hesitate, in the context of the fight against fascism, to use the accusation of homosexuality as a way to discredit Nazi leaders, planting suspicion in the public's mind. Ernst Röhm, leader of the

SA (Sturmabteilung, the stormtrooper assault section) and a notorious homosexual, was thus the target of a virulent media campaign organized by the *Münchner Post* (Munich post) or *Die Rote Fahne* (The red flag). In 1934, alongside the criminalization of homosexuality, its consideration as a "fascist perversion" became the new line of the Communist Party. German emigrants contributed largely to the spreading of rumors of widespread homosexuality within the Nazi Party, even though the Nazis' persecution against homosexuals was already in progress.

1933–45: The Persecution of Homosexuals Under Nazism
The pinnacle of homophobia in Germany was achieved under the Nazi regime. Even before its ascension to power, the Nationalsozialistische Deutsche Arbeiterpartei (National Socialist German Workers Party), the party of National Socialism, or Nazism, was known for its homophobic positions. During meetings in Munich, Hirschfeld was the target of extremely violent physical attacks. There was a certain ambiguity regarding the motive to the attacks, however, and gay movements were not wholly convinced of the Party's hostility toward them. This was due not only to Röhm's well-known homosexuality and his membership in the Bund für Menschenrecht (Union for Human Rights), but also to Hans Bluher's theories of *Männerbund* (which elevated the idea of the homosexual warrior) held by a minority of the Nazi party. Bluher, an associate of certain circles within the SA, and also a member of a homosexual group, Gemeinschaft der Eigenen (Community of the Self-Owners) had studied the organization of German youth groups such as Wandervogel ("migratory bird") and had deduced the value of homoerotic relations, sublimated by a devotion to the leader. If homosexuals were still questioning how the Nazis viewed them, however, a number of events would dissipate all doubts. The infamous Night of the Long Knives (June 1934) led to Röhm's elimination, as well as that of the SA. From then on, the Party's official position—as expressed notably by SS leader Heinrich **Himmler** supreme commander of the police, during his speech of February 18, 1937 before the generals of the SS—was one of repression and hate. Homosexuals, "**criminals** against the race," were an affront to the "vital" interest of the German people and needed to be "healed" or eliminated. Earlier, during the Nazis' first weeks in power in February and March of 1933, measures were taken

to put an end to "any and all" homosexual demonstrations: gay and lesbian movements were outlawed, publications suppressed, and meeting areas were raided. On May 6, 1933, Magnus Hirschfeld's Institut für Sexualwissenschaft (Institute for Sexual Knowledge), without a doubt the most symbolic place for European homosexuals between the wars, was pillaged and destroyed, while thousands of rare books and documents were fed to the flames. For German gays and lesbians, withdrawing oneself was a necessity: some emigrated, others married. All had to live in secret and in fear from then on.

The persecution of homosexuals took on different forms depending on the categories concerned. On February 10, 1934, a decree from the Ministry of the Interior ordered the regular surveillance of "corruptors of the youth" and gay prostitutes. A special office charged with homosexual affairs was created within the Gestapo. These measures were bolstered in September 1935 by the strengthening of Section 175, whose broadened interpretation included making simple homosexual desire a crime, and by the introduction of Section 175a, dealing with prostitution, the use of force, and the abuse of power or authority. Despite efforts to criminalize lesbianism, notably by the Nazi lawyer Rudolf Klare, it remained outside of the law. However, this does not mean that homosexual women were tolerated, but rather reveals proof of the contempt in which women were held: female sexuality was deemed to be easily controllable, by **violence** if necessary. This exemption for lesbians led to certain confusion; in annexed Austria, for example, lesbianism was punishable by five years' imprisonment. As well, lesbians were not free from being exposed, and a certain number were sent to concentration camps under various names such as "politicals" or "asocials." Meanwhile, the strengthening of Section 175 was accompanied by the creation of a new special bureau, the Reich Central Office, to combat homosexuality and abortion, and to register, file, and classify all homosexuals who were reported. In all, nearly 100,000 homosexuals were listed, under the direction of the SS Obersturmführer, Josef Meisinger, and over 50,000 were imprisoned. The fight against homosexuality was waged with a particular virulence within the Party itself, notably among the Hitler Youth and the SS. For a long time, the Wehrmacht maintained its own surveillance and repression procedures. Specific anti-homosexual campaigns were also led against opponents to the regime, as well as against certain individuals judged as being too burdensome. In 1937, Catholic religious orders were thus the target of a homophobic campaign, but the accusations, obviously forged, were not taken seriously by public opinion. Another campaign was launched in 1937, this time against those generals hostile to the annexation of Czechoslovakia; General Werner von Fritsch of the Wehrmacht was the victim of a set-up organized by Himmler, Reinhard Heydrich, and Hermann Goering, although he was acquitted of any crime.

However, there was never any question for the Reich concerning the extermination of all homosexuals. Himmler himself encouraged "medical" experiments designed to "cure" homosexuals, such as hormonal **treatments** and castration, with the idea of reintegrating them into the community, notably the **army**. But concentration camps were also presented as a vehicle for "reeducation": in Auschwitz and Sachsenhausen, homosexuals were required to report to the brothel. It is difficult to ascertain the exact number of homosexuals sent to the camps: habitual offenders, prostitutes, and pedophiles were the first victims. Many were never judged, while others saw their sentences arbitrarily prolonged. In any event, the "pink triangles" were forced to live in inhuman detention conditions. Near the lowest rung of the ladder (just above Jews), and often assigned the hardest labor, they were frequently separated from the other prisoners, many of whom were themselves homophobic. In all, the number of homosexuals who died in the camps is estimated to be between 5,000 and 15,000. If the use of terror by the police, the dehumanization of victims, and sentences disproportionate to the acts were particular to the repression of homosexuality under the Third Reich, the fact that Section 175 remained in place after the end of World War II was proof that the roots of German homophobia went beyond the racist and warlike ideology of Nazism.

From 1945 Onward: From Institutional Homophobia to Heterosexism

After the war, the former "pink triangles," often regarded with contempt, hesitated to testify against their captors and preferred to remain discreet as to the reasons behind their **deportation** or imprisonment. In fact, in what had become West Germany, Sections 175 and 175a were preserved and integrated into the new German Criminal Code, and gays were neither recognized nor compensated as victims of Nazism. It

wasn't until June 25, 1969 that homosexual acts between consenting adults over the age of twenty-one were decriminalized, and not until June 7, 1973 that the Bundestag reduced that age of consent to eighteen years of age. Nonetheless, **discrimination** still existed, since the age of sexual consent for heterosexual relations was lower, at fourteen years of age. The Catholic and Protestant churches were among the groups who were most hostile to any reform of Section 175; in the 1950s, they actively campaigned for the banning of all homosexual publications in Germany. And the persecution of homosexuals continued under Section 175: between 1950 and 1965, nearly 45,000 gays were imprisoned, compared to 10,000 under the Weimar Republic. Among the most famous trials, notable are those that took place in Frankfurt in 1950 and 1951; following the arrest of several male prostitutes, one came forward with a detailed notebook of his clients. As a result, police proceeded with massive raids in the city, leading to the arrest of over 100 people. However, Judge Kurt Romini, who presided over the trials, had made himself known as a prosecutor under the Nazi regime, where he was instrumental in convicting some 400 homosexuals in Frankfurt. After five men had committed suicide, the press soon put into question the methods used by the police, as well as the credibility of the main witness, who was ultimately sentenced to two and a half years' imprisonment; in addition, Judge Romini was transferred.

In what had become East Germany ("the GDR," German Democratic Republic), the situation was even more confused due to the opposing points of view between Soviet and East German leaders. While in the USSR, homosexuality continued to be severely repressed, Otto Grotewohl, East German prime minister from 1949 to 1964, had supported the abolition of Section 175 under the Weimar Republic. In 1948, a "compromise" was reached: Section 175 was preserved, but returned to its less severe definition dating from before 1935. Thus, the maximum penalty for convictions under Section 175 was reduced to five years' imprisonment from ten. Bills that proposed further reform of Section 175 were, after that, systematically rejected by the USSR. The use of homosexuality to political ends found new applications: the Minister of Justice, Max Fechner, who had participated in an uprising on June 17, 1953, was condemned to eight years' imprisonment as an "enemy of the state," under the pretense of having engaged in homosexual relations with his chauffeur.

In 1968, following the reform of Section 175, thereafter called Section 151, homosexual relations between men aged eighteen years or more were decriminalized. (The age of consent was lowered to sixteen in 1988.) Such legislative progress, however, cannot hide the fact that life for gays and lesbians in East Germany remained difficult: a gay and lesbian subculture was practically non-existent, and many men and women chose to enter into marriages of "convenience" rather than continue to live in fear. Gay and lesbian newspapers remained banned until 1988. In 1982, however, the first gay groups in East Germany began to emerge, some under the aegis of the Protestant Church. It is in this that there was a considerable difference between East and West Germany, where homophile groups had formed as early as the 1950s, and where, starting in the 1970s, gay and lesbian liberation movements, based on those in the United States, were founded. In East Germany, the last years of the Communist regime saw a progressive blooming of the gay scene, but the groups were closely watched by the Stasi (East Germany's secret police), which launched operations with names such as "Bruder" (brother) and "Aftershave" in order to infiltrate them. After reunification, Section 175 was finally, definitively abolished on June 11, 1994.

Homophobic prejudices in Germany, though largely in retreat, have not disappeared entirely. In February and March of 1991, Michael Bochow, in association with the GFM-GETAS Institute of Hamburg, completed a survey on anti-gay attitudes among some 1,000 residents each of the former East and West Germany. While 65% of West Germans and 69% of East Germans claimed to be indifferent to "someone's sexual orientation"—statistics which demonstrated progress compared to an earlier survey in 1974—there were still many who said they were in favor of social and professional discrimination against gay men. The proportion of those hostile toward homosexuals was notably higher among those who were members of a conservative political party or who were affiliated with a church, as well as those who had been lower in status in the former GDR. In total, at least one-third of the population was strongly hostile to homosexuals and another one-third was ambivalent. While the lessening of anti-homosexual attitudes can be linked to increasing secularization, individualist attitudes, and a decreased interest in the idea of moral standards, the persistence of homophobic prejudices is undoubtedly linked to the relatively low visibility of homosexuals, notably in the **media**, and the continued

importance placed on "traditional" male and female roles. The **AIDS** epidemic has furthermore contributed, as in other countries, to the revival of old fears. In 1983, the tabloid *Der Spiegel* ran the following headline: "AIDS, the fatal epidemic. The mysterious illness." Such proclamations opened the door to hysteria and the likening of the virus to a "curse from God." However, the last few years have seen significant progress: in June 2001, Klaus Wowereit (of the SPD), who had publicly announced his homosexuality, became mayor of Berlin. Since August 2001, homosexual couples are now officially recognized through the contracting of a "declared partnership," which affords almost the same rights as **marriage**, even if certain *Länder* (states) such as Bavaria are more hesitant. The very delicate issue of recognizing the "pink triangles" of the Nazi era has not yet been resolved. For the first time, on April 23, 1995, a representative of the gay and lesbian community was authorized to present a speech during official government ceremonies. A plaque in homage to gay and lesbian victims of Nazism was inaugurated in Berlin's Nollendorfplatz in 1989, and the construction of a monument is now completed. It wasn't until November 2000 that the German government officially apologized to gays and lesbians for the persecution they suffered under the Third Reich. However, to this day, only the Green Party has declared itself in favor of compensating homosexual victims of Nazism.

—*Florence Tamagne*

Anonymous. "A Lesbian Execution in Germany, 1721: The Trial Records." In *Historical Perspectives on Homosexuality*. Edited by in Salvatore J. Licata and Robert P. Petersen. New York: Haworth Press, 1981.

Anonymous. *Homosexuelle Frauen und Männer in Berlin 1850–1950*. Berlin: Hentrich, 1992.

Bochow, Michael. "Attitudes et appréciations envers les hommes homosexuels en Allemagne de l'Ouest et en Allemagne de l'Est." Translated by Pierre Dutey. http://www.europrofem.org/02.info/22con-tri/2.07.fr/livr_dwl/peur/dwlpeur7.htm (site now discontinued).

Burkhard, Jellonnek. *Homosexuelle unter dem Hakenkreuz*. Paderborn: F. Schönongh, 1990

Grau, Günther, ed. *Hidden Holocaust: Gay and Lesbian Persecution in Germany, 1933–1945*. London: Cassell, 1995.

Herzer, Manfred, ed. *Goodbye to Berlin? 100 Jahre Schwulenbewegung*. Exhibition catalogue. Berlin: Verlag Rosa Winkel, 1997.

Lautmann, Rüdiger, and Angela Taeger, eds. *Männerliebe im*

alten Deutschland, sozialgeschkhtliche Abhandlungen. Berlin: Verlag Rosa Winkel, 1992.

Leroy-Forgeot, Flora. *Histoire juridique de l'homosexualité en Europe*. Paris: Presses universitaires de France, 1999.

Plant, Richard. *The Pink Triangle: The Nazi War Against Homosexuals*. New York: New Republic Books/Henry Holt & Co., 1986.

Schoppmann, Claudia. *Nationalsozialistische Sexualpolitik und weibliche Homosexualität*. Berlin: Centaurus, 1991.

Steakley, James D. *The Homosexual Emancipation Movement in Germany*. New York: Arno Press, 1975.

Tamagne, Florence. *Histoire de l'homosexualité en Europe, Berlin, Londres, Paris, 1919–1939*. Paris: Le Seuil, 2000. [Published in the US as *A History of Homosexuality in Europe: Berlin, London, Paris, 1919–1939*. New York: Algora, 2004.]

—Armed Forces; Caricature; Censorship; Communism; Deportation; Discrimination; Eulenburg Affair, the; Fascism; Himmler, Heinrich; Hirschfeld, Magnus; Media; Medicine; Police; Scandal; Violence.

GHETTO

Beginning in the Middle Ages, the section of a city reserved for Jews was known as the ghetto. At that time, it was most often a forced place of residence, surrounded by walls with doors that were locked at night. The term, which dates from the beginning of the sixteenth century, stems from the *Ghetto Novo*, Venice's Jewish section. Jewish ghettos were discontinued, at least in Western Europe, after the French Revolution and through the nineteenth century, but in the 1920s, American sociologists from the Chicago School appropriated the word to refer to communities in American cities where those grouped by ethnicity or class, often victims of racial or social **discrimination**, came together, sometime voluntarily: for example, blacks, Italians, and the poor. The word "ghetto" suggests that its inhabitants are isolated—geographically, socially, economically, and even culturally—from the dominant society that surrounds them. After World War II and mostly since the 1960s, large North American cities have seen the formation of specific areas catering to an exclusively homosexual clientele (usually male), marked by a high concentration of bars, nightclubs, restaurants, and other commercial establishments. Homosexuals have often chosen to reside in these ar-

eas as well, thus creating urban sectors that sociologists, and even gays themselves, have started to refer to as "gay ghettos": for example, Greenwich Village and Chelsea in New York, Castro Street in San Francisco, West Hollywood in Los Angeles, and the "Village" in Montreal. The same phenomenon occurred in Europe: in the section of Paris known as the Marais, gay establishments have been common since 1979, and the area is now known as Paris's gay ghetto. Nevertheless, the expression also has negative connotations. In 1995, journalist Tim Madesclaire wrote that the gay ghetto is "the place where a minority is separated from the rest of society. This means that it is closed-in on itself, in a marginal condition. The ghetto acts as a geographic metaphor of the gay condition." A large number of gays, on the other hand, consider the Marais to be a liberating place where they can openly express their sexuality and live and act as they choose. For them, the ghetto is what makes a gay community.

Such opposing viewpoints is why the gay ghetto is today very much a disputed phenomenon in France, where some view any distinctions made between various groups (whether based on ethnicity, class, or sexuality) as a threat to the French "republican tradition" which emphasizes the unity and indissolubility of the national identity, and which tends to deny the existence (or at least to minimize the importance) of individual or group differences within that identity. For those who criticize it, the gay ghetto represents **communitarianism**, tribalism, and a "refusal of the universal," symbolizing the fragmentation of the French Republic and the degradation of urban life in Paris.

Thus, Jean-Robert Pitte, a professor at the Sorbonne in Paris, writes in *Le Quartier du Marais: Déclin, renaissance, avenir* (1997):

> Born in San Francisco, Amsterdam, and London, (gay) ghettoization has reached Paris....The development of ghettos is obviously dangerous, being so opposed to sociability and urbanity....Just as a nation, a city can only last if it allows different populations to live together and assimilates new arrivals and minorities....The real notion of city is negated when authorities accept and even encourage ethnic or more commonly cultural aggregation....No one dares to venture outside their minuscule territory.

Denunciation of the gay ghetto and communitarianism often leads to expressions of patented homophobia. In the 1990s, non-homosexual residents of the Marais led a campaign opposing the gay ghettoization of the area, believing that "no normally constituted citizen, being gay or heterosexual, can approve the multiplication of these specialized bars." Their complaints struck a chord with certain municipal authorities. In 1996, the **police** led a short-lived harassment campaign of gay bars, including the removal of rainbow flags adorning their storefronts. Suggesting that "grouped and almost systematic opposition to large dimensioned insignia could lead to hostile reactions," the police asked gay merchants to "moderate outdoor signage of their community belonging, which was the only way to ensure harmonious cohabitation with the neighborhood." In 1997, Pierre-Charles Krieg, mayor of the fourth borough in Paris, wrote that the affirmation of the Marais as a gay ghetto "would certainly be a windfall for extremists of all sides and a lucrative bargain for 'money makers' but also surely a sign of failure and hopelessness [at the expense of] this [gay] community." And Dominique Bertinotti, a councilwoman of the borough, declared: "In Paris, we have been pretending to ignore this phenomenon for years…. My position has always been very clear: I am hostile to it."

One must point out that not all critics of the gay ghetto are heterosexual. Arcadie, the main gay (then called "homophile") **association** in France from 1954 to 1982, and highly conservative in its attitude and politics (it specifically noted that homosexuals need to be "respectable" and "dignified"), systematically denounced the gay ghetto. In an article published in 1964 entitled "The Gravest Danger," a member of Arcadie denounced American society as "sick" and "poorly integrated" because it was composed of "a multitude of groups and sub-groups":

> Homosexuals from over there are in the mist of constituting a separate society, a small artificial world, very closed, very oppressive, where everything would be gay: not only bars, restaurants, cinemas, but also houses, streets (in New York, there are already streets that are inhabited almost exclusively by homosexuals), and wards…. A world where one could live one's entire life without seeing anyone other than other homosexuals, without knowing anything other than homosexuality. In Europe, this is called ghettos. And we violently reject this idea. We have nothing in common with that. We hate this false, ill-omened, grotesque conception of ho-

mosexuality…. Our ideal is a perfect integration of homosexual love in society, in all sectors. We must emphasize all that brings together the gay person and non-gays, not what separates him from them. It would be criminal on our part to artificially create a feeling of isolation among gays and to give them against their wills the false impression that they constitute an "isolated world."

At the time when he was dissolving the Arcadie in 1982, founder André Baudry also expressed his regrets: "Today certain gays [in France] want to build a ghetto, like in San Francisco. They isolate themselves from the national collectivity. Our doctrine was to meld with the collectivity."

But some gay radicals of the 1970s and 80s, even the rugged adversaries of Baudry and his conservative views, were also hostile to the concept of the gay ghetto. Members of the Front homosexuels d'action révolutionnaire (Revolutionary Action Gay Front; 1971–73) in Paris denounced what they called the "merchant ghetto," the gay bars and nightclubs of St-Germain-des-Prés and Rue Ste-Anne, contending that homosexuals were being confined there, and merchants were exploiting them economically. Jean Le Bitoux, a gay activist since 1968 and founder of the magazine *Gai Pied*, wrote at the beginning of the 1980s: "I believe that the worst thing for gays is ghettoization, in which they are making up their own culture, fabricating their own identity." Charles Myara, one of the organizers of Paris's Gay Pride in 1999, said: "After fighting the prejudices of which they were victims, gays have withdrawn into themselves. Gay bars have bloomed [in the Marais], followed by a large number of boutiques. Gays have created their own ghetto." In fact, a large number of homosexual men in Paris still refuse to live in the "closed circuit" (as they call the Marais), criticizing the gay conformity (in fashion, physical appearance, behavior, lifestyle) that they claim is prevalent there, and instead try to live their lives "outside the ghetto."

This last viewpoint is important in realizing that those who oppose the concept of the gay ghetto are not necessarily homophobic, given that homosexuals themselves are at times its harshest critics. In this we find a form of "gay homophobia," that is, a form of self-loathing, in those homosexuals who try to assimilate into the general population by losing or suppressing all visible characteristics of their lives as gay men or lesbians. Although being opposed to the gay ghetto may be perfectly legitimate, from a sincere republican perspective, this worry often seems to reinforce certain arguments of the homophobic rhetoric.

—*Michael Sibalis*

Galcerain, Sébastien, and Olivier Razemon. "Marais: la guerilla." *Illico* (December 1996).

"Gay Marais: Ghetto ou village?" *Le Nouvel observateur*. (February 28–March 6, 2002).

Huyez, Guillaume. "Dix Ans de ghetto: le quartier gay dans les hebdomadaires français," *ProChoix*, no. 22 (2002).

Levine, Martin P. "Gay Ghetto," *Journal of Homosexuality*, no. 4 (1979).

Mades-Claire, Tim. "Le Ghetto gay, en être ou pas?" *Illico* (1995).

Martel, Frédéric. *Le Rose et le noir*. Paris: Le Seuil, 1996. [Published in the US as *The Pink and the Black: Homosexuals in France since 1968*. Stanford, CA: Stanford Univ. Press, 1999.]

Pollak, Michael. "L'Homosexualité masculine, ou: le bonheur dans le ghetto?" *Communications*, no. 35 (1982). New Edition in *Sexualités occidentales*. Edited by Philippe Ariès and André Béjin. Paris: Le Seuil, 1984. [Published in the US as *Western Sexuality: Practice and Precept in Past and Present Times*. New York: Blackwell, 1985.]

—*Closet, the; Communitarianism; England; France; Germany; Heterophobia; North America; Peril; Rhetoric.*

GIDE, André

André Gide (1869–1951), an influential man of letters and a well-known pederast, was a prime target for satirists of his time. Often attacked for his lifestyle, Gide responded with a certain detachment; in this sense, he was probably not the writer most affected by homophobic attitudes, but nonetheless he was particularly vulnerable due to his notoriety. In fact, from the moment his homosexuality was known or suspected, he was the subject of numerous homophobic discourses.

Until 1924, André Gide was a lost soul who could still be saved. His many writings were certainly haunted by homosexuality; one only has to think of works such as *La Tentative amoureuse* (*The Attempt at Love*), *Les Nourritures terrestres* (*The Fruits of the Earth*), *Saül*, or *Les Caves du Vatican* (*Lafcadio's Adventures*). However, any subversive qualities were subdued under the pretense of fiction. In *L'Immoraliste* (*The Immoralist*), the sensory

exaltation of oases and young Arabs gave the impression of reckless hedonism, and the title was such as to denounce the protagonist. As a result, readers could feel reassured that the author was not sympathetic to that which was being portrayed. At worst, one could criticize Gide's unhealthy indulgence of an overly curious mind.

However, a few perceptive writer friends finally saw the direction in which Gide was going. In a letter from 1914, the poet Paul Claudel strongly urged him: "If you are not a pederast, why the strange interest in this subject? And if you are one, unfortunate; cure yourself and do not expose these abominations. Consult Mrs Gide." One week later, seeing Gide continue in the error of his ways, Claudel admonished him again, in this inimitable manner: "No, you know very well that the behaviors that you are talking about are neither allowed, nor excusable, nor respectable.... Moreover, Revelation teaches us that this **vice** is particularly hated by God. It is useless to remind you of **Sodom**, the *morte moriatur* of Leviticus, the beginning of the Epistle to the Romans, the *Neque fornicatores, neque adulteri, neque masculorum concubitores*."

Gide's friends—Claudel, François Mauriac, and Charles Du Bos among them—then found it necessary to try and prevent him from perverting the youth of France, but their efforts were unsuccessful. After a failed attempt to prevent Gide from publishing *Corydon*, author Jacques Maritain concluded with sadness: "Intelligence has crossed over to the devil."

In 1924, the "devil" published *Corydon*, which according to the author was "the most important of my books." In his defense of homosexuality, or more to the point pederasty (although the author included neither the inverted [passive types] nor effeminates, who were abnormal according to him, thus in keeping with homophobic prejudices of the time), the novel's eponymous character tries to convince his interlocutor of the legitimacy of his behavior. Written in the great tradition of moral and philosophical dialogues, the novel clearly demonstrated Gide's ideas and ambition, thus forcing critics to confront that which they had wanted to ignore in his work up until then. But as German novelist Klaus Mann noted, critics came to the conclusion "that Gide had generally gone too far this time. The press reacted either with icy silence or with rabble and obscene comments."

Before *Corydon*, campaigns instigated against Gide refrained from directly addressing his homosexuality, using euphemism or circumlocution instead. Thus in 1923, writer and activist Henri Béraud led an aggressive fight against what he called "La Croisade des longues figures" (The Crusade of the Long Figures)—specifically, a campaign against the growing influence of the literary magazine *La Nouvelle revue Française*, of which Gide was the patron—but Béraud had confined himself to generic morality arguments against Gide's harmful influence on youth. Novelist Roland Dorgelès, who had sided with Béraud, perhaps went a little further: "I condemn André Gide not only in the name of Catholic spirit that is mine, but in the name of my moral health. We are for fortifiers; he is for poison. He believes that he enlightens souls: what a mistake! He troubles them....Virtues are not what interest him, flaws are.... I understand it, of course: evil is more attractive than good, and this is why so many youths go to Gide."

But after *Corydon* and the books that followed, critiques of Gide's work became more explicit. For example, in writing about *Les Faux-monnayeurs* (*The Counterfeiters*), Paul Souday exclaimed: "Oh! There is no bluntness of terms here. A discreet, sheltered, and innocent reader could not, even under extreme circumstances, understand what it is all about. Nevertheless it is all too clear.... And that is enough; the measure is full." Robert Honnert, in turn, commented: "How could a man as subtle as Mr Gide not understand that he was much more interesting inhibited than emancipated?" And André Billy concluded: "That vice is a subject more appropriate for criminal court than **literature**." The publication of *Corydon* even gave rise to books in response to it, such as François Nazier's *L'Anti-Corydon* (The anti-*Corydon*), whose central tenet was circulated throughout Parisian circles: "Nature abhors Gide."

During this entire period, Gide was violently attacked in this way, and these ideas found a particular resonance in France during the dark years after 1940 when Germany defeated France. It was determined that those responsible for the defeat, scapegoats or otherwise, must be found at any cost. While former Prime Minister Léon Blum and a few other leaders of the Third Republic were being judged at the Riom Trial (1942–43), certain writers demanded that there be a similar cleanup of colleagues whose literary work during the interwar years contributed to France's defeat. The offensive, known as "querelle des mauvais maîtres" (The Quarrel of Bad Teachers), was launched by Guy

de Pourtalès. Gide was the first one targeted because the "pessimists, defeatists, immoralists, and corydons" had to be punished. Writer Camille Mauclair even demanded that this "poisoner of youth" be thrown in jail.

Such declarations in the 1930s might seem indifferent in the end, but in the context of the 1940s, they were especially dangerous, and pushed the writer into exile. A conspiracy was even concocted to justify "the hunt for Gide": a young man full of promise, who was of course unnamed, had committed suicide after having either read or met Gide. The story was more than doubtful, but it was meant to be symbolic of the distinguished man of letters' "perverted" influence over French youth. It was thus that the wounded nation's honor had to be avenged and necessary steps taken to oppose such harmful influences, and it is in the context of this exacerbated anti-Gidism that homosexuality was reinstated in Vichy France's penal code in 1942.

In truth, the homophobic attacks on André Gide came from very different communities, from the nationalist or Catholic right wing to the communist left wing that never forgave him for his 1939 travel book *Retour de l'U.R.S.S. (Return from the U.S.S.R.)*. Additionally, all kinds of opposing tactics were tried on him, from friendly sympathy to false indifference to hostile violence, by critics who were in fact less embarrassed by his pederasty than by his insolent way of living it and talking about it, as if it were legitimate.
—*Louis-Georges Tin*

Ahlstedt, Eva. *André Gide et le débat sur l'homosexualité; de L'Immoraliste (1902) à Si le grain ne meurt (1926)*. Gothenburg, Sweden: Acta Universitatis Gothoburgensis, 1994.

"Comptes rendus et dossiers de presse des livres d'André Gide," *Bulletin des Amis d'André Gide*. Also accessible online at http://www.gidiana.net (accessed January 8, 2008).

Cotnam, Jaques. *Inventaire bibliographique et index analytique de la correspondance d'André Gide*. Boston: G. K. Hall & Co, 1975.

Guérin, Daniel. *Shakespeare et Gide en correctionnelle?* Paris: Ed. du Scorpion, 1959.

Lepape, Pierre. *André Gide, le messager*. Paris: Le Seuil, 1997.

Lucey, Michael. *Gide's Bent: Sexuality, Politics, Writing*. New York/Oxford: Oxford Univ. Press, 1995.

Mann, Klaus. *André Gide et la crise de la pensée moderne*. Paris: Grasset, 1999.

GREECE, Ancient

From the eighth century BCE through to the Imperial Roman era in the second century CE, the Greek language did not have any significant terms for either homosexuality or heterosexuality. Greeks never defined sexual categories per se, including for those who had, as a common characteristic, an attraction to people of the same sex. Consequently, acts during this period that could be described as homophobic were not instigated against a unique, homogenous, and coherent group, but rather numerous and diverse types of behaviors, evaluated according to moral and social rules particular to Antiquity.

Greek society consisted of extreme hierarchal divisions, pitting men against women, the rich against the poor, citizens against slaves, paying clients against prostitutes, and land owners against peasants. Sexual relations were also deemed unequal, with one party more powerful than the other, and little room for individual expression. Practices that "conformed to the norm" were set in opposition to those "contrary to the norm": if the roles of the "socially dominant" and the "socially dominated" were reversed, the persons, whatever their gender, were the object of ridicule. The idea of a person having sexual relations with someone of the same sex was not considered objectionable in and of itself so much as on other criteria. Consequently, negative reactions to homosexuality could not be construed as specifically homophobic, because the same responses could be made against other "practices contrary to the norm," as with those between a man and a woman. It is in the context of the global condemnation based on that which is "contrary to the norm" that we can differentiate a specifically homophobic discourse, with all of its related characteristics and clichés.

Inasmuch as the Greek male was powerful and the Greek female was powerless, "homophobia" was expressed very differently against male homosexuals than lesbians. In ancient Greece, sexual intercourse between men often took the form of *paiderastia* (origin of the modern term "pederasty"), in which a mature male took up with a younger one, usually between the ages of twelve and eighteen. In these relationships, strict rules were obeyed; the younger object of desire (*eromenos*) must serve his older lover (*erastes*), who is moved by passionate desire. Physically, it was considered highly respectable for the *erastes* to insert his penis between the thighs of the *eromenos*; in this way, the *eromenos*'s physical integrity was kept intact. Society encouraged the seduction of *eromenoi* by *erastai*, but not vice versa.

Such relationships were brief and non-exclusive; adult males were still expected to marry even after having played the role of the *eromenos*, and even the *erastes*. A youth was permitted to engage in all kinds of sexual behavior, active or passive, with different partners; but if that youth continued to play the passive role as an adult, he was subjected to ridicule. Such is the case with the effeminate poet Agathon, whose relationship with Pausanias is ferociously attacked by Aristophanes in his play *Thesmophoriazusae* (*Women Celebrating Thesmophoria*), in language as violent as anything in the expression of homophobia. One characteristic of homophobic discourse in ancient Greece was the construction of the *kinaidos*, an effeminate male, whose passive role contrasted with the glorious image of the hoplite, the iconic Greek warrior.

What can explain the negative reaction against those in homosexual relationships that extend into adulthood, at the expense of **marriage**? Marriage produced children, thus perpetuating the human species so that one could attain immortality (according to Plato in *The Symposium* and *The Laws*); the refusal to reproduce was a refusal to attain immortality. The importance accorded to marriage by Greek society was also related to the ownership of land. In ancient Athens, one of the definitions of citizenship was the ability to own property (in addition, the duty to serve as a soldier). Only through marriage were land endowments allowed to be passed along; and by owning land, one was all that much more a Greek citizen. This again demonstrates that homophobia in ancient Greece was not the express disapproval of relations between men per se, but rather a means to penalize the refusal to obey Greek society's rules of conduct: in this case, marriage, which had the ultimate goal of perpetuating the human species and allowing members to become full citizens (by having access to land).

Relationships between women, on the other hand, were rarely the subject of contemplation compared to those between men. There is relative silence on the subject except for the choir compositions of Alcman, a poet of ancient Sparta from the seventh century BCE, and the *melica* (lyric) poetry of **Sappho**, both of which explored aspects of love and desire between women. Plato was one of the rare authors to refer to it, through dialogue by Aristophanes in *The Banquet*, in which he outlined a typology of sexual behaviors where "feminine homosexuality" was very briefly mentioned, without condemnation or judgment. But for the most part it appears, through the dearth of text and imagery of lesbians from this era, that ancient Greece's categorization of sexual practices simply excluded relations between women, perhaps in the belief that sexuality was a male prerogative.

For this reason, there were no laws condemning lesbians or any mention in historical material of women who were persecuted or targeted as a result. The caricature of the female homosexual, complete with masculine characteristics, only appeared late in Greek literature; and during the first century CE of the Imperial Roman era, a few satirical writings appeared which described certain non-standard, "monstrous" behaviors, including lesbianism. Also, the few terms to describe lesbians in ancient Greece (such as *hetairistria* and *tribas*) had pejorative connotations, and any literary discourse on female homosexuality turned lesbians into an abstract, notional figure, set apart from reality.

Finally, the archaic era may have been a short moment where love between women was part of the functioning of the city, but female homosexuality was not a preoccupation for men in ancient Greece, as it was deemed irrelevant to both male power and sexuality; relations between women were also not perceived as equal to those between men. Was this attitude the result of indifference or denial by silence? It is difficult to answer, given the fact that so few women's voices from the era were heard.

—*Sandra Boehringer* and *Luc Brisson*

Brooten, Bernadette J. *Love Between Women: Early Christians Responses to Female Homoeroticism*. Chicago/London: Univ. of Chicago Press, 1996.

Cantarella, Eva. *Selon la nature, l'usage et la loi. La bisexualité dans le monde antique*. Paris: La Découverte, 1991. [Published in the US as *Bisexuality in the Ancient World*. Second edition. New Haven, CT: Yale Univ. Press, 2002.]

Dover, Kenneth J. *Homosexualité grecque*. Grenoble, France: La Pensée Sauvage, 1982. [Published in the US as *Greek Homosexuality*. New edition. Cambridge, MA: Harvard Univ. Press, 1989.]

Halperin, David M. *Cent ans d'homosexualité et autres essais sur l'amour grec*. Paris: EPEL, 2000. [Published in the US as *One Hundred Years of Homosexuality, and Other Essays on Greek Love*. New York: Routledge, 1990.]

Winkler, John J. *The Constraints of Desire: Anthropology of Sex and Desire in Ancient Greece*. New York/London: Routledge, 1990.

—*Balkans, the; Essentialism/Constructionism; History; Italy; Peril; Sappho; School.*

GULAG

Beginning in 1934, tens of thousands of homosexuals were deported to the gulags, the generic name of Soviet penal labor camps, under the auspices of the NKVD (Narodunyy Komissariat Vnutrennikh Del; People's Commersiat for Internal Affairs), the leading secret state police organization in the Soviet Union, then later the KGB (Komitet Gosudarstvennoy Bezopasnosti; Committee for State Security). Earlier, on December 17, 1933, sexual relations between males, which had been decriminalized in the wake of the October Revolution of 1917, were re-criminalized throughout the USSR; on April 1, 1934, Article 154 of the Soviet penal code (which later became Article 121) was introduced, providing for sentences of up to five years in prison or penal camps. From that moment on, Soviet laws regarding homosexuality were entrenched and would not change for decades, until after the end of the Soviet Union in 1991 (homosexuality was decriminalized in post-Soviet **Russia** in May 1993). The experiences of homosexuals in the gulags is very poorly documented. One notes that Aleksandr Solzhenitsyn, the Nobel Prize-winning author, did not mention homosexuals in his acclaimed novels about the gulags such as *One Day in the Life of Ivan Denisovich*, no doubt adhering to homophobic Russian Orthodox tradition; the other big names of Soviet gulag literature are also silent on the subject, particularly Varlam Shalamov and Eugenia Ginsburg. The most renowned "121," as homosexual prisoners in the gulags were known, was the Armenian filmmaker Sergei Parajanov, condemned twice for homosexuality, in 1952 and 1974.

The gulag is important in the history of homophobia for the extreme degradation that prisoners suffered, akin to real sexual slavery. Let's recall that mass **deportation** to the gulags became a phenomenon in the 1930s and remained so until Joseph Stalin's death: there were 140,000 zeks (as prisoners were known) in 1930, 1 million in 1935, 2 million in 1941, and close to 3 million in 1950. Throughout the era of the gulags (there were still 900,000 zeks during the 1960s, after the death of Stalin), homosexuality was not uncommon in the camps, at least where prisoners were sufficiently fed to still have a libido. Prisoners were subject to additional harm if they were caught committing a homosexual act; other prisoners would force them to engage in sexual acts, thus making them sexual slaves. Young teenagers deported to the gulags starting in 1935 (youths were eligible for deportation at the age of twelve) were also used as sexual objects (the raping of teenagers in boot camps and preventive detention camps appears to have been frequent). The sexual abuse and rapes were often accompanied by beatings and torture.

According to Eduard Kuznetsov, who was released from the gulags in 1979 after being condemned to fifteen years in camp, many prisoners would engage in homosexual relations; of the eighty-three prisoners with him, eighteen were "passive" and thirty were "active," although it was commonly believed that only the "passives," *opouchtchennie*, were considered the true homosexuals. Being identified as an *opouchtchennie* was not necessarily someone that was condemned to the gulags for homosexuality (a "121") or even someone who considered himself homosexual; it could be a "pretty boy," a timid person, or even someone who lost a card game and could not pay his debt, or someone who broke the group's rules. And once named as an *opouchtchennie*, it was irreversible; the tag would follow prisoners from camp to camp. The concept of the *opouchtchennie*, which owes a lot to Russian Orthodox prejudices, has had a negative connotation throughout Soviet history. In the 1930s, *opouchtchennies* were housed in a separate building in the gulag that was managed by a type of "father pimp," who was supposed to maintain order and protect his "boys." Later, this relative measure of protection for them disappeared, and the *opouchtchennie* was condemned to live alongside the other prisoners, who would become his abusers. Not only was the *opouchtchennie* subject to death threats and torture, he was also relegated to the lower echelons of the camp hierarchy in terms of jobs (he could only have those jobs no one else wanted) or food (he did not receive any supplements of any sort). His belongings were marked (he was to use special flatware and

utensils at meal times). They were also referred to as "goats" and "roosters," derogatory terms that were the lowest of all **insults**, to the point that if used inappropriately, it could lead to the offender's murder. Similarly, a "goat" who had concealed his identity and thus been allowed to eat and live alongside other prisoners (the "bosses" and the "bitches") was deemed to have committed one of the most heinous acts, deserving of death. In this way the gulags clearly aimed to reinforce and sanctify the hierarchical system, as in other closed societies: those in power work to increase their power, while those without renounce their dignity. As acknowledged by Kuznetsov, who was not exempt from homophobia himself, the goat was the voiceless instrument without any sexual rights; it was only during sex that he was not a pariah. Exploiting the social and physiological fragility of homosexual prisoners, the gulag administration often tried to use them as informers. It was common for authorities to threaten such prisoners with allowing their fellow convicts to rape him unless he gave up the information they wanted.

Similar realities were apparent in women's camps, whose population greatly increased in the 1940s (female prisoners represented less than 5% of the total gulag population in the mid-1930s; this number rose to 25% in 1950). Virile women (referred to as *kobly*, or male dogs) took on masculine names and held dominion over other, more feminine women (*kovyrialki*). The relation was hierarchical as much as it was erotic, and roles were entrenched and could not be changed. Male criminals sometimes succeeded in penetrating women's camps in order to rape a *kobly*, who then had to commit suicide according to the group's law.

The first homosexual prisoner of the Soviet gulags to denounce the atrocity of the life for the opouchtchennie was writer Gennady Trifonov. In December 1977, he wrote an open letter to the Literaturnaya Gazeta (which, not unexpectedly, was never published) from his camp in the Ural Mountains: "I have experienced all that can be imagined in horror and nightmare; the situation of gays in Nazi camps was nothing compared to ours. Reduced to the state of animals, we dream of developing a mortal disease to have a few days of rest before death." Another former prisoner, condemned to three years in a gulag for the crime of homosexuality near the end of the Soviet era, reported that he witnessed the murder of ten homosexuals in the camp, most of them under conditions of extreme savagery. In the gulag at Sverdlovsk, one prisoner was killed by ten fellow inmates who, after raping him, jumped on his head with both feet.

Some Soviets living in exile, such as Mikhail and August Stern for example, saw in the gulag the origin of homosexual culture in Russia. While this is totally wrong, of course, it is certain that the gulag culture provided the basis of what would become the post-Soviet gay culture, marked by fear and **violence**; but its system was also emblematic of the homophobia that remains entrenched in current Russian society. It is telling that gay journalist and writer Yaroslav Mogutin, who had expressed interest in the history of homosexuals in the gulag, was forced to claim political asylum in the United States in 1995.

—*Pierre Albertini*

Amalrik, Andrei. *Notes of a Revolutionary*. New York: Alfred A. Knopf, 1982.

Kon, Igor S. *The Sexual Revolution in Russia*. New York: The Free Press, 1995.

Kuznetsov, Ednard. *Lettres de Mordovie*. Paris: Gallimard, 1981.

Mogutin, Yaroslav. "Gay in the Gulag," *Index on Censorship* 24, no.1 (1995).

Stern, Mikhail, and August Stern. *Sex in the Soviet Union*. London: W. H. Allen, 1981.

—*Communism; Deportation; Prison; Russia; Violence.*

H

HENRI III

The House of Valois line of the French monarchy came to an end on August 1, 1589, when King Henri III, at the age of thirty-eight, fell under the knife of Jacques Clément, a Dominican monk. Clément became a fanatic as a result of numerous outrageous pamphlets criticizing Henri III, who was abhorred by the Catholic League whose founder, Duke de Guise, was murdered on the king's orders. Henri III was a Christian who, according to critics, turned satanic by presiding over an inverted world order, a symptom of which—and not the least—was the sin of sodomy.

"Hermaphrodite," "sodomite," "bugger": in the semantic terrain of anti-royal homophobia, there were three levels of slander, referring respectively to unorthodox social behavior, criminal sexual practices, and a threat to Christianity. Memorialist Pierre de L'Estoile reported cases of the king's public transvestism, including an event where he was dressed as a female Amazon, and a series of celebrations in Blois in 1577, "where he was usually dressed as a woman, opened his doublet and uncovered his throat, wearing a string of pearls and three linen collars … as ladies of the court were then wearing." Several painted portraits of him depict the famous earring on his left earlobe, especially notable given the austerity of his clothing. In addition, the king frequently wore makeup, used a curling iron on his hair, and was fond of idle entertainments such as cup-and-ball, habits which appeared to many to hint at his homosexuality, but which were adopted by his fawning followers who shared his tastes, sartorial or perhaps even sexual: the famous "**favorites**." As for his same-sex interests—which the king himself seems to confess when he declares to know how to love only "with extreme"—there are epistolary signs, among them the end of this note addressed to his favorite Caylus:

"I kiss your hands with nothing but affection." One might interpret the **sterility** of his marriage to Louise de Lorraine-Vaudémont in the same manner; Louise loved him deeply, but Henri usually responded with polite indifference. In the end, the king's stigmatizing behavior was seen to endanger Christianity itself due to its suggestions of sexual and religious heterodoxies; this is apparent given that he was frequently referred to with the insulting epithet "*bougre*" ("bugger"), a term applied to homosexuals: the word *bougre* is a variation of "Bulgar," in reference to Bogomilism, the first Bulgarian **heresy** that took place in the country in the tenth century. The "Bugger King," then, is a heretic king, and vice versa. In the context of holy wars, the analogy is intentional, and was frequently referred to at the height of two periods of anti-Henri III propaganda. The first, which occurred at the beginning of his reign, 1574–76), was mostly enacted by Protestants; the second, after he reconciled with them, was instigated by the Catholic League in 1588-89. During this last period, King Henri was regarded the same: as a vain, effeminate sodomite. In one particular characterization, he was visually depicted as a hermaphrodite monster, with teats revealing his feminine lust, a fish's body, dragon wings expressing his bestiality, and rosary beads in his right hand as a sign of faith—or rather, bad faith, seeing that he conceals his allegiance to the cult of Machiavelli, whose picture appears in the mirror that he holds in his left hand.

Yet, a careful examination of evidence renders this criticism of the king invalid. Cross-dressing was a fashion in the French court, and L'Estoile correctly stated that there were fantasy-based masquerades. The flowery epistolary style of the king's correspondence, which led to malicious interpretation, was also in keeping with the popular style of the day. As far as the suggestion of relations between the king and his "favorites," there is no evidence to support it. Beginning in 1585, René de Lucinge, a Savoy diplomat and an ambassador to the court of Henri III, spent his time trying to confirm this suspicion, but he had the assistance of the Catholic League, making his testimony more than suspect. Queen Louise's inability to produce children was not due to her husband's abstinence, but the result of an unfortunate miscarriage in 1575, a situation which, according to observers, made the king desperate. Further, during his younger bachelor days, he had engaged in a number of affairs with women, which caused the Queen Mother to say affectionately that

Satirical portrait of Henri III. *Les Hermaphrodites*: "I am neither male nor female...." Sexual and moral duplicity join together in denouncing the king.

he was "a good stallion" whose dalliances should have produced at least one child out of wedlock. In his adulthood, he also engaged in impressive demonstrations of piety by performing acts of contrition, including self-flagellation sessions and exhausting processions. While his adversaries saw only hypocrisy, it is difficult to see any real evidence of heresy, of which homosexuality would be the most important element.

How then did Henri III end up as the "Bugger King" in the collective imagination? If his critics were homophobic, the cultural, political, and religious aspects of this metamorphosis are then greater than the specific issue of sexuality.

Well in advance of the great Versailles machinery, the last Valois king presided over a first attempt at domesticating or standardizing the moral behavior of the court, including advice on bodily hygiene and dinner table manners. However, the use of cutlery, soap, and a white powder for teeth, and the changing of clothes between day and evening, appeared to be eccentric to most, and went against the rustic tendencies that were common outside the immediate royal entourage; this eccentricity was somehow linked to sexual deviance. Added to this was a certain amount of anti-Italian xenophobia, given that Henri III's mother was Catherine of Medici, a source of great inspiration for him. The combination thus established presented another opportunity to discredit him politically. In choosing "favorites" from middle nobility, the king tried to bypass the influence of cliques from the high aristocracy, first and foremost, the House of Guise. As this was accompanied by an apparent will to distance himself from the royal persona, the resulting hostility of the high aristocracy was based on the idea that a king who hides himself must have something to hide. As for the then-frequent link made between the king and sodomy and, by association, heresy, idolatry, and witchcraft, it had the effect of making the king's piety seem less sincere and excluded him from religious matters, which were deemed better dealt with by the House of Guise. Under these conditions, one could say that Henri III was a victim of his adversaries' homophobia, one common and useful example of the polymorphic hostility expressed toward a king who was ahead of his time.

—*Laurent Avezou*

Chevallier, Pierre. *Henri III, roi shakespearien*. Paris: Fayard, 1985.

Godard, Didier. *L'Autre Faust, l'homosexualité masculine pendant la Renaissance*. Montblanc: H & O Editions, 2001.

Lever, Maurice. *Les Bûchers de Sodome*. Paris: Fayard, 1985.

Poirier, Gérard. *L'Homosexualité dans l'imaginaire de la Renaissance*. Paris: Confluences-Champion, 1996.

Solnon, Jean-François. *Henri III*. Paris: Perrin, 2001.

—*Favorites; France; History; Literature; Monsieur; Scandal.*

HERESY

Homosexuality has often been relegated to a form of heresy, and treated as such. In the Bible, St **Paul** identifies idolaters, effeminates, and pederasts (1 Cor 6:9–10) as those who have cut themselves off from God, and for whom the kingdom of God will thus be forbidden. Based on these affirmations, as well as the episode of **Sodom** (Gn 19) and the Apocalypse of John (Ap 21), it was determined that killing Sodomites by fire was the only means of confirming their spiritual death: the world needed to be purified of their presence. Middle Age **theologians** prolonged this Biblical tradition. For Thomas Aquinas, homosexual acts were an insult to God's willed nature and order; as such, sodomites were explicitly rejecting the Christian community in the same way as idolaters, pagans, and heretics; clearly, they were "heretics in love." Conversely, those accused of heresy were often referred to as sodomites and accused of acts **against nature**. These interpretations were based on the idea of the diabolical act. By definition, the devil acted "unnaturally" and was ready for all kind of excesses. The trials of those accused of witchcraft corroborated the trials of those accused of heresy and vice versa; in both cases, if found guilty, the penalty was that of purifying fire.

It was in this spirit of a return to the orthodoxy and purity of Christianity that the **Inquisition** was established at the beginning of the thirteenth century, and quickly entrusted to the Dominican Order. Today it is difficult to untangle the various reasons for condemnation, which often came about as a result of torture to loosen tongues, but one thing is clear: the war against homosexuality was also a fight to reinforce religious doctrine. The Manicheans, a Christian sect, were persecuted by the Byzantine empire before finding sanctuary in Bulgaria. Based on their apparent behavior, they were considered buggers, implying they were both sodomites and heretics. Similarly, the Albigensian sect, active at the beginning of the thirteenth century but also founded on ancient Manichean ideas, scorned matter, body, and procreation. Sexual relations were tolerated provided no procreation was involved; because of this, the Albigensians were suspected of favoring homosexual relations.

The Templars affair in the thirteenth century, in which a number of French Templars were arrested and charged with numerous heresies under the direction of King Philip IV as a means of ridding the country of the Templars, is a good example of the link between homophobia and accusations of heresy, as the order stood accused of both sodomy and idolatry at the same time. Their accusers obtained "proof" of unnatural acts through torture, a common practice. Under duress, many Templars admitted to having been kissed on the mouth when admitted to the order, or "having received a kiss on the arm, on the lower end of the spine, on the umbilicus and on the mouth by candidates." They also admitted that "if any heat moved them to incontinence, they had permission to spend it with other brothers," or even that "many among them, by way of sodomy, sleep sexually with each other." A few retracted their statements, but to no avail; such confessions were used as evidence of heresy, leading to dozens of Templars to be burned at the stake. The Vienna Council, which dissolved the order in 1312, justified it on the grounds that the Templars "had fallen in an abominable apostasy crime against our Lord Jesus Christ, in the detestable **vice** of idolatry, and the atrocious fault of sodomites and diverse heresies." The Council commission charged with the responsibility of examining the transgressions of the Templars eventually capitulated to the demands of King Philip IV. Still subject to torture, monks confessed crimes against nature in addition to heresy, according to Council texts. Whatever the truth was, one might think that heresy and idolatry were sufficiently serious offenses to justify their arrest, but in order to make the Templars disappear, Philip IV and his charges had to hit harder; the further accusation of crimes against nature added fuel to the fire. As a result, the king was justified in seizing their property, and Pope Clement V could abide by it without (too much) loss of face. It is important to note that homophobia was so anchored in the Church and the Civil Power's way of thinking that it was used to justify virtually any kind of arrest or punishment.

While the definition of crimes against nature was sufficiently clear, their link to other crimes that were much more of a threat to the Church, especially heresy, is difficult to understand. The fact remains, however, that those accused of these connected crimes, those so-called sodomites, were forced to endure torture, persecution, and in certain cases, being burned at the stake.

—*Thierry Revol*

Alberigo, Giuseppe, ed. *Les Conciles œcuméniques.* Vol. II-1: "Les décrets." Paris: Le Cerf, 1994.

Boswell, John. *Christianisme, tolérance sociale et homosexualité.* Paris: Gallimard, 1985. [Published in the US as *Homosexuality, Intolerance, and Christianity.* New York: Scholarship Committee, Gay Academic Union, 1981.]

Gaignebet, Claude, and Dominique Lajoux. *Art profane et religion populaire au Moyen Age.* Paris: Presses universitaires de France, 1985.

Lever, Maurice. *Les Bûchers de Sodome.* Paris: Fayard, 1985.

—Against Nature; Bible, the; Catholic Church, the; Damien, Peter; Inquisition; Judaism; Paul; Rhetoric; Sodom and Gomorrah; Theology; Vice; Violence.

HETEROCENTRISM. *See* Heterosexism

HETERONORMATIVITY. *See* Heterosexism

HETEROPHOBIA

It might seem paradoxical to reflect on a concept without proven linguistic existence. One dictionary defines heterosexuality as "the normal sexuality of the heterosexual," i.e. a characteristic of one "who feels a normal sexual preference for an individual of the opposite sex." Homosexuality, on the other hand, is defined as "tendency or behavior of homosexuals." These conventions are so widespread now as to be quasi tautological: the adjective "normal," used to characterize heterosexuality does not, in this instance, mean "habitual" or "common," but functions to underline the normality and conformity of the heterosexual. Facing so much normality, we can understand why no one asks if "homophobia" has its reciprocal. The notion of heterophobia will likely be thought of as superfluous, doubtful, incongruent, or at worst, completely suspicious.

Let us be clear that it does not work to impose a definition of the term heterophobia, which has already been interpreted in numerous ways (Jacques Tarnero makes it a synonym for racism, a form of hatred of the other), and whose real existence is problematic. Anyone who can grasp its reality and evaluate its importance can assume the indisputable existence of heterophobic practices. Unlike homophobia, heterophobia does not hold on to a discourse on axiological order, whether

for or against, as writer Erik Rémès suggested in a May 7, 2001 letter published in *Ibiza News.* He defined heterophobia as the "rejection or fear of heterosexuality, including a repulsion toward heterosexual fantasies, desires, and behaviors [as well as] discriminatory attitudes toward individuals of a heterosexual orientation." Heterophobia will be examined here as a theoretical concept in order to better question the absence of the term in a system that both legitimizes or discriminates against representations of sexuality: what is represented by this void, so to speak, and what new perspective does it reveal about the phenomenon of homophobia?

It is reasonable to assume that as a result of the physical and emotional **violence** perpetrated against homosexuals throughout history—which to this day can still result in all manner of stigmatization, imprisonment, and even death—that homosexuals might naturally feel as hateful and bitter toward heterosexuals in much the same way. How is it possible, then, that the reciprocal of this **discrimination**, i.e. heterophobia, has never taken hold? Isn't it strange that, with a few exceptions, homosexuals have not engaged in widespread reactionary violence as a result of their treatment, as has been the case of blacks through their history or for Jews following World War II and the Holocaust?

Certainly, it seems that in the history of homosexuals, liberation strategies have not included what could be construed as heterophobia. In fact, many gays and lesbians actively oppose the idea of heterophobia, which they believe contradicts the very values on which gay and lesbian identity is based, including a plea for **tolerance** toward all others, regardless of sexual preference. In this sense, to become heterophobic would invalidate their demands for equal rights, respect, and acknowledgment. Nevertheless, one can see traces of heterophobia in the behavior and discourse of certain gays and lesbians, whether it be verbal abuse (such as "heterocops" and "heterrorists," during the days of the FHAR, the Homosexual Revolutionary Action Front, a French activist group founded in 1971, or "breeders," in English); insults and caricatures that convey, under the guise of humor, a certain resentment; or myths and stories that create a "parallel universe." In this last case, heterosexuality can be excluded completely, such as in certain reformulations of the myth of the Amazons, or it can depict a world in which homosexuals possess the same phobic traits as their hetero counterparts: in his 1999 film *Shame No More,* director John Krokidas portrayed an idyllic small town whose inhabitants are all homosexual. When a male couple suspects their son is heterosexual, they are determined to return the young deviant back to normality. It should be mentioned that writings which are explicitly heterophobic are rare: one such case is Hervé Brizon's 2000 French novel *La Vie rêvée de sainte Tapiole* (The dream life of Saint Tapiole), a zany story about a gay militant terrorist who launches a plan to destroy the symbolic sites of heterocracy.

If there are indeed examples of real heterophobic responses in the world, however, we must note that they are not sufficient to legitimize heterophobia's presence in any significant way. Furthermore, we can observe that the theme of homosexual violence is an ambiguous subject in **literature** and in **cinema**. One is conscious of the fascination provoked by stories featuring gay killers (such as in Claire Denis's 1994 film *J'ai pas sommeil*, or *I Can't Sleep*) or by the stereotype of homosexual love stories that revolve around a crime (such as Alfred Hitchcock's 1948 film *Rope*). These examples illustrate the common depiction of homosexuals as evil, even **criminal** characters. However, they are not heterophobic because their behavior is not in response to heterosexuality as such. Furthermore, they sometimes commit violence against their will, as in Jean Genet's 1947 novel *Querelle of Brest* (the murder of the first Armenian lover), just as gays themselves are often the first targets of camp humor that takes the form of self-deprecation. Finally, for the most part, the depiction of alternative worlds that oppose the heterosexist universe have first and foremost a critical function; they do not represent a true agenda but are aimed solely at provoking a change in the audience's perspective, albeit fictional. This is what the character of Arnold does in Harvey Fierstein's 1978 play (and film) *Torch Song Trilogy* when, instead of arguing with his mother, he asks her to imagine a world in which heterosexuals are bombarded with discourses, books, and broadcasts that incessantly demand, "You've got to be gay!"

But this concept of marginalization in which victims engage in the same kind of behavior as they are subject to raises an essential point: even if homosexuals do not exact the same level of violence against heterosexuals in return, heterosexuals can still feel that they are victims of heterophobic demonstrations, which only increases their own resentment of homosexuals. Real or imagined, heterophobia is the result of a situation of inverse marginalization: to be refused entry at a gay bar, to be rejected by the uniformity of codes of the "gay milieu," or to see in a highbrow production or a political agenda signs of **communitarianism**. Homosexuality, as shown in debates surrounding Lesbian and Gay Pride or the **PaCS** (Pacte civil de solidarité; Civil solidarity pact) proposal in France, has been denounced as a threat again and again. Even if homosexuals do not respond in ways that are actually heterophobic, their response is sometimes violent, particularly in light of the cultural and political development of gay history. But regardless, heterophobia can never have the same impact as homophobia, as homophobics can act against homosexuals without having their own psychological or sexual identity questioned. In examining the heterophobic behavior of homosexuals, one would obviously see its pathological origins in their very sexuality; their heterophobia would be construed as reactive and the result of an unhealthy sexual identity.

It is this irreducible asymmetry that is the essential point of our reflective thinking on the subject: one can see in the notion of heterophobia, besides psychological questions or legal considerations, an intellectual interest before all else. The hypothesis of heterophobia has value only if it leads to the following question: Is it possible to radically question homophobia without thinking of the equal possibility of heterophobia, even if theoretical? Homophobia relies in great part, in fact, on a sense of impunity, of sexual legitimacy, manifested in the fact that the homophobe does not even think of the possibility that the violence might be mutual. It is violence itself, both physical and symbolic, that leaves no place for the victim to respond in kind; it is a one-way stigmatization, as if homosexuality were a handicap, a disability.

Lesbian and Gay Pride sometimes provokes the confrontational reaction of a "Hetero Pride." By contrast, being subjected to homophobia does not naturally provoke heterophobia in response. We have to applaud this if it signals the rejection by homosexuals of the idea that violence begets violence. But this is unlikely, and if heterophobia exists, it is better that it is talked about rather than left unspoken. Such a notion, currently not recognized in any legal way, is at present purely psychological and speculative, but at its core is a response to the very notion of homophobia: a way of legitimizing oneself. It is not possible to examine homophobic violence without examining the homophobe's sense of impunity, based on the idea that heterosexuality is the "normal sexuality" not be questioned by the "tendency" or "behavior" of those who love others of the same gender.

—*Jean-Louis Jeannelle*

Brizon, Hervé. *La Vie rêvée de sainte Tapiole*. Paris: Balland, 2000.

Franzini, Louis R., and Stephen M. White. "Heteronegativism? The Attitudes of Gay Men and Lesbians Toward Heterosexuals," *Journal of Homosexuality* 37, no. 1 (1999).

Krokidas, John. *Shame No More*. Short film, 1999.

"Le Miracle de l'hétérophobie," *Bang Bang,* no. 7 (2002).

Rémès, Erik. http://ericremes.free.fr/_textes/humeurs/humeur%201.html (accessed January 8, 2008).

Wittig, Monique. *Les Guérillères*. Paris: Minuit, 1969. [Published in the US as *Guérillères*. Urbana, IL: Univ. of Illinois Press, 2007].

—*Biphobia; Communitarianism; Criminal; Gayphobia; Ghetto; Heterosexism; Lesbophobia; Shame; Symbolic Order; Tolerance; Transphobia; Violence.*

HETEROSEXISM

Although the word heterosexism has only recently begun to appear in modern dictionaries, the concept itself is nothing new. It is clearly suggested in the writings of André **Gide**, as well as in the "Straight Mind" that writer and feminist theorist Monique Wittig talked about. It also appeared in the use of slogans such as "heterocops" or "heterrorists" used by early gay liberation activists; the word heterosexism itself was sometimes evoked in this period, but in a very limited way.

But in more recent years, in light of the various struggles for LGBT rights, the word and the concept have achieved greater legitimacy, especially when used in conjunction with terms such as heterocentrism and heteronormativity, which together force us to rethink rhetorical and practical devices of sexual domination.

It is not easy to define something on which little or no consensus exists, especially when its primary function is as a tool for social criticism. In any event, heterosexism can be defined as a vision of the social world that articulates the promotion of heterosexuality to the exclusion of homosexuality. It is based on the teleological illusion according to which man is made for woman and, chiefly, woman for man, an intimate conviction that serves as the necessary model of any hu-

man society. From there, attributing to heterosexuality the monopoly of legitimate sexuality, this dramatic social idea has the effect, if not the goal, of proposing in advance an ideological justification of the stigmatization and **discrimination** suffered by homosexuals.

Seen this way, this concept has the merit of distinguishing two realities that are often intertwined. As noted by French sociologist Eric Fassin, "actual usage wobbles between two very different definitions. The first hears the phobia in homophobia, that is, rejection of gays and of homosexuality. We are in the individual range of a psychology. The second sees heterosexism in homophobia: this time it is the inequality of sexualities. The hierarchy between heterosexuality and homosexuality returns to the collective register of ideology." From there, adds Fassin, "maybe in this case, like the distinction between misogyny and sexism, would it be clearer to distinguish between 'homophobia' and 'heterosexism' to avoid confusion between psychological and ideological acceptances? For my part, that is what I propose and practice." Under these conditions, people who claim "I am not homophobic, but …" (etc.), inasmuch as they refuse, for example, equality of rights between gays and heteros on questions such as marriage or adoption, will have to admit that they are at the very least heterosexist.

However, this distinction has the effect of reducing the link between stigmatization (homophobic) and discrimination (heterosexist). Worse, in reducing the semantic specter of the word homophobia, it gives the impression of limiting its necessary critical reach, that which Fassin justly wants to avoid: "In this case, talking about heterosexism rather than homophobia is not any more or less hypocritical or deft at making a euphemism of homophobic **violence** by calling it heterosexist." In short, the notion of heterosexism could possibly create more problems than it could solve.

Yet, in reality, it is the genesis of heterosexism that allows for the demonstration of its critical potential. Here, two different aspects must be looked at: the individual passage to heterosexuality (psychogenesis) and the collective conversion to heterosexism (sociogenesis). Psychogenesis of heterosexuality remains largely unexplained. If we agree with Freud's idea of the child's innate bisexuality, how can we explain the restrictions and limitations that intervene later in life? In respect thereof, one must without doubt grant a large place to social influences, evidently an influential factor in the psychic development of the individual. This is what is demonstrated by the work of anthropologists Clellen Ford and Frank Beach: "Men and women without conscious homosexual tendencies are a product of cultural conditioning along with gays that find heterosexual relations uncomfortable and frustrating. Those two extremes are the result of a distancing from the original intermediary way, where both sexual forms were manifested. In a society such as ours, a great part of the population learns not to react to homosexual stimulations and to avoid them until they cease to be a threat. At the same time, and equally by learning, a certain minority becomes very, not to say exclusively, sensitive to erotic attraction of the same sex." The psychogenesis of heterosexuality, after all, is greatly dependent on social learning.

We still have to explain, however, how a culturally acquired preference becomes a morally required value. So this sociogenesis of hegemonic heterosexuality constitutes the real heart of the problem. Despite the clarity of the work of LGBT historian Jonathan Ned Katz, especially in *The Invention of Heterosexuality*, the thesis he presents remains almost unthinkable for some. The negative reaction is a clear indication of the power of heterosexism which, as all cumulative ideology, prevents thinking outside the "normal" frame of thought. Of course, it is not for Katz, or for us evidently, to say that sexual relations between men and women are a historically dated invention. On the other hand, the uniqueness and, to be more precise, the symbolic predominance granted to those relations are not invariants or universals of human culture. On the contrary, everything leads to thinking that while the homosexual character, if we believe Foucault, was an invention of the medical community of the nineteenth century, the heterosexual character is a progressive construction whose emergence and evolution can be retraced.

To do this, one would have to consider Swiss writer Denis de Rougemont's *L'Amour et l'Occident*, published in English as *Love in the Western World*; perhaps it is time we had a book on heterosexuality in the western world, in which we would find the sudden appearance, around the twelfth century, of a new concept of sex and gender linked to established court ethics. It is at this time, still more than in the first centuries of Christianity's beginnings, that heterosexism and homophobia made their first joint appearance. Following this, one would clearly note a resurgence of heterosexist feeling in the second half of the sixteenth century and the first half of the seventeenth century, specifically in the new court

and fashionable parlor society of the Early Modern Age. Finally, another rise occurred around the end of the eighteenth century, from which we have not completely recovered. In a significant manner, it is to those three respective eras that these great myths of heterosexual culture belong: Tristan and Isolde, Romeo and Juliet and, to a lesser extent, Paul and Virginia, the eponymous characters of the 1787 French novel by Jacques-Henri Bernardin de St-Pierre.

It is, however, not sufficient to explain how this mythology of heterosexual amorous passion was constructed as a cultural absolute. We would be hard pressed to find examples of this in past eras, even the idea of which, to the Ancient, would have seemed highly unlikely; one would still have to demonstrate at the same time the systematic erasing of homosexual desire in this same culture: it is this **censorship**, through rereading and rewriting enterprises, to which all Christian society tied itself. This general sexual reform, which affected authors in Antiquity (e.g., **Sappho**, Anacreon, Pindar, Catullus, Virgil, Horace, Tibullus, Martial, and Petronius), was equally applied to modern authors such as Shakespeare, Michelangelo, and even Walt Whitman, in order to mask as much as possible the gay eroticism suggested in their works. Under these conditions, the representation of same-sex relations proved to be very difficult, and most of the time impossible, unless it conformed to social "**tolerance**" standards by presenting images that were either euphemistic or caricatures—in other words, in keeping with the dominant vision of homosexuality in the West.

That said, the social costs and effects of this ideology cannot be underestimated. In the heterosexist culture that grew out of the bourgeois society of the nineteenth century, traditional thoughts on marriage and parenting marginalized not only homosexuals, but also those who were not part of heterosexual couples: the "bachelor," the "old maid," and any others who give the impression of not ratifying the ideal of "the couple" or symbolically approving social order by seeming to foment social protest and "biological" disorder.

Inside this normative frame, however, daily life is not any more comfortable. Self-imposed constraints often transform collective agents of the social pressure into individual victims who come to regret their life choices, made in good part to satisfy social requisites for which they understand, generally too late, that they sacrificed youth, happiness, and liberty. Nevertheless, the cause of this everyday dissatisfaction and psychological misery that are the lot of many apparently "conforming" heterosexuals is often not identified, while symbolic violence, in the sense defined by French sociologist Pierre Bourdieu of the heterosexist system, is completely invisible and detrimental to the very same people whom it intended to benefit.

In this way, heterosexism appears like gender police, intended to call back to social order individuals of all kinds, whatever their sexual orientations, whether or not they are inside the defined frame. It would, however, be surprising that an ideology, so heavy and so onerous, could perpetuate itself in a mechanical way if persons did not see, rightly or wrongly, some benefits in it. Beyond purely pro-natalist interests, which were never threatened in diverse societies that made a more legitimate place for homosexual relations, heterosexism seems to guarantee the man who consents to it the mastering of the social world under the condition that he agrees to prove at a very young age, and all through his life, that he is neither a baby, a girl, nor finally a "gay." And for the woman, this heterosexual culture, where she apparently holds a psychologically valorizing position, as she sees herself being desired, courted, adulated, all while being completely enclosed, controlled, and dominated, seems to promise a marvelous happiness with Prince Charming and, at least the anticipation of a peaceful and reassuring **family** life in a society where complementarity of sexes would agree with equality of chances.

The problem is that sometimes the world breaches this fable. Far from being a principle of equality or reciprocity between sexes, heterosexism is a thinking system whereby the said conjugality, and even maternity, confirms male domination in sexual relations. It restricts women in the idea that their laudable and generous sweetness naturally earmarks them for service to man and family. At the same time, it confirms men in their feeling that women are naturally owed to them, according to the order of things and their "valor," an obscure conviction that confusedly justifies sexual aggressions and harassment of all kinds. This is perpetrated sometimes with complete peace of mind, and even, strangely enough, with a feeling of legitimacy that gives the impression of an extreme form of cynicism. In fact, we should perhaps see in this a sort of paradoxical naïveté, albeit one that is still inexcusible.

It is the cult of physical and sexual power, inherent to the constitution of male identity, at least as ordinarily conceived in our societies, which tends to valorize and so favor demonstrations of strength, as brutal as they can be, and which allows the comprehension of the remarkable co-relation, often not noted, between violence and masculinity. Most physical violence, sexual or not, is perpetrated by men who are conditioned by the social climate of masculinism. Heterosexism is altogether at the root of homophobia (toward gays), of sexism (toward women), but also in a more general way, at the root of numerous acts of violence (toward any person, whoever he or she is) whose ties with the masculine identity and culture of virile force do not show themselves at first glance, but this is why the most violent men are also often the most sexist, misogynistic, and, at the same time, the most homophobic. From this point of view, the fight against heterosexism will without doubt appear as a public issue, high on the agenda.

From this moment, we should focus on the deconstruction of heterosexism, which is the predominant logic of gender and sex promoted to the detriment of not just gays and women (let alone gay women), but also heterosexual men, who are often guided by the illusion of a badly understood social interest, as dominants dominated by their own domination. The "heterosexual social contract" that Wittig justly criticizes could give up its place to a new social contract with plural values, which grants complete legitimacy not only to gays and heteros, men or women, but also to bisexuals and transgenders that theoretical analysis and social practices, in their binary and exclusive logic, tend to obscure.

A final anecdote: in 1972, NASA put together a mission called "Pioneer" and sent a message into space intended for possible intelligent life forms that could receive it. On the message, which purported to be a figuration of "fundamentals" of our universe, appeared a map of the hydrogen atom, of the solar system, of our galaxy, and also of a couple, corresponding to an "average," determined by a computer, that is a man and a woman (of Caucasian race), the man raising his hand in a sign of peace, the woman standing modestly at his side. At the risk of straying from this surprising "average," the said scientists could also have represented lone individuals, hetero and gay couples, groups of friends, human beings, Asian, black, white, mixed-race, but they sacrificed this possibility, maybe even without noticing it, to heterosexist and racist prejudices that would want to see what is finally only a heterosexual middle-class couple from American suburbia, a kind of completely trite archetype of the human species. This is the ordinary illusion of metonymic reasoning or, to say it more familiarly, the story of the part that thought it was the whole. Finally we can suppose that the cosmic beings that will receive the message, in their supreme intelligence, will make do with a smile when they see this gross sham and will wait for better days to honor Earth by their visit.

—*Louis-Georges Tin*

Badinter, Elisabeth. *XY, de l'identité masculine*. Paris: Odile Jacob, 1992. [Published in the UK as *XY: On Masculine Identity*. New York: Columbia Univ. Press, 1995.]

Baret, Guy. *Eloge de l'hétérosexualité, pour le droit à la différence*. Paris: Les Belles Lettres, 1994.

Basow, Susan, and Peter Theodore. "Heterosexual Masculinity and Homophobia: A Reaction to the Self," *Journal of Homosexuality* 40, no. 2 (2000).

Beattie Jung, Patricia, and Ralph Smith. *Heterosexism: An Ethical Challenge*. New York: State Univ. of New York Press, 1993.

Beach, Franck, and Clellan Ford. *Le Comportement sexuel chez l'homme et l'animal*. Paris: Robert Laffont, 1970. [Published in the UK as *Patterns of Sexual Behaviour*. London: Eyre & Spottiswoode, 1952.]

Bourdieu, Pierre. "Sur le pouvoir symbolique," *Annales*, no. 3 (1977).

Burn, Shawn Meghan. "Heterosexuals' Use of 'Fag' and 'Queer' to Deride One Another: A Contribution to Heterosexism and Stigma," *Journal of Homosexuality* 40, no. 2 (2000).

Dorais, Michel, Pierre Dutey, Daniel Welzer-Lang, eds. *La Peur de l'autre en soi, du sexisme à l'homophobie*. Montreal: VLB, 1994.

Fassin, Eric. "Le 'Outing' de l'homophobie est-il de bonne politique?" In *L'Homosexualité, comment la définir, comment la combattre*. Paris: Ed. Prochoix, 1999.

Foucault, Michel. *La Volonté de savoir*. Paris: Gallimard, 1976.

Gide, André. *Corydon*. Paris: Gallimard, 1924. [Published in English as *Corydon*.]

Herek, Gregory. "Psychological Heterosexism and Anti-Gay Violence: The Social Psychology of Bigotry and Bashing." In *Hate Crimes: Confronting Violence against Lesbians and Gay Men*. Edited by Gregory Herek and Kevin T. Berril. London: Sage Publications, 1992.

"Hétérosexualité et lesbianisme," *La Revue d'en face*, no. 9–10 (1981).

Jackson, Stevi. "Récents débats sur l'hétérosexualité: une approche féministe matérialiste," *Nouvelles questions féministes*

17, no. 3 (1996).

———. *Heterosexuality in Question*. London: Sage, 1999.

Kantor, Martin. *Homophobia: Description, Development and Dynamics of Gay Bashing*. Westport: Praeger, 1998.

Katz, Jonathan. *The Invention of Heterosexuality*. New York: Penguin, 1995.

Kitzinger, Celia, and Mary Wilkinson. *Heterosexuality: A Feminism and Psychology Reader*. London: Sage, 1993.

Maynard, Mary, and June Purvis, eds. *(Hetero)Sexual Politics*. London: Taylor & Francis, 1995.

Onlywomen Press, ed. *Love Your Enemy: The Debate Between Heterosexual Feminism and Political Lesbianism*. London: Onlywomen Press, 1981.

Richardson, Diane, ed. *Theorizing Heterosexuality: Telling It Straight*. Buckingham: Open Univ. Press, 1996.

Rich, Adrienne. "La Contrainte à l'hétérosexualité et l'existence lesbienne." *Nouvelles questions féministes*, no. 1 (1981). [Published in the US as "Compulsory Heterosexuality and Lesbian Experience," *Signs* 5, no. 4 (Summer 1980).]

Rougemont, Denis de. *L'Amour et l'Occident*. Paris: Pion, 1939.

Straayer, Chris. *Deviant Eyes, Deviant Bodies: Sexual Re-Orientations in Film and Video*. New York: Columbia Univ. Press, 1996.

Tin, Louis-Georges. "L'Invention de la culture hétérosexuelle," *Les Temps modernes* (2003).

Wittig, Monique. *The Straight Mind*. Boston: Beacon Press, 1992.

—*Abnormal; Against Nature; Heresy; Heterophobia; Literature; Rhetoric; Symbolic Order; Violence.*

HIMMLER, Heinrich

Heinrich Himmler (1900–45)—who first came to prominence in Nazi Germany as commander of the Schutzstaffel (SS) (1929) and the Gestapo (1934), then as supreme chief of the German **police** (1936) and finally Minister of the Interior (1943)—was the main theorist behind official Nazi homophobia and the main instigator of the persecution of homosexuals by the Third Reich.

In a speech addressed to SS generals on February 18, 1937, Himmler revealed the principles of Nazi homophobia, which recycled popular prejudices to serve its racist and eugenist ideology. Presenting himself as a specialist on the topic, he insisted on relating homosexuality to a dangerous **contagion** that threatened the entire nation. In a Germany that had earlier been crippled by World War I, male homosexuality, as well as abortion, constituted an infringement on the "survival of the race" and hindered the expansion of the Reich and its conquest of a "vital space." Himmler also stressed the risk of a secret gay coalition at work in the heart of the state. Homosexuals—depicted as traitorous and weak—were seen as pursuing sexual solidarity at the expense of patriotism, and as such they were enemies of the state who had to be unmasked in order to prevent them from ruining the country. Homosexuals were thus most dangerous to a nationalist organization like the SS, which sought to protect all Nazi "virtues." For Himmler, homosexuality was the consequence of the mixing of races, most prevalent in urban centers; as a result, he vowed to protect those living in the German countryside (based on ancient Germania) from the "scourge" of homosexuality. Further, Germany's male youth needed to be protected from the gay temptation by the means of **sport**, work, and discipline; and, if needed, by encouraging the use of prostitutes and early marriages, and tolerating illegitimate births. He countered the Christian morality of the day (which he despised) with the seductions of a neo-pagan and Dionysiac society, albeit disguised with puritan and idealist accents. In this way, Himmler embodied the many faces of homophobia: in addition to the slighting associated with the "effeminate" gay stereotype, he added the fear of lower birth rates as a result of homosexuality, and a fear of widespread **degeneracy**, in a society obsessed with virility. One might also add personal factors: Himmler seemed to possess an irrational fear of and aversion to male homosexuality which, combined with a kind of voyeurism and a veritable joy in legislating the sexuality of others, would move him to put into practice his purifying fantasies.

The secret directive of Himmler, dated October 10, 1936, prioritized "the fight against homosexuality and abortion" which had started as early as 1933, with the Nazis' rise to power. The reinforcement of Paragraph 175 (the provision of the 1871 German criminal code which criminalized male homosexual acts), combined with the creation of new official organizations such as the Reich Central Office for the Combating of Homosexuality and Abortion, had the joint intention of creating files on known homosexuals, leading to increased arrests and—for certain categories of "criminals" such as prostitutes, "corrupters of youth,"

or repeat offenders—exile to concentration **camps**. Himmler was particularly obsessed with eradicating homosexuality within the Nazi party, the SS, and the Hitler Youth because he was conscious of the ambiguity instilled by the cult of virile camaraderie in these organizations. However, his attempts to "purify" the Wehrmacht were fruitless for a long time, due to the resistance of military authorities who were offended by his initiatives. In 1937, Himmler also fostered homophobic campaigns intended to purify the Catholic Church and the highest ranks of the **army**.

However, the extermination of homosexuals was not the objective of these campaigns, and Himmler himself contemplated the possibility of "rehabilitation" for those whose sexuality was considered "acquired" as a result of **debauchery**" or "seduction." He was very interested in the different methods advocated by doctors to "cure" gays, from psychoanalysis to hormonal **treatments**, and financed a number of experimental programs, including at Matthias Heinrich Goering's German Institute for Psychological Research and Psychotherapy, which reported a successful cure rate of seventy percent. After the beginning of World War II, however, the "rehabilitation" projects took a back seat, as Himmler became less interested in wasting time and money on "asocials." Thus, sending homosexuals to concentration camps became more systematic, and castration, notwithstanding the fact that it was disputed as a remedy for homosexuality, became the simplest means of sending "cured" gays to the front. Dr Carl Vaernet's criminal experimentations at the Buchenwald concentration camp, in which he tried to cure homosexuals by injecting synthetic hormones into their groins, were also encouraged by Himmler.
—*Florence Tamagne*

Himmler, Heinrich. *Discours secrets*. Paris: Gallimard, 1978.
Le Bitoux, Jean. *Les Oubliés de la mémoire*. Paris: Hachette, 2002.

—*Contagion; Decadence; Degeneracy; Deportation; Far Right; Fascism; Germany; Hirschfeld, Magnus; Medicine; Pétain, Philippe; Proselytism; Sterility; Treason; Treatment; Violence.*

HINDUISM

Before discussing homophobia in Hinduism, one must first address Hinduism itself. While it is generally presented as a religion, it is a mistake to discuss it solely on those terms. In fact, the definition of Hinduism covers a broad theological spectrum, from monism to polytheism (or pantheism). It also represents a rich historical culture that developed well before the strict monotheism of the Old Testament.

Instead of the term "religion," Hindus prefer to speak of *sanatana dharma*, or "system of eternal belief." There are six Hindu metaphysical systems called *darshanas* (or "visions of reality"), which are diametrically opposed to the feudal systems of Western Asia: *nyaya* (logicism), *vaisheshika* (atomism), *sankhya* (enumeration), *yoga* (transcendence), *mimansa* (interpretation), and *vedanta* (metaphysical speculation).

None of these systems refer to any god, or to a true metaphysic for that matter. Correspondingly, they are not linked to temporal morality. However, Hinduism contains a set of sacred, clearly organized principles, such as *karmakanda*, the full spectrum of rituals, and *dyana*, the full spectrum of knowledge. Morality and ethics are clearly separated; morality on the side of temporal duties and ethics on the side of eternal duties. Under this belief system, the origins of homophobia in Hinduism can now be explained insofar as it can be compared to homophobia in Western cultures. Hinduism does not hold any specific moral position on homosexuality, as it appears to be perceived as a voluntary, occasional practice engaged in by heterosexual men.

This is not to say that Hinduism does not address or in fact condemn those men who stray outside the sexual norm. The most ancient of Hindu's sacred knowledge, the *vedas*, mention the term *pandaka* (in the *Atharva veda*), which seems to designate a man with long, oily, wavy hair, and who wears jewelry and rings as a woman. Such a man is "effeminate," and in the *vedas*, the term is used as a curse: "May your son became *pandaka*."

Another striking word appears in the sacred Sanskrit epic the *Mahabharata*: the war prince Shikandi is called *napunsaka*, or he who does not penetrate, but it is difficult to ascertain if he does not want to penetrate or if he is unable to; his sexual behavior is at least uncertain. On the other hand, the *Mahabharata* also contains the term *kilba*, to describe the warrior Arjunas who, while in exile, cross-dressed in order to hide out at Princess Uttara's court; he also became her dance teacher. (At the same time, he refuses the sexual advances of her brother.)

Buddhist and Jain (a dharmic religion originating in Ancient India) sacred texts both mention the term tritika laingika, which can be translated as the "third sex." In fact, the Jain text includes more than ten categories of masculine gender, but these which roughly correspond to various physical types, such as those who are bald, or who do not have mustaches; as such, they are not really sexual definitions.

The only evidence of convergence between sexuality and gender identity in Hinduism, however allusive, appears in the *Shiva purana*, the text dedicated to the Hindu deity Shiva, in which Shiva is also called *Ardhanareshwara* (half-man). Shiva is a complex deity; like his symbol, the lingam, he is an ascetic who preserves his seed, but sometimes spreads it on the entire universe. In one of the sacred stories, he disperses sperm that is so hot it cannot even be collected by Agni, god of fire; it ultimately falls back into the Ganges, where six drops end up creating a divinity called Shanmukha.

In each of these definitions of men who contravene Hinduism's sexual standards, there is no question of an exclusive homosexual-type being. Sometimes the god changes himself into a woman (such as Vishnu becoming Mohini) who then adopts heterosexual behavior, thus eluding any stigma attached to homosexuality.

The only specific sanctions against homosexuality are mentioned in *Arthashashtra* (fourth-century BCE), the great treatise on economic policy, military strategy, and the state, and in the *Manusmriti* (third-century CE), the work of Hindu law and Indian society. In both texts, homosexuality is depicted as a negative, nonreproductive behavior, and both recommend severe penalties for those accused of it. Both texts consider sperm a "social resource" which must not be expended for means other than reproduction. If a man willfully engages in sexual activity that is not reproductive, this social resource is wasted, and for this he must be condemned. As the matriarch Gandhari declared to her husband in the *Mahabharata*, "Putha heen Pitah" ("No children, it is hell"); she then threatens him with going elsewhere to be inseminated. In this case, there is no morality here; it is a question of genetic inheritance.
—*Ashok Row Kavi*

Conner, Randy, David Hatfield, and Mariya Sparks. *Cassell's Encyclopedia of Queer Myth, Symbol, and Spirit*. New York/London: Cassell, 1997.

Kidwai, Saleem, and Ruth Vanita. *Same-Sex Love in India:*

Readings from Literature and History. Delhi: Macmillan India Ltd., 2002.

Pattanaik, Devdutt. "Homosexuality in Ancient India." *Debonair,* Anniversary Issue (2001).

———. *The Man Who Was a Woman and Other Queer Tales From Hindu Lore.* New York: Harrington Park Press, 2002.

—Buddhism; China; India, Pakistan, Bangladesh; Japan; Korea; Southeast Asia; Sterility.

HIRSCHFELD, Magnus

Magnus Hirschfeld (1868–1935), the German physician, sexologist, and advocate for the rights of homosexuals, was born to a Jewish family in Kolberg on the Baltic coast. He studied medicine in Munich and Berlin and traveled to the United States and North Africa before settling in Magdeburg, then Berlin, in the Charlottenburg quarter. It was the **suicide** of one of his patients, and his own sexual orientation, a day before the patient's wedding that led Hirschfeld to wonder about the "causes" of homosexuality. Taking inspiration from the works of K. H. Ulrichs in particular (which suggested the existence of a "third sex," defined as "a woman's soul in a man's body"), Hirschfeld published his first pamphlet, "**Sappho** und Sokrates" in 1896, under the alias Th. Ramien. In a subsequent publication *Die Homosexualität des Mannes und des Weibes* (1914) (*The Homosexuality of Men and Women* [2000]), he refined and developed his theory, based on numerous testimonies and thousands of questionnaires, that claimed the existence of *sexuelle Zwischenstufen* (sexual intermediaries) defined by four criteria—sexual organs, physical characteristics, sexual instinct, and moral aptitude—which allowed for the classification of human beings according to different degrees of hermaphroditism and intersexuality. According to Hirschfeld, homosexuality was congenital, not learned, and thus was not an "anomaly" but rather a "sexual variety" against which it is impossible to take action.

Not only a sexologist but also an activist, Hirschfeld cofounded the Wissenschaftlich-humanitäres Komitee (WhK; Scientific-Humanitarian Committee) in Berlin on May 14, 1897. The group was the first militant gay movement in Germany, aimed at defending the rights of homosexuals as well as working to repeal Paragraph 175 of the German penal code that criminalized homosexuality beginning in 1871. (Hirschfeld included

the story of the WhK's early years in his 1923 autobiographical work *Von einst bis jetzt* (From once up to now); in addition, he chronicled the rich Berlin gay scene in 1908's *Homosexuals of Berlin*.) In 1899, Hirschfeld also started a journal, *Jahrbuch für sexuelle Zwischenstufen* (Yearbook for sexual intermediaries), to publish new ideas about alternative sexualities (it was replaced in 1926 by *Mitteilungen des WhK* [Communications of the WhK], which was published until 1933). In order to fulfill its mission, the WhK led a lobbying campaign targeting the government and the **media**, printing thousands of information brochures, such as *Was soll das Volk vom dritten Geschlecht wissen* (What people must know about the third sex). In 1897, it started a petition demanding the abolition of Paragraph 175 which was signed by several high-profile people, among them doctors (Krafft-Ebing), politicians (Karl Kautsky, Eduard Bernstein), writers (Thomas Mann, Rainer Maria Rilke, Emile Zola), and scientists (Albert Einstein). Hirschfeld also was able to get a few left-wing politicians interested in his cause, among them August Bebel, one of the founders of Germany's Social Democratic Party, who subsequently raised the question of Paragraph 175 in the Reichstag in 1905, arguing that according to Hirschfeld's research, six percent of the population was homosexual or bisexual, meaning that thousands of Germans were at risk of being threatened by blackmailers, with no recourse due to Paragraph 175. However, politicians from both the left and right did not agree, both on moral grounds and the perceived will of the people, so the law remained in place.

But the **Eulenburg affair** of 1907–09, the country's biggest domestic scandal to date, put a temporary end to the actions of the WhK. Motivated by political revenge, a pro-imperialist journalist named Maximilian Harden accused anti-imperialist Prince Philipp of Eulenburg, close advisor to Wilhelm II, and Count Kuno von Moltke, a general in the German army, of being homosexual; the two were subsequently charged under the provisions of Paragraph 175. At the trial that followed in October 1907, Hirschfeld was called to the witness stand as an "expert"; he contended that Moltke's homosexuality was an "unconscious orientation," hoping this would be a means to break the government's hypocrisy on the subject. This strategy, however, was disastrous: in light of severe criticism, Hirschfeld was forced to retract his statement, causing support for his movement to decline by two-thirds (many of those withdrawing their support were homosexuals who now feared being exposed). In 1909, a bill (which was ultimately rejected) proposed extending Paragraph 175 to include lesbians, resulting in a temporary alliance between the WhK and certain feminist movements. However, it was not until the era of the Weimar Republic (1919–33) that the WhK had real influence again, the result of a favorable climate that also saw the blooming of Berlin's gay subculture.

In 1919, Hirschfeld founded the Institut für Sexualwissenschaft (Institute for Sexual Research) in Berlin, which soon became known worldwide as a research center that collected documentation on homosexuality as well as a place where homosexuals looking for medical or psychological support were welcomed. Among its prominent visitors were André **Gide**, René Crevel, and Christopher Isherwood. Hirschfeld's efforts also became international; he encouraged the formation of the British Society for the Study of Sex Psychology (1914) in England, and helped to found the World League for Sexual Reform (1928) at a congress in Copenhagen. In 1919, when film censorship did not yet exist in Germany, Hirschfeld worked with producer and director Richard Oswald, a specialist in social and educational **cinema**, on the first gay activist film, *Anders als die Andern* (Different from the others), which called for the repeal of Paragraph 175 by bringing public attention to the suffering of the "inverted" who commit suicide under the threat of blackmail (Hirschfeld co-wrote the film as well as appeared in it). While the film received many laudatory reviews and was a popular success, it was also subject to violent attacks from champions of moral order as well as anti-Semitic groups; numerous riots broke out where it was shown, which led **police** to ban it in certain cities, including Munich and Stuttgart. When cinematic **censorship** was instituted in Germany in 1920, the film was banned outright, and subsequently only shown to doctors or research-based organizations.

Hirschfeld also attempted to link the WhK with other gay movements, but he was sometimes treated with hostility (not without anti-Semitic elements) by groups such as Adolf Brand's Gemeinschaft der Eigenen (Community of Self-Owners), which thought Hirschfeld's model of homosexuality was effeminate, preferring instead the virile model of pederasty. Hirschfeld's relationship with left-wing parties, which had supported his efforts in Parliament, became unclear as well, as the Social Democratic Party and Communist

Party did not hesitate to use homophobic arguments in their efforts to combat fascism, against Ernst Röhm, commander of the SA and a homosexual of public record. For a while, Hirschfeld considered founding his own political party, but he was disappointed by the lack of support from the gay community. The year 1929 marked a turning point when the Social Democrats, Communists, and German Democrats had enough votes in the Reichstag to repeal Paragraph 175, but the rising Nazi Party managed to prevent it. The failure led to intense debates within the WhK, including severe criticism of Hirschfeld himself, leading to his resignation as a result. In 1933, Adolf Hitler's rise to power brought the ban of the WhK, as well as the apprehension of some members and the forced closure of the Institute for Sexual Research. Hirschfeld was outside Germany at the time, thus escaping certain death, but he had faced the wrath of Nazis and others throughout the 1920s. In Munich on October 4, 1920, he was beaten up and seriously hurt by a crowd armed with stones; in covering the story, the nationalist press regretted that he was not killed. In another incident two years later in 1922, a young man shot at him during a conference in Vienna. By 1929, Hirschfeld found it impossible to go out in public; the Nazis saw him as a typical agent of the Weimar Republic, and were relentless in their persecution of him. Taking refuge in France, he tried, without success, to re-start his Institute. Exhausted, he died in Nice in 1935.

As a pioneer of gay rights, Hirschfeld's notoriety resulted in countless affronts and personal insults. His love for publicity, as well as his sympathetic, medical-based opinions about homosexuals (who were usually treated as sick or as victims), made him subject to criticism. Claiming to be apolitical, he sometime lacked sound judgment, at times enjoining gays to vote for left-wing parties while also calling on right-wing parties that he hoped (unreasonably) would join his cause. However, one must place his actions and theories in the context of the period: confronted by hostile forces, in relative isolation—at its height, the WhK counted only 500 members—Magnus Hirschfeld was a gay activist ahead of his time, whose courage offered hope to thousands of gays, helping to make homosexuality a subject that one could then openly discuss on both a scientific and humanist basis.

—*Florence Tamagne*

Herzer, Manfred. *Magnus Hirschfeld, Leben und Werk eines*

jüdischen, schwulen und sozialistischen Sexologen. Frankfurt/
New York: Campus, 1992.

Wolff, Charlotte. *Magnus Hirschfeld: A Portrait of a Pioneer in
Sexology.* London: Quartet, 1986.

—Associations; Cinema; Deportation; Eulenburg Affair,
the; Far Right, the; Fascism; Germany; Himmler, Heinrich;
Scandal; Violence.

HISTORY

Until recently, homosexuality was not considered a legitimate subject for historians. Several factors contributed to this: for one, the preeminence of politics did not
predispose historians to be interested in behaviors that
were considered private and personal (at most, there was
mention of the "**unnatural** interests"—whether real or
imagined—of certain persons); on the other hand, academics were expected to share the general public's abhorrence of it (as Maurice Sartre said, "Whoever risked
taking too much interest in the issue could be suspected
of sympathies for it"). Such sentiment touches on the
historian's limited freedom: since the reform of Prussian
universities at the beginning of the nineteenth century, the Western university system was liberal in theory,
based on disinterested (affectively detached) research of
"truth," but all truth is not necessarily good to discover,
and academic discourse was seriously restrained, in any
given era, by what British philosopher John Stuart Mill
in 1859 called "the moral coercion of public opinion."
In any case, it must be stressed that between 1880 and
1960, historians discussed homosexuality in much the
same way as society had: as a defect going back to pre-
Christian Antiquity (such was the opinion of Henri-
Irénée Marrou and with him a number of Catholic
historians), as well as an aberration of religious, military,
or royal communities. Homosexuals were considered
weaklings (as exemplified by Edward II, James I, and
Philippe of Orléans), licentious, perverted, head cases,
or degenerates (biographers often joyfully connected
the subject to **pedophilia**, to complete at terarology,
whether it be Nero, Gilles de Rais, or Ernst Röhm). It
was said that when a particular personality was believed
to be gay or exonerated of the aberration, he was either "blackened" or "cleared" (thus the endless debates,
some continuing to this day, on the sexual preferences
of Julius Caesar, **Henri III**, Frédéric the Prussian, and
Adolf Hitler, to give some examples). It is clear that
references to "unnatural behavior" have been common
in homophobic **rhetoric** for centuries. We shouldn't
be surprised that evidence of homosexuality among
Prussian officers provoked French and British historians to issue salvos of wild ethno-psychology, which
were less objective science than exacerbated nationalism
during the course of the two World Wars. It is also important to note that the "Pederasty" chapter on Henri-
Irénée Marrou's famous *Histoire de l'éducation dans
l'Antiquité (History of Education in Antiquity)*, published in
1948, overflowed with hyperbole (featuring references
to "unnatural sexual relations," "**abnormal** acts," "villainous crimes," "absurdity and folly," "monstrous aberrations," and the "ravages of deviated sexual instinct").
One of the results of this common historical view of
homosexuality was the near-total silence—for more
than fifty years—on the subject of homophobic crimes
committed by the Nazis: given that homosexuals were
considered monsters in the eyes of most people (including historians), they were not conferred the status of
victims, despite their horrific treatment at the hands of
the Third Reich.

The sociology of the university played a role here, at
least in France: a large number of French historians who
taught during the postwar years had often been shaped
by **communism** or Christian democracy, which contributed to their disinterest in issues related to sexuality. Evidence of their persistent narrow-mindedness is
not lacking: in the 1950s and 60s, the poor reputation
accorded to French anarchist Daniel Guérin is much
more due to his homosexuality than to his leftist politics. Additionally, the exceptional historian Georges
Dumézil could not admit his homosexuality until near
the end of his life, in 1986. Examples of French historians contemptuous indifference include François
Bluche's derisive article on the "ultra mundane **vice**"
in the *Dictionnaire du Grand Siècle* (1990), and the con-
flation of homosexuality and pedophilia by Emmanuel
Le Roy Ladurie in justifying his hostility to the **PaCS**
(Pacte civil de solidarité; Civil solidarity pact) in *Le
Figaro* (October 19, 1998). The timidity of historians to
deal adequately with the issue of homosexuality gave
a platform to pseudo-historians and scandal mongers,
such as gay diplomat and writer Roger Peyrefitte; their
personal, historical chronicles with homosexual un-
dertones were principally disinterested in the historicity of their work; as a result, they were mediocre, and
then reinforced the idea that homosexuality was not a
serious or respectable topic for historical discussion.

It is in the field of ancient history, notably Greek history, that the taboo of studying homosexuality was first removed, but at the expense of a strictly homophobic exegesis. At the end of the nineteenth century, historians found it very difficult to pretend that Greek or Roman homosexuality had not existed: their positivist approach rested on reading original texts from the period, which exposed students to at times shocking passages (let us think of the works of Plato, Xenophon, Euripides, Plutarch, Cassius Dio, Virgil, Catullus, Suetonius, and the *Histoire Auguste*). Ancient history courses were thus, for a long time, the only places in society where non-medical discussion of homosexuality took place, and where homosexuality was presented as a social phenomenon (certainly, still aberrant, but on the other hand characteristic of a prestigious civilization). This discourse, however, was in fact as tortured as it was restricted: students were told (as E. M. Forster recalled of his years at Cambridge) that ancient Greek behaviors were "unspeakable," which prevented further discussion, or it was affirmed that Greek love was in fact not sexual, which had the double advantage of morally salvaging classical humanities and preventing contemporary homosexuals from claiming an ancient model. Without going as far as to lie, Marrou revealed the same kind of pedagogical trouble in the 1950s and 60s by exaggerating the spiritual dimension of Greek love, linking its physical manifestation to the "weakness of the flesh" in a very Christian way.

Under such biases, the historic reinterpretation of the issue of homosexuality was slow and extremely difficult. It started in British circles at the end of the nineteenth century, doubtless due to the importance of burgeoning gay subculture in large British universities. It is significant that the first modern historian to be interested in homosexuality was an Oxford professor, John Addington Symonds, who wrote *A Problem in Greek Ethics* in 1873 and published it in 1883: one of the first essays to defend homosexuality in the English language, Symonds stated that it was at the heart of Greek morality; further, that its warlike nature disputed Victorian views that it was effeminate, and that it was a healthy moral component that refuted claims that it was an illness. Nevertheless, censorship of such views was common: due to his poor reputation, Symonds was not elected to Oxford's poetry chair, and he published only ten copies of his essay in 1883; it was included in Havelock Ellis's book *Sexual Inversion*, published in 1897, but Symonds' dependents (Symonds had died in

1893) bought the entire print run to make it disappear, then demanded that Symonds' name be removed from the second edition of Ellis's book. After such a difficult birth, homosexual historiography was rare (Oxford and Cambridge did not become centers for gay studies again until after 1970). There were a few historical (essentially biographical) research projects on 1897–1933 Germany, given the role of Magnus Hirschfeld and his Scientific-Humanitarian Committee (which he established in 1897), but nothing had any legitimate scientific ambition, and in the end twentieth-century homosexual culture was documented less by history than by **literature**.

From the 1970s onward in Europe and North America, the situation changed due to many factors. The introduction of a politicized gay movement, various changes to the law, and the fact that the medical community no longer considered homosexuality an illness all contributed to removing academic prejudices against the subject and forcing historians to reflect on it from a new perspective. As a result of the growing interest in social history, particularly the history of women, the issues of sexuality and gender became more legitimate, as did the study of private lives, or what was called "the extraordinary lives of ordinary people" (micro-history based on studies of individual cases, a phenomenon which resulted in first-class works on the history of homosexuality which could serve as models for other sectors of historical research). In the United States in the 1960s and 70s, a renewed interest in the history of slavery provided analytical tools with which to better understand the resilience and resistance of a community subjected to legal, social, and psychological oppression. Everywhere, **anthropological** literature outlined the relatively common occurrence of homosexual rites in traditional societies (it was said that French academics' positive reception of the serious work of Bernard Sergent—1984's *L'Homosexualité dans la mythologie grecque* (*Homosexuality in Greek Myth*) and 1986's *L'Homosexualité initiatique dans l'Europe ancienne* (Initiatory homosexuality in ancient Europe)—was in part because Sergent "ritualized" Greek homosexuality, and in so doing, set it apart from contemporary concepts of it as hedonist). More and more historians stressed that homosexuality as studied could not be reduced to private behavior but had to be interpreted as a collective phenomenon, thus identifying a specific sociality that is always evolving. From this perspective, the investigative terrain of homosexuality is based on its long repression—religious, social, and legal—the heights of which may arguably have been attained by the Stalinist Soviet Union and Nazi Germany. But the history of homosexuality cannot be limited to this repression, as there have been positive experiences as well, particularly during the period between 1890 and the 1930s (e.g., the Weimar Republic). Furthermore, one ultimately discovers that each historical period constructed and reconstructed its own sexual identities and social roles, and also had its own concepts of what was lawful and unlawful; as a result, the main threat that the historian must watch out for is essentialist anachronism.

However, these indisputable advances, which allow for new perspectives on the entire history of sexuality, are poorly received at times by the historian establishment, particularly as a result of historians on the subject who are homosexual themselves and increasingly unwilling to hide their orientation. This provided a lazy defense for those embarrassed or made to feel guilty by these radically new studies: their authors were considered more militants than historians, or their research methods were considered unsound. The reproach is sometimes warranted, as in the case of John Boswell's 1980 book *Christianity, Social Tolerance, and Homosexuality*, which was tainted by a certain number of methodology errors; one must note, however, that the most severe criticisms against Boswell were leveled by gay historians, offering evidence that gay academics, whether their enemies like it or not, do not act in tandem with one another. On the other hand, the debate that surrounded this book was useful to help clarify the differences between "essentialists" (e.g., Boswell) and "social **constructionists**" (e.g., Michel Foucault). Conservative historians (the adjective having nothing to do with their political choices, given that some are actually socialist), at the same time, continued to expose their homophobic prejudices by repeatedly denouncing gay historians as pseudo-militants (or accusing gay and lesbian studies of excessive political correctness) and refusing to acknowledge the concept of "minority politics." In any event, it is difficult to reproach homosexuals for their interest in the history of their peers; as gay historian George Chauncey commented that if the hunger for historic knowledge is so strong among gays, it is because homosexuality's history has been negated for a long time. That is, it was not in school curriculums and it could not benefit from any oral transmission within the family, unlike what could happen in other marginal groups. In other words, if heterosexual historians who were, in theory,

"unprejudiced" had been interested in the topic or had done better research, gay historians wouldn't have had to do all the work. Finally, it is important to note that gay and lesbian studies are not by definition militant: social constructionists, by identifying the diachronic variability of sexual categories and by refusing to include great figures from the Middle Ages and Renaissance in the all-encompassing and stable category of a homosexual *sub specie aeternitatis*, contradicted a great number of gay militants who were anxious to include personalities like Richard the Lionheart and Michelangelo under their banner, and who are fearful that the "social constructionist" approach dominating current academic trends only serves to strengthen the Christian-based belief in conversion (reparative) therapy for homosexuals.

In any event, it is clear that the most important recent research on the history of homosexuals has been conducted in Britain and the United States (by, among many others, Allan Bérubé, George Chauncey, Madeline Davis, David Halperin, Jonathan Katz, Elizabeth Kennedy, Esther Newton, Eve Kosofsky Sedgwick, and Jeffrey Weeks). In particular, the power and wealth of the gay movement in the US has allowed for a comprehensive system of research tools, including oral, the establishment of historical centers and archives (e.g., the Lesbian Herstory Archives in New York and the LGBT Historical Society in San Francisco) and the publication of important books and documents (e.g., Jonathan Ned Katz's 1992 book *Gay American History* and the 1978 publication of the *Buffalo Women's Oral History Project* and the *San Francisco Lesbian and Gay History Project*). In the same way, under the influence of Foucault, the work of American historians on the subject of homosexuality is generally more sophisticated than elsewhere (and includes discussions on the definition of sexual activity, the vocabulary of identities, the sexual meaning of gender or cross-dressing, or class differences that cross into sexuality). Additionally, there are now gay caucuses present in almost all of the large American academic associations (such as historians, art historians, sociologists, and anthropologists) which encouraged the development of new study topics and scientific questions. In France, Florence Tamagne wrote the excellent *Histoire de l'homosexualité en Europe: Berlin, Londres, Paris, 1919–1939* (*The History of Homosexuality in Europe in the Inter-War Period: Berlin, London, Paris, 1919–1939*), but the fact remains that the best study on homosexuality in nineteenth-century France was published in Britain (*Homosexuality in Modern France,* published in 1996 under the direction of Jeffrey Merrick and Bryant T. Ragan Jr). Further, it is also revealing that the first in-depth work written on the history of the French gay and lesbian movement *Le Rose et le noir* was by a journalist and not a scholar in the strict sense. This being said, Chauncey has noted that even in the so-called "liberated" United States of the 1980s and 90s, numerous young historians decided not to make homosexuality the main topic of their study for fear of compromising their professional future. In the US and elsewhere, it remains easy for academic authorities, under the guise of scholarly study, to overlook openly gay historians for new positions, especially when candidates are numerous and almost of equal quality, which is often the case.

—*Pierre Albertini*

Bluche, François. "Relativité du vice ultramontain." In *Dictionnaire du Grand Siècle*. Edited by François Bluche. Paris: Fayard, 1990.

Boswell, John. "Revolutions, Universals, and Sexual Categories." In *Hidden from History: Reclaiming the Gay and Lesbian Past*. Edited by George Chauncey, Martin Duberman, and Martha Vicinus. New York: Penguin Books, 1990.

Celse, Michel, and Pierre Zaoui. "Négation, dénégation: la question des 'triangles roses'." In *Conscience de la Shoah, critique des discours et des représentations*. Edited by Philippe Mesnard. Paris: Kimé, 2000.

Chauncey, George, Martin Duberman, and Martha Vicinus. *Hidden from History: Reclaiming the Gay and Lesbian Past*. New York: Penguin Books, 1990.

Dowling, Linda. *Hellenism and Homosexuality in Victorian Oxford*. Ithaca, NY/London: Cornell Univ. Press, 1994.

Eribon, Didier. "Georges Dumézil, un homosexuel au XXe siècle," *Ex aequo*, no. 4 (1997).

———. *Michel Foucault*. Paris: Flammarion, 1989. [Published in the US as *Michel Foucault*. Cambridge, MA: Harvard Univ. Press, 1991.]

———. *Réflexions sur la question gay*. Paris: Fayard, 1999.

———. "Traverser les frontières." In *Les Etudes gay et lesbiennes*. Paris: Ed. du Centre Georges-Pompidou, 1998.

Fassin, Eric. "Politiques de l'histoire: *Gay New York* et l'historiographie homosexuelle aux Etats-Unis," *Actes de la recherche en sciences sociales*, no. 125 (1998).

Foucault, Michel. *Histoire de la sexualité*. Vol. 3. Paris: Gallimard, 1976–84. [Published in the US as *The History of Sexuality*. New York: Vintage Books, 1985.]

Guérin, Daniel. *Autobiographie de jeunesse*. Paris: Belfond, 1972.

Halperin, David. "Comment faire l'histoire de l'homosexualité masculine," *Revue européenne d'histoire sociale*, no. 3 (2002).

Katz, Jonathan Ned. *L'Invention de l'hétérosexualité* [1995]. Paris: EPEL, 2001. [Published in the US as *The Invention of Heterosexuality*. New York: Dutton, 1995.]

Kennedy, Elizabeth, and Madeline Davis. *Boots of Leather, Slippers of Gold: The History of a Lesbian Community*. New York: Routledge, 1993.

Marcus, Sharon. "Quelques Problèmes de l'histoire lesbienne." In *Les Etudes gay et lesbiennes*. Edited by Didier Eribon. Paris: Ed. du Centre Georges-Pompidou, 1998.

Marrou, Henri-Irénée. *Histoire de l'éducation dans l'Antiquité*. Paris: Le Seuil, 1948. [Published in the US as *A History of Education in Antiquity*. Madison, WI: Univ. of Wisconsin Press, 1956.]

Rupp, Leila J. "History." In *Lesbian Histories and Cultures*. Edited by Bonnie Zimmerman. London/New York: Garland, 2000.

Sartre, Maurice. "Les Amours grecques: le rite et le plaisir." In *L'Histoire, enquête sur un tabou: les homosexuels en Occident*. Paris, 1998.

Tamagne, Florence. *Histoire de l'homosexualité en Europe, Berlin, Londres, Paris, 1919–1939*. Paris: Le Seuil, 2000. [Published in the US as *A History of Homosexuality in Europe: Berlin, London, Paris, 1919–1939*. New York: Algora, 2004.]

———. "Homosexualités, le difficile passage de l'analyse des discours à l'étude des pratiques," *Revue européenne d'histoire sociale*, no. 3 (2002).

Tin, Louis-Georges, ed. *Homosexualités: expression/répression*. Paris: Stock, 2000.

—*Anthropology; Censorship; Essentialism/Constructionism; Greece, Ancient; Literature; Philosophy; School; Sociology.*

HOOVER, J. Edgar

J. Edgar Hoover (1895–1972) is one of the most enigmatic figures in the history of homosexuality and homophobia. As Director of the FBI for forty-eight years, he initiated the monitoring of gay organizations across the country in a relentless attempt to control their activities. Hoover and his Associate Director, Clyde Tolson, were proponents of **McCarthyist** tactics, and instrumental in helping to construct the concept of homosexuals as "an internal enemy" of the American machine. All the while, Hoover and Tolson were lovers for over forty years. If the evidence brought forward in Anthony Summers' 1993 book *Official and Confidential: The Secret Life of J. Edgar Hoover* leaves no doubt as to Hoover's sexual orientation, and despite reservations one might have with certain testimony, it remains nevertheless difficult to understand his paradoxical, hypocritical attitude. Even more, the exposure of Hoover's homosexuality by the American left was itself not exempt from accusations of homophobia, demonstrating the limits of its "sympathy" toward gay and lesbian issues.

There are a number of hypotheses that help to explain the paradox of Hoover's life; the most popular one establishes Hoover as a symbol of internalized homophobia, **self-hatred** that was manifested in his FBI directives against the first gay movements of the 1950s. Nevertheless, the exclusive and apparently harmonious relationship that he seems to have enjoyed with Tolson for four decades makes this hypothesis highly unlikely. One must then consider Hoover as a man of his generation, a senior member of the public service held to the important duty of social respectability. Moreover, his actions against homosexuals and particularly against the very first gay organizations must be viewed in light of other issues. Hoover's authorized harassment was equally directed against members of the American Communist Party and Henry Wallace's Progressive Party, as well as anti-segregationist militants. Hoover is most accurately a symbol of the construction of a federal totalitarian intelligence strategy, whereby the central administration attempts to extend its assigned limits by increasing its power and authority at the local level. That Hoover had gay associations targeted is a relatively well-documented fact; but to him, all collective dissident organizations were threats to the very legitimacy of the FBI's existence.

Thus, it is possible to hypothesize that Hoover's homosexual life was a purely private and individual issue, essentially based on the values of masculine friendship and fidelity; a personal homosexual experience that was clearly at odds with the approach taken by the early activists (such as Henry Hay, founder of the first Mattachine Society and former member of the Communist Party) to fight for acknowledgment of the collective gay experience (and who were generally regarded as leftist militants, the complete opposite of Hoover). The Hoover paradox then boils down to a generational issue that is relatively common in gay and lesbian history and marked by a process of discontinuity. Hoover could have very well considered that his

stable and "noble" relationship with Tolson had nothing to do with middle or working-class homosexuals, who were not necessarily in relationships nor seeking them, who engaged in interracial sexual relations, and who rubbed shoulders with or admired left-wing Beat Generation artists and addicts. During the 1950s, there was a growing apprehension of homosexuals as a coherent social group. That we, in retrospect, qualify his love life as homosexual is quite possible; however, to assume that this aspect should have influenced Hoover's social status and political convictions is purely anachronistic.
—*Pierre-Olivier de Busscher*

Powers, Richard. *Secrecy and Power: The Life of J. Edgar Hoover.* New York: The Free Press, 1987.

Reeves, Thomas. *The Life and Times of Joe McCarthy.* New York: Stein & Day, 1982.

Summers, Anthony. *Official and Confidential: The Secret Life of J. Edgar Hoover.* New York: G. P. Putnam's Sons, 1993.

—*McCarthy, Joseph; North America; Police; Treason; Violence.*

HUMOR

There is a story of two young seminarians who are cycling around in the seminary's courtyard while shrieking and laughing. Exasperated, the Father Superior opens the window and yells, "Stop shouting like that, or I'll have to put the seats back on your bicycles."

In France, the word *humour* is an Anglicism that first appeared in the eighteenth century, including in Diderot and D'Alembert's *Encyclopédie*. Up until the nineteenth century, the use of the term was generally associated with **England**; Victor Hugo once evoked "this English thing that is called humor." Nevertheless, the French adopted the word and used it to describe "a certain lively French wit," as stated in a dictionary of the times (the wit of Rabelais, for example), and even "witty Italian eloquence." Moreover, there exists the German term *witz*, which can be translated as "joke" or "witticism," and which gave way to Freud's interpretation of wit as "anger turned sideways."

The issue of whether humor itself can be "homophobic," as it can be anti-Semitic, is a difficult question. In the reverse of reality in which it operates, the expression of humor or witticism is at times ambiguous, and it is not always easy to definitively say that it is directed against this or that thing. Its nature is polyphonic; in reality, we hear several voices within it, and it would be simplistic to reduce it to a single voice. It is further complicated by the use of humor to taunt or razz someone, particularly when the object of derision is a peer, or even oneself. This is why homophobic humor has its place when it is told by homosexuals, in the same way that Jewish humorists make anti-Semitic jokes. When a particular group develops a specific type of humor about itself, it integrates—in a privileged way—the rejection felt by this group. There is a danger to this, however: in the telling of a "gay joke," whether by a gay person or not, representations may appear confused and warped, well beyond the intention of the one telling it. These representations have in common a psychological change which includes feelings the person himself refuses to admit. That is when homophobia—in the same way as anti-semitism—can play a role: it allows an environment in which one can conceal personal opinion.

One of the main characteristics of humor about homosexuals is that it can function with a simple *mention*. For many, the sole evocation of a gay person, without saying anything about him, is presumed to be hilarious. In many comedy sketches, or even in **songs** from the 1930s to the 1950s, a basic humor tactic consists of implying, during a lull in the dialogue, that one of the characters is gay, as in "Isn't he a little…?" followed by comical expressions and, hopefully, laughter from the audience. The stereotype of the male homosexual, preferably an effeminate **caricature**, has long been a familiar construction within heterosexual society, to the point that the development of sophisticated humor beyond it is not necessary.

According to psychologist George Weinberg (who introduced the first scholarly concept of homophobia in his 1972 book *Society and the Healthy Homosexual*), homophobia is mainly anchored in the fear felt by a heterosexual forced into the same proximity as a gay person. In a way, part of the inventiveness and creativity that is found in homophobic humor could be interpreted as the result of a will to *not think of* a situation that could potentially expose one to this risk.

> One day the amorino said to his mother:
> Why am I not dressed?
> If Baptiste sees me naked,
> my ass is done for.

In this small satirical quatrain about musician Jean-Baptiste Lully written in the seventeenth century, it is easy to see that the small amorino (a cherub) represents the innocent heterosexual threatened with rape by the crazed homosexual.

In an essay entitled "Homophobia Among Men" that appeared in the 1992 anthology *Men's Lives,* Gregory Lehne suggested that homophobia was primarily a masculine essence felt more by men than women. While debatable, this opinion seems to be confirmed when one observes humor whose subject is homosexuality. Such humor is often driven by fear, whether subtly or overtly; this fear may be defined further as the fear of passive penetration. In this way, a man who mocks homosexuals is in fact expressing his fear of losing his active sexual role, which is equated with a negation of his virility, a negation of himself. It is not so much the man who is having sexual relations with another man that is mocked in homophobic humor; it is he who assumes the passive role. For homophobes, what is most unthinkable about this *toevah* (abomination) that is described in the **Bible** is that this passive role could be a voluntary choice. Just as with the ritual sodomy of the enemy during Antiquity, the essential function of homophobic humor is to place an individual who is thought of as radically "other" in a position of being sodomized. Two situations can then result: either the individual is sodomized against his will under circumstances that can be more or less ludicrous (as is the case in the joke about Lully), or he presents signs of a comical will to be sodomized (as in the joke of the slow driver who, after the man in the car behind him yells, "Hey, move it or you'll get it in the rear," responds, "Promises, always promises").

In any case, being penetrated represents the most inconceivable situation for a heterosexual man, and one that can take on the most radical social or political significance. After all, one is always buggered by the unmentionable, the inhuman. For example, during the 2002 presidential campaign in France, an anti-National Front slogan read: "Now is not the time to move backward; the National Front is erect."

The image of the man with an "open ass" (which is the name of the Riprocte character in a comedy by Aristophanes) is common in Greek and Latin antiquity. Jokes in which this "open ass" is subject to all kinds of trials and tribulations are peppered throughout the works of Catullus and Martial as well as in Petronius's *Satyricon*. This humor, linked to male feminization and passivity, is an example of its scatological potential, which remains common to this day; when the premise is centered on male penetration, references to excrement are also prevalent. This leads to all kinds of suggestive situations and wordplays. A high percentage of jokes about gays are filthy in tone, producing ignominious images of sexuality, particularly anal, oral, or masturbatory. An example: the story of "the gay who worked at the sperm bank; he was let go because he was drinking on the job." Gay male jokes are, therefore, premised on a large inventory of potential situations, including mocked sexuality. This is equally valid, although less common, in humor that implicates lesbians. When the joke is not centered on the comical masculinization of the woman, or on related wordplays, it is centered on the premise of a strange, awkward sexuality that by nature is inferior to "real" coitus: "What do you call a lesbian with very thick fingers? Well-endowed."

Another obsessive fear rears its ugly head in gay jokes: that of **sterility** and the futile (i.e. non-procreative) spending of sexual energy, which homophobes see as typical of gay sexuality. In the traditional, heteronormative model of sexuality, homosexuals are viewed as outsiders, and as a result, are often caricatured and ridiculed as unrestrained, greedy, and non-reproductive. The "penalty" that is represented by the impossibility of homosexuals to have natural children thus offers this least funny form of humor: the tradition of mocking the "defectiveness" of others—for example, the short person, the humpback, the cross-eyed man—which is related to what Freud called the *Schadenfreude,* or "the pleasure derived from someone else's misfortune." An example: "What is the height of optimism? Two gays buying a baby carriage." This joke is without a doubt authentically homophobic in that the "humor" consists of pinpointing a defect in others which at the same time reveals the joker's apparent superiority. However, the reassurance provided by the inability of homosexuals to produce children is nonetheless insufficient to dissipate the fear of their propagation; as French writer Tristan Bernard said, "Even if they do not reproduce, we see more and more of them every year."

Generally, heterosexual humor that makes fun of gays—in the same way as humor that targets a racial minority—is a means to define an **otherness** that allows one, *a contrario*, to construct an identity. The homosexual *is not me,* the Jew *is not me.* This otherness refers to individuals whom we wish to be rid of or at least toward whom we feel only indifference. This

mechanism is benign on the surface, but can reveal itself to be pernicious, inserting itself into everyday language, to the point that offenders become unconscious of it over time. The universe of the male homosexual is associated with everything that is feared by "real men" in modern society: inadequacy in sexual fulfillment, lack of physical strength and vigor. In short, all that makes a man "not a man." An example: while serving a wine with a high alcohol content, a waiter might say, "It's a strong one, not the type of wine you'd serve at Gay Pride," without knowing the humor is homophobic.

Today, it seems that humor aimed at gays is changing. The classical representations of the feminized homosexual caricature ("the queen"), as well as the smutty gay jokes, seem less frequent than they were in the last decades, at least in Western society. The visibility of the gay community and its relative importance in contemporary culture are paving the way for a more refined humor that is made up less by sexual ignorance than by domestic clichés. Rather than the brutal, explicit jokes that make up the classic arsenal of gay-targeted humor, now we get: "How can you tell that your burglars were gay? All that had value is gone, and all that is left was tastefully rearranged."

Finally, homophobia itself has become a source for humor, which is based on non-mean-spirited situations about sexual differences rather than negative, satirical representations of sexual otherness. This kind of humor allows the audience on one hand to address its homophobia and on the other to laugh at itself. In the end, what if humor were the best therapy for homophobia?
—*Gilles Siouffi*

Blondel, Eric. *Le Risible et le dérisoire*. Paris: Presses universitaires de France, 1998.

Freud, Sigmund. *Le Mot d'esprit dans ses rapports avec l'inconscient*. Paris: Gallimard, 1953. [Published in the US as *Wit and Its Relation to the Unconscious*. New York: Moffat, Yard & Co., 1916.]

Flowers, Charles. *Out, Loud and Laughing: A Collection of Gay and Lesbian Humor*. New York: Anchor Books, 1995.

Labonte, Richard. *Tickled Pink: Lesbian and Gay Humor Fiction*. Boston: Alyson Publications, 1994.

Martin, Thierry. *Brèves gay de comptoir*. Paris: Montblanc, H & O Editions, 2000.

Minois, Georges. *Histoire du rire et de la dérision*. Paris: Fayard, 2000.

Sisser, Pierre. *Amour et humour gay*. Paris: Ramsay, 1995.

—*Caricature; Gender Differences; Insult; Literature; Rhetoric; Song; Violence; Vocabulary.*

I

IMPRISONMENT. *See* Prison

INDIA, PAKISTAN, BANGLADESH

In the Indian subcontinent, all sexual minorities—homosexuals, bisexuals, transgenders, *kothis* ("feminine men"), and *hijras* (considered members of the "third sex")—have been (and are still) subjected to social, cultural, religious, and political oppression because of who they are and their sexuality. Homophobia is very present in the region, even if it takes on different forms than its usual manifestation in the West. In the past, homosexual relations were tolerated or condemned depending on the situation, but in Indian society overall, at least until recently, homophobia has been as discreet as homosexuality.

According to Hindu philosophy, the world in which we live is but one of many universes existing in time and space. Nothing is absolute or permanent, except for the divine yet completely unfathomable principle *brahman*, which is the source of everything. Everyone lives many lives, passing from one to the next, which allows for many kinds of changes (e.g., gender, orientation, or identity); in this concept, the life one has lived determines what is to follow. Gender is not constant and is never an absolute part of an individual's identity because, like the body, it is simply an envelope covering the soul, which has neither gender nor sex. Thus, it is no surprise in Hindu mythology to find stories that evince a kind of sexual ambivalence, even if the dynamic is expressed in heterosexual terms. Sexual ambiguity and the fluidity of genders is a key part of this mythology.

The literary works of Ancient India often describe men with prostitute boys in non-pejorative terms, and whose roles in the daily life at court were perfectly normal. The *Kama Sutra* has an entire chapter on *auparashtika* (oral sex), in which the masters enjoy the fellatio performed by their male servants. The *Rajatarangini* (river of kings), the chronicles of the kings of Kashmir, describe the licentious mores of King Kshemagupta; in another historical text, the Tamil epic poem *Silappatikaram* (the jeweled anklet), a king of the Ganges plains pays tribute to a king of the Chera dynasty by giving him many gifts, including "a thousand *kanjuka* [boy prostitutes], with long flowing hair." Erotic drawings of women embracing can be found carved in relief on temple walls, as well as in miniature on paintings. According to ancient architectural treatises, a temple is not complete unless it has representations of erotic figures, because sensual pleasure (*kama*) is as important as earthly duties (*dharma*) and spiritual goals (*moksha*). In the *Valmiki Ramayana*, one of many mythological texts, the *rakshasa* women of King Ravana's harem make love together, and in the *Padma purana*, the king's two wives engage in sexual relations in order to give birth to a child after the monarch's death.

However, while philosophy might have recognized the essential diversity of things, society imposed an absolute submission to the sacred responsibilities (also *dharma*), the first responsibility of a man at the head of a Hindu **family** being to make children in order to perpetuate the cycle of life and to pay off the debt contracted at birth. Procreation was so important that the ancient legal texts (the *Dharmasastras*) specified severe punishments for men who did not fulfill this responsibility (castrated, impotent, or homosexual men were all grouped together under a generic term, *kliba*). Hence, the real question for Hindu gays and lesbians was **marriage.** Homosexuality could be ignored so long as it did not interfere with heterosexual marriage, which allowed one to procreate and thus fulfill one's *dharma*. Homosexuality, meanwhile, risked leading one to **debauchery** and **sterility.**

In the *Manusmriti*, which contains all the rules of conduct according to orthodox Brahmanism, a *kliba* is excluded from inheritance, sacrifices, and rituals. Sexual relations between men are forbidden, along with the following: wounding a priest, "inhaling liquors or other products that should not be consumed," incest, bestiality, anal and oral intercourse between men and women, sexual relations taking place in a cart drawn by a cow, sexual relations with a menstruating woman, and sexual relations during the day. Some of the punishments included bathing fully clothed, fasting, purification (by eating five products of the cow: its urine, dung, milk, curdled milk, and butter), and social ostracism through loss of caste. The *Manusmriti* also prescribes chastisement for women who have sexual relations with other women. If a young girl seduces and sleeps with another, she must pay a fine of 200 *panas*, plus double what the father of the "victim" would receive from the family of a future husband, as well as endure ten lashes of the whip. But if the perpetrator is a mature woman, the chastisement is even more severe. Her head is immediately shaven, two fingers are cut off, and she is made to ride across town on a donkey. The punishment of lesbians was thus manifestly more severe than that reserved for male homosexuals.

The *Narada purana* states that any transgression of the rules of caste, such as the spilling of semen outside of the vagina, will lead a man to *Reto-bhojana*, one of the many lower regions of the Hindu universe, where he must subsist by consuming semen, after which he will fall into *Vasakupa*, a deep, narrow, and greasy well where he must live for seven years, before being reborn as a lower life form. In the *Arthashastra*, an ancient secular text, a category exists called *ayoni* (non-vaginal sexual relations, with men or women), which are only lightly punished. In this case, relations between men are sanctioned against by heavier fines than those involving women. However, overall, homosexuality appears to be a minor offense. Thus, in the *Manusmriti* as well as the *Arthashastra*, certain homosexual offenses are less severely punished than some heterosexual ones, such as adultery with a person of a different caste.

Whatever the case, all of the ancient texts which describe sexual categories assigned a greater value to heterosexual relations than homosexual ones (which are often denigrated), insisted on the subordination of women to men, and, of course, justified the caste system. The texts also make reference to those who were effeminate, impotent, or otherwise inadequate. In short, this philosophy accepted and favored gender diversity, yet Indian society was founded on a strict masculine/feminine dichotomy, forcing people who did not conform to live on the fringes, or to conform in some small way to the heterosexual norms. Nonetheless, there were apparently no violent persecutions of homosexuals during these ancient times, and even fewer executions, unlike the Western world.

With the introduction of the Persian, Turkish, and Arabic cultures in the tenth century CE, the phenomenon of urbanization culminated in a concentration of the elite in the cities of the Indian subcontinent. The cosmopolitan flavor of these Muslim centers fostered homoerotic attitudes that became apparent in medieval stories, presented without any pejorative commentary. The booming cities and numerous markets created a culture of the bazaar, founded on interactions between men of all classes, castes, and communities. Men would also congregate in taverns, houses of entertainment, and brothels. Dargah Quli Khan's description of Delhi indicates that the tombs of Islamic saints were a favorite meeting place for men attracted by homoerotic relations.

Many consider the Qur'an's condemnation of homosexual relations to be without appeal; its condemnation is connected to the Hebrew peoples, Lot, and the destruction of **Sodom and Gomorrah**. At least eight passages explicitly condemn the sin of Lot's people. *Sharia*, the Islamic law based on the *ahadith* (traditions) and on the words of the prophet Muhammad, also condemns homosexuality. It is said that the Prophet declared that any man who has anal relations with a woman, man, or child will appear on the Last Day, stinking like a corpse; God would then nullify the man's good deeds on earth, and he would perish in the flames of hell. Al-Nuwayri, who compiled the *ahadith*, suggested that both the active and passive partners engaged in homosexual relations be stoned. He recounted, too, that the first caliph, Abu Bakr, had a sodomite buried head-down under the debris of a wall, as punishment for his crimes. Others advocated setting those condemned on fire or throwing them from the top of a minaret. However, the Hanafi school, which tended to be the dominant school of thought in India, was much less severe in the condemnations it pronounced on homosexuality. Besides, it was often difficult to establish one's guilt, as according to the *sharia*, at least four witnesses to the anal penetration in question were required.

During the twelfth century, the idea that the essence of God was unfathomable became prevalent, and that His beauty could only be perceived through the contemplation of His creations, which were the witnesses (*shadid*) to His magnificence. Within this perspective, the Sufis and other mystical poets of Persia often used homoerotic metaphors evoking the beauty of a young boy. This practice was severely condemned by many, most notably the Hanbali theologian Al-Jawzi, who considered this poetic and mystical discourse to be a mix of sodomy and idolatry, and thus doubly sinful.

By the nineteenth century, with the establishment of the British Empire in India, new laws founded on English legislation were introduced. These included the condemnation of fellatio and sodomy in Biblical terms, leaving no room for non-conformist identities or sexual conduct. The colonial government imposed its classification of acts "**against nature**," and the resulting anti-sodomy laws have remained valid to this day, even though English law was abolished in 1967. Section 377 of the Indian penal code stipulates that any person engaging voluntarily in "carnal intercourse against the order of nature" is subject to a punishment of up to ten years in **prison**.

British missionaries and educators in India often denounced the customs of marriage, family, and sexuality that they found to be primitive, permissive for men, and degrading to women. With Victorian morals as reference, they criticized arranged marriages, marriages involving children, the dowry system, polygamy, polyandry, and matrilineal family structures. They condemned the licentiousness of the Hindu gods, the homosexual relations of the Indian kings, and their indifference to the aspirations of their subjects. Indians raised in the Western way would take up the same colonial discourse, affirming that although Indian culture had originally been very close to that of Victorian culture, it had fallen into **decadence** during the Middle Ages. They would hasten to add that homosexuality was foreign to Hindu culture, and thus strongly condemn it, as in the West, then internalize the homophobia that was part of Victorian Puritanism. Monogamous, heterosexual marriage was idealized and presented as the only acceptable type of sexual activity.

In light of this, the British reproached the Muslims for their inclination toward unnatural vices, and accused them of having brought the "abominable **vice**"

into India since the start of their invasions, as early as the tenth century. The Urdu and Persian literary elite responded by working actively to purge the canon of any texts that evoked the "love of boys," which was now thought of as an "ignoble stain sullying their reputation." Some attempted to justify the homoerotic desires described in the *ghazal* (traditional Persian and Urdu lyrical poems) by explaining that, no doubt, the poets had thought the evocation of a woman to be inappropriate for poetry about love. More often, though, the explanation simply said that the poem was really addressed to God.

In reality, Section 377 has, to date, rarely been used in India to punish homosexual relations between consenting adults. Among the thirty-six cases tried since the law's inception, most have concerned matters of rape. However, the **police** use it in conjunction with other laws concerning vagrancy, begging, and indecency, and often to bully or blackmail homosexuals surprised in parks or other public places. The law is also invoked to further condemn defendants accused of rape or murder. As well, the absence of any mention of penetration or the penis has permitted the law to be used to intimidate lesbians, particularly in cases of women who have run away together, or whose relationship has become public.

Police harassment constitutes a large part of modern homophobia in India. It is difficult to estimate the number of cases of extortion that homosexuals are subjected to, given that there are obviously no police records on the topic. The fear of being **outed**, which could be disastrous for some, forces many homosexuals to simply give in to such demands without a fight. As well, the police regularly carry out raids on known gay pick-up spots and make arrests; verbal, physical, and sexual assault are common police practice. Although such treatment exceeds the boundaries of the law, the police can usually count on the support of the state. Further, they rarely target the affluent or the educated, people who would most likely be able to defend their rights; instead, they focus on people of modest means, unable to oppose authorities and even less able to make their situation public, all of which make them an easy target for police harassment.

Given their visibility, *hijras* and *kothis* are faced with a similar situation. The *hijras* form organized communities that include castrated men as well as transsexuals, transvestites, homosexuals, and hermaphrodites. They are often despised, badly treated, and exiled from the mainstream, even though they are supposed to have a recognized place in Indian society, especially at weddings, births, and festivals. Unfortunately, few employment opportunities are available to *hijras*, so many must turn to begging or prostitution. For many homosexuals of the working class, becoming a *hijra* is one of the few options socially open to them. However, the confusion that exists in popular culture between homosexuals and *hijras* is an unfortunate by-product of social homophobia, which refuses to recognize homosexuality as legitimate. Meanwhile, the *kothis*, who are biological men who adopt feminine identities but without castrating themselves or cross-dressing, suffer less than the *hijras*; however, their feminine mannerisms, highly visible, also make them easy targets for the police.

State-supported police intimidation encourages a culture of silence and intolerance, practiced by many levels and institutions of Indian society. Often, the sexual minorities themselves refuse to acknowledge their own marginalization and oppression, because doing so would increase their feelings of fear and **shame**. Most Indian families prepare their children for heterosexual marriage from the start, and the pressure to marry begins early. Sexuality is not a topic of discussion in public or at home, and the refusal to marry is a serious offense within families, particularly for women who have limited personal and financial autonomy. Often, duress and violence are used in order to force consent. A homosexual relationship can be tolerated, so long as it is disguised as nonsexual and does not get in the way of marriage and procreation. Under these conditions, many homosexuals enter into heterosexual marriages and subsequently go on to lead double lives.

In 1987, the marriage of two women police officers in the Madhya Pradesh Special Armed Force, Leela Namdeo and Urmila Srivastav, rocked public opinion and made newspaper headlines, resulting in both women being immediately fired from the service by reason of "unjustified absences" and "conduct unbecoming a servant of the State." Recently, a new and extremely troubling phenomenon has appeared: joint **suicides** by lesbian couples. Most are women in small towns or villages who declare their mutual commitment, but despair of ever being allowed to openly love each other or live together. In 1996, the film *Fire* caused a huge controversy over its story of a homosexual relationship between two married women within a Hindu family, in an environment filled with traditional symbols. In protest, activists from the right-wing polit-

ical party Shiv Sena invaded theaters showing the film in Mumbai, Delhi, and Calcutta. Moreover, Shiv Sena found many allies within Indian **feminist** groups who also opposed the film, which according to them was guilty of "doing a disservice to the cause of women."

In Indian society, lesbians generally encounter more problems than gay men. With public space being largely masculine, homosexual men can at least find a place, however limited and perilous it may be. But lesbians are in general relegated to the private sphere, the only place where female sexuality (hetero and homo) is allowed to express itself. In addition, defenders of the heterosexual patriarchy are able to control and contain female sexuality through violence and intimidation. In such an environment, there is even less room for a bisexual identity to develop, **biphobia** being as common among homosexuals as it is among heterosexuals. Nonetheless, bisexuals are slowly becoming more visible, but often come out of one **closet** simply to enter another.

More and more homosexual men and women are being subjected to aversion **treatment** and therapy, a sign of the homophobia within India's psychiatric community. Even though patients undergo treatment voluntarily, their "consent" is rarely well-informed. At best, these treatments violate the subject's right to privacy, and at worst are a form of torture. There is also a growing trend in newspaper advice columns, in which unqualified "experts" and various celebrities dispense homophobic counsel to would-be homosexuals. Such advice includes consulting a doctor, resisting desires, or seeking out the company of the opposite sex.

Researchers and scholars have until recently remained noticeably silent on the issue, even in those fields related to Marxism, feminism, and post-colonial studies. However, in order to keep up with Western **media** and so as to not appear too backwards, the English-language press has progressively been covering the Indian gay rights movement more favorably. At the same time, the national-language press tends to be increasingly hostile to anything seemingly related to "Western influences," clearly revealing its homophobic and indeed sex-phobic prejudices. Newspaper articles condemning lesbianism in India, which connect it to Western influence, seem to neglect the fact that lesbian marriages and suicides involve women from the lower classes who do not speak English, and thus have no connection with the said Western phenomenon.

Pakistan, which has had a long common history

with India, also retained Section 377 in its penal code, declaring homosexual relations punishable by a sentence of ten years in prison and corporal punishment that can include as many as 100 lashes of the whip. In Pakistan, since the re-establishment of Islamic law (*sharia*) in 1990, homosexual acts have been punishable by stoning. As in India, the law is rarely invoked, but it makes the blackmail, ransoming, and harassment of homosexuals more likely. Homosexuals arrested are also sometimes raped. *Jamaat-e-Islami*, a right wing Islamic political party, has re-affirmed the illegality of homosexuality, stating that it "will not be accepted, not by the State, not by Islamic society." Obviously, and despite this, homosexuality has not disappeared from Pakistan, but it has been banished to the shadows and silence. Nonetheless, in the northwest region of the country, the Pashto culture permits men to take younger men as lovers, yet without being perceived as homosexual.

Like Pakistan and India, Bangladesh condemns homosexual relations through Section 377, which are punishable from ten years in prison up to a life sentence. Here again, the police invoke the law solely for extorting blackmail and harassment, and homosexual men are sometimes subjected to sexual aggression by the police or by street ruffians, known as *mastaans*. Bangladeshi society as a whole lives in denial of homosexuality, most notably the media, which never mentions the subject. Thus in Pakistan and Bangladesh, as in India, the same law against homosexuality—a legacy of English colonialism—remains in place despite the fact that Britain itself long ago abolished it.
—*Mario D'Penha*

Bakshi, Sandeep. "Soupçon d'un espace alternatif: étude de deux films du cinéma parallèle en Inde," *Inverses* (2002).

Dowsett, Gary. "Men Who Have Sex With Men In Bangladesh," *Pukaar* 27, Naz Foundation International (n.d.).

Fernandez, Bina, ed. *Humjinsi: A Resource Book On Lesbian, Gay and Bisexual Rights in India*. Mumbai: India Centre for Human Rights and Law, 2002.

Humsafar Trust, The. "Looking Into the Next Millennium." Conference report. Mumbai: Humsafar Trust, 2000.

International Lesbian & Gay Association. "World Legal Survey." ILGA, 1999. http://www.ilga.org (accessed April 21, 2008).

Murray, Stefen O., and Will Roscoe, eds. *Islamic Homosexualities: Culture, History and* Literature. New York/ London: New York Univ. Press, 1997.

Nanda, Serena. "Hijiras as neither Man nor Woman." In *The Lesbian and Gay Studies Reader*. Edited by Henry Abelove, Michèle Aina Barale, and David Halperin. New York/ London: Routledge, 1993.

Pattanaik, Devdutt. "Homosexuality in Ancient India," *Debonair* (Anniversary issue, 2001).

———. *The Man Who Was a Woman and Other Queer Tales From Hindu Lore*. New York: Harrington Park Press, 2002.

People's Union for Civil Liberties-Karnataka. *Human Rights Violations Against Sexuality Minorities In India*. Bangalore: PUCL-K, n.d.

Ratti, Rakesh, ed. *A Lotus of Another Color: An Unfolding of the South Asian Gay and Lesbian Experience*. Boston: Alyson Publications, 1993.

Renouard, Michel. *Les Castrats de Bombay*. Quimper, France: Ed. Alain Bargain, 1997.

Vanita, Ruth, and Saleem Kidwai. *Same Sex Love in India: Readings from Literature and History*. Delhi: Macmillan India, 2002.

—*England; Heterosexism; Hinduism; Islam; Lesbophobia; Middle East, the; Police; Psychiatry; Shame; Violence.*

INQUISITION

The original Inquisition refers specifically to the Catholic tribunal established by Pope Innocent III in the twelfth century, necessarily religious both in its origins and its structure, whose purpose was to protect the purity of the doctrine of the faith (in broad terms, it refers to the judgment of heresy by the Roman Catholic Church). This court carried out research (*inquisitio*) detailing various infringements of the faith, and crimes of **heresy** and apostasy through all of Christianity; such acts were punished through what became known as the *auto da fé,* the ritual of public penance of condemned heretics and apostates. Faced with a massive increase in all forms of heresy, Pope Lucius III called together a synod at Verona in 1184, during which he proclaimed a Constitution that assigned bishops to the duty of maintaining the faith. The resulting papal bull known as *Ad abolendam* became the founding text of the first Inquisition, known as the Episcopal Inquisition. As of the thirteenth century, the Medieval Inquisition (or Papal Inquisition) was established as a specific, unique, and universal court to deal with heretics. In the papal bull entitled *Ille humani generis* of February 8, 1232, Pope Gregory IX assigned the Dominican Order to the task of repressing heresy, who were later joined by the Franciscan Order.

On Friday October 13, 1307, Philip IV the Fair, the King of France, as part of a scheme to plunder his rivals, ordered the arrest of approximately 140 members of the Knights Templar, a 200-year-old military order that supposedly answered only to the Pope, thus beginning one of the largest trials of the Middle Ages. The king undertook this after confiding in his Dominican confessor, the Inquisitor General of the Kingdom, Guillaume de Paris, and without first consulting Pope Clement V. Among the main charges against members were the denial of Christ, idolatry, and profanation. The inquisitors interrogated them, often accompanied by torture, about one of the Knights' rituals in particular: one that involved kissing a superior's anus through his uniform, followed by kissing the bare navel, then the mouth. One of the accused revealed the obligation of a fourth kiss, on the penis. Between October 14 and mid-November of 1307, the accused were interrogated about their homosexual practices, given that relations with women were formally prohibited by the order. Of the 140 arrested, seventy-six confessed to having practiced sodomy, and some even added that it was part of the rules which new members had to follow: "… and if any brother should come to him to be bawdy with him, he should submit and endure without repugnance: as he is commanded to do so by the statutes and laws of his order" (excerpt of a letter from Commissioner Odard de Molinier to Philip IV, about the Templars at Beaucaire). One hundred and two members acknowledged that the kiss on the anus was a prelude to sodomy. Pope Clement V, under pressure from Philip IV, issued a papal bull on November 22, 1307, which ordered the arrest and subsequent interrogation and torture of members in England, Castile, Aragon, Sicily, and Italy, as well as the seizure of their property. The goods confiscated were sequestered by Philip IV's men, despite the formal opposition of the Pope. On March 18, 1314, the four leaders of the Knights Templar, including the Grand Master of the Order, Jacques de Molay, were brought to the public square of Notre Dame in Paris. There, de Molay publicly retracted his confession, followed by Guillaume de Charrai. That very evening, both men were sent to be burned at the stake on a small island in the Seine River, between the King's garden and the Augustinian monastery. In total, fifty-nine members were burned at the stake that year, nine in Senlis and a large number in Provence.

Less than two centuries later, in Spain, a new tribunal would carry out the Catholic Church's repressive work against homosexuals. With the signing of the papal bull of November 1, 1478 (*Exigit sincerae devotionis affectus*), Pope Sixtus IV gave life to the Spanish Inquisition. The request had come directly from the Catholic monarchs Ferdinand II of Aragon and Isabella of Castile as a means to maintain Catholic orthodoxy in their kingdoms; this would be the most unique characteristic of this new court, that which brought together papal will with that of Spanish political powers at the highest level. The court was constituted as a council under the name *Consejo de la Suprema y General Inquisition*. It originally had four members, all ecclesiasts, one of whom held the title of Inquisitor General.

It is not known today what pushed Pope Clement VII, by a decree on February 24, 1524, to entrust the repression of sodomy within the Aragon peninsula to the sole tribunal of the Inquisition. The decree made explicit mention of the homosexual habits of the Moorish minority, and of the threat of "putrid contamination of the healthy faithful by these few black sheep." The repression of Aragon homosexuals in Spain began later, under the reign of Philip II (beginning in 1560) and would continue unabated until the end of the seventeenth century.

The Spanish Inquisition made a distinction between "perfect" sodomy (where it involved two males) and "imperfect" sodomy (when it took place within a heterosexual relationship); however, nine cases out of ten concerned homosexual relations. Later, the tribunal's jurisdiction over matters of sodomy grew to also encompass those on ships, which maintained regular connections to the region, as well as those populations on the new continent, which were subject to the tribunal at Cartagena de Indias (Colombia), established in 1610. Between 1560 and 1630, the three Aragon tribunals (in Barcelona, Valencia, and Zaragoza) investigated the majority of those accused, who were most often clergymen or peasants. Other groups were also singled out: sailors, slaves, students, and shepherds. They all shared in common a tendency for social instability and had few local roots. However, this did not prevent a few nobles from finding themselves at the mercy of the court. The Moors, targeted by Pope Clement VII's decree of 1524, only made up a small percentage of those accused (8.2%) between 1560 and 1609 (the date when they would be expelled from the country). The number of foreigners indicted, on the other hand, was significant: Italian sailors from coastal ports, French travelers in Catalonia, Portuguese, and Turks. Homophobic repression and xenophobia were closely linked; this association ensured that the tribunal would have the people's approval, by denouncing those with whom the general public also had issues. A large number of the accused were arrested in the two large cities of Barcelona and Valencia, which were ports of arrival and departure for many commercial ventures and a common ground for misfits, vagabonds, slaves, and servants of all kinds. The suppression of lesbians was also carried out, but a June 1, 1560 decree by the Suprema (the Council of the Inquisition) restricted this accusation to those who, during their liaisons, made use of an instrument. Cases involving women were rare.

The power of the Spanish Inquisition was reinforced under the reign of Charles V (1517–56) and that of his son, Philip II (1556–98), giving the tribunal latitude to proceed with arrests without any consideration of either territorial or juridical limits. This situation was exploited by those in power, whereby those who were perceived as enemies were accused of sodomy and subsequently arrested. The sodomy trial of Pedro Luis Galceran de Borja (of the Borgia family), Grand Master of the Order of Montesa, in 1572 was a perfect example of an attempt at the political elimination of an aristocrat by bitter adversaries. Another trial indicted a very influential person, Philip II's secretary Antonio Perez, who was accused of having ordered the assassination of Juan Escobedo, secretary to the king's half-brother, Don Juan of Austria. Perez fled and took refuge in Aragon; however, another trial was launched against him in absentia, this time accusing him of the multiple crimes of sodomy, **Judaism**, and hostility toward the Spanish Inquisition. (The new sodomy charge was supported by the damning testimony of a young page, Antón de Añón.) The trial set in place a manhunt that was stymied when the fugitive escaped to France. Once again, the crimes of homosexuality and **treason** were invoked together to ruin the reputation of a man who had fallen into disgrace.

The average length of a trial against an accused homosexual was six months and fifteen days, a period that varied based on how quickly the accused admitted to the offense. For de Borja, mentioned above, the interval was several years, and the cost to his wealth was considerable; in fact, the expenses for keeping him detained were paid out of his own pocket. During the entire time, he was kept in a prison cell in a secret location. The trial's procedure, also secret, never allowed him to learn the identity of those who had denounced him and were testifying against him.

Contrary to popular belief, torture was a normal part of the investigation and never used as a punishment. In the perspective of the time, its use allowed the Spanish Inquisition to uncover the "truth" in those cases where there were insufficient witnesses or where the accused denied the charges. One of the most common forms of torture involved the pulley, whereby the subject was suspended by his hands, a weight was tied to his ankles, then he was raised and dropped in heavy jerks; another was the garrote, in which the subject was tied down to a device and a rope placed around his neck which is increasingly tightened (it was also used as a means of execution). An accused who was able to resist torture had a good chance of being freed and his trial suspended.

Those found guilty or who admitted their guilt incurred a punishment of 200 lashes of the whip and would be sentenced to the slave galleys for three to seven years (the average being six years and eight months), followed by an equivalent amount of time in exile. The court would deliver the sentence in a room in the palace of the Spanish Inquisition or as part of an *auto da fé* taking place in a central location in the city. Only those sodomites sentenced to death would appear before an *auto da fé*, a lavish and well-attended public ceremony, the purpose of which was to illustrate the example not to follow. The Holy Office would be there in full, enjoying privileges over the rest of the Church hierarchy as well as civil authorities. The condemned wore the *coroza* on his head, a sort of miter decorated with the flames of hell, as well as the *sambenito*, a yellow tunic painted with St Andrew's cross in red, on which would be written his name and his crime, also surrounded by flames. The death sentence would be assigned to those homosexuals convicted of repeated offenses, which in fact made up a good number of the accused. The capital punishment, known as *relaxe* (because the tribunal relaxed, or relinquished, responsibility for the punishment to the secular arm, the only group permitted to mete out death), would follow about twenty-four hours after the *auto da fé*. The unfortunate individuals would be burned at the stake, which generally took place outside the walls of the city. If the condemned converted or repented, he was often strangled to death by the executioner before being put to flame.

The darkest period of this response to sodomy lasted about two decades, from 1570 to 1590. But the virulence of this repression lessened under the 1621–65 reign of Philip IV and the government of his favorite, the Count-Duke of Olivares, whose priorities seemed to be quite different from those of the Inquisitors. As a result, no homosexual was sentenced to death after 1633. In fact, compared to other European countries, very early on, Spain stopped punishing homosexual acts by death or torture. In Aragon, a few sodomy trials were still carried out, but by the royal court. The punishments were more severe in these cases; for example, following the trial of the Marquis d'Aytona's cooks in Valencia in 1581, a fifteen-year-old convicted of being a "passive sodomite" was "made to sit on a burning grill."

In the New World, royal orders issued on January 25 and February 7, 1569, excluded Natives from being subject to the juridical power of the Spanish Inquisition. Native Americans were thus spared from the tribunals established in Mexico (1568) and Peru (1569), but not in Brazil, where proponents of the Portuguese Inquisition would make regular visits beginning in July of 1591; as a result, about forty trials for sodomy took place. Prior to this, the Dominican theologian Francisco de Vitoria (1480–1546), one of the greatest defenders of the Native cause (along with Bartolomé de las Casas), nevertheless stated that it was the duty of the Spanish to ruthlessly fight against the abominable homosexual habits of the Natives. Their practice of sodomy was rejected by the conquerors in the same way as their cannibalism and rites of human sacrifice. According to de Vitoria, these practices condoned what he considered a just war against the chaos and sin that went against the natural order.

Overall, the Inquisition constituted one of the darkest chapters in the history of homophobia, as well as the Church. However, the myths surrounding the Inquisition are arguably larger than the facts: the number of those burned at the stake was less than many imagine, although the persecution of homosexuals, and the ever-present threat of execution, certainly made life extraordinarily difficult for them.

—*André Fernandez*

Bennassar, Bartolomé. *L'Inquisition espagnole XVe–XIXe siècle.* Paris: Hachette, 1979.

———. *Histoire du Brésil 1500–2000.* Paris: Fayard, 2000.

Burman, Edward. *Supremely Abominable Crimes: The Trial of the Knights Templar.* London: Allison & Busby, 1996.

Carrasco, Raphaël. *Inquisición y Represión sexual en Valencia.* Barcelona: Laertes, 1986.

———. "Le Châtiment de la sodomie sous l'Inquisition (XVIe–XVIIe siècle)," *Mentalités,* no. 3, Paris (1989).

Fernandez, André. *Au nom du sexe: Inquisition et répression sexuelle en Aragon (1560–1700).* Paris: L'Harmattan, 2003.

García Cárcel, Ricardo, and Doris Moreno Martinez. *Inquisicío.* Madrid: Historia critica, 2000.

Mott, Luiz. *Justitia et Misericordia: a Inquisição portuguesa e repressão a nefando pecado de sodomia.* Paris: CIDH, 1990.

Spencer, Colin. *Histoire de l'homosexualité, de l'Antiquité à nos jours.* Paris: Le Pré aux Clercs, 1998. [Published in the US as *Homosexuality in History.* New York: Harcourt Brace, 1995.]

Vainfas, Ronal. "Tropico dos pecados: moral, sexualidad e inquisição no Brasil." In *Dicionário do Brasil Imperial.* Rio de Janeiro: Campus, 1989.

—*Against Nature; Bible, the; Catholic Church, the; Damien, Peter; Debauchery; Heresy; Latin America; Paul (of Tarsus); Sodom and Gomorrah; Spain; Theology; Vice.*

INSULT

Insult is an essential component of the phenomenon of homophobia. Even though the subject is sometimes complex and not easily defined, there have been suggestions that homophobic insults ought to be penalized by the law. French philosopher Didier Eribon's analysis of the power of insult argues strongly in favor of this position.

Insults usually target an individual's abnormality or inferiority, or that of a group of individuals in comparison to others. But more fundamentally, insults play a role in the construction of the identity of the person to whom they are addressed—an identity that is *necessarily* inferior. This occurs whether the insult is explicit or implied, or when even the suggestion of **violence** is perceived as a legitimate threat.

The depth of an insult's effect depends on its recipient's knowledge that he or she can, at any moment, be assigned to a position of inferiority; it is also based on exclusionary values deeply ingrained in everyday language. For gays and lesbians, the experience of this language has the additional consequence of instilling insurmountable feelings of **shame**, fear, and social inferiority.

Through the use of insults, language is a powerful

vehicle for homophobia. But words are not simply occasional tools of aggression. By and large, they translate
and perpetuate the representation of an arbitrary social
hierarchy determined by sexual orientation. Moreover,
this does not only include formulas that are *objectively*
violent ("dirty fag," "rotten dyke"), but also, in a more
global sense, the whole of discourse that elaborates,
justifies, or expresses **discrimination** against homosexuality. This being said, from a theoretical point of
view (to the extent that this concept could be applied
to any number of diverse situations), it becomes possible to realistically consider the possibility of outlawing homophobic insults.

Before doing so, however, one must first be able to
distinguish, on one hand, the critique and scientific
deconstruction of a discourse that elaborates on the
concept of discrimination and, on the other, the law's
potential to criminalize homophobic insults. In effect,
laws in many countries already protect gay and lesbian citizens from discrimination, violence, and hatred;
many of these laws were originated to combat racism,
and "sexual orientation" was later added as a category.
In order for such laws to evolve to further protect gays
and lesbians from homophobic insults, they would
need to specify the prohibition of libel that evinces
a homophobic character, or as it has been defined in
France, "any allegation or imputation of a fact that casts
a slur on or undermines the consideration of a person
to whom it is directed"; as well, any insult of a homophobic nature, that is, "any offensive expression, term
of derision, or invective not at all based in fact."

From this perspective, the law cannot be reasonably
invested with the mission of eradicating homophobic
insult completely. But as a first step in the right direction, it can push for the cessation of one of homophobia's most insidious manifestations, especially by
educating the public that it is not only inappropriate,
but unacceptable. France became a pioneer in this area
in 2004, when the French parliament adopted legislation that criminalized the insulting of homosexuals or
women, punishable by up to one year in prison.
—*Daniel Borrillo and Thomas Formond*

Borrillo, Daniel. *L'Homophobie*. Paris: Presses universitaires
de France, 2000.

———. "L'Homophobie dans le discours des juristes." In
Homosexualités: expression / répression. Edited by Louis-
Georges Tin. Paris: Stock, 2000.

———, and Pierre Lascoumes, eds. *L'Homophobie: comment
la définir, comment la combattre*. Paris: Ed. Prochoix, 1999.

Burn Shawn, Meghan. "Heterosexuals' Use of 'Fag' and
'Queer' to Deride One Another: A Contribution to
Heterosexism and Stigma," *Journal of Homosexuality* 40,
no. 2.

Delor, François. *Homosexualité, ordre symbolique, injure et discrimination: Impasses et destins des expériences érotiques minoritaires dans l'espace social et politique*. Brussels: Labor, 2003.

Douglas, Mary. *De la souillure*. Paris: La Découverte, 1992.
[Published in the UK as *Purity and Danger: An Analysis of
Concepts of Pollution and Taboo*. London, Routledge & K.
Paul, 1966.]

Eribon, Didier. "Ce que l'injure me dit." In *L'Homophobie:
comment la définir, comment la combattre*. Reprinted in
Papiers d'identités. Interventions sur la question gay. Paris:
Fayard, 2000.

———. *Réflexions sur la question gay*. Particularly, "Un
monde d'injures. Paris: Fayard, 1999. [Published in the
US as *Insult and the Making of the Gay Self*. Durham, NC:
Duke Univ. Press, 2004.]

Goffman, Erving. *Stigmate, les usages sociaux des handicaps*.
Paris: Minuit, 1975. [Published in the US as *Stigma: Notes
on the Management of Spoiled Identity*. Englewood Cliffs,
NJ: Prentice-Hall, 1963.]

—*Abnormal; Discrimination; Humor; Rhetoric; School;
Shame; Violence; Vocabulary.*

INVERSION

In the analysis of the social structure of homophobia,
the issue of homosexuality as sexual "inversion"—i.e.
a deviation from the sexual norm, in which gay men
have female characteristics and vice versa—is a complex
subject. The "right" to male effeminacy—the physical
behavior behind the stereotype of the "queen," and
once defined as a pathology by medicine—has been
regularly defended by homosexuals over time, from the
first German movement at the end of the nineteenth
century, to the gay liberation trend of the 1970s, to the
AIDS-related activism of ACT UP in the 1980s. The
quasi-technical term "inversion" was even the title of
one of the first gay magazines in France, during the
inter-war period.

The image of the invert was not a medical "invention" at all, however. Historical works on eighteenth-century France and England clearly show that
the first gay "subcultures" were based in part around

The cover of a novel by Dr J. de Cherveix, *Amour inverti*, published in 1907.

effeminacy and transvestism, almost a century before doctors would begin looking for the morphological, physiological, or psychological characteristics of the opposite sex in homosexual men and women.

The medical theories constructed around the idea of inversion refer to Austro-German psychiatrist Richard von Krafft-Ebing's classifications of homosexuals, gay German sexologist Magnus **Hirschfeld**'s theory of a third sex, and research based on organotherapies and **endocrinology**. All of these have their origins (more or less) in the writing of nineteenth-century lawyer and gay pioneer Karl Heinrich Ulrichs of Germany, the first "militant" for the gay and lesbian cause, who between 1864 and 1879 published a series of essays justifying "Uranian" love (that is, homosexual), with the argument that men in these kinds of relationships possessed "a female psyche in a male body."

But the issue of inversion goes far beyond the role played by medicine in the social construction of homosexuality and homophobia. Over time, changes in the representations of the masculine and feminine genders resulted in many people no longer thinking of and/or perceiving themselves as being completely man or woman, based on their attraction to people of the same sex. Medicine merely provided confirmation (and not without contradictory debate) of this representation which many homosexuals already had of themselves.

However, by presenting this idea as "scientific truth," medicine helped to perpetuate the stereotype of the "queen."
—*Pierre-Olivier de Busscher*

Charcot, Jean-Martin, and Victor Magnan. "Inversion du sens génital et autres perversions sexuelles," *Archives de neurologie,* no. 7,12 (1882).

Kennedy, Hubert. *Ulrichs: The Life and Works of Karl Heinrich Ulrichs, Pioneer of the Modern Gay Movement.* Boston: Alyson Publications, 1988.

Lhomond, Brigitte. "Un, deux, trois sexes: l'homosexualité comme mélange." In *Actes du colloque international Homosexualité et Lesbianisme: mythes, mémoires, historiographies.* Edited by GREH et al. Lille: GayKitschCamp, 1989.

Rosario, Vernon. "Inversion's Histories/History's Inversions: Novelizing Fin-de-Siècle Homosexuality." In *Science and Homosexualities.* New York/London: Routledge, 1997.

Spiess, Camille. *L'Inversion sexuelle.* Paris: L'Athanor/L'En Dehors, 1930.

—*Biology; Caricature; Degeneracy; Endocrinology; Ex-Gay; Fascism; Gender Differences; Genetics; Himmler, Heinrich; Hirschfeld, Magnus; Literature; Medicine; Medicine, Legal; Perversions; Psychiatry; Psychoanalysis; Transphobia; Treatment.*

INVISIBILITY. *See* Closet

IRELAND

On September 10, 1982, a thirty-two-year-old man was killed in a municipal park in the city of Dublin by a group of youths who, on their own admission, were out gay bashing. Several members of the group declared as well that they had beaten up twenty "poofs" in the weeks prior to the murder of Declan Flynn, and that they had hunted down over 150 homosexuals the year before.

During the trial of Flynn's murderers, Anthony Maher, a young eighteen-year-old man, declared, "There were a bunch of us out beating up queers for the past few weeks. But we didn't want to kill Mr Flynn. I thought he was just a gay who was there in the park to meet other gays." This was the strategy of his defense, paradoxical, but it paid off all the same in the end. He also pretended to have believed that Declan

Flynn was a heterosexual, in order to present his action as an error, a misunderstanding, regrettable for all that, because he would, of course, have never killed a heterosexual. On March 8, 1983, six months after the murder of Declan Flynn, the five murderers were brought before Dublin's Central Criminal Court. The judge, Mr Gannon, suspended their sentences. That night, the murderers, their families, and their friends organized a march with torches to celebrate the victory at the very scene of the crime. A few months later, the same judge ordered a sentence of six months in jail for the theft of a purse. With this judgment, the Irish authorities seemed to officially ratify a violent homophobic act. Nevertheless, the government was severely criticized in the aftermath, and the whole process launched the gay pride movement in Ireland, as it revealed the treatment that homosexuals could expect in this country, under the "protection" of justice.

The **decriminalization** of homosexual relations in Ireland did not take place until June 1993. Prior to that date, sexual relations between men constituted a crime punishable by **prison**, though the law did not take into account relations between women. The history of homophobia in Ireland is completely hidden by the history of English colonization, as well as by the close and complexities between the state and the Catholic Church.

The first significant civil law against homosexuality in England appeared in 1533 under Henry VIII. The Buggery Act made sodomy a crime punishable by death, and despite being abrogated and reinstated several times during the years that followed, it was finally reactivated and extended to all British colonies in 1563 by Elizabeth I, the daughter of Henry VIII. The Buggery Act was adopted, often word for word, by the first thirteen colonies of America, and sodomy was thus punishable by death. The fist Irish victim was the Bishop John Atherton who, in an ironic tragedy, after noting that the law did not apply to Ireland organized a "Campaign to save Ireland from sodomy." However, this campaign was so effective that he would pay for it with his own life, himself accused and found guilty of sodomy.

The monastic and penitentiary tradition in Ireland had already influenced the English thinking. Manuals of penance circulated in the puritan Irish Celtic Churches, and their influence was known as far as England, France, and Germany from the early Middle Ages. Every homosexual act was ranked as being more or less sinful, according to its character. The base chastisements were the exclusion from the sacrament, automortification (the youngest being hit by rods by older clerics), and a diet of dry bread and water on holy days, with the main difference between punishments being the duration of their application.

After England's colonization of Ireland, the Church was able to increase its hold on the Irish people. The only choice thereafter was the following: allegiance to the crown or allegiance to the Catholic Church. Catholicism became the only possible expression of Irish autonomy. Over time, Irish nationalism would become more and more closely tied to the teachings of the Irish Catholic Church and, in 1919, canon law became the principal influence on the constitution and the government of the first Irish Republic.

Homosexuality was actively fought within the Irish Republican Army (IRA). During the 1970s and the early 80s, those IRA members imprisoned in the North's H-Blocks literally ostracized those of their comrades who they perceived as homosexuals. To this effect, Brend' McClenaghan recounts: "When I would come down into the 'ablutions' room, the men would back away from the sinks, showers, and urinals, keeping away from me until I left." These homosexual prisoners were forced to leave the "republican" quarters of the prison, in this way losing their status of political prisoner that the members of the IRA could claim. Interestingly, Sinn Fein, the political party with close ties to the IRA, was the first to adopt a policy of equality for gays and lesbians at the end of the 90s.

Several centuries earlier, in his *Summa Theologica*, St Thomas Aquinas, whose ideas still today constitute the foundation of the Catholic Church's position against homosexuality, claimed to have established a rational basis for anti-homosexual prejudice by making the greatest hedonistic crime the sin **against nature**. According to this **philosophy**, reason designates procreation as the unique goal of sexual activity, and this condemnation of homosexuality became the source of all theological discussion on the subject.

The first Irish government in 1919, not content to simply renew this philosophy in harmony with the powerful Catholic Church of the era, decided instead to maintain the English laws against homosexuality, inherited directly from the Buggery Act of 1533. The Labouchere Amendment in 1885, which criminalized "acts of gross indecency between men," was adopted into Irish law, as well as the 1861 Offences Against the

Person Act. These were the same laws used to condemn the Dublin-born Oscar **Wilde** to two years of hard labor. The **police** and the law in Ireland were undoubtedly less brutal than in England, but these laws still set the tone for the lives of Irish homosexuals throughout the twentieth century.

But homophobia also acted through socio-economic **discrimination**, which is still justified today based on the archaisms of canon law. Though modeled after the concept of cohabitating heterosexual couples, gay and lesbian couples could not enjoy the same economic benefits that married couples are legally granted in regards to taxes, insurance, pension, legacy, and mortgage.

In the years leading up to **decriminalization** in 1993, as in many other countries, **AIDS** began to foster homophobic discourse and practices. In Ireland, unlike many other countries, homosexual relations were still illegal, so the implications of AIDS were different. Given that in other countries certain conservatives were trying to propose new homophobic so-called "public health" laws to protect the population from AIDS, why would the Irish government want to abolish the law of 1885?

The fact that the laws of 1861 and 1885 were abrogated in the context of the AIDS epidemic, during a time when hostility against homosexuals was undoubtedly at its highest in Ireland, reveals nonetheless what kind of impact AIDS had on the legitimacy of the gay movement in Ireland. The high number of gays who contracted AIDS in the USA was often used to justify obstructions of personal freedoms, for example when the bathhouses were closed in San Francisco in 1984. However, in Ireland, AIDS during these years affected drug addicts far more than it did gays, and thus could not justify maintaining **criminalization**. The Gay and Lesbian Equality Network joined the campaign for decriminalization and quickly made AIDS into "another reason for the abolishment and not the conservation of those laws actually in place." In Ireland, AIDS would not hinder the struggle for the reformation of the laws and for equality.

In 1993, when homosexuality was decriminalized and the age of sexual majority was made the same for everyone, it was often said that no one had been prosecuted under the Labouchere amendment in over forty years. This was false. Throughout the 1970s, David Norris, a lawyer who would later become a senator, and Mary Robinson, a barrister who would go on

to become president of the Republic, both defended many men arrested by police under compromising circumstances. "But I do remember very clearly the humiliation caused to those accused even when we secured their acquittal," declared Norris in a speech before the Senate in June 1993, during the debate on decriminalization. "In particular, I recall one occasion when a young man was forced to repeatedly describe in detail an act of fellatio in which he had engaged, the judge amusing himself by making **humorous** remarks to the huge enjoyment of those in the body of the court."

In 1974, Norris took the Republic of Ireland to the Supreme Court of Justice in order to prove that the dispositions of Irish law violated human rights, and that they were then unconstitutional. In his verdict, the judge, Mr McWilliam, responded that he could not grant Norris' request because of the Christian and democratic nature of the Irish Republic. The appeal to the Supreme Court was similarly rejected, so Norris decided to take his case to the European Court of Human Rights. This court ruled in his favor in 1988, but it would be five years later before legislators would modify Irish law.

Nevertheless, lesbians and gays were not absent from the Irish cultural revolution. During these movements of national pride that led to the creation of the Republic, many gays and lesbians were able to express themselves, albeit discreetly. The most famous example is the work of Roger Casement, the *Black Diaries*, which stood on municipal library bookshelves for decades. Casement, an Irish knight who converted to the cause of the Republic, was arrested and tried for **treason** after the 1916 revolution. During the trial, the English government circulated the diaries in order to establish his guilt. The journals describe the author's homosexual encounters with the same economical tone in which he might have recorded his daily expenses. Casement was hung for treason, and even to this day, certain intellectuals question the authenticity of the diaries, most of their arguments very clearly based on homophobic sentiment and prejudice.

Other figures of great importance during the development of Irish culture were openly gay, lesbian, or bisexual, or had clearly expressed homosexual desires in their works, for example novelist Kate O'Brien; Micheal McLiammoir, the actor who founded the Gate Theatre; the Celtic Revival poet Eva Gore-Booth; or novelist Brendan Behan. One of the charismatic leaders of the 1916 Revolution, Padraig Pearse, expressed his homosexual desires in his poetry, and was lauded for it. In addition, when Micheal McLiammoir died in 1978, the president of the Republic attended his funeral and publicly presented his condolences to McLiammoir's long-time partner, Hilton Edwards—and this in a nation where homosexual relations constituted a crime, and would still for another fifteen years.

—*Brian Finnegan*

Collins, Eoin, and Ide O'Carroll. *Lesbian and Gay Visions of Ireland*. New York: Cassel, 1995.

Horgan, John. *Mary Robinson: An Independent Voice*. Dublin: The O'Brien Press, 1997.

Inglis, Brian. *Roger Casement*. London: Penguin Books, 2002.

Irish Council For Civil Liberties. *Equality Now for Lesbians and Gay Men*. Dublin: ICCL, 1990.

Marcus, David. *Alternative Loves: Irish Gay and Lesbian Stories*. Dublin: Martello Mercier, 1994.

Mitchell, Angus. *Amazon Journal of Roger Casement*. Dublin: Anaconda Editions, 1997.

Philpot, Ger. "Martyr in the Park," *GI Magazine* (2001).

Rose, Kieran. *Diverse Communities: The Evolution of Lesbian and Gay Politics in Ireland*. Cork, Ireland: Cork Univ. Press, 1994.

Staunton, Denis. *Micheal MacLiammoir*. London: Absolute Press, 1997.

—*Armed Forces; Decriminalization; England; North America; Theology; Violence; Wilde, Oscar.*

ISLAM

Considering today's context of a Western perception of Islam which produces constant fundamentalist discourse filled with racism, it is important to keep a few things in mind before exposing the manifestations of homophobia in the Muslim religion. First and foremost, it would be prejudiced to speak of Islam in general, as the religion is divided into multiple branches, whose positions on many questions can be quite divergent. Moreover, it should be remembered that there are always differences among the fundamental texts of a religion, the laws decreed by that religion, and individual religious practices. In addition, the physical range of Islam is so vast (from Morocco to Indonesia) and consists of such a socio-cultural and historical diversity that it has produced multiple modes of reli-

gious interpretations and practices. Finally, the modern emphasis on the rigorist and puritanical tendencies of Islam most assuredly stems from the dynamics of intercultural relations between the East and the West; more precisely, from the reaction to the colonial periods. This rise in fundamentalism is thus not simply the product of an indigenous culture; rather, it is instead primarily a reactionary movement to the West. All this must be kept in mind when reading the following pages.

The Origins of Islam

There are certain fundamental elements of Islamic knowledge. To Muslims, the Qur'an (meaning, the "Revelation" or "Recitation") is the word of God revealed to the prophet Muhammad between 610 and 632 CE. These words, memorized by the prophet's companions and sometimes partially preserved in written form, were collected and compiled into a single definitive text around twenty years after Muhammad's death, following a long review of the various versions. To Muslim believers, the resulting text (the Qur'an), has a sacred and intangible character because it is the word of God. Because of this, it is the primary source for their religion. Aside from the Qur'an, there is another corpus of referential texts: the *Sunnah*, or "Prophetic Tradition," which, when necessary, covers those topics on which the Qur'an is silent, or alternately expands on its verses. These are a collection of rules based on the examples of the life of the Prophet—the Qur'an having put forth Muhammad as a "good model." The Prophet's actions and words, the *ahadith* ("narrations"; or in singular form, *hadith*) from which spring the *Sunnah*, were first preserved by his companions, then by a succession of sometimes numerous informants, until they were fixed in writing, compared to one another, then selected and compiled between 870 and 915 into the collections which remain unmodified to this day. The authenticity of some of these *ahadith* has been contested, and in certain cases it is obvious that some are an attempt to impose a particular point of view by unduly attributing it to the Prophet. From these two sources, the Qur'an and the collections of *ahadith*, sprang the *sharia*, Islamic law (literally meaning "path," "way," or "itinerary"), which consists of a corpus of jurisprudence. To Muslims, the *sharia* is not a vulgar human creation, but the expression of divine will. This makes it something immutable, of which modification is forbidden. That said, the *ahadith* are sometimes equivocal, and their interpretations have drawn numerous divergences. Moreover, *sharia* simply does not have answers for all situations that can arise in daily life. Because of this, many schools of thought, each proposing different methods of interpreting the founding texts as well as answers to countless new questions, have progressively come into being. There are four schools: Hanafi (the most liberal doctrine), Shafi'i, Maliki (more austere than the two previous), and Hanbali (the most rigorous). All four were founded over the course of about a century (from 767 to 855) and have progressively elaborated a voluminous corpus of **jurisprudence**: the *fiqh*. So what, then, do the Qur'an, the *ahadith*, and the different schools have to say about homosexuality?

The Qur'an

The term homosexuality does not exist in the Qur'an. On the other hand, the story of Lot's people, which retells that of **Sodom and Gomorrah** from Genesis (19:1–23), appears in the Qur'an thirteen times (7:80–84; 11:69–83; 15:51–77; 21:71–75; 22:42–43; 25:40; 26:159–175; 27:54–58; 29:28–35; 37:133–138; 50:12–13; 54:32–40; 60:10; the first number indicating the *sura*, or chapter, and the second is the verse); however, the two cities are never named. In the Qur'an, the destruction of Lot's people by "a rain of stones" is presented as a "sign" of divine power and as the sanction incurred by those who do not believe in God, and who disobey Him. It is because "Lot's people" did not listen to their prophet's warnings, who informed them of God's commandments and suggested they stop their dealings, that they were destroyed. It is made clear that this radical sanction punishes them for having accused Lot of "lying," for having denied God's existence through their refusal to submit to his commandments, and for having challenged Lot to give them proof of the Lord's existence (22:42–50; 50:12–13; 54:33–40). More than their behavior, it is undeniably the accusation of "lying" and their defiance that triggered the divine wrath.

Lot's warnings include an explicit condemnation of sexuality between men, but the "misdeeds" committed by his people numbered far more than just that. Verse 165 of *sura* 26 makes it known that the men were not simply attracted to other men, but also to adolescents, young boys, and even male animals, as the formula used to designate their partners is quite ambiguous: "Of all the creatures in the world, will ye approach males." Nonetheless, the other verses only indicate that the

men "approach" other men, instead of their "wives" or "women," and that they "act senselessly" (27:55) to "practice [their] lusts" (7:81). Verses 58–77 of *sura* 15 also indicate that Lot's people attempted to "disgrace" God's "messengers," who had come to save Lot before the destruction of the city (15:320). We can turn to the book of Genesis (which is much more explicit than the Qur'an on this aspect of the story) to better understand the implications: the people of Sodom wanted to have "carnal relations" with the "messengers," and they threatened to use violence to achieve this end. Thus, Lot's people attempted to rape angels. As well, verses 28 and 29 of *sura* 29 indicate that Lot's people also practiced other reproachful actions, such as highway robbery:

> 28 And (remember) Lot
> behold, he said to his people:
> "Ye do commit lewdness,
> such as no people in Creation (ever) committed
> before you.
> 29 "Do ye indeed approach men,
> and cut off the highway?
> and practice wickedness (even) in your councils?"

In the majority of verses, sexuality between men is presented as the most significant "misdeed" of Lot's people—it is an "abomination" that had never before been committed.

In the Arabic version of the Qur'an, the term *fahisha* (generally translated as "lewdness" or "shameful deed"), is used in the verses concerning Lot's people. Because of this, some writers see it as a veiled allusion to sodomy between men, but the expression has a much wider meaning, because it also can imply heterosexual sexuality out of wedlock. In this sense, verse 16 of *sura* 4 commands Muslims to "punish" (in the sense of "do harm" or "mistreat") those who give in to "lewdness":

> 16 If two men among you are guilty of
> lewdness,
> punish them both.
> If they repent and amend, Leave them alone;
> for Allah is Oft-returning,
> Most Merciful.

According to scholar Pinhas Ben Nahum, this verse has traditionally been interpreted as a condemnation of sodomy between men, though many (like Joseph Schacht) believe that an allusion to sodomy is quite unrealistic and that this passage is about extramarital heterosexual sexuality. If one admits this second hypothesis, then the Qur'an sets out no earthly sanctions against sodomy between men. However, if the first hypothesis is accepted, then the Qur'an condemns those who practice it to public prosecution and conviction, though with no specific mention as to the nature of the punishment. Regardless, those who imitate "Lot's people" are qualified as "evil," "lewd," and "immoral" (21:74; 7:79–81). Note that at no time is there any mention of sexuality between women.

Despite this reprobation, the Qur'an repeats often enough that God is "gracious and merciful." The verse above even states that he who repents and gives up the practice must be forgiven. He will earn God's forgiveness and will be able to reach paradise, as opposed to those who refuse and "cry out lies." Similarly, as pointed out by an anonymous author, the Qur'an is not lacking in ambiguity, as it promises to believers a paradise where they will be served by "youths of perpetual freshness" (56:17; 76:19) as "handsome as pearls well-guarded" (52:24).

To better understand the equivocal character of this reprobation, one has to understand the place of sexuality in the Muslim religion. In paradise, it is omnipresent—the faithful receive *houri* for wives (magnificent young women, eternally virginal) and beautiful young boys as servants. Orgasms are permanent and erections are perpetual. On earth, sexuality is simply a taste of the pleasures to come in paradise, and does not carry with it the same guilt as it does in Christianity. However, as Maarten Schild points out, this can be a source of social disorder and must be channeled into **marriage**, which is presented as "the expression of divine harmony and of the complementarity of the sexes." *Zina* (or "fornication," that is, extramarital sex) is severely reprimanded. The Qur'an suggests a punishment of up to life imprisonment for women who have committed "a lewdness" (4:15), and the "adulterer and adulteress" each must endure 100 lashes of the whip (24:2). But the woman who affirms five times that "[her accuser] is most surely one of the liars" must be pardoned (24:8). Penal procedure is very strict: four healthy adult Muslim men must have witnessed the acts and be capable of providing anatomical detail—near impossible conditions to meet. Otherwise, the guilty person must confess to his (or her) "crime" so that the punishment

can be enforced. Those "who launch a charge against chaste women, and produce not four witnesses" will be "[flogged] with eighty blows of the whip" (24:4). These slanderers, considered "perverts" like Lot's people, are destined for Hell (24:23). Islamic scholar Sadok Belaïd correctly points out that the presence of four witnesses presumes that the issue is a public matter, conferring a gravity on the situation. The same procedure is used for those "guilty" of sodomy between men. Naturally, the application of sanctions in this way is practically impossible. Moreover, given the punishment reserved for *zina* (incarceration for life and flagellation with no chance of avoiding this by repenting), Jim Wafer, writer on Islam and homosexuality, states that the simple injunction to "chastise" those who practice sexuality between men, without any further details, seems to be moderate by comparison. This difference in treatment suggests that *zina* only applies in the heterosexual sense in the Qur'an, and that sexuality between men is less serious than heterosexual sexuality out of wedlock.

The Ahadith

The *ahadith* provide a very different sort of prescription. They make reference to Lot's people mainly through the usage of the term *liwat*, derived from the word Lot and which signifies "the doings of Lot's people." But what is the exact meaning of this word? *Liwat* is often translated as "homosexuality," but Arno Schmitt has demonstrated through his own contextual analysis that this translation is inexact. *Liwat* refers to sodomy, that is, the sexual act, and not to sexual orientation, nor to a personal characteristic shared by all people who practice sodomy, nor to a sexual identity. The sodomized partner can also be a woman, but the *ahadith* specify the partner's sex. *Liwat* can also designate by extension a practice substituting for sodomy, *tafhid*, which is the thrusting of the penis between a man's thighs. *Luti*, meaning the "active" partner, signifies "performing sodomy by means of a boy," but not with a boy. The "passive" partner, the *ma'bun*, is considered an instrument, inferior, a non-man—all terms implying abnormality. Other equivalents to *luti* are: *fa'il*, "active one," or "he who does it"; *sani*, "he who does it," the "worker," or the "laborer"; *'ala*, "the one on top"; and *dabbab*, "he who climbs on someone to dominate." Some equivalent terms to *ma'bun* are: *maf'ul*, the "passive one"; *asfal*, "the one on the bottom"; *madbud 'alaihi*, "he upon whom the other person climbs"; *malut bihi*, "he who is sodomized"; and *manyak*, "he who is penetrated," or "queer," in modern Turkish slang. All of these words make reference to the idea of penetration. Thus, it is not homosexuality as it is known today that the Qur'an and the *ahadith* sanction when they refer to *liwat* and its derivatives, but simply the practice of sodomy between men. Neither fellatio nor mutual masturbation between men, nor sexual practices between women are implied by these terms. This is partly confirmed by the fact uncovered by Frédéric Lagrange, that fellatio is not mentioned at all in the *fiqh* (Islamic jurisprudence). The words which refer to sexuality between women are *sahek, sihak*, and *musahaka*, and are generally translated by "lesbianism," or "tribadism," which is the best translation because this word, of Greek origin, is derived from *tribein* ("to rub"), thereby making reference to the action, and not to an identity. *Sahak* does not appear at all in the *ahadith*.

Those *ahadith* dealing with "the doings of Lot's people" are noticeably plentiful. They have been compiled by Al-Nuwayri into a work entitled *Nihaya*. In the book's commentary, the anonymous author previously mentioned writes:

> The prophet is said to have stated that his biggest
> fear for his community were the practices of Lot's
> people (though he is known to have expressed
> the same idea about wine and feminine seduction;
> *Nihaya*, II,198). To him, the active person and the
> passive person must both be killed (*yutal/uktulu l-
> fa'il wa-l-maful bi-hi* …), or, more precisely, subjected
> to the prescribed chastisement for one guilty of
> *zina*, the fornicator, which is to be stoned.

Later on, he adds the following about *sahak*: "On this topic, there is one *hadith* according to which it is considered the same as *zina (sihak al-nisa' zina bayna-hun-na)*."

Unlike the Qur'an, the *ahadith* clearly liken sodomy between men and sexuality between women to *zina*, to the point where the punishment prescribed for sodomy between men is the same here as for "fornication" in the heterosexual sense—though no punishment is specified for sexuality between women. In the *ahadith*, *zina* is the focus of two sanctions not to be found in the Qur'an: stoning and banishment. Stoning is a punishment of Jewish origin (Dt 22:22). Its application is considered by the *fuqaha* (jurists of the tradition) to be inherent to the Qur'an and as such is applicable to all Muslims guilty of *zina*; although, this interpretation in particular has been contested. According to Belaïd, the Prophet had never ordered this punishment except in exceptional circumstances (to dictate the chastisement of a Jewish adulteress), and that this was not meant to establish a formula applicable to all Muslims. The *fuqaha* have clearly decided otherwise. According to Jehoda Sofer (author of "Sodomy in the Law of Muslim State"), another *hadith* proposes different sanctions for those "guilty" of *liwat*: stoning, if the individual is married or is cohabitating with a concubine (a union between the master and his slave); 100 lashes of the whip accompanied by a year's banishment if he is unmarried. (Note that it is not the individual's role in the sexual relation that dictates the punishment, but his marital status.)

In another *hadith*, the Prophet is also said to have condemned "those men who take on a feminine appearance and women who take on a masculine appearance," then commanded the believers to "chase them from their homes," without specifying any duration for this banishment, nor if it should be accompanied by corporeal punishment. This simple sanction of banishment contrasts sharply with the physically abusive punishments indicated in the previous paragraph. The disparity between punishments is so considerable that one is led to think that it is not actually sexuality between people of the same sex that is being condemned in the *hadith*. However, this is exactly what scholar François-Paul Blanc says when he suggests that it targets the homosexual man or woman. Aside from those qualifications previously formulated for the use of the term "homosexuality" as a translation for the expressions used in medieval Arabic, it would seem that a man taking on the appearance of a woman and a woman taking on the appearance of a man do not necessarily indicate that the individual has had sexual relations with a person of the same sex. On the other hand, this same *hadith* does clearly sanction any crossing of gender lines by one's appearance and dress—transvestism being the explicit target. The duality of the sexes, and more generally, the sexual dichotomy of a world divided into two opposing and complementary genders is considered the work of God, to the point where the transgression of this duality is thought to be an affront to the divine order and even a "revolt against God" (as Abdelwahab Bouhdiba explains it in *La Sexulaité en Islam*). Despite there being a notable distinction between a person's attire and their sexuality, it is highly probable that outward appearance was thought to be an expression of having crossed the line in terms of sexual relations with someone of the same gender. In this case, the *hadith* in question only punishes the "passive" man and the "active" woman, not the "active" man and the "passive" woman. In this way, it is the expression of this sexuality that is being punished, rather than the sexuality itself.

Numerous *ahadith* also warn against the allure of young boys, reputed to be even more seductive and tempting than the *houri*, the magnificent virgins of paradise. According to Wafer, the Prophet is said to have identified three types of *liwat*—action *liwat* (seen as "criminal"), looking *liwat*, and touching *liwat*—and that they should not all be considered equal. Wafer states that the warning against touching and looking is to prevent the believer from living in temptation (of sodomy, that is), and not to quell the amorous affection between a man and a youth. The same repression of carnal desire is expressed in a *hadith* which postulates that a simple kiss given "with lust" to an adolescent will be punished in the hereafter by a thousand years of *jahannam* (damnation). According to Bouhdiba, this interpretation of these *ahadith* has led some *fuqaha* (jurists) to recommend a strict segregation of mature men from the youths—and that men should abstain from even looking at adolescents or sitting next to them. This is comparable to the recommendation that men avoid the presence of women, because of the three forms of *zina* pronounced by the Prophet: *zina* of the eye, *zina* of the touch, and *zina* of the ear. By virtue of these *ahadith*, some *fuqaha* have prescribed a rigid segregation of the sexes—men must avoid looking at, touching, or listening to women. These various types of *zina* and *liwat* are not assigned any earthly punishment, but they do lead to Hell. Nonetheless, according to Wafer, the Egyptian mystical poet Ibn al-Farid (1182–1235) tells that the Prophet himself is said to have loved a man named Mu'adh ibn Jabal, and that he is supposed to have said, "O Mu'adh ibn Jabal. I love you so much." Arno Schmitt stated that the Hanbalite jurisconsult Ibn al-Jawzi (who died in 1200) wrote: "He who declares never having felt desire [while looking at a magnificent adolescent] is a liar, and to believe him would be to make him an animal, not a human being." Arabic society during the beginnings of Islam attributed a strong power of attraction to the beauty of young boys, but the Prophet made a visible effort to master carnal urges. Schmitt adds to this:

But to desire is not to do. And more than one devout Muslim has resisted and found comfort in the words of the Prophet: "He who loves passionately yet remains chaste is a martyr" (i.e. he will go directly to paradise).

So which of these punishments were actually meted out for sodomy between men and for sexuality between women during the time of the Prophet and the first caliphs (who succeeded him in the task of guiding the believers)? Death by stoning seems to have only been enacted once by Muhammad for a heterosexual Jewish woman. However, afterwards, the caliphs extended this measure to Muslim subjects. The anonymous author states that specific cases of the stoning of *lata* (plural of *luti*, "sodomites") were reported by al-Nuwayri and al-Jahiz during the first century of the Muslim era (seventh century of the Christian era): Abu Bakr (first caliph, 632–34) is said to have condemned a homosexual to being buried under the rubble of a wall and ordered all others who carry out such practices to be burned alive. For his part, Ali ibn Abu Talib (fourth caliph, 656–61) is said to have stoned one *luti* and to have thrown another one head-first from the top of a minaret. Expanding on the Prophet's condemnation, Abd-Allah ibn Umar (son of the second caliph, 634–44) suggested that these people would be reborn as monkeys or pigs.

While the practice of stoning has been proven by historians, the possibility that anyone had been burned alive has been strongly contested because burning at the stake was not part of Muslim tradition.

Schools of Jurisprudence
So what do the schools of legal thought, Hanafi, Shafi'I, Maliki, and Hanbali, have to say? According to Wafer, they consider both sodomy between men and sexual practices between women to be illicit, but there is a diversity of opinions among the jurists on what the Prophet believed. He adds that certain *fuqaha* tend toward exaggeration in their denunciation of sodomy: "When one man mounts another man, God's throne trembles, the angels look on in horror and say: Lord, why do you not command the earth to punish them and the sky to rain brimstone down upon them." The various schools disagree on the severity of the sanctions to be imposed on those who engage in sodomy between men, and on the attitude to adopt regarding sexuality between women. The differences are about

whether or not sodomy between men should be considered the same as *zina*, which would justify a different punishment. Sexuality between women is not generally considered *zina* because, in the thinking of the *fuqaha*, it excludes penetration. However, it remains a serious "sexual sin," deserving of at least a lesser punishment and subject to discussion.

In general, in all cases where *zina* is not proven but where the behavior is still in the realm of "sexual sins," *ta'zir* is invoked—punishments which were not as strict as those set out by the Qur'an and the *ahadith* for *zina*. The precise punishment is left to the discretion of the judge. It can be as light as a simple reproving look or fewer than thirty-nine lashes of the whip (the lightest punishment set out for *zina*, that of *zina* with a slave); alternatively, it could be up to 100 lashes of the whip (being the punishment for *zina* of free people). In cases of proven *zina*, stoning is only applicable under certain conditions: that the person indicted is *muhsan* (i.e. having engaged in coitus within a present or previous legal marriage), is free, past puberty, and of sound mind. A non-*muhsan* person (who has never had coitus while married), pre-pubescent, queer, or a slave guilty of *zina*, is to receive flagellation. Thus, it is not the act committed (heterosexual adultery, sodomy between men, being "active" or "passive," etc.) that determines the punishment, but the fact of whether or not a person had had intercourse while married, was master or slave, or was above or below the age of puberty. The distinction between *muhsan* and non-*muhsan* comes from the worthiness conferred by marriage, as well as in the increased responsibility for the guilty party. This is because the "crime" committed by a person who is *muhsan*, as Blanc points out, endangers the institution of family. The schools of thought also argue over the necessity of adding a penalty of one year's banishment for cases of *zina*, which refers back to the *ahadith*.

According to Sofer, the Hanafi school of thought originally believed that sodomy between men did not constitute *zina*, and that it should not then be punished as such—the judge has to choose between the punishments of imprisonment or flagellation, according to Muhammad al Hussein as-Saibani, one of the founders of this school. Wafer added that the rejection of corporal punishment stems from the following *hadith*: "The blood of a Muslim should not be spilled except for the reason of adultery [meaning *zina*], of apostasy, or of homicide." The Hanafi followed this interpretation for over 700 years. Sofer stated that the jurists then began to draw closer in line to the other Sunni schools of thought—in 1936, Ibrahim al Halabi prescribed death by stoning for sodomy (with a man or a woman) if the individual is *muhsan*, and a whipping if he was not.

Blanc identified that within the Maliki school, sodomy between men earns the same type of punishment as *zina*, but with increased severity as prescribed by Al-Qayrawni (an eminent jurist of the Maliki school), who calls for both *muhsan* and non-*muhsan* to be stoned. Khalil, another prominent Maliki judge, adds that stoning should also be extended to slaves and non-Muslims, but that acts "against nature" between women are not *zina*, and that the punishment for these should be determined by a judge.

According to Sofer, al-Shafi'i (767–820), the founder of the Shafi'i school, had two different opinions on the subject: on one hand, he recommended death by stoning for both partners, *muhsan* or not; on the other hand, death by stoning for the *muhsan* and 100 lashes of the whip accompanied by one year of banishment for the non-*muhsan*. Most jurists following in his footsteps opted for the second choice.

Wafer points out that the Hanbali school of thought requires a severe chastisement for sexuality between men. Referring to the "rain of stones" that struck down Lot's people, they call for death by stoning. Some even believe the "guilty" party should be buried alive or thrown from the city's highest building, after the practices of the first and fourth caliphs.

Despite the severity of these punishments proposed by Muslim judges, bear in mind that the procedural requirement of four witnesses capable of describing the facts, makes these punishments practically inapplicable, and instead they simply play the role of a deterrent in the Muslim ethos. According to Stefen O. Murray, this infers that Islam (unlike Christianity) is characterized by the "will not to know" what individuals are doing. Nonetheless, the reprobation is immense—Hell is promised to those men and women who so much as experience carnal desire for a person of the same sex. This way, Islam defers the individual to God's chastisement, instead of earthly punishment.

The Muslim States

Most Arab states have declared Islam to be the national religion, and *sharia* as the principle inspiration for their legislation. Generally, though, secular laws inherited from colonial days have been adopted as legislation for almost all aspects of society—with the notable exception of the family, where the laws on personal status are based on *sharia*, completely or in part, which leads to considerable differences from country to country.

Today, Saudi Arabia, Iran, Mauritania, Sudan, and Yemen all apply *sharia* and have provisions in their penal codes for death by stoning, flagellation, banishment, and *ta'zir*. The same was true of Afghanistan under the Taliban regime. Other countries take their inspiration both from *sharia* and secular law, detailing punishments of imprisonment and fines, sometimes accompanied by corporal punishment. In these, traces of the criminal codes of Western colonizers are mixed with elements of *sharia*, because the concept of a fine did not previously exist in Islam. Other countries still, like Turkey and Egypt, have adopted a secular law with no criminalization of sexuality between people of the same sex, though this has not prevented police harassment under other contexts. For example, fifty-two men were arrested in 2001 in Cairo aboard a floating gay nightclub. The invocation of the sacred founding texts by certain nations and other fundamentalist groups (who advocate a return to Islam's roots) has served to legitimize and incite the violent repression of homosexuality. As well, these movements present homosexuality as a symbol of Western decadence that they are called on to fight. Sheik Omar Bakri, an alleged spiritual leader for Al Qaeda, regularly calls for the murder of homosexuals in his preaching. Amnesty International has indicated that in those countries where *sharia* is enforced, people are essentially sentenced to death by stoning and flagellation, and that the accusation of "fornication" with a partner of the same sex is used frequently to reinforce condemnation of political opponents. Given the rigidity of Islamic criminal procedure, it is obvious that these condemnations are only made possible either by the arrangement of false testimonies, or through extortion.

—*Christelle Hamel*

Amnesty International. *Briser le silence. Violations des droits de l'homme liées à l'orientation sexuelle.* 1999.

Anonymous, "Liwāt." In *Encyclopédie de l'islam.* Paris: Maisonneuve & Larose, Leiden E. J. Brill, 1977–86.

Belaïd, Sadok. *Islam et droit, une nouvelle lecture des versets prescriptifs du Coran.* Tunis, Tunisia: Centre de publication universitaire, 2000.

Bellamy, James A. "Sex and Society in Islamic Popular Literature." In *Society and the Sexes in Medieval Islam.* Edited by Afaf Lufti al-Sayyid Marsot. Malibu: Udena, 1979.

Ben Nahum, Pinhas. *The Turkish Art of Love.* New York: Panurge Press, 1933.

Bouhdiba, Abdelwahab. *La Sexualité en islam.* Paris: Presses universitaires de France, 1975–98. [Published in the UK and the US as *Sexuality in Islam.* London/Boston: Routledge & Kegan Paul, 1985.]

Le Coran. Translated by Denise Masson. Paris: Folio, 1967–93.

Duran, Khalid. "Homosexuality and Islam." In *Homosexuality and World Religions.* Edited by Arlene Swidler. Valley Forge: Trinity Press International, 1993.

Lagrange, Frédéric. "Male Homosexuality in Modern Arabic Literature." In *Imagined Masculinities: Male Identity and Culture in the Modern Middle East.* Edited by Mai Ghoussoub and Emma Sinclair-Webb. London: Saqi Books, 2000.

Murray, Stefen O. "The Will not to Know: Islamic Accommodations of Male Homosexuality." In *Islamic Homosexualities: Culture, History and Literature.* Edited by Stefen O. Murray and Will Roscoe. New York/London: New York Univ. Press, 1997.

Schacht, Joseph. "Zinā." In *Encyclopédie de l'islam.* Paris: Maisonneuve & Larose, Leiden E. J. Brill, 1977–86.

Schmitt, Arno. "Different Approaches to Male-Male Sexuality/Eroticism from Morocco to Uzbekistan." In *Sexuality and Eroticism Among Males in Moslem Societies.* Edited by Arno Schmitt and Jehoda Sofer. New York/London/Norwood: Harington Park Press, 1992.

Sofer, Jehoda. "Sodomy in the Law of Muslim States." In *Sexuality and Eroticism Among Males in Moslem Societies.* Edited by Arno Schmitt and Jehoda Sofer. New York/London: Harrington Park Press, 1992.

Schild, Maarten. "Islam." In *Sexuality and Eroticism Among Males in Moslem Societies.* Edited by Arno Schmitt and Jehoda Sofer. New York/London: Harrington Park Press, 1992.

Wafer, Jim. "Muhammad and Male Homosexuality." In *Islamic Homosexualities: Culture, History and Literature.* Edited by Stefen O. Murray and Will Roscoe. New York/London: New York Univ. Press, 1997.

—*Africa, Central & Eastern; Bible, the; Judaism; Maghreb; Middle East, the; Sodom and Gomorrah; Southeast Asia; Violence.*

ITALY

Antiquity

There is no Latin word signifying homosexuality or heterosexuality. The Romans, like the Greeks, neither created nor conceived of a sexual category that would indistinctly encompass men and women from all levels of society, with the common characteristic of being attracted to members of the same sex. Social norms dictated that any relations were first and foremost relative to power and status. Consequently, those reactions which would today be qualified as "homophobic" belong to a more general kind of display targeting those who disobey this division of social roles and the moral rules specific to the Roman world.

In Rome, an individual's shaming would begin as soon as the public began to suspect a deviation. But what kind of deviation could still be unclear. In such a small community, where everyone knows each other, conversations could glorify or ruin a person's social standing. As far as it concerned men, pejorative clichés that today would be called homophobic would never identify a homosexual as such (since Roman society had no concept of this definition), but would instead apply to a figure of authority who had earned some infamy, thus proving his incapacity to fulfill those functions reserved for free, adult, male citizens. The Romans' chief preoccupation was that one's behavior corresponded with the collective moral standards. A person's sexuality, regardless of orientation, was not an immediate or isolated part of one's identity, according to these standards. Naturally, the collective supervision extended all the way into the bedroom. But the deviations of an unorthodox libido would be denounced only if they violated this order and kept a person from being able to function in the forum or the **army**.

Deviance, in Rome, had nothing to do with being a homosexual. The modern image of a "man covered in women" was as frowned upon by the Romans as a "man covered in men." Someone who spends his days in the public baths looking for a good time was considered an example of a waste of masculine energy that could have been put to better use in the service of glory. Being the active partner (to use the modern language) was not as humiliating as being the passive partner; though being active was not viewed well if the sexual activity turned to obsession or worse, to prostitution. Two Latin words designate the behaviors described in poetry: *pathicus*, to indicate a man who submits to another man, and *pedicator*, to indicate a man who imposes sodomy upon another man (or woman, too). Either a person services another and in doing so becomes like a slave, or a person humiliates another with a symbolic punishment: in both cases, it is debasing.

Moreover, those same people who would denounce the sexual eccentricities of their enemies would often enjoy relations with young slaves, whose sensuality was seen as the height of eroticism. Battalions of young pages, hairless, perfumed, and made-up, provided delights to their masters in their posh abodes—funeral inscriptions attest to the pleasures experienced by the head of the house with his dear and preferred boy (his *puer delicatus*), whose premature death left him inconsolable. Nothing would stop a Roman man in the forum from condemning the sexual practices of so and so with someone else, while just several hours later, this same Roman would be enjoying the kisses of his favorite slave during a relaxed banquet. Roman civilization was compartmentalized into different activities according to the time of day. The morning was reserved mostly for public duties (receiving friends and protégés and organizing war, politics, and diplomacy), while the evening (which began during the afternoon, after a relaxing trip to the baths) was devoted to the comforting mellowness of food, music, and eroticism. This complementary approach to life is what defined the Roman man. Roman sexual morality may appear to be repressive, but only if one overlooks this dichotomy between the *duritia* and the *mollitia*, effort and languor.

The types of attacks that blow a rival's idiosyncrasies out of proportion (for example, Marcus Antonius when targeted by Cicero) or the aberrations of an emperor (Tiberius or Nero) are still in use today in homophobic stereotypes. Saying that an enemy throws parties with excessively masculine (or just the opposite, excessively effeminate) young men, is meant, and construed, as a derogatory **insult**. In the same way, an orator or a satirist might attack a rival's gluttony, spending habits, or cowardice. This kind of discourse simply compounds the cultural clichés. Here can be found the origins of many of homophobia's enduring stereotypes, where the homosexual is relegated to the periphery of a respectable community; the homosexual is seen as artificial, superficial, vain, and most of all, insatiable. The less he has, the more he wants, but also, the more he has, the more he wants. His ungratefulness is proven in every way (sexual obsession, gluttony, waste of legacy, etc.), making him into an immoral being, incapable of starting a **family** or of defending his nation. Sexual marginality was scandalous to the Romans because to them it was a sign of a political or civil marginality: this magistrate or that emperor was considered debauched because, by the cultural logic of the time, their image did not integrate well with the criteria for civilization. They were not branded as homosexuals—above all else they were considered morally mediocre or useless, and this is what made their sexuality degrading, especially their relations with the masculine sex. The men, targets of public reproach, have relations with other men or with boys, but these relations would be considered obscene and fail to be part of a refined and amorous conviviality. The standards of amorous refinement are met only by the superior forms of masculine relations, notably a boy's kisses, which are soft as honey and represent an exchange of erotic breath, without the laborious and dirty drudgery of penetration. In conclusion, if homophobia existed at all in ancient Rome, it was inseparable, then, from the euphoric mastery of pleasure that a man experiences with a boy.

On the other hand, a relationship between two women was never considered to be equivalent to a relationship between two men. While certain types of sexuality between men were socially admissible, there were no scenarios at all where the practices classified today as "feminine homosexuality" would have been acceptable to the Romans.

In Greece, sexual relations between women were perceived as falling outside the realm of sexuality. However, in Rome, the contrary was true: most texts touching on the subject describe only the sexual character of this behavior, removing all other aspects one might expect from a relationship (affection, exchange, pleasure, etc.). A women's desire for another woman was, in the first texts making mention of the subject, presented as a mistake (in a fable about Phaedra, it was due to an error by Prometheus, who had drunkenly created certain humans the wrong way) or part of a temporary condition intended to be corrected (in a passage from Ovid's *Metamorphoses*, one of two women had been transformed into a man). Little by little, the reactions of rejection and disgust became more explicit: the *tribade* persona appeared and became the object of caricature and mockery (the Latin term *tribas*, based on the Greek verb *tribein*, means "to rub," but the creation of this word also demonstrates how the invention of

this practice was attributed to another culture). Martial and Juvenal, first-century satirists, position their female characters as women with no self-control (the concept of excessiveness is recurring, temperance being the mark of a civilized person), drunken and indecent. Philaenis (described in poet Martial's *Book VII* [67]) is endowed with exceptional strength and displays a degrading hyper-sexuality. It is said of these women that they "act like men" without really succeeding, while the situation of the other partner is never taken into account.

This kind of discourse, which today can be qualified as homophobic, is deeply rooted in the Roman attitude toward women in general. What was most shocking and fearful about a woman loving women was the fact that in doing so she transgresses the role assigned to her by Roman sexual morality. This fear can be explained by the fact that in Rome, women had a more important social role than they did in Greece—they were in charge of educating children, which included inculcating Roman values. More involved in daily life, women represented a danger to these values if, in addition to their social and familial activities, they decided to exert the same autonomy over their sexuality.

The greatest difference between homophobic discourse targeting men and that targeting women lies in the fact that there is no mention of any real cases of women who were prosecuted or subjected to persecution, nor are there any juridical writings condemning sexual relations between women. The issue was raised in cases of adultery (such as in Seneca the Rhetorician's first-century *Controversiae* [I, 2, 23]), but it concerned marriage and the rights of the husband, and not specifically feminine homosexuality as such. Thus, no conclusion can be made.

While it was possible to launch accusations (founded or not) against men, invectives against *tribades* remained within the realm of fiction. One of the characteristics specific to the "**lesbophobic**" discourse in Rome was that it operated only in self-referential isolation, acknowledging itself only through sly winks and innuendo, and never referring to anything real. As a result, relations between women were presented as impossible, something prodigious or monstrous.

From the Middle Ages to the Modern Day
By the beginning of the Middle Ages, the repression of homosexuality was taking place at the municipal level, as the freedom from imperial power began to permit

the development of local autonomy. Prosecuting the "crime" of sodomy was of interest to municipalities for two reasons. Firstly, this allowed an area to increase its resources as a result of confiscating a sodomite's assets, a practice common in the majority of Italian communes beginning in the fourteenth century. Secondly, it allowed the communes to demonstrate their independence from papal authority, though collaborations with the **Inquisition** were common. This repression would last throughout the Renaissance, during which all the large cities would prosecute sodomites, including such figures as Leonardo da Vinci and Benvenuto Cellini.

An episode that is emblematic of the political exploitation of homophobia took place during the Middle Ages, with the conflict between the Guelphs (primarily *bourgeois*—bankers, merchants, etc.—who favored the Pope and had ties with monastic orders) and the Ghibellines (supporters of Frederick II). The papacy launched accusations of sodomy against those imperial forces with which they were at war, and the Guelphs were particularly insistent on the execution of **heretics**, sodomites, and other offenders of morality. The conflict was bloody, as much in terms of the individual prosecution of Ghibellines accused of sexual laxity as in terms of the collective battles. An arbitrary link between the moral and the political was constructed. The political expansion of the Church was legitimized (at least internally) by the necessity of spreading the moral and religious doctrine. And as morals and politics had become inseparable, reducing the conflict to a mere political level was simply not supportable by the papacy and the Guelphs, who needed to attribute to their Ghibelline adversaries a degraded moral dimension against which to fight. In this way, the Guelphic and papal conquest fabricated its justification of a moral struggle against sodomy (the worst crime of the era), as a means to pursue its political objectives.

Decriminalization progressively took hold after the end of the eighteenth century. It began first in Tuscany under the reign of Grand Duke Leopold, then in all of Northern Italy after the promulgation of the Napoleonic Code. Charles Albert's Code of 1837 for Piedmont-Sardinia was extended to all of his possessions after the creation of the Kingdom of Italy in 1870 by the House of Savoy. No punishment existed for homosexuality after decriminalization had successively reached all the Italian regions with the creation of the Kingdom. This decriminalization was also accompanied by a less repressive social climate.

Benito Mussolini did nothing to change this situation at first. In 1930, he even maintained that, given that Italians were naturally virile and non-homosexual (as opposed to degenerate foreigners), it would not be necessary to fashion laws against homosexuality. Another important factor motivated his refusal: Italy's economic need for the substantial influx of money brought by homosexual tourism. Moreover, in the Hitlerian ideology, Latins, like Slavs, were considered an inferior race. In this light, the Latin European and South American Fascist countries integrated racial conceptions to a far lesser extent and had little reason to believe that homosexuals were a danger to the race. After the creation of the Rome-Berlin axis in 1936, Mussolini promulgated anti-homosexual decrees, under Nazi pressure, in this way breaking with the relatively liberal Latin tradition. **Fascist** logic seeks to eliminate all political opposition. In this way, it differs from the Nazi logic, which was to eliminate all people thought to be a threat to the race. Thus, homosexuals came to be considered political criminals. Their punishments under the Fascists were imprisonment, exile to remote regions (usually islands), and loss of employment.

By the end of the twentieth century, as in other Western countries, the first signs of a civil recognition for same-sex couples began to appear (as they did for decriminalization), mostly at the municipal level. In this way, on June 28, 1992 in Milan, ten gay and lesbian couples were married in a series of public civil ceremonies in the Piazza del Duomo. Some municipalities have passed laws providing for civil unions and several regions have formerly supported efforts for national law on civil unions.

Still today, contrary to many of its European neighbors, Italy has no national legal framework dealing with same-sex couples, but a draft bill to recognize domestic partnerships was proposed in 2006. The bill faced considerable opposition and was stripped from reaching the floor for a vote, but in 2007, it was merged with other civil union proposals, and the Senate's Judiciary Committee has been discussing a new draft. The country is also one of seven European nations that have no national anti-discriminatory laws in regards to sexual orientation; however, in 2004 Tuscany became the first region to ban discrimination against homosexuals, and the region of Piedmont has since followed suit. Finally, the Vatican's views on the subject of homosexuality remains highly influential.

—*Sandra Boehringer, Thierry Eloi, and Flora Leroy-Forgeot*

Brown, Judith. *Immodest Acts: The Life of a Lesbian Nun in Renaissance Italy.* New York/Oxford: Oxford Univ. Press, 1986.

Canosa, Romano. *Storia di una grande paura: la sodomia a Firenze e Venezia nel quattrocento.* Milan: Feltrinelli, 1991.

Cantarella, Eva. *Selon la nature, l'usage et la loi. La bisexualité dans le monde antique.* Paris: La Découverte, 1991. Originally published as *Secondo natura.* (Rome: Riuniti, 1988). [Published in the US as *Bisexuality in the Ancient World.* New Haven: Yale Univ. Press, 1992.]

Dupont, Florence, and Thierry Eloi. *L'Erotisme masculin dans la Rome antique.* Paris: Belin, 2001.

Gnerre, Francesco. "Littérature et société en Italie," *Inverses,* no. 2 (2002).

Leroy-Forgeot, Flora. *Histoire juridique de l'homosexualité en Europe.* Paris: Presses universitaires de France, 1997.

———, and Caroline Mécary. *Le Couple homosexuel et le droit.* Paris: Odile Jacob, 2001.

Lupo, Paola. *Lo Specchio incrinato: storia e immagine dell'omosessualità femminile.* Venice: Marsilio, 1998.

Rocke, Michael. *Forbidden Friendships: Homosexuality and Male Culture in Renaissance Florence.* New York/Oxford: Oxford Univ. Press, 1996.

Ruggieriero, Guido. *The Boundaries of Eros: Sex, Crime, and Sexuality in Renaissance Venice.* New York: Oxford Univ. Press, 1985.

Williams, Craig, A. *Roman Homosexuality: Ideologies of Masculinity in Classical Antiquity.* New York/Oxford: Oxford Univ. Press, 1999.

—*Art; Catholic Church, the; Damien, Peter; Decadence; Essentialism/Constructionism; Fascism; Greece, Ancient; Heresy; History; Literature; Pasolini, Pier Paolo; Sappho; Theology.*

J

JAPAN

Homophobia in Japan is a complex issue, the origins of which are both ancient and recent; the real debate is on whether the phenomenon is indigenous to Japanese culture or imported from elsewhere. Today, a certain number of Japanese homophobes still insist that China is to blame for the first appearance of homosexuality in Japan, with the establishment of Buddhist monasteries in the eighth and ninth centuries. Opponents of this view however, respond that it is actually *homophobia* that, in many ways, was imported. In this view, homophobia in Japan first appeared in the sixteen century under the influence of Jesuit missionaries, and again during the nineteenth century, in the wake of Japan's opening up to Western powers. The truth, however, as writer Tsuneo Watanabe demonstrated so well, is much less black and white.

Japan's rich homosexual history began between the ninth and twelfth centuries among the monastic class, then the warrior and the bourgeois classes at the time of the Edo period, beginning in seventeenth century. It was among the samurai of the fifteenth through seventeenth centuries that sexual relationships between men more clearly developed, or more precisely, between an older man and a young page (*kosho*), homosexuality being exalted as "the flower of the *bushido*," or the flower of "the way of the warrior." Love between two men, who had no interest in reproduction, was considered less burdened and more pure than the love between a man and a woman. Later, in Edo's bourgeois milieu during the time of Tokugawa (between the seventeenth and nineteenth centuries), homosexuality was often expressed through effeminacy (the usual word for homosexual being *Yokama*, or passive and effeminate) and prostitution. In this respect, the theater played a central role, contributing to Japanese gay culture by way of the *onnagata*, where the very popular actors who specialized in playing female roles in kabuki often offered themselves as prostitutes to customers following the performances. Homosexual practices in ancient Japan appeared to have been rather widespread, so much so that it would have been possible to consider bisexuality the norm; however, this is clearly refuted by the fact that female prostitutes greatly outnumbered male ones. It also must be noted that, if ancient Japanese culture was highly **tolerant** toward male homosexuality, its views of lesbianism were quite the opposite: female sexuality that served no male pleasure and that did not lead to the conception of a child was considered totally unacceptable.

The first great wave of homophobia in Japan coincided with the arrival of Jesuit missionaries in 1549; François Xavier saw the "crime of **Sodomy**" everywhere he looked. During a visit to a Zen monastery, he discovered with horror that "among the bonzes [monks], the **unnatural** and abominable **vice** was so popular, that they committed it without any **shame**." He immediately began to scold them, which provoked nothing but surprise and laughter. Later in his visit, Xavier realized that the *samurais* and the *daimyos* (feudal lords) shared the same morals as the bonzes. He then explained to them that the three great sins were infanticide, idolatry, and the "abominable sin," to which his audience reacted disdainfully. A *modus vivendi* was established; commoners contented themselves with jeering at the missionaries in the street: "Look! These are the men who say that we are not to sleep with boys!" Watanabe contends that there is no doubt that the Jesuits' ultimate failure in Japan, starting with their harsh persecution at the hands of the Japanese in 1597, was largely due to their virulent homophobia.

That being said, indigenous homophobia began to develop at the end of the Tokugawa period (eighteenth to nineteenth century), when Japan adopted a policy of national isolation. Certain *shoguns* tried to forbid male prostitution, which they saw as a cause of social disorder associated with sympathetic suicide (too often, a lover would commit *seppuku* upon his beloved's death) or crimes of passion (jealously often ended in a blood bath, as depicted in Nagisa Oshima's 1999 film *Taboo*). Furthermore, Take, a woman who not only passed herself off as a man but also as a judge, was found guilty of the "corruption of public morals" in the 1830s and forced into exile. There is thus the impression that Japanese homosexual culture was already beginning to crumble by the time Western powers were forcing Japan to open up (1853).

Whether or not that is true, homophobia in Japan intensified with the arrival of Westerners and the imperial restoration of Meiji in 1868. Just like their sixteenth-century predecessors, nineteenth-century missionaries were scandalized by the spectacle of sexual behavior they discovered, and the casual attitude many Japanese displayed toward sodomy. As a result the imperial Japanese government, rather self-conscious with regard to the West, endeavored to adopt the morals of the large Western powers in order to make Japan respectable in the eyes of the world. Thus, homosexuality in Japan was then considered an archaic and unhealthy tradition that was best abandoned, as were mixed baths, which had so scandalized the British. The Meiji period (1868–1911) was marked by the adoption of strict sexual standards, and the promotion of absolute sexual identities (e.g., men must not have any feminine traits, and women must submit to the "good wife and wise mother" maxim). An 1873 law, reestablishing an 1841 prohibition, called for ninety days of **imprisonment** for anyone who committed the crime of "sodomy"; the law was relaxed in 1883 and the incrimination of sodomy was replaced, under the influence of the French, by the more vague category of "indecent assault": for example, the seduction of a sixteen-year-old minor, regardless of gender, became punishable by two months of hard labor. Above all, social intolerance of homosexuality increased dramatically, as proven by a media campaign in 1899 against the "bad morals" of certain students at the University of Tokyo (with one newspaper reminding readers that "homosexual acts are punished as crimes in every civilized country" and demanded that it be the same in Japan). It was no surprise that the Meiji period saw the disappearance of the *samurais*, who transformed themselves into businessmen

and administrators, and the decline of the *kabuki* tradition, limited to solely presenting an ancient repertoire. However, the westernized **armies** of Meiji, Taisho, and Showa (Hiro Hito) preserved a part of the *samurai's* homosexual heritage. The best in Meiji's army came from the province of Satsuma, whose warriors were particularly famous for their "Spartan" homosexual traditions, and the idea of the sympathetic suicide, often adopted by *kamikazes* attested to the survival or resurgence of a certain military love of men. To this day, a part of the nationalist intelligentsia in Japan has maintained nostalgia toward the *bushido* ("the way of the warrior") and, in certain cases, its erotic content. Such was the case of author Yukio Mishima (1925–1970), who was much attached to a part of his paternal lineage, populated with *samurais*, and through it, to an ascetic and masculine ideal. His novel, *Confessions of a Mask*, loosely based on his own life, is representative of the taboo that became homosexuality in World War II-era Japan. In the book, the young hero's trials are no less difficult than those of an adolescent "queer" in Great Britain during the same period. The American occupation of Japan from 1945 to 1952 replayed similar mechanisms from the Meiji period: homosexuality was banned in the American army beginning in 1943, and once again the winner's homophobia was imprinted upon the loser's subconscious.

The redefinition of sexual identities in Japan, established during the Meiji-era 1870s remains largely intact to this day; it can be at least partially attributed to the conservative traditions of Japan's imperial governments. Thus, although the notion of sin has never taken root in Japan, social constraints against homosexuality have become even more prevalent than in the West. Family pressure in favor of **marriage**, regardless of the participants' sexual orientation, is considerable: in general, Japanese gays and lesbians bow to this un-written rule, placing themselves under the socially protective umbrella of heterosexual marriage. Since the Meiji Restoration, and notably since the Imperial Rescript on Education of 1890, **school**, **family**, and society in general teach that "all Japanese are similar" and therefore must all be alike. Accordingly, homosexuality is not bad for moral or religious reasons, but because it is different from the norm (for example, according to Japanese law, it is not a sexuality, but rather a "simulacrum of sexuality"). It is understandable that under these conditions, coming out is quite difficult. For one, anyone "accused" of being a homosexual is often ridiculed, although the physical manifestation of gay bashing remains rare; additionally, openly declaring oneself as different, is to break with the fabric of daily "normalcy" and aspire to an individualism that is totally foreign to traditional Japanese culture. Homosexuality is also often something which no one speaks about openly in Japan. To shed light on the pervasiveness of this taboo, it should be noted that even if Japanese law does not forbid gays and lesbians from serving in the armed forces (the Self Defense Force, established in 1954), no Japanese military personnel ever dared reveal his or her homosexuality before 1998.

In the 1990s under the influence of the West, the plight of homosexuals in Japan began to change. Some courageous gay and lesbian groups, the most important being OCCUR, have been leading a fight for legislative change in Japan. In 1997, after seven years, OCCUR won a court case against the Metropolitan Government of Tokyo, which had excluded gays and lesbians from getting rooms at the Tokyo Youth Hostel. Today, the fight against homophobia in Japan centers on a critical revision of the moral code set up at the end of the nineteenth century, which will improve the lives of women as well as gays and lesbians.

—*Pierre Albertini*

Leupp, Gary P. *Male Colors: The Construction of Homosexuality in Tokugawa Japan*. Berkeley: Univ. of California Press, 1995.

McLelland, Mark. *Male Homosexuality in Modern Japan: Cultural Myths and Social Realities*. Richmond, UK: Curzon Press, 2000.

Pflugfelder, Gregory. "Strange Fates: Sex, Gender, and Sexuality in Tonkaebaya Monogatari." *Monumenta Japonica*, no. 47 (1992).

Saikaku, Ihara. *The Great Mirror of Male Love*. Stanford: Stanford Univ. Press, 1990.

Suvilay, Bounthavy. "Le Héros était une femme: le travestissement dans le manga." *ProChoix*, no. 23 (2002).

Watanabe, Tsuneo. "Une hypothèse sur l'attitude anti-homosexuelle spécifique aux sociétés modernes." *Research Report of Kochi University* 30 & 31 (1981–82).

———, and Junichi Iwata. *La Voie des éphèbes, histoire et histoires des homosexualités au Japon*. Paris: Trismégiste, 1987. [Published in the UK as *The Love of the Samurai: A Thousand Years of Japanese Homosexuality*. London: GMP, 1989.]

—*Buddhism; China; Comic Books; Korea; Southeast Asia.*

JUDAISM

Jewish reprobation of homosexuality is based on three passages from the Torah: Leviticus 18:22 ("You shall not lie with a male as one lies with a female; it is an abomination"), Leviticus 20:13 ("If there is a man who lies with a male as those who lie with a woman, both of them have committed a detestable act; they shall surely be put to death"), and Deuteronomy 23:18 ("There shall be no temple harlot among the Israelite women, nor a temple prostitute among the Israelite men"). The first Jewish interpretation of biblical laws stems from the Targum, an ancient Aramaic paraphrase or interpretation of the Hebrew Bible read in Palestinian synagogues at the beginning of the Common Era. Leviticus 18:22 is interpreted literally, while Leviticus 20:13 specifies only that stoning is a suitable punishment. However, the Targum of Deuteronomy 23:18 does away with the obsolete terminology of sacred prostitution; one of its critical revisions (*onkelos*) reformulates the interdict this way: "None of the sons of Israel shall take a serf for a wife." In short, these sources speak briefly to what they consider to be a Canaanite or Egyptian **vice** that has nothing to do with Israel. Moreover, according to Jewish legend, when the Bible refers to the Egyptian named Putiphar as a "eunuch," it is because he acquired Joseph for sexual purposes, and was emasculated by a divine miracle (Targum PsJ Gn 39:1 and LvR § 86).

During these ancient times, the episode involving the city of **Sodom** (Gn 19) was originally not connected to Palestinian ideas of "sodomy." The city's vice was mainly the result of brazen greed due to its riches, which led to the poor treatment of travelers there, as indicated in Ezekiel 16:49 and Flavius Josèphe.

Ancient Judaism

The ancient texts preceding the time of the Mishnah and the Talmud offer some interpretations of homosexuality. Ancient texts produced in Eretz-Israel (land of Israel from biblical times) purport that homosexuality was a non-Jewish tradition, and instead originated among those who also resorted to prostitution and composed hymns to the glory of sodomy (LvR ad Gn 18:3–4). The texts also state that certain pagan kings took themselves for gods and, as punishment, God cursed them to sexual submission *modo foeminarum* (like that of a woman). However, some believe, on the basis of the word "abomination" in Deuteronomy

32:16, that the Israelites of the desert also succumbed to this "vice," as they too yielded to idolatry. In the same vein, some sages judge that God had condemned their ancestors to exile from Babylon for four inseparable crimes: idolatry, social injustice and violence, sodomy, and adultery. There are three interpretations to be taken from this: for one, homosexuals existed elsewhere other than among the nation of Israelites; for another, if homosexuals did exist among them, they are subject to punishment for a range of sins against the social and sacred "order" established by the Creator; and finally, the unity of ancient Judaism held more to "orthopraxis" than to orthodoxy, and more to a concern for correct action than to fair and just thought. Based on these facts, the texts condemn the act of homosexuality, but ignore the rights of the individual.

Further, ancient Jewish writings in Greek, stemming from the Diaspora, reveal a dread of the Hellenic **tolerance** of homosexuality. *Letter of Aristae,* Section 152 (second century BCE), likens relations between men to incest, and concludes, "But we have remained apart from such things." This literature reflects a Judaism that, by mixing in many Greek moralists and claiming ethical superiority, intended to reform morality. This is present in the *Sibylline Oracles* (Sib Or 3:185), which pronounce Jews to be unscathed by this deviation (Sib Or 3:596; 5:430). It is suggested by Pseudo-Phocylides, a contemporary Jewish moralist of St **Paul**: "A boy should not grow curls on his head, should not braid his hair, and should not tie his locks into a bun; do not grow long hair on a man, it is only fit for pretty women. Of a young boy, keep watch on his adolescence, for many passionately search for male love" (v. 210–14; v. 3. 190–94). This text, like Apuleius's *Metamorphoses,* confirms the importance of hair in the sexual excitement of Antiquity (1 Co 11:1–16). And Joseph confirms the Jewish condemnation of homosexuality, in the name of the **Bible** (AJ 3:275; 4:301; CA 2:199, 215, 273); he likens the homosexual to those who choose castration: both, refusing to procreate, are "murderers of children" (AJ 4:291).

Philo of Alexandria (20 BCE–50 CE), in his monumental commentary on the Hebrew Bible, does not deal much with the problem of homosexuality. But for him as well, the homosexual act, because it is **sterile**, infringes on the commandment of procreation, "Go forth and multiply" (Gn 1:28). His other arguments relate to stoicism, and to the principle of "nature," whereby pederasty forces the male into feminine conformity. Evoking Greco-Roman banquets, he mocks the clothing, hairstyles, makeup, and perfumes that identify the "**favorites**" (Szesnat). Further, he states that the (active) pederast corrupts youths, and that his immoral passions drive him to ruin, both financial and in the loss of interest in civic life.

The Talmud & Its Ancient Interpreters

Often neglected, the preceding testimonies are the matrix of the Talmudic age. The Mishnah (Sanh 7:4), the first written recording of the Oral Torah of the Jewish people, places homosexual acts among the crimes punishable by stoning, and among the thirty-six transgressions punished by "spiritual excision" (Ker 1:1), a phrase that resulted in divergent judicial interpretations. The Talmud renews the link between homosexuality (incest!) and two other capital crimes: idolatry and homicide (Sanh 74a). If sodomy is "**against nature**," then the interdict applies to everyone, not only Jews (Sanh 58a); but with this issue, minors escape all penalties (Sanh 54a) and, as the Bible makes no mention of lesbian relations, lesbians are subject only to flagellation. Thus, the motive behind the reprobation of homosexuality is the concept of "nature" and the defense of the family order and other social structures with afflicted subjects at risk of resorting to idolatry, that is, in danger of subverting the order of creation imposed by the one God. For his part, the Jewish philosopher Maimonides (1135–1204) makes the distinction between active and passive homosexuality (*Sefer Hamitzvot* [The Book of Commandments], in the 350th Negative Commandment). In the centuries since, the *responsa*, the collection of opinions establishing jurisprudence with regard to all aspects of Jewish life, has also endeavored to determine responsibilities in this matter.

In the fourth century, Rabbi Judah said: "an unmarried man may not keep livestock nor two unmarried men share the same blanket; but the Sages permit it" (Kid 4:14). After these last texts, followed by Maimonides, the Talmud (Kid 82a) determines this precaution against homosexuality to be useless. Similar to Rabbi Judah, Rabbi Joseph Caro (1488–1575), in an effort to squelch debauchery, states that two males should not remain alone together. However, Rabbi Joel Sirkes (1561–1640) considers homosexuality to be non-existent among Polish Jews. This idea that homosexuality is non-existent in Judaism thus persists, despite the claims of homoerotic, medieval Jewish poetry to the contrary (Schirmann). In truth, there is no evidence in Jewish history of any cruel repression of "sodomites." Living in the Diaspora under the laws of the *goyim* (Gentiles), Judaism had no opportunity to apply its own laws; further, since the time of the Pharisees, Judaism has been averse to all forms of the death penalty: the Halakha, the body of Jewish law, has always been flexible enough to avoid this. Finally, a widespread opinion that still remains, attributed to Immanuel Jakobovits, retired chief rabbi of the British Commonwealth, challenges the primacy of love put forth by certain Christian circles: "Jewish law states that no hedonistic ethic, even one called 'love,' can no more justify the morality of homosexuality than it can legitimize adultery or incest, no matter that such acts can be carried out by reason of love or mutual consent."

Evolutions

"To say the Jewish people are a chosen people is to say that they have an infinite and permanent responsibility towards others" (Bernheim, 44). This is the underlying conviction behind Judaism's opinion on homosexuality. Three factors have revived this issue: homosexuality's "coming out," including among Jews, post-Freudian research on sexuality, and the introduction and spread of **AIDS**.

On this observation, Judaism and its diverse currents do not all agree on homosexuality. "Orthodox" Judaism would content itself with the repression of homosexuals were it not, in fact, subject to state legislation. "Moderate" (or conservative) Judaism does its best to reconcile the imperatives of the Halakha and the humanist values of the Jewish tradition, specifically the attention to man as he is. The latter tends to recognize the homosexual identity, but Jewish debates on the subject in the United States between 1990 and 1992 resulted in an open, if tenuous agreement (Dorff, *Epître de l'amour* [*This is My Beloved, This is My Friend*]); access to the rabbinate remained closed to avowed homosexuals, but the movement was resolutely committed to the fight for the recognition of gay rights in society. As of 2007, the Jewish Theological Seminary of America ordains gay and lesbian rabbis and accepts openly gay and lesbian students. Some, playing on the Talmudic principle (BK 28b) that one who is *forced* to break the laws of the Halakha cannot be held guilty, excuse homosexuality, based on the idea that it is impossible to subscribe to "normality." This point of view

also prevents homosexuals from being condemned to perpetual chastity, as sexuality is a gift from God, who insists upon its blossoming. "Reform" (liberal) Judaism starts from yet another principle: that the Bible, the Talmud, and its interpreters are informed by bygone historical circumstances, and it is necessary to revise the Halakha in view of new information on sexuality available.

The Jewish arguments on the nature of homosexuality itself do not necessarily divide along these same Judaic lines. A perceptive examination by a rabbi inspired this observation: the gay Jew faces "the religious split, which relegates him to the domain of the interdicts; the familial split, which confronts him with silence; and the community split, which makes of him a pariah" (Bernheim, 80). Others still declare homosexuality to be as a psychiatric disorder and call for compassion and understanding (Jakobovits, "AIDS: A Jewish Perspective"). However, others believe that any such permissiveness will bring about other excesses, such as the legitimization of cannibalism. As such, a combination of these beliefs would advocate the care of those stricken with AIDS, in the name of the law (Lv 19:16), but at the same time rail against the conduct that led to the infection in the first place. Perhaps, some might add, those who are afflicted with the contagion will be moved to repent their past, and thus become even more worthy of mercy (Rosner). In any event, some say, if AIDS is not a form of divine punishment, it is the consequence, the price to be paid for the tendencies of a permissive society.

These viewpoints do not cover the whole of Judaism. They have, however, driven certain gay and lesbian Jews to affirm their difference. Today, gay synagogues exist in various cities. And since 1977, Beit Haverim, the French Jewish LGBT organization, describes itself as "[gathering together] Jewish gays and lesbians from Paris and its suburbs," though the Consistory (the governing body of Jewish congregations in France) does not recognize it as a Jewish association. Defining themselves on clearly liberal Jewish sources, these gay institutions maintain a two-fold position: demanding the recognition of the gay identity in Judaism, and providing a refuge for gays and lesbians in the face of the rejection by the Orthodox community.

According to Daniel Boyarin, it is during the twentieth century that homosexuality has finally been categorized: "If Foucault could write 'our time has inaugurated sexual heterogeneousness,' we can also claim that our time has inaugurated, and almost in the same way, racial heterogeneousness" (Boyarin [1994], 239). Judaism, too, has been categorized. From this point of view, the Jewish community, often subject to widespread discrimination, goes hand and glove with the gay community (Dorff, *Epître* [*This is My Beloved*]). At its heart, Jewish culture is not necessarily inclined toward homophobia, but it seeks a balance between the Halakha and the human (Bernheim), and between religious standards and a profound sense of human rights—a sense that is nourished by both the Halakha and the Bible itself.

—*Claude Tassin*

Beck, Evelyn Torton, ed. *Nice Jewish Girls: A Lesbian Anthology*. Boston: Beacon Press, 1989.

Bernheim, Gilles. *Un rabbin dans la cité*. Paris: Calmann-Lévy, 1997.

Boyarin, Daniel. *A Radical Jew: Paul and the Politics of Identity*. Berkeley: Univ. of Califomia Press, 1994.

———. *Carnal Israel: Reading Sex in Talmudic Culture*. Berkeley: Univ. of California Press, 1993.

Dorff, Elliot N. "Conservative Judaism." In *Encyclopedia Judaica*. CD-ROM Edition. 1997.

———. *Epître de l'amour*. Paris: Nadir, 2000. [Published in the US as *This is My Beloved, This is My Friend*. New York: Rabbinical Assembly, 1996.]

Jakobovits, Immanuel. "AIDS: A Jewish Perspective"; "Homosexuality." In *Encyclopedia Judaica*. CD-ROM Edition. 1997.

Leneman, Helen. "Reclaiming Jewish History: Homoerotic Poetry of the Middle Ages." *Changing Men*, no.18 (1987).

Rosner, Fred. "Medical Ethics of Judaism." In *Encyclopedia Judaica* II. 2000.

Schirman, Jefim. "The Ephebe in Medieval Hebrew Poetry." *Sefarad* 15. (1955).

Shoheid, Moshe. *A Gay Synagogue in New York*. New York: Columbia Univ. Press, 1995.

Szesnat, Holger. "Pretty Boys in Philo's *De Vita Contemplativa*." *The Studia Philonica Annual* 10 (1998).

Wigoder, Geoffrey, ed. "Judaïsme conservateur"; "Judaïsme orthodoxe"; "Judaïsme reformé." In *Dictionnaire encyclopédique du judaïsme*. Paris: Le Cerf, 1993.

—*Against Nature; Bible, the; Greece, Ancient; Paul (of Tarsus); Sterility; Theology; Vice; Violence.*

JURISPRUDENCE

The consideration of homosexuality by the judicial system has been a constant in French law in particular since the mid-nineteenth century; not only homosexuality itself but "problems" arising from it as well. Historically in France, it is in criminal law that this attitude first came to be adopted. Whereas in 1810, the law specifically stated that sexual relations between persons of the same gender would not be penalized, French judges beginning in the 1850s started to identify homosexuality in particular as an aggravating circumstance in certain cases, such as relations between adults and minors. If today in France this attitude toward homosexuality no longer seems prevalent in criminal matters, it still appears in civil law cases, particularly in family law, with regard to divorce and parental rights.

During the first half of the twentieth century, in some divorce cases, the judicial system cited the husband's homosexuality as grounds for the dissolution of marriage. For example, in one case in 1909, a divorce was granted where the husband was declared at fault for having "gravely abused" his wife by maintaining, with another man, "a passionate friendship that dominated him to the point of making him indifferent and even hostile to his wife." An implied representation of his homosexuality was even included in the court documents, in which the husband was portrayed as weak, unfaithful, and a traitor, not only to his wife, but also to her **family**. We must note the shift from the initial grievance against his relationship with another man to that of a socially perverse, unbalanced, and abnormal individual, using the language used by the **medical** profession at the time to describe homosexuals. The French Court of Appeal, referring to "relations that were manifested in such a strange way" with regard to the husband's "tenderness, too similar to that of a woman," was also inspired by medical arguments when it considered that the husband's calls to his lover "reveals the exasperation of a pathological sensitivity, a type of hysteria of the brain."

Since the 1940s, there have been more judicial decisions in civil cases of this sort, each one revealing, in essence, that the judge in question determined the existence of a specifically *homosexual* offense, which could be used as grounds for divorce even if the other duties and obligations of marriage were upheld. A spouse's homosexuality is not considered among the issues traditionally linked to a couple's sex life, but rather exclusively as an offense. Furthermore, a husband's "homosexual penchants" can be reason to forgive the wife's refusal to have sexual relations with him, as well as the revelation of "indiscretions" (gossip) with others regarding the husband's "homosexual adventures."

With regard to the proprietary consequences of divorce, jurisprudence admits that, based on the grounds of civil liability, the circumstances of a husband's homosexuality may be grounds for a wife to request financial compensation for damages, emotional or otherwise. Such decisions thus accept that the husband's "publicly known homosexuality" causes obvious and reparable moral wrong to the wife. As an offense according to civil liability, legally speaking, the husband's homosexuality is therefore considered to be a "lapse in conduct."

When it comes to the issue of exercising parental authority in divorce cases in France, since the 1980s homosexuality has constituted a "valid" reason for which a parent can be deprived of his or her rights, or at least have those rights restricted; this has been solely the arena of jurisprudence, in the absence of any specific legislation. The restriction of parental rights on these grounds has been demonstrated in numerous ways, including the refusal to grant shared custody, the refusal to acknowledge the homosexual parent's home as the child's primary residence, or even by the limitation or outright denial of visitation rights. These homophobic decisions by the judicial system have the effect of causing shame and embarrassment to the homosexual partner or parent. Jurisprudence, in treating homosexuality as a "serious offense" (and hence detrimental) with regard to a healthy marriage or child-rearing, thus equates it with parental crimes such as kidnapping or abuse.

In determining place of residence for a child of divorce, homosexuality is always regarded as a decisive circumstance; whether the judge feels that the parent's sexual orientation or same-sex relationship is not compatible with a child's best interests. As for visitation rights, these are an extension of the previous themes: the circumstance of homosexuality is considered relevant by those judges, who, *a priori*, are hostile to it. If visitation rights are granted to the homosexual parent, it is, hypothetically, "despite" the parent's homosexuality and based on the understanding that it will not to be detrimental to the children.

The judicial system's use of homosexuality as grounds for divorce or as a reason to limit or deny parental rights is, on one level, nothing more that a reflection of how society views homosexuality. However, it also reminds us of prevalent attitudes within the judicial system with regard to homosexuality, and reveals the predominant role played by jurisprudence in the construction of a stigmatized *homosexual* difference that is evident in society, even in countries where homosexuality itself is officially legal.

—*Daniel Borrillo and Thomas Formond*

Comstock, Gary. "Developments: Sexual Orientation and the Law," *Harvard Law Review* 1541–54, no. 102 (1989).

Danet, Jean. "Le Statut de l'homosexualité dans la doctrine et la jurisprudence françaises." In *Homosexualités et droit.* Edited by Daniel Borrillo. *Les Voies du droit.* Paris: Presses universitaires de France, 1999.

———. "Discours juridique et perversions sexuelles (XIXe et XXe s.)." In *Famille et politique.* Vol. 6. University of Nantes, France: Center of Political Research, Faculty of Law and Political Science, 1977.

Duberman, Martin, and Ruthann Robson, eds. *Gay Men, Lesbians and the Law (Issues in Gay and Lesbian Life).* New York: Chelsea Publishing, 1996.

Formond, Thomas. "Les Discriminations fondées sur l'orientation sexuelle en droit privé." Doctoral thesis in private law. University of Paris X, Nanterre, France (September 2002).

MacDougall, Bruce. *Queer Judgment: Homosexuality Expression and the Courts in Canada.* Toronto/Buffalo/London: Univ. of Toronto Press, 2000.

Newton, David. *Gay and Lesbian Rights: A Reference Handbook.* Santa Barbara, CA: ABC-CLIO, 1994.

Peddicord, Richard. *Gay and Lesbian Rights: A Question—Sexual Ethics or Social Justice?* Kansas City: Sheed & Ward, 1996.

Watts, Tim. *Gay Couples and the Law: A Bibliography.* Public Administrations Series P-2810. Monticello, IL: Vance, 1990.

—*Criminalization; Decriminalization (France); Discrimination; European Law; Family; Marriage; Parenting.*

JUSTINIAN I

The period under the reign of Byzantine emperor Justinian I (527–565 CE) was one which greatly repressed homosexuals, called *arsenokoites* or *androkoites.*

Repression of male homosexuality was nothing new in the Eastern Roman Empire; sexual relations between women were known and attested to in historical sources, and there existed legislation that, in a general sense, condemned relations that were "**against nature**." However, Justinian's repression of male homosexuality was particularly solemn and severe, so much so that it had a significant impact on the population, and is referred to in the writings of Byzantine chroniclers at the time. Justinian's policies in fact constitute a turning point in what we can today call the history of homophobia.

The concentration of legislation regarding male homosexuality during Justinian's reign, including provisions for the punishment of male homosexuals, sheds light on the extent to which sexual relations between men became a state issue during this period. Such legislation consisted of a number of legal documents, but it is *Novella 141*, dating back to 559 CE, which established the most complete legal framework for the repression of homosexuality; addressed to the residents of Constantinople, the document was only concerned with sexual relations between men. The Christian context of this law was quite clear, as well as the arguments and terms it used offer insight into the political motives behind the oppression of homosexuals. Justinian justified the law by stating his desire to avoid the wrath of God; it was common in Byzantine texts to claim that disasters such as famine, earthquakes, and plague, as well as devastation brought about by the barbarians, were all consequences of God's vengeance. According to Justinian, male homosexuality caused God's wrath to visit upon what he now considered **Sodom**, where inextinguishable fires raged; and Justinian's laws would effectively put out these fires. Thus his laws, which represent the punishment of Sodom, have a pedagogical aspect. The laws had to serve as a lesson to the citizens of the Empire by revealing the sacrilegious character of homosexuality. In justifying his measures, Justinian called attention to the condemnation of homosexuality by both the apostle **Paul** and the state, and underlined its unnatural character by stating that it was something that even animals did not partake in. Specifically, according to Justinian's law, men who "corrupt[ed] themselves" had to cease to do so, let their "illness" be known to the "Patriarch," and then make penance; those who did not would "be pursued, and ... suffer the worst of punishments." One might believe that this punishment would be death, but according to Byzantine chronicler Procopius, those accused of homosexuality were publicly denounced, and the guilty were castrated and put on public display. He specified that in the beginning, these measures were used as an excuse to control the Greens, a faction that opposed Justinian, as well as others who offended the state. However, Procopius's statements must be taken in stride, given that they were polemical. Nonetheless, it is quite possible that accusations of homosexuality and the practice of castration were used as political weapons. Procopius stated the example of a young man named Basianos, whom Theodora, Justinian's wife, accused of homosexuality simply because he offended her. She had him castrated, put to death, and then confiscated his possessions.

Other Byzantine authors confirm the wide implementation of this homophobic law, which even extended to men of the cloth. Jean Malalas and Theophanous told the story of two bishops, Isaiah of Rhodes and Alexander of Diospolis in Thrace, who, around 528, were accused of homosexual practices. They were brought to Constantinople, where they were judged, deposed from their Episcopal positions, and condemned. According to Theophanous, they were castrated and put on display throughout the city, while a crier declared, "As bishops, you must not soil your honorable cloth." Malalas noted that "those who suffer from the desire for men" lived in constant fear of the severe measures taken by Justinian. In fact, a good number were arrested and died as a result of their castration.

This official attitude toward homosexuality must be examined in the context of other legislation under Justinian I, which was also harsh when dealing with issues relating to the **family** and morals. For example, men who suffered from impotence had their matrimonial rights reduced, and in 542, divorce by mutual consent was suppressed. The influence of Christian morality played a certain role, as demonstrated by Justinian's numerous references to the **Bible**; we cannot underestimate his fear of divine punishment: earthquakes were both frequent and often quite devastating in the Byzantine Empire, and Constantinople was particularly at risk. The Empire also suffered from a widespread epidemic of the plague, and famines and barbarian raids occasionally struck its provinces.

When all is said and done, Justinian's policies—by their extensiveness and their severity, as well as the fear they generated—mark an essential moment in the history of homophobia. The spectacle of castrating and publicly displaying those condemned are particularly cruel examples of how far the state was willing to go in order to deal with homosexuals. In its view, homosexuality was clearly outlawed, and everyone needed to know.

—*Georges Sidéris*

Cedrenus, Georgius. *Corpus Scriptorum Historiae Byzantinae.* Edited by I. Bekker. Vol. 1. Bonn: 1838.

Corpus Iuris Civilis. Vol. 3. Edited by R. Schöll, G. Kroll, and W. Kunkel. 6th ed. Berlin: 1959.

Malalas, Jean. "Ioannis Malalae Chronographia." *Corpus Fontium Historiae Byzantinae* 35. (2000).

Procopius. "Anekdota" In *Procopii Caesariensis Opera Omnia.* Vol. 3. *Historia quae dicitur Arcana.* Edited by J. Haury Leipzig, 1906. G. Wirth, 1963.

Sidéris, Georges. *Les Anges du Palais. Eunuques, sexes et pouvoir à Byzance (IVe – VIIe s.).* Paris: Brepols, 2003.

Theophanous. *Theophanis Chronographia.* Vol. 1. Edited by C. de Boor. Leipzig, Germany: Teubner, 1883.

Further Reading:
The Institutes of Justinian: Text, Translation, and Commentary. J. A. C. Thomas. New York: American Elsevier Publishing Company, 1975.

—*Against Nature; Bible, the; Damien, Peter; Judaism; Paul (of Tarsus); Sodom and Gomorrah; Theodosius I; Theology.*

K

KOREA

There are no dictionaries of Korean language which contain the word "homophobia"; however, out of eighteen dictionaries consulted, seventeen define homosexuality as "a sexual **perversion**." The effects of homophobia and heterosexism, just like sexism or racism, are not always apparent but are nonetheless hostile, and in fact, attacks against homosexuals seem to be on the rise in Korea.

Documents that reveal the traditional negative attitude toward homosexual relations first appeared during the era of the Joseon (or Yi) dynasty that ruled the country for over 500 years, from 1392 to 1910 CE. Prior to this, the Goryeo dynasty (918–1392) had promoted **Buddhism**, but the new rulers accused their predecessors of **debauchery** and homosexuality, and imposed their own form of neo-Confucianism that favored the familial hierarchy, male domination, the separation of the sexes, and sexual purity. It was during the reign of Sejong (1418–50), the fourth king of the Joseon dynasty, that homosexual relations were condemned for the first time, when he imposed a punishment of 100 lashes on concubines believed to have had sexual relations with other concubines. In the eighteenth year of his reign, when his son's wife was caught in bed with one of his concubines, he banished her from the royal court. She was subsequently murdered by her father, who then committed suicide.

In practice, the political application of Confucianism in Korea appeared around the seventh century. The principle of obedience to the king evolved, thanks to the sexual ideology of the yin/yang duality, into the more general obedience to the male; as an adjunct to this, the idea of relations between people of the same sex (yin/yin or yang/yang) was thus viewed as **against nature**. Under the Joseon dynasty, the pressure to be heterosexual brought forth a system of familial succession that was doubly stringent: only a male could occupy the role of head of the **family**; and in the absence of a son, the family line would be extinguished, much to the horror of parents and elders. As to the elevation of his social status, the son occupied a preeminent place in the family structure and assumed the role of the father after his death. Thus, an act that went against the paternal authority violated not only the natural order, but also that of society.

Even today, the preference for male children, which has historically resulted in selective abortion and the infanticide of female babies, creates an imbalance in the gender ratio, although it has improved over the years. In 2006, there were 107 male babies to every 100 female; while this imbalance is still above the normal standard, in the 1990s it was even more pronounced. Further, in the case of parents having a third or fourth child, the ratio was 179 and 205 (respectively) boys to 100 girls in 1995. Taking into account all aspects of daily life, Confucianism and the yin/yang ideology generally view sexuality in a negative light (a view shared by **Christianity**). However, homosexual relations were in fact common at one time, and even enjoyed a certain level of social acceptance among the yangban (the class of scholarly elite) and the namsandang (troupes of men, artists, and acrobats who would travel from village to village). The young men who accompanied the namsandang, called midong (beautiful boys), would dress attractively, often (though not always) wearing girls' clothing. However, if a midong reached marrying age but wished to maintain his effeminate status, he would be considered an undesirable, perverted, and strongly stigmatized as a result. In the same way, homosexuality proper was rejected; it was considered a social problem, and those who practiced it were accused of threatening the ideology of the genders by deviating from heteronormativity (a situation that it not uncommon today).

In the nineteenth century, Catholicism was introduced to Korea not by priests, but by books imported by scholars. By disseminating knowledge in this way rather than preaching, Christianity succeeded in spreading quickly. In the beginning, Christians had difficulty convincing the public that sexuality was for procreation only and that homosexuality was a **sin**, but eventually the concepts took hold. Today, religious communities in Korea are composed of fundamentalists who, through their missions, tirelessly spread virulent homophobic messages through television, radio, newspapers, and the Internet.

In the twentieth century, Korea underwent numerous changes: first, occupation by Japan (1910-45); then the division of the South, provisionally under American control, from the North, under Soviet control, in the aftermath of World War II; and finally, the Korean War (1950-53). North Korea's isolationism makes it difficult to confirm what life is like there for homosexuals, but it is understood that homosexuality is considered a social plague, as it was in other, now former **communist** countries. In the South, after having undergone many hardships, the government propelled the country into the industrialized age, where any appearance of deviation from the national agenda is strongly discouraged.

In the 1960s, a homosexual subculture emerged in Nakwon (Paradise), a district (*dong*) in Seoul; during this same period, many new derogatory expressions were coined, including *pogal*, formed by reversing *kalbo*, the latter a vulgar word for prostitutes as well as any person engaging in debauchery; and *dongseong yeon'aeja*, meaning a man who makes love only with men. Up until contact was made with the Western gay world, the word "homo" was occasionally used by homosexuals themselves, then by heterosexuals as an insult. The term "gay" was also used, but usually to designate a transgender person. The most popular word is still *iban* ("different person"), referring to the homosexual identity (just like "queer" in the West). The origins of *iban* are not known, but the term is a play on the word *ilban* (ordinary person).

During the 1970s, medical theories around homosexuality gained currency, especially after the publication of a study that suggested that the low number of homosexuals in South Korea was the result of the country's sexual maturity and its yin/yang culture. Through the reaffirmation of gender norms and the importation of Western ideas regarding **inversion**, Korean **psychiatry** determined that homosexuality was dysfunctional and socially unacceptable, at the same time that western medicine was changing its tune and no longer connecting homosexuality to mental illness.

Social **discrimination** and legal repression eventually gave rise to new sexual identities in South Korea, and a new culture of public expression began to develop. When LGBT activists started favoring homosexual visibility in the 1990s, the homophobic responses simply got louder, reaffirming the claim that homosexuality was a **peril** to the stability, morality, and health of Korean society. From that point on, homophobia was no longer an abstract belief; it became more and more a religious doctrine, a political conviction, a discriminatory practice, and a scientific fallacy based on "tradition" and "natural" law.

Today, although military service is mandatory for all young males, sodomy is condemned by the **armed forces**. Enlistees are often subjected to psychological screenings regarding sexual preference; those found to be homosexual may be institutionalized, or else dishonorably discharged. In 1997, the first Festival of Queer **Cinema** in Seoul was closed down by the police, which considered it illegal and obscene (it took place successfully the following year). South Korea's first gay magazine, which launched in 1998, has been consistently prohibited by the Korean Publication Ethics Committee from being sold to minors. In 1999, a school textbook described gays as carriers of **AIDS** and as sexual perverts. Anti-AIDS policies in South Korea are, for the most part, anti-gay policies; associations fighting against AIDS are supposed to fight the disease, but in fact mostly fight against the "spread" of homosexuality by promoting homophobia and strictly conservative sexual morals. In 2000, a famous South Korean actor, Hong Suk-chon, came out of the closet, but the very next day, he was fired by the television network that employed him (in 2003, however, Hong began a promising return to film and television).

In 2001, the Ministry of Information and Communication adopted a system which classified LGBT sites as "harmful **media**," requiring that they be filtered on all computers accessible to youth, that is, in **schools**, libraries, and Internet cafés. In the criteria defining indecent websites, homosexuality is classified under the category of "obscenity and perversion." The first case of legal action was in November 2001, against the owner of South Korea's first and largest gay web-site; he was threatened with two years in jail unless he labeled his site as "harmful" and installed filters (with a price tag of $10,000 US).

Despite this negative legacy, discussions on the subject of homosexuality are at least now tolerated in day-to-day life, and anti-discriminatory measures are being put into place. And in April 2003, the Korean National Human Rights Committee ordered that anti-gay language be removed from the Youth Protection Act, which had been originated to protect youth from evils such as homosexuality. Even today, people believed to be homosexual are becoming targets of physical violence.

—*Huso Yi*

Herdt, Gilbert. *Same Sex, Different Cultures: Exploring Gay and Lesbian Lives.* Boulder, CO: Westview Press, 1997.

Murray, Stepheno. *Homosexualities.* Chicago: Univ. of Chicago Press, 2000.

Dong-Sae, Han. "Sexual Perversions in Korea," *Journal of Korean Neuropsychiatry* 9, no. 1 (1970).

Chung, In-Ji, Jong-Seo Kim, and Bo-In Hwang. *Sejong Shilrok* [History of Sejong the king, from 1418 to 1450] (n.p, n.d.).

Yi, Huso. "Homosexuality in South Korea," In *The International Encyclopedia of Sexuality.* Vol. 4. Edited by Robert T. Francœur and Raymond J. Noonan. New York: Continuum, 2001.

——. [Korean translation of *Is It a Choice?: Answers to 300 of the Most Frequently Asked Questions about Gay and Lesbian People*]. Seoul: Park Young-Yul Publisher, 2000.

—*Buddhism; China; Communism; Japan; Southeast Asia.*

L

LATIN AMERICA

When Latin America was discovered by Spain, and, in the case of Brazil, by Portugal, at the end of the fifteenth century, the two European countries were experiencing the most intolerant period in their respective histories with regard to the "abominable" sin of sodomy. At that time, more than a dozen tribunals of the Holy Office of the **Inquisition** were established in the Iberian Peninsula, and among its decisions, declared sodomy as heinous a crime as **treason** or regicide. In Spanish America, a good number of tribunals were also set up in Mexico, Peru, and Colombia. In Brazil, visitors and "friends" of the Holy Office made regular inspections in all parts of the Portuguese colony, denouncing and arresting sodomites as they were discovered. The **sin** of sodomy was one of the rare crimes for which the first governors of Brazil could impose the death penalty without having to first consult the king of Portugal.

Still today, in Latin America, homophobia is strongly entrenched in Iberian male chauvinism, whose presupposed ideologies are inspired by tracts on moral **theology** dating from the time of the conquests: "Of all the sins, sodomy is the most shameful, the dirtiest and the most corrupt, and there is no other that is as regrettable in the eyes of God and man. Because of this sin, God flooded the Earth, and for this sin, he destroyed the cities of **Sodom and Gomorrah**. Because of sodomy, the Knights Templar were destroyed in all of Christendom in a single day. This is why we ordain that all men who have committed such a sin be burned and reduced to ash by the fire, in such a way as there remain no memory of their body or tomb." During this time, homosexuals were persecuted by three different tribunals: the king's justice, the Holy Inquisition, and the bishop.

When they arrived in the New World, the Spaniards and Portuguese discovered a great diversity of peoples and civilizations whose practices were very different from the Judeo-Christian cultural matrix, and even sometimes diametrically opposed with regard to nudity, the concept of honor, virginity, incest, polygamy, divorce, and especially homosexuality, transvestism, and transsexuality.

The *História General y Natural de las Indias* reveals that as early as 1514 the native taste for the *vitium nefandum* was everywhere, in the Caribbean islands as well as in the territories of *Tierra Firme*. The conquistadors were profoundly scandalized by the sculptures and idols venerated by the native population, which included explicit representations of homoerotic relations. Whether in Mexico, Central America, or South America, whether in the Andes or the Amazon, the Europeans repeatedly referred to the natives as "sodomites" in their journals, whether male or female. As well, a good number of chroniclers associated sodomy with irreligiousness: according to one, "As the natives do not know the real God and Father, they commit every day the worst of sins: idolatry, human sacrifice, ingestion of human flesh, speaking with the Devil, sodomy, etc."

This is not to say that all Native American cultures in this region looked favorably upon love between persons of the same gender. According to Franciscan chroniclers, the Maya and the Aztecs believed that "the patient sodomite is abominable, *nefandum* and detestable, deserving of contempt and ridicule." It is interesting to note a contradiction observed in pre-Columbian civilizations: on one hand, they believed in an extremely Dionysian mythology, valuing hermaphrodism and homosexuality, but on the other, engaged in a rather repressive, Apollonian moral practice that allowed for the death sentence in certain cases of homoseuxal activity. Nevertheless, as Venezuelan historian Antonio Raquena, author of groundbreaking studies on homosexuality in the New World, stated in 1945, "Accepted or excluded, honored or severely chastised depending on the nation where it is practiced, homosexuality was present from the Bering Strait to the Strait of Magellan."

In the history of homophobia in the New World, 1513 stands as a particularly tragic date. As described by the sixteenth-century historian Pietro Martire D'anghiera, upon discovering many homosexual natives in the Isthmus of Panama, conquistador Vasco Balboa had forty of them arrested and subsequently devoured by his hounds. In 1548, even homosexual European colonists could not escape institutional persecution: in Guatemala, seven sodomites were arrested, among whom were four clerics. However, at the moment they were tied to the stake, they escaped punishment thanks to an uprising of the local populace.

The first deportation to the Americas for reason of sodomy took place in 1549, when a young Portuguese man, Estêvão Redondo, ex-servant of the governor of Lisbon, was permanently exiled to northeastern Brazil. Some twenty years later, in 1571, the tribunals of the Holy Inquisition took up residence in Mexico and in Peru and later in 1610, in the city of Cartagena in Columbia. However, in these Spanish colonies, contrary to the Portuguese colony of Brazil, the Holy Office did not have the power to persecute the sin of sodomy, as it fell under the king's justice and that of the bishop.

In Brazil, between 1591 and 1620, some 283 men and women were charged with sodomy, with forty-four condemned, many of whom were sentenced to the king's galleys or deported to the far reaches of Africa or **India**. Among the twenty-nine lesbians denounced, five suffered financial and spiritual punishment, three were deported, and two were sentenced to public flogging. (Under the initiative of the International Gay and Lesbian Human Rights Commission, Filipa de Sousa, the most famous of these lesbians, was remembered centuries later with the establishment of an international human rights award in her name.) In 1646, the Portuguese Inquisition decriminalized lesbianism, but although lesbians could now escape the death penalty, they continued to be persecuted by royal and Episcopal justice.

Documents, meanwhile, confirm the executions of two young homosexuals in Brazil. In 1613, in St-Louis du Maranhão, by order of French invaders under the instigation of Capuchin missionaries, a Tupinamba native, known for being *tibira*, or a passive sodomite, was tied to the mouth of a cannon, his body shred to pieces by the mortar, "to purify the Earth of their evils." Then in 1678, in the Sergipe region of northeast Brazil, a young black slave "was flogged to death for having committed the sin of sodomy with a white soldier."

However, it was in Mexico that the persecution of native Latin American sodomites was the most violent during the colonial period. In 1658, 123 *mariquitas* living in the capital region were exposed; nineteen were arrested and fourteen were burned. One of the condemned, a boy under the age of fifteen, escaped the flames, but he nonetheless received 200 lashes and was condemned to six years of hard labor. In 1673, another persecution took place, this time in the region of Mixoac, where seven mulatto, black, and mixed-race *sométicos* were burned at the stake.

With the end of the Portuguese and Spanish Inquisitions, the tribunals of Holy Office disappeared from Latin America: from Mexico and Peru in 1820 and from Cartagena and Brazil in 1821. Though the *Monstrum horribile* was officially destroyed, attitudes were not. To this day, the spectre of the Inquisition remains alive throughout Latin America, not only in an ideology that is moralist and intolerant toward sexual minorities, but also in the very makeup of the local governments, whose traditional roots come directly from the merciless friends and commissioners of the Holy Office.

Taking inspiration from the Napoleonic Code, the majority of the new Latin American nations eventually decriminalized sodomy. However, prejudice and **discrimination** against homosexuals continued during the nineteeth century, specifically against sexual "passivity." Under the pretext of curbing indecency or prostitution, and in the case of transvestites, ideological falsity, many homosexuals continued to be blackmailed, incarcerated, and tortured by agents of the new police order. Thus, homosexuals moved from the clutches of the Inquisition to those of the **police**. At the same time, many doctors and scientists showed their so-called good will, shielding women and "inverted" men from **prisons** and police stations, by testing their cures for homosexuality in clinics and hospitals. However, in so doing, they effectively acted as the watchdogs of official **morality**. With regard to "curing" the *maricones*, they were sometimes subjected to torturous therapies, including electric shocks, high doses of hormones, dangerous drugs, and even transplantation of monkey testicles—all of which, of course, met with little success.

In the twentieth century, marginality, secrecy, self-loathing, violence, and even assassination had become the daily bread for millions of gay, lesbian, bisexual, and transgender Latin Americans who were rejected by their families, humiliated in the streets, and refused **work**. In Brazil, home to more than seventeen-million homosexuals, research has revealed that among all social minorities, gays and lesbians are by far the most hated. The continuum of discrimination spans from verbal insults to homophobic murders, and from public violence to arbitrary incarceration. To this day, Mexican gays are still nicknamed the "forty-one," an allusion to the forty-one homosexuals arrested one night in 1901 and subjected to shameful punishments.

Today, according to the *Spartacus International Gay Guide*, gay cruising areas and gay-friendly bars and businesses exist in every Latin American and Caribbean nation. Nonetheless, the sporadic existence of LGBT rights groups—in roughly only half of these countries—attests to the fact that progress is still yet to be made with respect to gay rights.

Despite the great socio-economic and cultural diversity of the region, Latin America's history is marked by the extreme virulence of male chauvinism and homophobia that, reinforced by the omnipresent, Christian church-influenced familial control, inhibits the gays from coming out, which in part explains the precariousness of LGBT rights groups. The stigmatization is so strong, in fact that it is often said that "one must be very macho in order to be gay in Latin America." (The word *marica* and its regional variants, *mariquita*, *mariquinha*, and *maricona*, are used everywhere in Latin America, including in Brazilian Portuguese, and are the most frequent insults aimed at homosexuals.) The same hostility also affects lesbians, who are often victims of severe acts of violence committed by members of their own families, or by male ex-lovers/spouses, motivated by misogynistic and **lesbophobic** ideology that interprets the love between two women as an outrage and a threat to male chauvinist hegemony.

Among the countries of Latin America, the Republic of Cuba has unfortunately distinguished itself during the 1960s through government-sanctioned violence and persecution of homosexuality, being deemed a sign of capitalist **decadence**. Many books and films, such as Tomás Gutierréz Alea's 1993 film, *Fresa y chocolate* [*Strawberry and Chocolate*], and Reinaldo **Arenas**' 1992 book, *Antes que anochezca* [*Before Nights Falls*; adapted to film in 2000], reveal Cuba's homophobic intolerance during this period. Today, though there is no information on any organized gay movements in Cuba, it is well known that in its urban centers at least, lesbians and gays are gaining freedom, benefiting from the relative **tolerance** of authorities. (This new attitude of respect with regard to sexual orientation or questions of gender was publicly observed during official UN meetings held during the World Conference on Women in Beijing in 1995, where Cuba was the only Latin American country to defend every anti-discriminatory reference founded on sexual orientation.)

Despite a general ideology in Latin America strongly influenced by male chauvinism, which historically led to particularly violent homophobic acts, 1969 saw the creation of the first gay rights group, later called the Frente de liberación homosexual, in Argentina. In 1978, similar associations were founded in Mexico and Brazil, followed by Peru, Colombia, and Venezuela in the 1980s; and during the 1990s, LGBT movements began to organize in Chile, Uruguay, Puerto Rico, and Jamaica. However, in countries such as Chile, Cuba, Ecuador, and Nicaragua, and the US territory of Puerto Rico, homosexuality was still considered a crime until the mid-1990s. Even now, at the beginning of the twenty-first century, Puerto Rico retains anti-sodomy laws. Ecuador, on the other hand, has become an example of social modernity, becoming the second country in the world, after South Africa, to explicitly include in their constitution a ban on discrimination based on sexual orientation. With regard to city and regional jurisdictions, in the 1990s, Buenos Aires and Rosario in Argentina, and the state of Aguascalientes in Mexico, as well as over seventy cities in Brazil, have adopted laws against discrimination on the basis of sexual orientation. (Mexico even has an openly lesbian deputy seated in the Chamber of Deputies.) And massive pro-gay demonstrations are becoming more common in many capital cities in South America. For example, more that 1 million people attended the 2007 Gay Pride parade in São Paulo, Brazil.

Nonetheless, there still exists in every Latin American and Caribbean country highly moralistic and repressive legislation, which generally is applied most rigorously against gays, lesbians, and transsexuals. Some examples: homosexuality is often considered an "aggravating circumstance" and transvestism a crime of "indecency" or "impersonation." Gays and lesbians also still do not have access to the institution of **marriage**, as the civil codes and constitutions of these countries constrain the definition of marriage to heterosexual couples.

As a consequence of colonialism and slavery, gays, lesbians, bisexuals, and transvestites in the majority of Latin American and Caribbean countries are still subjected to a high degree of physical violence and moral pressure. In every region of Brazil, for example, one can hear the "*Viado tem que morrer!*" (the fag must die); while elsewhere on the continent, parents publicly proclaim that they would prefer their son be a thief, or their daughter a prostitute, than gay or lesbian. Catholic Church bishops and more recently with even more fervor, fundamentalist Protestant Church pastors have violently attacked gays in the **media** and in their sermons, censuring anti-AIDS campaigns aimed at homosexuals and supporting obstacles to same-sex civil partnerships. Many of these sects also conduct clinics to cure homosexuality. In some countries of the Caribbean, anti-sodomy laws from the colonial period still persist, and in recent years, have led to official homophobic measures forbidding, for example, the landing of gay passengers from cruise ships in the area.

Worse still: homophobic murders. In practically every country of Latin America, homosexuals and transvestites continue to be attacked and killed in a totally revolting climate of impunity. These crimes are made worse by the identity of the perpetrators: many of the homicides are carried out by death squads, the police or, more recently, neo-Nazi groups. Despite the unavailability of regional statistics on hate crimes, there is information on homophobic homicides in two of Latin America's largest countries. In Mexico, according to the *Comisión Ciudadana de Crímenes de Odio por Homofobía*, 213 homophobic murders were reported between 1995 and 2000, although the actual number is estimated at roughly three times as much. In Brazil, according to the *Grupo Gay da Bahia*, between 1980 and 2000, 1,960 homophobic murders were reported, of which 69% of the victims were gay, 29% were transvestites, and 2% were lesbians; this translates to an average of one homophobic murder in Brazil every two days.

In sheer numbers, it is in Latin America and the Caribbean that the greatest number of homophobic crimes are committed, evidence of its ties to its homophobic past, a sad fact in a region that boasts a vibrant and diverse homosexual culture and shows a remarkable exuberance and *joie de vivre*.

Under these circumstances, there was certainly a need for the International Day Against Homophobia, launched by Louis-Georges Tin, and celebrated in many countries in Latin America, including Brazil, Chile, Cuba, Panama, Peru, and Venezuela. Moreover, the day has been officially recognized by public authorities in Costa Rica and Mexico.

—*Luiz Mott*

Azoulai, Martine. *Les péchés du Nouveau-Monde: les manuels pour la confession des Indiens, XVIe–XVIIe siècle*. Paris: Albin Michel, 1993.

Balutet, Nicolas. "Le Mythe des géants sodomites de Patagonie dans les récits de voyage des chroniqueurs des Indes occidentales." *Inverses*, no. 2 (2002).

Burg, Barry Richard. *Sodomy and the Pirate Tradition: English Sea Rovers in the Seventeenh-Century Caribbean*. New York: New York Univ. Press, 1995.

Carrier, Joseph. *De las Otros: Intimacy and Homosexuality Among Mexican Men*. New York: Columbia Univ. Press, 1995.

Cardin, Alberto. *Guerreros, chamanes y travestís. Indicios de homosexualidad entre los exóticos*. Barcelona: Tusquets, 1989.

"Comisión Ciudadana de Crímenes de Odio por Homofobia," In *Reporte de crímenes 2000*. Mexico: 2001.

Delon, Michel. "Du goût antiphysique des Américains." *Annales de Bretagne*, no. 84 (1977).

Inter-Church Committee on Human Rights in Latin America. *La Violencia al Descubierto: Represión contra Lesbianas y Homosexuales en America Latina*. Toronto: 1996.

Goldberg, Jonathan. "Sodomy in the New World: Anthropologies Old and New." *Social Text*, no. 9 (1991).

Green, James. "Beyond Carnival: Male Homosexuality in Twentieth-Century Brazil." *Journal of Homosexuality* 42, no. 4 (2002).

Lancaster, Roger N. "Subject Honor and Object Shame: The Construction of Male Homosexuality and Stigma in Nicaragua." *Ethnology*, no. 27 (1988).

Mathy, Robin M., and Frederic L. Whitam. *Male Homosexuality in Four Societies: Brazil, Guatemala, the Philippines, and the United States*. New York: Praeger, 1986.

Mendès-Leite, Rommel. "Les Tropiques et les péchés: mésaventures des sodomites." In *Sodomites, invertis, homosexuels: perspectives historiques*. Lille: GayKitschCamp, 1994.

Mott, Luiz. *Epidemic of Hate: Violation of Human Rights of Gay Men, Lesbians and Transvestites in Brazil*. San Francisco: International Gay and Lesbian Human

Rights Commission, 1996.

———, and Marcelo Cerquiera. *Causa Mortis: Homofobia*. Salvador, Brazil: Editora Grupo Gay da Bahia, 2001.

Murray, Stephen. *Male Homosexuality in Central and South America*. San Francisco: Instituto Obregón, 1987.

Ordonez, Juan P. *Ningún Ser Humano es Desechable: Limpieza Social, Derechos Humanos y Orientación Sexual en Colombia*. San Francisco: IGLHRC, 1995.

Ramos, Juanita, ed. *Compaðeras: Latina Lesbians, an Anthology*. New York: Routledge, 1994.

Vainfas, Ronal. *Tropico dos pecados: moral, sexualidad e inquisição no Brasil*. Rio de Janeiro: Campus, 1989.

Williams, Walter. *The Spirit and the Flesh: Sexual Diversity in American Indian Culture*. Boston: Beacon Press. 1986.

Young, Allen. *Gays Under the Cuba Revolution*. San Francisco, Gay Fox Press, 1981.

—Anthropology; Arenas, Reinaldo; Gender Differences; Heterosexism; Inquisition; Police; Spain; Violence.

LAW. *See* European Law

LEDUC, Violette

Violette Leduc (1907–72) was a bisexual novelist and memoirist in France whose work specialized in women's issues, including lesbianism. In her first autobiography *La Bâtarde* (*The Bastard*) (1964), which became her best-known book, she noted that she was born an illegitimate child to a servant girl; her work was borne out of the hopelessness of not being loved, as well as the anguish of self-doubt, but the notoriety associated with her affairs with both men and women did not ultimately mollify her career. Leduc was "a homely woman," according to Simone de Beauvoir—a "bastard," poor, alone, long unrecognized as a writer, and involved sexually with persons of both genders. She was "the sum of all intrusive marginalities," according to Carlo Jansiti, who wrote her biography. Even if it is overly simplistic, as suggested by Leduc scholar Catherine Viollet, to see her work as "purely autobiographical," Leduc's life and writing are interwoven to such a degree that both Leduc the woman and Leduc the writer were subjected to severe criticism; but were all of these critics homophobic?

She was certainly confronted by homophobia early in her life. Her first love affairs were homosexual: in 1925, she fell in love with an undergraduate classmate, Isabelle P. (as documented in her autobiographical novel *Thérèse et Isabelle,* 1966), then with a female supervisor, Denise Hertgès (represented by the character Cécile in *Ravages,* 1955, and Hermine in *La Batârde).* This last liaison provoked her expulsion from college, for reasons of "morality," in 1926. For her mother, though, being homosexual was less ignominious than being an "unwed mother," and this maternal permissiveness might have eased Leduc's own acceptance of her homosexual tendencies. In spite of this, Leduc also had heterosexual liaisons, while her relations with lesbians remained ambiguous. In a letter to Beauvoir, for whom she felt an unrequited passion (she is the "Madame" in *L'Affamée* [Starved], 1948 and also features in *Trésors à prendre* [Treasures to take]*,* 1960), she explained that "women are too weak, too dull to impose their state as a couple when they are not disguising themselves as men." Was this self-denigrating remark a defensive reaction against potential homophobic attacks? It is unlikely, given that Leduc did not hide her admiration for homosexuals such as writer Maurice Sachs, French leftist Daniel Guérin, and Jean Genet (as detailed in the second installment of her autobiography, *La Folie en tête* [*Mad in Pursuit*], 1970). Further, it is not so much the fact that she liked women or surrounded herself with gay men that triggered enmity, but rather her intransigent character: it is possible that her apparent self-hatred transformed into a form of misogyny.

In reality, attacks of a homophobic nature were more specifically aimed at her work than her personal life. The example of her novel *Thérèse et Isabelle* is enlightening; it was initially supposed to be the beginning of her 1955 novel *Ravages* but was dropped as part of 150 pages excised by the publisher Gallimard for being too daring. The novel was inspired by Leduc's real-life passion for her classmate Isabelle, describing the relations between the two young girls with precision. Leduc contended that she was not looking for scandal by writing about the affair, but her "unashamed sincerity" at first offended Beauvoir, who proofread Leduc's manuscripts: "Certain pages are excellent … but as far as publishing this, it is impossible. It is a story of lesbian sexuality as blunt as Genet's work." As for Gallimard, its editors read it as an "enormous and precise obscenity" which had to be censored in order "to suppress its eroticism and keep its affectivity." (The elaborate descriptions of a penis and an abortion also disturbed the editors, but it was the lesbian scenes that were the most scandalous.)

Ravages was thus published in a purged edition in 1955, but Leduc's search for "the magic eye of a breast … the meat of a woman's open sex" remained dear to her heart: "Continue to write after such a denial? I cannot. Hives are coming through my skin at every moment." In 1964, she inserted part of *Thérèse et Isabelle* into the manuscript of *La Bâtarde,* but as Catherine Viollet revealed, this came at the price of self-censorship, as demonstrated by the pages that were stricken out by the author; the rest was published as *Thérèse et Isabelle* in 1966. During this time, homophobic critics became a real problem for the writer. She began to doubt the validity of her writings: "I wouldn't dare … my writing will be disgusting without my meaning it to be" (*La Folie en tête*). She even got to the point where she wondered if "she hated lesbians"; in *La Chasse à l'amour* (The hunt for love), the final installment of her autobiography published posthumously in 1973, she characterized them as sad and "frenzied."

The homophobic criticism of Leduc was puzzling given the abundance of literature portraying lesbians as early as the nineteenth century. Why then were Leduc's writings rejected? According to Leduc biographer Colette Trout Hall, it was because the writer strayed from Baudelaire, Balzac, or Proust's images of the "vicious and damned" female couple. Leduc defined the characters of Thérèse and Isabelle as "too authentic to be vicious," which put into question the traditional representation of lesbianism based on male erotic fantasies. She was the first female writer to assert the value of a lesbian sexuality described from a woman's perspective. While amorous friendship between women was tolerated—the "psychic love" described by lesbian scholar Lillian Faderman—the purely sexual aspect remained taboo, as was well illustrated by the editors' remarks on eroticism and affectivity. Thus, it is possible to describe the censorship exerted against Leduc as not only homophobic, but also anti-feminist.

Just as Leduc herself, a woman who loved women but who felt no empathy for lesbians, her work met a paradoxical fate. In the 1950s, it was the lesbian love scenes that subjected her to censorship; then in the 1970s, she was of no interest to either scholars or feminists because there was no underlying ideology to her lesbianism, contrary to Hélène Cixous or Monique Wittig. For Leduc, desire encompassed women, men, and even nature; it was, above all else, poetry. She "exposes love or even desire's irreducibility to a sexual tendency" (writer and translator René de Ceccatty). Thus the Leduc paradox:

while her writings did not find a large audience prior to 1964—due at least in part to a form of homophobia or even **lesbophobia**—it was the author's own lack of homophilia or lesbophilia that diverted interest in the study of her work before the 1980s.
—*Anne-Claire Rebreyend*

Faderman, Lillian. *Surpassing the Love of Men: Romantic Friendship and Love between Women from the Renaissance to the Present.* New York: Morrow, 1981.

Jansiti, Carlo. *Violette Leduc.* Paris: Grasset, 1999.

Leduc, Violette. *Thérèse et Isabelle. Texte intégral.* Postface and notes by Carlo Jansiti. Paris: Gallimard, 2000.

Trout Hall, Colette. *Violette Leduc, la mal-aimée.* Amsterdam: Rodopi, 1999.

Viollet, Catherine. "Violette Leduc. Les ravages de la censure." In *Genèse textuelle, identités sexuelles.* Paris: Du Lérot, 1997.

—*Censorship; Lesbophobia; Literature; Radclyffe Hall, Marguerite; School; Shame; Scandal.*

LESBOPHOBIA

Why use the term "lesbophobia" when the term "homophobia" concerns homosexuals of both genders? If identity were a similar condition between gays and lesbians, then the distinction would be superfluous. However, this is not the conclusion reached by the French Coordination lesbienne nationale (CLN; National Lesbian Committee). Its study of accounts of homophobia aimed at lesbians, as individuals or as a social group, reveals characteristics that are specific to lesbophobia.

The first is the eclipsing of lesbians in culture and history, as attested by Marie-Jo Bonnet in her work *Les Relations amoureuses entre les femmes* (Love affairs between women). When historians make mention of lesbianism, it is often distorted, reduced to either its sexual or emotional dimension, in contrast to socially recognized pederasty of Greco-Roman society. Even today, the eclipsing of lesbianism by the media is frequent. The presentation of lesbian books or films often neglects to mention the emotional aspect of the relationship between two women. For example, the film *Go Fish* (1994) was "interpreted" by certain newspapers as the "sentimental adventures" of four young women without mentioning the lesbian content, which was quite explicit. French television and press quite readily choose to overlook lesbians, even during the Lesbian and Gay Pride celebrations, despite the banners carried by groups such as Fierté lesbienne (Lesbian Pride) and the CLN. Even without media **censorship**, public opinion nonetheless perceives homosexual culture and community as being essentially male. The little interest given to lesbian culture and organizations contrasts significantly with the abundance of articles devoted to "gay [male] power." This constitutes a sexist manifestation of the second-class status assigned to women in patriarchal society. Thus, the eclipsing of an individual or a legal entity with the intention of denying their existence is an act of **discrimination** which leads to harmful exclusion.

Lesbophobic stigmatization is also specific: if gay men are likened to **pedophiles**, then lesbians are discredited by their representation as "*rabatteuse du porno*," a French term to describe a woman who finds other women for her and her male partner to have sex with. ("*Rabbateur*" is a dog that leads the prey to the hunter.) When its existence is not denied, sex between women is often considered secondary, simplistic and an object of pornographic voyeurism for heterosexual men. Displayed with impunity, this **caricature** of lesbians is defamatory. Consequently, lesbian militants have discovered their names and telephone numbers in pornographic magazines, while certain magazine stands stock *Lesbia Magazine* (a lesbian, cultural, feminist magazine) in the pornography section.

Lastly, if **violence** against lesbians punishes the sexual transgression of masculine/feminine roles, as does violence against gays, the underlying meaning of the aggression differs: essentially, gay men are punished for not exercising their virile power over women, whereas lesbians are chastised for their sexual independence from men. The attacks are aimed at their female gender, their androgynous appearance and their non-submission to the heterosexual and patriarchal order. Examples of this type of violence are easy to find: family rejection, harassment from neighbors with insinuations of a supposed usurpation of the male role, and punitive rape. Further evidence can be gleaned from a sampling of **insults**: from one woman's father, "I'd have preferred that you were a whore"; from a neighbor, "Why don't you go and have some balls sewn on?" In each case, the lesbophobia involves an intensification of sexism.

In order to effectively resist, it is not enough to add the term "sexist" to the term "homophobic." The former concerns all women; the latter, more often than not, brings to mind attacks against gay men only; whereas hate directed toward lesbians encompasses both phenomena, because they suffer discrimination as women in a male-dominated world and as homosexuals in a heterosexual society.

The universalist argument for the mixing of gays and lesbians that opposes the non-mixing argument is, therefore, an illusion. The mixing of men and women only in terms of "men" or "homosexuals," denies the social hierarchy of the sexes, the cultural, political, and economic supremacy of men, and the resultant sexist and lesbophobic discrimination. It disqualifies feminist and lesbian demands. Thus, neutralized in the male universe, lesbians have no way to escape invisibility and defend their dignity and rights other than by revealing the specifics of lesbophobia and demanding it be countered with preventative and strict antidiscrimination legislation.

This analysis is supported by numerous European and North American studies, as well as by foundational texts from lesbian-feminist and/or radical culture. Numerous examples of chastisement and ostracism for refusing to submit to male rule can be found in *The Proceeding of the International Tribunal on Crimes Against Women*. As noted in this report, a Norwegian lesbian is hospitalized and submitted to "re-education," in which coitus with her ex-husband is imposed daily, despite her vomiting; in Germany, judges and journalists take advantage of the trial of two lesbians who murdered a husband to attribute to lesbians a frequent penchant "for all types of murders, suicides, and assassinations," which leads the report's narrator to conclude:

> Discrimination against lesbians represents the extreme sexual oppression practiced against women. In this instance, men's fear that women be sexually independent illustrates itself the most clearly. By their lifestyle, lesbians represent a threat to those very foundations of patriarchal society: **marriage** and **family**. Since women are not supposed to develop their own sexuality, sexual needs in which men are not concerned are forbidden.

In her book *Homosexuality: Power and Politics*, Susan Hemmings writes of the lesbophobic campaign that preceded the decline in gay rights and the increased scarcity of salaried jobs for women in England from

1979 onward: after a female Labour Party candidate who was suspected of being a lesbian and was forced to come out publicly, a newspaper published the following comment: "The Lord gave us two sexes with a mutual attraction in order to perpetuate the race and those men and women who seek to pervert this plan go against God's will"; *The Evening News* denounced the idea of artificial insemination for lesbian couples, expressing the horror of imagining a child raised without a father. In an article titled "Boys Will Be Boys," a journalist for the *Daily Express* attacked a school teacher because she taught "ten ways to fight sexism at school," thus compromising her career. In this campaign, anti-feminism becomes linked to anti-lesbianism. In an essay entitled "Des droits à reconnaître" (Rights to be recognized), Quebecois lesbians underline the role institutions play in such waves of reaction: the hospital where a medical team attributed a woman's problems to her lesbianism; the court that revoked a lesbian mother's custody of her child by associating lesbianism with sexual **perversion**, etc.

Irene Demcsuk and Linda Peers remind us that medical and psychoanalytical language are implicated in the pathologization of lesbianism. Even if this supposed sickness no longer appears in the nosography, the stigma is still conveyed socially and remains present in people's minds. In order to explain this discrimination, the authors call into question "the constraint of heterosexuality," "a constraint whose function is to ensure the patriarchal control of women's bodies." They borrow this concept from Adrienne Rich, for whom "heterosexuality is neither a fact of nature, nor an innate characteristic, but a social construction affected by the relations of the sexes and by the domination of women by men." This "constraint to heterosexuality" is, according to them, ideological: "**Heterosexism**" is the "patriarchal ideology founded on the presumption that all individuals must be heterosexual under threat of being presumed immoral, perverse, deviant, sick, deficient and, therefore, inferior."

If this definition applies to gays as well as lesbians, it seems to apply more to the latter in that it reveals the sexist component of homophobia. The foundational texts of lesbian-feminist culture illustrate the systemic functioning that produces this ideology, though neither terms "heterosexist" nor "lesbophobia" are to be found anywhere in them. In the tradition of Kate Millett, Nicole-Claude Matthieu, and Christine Delphy, Collette Guillaumin's materialist feminism denounces

the multiple ways that the class of men oppresses the class of women by way of "sexing," that is, the private appropriation of each woman by a husband or father and the collective appropriation of all women. Monique Wittig's materialist lesbianism calls into question the categories of "man" and "woman" themselves: "The categories in question function as primitive concepts in a conglomerate of various disciplines, theories, trends, and ideas that I would call 'straight thought.' … It's a question of woman, man, difference, and the whole series of concepts that are affected by this marking, including concepts such as history, culture, and reality." Wittig emphasizes the political finality of this conceptual structure: "Heterosexuality is the political system in which we live, based upon the enslavement of women." Consequently, the woman who loves another woman and who does not belong to a man must "consider herself a fugitive, an escaped slave, a lesbian." This leads Wittig to state: "It would be wrong to say that lesbians live, associate, and make love to women as the term woman exists solely in heterosexual systems of thought and economic systems. Lesbians are not women."

These analyses allow us to better understand, whether we want to or not, why lesbianism is intolerable for patriarchal society and in what ways it is subversive. They offer an adoptive strategy in order to combat lesbophobia. Monique Wittig's strategy seeks "a total conceptual re-evaluation of social fabric": "The transformation of economic relationships is not enough. We must implement a political transformation of key concepts, that is to say, those concepts which are strategic for us." Wittig's lesbian consciousness is not aimed at transgression, but rather the abolition of the gender and sex upon which the notion of universality itself is based. Her strategy also consists of reinventing language and literary genres that subvert heterocultural heritage, in order to offer women (and men?) examples of what writing, fiction, and a lesbian-specific utopia could be.

As stakeholders in this revolutionary current, radical lesbians pursue the deconstruction of the heterosexual system with the objective of abolishing it. For them, "the constitution of a lesbian community represents the basis of a political force, and not a simple expression of identity." It is for these reasons that, since the 1978 split, some radical lesbians keep their distance from the "hetero-feminists" who do not call into question the supremacy of heterosexuality as the foundation of patriarchy and the oppression of all women. If the imprint of materialist lesbianism and radical lesbianism is real in European and North American society, lesbian activism has diversified and, some would say, compromised itself in homosexual reformism in order to obtain social recognition and equal rights.

In France, because of the plurality of groups and a non-monolithic political conscience, the CLN has pragmatically decided to promote lesbian visibility and the defense of their rights as citizens. This translates, notably, into the active presence of CLN representatives in the offices of the Collectif national pour les droits de la femme (National Collective for Women's Rights), in the coordination of the European Women's Lobby, and by its participation in the World March of Women. Their work organizes around understanding lesbophobia as the ultimate expression of sexism and in revealing the need for mutual support between heterosexual women and lesbians. The positive results of this approach attest to the fact that only patient explanation of our common oppression can reverse the systemic heterosexism instilled within each and every one of us.

The struggle against lesbophobic attacks also progresses through solidarity with gay men, who, if they benefit from the privileges of the dominant class because they are men, are still oppressed because they too suffer from heterosexual constraint. If collective action aims to integrate sexual orientation into anti-discriminatory legislation, it is imperative that political prevention and laws take into account the sexist dimension of lesbophobia. This explains why the CLN wishes to bring, beyond the collective goal, its own amendments to the law where necessary. As legal expert Anne Le Gall states, "You can have neither discipline, nor way of expression, nor mystique even, nor transcendence, nor a relationship with another if you are not an autonomous individual, including on the legal, social and political level as brought about by *law*; and a law which applies to men as it does to women."

—*Raymonde Gérard*

Coordination lesbienne nationale. "La Lesbophobie en France" report (March 2001).

Bonnet, Marie-Jo. *Les Relations amoureuses entre les femmes*. Paris: Odile Jacob, 1995.

Delphy, Christine. *L'Ennemi principal*. Paris: Syllepse, 1976. [Published in the UK as *The Main Enemy*. London: Women's Research and Resources Centre Publications, 1977.]

Guillaumin, Colette. *Sexe, race, et pratique du pouvoir—L'idée de nature*. Paris: Côté-Femmes Editions, 1992. [Published in English as *Racism, Sexism, Power and Ideology*. New York: Routledge, 1995.]

Lesselier, Claudie. "Formes de résistance et d'expression lesbienne: dans les années 1950 et 1960 en France." In *Homosexualités: expression/répression*. Edited by Louis-Georges Tin. Paris: Stock, 2000.

Millett, Kate. *La Politique du mâle*. Paris: Stock, 1971.

Matthieu, Nicole-Claude. *L'Anatomie politique*. Paris: Côté-Femmes Editions, 1991.

Rich, Adrienne. "La Contrainte à l'hétérosexualité et l'existence lesbienne." *Nouvelles questions féministes*, no. 1 (1981). [Published in the US as "Compulsory Heterosexuality and Lesbian Experience," *Signs* 5, no. 4 (Summer 1980).]

Russel, Diana E. H., and Nicole Van de Ven. *The Proceeding of the International Tribunal on Crimes Against Women*.

Wittig, Monique. *La Pensée straight*. Paris: Balland, 2001.

—*Biphobia; Gayphobia; Heterophobia; Heterosexism; Radclyffe Hall, Marguerite; Rhetoric; Sappho; Transphobia.*

LITERATURE

There is a persistent assumption that literary milieus are free of the rigors of homophobia and among the few venues in which homosexuals can freely express themselves. However, this popular opinion misunderstands the conditions under which most literary works of the past were produced. It neglects to take into consideration the fate suffered by homosexual authors from different eras, such as Théophile de **Viau**, Oscar **Wilde**, and Reinaldo **Arenas**. Far from being spared from homophobia, on the contrary, they were particularly exposed to it, due to their notoriety as writers. In reality, many authors suffered from this experience. Beyond those who were charged with crimes, found guilty, and jailed, one must also include those who were never apprehended nor condemned, but who nevertheless had to suffer the hardship of social and moral constraints exercised against them because of their homosexuality; these writers include Giacomo Leopardi, Nikolai Gogol, Tennessee Williams, Thomas Mann, Julien Green, and **Radclyffe Hall**, an open lesbian who was forced to endure the ordeal of **scandal** as a result.

Homophobic discourses and practices in the literary

world have not been thoroughly explored by scholars, and while it is surely difficult to propose a unified hypothesis on the subject, it is possible to shed light on it. Homophobic logic in literature operates on two distinct levels: by authors who claim to unmask homosexuality in order to properly denounce it in accordance with morality; and by literary editors who try to mask homosexuality when it appears in the works of others, again in accordance with morality.

For authors, this logic results in the production of a discourse against homosexuality, while for editors, it is the dismantling or transformation of a work to make homosexuality appear less attractive. Discursive production on one hand, reduction on the other; it is not uncommon for such seemingly opposite mechanisms to be complementary to one another while working toward the same goal. As a consequence, one can say that a homophobic poetics exists on one hand, and a philological homophobia on the other; both contribute to the assignment of homosexuality to a predetermined literary space.

From the Homophobic Poetic …

This poetics of homophobic discourses through the centuries has succeeded in adjusting its literary means to its ideological objectives. In this way, it has often employed the genre of satire in order to intensify the vigor of its homophobic attacks. Generally, such satires portray their subjects in a negative light by saddling them with morals that are judged loathsome; further, it tends to draw on archetypal homosexual behavior, dwelling on small details of character which claim to be revealing. One common means was to depict homosexuality in the guise of the effeminate man or the manly woman. Added to this was a cheerful narrative tone, thereby giving the appearance of levity to comments and situations that were often quite heinous. Satire was thus the faux mirror of "truth" which allowed the symbolic and joyful killing of stigmatized persons.

This is how **Henri III** of France was denounced by numerous poets in the sixteenth century, such Pierre de Ronsard and Agrippa d'Aubigné, who devoted numerous lines of *Les Tragiques,* in which he evoked "the effeminate gesture, Sardanapale's eye / … as at first, everyone was in difficulty / if he say a woman King or a man Queen." Similarly, in the following century, Cardinal Mazarin became a favorite target of satirists when he was accused of **vice**, a fact which French

dramatist Paul Scarron, in his famous *Mazarinade,* did not hesitate to shout from the rooftops. According to Scarron, Mazarin would be "Sodom's wand sergeant / exploiting the realm everywhere / Devil buggering, buggered devil / and bugger to the highest degree / bugger with hair and bugger with feather / bugger in big and small volume / Bugger sodomizing the State / and bugger with the most carats.…" Whether the accusation of homosexuality was true or not, these satires permitted of the subject's symbolic beating or murder, regardless of his status.

That said, homophobic satire remained common throughout the twentieth century, mostly in light-hearted stage comedies which evoke over-the-top queens or young men who are "a little like that." In fact, the homosexual (the gay man, because the lesbian does not appear often in these representations) is frequently present, but always in a secondary role. He has a definite function: he is the proscribed entertainer on duty, performing the same function as the idiot in medieval theater, or the harlequin in the *commedia dell'arte.* Beyond provoking laughter, this character is a deeply anguished figure, and he exorcises this anguish by laughing at the top of his voice. The "queen" character is easily recognizable by his mannerisms, his melodramatic responses, his limp wrists, and his eccentric, colorful clothes: the social stereotype becomes a theatrical and literary type, unless it is the reverse. Even if theatrical history grants little importance to such plays, they nonetheless played an important role in the popular cultural representation of homosexuals; many audience members were only acquainted with homosexuals through their appearance in such plays. Under these conditions, and in the context of homophobic satire, homosexuality was necessarily depicted as a comical yet distressing reality, familiar yet troubling, as shown in Jean Cau's 1973 play, in which the protagonist learns that his wife is having an affair with his best friend and, at the height of his misery, that his son "is like that," the "illness" having spread throughout the entire country; hence the play's title, *Pauvre France* (Poor France). But the pinnacle of the genre was reached with Jean Poiret's 1973 play *La Cage aux Folles,* in which French actor Michel Serrault appeared over 1,500 times (a film version was released in 1978, followed by a stage musical a few years later, both enjoyed incredible commercial success in France, the United States, and elsewhere). Its two characters, the same-sex couple Renato and Albin, a.k.a. Zaza (a drag queen), were touching but pathetic; at the same time, the popularity of the play (and film) largely served to perpetuate stereotypes, contributing further to popular homophobia.

Besides satire, the homophobic poetic also developed two other trends: one, the religious, moralizing sermon, and the other, didactic, scholarly literature. These two trends have radically different approaches. The moralizing discourse willfully employs maxims, biblical references, and hyperbole to support its themes; the scholarly discourse is more tempered, using rigorous terminology and methodology to further its claims. What unites these two styles, however, is their serious and somber approach to their subject, unlike satire. From St Thomas Aquinas' *Summa théologica* to André Breton's "Recherches sur la sexualité" (Research on sexuality), from Father Garasse's *La Doctrine curieuse* (The curious doctrine) to Etienne Pivert de Senancour's *De l'amour* (On love) to Pierre-Joseph Proudhon's *Amour et marriage* (Love and marriage), these works found ways to perpetuate, even if incidentally, the most obscurant prejudices toward homosexuality. Voltaire himself, in his *Lettres sur la justice* (Letters on justice), saw in sodomy "a low and disgusting **vice** whose real punishment is scorn," a passing of judgment that he confirmed in the article "Amour socratique" (Socratic love) in the *Dictionnaire philosophique* (The philosophical dictionary), while at the same time admitting that it did not warrant **prison.**

In novels, however, homophobic discourse revealed itself to be more difficult to analyze due to distortions introduced through the device of fiction. At the end of the nineteenth century and the beginning of the twentieth, a series of popular novels was published in France in which homosexuality was presented in a stereotyped, unhealthy way, albeit seductive at times: novels such as Gabriel Fauré's *La Dernière journée de Sapphô* (The last day of Sappho) (1901), Dr J de Cherveix's *Amour inverti* (Inverted love) (1907), Charles-Étienne's *Notre Dame de Lesbos* (1924) and *Léon dit Léonie* (1922), Victor Margeuritte's famous *La Garçonne* (The bachelor girl) (1922), Willy and Menalkas's *L'Ersatz d'amour* (The ersatz of love) (1922), and Charles-Noël Renard's *Les Androphobes* (1930). These novels superimposed successive layers of the homophobic imagination: the ancient courtesan with doubtful morals, the **heretic** from the Middle Ages, the **debauched** aristocrat from the Ancien Régime, the androgyne of the nineteenth

century, and the invert—the figure of the third sex, as described in pseudo-scientific theories of the era: all of these types and more appeared through the artistic gaze of a languid prose that seemed to take pleasure in evoking what it was in fact stigmatizing.

To this effect, Marcel Proust's master work *A la recherche du temps perdu* (*Remembrance of Things* Past) constitutes a particularly emblematic case due to its essential ambiguity. In his novels, homosexuality is tied to the dark legend of **Sodom and Gomorrah;** it appears as a trait of slavish servants such as Jupien, and decadent aristocrats such as Charlus, and is depicted as it meanders tortuously in a somber and long descent to Hell, which ends in the final revelation of *Temps retrouvé* (*Past Recaptured*), when all of the inverts finally drop their masks and reveal their degradation. As complex and seductive as these characters might seem, they are nonetheless branded by the ancestral curse which appears to weigh heavily on them.

In this respect, the literary prism through which the narrator depicts homosexuality is clearly linked to all three genres of the homophobic poetic: satire, moral and religious tradition, and finally, medical opinion of the time that understood **inversion** to be a disease, an opinion shared by hallowed dissertations on the subject of *Sodom and Gomorrah*. But in reality, *Temps perdu* is neither a satire, nor a moral or science-based discourse: it is a work of fiction that orchestrates a number of social discourses in a polyphonic ensemble, which can be read in multiple ways.

However, this vision of homosexuality, thoroughly negative though refined—by a gay author, no less—certainly annoyed André **Gide**, himself a homosexual: "This offending of the truth is likely to please everyone: the heterosexual, whose warnings it justifies and whose loathings it flatters; and the others, who will now have an alibi and who will benefit by their scant resemblance to those whom he portrays. In short, given the general tendency to cowardice, I do not know any writing which is more likely than Proust's *Sodom* to encourage wrong-headed thinking." And according to Gaston Gallimard, Gide even said to Proust: "You have driven back the question to where it was fifty years ago." As a matter of fact, before Proust's homosexuality was known, his work was understood as that of an austere moralist. "To repress a vice, one must have the courage to denounce it by making it odious," Paul de Bellen wrote about him in the anti-Semetic periodical *La Libre Parole,* completely satisfied with

At the end of the nineteenth century, and the beginning of the twentieth, a whole body of literature took aim at homosexuals, generally presented as intersexual, degenerate, and decadent beings.

the "odious" portraiture of inverts created by Proust. For Roger Allard, the work's greatest merit was that it "breaks the aesthetic charm of sexual inversion." And for Paul Souday, Proust was to be commended because he "does not directly describe these delinquents' excesses, but studies their psychology in relation to their **vice**." In all, homophobic prejudices felt completely reassured by *Temps perdu*.

However, Proust himself, and Gide most assuredly, made homosexuality fashionable in the world of letters. In fact, in 1926, Eugène Montfort, in the French periodical *Les Marges,* launched an investigation into the preoccupation with homosexual themes in literature. Writers who were questioned on the subject— Henri Barbusse, François Mauriac, and Pierre Drieu la Rochelle, among others—noted with disdain an increase in interest in this topic in contemporary novels. In order to fight it, it was determined that it was no longer sufficient to merely unmask homosexuality, given that it dared to show itself spontaneously and without any modesty; what had to be done was just the opposite.

… to Philological Homophobia
Hiding homosexuality is the other great recourse of homophobia in general. Rather than condemn it outright, certain opponents of homosexuality used subtle yet no less effective means related to philology to deal with its appearance in literature, including reforming pagan works of the literary pantheon long after they were written: those Greek and Roman authors, renowned and consecrated, who wrote immodestly about same-sex relationships.

Concealment of texts was the first technique. The most troubling ones were often hidden away in oubliettes; unless some miraculous exhumation occurs, we will never see them. We can at the most dream of those lost treasures that time's furor has very often destroyed. The second technique: mutilation; usually the original versions of texts, which were then censored. This is how the works of **Sappho**, Anacreon, Pindar, Catullus, Virgil, Horace, Tibullus, and Martial were sanitized in order to be made more acceptable (i.e. heterosexual). The third technique: falsification, in which the text was not maimed but rather modified in order to remove any implications of homosexuality, a task that was often as simple as changing pronouns from "he" to "she."

This is the manner in which Michelangelo's poems

were treated. For sixty years, his heirs hid his manuscripts; finally, the texts were published, but the love sonnets addressed to his lover Tommaso dei Cavalieri were either censored outright, or the identity of the person addressed was neutralized or feminized. This is how the line "I am prisoner of an armed rider" became "I am prisoner of a heart armed with virtue." It was only in 1897 that a German scholar, Karl Frey, finally restored the original text. Michelangelo's work was thus concealed, mutilated, *and* falsified.

These techniques serve to heterosexualize both the text and the author. On a subtler level, however, it is sometimes possible to obtain just as effective a result by using hermeneutic tools (methods that seek to interpret the true final essence of the text) instead: it suffices to interpret, and to alter not the text so much as the judgment of the future readers. Published in 1609, Shakespeare's *Sonnets* constitute an enlightening example of this; the first 126 love poems are addressed to a young man, and the twenty-four which follow are addressed to the mysterious and somber "Dark Lady." In 1640, John Benson published a new edition of the *Sonnets* in which he transformed *he* and *his* into *she* and *her*. But inasmuch as the original text was already accessible to the public, his awkward philological intervention risked attracting attention to the same-sex phenomenon that he hoped to conceal. More slyly, similar literary revisionists in the century that followed explained to readers that Shakespeare's odd use of pronouns was a peculiar verbal usage of the Elizabethan era. Samuel Taylor Coleridge, who was more embarrassed by the *Sonnets* than anything else, at first affirmed that the poems indeed evoked a young man, but that it was without real love; then he declared the contrary, that they were about love, but were not *really* addressed to a young man; Shakespeare had used the masculine pronouns in order to mislead readers! As for François-Victor Hugo—who also took a turn at translating the poems—he imagined that the pieces addressing the young man were written by a weeping female lover, of whom we see no trace in the work.

Evidently, these *Sonnets* caused problems not because they were about gay love (which would have been sufficient cause to throw them into the bowels of the libraries), but because their author was William Shakespeare. To suggest that the Great Shakespeare could be a sodomite was nearly blasphemous, given that he was already regarded as the most important man of letters. Those in agreement with this perspective, seized by a strong **heterosexist** will, subsequently tried to restore his reputation and integrate him by force into the community of "good people," using inventive and imaginative techniques.

This example is far from being an isolated one. The diverse practices of concealment, mutilation, falsification, and reinterpretation were often used to heterosexualize writers long after their death. We would also be wrong to believe that such techniques belong to another era; although they are increasingly untenable, evidence of similar homophobic attempts at literary revisionism appeared throughout the twentieth century. But today, the most current means is without doubt euphemization. In this way, the numerous lesbian aspects of Colette's work, not only in *Le Pur et l'Impur* (*The Pure and the Impure*) but in the *Claudine* novels as well, are only vaguely evoked, at least in France. Even with Proust's critics, homosexuality was often made relative: it was determined to be only a marginal theme, and not a very interesting one, either. (One critic claimed that Proust was "heterosexual in his soul"!)

But euphemization is still derived from hermeneutics. So nowadays, those who still insist on this homophobic effort will rely less on such coarse interpretive tools; they will employ more political arguments instead. For example, when a writer's homosexuality is mentioned to clarify his or her work, they will try to smother the discourse by providing suspect objections ("Isn't this gay or lesbian **communitarianism**?"; "Should we not respect the author's **privacy**?") on the other hand, the private lives of heterosexual authors are almost always taken into account when explaining their oeuvre.

Thomas Mann's reticence in discussing his homosexuality might legitimize the reticence of critics after his death. But considering the author of *Death in Venice* ordered that his diaries not be opened until twenty years after his death, claims that Mann's closetedness was a reason to *not* read his work as homosexual seems more like an avoidance strategy, especially given this biographical "detail" does indeed shed light on certain of Mann's works. Similarly, the posthumous publication of Roland Barthes' *Incidents* raised earnest critiques where people saw a kind of post-mortem **outing**. But in reality, this text was a revelation for no one: his earlier *Fragments d'un discours amoureux* (*A Lover's Discourse*), in spite of its sensual and poetic abstraction, succeeded in deceiving only a few, while in *Roland Barthes par Roland Barthes* (*Roland Barthes by Roland Barthes*), the author clearly revealed himself, albeit with some reservations.

Viewed generally, instances of homophobia in the world of letters might seem infrequent. This false impression is in fact due to its means of expression; it essentially acts by working negatively and subtly, which makes it invisible and thus that much more effective: self-censorship and prudence have led numerous authors over the years to abandon or refuse to publish works featuring homosexual content. One only has to think of E. M. Forster's *Maurice* (written in 1913–14 but finally published in 1971, a year after Forster's death), Federico García Lorca's *Sonetos del amor oscuro* (Sonnets of dark love), Umberto Saba's *Ernesto,* Jean Cocteau's *Le Livre blanc* (*The White Book*), or Roger Martin du Gard's *Lieutenant-colonel de Maumort*. And when other homosexual-tinged works were brought into the world, they were often concealed, mutilated, falsified, and otherwise ignored. Under these conditions, the literary space as constituted could seem surprisingly neutral and seemingly exempt from homophobia (in addition to being exempt from homosexuality). Rarefied from then on, depictions of homosexuality were relegated to moral satires or science-based discourses, insofar as they were able to present the subject as unfavorably as possible.

Starting with the twentieth century but particularly in the last few decades, political and social conditions have allowed the emergence of a homosexual literature in which allusion, euphemism, and paraphrasing are no longer mandatory. Heroes of such works are no longer necessarily condemned to misfortune (Julien Green's *Sud*), delinquency (Jean Genet's *Journal du voleur*) or to **suicide** (Roger Martin du Gard's *Un taciturne* [The silent one]). Further lesbian literature is finally starting to assert itself and be recognized for what it is. In such works, homosexuality not only appears without apology, a certain number of them in fact attempt to vigorously oppose homophobia. This was the intention of Gide's *Corydon,* his "defense" of homosexuality published in 1924; it is also the goal of an anthology of poems edited by Scott Gibson entitled *Blood and Tears: Poems for Matthew* **Shepard**. But what seems true, or at least possible, in most Western countries is certainly not the case in the rest of the world. In these regions, the freedom to write on the subject, as on many others, remains a distant horizon.

—*Louis-Georges Tin*

Bristow, Joseph. *Sexual Sameness: Sexual Difference in Gay and Lesbian Writing.* London: Routledge, 1992.

Dollimore, Jonathan. *Sex, Literature and Censorship.* Cambridge, UK: Polity Press, 2001.

Jay, Karla, and Joanne Glasgow, eds. *Lesbian Texts and Contexts: Radical Revisions.* New York: New York Univ. Press, 1990.

Larrivière, Michel. *Les Amours masculines, l'homosexualité dans la littérature.* Paris: Lieu commun, 1984.

Marks, Elain, and George Stambolian. *Homosexualities and French Literature.* Ithaca, New York/London: Cornell Univ. Press, 1979.

Laurent, Emile. *La Poésie décadente devant la science psychiatrique.* Paris: Maloine, 1897.

———. *Les Marges* 35, no. 141 (March 1926). New edition edited by Patrick Cardon in *Cahiers GayKitschCamp,* no. 19. Lille: 1993.

McFarlane, Cameron. *The Sodomite in Fiction and Satire, 1660–1750.* New York: Colombia Univ. Press, 1997.

Munt, Daily, ed. *New Lesbian Criticism: Literary and Cultural Reading.* London: Harvester, 1992.

Robinson, Christopher. *Scandal in the Ink: Male and Female Homosexuality in Twentieth Century French Literature.* London: Cassel, 1995.

Rosario, Vernon. "Inversion's Histories/History's Inversions. Novelizing Fin-de-Siècle Homosexuality." In *Science and Homosexualities.* New York/London: Routledge, 1997.

Salducci, Pierre, ed. *Ecrire gai.* Québec: Stanké, 1999.

Tin, Louis-Georges. "La Littérature homosexuelle en question." In *Homosexualités: expression/répression.* Paris: Stock, 2000.

Woods, Gregory. *A History of Gay Literature, the Male Tradition.* New Haven, CT/London: Yale Univ. Press, 1998.

—*Arenas, Reinaldo; Art; Comic Books; Censorship; Cinema; Dance; Duras, Marguerite; Gide, André; Humor; Leduc, Violette; Music; Pasolini, Pier Paolo; Radclyffe Hall, Marguerite; School; Song; Viau, Théophile de; Villon, François; Wilde, Oscar.*

LOBBY

The word "lobby" is often invoked in France in a homophobic context when it is used to criticize the actions of the so-called "gay lobby." For example, a March 16, 1999 article on the subject of gay **parenting** entitled "La Contre-attaque du lobby homosexuel" (The counterattack of the homosexual lobby) published in the French Catholic newspaper *Présent* was accompanied by an illustration of two men welcoming a small child by saying, "Don't be afraid, you can see we're welcoming you with open … sheets."

Unfortunately, the homophobic use of the expression "gay lobby" is not limited to the **far right**. During the heated debates in France on the **PaCS** (Pacte civil de solidarité; Civil Solidarity Pact) proposal, it was often heard coming from the mouths of French members of parliament. For example, Guy Teissier, a Liberal Democrat, declared that PaCS "was invented by a gay MP to satisfy the demands of the gay lobby and to honor an electoral promise made to the gay community" (September 10, 1998). In a free bimonthly distributed in the 8th and 9th arrondissements of Paris, MP Pierre Lellouche of the RPR (Rally for the Republic) wrote: "PaCS is a string pulled by a lobby, taken up by the Left, and which, little by little, is being wound into an uncontrollable ball: **family,** society as a whole, the role of the state, solidarity, personal property and welfare…. The most scandalous fact is that this text, which is a tragedy for the well-being of our society, is presented as being modern." Similarly, in a widely distributed flyer, the French association Avenir de la culture (Future of the Culture) stated with regard to PaCS that "it's obvious that the offensive by the gay lobby will spearhead the destruction of the essential principles of our civilization."

Just like the concept of the gay "**ghetto**," the homophobic accusations of gay lobbying are premised on the idea that gay and lesbian **associations** work on the basis of **communitarianism**. On the other hand, contrary to the "ghetto" argument, lobbying is also premised on describing the gay and lesbian movement as a special interest group whose demands are detrimental to the greater public interest, whose aim is to influence society. The word is frequently used to refute the legitimacy of the associative or militant action surrounding an issue, which implies that gay associations achieve certain goals by bribing politicians or through other underhanded methods. This strategy is very close to that used historically against the Jews and the Freemasons, making use of the **rhetoric** of conspiracy. Just as the Jews were accused of plotting (as exemplified by "The Protocols of the Elders of Zion," a 1903 Russian article detailing a Jewish plan to achieve world domination that was later revealed to be an anti-semitic literary forgery), homosexuals are depicted as gathering in secret in order to plan the destruction of society and civilization, as demonstrated by a pamphlet entitled *The Gay Manifesto*, widely distributed in 1999 by the Miami-Dade chapter of the Christian Coalition in the United States, which revealed this alleged conspiracy as hatched by gays and lesbians.

However, the reality of gay "lobbying" is quite the opposite. In France during the PaCS debates, the only meaningful lobby that was hard at work was the conservative, anti-gay/pro-life lobby, a sufficiently powerful and well-financed group with the means to conduct a letter-writing campaign to over 35,000 French mayors seeking their support. The group Avenir de la culture, representing one simple link in the chain, was able to send out a petition to hundreds of thousands of French citizens warning them against the "sodomites" and their pernicious plans. An influential group capable of organizing mass demonstrations premised not on progress but on **discrimination**, the anti-gay lobby also had the means to organize and finance the transportation of hundreds of demonstrators from all over France into Paris. Each demonstrator received a high quality T-shirt with the slogan "PaCS OUT" at an estimated cost of $400,000.

As for the gay lobby, if it truly existed, right-wing MPs would not have succeeded in blocking the French government's motion for the PaCS proposal on October 9, 1999, nor would left-wing members, who held the majority in the National Assembly, neglect to show up for the vote. Despite all that has been said by conservatives, the gay lobby in France proved its non-existence by this very act. On the other hand, something else came of October 9: PaCS proponents who had not been initially concerned about the mo-tion, believing that the gay lobby had it taken care of, were shocked into mobilization. As a result, a coalition of gay organizations came together to establish the Observatoire du PaCS, dedicated to the resurrection of the civil union proposal. Members dissected the successful methods used by the anti-PaCS lobby, then adapted them for their own use. Thus, the inaction of the gay lobby on that day was a call to arms, permitting a mobilization of political will. Is this how a lobby is born? Only history will tell. Whatever the case, by its pejorative connotations, the term "lobby" is still used in homophobic rhetoric to discredit the legitimacy of the gay and lesbian movement. What remains to be seen is if this presumed lobbying, whose objective is to fight against **violence** and discrimination, will one day be understood for what it is: the noble principle of political action and democracy at work.

—*Caroline Fourest*

Boutin, Christine. *Le "Mariage" des homosexuels? CUCS, PIC, PACS et autres projets législatifs.* Paris: Critérion, 1998.

Bull, Chris, and John Gallagher. *Perfect Enemies: The Religious Right, the Gay Movement, and the Politics of the 1990s.* New York: Crown Publishers, 1996.

Clamen, Michel. *Le Lobbying et ses secrets: guide des techniques d'influence.* Paris: Dunod, 2000.

Goldstein, Kenneth M. *Interest Groups, Lobbying and Participation in America.* New York: Cambridge Univ. Press, 1999.

Herman, Didi. *The Antigay Agenda.* Chicago/London: Univ. of Chicago Press, 1997.

—*Anti-PaCS; Communitarianism; Ghetto; Heterosexism; Peril; Proselytism; Rhetoric; Universalism/Differentialism.*

M

MAGHREB

Law & Politics

The Maghreb, which means "place of sunset" or "western" in Arabic, generally refers to the Northern African region of Morocco, Algeria, and Tunisia. Laws governing sexuality represent some of the most extreme manifestations of homophobia there. Sexual relations between persons of the same gender are considered crimes in the same category as "indecent assaults." In Morocco, homosexuality, defined in Section 489 of the penal code as an "immodest or unnatural act with an individual of one own sex," is punishable by six months to three years in **prison** or a fine of 120 to 1,200 dirhams (about $15 to $150 US). Sections 333 and 338 of the Algerian penal code provide a penalty of six months to three years in prison and a fine of 1,000 to 10,000 dinar (also $15 to $150 US) "when the public offense to modesty consists of an unnatural act with an individual of the same sex." In Tunisia, homosexuality as such is not illegal but Section 230 of the penal code stipulates that "sodomy … is punished by a jail term of three years." These laws compel citizens to heterosexuality and consider any homosexual to be a dangerous delinquent in society. Under these conditions, even talking about one's same-sex attractions or practices puts one at risk not only of being rejected and stigmatized by society, but also of being reported to the **police**. In the same way, those who frequent known gay meeting places risk being arrested during police raids, whose frequency varies depending on the current political climate—specifically, the will of politicians to "declare war on sexual deviations," associating the fight against homosexuality with the fight against crime in general; raids are also conducted as a function of the homophobic rhetoric of fundamentalist Muslims in each of these countries. This makes Algeria the country where, beyond legislation, homophobic practices of all types are the most blatant in the region. In fact, many of the foreign-born homosexuals who

flee their homeland and claim refugee status in France are Algerian. However, one also notes that in Morocco, in 1988, the publication of an article by Latefa Imane and Hinde Taarji in *Kalima* on male homosexuality and prostitution among the street kids of Marrakech was followed by numerous arrests and the banning of the magazine. Then in the spring of 2001, Casablanca's police chief organized a whole series of arrests of homosexuals; he later boasted in *Bayane Al Yaoum* about his extraordinary efficiency in the fight against crime, as the number of arrests for "sexual deviancy" had greatly increased "due to" his intervention. As for Tunisia, information is unfortunately nonexistent.

The criminalization of homosexuality serves to perpetuate it along the same lines as prostitution or theft, resulting in the situation in which homosexuals who are victims of **violence** are unable to assert their legal rights, and as a result, their perpetrators go unpunished. In 1995, in an internal report of the Morocco Association for the Fight Against **AIDS**, Latefa Imane revealed that "young [male] prostitutes, particularly the most effeminate, are the source of a very lucrative commerce between prison guards and other prisoners," with victims being unable to complain about their aggressors or pimps. One can also note that in all three countries, the protection of homosexuals' human rights is nowhere to be found on the government agenda. The necessity for homosexuals to hide in the Maghreb creates an invisibility that leads one to think perhaps that homosexuality does not exist in the region, and that it is perhaps a Western phenomenon. In this way, resisting Western imperialism uses the words of homophobic discourse.

Family Against Homosexuality

These laws also depict homosexuality as an act of disgrace by men and as an act of rebellion by women; to better understand these notions and their implications, one has to consider the typical family in the Maghreb. Parents and children constitute a small unit within a larger group based on agnatic, or male-descended, lineage. This lineage is synonymous with family and honor, and the family name—the father's name—is the incarnation of this honor. Loosely, honor is defined in this sense by a set of codes that outline the respective roles of men and women and establish sexual norms. The perpetuation of the family and the family name requires male progeny; male honor is achieved through **marriage**, fathering male children, and, of course, heterosexuality.

Under these conditions, a boy's homosexuality, when it is claimed publicly as an identity, particularly if it is "feminine" as a result of the "passive" practice of sodomy, constitutes an affront to the familial lineage, a disgrace that cannot be tolerated; it has been said that it is considered a transgression more serious than rape or pedophilia, although this classification thankfully cannot be verified in legislation. The lost honor must be re-established by the men of the family, first by the father and brothers. Such a re-establishment can only be done by the social death of the homosexual subject, who is forced to abandon all sexual practices and face numerous sanctions, humiliations, and, finally, systematic exclusion from the family.

After being beaten, insulted, and sometimes even raped by his brothers as punishment, the homosexual boy is thrown into the street and banished by his family; he is informed that he "will have no inheritance rights" or that he will be "stricken from the family book." After being designated as a person unworthy of being considered a "real man," and losing his dignity, pride, and honor, the homosexual boy is effectively treated as a "half-man," while the homophobes who scorn him are "men of honor" and "real men."

The treatment of lesbians is slightly different as, on one hand, a girl's status in the family is not as highly valued as that of boys and, on the other, sexuality is strictly defined by male penetration. This means that since the perpetuation of the family lineage does not depend on the daughters but rather on the sons, lesbianism is not a threat to it. Further, from the perspective of sexuality, the honor of a woman rests on the preservation of her virginity until her wedding day. It follows that lineage is not endangered by lesbian sexuality when it is confined to the premarital period. In fact, the lesbian figure makes people smile, and lesbianism is simply not thought of as an existing or even possible sexuality: the lesbian is thus almost absent from the collective imagination. Of course, when a lesbian openly opposes

marriage or presents herself with masculine characteristics, lesbianism becomes an act of insubordination to heterosexual order on the one hand and to the hierarchy of sexes on the other. When viewed in this way, the moral condemnation of lesbianism is no less virulent than that of male homosexuality. Physical violence and forced marriage (in other words perpetual rape) are but two means to punish this ill-advised representation of sexual freedom and autonomy from men. However, avoiding marriage is particularly difficult for women in the Maghreb given that few of them have access to jobs and thus financial autonomy. Further, one of the means to control women in the region is to restrict their freedom of movement, which means that lesbians are more at risk of isolation than their male counterparts. **Lesbophobia** is then manifested not by the exclusion of lesbians from their families or their incarceration, but by the negation of lesbian sexuality and deprivation of their freedom through forced marriage.

Homophobia in the Maghreb also associates homosexuality with an illness that must be treated by either a psychiatrist, an *imam* (whose wise counsel will bring back the "lost" being to God's way), or a *fquih* (a learned man acquainted with the *suras* of the Qur'an and how to prepare amulets to exorcize the "possessed"), who will eventually rid the homosexual of the *djnoun* (invisible and sometimes harmful beings) that possess him and drive him "crazy." Homophobia is also expressed in pejorative terms referring to homosexuality and homosexuals, which are frequently used as insults.

Homophobia Legitimized by Religion

Homophobia appears in Qur'anic texts and in the *ahadith* (compilations of acts and words attributed to the prophet Muhammad). The Qur'an does not mention female homosexuality at all, but quite clearly condemns male homosexuality. In *sura* 7, verses 80–81, there is a reference to the prophet Lot who said to his people: "Are you partaking of this abomination which none before you in the world has committed? You approach men in preference to women to spend your passions. You are a people of perverts." (See also *sura* 27:54–55 and *sura* 26:165–66.) Those among Lot's people who did not want to listen to the prophet's warning were exterminated by God's action, which leaves no doubt as to **Islam**'s view of male homosexuality. The *ahadith* are, for their part, more explicit about the punishment which must be inflicted on those guilty of sodomy between men: both the "active" and the "passive" must suffer the penalty reserved for all who are guilty of *zina* (sexuality outside marriage), i.e. death by stoning. Lesbianism for its part is almost not mentioned in the *ahadith,* though one of them also assimilates it to *zina.*

While Muslim orthodoxy very explicitly condemns homosexuality, one nevertheless observes that homosexuality is widely popular and "tolerated" as long as it remains confined to silence. Further, the interpretation of the Qur'an and the *ahadith* gives rise to divergent legislation among countries that apply the *sharia* (Islamic law based on the Qur'an and the *ahadith*). While the countries of the Maghreb do not apply the *sharia,* they nonetheless give tacit support to heinous rhetoric, even assassinations committed by fundamentalist Muslims. This seems to prevail mostly in Algeria, but in May 2001, the online publication *Kelmaghreb* featured an interview with Egyptian sheikh Al Mitaani, professor at the Al-Azhar University in Cairo originally published by the internationally distributed Arab newspaper *Al-Majalla,* which demonstrated that these arguments are popular beyond any border despite legislation specific to each country. Al Mitaani presents female homosexuality as a "rebellion against divine law" and a "negation of human nature created by God" that must be punished by locking up "these women … until their death." On the subject of male homosexuality, he affirms that "if it is proven that a man is really a homosexual pervert … one has to purify life by getting rid of him, in killing him by applying religious principles." The assassination and blackmail of homosexuals, as testified by Algerian refugees in France, show that homosexuals are a prime target of the Armed Islamic Group, even though it is impossible to determine the identity of those responsible or the extent of these crimes and persecutions (which would imply revealing the identities of victims and expose their families and investigators to too great a danger). There is nonetheless some information on the methods used to persecute homosexuals. The French association ARDHIS, an association working for the rights of foreign homosexuals and transsexuals to immigrate and stay in the country, was tracked by fundamentalist Muslims in Algeria, who visited the association's website and then proceeded to harass and threaten those whom the agency were helping. ARDHIS also reported that many Algerians for whom it had obtained immigrant status were reported by their own families to the Armed Islamic Group because they had refused

to marry. An Algerian lesbian, supported by the French section of Amnesty International, obtained asylum on the basis that she had been physically attacked in Algeria by a Muslim fundamentalist who had deemed her clothing to be too masculine. For my part, in 1999 I met a gay Kabyle (an ethnic group in Algeria) who revealed that he knew young gays who had been massacred in Algeria during a masquerade party, most likely by members of the Armed Islamic Group. Finally, it should be noted that the first person to obtain political asylum in France based on his sexual orientation was an Algerian transsexual who had been persecuted by the Algerian army and threatened with death by fundamentalist Muslims.
—*Christelle Hamel*

Anonymous. "Liwat." In *Encyclopédie de l'islam.* Edited by C. E. Bosworth et al. New edition. Vol. 5. Paris: Maisonneuve & Larose, Leyde E. J. Brill, 1986.

Chebel, Malek. *Encyclopédie de l'amour en islam.* Paris: Payot & Rivages, 1955.

Courtray, F. "La Loi du silence. De l'homosexualité a milieu urbain au Maroc," *Gradhiva,* no. 23 (1998).

Hamel, Christelle. "Questions d'honneur: l'homosexualité en milieu maghrébin." In *Dissemblances. Jeux et enjeux du genre.* Edited by Agathe Gestin, Rose-Marie La Grave, Éléonore Lépinard, and Geneviève Pruvost. Paris: L'Harmattan, 2002.

Schmitt, Arno, and Jehoda Sofer, eds. *Sexuality and Eroticism Among Males in Moslem Societies.* New York/London: Harrington Park Press, 1992.

Wafer, Jim. "Muhammad and Male Homosexuality." In *Islamic Homosexualities: Culture, History and Literature.* Edited by Stefen O. Murray and Will Roscoe. New York: New York Univ. Press, 1997.

—*Gender Differences; Heterosexism; Islam; Middle East, the; Police; Violence.*

MARRIAGE

During the 1990s in many European countries, from Scandinavia to Spain by way of the Netherlands, Belgium, and France, as well as North America and elsewhere, the almost simultaneous emergence of the demand for "gay marriage" presents a new step in the logistics of freedom. It is true that this policy has encountered setbacks, particularly in the United States and there is no doubt that its successes are partial, as in France. Nonetheless, the leap from **tolerance** to recognition may be of an historical importance comparable to that which, in many countries, led from repression to tolerance.

However, this moral progress has coincided, paradoxically, with a spectacular resurgence of intolerance in France, the United States, and elsewhere. We wanted to believe that homophobia would vanish with legal liberalization, to exist more as a relic of the past, an obscurant image projected by distant cultures, all the more reassuring due to its exoticness. Some doomsayers based their opposition to liberalization on our enlightened societies' newfound tolerance as a way to discourage any gay policies. According to these well-meaning conservatives, any demands seemed not only contradictory, but useless (what's the use of fighting a homophobia that has reached the terminal stage?) and dangerous (why take the risk of awakening a dormant homophobia?).

By exposing this contradiction, the debates on gay marriage proved the minstrels of apathy to be both wrong and right. Wrong because homophobia had never vanished; it had only changed faces, **rhetoric** and logic, but not its target. In reality, homophobia is like racism: it has no consistent face, it is better to pursue its incarnations. Racism can define a race, as homophobia does homosexuality, by way of **biology**, or contrarily, by culture. Whether black or gay, both groups can be criticized for their acceptance of assimilation or their desire for segregation, their policies of integration or their **communitarianism**. Throughout its transformations, homophobia, like racism, has only one constant, its reactionary opposition to progressive policies pertaining to minorities, and in this case, gays and lesbians.

It must be recognized that the doomsayers were also somewhat correct: the demand for gay and lesbian marriage effectively generated a revival in homophobia. The example of France is illuminating: during an **anti-PaCS** demonstration in January 1999, there were cries to "Burn the fags." And we know the litany of such slogans isn't limited to the streets. Unsurprisingly, PaCS (Pacte civil de solidarité; Civil solidarity pact) awoke monsters in the extreme **right-wing** media. On page one of the French newspaper *Présent*, linked to the right-wing National Front, there appeared a cartoon showing two gay men welcoming a child with "open sheets." Other monsters reared their heads at the Assembly (where one Member of Parliament advocat-

ed the signing of a PaCS agreement in a veterinarian's office), or at the Palais Bourbon (for one senator, the acronym meant "Practice of AIDS Contamination").

Let's not for a moment believe that such blunders, frequent in the political setting, do not have their intellectual counterparts; and without mentioning minor figures, such blunders are pronounced by those who we would have hoped were more enlightened. In the pages of Figaro, historian Emmanuel Le Roy Ladurie brandished the specter of **pedophilia** (which, according to him, has risen since 1980, but was absent under the Vichy regime), legal expert Pierre Legendre, in an interview published in *Le Monde*, repeated his condemnation of "homosexualism" (which carries, according to him, a "hedonistic logic inherited from Nazism"). The debate on gay marriage that engenders such symmetrical fantasies from a homophobic revisionism, has, strangely enough, forgotten the **deportation** of gays and lesbians to Nazi concentration camps.

How is it possible to understand such outbreaks and such virulence? How can we analyze homophobia's fall and rise? Is the debate on registered partnerships nothing more than a factor of homophobia, or is it the catalyst? It could be said that society's latent homophobia has again found a way to express itself. What is currently being expressed has always been present, of that there is no doubt. However, are we not missing the essential point? In reality, throughout the course of these debates, something quite new is emerging. "Gay marriage" not only reveals homophobia, it creates it. Let's not reduce homophobia to a non-historical constant, nor relegate contemporary manifestations of homophobia to any universal and timeless psychological trait. This would effectively mean explaining homophobia as the rejection of homosexuality, as part of an unchanging human nature. Such a tautology relies on the historical specificity of the present; it forbids the understanding of change and, by the same token, prevents the imagining of political liberation.

A comparison between two debates, and therefore between two societies, allows us to dispense with the illusion that the same story is always repeating itself. Even when the debates are simultaneous, or nearly so, it's always a different story being heard. In France, as is well known, the debate regarding PaCS went "beyond PaCS." The statute only spoke of the couple, but the controversy centered mostly on children. In order to deny same-sex couples the right to **adoption** or medically assisted procreation, certain individuals declared themselves disposed to offer them certain advantages, practical or symbolic—a quasi-marriage.

In contrast, in the United States the battle over gay marriage did not concern offspring and centered on the union itself: the anthropological foundation of culture was marriage. In fact, the law adopted in reaction against a decision by the Supreme Court of Hawaii, which threatened to open the door to same-sex marriage, is called "The Defense of Marriage Act." In France, the sanctification concerned offspring, while in the United States, it concerned marriage. In other words, in these parallel debates on either side of the Atlantic, homophobia did not crystallize around the same issue.

Considering the diversity of national contexts, is it possible to explain the simultaneous resurgence of homophobia that accompanied the parallel demands for equal status for same-sex couples? If we must abandon the simple explanation of a spontaneous, universal, even natural homophobia, we must therefore ask ourselves what provokes homophobia in such diverse cultures during these controversies. And it is here that we need to specify exactly what it is we are discussing when we speak of "gay marriage."

At the risk of being paradoxical, let's first assume that it isn't (or at least, not exactly) a marriage between two homosexuals. Remember that our societies have always been somewhat accommodating; and let's put aside the contested historical example of the "same-sex unions" of pre-modern Europe, studied by the historian John Boswell, for it is uncertain whether it is advisable to see this as the ancestor of "gay marriage." However, many homosexuals have been getting married for a long time in our societies—to someone of the opposite sex. Marriage was, for a man or a woman, at best a hope to reform his or her ways, and at worst, a means to hide them from the world. And this does not even touch upon the question of forced marriages. In English, it is the gay man's "beard." As therapy or hypocrisy, this model has its celebrities, starting with André **Gide**. In this model, homosexuality remains outside marriage while homosexuals enter into it.

Let's suggest, however, that in this context the issue is not really gay marriage. It was evident in France during the debate over PaCS that the counter-proposition of a status reserved for homosexuals provoked less anxiety that the opening of a common status to all couples, be they same-sex or opposite sex. It may not have been by chance that the first legislative successes, in Scandinavia,

rested upon the segregation of the sexualities. It was a line of least resistance drawn, first in Denmark, then in Norway and Sweden, by the proponents for homosexual marriage, since it was really a question of a marriage for homosexuals. Even then, what failed in the State of Hawaii succeeded in Vermont: in the first case, the issue was the opening of marriage to homosexuals; in the second case, it was a status equivalent to marriage, reserved for homosexuals.

So it isn't marriage between homosexuals that sets off homophobic virulence, nor does marriage for homosexuals. The real issue of "gay marriage" is the marriage itself. That is to say, its opening, at the same time to homosexuals, by way of same-sex couples, and to homosexuality. The reason is two-fold: it is based, on the one hand, on the ordering of sexuality and, on the other, by the ordering of sex. And it is precisely the link between the two that is being played out in the issue of marriage. Because, when it comes to marriage, we are tampering with the legitimate standard.

It is, therefore, a question of sexuality. What causes fear isn't homosexuality itself but rather its normalization. In the United States, the slogan "God hates fags" is not only shouted at the most eccentric of transvestites, but also at the most conventional of couples. In other words, the commonplaceness of homosexuality causes as much fear as do its most radical provocations. Michel Foucault succeeded in surprising by evoking "all that can be disturbing in affection, tenderness, friendship, fidelity, camaraderie, companionship," whereas the cliché of "two young men who meet in the street, seduce each other with a look, place a hand on each other's buttocks and have sex in less than fifteen minutes" is reassuring. Homophobia would, therefore, be manifest in reaction to the "lifestyle," rather than against the "sexual act." Recent events confirm this: in the television adaptation of *Tales of the City* (1993), it is the chaste kiss between two men, in a very 1950s style, which provoked the most virulent reactions. It is the innocence of Armistead Maupin's characters that made the American Moral Majority tremble.

If this commonplaceness frightens, it is precisely because it disrupts the status quo with its obviousness. The heterosexuality of marriage went without saying, but this is no longer the case. Homosexuality forces one to reconsider marriage as a heterosexual institution, if not a heterosexist one. In other words, homosexual marriage imitates heterosexual marriage in order to reform it, to engage it in an egalitarian logic.

And it is here that anxieties about the ordering of sex and sexuality cross. Was it not said in France, in opposition to homosexual affiliations, that it is the **difference** between the sexes that needed to be preserved? And in the United States, are not the political movements opposed to abortion the same that are opposed to gay marriage? Did anti-feminists not declare that the amendment to the Constitution regarding the equality of the sexes, if it were adopted, would eventually lead to gay marriage?

In short, gay marriage forces us to rethink the norm. If homosexuality is no longer confined to tolerable subversion, which is ultimately reassuring, then the heterosexuality of marriage can no longer be justified as the norm. The most solid foundation of **heterosexism**, and also of sexism, has been shaken. We have dared touch marriage? No one should be surprised when homophobia rages.

—*Eric Fassin*

Andenaes, Mads, and Robert Wintemute, eds. *Legal Recognition of Same-Sex Partnerships. A Study of National, European and International Law*. Portland, OR: Hart, 2001.

Baird, Robert M., and Smart E. Rosenblaum, eds. *Same-Sex Marriage: The Moral and Legal Debate*. New York: Prometheus Books, 1997.

Borrillo, Daniel, Eric Fassin, and Marcela Iacub, eds. *Au-delà du PaCS. L'expertise familiale à l'épreuve de l'homosexualité*. Paris: Presses universitaires de France, 1999.

———, and Pierre Lascoumes. *Amours égales? Le PaCS, les homosexuels et la gauche*. Paris: La Découverte, 2002.

Fassin, Eric. "Same Sex, Different Politics: Gay Marriage Debates in France and the United States." *Public Culture* 13, no.2 (2001).

———. "L'Inversion de la question homosexuelle." *Revue française de psychanalyse* 1 (2003).

———. "Usages de la science et science des usages. A propos des familles homoparentales," *L'Homme*. Special edition, "Question de parenté" (2000): 154–155.

Foucault, Michel. "De l'amitié comme mode de vie." 1981. In *Dits et écrits, 1954–1988*. Vol. 4. Paris: Gallimard, 1994.

Gleizes, Henri. "L'Etat de droit et les mœurs, à quand le mariage des homosexuels?" *Permanences, revue mensuelle de formation civique et d'action naturelle selon le droit naturel et chrétien*, no. 340 (1997).

Leroy-Forgeot, Flora, and Caroline Mécary. *Le PaCS*. Paris: Presses universitaires de France, 2000.

———. *Le Couple homosexuel et le droit*. Paris: Odile Jacob, 2001.

Sullivan, Andrew. *Same-Sex Marriage: Pro and Con*. New York: Vintage, 1997.

Warner, Michael. *The Trouble with Normal: Sex, Politics, and the Ethics of Queer Life*. Cambridge, MA: Harvard Univ. Press, 1999.

—Adoption; Anti-PaCS; Associations; European Law; Heterosexism; Jurisprudence; North America; Parenting; Rhetoric.

McCARTHY, Joseph

American Republican Senator Joseph McCarthy (1908–57) became the figurehead of the anti-Communist crusade in the United States between 1947 and 1954. This period, known simply as "McCarthyism," was the equivalent of a witch hunt throughout American society against those who were perceived by conservative forces as "anti-American," with presumed ties to the Communist Party and the Soviet Union. In fact, McCarthyism really started before McCarthy himself: simply put, it is the manifestation of a systematic and hateful expression against perceived dissent. More specifically, McCarthyism was the direct result of action to rout out would-be communists by the Federal Bureau of Investigation (FBI), which since 1924 had been directed by J. Edgar **Hoover,** who discovered his administration's *raison d'être* in this movement.

In the Cold War context of 1947 under the influence of President Harry Truman, a US senatorial commission was set up to investigate the "allegiance" of federal employees. The target of this commission was those who were found to be supporters of totalitarianism, **fascism**, or **communism**. The FBI got involved, helping to coordinate the investigation of all federal agencies. Following McCarthy's infamous speech in Wheeling, West Virginia in 1950, in which he produced a list of people he claimed were known Communists working for the state department, the process became more radical. A few days later, Deputy Undersecretary of State John Peurifoy was called as witness by the commission. When asked about the number of employees who had resigned from the department since 1947, Peurifoy answered, "Ninety-one," but added that most were homosexual. From then on the homosexual figure, the "pervert," was directly linked to the communist figure, the "red." For the first time in American history, homosexuality became a major political issue. The logic of the McCarthy-esque rhetoric on homosexuality was simple: homosexuals were individuals with weak characters, and thus particularly susceptible to blackmail, and more apt to belong to clandestine circles that were subject to foreign influences; as a result, homosexuals were "predestined" to be traitors to the nation. Under these conditions, it was determined that all jobs having to do with the nation's security must be closed to them, particularly those under the federal administration. It is this logic that would prevail with the approval of the Immigration and Nationality Act of 1952, which closed American borders to "sexual deviants," and President Dwight Eisenhower's order in 1953 making "sexual **perversions**" an acceptable reason to exclude someone from working for the federal government.

McCarthy's personal downfall in December 1954, which was arguably instigated by his ill-fated 1953 inquiry into the US **Army** (nothing came of the investigations) as well as recurring rumors about his close collaborator Roy Cohn's homosexuality (which were later proven true), did not change the American public's negative views on homosexuality. The issue remained at the heart of American public debate; further, the FBI's mission to control the lives of homosexuals continued, and **discrimination** toward gays and lesbians gained a legal foothold.

It is estimated that between 1947 and 1950—before the apex of McCarthyism—more than 1,700 candidates for federal jobs were rejected because of their homosexuality; as well, more than 4,000 from the armed forces and closed to 500 government workers were fired. Between 1950 and 1953, historian John D'Emilio places the number of gays and lesbians fired from the federal administration at forty to sixty a month. Moreover, beginning in 1950, McCarthyism went beyond a simple "clean-up operation" to rid the civil service of homosexuals; it evolved into a national "panic" against homosexuals and their immoral ways. A year earlier in 1949, *Newsweek* magazine described homosexuals as "sexual murderers." Soon, across the country, the **police** intensified raids on gay and lesbian bars and public cruising areas, and disseminated the names of those arrested. In certain states such as Idaho, obsolete anti-sodomy laws were revived, permitting the imprisonment of those convicted. And on a sordid, anecdotal note, in 1954 following a homophobic murder in Miami, a local newspaper advocated that

gays themselves should be punished in such instances because they incite "normal" persons to commit such actions.

Beyond America, the McCarthy politic against gays and lesbians had consequences in Canada and the United Kingdom. There, too, anti-homosexual campaigns were focused on those working for the government in the name of "the enemy within." In Canada, the movement was short-lived, but nonetheless led to a number of anti-immigrant measures similar to those adopted in the United States. More paradoxically, in the United Kingdom, it was precisely the McCarthy crisis that led to the constitution of the Wolfenden Commission in 1954, charged with investigating the problems of homosexuality and prostitution after a succession of high-profile men were convicted of homosexual offences. The commission's resulting report was published in 1957, which surprisingly recommended that "homosexual behaviour between consenting adults in private should no longer be a criminal offence," the first positive political action that would lead to **decriminalization** a decade later.

In the United States, the consequences of McCarthyism forced the emerging gay activist movement (e.g., the Mattachine Society, the Daughters of Bilitis) to keep a low profile, going as far as to cooperate with authorities on issues such as cruising in public places. Attempts at a more radical militancy among gay activists, which had nonetheless led to the foundation of the Mattachine Society, would not reach its apex until the **Stonewall** revolt in 1969. Still, certain debates from the era of McCarthyism remain topical to this day, such as that related to the presence of gays and lesbians in the military.
—*Pierre-Olivier de Busscher*

D'Emilio, John. *Sexual Politics, Sexual Communities*. Chicago/London: Univ. of Chicago Press, 1983.

———. *Making Trouble: Essays on Gay History, Politics, and the University*. New York/London: Routledge, 1992.

Reeves, Thomas. *The Life and Times of Joe McCarthy*. New York: Stein & Day, 1982.

—*Armed Forces; England; Hoover, J. Edgar; North America; Peril; Police; Treason; Turing, Alan.*

MEDIA

In the past, media has treated homosexuality in three

different ways: with silence, condemnation, and mockery.

In the nineteenth century, newspapers did not mention homosexuality, but if they did, it was with contempt: common references to it included "shameful acts," "vile morality," and "abominable commerce." The first major media frenzy over homosexuality in France happened when the Count de Germiny was arrested attempting a pickup at a street urinal on the Champs Elysées in 1876). For many English, it was "the unnameable **vice**, the unspeakable vice, *inter Christianos non nominandum.*" first put forward by professors, which meant that it was not to be discussed in classes or as part of any serious scientific discourse. In the 1920s, the *Times* of London published only one or two short articles on the subject each year (in some years, homosexuality was not mentioned at all) and, in the 1930s, the same newspaper no longer even used the word "homosexual": homosexuality was now described as a "grave offense against morality," and gay bars were "bars with a peculiar reputation." In 1929, during the second conference of the World League for Sexual Reform held in London, the "taboo attitudes" of the press were denounced: the previous year, the *Daily Express* believed it had the right to write about the **Radclyffe Hall** affair: "There are certain vices in the world which, as they cannot be cured, must be endured, but in silence." It must be said that in Anglo-Saxon countries, virtually all publications about homosexuality were subjected to obscenity laws, the most famous being the 1873 Comstock Law in the United States.

In France, the taboo against homosexuality was also very strong, even within the leftist press. When André **Gide** published *Corydon,* his book on homosexuality and its place in the world, without publicity in 1924, the satirical newspaper *Le Canard enchaîné* (The chained-up duck) published a significant news item: "Mr. André Gide wishes to announce that he does not give copies of his book (which can lead to **scandal**) either to critics or to his friends. This is good! But why not do that same favor to booksellers?"

The taboo also concerned images of homosexuality. The famous British satirical weekly *Punch* hardly published any gay cartoons between 1919 and 1939. Over in Hollywood, the Production Code (also known as the Hays Code), written in 1930 by a Presbyterian (Hays) and a Jesuit (Father Daniel Lord) and then adopted by the Motion Pictures Producers

and Distributors Association (later the Motion Picture Association of America), identified morally acceptable and unacceptable content for motion pictures, making cinematic representations of homosexuality virtually impossible (it specified that "sexual **perversions**, even as an allusion, are forbidden"); the code remained in effect for over thirty-five years, until 1967, although in 1961, a revision of the code allowed for representation of "sexual aberrations" but only with "**discretion**, precaution and moderation." That same year, the San Francisco public broadcaster KQED presented *The Rejected*, a one-hour "frank and outspoken appraisal of homosexuality" featuring Margaret Mead and others, regarded as the first television program on the subject anywhere in the world. But French television was for a long time terrified of the homosexual question: in 1973, an episode of the popular program *Les Dossiers de l'écran* on the subject of homosexuality was postponed on request from government authorities; it was postponed again in 1974, this time by Arthur Conte, the CEO of the program's broadcaster, ORTF. It was only in January 1975 that the program was finally aired, with an audience of 19 million viewers.

The increase in homophobic attitudes around the last third of the nineteenth century meant that gays were consistently referred to in the media as perverts, murderers, **criminals**, and traitors. It must be said that articles on homosexuals were considered good for business, as proven by the media hype in France in 1903 over the Adelswärd-Fersen affair, whereby Jacques d'Adelswärd-Fersen, a young aristocrat, was tried for hosting orgiastic "black masses" in his apartment which involved underage boys, and then in 1908 over the Renard affair, in which a hotel concierge was accused of killing his employer due, in large part, to the fact of his homosexuality. The media became the mouthpiece for all discriminatory discourses, paraphrasing the opinions of psychiatrists that homosexuals were sick; of **police** that they were criminal; and of clergy that they were morally dangerous. One might also state that the consideration of homosexuality as an illness (particularly as a result of scandals, such as those in Britain involving Oscar **Wilde**, Guy Burgess, and Lord Montagu) was largely the work of the media (as well as cinema, which frequently suggested that homosexuality was criminal, as in Hitchcock's 1948 film *Rope.*

Inappropriate references to homosexuality by the media continued into the 1960s. In 1962, an article in London's *Sunday Pictorial* explained "how to flush out a homosexual." In 1963, a headline in the *New York Times* read: "Homosexuality, by being more and more open in New York, creates general anxiety." And in 1967 on *CBS Reports,* during one of the first network television programs on the subject, journalist Mike Wallace dared to opine that "the average homosexual … is incapable of having a long-lasting relationship such as heterosexual **marriage**." Finally, in 1971 in France, when Ménie Grégoire devoted one of her RTL radio programs to "the painful problem of homosexuality," only psychiatrists and church leaders were invited to participate. It would appear that most media believed that one could talk about homosexuality provided that it was condemned; some believe it to this day. In fact, tabloids have maintained their taste for this stigma; the well known Australian-American magnate Rupert Murdoch—chairman and CEO of the News Corporation, which owns the Fox network and the *New York Post*—is on record as being anti-gay, and many tabloid editors believe that homophobic articles are means to link their newspaper to popular opinion. Tabloid treatment of this subject is, unsurprisingly, in poor taste, and often focuses on **outing** or general speculation of whether certain celebrities are gay.

Satirical **caricature** was also used by the media to depict homosexuality. The earliest examples are from the English press in the eighteenth century, when the "molly" tied to the whipping post and the "fop" with his limp wrist were recurring images; and from France at the beginning of the nineteenth century, which included insulting representations of well-known figures such as Jean Jacques Régis de Cambacérès—the homosexual lawyer responsible for the Napoleonic Code who was also behind the decriminalization of homosexuality in France—such as one in which he turns his back on women and plays with a turkey. The apex of caricature's popularity was the period beginning with the **Eulenburg affair** in 1907 (which inspired numerous drawings in Germany and France in which homophobia was a little bit mixed with anti-militarism) until the 1960s. During this period, the satirical press in the 1920s and 30s in France thus denounced the "sentimental **heresy**" and the "German vice" (in 1933, *Fantasio* magazine presented Hitler as a lost queen). In England, "polari" (gay slang) was introduced in BBC entertainment programs at the end of the 50s. It is true that the "queen," the "queer," and the "fag" were the basis for hundreds of jokes and caricatures, complete

with high voices, limp wrists, and effeminate gestures, passed down from the music hall to high school, barracks, and barrooms, giving heterosexuals the impression that homosexuals were ridiculous and defective. This less-than-sympathetic approach to comedy has never quite disappeared, either: it could be found in *La Cage aux Folles* and in the popular BBC television series *Are You Being Served?* (1972–85), as well as present day, in the obnoxious jokes of the French program *Les Grosses têtes*.

On the flip side, the first attempts at building the gay press, between 1896 and 1960, were thwarted by homophobic **censorship**. The earliest known one took place in Wilhelmine Germany in 1896–97, by the aesthete Adolf Brand, whose *Der Eigene* was the first homosexual magazine in the world; it survived an arduous beginning until it ceased publication in 1931, after constant harassment by the Nazis. Another attempt, but less successful, was the literary monthly *Akademos* in France in 1909, which lasted less than a year. It was in the Weimar Republic in the 1920s, however, that the gay press took on an exceptional vitality alongside the German gay movement: several successful periodicals appeared, including *Die Freundschaft* (1919), *Die Insel* (1922; by 1929, it had a circulation of 150,000), and *Die Freundin* (1924). These publications offered all types of information for readers, including a large number of classified ads; nonetheless, they became the target of a Christian crusade *"gegen Schund und Schmutz"* ("against smut and filth"), led by Pastor Reinhard Mumm, which helped to bring about prohibitions between 1928 and 1931; what was then left of the gay press in Germany ended up being stamped out by Nazism.

In the United States, the earliest publication was *Friendship and Freedom,* spearheaded by Henry Gerber in Chicago in 1924, but it published only two issues before police intervened. It was not until Los Angeles around 1950 that the next wave of gay press appeared, around the same time as the establishment of the Mattachine Society, the first American gay activist association: *Vice Versa,* founded in 1947, was the first American lesbian periodical, and *One,* founded in 1953, the first "queer" periodical. But within a year, *One* had to deal with the issue of the US Postal Service's refusal to transport the magazine, which it found pornographic; the publishers of *One* took the postal service to court, and in January 1958, after a protracted battle, the Supreme Court ruled in their favor.

In France, *Inversions*, launched in November 1924, was condemned for "indecent behavior" in quick succession by the Court of Instance (March 1926), then the Paris Court of Appeal (October 1926), and finally the Court of Cassation (March 1927), the latter of which ruled that "indecent behavior" could exist without stylistic obscenity: on the topic of homosexuality, the horror is not in the words, but in the act itself. The very courageous and militant *Futur,* launched in 1952, was forbidden from being displayed in stores, and was forced to suspend publication from March 1953 to June 1954. After it resumed, France's Council of State intervened on December 5, 1956, ending it for good. In its ruling, the council stated: "A publication that defends and emphasizes homosexuality in the name of absolute liberty of the individual and the liberty of sexual practices is a publication whose goals contradict ordinary morality." In 1954, the first issue of the very proper *Arcadie,* the main gay magazine in France prior to *Gai-Pied,* was also prohibited from display and sale to minors, which remained in effect until 1975. In addition, its editor, André Baudry, was even arraigned for indecent behavior in 1955.

If things improved in the 70s and 80s, they only did so slowly and partially. One must first note the continued reluctance of radio and television programs to discuss the issue of homosexuality, which can be explained by several factors: the perceived lack of legitimacy of the subject, despite the Stonewall riots and gay liberation; the obsession with not wanting to upset the audience, which producers believed would be shocked by such material; and the unwillingness of most homosexuals to speak "on record." While the **AIDS** epidemic, the growing number of gay organizations, and the success of Lesbian and Gay Pride have radically changed perceptions of homosexuality over the last twenty years, media homophobia is nonetheless always present. It is revealed when a journalist equates homosexuality with pedophilia or makes a point of emphasizing the homosexuality of a particular criminal; it is also revealed when a newsroom neglects stories pertinent to gays and lesbians (for example, the Gay Games, which are virtually ignored by mainstream sportscasters). Outside the West, the situation is worse: Igor Kon, who has written extensively on sexuality in Russia, has made note of the rigid homophobia of the Soviet press of the 1980s and the Russian press of the 90s, where homosexuality was (and still is) linked to everything that is loathed: Bolshevism, Zionism, Western democracy

and sometimes all three at the same time!

The increasing visibility of homosexuals in the West in the 1970s provoked a significant media backlash among Conservative Christians: it started in the United States around 1977 with Anita **Bryant**'s crusade in Florida ("Save Our Children") and continued throughout the Reagan years of the 1980s, when AIDS was deemed "God's punishment." Publications of the American Christian far right multiplied, aiming to present the uncultured public at large with stereotyped and negative images of homosexuality, fueled by pseudo-scientific data on the subject. For members of this so-called "Moral Majority," one of their most important beliefs is that homosexuals can never be happy in their lives (because of their promiscuity and their inability to have stable relationships); as a result, they need to be "cured." Of course, there is no mention that the unhappiness of homosexuals might have something to do with the negative social conditions imposed on them, including Christian homophobia.

In France in the 70s, the conservative newspaper *Le Figaro* was highly homophobic, sometimes revolting, as in the obituary of novelist Jean-Louis Bory by Renaud Matignon in June 1979: "He perverted all of the pseudo intelligentsia, making leftists out of buffoons, buffoons out of leftists, and converted little boys." As for the gay press, the country made another attempt at silencing it as recently as March 1987, when Charles Pasqua, Minister of the Interior, requested that the 1949 Protection of Minors Act be applied to *Gai-Pied.* In the end, after much outrage, Pasqua relented. However, the Christian homophobic lobby did not disappear as a result: it made itself heard in the 90s during debates on AIDS prevention (should television programs show gays kissing each other?) as well as the PaCS civil-union proposal and other new rights for gays and lesbians. A conservative association created in 1986, Avenir de la culture (Future of the Culture), linked to the Brazilian group TFP (Tradition, Family, and Property), condemned gays and lesbians to their secular invisibility and conducted massive protest mailing campaigns whenever they appeared on television, including during AIDS awareness campaigns. The homophobic family-oriented lobby was worried by the growing visibility of gays and lesbians and their roles as trendsetters, particularly among youth. The vehement public debate on the concept of the gay **family** in the 90s was thus an upheaval and a challenge: conservatives felt compelled to foment public opinion against gay

parenting in spite of the seemingly favorable image of gays to the contrary. The result was a number of large, **anti-PaCS** demonstrations which used the media as a platform for their inflamed calls to respect "nature" and gender **difference** (whose apex was reached when conservative writer Guy Coq monopolized the conversation on the set of a news program on France's public television network FR3, in front of its dumbfounded host, in November 1998). But the most important of these demonstrations, on January 30, 1999, turned out to be an abysmal failure: where the organizers were hoping to use the media to their advantage, the plan backfired, revealing only the protestors' backward fears and beliefs ("Gays to the pyre!").

The positive evolution of the media was instigated in part by gays and lesbians themselves. Conscious that homophobia is constructed and circulated by media, gays organized themselves into lobby groups, particularly in the United States. The **Stonewall** riots of 1969 were a decisive factor in this, given that Stonewall was a turning point in American gay history when homosexuals could confirm that they were victims of a palpable censorship by the press (the riots garnered only a few square inches on page thirty-three of the *New York Times*). As a result, they knew they had to fight to present themselves without distortion to the general public; they adopted the tactics of anti-Vietnam protesters and civil rights activists, which consisted of creating "events" through demonstrations, marches, and parades. In 1973, the Gay Activists Alliance (GAA), founded in New York in 1969 by the moderate wing of the Gay Liberation Front, met with executives of the ABC television network to discuss gay and lesbian stereotypes on its programs. The same year, the self-styled Gay Raiders interrupted a broadcast of the *CBS Evening News*. In 1973, a dissident group of the GAA formed the National Gay and Lesbian Task Force, which organized a publicity boycott of the ABC drama series *Marcus Welby, M.D.*, which it accused of presenting homosexuality as a disease. In 1985, GLAAD (Gay and Lesbian Alliance Against Defamation) was created in New York to protest the manner in which mainstream media covered the AIDS epidemic. By this time, the hysterical panic over AIDS had incited the same reaction in the American press, which frequently referred to its "innocent victims," subtly dividing heterosexuals and children from homosexuals; it was also bent on outing celebrities who were afflicted, such as Rock Hudson. In the long run, GLAAD's action was

a complete success; AIDS is no longer "the gay disease." Today, GLAAD is the primary gay media watch dog and lobby group in the US: among its victories, it convinced the *New York Times* to use the word "gay" instead of "homosexual," in 1987; it also won the approval of executives at Disney/ABC to authorize the coming out of lesbian actor Ellen DeGeneres's character on her comedy series *Ellen*, which became *the* television event of 1997, and landed DeGeneres on the cover of *Time* magazine (she also came out personally at the same time).

The origins of the gay organization ACT UP (AIDS Coalition to Unleash Power) are essentially linked to a media fight. The movement was created in 1987 by New York activists in response not only to the unwillingness of the Reagan administration to acknowledge the AIDS crisis, but also to the general prejudice of mainstream media (one of the founders, Vito Russo, was a specialist on the representation of gays and lesbians in movies, as documented in his book *The Celluloid Closet*). ACT UP's strategy, in the US and the rest of the world, was spectacular: demonstrations became street theater and agitprop, as members noisily harassed politicians and drug companies and chained themselves in the most unexpected public places, such as Wall Street in 1989. It created powerful images that were disseminated through the media, such as the pink triangle with the slogan "Silence = Death" or, in Paris, a giant condom placed on the obelisk of the Place de la Concorde in 1993. This strategy provoked a mixture of fascination and resistance: for a long time, mainstream media presented ACT UP as an irrational and extremist organization, and government authorities even tried to use the police, the FBI, and the justice system to intimidate members. But, generally, ACT UP succeeded in modifying mainstream media's behavior: it became much more interested in gay and lesbian issues; there was less censorship of gays and lesbians. Reporters chose their words more carefully while media owners discovered the power of the gay audience, which not only is generally wealthier (and hence attractive to advertisers) but will also not hesitate to boycott a product or program if they are believed to be anti-gay. In England, responsibility for watching the media on gay and lesbian issues is essentially shared between two groups: Stonewall (an LGBT organization which underlines the inequalities gays and lesbians endure) and OutRage! (a queer rights direct action group which denounces homophobia in all its forms). One of the founders of OutRage!, Peter Tatchell regularly outs bishops and politicians, and distributes pamphlets to high school kids entitled "It's OK to be Gay." He has also interrupted an Easter service presided over by the archbishop of Canterbury, and attempted to make a citizen's arrest of the arch-homophobe Robert Mugabe, president of Zimbabwe.

In France, the gay movement of the 70s was mainly comprised of media protests. On March 10, 1971, Ménie Grégoire's program on the radio network RTL was interrupted by lesbians, and this event led directly to the creation of the Front homosexuel d'action révolutionnaire (FHAR; Homosexual Front for Revolutionary Action). After much misgiving, mainstream press eventually became interested in gays and lesbians, although not without a struggle. *Libération*, founded in 1973, was the first daily in France to seriously acknowledge the gay phenomenon (even bragging of publishing "more information on homosexuality in eight years than the whole French press in a century"); this attention, however, resulted in charges of "indecent behavior and incitation to **debauchery**" in 1979. Things went sour after that: in the 80s, articles in *Libération* made frequent references to the "gay cancer" in relation to AIDS, and between 1997 and 2001 it was curiously ambivalent on the question of gay rights. *Le Monde*, which in 1960 had not uttered a single word of denunciation for the **Mirguet** amendment (which proclaimed homosexuality to be a social scourge), acknowledged the importance of the gay vote just after François Mitterrand's presidential victory in 1981. It continued its editorial evolution through the 1990s to the point that it is now considered very progressive on the topic, something that does not please all of its readers.

Finally, it should be noted that gay journalists who work in mainstream media now feel it is less necessary to hide their sexuality than before; their ability to access positions of power proves and highlights the decline of homophobia in the media (at least in the West). In 1990, Jeffrey Schmalz, assistant editor of the *New York Times*, revealed his homosexuality; in 1990, the National Lesbian & Gay Journalists Association was formed and, three years later, counted over 1,000 members. In Great Britain, there are growing numbers of visible gay and lesbian journalists who work for respected newspapers (*The Guardian, The Times, The Independent*) or major television stations (BBC, Channel 4, ITV).

There remains an under-representation and perhaps misrepresentation of gay and lesbian characters in television, although this is changing. Great Britain has proven itself to be progressive in this area; a frank television miniseries adaptation of Evelyn Waugh's *Brideshead Revisited* was produced in 1981 (and was a cult hit in the US); more recent gay successes include *Queer as Folk, Absolutely Fabulous,* and openly gay chat show host Graham Norton. In the US, the most well-known and perhaps most controversial example, discussed earlier, was *Ellen*. While none of the main characters on the hit sitcom *Friends* was gay, the ex-wife of one of them was a lesbian, which was always treated matter-of-factly. *Will & Grace* was the first comedy series to feature a gay man as a lead character; throughout its run, it was a major hit with gay and straight audiences alike. Perhaps as an indication of how far things have swung: in 2008, audience members, most of them straight women, protested that two gay male characters on the CBS soap opera *As the World Turns* weren't being portrayed as frankly as a heterosexual couple would.

—*Pierre Albertini*

Alwood, Edward. *Straight News: Gays, Lesbians and the News Media.* New York: Columbia Univ. Press, 1996.

Chauncey George. *Gay New York: Gender, Urban Culture and the Making of the Gay Male World, 1890–1940.* New York: Basic Books, 1994.

Gross, Larry. "Sexual Minorities and the Mass Media," In *Remote Control: Television, Audiences, and Cultural Power.* Edited by Hans Borchers et al. London: Routledge, 1990.

Howes, Keith. *Broadcasting It: An Encyclopaedia of Homosexuality on Film, Radio, and TV in the UK, 1923–1993.* London: Cassel, 1999.

Russo, Vito. *The Celluloid Closet: Homosexuality in the Movies.* New York: Harper & Row, 1987.

Sanderson, Terry. *Mediawatch: The Treatment of Male and Female Homosexuality in the British Media.* London: Cassell. 1995.

Signorile, Michelangelo. *Queer in America: Sex, the Media and the Closets of Power.* New York: Random House, 1993.

Steakley, James D. "Iconography of a Scandal: Political Cartoons and the Eulenburg Affair in Wilhelmin Germany," In *Hidden from History: Reclaiming the Gay & Lesbian Past.* Edited by George Chauncey et al. New York: New American Library, 1989.

Tamagne, Florence. *Histoire de l'homosexualité en Europe, Berlin, Londres, Paris, 1919–1939.* Paris: Le Seuil, 2000. [Published in the US as *A History of Homosexuality in Europe: Berlin,*

London, Paris, 1919–1939. New York: Algora, 2004.]

Weeks, Jeffrey. *Coming Out: Homosexual Politics in Britain, from the Nineteenth Century to the Present Time.* London: Quartet Books, 1977.

—*Art; Caricature; Censorship; Cinema; Literature; Outing; Publicity; Scandal.*

MEDICINE

In order to ponder the homophobia of medicine, or medical practices which contribute to the rejection of homosexuality by society, one has to take into consideration its ambivalent process, in which scientific statements are sometimes exclusionary and sometimes, on the contrary, favor inclusion. As a sign of this ambivalence, some of the most important players of the first gay movement at the beginning of the twentieth century, like German sexologist Magnus **Hirschfeld**, produced a medical discourse whose theoretical framework was no different from that of doctors who were trying to "eradicate" homosexuality either by **treatment** of individuals or through eugenic measures.

Thus, to understand the history of the relations between medicine and homophobia, it is necessary to follow several clues which lead to paradoxical conclusions. One must first understand the social and scientific conditions existing at a given moment in history, such that homosexual practices and/or the homosexual individual become legitimate scientific objects for study by medicine. When this is the case, this phenomenon evolves within a particular context of the history of medicine, which, after undergoing a number of mutations, became a privileged ancillary of the state (with demography being born at the same time) in the "management of populations." As the science of the human body, medicine is called upon to address the usage of the sex organs, thereby bringing to the fore the same notion of "sexuality" as that stressed by Michel Foucault. From then on, its discourse is structured around two objectives: one that favors reproduction and the other which ameliorates the quality of its "result," Malthusian theses offering a radical variation where it is a question of considering only "good reproduction." This context then allows for the comprehension of the axes of questioning which provide many opportunities for the expression of homophobia: homosexuality is a diversion from the finality of the sexual act, and in the same way as onanism or masturbation, it compromises the possibilities for future reproduction or, at least, it may alter the quality of the result of any reproduction.

This matrix of the medical discourse allows us to proceed to the level of scientific statements, which can be found in **psychiatry** by the end of the nineteenth century. "Contrary" to the genetic instinct of the human species, homosexuality is then perceived as troublesome, the responsibility for which is not incumbent on individuals who find themselves so afflicted. Just like **suicide**, homosexuality cannot result from choice, in the sense that even the most criminal mind cannot "choose" to oppose his vital impulses. It followed, then, that the result of "naturalizing" homosexuality was to pathologize it. It is in this naturalizing/pathologizing context that a paradoxical alliance between the nascent gay militancy and medicine was constructed. And, in the context of imperial Germany, which imprisoned men who engaged in sexual relations with one another, medicine advanced arguments which depicted the homosexual as a victim of a pathology who was more in need of compassion than punishment.

A century later, the same paradox appeared in the context of **genetics**. Research into the genetic causes of homosexuality was the direct result of this science during the nineteenth century, which found the origin of sexual **perversion** in the hypothesis of morbid heredity, linked by the theory of **degeneracy**. Following eugenics-oriented research in the 1940s, the genetics approach to homosexuality obtained its seal of approval at the end of the twentieth century, thanks in part to the support of American gay and lesbian activists who, when confronted by advocates of the religious right, interpreted these findings as proof that homosexuality was also the "work of God," or at least of nature. Further, for many gays and lesbians, their perception of their own homosexuality was that it was not a question of choice, and even less a social construction. Genetics thus provided a biological rationale that satisfied not only gays and lesbians but also homophobes who envisioned its eugenic applications which would allow, for example, a prenatal genetic diagnosis of sexual orientation.

At this time, these findings compel one to ask the question of the role of medicine regarding homosexuality from a more general perspective. The process through which common-sense facts (e.g., "Certain people have sexual practices with people of the same sex") mutates into a "scientifically true" medical category (i.e. "homosexuality") tends to construe the fact of "being different" as a form of absolute **otherness**. This situation is similar to the scientific construction of the notion of race; in this sense, homophobia is directly related to racism in an analysis of the political and social uses of science.

In this framework, it is not possible to consider a non-homophobic medicine, other than through a means that renounces the consideration of homosexuality as an object in order to better construct the homosexual as a subject. This would also imply the renouncing of a number of certain scientific facts and, more particularly, research into the biological causes of homosexuality. This concept was at the heart of a movement that first started in the United States in the 1960s when American homophile **associations** promoted the idea of homosexual "well being," which encouraged the flowering of an individual vis-à-vis sexual orientation in light of the risks of depression, alcoholism, and **suicide** due to his homophobic environment. Further to this, and in the same perspective, gay community health centers and gay physicians' groups such as the Association des médecins gais (Association of Gay Doctors) in France were established. Finally, it is in this context that the gay community's response to the **AIDS** epidemic in the 80s was constructed, at the level of prevention as well as taking care of the sick.

—*Pierre-Olivier de Busscher*

Aron, Jean-Paul, and Roger Kempf. *La Bourgeoisie, le sexe et l'honneur*. Brussels: Complexe, 1984.

Bullough, Vern. *Science in the Bedroom: A History of Sex Research*. New York: Basic Books, 1994.

Dynes, Wayne R., and Stephen Donaldson. *Homosexuality and Medicine, Health and Science*. New York: Garland, 1992.

Foucault, Michel. *Histoire de la sexualité*. Vol. I : "La volonté de savoir." Paris: Gallimard, 1976. [Published in the US as *The History of Sexuality*. New York: Pantheon Books, 1978.]

Lantéri-Laura, Georges. *Lecture des perversions: histoire de leur appropriation médicale*. Paris: Masson, 1979.

Rosario, Vernon, ed. *Science and Homosexualities*. New York/London: Routledge, 1997.

—*Biology; Degeneracy; Endocrinology; Ex-Gay; Fascism; Genetics; Himmler, Heinrich; Hirschfeld, Magnus; Inversion; Medicine, Legal; Perversions; Psychiatry; Psychoanalysis; Treatment.*

MEDICINE, LEGAL

Legal medicine, which deals with the application of medical knowledge to legal problems and proceedings, was arguably the first medical discipline to consider itself an "expert" on the issue of homosexuality, especially during the period of transition between the religious control of sexual practices and the medicalization of homosexuality by the **psychiatric** community in the second half of the nineteenth century. The treatment of the homosexual question by religious forces was manifested in the outright condemnation of homosexuality by the church, and by the states that were, at least in European monarchies, the secular arm of divine law. The goal of legal medicine was to prove the existence of homosexual practices; in this sense, and contrary to subsequent research, this field of medicine did not propose any analysis of the causes of homosexuality, nor any **treatment** for it, and even less, it did not construct the "homosexual" (or pederast, as the word homosexuality had not yet been invented) as a specific entity. Its only goal, as an expert science of the body, was to unearth evidence of sexual activity between two individuals of the same sex. In societies that did not legally repress homosexuality, such as post-revolution France, the work of legal medicine was allowed to continue, including complementary research into criminal situations such as prostitution, blackmail, and violent crimes.

Three studies marked this disciplinary field in an important way: Paolo Zacchias, in Italy, at the beginning of the seventeenth century; J. L. Casper, in Germany at the beginning of the nineteenth century; and the Frenchman Auguste Ambroise Tardieu, a professor of legal medicine at the Université de Paris in the mid-nineteenth century. Their findings share a similar structure, combining a "sociological" dimension that described the social habits of those "guilty" of homosexual practices (a discourse which usually included a "sociology" of the gutter, as nineteenth-century theorists were pleased to describe it) and a physiological dimension based on the idea that the body's organs which were used for activities that were not "natural" were irreparably damaged. This latter concept had similarities to physiological studies of rape, whose objective was to find tangible signs of constraint during sexual intercourse. Tardieu's study of pederasts was, incidentally, part of a more general document dealing with indecent assault and rape.

In addition to its position as an auxiliary science supporting the religious and/or legal repression of homosexuality, the discourse around legal medicine largely contributed to the legitimization of certain negative representations of homosexuality in **medicine** and, more significantly, in society. Due to the criminal activity that homosexuals must naturally deal with, legal medicine postulated that homosexuality could only be understood in the sordid context of nightlife, between ports of call and brothels, where prostitution, blackmail, racketeering, **treason**, and exploitation were common occurrences. This link—which caused Tardieu to remark that pederasty (read homosexuality) was the school where the most audacious criminals were trained—was renewed at the beginning of the twentieth century by Cesar Lombroso, the Italian criminologist who theorized that criminality was inherited; he further suggested there were connections between "born criminals" and "born inverts," which allowed for the construction of all discourses on the social danger of homosexuality (which Jean Genet would later use to his advantage in his revolt against society).

What's more, according to legal medicine, the highest proof of homosexuality is the dilation of the anus (in spite of Tardieu's claims of another: penises that have been twisted and thinned out by repeated penetration of an orifice that is too narrow "by nature"). According to this view, passive anal penetration is represented physiologically by an anus with a relaxed sphincter that is formed like a funnel, and buttocks that take on feminine characteristics; such penetration is then associated with homosexuality. In this, the French insult *"enculé"* (referring to a man who is "fucked in the ass") finds its scientific basis; moreover, these feminine characterizations of the invert's nether regions, often accompanied as well by a slight development of the chest and an atrophy of the penis, prefigure theories on **inversion**, which will represent homosexuality only in terms of gender inversion. In this sense, legal medicine invented the homosexual body, anchoring differences of behavior in flesh, following a process similar to that of colonial medicine and physical **anthropology** which, during the same era, invented the idea of race.
—*Pierre-Olivier de Busscher*

Aron, Jean-Paul, and Roger Kempf. *La Bourgeoisie, le sexe et l'honneur.* Brussels: Complexe, 1984.

Bonello, Christian. "Du médecin légiste à l'aliéniste. L'homosexualité sous le regard de la médecine au XIXe s." In *Homosexualités: expression/répression.* Edited by Louis-Georges Tin. Paris: Stock, 2000.

Carlier, François. *La Prostitution antiphysique* (1887). Paris: Le Sycomore, 1981.

Casper, Johann Ludwig, ed. *Traité pratique de médecine légale.* Paris: Baillière, 1862.

Chevalier, Julien. *L'Inversion sexuelle.* Paris: Stock, 1893.

Coutagne, J. P. Henry. "Notes sur la sodomie." In *Lyon médical.* Lyon: Henri Georg Libraire, 1880.

Martineau, Louis. *Leçons sur les déformations vulvaires et anales produites par la masturbation, le saphisme, la défloration et la sodomie.* Paris: Ed. A. Delahaye et E. Crosnier, 1884.

Ritti, Antoine. "De l'attraction des sexes semblables," *Gazette hebdomadaire de médecine et de chirurgie* (January 4, 1878).

Schwartz, Léon. "Contribution à l'étude de l'inversion sexuelle." Medical thesis presented at Montpellier, 1896.

Tardieu, Ambroise. *Etude médico-légale sur les attentats aux mœurs.* Paris: Ed. Baillière, 1860.

—*Biology; Criminal; Degeneracy; Endocrinology; Ex-Gay; Fascism; Genetics; Hirschfeld, Magnus; Inversion; Medicine; Perversions; Psychiatry; Psychoanalysis; Treatment.*

MIDDLE EAST, the

Geographically speaking, the region known as the Middle East is not strictly defined. It covers an area that stretches from the Mediterranean Sea to the Gulf of Oman, from Turkey in the west to Iran in the east. Out of a core of sixteen countries that are defined as belonging to the Middle East, twelve are overwhelmingly Arab in population. This region, unsurprisingly, reveals clear differences in general practices and attitudes, especially with regard to homosexuality. This can be largely explained by two factors: religion and the influence of the West. In the Middle East, religion is a dominant force, be it **Islam**, **Judaism**, or **Christianity**. Social practices and attitudes are largely determined by these forces; as a result, in various countries in the region, religious minorities have conformed to the social norms of the majority. The degree of openness to foreign cultures in any given country, however, has a direct impact on the degree of homophobia experienced there, in that notions of LGBT identities are largely tied to European and North American ways of thinking.

Taken as a whole, the Middle East is one of the most hostile regions in the world for homosexuals; of the nine countries in the world where homosexual acts are punishable by death (as of 2008), four are in the Middle East: Saudi Arabia, United Arab Emirates, Iran, and Yemen, to which we could add Afghanistan, Pakistan, Sudan, and Chechnya, bordering states that also participate in the region's cultural dynamic. (Despite the concentration of capital punishment for homosexual acts in this region, it is interesting to note that the highest number of homophobic murders occurs in Brazil.) The facts are overwhelming if one also takes into consideration other countries in the region where informal, social homophobia is rampant despite the lack of statistics, on the murder of homosexuals for instance. Moreover, we must assume that the populations of the Middle East have long since learned to avoid the rigors of law, which are severely applied but less often than one would think, given the legal inefficiencies of many countries in the region. And as homophobic as these states may be, their hostility toward gays and lesbians should not be thought of as inevitable and irreversible. Far from being the "natural" expression of local societies, on the contrary, this attitude is only part of a history that still remains to be retraced.

In fact, since Antiquity, the Middle East has been home to homosexual or pederast cultures that flourished greatly, not only during the ancient Persian era, but also afterwards, under Islamic-Arab domination. Verses proclaiming love for young men appeared in the work of certain poets who are among the greatest Arabic authors, such as Abu-Nuwas and Hafez Shirazi. Moreover, the ascetic sect of Sufism gave birth to many mystical texts that were strongly homoerotic, in which the love of God and the love of youths appear to follow common paths, such as in the writings of Mansur al-Hallaj, Jalal al-din Rumi, and Umar Ibn al-Farid. Many writings depicted beautiful young men (*fata, mourahíq*) and dainties (*ghilman*) who aroused the desire of men, princes, and kings, as in *Gulistan* by Shaykh Sa'di, or in *One Thousand and One Nights*, which was collected over many years and included the work of many different authors; some stories in it featured amorous relations between women, an event rare enough to be noted. But this sensual, erotic **literature**, still present in the *ghazal* (lyrical poems of the Persian and Urdu traditions), is not well known given that it was often voluntarily hidden or diligently expurgated by **censorship** in eras that followed. However, barely thirty years ago, Iran still had a relatively lively homosexual community (something that current Iranian President Mahmoud Ahmadinejad, who claims that there are no homosexuals in Iran, would be loath to admit). Contemporary

hostility toward gays and lesbians thus corresponds to the rise of **Islam**, especially to Islamic fundamentalism, in a reactive logic in relation to the West, whose power is perceived as more and more imperialist, menacing, and hostile. Fundamentalism appears as a means of resistance in the name of identity and, in this context, despite native traditions, homosexuality cannot be perceived as anything other than a foreign import linked to Western gay and lesbian movements; in other words, it is necessarily bad. It is possible to turn a blind eye to the discreet practices of a few homosexuals, but any activity that takes place out of the shadows is considered an intolerable affront. In Muslim nations, the hostility toward homosexuals is thus a dynamic of opposition, propagated of course by religious and nationalist dogma that is highly critical of the West in general, and the United States in particular.

These few details will doubtlessly allow for a better understanding of the foundations of contemporary homophobia in the Middle East. For a start, if we consider the two factors which have an impact on Middle Eastern attitudes on homosexuality—Islamic fundamentalism and the influence of the West—the region can be divided into three groups: those states dominated by Islam and generally opposed to Western influences; Turkey and Cyprus, whose populations are essentially composed of non-Arab Muslims and Christians, more open to Western influences; and Israel, a mainly Jewish country, and very much influenced by Western culture.

The Muslim States

The predominantly Muslim countries of the Middle East are generally defined as the following: Bahrain, Egypt, Iran, Iraq, Jordan, Kuwait, Lebanon, Oman, the Palestinian territories, Qatar, Saudi Arabia, Sudan, Syria, the United Arab Emirates, and Yemen. Official information concerning homosexuality in these countries is quite limited.

These Muslim societies are regarded in the West as sexist, in that women are largely subordinate to men in practically every field. They are also heterosexist in that they value exclusively the heterosexual model. The members of the same family always live together, have practically no privacy, and often children only leave the household when they get married. Interaction between the sexes is very limited, though it varies according to the country, each person having his or her strictly defined social role. In the Muslim world, homosociality is the norm. Gestures of affection between men or between women are common, and can be made publicly, as long as they have no sexual connotation. For a Westerner, the rarity of women in public places and the physical displays of affection between men can appear surprising. But as long as a man acts in a masculine manner, he is honored and respected (even if he privately penetrates another man); if he acts in a feminine manner, or if he adopts the "passive" role, he is dishonored and considered to be a degenerate. In these societies, gender and sex categories are defined in relation to power structures, to positions of dominance and subordination, and to normal or deviant behavior. Under these conditions, homosexuality is not linked to an identity (gay or lesbian), but rather to a behavior (inappropriate acts that do not conform to gender or status). If we define homophobia as the American psychologist George Weinberg did—i.e. the fear of being in a closed space with homosexuals—the term may be inappropriate for these societies since individuals live in close contact with those of their own gender. What the Muslim man fears most is that he not be perceived as a true man. Thus, the term "homonegativism," which defines the tendency to oppose homosexuality on moral grounds, may be more appropriate.

In Muslim states, the distinction between what can be done in public or in private is more rigorous than in the West. Most often, homosexuality, and sexuality in general, are subjects that are not spoken of in public, sexual education being, for the most part, nonexistent. Thus, basic knowledge on issues relating to sexuality (including homosexuality and other subjects such as the prevention of HIV) is, in general, lacking; this ignorance obviously feeds homonegativism.

The homosexual issue is not perceived the same way depending on if it is expressed in public or in private. In private, sex between men is more or less accepted, as long as it is kept quiet and certain rules are obeyed. In fact, there are many Muslim men who have engaged in homosexual practices at one time or another in their life. For the rest, certain sexual relations between men of different ranks are permissible, notably between older, wealthy men and younger, poorer men. Homosexual practices, sometimes for money or other favors, are common among young men before **marriage**. But in public, social pressure is enormous, as is the price to pay for deviant behavior. Under these conditions, most men end up getting married, all the while continuing to have occasional homosexual encounters. Despite the regularity of these practices, for these men, the homo- or bisexual issue does not constitute a particular identity.

With regard to sexual relations between women in the Muslim world, information is even more scarce. In the most conservative Muslim countries, women are confined to the home, and even in more liberal countries, according to the dominant thought, women are not supposed to have any independent sexual desire: they must content themselves with satisfying their husband's desires. All sexual contact between a woman and a person other than her husband is rigorously condemned. In many Middle Eastern countries, the "honor" killings of women and girls by members of their own family are intrinsically linked to inappropriate female sexuality: adultery, premarital sex, and homosexuality.

An interesting fact is that in certain countries, transgenders are relatively tolerated in public and are not confronted by the same hostility as are homosexuals. Male actors and dancers can adopt feminine attitudes. In Iraq, there are the *mustergil*, biological women who dress as men in order to free themselves of the many restrictions normally imposed on women; this phenomenon appears to be partially tolerated by the community. Similarly, in Oman, there are the *xaniths*, who are perceived as "botched" men, or a sort of third gender. These are biological men who have homosexual relations, but who are allowed to marry; they dress and act in public according to social norms that are halfway between male and female. In other countries, the situation is also sometimes paradoxical. In Iran, for instance, where homosexuality risks execution, sex change operations are completely legal, even partially funded by the state. Such operations are also legal in Turkey.

There are no officially recognized LGBT organizations in Muslim nations of the Middle East, but there are associations that meet rather clandestinely. In general, meetings are held in private homes; if they occur in public places, they are normally disguised in order to not attract the wrath of authorities. In Dubai in 2005, twelve men were jailed after being arrested preparing for a gay commitment ceremony. Gay meeting places are strictly underground, with a few exceptions. These meeting places are usually not exclusively gay, otherwise they are extremely discreet. In a recent edition of the *Spartacus International Gay Guide,* the listing for Egypt includes cruising areas and many bars and hotels in large cities, including Cairo, where there is also a dance club and an escort service. The listing for Jordan mentions only two bars, one dance club, and a restaurant in the capital city of Amman, and a few cruising areas. In Lebanon, in the city of Beirut, there are two dance clubs, a bathhouse, and a few cruising areas. In effect, there are very few gay and lesbian places listed, and these are countries that are more open to Western influences. In these countries, it is still possible to meet people who can clearly assert their gay or lesbian identity. But sexuality cannot be freely spoken of in the **media**, and homosexuality in particular usually appears in the context of one **scandal** or another. In such cases, the "criminals" are described in demeaning terms. There are numerous websites on homosexuality in Muslim countries of the Middle East, but it is significant that the majority of them—if not all—are hosted by Western service providers (e.g., Al-Fatiha, the Gay and Lesbian Arabic Society [GLAS], and Huriyah).

Many of these countries apply Islamic religious law, or *sharia*, the basis by which homosexuality is condemned by fundamentalists. Homosexual acts, both male and female, are now illegal in every Arab country in the Middle East, with the possible exception of Iraq, where homosexuality was legal until 2001, when under pressure from fundamentalists it was criminalized by Saddam Hussein; its legal status is unclear at present, but this has not prevented religious militias in the ongoing civil war from actively murdering homosexuals.

Amnesty International and the International Gay and Lesbian Human Rights Commission report on the severe lack of human rights in general in most of these countries, and the lack of rights concerning homosexuality in particular. Foreigners perceived as being gay are authorized to leave the country if they wish to avoid punishment. In Qatar, many foreign workers were thus expelled in 1997 because of their perceived homosexuality. In 2001, fifty-two men were arrested in Egypt for "debauchery" and tried under a special "emergency court," denying their right to an appeal under human rights law. Moreover, in Iran, the death sentence has been pronounced many times in recent years for men found guilty of homosexual acts. Similarly, in Saudi Arabia, three men accused of sodomy were decapitated in January of 2002. In Afghanistan (which lies on the periphery of what is defined as the Middle East), before the fall of the Taliban regime, Mohammad Hassan, Governor of Kandahar, declared, "We have a dilemma: according to certain wise men, we must take these people to the roof of the highest

building and throw them over the side, but for others, we must dig a hole next to a wall, place them inside the hole, and knock the wall over in order to bury them alive." It was this second solution that was chosen on February 25, 1998, for three men accused of sodomy; a military tank knocked a stone wall over top of them. Miraculously, they survived their many injuries, and in his great goodness, Mullah Omar granted them his mercy (although two of them died the next day). However, in another incident on March 22, Abdul Sami, aged eighteen, and Bismillah, twenty-two, were less fortunate: they died under the rubble.

Charged with "debauchery with men," fifty-two Egyptians were arrested on May 11, 2001 in a nightclub. Egyptian legislation provides for up to five years in prison for such a "crime."

The precision of Mohammad Hassan's ideas on the various forms of punishment possible for homosexuals was echoed by Ayatollah Musava Ardelsili of Iran. During a speech at the University of Tehran, he declared,

> For homosexuals, Islam has prescribed the most severe punishments. After guilt has been established according to the dictates of *sharia*, the individual must be seized, be kept standing, and divided in two with a sword to either cut off his head, or split him completely in two. He (or she) will fall…. After his death, a pyre must be prepared, the body placed on it and set on fire to burn it, or brought to the top of a mountain and thrown from a cliff. Then the body parts must be collected and burned. Or a hole must be dug, a fire started in it and he must be thrown in alive. We have no such punishments for other crimes.

Obviously, the worst doesn't always happen, and **dis-**

cretion on the part of homosexuals generally allows them to avoid punishments prescribed by the law. But it is clear that these conditions often create a climate of constant anguish. As for those who adopt a more visible gay or lesbian identity, they often attempt to flee their native country in order to escape familial and social pressure. In this way, many Palestinian homosexuals seek refuge in Israel as a result of death threats received from family or authorities. Many Muslims have sought political asylum in the West on the basis of their homosexuality, but as Western immigration laws are becoming more restrictive, most are sent back to their country. In reality, these experiences represent only the tip of the iceberg, since instances of **discrimination** and harassment on the basis of sexual orientation are essentially hidden due to the taboo surrounding the subject.

With regard to hospitalization and forced **treatment** of homosexuals, information is rarer still. The fact is usually kept secret, but the practice is nonetheless admitted, at least in the Palestinian territories where many people were hospitalized in order to change their sexual orientation.

The situation in Iran is particular: a few decades ago, during the time when the country was more open to Western influences, the attitude toward gays and lesbians was more "favorable" than in other Arab countries. With the Islamist revolution, however, the prohibition against homosexuality has become more rigorous, the punishments more violent. At the same time, many of the political parties in exile have expressed their support for gay and lesbian rights.

In Muslim nations of the Middle East, all publications must endure some form of censorship. Publications concerning homosexuality are censored in Egypt and in Kuwait, as are Internet sites in Jordan and the United Arab Emirates. In Lebanon, the owner of an Internet service provider was prosecuted because he had hosted a gay website, and the director of the local Association for Human Rights who came to his aid was also prosecuted.

Turkey & Cyprus

In Cyprus, the population is made up of Greek and Turkish communities. The Greeks are, for the most part, **Orthodox** Christians, and the Turks are Muslim. The Church of Cyprus, largely conservative, exercises great influence over social issues such as sexuality, and its leaders have violently opposed homosexuality. In both Cyprus and Turkey, religion plays an important

role in every aspect of social life, but Western influences are also felt rather strongly. Social attitudes in these countries are generally more liberal than in the Muslim states, and the rules concerning sexuality appear to be less strict. As a result, the segregation of the sexes is rarer in Turkey than in Arab countries, and its socio-cultural climate favors the development of gay and lesbian identities, more or less comparable to those in Europe and North America.

Turkish society has a mix of both Western and Eastern standards for sexuality in general, and for homosexuality in particular. Huseyin Tapinc, who has written on male homosexuality in Turkey, distinguishes four types: 1) the heterosexual male who practices mutual masturbation with another man, but refuses all oral or anal sex with him; 2) the heterosexual male who always maintains the active role in relations with passive homosexuals, thus not endangering his heterosexual identity; 3) the homosexual male who has relations with a "passive" homosexual (contrary to the preceding types, in this case both partners more or less adopt a gay identity); and 4) the male who definitively assumes a gay identity, and for whom distinctions between active and passive do not hold any social pertinence.

In Cyprus, there are numerous LGBT beaches, bars, and discotheques, even if most of them are not exclusively gay. There is also a website (Archimedes) containing information on various types of LGBT services. Since 1993, there is also the Cypriot Gay Liberation Movement, which has actively fought to modify anti-gay laws. However, in the Turkish Republic of Northern Cyprus, a separatist republic located in the northern region of the island of Cyprus (and which is only recognized by Turkey), homosexuality remains illegal.

Since the 1970s, there has been a visible gay subculture in major cities in Turkey, notably Istanbul. Areas where gays and lesbians can congregate include stores, restaurants, hotels, sports venues, and cinemas; some are exclusively gay, others not. The most important gay organization in Turkey, Lambda, was created in 1993; it has a website, organizes weekly get-togethers, and publishes a monthly magazine. Further, the democratic and radical Green Party in Turkey has supported the gay and lesbian movement there since the 80s, and has been in favor of promoting HIV prevention, which requires a growing vigilance. Turkish homosexuals are often able to resist the pressure to get married and even reveal their homosexuality to their families. Parents sometimes learn to accept their child's homosexuality, but there are still many who cut off all ties to their child because of their sexual orientation.

Cyprus has experienced a major evolution with regard to homosexuality in recent years. Homosexuality was only decriminalized in 1998, and only because Cyprus stood to lose its prospective membership to the European Union if it did not; prior to this, men prosecuted for this offense risked up to fourteen years in prison. The decriminalization nonetheless created a discriminatory situation on the age of consent in relation to heterosexuals; it would not be until 2002, under pressure again from the European Union, that a new universal age of consent was established at seventeen years of age. In Turkey, homosexuality has been decriminalized for many years, however in both countries, only so long as it is behind closed doors; when it is expressed in public, it is perceived as indecent and can be pursued legally under one pretense or another.

Moreover, despite their legal status in Cyprus, homosexuals are often the victims of human rights violations. Scenes of physical homophobic **violence** are widespread, and gays often fear losing their jobs. There is at least one known case whereby a man was refused entry into the Cypriot **army** because of his sexual orientation. Furthermore, even the suspicion of homosexuality appears to be sufficient grounds to refuse an immigrant, and thus send him back to his country.

Similarly, despite the legality of homosexuality in Turkey, authorities display no **tolerance** whatsoever on the question. In Istanbul in 1993, a gay and lesbian conference was forbidden, and the foreign delegates were arrested. In 1994, in a city in southern Turkey, public kissing between two men was officially banned. The Turkish army does not admit homosexuals into its ranks. And at the end of the 80s, the **police** beat and arrested many homosexuals, many of whom were subsequently sent to psychiatric institutions; moreover, the police took it upon themselves to inform these individuals' employers, who fired them. Sex changes have been legal in Turkey since 1988, and transsexuals and transvestites are quite visible in Istanbul, which is behind the motivation for serious police assaults against them; in many instances, their homes were torched and the individuals beaten and arrested. By the end of the 90s, many international human rights organizations denounced the use of torture by Turkish police. As for the Turkish media, their attitude on homosexuality has been rather ambiguous. Homosexuals are often depicted in an unfavorable light, and information

is sometimes censored by authorities; many books on homosexuality have been banned.

Israel

Israel's population is composed mostly of Jews, but includes a not insignificant number of Muslims and Christians. The numerous immigrants have brought with them values from around the world. The Jewish community in Israel is very heterogeneous, complex, and dynamic, and it is difficult to discuss it in general terms. Non-religious Jews have been influenced by social evolutions in the West; in secular areas, sexuality, homosexuality, and issues related to **AIDS** can be discussed publicly, and attitudes on sex and gender are relatively close to those in the West.

Religion is a central fact of life in Israel, but the nation's values and norms are surprisingly diverse. To a certain degree, the majority of Israelis consider themselves to be believers. The most conservative positions are held by the ultra-Orthodox: they adhere strictly to Jewish laws, which accord homosexuality an inferior status. That being said, they live apart from the rest of Israeli society, in communities where there is a clear segregation between the sexes and where roles are assigned according to gender. In these ultra-Orthodox communities, sexuality is not discussed in public, and remains an intimate subject.

Arab Israelis also make up a separate community, and constitute the country's largest minority. They are partly Muslim and partly Christian. In Arab Israeli communities, sexual segregation is less strict than in Muslim countries, but the separation of the sexes and homosociability are still a reality. Social modernization is still possible, but attitudes toward homosexuality remain very conservative, comparable to those in Muslim states and, to a certain degree, Orthodox Jewish communities.

During the last decades, however, gays and lesbians in Israel have succeeded in obtaining a more visible place in the public sphere. Public demonstrations such as those organized by the Association of Gays, Lesbians, Bisexuals and Transgenders (AGUDAH), the Jerusalem Open House, and the Israel Center for Social and Economic Progress give the impression of progress made in improving the general public's attitude toward homosexuals. However, harassment and intimidation are not uncommon occurrences.

Transgenders have organized themselves within the LGBT community. Many transsexual singers enjoy large audiences, but most limit themselves to smaller, more closed circles for fear of reprisals. Sex changes are legal, but regulations are so strict that individuals rarely undergo surgery.

Gay and lesbian issues are openly debated throughout secular Jewish media, often in a favorable light; conversely, in religious media, homonegativism is the norm, so much so that these issues are never discussed.

Separation between state and religion is clearer in Israel than in most Muslim countries, but it is not complete. There are certainly some openly gay or lesbian politicians, and heterosexuals who openly support gay and lesbian rights, however, by the same token, many political and religious leaders have spoken out against homosexuality. It is clear that the political and judicial systems in Israel are subjected to constant pressure from conservative elements in Israeli society.

The legal system does not penalize homosexual relations, and in fact Israel is the only country in the Middle East to have laws protecting gays and lesbians from discrimination. During the last few decades, many legal proceedings have determined that same-sex partners are entitled to the same rights as heterosexual partners. The city of Tel Aviv has begun registering same-sex couples, but they are not recognized by Israel's government, marriage being under the domain of religiously inspired laws. In 2007, Jerusalem registered its first gay couple. Certain legal battles concerning gay parents have been fought and won, including the right to **adoption** by same-sex couples.

Over the last few years, authorities in Israel have demonstrated a more favorable attitude, though there remains a void between progressive legislation and individual practice. Thus, gays and lesbians are admitted in the army, but once there, are often confronted by hostility. Similarly, the police cooperate with the gay and lesbian community, but individually, officers are sometimes very homophobic.

—*Daniel Weishut*

Abû-Nuwâs. *Le Vin, le vent, la vie, poèmes traduits de l'arabe et présentés par Vincent-Mansour Monteil.* Arles, France: Actes-Sud, 1998.

Al Fatiha—Foundation for LGBT muslims and their friends. http://www.al-fatiha.net (accessed April 23, 2008).

Amnesty International. http://www.amnesty.org (accessed April 23, 2008) and http://www.ai-lgbt.org (accessed April 23, 2008).

Archimedes. http://www.geocities.com/westhollywood/heights/4639 (site now discontinued).

Chaline, Eric, ed. *Gay Planet: All Things For All (Gay) Men.* London: Quarto Publishing, 2000.

Dunne, Bruce. "Power and sexuality in the Middle East," *Middle East Report,* no. 206 (Spring 1998).

Gay and Lesbian Arabic Society (GLAS). http://www.glas.org (accessed April 23, 2008).

Gay, Lesbian & Bisexual Nation of Cyprus (GLBCY). http://www.geocities.com/westhollywood/village/5297 (site now discontinued).

Gay.org.il. Home page for LGBT organizations (site now discontinued) .

Gogay. Israeli LGBT website. http://www.gogay.co.il (accessed April 23, 2008).

Ghoussoub, Mai, and Emma Sinclair-Webb, eds. *Imagined Masculinities: Male Identity and Culture in the Modern Middle East.* London: Saqi Books, 2000.

HOMAN. Iranian LGBT organization. http://www.homanla.org (accessed April 23, 2008).

Huriyah. Magazine for Muslim LGBTs. http://www.huriyahmag.com (accessed April 23, 2008).

Lambda-Istanbul. http://www.qrd.org/qrd/www/world/europe/turkey or www.lambdaistanbul.org (accessed April 23, 2008).

International Gay and Lesbian Human Rights Commission (IGLHRC). http://www.iglhrc.org (accessed April 23, 2008).

International Lesbian and Gay Association (ILGA). http://www.ilga.org (accessed April 23, 2008).

McKenna, Neil. "Turkish Police Target Transvestites: A Gay Movement Grows," *The Advocate,* no. 582 (n.d.).

Murray, Stephen O., and Will Roscoe. *Islamic Homosexualities: Culture, History and Literature.* New York: New York Univ. Press, 1997.

Schmerka, Blacher Philippe: "Tête de (gay) turc." In *La Haine de soi, difficiles identités.* Edited by Esther Benbassa and Jean-Christophe Attias. Paris: Ed. Complexe, 2000.

Schmitt, Arno, and Jehoda Sofer, eds. *Sexuality and Eroticism Among Males in Moslem Societies.* New York: Harrington Park Press, 1992.

Shirâzi, Hâfez. *L'Amour, l'amant, l'aimé, cent ballades traduites du persan et présentées par Vincent-Mansour Monteil.* Arles, France: Actes Sud, Sinbad/Unesco, 1998.

Tapinc, Huseyin. "Masculinity, Feminity, and Turkish Male Homosexuality." In *Modern Homosexualities: Fragments of Lesbian and Gay Experiences.* Edited by Ken Plummer. London/New York: Routledge, 1992.

Weishut, Daniel. "Attitudes Towards Homosexuality: An Overview," *Israel Journal of Psychiatry and Related Sciences* 37 no. 4 (2000).

———. "Attitudes Toward Homosexuality: A Study on

Israeli Students," *Israel Journal of Psychiatry and Related Sciences* (n.d.).

Yuzgun, Arslan. "Homosexuality and Police Terror in Turkey," *Journal of Homosexuality* 24, no. 3 (1993).

—*Associations; Censorship; Heterosexism; India, Pakistan, Bangladesh; Islam; Judaism; Maghreb; Media; Orthodoxy; Police; Violence.*

MILITARY. *See* Armed Forces

MINIONS. *See* Favorites

MIRGUET, Paul

Paul Mirguet (1911–2001) is best remembered as the architect of a 1960 amendment that declared homosexuality a "social scourge," marking the apex of political homophobia in twentieth-century France.

Mirguet was a third-class parliamentarian and his career as member of parliament was extremely short (1958–62). Nothing prepared him to enter politics: he was born in 1911 to a peasant family in Moselle on the border between France and Germany; armed with only a primary education, he worked in a small refrigeration business selling meat when he was very young. World War II completely transformed his existence: Mirguet, who opposed the de facto annexation of Moselle by the Third Reich, joined the Resistance, specifically the FFI (French Forces of the Interior) in Indre; by 1944, he was head of the Resistance in Berry Creuse. He was an effective operator who was of enormous help to the Allies. At liberation, his professional interests took over again: he was, for a time, director of meat services in the Ministère du Ravitaillement (Ministry of Supplies) and in 1956–57, played an important role in a reconstruction project for La Villette's slaughterhouses on the outskirts of Paris. (The project was a ruinous catastrophe and is now a park.) He was elected as member of parliament for the Gaullist UNR party in 1958, winning his constituency from a Christian-Democrat, Joseph Schaff; four years later, he was defeated by his predecessor and never served in office again. He died largely forgotten in May 2001.

The actions of Mirguet the politician were very limited and generally uninspired; they included defending the interests of coal workers and butchers, in which he revealed an anti-American streak and evoked a Western civilization that was at **peril**. He made his mark on July 18, 1960, however, when his motion in the National Assembly directing government to take "all measures needed to fight homosexuality" was passed, resulting in homosexuality being officially declared a "social scourge" and thus equating it on the same level as other social ills such as alcoholism and prostitution. Mirguet first introduced his amendment to the parliament in a few sentences: "I think that it is not necessary to insist at length, as you are all conscious of the seriousness of this scourge that is homosexuality, against which we have the duty to protect our children." (One might note in passing the popular association of homosexuality with **pedophilia** during the era.) "At the moment when our civilization, dangerously in a minority when compared to the rest of the world, becomes so vulnerable, we must fight against all that can diminish its prestige; in this area as in others, France must lead by example." (Mirguet, blamed declining birth rates on homosexuals and feared that Western civilization would be eclipsed by the surging population of the Third World in this period of decolonization.) Mirguet's homophobic prejudices perhaps came from his upbringing (Moselle, part of Alsace-Lorraine, prohibited homosexuality as part of the German Empire from 1871 to 1918) and from his electorate (it seems likely that he sought the support of Christian-Democrats).

The vote was held at the end of a night session (it is one point in common between the Mirguet amendment and the Labouchere amendment, approved by the British Parliament in 1885, which had horrible consequences for homosexuals in Britain), and almost without debate. It is clear that the members of parliament voting on the Act were mostly concerned with the naming of alcohol as a "social scourge," and that those who voted no or abstained did so not out of concern for the plight of homosexuals, but to protect the interests of the alcohol lobby. The next day, the newspaper *Le Monde*'s coverage of the vote included only a few lines about it, and did not mention homosexuality: "The National Assembly authorizes the government to restrain by order the privilege of grower-distillers." It is clear that, for almost all, particularly Communists, Christian-Democrats, and Gaullists, homosexuality was, if not a "social scourge," at least a disease against which it was acceptable to take legislative measures. As a result, no one addressed the National Assembly to either oppose the amendment or defend the rights of homosexuals. In fact, Mirguet's proposition was essentially received with laughter in the National Assembly, a reminder that homosexuality was not a legitimate political issue in 1960 France. Moreover, wanting to return some measure of dignity to the debate, Member of Parliament Marcelle Devaud (UNR), who was also the president of the Commission on Social Affairs, had the following reaction: "I do not find it particularly funny…. Be assured that I am not at all embarrassed to speak about these things as they exist. It is natural to speak of them in order to fight them."

The infamous Act was signed into law on July 30 by President Charles de Gaulle and cabinet ministers Roger Frey, Edmond Michelet, Pierre Chatenet, Wilfrid Baumgartner, and Bernard Chenot. *Le Monde* made no comment; *Paris-Presse* published Mirguet's photo with a heroically-styled caption that included the fact that "he is the first to request measures against homosexuality." Only the gay association Arcadie protested the amendment in a letter to Mirguet. In response, Mirguet stressed his worries as the head of a family (he was married and had two children) and pretended that he had not asked the government to issue repressive measures but rather medical ones. Nevertheless, a few months later, penalties in cases of "*outrage public à la pudeur*" (a crime that first appeared in the French penal code in 1810, regarding instances of "causing a public scandal by gestures or obscene exhibitions") of a homosexual nature were increased. The law had broad ramifications, and the gay community in Paris, still in its infancy, was severely affected by the change; the club associated with Arcadie had to end its Sunday afternoon tea dances and the magazine suspended its classified ads.

As the years passed, Mirguet was, without a doubt, less and less proud of his amendment. Isolated and ineffective, in January 1975, he nevertheless took part, in a televised debate on homosexuality on the program *Dossiers de l'ecran*. Times had changed. Gay author and journalist Jean-Louis Bory ate him alive, and even the priests and doctors on the panel were against him. Finally, in a fitting irony, in 1972 a contemporary gay periodical named itself in reference to Mirguet's passion: *Le Fleau social* (The social scourge).

—*Pierre Albertini*

Mirguet, Paul. *Viandes et réalités économiques et politiques.* Paris: Brunétoile, 1957.

———. *Programme de réformes et d'action politique pour une France libre et sociale.* Metz, France: Reinert, 1973.

—*Abnormal; Criminalization; France; Heterosexism; Politics.*

MONSIEUR

It was no secret at the court of Versailles that Philippe d'Orléans (1640–1701)—known as Monsieur, brother to Louis XIV—was obsessed since childhood by a fantasy of cross-dressing. He adored ribbons, lace, and jewelry, and would have willingly worn a dress if it had not been prevented by his rank. The influence exerted on him by his lover, the Knight of Lorraine, did not contradict the other traits of his character, which included a rather gaudy piety, an obsession with precedence and etiquette, and an unapologetic frankness, which allowed him to tell his second wife that he was comparable to **Henri III** (who was regarded as homosexual) "in every respect."

Monsieur suffered from comparison with his wives. The first, Henrietta Anne Stuart of England, was well known for her beauty and charm, but died at the age of twenty-six in 1670, which was thought to be due to poison, blamed, without proof, on her husband's **favorite**, Phillip of Lorraine. After having been eclipsed in popularity by his first wife, Monsieur was subsequently crushed by his second, the thunderous Elizabeth Charlotte, also known as Princess Palatine, who married Monsieur against her will in order to further the ambitions of her father, Charles I Louis of Hanover. She swayed between affection, repugnance, and commiseration toward her husband, whose conjugal duties resulted in three children; in turn, he, after failing to transform her into a subservient court doll, treated her with a respectful indifference. As talk of his indiscretions with favorites increased, Monsieur's star within the French court rapidly began to fade: "Monsieur is debauched, and his only interest is … in recommending his favorites and obtaining from His Majesty all sorts of good treatments and favors for them. As for his children, he doesn't think of them" (1686). In the end, with all things considered, his biggest failure was to allow himself to be persuaded by his favorites at the expense of his family; in other words, he began to correspond too closely to the archetype of the effeminate, becoming a futile and easily influenced man, and as such someone "more to pity than to hate." At the same time, Elizabeth Charlotte became enamored with his elder brother, Louis XIV, who delighted his sister-in-law, who, according to one of her friends, had "never been married" in the true sense, given Monsieur's predilections.

The fate of Monsieur lay in an unavoidable confrontation with Louis XIV. In Louis's eyes, haunted by the precedent of his uncle Gaston d'Orléans (eternal challenger to the crown of his brother, Louis XIII), it was imperative for him to politically neutralize his troublesome *puisne* ("inferior"). To keep him at a disadvantage, Louis encouraged his brother in his "peculiar" inclination, which prevented him from having any power or influence in the court. On at least two occasions, however, this position was tested. In 1656, the court expressed its concern when an illness nearly took Monsieur's life, much to the consternation of the king. Then in 1677, Monsieur enjoyed military success in the war with Holland. If the glory he attained there did not cause him to lose his brother's affection outright, it at least awoke the king's mistrust: as a result, Monsieur was never again allowed to participate in a military campaign. By the end of the seventeenth century, evidence of Monsieur's behavior came to affect the reputation of his son, the Duke of Chartres, and the future Regent. The atavistic **perversion** attributed to the Orléans would end up feeding the antagonism fated to last among the elder and the younger branches of the royal family.

—*Laurent Avezou*

Erlanger, Philippe. *Monsieur, frère de Louis XIV* [1953]. Paris: Perrin, 1981.

Godard, Didier. *Le Goût de Monsieur, l'homosexualité masculine au XVIIe siècle*. Montblanc: H & O Editions, 2002.

Princesse Palatine. *Lettres de Madame, duchesse d'Orléans*. Paris: Mercure de France, 1981.

—*Against Nature; Debauchery; Favorites; France; Henri III.*

MORALITY. *See* Abnormal; Debauchery; Philosophy; Theology; Vice

MULTICULTURALISM. *See* Communitarianism

MUSIC

The study of homophobia in music is not without dif-

ficulties; the novelty of the problematic and the scarcity of studies available prevent any clear synthesis of ideas. More specifically, the art of music is often resistant to the transmission of signification. Despite this, homophobia in music will be discussed here in a wide number of subject areas, including texts put to music, opera plots, public attitudes, and the positions of musical historiography.

Like all other social groups, composers were victims in their time of the different forms that homophobia could take through the centuries. Here are some symbolic examples.

In **Ancient Greece**, where relations between active adults and passive young boys were valorized, the dramatist and musician Agathon was caricatured by Aristophanes in his *Thesmophoriazusae*: it is the feminine aspect of a mature man that is stigmatized. In reverse, in the Christian world, particularly in the exclusively masculine one of masters charged with sacred music in churches, "affairs of morality" between teenagers and adults were repressed. In seventeenth-century France, Jean-Baptiste Lully, director of the king's music and a notorious homosexual, was regularly the target of hurtful lampoons. Songwriters erupted against him in 1685, at the moment when Louis XIV, incited by the Jesuit Louis Bourdaloue to take severe action against sodomites, had Lully's page Brunet arrested, whipped, and jailed because he was sharing the musician's bed. As a sign of the inequality of punishment according to social hierarchy, Lully only received royal disgrace. **Songs** directed against the musician linked his homosexuality to his obscure extraction ("Jean-Baptiste is the son of a miller / He could not deny it / He only rides as a miller / Always on the back of it"), as well as his foreign origin, i.e. "Italian **vice**" ("Lully, this great musician / Still greater Italian / Chose by adventure / An unnatural musical note") and even the supposed behavior of the Jesuits, his persecutors ("La Chaise said to Bourdaloue, / Father, why are we suffering / That this naughty Baptiste / Acts as a Jesuit"). For Pyotr Ilyich Tchaikovsky, on the other hand, the homophobia of his social milieu seems to have been fatal. His death, which was attributed to cholera, is now widely believed to have been a **suicide** to avoid the **scandal** which would have been provoked by the revelation of his liaison with a young man of high society. On a less tragic tone, in the twentieth century, one must attribute the self-censorship of composers such as England's Ethel Smyth, who hid her lesbianism in her autobiographical writings, to the heterosexist social context at the time.

Homophobia directed against gay composers was not only expressed in the **violence** that they sometimes had to endure: it was also present in writings on the period. Sometimes the sentiment was pure hatred, such as *Une Histoire de la musique* (A history of music) by Lucien Rebatet, published in 1969; the composer Reynaldo Hahn was introduced this way: "Born in Venezuela with a German Jewish father, he never hid his penchant, and remained to his final days the stunning figure of an old invert with wig, monocle, and corset. He was no less reactionary in his taste; his catalogue, with the exception of Mozart, was the worst and dullest music that one could have made in a century and a half."

The majority of music biographers wishing to present their gay subjects sympathetically, however, were nonetheless influenced by a heterosexist distortion of reality, in order to disguise or euphemize the composer's personal life. While deliberate in the case of Tchaikovsky, this distortion sometimes appeared to be unconscious. In his 1933 monograph on Arcangelo Corelli, Marc Pincherle stressed that in 1682, when Corelli was twenty-nine, "Matteo Fornari, his student and friend, appeared at his side as second violin, and who in the future would virtually never leave him." Pincherle made it clear that Fornari lived with Corelli, who bequeathed him his musical instrument and charged him with publishing his *Opus 6* after his death. Pincherle concluded by being amazed by the absence of women in the musician's life: "Music, painting and friendship seem to have completed his life."

For a composer as important as Handel, such an illusion could not be maintained for long. Cutting the conclusions of some researchers (such as Gary C. Thomas) short, Jonathan Keats affirmed: "The hypothesis that makes [Handel's] definitive celibacy a proof of homosexuality is unsustainable in the context of the eighteenth century, where the itinerant life of so many musicians made marriage an obvious interference." That the "context" in question was made up of renowned homosexual circles, such as those of Cardinal Ottoboni in Rome or the Count of Burlington in England, does not seem to become apparent to Keats, nor the fact that numerous homosexuals were married, such as Lully. More amazingly, Keats founded his conviction of Handel's heterosexuality on "the music of his operas, cantatas, oratorios, that express love with a maturity and complexity worthy of competing with Mozart and Wagner."

Interpreters and, in particular, singers, whose bodily instrument was made a spectacle for the public, were especially vulnerable to heterosexist violence. Women, who were not numerous and were made invisible in the world of musical creation, were at the forefront in this regard. Female opera singers, in the same way as actresses, were simultaneously adulated and scorned, considered as artists and relegated to prostitutes. The mixture of voyeurism and hypocritical moral reprobation in the stories of their love lives was particularly flagrant in the case of Sophie Arnould, the great interpreter of Rameau in the eighteenth century, whose bisexual adventures were the delight of the readers of *Correspondance littéraire* or *Mémoires secrets*, which were newsletters detailing the personal lives of writers and artists in eighteenth-century Paris.

With regard to male singers, the castrati were principally stigmatized. It was less a case of detailing the private adventures of a *musico* than crying out in indignation over the temptations of these accomplished virtuosi who often possessed an androgynous beauty. Montesquieu, in his *Voyages*, noted that "in Rome, women do not play in theater; they are castrati dressed as women. This has a very bad effect for moral behavior: as nothing (that I know of) inspires more philosophical love for Romans." In an *Essay on the Operas* dated in 1706, the English critic John Dennis became indignant: "When I affirm that an opera in the Italian fashion is monstrous, I cannot exaggerate; I even add that it is so prodigiously unnatural that it could not be born from any other country, except the one reputed throughout the world to prefer monstrous and abominable pleasures to those which are in accordance with nature."

Old musical works rarely treated homosexuality in a direct way. Let's quote the polyphonic song by Clément Janequin, published in 1540, which evoked with certain benevolence the margins of normative sexuality: "The hermaphrodite is strange in figure / Wanting to make use of man and woman. / But the one that we will call loathsome / Who is missing one or the other nature." In general, homosexual subjects appeared in the lesser known repertoires which evaded **censorship**, such as songs of the street. A homophobic attack against a person of prestige was often a political weapon, frequently endorsed by those in higher authority. For example, Cardinal Mazarin was accused not only of sodomy but also adultery, with Anne of Austria, and **pedophilia** with young Louis XIV: "Sire, you are but only a child / And they steal from you with impunity; / The Cardinal fucks your mother / Lère la, Lère lan lère, / Lère la, Lère lan la. / Even it is said that he protested / That he fucks your majesty / Just as Monsieur his brother / Lère la, Lère lan lère, / Lère la, Lère lan la." There was also rambling about Marie Antoinette's bisexuality: "This lady, gentlemen / Was worth it: / She was the princess of Henin; / As she is a lesbian and hustler / She was chosen as the queen."

Opera was the privileged place for the depiction of amorous expressions. The heterosexist standard was the norm (Charles Gounod's Sappho is heterosexual, and Bedrich Smetana's Dalibor became heterosexual over the course of the opera), even if examples of virile friendship (Gluck's *Iphigénie en Tauride*, Bizet's *Les Pêcheurs de perles* [*The Pearl Fishers*]) are recurrent. The expression of homosexuality, even muted, was rare; there is evidence of it in the eighteenth century, however, in the tragedies of Jesuit colleges that excluded love and valorized masculine friendships (Marc-Antoine Charpentier's *David et Jonathas*) or among the baroque fantasies of Venetian opera: in *La Calisto* by Francesco Cavalli, the reference to Diana's lesbian behavior was explicit, but heterosexual morality was safe, since it was Jupiter, under the disguise of the goddess, whom we see receiving the caresses of a young nymph. In the twentieth century, English composer Benjamin Britten wrote numerous operas in which gay characters appeared. While they were often worrisome (*The Turn of the Screw*) or destined to a tragic fate (*Billy Budd, Death in Venice*), Britten at least knew how to powerfully evoke the homophobia of the hostile crowd (*Peter Grimes, Albert Herring*).

The common thread of impersonations in opera plots resulted in ambiguous effects. In *Fidelio* by Beethoven, Leonore is constantly dressed as a male prison guard; based on this appearance, she is loved by Marzelline (one first sees them as a man and a woman, but understand them as two women), then frees her husband Florestan (whom one first sees as two men, but understands them as a man and a woman). On the other hand, the tradition that demanded that the roles of young men be played by female singers and, in the baroque era, old women by tenors, also allowed the presentation of same-sex couples, if not part of the plot, then at least on the stage. But the resulting effect, highly dissymmetrical, shed light on the sexism at work in this kind of representation: the female couple was a sensuous source of intrigue for male audiences (*Le Chevalier à la Rose* by Strauss) whereas the male couple could only be comical (*Platée* by Rameau). To this, we must ask, what of the roles of the castrati in baroque opera given to female singers? The distribution that was almost exclusively feminine (*Alcina* by Handel, *Orfeo ed Eridice* by Gluck), and the lesbian atmosphere that arose from it, evidently embarrassed some critics, who demanded male counter-tenors in such roles, to be more "realistic."

During the last half-century, homosexuality and homophobia were expressed more openly in the musical field. Singers were frequently victims of homophobic legislation, like Charles Trenet, jailed for one month in 1963 for "corruption" of minors (specifically, four nineteen-year-old males). Conversely, singer Anita **Bryant** in the United States launched a crusade in the 1970s against gay and lesbian rights. But mostly, many songs clearly evoked the subject of homosexuality. French singers in particular became more overt in their homophobia, such as Maurice Chevalier, who imitated fellow singer Félix Mayol with cruelty, or Michel Sardou who, in "J'accuse" (lyrics by Pierre Delanoë, 1976), blamed homosexuals for every ill ("I accuse men of believing hypocrites / Half fags, half hermaphrodites / Who pretend to be rough to dig in butter / And kneel as soon as they are scared"); previously, he attacked homosexuality in the army or boarding school ("Le Rire du sergent" [The Sergeant's laughter], "Le Surveillant général"). While in 1972, Charles Aznavour preached **tolerance** in "Comme ils dissent" (known in English as "What Makes a Man a Man") ("None has the right in truth / To blame me, to judge me / And I spell it out / That it is truly nature which / Is the only guilty if / I am a man, eh / As they say"); the image he projected of the homosexual was nonetheless a wretched caricature.

With the advent of numerous rock stars with an androgynous stage presence beginning in the early 70s (such as Mick Jagger, Prince, David Bowie, Lou Reed, and Iggy Pop), their most often heterosexual lyrics contrasted with the cultivated ambiguity of their physical appearance (costumes, makeup) that was more challenging than demanding. Let us cite, however, openly gay singer Elton John's strong position against homophobia (his song "American Triangle" was about the murder of Matthew **Shepard** in Wyoming in 1998), which made his defense of rapper Eminem, who has been accused of homophobia, that much more striking. However, homophobic violence is part of Eminem's image, and the debates over it effectively contribute to his media coverage.

Speaking of rap, its tendency for misogyny and casual violence, which helps to construct the virile posture of the malcontent, makes it ripe for homophobia as well, as demonstrated by the French rapper Rohff in "Rap de barbares": "From what they say most rappers think they are bad boys / For my part I do not mix strings with underwear / It is not shitty rap, I am not queer / I rap for those that try hard, I bugger the cops" (*Mission suicide,* 2001). For Passi, another French rapper, homosexuals represent Western society's drift: "The old ones have Viagra, whores want social security, pedophiles are still at work / In the street your son sees two gays kissing" (*Genèse,* 2000). The machismo and homophobia that appear in ragga, under the influence of rap, are presented as a reaction against the more humanist reggae discourse, and as resistance to commercial recuperation. One has to stress finally that, in these collections, only male homosexuality is questioned. Lesbians are once again invisible and women are only presented as desired and hated objects, without an autonomous sexual life.

Outside of lyrics, musical styles and types of instruments can be used as markers of homosexuality or heterosexism. Repertoires as diverse as opera or techno are associated with gays, while sexism is often very present in classical orchestras, even more so in jazz or rock groups. In classical music, the gender split happens mainly between the feminine strings (chiefly the harp) and the masculine winds (particularly brasses). In jazz or rock, unless they are part of an all-female group, women are usually reduced to the role of singers: to play an instrument, such as sax, guitar, or drums, is already a transgression of the norms. Here again, the most traditional phenomena of construction of masculinity and femininity are at work.
—*Raphaëlle Legrand (thanks to Philippe Blay, Théodora Psychoyou, Catherine Rudent, Alice Tacaille, and Louis-Georges Tin)*

Bonnet, Marie-Jo. *Les Relations amoureuses entre les femmes.* Paris: Odile Jacob, 1995.

Brett, Philip, Gary C. Thomas, and Elizabeth Wood, eds. *Queering the Pitch: The New Gay and Lesbian Musicology.* New York: Routledge, 1994.

Brett, Philip. "Britten's Dream." In *Musicology and Difference: Gender and Sexuality in Music Scholarship.* Edited by Ruth A. Solie. Berkeley: Univ. of California Press, 1993.

———. "Musicality, Essentialism, and the Closet." In *Queering the Pitch: The New Gay and Lesbian Musicology.* New York: Routledge, 1994.

De Gaulle, Xavier. *Benjamin Britten ou l'impossible quiétude.* Arles, France: Actes Sud, 1996.

Duneton, Claude. *Histoire de la chanson française.* Vol. 1. Paris: Le Seuil, 1998.

Garber, Eric. "A Spectacle in Color: The Lesbian and Gay Subculture of Jazz Age Harlem." In *Hidden from History: Reclaiming the Gay and Lesbian Past.* Edited by George Chauncey, Martin Duberman, and Martha Vicinus. New York: Meridian, 1990.

La Gorce, Jérôme de. *Jean-Baptiste Lully.* Paris: Fayard, 2002.

Lischke, André. *Piotr Ilyitch Tchaïkovski.* Paris: Fayard, 1993.

Thomas, Gary C. "Was George Frideric Handel Gay? On Closet Questions and Cultural Politics." In *Queering the Pitch.* New York: Routledge, 1994.

Segrestaa, Jean-Noël. "L'Opéra des gais," *Trangul'ère,* no. 2 (2001).

Solie, Ruth A., ed. *Musicology and Difference: Gender and Sexuality in Music Scholarship.* Berkeley: Univ. of California Press, 1993.

Wood, Elizabeth. "Lesbian Fugue: Ethel Smyth's Contrapuntal Arts." In *Musicology and Difference: Gender and Sexuality in Music Scholarship,* edited by Ruth A. Solie. Berkeley: Univ. of California Press, 1993.

———. "Sapphonic." In *Queering the Pitch: The New Gay and Lesbian Musicology.* New York: Routledge, 1994.

Discography

Baccardi, Pit, Disiz La Peste, ROHFF et al. "Rap de barbares," *Mission suicide* (2001).

Britten, Benjamin. *Albert Herring.* DECC 421 849-2LH2.

———. *Billy Budd.* Erato 3984 21631-2.

———. *Peter Grimes.* Chorus and orchestra of Covent Garden. EMI 7 54832 2.

———. *The Turn of the Screw.* Philipps 446 325-2.

Cavalli, Francesco. *La Calisto.* HMC 901515.17.

Charpentier, Marc-Antoine. *David et Jonathas.* HMC 901289.90.

Eminem. *The Marshall Mathers LP* (2001), Aftermath Records 493 062-2.

Elton John. "American Triangle," *Songs of the West Coast.* Mercury 586 330-2.

Lunatic. "Le Son qui met la pression," *Mauvais œil* (2000).

Passi. "7 société va mal," *Genèse* (2000).

ROHFF. "Rap info," *La Vie avant la mort* (2001).

Sardou, Michel. *Intégrale 1965–1995.* Vol. 2, 4. Tréma.

Smetana, Bedriich. *Dalibor.* Supraphon. SU 0077-2 632.

—*Art; Comic Books; Bryant, Anita; Cinema; Dance; Gender Differences; Heterosexism; Literature; Rhetoric; Sappho; Song.*

N

NATURE. *See* Against Nature

NORTH AMERICA

In order to understand the issue of homophobia in North America, it is necessary to analyze the sexual culture of its complex society, the result of migratory waves of people from other parts of the world, many whom were conservative and dominated by religious forces. As a result, it could be said that there is not one, but rather many homophobic attitudes in North America, each relating to cultural constructions that have little in common with each other and yet overlap and reinforce one another. This reality is particularly acute in the United States, the most popular destination for immigrants in the nineteenth and twentieth centuries. By contrast, Canada, with its smaller population dispersed over a wide area, and whose politics have long been influenced by its historical relationship to Britain, experienced a more "European" evolution in the sense that the issue of homosexuality did not provoke a multiplicity of opposing viewpoints. It is thus best to undertake a separate analysis of these two countries, while keeping in mind that the extraordinary political and economic power of the United States regularly holds sway over Canada, including its attitudes on various social issues.

United States
The seventeenth-century colonization of what became the United States gives us insight into the issues that became the founding basis of homophobic attitudes there. The first two colonies to be established in the territory can in fact be considered two opposing models of colonization, each having different consequences on the construction of the representation of sexuality.

The first of the two, Virginia, is a model of economic colonization, founded on an agricultural crop hitherto unknown in Europe, namely, tobacco. This specialization led to an immigration flux made up primarily of young men, which resulted in a hyper-masculine colonial society that was both adventurous and violent. In this context, the low female population created the social conditions that not only allowed prostitution to flourish, but also for men to have sexual contact with each other, most often in hierarchical relationships similar to those in prisons and penitentiaries, with no particular ramifications on their "sexual orientation." Under these circumstances, then, homosexual relations were possible. At the same time, however, issues in this nearly-all-male society regarding masculinity became greatly exacerbated, allowing for the development of machismo attitudes, which included the disrespect of the "passive" partner in sexual relationships, whether male or female. Thus, we see the appearance of seemingly paradoxical behaviors in which a man may seek a "passive" same-sex partner while at the same time is willing to exact **violence** against those whom he perceives as being anti-masculine; i.e. homosexual.

Conversely, New England, the second colony established in the territory, was chiefly populated by English Pilgrims fleeing the repression of the Anglican Church. The immigrants were primarily made up of families, and thus there was no significant gender imbalance as there was in Virginia. However, New England's sexual culture was forged on radical Calvinist values, and the public sphere, while accepting distant supervision by England, was structured on a theocratic model. In this context, homosexuality was obviously a serious sin, all the more so as the logic of the return to the purity of the Holy Gospels, and more particularly the Old Testament, inherent to the constitution of Puritan Protestant sects, which considerably reinforces the Hebraic interdict of homosexuality written in Deuteronomy.

These two models—the violent machismo of a hyper-masculine culture and the religious fundamentalism of a Puritan society—serve as the basis for the construction of contemporary American homophobia; in fact, these models recur at regular intervals throughout the history of the Union. For example, in the late nineteenth century, new immigrants arriving from Ireland and Italy (the Virginia model: mostly male and immigrating primarily for economic reasons) as well as Orthodox Ashkenazi Jews (the New England model: usually families, in this case the result of the pogroms in Europe) brought with them their cultural biases against homosexuals.

Add to this matrix two important elements: firstly, the multi-ethnic factor. Unlike the Old World, the United States is made up of many different ethnicities and cultures. As in **Latin America**, North American colonizers encountered native populations already present on the continent. Also, because slavery was legal until the Lincoln presidency, there was a significant surge in people coming from sub-Saharan Africa, particularly concentrated in the southern states. Additionally, as a new economic force began as early as the nineteenth century, the United States was a constant center of attraction for immigrants from countries well beyond Old Europe, such as Asia and Latin America. Finally, the United States, in its imperialist and expansionist mode, took on territories belonging to other cultural spheres, such as Hawaii. In this sense, the construction of masculinity and sexuality is the result of multiple cultural shocks wherein each ethnic community possesses its own values, all the while being confronted with the representations and standards of other communities within the dynamics of economic and political domination. To cite one example, the homophobia present in the urban African- and Latin-American subcultures of today, as suggested in the homophobic lyrics of certain hip-hop and rap artists, can be interpreted as an of intensification of the values of virility of certain economically and culturally marginalized communities, reinforced by the dominant visibility of the "Anglo-Saxon" (i.e. white) gay community. This attitude has a doubly tragic consequence, intensifying the hatred toward "white fags" and possibly leading to physical violence or murder, while making it difficult for the African- or Latin-American individual discovering his attraction for a person of the same gender to construct his own identity, producing an increased risk of depression and self-destructive attitudes. Conversely, the multicultural experience of America has also had some positive effects on homosexuals: for example, Harlem in the 1920s became a safe harbor for gays at a time when African-American culture rarely stigmatized homosexuality; and the first attempt in the United States to recognize same-sex **marriage** occurred in Hawaii, linked at least in part to the customs of its peace-loving native population.

The other factor that has influenced the construction of American homophobia is political in nature. The world's economic leader since 1914 and its most powerful political force following the end of World War II in 1945, the United States has often modeled itself as a fortress under siege. In this context, the population's ethnic diversity at times has instigated a fear of the "enemy within." For example, during World War II, Americans of Japanese descent were deported to internment camps for fear of their ties to Japan. This sentiment also manifested itself in anti-communist panic during the Cold War, and at the same time linked the fate of homosexuals to that of the "Reds." The "pervert," perceived as the nation's weakest link and susceptible to blackmail because of his "immoral" activities, became the ideal target of communist agents who had infiltrated the country. Because of this, in the eyes of the government at all levels, homosexuals were incompatible with any public duty. This analysis, which is at the heart of gay history during McCarthyism in the 1950s, has since been constantly reinforced by the American religious right, which plays on supposed links among atheists, communists, and homosexuals. McCarthyism is also the phenomenon that has fostered the main obstacles hindering the acceptance of homosexuality in America; obstacles that, to this day, are still at the forefront of the battles being fought by the American gay and lesbian movement.

First, it is necessary to determine the make-up of the modern gay and lesbian identity. Certainly, the construction of the gay identity began well before the Cold War. However, it was grounded principally in the reality of the white middle-class in large urban centers. Conversely, the witch-hunts brought about by McCarthyism helped make tangible a unified homosexual "condition." Each practicing homosexual, regardless of ethnic origin, social class, or location, became a "pervert" in the eyes of the federal government, and as such an "enemy within," excluded from public service and a target of FBI surveillance. This treatment had the effect of unifying gays and lesbians across all cultures and classes who, from that point on, shared a common identity. Ironically, it is in this context of repression that the first "homophile" organizations, the Mattachine Society and the Daughters of Bilitis, formed; it is also in this context that San Francisco became the nation's gay mecca, a role reinforced by the city's position as the destination for military personnel dishonorably discharged from services because of their homosexuality. In this sense, in the construction of the gay and lesbian identity and the subsequent emergence of gay militancy in the United States, McCarthyism played a role similar to that played by nineteenth-century **psychiatry** in the history of homosexuality in Germany.

Less optimistically, the period of the 1950s also gave birth to conservative alliances that formed the basis of the powerful religious-based American right that helped to bring Ronald Reagan, George Bush, and George W. Bush to power. It is not only the Republican Party that has benefited from such groups, however. In fact, since the American Civil War, many Puritan evangelical organizations have, in a way that seems paradoxical to European observers, supported the Democratic Party. By rejecting Republican President Abraham Lincoln because of his anti-slavery policies, and because of a mistrust in government in general, the most sectarian religious populations of the South and agricultural Center allied with the unionized working-class populations of the North around the Democratic Party; decades later, this alliance helped form the basis of President Franklin Roosevelt's rise to power and subsequent re-elections. Yet, the Republican party line on questions of morality as generated by Joseph **McCarthy** in the 1950s, followed by President John F. Kennedy's policies regarding racial segregation, marked the beginning of the end of this alliance's support for the Democratic Party. Moreover, in the late 60s and early 70s, the Democrats were forced to strengthen their left-wing agenda or risk the alienation of those in the hippie and pacifist movements, a move that made alliances between religious conservatives and social democrats all the more distinct. It is solely the issue of morality that, in the 70s, allowed various conservatives groups to come together under the banner of the Republican Party.

In fact, between the religious groups and the Republican Party, neither economic issues, nor the

state of the union, nor racial issues could generate a unified dynamic. Even more, these three issues were, and remain, important factors of disagreement within the conservative clan. The question of morality, then, focused on the sacredness of the American "family" and became the point of convergence that allowed for the realignment of the American electorate, resulting in the 1980 election of President Ronald Reagan. During the campaign, three central issues emerged: the legalization of abortion, aid to single mothers, and rights for gays and lesbians. These issues, to one which might add gun control and the death penalty, make up the basis of the religious-conservative right that kept the Republican Party in power for twelve years between 1980 and 1992. As such, the question of gay rights remained part of the ongoing American political debate, exacerbated through the decade of the 80s by the **AIDS** epidemic which, amid a slew of archaic and outrageous characterizations—at best, the expected result of sexual disorders; at worst, divine retribution—intensified and entrenched various political positions on the subject, and reinforced the institutionalization of homophobia. The vehemence of the debates regarding gay rights during this period was also evident in other gay-related issues, such as the 1986 Supreme Court ruling upholding the constitutionality of state anti-sodomy laws (which the Supreme Court would rule as unconstitutional in 2003); legal recognition of same-sex partnerships; and gays and lesbians in the **armed forces**. One notable consequence was the increasing radicalization of the gay and lesbian movement, spearheaded by queer political groups such as ACT UP, Queer Nation, and the Lesbian Avengers.

The Democrats' return to power in 1993 under President Bill Clinton seemed to soothe tensions surrounding the question of gay rights. The Clinton administration's decisions were timid and ambiguous at times (particularly the "Don't Ask, Don't Tell" policy regarding gays and lesbians in the armed forces), but the spread of AIDS to heterosexual communities, and the emergence of a conservative gay lobby within the Republican Party, have also helped to defuse the virulence of the debates on the issue. An example of the growing contingency of those who support to the rights of gays and lesbians was the enormous public outrage, extending beyond the gay and lesbian community, in response to the barbaric murder of Matthew **Shepard**, a twenty-one-year-old man who was tortured and killed in Wyoming in 1998 because he was gay. The somewhat ambiguous position on homosexuality taken by George W. Bush during his first presidential campaign in 2000, despite attempts to the contrary by the Republican Party's right-wing as well as ultra-conservative candidate Pat **Buchanan**, may have also given the impression that a new page, composed of appeasement and normalization, was being written in the United States for gays and lesbians.

Nevertheless, the issue of homosexuality still provokes particularly strong opposition in the American political sphere. It is in this sense that, in the strictest of terms, homophobia in the United States is political. Conversely, the experience of gays and lesbians in Canada is closer to the European experience, despite the close proximity and decisive influence of its powerful neighbor to the south.

Canada

The history of homophobia in Canada is neatly summarized by gay Vancouver activist Doug Sanders: "The problem in Canada is not one of persecution, but rather of the dominant opinion that gays do not exist." Despite a history that one could assume was similar to that of the United States, different factors have, in fact contributed to the experience of homophobia in Canada.

The religious factor is one difference. Unlike the US, the number of Evangelical Protestants in Canada has always remained low. As of 2005, it represented only six percent of the population, versus twenty-two percent in the United States. Despite the importance of the Anglican and Catholic religions—reinforced by the historically difficult coexistence between English and French Canada—there is no obsessive desire to create a morally pure society, free of all sin, as is the case with Puritans.

Secondly, Canadian social policy, similar to the European standard (which features state intervention in the economy and the workplace), has not created inequalities among ethnic communities on the same scale as the United States. A major historical ethnic conflict, that between English and French Canada, did not have an impact on the issue of homosexuality.

Finally, Canada's low profile on the international political stage has meant that homosexuals have never been considered a threat to Canada's political stability or social fabric, as they have in the United States.

All these conditions have led to a relatively smooth history for gays and lesbians in Canada, despite the fact that homosexuality was criminalized until 1969, just as it was in the United Kingdom (1967). In the era preceding its legalization, the 1950s was the only decade that could be characterized as particularly homophobic, in part due to the influence of McCarthyism to the south. In 1952, the Immigration Act was adopted, forbidding homosexuals from entering the country; further, a special unit of the Royal Canadian Mounted Police was created to compile a list of all known homosexuals, particularly those working in the Canadian civil service in Ottawa. The official response to homosexuality softened in the years to come; the Klippert Affair (in which George Klippert became the last person in Canada to be arrested, charged, and imprisoned for homosexual acts) revealed that a strict application of Canadian laws could result in life imprisonment, leading ultimately to decriminalization in 1969, despite the disapproval of the Opposition, the Conservative Party.

The history of homosexuality and gay rights in Canada coincides with gay and lesbian liberation experienced elsewhere; Canada has also taken a leading role in certain issues affecting gays, such as **suicide** prevention among young gays and lesbians. However, as an example of its susceptibility to American and British influence, Canada saw its conservative right wing rise up in the wake of its American counterparts led by President Ronald Reagan in 1980, followed closely by Margaret Thatcher in the United Kingdom. Earlier, in the 1970s, Canada's religious conservatives were buoyed by Anita **Bryant**, who decided to extend her anti-gay crusade beyond the American border, finding support not only in Canada's evangelical communities but also in the Catholic Church, which has always been particularly powerful in French-language Quebec. During the 1976 Montreal Olympics, this religious-conservative attitude toward homosexuals took the form of a police operation called *ville propre* (clean city), in which police raided gay bars and bathhouses in both Montreal and Ottawa, leading to the arrest of dozens and the seizure of bathhouse membership lists. This "war against bathhouses" remained one of the most popular methods used by Canadian authorities to fight homosexuality (based on the illegality of public sex) throughout the 70s; at the same time, the Parti Québécois, which held power in the province of Quebec, added sexual orientation to the Quebec Charter of Human Rights and Freedoms in 1977.

Meanwhile, English-speaking Canada, more conservative and more sensitive to the sirens of the new American right, pursued its administrative harassment of gays and lesbians by searching the offices of *The Body Politic*, a militant gay newspaper based in Toronto, and by attempting to forbid the paper's distribution, under the pretense that it incited **pedophilia.** These operations had the opposite effect, however: it only strengthened the gay and lesbian movement, which had been in a period of relative lethargy since the early 70s.

Whatever the attraction English-speaking Canada may have had for Reagan-era religious conservatism, the experience of French-speaking Canada (Quebec) and its fierce protectionist policies, which resulted in referendums on its potential separation from the rest of Canada, probably precluded the entrenchment of a serious English-Canadian right wing along the lines of that in the United States. Thus, these influences remained superficial, without any deep ideological foundations, and as a result, institutionalized homophobia did not take root in Canada as it did south of the border. Conversely, the new right's rhetoric acted as a foil of sorts for the French-Canadian community, who saw it, not without reason, as a form of Anglo-Saxon imperialism; as a result, this allowed for the establishment of a relatively pro-gay policy in a province with strong historical ties to Catholicism. Still today, the Montreal gay and lesbian community, centered around Ste-Catherine Street, is probably one of the most active and best-integrated communities in North America.

On June 7, 2002, Quebec approved a law which recognized same-sex couples and their right to **adopt**. Remarkably, the law was passed unanimously. When the legislation was first introduced, however, more conservative members of parliament had been strongly opposed to the idea; however, after meeting with various gays and lesbians, including families and parents, they were convinced otherwise. Certainly, the Catholic Church remained opposed to the legislation until it was passed, but as Quebec Justice Minister Paul Bégin said, "What was at the center of the debate was love; and the priests never spoke of love."

—*Pierre-Olivier de Busscher*

Adam, Barry D. *The Rise of a Gay and Lesbian Movement.* Boston: Twayne Publishers, 1987.

———, Jan Willem Duyvendak, and André Krouwel, eds. *The Global Emergence of Gay and Lesbian Politics: National Imprints of a Worldwide Movement.* Philadelphia: Temple, 1999.

Bérubé, Allan. *Coming Out Under Fire: The History of Gay Men and Women in World War Two.* New York: Free Press, 1990.

Chauncey, George. *Gay New York: Gender, Urban Culture, and the Making of the Gay Male World, 1890–1940.* New York: Basic Books, 1994.

D'Emilio, John. *Sexual Politics, Sexual Communities: The Making of a Homosexual Minority in the United States, 1940–1970.* Chicago: Univ. of Chicago Press, 1983.

Duberman, Martin. *Stonewall.* New York: Dutton, 1993.

———, George Chauncey, and Martha Vicinus, eds. *Hidden from History: Reclaiming the Gay and Lesbian Past.* New York: Meridian, 1989.

FitzGerald, Frances. *Cities on a Hill: Journey Through Contemporary American Cultures.* New York: Simon & Schuster, 1986.

Fout, John, and Maura Shaw Tantillo, eds. *American Sexual Politics: Sex, Gender, and Race Since the Civil War.* Chicago: Univ. of Chicago Press, 1999.

Katz, Jonathan. *Gay American History: Lesbians and Gay Men in the U.S.A.* New York: Harper & Row, 1985.

Kinsman, Gary. *The Regulation of Desire: Sexuality in Canada.* Montreal: Black Rose Books, 1987.

Miller, Neil. *Out of the Past: Gay and Lesbian History from 1869 to the Present.* New York: Vintage, 1995.

McLeod, Donald. *Lesbian and Gay Liberation in Canada: A Selected Annotated Chronology, 1964–1975.* Toronto: ECW, 1996.

Sylvestre, Paul-François. *Bougrerie en Nouvelle-France.* Hull, Quebec: Editions Asticou, 1983.

—*Armed Forces; Bryant, Anita; Buchanan, Pat; Ex-Gay; Hoover, J. Edgar; McCarthy, Joseph; Protestantism; Shepard, Matthew; Stonewall.*

OCEANIA

The Largest Sexual Laboratory in the World

Oceania stretches across much of the southern Pacific Ocean, from the Malaysian archipelago in the west to Polynesia in the east, and from Micronesia in the north to Australia in the south. The region is characterized by a notable cultural, religious, and racial diversity.

The most important element of Oceania is its geography, which is without a doubt the source of this diversity. The region contains thousands of islands spread over the entire area; the distance between them, as well as numerous mountains or maritime barriers between neighboring tribes, explains how various cultures in the region evolved in different manners. For example, on the main island of New Guinea, one-quarter of the all languages in the world are spoken here, including some that are used by a single village. And even though Indonesia is now the largest Muslim country in the world and despite the lasting influence of Christian missionaries in the South Pacific in general, its earliest form of religion consisted of a myriad of local cults and animist traditions. Further, Oceania is, without a doubt, the largest sexual laboratory in the world. For centuries, anthropologists have been attracted to this region, so rich and so "exotic," particularly with regard to sexual practices and the construction of gender. Literature on sexuality in Oceania is plentiful; however, references to homophobia or to any similar taboo are strangely rare. Does this mean that homophobia as it is conceived in the West does not exist in the region? Or is it that this is a blind spot particularly revealing of anthropological research? Both of these two explanations may be valuable. Anthropological literature reveals evidence of homosexual practices in the region. For example, homosexual rites are practiced in the region of Melanesia, which stretches over 3,100 miles, from the east coast of Indonesia to the Fiji islands. However, while widespread, these rites are not present everywhere in Melanesia; they are practiced mainly in the lowlands, on the coasts, and in inland communities. These practices are also present in numerous Australian tribes.

Traditional Cultures

Despite important differences among rites that are practiced, it is possible to identify certain general commonalities. In the communities where these rites occur, sperm is considered as the main source of male power, and the insemination of young men is a mandatory rite of passage for all men without exception; it is considered the main means by which boys can become powerful men, and as such, has a high social and ritualistic value. As noted by anthropologist Gilbert Herdt, ritual homosexuality is mainly practiced among the most warlike clans and those that have a headhunting past.

It is equally interesting to note that this homosexual practice is in no way associated with fetishism or cross-dressing, susceptible to subverting gender categories. Further, it is traditional that all young men engage in these practices for years, first in the role of "receiver" and then later as "giver"; these practices do not exclude relations with women or, later on, heterosexual **marriage**. The situation is thus very different from the Western concept of homosexuality as effeminate and devoid of heterosexual relations.

Sexual relations described by Herdt and other anthropologists follow precise rules in agreement with traditional rites and laws. In Melanesia at least, ritualized homosexual relations are usually based on age, whereby the younger one always plays the role of "receiver." Herdt reminds us, however, that ritualized or not, this homosexuality always implies sexual excitation, at least for the "giver." (By contrast, homosexual relations between equals are less common, and accounts of lesbian relations are rarer still.) This ritual homosexuality is not only tolerated, it is valorized as an essential means to produce a complete man. Under these conditions, homophobia as we know it does not appear in these societies.

Colonial & Post-Colonial Oceania

Then, the great explorers led the way for the Europeans to preside over Oceania. At the beginning of the twentieth century, the region was under the thumb of colonial powers, divided among England, France, Germany, the Netherlands, Portugal, Spain, and later Australia, Japan, Java, New Zealand, and the US. Europeans established colonial administrations, new laws (and particularly anti-sodomy ones), and religious missions. One of the first effects of the Europeanization was the impact of the missionaries' homophobia on indigenous masculinity, particularly in places where ritual homosexuality had been highly valorized until then. Tribes and indigenous cultures suffered greatly from this intervention, which provoked irreversible changes. As a result, rather than abandon their ancient traditions, many clans started to conduct their initiation rites in secret and concealed their sacred objects from the invaders; even today, they maintain a total silence around the secret "affairs" of men and women, even in Australia.

This colonial heritage clearly appears in the institutions and laws of the countries of Oceania. Male homosexuality is now illegal in several countries where ritual homosexuality was practiced in times past, particularly Papua New Guinea. Paradoxically, homosexuality is not illegal in Indonesia, which is the most populous Muslim state in the world, nor in Vanuatu or French Polynesia, where French law applies.

The last quarter of the twentieth century was an era of decolonization, reforms, and the dismantling of homophobic laws. Australia and New Zealand decriminalized homosexuality in 1975 and 1986 respectively, introduced laws against **discrimination**, and have equal opportunity policies with regard to gays and lesbians in the military and police force. However, although same-sex couples may now be recognized by law in New Zealand through civil unions, discrimination persists. In New Zealand, for instance, gay men are not allowed to give blood, and in Australia, same-sex commitment ceremonies do not constitute any legal

semblance of marriage. Further, in spite of legislative advances, homophobic biases are still used in courtrooms. The most renowned example is without doubt Australia's notorious "homosexual advance defense," in which a person accused of a crime alleges that he acted either in self-defense or under provocation in response to a homosexual advance made by another person. (It is known in the US as the "gay panic defense.") While it is not formally recognized by Australian law, it has been used to attain acquittals or lenient sentences for trials for homophobic murders, in the states of Victoria, New South Wales, and South Australia. One example was Malcolm Green, who in 1997 was acquitted of murder and instead convicted of manslaughter, as the court agreed that he acted in self-defense in response to unwanted homosexual advances.

In 1994, the Australian organization Gay Men and Lesbians Against Discrimination (GLAD) published the results of a survey on the gay and lesbian population of the Australian state of Victoria. Seventy percent of the 492 lesbians and 69% of the 510 gay men questioned reported they had been the victim of insults, threats, or violence due to their sexuality. In addition, 11% of the lesbians and 20% of the gay men had been physically assaulted, and 2.6% of the lesbians and 5.5% of the gay men had been assaulted by **police**. Further, many countries in Oceania have had to deal with the tragic problem of homophobic murders. In Fiji in 2001, the country's Red Cross director John Scott and his partner Greg Scrivener, both from New Zealand, were brutally murdered by a man wielding a machete; at the time of the perpetrator's arrest, the police commissioner claimed that the young man had been "exploited" by the couple. Paradoxically, in 1997, Fiji had become the second country in the world (after South Africa) to explicitly protect against discrimination based on sexual orientation in its constitution. Although the constitution's position has been precariously tested by two military coups since then, it would appear that consensual sex between gay men is not an issue for the police, however, it is still illegal.

As we go forward in the new millennium, things seem to be progressing for homosexuals in Oceania, and since the end of the twentieth century, homophobia, at least that which the law can sanction, appears to be receding. Today in Australia, Sydney is a world capital for gays and lesbians, and homosexuals are permitted to join the military. In 1999, New Zealanders elected Georgina Beyer, a woman of Maori origin, as a Labor MP for Wairarapa, becoming the first trans-sexual person in the world to sit in a national parliament. Recent years have also seen the emergence of new perspectives, the most striking example being the Gay and Lesbian Mardi Gras celebration in Sydney, which started in 1978 as a response to homophobia. Today, the parade attracts close to half a million spectators and is one of the world's largest gay and lesbian events.

Homophobic prejudices, however, still exist in Oceania. Churches and religious associations escape anti-discrimination laws. Certain indigenous cultures, once tolerant of homosexual practices, are today less so because of colonial influences, and homophobic murders remain a troubling problem.

—*David Plummer*

Aldrich, Robert, and Garry Wotherspoon, eds. *Gay Perspectives: Essays in Australian Gay Culture*. Sydney: Univ. of Sydney Press, 1996.

Beyer, Georgina, and Cathy Casey. *Change for the Better: The Story of Georgina Beyer*. Auckland: Random House, 1999.

Comstock, Gary. "Developments: Sexual Orientation and the Law," *Harvard Law Review*, no. 102 (1989).

Gay Men and Lesbians Against Discrimination (GLAD). *Not a Day Goes By: Report on the GLAD Survey into Discrimination and Violence Against Lesbians and Gay Men in Victoria*. Melbourne: GLAD, 1994.

Herdt, Gilbert. "Ritualised Homosexual Behaviour in the Male Cults of Melanesia, 1862–1983." In *Ritualised Homosexuality in Melanesia*. Berkeley: Univ. of California Press, 1993.

Hodge, Dino. *Did you Meet any Malagas? A Homosexual History of Australia's Tropical Capital*. Darwin, Australia: Little Gem Publications, 1993.

International Lesbian and Gay Association, Brussels. *World Legal Survey*. http://www.ilga.org (accessed April 23, 2008).

Murray, Stephen O. *Oceanic Homosexualities*. New York: Garland, 1992.

New South Wales Attorney General's Department. *Review of the "Homosexual Advance Defence."* Sydney: New South Wales Attorney General's Department, 1996.

Plummer, David. *One of the Boys: Masculinity, Homophobia and Modern Manhood*. New York: Haworth Press, 1999.

———. "Policing Manhood: New Theories about the Social Significance of Homophobia." In *Sexual Positions: An Australian View*. Edited by Carl Wood. Melbourne: Hill of Content-Collins, 2001.

Sandroussi, Jewly, and Sue Thompson. *Out of the Blue: A Police Survey of Violence and Harassment against Gay Men and Lesbians*. Sydney: New South Wales Police Service, 1995.

Tomsen, Stephen. "Hatred, Murder and Male Honour: Gay Homicides and the 'Homosexual Panic Defence'," *Criminology Australia* 6, no. 2 (1994).

———. "Was Lombroso Queer? Criminology, Criminal Justice and the Heterosexual Imaginary." In *Homophobic Violence*. Edited by Gail Mason and Stephen Tomsen. Sydney: Hawkins Press, 1997.

Wotherspoon, Gary. "Les Interventions de l'Etat contre les homosexuels en Australie durant la Guerre Froide." In *Sodomites, invertis, homosexuels: perspectives historiques*. Edited by Rommel Mendès-Leite. Lille, GaiKitschCamp, 1994.

—*Anthropology; Essentialism/Constructionism; Southeast Asia.*

ORTHODOXY (Christian)

Orthodox or Eastern Christian Churches claim to be the authentic Christianity, having received the true faith during the first seven ecumenical councils between 325 and 787 CE. Polycentric, Episcopal, and council-minded, the Orthodox Church is made of nine Patriarchates (first, Constantinople, Alexandria, Antioch, and Jerusalem, with Rome; then, Moscow, Georgia, Serbia, Romania, and Bulgaria), three auto-cephalic Archdioceses (Cyprus, Albania, Greece), and three metropolises (Poland, the Czech Republic, the US); in all, between 150 and 350 million believers. It is the second largest Christian church in the world after the Roman Catholic Church. Mainly and originally Eastern, orthodoxy has grown around the world from the sixteenth century due to political crises in the Byzantine and Slavic world. Assuming universality, the Orthodox Church continues to claim a moral authority on the societies that it oversees.

It would be paradoxical if orthodoxy was less homophobic than its Roman rival but that is not the case. The Orthodox Church purports to maintain a faith common to Latins and Orientals before the 1054 schism. The condemnation of homosexuality in all its forms is one area of agreement with the views of Rome, as proven by Moscow Patriarch, Alexius II of Russia's public declaration for united action with Rome against **decriminalization** and "banalisation" of homosexuality and other "lay violations" of divine law. He wrote to Pope John Paul II about the European Union's Charter of Fundamental Rights in 2000: "The criteria of division of citizens pursuant to their sexual orientation does not appear to us as inherent to human nature, also the introduction of this criterion does not appear justified." A position against homosexuality is easily agreed upon through the churches, even divorce and conjugal sex (considered polemic against the Catholic Augustine penchant) are contentious topics. But faced with liberal **Protestantism**, particularly American Protestantism, orthodoxy is threatening to leave the too "inclusive" ecumenical movement if it admits homophile churches or "gay Christians." *A priori,* it is inconceivable to bless a gay couple (Orthodox Press Services, no. 65, February 1982): priests and "pseudo spouses" would be excommunicated.

By forbidding homosexuals all sexual expression, orthodoxy demands that they renounce this constitutive part of their self and the fulfillment of love, if faithful, while this relation is legitimate for married heterosexuals. The rise of modern theologians more "open" to the reality of a profound sexual orientation (psychological or biological), previously rejected by ecclesiastic authorities, does not change anything: in the past it was a diabolical tendency; new homosexuality remains a pathology in the classical sense of "passion" (demanding to be prevailed over by reason, but also by penance and prayer) and also in the modern sense of illness or mental alteration. Gays, who "are not only that" (being "reasonable souls"), are forced in conscience to absolute chastity with the help of the competent therapist and the sympathetic spiritual father.

Orthodoxy is guaranteed by Canons or codes of laws fixing sexual norms and forbidding the practice of all forms of carnal homosexuality. The local Council of Elvira (Spain, c. 300) and the ecumenical Council of Ancyra (Turkey, 314, Canon 16) are valid eternally due to their essential link to faith. The proof is in the interdictions of the Law (Deuteronomy, Leviticus) confirmed by the destruction of **Sodom and Gomorrah**. St **Paul**'s epistles and St John's Apocalypse (chapter twenty-one: fire for fornicators and idolaters) have definitely established this interpretation, along with the Apostles' Didache. The Church punishes with long and humiliating penances, even by excommunication, the sins of *arsenokoitai* (coupling of males) and of *paido-phtoresis* (corruption of boys) with threats of damnation. The Fathers have placed the seriousness of homosexual acts (according to age, practices, roles, and frequency) among masturbation, bestiality, incest, adultery, or fornication. The illegitimacy of the act is double, because there is both fornication and gender anomaly. If intercrural coitus is worth eighty days of penance, St Basile of Caesarea (fourth century) condemned simple sodomy and adultery to fifteen years of penance, eighteen years according to his contemporary St Gregory of Nyssa (Canon 4), and homosexual sodomy demands a penance of thirty years according to the seventh of Basil's ninety-two canons ("of those who have sinned **against nature** and other great sinners"). St John Chrysostom, Archbishop of Constantinople (347–407), considered the death of a young consenting sexually passive man a benefit compared to the damage they cause to themselves, damage, according to him, which is equal to several deaths. Excluded from the priesthood, they also must be prevented from marrying, according to Lucas Chrysoberges, Patriarch of Constantinople between 1154 and 1170, probably to avoid causing damages to their new relatives.

Incidentally, if "sodomy" is compared to witchcraft and idolatry, it is because it constitutes from this perspective a challenge to the order of creation. As any universalism, orthodoxy tries to rationally justify the revelation: its **anthropology** defines sexuality as a device second to "Love." Due to its biological **sterility**, which seems to negate the sexual complementarities of genders created *ad hoc* by God (sexuation originally for the good of man), homosexuality seems incompatible with faith and it is even compared to "bestiality" (it is the same word in Serbian). Human destiny becomes part of the divine project of creating a free, and mortal, being of flesh. The real **philosophy** (a Byzantine mix of neo-Platonism and Stoicism) that leads to faith establishes the idea of a "natural" norm of morality and sexuality, to which homosexuality is foreign. In substance, orthodoxy wobbles between a neo-Platonism hostile to sexuality as such, always blemished with "carnal pleasure" (John Chrysostom's tradition, heir to early Christian scholar Origen on this subject), and a conception which legitimizes the pleasure in marriage (Council of Gangres, 340), without dissociating it from the possibility of procreation. The spouses must evolve toward tenderness. It is the chaste relation between the Church and Christ that serves as an analogically perfect model. The soul's domination of the body and reason's domination of passion lead to the limitation of sexuality.

Refusing to cooperate with God, homosexuality would express an "irrational" desire for sensual delight. On these grounds, it is classed among Hedonist deviances, as sodomy in general or masturbation. Traditionally and still often today, theologians and canonists do not meditate on homosexuality, its nature or its origins. For them, God and nature desire reproduction and impart a healthy instinct to man; pure homosexuality does not exist or would be an accidental monstrosity. It is issued from an over-abundance of usurping sensitivity. Incidentally, it is generally confused with Greek—and therefore pagan—pederasty and Eastern pedophilia, which allows it to be seen as a release of excessive adult emotions, while remaining male (as long as he is the active partner), and a teenage naiveté. Inversely, orthodox thinkers have difficulty imagining the "passive" as other than forced, raped, or abused at an easily influenced (biological or mental) age. The "effeminate" passive adult in traditional societies is considered a prostitute (which can be the case) and generally incurs more social slight, even if the Church does not make any distinction: in all cases, it is considered profanation of masculinity. The boy or young man, if he is androgynous, is a worry for canonists and authors of monastic rules: naturally seductive, he fatally gives rise to sexual desire in the cloister and is a privileged tool of the devil. Ascetic privation, sexual ambiguity, and its availability in male milieus seem sufficient to explain the exceptionality. If it is occasional, it is a **perversion** of taste.

Russian St Nilus of Sora (sixteenth century) and the *Pedalion* (*The Rudder*), a codification of Canon law by St Nicodemus of the Holy Mountain, according to Plato, stigmatize "that which no quadruped beast would dare to do" as an abuse of our unconfined imagination. They do not express a zoological reductionism (if there is nature, it is in one sense "analogical"), but a reminder of the requirement for the free being to submit his sexuality, potentially overflowing, to what gives it sense, reproduction, and to imitate the temperance of seasonal animal coupling.

From this came the idea that homosexuality would be a biological threat to humanity. The taking root of the **vice** (to which is linked the attraction of pleasure, as man is sensual and seeks it infinitely) would discourage men from the use of women in procreation: homosexuality and sodomy would invade Christianity, according to Chrysostom in his work *Against Opponents of Monastic Life*. Justinian justified his code by his concern to prevent "natural" catastrophes and epidemics, derived from the hand of a vengeful God. His mission was to protect society from the collective punishment but also to scare sinners who were destroying themselves morally and damning themselves. Sodom was the dramatization and justification for Justinian's preventive legislation. The idea of the threat to the species leads to the homosexual being scapegoated for his irresponsible egotism as much as his lustfulness. Heir to the Byzantine tradition, the *Pedalion* sees homosexuality as a form of excess and also revives medical myths of psychosomatic harm caused be masturbation and sodomy.

Largely taboo, due to the fear of **scandal**, the subject that had remained confined to canonic and penitential literature appeared marginally in Russian Christian thought of the twentieth century and in emigration. Freudian **psychoanalysis** and psychopathology served as scientific paradigms and cautioned as to the idea of "nature" and definite roles of gender, without the homosexual being an approved third sex or being authorized to live his nature, as he is not of original nature. But "personalism" frees the person, by showering him with his moral freedom and transcendence in relation to unmastered desire, in the tradition of Kant.

If Russian Orthodox theologian Paul Evdokimov (1901–70) was inspired by Jung in general, he forgot the psychiatrist's generous positions. The sole mention of homosexuality in his *The Sacrament of Love* reduces it to a manifestation of sexual nihilism, of excessive masculinization of the world, of a refusal of femininity (magnified by the Virgin), and moreover of God: "This too masculine world, where feminine charisma does not play any role anymore, where woman becomes masculine, is more and more a world without God, because it is without Mother-Theotokos [Mother of God], and God cannot be born there. It is symptomatic that this ambiance, **debauchery** of children, incest and homosexuality affirm themselves openly." So homophobia is once again based on the uncompromising imperative of reproduction: by his refusal of the world, of creation, the homosexual egotistically and viciously refuses to participate in the renewal of humanity for his "mechanical" and absurd pleasure. It is symptomatic that Evdokimov put the refusal of woman and paternity alongside **pedophilia**: the homosexual is thus a rapist, almost an abortionist of children, and of Jesus himself. The sexual nihilism would be an aspect of rhetorical and practical atheism at work in the modern world, particularly in the West, that gives it too much freedom of expression.

As for Freud, his "pansexualism" is rejected with disgust, while his arguments on homosexual immaturity are used. Evdokimov places those theories in parallel with the debauchery of children and incest in presupposing an infantile regression and an incapacity to meet his normal object. It is symptomatic that those theologians who show themselves to be "progressive" toward the status of women, such as Evdokimov, Oliver Clément, and Elisabeth Behr-Sigel, also propose their services as *moderns* in the critique of homosexuality and show a compensatory aggressiveness. The same ones stress the misogyny of a part of Christian culture, plead for a historic-contextual interpretation of prohibitions of impurity in Leviticus, and describe St Paul as an ignored progressive, but do not think to proceed with this type of rereading on homosexuality. Anti-Catholic and interested in recruitment, this orthodox lyricism of female charisma, often antifeminist at its base, is as suspicious as its bogus rehabilitation of sexuality, which at numerous levels is nothing but disguised conservatism. In his *Questions sur l'homme* (Questions on man), Clément expressed the old anxiety about the reversal of cosmic order brought about by lesbianism: "Violence creates a type of homosexual and domineering Amazon, and ignorance of the disciplines of metamorphosis, once the old levees are broken, only frees the instincts of very ancient magic."

Since gay liberation, the Orthodox Church rejects, whenever possible, the **decriminalization** and any judicial, social, or scientific commonplaceness of homosexuality. American Orthodoxes distinguish themselves by their controversial conservatism. British psychotherapist and theologian Elizabeth Moberly opposes with "compassion" any normalization of "an incapacity of the child to bond with the parent of the same sex" and a "blocking of development" certainly widespread, but as pathological and curable as the flu! This sad problem demands patience and therapy, but the eroticization of this deviance of desire would be, for Moberly, the worst of all things. William Basil Zion goes into rapture over Moberly's depth and criticizes the Jesuit John McNeil for his neo-Thomist homophilia and John Boswell for his erroneous interpretation of the bases of patristic homophobia. A caricatured vision of the gay **ghetto** serves to reduce homosexuality (accused of the refusal of **otherness**, i.e. of woman) to eroticism, promiscuity, **AIDS**, narcissism, and mental instability, rendering meaningless all acknowledgment of gay "couples" or of their "love." Gay liberation would be a victimization of irresponsible hypocrites, while the role played by Christian stigmatization in the critiqued behaviors is never mentioned.

The Archbishop Chrysostom of Cyprus led without much effect a large campaign in April and May 1998, recommending to Cypriots to prefer state homophobia (seven years in **prison** for consenting adults since 1899) to adherence to the European Union, if the price were a legal protection of homosexuals and their orientation, which is only "debauchery." The Romanian Church obtained from parliament an ambiguous abrogation of dispositions condemned in Europe. In Greece, the concordant Church could not prevent decriminalization (1951) and the lowering of the sexual majority (fifteen years old), but has largely maintained its moral condemnation. The Metropolis of Attica rejected, in the name of St Paul, perversions that preclude access to the realm of God and is indignant of the growing equality of treatment between gay couples and heterosexual couples.

State **communism** in Slavic and Balkan countries forbade the Church from taking a public position on social questions, but with the fall of communism, the Church joined the state on the idea of a social morality to direct adult desires and life choices toward a "normative" nature. The Serbian Church approved the homophobia of three quarters of the population, brought up between communism and religion, and incited violent demonstrations by nationalists, monarchists, and reactionaries against **tolerance** toward gays. In 2001, Belgrade's first gay pride gave rise to violence from Milosevic and Greater Serbia partisans, valorized on posters calling on "the Orthodox to mobilize for a spiritually healthy Serbia and against anti-Christian homosexual immorality." In 2001, the social doctrine of the Russian Church defined homosexuality as a "sinful alteration of human nature"; further, it proposes stigmatization, by requiring that the state remove gays from all pedagogical and military authority.

Lesbianism, traditionally forgotten, is now condemned, due to the popularization of the theme. The status of women (excluded from the priesthood) and the joint horror of sodomy and homosexuality manifest the heterosexist character of orthodox religion. The critique of Western Augustinian ways, such as the guilt complex over sex and the Orthodox pretensions about limiting **marriage** to procreation, reveal their intolerance for the **discrimination** of adult love and the need for the social legitimization of sex. Orthodoxy is a prisoner of a need for cosmic order and Trinitarian symbolism that makes "gender" so essential to the point of alienating the person in the name of his or her transcendent vocation. A miraculous election to self-restraint, the radical crucifixion of carnal desire: such is God's project for the gay Orthodox.

—Nicolas Plagne

St Clement of Alexandria. *Le Pédagogue.* Paris: Sources chrétiennes, 1960–70.

St Nicodermus of the Holy Mountain. *The Pedalion* or *The Rudder.* Athens, 1953.

Evdokimov, Paul. *Le Sacrement de l'amour.* Paris: Desclée, De Brouwer, 1967. [Published in the US as *The Sacrament of Love.* Crestwood, NY: St Vladimir's Seminary Press, 1985.]

Meyendorff, John. *Le Mariage, une perspective orthodoxe.* Paris: YMCA, 1986. [Published in the US as *Marriage: An Orthodox Perspective.* Crestwood, NY: St Vladimir's Seminary Press, 1975.]

Moberly, Elizabeth. *Psychogenesis: The Early Development of Gender Identity.* London: Paul Kegan, 1982

———. *Homosexuality: A New Christian Ethic.* Cambridge: James Clarke, 1983.

Stern, Mikhail, and August Stern. *La Vie sexuelle en URSS.* Paris: Albin Michel, 1979.

Zion, William Basil. *Eros and Transformation: An Eastern Orthodox Perspective.* New York: Univ. Press of America, 1984.

—Balkans, the; Bible, the; Europe, Eastern & Central; Heresy; Inquisition; Justinian; Russia; Sodom and Gomorrah.

OTHERNESS

The concept of otherness is relatively recent in the history of homophobia, yet it is becoming increasingly dominant and widespread among philosophers, priests, psychoanalysts, and anthropologists alike. According to this view, homosexuality is the fear of true otherness in its embrace of similitude and narcissism. Where did such an idea originate?

Without a doubt, it was not in the Old Testament: Eve born of Adam, woman of man, certainly does not appear to be an example of otherness. As for **Sodom and Gomorrah**, it is the "cry of their abominations" (injustice and inequity, according to Genesis), their distortion of the common law—and not their rejection of otherness—which distinguishes them from all other cities, and calls upon them divine retribution. Of course, we need not even mention Lot, the only fair man of Sodom, whose act of incest with his two daughters is definitely no great lesson in otherness.

Nor in the New Testament will one discover arguments centered on the notion of "neighbor," which is a form of the "other." Even under **Paul**, the condemnation of "uncleanness, fornication, and lewdness" (2 Cor 12:21) is still based on deviation from the law, and not any particular relationship with the Other. In this way, the criticism of homosexuality as being anti-"other" could not have originated in Scripture.

With regard to **philosophy**, we can focus on modern philosophy's role, given that ancient philosophy, from Plato to Roman Stoicism, appears to be indifferent to the notion of otherness, and in fact, speaks favorably to the idea of love (or friendship) for the same or similar. In modern philosophy, there is a notable importance accorded to gender **differences** by philosophers such as G W. F. Hegel or Emmanuel Lévinas, and with it, the seed of modern homophobia which depicts homosexuality as the fear of the Other. Yet, according to both Hegel and Lévinas, the idea of the Other is as much based on biological differentiation as it is against it. Moreover, the modern concept of the Other could just as well lead to an opposing theory: homosexuality could be interpreted to mean the primacy of a look toward the Other, and the subsequent choice to present oneself as an *object* for others. This, notably, is Jean Genet's "Sartrian" interpretation: the genesis of homosexuality, of "pederasty" as Sartre would say, is situated in the man who discovers his truth in "being for others."

In the world of **psychoanalysis**, the anti-otherness arguments appear to be more serious. It was Sigmund Freud who, before all others, considered homosexuality to be a "narcissistic love" and as an inability to grasp the difference of the sexes by assuming the castration of the mother. This legitimized the terms "**inversion**" and "**perversion**," relating the male homosexual urge as an identification with the mother, and consequently, an inability to attain the symbolic Other. However, things then become complicated. Firstly, the distinction that Freud makes between "narcissistic love" and "anaclitic love" is not only internal to heterosexuality, but also totally exempt of any value judgment: anaclitic love could just as easily be that with the "mother" figure or with the "whore," which would not be any great doorway to the Other. Secondly, Freud later recognized that secondary narcissism (which allows narcissism to become narcissistic love, thus preserving the exteriority of the object) may play an essential role as a secondary defense against any death drive. Thirdly, because Freud occasionally found (notably in cases of female homosexuality) the inversion of narcissistic love into love by support, homosexuality becomes a form of privileged access to the idea of the Other (by way of identification with the father). Jacques Lacan emphasized this point: if it is gender differences that evoke the constituent separation between the imaginary and the symbolic, then these differences are themselves an effect of the symbolic. In other words, the symbolic place of the Other can be represented equally by either a masculine or feminine image. If popular psychoanalysis (or its American interpretation) appeared to fix the homosexual to the image of sameness, a more serious reading of Freud's psychoanalytic theory (for example, Lacanian) may free the homosexual, or at least re-situate him at the same level as the heterosexual with regard to his complex relationship to the Other.

Finally, very little will be said concerning **anthropological** arguments that reduce homosexuality to a form of "altruicide," as the extravagance of such arguments is blatantly apparent. For over a century, empirical ethnography has continuously collected reports of homosexuality in various cultures, from the most open societies to the most closed, but it is difficult to see how one could deduce the slightest anthropological constant that would link the sameness of the sexual relationship to the exclusion of the Other. As for structural anthropology—based on Claude Lévi-Strauss's idea that people think about the world in terms of binary opposites—this concept of homosexuality does not appear to infringe on Lévi-Strauss's fundamental principle: that the foundation of all culture or civilization does not rest on that which it forbids, but on the fact that it forbids, and on the structure of that forbiddance.

In any case, one can see that there is no serious argument substantiating the reduction of homosexuality to the sphere of sameness. If such a reduction remains in vogue, it would be due to the pure and simple effect of its signifier, produced by the term homosexuality itself, which translates literally as "sexuality of the same." Important in this regard is the circularity of the signified or the referent, to which almost all homophobic

arguments of this kind resort: theology could then claim to represent **psychoanalysis**, psychoanalysis to represent anthropology, anthropology to represent philosophy (it is notably easier to understand the specific homophobia of certain followers of Lévi-Strauss by the allegiance of their teacher to Jean Jacques Rousseau, than by its anthropology proper), and finally, philosophy itself relying on the professions of faith by Savoyard curates. Expressed otherwise, the signified no longer really matters; what matters henceforth is only the signifier, the "as-its-name-states."

However, perhaps the word "henceforth" is too strong, since from the beginning, homosexuals did not fit into that compartment of nosology to which they are assigned, their supposed "love of the same" reduced to nothing more than an effect of a signifier. An example to this effect is the fact that Richard von Krafft-Ebing, the German psychiatrist and quasi-inventor of the nosological term of homosexuality as an example of sexual deviance, constantly referred to the concept of "true homosexuality" in order to contrast it with the overly vague notion of "psychosexual hermaphroditism." Thus, otherness is derived from the concept and not from the factual; and the denial of the Other by the homosexual is not a theory, but rather a simple analytical proposition.

From this perspective, it is best to be wary of the pseudo-scientific term of "homosexual," which is the true crux of all modern homophobic ideas that originate from otherness; as well, we must be equally wary of the concept of homophobia itself that is derived from it. Its proponents may think it is an idea of great strategic value but, when heard literally, always risks legitimizing the very foundation of what it claims to denounce.

—Pierre Zaoui

Freud, Sigmund. "Contributions à la psychologie de la vie amoureuse" and "Pour introduire le narcissisme." In *La Vie sexuelle*. Paris: Presses universitaires de France, 1969.
———. "Le Clivage du moi dans le processus de defense." In *Résultats, idées, problèmes* II. Paris: Presses universitaires de France, 1985.
———. "Sur la psychogenese d'un cas d'homosexualité feminine." In *Névrose, psychose et perversion*. Paris: Presses universitaires de France, 1973.
Krafft-Ebing, Richard von. *Psychopathia sexualis*. Paris: Payot, 1950. [Published in English as *Psychopathia Sexualis*.]
Lacan, Jacques. "La Relation d'objet." In *Séminaire* IV. Paris:

Le Seuil, 1994.

Mendès-Leite, Rommel. *Le Sens de l'altérité. Penser les (homo)sexualités masculines.* Paris: L'Harmattan, 2000.

Sartre, Jean-Paul. *Saint Genet, comédien et martyr.* Paris: Gallimard, 1952.

—*Gender Differences; Philosophy; Psychoanalysis; Universalism/Differentialism.*

OUTING

The term "outing" appeared in the United States at the beginning of the 1990s to describe the action led and conceived by New York journalist Michelangelo Signorile, who is considered by many to be the father of this practice. Neither the idea nor its application were really a first, but the application benefited then from an unprecedented impact, provoking an important media debate which, in a few months, crossed oceans to reach Australia as well as Europe (including Germany, France, Great Britain, and the Netherlands).

Defining the principle or the practice of outing is not easy, as the conferred meaning can vary widely. According to those who currently use the practice, outing consists of revealing the homosexuality of a public figure who is trying to hide it and, by this, validating the stigma associated with it, while stressing the silence imposed on gays. Certain advocates have preached it or exercised it based on a more precise definition, concerning personalities who not only choose to "remain in the **closet**" but also encourage homophobia by their stated positions or affiliations. In both cases, the partisans of outing think that this is the way to fight homophobia: by fighting the silence and invisibility which play into the hand of oppression, or by making public the contradiction of those who, by their positions, promote the **discrimination** of gays and lesbians. However, there have been numerous opponents who consider outing to be a practice that attacks personal freedom and is thus homophobic. Because homosexuality in our society is stigmatized and the object of discrimination, to reveal the homosexuality of those who wish to remain silent submits them to discrimination. And this ambiguity is the basis for divisions on this subject, which oppose partisans and enemies of outing.

However, this ambiguity is partly removed if one takes into account contexts and intentions that lead to the revelation of the homosexuality of a third party. For many decades, the repression of gays in Western countries has fed on multiple forms of denunciation, including information that made **deportation** of gays possible in Germany and elsewhere, persecutions by McCarthyism in the US, and blackmailing practices which lasted throughout the century in many different countries. In all cases, the informant acted according to a homophobic logic that aims to bring prejudice to the targets. Reciprocally, the advocates of outing are gays who consider that they are acting in the cause of gay liberation. This is why, first at the level of intentions, it is important to distinguish whistle-blowing practices with discriminatory objectives from outing as conceptualized at the end of the 1980s in certain Western countries. One must then take into account the context in which the public revelation is made and the consequences that can result for the persons concerned. In certain cases, the risk taken is of a penal nature, in others, of social nature: denunciation practices are generally made in the first context, and outing in the second.

The practice, which consists of revealing the homosexuality of public figures in order to advance the gay cause found one of its first tenants in Germany at the beginning of the twentieth century in the person of Adolf Brand, founder of what is considered the first gay magazine, *Der Eigene* on different occasions, he revealed the homosexuality of those involved in the implementation of homophobic policies. That said, the context of the era was marked by numerous **scandals**, affairs, and legal actions, which were widely echoed in the press, forcing individuals out of the closet under constraint of imposing legal risks. If it is possible to see there, with certain authors, the ancestor of outing as it will be defined later, one must also take into account the fundamental difference in context.

In its contemporary form, the practice of outing requires the existence of a group who applies and demands the principle of visibility for gays. However, it was not present during the first period of the history of the gay liberation movement. Its rhetorical formulation is surely advanced in an article by the American author Taylor Branch, published in 1982, but it is only at the end of the 80s that it appeared in the US, in the context of **AIDS**. Unquestionably, it is a situation of double jeopardy where gays and lesbians were simultaneously confronted by the epidemic and homophobia, which made the spirit of outing possible. The first to implement it were militants in the fight against AIDS: Larry Kramer in New York; Wayne Harris and Tom Schoedler of ACT UP-Portland regarding Senator Mark Hatfield; Michael Petrelis, who revealed the homosexuality of tens of members of Congress, among them Steven Gunderson; and, naturally, Signorile, who was at the origin of the media storm that outing provoked at the beginning of the 90s.

Born in Brooklyn in 1960, Signorile joined ACT UP-New York at the end of 1987 and quickly integrated its media committee, where he learned activism and familiarized himself with **media** logic. In 1989, after quitting the group, he was invited by Gabriel Rotello (another ex-ACT UP member) to join a new gay magazine, *OutWeek,* where he took charge of a section on the treatment of gays in the media and, particularly, in the entertainment press. Signorile was the first to out someone without having yet conceptualized the practice when he revealed the homosexuality of right-wing millionaire Malcom Forbes after his death in March 1990. *Time* magazine condemned the process, qualifying it as "outing," thus inventing the term which militant gays would adopt. Certain media saw it as a method worthy of **McCarthy**, but these criticisms were nothing compared to those yet to come. In the spring of 1991, Signorile was again attacked (particularly by the *Village Voice*) when an OutPost poster campaign appeared on New York walls. The posters showed photographs of Hollywood stars, accompanied by the caption: "ABSOLUTELY QUEER." In August 1991, Signorile published in *The Advocate* (*OutWeek* had disappeared) an article that put fire to the powder keg: he revealed the homosexuality of Pete Williams, who was Pentagon spokesman at a time when gays were victims of a veritable witch hunt in the American **army**. While many agree with the unacceptable character of Williams' position, the practice of outing again provoked true hostility, including in certain gay groups such as the International Lesbian and Gay Association, which officially condemned it. As for the media, there was an angry outcry. If many journalists attacked Signorile with such virulence, it was because some of them were the privileged target of his attacks: those who, according to him, kept the homosexuality of public figures quiet in order to better hide their own.

In France as well, reactions were very quick: articles on outing appeared in both the gay and general press. In less than eighteen months, *Gai-Pied* published

three articles on the phenomenon (on November 8, 1990; September 19, 1991; and March 6, 1992). The positions expressed were generally hostile, in spite of Didier Lestrade's articles that attempted to make this practice comprehensible and acceptable for the French readers. The only **association** to be favorable to the practice was ACT UP-Paris: it officially adopted the principle of outing on March 19, 1991, after three weeks of heavy debate. The definition which it gives of outing is the following: "Outing consists of making public the homosexuality, the sero-prevalence or the illness of a figure in the arts, the media or in political circles. Outing also consists of revealing the real causes of death of a public figure who preferred to keep his or her AIDS secret." The association justified this choice with the argument that homophobia "was right down AIDS' alley," and one can only fight homophobia through visibility (voluntary or forced). In this way, to essential gay visibility, ACT UP-Paris added the visibility of seropositives and the ill, with the main reference to the case of American politician Tom Duane who, under pressure from activists, chose to personally reveal that he was HIV positive. But on this theme, resistance was redoubling (including in the US, where the outing of seropositivity was very rarely preached and never practiced), the respect of medical confidentiality having always been one of the main demands of militants in the fight against AIDS.

It must be noted that, according to the definition it gave, ACT UP-Paris chose not to limit the practice to gays who encouraged homophobia. Nevertheless, the only outing that it attempted (but did not complete) is the case of a gay man who had taken positions that were, at the very least, homophobic (the association voted twice before for the outing of public figures, which it would not act on). This is the case of a Union pour la démocratie française (UDF; Union for French Democracy) member of parliament, reproached for having taken part in an **anti-PaCS** demonstration organized by Christine **Boutin** on January 31, 1999. A few days later, the association wrote to him and demanded that he "publicly announce his homosexuality and condemn homophobia." When the MP refused, the association informed the media of its doings and promised to reveal the name of the person later. The media were more often unfavorable to outing, talking of "blackmailing" and of "informants" without being embarrassed by the contradiction of invoking "privacy" while breaking this principle on many other occasions, including on the topic of a celebrity's homosexuality. Even in the gay press, the contradiction is sometimes blatant. So, to give only one example, a journalist wrote in his regular column in gay magazine *Ex aequo*: "Evidently we all are against outing, we also think that it is a serious interference in individual freedom," (no. 14, January 1998); one year later, on the topic of the producer of a film judged to be despicable, the same journalist wrote, "I could not help but think of the producer's homosexuality. As, according to converging rumors, [he] would be gay" (no. 26, March 1999).

The ambivalence of journalists who, on one hand, condemn (sometimes violently) outing and, on the other, do not hesitate to describe the intimate activities of heterosexual public figures, from artists to state leaders (whose wives have to face the media in France and the US), reveals, in the end, the inequality of media or social treatment reserved for homosexuality, which precisely motivates the practice of outing initiated by Signorile: it is in opposition to the silence of homosexuality in the entertainment press that he decided to reveal the homosexuality of public figures. The argument that justifies this silence and is put forward by those opposed to outing is that of "respect of privacy." Because it is part of the private sphere, homosexuality should not be evoked publicly by others than those concerned; outing would then infringe on an individual's freedom and a basic rights.

However, without refuting the principle itself of a right to "privacy," one is forced to observe that homosexuality does not belong solely in this domain, particularly and mainly due to the social construction from which it results and, more precisely, due to the homophobic logic that submits gays (or at least part of them) to discrimination and regulates them to an inferior social category. For some, the argument of "respect of privacy" opposed to outing, because it is applied to gays only (who would contest that the President or Prime Minister's heterosexuality be made public?), translates and maintains the unequal and demeaning treatment reserved for them. And it is with the only intention of reestablishing an equality of treatment that journalist Gabriel Rotello, for example, defends outing, which he has unsuccessfully tried to rename "equalizing."

So, must any journalist evoking the homosexuality of a public figure be considered to be practicing outing, independently of the way he delivers information? A recent media event suggests that we should answer this question in the affirmative. The publicity

surrounding the proffered threat by ACT UP-Paris in 1999 offers a new visibility to the method of outing in France and seems to have inspired a representative of Rassemblement pour la République (Rally for the Republic, a right-wing political party), Jean-Luc Romero, who claims to be the victim of it and decided to alert the media to protest against the mention of his homosexuality in a gay magazine. As a matter of fact, in an article published in October 2000 on the next municipal elections in Paris, a journalist mentioned the decision of Philippe Séguin to choose a candidate who had a chance of winning the gay vote for the right-wing list presented in the Marais (the gay area of Paris). He added: "This is the common point of all those whose names are circulated. Roselyne Bachelot, appreciated by gays, or Romero, gay himself." The ramifications of this incident in the media were out of proportion with the intention of the journalist. Romero recounted the incident one year later when he wrote a book on what he described as the "first outing of a French politician," in which the information that was judged objective and neutral by the journalist took on a negative and vicious tone that made the journalist come across as homophobic. However, a few months later, Romero apparently made an outing similar to the one he complained of having been subjected to, in an interview published on August 1, 2002 in *Actions-Gay* (a free local gay paper, altogether similar to the one that Romero had accused). Asked about the fact that Renaud Donnedieu, a UDF member and then minister in the first Raffarin government (2002–04), had not been recalled to his job, Romero answered that it was all the same to him and, anyway, he preferred "people like Aillagon," who "assume," which apparently suggested that Donnedieu was a gay man himself. But this interpretation was later denied by Romero himself, his discourse containing, according to him, "manifestly no evidence" on Donnedieu's sexuality. In the end, according to Romero, there had not been any outing. These examples illustrate the ambivalence that characterizes the definition of outing (whether it is seen as a means of freedom or a weapon of oppression) and the different ways in which this ambivalence is manifested.

—*Christophe Broqua*

ACT UP-Paris. *Le Sida*. Paris: Ed. Dagorno, 1994.

Fassin, Eric. "Le *Outing* de l'homophobie est-il de bonne politique? Définition et denunciation." In *L'Homophobie*, *comment la définir, comment la combattre?* Edited by Daniel Borrillo and Pierre Lascoumes. Paris: Prochoix, 1999.

———. "'Out': la métaphore paradoxale." In *Homosexualités: expression/répression* Edited by Louis-Georges Tin. Paris: Stock, 2000.

Gross, Larry P. *Contested Closets: The Politics and Ethics of Outing.* Minneapolis: Univ. of Minneapolis Press, 1993.

Johansson, Warren, and William A. Percy. *Outing: Shattering the Conspiracy of Silence.* New York: Harrington Park Press, 1994.

Lestrade, Didier. *ACT UP: une histoire.* Paris: Ed. Denoël, 2000.

Mohr, Richard. *Gay Ideas: Outing and Other Controversies.* Boston: Beacon Press, 1992.

Murphy, Timothy F., ed. *Gay Ethics: Controversies in Outing, Civil Rights, and Sexual Science.* New York: Haworth Press, 1994.

Romero, Jean-Luc. *On m'a volé ma vérité: histoire du premier outing d'un homme politique français.* Paris: Le Seuil, 2001.

Signorile, Michelangelo. *Queer in America: Sex, the Media and the Closets of Power.* New York: Random House, 1993.

Tamagne, Florence. *Histoire de l'homosexualité en Europe, Berlin, Londres, Paris, 1919–1939.* Paris: Le Seuil, 2000. [Published in the US as *A History of Homosexuality in Europe: Berlin, London, Paris, 1919–1939.* New York: Algora, 2004.]

—*Associations; Closet, the; Discrimination; Media; Politics; Privacy; Scandal.*

P

PaCS. *See* Anti-PaCS

PARENTING

At a time when attitudes are evolving and homosexuality is increasingly perceived as just one sexuality among many, an indisputable discomfort still remains around the topic of same-sex parents. Denmark was the first country to acknowledge gay couples; in 1989, it approved its Registered Partnership Act that granted the same rights to gay couples as heterosexual ones, with the exception of **adoption**. Norway adopted similar legislation in 1993, followed by Sweden in 1995 and Iceland in 1996, but all of them also excluded adoption rights. (Iceland does, however, allow the adoption of a same-sex partner's existing children.) In 1995, the Constitutional Court of Hungary granted gay common-law spouses the same rights as heterosexual ones, but once more excluded the right to adopt. In 1999, France jumped on the bandwagon with the PaCS civil union legislation that acknowledged gay common-law marriage. The pattern was clear: while great progress was made by Western countries to recognize same-sex couples, legislation consistently refused to include their right to adopt children.

Things started to change, however. In 2002, the provincial parliament of Quebec, Canada unanimously approved a law granting gay couples the right to adopt. In Canada, adoption by same-sex couples is now legal in the provinces of British Columbia, Manitoba, Newfoundland and Labrador, Nova Scotia, and Saskatchewan, the Northwest Territories and Nunavut. It is illegal in New Brunswick and only stepchild adoption is legal in Alberta; the law is ambiguous in the Yukon. Across the national border, the US states of Vermont and New Jersey also legalized adoption by same-sex couples. In 2000, the Spanish region of Navarre passed legislation acknowledging the legal equality of common-law couples, whether gay or straight; such couples enjoyed the same rights and privileges as those who were married, including the right to adopt. Gay adoption was legalized throughout Spain in 2005 when same-sex marriage was legalized. In the Netherlands, same-sex couples have had access to civil marriage and could adopt since 2002. Sweden approved in 2002 an act allowing gays to adopt children. (Gay marriage is not yet legal in Sweden, although registered partnerships have been legal since 1995. The Swedish Church permitted the blessing of same-sex marriages in 2007, but a law has not yet been passed.) **England** followed suit in 2005, and Belgium in 2006.

Despite these advancements, however, a report by the International Gay and Lesbian Human Rights Commission in 2000 outlined the many difficulties encountered by gays and lesbians on the issue of parenting. These can range from custody problems after a divorce when one partner reveals that he or she is gay, to the systemic exclusion of gays and lesbians from reproductive techniques available, to the outright illegality of adoption by homosexuals. In France, progressive thinkers believe that one's sexuality has no bearing on their competency as a parent, but most political parties are united in refusing to contemplate legal changes that would grant children raised by same-sex parents the same protections as others, with the remarkable exception of the Green Party, which in 2001 adopted a motion recommending the "reform of family law, excluding all discriminations."

Words
If we speak of homophobia, we cannot overlook the historic homophobic attitudes relating to homosexuals and children. For many, gay parenting is the line

that should not be crossed, a horror that will ultimately lead to the entrenchment of the gay couple. There have been several types of arguments against the right of gays and lesbians to adopt:

1. The desire of homosexuals to have children is innately suspicious.

In the French debates over the controversial PaCS proposal, the following pronouncements were made: "[Homosexuals] only want children because it is fashionable; for them, children are consumption objects, and they want them in the same way we keep a cat or a dog" (Charles Melman); "They want children to satisfy their perverse and fetishist needs" (Jean-Pierre Winter); "Gay couples try to normalize their relationships through adoption" (Nazir Hamad). Another psychoanalyst, Daniel Sibony, wrote: "The principle of pleasure will crush the symbolic…. To have a good self-image—an open, liberal self without prejudice—must we create situations where kids are sacrificed? When adults get drunk on their image, children take the rap."

2. It is not in the child's best interest.

The welfare of children is a fundamental in French law (Civil Code, Article 287) and it is regularly set in opposition to homosexuality. According to many, the legal recognition of gay couples and their right to adopt would be to the detriment of the child; there are numerous legal scholars and psychoanalysts who still agree on this point. The child needs both a father and a mother, nothing more, nothing less. Some go so far as to predict a dire future for children raised by same-sex couples. On the subject of the "symbolic wound" of the child with gay parents, Jean-Pierre Winter writes: "We fear that it translates, from the first generation to the second, even the third generation, into an arrest of the transmission of life: by dementia, death or **sterility**." Nothing less. Dozens of long-term studies conducted with a certain historical perspective (because children studied are now adults, even parents themselves) show that children raised by gay and lesbian parents do not develop any more developmental troubles than children raised in more "traditional" families. That said, these studies, nevertheless done according to rigorous protocols and published in specialist, professional, and family magazines, are regularly denigrated. Every time a study reveals that the children of gay parents are healthy and happy, the study is dismissed as militant

and thus invalid. On the other hand, purely rhetorical texts, unfounded on any clinical experience and not based on any field study or samples, which affirm that children raised by same-sex parents are in danger, are not, for their part, ever suspected of militancy. Such being the case, to be in the majority, authors of these texts are nonetheless militants: militants of the established norm.

Certain psychoanalysts in France were concerned that the model proposed by PaCS would render Freud's theory of the universality of the Oedipus complex obsolete. Psychoanalyst Simone Korff-Sausse wrote: "With PaCS, the gay couple becomes a model. That said, this model makes the classic model of identity construction, that is Oedipus, obsolete. **Psychoanalysis** demonstrated that the Oedipus structure is a universal principle that set everyone's relation to the two **differences** that constitute identity, that is, the difference between the sexes and the difference between the generations." One can wonder here if the point is directed to the child's interest or the theory's. More generally, most arguments, when they acknowledge that parenting abilities may have nothing to do with one's sexuality, no longer refer to the "child's best interest," which—they finally admit—is not threatened; rather, it is all of society that is. Approving gay parenting would put society at **peril** and undermine its foundations.

3. It is not in society's best interest.

A recurring theme raised by those opposed to gay parenting equates homosexuality with the negation of the difference of the sexes; a negation of **otherness**, even a denial of the other sex. These ideas regularly appear in the writing of Tony Anatrella, who claims: "In the first case (heterosexuality), society's interests are healthy, while they are nonexistent in the second (homosexuality)…. Society cannot be anything other than heterosexual…. This is the only way that society can organize itself and survive throughout history." For Anatrella, heterosexuality is an adult sexuality and is synonymous with the "difference between the sexes." He denies gays, reduced to their sexual behavior, access to this difference.

With this accusation of denying the difference between the sexes, one can see the rise of another fear, that of a world where sexual reproduction is no longer essential. The impossibility of thinking about the disjunction between procreation, sexuality, and lineage leads to the projection of fearful representations on gay parents. Gay parenting is thus perceived as a first step toward a world definitely split between the masculine and the feminine, with no possibility of the two ever meeting. Fears expressed by anthropologist Françoise Héritier on reproductive cloning seem to echo the same sentiment: "Appeal to the other sex wouldn't be essential anymore to reproduce, which would lead to the loss of the social link of man and woman via sexual encounter…. It is to prevent this drift that governments have forbidden reproductive cloning." Talking about PaCS, Korff-Sausse wrote: "Why risk otherness when one can revel in the comfort of the same?" Here, gay parenting and cloning are introduced with the same fright: "The family institution defines, on the social plane, this organizing principle by regulating the working between the two couples of fundamental opposition: man-woman, child-adult. The new model, that is, of PaCS as well as cloning, advocates the union of two fellow creatures or the creation of same by same, and abandons the necessity of the association of two who are dissimilar…. PaCS and cloning obey the same principles." As well in these discourses, the concept of parenting is interchangeable with fertility, and homosexuality is equated with sterility; thus, the reasoning goes: "Nature does not allow a gay couple to reproduce, so they cannot be parents."

The interest of the entire society, through its social order—its **symbolic order**—seems threatened by a non-traditional concept of family, i.e. the possibility that a child could have two fathers or two mothers. It seems difficult for some to think of parentage as separate from conception; to think of it based on commitment and responsibility and no longer on biological plausibility. The terms of father and mother are always represented as players in reproduction, even in adoption scenarios. Those who do, like sociologist Irène Théry, observe that only biological signifiers can identify a man as father and a woman as mother, dismissing the possibility of gay legal or social parentage. Psychoanalyst Corinne Daubigny fears that the adoption of a child by a gay couple would trigger the anger of the child's original parents for having given him or her up in the first place, which Daubigny blames on laws which allow gay adoption.

The Deeds
Beyond rhetoric, there were also deeds that were issued forth which served to discriminate against gays and lesbians who either are already parents or wish to become so. We can find evidence of this in three types of decisions.

First, decisions linked to the exercise of parental authority. The 1993 French law on parental authority sets out a joint exercise of parental authority in case of separation. Such being the case, when one of the parents is gay, at best the judge will hesitate to assign the child's principal residence to the gay parent; at worst, the judge will decree that visits between the child and the gay parent occur in the presence of a third party. Certain rulings on visitation rights are accompanied by restrictive conditions, such as prohibiting the child from being in the presence of the partner. On this subject, it is interesting to note a paradox: a gay father without a partner may be at risk of being seen as unstable, leading a nightlife that is incompatible with family life; at the same time, a gay father with a live-in partner for a number of years, which should be seen as more reassuring, is also perceived negatively.

Then there are decisions linked to the agreement to adopt. France's law on adoption, in place since 1966, allows married couples or any person who is at least twenty-eight years old to seek an agreement in order to adopt a child. The General Council must make inquiries to insure that the candidate satisfies conditions from a psychological, emotional, and educational point of view. The law does not specify that the candidate, if not married, must live alone or what his or her sexual preferences must be. The Council of State attempts to limit decisions made by the General Council that it finds arbitrary; for example, it has been known to intervene and reject applications based solely on the person's unmarried status. But this has a different meaning, given that sexual orientation is not mentioned, when the applicant is openly gay. "Lifestyle choice" and the absence of the other sex are calculatingly evoked in order to justify refusal, even if the candidate "possesses sure human and educational qualities" (Mangüé, State Council, October 9, 1996). As lawyer and philosopher Flora Leroy-Forgeot wrote, the refusal to give serious consideration to adoption applications by gays and lesbians is an essentially political act. Their competencies are never challenged, even though there is an implied parallel between homosexuality and an inability to parent. For authorities, the link between homosexuality and the denial of adoption rights is always done through categorization. Those who process adoption applications deny this, insisting that the applicant's homosexuality is not an issue, while at the same time basically evoking it as the motive for refusal, going so far as to specify that "to concede that the legality of the refusal of agreements in the present case hearkens back to the implicit yet necessary condemnation of all adoption requests from gay persons to failure" (Mangüé, State Council, October 9, 1996). This situation creates a real vicious circle. Gays and lesbians know that if they want to have a family by adopting, they will have to conceal their orientation. Social services know it, and suspect that any applicant who is not married may be homosexual; and certain French politicians, like Renaud Muselier, want to prohibit adoption by applicants who live with a person of the same sex. (Such legislation, if it is adopted, would automatically lead to violations of **privacy**.) Forced to say "I" when they are really "we," gays and lesbians who wish to adopt a child as a couple cannot count on the help of social workers and other authorities. Belgium has a very different point of view, however. Psychologists who investigate requests by lesbian couples for artificial insemination take into account the couple's stability, and the way each partner handles her homosexuality in relation to society and her own family, as favorable criteria for parenting.

Finally, there are decisions related to adoption of a partner's child, or so-called stepchild adoption. In the past, such adoptions were only possible for married heterosexual couples, but these requirements are being filtered out as more and more countries grant full adoption rights to homosexuals. In France, adoption law nevertheless allows a person who raised a child to adopt him or her if the birth parents consent to it and if the child, if older than thirteen, equally consents. In this situation, the adoptive parent is added to the original parentage, but parental authority is transferred solely to the adoptive parents. Such an adoption, designated elsewhere by the phrase "adoption by the second parent," may constitute a solution that would entrench the relationship between a child and his or her legal parent's partner. One could think that such a device, when all stakeholders consent, does not present particular difficulties. In reality, however, its success depends in large part on the personal (and possibly homophobic) convictions of the judge overseeing the case. In 2000, a woman requested to adopt her partner's child, whom they had raised together since birth; the child, of full age, wished for this adoption as did his mother. There was no other parent who could oppose

it. But the judge ruled against this child having two mothers (High Court, Colmar, June 28, 2000) based on the rationale that adoption would be diverted from its purpose. On appeal (Administrative Court, Colmar, February 16, 2001) the ruling was reaffirmed on the rationale that "in the actual state of French society, the family model of reference is the couple constituted by a man and a woman." **Jurisprudence** reveals that the personal opinion of judges, whether homophobic or not, is part of the issue.

Notwithstanding, PaCS has paved the way for a remarkable evolution in France. The same-sex couple acquired "freedom of the city" status in Paris (akin to the key to the city). The traditional family model has integrated the reality of gay families more and more. One political party, the Greens, has endorsed propositions of the Association des parents gays et lesbiens (APGL), particularly adoption by common-law couples (whether gay or straight), and status for social parents. In response, we are seeing a stiffening of General Counsels for whom sexual orientation becomes a sufficient reason to refuse applications to adopt.

In February 2002, in the legal case of *Fretté v. France* (whereby a gay man, Philippe Fretté, sued the government of France after his adoption application was turned down when he revealed in an interview with a case psychologist that he was gay), the European Court of Human Rights refused to condemn France for violation of Sections 8 (right to personal and family privacy) and 14 (prohibition of discrimination) of the European Convention for the Protection of Human Rights. Even though the decision was close (four against three), it has been used as a cautionary note for those prospective gay adoptive parents who would disclose their homosexuality during investigations. On June 6, 2002, the same day that the Council of State was confirming its decision in the Fretté case, Sweden and the Canadian province of Quebec were integrating the rights of same-sex couples into their adoption laws.

New family law provisions are thus essential; more and more scholars and family professionals are convinced of the need to legally define notions of parenthood that go beyond the boundaries of biological reality. These reforms will have to allow for provisions based on the ethics of responsibility and not merely blood relationships. In order to take into account all potential forms of family—whether it be traditional, blended, gay parent, single parent, or foster—it will have to enlarge its definition of parent. In order to do

that, it will have to encompass three aspects of the parental structure: biological, with knowledge of a child's origins; legal, which gives a child a genealogical inscription distinct from the biological; and social, which allows a child to maintain ties with the people who raised him or her. Making equal space for these three aspects would be in the best interests of all children.
—*Martine Gross*

Anatrella, Tony. "A propos d'une folie," *Le Monde* (June 26, 1999).

Association des parents gays et lesbiens. *Petit Guide bibliographique à l'usage des familles homoparentales et des autres.* Paris: APGL, 1997.

Borrillo, Daniel, Eric Fassin, and Marcela Iacub. *Au delà du PaCS.* Paris: Presses universitaires de France, 1999.

Daubigny, Corinne. "Le Couple homosexuel et la tentation de l'adoption," *La Croix* (June 13, 2001).

Coursaud, Jean-Baptiste. *L'Homosexualité entre préjugés et réalités.* Toulouse: Les Essentiels Milan, 2002.

Gross, Martine, ed. *Homoparentalités, etat des lieux.* Paris: ESF Editeur, 2000.

Héritier, Françoise. "Privilège de la féminité et domination masculine," *Esprit* (March–April 2001).

Korff-Sausse, Simone. "PaCS et Clones, la logique du même," *Libération* (July 7, 1999).

Leroy-Forgeot, Flora. *Les Enfants du PACS, réalités de l'homoparentalité.* Paris: L'Atelier de l'Archer, 1999.

Minot, Leslie. "Conceiving Parenthood: Parenting and the Rights of Lesbian, Gay, Bisexual and Transgender People and Their Children." A report of the International Gay and Lesbian Rights Commission (2000).

Nadaud, Stéphane. *L'Homoparentalité, une chance pour la famille?* Paris: Fayard, 2002.

Patterson, Charlotte. "Children of Lesbian and Gay Parents: Summary of Research Findings," *Lesbian and Gay Parents: A Resource for Psychologists.* American Psychological Association (1995).

Rihal, Hervé. "L'Intérêt de l'enfant et la jurisprudence du Conseil d'Etat concernant les agréments en matière d'adoption," *RD sanit. Soc* 33, no.3 (1997).

Sibony, Daniel. "PaCS: cette homo-famille qui gene," *Libération* (October 30, 1998).

Théry, Irène. "Différence des sexes et différence des generations," *Esprit* (December 1996).

Winter, Jean-Pierre. "Gare aux enfants symboliquement modifies," *Le Monde des débats* (March 2000).

—*Adoption; Anti-PaCS; Discrimination; European Law; Family; Heterosexism; Jurisprudence; Marriage; Pedophilia; Sterility; Symbolic Order.*

PASOLINI, Pier Paolo

Pier Paolo Pasolini (1922–1975), Italian director, screenwriter, essayist, poet, critic, and novelist, was without a doubt the first intellectual in his country to consciously make his way into the mass communication world of postmodern culture. He was one of the rare artists of his time who was able to pursue his craft without having to abandon his integrity, ideological radicalism, or authority. Regardless of what can be thought of his political positions, it must be said that, well before any of his peers, and without any cynicism, Pasolini knew how to take advantage of particular popularity of newspapers and television—representing for the first time a "mass" public, to express his own truth; a truth that was in large part incompatible with that normally represented by the **media** of the time, or even today. But this same media demanded a price for Pasolini's transgressions, making him out to be a "case," a "phenomenon," and a "**scandal**," by trying to simplify in the extreme his subversive vocation and reduce it to a "difference" *a priori* pathological, to be cured or punished.

Pasolini's homosexual identity and the social condemnation that he provoked certainly played a major part in his relationship with the public, which can be described as that between a man who was dedicated to a critical and transgressive performance, and a public that was largely desirous of exorcising this transgression. From 1949, well before he became a celebrity, Pasolini decided to no longer hide his sexual orientation. More importantly, at a certain moment, this "perverse" desire became a decisive element of his art, a recurring and sometimes central theme (be it in the films *Orgia*, *Teorema*, or *Petrolio*), but also, and more subtly, an ideological crux that is present in all his work, aligning it to his biography and giving it meaning. For Pasolini, homosexuality was not a mark of difference in relation to others, but rather the sign of a radical opposition to others: "Pasolini always preferred **Otherness** to **Difference**," said Italian literary critic Carla Benedetti. Without limiting himself to simply demanding dignity and equal rights for gays and lesbians, and even, more often than not, by ignoring these aspects (considered useless or vain) gay consciousness was at work at the heart of his reasoning: it informed any views he expressed, and thus, for those with whom he spoke, it was a fundamental idea, impossible to put aside or bypass. For Pasolini, he knew it: "What they have always condemned was not so much the homosexuality as it was the writer for whom homosexuality could not be used as a method of pressure, of blackmail, to make him toe the line. In reality, the scandal stemmed not only from the fact that I did not silence my homosexuality, but also from the fact that I totally refused to be silenced."

It is most definitely the central character of the "perverse" desire in Pasolini's action that explains why homophobic features, both obvious and veiled, so often surfaced in the legal saga that accompanied him his entire life, and even after his death. With regard to the very violent and numerous assaults committed on him by hoodlums (so many in fact that, at one point, Pasolini no longer even bothered to report them), homophobia was expressed in a classically **fascist** manner, as attested by the violent attack that occurred in the Barberini movie theater in Rome during the premiere of his 1961 film, *Accatone*, accentuated by punches, screams of "bastard!", and the throwing of vegetables, specifically fennel (*finocchio*), upon which newspapers commented, "The message was perfectly clear." (The term *finocchio* is the Italian slang equivalent to "fag," and makes historical reference to the act of throwing fennel seeds at the feet of those condemned to the pyre in order to mask the smell of burning human flesh.)

In the legal arena, on the other hand, homophobia was the result of hidden standards. From 1949 to 1977, Pasolini was submitted to thirty-three legal procedures: he was accused mostly of pornography, obscenity, gross indecency, and affront to the state religion. But aside the numerous police reports, denunciations for presumed soliciting and **exhibitionism** during trials, the other accusations always contain a homophobic undercurrent that often emerged in the form of more or less explicit moral **censorship**. The San Felice Circeo episode of November 1961 is a classic example of the way homophobic fantasies seek to represent the artist's "imbalance": a young gas station attendant accused Pasolini of having attempted to rob him, wearing black hat and gloves, and brandishing a pistol loaded with golden bullets. "At a certain level of cultural underdevelopment, people tend to confuse the author with his characters," Pasolini commented. "He who describes a thief is a thief," he continued, in reference to the

novel *Ragazzi di vita*, published in 1955, which Pasolini had set in the world of small-time Roman delinquents. Incapable of proving armed robbery, the indictment focused its attention on the hypothesis of sexual assault: the prosecution ordered a psychiatric assessment, which described the accused Pasolini as "a sexual abnormality, a homophile in the most absolute meaning of the word … an abnormality so deep that he consciously accepts his abnormality all the while demonstrating himself to be incapable of being affected by it as such. A homosexual exhibitionist and voyeur … a subject whose instincts are fundamentally flawed and showing profound signs of insecurity."

In the story of Pasolini's persecution, two episodes most definitely stand out: the first and the last in the series. On October 22, 1949, Pasolini, who, at the time, was teaching **literature** at a college a few kilometers outside of Casarsa, in Friuli, was denounced by local *carabinieri* for corrupting minors and performing acts of obscenity in a public place. During the previous year, Pasolini was an active communist militant, serving as Secretary of the Santo-Giovanni-de-Casarsa section of the party; his political adversaries, especially the Christian Democrats, cried scandal. The leaders of the Friuli Partito Communista Italiano (PCI, Communist Party of Italy) decided to expel Pasolini from the party without even verifying if the accusation was founded. The academic officials of the college fired him, despite protests from the parents of Casarsa students who wanted him to continue teaching. His father, an ex-officer in the Italian army, reacted violently to his son's situation forcing him to flee to Rome with his mother. Ostracism came not only from the clerical and fascist right, but the conservative left as well: from that moment onward, public opinion would feel it was justified to "confuse the accusations of obscenity, or of contempt of the city gods, laid against the work, with those of corruption of minors attributed to the writer's life," said writer Franco Fortini.

If this first and very precocious homophobic episode is emblematic of Pasolini's life, the second tends to explain his assassination. On the night of November 1, 1975, on an esplanade in the region near the seaplane base of Ostia, Italy, Pasolini was assassinated by seventeen-year-old Pino Pelosi who, after having savagely beaten his victim, drove over the body several times with his car. After his arrest, Pelosi defended himself by saying that he had reacted to an assault by the Pasolini who, after having picked him up at Rome's central station, had insisted on being repaid through sex. Italian television, on the evening of November 2, described the assassination as a sordid crime, typical of the homosexual world. Most media reports failed to mention the many clues discovered at the crime scene, which implied the presence of other individuals and, possibly, an actual trap. (In fact, Pino Pelosi was condemned in 1976 for involuntary homicide with unknown accomplices; the following year, the Court of Appeal affirmed the sentence, but concluded that there was insufficient evidence to indict any accomplices.)

What remains to be touched upon, as it is an important fact, is the sadomasochistic aspect of Pasolini's relationship to the homophobia that surrounded him. According to Italian writer Alberto Moravia:

> Over time, to the diffused idea in every social **class** in Italy that it is, so to speak, lawful to kill homosexuals, has been added, in this precise case, the other terrible idea according to which Pasolini could not have ended his days in any other fashion: Pasolini had to die.…We were, most likely, not very far from the truth when we said that, over time, in Pelosi's subconscious, and that of his "accomplices," grew the obscure conviction that not only was it possible, but it was necessary to kill Pasolini.

Moravia's words hide the particular relation that, in the scene of this persecution, the victim and the assassin are inextricably linked one to the other, making the crime possible if not inevitable. A conformist, profoundly violent society, hungry for condemnations, could not help but fiercely and unrelentingly hound a victim who was not only nonconformist and rebellious, but destined to falter, and desirous of being symbolically punished: in short, Pasolini was an ideal victim.

Pasolini always enjoyed the vocation of the persecuted innocent—"There are no limits to the pleasure of being humiliated/especially when we feel we are innocent"—which often revealed itself through his taste for retort, despite the disapproval of others. Evoking his soccer years, he stated, "I only played well when we were elsewhere, before a hostile public." It is known that organized societies always look for their examples among those citizens who, for one reason or another, are considered to be "turbulent" and "different"; Pasolini, the epitome of difference, was driven by masochistic urges of expiation, themselves linked to a frustrated desire of omnipotence, to an original,

narcissistic wound—in short, to a feeling of metaphysical exclusion from the world that made up his psychic identity. The perfect "scapegoat," as he once defined himself, Pasolini was powerfully attracted, since childhood, to the idea of sacrifice: "In my daydreams, there appeared the explicit desire to imitate Jesus.… I saw myself suspended from the cross, nailed there, my loins barely covered by a light veil. On each side of me, there was a large crowd watching me. This public martyrdom finally transformed itself into a voluptuous image." Of scenes of martyrdom, we know, his works are full, from *Accattone* to *Ricotta*, by way of *Porcile* and *Il vangelo secondo Matteo* (*The Gospel According to Saint Matthew*). Pasolini's innate talent for critical self-exhibition found itself confronted by homophobic aggressiveness, resulting in a long psychodrama, a cruel performance, and a martyrdom that was both symbolic and real.

—*Gian-Luigi Simonetti*

Betti, Laura, ed. *Pasolini: cronaca giudiziaria, persecuzione, morte.* Milan: Garzanti, 1977.

Benedetti, Carla. *Pasolini contro Cahnno. Per una letteratura imputa.* Turin: Bollati Boring-hieri, 1998.

Casi, Stefano, ed. *Desiderio di Pasolini. Omosessualità, arte e impegno intellettuale.* Turin: Sonda, 1990.

Contint, Gianfranco. "Testimonianza per Pier Paolo Pasolini." In *Ultimi esercizi ed elzeviri (1968–1987).* Turin: Einaudi, 1988.

Fortini, Franco. "Poesia e corruzione." In *Attraverso Pasolini.* Turin: Einaudi, 1993.

Naldini, Nico, ed. *Lettere 1940–1954.* With a chronology of his life and works. Turin: Einaudi, 1986.

———, ed. *Lettere 1955–1975.* Turin: Einaudi, 1988.

Schwartz, Barth David. *Pasolini Requiem.* New York: Pantheon Books, 1992.

Siti, Walter. "Tracce scritte di un'opera vivente." In *Pier Paolo Pasolini, Romanzi e racconti.* Edited by Silvia de Laude and Walter Siti. Vol. 1. Milan: Mondadori, 1998.

—*Censorship; Cinema; Italy; Literature; Scandal; Violence.*

PAUL (of Tarsus)

Paul of Tarsus (c. 5–65 CE) was a Jew who persistently persecuted early Christians until his conversion to the new religion, after which he became one of its most fervent and rigid disciples. In the New Testament, his doctrine actions are predominantly described in the

Acts of the Apostles and in his own letters (or epistles) that he sent to the churches he founded.

Paul of Tarsus's writings are both mystical and moral, expressing interest in the figure of Christ and the relationship between the individual and God. A good deal of Christian **theology** is based upon his writings, in which he proposes an austere philosophy and severe judgment of humanity and its vices, including homosexuality. Homosexual acts are considered sinful as they represent a **perversion** of human existence and nature, created and willed by God; thus, Paul introduces the concept of "unnatural," a concept largely taken up afterward, and until now, by representatives of the various Christian churches in order to justify their violence against homosexuals and homophobic ideals.

According to Paul, relations between people of the same gender are especially condemnable because they represent a relic of an ancient pagan humanity, with laws foreign to those of Christ, and thus, impure. The condemnation of homosexual acts, thus established upon religious and moral principles, at the same time became a condemnation of those persons who practiced these acts; the distinction between them (acts/ person) was considered too subtle to be truly efficient and avoid abuses.

It is difficult anyway to understand how it is less homophobic to condemn homosexual acts rather than the individuals who practice them—hate the sin, love the sinner—and how this could constitute a sign of "compassion."

—*Thierry Revol*

Boyarin, Daniel. *A Radical Jew: Paul and the Politics of Identity.* Berkeley: Univ. of California Press, 1994.

Hubaut, Michel A. *Paul de Tarse.* Paris: Desclée, 1989.

McNeill, John. *L'Eglise et l'homosexuel, un plaidoyer.* Geneva: Labor & Fides, 1982. [Published in the UK as *The Church and the Homosexual.* 4th ed. Boston: Beacon Press, 1993.]

Nouveau Testament: traduction œcuménique de la Bible. Paris: Le Cerf/Les Bergers et les Mages, 1983.

Saitrey, Henri-Dominique. *Histoire de l'apôtre Paul, ou Faire chrétien le monde.* Paris: Le Cerf, 1991.

Thévenot, Xavier. *Homosexualités masculines et morale chrétienne.* Paris: Le Cerf, 1985.

—*Against Nature; Bible, the; Heresy; Judaism; Sodom and Gomorrah; Theology; Vice.*

PEDOPHILE. *See* Pedophilia

PEDOPHILIA

Pedophilia, whether homosexual or heterosexual, is a behavior that has only been recognized as much in Western society for a short time. In fact, as has been rightly noted by French historian Philippe Ariès, the notion of pedophilia is necessarily predicated on the notion of children (i.e. as different from adults), with rights of their own. On the other hand, since the early days of Antiquity, sexual relations between men, and to a lesser extent between women, have been the subject of debate in Western society. Now that it is agreed that children have rights and that they must be protected, the distinction between homosexuality and pedophilia has become more precise, even if the confusion that aims to assimilate homosexuals with "corruptors of youth" (to use a term from the nineteenth century) arises with regularity in homophobic rhetoric.

Greek antiquity, in particular Socratic-Platonic philosophy—to use terminology dear to Michel Foucault—"problematized" the relationship between the *éraste* and his *éromène.* The *éraste* is an adult who engages in sexual relations with his *éromène,* who is a *païs,* that is to say a boy around the age of puberty. This particular relationship is called pederasty (*païd-erastes*), a term which, in current usage, is often synonymous with male homosexuality. Pederasty during Antiquity was a completely codified relationship between free individuals, with no social stigma whatsoever, and which usually ended once the facial hair of the *éromène* started to grow.

If the relationship continued past this point, it was then considered a homosexual relationship between two adults, and thus the object of mockery, as can be interpreted in certain comedies written by Aristophanes; this, of course, is a curious paradox given that presently, in many respects, the situation is reversed. Moreover, homosexual prostitution that led to the loss of civic rights for the prostitute, or the use of violence to force a child to have sexual relations, were behaviors that were fully condemned in this society.

The arrival of Christianity saw the merging of homosexuality and homosexual pedophilia into the term "crime against nature," punishable by being burned at the stake. It is only progressively, with the emergence of the notion of childhood, that distinctions in the response to this crime begin to appear. The church was primarily concerned with the sexual practices of its faithful, and it is the church that made the first distinctions between the sexual practices of adults and those of children, particularly with regard to penitence. In the handbooks used by confessors, which are an unlimited source for understanding sexuality of the period, one can read that the recommended penitence for sins of the flesh were less severe for children than they were for adults.

While the French Revolution accorded rights to homosexuals by the nineteenth century, **medicine** and law very quickly took over the church's responsibility for the treatment of what became known as "**perversion**." Parallel to this, the idea of childhood developed, as well as the idea of alleviating the suffering of minors in general which became coupled with a new preoccupation: the protection of youth. The fact that very young children were put to work in workshops and did not receive a proper education was condemned by doctors and philanthropists, who also felt that promiscuity between children and adults was harmful. In France in the mid-nineteenth century, Ambroise Tardieu, a forensic physician and a professor of legal medicine, exposed the problem of abused children. At the same time in Germany, Richard von Krafft-Ebing, the Austro-German psychiatrist, wrote in his seminal work *Psychopathia sexualis* of his revulsion for pederastic adults and their corrupting influence:

> The innocent souls who are these abandoned children have been led astray, and whom fate has delivered into the hands of an active pederast, who seduces them and then leads them to horrible work in order to earn a living, either as kept boys or as male prostitutes working the streets, with or without a procurer.

These pederasts linked to criminal activity were not the only ones accused of corrupting minors, however. Homosexuals in general were denounced by doctors and others during this period, again in the name of protecting youth.

Today, the distinction between homosexuality and pedophilia is clearer, as much scientifically as it is legally. In most countries homosexuality is no longer considered a crime or an illness. The issue of limits with regard to age, however, remains unclear. If an adult has sexual relations with a prepubescent child, no one—whether doctor, judge, or homosexual—would contest the suggestion that the act was reprehensible and pathological. However, consensus is less obvious when a homosexual relationship occurs between an adult and an adolescent.

In many countries, the law is rather transparent: in France, for instance, it is considered that, past the age of fifteen, an adolescent is free to make his or her own sexual choice, be it homosexual or heterosexual. This disposition in French law dates back to 1982, when a subsection of the civil code established an age of consent between homosexual or heterosexual partners. However, in the eyes of the law, one is still a minor at the age of fifteen, and an adult can be condemned for corruption of a minor if the parent makes a complaint, a circumstance that can be aggravated if the adult holds a position of power over the youth (e.g., a teacher and pupil or a coach and athlete).

Psychologists and psychiatrists distinguish between pedophiles and homosexuals. The homosexuality of those who claim that it causes them to suffer is considered a problem requiring treatment; on the other hand, if a homosexual patient does not request help, no one can force him to seek treatment. Such is not the case for condemned pedophiles, whose treatment is often made mandatory by the judicial system, even if such treatment appears to be impossible in the eyes of psychiatrists. However, the idea that a person's homosexual orientation can be established as early as adolescence offends certain therapists who remain convinced that homosexuality cannot be set in stone at such a young age and consider such practice by adolescents to be pathological; even more so when the adolescent's partner is an adult, who is then considered to be a corrupting influence.

Clouding the issue even further is the fact that the relationship between homosexuality and pedophilia is promoted by those engaging in homophobic arguments, who also insinuate themselves into certain scientific research. Children raised by homosexual couples are the poster children of this phenomenon: they are the subject of a good many studies—proof that they are given particular attention by science, which sometimes attempts to delineate the risks of these children being sexually abused, particularly when their parents are two men, as if homosexuality naturally leads to pedophilia.

Obviously, in the context of the recent debates on gay marriage, this insinuation of the links between homosexuality and pedophilia has been made by those determined to oppose gay marriage at any cost. In her book *Le "Mariage" des homosexuels?* (Marriage between homosexuals?), conservative French politician Christine **Boutin** wrote: "Where will we draw the line, for an adopted child, between homosexuality and pedophilia?" On the same note, in March of 1999 a caricature appeared in the French newspaper *Présent* in which a male couple proposes to a young boy to receive him "with open sheets." In another example, as if it were necessary, a well-distributed leaflet by a French association called Avenir de la culture (Future of the Culture) began with the following terms: "It's a revolution. Do you want an old homosexual couple at the door of the school tomorrow, waiting for your children or grandchildren to come out?" Or this slogan from a demonstration in France against the PaCS (Pacte civil de solidarité; Civil solidarity pact) domestic union proposal: "The homosexuals of today are the pedophiles of tomorrow." In each of these examples, the intent was to extend the stigmatism of pedophilia to homosexuality itself.

Certainly, the phonetic proximity between pedophilia and pederasty (the latter being long synonymous with male homosexuality) facilitates this confusion; and by this fact, there are many who, in all innocence, confuse the two subjects as a result. However, specific declarations of this kind, especially when they are made by someone who is a member of parliament (and now a government minister) like Boutin, are obviously deliberate, and baldly homophobic.

—*Roger Teboul*

Ariès, Philippe. *L'Enfant et la vie familiale sous l'Ancien Régime.* Paris: Le Seuil, 1973.

Boutin, Christine. *Le "Mariage" des homosexuels? CICS, PIC, PACS et autres projets législatifs.* Paris: Critérion, 1998.

Buffière, Félix. *La Pédérastie dans la Grèce Antique.* Paris: Les Belles Lettres, 1980.

Foucault, Michel. *Histoire de la sexualité.* Vol 1: *La Volonté de savoir.* Paris: Gallimard, 1976; Vol. 2: *L'Usage des plaisirs.* Paris: Gallimard, 1984; and Vol. 3: *Le Souci de soi.* Paris: Gallimard, 1984. [Published in the US as *The History of Sexuality.* Vol. 1: *An Introduction.* New York: Vintage, 1990; *The History of Sexuality.* Vol. 2: *The Use of Pleasure.* New York: Vintage, 1990; and *The History of Sexuality.* Vol. 3: *Care of the Self.* New York: Pantheon Books, 1988.]

Gauthier-Hamon, Corinne, and Roger Teboul. *Entre père et fils: La prostitution homosexuelle des garçons.* Paris: Presses universitaires de France, "Le Fil rouge," 1988.

Krafft-Ebing, Richard von. *Psychopathia sexualis.* Paris: G. Carré, 1895. [Published in English as *Psychopathia Sexualis.*]

Laufer, Eglé. "La Cure d'Anne." In *Adolescence.* Vol. 7, no. 1. Paris: GREUPP, 1989.

Laufer, Moses. "Homosexualité à l'adolescence." In *Adolescence.* Vol. 7, no. 1. Paris: Editions GREUPP, 1989.

Lever, Maurice. *Les Bûchers de Sodome.* Paris: Fayard, 1985.

Nadaud, Stéphane. *Homoparentalité: Une nouvelle chance pour la famille?* Paris: Fayard, 2002.

Sergent, Bernard. *L'Homosexualité dans la mythologie grecque.* Paris: Payot, 1984. [Published in the US as *Homosexuality in Greek Myth.* Boston: Beacon Press, 1986.]

Tardieu, Ambroise. *Etude médico-légale sur les attentats aux mœurs.* Paris: J. B. Baillère & fils, 1858.

—*Abnormal; Debauchery; Family; Gayphobia; Perversions; Parenting; Rhetoric; School; Vice.*

PERIL

Homosexuals, according to the homophobic worldview, are paradoxically both inferior and dangerous. They are a danger to the **family**, the country and to humanity, and dangerous, as well as contagious, to children. The myth of the homosexual "peril" as a deadly, imminent, and generalized threat appears in the medieval interpretation of the biblical episode of **Sodom and Gomorrah**, and survives to this day, confirmed once again by the parliamentary debates that accompanied the vote on the French law **PaCS** (Pacte civil de solidarité; Civil solidarity pact). The supposed cause of "peril" today has turned from homosexuality *per se*—so far tolerated as long as of subordinate status—to the frightening prospect of legal and social equality of the sexes and of sexual orientations. As quoted by a Catholic group in 1998: "A society that places homosexuality and heterosexuality on the same footing is only working towards its own disappearance and could greatly compromise child education." The turn toward equality has not silenced this refrain, whose presence has even increased, whether explicitly or in the background, not only in the public mindset but also, notably, in the political discourses—pseudo psychoanalytical or anthropological—that have begun to appear in the press.

The peril discourse selects themes without appearing to maintain any coherence: when singular, it is to the collective what the discourse of sin is to the individual. In a rather contradictory measure, homosexuality is a practice that appears to be both **against nature** yet capable of transmitting itself. This **contagion** is always thought to be one way, i.e. from homosexuals to heterosexuals, and never the reverse. Though widespread, heterosexuality has never been perceived as being a contagious practice. Throughout history, the myth of sexual peril in all its forms has known many moments of crystallization: it has justified purges against sodomites, women of more unbridled sexuality, and more generally, against the many manifestations of erotic "deviance." In each particular case, we find a common schema, sometimes under the guise of religion, sometimes under a more secular form: the earthly punishment of scapegoats anticipates and prevents a divine punishment of all, which is indiscriminate and, therefore, more frightening. This philosophy originated in thirteenth-century discourse regarding sodomites and heretics, the two so often confused with each other. In a very different form, it was also resurrected in Nazi Germany: the **treatment** reserved for inverts was meant to prevent the collective **degeneracy** of the Aryan race. In the United States, under McCarthyism, the nebulous illusion of peril wore the veil of a generalized homosexual "conspiracy" (nowadays, one would speak rather of a gay "**lobby**").

"Sexual panics" often return during times of conflict (the moment when those in power need to find internal enemies in order to "discipline" the national population or to distract it from the real issues). Collective and visible, the existence of homosexuals would "contaminate" society as a whole through a general "softening" of morality, which would compromise the "good health" of civilization, notably by reducing the fierceness of soldiers in battle. Today, in the sense that threats of war on Western nations are distant, homosexuality appears more as a purely egotistical "behavior" which, being part of a "value-destroying" contemporary hedonism, seeks only the narcissistic satisfaction of its own immediate pleasure. It forgets the hard task of reproduction that is the responsibility of courageous heterosexuals, whose method of mating is intrinsically linked to the general interest.

In a barely more euphemized version, the call for equality of the sexes and of same-sex couples would also be guilty of wanting to "disestablish the **difference** between the sexes." This difference being understood as the fundamental difference that allows us to conceive of all other differences; it is the whole of the "**symbolic order**" that would be threatened with extinction, and with it language, the possibility of recognizing others, and finally society itself. Children in gay families would be deprived of all references to "**otherness**" and, being incapable of "accessing the symbolic," would risk falling into inhumanity, bringing future civilization with them.

Until now, the dominant strategy of the contemporary gay and lesbian movement has been to emphasize the ridiculousness of these homophobic fantasies, for example, the strangely simplistic character of an "otherness" systematically centered on the differences in genital organs. It has been suggested that if there is in fact a symbolic order (a condition permitting members of a society to understand each other and coordinate), such an order is neither unchanging nor eternal. As a contingent product of history and political struggles, it is susceptible to being changed by that history and by present or future struggles. It has been argued that the fear of a "psychological unstructuring" of children of gay families and—by extension, of all "future generations"—was based upon a naively heterocentric projection of adults who have been trained to believe in the "natural" character of the heterosexual family. This is the final bastion of the mystery of blood: to imagine that a young child, free of all socialization, can expect a father (strict and dominating) and a mother (kind and understanding), and that the sight of two same-sex parents will cause irreversible harm and atrocious psychological problems. Incapable of imagining any alternative social reality, homophobic thought projects its own imagination into the newborn's mind. In short, defenders of gay rights and intellectuals concerned with social justice have stated that the homophobic sentiment of disorder and the fear of the "homosexual threat" do not come from objective reality, but rather from a subjective lack of perceptual categories that allow one to conceive of the possibility of a different order.

An Internal Threat
However, homosexuals should not allow their understandable desire for legitimization to minimize the subversive charge that their demands and their collective existence bring to bear against the heterosexist social order. For too long a list of euphemisms would eventually render them as unintelligible as that homophobic

resistance to sexual equality. In order to avoid this risk, it is necessary to take the discourse of peril seriously and try to ascertain the real threat of mythical peril in a transfigured form. What exactly do sexual equality and sexual orientations "threaten with extinction"? What does legal recognition of same-sex couples put into "peril"? Not "civilization" itself, but heterosexist civilization; not the "symbolic order," but the homophobic symbolic order. Not only the dominant ideology, but also the entire structure of social relations that is legitimized by presenting the "socio-sexual" hierarchies and inequalities as natural. The threat, therefore, is a political one; the "peril" that homophobes perceive is real. It concerns the disappearance of their sexual, institutional, symbolic, and epistemological privileges.

Yet, the fear of homosexual demands cannot be reduced to an awareness of their capacity to question political privilege. Contrary to other forms of racism, notes Leo Bersani, "homophobia is entirely a reaction to an internal possibility." While "even the worst racist could never fear that blacks would have the seductive power to make someone black," the myth of peril finds its strength in the fantasmatic fear that gay and lesbian affirmation will lead to the "recruitment" of heterosexuals. Gay peril is also, therefore, an internal threat. At the beginning of the 1990s, the debate launched in the United States by President Clinton on allowing "openly homosexual" individuals to enter or remain in the **army** revealed a fear that this reform would engender a form of contagion. According to Bersani, this phobia of male homosexual contagion reveals repression not of a "homosexual" desire *per se*, but of the "overwhelming pleasure" of the feminine jouissance "as the male body has fantasmatically lived it," "as the seemingly suicidal ecstasy of taking his sex like a woman" and which the body anticipates in the fascinating perspective of its own recruiting. In this sense, the myth of homosexual peril transforms, in political terms, an internal tension into homosexual desire.

The political affirmations of contemporary gay and lesbian movements have troubled collective opinions and self-imaging by claiming to put a name and "identity" on age-old practices that were historically tolerated as long as they remained clandestine and secondary. In a rather classic paradox, this "negative freedom," which allowed one to be and do whatever one wished under the shelter of secret practices and love without a name, found itself threatened by "liberation," leading to phases of collective tension; a response, in the first instance, to the assertion of identity. Using the example of the army, Bersani notes that "the inherent homoeroticism of military life certainly risks being revealed to those would want to both deny it and continue to take advantage of it, if active homosexuals publicly proclaim their preference." More radically, it is the entirety of "homo-social" relations that homosexual affirmation threatens to "desublimate" by revealing the homosexual eroticism within these relations, often are tacitly exploited in everyday interactions (consider, for example, the sublimated sexual tension that in the "frank and virile camaraderie" of men).

Finally, just as spelling mistakes, if they are too numerous, threaten to drastically change spelling (unlike an error in counting, which, in itself, has no consequence for mathematical truth), homosexuality threatens, if it is too radically emancipated, to "deinstitutionalize" heterosexuality. That is to say, to rob it of its socially dominant status. The "peril," therefore, is not simply in the minds of homophobes, but in the reality of a political relation that is under construction. It does not concern "society," but rather a certain structure of oppression. If the "spontaneous" impression that there are "more and more" homosexuals corresponds to an optical illusion repeated from generation to generation, this illusion depends on a rather well-founded awareness of the risks such a "spontaneous generation" poses to heterosexual privileges. Thus, we could conclude by saying that after further examination of the social logic at work, there is no possible doubt: gays and lesbians are, in fact, dangerous.

—*Sébastien Chauvin*

Bersani, Leo. *Homos*. Paris: Odile Jacob, 1998. [Published in the US as *Homos*. Cambridge, MA: Harvard Univ. Press, 1995.]

Borrillo, Daniel. "Que sais-je?" *L'Homophobie*. Paris: Presses universitaires de France, 2001.

Bryant, Anita. *The Anita Bryant Story: The Survival of Our Nation's Families and the Threat of Militant Homosexuality*. Old Tappan, NJ: Revell, 1977.

Bull, Chris and John Gallagher. *Perfect Enemies: The Religious Right, the Gay Movement, and the Politics of the 1990s*. New York: Crown Publishers, 1996.

Fortin, Jacques. *Homosexualités: l'adieu aux normes*. Paris: Textuel, 2000.

Herman, Didi. *The Antigay Agenda*. Chicago: Univ. of Chicago Press, 1997.

Hirschman, Albert O. *Deux Siècles de rhétorique réactionnaire.* Paris: Fayard, 1991.

Hocquenghem, Guy. *Homosexual Desire.* New ed. Paris: Fayard, 2000. First published in 1972.

—Abnormal; Communitarianism; Contagion; Debauchery; Heterosexism; Otherness; Proselytism; Rhetoric; Sodom and Gomorrah; Sterility; Symbolic Order; Theology.

PERVERSIONS

"Sexual perversion" was the generic term used in psychiatry during the second half of the nineteenth century to describe all sexual practices and attractions that did not lead to reproduction. The work of German psychiatrist Richard von Krafft-Ebing to classify "perversions" is at the center of this definition. In his study *Psychopathia Sexualis*, he determined a typology of four different categories of sexual deviance, defined by flawed sexual desire (e.g., homosexuality, bestiality, fetishism), behavioral anomaly of the sexual instinct (e.g., sadism, masochism), diversion of other physical

Starting at the end of the nineteenth century, the theme of sexual perversion was frequently found in literature dealing with homosexuality.

functions to a sexual end (e.g., urophilia, scatophilia), or finally, the limiting of sexual behavior to practices perceived as "preliminary" (e.g., voyeurism, **exhibitionism**).

However, despite the enormous list of perversions identified by Krafft-Ebing, homosexuality served as the theoretical model upon which he constructed the base of his scientific theory, and which furthermore was most often associated with other perversions in his clinical descriptions (e.g., homosexuality and sadism, homosexuality and fetishism, etc.). In this manner, homosexuality is depicted as the "mother" of all perversions and, as such, it is not surprising that the terms "homosexual" and "pervert" became almost synonymous among homophobes.

Without reverting to the concept of perversion in analytical theory—which, after the works of Freud, have very little to do with the psychiatric concepts of the nineteenth century—"sexual perversions," as understood by Krafft-Ebing, were an important part of the vocabulary of contemporary sexology, but were also pornographic, thus reinforcing the enduring negative representations of homosexuality as "perverse."
—*Pierre-Olivier de Busscher*

Charcot, Jean-Martin, and Valentin Magnan. *Inversion du sens génital et autres perversions sexuelles* [1883]. Paris: Frénésie Editions, 1987.

Danet, Jean. "Discours juridique et perversions sexuelles (XIXe et XXe s.)." *Famille et politique.* Vol. 6. Center for Political Research, University of Nantes. Faculty of Law and Political Science, 1977.

Krafft-Ebing, Richard von. *Psychopathia Sexualis: Etude médico-légale à l'usage des médecins et des juristes.* Paris: Payot. 1950. [Published in English as *Psychopathia Sexualis.*]

Lanteri-Laura, Georges. *Lectures des perversions: histoire de leur appropriation médicale.* Paris: Masson, 1979.

—Biology; Degeneracy; Fascism; Endocrinology; Ex-Gay; Genetics; Himmler, Heinrich; Hirschfeld, Magnus; Inversion; Medicine; Medicine, Legal; Pedophilia; Psychiatry; Psychoanalysis; Treatment; Vice.

PETAIN, Philippe

There is no doubting the homophobia of Philippe Pétain (1856–1951), the French general who eventually became the Chief of State of Vichy France from 1940 to 1944 following the military defeat of France by Nazi Germany during World War II. His homophobia is not surprising for a man of his generation, given his origins and experiences: he had a rural Catholic childhood, and his family included extremely pious grandparents as well as two uncles who were clergymen. He studied at the "free" college in St-Omer, but overall he led a rather stern life, and maintained ties to the Church and the conservative right from his youth until his death. Moreover, Pétain was known for his numerous affairs (married late in life in 1920, he had many young girls and married women as lovers until the 1940s). Without a doubt, heterosexuality was for him self-evident, and he was often boorish in his homophobia. On one occasion in 1916, Pétain refused to have the writer Pierre Loti at his table because "that little pretentious and painted old man" had eye makeup and wore rouge. He even wrote to the French Minister of Marine that Loti, who was a naval attaché at the time, "would probably be more useful in Morocco with [Hubert] Lyautey," a French general who was Resident-General of Morocco at the time, a perfidious allusion to the latter's morals. Pétain's prejudices poisoned his relationship with Lyautey in 1925–26, when Pétain himself was sent to Morocco to put down a rebellion led by Abdel-Krim. During the Nazi occupation, his homophobic attitude came to light again when he and his wife nicknamed Abel Bonnard, one of the Ministers of Education in the Vichy regime, "*Gestapette*" (Gestapo-fag).

Pétain's homophobia, which probably was not that much different from millions of French of his generation, became very clearly political beginning in June 1940, when he signed an armistice with Nazi Germany giving them control over the north and west areas of the country, including Paris and the entire Atlantic coastline, but leaving the remaining two-fifths unoccupied, which became Vichy France. Homophobia was at the heart of Vichyist criticism of moral liberalism and hedonistic individualism stemming from the French Revolution, resulting in a lowered birthrate and moral **decadence**. The relative visibility of homosexuality during the 1920s and 30s was, according to the Vichy right, the very incarnation of the moral decay that had pervaded the French Third Republic (1870–1940); the fact that there were known homosexuals in the entourage of French Prime Minister (until 1940) Edouard Daladier, in particular his Chief of Staff Edouard Pfeiffer (apparently a sadomasochist),

was no doubt fuel for the fire. The mortal sin of the Third Republic was that the "spirit of enjoyment had won over the spirit of sacrifice"; Pétain clearly felt this way, telling writer Henri Bordeaux in July 1943 that he had been beaten by "every pleasure seeker and every advocate of the Third Republic." It appears that, as far as Pétain was concerned, homosexuality, in its search for a pleasure that is disconnected from the **family** as well as from society is a form of that abominable individualism, "which is exactly that from which we almost died." (In light of his stern pronouncements, it is rather amusing to note that Pétain's sexuality, as heterosexual as it was, was never focused on procreation: he had a multitude of affairs but never fathered any children.) Everyone in the marshal's entourage (Raphaël Alibert, Dr Ménétrel, the admirals) were united in their reactionary, conformist (steak-and-cigar, white-collar oafs), and strongly Catholic homophobia (which is very similar to the type of homophobia exhibited decades later by French politicians Philippe de Villiers, Charles Millon, and Christine **Boutin**). The concern for setting the right tone often prevented the explicit mention of homosexuality, but it was no less implicit in all the great texts of Vichyist ideology. In fact, it was a popular target in the majority of Vichy arguments on youth and **literature**: French writer René Gillouin, a friend and supporter of Pétain who, even before World War II, denounced the morals of **Gide**, Cocteau, and Parisian literary circles, saw in homosexuality the cause of the end of the Third Republic in 1940; according to him, the sinister influences of homosexuality caused the French to become "a people ravaged by alcoholism, rotted by eroticism, [and] eaten away by a falling birthrate." Writer René Benjamin, a pamphlet-waving admirer of Charles Maurras (head of the monarchist, counter-revolutionary movement Action Française), chose to combat "art that believes that the purest of the pure is to reveal that which the moral **police** still hides temporarily." Moreover, the Vichy regime's family- and pro-birth-oriented arguments were, in the cultural context of the time, implicitly homophobic: united in its conservative viewpoint, the Vichy exalted the "eternal feminine," the complementary nature of the sexes (in a perfectly misogynist way), and the patriarchal structures that were so dear to French philosopher Gustave Thibon.

Despite its homophobia, Vichy did not deport homosexuals from France; the only homosexuals to be deported were the Alsatians from Moselle, according to the instructions of the German penal code between 1940 and 1944. However, Vichy homophobia still had disastrous consequences for French homosexuals because in 1942, Pétain set the stage for the return of legal **discrimination**. In fact, the law of August 6, 1942, for the first time since 1791, specifically criminalized homosexual relations: it created a new article in the penal code, Article 334, which specified imprisonment of those who committed same-sex "acts that were shameless and **unnatural**" with a minor under the age of twenty-one years. The worst part, however, was the fact that the anti-gay article was maintained under President Charles de Gaulle after France was liberated after the war: the order of July 27, 1945 redefined it as Article 331, paragraph 2 of the penal code, which remained in effect until 1982. In more recent years in France, the very slow "de-Pétainization" of the country must be taken with a grain of salt: the Christian Democrats and the Communist Party, both of which emerged from World War II stronger, were just as homophobic as was Vichy; and in its views toward society, Gaulist thought is very similar to Pétainism (it is doubtlessly what motivated Pétain in July 1944 to state: "Fundamentally, we have the same ideas"). We must also remember that many Gaulists, Communists, and resistant Catholics contributed to the belief that Nazism was a homosexual movement and helped to hide the persecutions of the "pink triangles" during the war, thereby increasing the symbolic stigmatization of homosexuality. It is clear that, as far as gays and lesbians were concerned, 1944 did not bring about any real form of liberation.

—*Pierre Albertini*

Borrillo, Daniel, ed. *Homosexualités et droit*. Paris: Presses universitaires de France, 1998.

Griffiths, Richard. *Pétain et les Français, 1914-1951*. Paris: Calmann-Lévy, 1974. [Published in the UK as *Marshal Pétain*. London: Constable, 1970.]

Gury, Christian. *L'Honneur retrouvé d'un officier homosexuel en 1915, suivi de Grande guerre et homophilie*. Paris: Kimé, 2000.

Lottman, Herbert. *Pétain*. Paris: Le Seuil, 1984. [Published in the US as *Pétain, Hero or Traitor: The Untold Story*. New York: W. Morrow, 1985.]

Muel-Dreyfus, Francine. *Vichy et l'éternel féminin*. Paris: Le Seuil, 1996. [Published in the US as *Vichy and the Eternal Feminine: A Contribution to a Political Sociology of Gender*. Durham, NC: Duke Univ. Press, 2001.]

—*Armed Forces; Boutin, Christine; Decadence; Deportation; Discrimination; Far Right; Fascism; France; Police.*

PHILOSOPHY

At first glance, homosexuality, and by extension homophobia, seem to both be secondary problems for traditional Western philosophy. Because the problems of morality in general should be of no concern to the main body of philosophy, the few recorded remarks on the subject by well-known philosophers are considered extremely marginal in the majority of the great metaphysics of morality or the great philosophies of domestic life. Even the last works of Michel Foucault or the philosophies influenced by **psychoanalysis** (such as Sartre, Marcuse, and Deleuze) do not fundamentally depart from this rule of thumb: they are neither homophobic nor anti-homophobic. Perhaps philosophy's real problem (and doubtlessly its real shame) lies in its relationship with women and sexuality in general rather than its relationship with the more specific issue of homosexuality.

More to the point, it could be said that the term homosexuality covers a concept and a reality that were historically constituted at the end of the twentieth century, thus too recent for it to be an appropriate subject for philosophy, which is principally concerned with rediscovering eternity, permanence, or at least the continuity of certain problems throughout the centuries. Take, for example, the question of whether a culture such as **Ancient Greece**—where Western philosophy was born, and which at times praised the love between boys, but also condemned sodomy—is homophobic. In philosophy, such a question makes no sense, primarily because the concept of homophobia, and the homosexuality it presupposes, are not well analyzed. The relation to boys is one thing, the relation to sodomy is another, and one cannot confuse the two under the same concept. There are even things for which there are no concepts in philosophy. Thus, like the notion of racism, homophobia has difficulty attaining the full dignity of an established philosophical concept.

In any case, it would be necessary to acknowledge that the falsely trans-historical question of homosexuality (or sodomy, abuse, or love "**against nature**," depending on its various designations throughout history) is not a central question of philosophy, and thus it is not possible to speak of a homophobia that is specific to philosophy. And it would be difficult to highlight the homophobia of specific philosophers, taking into consideration the context of the specific era, without it tainting philosophy's overall image.

It is nonetheless difficult to leave it at this first analysis and to believe that philosophy, following the example of **literature** and unlike religion or **psychiatry**, is as estranged from homophobia as it claims to be. There are three facts which suggest otherwise. Firstly, from **Sappho** to Renaud Camus, there has long existed an overtly homophile literature, running alongside—and behind—a literature that was completely homophobic, from Aristophanes to Michel Houellebecq. At the same time, there has been no trace of a homophile philosophy (the marginal Diderot, Sade, and Deleuze perhaps being exceptions), whereas we find many condemnations, admittedly marginal but no less abundant and violent, of homosexuality in philosophy; and nowhere is it justified or praised, at least among the most well-known philosophers. Once again, neither Sartre nor Foucault could be said to be homophile philosophers based on their work, regardless of what their political engagement may have been toward the homosexual cause. This fact is in no way a criticism of them, but it is nonetheless a fact, and a curious one: if the question of homophobia/homophilia is extrinsic to philosophy, why then when it engages on the subject, is it always porous to hate and not to love?

Secondly, it is equally surprising that philosophy, which prides itself on posing questions on subjects that the general population takes for granted, had continuously refused to see any interest in homosexuality as a subject matter. It is for example customary, at least presently, to pay tribute to Aristotle for having conceived of slavery as a problem for philosophy and thus challenging its legitimacy. In the same manner, it is possible to identify Nietzsche as one of the first to voice the problem of the "Jewish question," and more specifically, in a tragically prophetic way, the question of the future of Jews in Europe. But who has done this for homosexuality? When homosexuality specifically becomes a problem for Plato in his *Laws*, he is less concerned with its nature or its consequences than with its eradication. Twenty-five centuries later, in a remarkable 1996 work entitled *Le Savoir grec* (published in English as *The Greek Pursuit of Knowledge*), edited by Jacques Brunschwig and Geoffrey E. R. Lloyd, such a question is just as absent, whereas the relationship between the *eromenes* (boys) and the *erastes* (adult men)

was for decades at the heart of the Athenian concept of learning. In other words, it is sometimes the philosophers themselves (or rather their translators or contemporary commentators) who, often under the cover of the non-conceptual character of homosexuality, use it as a simplistic and non-problematic concept.

Thirdly, and doubtlessly most important: philosophy returns periodically to the issue of homosexuality at key points in its history in order to redefine progressively harder and more repressive positions on the subject. It first occurs in the fourth century BCE with Plato's *Laws*, when the Athenian conceives of the different possible ways to rid society of the Spartan "plague" of sex between men. Then in the thirteenth century with Thomas Aquinas' most famous work *Summa Theologica*, in which the Dominican philosopher attempts to confirm, not simply from St Paul and St Augustine but at least as much as Aristotle, the existence of reason and nature, and that the "sin against nature" is "the greatest of all sins." And it occurs again in the eighteenth century, when Rousseau simultaneously synthesizes homophobias of the past under the figure of a homophobia of sentiment that serves as a bridge between the blessed moment of the Enlightenment and more modern reactions when, from Hegel to Levinas, philosophy will attempt to establish the figure of **otherness** and of the biological **differences** between the sexes, establishing at the same time the foundation of the contemporary homophobic *doxa*: that homosexuality is the fear of the Other.

It is thus quite remarkable that at each of the key points in time, philosophy, of its own accord, nonetheless anticipated the hardening of the political repression of "unnatural practices." Plato foresaw the crumbling of the Athenian and Aristocratic model of pedagogical love: henceforth, and for all Antiquity, philosophical morality would have to be a morality of the masses, "naturally" heterosexual. Moreover, Aquinas anticipated the violent means used during the Inquisition that would be invented (at least compared to a certain indifference during the High Middle Ages) in order to protect good Christians from sodomites. Finally, Rousseau foresaw (in truth, more so than Freud and all the social sciences, the fantastical **anthropologies** and homophobia of today) by elaborating upon his concept of civil equality over the "natural" inequality of sentiment and the domestic sphere.

At this second level of analysis, everything would seem to be strangely reversed: it is no longer the prevalent idea that homosexuality is foreign to philosophy; rather, philosophy appears to have had a role in the waves of homophobia that occurred periodically, in a similar way that religion has or, more recently, psychiatry. We should not content ourselves with such a simplistic reversal. First of all, in addition to the three instances mentioned earlier, there are at least two others in which philosophy has doubtlessly played a key role in the social acceptance of "unnatural sexualities": the Enlightenment, and the period of the 1970s (notably in France) and 80s (notably in the United States), because the very concepts of the philosophical arguments during these periods, in which certain forms of homophobia can be read (whether admitted or not), could have just as well been used in the battle for gay and lesbian liberation (with the exception of Rousseau). Thus, it is both because of and despite Plato that the figure of Socrates never appeared as a particularly homophobic figure. Similarly, Aquinas' argument is so tortuous that it almost appears to be a criticism of itself, and concludes with the violent and seemingly anti-philosophical harshness of a St **Paul** or even a St Augustine. Finally, it is not necessary to have to rely on Hegel's conceptions of the Other, or accept Levinas' criticism of the identification of homosexuality as the love of the same: whether consciousness or transcendence, the Other is, all the same, a little more (or a little less!) than a biological gender, and Levinas and Hegel learn at least to untangle themselves from this biological *unthought* as much as to rely on it.

In short, it is not possible to clearly answer the question of whether a specifically philosophical homophobia exists. But for all that, the worm is still in the fruit. There is no philosophical innocence with regard to this question. We thus have the right to ask ourselves what, in philosophy—specifically speaking, short of the metaphilosophical opinions of philosophers—*could* produce a homophobic conception of sexuality. We are within our rights to take philosophy for what it is or claims to be, that is to say not a simple vehicle among others in the history of ideas, judgments, and interdicts, but a veritable *cause* of or *foundation* for certain forms of homophobia. In other words, in trying to not be duped by the effects of rhetoric—since the more directly violent or explicit is not necessarily the most philosophically pertinent—what intrinsic part of philosophy, what specifically philosophical reason, could serve as the foundation for homophobia?

Very roughly and succinctly, it is possible to out-line four responses in relation to four great periods in Western philosophy: Greek, Christian Medieval, Enlightenment, and modern philosophy.

Greek Philosophy: Political Homophobia

We are familiar with the conception of Socrates as a boy chaser, a legend that is defended for both sympathetic and hostile reasons. It is the Socrates as conceived by Fourier and Proust, but even before that, though in an inverse perspective, the Socrates of Aristophanes and certain neo-Thomists. And yet, it is not quite the true philosophical Socrates, the one described by Plato. In the *Symposium* (Banquet), notably, Socrates appears as the very image of abstinence, resisting every "trap" set by the beautiful Alcibiades. And the words of Diotima, which he claims to relate, thus appear to be the perfect counterpoint to the apology of love between youths expressed by Phaedrus and Pausanias. For Plato's Socrates, there is an immediate dynamic of Eros that drives beautiful bodies towards beautiful souls, and beautiful souls to the "science of beauty," following which the sage naturally comes to "look at the beauty of the body as little else." With Socrates, we are thus well beyond a mere defense of Platonic love: neither homosexuality, nor even, at the other end of love, homophilia. It would go the same way in *Phaedrus*, though following other arguments: the overly satisfied lovers will leave their bodies "without wings" on the day of their death. In any case, with Plato, we can note that it is possibly less in the homosexual or homophile relationship that philosophy is introduced than in his "internal criticism" as it were: the philosopher is not the inaugural lover of youths; he is the one who renounces it.

It is not possible to see in this dialectic of love even the slightest foundation of the homophobia to come in Hellenic Greece; if, at that time, Plato claims to go beyond physical, and even moral love, there is at the same time no evidence of general condemnation, and, in the beginning, the love between male youths always succeeded more than the love of women (heterosexuality and Sapphism combined). However, the tone changes completely with *Laws*, even if Plato still defends the love of the same over the love of difference, and even if his specifically philosophical misogyny remains stronger than his newfound homophobia. This time, it is no less than to legally and religiously consecrate the "unanimous, public voice," i.e. the voices of free men and slaves, women and children, which asserts that in homosexual acts, "there is no sanctity, they are rather the object of hate for Divinity, and the most villainous thing among the most villainous things." Plato, calling upon slaves, women, and children to condemn male homosexuality! What on earth happened?

This argument from an aging Plato, having become more "feminist" and more pious, is absurd: on one hand, because his tastes have not changed; once again, he continues to affirm friendships between those who are similar over those who are different. On the other hand, because this argument is no more religious than those preceding it; quite the contrary, Plato claims to use religion to his own ends, dictated only by philosophy (at least as seen by modern sentiment, if not more blasphemous). What has changed is the new object of Plato's fancy: political legislation. He says it himself: if sexuality between men were a marginal practice, there would be no need to legislate. In other words, homosexuality is only condemnable when it goes against common interests of the state; and having become a common practice, it goes against its better interests by losing, by wasting the *seed* that is vital to its reproduction and development. Thus, in a certain way, we witness the invention of a homophobia that is neither religious, nor psychological, nor morally obedient, but specifically political or, more precisely, specific to political philosophy. What is at stake is the seed, that is to say the species and the politic of the species; in other words, the question of knowing just how far political philosophy must support the universality of common practices. At stake is the universality of the concept applied to politics, the specifically political idea that there can be no politic unless it belongs to all. Thus, Plato is not inconsistent; he has not "changed."

In this regard, even Aristotle's more specifically "moral" criticism appears much more inoffensive and much less specifically philosophical. His description is no less violent. Reflecting on the different causes of intemperance, he draws up a list in *Nichomachean Ethics*: "the habit of plucking out the hair or of gnawing the nails, or even coals or earth, not to mention homosexuality…." But one cannot stop at the effect of this list alone. On one hand, because by "homosexual," Aristotle means the *ubrizomenoi*, literally "those who were abused during childhood," commonly the sodomites. On this, he does not distinguish himself from the common opinion of Greeks who often condemned sodomy; he does not invent any specifically philosophical homophobia. On the other hand, because through

the violence of devalorization, a form of intemperance appears: the habit does not come from sodomites, as they have been "abused" as children and, as a result, "to have these various habits is beyond the limits of **vice**," and thus, conversely, succeeding in mastering them is not a question of temperance as such. More brutally speaking, the Aristotelian fantasy of the *learning* of homosexuality seems less directly homophobic than the Platonic fantasy of the possible political "unlearning" of sodomites.

What then allows Aristotle, not to dissolve (since he fundamentally continues to subscribe to an "artificialist," "against nature" conception of sodomy in regards to an alleged universality of desire), but to neutralize the violence of Plato's legislative utopia? Precisely the emphasis placed on the allegedly unnatural (*paraphusin*) character of sodomy: by being beyond nature, homosexuals are also beyond the limits of vice and virtue, and thus on the periphery of politics rather than at its heart. The argument of homosexuality as "against nature," thus "naturally" rare, reduces the risk (or the fantasy) of a (male) homosexuality that is so desirable that it would spread throughout society like wildfire. This does not totally exonerate Aristotle: at the price of reworking the universal idea (which no longer applies to everyone, but rather the greatest possible number), the specifically philosophical desire of the metaphysics of universal morality is maintained (or perhaps more accurately "the most universal as possible"), but this time rejecting the issue of particular sexualities in its shadows and examples in passing.

The desire of a morality that is as universal as possible would thus be maintained throughout all Hellenic philosophy, far from all empathic comprehension, but also far from all condemnation of "deviant" sexualities—to which Foucault would respond, "No, the Greeks were not so great"; that is to say, long after Aristotle, and in the name of the possibility of a common morality, the standard would become more problematic than exceptional, abandoning the *de facto* sodomites to the contingent violence of the common standard but protecting them all the same by the indifference granted to their specific sexuality.

Medieval Christian Philosophy: Homophobia "by Nature"

For lack of space, it is not possible to explore the twists and turns of a Christian philosophy weighed down by **theology** on one hand and strict politics on the other. To look at two great figures of medieval Christian philosophy, St Augustine and St Thomas Aquinas (if we arbitrarily accept that Augustine was a medieval philosopher), it seems, rather curiously, that everything gets overturned: it is no longer Platonism and its finicky universalism that will serve as the foundation for virulent homophobia, but Thomist Aristotelianism and its apparently more moderate conception of the universality of nature.

Certainly, when Augustine confronts the question of "impurity" (i.e. unnatural sexuality) head-on in *Confessions* (Book III), he is no miser with his condemnation: "The crimes **against nature** deserve everywhere and always detestation and punishment, as befalls Sodomites. When all peoples would commit them, they would fall, accusable in the same manner, under Divine law, which has not made men for such usage. In fact, it is to infringe upon the social order required by God and us, to dirty the natural institution, the work of God, by a perversion of **debauchery**." But we can note at least two things. On one hand, there is a change in relation to Plato. The detestation ceases entirely to be based on a specifically political argument: it is "in the same way" as individuals that entire peoples could be accused of sodomy. In other words, sodomy is no longer dangerous to social and natural order. Certainly, it remained so, but at the same level as many other crimes like those against custom or the assaults described immediately following in the text. On the other hand, what is at stake here for Augustine is to search for "a time and a place" where it is possible to love God and God alone. In other words, the first and primary crime of sodomy is to turn us away from that love. For this reason, it can only be taken as part of a much more general criticism of sensual pleasure and sexuality itself. In this respect, all that remains is to compare this condemnation of sodomy with Augustinian descriptions of the sexual pleasure experienced in the legal relationship of **marriage**, and more so with descriptions of a pregnant woman in a union—identified in the matter, that is to say, by a Platonist, at the outer reaches of nothingness—to convince oneself that his problem is not at all homophobia, but sexuality in general, all the way down to its acceptable Christian forms, as historian Peter Brown so perfectly demonstrates.

It would thus appear that it is Augustine's Platonism that, given his strict universalism, does not really dwell on the specific practices of each person in order to develop them all within the same repulsion, and which at the same time prevents a specific homophobia from

developing during the first centuries of the Middle Ages (as much as we can believe in the causality of ideas).

On the contrary, it is in the Aristotelianism of Thomas Aquinas that the sin against nature (e.g., masturbation, sodomy, love for the same sex, or aberrant sexuality) once again becomes a specific issue. He dedicates the two last articles of his *Quaestio* on temperance, and refers to it again as an example in other problems. All of Aquinas' issues, as a good Aristotelian, are in effect to classify the sins of intemperance and measure their various degrees of gravity. In this sense, it is no longer religion that is revealed but rather philosophy that will force Aquinas to classify sins against nature as the worst of the sins of intemperance, regardless of the arguments of authority (such as Augustine) that he invokes in his solutions to better support his thesis. It is a theory that is philosophical, not theological, to state: "The specific nature of the species is tightly bonded to each individual, bonds stronger than between individuals. Therefore, sins against the nature of the species are more grievous." Similarly: "The gravity of a sin depends more on the abuse of a thing than on the omission of the right use." More precisely, it is the re-using of a Christianized Aristotelianism that constitutes the politic on nature that is at play: to go against nature (i.e. as conceived as a work of God) is worse than going against God's direct Commandments. In other words, it is not the Revelation that forces philosophy to submit itself to its "homophobic" commandments; on the contrary, it is philosophy that forces the specifically Christian revelation to harden its homophobia—here, the relation of philosophy to theology no longer appears as ancillary, regardless of what Aquinas might say, for the argument, in the strictly philosophical sense, appears quite leaden: if temperance supports itself on natural needs, these being linked to the reproduction of the species (the "good desires," according to Aquinas), then sodomitical or homosexual desires (he makes a clear distinction between them, the first being the worst) must logically be the worst sins.

At the same time, we should not definitively condemn Aquinas. First of all, because it is *by his own action* that he allows his objections to be used against him: either religiously (only charity, and not the idea of nature, is a condition of faith), or rationally (if it happens in nature, how can it be qualified as unnatural?). Thus, we find the grandeur of rational, argumentative philosophy leaving the door open to criticism.

Further, by supporting himself on a badly understood Aristotelianism in the details (for Aristotle, sodomy is not brutishness, but habit, and as far as he is concerned, it is not a vice), but well understood in the principle (nature, being the practice and opinion of the greatest number, is the only possible source of norms), Aquinas, despite himself, effectively shows the point to which arguments on homosexuality are reversible: an attack on desire in general (Platonism) can depict homosexuality as either the worst of plagues, for it is the most desirable (Plato), or as a sin that is as guilty, and thus innocent, as all others (Augustine). Even here, whereas Aristotle seems to calm Plato's legislative fervor, it is to the contrary that Thomas the Aristotelian will help to launch the great systematic hunt for sodomites that will last at least until the Nazis. Certainly, it required a lot of philosophy, and not simply religion, to put so much work into such **violence**.

The Philosophy of the Enlightenment: The Reactive Homophobia of Sentiment

At last, the Enlightenment arrived. It is a cliché of a certain Republican philosophy which has not solved all of its problems with homophobia. But how can we think otherwise upon seeing the texts? First of all let us look at the Scottish Enlightenment. Nothing is stronger than David Hume's criticism of nature, as well as of the idea that homosexuality could be unnatural: on one hand, we do not know what nature "wants," as it is a simple principle of habit and convention; on the other, nothing can happen against nature (refer to Hume, *A Treatise of Human Nature*). Homophobia finds itself beforehand reduced either to its individual private character or to religious prejudice. It is nevertheless on this basis of **utilitarianism** that Jeremy Bentham's essay entitled "Paederasty," which expels homophobia from all rational philosophical discourse, could be constituted on philosophical grounds.

It is almost the same in France, notably with Diderot and Sade, but, importantly, with less convergent arguments. With Diderot, the essential argument rests in fact in the passage from a normative naturalism to a descriptive naturalism: the passage from one nature, understood as a unique and coherent form or as a law of the greatest number, to another nature, understood as a continuous but polymorphic unit, including the whole of its manifestations and its criticisms. Bordeu, a character in Diderot's *Le Rêve de d'Alembert* (*D'Alembert's Dream*), is quite clear on this point: "Life is aggregate,

sensitivity is elemental." From this perspective, one element could never reasonably judge another.

Conversely, Sade's argument, in his political treatise *Français, encore un effort si vous voulez être republicains!* (French, try harder if you want to be republicans!), rests in a hyper-normative naturalism: nature is law, and law is prohibitive, but precisely like nature, that is to say as desire and liberty, and not as collective institution; therefore, few positive laws are needed if we wish to allow the laws of nature to speak. In this regard, since homosexuality exists despite the institution, it conforms to nature; not only is it not evil, but it is good. And to take up an argument similar to that of Phaedrus in *Symposium*, at the opposite extreme of clichés of revolutionary virility, Sade qualifies his argument by saying: "look at Sparta."

Thus, what interests us in these two apparently contradictory arguments, is that they designate a common enemy: Rousseau and his naturalism of sentiment. To situate, in effect, nature in sentiment, and not in the aggregate or in an empirically natural law, is to revive the old argument of "against nature." Certainly, in Book II of *Confessions*, it is at the sole level of private and personal sentiment that Rousseau tells his sad adolescent experience with seduction: "This adventure caused me to safeguard myself in the future from the enterprises of the Horsemen of the wrist, and the sight of those who appeared to be, reminding me of the air and the movements of my appalling Moor, has forever inspired in me so much horror, that I had difficulty in concealing it." But it is not only that. This "horror" and "disgust," as he mentions before, do not alone burden the whole of his supposedly more philosophical texts: it is also his frightening description of the children of the Swiss bourgeoisie in his *Lettre à d'Alembert sur les spectacles* (Letter to Monsieur d'Alembert on the Theatre); it is the allusions to Lesbos in *Émile* as an example of totally corrupt morals in Book IV of *Confessions*. But mostly, with Rousseau, at the strictly conceptual level, the feeling of the voice of nature never remains simply private: it is on the contrary the very place for the expression of the principle for morality and education, the very place of the general will for politics. With Rousseau, this subjective, sincere truth is not discounted or second-rate, useful only for the margins of specifically philosophical discourse: it is the heart of all truth. In other words, it is not Rousseau's particular, specifically aphilosophical and possibly painful, experience that sustains his homophobia; it is his own philosophy as a philosophy of nature which places the allegedly natural sentiment at the heart of political decision and moral education. During the century of Enlightenment, which finally sees a better situation for the "*chevaliers de la manchette*" (a French phrase for homosexuals at the time), Rousseau thus succeeds in unifying the political homophobia of the Ancients with the homophobia "by nature" of the Medievals under the aegis of the natural sentiment "that does not mislead": "As if a natural hold was not necessary to form social ties: … as if it were not the good son, the good husband, the good father that make up the good citizen." (Nietzsche called Rousseau a "moral tarantula.")

We could even say, perhaps unfairly, that Rousseau contaminates Kant himself, whose formal morality—founded on the respect of the human person determined *a priori*, thus independently of any empirical specificity (sexual or otherwise)—is in essence foreign to all homophobia in the same way as to all racism in general. Kant later does not restrain himself from writing—following his beautiful definition of a "sexual community" that almost justifies same-sex marriage through the "reciprocal use that a man can make of the sexual organ and faculties of another person"—that this usage is either "natural" or "contrary to nature," that is to say "with a person of the same sex or an animal of another species"; he comments, "These transgressions of the laws, these vices contrary to nature, that they say are unnamable, are insults to the humanity within our persons that no restriction or exception could save from complete reprobation." It is thus necessary to be unfair: this is not truly Kant, it is once again Rousseau.

Modern Philosophy: Bio-Anthropological Homophobia
Let's go a little further. Rousseau does not content himself to synthesize the foundations of two great philosophical arguments of the past to become homophobic; he establishes the basis for specifically modern homophobia, which will surreptitiously run from Hegel to Levinas in the form of the primordial bio-anthropological affirmation of gender differences. It is in fact once again Rousseau who invents, in part, the figure of the love of the Other based on the biological difference between the sexes; that is to say, it is not the legitimization of heterosexuality (this legitimization has barely any history), but the idea that the anthropological basis of our relations with others is situated in the unquestionable biological difference between the sexes. "Neither nature nor reason can make a woman love in man what resembles her, nor is it by taking his mannerisms that she must seek to be loved"; and vice versa.

Similarly, there is around this time a profound rupture of the archaic model of "against nature." It is no longer a question of condemning the love of persons of the same sex as a deviance or a difference from nature, but rather to see in such a love the incapacity to conceive of another same-sex person as a veritable figure of Otherness. Homosexuality no longer contravenes the homogeny of nature, nor does it any longer "pervert" (in the sense of diverting) "natural" desire; further, its condemnation is no longer based on its veritable defense of homophilia (love of the same). Homosexuality's essential fault is, on the contrary, to lack the primordial heterogeneity of nature, its primary otherness, that can only be given in the form of the male-female relation, before any love of the same. It is thus no longer "nature" as such that is corrupt, it is its opposite: the foundation of a good socialization with those who are similar; the foundation of good rapport with all others (the sin of the Jesuit and of the convents, sin of all institutions that are too masculine or too feminine). For Rousseau, the calamitous Sophie must not only be the *first* other of Emile but also she must *primordially* be the foundation for his later relations with other men.

It is in this breach that, to a greater or lesser degree, the two great modern philosophies of the Other (that of Hegel and Levinas) will commit themselves. Hegel states it explicitly in the *Encyclopedia of the Philosophical Sciences*: the differences between the sexes is what allows the "awakening" of the human soul, its exit from the "sleep" of simple, fixed singularity, and its first step towards substantial universality. In other words, only the sexual act between biologically different sexes, by permitting to find oneself in the other, offers the soul the real possibility to go from its being-in-self to being-for-self. This moment in the differences between the sexes is only an initial one, but it is crucial, and seems to appear in the *Encyclopedia*, through the central role played by the Master and the Slave dialectic, and in *The Phenomenology of Spirit*, which only reasoned at the level of consciousnesses. If we allow ourselves to extrapolate the Hegelian text, we would willingly say (as he does not speak of it explicitly): homosexuality is the simple and non-dialectal fixity of the first years of life; the homosexual, forever locked away in his being-in-self, will never have access to the other, i.e. human being. That is to say not to the All Other, abstract and empty, but to the real other, rich in determinations that make up individuals.

From a completely different perspective, it is by following the same device excluding all primordially homosexual otherness that Levinas constitutes, over a century later, his phenomenology of the transcendence of the Other. He states it explicitly when he tries to once again find the—if not primordial, at least "intimate"—core of our relationship to the Other as essentially inappropriable: "And the Other, whose presence is discreetly an absence, and through which is accomplished the hospitable welcome *par excellence* that maps out the space of intimacy, is Woman. Woman is the condition of reverence, the interiority of hearth and home." In other words, at the intimate level, of sexual love and faithful love—the love "at home"—it is only Woman (for Man) who can constitute a viable and human relationship to the Other, a gentle immanence in the hard and imperative transcendence of the Other. What Levinas barely explains later in his criticism of Buber: "The I-you where Buber perceives the category of the interhuman relationship is not the relationship with the interlocutor, but with female otherness." It could not be any clearer: love and sex cannot be human unless they graft themselves onto the biological difference between the sexes.

However, here again, we cannot too quickly qualify all of Hegelian or Levinasian philosophy of otherness as homophobic. It is not at the level of Reason fulfilled, but in his unique analysis of the "ages of life" that Hegel takes the issue of gender differences into consideration; and from this point of view, we could rightly say that it is not at the level of his philosophical system (in which the specifically biological has no place), but at the level of its foundations, its material phenomenology (specific to the *Encyclopedia*) that traces of homophobia clearly intervene. Similarly, for Levinas, it is not in his primordial constitution of ethical otherness that we can speak of homophobia; at this level, the absolute transcendence of others, which forces me to close our eyes, absolutely forbids us from simply distinguishing between man and woman, or even more, the child (even though Levinas says the Son, but this time no doubt religiously and not philosophically, with regard to Abraham's sacrifice). At the level of a phenomenology of the "home" (which for him has none of the fundamental nature given to it by Heidegger in the last phase), to speak of Levinasian homophobia—to say that the homosexual denies the Other—is to have no understanding of what Levinas means by this.

To have a little fun, we could even find in Hegel some serious arguments to make an apology (at the opposite spectrum from the Greeks) if not for a homosexuality, at least for a homophilia, that is specifically adult, once rid of the heterosexual arousals of youth. And in Levinas as well, we could find arguments to support the happy homosexuality of certain married men (no more despicable than anything else); they alone possibly know how to surrender to the absolute experience of otherness, it being purged of the "discretion" of the domestic sphere.

These last lines are not written in order to wash Hegel and Levinas (and through them, philosophy itself) of their homophobic "excesses"; once again, it would not seem to be a question of such. Simply, let us recall for a last time our thesis: philosophy is rarely homophobic, but when it is, it is only in the margins; however, since there is evidence that philosophy has indeed been homophobic, it is necessary to recognize that it is possibly for specifically philosophical reasons, and not as a mask for some common sense or a given religion, no more than as an ideology of a secretly repressed urge, idiosyncratic and thus pre-philosophical. Hegel does not seem to be homophobic because he was a German Protestant bourgeois at the beginning of the nineteenth century; nor does Levinas because he was a Jewish bourgeois from before the sexual revolution. They were philosophically homophobic because they were philosophers. And in this sense, they appear to be even more homophobic than Kant, for example, who uses much harsher words. It is not at the level of discourse, but at the very level of the concept that philosophy should question itself on its potential homophobia. This is an acknowledgment which may perhaps remind philosophers in general to show some modesty on this "despicably" strategic question of homophobia, given the philosophically uncontestable grandeur of these two "cases"; and what is more, to exhort them to correct their incorrigible temptation to absolve themselves beforehand of what is real in the name of their assumption of understanding it. Hegel himself foresaw it: philosophy must guard itself from becoming edifying; one does not give lessons and expect to get away with it.

—*Pierre Zaoui*

Aristotle. *Ethique à Nicomaque* (VII, 5). Paris:Vrin, 1986. [Published in English as *Nicomachean Ethics.*]

Augustine, Saint. *Confessions* (notably III, 8, 15). Paris: Le Seuil, 1982. [Published in English as *Confessions.*]

Bentham, Jeremy. *Essai sur la pédérastie*. Lyon: Presses universitaires de Lyon, 1982. [Published in English as "Paederasty."]

Brown, Peter. *Saint Augustin*. Paris: Le Seuil, 1986. [Published in the US as *Augustine of Hippo*. Berkeley: Univ. of California Press, 2000.]

Brunschwig, Jacques, and Geoffroy Lloyd. *Le Savoir grec*. Paris: Flammarion, 1996. [Published in the US as *Greek Thought*. Cambridge: Belknap Press, 2000.]

Diderot, Denis. *Le Rêve de d'Alembert*. Paris: Bordas, 1990. [Published in English as *D'Alembert's Dream.*]

Hegel, Georg Wilhelm Friedrich. *Encyclopédie des sciences philosophiques* (notably book III "Philosophie de l'esprit," § 398 and 412). Paris:Vrin, 1988. [Published in English as *Encyclopedia of the Philosophical Sciences.*]

Hume, David. *Traité de la nature humaine* (notably I, II, III). Paris: Garnier-Flammarion, 1995. [Published in English as *Treatise of Human Nature.*]

Kant, Immanuel. *Doctrine du droit* (III, 1, § 24). Paris:Vrin, 1985. [Published in English as "The Science of Right."]

Levinas, Emmanuel. *Totalité et infinité*. Paris: Martinus Nijhoff, 1971 (notably page 166 and *s*). [Published in English as *Totality and Infinity.*]

Plato. *Phèdre*; *Banquet*; *Lois*. Paris: Gallimard, "Pléiade," 1988 (notably 838 *c* and *s*). [Published in English as *Phaedrus*; *Symposium*; and *Laws.*]

Rousseau, Jean-Jacques. *Confessions* (II); *Emile ou de l'éducation* (III–V); *Lettre à d'Alembert*. Paris: Gallimard, "Pléiade," 1964. [Published in English as *Confessions*; *Emile*; and *Letter to D'Alembert.*]

Sade, Donatien Alphonse François (Marquis) de. *Français, encore un effort si vous voulez être républicains*. Paris: Presses de la Renaissance, 1972.

Thomas Aquinas. *Somme théologique* (notably I.II, q. 94, II.II, q. 142, and q. 154). Paris: Le Cerf, 1999. [Published in English as *Summa Theologica.*]

—*Against Nature; Biology; Essentialism/Constructionism; Heterosexism; Medicine; Otherness; Psychiatry; Psychoanalysis; Symbolic Order; Theology; Universalism/ Differentialism; Utilitarianism; Vice.*

POLICE

In Western countries, the police have long played a central role in the harassment of gays and lesbians and in the construction of the negative image of homosexuals. This role deserves close study, because it sheds light not only on the gay condition at its darkest but also the internal functions of the police and the liberties they often took with the law.

Police repression of homosexuality is an old reality which goes back at least to the seventeenth century. In **France**, it began with the creation of the Paris police in 1667 under Lieutenant General (i.e. chief) Gabriel Nicolas de la Reynie. Henceforth, Parisian sodomites risked being arrested and possibly imprisoned. Inside the police force, a vice squad was created in 1725 by Nicolas Jean-Baptiste Ravot d'Ombreval; two members, Simonnet and Haymier, were specifically assigned to follow and subsequently arrest homosexuals (they collected bonuses according to their results, but very early on began blackmailing those they were arresting, in keeping with a long tradition of police corruption). They maintained a network of several dozen informants or "*mouches*" (flies), recruited from among the lackeys and male prostitutes who previously had dealings with them, being both informers and corrupt abetting agents, enticing the "*infâmes*" (the "vile ones"), whom they delivered into the hands of the police. Thanks to these collaborators—which also included some virtuous types who agreed with the police's actions, such as Abbot Théru, who helped to spy on their behalf at the College of the Four Nations—the police uncovered several covert homosexual networks; as a result, the capture of pederasts became a daily event. There were also routine police raids of known homosexual meeting places, such as the Jardin des Tuileries (the main cruising area for the Ancien Régime of Paris, which was socially very mixed), the banks of the Seine (where lackeys worked the streets), the Jardin du Luxembourg, and the former St Antoine's Gate, as well as numerous nightclubs which were equipped with small private rooms. Police interrogations were relatively thorough: they tried to establish the origin of the "corruption" or the "initiation to **vice**"; they inquired as to the precise nature of the acts committed; they maintained a rigorous record of instances of "sexual intercourse," "hand jobs," and ejaculations. Those arrested (who were often shaking with **shame**) were made to swear that they would "mend their ways" and to sign a letter confirming their guilt. Punishments varied from reprimand to imprisonment (between eight days to two months on average, but this could be prolonged at the request of families on the condition that they paid the additional cost for keeping them there). Court proceedings were rare, and death sentences were rarer still (the last two men so condemned, and subsequently burned alive for acts of sodomy not aggravated by violence and murder, were Jean Diot and Bruno Lenoir, a shoemaker and a laborer, arrested after being caught having sex on Rue Montorgueil in January 1750). The degree of severity by police, not surprisingly, depended on the social standing of those arrested: noblemen caught in the act were, at most, lightly reprimanded; clerics were referred to their superiors, who generally let the incident slide; heads of families and teenagers were lectured for long periods, but released rather quickly; and as for commoners, they ended up in the notorious Bicêtre prison. This enormous amount of activity allowed police to report to the Minister of Paris (the secretary of state for the king) an estimate of the number of Parisian "sodomites" (20,000 were reported in 1725 and 40,000 in 1783) and also provided lists of homosexuals in the upper class, as revealed by their servants.

Police activity of the same nature occurred in London during the same period. Starting in 1699, police made raids on molly houses (taverns or private rooms where homosexuals could congregate). The most famous of these operations took place in 1726, when dozens of people were arrested at Mother Clap's bawdy house in Holborn. The proprietress and her customers were placed in the stocks, where they were at the mercy of furious crowds; a number of sodomy trials ensued, and three people were condemned to hanging. Besides, the English police, just as the French, had no qualms about setting traps and using abetting agents.

The French Revolution decriminalized homosexuality in 1791; the Napoleonic Empire confirmed this decriminalization in its penal code of 1810. Henceforth, and until 1942, French law did not specifically repress homosexuality. But this did not prevent the French police from continuing to entrap and harass homosexuals, using increasingly inventive methods. Indeed, they were faced with a phenomenon which was no longer **criminal** in the eyes of the law but which was still considered monstrous according to public opinion. This was evident in the discourse of magistrates, which was embellished with such phrases as "shameful passions," "immoral act," and "facts that shock nature." Napoleon, however, thought that sodomy was a concern for police, not the justice system, offering the immense advantage of settling scandalous affairs without publicity. In 1804, during a search, Paris police came across love letters exchanged between two men; the police prefect decided to imprison them for seven weeks and then to separate them (one was sent to Belgium and the other one to Etampes [near Paris]). Further, between 1810 and 1813, a man named Pierre Barbier was kept under lock and key in Dourdan for "pederasty and **debauchery**" without being charged with a crime.

For the most part, police activity was developed and carried out in an extrajudicial manner; only the fight against **pedophilia** relied on substantial legislation, namely the 1832 measures with respect to "indecent assault without violence" on minors eleven years old or younger (the age was increased to thirteen in 1863). It is clear that the arbitrariness of the police was facilitated by public prejudices, the shame of the person being questioned, and the public's lack of judicial knowledge. It is also evident that many people—perhaps a majority of France's population—in the nineteenth and twentieth centuries believed in good faith that homosexuality was in fact illegal in their country; in 1975, the French archaeologist and historian Paul Veyne noted the shocked comment of a villager in Vaucluse, after the famous "Les Homosexuels" episode of the program *Dossiers de l'écran* was broadcast: "They said on television that it was allowed." The police were as interested in homosexuals as they were in prostitutes (prostitution was not an offense either), essentially in the name of the fight against "indecency" (Paragraph 330 of the penal code), with the wide support of the public (the police assured them that they would "keep the streets clean"). But while police regarded female prostitution as a minor "pain," they considered homosexuality a monstrous aberration, which explains the vehemence of their handling of pederasts who fell into their hands. As for homosexual prostitutes, the police considered them the dregs of society and the "anteroom to crime," according to François Carlier, leader of the vice squad between 1860 and 1870, in his *Etudes de pathologie sociale: les deux prostitutions* (Studies of Social Pathology: The Two Prostitutions) in 1887. The police were also interested in homosexuality when a pederast was charged in a criminal case: inquiries into the subject's morality gave his neighbors and janitors an opportunity to express their prejudices and personal resentment against him in ways that could profoundly influence the handling of the case. These testimonies weighed heavily on the verdicts; whether the verdicts were delivered by a judge or a jury, the homosexuality of the accused was always an aggravating circumstance.

The Second Empire of Napoleon III clearly marked a hardening of police and judicial positions on homosexuality. It was during this era that the "danger of pederasty" became a popular topic, partially under the influence of Ambroise Tardieu (who associated homosexuality with crime and child abuse), and because homosexual activity involved the mixing of social classes in ways that seemed increasingly unhealthy. As a result, the police resumed its tactic of traps and "raids" on cruising areas and, in the 1880s, charges of public indecency were almost exclusively leveled at homosexuals. By the end of the nineteenth century, the vice squad became even more powerful, as well as corrupt. Police raids took place around urinals and other well-known places of soliciting, such as the arches of the Palais Royal, the Jouffroy, Panoramas, and Verdeau passageways), as well as cafés and public dances that were frequented by gays. The urinals in particular, located on Paris sidewalks, used by homosexuals as a discreet place for contact, were subject to police surveillance. Christian Gury offered insight into police efforts on the Champs-Elysées when he described the arrest of the Count de Germiny in 1876: several undercover policemen spent time observing the interactions of the men who gathered there, before jumping on the "delinquent" and proceeding to arrest him. This police harassment was crucial in many respects: it made gay encounters very difficult, further complicating lives that were already difficult; it strengthened the public's opinion of homosexuality as abominable and degrading; and it facilitated all forms of blackmail. The police also raided theaters, if "good moral standards" were offended; when Colette publicly kissed her partner Missy onstage at the Moulin Rouge in 1907, a riot ensued, resulting in a police raid.

The ability of police to compile records on homosexuals was strengthened by the restructuring in 1894 of the vice squad, which was now charged with the task of compiling "moral standards files" on the personalities of "all Paris." In particular, the vice squad increased surveillance records of the most notorious homosexuals, as well as public houses and other businesses specializing in this type of clientele, from which the police could draw information and, no doubt, hush money as well. Police reports were not above entertaining rumors or innuendo, either; of the famous feminist Madeleine Pelletier, a police index card read: "She is known to have special customs and is represented in the circles which she patronizes as a tribad [lesbian]." Of course, police files on gays and lesbians went beyond the vice squad and the capital of Paris; its practice would remain in effect until 1981, with dramatic consequences in Alsace and Moselle between 1940 and 1944 in particular: while Pierre Seel (the only French person to testify openly about being deported during World War II due to his homosexuality) was arrested by the Gestapo, it was because the Alsatian police had originally registered him as a pederast in the 1930s.

The last time police interventionism against homosexuality increased significantly in France was during World War II. The 1942 Vichy legislation created the offense of an "unchaste and unnatural act with a minor less than twenty-one years old of the same sex as the subject," which was upheld by Charles de Gaulle in 1945; it was used to criminalize many sexual relations which had been tolerated in the pre-war years. Further, Gaullist and Christian Democrat familialism provoked a postwar ban on transvestism and on any homosexual contact in public places, once more giving police more reason to intervene. The **Mirguet** amendment of 1960 proclaimed homosexuality a "social scourge," which resulted in nearly doubling the punitive measures brought against gays found guilty of public indecency. By the beginning of the 1970s, police raids of gay establishments were still frequent, and were harshly denounced in the famous leftist manifesto entitled *Tout!* on April 23, 1971. (It is at this same moment that the first gay activists coined the insult "hetero-cop.") During the 1970s, the police regularly made the rounds of bars and cinemas considered to be places where public gay sex occurred, and made arrests. A decade later, the **AIDS** epidemic gave them another reason to intervene in the most "hard-core" gay bars, notably when the decision to close backrooms was made in 1984–85.

In other countries, there was even heavier police activity regarding homosexuality, particularly where it was illegal. In **England**, police actions against gays, prevalent as early as the nineteenth century, intensified in the 1930s and 40s, when the most flamboyant homosexuals were tossed out of pubs and arbitrarily accused of soliciting, as described by Quentin Crisp in his diaries. Homosexuality's criminalization also encouraged informants and blackmail, i.e, a moral corruption very foreign to the fair-play values and transparency generally associated with the British identity. In particular, the police (or "bobbies") were merciless against those engaged in "cottaging" (sexual touching in public places, so named because the public toilets in parks resembled cottages), resulting in the arrest of thousands of people a year during the 1950s, and using more and more abetting agents. The victims of these interventions were often shocked and ashamed, given that in England, respect was a key social value, and an accusation of buggery or gross indecency could have huge social and human consequences (actor Alec Guinness, arrested in Liverpool in 1946, was only able to save his burgeoning career by giving police a false name). In the 1950s, the obsession of police with this issue was such that the entire country, in spite of its liberal traditions and the guarantees of personal freedom it had advocated for centuries, was within a hairsbreadth of becoming a police state on this question. Between the late 1930s and 1955, the number of men arrested for homosexual offenses increased by a factor of six. There were three people responsible for this trend: Sir Theobald Mathew, a devout Catholic who became the Director of Public Prosecutions in 1944; Sir David Maxwell Fyfe, Home Secretary in the Churchill cabinet from 1951–54; and Sir John Nott-Bower, who became commissioner of the London Metropolitan Police in 1953. Despite the partial decriminalization of homosexuality in 1967, the fight against gay public sex by police continued, with a predictable voracity during the Thatcher era of the 1980s, with some strange consequences: in 1985, gay pop singer Jimmy Somerville was arrested in Hyde Park for gross indecency by a policeman, who allegedly then asked him for an autograph for his daughter.

In Germany, the police showed themselves to be relatively tolerant in the 1920s, particularly in Berlin, where they came to an agreement with prominent gay leader Magnus **Hirschfeld** to allow homosexual establishments to prosper; the advent of the Nazi era in 1933, however, obviously changed this: between 1937 and 1939, raids in bars, parks, and other meeting places resulted in the arrest of 95,000 gays, who were then subject to the whims of the Gestapo. Following World War II, West Germany resumed the harassment of homosexuals (with the blessing of Chancellor Konrad Adenauer, a devout Catholic) until the abrogation of Paragraph 175 in 1969.

The police were also very active in the United States, even if anti-gay legislation was not the same in every state. It is necessary to state that the Federal Bureau of Investigation (FBI) played an increasing role on the subject from 1937 on: J. Edgar **Hoover**, the FBI's director between 1924 and 1972 (and himself a closeted homosexual), compiled files on those regarded as sex degenerates and sex offenders (the most famous of these were on writers Allen Ginsberg, Tennessee Williams, James Baldwin, and Truman Capote). In 1953, the compilation of these records was strengthened by President Dwight Eisenhower's Order 10450, which authorized the dismissal of federal civil servants on grounds of sexual **perversion**. The FBI relied on informers' networks, infiltration agents, *agents provocateurs*, and large-scale phone-tapping and mail diversion tactics (it can be noted in this respect the links between the police and the US Postal Service: postal workers did not hesitate to name homosexual coworkers to their employers). As a result of this activity, Hoover accumulated a vast amount of information on suspected homosexuals, including politicians whom he blackmailed, thereby increasing even further the FBI's immense power. Added to this practice was the harassment and surveillance of homosexuals in parks and bars and the outlawing of transvestism; many gays and lesbians were arrested, and often these arrests were accompanied by **violence**, sometimes rape. All of this activity exasperated the burgeoning gay community, culminating in 1969 with the **Stonewall** riots in New York. During the 1970s in the aftermath of Stonewall, police violence seemed to recede, but it did not totally disappear: the crucial events of 1978 in San Francisco revealed that police bias remained firmly on the side of homophobia. Dan White, who murdered pro-gay rights mayor George Moscone and openly gay councilor Harvey Milk at San Francisco City Hall, was himself a retired San Francisco police officer. When White was shockingly only convicted of manslaughter, the city's gay community went on the rampage; in response, the police raided Castro Street in the heart of the gay community, destroying several gay bars and businesses in the process. Even today, particularly outside of the major urban centers, many homosexuals in the US who are victims of assault do not lodge a formal complaint, for fear of how the police will treat them.

Nevertheless, the relationship between homosexuals and the police in the West has generally improved since

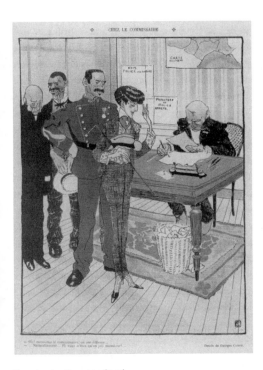

Drawing by Georges Carré.
A young man arrested by the morality squad: "But, Captain!
I am defamed … naturally…. And you are such a handsome
man!…"

1970. In France, as early as the Pompidou-Giscard years, the gay movement's increased importance ensured that the police could no longer resort to its authoritarian tactics of the past. The FHAR (Front homosexuel d'action révolutionnaire; Homosexual Revolutionary Action Front), for instance, was relatively protected by its political connections with the far left, but it was not until the election of François Mitterrand in 1981 that turned back centuries of police suspicion and arbitrary power. The Deferre *circulaire* (notice) of June, 1981 drafted by Maurice Grimaud, Prefect of Paris Police, director of the cabinet of the home secretary, was sent to all police services stipulating that "no **discrimination**, let alone suspicion should weigh upon people based only on their sexual orientation." In the United States, the 1974 Privacy Act forbade police and other authorities from breaking the First Amendment (in 1998, under the authority of this law, a gay librarian named Daniel C. Tsang won a lawsuit against the CIA, which was ordered to stop spying on him and pay him $46,000 in legal costs). Another positive phenomenon was the coming out of numerous gay and lesbian police officers; on November 22, 1981, Sgt. Charlie Cochrane

became the first New York policeman to publicly reveal his homosexuality). However, police continued homophobic actions in states where laws prohibiting sodomy still existed (all of which were struck down by 2003), and sometimes even in so-called "liberal" states (Amnesty International listed several cases of homosexuals being poorly treated by police in the state of New York in the 1990s). In the United Kingdom, the law still allows the British police to intervene when gay sexual relations include more than two participants or is "tainted" by sadomasochism (as shown in the 1993 Hoylandswaine affair, when police raided a private gay party, and the 1998 Bolton Seven affair, in which two men were charged after making a private porn movie). But despite this, there has been a general liberalization in Britain too: in 1990, gay British policemen created the LAGP (Lesbian and Gay Police Association), and, since 1998, some district authorities began recruiting gay police officers in an effort to combat the homophobic traditions of the profession and to make the police more effective in dealing with gay bashing incidents. The British police were inspired by the Dutch model: the Netherlands indeed offered a rare and early example of a determinedly gay-friendly police.

In countries where homosexuality's legal status is either vague or negative, police continue to harass their gay and lesbian populations. Police in Romania, under the repressive communist government of Nicolae Ceaucescu, were well known for their arrest, beating, and torture of homosexuals. The Serbian police barely defended Belgrade's participants in the country's first Gay Pride on June 30, 2001, when hooligans assailed them. Homophobic police behavior is also common, and often brutal, in Turkey and Albania, in several countries of **Latin America** (Brazil, Venezuela, Peru, Costa Rica), in most Muslim countries, in many countries of **Africa**, and in **India** and **China**. Almost everywhere, transvestites and effeminate gays seem to be particularly vulnerable targets of police aggression.
—*Pierre Albertini*

Amnesty International. *Breaking the Silence: Human Rights Violations Based on Sexual Orientation.* London: Amnesty, 1997.

Buhrke, Robin A. *Matter of Justice: Lesbian and Gay Men in Law Enforcement.* New York/London: Routledge, 1996.

Carlier, François. *Etudes de pathologie sociale: Les deux prostitutions.* Paris: E. Dentu, 1887.

Gury, Christian, *L'Honneur perdu d'un politicien homosexuel en*

1876. Paris: Kimé, 1999.

———. *L'Honneur perdu d'un capitaine homosexuel en 1880.* Paris: Kimé, 1999.

Leinen, Stephen. *Gay Cops.* New Brunswick: Rutgers Univ. Press, 1993.

Lever, Maurice. *Les Bûchers de Sodome.* Paris: Fayard, 1985.

Peniston, William A. "Love and Death in Gay Paris: Homosexuality and Criminality in the 1870s." In *Homosexuality in Modern France.* Edited by Jeffrey Merrick and Bryant T. Ragan Jr. Oxford: Oxford Univ. Press, 1996.

Rey, Michel. "Police et sodomie à Paris au XVIIIe siècle," *Revue d'histoire moderne et contemporaine.* Paris (1982).

Seel, Pierre. *Moi, Pierre Seel, déporté, homosexuel.* Paris: Calmann-Lévy, 1994.

Sibalis, Michael David. "The Regulation of Male Homosexuality in Revolutionary and Napoleonic France, 1789-1815." In *Homosexuality in Modern France.* Edited by Jeffrey Merrick and Bryant T. Ragan Jr. Oxford: Oxford Univ. Press, 1996.

Tamagne, Florence. *Histoire de l'homosexualité en Europe, Berlin, Londres, Paris, 1919–1939.* Paris: Le Seuil, 2000. [Published in the US as *A History of Homosexuality in Europe: Berlin, London, Paris, 1919–1939.* New York: Algora, 2004.]

Tsang, Daniel C. "US Government Surveillance." In *Gay Histories & Cultures.* Edited by George E. Haggerty. New York/London: Garland, 2000.

Weeks, Jeffrey. *Coming Out: Homosexual Politics in Britain, from the Nineteenth Century to the Present Time.* London: Quartet Books. 1977.

—Armed Forces; Criminal; Criminalization; Deportation; Gulag; Hoover, J. Edgar; McCarthy, Joseph; Mirguet, Paul; Pétain, Philippe; Prison; Stonewall; Violence.

POLITICS (France)

The subject of homophobia in politics is immense. It is also a difficult one to define, given the necessity of talking about it in terms of institutionalized homophobia, political parties, and elected officials, including politicians who are either suspected of being homosexual or who publicly declare their homosexuality. Regardless, while recent French political history has been subject to an obvious and sometimes violent homophobia—particularly around the debates over the **PaCS** (Pacte civil de solidarité; Civil solidarity pact) civil union proposal and the issue of gay **parenting**—questions remain unanswered about its appearance in earlier times.

First of all, let us note that France's political milieu, from the French Revolution of 1789 to more recent times, has been dominated by men, even after the introduction of laws on gender parity. It is men who developed the country's political culture and its rites and rituals (long before political parties allowed women as members) and monopolized national representation and government. History has shown that single-gender social groups such as the **army**, **prisons**, or even convents, were conducive to the development of homosexual relationships. Can the same be said for the political milieu, which has remained almost exclusively masculine for so long? The proof remains elusive but we can assume, without fear of error, that some legislators and members of government were homosexual. And it is not unthinkable that among the few women who entered French politics since 1944, some may have been lesbians. However, it remains that until recently, homosexuality among politicians was a well-kept secret shared by only a few initiates.

In fact, national representation in France is portrayed as the guardian of **family** and **heteronormativity**. The model of the (male) politician has long been depicted as a father figure who upholds the Civil Code (the basis of French law), which has made the family, and by association, **marriage**, one of the fundamental pillars of society. The idea remains to this day; even though the right to divorce was adopted in 1884 (first added to French law after the Revolution, it was abrogated during the Restoration), over 100 years later, the announcement in the 1990s by former French Prime Minister Michel Rocard that he was divorcing created quite a stir. It was clear that a male politician in France, even at the end of the twentieth century, needed to be married and, as much as possible, be a father. It was this idea that also spurred then-presidential candidate François Mitterrand, during France's 1981 national election (which he would win), to advise the young, single ministerial hopefuls in his entourage that they must be married if they were to receive a portfolio in his government. Under these circumstances then, how is it possible for politicians to engage in relationships other than those established as the "norm," even if that norm is discreetly transgressed, as evidenced by Mitterand's well-known but unspoken "other family," the result of an affair?

What was essential then was that the politician must serve as a model to the "good people." Homosexuality was considered even more taboo than extramarital relations. But of course, French politicians were not all exclusively heterosexual. And thanks to Jean Jacques Régis de Cambacérès (1753–1824)—the French statesman and author of the Civil Code who, history tells us, was himself homosexual—sodomy ceased to be considered a crime. From its birth as a modern democracy, France no longer penalized homosexual relations, but did find it appropriate to ensure the clear division between genders in public life. Thus, by an order of November 7, 1800, it was forbidden for women to dress as men without the prefect's authorization. However, until World War II, save for another order that forbade those dressed in the clothing of the opposite gender from attending public events or celebrations, men were not tried for transvestism.

In truth, French legislators ignored homosexuality until 1942; until then, it was up to the police and the legal system, in the name of respecting "good character," to pursue anyone whose behavior was deemed to be "deviant" and put them on file. The fact that during World War II, the French state under the Vichy government introduced a law criminalizing homosexuality is not, *a priori*, surprising; in Vichy France, moral order was triumphant. However, it may be surprising that the law was not repealed after the war, when the Republic was restored, though one must remember that the years and, in fact, decades following France's liberation were marked by a desire to uphold the idea of the "family," a belief shared by the entire political spectrum from the Mouvement républicain populaire (Popular Republican Movement) to the Communist Party. It is in this context that the **Mirguet** amendment was passed in France in 1960, which officially turned homosexuality into a "social scourge." During this time, homosexual rights were not an issue; the question was not the object of debate in Parliament, and in society at large, there was no discussion of the need to evolve. The major gay movement in France, Arcadie, was resolutely reformist—certainly, it criticized existing laws and demanded their repeal—but it was locked in the dilemma of the period that tended to separate public and **private** life. Even though Arcadie lobbied politicians for change, it did not make homosexuality a specifically political question. An abrupt change came about, however, in 1968, when gay and lesbian associations finally presented and defined themselves as political.

The pressure exerted by these new groups had an impact on politicians, to the point that the progressive

Illustration for *Les Enfants de Sodome à l'Assemblée nationale ou Députation de l'ordre de la Manchette aux représentants de tous les orders ...*,1790. A practical joke of the Revolution that, despite its outrageous demands and burlesque humor, is nothing less than a sincere plea for sexual freedom.

parties, notably the Socialist Party, seriously listened to their demands. "Until the 1980s," wrote Jean Danet, "homosexuality's social situation had this consequence: the affective relationship between two persons of the same sex did not solicit much legal intelligence." Homophobia, as defined by Daniel Borrillo, was "liberal": homosexuality was tolerated if it remained discreet. It remained, however, that the law discriminated against homosexuals. In 1982, a year after the Socialist Party was elected to power, it corrected the situation (despite a strong resistance from conservative politicians) by revising Article 331 of France's Penal Code, which had been originally written by the Vichy regime during World War II, maintained by the restored Republic, and made even worse in 1980 (with the addition of a paragraph that allowed for the punishment of relations between minors). Following the vote on the law on August 4, 1982, homosexuality could no longer be suppressed. Thereafter, political battles regarding homosexuality in France shifted to the fight for the legal recognition of same-sex couples, who did not enjoy the same rights as unmarried heterosexual couples.

This new debate, which started in the 1990s, revealed that homophobia, both in the political world and in French society in general, was more than latent. A petition was presented by family associations to some 36,500 French mayors demanding that potential contracts between same-sex couples not be registered. The huge anti-PaCS demonstration of January 31, 1999—against the controversial civil union pact proposed by the government which granted rights (short of marriage) to unmarried couples, gay or straight—brought out tens of thousands of French citizens mobilized by **right-wing** associations and **Catholic** and fundamentalist groups. In Parliament, discussion of PaCS revealed that while the question divided most politicians along party lines, there were even those on the left who were difficult to persuade. During its first reading in the National Assembly, in fact, the proposition was rejected due to insufficient participation by the majority in session. Among other things, the debate unleashed in some politicians an explicit homophobia notable for its vulgarity ("Homosexuals, I piss in their asses," was the declaration of Union pour la démocratie française (UDF; Union for French Democracy) Member of Parliament Michel Meylan) and provocation (according to UDF Senator Emmanuel Hamel, "PaCS" was short for "Practice of AIDS Contamination").

The debate in France on PaCS, and the one on gay parenting that followed, had the effect of re-politicizing the question of homosexuality. While those on the left (with a few exceptions) generally supported PaCS, the question of gay **parenting**, in particular **adoption** by same-sex partners, was more nebulous. A parliamentary petition to forbid adoption by homosexuals, launched by Member Renault Muselier, was signed only by members of the right; however, very few on the left openly opposed it.

As a result of such debates, certain French politicians decided it was time to publicly declare their homosexuality. Though the number who have come out remains small, some have offered personal accounts of their experiences, particularly in the context of their political affiliation. Nonetheless, as a rule of thumb, elected officials in France remain discreet about their private lives, especially when those lives are not traditional. This issue brings up the question of **outing** public personalities, especially when they take homophobic positions or associate themselves with homo-

phobic demonstrations such as the 1999 anti-PaCS protest. The political world, with a few exceptions, remains guarded on emerging social issues, and on homosexuality in particular. Even if the sociology of France's political world has evolved (in 1999, *ProChoix* magazine counted 171 MPs who were not married), in general, elected officials remain wary of offending their constituents. But what about the "gay and lesbian vote"? Does it exist in France? Conversely, what about openly homophobic politicians and the impact of their views on voters? These questions are not easily answered, although numerous homophobic officials have been reelected.

In the end, the political milieu in France is neither more nor less homophobic than any other. What is clear, however, is its resistance to change in relation to society as a whole, regardless of political affiliation.
—*Françoise Gaspard*

Adam, Barry D. *The Rise of a Gay and Lesbian Movement.* Boston: Twayne Publishers, 1987.

———, Jan Willem Duyvendak, and André Krouwel. *The Global Emergence of Gay and Lesbian Politics: National Imprints of a Worldwide Movement.* Philadelphia: Temple Univ. Press, 1999.

Borrillo, Daniel. *L'Homophobie.* Paris: Presses universitaires de France, 2000.

———, ed. *Homosexualités et droit.* Paris: Presses universitaires de France, 1998.

Butler, Judith, and Joan Scott, eds. *Feminists Theorize the Political.* New York/London: Routledge, 1992.

D'Emilio, John. *Sexual Politics, Sexual Communities: The Making of a Homosexual Minority in the United States, 1940–1970.* Chicago: Univ. of Chicago Press, 1983.

"Femmes travesties, un 'mauvais genre'," *Clio* (1999).

Front homosexuel d'action révolutionnaire. *Rapport contre la normalité.* Paris: Champ libre, 1971.

Gay Left Collective. *Homosexuality: Power and Politics.* London: Allison & Busby. 1980.

Gury Christian. *L'Honneur perdu d'un politicien homosexuel en 1876.* Paris: Kimé, 1999.

Marotta, Toby. *The Politics of Homosexuality: How Lesbians and Gay Men Made Themselves a Political and Social Force in Modern America.* Boston: Houghton Mifflin, 1981.

Mécary, Caroline, and Géraud de la Pradelle. *Les Droits des homosexuel(les).* Paris: Presses universitaires de France, 1997.

Tamagne, Florence. *Histoire de l'homosexualité en Europe, Berlin, Londres, Paris, 1919–1939.* Paris: Le Seuil, 2000. [Published in the US as *A History of Homosexuality in*

Europe: Berlin, London, Paris, 1919–1939. New York: Algora, 2004.]

Weeks, Jeffrey. *Coming Out: Homosexual Politics in Britain. from the Nineteenth Century to the Present Time.* London: Quartet Books, 1977.

—*Adoption; Criminalization; Decriminalization (France); Favorites; France; Henri III; Marriage; Mirguet, Paul; Monsieur; Outing; Parenting; Privacy.*

POPE JOHN PAUL II. *See* Catholic Church

PORTUGAL

Legislation in Portugal prior to the nineteenth century was modeled on the Visigothic Code, or *lex gothorum* in its *vulgata* version, a set of laws established by Chindasuinth, the Visigothic king of Hispania, in the seventh century. It is here that the penalty for the act of sodomy appears for the first time, and was maintained in the *Ordenações Afonsinas* of 1446–47, the *Ordenações Manuelinas* of 1521, and the *Ordenações Filipinas* of 1595. Despite the lack of substantial documentation available today, it is reasonable to suspect that condemnations for sodomy were only rarely applied during the Middle Ages, in particular the sentence of being burned at the stake. Likewise, the Portuguese **Inquisition**'s relentless persecution of sodomites between the sixteenth and eighteenth centuries was characterized by the "quality" of trials rather than the quantity. Generally, the main victims were Jewish *conversos* (converts) accused of covertly pursuing their religious practices; the accusation of sodomy was mostly directed at "old Christians" who could not be included in the genealogical lists of either the *conversos* or "new Christians," and who could not be suspected of Crypto-Judaism. This accusation was the perfect means by which authorities could eliminate not only true sodomites, but also the alleged enemies of the Inquisition or the Church, notably intellectuals and scientists. On the other hand, the function of social control is doubtless: many of the condemned were monks, slaves, or colonists in Brazil.

Sodomites were condemned by *auto da fé* (act of faith) (the solemn proclamation of public penance of condemned heretics during the Middle Ages issued by the Inquisition) from 1551 to at least 1752, but for the most part it was the seventeenth century that was the Inquisition's golden age: during this time, moral sanction often served as a pretense for political persecution. Formally, the Inquisition represented the interests of the Spanish Crown, which governed Portugal from 1580 until 1640 as an all-powerful entity within the Portuguese state. One of the revolutionaries of 1640—the year that Portugal substantially attained its independence—was D. Rodrigo da Cunha, Count of Vila Franca; his morals made him very vulnerable to the Inquisition and he became its most famous victim. Condemned to life imprisonment in 1652, he died after twenty-one years of incarceration.

The Inquisition shaped homophobia until the dictatorial regime of the Estado Novo (Portuguese for "New State") (1926–74), when modern **medicine** used scientific arguments to reinforce theological morality as interpreted by Catholic fundamentalism. Portuguese **psychiatry** followed the tendency to pathologize homosexuality since the nineteenth century, but it was Portuguese neurologist Egas Moniz, 1949 Nobel Prize winner for the discovery of the prefrontal leucotomy (the precursor of the lobotomy), who was the biggest influence on medical and legal attitudes toward homosexuals in Portugal. His 1901 treatise *Una Vida sexual (fisiologia e patologia)* (The physiological and pathological aspects of sex life), which has been published in numerous editions, is a monumental example of scientific-based homophobia. In it, Moniz affirms his knowledge of the first well-organized homosexual communities, such as the one in Berlin, as well as the work of Karl Heinrich Ulrichs, the nineteenth-century German writer and pioneer of gay rights, whom he cites only in order to condemn him. The Portuguese First Republic, as the period between the October 5th revolution of 1910 and the coup d'état of 1926 was known, was a time of openness on many levels; nonetheless, one of its presidents, Teixeira Gomes, was forced to resign in part because of his homosexuality, to which he admitted in his writings.

Clearly homoerotic literature appeared in Portugal in the 1920s, written not only by Fernando Pessoa (the poet and writer who has been referred to by Harold Bloom as being among the most representative poets of the twentieth century) but also by António Botto and Judite Teixeira, writers who were also the victims of a smear campaign led by the Lisbon Students' Fascist League. Even though Pessoa and others came to their defense, they were eventually forced into self-imposed exile due to the pressure of public hostility, which had become unbearable after the country's dictatorship was installed in 1926. Earlier, Botto was expelled from his job at the Ministry of the Colonies and, under pressure from the Catholic Church, his request for a return from exile was refused; both died destitute in 1959. The cases of Botto and Teixeira left a deep and lasting mark on Portugal's writers, who became adept at self-censorship in addition to the official **censorship** instituted by the dictatorship. Until 1974, the expression of homosexuality in Portuguese **literature** could only be made through allusion or by using very discreet codes.

The story of the anonymous victims of homophobia during the Estado Novo dictatorship, whether social, medical, religious, or legal, remains to be told. However, it is known that verbal and physical assaults of homosexuals by **police** were common, at least until the 1960s, and victims were also subject to public humiliation. On occasion, in order to conceal a "disgraceful" relative, higher-class families would resort to committing them to psychiatric hospitals. Other procedures, such as being sent to a penal colony or being placed under house arrest, were reserved for members of the lower classes who had become too notorious due to their "indecent exposure" or "sexual offence."

Highly influenced by French criminal law, Portugal's 1886 penal code foresaw the application of measures against "all those who habitually practice **vices against nature**," meting out punishment for "the sexual assault of a person of one sex or the other." Anti-homosexual legislation remained in force until the penal code was revised in 1982, when all sexual relations between those aged sixteen years or older were decriminalized. The overthrow of Portugal's dictatorship by a military coup eight years earlier in 1974 had created the formal conditions for freedom of association and expression, setting the stage for the emergence of the first LGBT organizations in the country. At the same time, however, right-wing political forces were always opposed to the formation of such groups; for example, General Galvão de Melo, a prominent member of the National Salvation Junta that overthrew the Estado Novo, gave a virulent speech against early attempts in Portugal to create a gay and lesbian movement. As for left-wing parties, the discourse was not much more favorable; while politicians and unions monopolized civic activities, LGBT movements were accused of dividing, weakening, and demoralizing the workers' movement with demands that diverted attention from more important

battles, bringing into question the dignity of homosexuals as well. In a remarkable way, certain members of the **Communist** Party even used homosexuality against its political enemies, renewing a long and tiresome homophobic tradition among communists. Prior to the end of the Estado Novo, Júlio Fogaça, one of the Communist Party's disgraced leaders, was denounced as a homosexual and imprisoned with the connivance of the party. Today, it is mostly the Council of Catholic Bishops that adopts the most homophobic positions in Portugal; the Council vigorously opposed the 2001 Uniões de Facto (Civil Union Act), which opened the door to the possibility of same-sex **marriage**, yet to be made legal.

Moreover, recent studies have shown that homophobia remains rather widespread in Portuguese society in general, including in the gay and lesbian community itself, notably with regard to the perceived poor public image of homosexuals, which makes it difficult to assert a proud lifestyle outside of the closed circles of the **family** or the **ghetto**.

—*Fernando Cascais*

Assunçào, Aroldo, and Luiz Mott. "Love's Labors Lost: Five Letters from a 17th Century Portuguese Sodomite." In *The Pursuit of Sodomy: Male Homosexuality in Renaissance and Enlightment Europe.* Edited by Kent Gerard and Gert Hekma. New York: Harrington Park Press, 1989.

Cascais, Fernando. "Como quem não quer a coisa," *Fenda (In)Finda* (1983).

———, ed. *Indisciplinar a Teoria. Estudos Gays, Lésbicos e Queer.* Lisbon: Fenda, 2004.

Mendoça, José L. O., and Antonio Moreira. *História dos principais actos e procedimentos da Inquisição em Portugal.* Lisbon: Imprensa Nacional/Casa da Moeda, 1980.

Moita, Maria Gabriela. *Discursos sobre a homossexualidade no contexto clinico: A homossexualidade dos dois lados do espelho.* Doctoral thesis. Porto, Portugal: Instituto de Ciências Biomédicas de Abel Salazar, 2001.

Mott, Luiz. "Portuguese Pleasures: The Gay Subculture in Portugal at Inquisition's Time." In *Homosexuality, Which Homosexuality?* Edited by Dennis Altman, Carole Vance, Martha Vicinus, and Jeffrey Weeks. Amsterdam: Free Univ. Press, 1989.

———. "Justitia et Miscricordia: a Inquisição portuguesa e repressão a nefando pecado de sodomia." Paris: CIDH, 1990.

Pessoa, Fernando. *Aviso por causa da moral.* Lisbon: Hiena Editora, 1986.

—*Fascism; Inquisition; Latin America; Medicine; Police; Spain; Violence.*

PRISON

As of June 1, 2002, 54,950 individuals were being detained in French prisons, of which 52,979 were men (96.4%) and 1,971 were women (3.6%). This over-representation of men in the spheres of delinquency and criminality has led to various interpretations in terms of social relations of the sexes. Because of their socialization, men are generally more exposed to taking risks, to tests of strength, to domination and **violence**; they are more present in the public sphere, on the outside. Such is the predominant example of the male image as he should be, conveyed by numerous ideas, attitudes, and behaviors. On the other hand, representations of the "eternal feminine" reflect internal, private, and domestic spheres, a reduction in risk and violence, and reason and/or wisdom.

These representations are promoted by various institutions of socialization—**family**, **school**, the **army**, the **workplace**, and prison—which Michel Foucault designated as a continuum within the scope of a disciplinary society. The internalization of these respective models—in the form of *habitus*—anchors dispositions toward specific practices and behaviors; with regard to male delinquency, this internalization exposes men to a greater risk of committing certain offenses, and at least partially explains their over-representation in prison as compared to their female counterparts.

Further, many young males believe that "doing time" makes one a man. Thus, going to prison becomes a rite of initiation, according to Canadian sociologist Erving Goffman. Perceived as a form of masculine validation, incarceration becomes a sign of belonging, as well as a source of secondary advantages in the eyes of one's peers. As a sign and symbol of courage, strength, and violence, prison sometimes operates as a label, a distinction, even a "sign of nobility" that validates and consecrates a masculine identity. It becomes a form of nobility and allows one to amass a certain form of capital; as a result, many do no fear going to prison, which they see as some kind of symbolic vocation which itself inspires fear in others.

In a certain way, this transgression of what is ordinarily threatening allows one to position oneself as threatening and thus reverse the stigmatism of prison,

turning it into a source of validation in certain social contexts. Thus, we go from the threat of prison to the threatening inmate: prison accords one the status of a big shot, a tough guy, based on supposed courage, strength, and virility.

While the subsequent commonplaceness and sacredness of prison among certain young men demonstrates that its initial meaning can be changed, for most men prison still represents a threat on another level, especially with regard to their sexual identity. In fact, the unisexual reality of the prison environment forces them to prove that they are men—"real" men, and not "fags"—because there is a belief that there is a great deal of homosexual activity in prisons, and inmates must defend themselves against it. The virility of the outside world is thus reinforced in the prison setting. Inmates must demonstrate that they believe that homosexuality is degrading, and as a result are exaggerated in their homophobia. To participate in the condemnation of homosexuality is to signify that it is dishonorable for oneself. This stigmatization of homosexuality recalls the "fear of the other within us" that must be rejected and expelled; it also expels the fear of the same within. The worrisome similitude that threatens the sexualized identity must be converted into a "strangeness"; as a result, homosexuality is rejected in a process that comes under the domain of the "scapegoat," as described by French philosopher René Girard.

In this sense, homophobia meets the notion of **heterophobia**, of which it is a variant. According to French sociologist Albert Memmi, heterophobia signifies "a diffused and aggressive fear of others." Prison can be perceived as a "house of men" where social relationships and hierarchies are constructed around virility. If there are instances of sexual activity between men in detention areas, they are often the object of a battle of strength and dominance, and are not considered by those involved to be homosexual activity per se, but rather a substitute for heterosexual relations. Such relations seem to be structured on the dual and unequal logic of the "buggerer" and the "buggered," thus whoever is "active" in these sexual relations does not consider himself homosexual, whereas the one who is "passive" is considered to be so, in the sense that he occupies the role of the woman. The taboo and the denial of sexuality in prison is akin to the denial of abuse, in that we can wonder to what extent prison authorities support this. For example, it is well known that sex offenders are the targets of continuous bullying, violence, and rape in prison. Under these conditions, homosexuals, or those perceived as such, are particularly subject to punitive rape, because, as a homosexual, he "was asking for it." In other areas, transvestites were the victims of sexual abuse by prison guards. In the majority of cases, when complaints were filed, the facts were watered down and punishment did not equal the gravity of the crime.

The phenomenon is even more striking in countries where homosexual acts are officially condemned by law, or officiously pursued by **police**. When, after a raid or trial, a homosexual prisoner is sent to prison, other inmates—who quickly discover the reason for his imprisonment (often due more or less to involuntary indiscretion of the authorities)—feel justified in committing violent acts against the newcomer, who often becomes the prison's resident whipping boy, sexual slave, or scapegoat who can be humiliated, exploited, assaulted, or even killed with impunity; as a result, the dominant inmates obtain a symbolic advantage over the inherent social mechanisms and hierarchies within the prison milieu. Thus, the homosexual inmate is doubly condemned: first by the judges or police who sent him to prison, then by his fellow prisoners. This trait is common in prisons of all sizes in all areas of the world, including concentration **camps** and Soviet **gulags**, constituting a very specific phenomenon.

Apparently, what is considered rape in the outside world is not qualified as such in prison, in the sense that the victims are not considered persons within society, but rather as individuals outside of society. This process tends to legitimize unacknowledged abuse and make it commonplace. If penal institutions are uncomfortable around the question of sexual abuse in prisons—in the same way that they are with regard to the problems in the prevention of sexually transmitted diseases—it is also that they are embarrassed by the question of sexuality, which they have repressed for decades while pretending to deal with it. This explains why France's penitential reform of April 2, 1996, according to which "an inmate who commits an obscene or offensive act in view of others is committing a second degree offence," is still in force. Reducing sexuality to an "obscene act" seems anachronistic, but as far as most prisons are concerned, sexuality remains a dirty, shameful, and punishable thing. In one instance, an inmate in France was sentenced to thirty days in solitary confinement for being caught kissing a visiting woman. In another in-

stance, in 1998, an inmate received a ten-day sentence in solitary confinement for presenting a signed petition to the Observatoire international des prisons (a French NGO that monitors prison conditions worldwide) requesting "the right to intimacy in detention." Inmates are thus treated as children, as if they were not entitled to a dignified sexuality.

Paradoxically, many prisons have either implemented or are considering family units for inmates that would allow for the possibility of conjugal visits. In fact, in 1991, the European Committee for the Prevention of Torture and Inhuman or Degrading Treatment or Punishment requested that the French penitentiary administration allow inmates to receive prolonged visits in order to pursue familial and affective relationships (including sexual relations) "in conditions that respect human dignity." The European Commission of Human Rights has repeatedly expressed "that it is essential to the respect of family life" that prisons allow inmates to maintain "contact with their immediate family," that sexuality is an integral part of a person's physical and mental health, that "the development and accomplishment of the personality demand the possibility of developing different types of relationships, including sexual relationships with other persons." In September 1997, the Parliamentary Assembly of the Council of Europe launched a call to "lighten the stigmatism and the perverse effects linked to detention" and incited its member nations to improve the visiting conditions for spouses and their children by "setting up appropriate areas for intimacy." Further, the Council of Europe added, "A study on sexuality in prisons demonstrated that, based on pilot projects in the United States, Canada, Denmark, Sweden, and Mexico, conjugal visits, when based on cultural habits, have positive repercussions on discipline within the establishment." In this sense, permitting sexual relations within the context of prison is a disciplinary measure, a means to maintain order among the prison population. By the same token, the denial of sexual relations in prison hampers all attempts at the prevention of sexual abuse, as well as sexually transmitted diseases, and reinforces homophobic attitudes and behaviors.

It remains that if homophobia is distinct in prison, it is not only due to the specificity of the prison setting, but also, and perhaps most of all, to the disposition acquired on the outside and internalized within: the experience of homophobia in prison only serves to reveal the permanence of a homophobic culture present outside prison walls which updates itself and shows itself in various ways in the fertile ground of the prison environment.

—*Michaël Faure*

Faure, Michaël, Lilian Mathieu, and Daniel Welzer-Lang. *Sexualités et violences en prisons.* Lyon: Observatoire international des prisons/Aléas, 1996.

Foucault, Michel. *Surveiller et punir: naissance de la prison.* Paris: Gallimard, 1975. [Published in the US as *Discipline and Punish: The Birth of the Prison.* New York: Pantheon Books, 1977.]

Girard, René. *Le Bouc émissaire.* Paris: Grasset, 1982. [Published in the US as *The Scapegoat.* Baltimore: Johns Hopkins University Press, 1986.]

———. *La Route antique des hommes pervers.* Paris: Grasset, 1985.

Herzog-Evans, Martine. *L'Intimité du détenu et de ses proches en droit comparé.* Paris: L'Harmattan, 2000.

Lesage de la Haye, Jacques. *La Guillotine du sexe.* Paris: Les Editions de l'Atelier.

Memmi, Albert. *Le Racisme.* Paris: Gallimard 1982 and 1994. [Published in the US as *Racism.* Minneapolis: Univ. of Minnesota Press, 2000.]

Monnereau, Alain. *La Castration pénitentiaire.* Paris: Ed. Lumière et Justice, 1986.

—*Armed Forces; Deportation; European Law; Gulag; Police; Violence.*

PRIVACY

The protection of homosexuality through the right to one's privacy, which both the French Civil Code and the European Convention on Human Rights specifically address, has had limited results to date. Traditionally, the notion of privacy has three distinct components: the right to freedom from interference in the private sphere; the right to keep certain personal information secret; and, finally, the right to freely make choices concerning one's own life. That said, each in their own way, French law and the European Court of Human Rights both contributed to confine the emotional and sexual life between individuals of the same sex to the strict sphere of privacy—the "secret" of the bedroom, as it were—thus reinforcing the idea that homosexuality ought to remain hidden. In fact, while the European court played a major role in condemning the **criminalization** of same-sex relations between consenting adults, it has, on one hand, considered that "sexual life" is in the domain of privacy protected by the Convention, but on the other, has to this day refused gay and lesbian couples the right to have families, which is also set out in this same Convention. This being said, there have also been some promising decisions set down by the Court in recent years: the notion of privacy has been extended to relationships other than those that are strictly intimate, and protection of family life has been extended to the relationship between a gay or lesbian parent and his or her child.

For its part, French law perpetuates a representation of a sexual orientation that is tinged with disgrace. This appears firstly in jurisprudence when it rules that revelations (or even allegations) of an individual's homosexuality violate that individual's right to privacy. In this manner, the "honor" and "reputation" of the individual are purportedly being protected. In accepting homosexuality as a valid circumstance whereby an individual's reputation may be irreparably damaged, a judge actively participates in, if not the construction, at least the perpetuation of a negative and degrading social representation of homosexuality. Further, the restriction in accessing the identity of the partner in a **PaCS** (Pacte civil de solidarité; Civil solidarity pact) agreement, and the impossibility of selecting PaCS participants by their gender (even for statistical purposes) under pretext of protecting a "homosexual vulnerability" reinforce the idea that homosexuality must be occulted. Used ostensibly to protect concerned individuals from disgrace, the notion of privacy is today at risk of perpetuating the idea of the impossibility of being openly gay or lesbian.

From a strategic point of view, shouldn't the preservation of "gay privacy" by law "at all cost" in order to protect an individual from various prejudices be complemented by a denunciation and condemnation of these prejudices as irrational? It would contribute not only to the transformation of social representations of homosexuality, but also to the more effective protection of individuals, regardless of their sexual orientation.

—*Daniel Borrillo and Thomas Formond*

La Pradelle, Géraud de, and Caroline Mécary. *Les Droits des homosexuel(le)s.* Paris: Presses universitaires de France, 1998.

Schutter, Olivier de. "Fonction de juger et nouveaux aspects de la vie privée." In *Homosexualités et droit*. Edited by Daniel Borrillo. Paris: Presses universitaires de France, 1999.

—*Closet, the; Communication; Criminalization; Decriminalization; European Law; Insult; Jurisprudence; Outing; Scandal; Vice.*

PRIVATE LIFE. *See* Privacy

PROSELYTISM

"We must condemn gay proselytism."
—Jean-Marie Le Pen, leader of France's National Front party, 1984

The concept of proselytism, defined here as the zeal employed by those who spread the "faith" in order to gain converts, is one of the most common spaces of homophobic **rhetoric**. Through the pejorative connotations tied to this term, homosexuality is depicted as some underground sect that wishes to spread its insidious ways through various social classes, if not entire nations. In this manner, it becomes increasingly obvious that homosexuality is a universal plot whose objective is to corrupt morals in order to weaken the general public, so that it may better dominate and exploit it. Moreover, this concept of gay proselytism becomes a means to explain the paradoxical "proliferation" of homosexuals despite their inability to produce their own children: "They may not reproduce, but there are more of them every year," French writer Tristan Bernard once said. Regardless, under different forms, this concept was especially useful during periods of "witch hunts" in order to justify various purges of homosexuals: for example, the campaign at the end of the Middle Ages against the *bougres* (Bulgars) (the term originally designated a "**heresy**" that originated in Bulgaria), or in the twentieth century, most notably in Nazi Germany, but also in the Soviet Union, and in the US under McCarthyism.

The metaphor of gay proselytism is linked to the idea of a counter-religion—heretical, of course—which attempts to spread a faith that goes **against nature**. Even if it appears archaic, this phraseology is still nonetheless common today, particularly among the American religious right, in the fundamentalist circles close to

Opus Dei, and in certain Christian, Charismatic, and radical movements. In 1998, during the annual conference of the Concerned Women for America, Wilma Leftwich suggested the existence of an international plot to "abolish the sovereignty of the United States, forbid Christians from practicing their religion, and reduce the American population through the general accessibility of abortion, the sterilization of women with many children, and the promotion of homosexuality." Similarly, in a book by conservative politician William Dannemayer entitled *Shadow in the Land: Homosexuality in America*, often cited by the religious right, gays and lesbians are portrayed as a sort of "army of Genghis Khan"; the author further states, "We must defeat militant homosexuality, or else it will overwhelm us." In a similar vein, right-wing French politician Christine **Boutin** (who led the charge against the **PaCS** civil union proposal) wrote in her book *Le "Mariage" des homosexuels?* (The "marriage" of homosexuals?) of the "followers of homosexuality," describing a sort of homosexual cult and even a "homosexual propaganda," terminology that recalls medieval concepts in which sodomites are the most frightening members of pernicious sects seeking to recruit new initiates; from this, a number of expressions emerged, such as "the heresy of love," which to a certain extent are still used today.

But starting in the nineteenth century, the religious and moral paradigm making sodomy a sin or **vice** was increasingly challenged by the medical and psychiatric discourse that views homosexuality as pathological (a concept whose historical development was analyzed by Michel Foucault). Under such conditions, these new **medical** theories in which homosexuality was considered innate could have undermined old moral and religious beliefs which construed homosexuality as an acquired disposition under pernicious and proselyte influences. But in reality, both views were able to coexist, whereby homosexuals were now paradoxically perceived as ill and perverted individuals seeking to "teach" their illness to others. In fact, far from being dismissed by the "scientific" discourse, the accusation of proselytism seemed to be confirmed by certain medical theories that clearly distinguished the inversion, mental pathology, or congenital defect from the **perversion**, which would be a type of voluntary illness, a deliberate inversion of the self, and of others. But where the inverts should be pitied, the perverts—who are future corrupters—are the real threat by virtue of their proselytism. With this medicalization of the notion of perversion—soon to be assumed (though not without ambiguity) by **psychoanalysis**—gay proselytism was thus disqualified by both religious morality and medical discourse, which mutually reinforced each other in the construction of a new homophobic rhetoric.

In France, this new rhetoric was expressed emblematically in **literature**, which has historically often been criticized as one of the principle vehicles for gay proselytism. In a vehement essay, Paul Souday, literary critic for *Les Temps*, railed against André **Gide**'s *Les Faux Monnayeurs* (*The Counterfeiters*) and this increasingly intolerable "tendency"; and in 1926, the French magazine *Les Marges* launched a general inquiry into the "homosexual preoccupation" in French literature of the time, to which many authors, such as François Mauriac, Pierre Drieu La Rochelle, Henri Barbusse, and Willy (pseud.), responded. For many of them, this growing "preoccupation" was in fact a form of proselytism. Barbusse, for example, spoke of a "phalanx of decadent homosexuals." Gérard Bauer said, "It cannot be denied that homosexuals have currently become more assured and have adopted an audacious proselytism," which he attributed for the most part to the influence of Proust. Others pointed to other areas as the cause of this problem. Thus, according to Pierre Dominique, "the extreme freedom of modern morals, and the weakness or nonexistence of religious morals, either natural or civic, open the way to this proselytism. As a result, many people who are physiologically normal become, under the actions of the odd apostles, homosexuals by curiosity." Camille Mauclair denounced these "apostles of vice obeying a desire for a public ministry concomitant with their mental and sexual state. The invert wants to convert; for this, (he needs) a special literature." For this reason, according to Charles-Henry Hirsch, "Doctors and legislators should work together in order to stave off the propagation of this disgusting aberration: a mental home for the irresponsible, **prison** for the conscious corruptors." These few examples, which accurately reflect the mindset on this question and, notably, the link between **inversion**, perversion, and conversion, illuminate the vividness of social discourse surrounding gay proselytism, as well as the singular expression of moral and medical conceptions on this issue.

This vision continued into the twentieth century, giving way to terrible persecutions, notably under the Third Reich. In fact, in its medico-moral formulation, the homosexual question constitutes a significant preoccupation for SS leader Heinrich **Himmler**, who intended to save Aryan youth from a proselytism whose insidious audacity threatened to debase the entire nation: as a result, he attempted to "cure" those who could have been gay, and sent the others to concentration **camps**. This concept arose in Communist ideology as well, often with formulations that were comparable in their **violence** and their consequences, as well as in numerous speeches during the **McCarthy** years in the US. Of course, the idea is not to compare entirely different regimes, but to underline the remarkable recurrence of the same argument in completely different contexts, each of them linked by an exacerbated, imperious nationalism that was concerned with preserving and increasing, at any expense, the power of the nation, even if this meant the sacrifice of individual freedoms on the altar of *ratio sexualis*.

However, in addition to nationalist, authoritarian, or dictatorial regimes, accusations of gay proselytism have also been heard in more liberal nations, which had the effect of extending the reach of homophobic condemnations that were already present. This tendency is premised on the idea that homosexual practices are often difficult to prove and condemn, especially where they are not officially outlawed. By suggesting the existence of gay proselytism, however, many pro-homosexual actions and views, notably in gay newspapers, can be condemned in complete legality, thus relativizing the degree of liberty enjoyed by *de facto* homosexuality in many countries where it is legal.

In France, although the **army** no longer forbids homosexual practices, any soldier accused of gay "proselytism" is excluded from the possibility of promotion. Similarly, though homosexual practices have been progressively decriminalized in England since 1967, Section 28, passed into law in 1988 and repealed in 2000, forbid the "promotion" of homosexuality in schools ("promotion" here means any view on the subject that does not *a priori* underline the reprehensible character of this practice). In the same vein, in 1996, under European pressure, the Parliament of the new Romanian democracy voted to **decriminalize** homosexual relations. However, Article 200 stipulated that "any person having incited, by seduction or any other method, another to have homosexual relations with them, having formed propaganda **associations** or having, in any way whatsoever, proselytized to this end," is subject to imprisonment for up to five years.

This law was potentially more repressive than before, as even if it no longer condemned the acts, it punished incitement, seduction, associations, views, intentions—in short, any semblance of gay life. Article 200 was repealed in 2001.

Under these conditions, accusations of proselytism work in the same way as accusations of indecency, sexual assault, and indecent offense, resulting in the criminalization of homosexuality when in fact it is not legally criminalized. Though, *a priori*, they appear as a euphemized form of homophobic rhetoric, these repressive views are in reality even more harsh, as they allow for a vague and arbitrary legal interpretation, whereby an overzealous police force could interpret any and all examples of homosexuality as being a form of proselytism, and therefore criminal.

Given this problem of interpretation, the very definition of gay proselytism comes into question. Moreover, during the last twenty years, a new front has appeared in the rhetoric of proselytism: in addition to the notion of sexual proselytism, there is now also the concept of cultural proselytism as a result of the increasing visibility and self-confidence of gay and lesbian culture. It is by no means a fluke that such accusations often crystallize around Gay and Lesbian Pride parades. From this perspective, it is not just sexuality that is being condemned, but also political opinions and a particular **philosophy**.

This new proselytism appears to its critics as more dangerous than its predecessor. At least "back then," gay propaganda was shameful and miserable, originating in the slums and the shady districts, limiting itself to sex. Today, it is displayed in the full light of day, on the streets, on television and in movies…. In short, "Sodom claims the right of the city," according to Hervé Lécuyer in a 1998 article published in *Economica*. This new form of gay proselytism is thus even more effective in that this culture looks happy; therein lies the rub. It is this concept that some Christian movements find the most difficult of all, particularly those in the American **ex-gay** movement, as Tim LaHaye expressed in his evocatively titled book *The Unhappy Gays*. According to STRAIGHT (Society To Remove All Immoral Godless Homosexual Trash), a Christian association that promotes **heterosexism** and fights homosexuality, gays are in fact SAD (Sodomites Against Decency), i.e. fundamentally miserable (in every sense of the word). Similarly, in France, in an essay entitled "Ne deviens pas gay, tu finiras triste"

(Don't become gay, you'll end up sad), the anonymous author, a "repentant" homosexual, concludes by affirming, "I am talking about the strangers who protect the illusion that homosexuality is a road like any other towards happiness and, more than protecting it, seek to spread it." In this manner, gay proselytism that spreads the idea of pride and happiness is thus deceitful and wholly intolerable. Beyond then the question of sexual "recruitment"—which today is generally regarded as absurd—if by affirming their freedom, rights, and culture, gays and lesbians are proselytizing, then yes, it is necessary to recognize the existence of gay proselytism, which is fully comparable to every cultural, social, or political movement in general. In this sense, the affirmations of every minority—be it regional, black, Jewish, Arabic— can naturally be construed as proselyte actions. The dominant culture enjoys the epistemological privilege of self-transparency, which allows that culture to denounce any alternative, heterodoxy, or minority proposition as propaganda; by the same token, its own majority position is considered "natural," obvious, and self-evident. Consequently, the argument of gay proselytism reveals that those who use it wish to impose a **symbolic order** laced with obvious yet hidden heterosexist commands. At the same time, the same argument obscures the undeniable fact of heterosexual proselytism, an inconsistency which André Gide revealed in *Corydon*:

> Just think how in our society, in our behavior, everything predestines one sex to the other; everything teaches heterosexuality, everything urges it upon us, everything provokes us to it; theater, literature, newspapers, paraded examples provided by our elders, the ritual of our drawing rooms and our street corners. *Given all that, failing to fall in love is a sign of ill breeding!* crows Dumas *fils* in his preface to *La Question d'argent*. Yet if a young man finally succumbs to so much collusion in the world around him, he refused to grant that his decision was influenced, his desire manipulated if he ends up making his choice in the "right" direction! And if, in spite of advice, invitations, provocations of all kinds, he should manifest a homosexual tendency, you immediately blame his reading or some other influence (and you argue in the same way for an entire nation, an entire people); it has to be an acquired taste, you insist; he must have been taught it; you refuse to

admit that he might have invented it all by himself.

Therefore, in the idea that heterosexuals are in fact unconscious proselytizers, the accusation of proselytism could equally be laid against both parties: yes, gays and lesbians are proselytizers, but heterosexuals are even more so, without knowing it. In reality, however, the issue is not who proselytizes the most, because proselytism does not designate an objective, but a value judgment. Through the argument of proselytism, there is a symbolic struggle for dominance whose legitimacy is the fundamental question. The pejorative connotations tied to the term presuppose an illegitimate content. Therefore, there are two possibilities: either homosexuality is legitimate, and its social, cultural, and political expression is as well, or homosexuality is illegitimate, and its social, cultural, and political expression is in fact nothing but abusive proselytism. And that, generally, is what conservatives such as Christine Boutin stumble over when they affirm, rather symptomatically, that "A right to homosexuality … does not legitimize gay proselytism." In reality, however, it is clear that Boutin's concept of this "right to homosexuality" is based on a logic of **tolerance**; that is to say, she does not recognize it at all as a right. Therein is the rub. If homosexuality is merely tolerated, gay and lesbian rhetoric will always appear to be a form of proselytism, necessarily abusive and condemnable, as Jean-Marie Le Pen would have it. If homosexuality is a legitimate disposition, the very idea of gay proselytism must be taken for what it is: a concept that is politically dangerous, but intellectually ridiculous.

—*Louis-Georges Tin*

Boutin, Christine. *Le "Mariage" des homosexuels? CUCS, PIC, PACS et autres projets législatifs*. Paris: Critérion, 1998.

Foucault, Michel. *Les Anormaux, Cours au Collège de France*. Paris: Gallimard, Le Seuil, 1999. [Published in the US as *Abnormal: Lectures at the Collège de France, 1974–1975*. New York: Picador, 2003.]

Fourest, Caroline. *Foi contre choix, la droite religieuse et le mouvement "prolife" aux Etats-Unis*. Paris: Ed. Golias, 2001.

Gide, André. *Corydon*. Paris. Gallimard, 1926. [Published in the US as *Corydon*. Urbana, IL: Univ. of Illinois Press, 2003.]

Herman, Didi. *The Antigay Agenda*. Chicago/London: Univ. of Chicago Press, 1997.

Himmler, Heinrich. *Discours secrets*. Paris: Gallimard, 1978.

Krinsky, Charles. "Recruitment Myth." In *Gay Histories and Cultures*. Edited by Georges E. Haggerty. New York/London: Garland, 2000.

Lever, Maurice. *Les Bûchers de Sodome*. Paris: Fayard, 1985.

Les Marges, Mar–Apr 1926. Re-edited in *Cahiers GaiKitschCamp*. Lille, no. 19 (1993).

Rich, Adrienne. "La Contrainte à l'hétérosexualité et l'existence lesbienne." *Nouvelles questions féministes*, no. 1 (1981). [Published in the US as "Compulsory Heterosexuality and Lesbian Experience," *Signs* 5, no. 4 (Summer 1980).]

Sébastien. *Ne deviens pas gay, tu finiras triste*. Paris: Ed. François-Xavier de Guibert, 1998.

Tin, Louis-Georges. "L'Invention de la culture hétérosexuelle," *Les Temps modernes*, 2003.

Wittig, Monique. *La Pensée straight* [1980]. New edition. Paris: Balland, 2001.

—*Closet, the; Contagion; Exhibitionism; Heresy; Heterosexism; Himmler, Heinrich; Peril; Perversion; Rhetoric; Sterility; Theology; Tolerance; Vice.*

PROTESTANTISM

Because Protestantism was based on the theological and moral criticism of the Catholic clergy's "abuses," it was hardly predisposed to be lenient toward sodomites. The comparison of Catholic Rome to the town of Sodom was a common theme in the rhetoric of the Protestant Reformed Church of France, theologians such as John Calvin and Martin Luther, humanists such as Henri Estienne, and poets such as Agrippa d'Aubigné, who violently criticized France's King **Henri III** (widely believed to be homosexual) in *Les Tragiques*; they did not want to miss a chance to deplore the corruption of morals, in particular the influence of sodomites. A famous **scandal** was caused when Théodore de Bèze (1519–1605), an early Calvinist reformer in France, wrote verses that referred to his roguish preference for Audebert, his **favorite**, rather than Candida, his mistress. The reaction was such that de Bèze was made to issue a resounding criticism of himself, condemning these thoughts as temporary distractions—the fruits of a sinful soul—before he was permitted to become Calvin's successor as head of the Geneva Academy and the Protestant Churches of Switzerland and France. Further, during the sixteenth and seventeenth centuries in Protestant Geneva, several men and women were beheaded, hanged, or drowned because of their alleged acts **against nature**. Meanwhile in England in 1533, King Henry VIII, the monarch behind the Anglican schism, promulgated the Buggery Act, a sodomy law that was the first civil legislation against homosexuals in the country, which entrenched England's homophobic legislation; it was declared perpetual some years later by his daughter, Elizabeth I. Protestant homophobia lived on for centuries thereafter; in 1930, Théodore de Felice of France wrote in *Le Protestantisme et la question sexuelle* (Protestantism and the sexual question): "The aversion for the opposite sex, demonstrated by homosexuals, clearly classifies them among the ill, and moreover among the dangerously ill, because they constantly search for new partners whom they will make abnormal in turn." Likewise, in 1936, Georges Portal showed how difficult it was to reconcile Protestant ethics and homosexual life in a novel entitled *Un Protestant*. Under these conditions, it is clear that the climate of moral austerity imposed by the Protestant religion in general was hardly conducive to recognizing any type of sexual pluralism.

Today, however, compared with the Catholic tradition, the philosophy developed by Protestant thinkers is characterized by a somewhat more favorable position on homosexuality. The Protestant interpretation of the **Bible** on this question differs appreciably from the Catholic perspective. And even if homosexuality's status varies from one Protestant group to another, it is nonetheless quite remarkable that pastors have been blessing same-sex unions for a long time. Several reasons can explain this.

First of all, the explosion of Protestant groups and the limitations of the Protestant hierarchy allowed the development of a certain autonomy on questions of morality. Characteristically, the very Catholic writer Paul Claudel wrote a reproachful letter to André **Gide**, dated March 9, 1914: "You are especially a victim of … your Protestant heredity, which has accustomed you to look only within yourself for the rule of your actions."

Also, the notions of personal freedom and the protection of one's right to **privacy** are fundamental in Protestant culture. This reformist religion had to harshly assert its right to exist; as a result, the freedom of thought, consciousness, and expression were considered essential rights. This concept of individual autonomy included protection from state intervention in the public sphere. The protection of privacy, which became fundamental in predominantly Protestant countries, thus figured in Protestant arguments favor-

ing the **decriminalization** of homosexuality. The reformist culture took into consideration the danger of becoming a scapegoat on this issue, mainly because Protestants had long been the targets of their political and religious opponents. Thus today, arguments favoring same-sex **marriage** resemble arguments in support of Protestants during the Middle Ages, who were considered second-class citizens at the time. As such, we can agree with judicial sciences professor Daniel Borrillo that marriage is an institution that allows the political integration of various constituents of the population. What is most at stake in this parallel, in the recognition of minorities in order to counteract negative influences, is the consciousness and acceptance of social pluralism.

Finally, in Protestantism, celibacy is not mandatory for its clergy, and the issue of sexual "difference" is not considered major. While the concepts of the heterosexual couple and the **family** are closely related in Catholicism (the purpose of the union of two people is reproduction), they are more distant in the Protestant context (the purpose of the couple is the couple itself). Thus, the distinction between the notions of couple and family evolved faster in predominantly Protestant countries, where marriage is perceived as a contract between two people, unlike the Catholic perspective, which considered it a sacrament.

The Renaissance and the Reformation, in a context of political, sociological, economic, and cultural disruption, promoted the contractual approach to marriage which influenced French revolutionaries, who as a result established secular marriage, by which marriage was no longer perceived as a divine sacrament. The Protestant world also offered a much more favorable breeding ground than Catholicism for the emerging concept of human rights, eventually allowing the recognition of same-sex unions.

It is, however, necessary to qualify that at the present time, Protestant congregations that celebrate these marriages remain rare; most of them celebrate only blessings. Moreover, depending on the country, these marriages are not recognized by the state in the same way as heterosexual marriage is; furthermore, in certain countries, such as France, legislation requires a civil marriage before a religious rite, and because French civil law does not recognize same-sex marriage, a religious gay marriage is impossible.

The first models of same-sex unions in contemporary Europe were legalized in Denmark (1989), Norway

(1993), Sweden (1994), and the Netherlands (1997), all of which are predominantly Protestant countries. Also, Iceland's 1996 law legalizing civil unions and the Netherland's 2002 law granting same-sex couples the right to adopt (the same year same-sex marriage became legal) are positive developments with regard to LGBT **parenting**.

In Europe, and more particularly in Scandinavian countries, Protestant congregations, with their considerable political influence, gradually considered the spiritual demands of gays and lesbians. In 1997, the Northern Protestant Church of Germany decided to legitimize the blessing of gay unions for the first time. Also, Lutheran priests in Stockholm have been blessing same-sex couples for some years now.

In France, recent Protestant tradition has also been to bless same-sex unions. The first such blessed unions were in fact celebrated in 1974; however, such blessing confers neither rights nor duties toward either parties, and as such the act only has moral and spiritual meaning. In the United States, several Protestant congregations celebrate same-sex unions. These religious ceremonies have all the similarities of a church wedding; websites and other sources offer practical advice on the various types of ceremonies available, as well as information on businesses that specialize in organizing gay marriages. The Unitarian Universalist Church, a liberal-minded North American movement, has been blessing gay couples since the 1970s. The Universal Fellowship of Metropolitan Community Churches first gained notice by marrying several same-sex couples during New York's Gay and Lesbian Pride in 1994 (which commemorated the twenty-fifth anniversary of **Stonewall**). These religious same-sex celebrations contributed to the religious "revitalization" of the faiths, at a time when gays and lesbians felt they were being ignored, if not opposed, by traditional congregations.

Nevertheless, the degree to which the consecration of gay unions is accepted varies depending on the congregations and countries. For example, in Denmark, 33% of those polled were in favor of allowing traditional religious marriage for gays and lesbians, and 21% believe in a religious ceremony specific to same-sex couples; however, the majority of those surveyed were opposed to any religious same-sex ceremonies whatsoever.

Moreover, in the United States, while numerous Protestant movements sided with gays and lesbians, there were others that took part in violent homophobic crusades related to the religious right and/or the Moral Majority. These movements, which have existed in one form or another since the days of **McCarthyism**, have been reenergized in recent years, beginning with Bill Clinton's presidency, who, in spite of himself, triggered an unprecedented storm of controversy when he tried to abolish the laws forbidding gays and lesbians from serving in the **military** (resulting in the compromised policy of "Don't Ask, Don't Tell"). The issue of gay **marriage** also aroused new resentful and violent homophobic campaigns led by evangelicals. Many of those who had previously worked on behalf of campaigns against abortion or civil rights gladly joined this new battle which attracted much media attention; among them was televangelist and onetime presidential candidate Pat Robertson who, in 1998, during a broadcast, announced that God would send a tornado or a meteorite upon the city of Orlando if gays and lesbian shops there continued to display their rainbow flags; and Pat **Buchanan**, another broadcaster and politician who widely contributed to the spread of homophobic ideas within the Republican Party before becoming the Reform Party's candidate in the 2000 presidential election.

With a more or less ecumenical base, the Christian Coalition of America circulated a vehemently homophobic video mixed with medical and moral rhetoric entitled *The Gay Agenda*. The video, which sold 60,000 copies in less than three months, was excerpted widely on Christian television programs and was distributed free to all members of the country's House of Representatives. This same Christian Coalition also published a pamphlet entitled *The Gay Manifesto*—reminiscent of the anti-Semitic *Protocols of the Elders of Zion*—a gross forgery on the malefic "plot" of homosexuals to take over the world. In 1995, *Newsweek* magazine published the unfortunate results of a survey in which 21% of Americans, and 43% of Evangelical Christians, stated that they believed that the gay and lesbian movement was "Satan incarnate." Finally, there are some religious currents, such as the Christian Reconstructionists, that demand capital punishment for those who engage in practices against nature.

Such discourses are not without impact in a country where, until recently, many states still upheld religious-based anti-sodomy laws which, until a fateful Supreme Court decision on June 26, 2003, they certainly had no intention of abolishing. And on the "question of the year," as the debate of gays in the military was called,

Bill Clinton was forced to compromise, confirming the exclusion of gays and lesbians. Further, certain states which had initially favored same-sex marriage decided to renege on their commitment, while others approved laws forbidding any legislation to this effect; boycott campaigns were launched against companies or **media** deemed to be "favorable" to homosexuals; hiring **discrimination** policies were put in place, notably in **schools**, in the name of the "interest of the child"; "reparative therapies" proposed by **ex-gays**, a mix of **psychoanalysis** and wayward religion, multiplied; and most disturbingly, homophobic murders remain common if not more numerous. These recent examples of homophobia can be linked to strong religious sentiment, including among some Protestants, which constantly refers to biblical sources and puritanical traditions, and which does not hesitate to contend that "God hates fags."

Under these conditions, the attitude of Protestants on the issue of homosexuality is naturally difficult to generalize, given that Protestantism has promulgated some of the most liberal statements on the subject, as well as some of the most repressive. This contradiction can be explained in that the homophobia which flows through Protestant culture in fact stems from underlying and diverse causes which widely surpass strict religious faith. In the end, religious homophobia is not simply a question of religion.

—*Flora Leroy-Forgeot and Louis-Georges Tin*

Abelove, Henry. *The Evangelist of Desire: John Wesley and the Methodists.* Stanford: Stanford Univ. Press, 1990.

Aubigné, Agrippa d'. *Les Tragiques* [1616]. Paris: Gallimard, 1995.

Ben Barka, Mokhtar. *Les Nouveaux rédempteurs: Le Fondamentalisme américain aux Etats-Unis.* Paris: Les Editions de l'Atelier, 1998.

Bèze, Théodore de. "Son affection pour Candide et Audebert" [1548]. *Anthologie de la poésie du XVIe siècle.* Edited by Jean Céard and Louis-Georges Tin. Paris: Gallimard, 2003.

Bull, Chris, and John Gallagher. *Perfect Enemies, The Religions Right, the Gay Movement, and the Polilics of the 1990's.* New York: Crown Publishers, 1996.

Cecco, John de, ed. *Bashers, Baiters and Bigots: Homophobia in American Society.* Binghamton, NY: Harrington Park Press, 1985.

Estienne, Henri. *Apologie pour Hérodote* (1566). Paris: Liseux, 1879.

Felice, Théodore de. *Le Protestantisme et la question sexuelle.* Paris: Librairie Fischbacher, 1930.

Fourest, Caroline. *Foi contre choix, la droite religieuse et le mouvement "prolife" aux Etats-Unis.* Paris: Ed. Golias, 2001.

Gide, André. *Si le grain ne meurt.* Paris: Gallimard, 1926. [Published in the UK as *If It Die.* London: Secker & Warburg, 1950.]

Herman, Didi. *The Antigay Agenda.* Chicago/London: Univ. of Chicago Press, 1997.

Leroy-Forgeot, Flora. *Histoire juridique de l'homosexualité en Europe.* Paris: Presses universitaires de France, 1997.

———. *Les Enfants du PACS.* Paris: L'Atelier de l'Archer, Presses universitaires de France, 1999.

———, and Caroline Mécary. *Le Couple homosexuel et le droit.* Paris: Odile Jacob, 2001.

Percey, William A. "Protestantism." In *Encyclopedia of Homosexuality.* Edited by Wayne R. Dynes. New York: Garland Publishers, 1990.

Portal, Georges. *Un protestant.* Paris: Denoël, 1936.

Puff, Helmutt. *Sodomy in Reformation Germany and Switzerland, 1400–1600.* Chicago: Chicago Series on Sexuality and Society, 2003.

Schouten, H. J. "La Soi-Disant Pédérastie du réformateur Jean Calvin," *Arcadie,* no. 105 (1962).

—*Bible, the; England; Germany; North America; Europe, Northern; Judaism; Orthodoxy; Switzerland; Theology.*

PSYCHIATRY

During the second half of the nineteenth century, psychiatry seized upon the question of homosexuality in order to reconstruct it as a mental illness. This appropriation lasted a very long time, during which psychiatry remained the preeminent paradigmatic discipline for the medicalization of homosexuality. Psychiatry was responsible for the essential theoretical data that has been generally accepted by other medical disciplines; this data relates to such issues as the pathological nature and innate character of homosexuality, its hereditary risk, and the concept of gender **inversion**. As well, psychiatry was responsible for many proposed **treatments**, which include aversion therapy, electroshock therapy, lobotomies, hypnosis, psychotherapy, and everything else that resulted from analytic therapy becoming increasingly instrumental among psychiatrists. Most of all, these theories and treatments enabled psychiatry to assume enormous control over homosexuals within its care, both male and female. Certainly, the genetic theories led to the forced **sterilization** of some individuals, and the hormonal hypothesis resulted in the death of some subjects used as guinea pigs, but neither of these instances negated the fact that psychiatry held sway over homosexuality around the world for nearly a century. It was consistently the psychiatrist to whom the adolescent or adult who felt an attraction to persons of the same sex would be referred, not only by those around him or her, but also by his or her own volition. As a consequence, the removal of homosexuality from the American Psychiatric Association's list of mental illnesses in 1973 is a profound moment in the history of gay liberation, almost as important as **Stonewall**.

Since the emergence of the concept of "alienism" (the study or treatment of diseases of the mind) in the eighteenth century, homosexual relations have been the object of particular attention by psychiatrists. Nevertheless, until the second half of the nineteenth century, these types of relations were, at most, perceived as a "distasteful" behavior that could certainly be caused by mental illness, in the same way that alcohol abuse, or even an overabundance of heterosexual intercourse, could. Further, masturbation, considered the great "sexual" scourge that invariably led to insanity and death, received far more attention from the medical community during this period.

Conversely, the last quarter of the nineteenth century saw a reversal of this trend, when homosexuality became a major subject of concern for psychiatry. The theory of **degeneracy** (put forward by Austrian-French psychiatrist Bénédict Augustin Morel), the publicity arising from various criminal or political scandals involving homosexual relations, and the transformations in the structure of gender relations all paved the way for psychiatry's interest in the subject of homosexuality. In fact psychiatry superseded the discipline of **legal medicine** which at one time was the principal medical branch involved in work on homosexuality, and was more able to propose etiology and treatments.

The central figure in psychiatry's appropriation of homosexuality was Richard von Krafft-Ebing, the Austrio-German psychiatrist. His famous work *Psychopathia Sexualis*, a study of sexual perversity, was first published in 1886, then constantly updated throughout the next century, even after his death by his disciple Albert Moll. It was a bestseller from the start,

a success that went well beyond professional medical circles. Its analysis of homosexuality can be summarized in three major points:

1. Homosexuality is a sexual **perversion** among others, following the example of fetishism or sadomasochism, but at the same time it constitutes a theoretical model for all other perversions. In this sense, it is a mental illness for which the individual cannot be held responsible.

2. Homosexuality is congenital, that is to say innate, and its etiology inscribes itself in the framework of pathological heredity within the theory of degeneracy. Thus, it is the product of the progressive delinquency of a family line.

3. Rarely curable, the clinical manifestation of homosexuality recalls an inversion of gender, even if the majority of homosexuals preserve the appearance and psychic life of their gender.

In the book, all the keynotes of scientific homophobia—homosexuality's pathological nature, heredity, gender inversion—were present and elaborated upon. If Krafft-Ebing appears to be a doctor whom we cannot easily qualify as being virulently homophobic—unlike sexologist Auguste Ambroise Tardieu and his treatise, or the criminal intentions of the Nazi medicine—he is nonetheless the one who defined the three points above that would subsequently allow medicine in general, and psychiatry in particular, to be the privileged technology used to control and socially exclude homosexuals. Moreover, paradoxically, Krafft-Ebing's concepts were considered progressive by the homosexuals of his time, many of whom risked imprisonment in their countries, in imperial Germany in particular. In a way, this phenomenon came from the ambivalence felt by the very first gay movement and its leader, sexologist Magnus **Hirschfeld,** who considered the effeminate homosexual to be an "accident of evolution," thus allowing psychiatry to gain a better foothold on the issue, being that it was accepted by homosexuals themselves. Psychiatrists Jean-Martin Charcot and Valentin Magnan, at the frontier between psychiatry and neurology, pushed the etiological issue further by suggesting a cerebral cause for the "inversion of genital awareness." For Magnan, along with nymphomania, satyriasis, and **exhibitionism**, homosexuality was the result of spinal-cerebral dysfunction. This is the first mention of the idea of the "homosexual brain," which would be used to justify lobotomy as a treatment for homosexuality; today, it is again the subject of attention as a result of the published work of British neuroscientist Simon LeVay on the hypothalamus of gay men. The return of a theory of a cerebral cause for sexual orientation—by an openly gay researcher no less—in order to once again justify the "natural" character of homosexuality, reveals the longevity of psychiatric concepts that originated in the nineteenth century, proving once again the paradoxical dimensions of medicine with regard to homosexuality, both a justification for repression and a means of liberation.

—*Pierre-Olivier de Busscher*

Bayer, Ronald. *Homosexuality and American Psychiatry: The Politics of Diagnosis*. Princeton, NJ: Princeton Univ. Press, 1987.

Bonello, Christian. "Du médecin légiste à l'aliéniste. L'homosexualité sous le regard de la médecine au XIXe siècle." In *Homosexualités: expression/répression*. Edited by Louis-Georges Tin. Paris: Stock, 2000.

Bullough, Vern. *Science in the Bedroom: A History of Sex Research*. New York: Basic Books, 1994.

Charcot, Jean Martin, and Valentin Magnan. *Inversion du sens génital et autres perversions sexuelles* (1883). Paris: Frénésie Editions, 1987.

Duberman, Martin, and Ellen Herman, eds. *Psychiatry, Psychology, and Homosexuality (Issues in Lesbian and Gay Life)*. New York: Chelsea House Publishing, 1995.

Krafft-Ebing, Richard von. *Psychopathia sexualis. Etude médico-légale à l'usage des médecins et des juristes*. Paris: Payot, 1950. [Published in English as *Psychopathia Sexualis*.]

Foucault, Michel. *Histoire de la sexualité*. Vol. I : "La volonté de savoir." Paris: Gallimard, 1976. [Published in the US as *The History of Sexuality*. New York: Pantheon Books, 1978.]

Lanteri-Laura, Georges. *Lectures des perversions: histoire de leur appropriation médicale*. Paris: Masson, 1979.

Steakley, James. *The Homosexual Emancipation Movement in Germany*. New York: Arno, 1975.

—*Biology; Degeneracy; Endocrinology; Ex-Gay; Fascism; Genetics; Hirschfeld, Magnus; Inversion; Medicine; Medicine, Legal; Perversions; Psychoanalysis; Psychology; Treatment.*

PSYCHOANALYSIS

In 1973, the philosopher Gilles Deleuze wrote to Michel Cressole, founding member of the Front homosexuel d'action revolutionnaire (FHAR; Homosexual Revolutionary Action Front), these few words: "Subject of an intimate joke, how can the boys of FHAR, the girls of MLF [Mouvement de liberation des femmes; Women's Liberation Movement], and so many others, get analyzed? Doesn't it bother them? Do they believe in it?" At first glance, we can easily understand the joke, given that the different psychoanalytical vulgates seem to have rivaled each other in homophobia with a fury that borders on the comical. Since its invention, from Freud to Ernest Jones to Tony Anatrella and Daniel Sibony, the different currents of psychoanalysis have never ceased to explain:

First, that **inversion**, then homosexuality, is a regressive form of sexuality (infantile fixation of a partial urge and Oedipal identification with the mother or the father) serving as an etiological factor for a majority of mental "illnesses" (**perversion** by non-repression of the partial urge, hysteria and neurosis by partial identification, and psychosis, paranoia mostly, by debarment or denial of the Name-of-the-Father). Second, that homosexuality represents the structure of perversion *par excellence,* that is to say the reverse of neurosis (he who does not repress), this meaning being often confused with its moral meaning (he who ignores pity and wishes bad for the sake of bad through an alliance between cruelty and erotic urges, according to the Freudian theory of sexuality). Third, that it is nonetheless possible, even if difficult, to try to "treat" homosexuals, on condition that they be "sincere" (which Freud's patients were not), be it without their consent (in the United States, the most reactionary psychoanalysts built clinic-prisons to this effect). Fourth, that the suffering of homosexuals does not come from the society that represses them or from arbitrary moral standards that degrade them, but rather from themselves and their own history with the Oedipus Complex. Therefore, they cannot have any legitimate political demands: it is a private affair. Fifth, that, in a sense, homosexuality does not truly exist, as homosexual desires are not true desires, they are but a substitute of other oedipal desires of heterosexual essence: what the homosexual female desires is the phallus, what the homosexual male desires is his mother, to the point of identification (for sodomy), or the breast as partial object (for fellatio). Sixth (and it is a beauty), that homosexuals can nonetheless take an active role in "the general interests of humanity," but on the specific condition that "they fight their tendency to exercise their sexuality," as Freud said with regard to the case of Daniel Paul Schreber.

In short, if it is true that the Unconscious ignores contradiction, we must admit that psychoanalysis is not any more familiar with it: homosexuality would thus be the source or the symptom of illness (neurosis and psychosis), all the while being the opposite (a perversion); therefore, it is not completely an illness, although it can be treated; and it thus does not truly exist (neither politically, nor truly in a private way), but it *must* be sublimated. What a joke! More so that psychoanalysis, atheist in its origins, thus seems to imitate the worst religious casuistry: How can one welcome homosexuals while pushing them away? How can one condemn them (they are perverse) and forgive them as they know not what they do (they are ill)?

And yet, despite all these tortures, all these poisons, it is quite difficult to brand, univocally and without distinction, psychoanalysis as homophobic. First of all, it has mended its ways—as a business of sexuality, it has had to adapt to the evolution of morals in Western societies: the offices of analysts are well frequented, and of their own accord (the Freudian fashion of accepting perverts by request of the Father being rather outdated), by homosexuals, some of whom, in all good conscience, do not hesitate to open up shop. Thus, in the middle of an ocean of psychoanalytical homophobia, there have certainly been islands of explicit anti-homophobia (isolated at first, such as Georg Groddeck or Otto Rank, but more numerous today). But first and foremost, deep down, it is not certain that psychoanalysis had been constituently homophobic since the beginning, and that, for at least three reasons.

The first holds to a historical principle of justice: we cannot blame all of psychoanalysis for the prejudices of the bourgeoisie of the early twentieth century, and it would be a caricature to present it solely under its repressive or rigidly conventional view of homosexuality. Not only did it sometimes constitute a place of defense, of listening, and of self-reconstitution for many homosexuals, but, significantly, it is not certain that this "theory" is necessarily homophobic: by over-reading the analyses of homosexuals, overt or supposedly repressed, we forget to read the analyses of others, which often are not worth much more; in other words, "true"

psychoanalysis is more Augustinian than Thomistic, for it is all sexuality that it envelopes in the same suspicion (and in the same familialist conception). The second reason is both more speculative and more tactical: Is it certain that psychoanalysis has the exclusive effect of "normalizing" and "depoliticizing" homosexuality? By recognizing both the universality of homosexual urges and the universality of every urge to turn away from its initial objective, does it not on the contrary tend—in spite of itself or not—to establish the fundamentally subversive character of all freely affirmed sexuality? As to the third reason, it is essentially strategic. It may be in the best interest of gay, lesbian, bisexual, queer, or transgender movements, who oscillate between the wish for normalization and subversive intention, to maintain, one way or another, contact with a practical and theoretical discipline which, since its beginnings, has also constantly managed to deal with oscillation, analogous rather than identical—sacrifice the pleasure to save the desire (as Deleuze would say) or sacrifice the false desire of pleasure to save the true joys (as Foucault would say).

Let's attempt to examine these reasons one by one, keeping in mind the undeniable fact that psychoanalysts have been and are for the most part publicly homophobic. Thus, during the debates on **PaCS** (Pacte civil de solidarité; Civil solidarity pact), they were the first to oppose the recognition of same-sex couples and gay **parenting**; few among them expressed any wish for a professional prohibition that should have stopped them from intervening in these political issues *as psychoanalysts*.

From History to Theory
The first meetings between nascent psychoanalysis and the loose conglomeration of homosexual practices, fantasies, and urges were bad encounters and would no doubt bias the future of their relationship (or non-relationship) for a long time. First of all, psychoanalysis was born at the conjunction of a dominant, doubly homophobic discourse: the nosographic discourse of German **psychiatry** and the moral discourse of the Viennese and German bourgeoisie. In this sense, it initially only repeats prejudices that come from elsewhere. Secondly, it is inevitably under the sign of suffering or mental disorder that the first forms of homosexual urges present themselves to Freud: healthy, overt homosexuals have no need to submit themselves to his new form of "cure." From which, by not thinking about it

too much, derives the easy identification of homosexuality with unhappiness and illness: it was not Freud who invented the patient Dora's respiratory troubles and attempted **suicide**, nor "young Viennese homosexual woman's" provocations, nor Schreber's transsexual delusion (it would be "lovely" [*recht schön*] "to be a woman succumbing to intercourse") or his dream of receiving God's rays in his rear. Thirdly, it does not appear to be Freud who, on his own initiative, tries to "treat" homosexuality, the request seems mostly familial: it is families, and notably the fathers, of Dora, the young homosexual female, or of Little Hans, who ask Freud to "cure" them. At this level, the bias lies with the liberal and commercial nature of psychoanalytical **treatment**: it is difficult for a nascent enterprise to be too choosy on the origins or the request (in the economical sense), even if said request runs against his professional principles (it is the patient's request that must take precedence)— that is the law of business. During the International Psychoanalytical Association (IPA) conference, Jones appears to even generalize somewhat on this "economical" principle of the specific familial request in regards to the "general social request" by declaring that in everyone's eyes, homosexuality is a "repugnant crime: if one of our members committed it, it would discredit us all) (cited by Roudinesco and Plon).

Homophobia inherited from psychiatry the desire for bourgeois credibility and commercial interest, confirmed repeatedly and for very little by the objective suffering of their analysands, it is understood that the essence of the psychoanalytical movement, since Jones and Karl Abraham, actively relayed by Anna Freud, until the sexual revolution of the 1960s and 70s, has gotten busy not only to forbid homosexuals from becoming psychoanalysts but, even more, to convert them to heterosexuality. Nothing strictly psychoanalytical in that, only the appearance of sinister (unconscious?) calculations in regards to money, parish, and power, making psychoanalysts the new priests of the heterosexual **symbolic order**.

By reasoning thusly, however, they not only betray the patients who had trusted them, but also their own theory. We must recognize that this conversion of psychoanalysts into zealous missionaries of heterosexuality operated at the expense of the otherwise profound ambiguities of Freudian theory, if we strip it of its exogenous, and possibly infantile prejudices, "infantile" in the measure that Freud seems to have evolved with time; what remains is his famous, but late, letter of April

9, 1935 to an American mother who wanted him to treat her son: "Homosexuality is assuredly no advantage, but it is not a thing to be ashamed of, no **vice**, no degradation, it cannot be classified as an illness…. It is a great injustice to persecute homosexuality as a crime, and a cruelty too." And doubtlessly "exogenous" prejudices, for the essence of the first Freudian analyses revolved around two blind spots: Firstly, is it the homosexual urge as such or its repression that is the pathogen? Secondly, what is the definition of "normal" in the "normal" oedipal elimination (which the homosexual cannot achieve, being stuck at the anal or phallic stages of pre-genital sexuality)? A veritable moral law of civilization that would require the repression of all partial urges or a simple statistical and descriptive standard without moral connotation? If we settle these alternatives each time on the first sense, we dive into militant homophobia; if we settle each time on the second sense, then we agree with Wilhelm Reich, and there is no longer any homophobia, but then there is no psychoanalysis either, as its first essential foundation is shattered: castration or the primacy of the phallus.

But Freud does not fully settle on one or the other. For the first alternative, he effectively says (with regard to Schreber, for example) on the one hand that the "weakness" of homosexuals stems from the fact that they "have never been able to free themselves of this need that the object must have the same genital organs as they do," thus it is the homosexual urge in itself that is a "fixation" or "regression" in the adult and, on the other hand, that the weakness stems from repression itself, and thus paranoid homosexuals become so by seeking "to *defend themselves* from such a sexualization of their instinctual social investments"; the illness thus stems from a maladjusted defense and not from the urge. And it is the same for the second alternative: on one hand, it is an almost moral abnormality when Freudian analysis transforms itself into a theology of desire: the desire *must* eliminate Oedipus by accepting castration in order to be able to love (it is notably the case in Freud's *Three Essays on the Theory of Sexuality* and in his analysis of Little Hans), on the other hand, it is an absolute infra-moral abnormality and thus purely statistical, since the homosexual who identifies with his mother will love others as she loved him and thus as well, or as bad, as the others (which is the case, notably, in *Group Psychology and the Analysis of the Ego*, and once again in the analysis of Little Hans). So, the essence is that Freud does not settle, and even seems to forbid himself from settling, thus letting castration appear as the common horizon of all sexualities, perversions (of which homosexuality is the archetype), thus no longer appearing in this *entre-deux* as an abnormality, but as the simple "reverse of the neurosis" (the cost of heterosexuality and not of civilization). Neurosis and perversion thus no longer constitute the terms of a judgment that distinguished the normal from the pathological, but the simple terms of a choice, amoral and unconscious: the "choice of object," the choice of the object of desire. And certainly, we could still refute this whole theory of castration, and therefore psychoanalysis itself (there may even be some good reasons to do so), but this time, in no way in the name of any type of homophobia in its theoretical suspense, Freudian-style psychoanalysis is beyond all homophilia, as all homophobia, and even the notion of "infantile regression" is no longer homophobic because it is, fundamentally, the peculiarity of all pleasure.

Consequently, on this point, we must certainly not "burn" Lacan, but rather honor him for having rehabilitated the reading of Freud, notably against American hyper-normalists, and for having sought to rid Freud himself of his prejudices, which made him almost systematically opt, less at the level of theory than of discourse and practice, for terms that are morally connoted as "weakness," "powerlessness to," "resistance to get well," et cetera. Thus, in regards to the rupture of the analytical relationship with the young Viennese lesbian, Lacan notes: "Regardless of Freud's opinion, we are far from blaming everything on the deadlock in regards to the patient's position [in the transfer]. His intervention, his conception, his prejudices on the position, must have something to do with the situation's breakdown." What then, according to Lacan, are these prejudices on the young lesbian's transferential position? Of having mistaken the imaginary position for the symbolic position, the transfer, and thus the analytical relationship, have no impact on the imaginary level but only on the symbolic level. And thus, regardless of who is male or female in reality, all that counts are the symbolic positions occupied in the structure: a transfer, and more generally a relationship, is always possible because the "perversion" is no less a structure than the neurosis. Homosexuality is thus no more, no less "normal" than heterosexuality because neither of them is [normal]; in a sense even, neither of the two exists—there exists only difference, the Other.

From this point of view, those psychoanalysts who want to forbid legalization (same-sex **marriage**) or lineage (gay **parenting**) in the name of the preservation of symbolic order, just as those who stigmatize these forms of normalization in the name of the subversion of this same order, have no idea what they are saying; specifically, if symbolic order can be odiously threatened or supported in a conformist manner by imaginary identifications, it is simply not a symbolic order; as per the Lacanian way of speaking, "it would be known." To state it more simply, **gender differences** and the primacy of the phallus that symbolically constitutes them, if they are essential, are only essential because they are, in fact, symbolic: anyone can "choose" to identify themselves with any place, the only thing that is important for one's own health is being able to hold to it. Thus, the gay or lesbian's ethics would also consist of "not retreating before the legitimacy of one's desires" by admitting only which place he or she occupies (phallic or spayed, active or passive). It is not very elegant, certainly, but this is not a question of homophobia, but rather misogyny, and then some.

On this count, we can no longer speak of homophobia, neither with regard to gays nor lesbians, because the reign of the significant symbolic King, the Phallus, only assigns the places, as the God of St **Paul**, that is to say "without distinction of persons" nor anatomies. In this sense, the aging (and often very obscure) Lacan uses droll phrases, like a match to the Deleuzian joke (they are obviously laughing at the same thing), to explain that the symbolic Phallus, which he calls *touthomme* [allman] or the *touthommic* "race," expresses its truth in the sexual act that it institutes and not in the relationship of the same name that does not exist:

> Would we presume that of *allman,* if there remains a bi[o]logical trace, it is but of a race to Thomosize ourselves, and nothing else at all…. It is constituted from the way the order of discourse transmits symbolic places, those by which are perpetuated the race of masters and no less the slaves, of the pretentious as well, to which must be added in response that of fags, of the boring, and I would add that they not go without the bored.

To see in this the slightest indication of homophobia would not only be to lack humor, but to think the moon is made of green cheese, given that, to the contrary, the homophobic argument is pinned down (and certainly as is any univocally homophile discourse):

one only sees "dirty fags" when one takes oneself for a little master, and one only believes oneself capable of judging the Other when one's own knowledge judges oneself, and does so harshly; in Lacanian terms, psychoanalysts are also assholes.

What is a Pervert?

Is that to say that, thanks to Lacan, psychoanalysis could finally in truth be washed of all suspicion of homophobia, and that all there remains is to scorn, in the name of their "stupidity," those who still believe they can find in it the foundations of a *real* (thus political and legal) heterosexual Order and not a symbolic one (thus falling under a completely different law)? Not quite, and that, at least in France, is because of Lacan himself, who was not outdone on the question of the "discourse of the master." And the fact that he knew it and added to it, no doubt in order to not overly enjoy it, does not totally exonerate him. More precisely, if Lacan succeeded in illegitimizing all homophobic discourse and claims by subscribing gender differences to symbolic order, just as with the un-analyzable mix of seriousness and humor he used to speak of it, if he thus succeeded in saving psychoanalysis (unwillingly: obviously, he could not have cared less) of the accusation of being homophobic by sacrificing past and future psychoanalysts, he nonetheless permitted some of them to find themselves, for better or for worse, on a relatively homophobic basis. And that, for three reasons.

First of all, he himself transgressed the limits he imposed on his own discourse, that is, to be but the "frenzy of science" and thus to be able to intervene only on *an individual basis* with *each* of those who are in search and having difficulty before the truth or their truth—scientists, neurotics, perverts, the insane—but never in a discourse for everyone, never for all. As far as we are concerned here, if the symbolic structure is truly independent of reality because it founds it as real, that implies that there may be a truth to certain particular homosexual and heterosexual histories, but that there is no sense in conceiving of a generic homosexual relationship, and even less of a general relation between homosexuality and heterosexuality. But, he could not help himself: he gained a following, he spoke to everyone of the Pervert and the Master, in Vincennes University, before the ORTF (French bureau of television and radio broadcasting), everywhere. Doing this, he reopened Pandora's Box: psychoanalysts had to speak up, to intervene politically, they were the

specialists of the Thing. So, what would require a prioritized intervention today if not the stakes in gender differences and, more precisely, gay and lesbian claims or demands? All of Lacanism should learn to keep quiet on these stakes: it is none of its business. But Lacan transgressed, and it is necessary to resemble the master: today's psychoanalytical homophobia is no longer an interest, as mercantile and sordid as it may be, it is a symptom, and, in many ways, that is even less forgivable.

Secondly, he himself gave the key to this pillaging of symbolic order in the field of politics by his immoderate use of capital letters and play on words. To say Name-of-the-Father, the Phallus, the Signifier, or the Other, was to necessarily open the doorway to the imaginary at the very moment when we claimed to close it, because contrary to what it may be in German, using a capital letter in French or in English is to refer naturally to people and figures, and to acts that are imaginatively identifiable by those people and figures. Lacan wanted to say that the proper noun, the Name-of-the-Father was never more than a noun, a manna, which distributed itself into every meaning, anonymously: "To imply that the Name-of-the-Father is God. It is how psychoanalysis, successfully, proves that the Name-of-the-Father, we can just as well do without it, on the condition that we use it." But, by using the capital letter, he once again set it up—in spite of himself or cynically—as a divine being and, thus, largely contributed to its mystification. After that, the perverse structure logically became the structure of the Perverse, the homosexual drive logically became the drive of the homosexual, the very incarnation of the "more ecstasy," and, sadly, symbolic order incarnated itself in the Order of Symbols that must be saved at all cost as it has become incarnate in the law of the state. It is the same for plays on words: with Lacan, they inaugurally and subtly serve not to express, but to imply, at the risk of the one listening: but overused alone, they are nothing more than linguistic habits or slogans, circulating the symptoms more than revealing them. Would not the puns run the risk of having homophobic effects among all those who learned to repeat them before learning to understand them? To play the game of playing on words, we could easily say that Lacan, after repeating the same old song, taught some of his disciples to better unsheathe words, certainly to better stab themselves in the foot (or better yet, their patients), but the damage appears to have been done, for today, they only intervene, at least publicly, to prevent real desires from seeing the light of day.

Thirdly, and it is the worst and the most serious criticism: because of his compulsion for reactionary posturing (specifically, in reaction to the supposed illusions of others), Lacan simply taught (or re-taught) psychoanalysis to summarily ignore reality in the very name of the only reality created by symbolic order and to sacrifice the health expected by the ones on the altar of Truth implied by the Other. Thus, he notably taught psychoanalysts who claim to adhere to this theory to turn away from the trivial sufferings of reality, from the "social," or simply comforted them in their comfortable and cynical indifference. With Lacan, psychoanalysis, at least born from the attention to the suffering of the analyst's subjects, finished by affirming itself on the scorn for all the suffering inside and outside of the office, suffering that, against his whole theory, cannot be called anything else but absolutely real and that he only took to be symptoms, in themselves indifferent. Certainly then, Lacan had courage to oppose himself, thanks to this indifference and this refusal to fight the symptom, to the Puritan (and homophobic) stupidity of the psychoanalytical majority; and he even went so far as to tell his own disciples or students at Vincennes that if they sought a teacher, they would certainly find one. And of course, the good souls who make money from the suffering of others are often overwhelmingly stupid. But, in the end, courage is never anything more than a simple, narcissistic fantasy, which, by definition, cannot transmit itself, but is constituently *depoliticizing*: it is Lacan, from the bottom of his own revolution, who taught or reminded others that there was no good psychoanalytical policy unless you were reactionary. From this point of view, the way that psychoanalysis in general, and Lacanian psychoanalysis in particular, totally missed, or almost, the political stakes of the FHAR social revolt, of the **decriminalization** of homosexuality, of PaCS, and especially AIDS, says a lot about his contemporary shortsightedness.

For these three reasons, try as we might to save psychoanalysis from homophobia thanks to Freud, for lack of saving psychoanalysts thanks to Lacan, in the end, even Lacan may not quite be savable, and it may be necessary to throw him out with the bath water. And that, not because he was not a "friend" of the Homosexual Cause (to criticize him for it would be ridiculous, or worse, it would be very "Lacan": the symptom of an inadmissible scorn for the suffering of

"private" homosexuals). Even less because he would have been the great demystifier of the illusions tied to all sexual affirmation (here, on the contrary, he could have done a pious deed). But, in the end, simply because he may have traded philosophical megalomania for analytical phobia, thus leaving psychoanalysis in the hands of the reactive phobias, including homophobia, that is to say the phobia of the protesting "Pervert," the militant homosexual.

The Huge Labyrinthine System of Homosexualities

Thus, there is doubtlessly nothing to expect from psychoanalysis as such, at least in regards to gay and lesbian struggles. But to definitively turn our backs on it would be the greatest risk: to forget from where, from which huge labyrinthine system constructed on multiple contradictions, such a renouncement would take its sense. For, as apolitical and phobic as psychoanalysis may be, it remains that the different gay, lesbian, or queer associations and communities continue to confront the same contradictions that psychoanalysis has the merit of having revealed, for lack of having resolved them. Notably, these: How can one promote the very notions of homophobia and differences in genders while renouncing all notions of homosexuality and gender differences, even symbolic? How, concerning AIDS, can one claim to clean up one's own back yard in regards to certain unsafe practices (bareback, etc.) without revisiting, one way or another, the question of the relation between desire and law, as much as between love and ecstasy? How can one claim to both affirm the nature of one's sexual identity *and* its transgender free usage while renouncing the very notion of "unconscious choice of object," which best expresses this ambivalence? How can one disown any reference to the Phallus-king without simply and foolishly denying the absolutely real abyss that separates gay sexuality from lesbian sexuality? Or how can one renounce all ideas of perversion, in the sense of diversion and specific structure of desire, without surrendering homosexual communities to a certain petite bourgeoisie Puritanism ("We are normal!") or without dissolving the very notion of community (since there would no longer be anything specific)?

It is probable that there is no unambiguous answer to these questions. Simply, at this level, a certain usage or a certain poaching of psychoanalysis may help to continue the analysis, and thus to remember that in the battle of sexualities, as in any battle, alliances and ruptures are as often internal as external, and it would no doubt be a mistake to forego them. With his inexhaustible and mean humor, Lacan, ever the same, questioned himself thus: "Are we equal to what we appear to be called to bear, by Freudian subversion, i.e. the being-for-sex? We do not seem very willing to hold the position. Nor much gayer. This, I think, proves that we are not quite there yet." We could look closely, and we could replace "Freudian" with "militant homosexual": despite himself and in spite of everything, it may well be a warning for everyone.

—*Pierre Zaoui*

Anatrella, Tony. *La Différence interdite*. Paris: Flammarion, 1998.

———. "A propos d'une folie," *Le Monde* (June 26, 1999).

Ellis, Havelock. *Sexual Inversion* (1897). New York: Arno Press, 1975.

Eribon Didier. *Une morale du minoritaire. Variations sur un thème de Jean Genet*. Paris: Fayard. 2001.

Fassin, Eric. "L'Inversion de la question homosexuelle," *Revue française de psychanalyse*, no. 1 (2003).

Freud, Sigmund. *Trois Essais sur la théorie de la sexualité*. Paris: Gallimard, 1962. [Published in English as *Three Essays on the Theory of Sexuality*.]

———. *Cinq Psychanalyses*. Paris: Presses universitaires de France, 1954. [Published in the US as *Five Lectures on Psycho-analysis*. New York: Norton, 1977.]

———. "Sur la psychogenèse d'un cas d'homosexualité féminine." In *Névrose, psychose et perversion*. Paris: Presses universitaires de France, 1973.

———. "Psychologie des foules et analyse du moi." In *Essais de psychanalyse*. Paris: Payot, 1981

———. "La Sexualité dans l'étiologie des névroses." In *Résultats, idées, problèmes I*. Paris: Presses universitaires de France, 1984.

———. "Sur les transpositions de pulsions plus particulièrement dans l'érotisme anal." In *La Vie sexuelle*. Paris: Presses universitaires de France, 1969.

———. *Correspondance 1873–1939*. Paris: Gallimard, 1966.

Groddeck, Georg. *Le Livre du ça*. Paris: Gallimard, 1967. [Published in the US as *The Book of the It*. New York: International Universities Press, 1976.]

Haldeman, Douglas C. "Gay Rights, Patient Rights: The Implications of Sexual Orientation Conversion Therapy," *Professional Psychology: Research and Practice* 33 (2002).

Hocquenghem, Guy. *Le Désir homosexuel* (1972). Paris: Fayard, 2000. [Published in the US as *Homosexual Desire*. Durham, NC: Duke Univ. Press, 1993.]

———. "Les Homosexualités," *Clinique lacanienne*, no. 4 (2000).

———. "L'Inconscient homosexuel," *La Cause freudienne* (1997).

Lacan, Jacques. "La relation d'objet." In *Le Séminaire, livre IV*. (Notably chapters 6–8.) Paris: Le Seuil, 1994.

———. "Les concepts fondamentaux de la psychanalyse." In *Le Séminaire, livre XI*. Paris: Le Seuil, 1973

———. *Autres écrits*. Paris: Le Seuil, 2001.

———. "Le Troisième sexe," *La Mazarine* (March 13, 1999).

Prokhoris, Sabine. *Le Sexe prescrit, la différence sexuelle en question*. Paris: Champs Flammarion. 2000.

Roudinesco, Elisabeth, and Michel Pilon. *Dictionnaire de la psychanalyse*. Paris: Fayard, 1997.

Tort, Michel. "Homophobies psychanalytiques," *Le Monde* (October 15, 1999).

———. "Sur la différence psychanalytique des sexes," *Les Temps modernes*, no. 609 (2000).

—*Abnormal; Ex-Gay; Heterosexism; Inversion; Medicine; Otherness; Perversions; Psychiatry; Psychology; Shame; Symbolic Order; Treatment; Vice.*

PSYCHOLOGY

Psychology is the science of the mind or mental phenomena, but the word's origin, which is Greek, means "study of the soul." Psychology is a social science whose development has been greatly influenced by a number of disciplines, including **philosophy**, **biology**, physics, cognitive sciences, **sociology**, and **medicine**. Despite its diverse origins, however, psychology has adopted the scientific method as its primary means of investigation.

From this perspective, the study of human sexuality has been constructed as a legitimate object of scientific research: this process has led to what Foucault called *scientia sexualis*. The first studies in this field of sexuality in general, and homosexuality in particular, were largely influenced by the dominant social norms that condemned deviant sexual behavior and turned homosexuality into a pathology (Richard von Krafft-Ebing). However, certain researchers and political activists of the time who did no conform to the social norm, such as Havelock Ellis and Magnus **Hirschfeld**, tried to oppose this orthodoxy. Thereafter, such researchers pursued their own work in this field, notably biologist Alfred Kinsey and his colleagues. Kinsey demonstrated that homosexual behavior was far from rare, and proposed a concept of sexuality as a continuum ranging from exclusively heterosexual behavior to exclusively homosexual behavior. Similarly, in her studies on the relationship between sexuality and psychopathology, Evelyn Hooker demonstrated that, in this regard, homosexual men do not distinguish themselves from heterosexual men. There was some scientific "proof" indicating that homosexuality was neither an anomaly nor a pathology; however, most psychiatrists and psychoanalysts (such as Edmund Bergler and Charles Socarides) were persuaded of homosexuality's psychopathological character. And yet, the father of **psychoanalysis**, Sigmund Freud, did not consider homosexuality to be a pathology.

A significant step was achieved in 1973 when the American Psychiatric Association voted in favor of removing homosexuality from the Diagnostic and Statistical Manual of Mental Disorders. But for some, this resolution was motivated more by political pressure from gay and lesbian associations than by any careful consideration of medical evidence. Regardless, even though homosexuality is no longer officially considered a mental illness, some therapists continue to advocate renovation therapies for their gay patients. For them, the problem is homosexuality itself, rather than its potential lack of social acceptance.

The systematic analysis of attitudes on homosexuality (measured through questionnaires) has been an important means of investigation in many of psychology's sub-fields, and its notions of homophobia and **heterosexism** are largely taken from this. The American psychologist George Weinberg, a heterosexual therapist, used the term "homophobia" to describe what he called "the fear of finding oneself in proximity to a homosexual," as well as the feelings of self-loathing experienced by some homosexuals. Others preferred terms such as "heterosexism," which draw attention to social attitudes and institutions that, in a diffuse manner, contribute to the domination of homo-, bi-, or transsexual individuals. More recently, American psychologist Gregory Herek proposed the term "sexual prejudice" to designate "any negative attitude based on sexual orientation, whether the person targeted is homo-, bi-, or transsexual."

Numerous psychological studies and theories are interested in the causes of homosexuality and, for the moment, biological and genetic theories seem to be in vogue, in lieu of psychoanalytical and behaviorist

formulations. These approaches clearly appear to be heterosexist, in that they only seem to be searching for a way to explain the deviance. What would seem to require explanation, is homosexuality itself and not sexuality in general, or heterosexuality in particular. However, homo-, bi-, or transsexual psychologists are attempting to change that perspective, becoming interested less in the causes per se than in the means of the development of personal identities. Other psychologists criticize the essentialist approach of the notion of sexual orientation by suggesting that our conventional categories, such as lesbians, gays, and bisexuals, are inadequate.

In North America, psychology is only now beginning to examine the evident heterosexist biases in clinical publications, research, and practices, as demonstrated by the American Psychological Association ("Division 44/Committee on Lesbian, Gay and Bisexual Concerns," 2000; Herek, Kimmel, Amaro and Melton, 1991). The association also sided with gays, lesbians, and bisexuals in political and legislative fields (Committee on Gay and Lesbian Concerns, 1991). However, the lack of financial support and the remaining stigma attached to research on these questions has meant that heterosexism has not yet been completely eradicated from the field of psychology.
—*Roy Gillis*

Bayer, Ronald. *Homosexuality and American Psychiatry: The Politics of Diagnosis*. New York: Basic Books, 1981.

Bergler, Edmund. *Counterfeit Sex*. New York: Grune & Stratton, 1951.

Committee on Lesbian and Gay Concerns, American Psychological Association. *American Psychological Association Policy Statements on Lesbian and Gay Issues*. Washington, DC: American Psychological Association, 1991.

Broido, Ellen M. "Constructing Identity: The Nature and Meaning of Lesbian, Gay, and Bisexual Identities." In *Handbook of Counseling and Psychotherapy with Lesbian, Gay, and Bisexual Clients*. Edited by Ruperto M. Perez, Kurt A. Debord, and Kathleen J. Bieschke. Washington, DC: American Psychological Association, 2000.

"Division 44/Committee on Lesbian, Gay and Bisexual Concerns Joint Task Force on Guidelines for Psychotherapy with Lesbian, Gay, and Bisexual Clients. Guidelines for Psychotherapy with Lesbian, Gay, and Bisexual Clients," *American Psychologist* 55 (2000).

Duberman, Martin, and Ellen Herman. *Psychiatry, Psychology,* and Homosexuality (Issues in Lesbian and Gay Life). New York: Chelsea House Publishing, 1995.

Ellis, Havelock. Sexual inversion (1897). New York: Arno Press, 1975.

Foucault, Michel. Histoire de la sexualité. Vol. 3. Paris: Gallimard, 1976–84. [Published in the US as The History of Sexuality. New York: Vintage Books, 1985.]

Freud, Sigmund. "Letter to an American Mother," American Journal of Psychiatry (1951).

Haldeman, Douglas C. "Gay Rights, Patient Rights: The Implications of Sexual Orientation Conversion Therapy," Professional Psychology: Research and Practice 33 (2002).

Hamer, Dean H., and Peter Copeland. The Science of Desire: The Search for the Gay Gene and the Biology of Behavior. New York: Simon & Schuster, 1994.

Herek, Gregory M. "Psychological Heterosexism and Anti-Gay Violence: The Social Psychology of Bigotry and Bashing." In Hate Crimes: Confronting Violence against Lesbians and Gay Men. Edited by Gregory M. Herek and Kevin T. Berrill. Thousand Oaks, CA: Sage Publications, 1992.

———. "The Psychology of Sexual Prejudice," Current Directions in Psychological Science 9 (2000).

———, Douglas C. Kimmel, Hortensia Amaro, and Gary B. Melton. "Avoiding Heterosexist Bias in Psychological Research," American Psychologist 46 (1991).

Hooker, Evelyn. "The Adjustment of the Overt Male Homosexual," Journal of Projective Techniques 21 (1957).

Hirschfeld, Magnus. Transvestites: The Erotic Drive to Cross Dress [1910]. Amherst, NY: Prometheus Books, 1991.

Kinsey, Alfred C., Walter B. Pomeroy, and Clyde E. Martin. Sexual Behaviour in the Human Male. Philadelphia: Saunders, 1948.

———and Paul H. Gebhard. Sexual Behaviour in the Human Female. Philadelphia: Saunders, 1953.

Krafft-Ebing, Richard von. Psychopathia Sexualis: A Medico-Legal Study. Oxford: F. A. Davis, 1898.

Leahey, Thomas H. A History of Psychology: Main Currents in Psychological Thought. Upper Saddle River, NJ: Prentice Hall, 1997.

Socarides, Charles. The Overt Homosexual. New York: Grune & Stratton, 1968.

Weinberg, George. Society and the Healthy Homosexual. New York: St Martin's Press, 1972.

—Abnormal; Anthropology; Biology; Essentialism/ Constructionism; Heterosexism; Hirschfeld, Magnus; Medicine; Philosophy; Psychiatry; Psychoanalysis; Sociology.

PUBLICITY

Publicity and advertising can be topical, fantastical, ideological, and even political, but most of all, they are economic objects. It is this essential characteristic that structures how publicity and advertising represents homosexuality, a fact that it doesn't hide either. In October 2000, when questioned on the relationship between advertisers and homosexuality, Gilles Moreau, strategic planner for Publicis, responded: "I suppose that in France, [advertisers work from] an old base of mistrust, overcautiousness even. We don't want to offend certain customers, nor do we want a message to be detrimental to the trademark." In this, he euphemistically expressed the marketing "worries" that exist in the constructs of advertising which, in their unwillingness to "offend" the public, are potentially homophobic. This position, however, cannot begin to describe the enormous variety of positions taken by advertisers in media; although it is apparent that in targeting a particular market (i.e. in order to seduce the greatest number of consumers), the representation of homosexuals in publicity and advertising follows the social evolution (or lack thereof) of the image of homosexuality. In this way, advertisers adopt the prevailing ideology that is, depending on the times, if not homophobic, then at least **heterosexist**. In this sense, we can distinguish three significant periods in the representation of homosexuality in publicity and advertising. From the very first advertisements through to the end of the 1950s, homosexuality was either ignored or hidden; from the 60s to the early 90s, it was caricatured. Since then, however, homosexuality has been reified. Hidden, caricatured, and reified: so many forms assumed by an oft-present homophobia that never speaks its name.

Hidden

From advertising's early days until the end of the 1950s, homosexuality did not exist, at least explicitly. A social taboo, it was unthinkable in advertising, which focused on representations that were deemed "acceptable" by the "greatest number." The concept of marketing itself, which originated in the United States in the 50s, dictates this same law of the masses. In order to construct efficient advertising messages, marketing draws from the patriarchal culture of Western countries that place the nuclear **family** at the core of their values, and in which there is no room for homosexuality. Thus, under the aegis of marketing, we can see in the messages that advertising offers a social world that, while not an exact photocopy, is a construction of the values that exist in Western societies, as well as the taboos that shape them. Thanks to the magic of language (whether verbal or otherwise), there is no communication that is transparent; even, and perhaps especially, to the one who expresses it. If showing "values" is the intended goal, and if they are consequently more or less explicit, then taboos show through just as well—not at the explicit level of the message's meaning, but at the implicit level where the semiotics of diverse connotations occur. Thus, homosexuality is unconsciously present in the advertisements of this period, like a sort of Freudian slip of reality that does not yield to its own denial.

Thus we see, as early as 1916, the company Procter & Gamble—emblematic of traditional American culture—produced an advertisement for its product Ivory Soap that appeared in *National Geographic*: a perplexing representation of athletes after a game who are looking at one another while washing. The caption is also rather ambiguous: "Not the least of the pleasures of a hard game is the bath that follows it. For it is just after the final whistle when you realize for the first time how warm you are and how your skin is chafing, that the cooling, soothing, refreshing qualities of Ivory Soap are most appreciated." The scene takes place in the locker room, a place of many homoerotic fantasies. There is also a man who is bending over with his back to the others, as if he were picking up his soap; the slogan says it all: "Ivory soap … it floats." Beneath the superficial promotion of heterosexual virility (i.e. the athlete), there are a number of signposts that lead us to see a highly sexualized representation of relations between men. It is once again in the locker room, but not in the showers, that underwear-maker Arrow chose to depict its models. In its 1933 campaign to promote a line of underwear's new array of colors, the ad's slogan is rather surprising: "And now, the Shorts with the Seamless Crotch Go Gay! (But Not Too Gay)." The caption, and notably the use of parentheses, can be interpreted at different levels. The ad's text (aimed at the department store purchasing managers) further explains that the colors are "not too outlandish" ("Gypsy's Delight" or "Tropical Sun"), but are instead "he-man." But while the word "gay" was used by homosexuals to refer to themselves as early as the 1920s, it is uncertain whether the word as used in the Arrow ad was meant to suggest a homosexual component, whether consciously or not.

A 1978 French ad for DAF Trucks. Its message, *"Il suce pas, lui"* (It doesn't suck) has a double meaning: this truck does not consume a lot of fuel, but also it is not a vehicle for "fags," but rather real men....

These two examples are characteristic of this paradox between the spoken and unspoken, which is revealing of the status of homosexuality in the societies that produce these messages. It will not be long before the homophobia present in this paradox expresses itself explicitly: from the 60s to the 90s, advertising and publicity become openly and, it could be said, nonchalantly homophobic.

Caricature

With the 1960s and the mass popularity of television, the nature of advertising and publicity changes: advertising enters the era of the narrative, whose different genres it will exploit. From this point of view, the figure of the homosexual is systematically set in the medium of the comical, from satire to burlesque. This period marks advertising and publicity's most overtly homophobic years, during which we see the frequent appearance of caricatured figures such as the "queen" and the "transvestite." These humiliating clichés are regularly used to describe and stigmatize homosexuality as a "monstrosity" (in the etymological sense) which the public is supposed to look upon with both amusement and consternation. The face of the transgender becomes a sort of metonym for homosexuality. A good example is a television commercial for Hamlet cigars from 1987. In a horror film setting, the camera explores the sheet-covered body of a Frankenstein-like creature, which suddenly sits upright and looks timidly under its sheet. What it discovers visibly troubles it: we see it swallow nervously and we hear sad music in the background. Then the creature reaches for a cigar, no doubt to console itself over its terrible discovery; it crosses its legs and we discover that it is wearing stockings and high heels. Under the guise of **humor**, then, the transgender is explicitly (and literally) depicted as a monstrosity.

When the homosexual is not playing the role of the funny, sympathetic clown, he intervenes in narratives constructed around the motive of *trompe-l'oeil* and the "mistake," from which the discovery of the "monster's" true "nature" provokes various levels of panic. For example, in a Bouygues Telecom campaign for its pre-paid telephone card that offers "no long-term commitment" depicts a man who discovers that his young bride is, in reality, a young groom. Homosexuality is thus cast down to the domain of the **abnormal** or pathological.

It is precisely this "abnormality" that interests advertising agencies seeking originality, in the hopes of distinguishing themselves from the masses. It is a strategic choice of representation, and not simply a matter of unfortunate and unintentional consequences. A common response from advertising agencies when confronted on their homophobic tendencies is to describe it as an inevitable consequence of the brevity of the medium, which must say a lot in very little time and with few words and images. Arguing the necessity of having to use analogy and metaphor, which "represent more quickly and better," advertising agencies attempt to depoliticize a construction that is nonetheless eminently ideological. However, there is a phenomenon that has recently arrived to counter such an argument: the emergence of gay and lesbian-targeted marketing, in response to the evolution of the gay and lesbian community in Western nations that is not only political, but affluent. In this regard, advertisements that specifically target gays and lesbians are rarely in the realm of the burlesque and instead present less "metaphorical" representations of homosexuality: they are, therefore, possible. A significant example is a 1997 Johnnie Walker Red campaign using gay men. A print advertisement shows a "bunch of buddies" who are multicultural, and whose physical appearance does not allow us to distinguish them from other men their age. The politically charged slogan states, "For the last time, it's not a lifestyle, it's life." The advertisement thus criticizes the traditional message popularized by advertisers that homosexuality is a "lifestyle" choice. In this, we have the beginnings of a discourse that chooses to oppose the usual discourses on homosexuality.

Reification

The strategy of the photographic "negative" is one of the responses to the inherent paradox of the relationship between advertising and homosexuality, most notably since the early 1990s. This paradox holds to the advertising discourse. In fact, for advertising agencies, it is a schematic way of attracting the greatest number of potential consumers and, consequently, not to offend any. In this manner, the publicity work can be deconstructed by way of an economic logic (target the largest possible number of consumers) and a **rhetorical** logic (develop a message that reaches the greatest number of those targeted). The latter requires the construction of a politically correct discourse that is at the same time based on the *doxa,* or popular opinion. As such, homosexuality is doubly troubling: on one hand, the gay and lesbian community has emerged as a social group with a large purchasing power that cannot be ignored; on the other, advertising agencies may fear that communication aimed at this group will harm their product's image, a fear which is nothing more than a reflection of the ongoing homophobia that continues to affect the general social discourse. Unless one adopts a "niche" strategy, that is to say choosing to directly market to a specific social group (in this case, gays and lesbians) without worrying about the masses, the problem becomes one of how "to speak of it without speaking of it."

Regardless, in the new era, homosexuality and homosexuals become objects that sell, whether it is explicit or implicit, the latter consisting of using certain attributes of homosexuality without identifying them as such. The proposed response to the paradox presented above is, in this case, the "double discourse." The subject's reification is, in this way, more radical: homosexuality and some of its alleged attributes of sensuality and sexuality are exploited to present a more nefarious image of a product. Those that opt for this strategy of "radical differentiation" offer a series of clichés that risk insulting and even endangering the gay and lesbian community.

This strategy of the "double discourse" moves the localization of homophobia, which appears not to be in the statement itself but in the minds of those creating the ads. The apparent **tolerance** of homosexuality, which seemed to be a trend in advertising throughout the 90s, can barely hide the queasiness, the phobia even, of advertisers on the question of homosexuality. Admittedly, gay culture is fashionable, and advertisers, always on the lookout for the latest craze, are constantly testing the waters. As a result, numerous commercials and print ads—for Dim (a lingerie and underwear company), Coca-Cola, Minute Maid, and Club Med—use the esthetic codes of the gay community, the festive and trendy connotations of the *gay attitude*. But if asked to confirm this, advertisers would deny it, finding numerous ways to justify their esthetic choices without ever having to admit to the theme of homosexuality.

As for the strategy of "radical differentiation," it is used by a number of fashion labels that appropriate the image of homosexuality to sell their products. This appropriation is one argument among others in the glamour rhetoric developed by these companies. It was initiated in the late 1980s by Calvin Klein, who wanted to sex up the image of his company. This tendency reached an apex in 2000 with the trend of "porno chic," whereby companies appropriated the same-sex imagery of gay porn. (Notably, Christian Dior focused many of its advertisements during this time on images of female couples in erotic positions.) Here, homosexuals were employed under the prism of "hypersexuality," a cliché that purports to explore the nefarious nooks and crannies of sexuality, such as pornography, prostitution, or pederasty. For example, one Calvin Klein campaign suggested a casting session for a porno film: young-adult men are questioned on camera by a man whose face we never see; the tone of his voice, as well as the suggestive nature of his questions, suggests that the (older) interviewer has a sexual interest in the (much younger) models.

But it is lesbians, largely absent from advertising and publicity over the years, who are most commonly represented in advertising's fantasy of homosexual "hypersexuality." In these representations, the lesbian is the devastatingly beautiful and sensuous woman not unlike the one who populates heterosexual pornographic imagery. Thus, lesbians presented in this way persist in feeding the old male fantasy about female homosexuality: it is no more than an erotic crutch for chauvinistic sexuality. Such same-sex representations do not subvert the heterosexist vision of the world; in fact, they affirm it.

In all, publicity and advertising are riddled with a rampant homophobia which more often than not mirrors the homophobia of our times.

—*Samira Ouardi*

Chasin, Alexandra. *Selling Out: The Gay and Lesbian Movement Goes to Market*. New York: St Martin's Press, 2000.

Commercial Closet Association. http://www.commercial closet.org [US website compiling a large number of advertisements with a gay or homophobic theme] (accessed March 14, 2008).

Leigh, Daniel, Bhat Subodh, and Daniel Wardlow. "The Effects of Homosexual Imagery in Advertising on Attitudes Towards the Ad," *Journal of Homosexuality* 31, nos. 1-2 (1996).

Maingueneau, Dominique. *Analyser les textes de communication*. Paris: Dunod, 1998.

Kates, Steven. *Twenty Million Customers: Understanding Gay Men's Consumer Behaviour*. New York: Haworth Press, 1998.

Lukenbill, Grant. *Untold Millions: Positioning Your Business for the Gay and Lesbian Consumer Revolution*. New York: Harper Business, 1995.

Minot, Françoise. *Quand l'image se fait publicitaire. Approche théorique, méthode et pratique*. Paris: L'Harmattan, 2001.

Mitteaux, Valérie. "Les Marques *gay friendly* mais toujours honteuses," *Culture Pub*, no. 2 (2001).

Yarts. "Les Gays à la niche." http://www.yarts.fr (site now discontinued).

—*Art; Comic Books; Caricature; Cinema; Family; Heterosexism; Media; Rhetoric.*

R

RADCLYFFE HALL, Marguerite

When *The Well of Loneliness* was published in **England** in 1928, poet and writer Radclyffe Hall (born Marguerite Radclyffe-Hall in 1880) was already famous not only for her work *(Adam's Breed* had received many literary awards) but also for her lifestyle. While her first lover was an amateur singer named Mabel Batten (whose nickname was "Ladye"), who died in 1915, the great passion of her life was for sculptor Una Troubridge, who was married to Admiral Ernest Troubridge at the time they met. An emblem of the New Woman, the feminist ideal that emerged in the late nineteenth century, "John" (as she preferred to be known, except as an author) commonly wore men's clothing and short hair beginning around 1920, whereas Troubridge had a more feminine demeanor. Both readily frequented chic lesbian circles, such as Natalie Barney's literary salon in Paris, or Edy Craig's more remote circle in Rye, England. In 1920, Hall was accused by Sir George Fox-Pitt of immorality for breaking up Admiral Troubridge's marriage; she successfully sued him for slander. If the couple appeared scandalous in the eyes of the public as a result, both women nonetheless held decidedly conservative political opinions. A convert to Catholicism, Radclyffe Hall's ideals were very close to that of **Fascism** in the 1930s, and she chose to set up residence in Florence in Fascist **Italy** with Una.

In her first works, such as *The Unlit Lamp* (1924), Radclyffe Hall broached the subject of lesbianism in a veiled manner. She then, however, considered the notion of writing a book on what was known as "**inversion**," which would reveal the suffering endured by lesbians to the public. Written between June 1926 and April 1928, *The Well of Loneliness*, a melodramatic novel that was greatly influenced by the work of sexologists such as Havelock Ellis and Richard von Krafft-Ebing, retraces the painful destiny of Stephen Gordon, a young, mannish lesbian—the very example of the "congenital homosexual"—whose life was marked by "difference," solitude, and exclusion.

Published on July 27, 1928 by Jonathan Cape, the book initially received a lukewarm response. But three weeks later on August 19, the *Sunday Express* published on its front page an inflammatory article by its editor James Douglas entitled "A Book That Should Be Banned," in which he stated: "I would prefer to give a healthy lad or lass a vial of prussic acid [cyanide] rather than this book. The poison kills the body, but moral poison kills the soul." A photograph of the writer, in one of her most masculine poses, accompanied the article, as if to provide further evidence against the author. Very quickly, the controversy over the book took on a national scale. The ground was fertile: since the end of World War I, there was a common belief that female homosexuality was on the rise. A growing amount of **literature** echoed the positions that were widespread in public opinion: that there were increasing numbers of female bachelors, evidence of a **contagion** rooted, in part, in the feminist movement. The image of the "flapper," the free-spirited, independent girl who took charge and lived life to the full, was sometimes associated with the lesbian. In 1921, a bill seeking to criminalize lesbianism was passed by the House of Commons, but subsequently rejected by the House of Lords, which ironically argued that it was necessary to preserve the innocence of women who knew nothing of such practices, and whose curiosity could have been aroused by the passage of the law. Within this context, the controversy over Radclyffe Hall's novel provided an opportunity to make an example.

Following the negative reaction of the press, her publisher Jonathan Cape immediately sent a copy of the book to British Home Secretary William Joynson-Hicks in order to get his opinion on the novel's obscene character. On August 21, Joynson-Hicks, reputed for his Puritanism and intransigence, ordered an immediate stop to publication. The following day, the book was removed from sale, but Cape took it upon himself to pursue publication by way of France, through Pegasus Press. Upon their arrival in England, the Parisian copies of the book were seized by customs. The publisher was charged with obscenity and went to trial on November 9, 1928 in the Bow Street Magistrates' Court in order to determine whether the books were to be destroyed or not.

Since the beginning of the **scandal**, a number of intellectuals had mobilized in order to defend the book. E. M. Forster and Leonard Woolf had thought to publish a letter of protest, but the plan was in part sabotaged by Radclyffe Hall herself, who insisted that the book's artistic merit be underlined, a point on which many authors displayed a profound wariness. During the trial, despite numerous withdrawals, forty well-known personalities, a good number of them bi- or homosexual, declared themselves willing to defend the work. It was not to be. After the first witness, writer Desmond Macarthy, had refuted the book's obscene character, Judge Biron, who had already revealed his hostility, rejected all subsequent witnesses. The defense's efforts to demonstrate the novel's scientific and profoundly moral character met with little success. On November 16, Biron declared that the book, which in his opinion referred to "unnatural acts of the most horrid and disgusting obscenity," was to be destroyed. On November 22, a letter of protest appeared in the *Manchester Guardian* signed by forty-five intellectuals, but to no avail. On December 14, the attorney general, Thomas Inskip, confirmed the decision on appeal.

The Well of Loneliness had a profound impact on many lesbians who found, in Stephen Gordon, both a symbol and a model. Banned in England until 1949, the book continued to be available in the United States, where it became a bestseller. In France, a play inspired by the novel, published by Gallimard, was presented in Paris, albeit without the author's consent. Radclyffe Hall and Una Troubridge, profoundly upset by the scandal, chose to leave England in 1929. The rampant condemnation of the novel had marked the apex of **lesbophobia** in pre-World War II England: behind the accusation of obscenity, there was the personal criticism of a woman whose appearance and life-

style transgressed the hierarchies linked to gender and threatened patriarchal society. However, in the same year that *The Well of Loneliness* was published, Virginia Woolf published *Orlando,* a tribute to her close friend Vita Sackville-West, and Compton MacKenzie published *Extraordinary Women,* a satire about the aristocratic lesbian community, both without issue.

—*Florence Tamagne*

Baker, Michael. *Our Three Selves: A Life of Radclyffe Hall.* London: Hamish Hamilton, 1985.

Cline, Sally. *Radclyffe Hall: A Woman called John.* Woodstock, NY: The Overlook Press, 1998.

Dickson, Lovat. *Radclyffe Hall at the Well of Loneliness.* London: Collins, 1975.

Souhami, Diana. *The Trials of Radclyffe Hall.* London: Weidenfeld & Nicolson, 1998.

—*Censorship; Contagion; England; Lesbophobia; Literature; Media; Scandal; Wilde, Oscar.*

RHETORIC

In the past, homophobic rhetoric was rather simple. Certainly, it had access to a rich vocabulary: sodomite, uranist, fag, queer, poof, lesbo, butch, carpet muncher, dyke, et cetera, but it had a rather rudimentary syntax, reduced to a few **insults** ("Damned queer!"), curses ("May their blood fall upon them!"), and maxims ("All lesbians need is a good fuck"). It never went beyond the limitations of the sentence, for a sentence was all that was needed. Homophobic statements were made, and people agreed with them. Obviously, the simplicity of these statements took nothing away from their strength and efficiency; quite the contrary, in fact. Simply, there was no need to say anything more.

Now, over the past century, and notably in recent years, homophobes have felt the need to improve their rhetoric. Not that it is necessarily more violent or virulent than before, but it is clear that it is now more sophisticated than it once was: its syntax has been fleshed out, its concepts have become more refined. Mostly, it has become more self-conscious, which reveals its new reality in rhetorical space. Until now, homophobic rhetoric was considered not mere opinion but rather the truth, shared by all. In recent years, however, this rhetoric is now challenged on a regular basis, which has caused a certain uneasiness in homophobic discourse, but rather than recede, it has begun to mutate. Specifically, homophobes have modified their linguistic tools in order to continue to justify their presupposed ideology, and to remodel their social image in order to fight their political enemies. Without sacrificing its pathos, fantasy, or emotion, it is now more rational and argumentative. Homophobic rhetoric now has new clothes.

But just what is this homophobic rhetoric? Truth be told, it is difficult to encapsulate. It is not a stable lexical corpus spoken by an identifiable social group, such a Christian, Marxist, or psychoanalytical rhetoric, each with its own official doctrine, references, and known advocates. Homophobic rhetoric is more akin to a grouping of scattered snippets, phrases, and heterogeneous formulae used in different manners and milieus, by everyone in general and no one in particular, and sometimes even by people who are not homophobic or do not consider themselves to be, but are simply thoughtless. In short, this discourse is both omnipresent and evanescent, but it can at least be objectified and brought back to the everyday sources from which it draws its arguments.

The Sources of Homophobic Rhetoric
Sources of homophobic rhetoric, to use the vocabulary of rhetorical analysis, are more or less reserves where those employing it can find the necessary "evidence" to prop up their ideas.

Pseudo-theoretical sources are the "intelligent" armor of homophobic discourse. Their relative importance in the argumentative device has continuously increased over the last few years in order both to euphemize and reinforce the most conservative points of view. Used in this way, they give arguments the appearance of neutrality so they can be perceived as objective, scientific, and consequently, truthful. Thus, even the most violent, partisan positions may be successfully understood as expert arguments. However, the sciences and disciplines that are most frequently referred to by homophobes have changed. Formerly, homophobic rhetoric was based mostly on theological, moral, or medical sources, such as **sin, debauchery**, nature/**against nature**, illness, and defect. However, today, the themes most commonly invoked are **psychoanalytical, sociological**, and **anthropological**, such as narcissism, **perversion, otherness, symbolic order**, and **gender differences**. As a sign of the times, when Catholic authorities periodically wish to issue a

new condemnation of homosexuality, they judiciously avoid the violent images used frequently in the past, such as **Sodom and Gomorrah** consumed by fire; now they resort to concepts belonging to psychoanalysis, whose arguments they once judged as too permissive and obscene.

However, homophobic rhetoric also borrows from less sophisticated discourse: the "common" sources, which stem more from general opinion than official science.

Without question, the most obvious source is **heterosexism**. It is, more or less, the profound belief in a heterosexual teleology of desire, which finalizes, *a priori,* the individual: save for an accident or malignant influence, all children are and will be heterosexual, man is made for woman, and especially, woman is made for man. These implicit certainties are founded on a sort of popular anthropology that links **theology, biology**, and psychoanalysis: it is the image of an improbable heterosexual fantasy, a genuine heterosexism that implicitly excludes all homosexual desire. At best, homosexuality is only a phase, a passage before giving in to complete heterosexuality; at worst, it is a "fatal accident" along the way. Homophobia is the inevitable result, which in this regard is the fear that homosexuality endangers the heterosexual finality of desire, at all levels: the rampant scourge that threatens the individual, the couple, the **family**, the nation, and even the human race, which, as a result of **sterility** brought on by the homosexual **contagion**, could well disappear from the face of the Earth. In this, more than merely marginal, homosexuals are perceived as traitors, because they are opposed to the group, and as such they represent a universal threat.

This rhetoric is often based on a fundamental misogyny with which it is closely linked. From this perspective, since there is nothing worse for a man than to resemble a woman, the image of the male homosexual is obviously one of effeminacy, and thus subject to scorn and jeers. Conversely, if a lesbian seems more masculine, it is considered an arrogant and scandalous sham, since she refuses to remain in the place assigned to her by society. And yet, the stereotypes of homophobic rhetoric are singularly reversible and malleable. If the homosexual male is criticized for not being virile enough, he will eventually be criticized for being too virile, and his taste for **sports**, such as bodybuilding, is regarded as manifestly artificial and inauthentic. Whereas the lesbian, if she is feminine, she is too feminine to be real; her charms are pernicious and diabolical. Man must be virile, but not too much or too little, and woman must be feminine, yet not too much or too little. However, if gay men and women confine themselves to the middle ground of virility or femininity, it is even worse: they are suspected of wanting to blend into the masses in order to better trick the rest of society. On some levels, heterosexist opinion in fact prefers the "queen," who is more recognizable and thus more reassuring. In short, nothing will ever be satisfactory.

Homophobic rhetoric is often based on xenophobic arguments as well: historically in **France** it was known as the "Italian **vice**" in the sixteenth century, the "English vice" in the eighteenth and nineteenth centuries, and the "German vice" in the early twentieth century. In this manner, homosexuality was always a foreign intrusion, belonging to the "other," but not just any: it tended to be the nation's foremost rival, depending on the era. Such arguments were thus a vehicle by which a nation could vent its hostility and hatred; a form of symbolic compensation that reduces an otherwise threatening power to the level of sexual perversity. But is this convergence of homophobic and xenophobic arguments a thing of the past? It is doubtful. In **Africa**, homosexuality is often presented as a white man's vice, an opinion that also became apparent in the (lack of) early responses to **AIDS** in Africa, where it was thought to be a homosexual issue, and therefore, a white issue. Specifically, the hatred of whites and the scorn for homosexuals mutually reinforced one another. Similarly, in contemporary France, while homosexuality itself is not considered an "American vice," the gay and lesbian lifestyle, linked to Anglo-Saxon **communitarianism**, is perceived as a terrible American influence that endangers France and its Republican model. Conversely, on the other side of the Atlantic, gay and lesbian studies are often criticized for being overly French-centric, too influenced by the words of thinkers such as Foucault, Derrida, or Cixous, the objective being to disqualify their intellectual legitimacy. Finally, homophobic rhetoric is sometimes in harmony with hatred according to class: for the nineteenth-century proletariat, homosexuality was a "bourgeois vice"; for the bourgeois, it was a symptom of the "always immoral" working classes, or the "obviously **decadent**" aristocracy. Today, these watered-down social representations are finding a resurgence of sorts, for example, in the discourse of certain suburban youths who see in gay and lesbian culture a type of bourgeois luxury that

is typical of the well-to-do; it is also a form of shameful social distinction, as depicted by numerous well-known reggae artists for whom homophobic discourse is a recurring strategy that allowed them to reaffirm their own masculinity as "natural." Similarly, in the 1980s, the rise of AIDS reactivated old arguments of hatred and fear directed at gays, this "high-risk" population having been justly punished. "AIDS cures fags" became a familiar slogan of the religious right in the United States (of course, in this instance, "cures" means "kills"). Throughout the world, there have been many who advocated compulsory testing and tattooing of homosexuals, as well as "AIDS-atoriums" and quarantine. Under these conditions, AIDS has provided an opportunity for homophobes to justify and reinforce the argument of exclusion of homosexuals. In another way, the debates on the **PaCS** civil union agreement in France also gave rise to arguments of social hatred, putting into question the alleged financial affluence of homosexuals, as well as their outrageous fiscal demands that would be, of course, to the detriment of the French taxpayer: "Are we going to pay for the fags?" became an often-heard slogan. However, in the US, these arguments are not diminishing: just like Jews, homosexuals are often represented as an overpowerful minority that dominates Hollywood ("the gay Mafia"), the **media**, the economy, and **politics**. In this view, demands by homosexuals for equal rights (by striking down anti-sodomy laws, for example, or recognizing same-sex **marriages**) are construed as exorbitant privileges that must be denied, as their hegemonic power is already too well established.

The Strategies of Homophobic Rhetoric
All of these kinds of rhetoric constitute the basis of the homophobic argument, but they must still be structured according to various strategies that are, themselves, rhetorical traps.

First of all, the strategies of definition. In this discourse, homosexuality is often defined in an authoritarian, albeit subtle, way: etymologically, it is said to be the love of the same, narcissism, self-centeredness. It is thus a refusal of, among other things, **otherness**, closure, the **ghetto**. Once put into play, this strategy allows one to roll out all the desired consequences from a simple definition, locking homosexuals in their presumed essence. Once it has been set down, whether explicitly or implicitly, the definition can become a dangerous weapon, a moral absolutism, a principle of both vision and division of the social world. Cleverly, this definition is surreptitiously linked to other completely different and heterogeneous realities; homosexuality thus becomes synonymous with such disparate subjects as pederasty, **pedophilia**, **perversion**, debauchery, drugs, AIDS, and sterility.

Next, the simple injunction. With regard to the strategies of definition, it does not define what homosexuality is, but what it should be. It is the injunction of virility, femininity, discretion, chasteness, the sublimation of sexual desire; as such, the homophobic argument is a normative argument. Internalized since childhood, the rules it decrees have a power of considerable mental coercion. More subtle, but no less efficient, is the double injunction. This rhetorical strategy consists in successively uttering contradictory injunctions according to the necessity of the time. Thus, the injunction of normalcy was for a long time the privileged motive of homophobic discourse. But when, by chance, homosexual activists began working for the legal recognition of gay and lesbian couples, this demand was criticized because it was believed to endanger the social norm. Thus, those who had themselves exhorted homosexuals to act "normally," now criticized their willingness to be socially integrated, and urged them to become even more subversive. The debate on gay **parenting** reveals similar results: homosexuals are often accused of being "selfish" by refusing to participate in the reproduction of the species; but when gay men and lesbians demand the right to artificial insemination and/or to **adopt**, these too are deemed as "selfish." In short, whether they wanted children or not, homosexuals are selfish; whether they complied to injunctions or not, they are always at fault. If they live their lives openly, they are asked to be discreet, but if they are discreet, it is because there is something shameful, unnameable going on. One way or another, the dialectics of the debate are locked.

Another strategy: guilt. In fact, homophobic discourse can, for the most part, count on the rhetorical effects of **shame** that it engenders and maintains: through their fear of being stigmatized, many gays and lesbians are willing to endure the most violent insults without saying a word. And even when they believe they have rid themselves of this feeling of shame, it subsists nonetheless in a mitigated form that renders them particularly susceptible to an uneasy conscience, self-censorship, and the argument of the perverse, so characteristic of reactionary discourse. As a result, they renounce certain fundamental freedoms, so that they

will not embarrass, shock, or jeopardize this moral or symbolic order that is so easily used against them. They will also accept the most extravagant reversals: excluded from groups, and as victims of intolerance, they will allow themselves to be accused of intolerance and exclusion; forced into secrecy, they will accept the criticism of duplicity; fighting against homophobia, they will be accused of fanning the flames. The tactical advantage of these rhetorical strategies is only too evident as they force these people to exclude themselves from the field of legitimate demands and discourse.

The final strategy of homophobic rhetoric consists of denying oneself as such. This denial, better known in its most vulgar form, "I'm not homophobic, but …" has many levels of expression. The most radical is revisionism, such as those who have long denied the historical fact of the **deportation** of gays and lesbians, and who, logically, deny the homophobic character of this denial. Less extreme, yet more common, is belittling. Those who engage in it do not ignore homophobic practices, but they relativize them in a friendly and happy manner: they argue that bullying in the schoolyard is only children at play; that **discrimination** exists but there are so many more important problems. In this logic, a form of optimism, or ignorance, leads some people—sometimes in good faith—to become apostles of demobilization by advancing dubious affirmations: according to them, homophobia is something that happens in distant, backward countries, or is a thing of the past. If it does exists, it can only be residual and it will soon be erased by inevitable moral progress, which is continuous and irreversible; as a result, the incessant demands of gay and lesbian activists are inappropriate, even unpleasant.

Confronted by the demands of gays and lesbians, those who engage in homophobic rhetoric have had to change its ways and euphemize its arguments, all the while toughening them by grounding them in the social sciences. Such rhetoric, in this process of modernization as it were, also retains its historical and structural affinities with heterosexism, misogyny, xenophobia, and all the discourses of social hatred in general. For all this, it remains a diffuse, difficult, and delicate object because, in the end, it is less a discourse than a linguistic climate whose everyday effects are felt even in the absence of effective expression. This is a crucial point, which is doubtlessly difficult for those who have never experienced it to understand, but, in fact, social homophobia creates the symbolic conditions of perma-

nent moral insecurity, whose insults or anathema are
nothing more than secondary symptoms. Thus, beyond
the various words spoken here and there, and without
mentioning the physical **violence** that often accompanies them, homophobic rhetoric resides less in the
overt discourses than in the possible ones, which force
those who are their potential targets to be constantly
wary of them in order to better avoid, anticipate, reject,
or internalize them—a daily task that weighs heavily
on morale. However, homophobic rhetoric has perhaps finally started to reach its limits: in the end, in
the absence of all rationality, it can only resort to tautological redundancy ("Come now, a man is a man!")
or esoteric transcendence (i.e. God or moral, symbolic,
or natural order). Regardless, those who still cling to
homophobic rhetoric feel the need to constantly justify it and themselves, which is a small victory, but a
victory indeed.

—*Louis-Georges Tin*

Angenot, Marc. *La Parole pamphlétaire.* Paris: Payot, 1982.

Delor, François. *Homosexualité, ordre symbolique, injure et discrimination: Impasses et destins des expériences érotiques minoritaires dans l'espace social et politique.* Brussels: Labor, 2003.

Eribon, Didier. *Réflexions sur la question gay.* Paris: Fayard.
1999. [Published in the US as *Insult and the Making of the
Gay Self.* Durham, NC: Duke Univ. Press, 2004.]

Goffman, Erving. *Stigmate.* Paris: Minuit, 1975. [Published
in the US as *Stigma.* Englewood Cliffs, NJ: Prentice-Hall,
1963.]

Grahn, Judy. *Another Mother Tongue: Gay Words, Gay Worlds.*
Boston: Beacon Press, 1990.

Hirschman, Albert O. *Deux Siècles de rhétorique réactionnaire.*
Paris: Fayard, 1991. [Published in the US as *The Rhetoric of
Reaction.* Cambridge: Belknap Press, 1991.]

Larguèche, Evelyne. *Injure et sexualité.* Paris: Presses universitaires de France, 1997.

Mackinnon, Catharine. *Only Words.* Cambridge/London:
Harvard Univ. Press, 1996.

Reboul, Olivier. *Langage et idéologie.* Paris: Presses universitaires de France, 1980

———. *La Rhétorique.* Paris: Presses universitaires de France,
1983.

—*Abnormal; Anthropology; Caricature; Heterosexism;
Humor; Insult; Literature; Otherness; Proselytism;
Psychoanalysis; Symbolic Order; Violence; Vocabulary.*

RIGHT WING. *See* Far Right

RUSSIA

Starting in 988 CE, Christianization had the effect of
introducing Byzantine sexual morality into Russia.
Both **Orthodox** canonic law (*nomokanon*) and the
Bible forbid *muzhelozhestvo* ("the position of man on
man") and *sodomsky grekh* ("the **sin** of **Sodom**"), giving Russian homophobia its Christian foundations:
the first Russian *nomokanon* refers to **Justinian**. The
sexual morality of Eastern pagan Slavs, according to
erotic folklore (assembled in the nineteenth century by
Afanassiev and **censored**), illustrates a great freedom
and acceptance of homosexual practices that the former
civil laws had never penalized. Russian princes referred
sexual issues—sins that are a matter of penitence—to
the Church and its tribunals. Absent from the accounts,
but largely practiced and tolerated (albeit with resignation), homosexuality was rarely reprimanded, except
when it was linked to **heresy**, or when an ecclesiastic
dignitary's homosexuality became public knowledge.
But the first penitential in Russia in the thirteenth
century, based on the beliefs of Archbishop Nifont of
Novgorod in the twelfth century, was rather lenient on
the subject of sodomy.

The notion of sodomy includes all perversions of
marriage, attesting to the interpretation of the story
of Sodom as punishment for lustfulness and shamelessness. Ordained first of all for purposes of procreation, sex must be limited to face-to-face penetration
between a man and a woman, lest it violate "nature"
and the Divine order. The homosexual act is doubly
sinful, according to orthodoxy. Male **perversion** (*mu-
zhebloudiye*) can encompass masturbation (*rukobloudiye*),
also referred to as perversion by the hand (in Greek,
malakid). Penitence depends on the age and marital
status of the sinner, being more severe for older, married men, but more lenient for youth, who are excused
on the basis of lacking self-control over sexual urges.
From this perspective, debauchery between young
women could be nothing more than masturbation and
seemed minor in relation to heterosexual non-procreative fornication, which was a threat to marriage and
potential offspring.

Homosexual practices bothered the upper clergy
especially as a form of commonplace sexual license
involving monks, who until the seventeenth century

were suspected of engaging in unnatural relations with young male servants, beggars, prostitutes, and "hairless" visitors, despite divine interdicts and monastic vows. The troubling beauty of these young men was considered the ultimate ruse of the Devil to corrupt these monks, according to those who wrote the rules. Nilus of Sora, a fifteenth-century hermit, wrote: "Distance yourself from the company of young men with beautiful and feminine faces; do not look upon them, for it is a net laid down by the Devil to catch monks, as one Father said. If it is possible, do not unnecessarily remain alone with them, said Basil the Great, for there is no thing more important than your soul...." To staunch this desire, Nilus threw nothing less than Christ's sacrifice (which does not provide forgiveness for this vice) into the balance, and was desolate as a result: "We are agitated by unnatural things that are alien even to animals."

The birth of the autocracy was accompanied by a synthesis of legal, moral, and religious matters as well as their placement under the authority of the Russian tsar. The pronouncements of the Council of the Hundred Chapters of 1551, presided over by the young Ivan IV, told of bisexual activities during large pagan feasts that transgressed the Church's interdicts, and denounced the **inversion** of natural sexual roles: "Men and youths ... dress in women's clothing." The *Domostroy,* a sixteenth-century Muscovite set of domestic rules (which was later denounced in the nineteenth century), expressed the mentality of wealthy boyars (aristocrats) and their inherent demand for self-control. Its misogyny and patriarchal conservatism were also revealed in its condemnation of unnatural morals. Chapter eight of the *Domostroy*, which explains "how the Christian cures himself of illness and all suffering," deals with illness of the soul and perdition. The sin of Sodom is mentioned, alongside infidelity, and full of passionate excessiveness, including pleasure, swearing, blasphemies, and demonic attitudes and gestures, licentious games, dances, and instrumental music that evoke superstition and magic.

Russian sources are silent on the question of sexual freedom in Muscovite society, but it scandalized foreign visitors, particularly the apparent predilection for zoophilia and homosexuality. Russian "barbarism" was manifested in general impudence (e.g., promiscuity in mixed steam rooms, obscene puppet shows for children) and lasciviousness, and also by drunkenness. The German envoy Adam Olearius, in his *Voyage à Moscou* (Journey to Moscow) (1659), observed: "They

practice all sorts of perversions and even sins **against nature**, not only with men, but also with beasts." Homosexuality was thus associated with depictions of savagery, demonstrating how overdue social control by religion and morality was (an ambition set into motion in the West by the Reformation and Tridentine **Catholicism**).

The first non-religious criminalization of *muzhelozhestvo*, which appeared in Peter the Great's military regulations of 1706, was not a civil law. Peter, himself bisexual, was nonetheless inspired by the discipline displayed by his Swedish enemies, and sought to expunge homosexual practices from his army. Homosexuals were subject to being burned on the pyre, although ten years later, the penalty was reduced to ten years in exile. The rule did not apply to high-ranking military leaders of the nobility, Souvo and Koutouzov, even though their habits were known.

The Code of Laws of 1830 and the new penal code of 1832 (Article 995) punished sodomy (now referred to under its biblical name) with four to five years of exile in Siberia. Another law, Article 996, doubled the sentence in cases of rape or abuse of a minor or the feeble-minded (once again, this was borrowed from the Germanic Protestant world). Another, earlier attempt at criminalization dated back to 1813, a time when Tsar Alexander I was a champion of the anti-French cause, which may have entailed his opposition to the Napoleonic Code's decriminalization of sodomy; Alexander's document invoked the Bible, as the tsar was going through a mystical period. But the law was not applied due to its prudish impreciseness (is it generally homosexuality it objects to, or specifically anal penetration?) and the difficulty establishing factual evidence. But it had an ideological function, both internally and externally: to compensate for the absence of a constitution by a moralizing excessiveness, and to present the Russian state as a paragon of virtue compared to the liberal West, during a time when the state tightened the alliance between the throne and the Church and proclaimed the "national and orthodox" nature of the autocracy. In 1845, the *muzhelozhestvo* became an "unnatural vice," and punished with exile, hard labor, and property seizure. The paradox: the principal ideologist and minister of the time, Ouvarov, was gay.

As for members of the elite who were found to be homosexual, they were not subject to public scandal or legal trouble, but rather discreetly and temporarily exiled in order to undo any visible links. However, the absence of a precise qualification for *muzhelozhestvo* rendered the 1845 law more or less null and void. In 1872, the Russian senate defined "pederasty" and "sodomy" as homosexual anal penetration in one of its first acts. The idea of equal treatment for heterosexual sodomy shocks some: according to certain distinguished protesters from Kharkov, "sodomy has a less corrupting effect on a female than on a male." By the end of the century, the first debate on homosexuality and the law between lawyers, doctors and priests pitted moralizing conservatives against moderates and liberals influenced by Western **psychology** and **medicine**, then by nascent **psychoanalysis**. The church and the state refused to secularize sexual rights, despite arguments that demonstrated the uselessness of the law: abolition was inconceivable, as it would appear to sanction the **decadence** of the liberal West. The autocratic moral order cut off any opportunity for rational discussion. The intrusion into the private sexual activities of consenting adults seemed lawful, given that male homosexuality (the only type conceived)—likened to bestiality and rape—aroused a deep-rooted fear of a reversal in the social order. In 1903, a commission proposed to remove bestiality from the law but not sodomy between consenting adults. But biblical references were being replaced by naturalist, anthropological arguments. The analogy of homosexuality with rape, the corruption of minors, or the abuse of the weak seduced the imagination, but it had its limits (who was raped?) and was not deemed to be pertinent where rational law was invented. The basis for **criminalization** was religious, but the most modern lawyers were now making a distinction between morality, law, and religion. The great liberal lawyer and criminologist Vladimir Nabokov (father of the famous writer of the same name) wrote a paper in 1903 in which he argued that private sexual relationships should not fall under the law of the state, provided they were adult and consensual; he went from personal disgust to sincere **tolerance** on the subject.

Control of the press in Russia explains why homosexuality was never exploited politically or socially. The aristocracy and monarchy were untouchable, but conservative historian Sergei Soloviev, head of the Hegelian School of Law, stigmatized Prince Meschersky, director of the reactionary journal *The Citizen*, as "Prince Sodom, citizen of Gomorrah" (which played on the phrase "Prince Minine and the bourgeois Pojarskii," referring to the Moscow liberators of 1612 and na-

tional heros, Prince Pojarsky and Minin, a butcher). Meschersky showed great affection for his favorites at court, and Soloviev, son of an Orthodox priest, saw in him the tradition of vice that foreign travelers to Russia had noted in the sixteenth century. Conservatives considered open homosexuality of the elite to be a discredit to the regime.

The radical progressives were no less severe toward homosexuality. In a letter to fellow writer Leonid Andreyev, Maxim Gorky severely criticized the esthetics of homosexuality as described by Mikhail Kuzmin, author of the first homophile Russian novel *Wings* (published in 1906), which provoked an enormous **scandal**. Meanwhile, poet and playwright Viacheslav Ivanov affirmed: "They are slaves of the old fashion, people who cannot restrain themselves and who confuse liberty and homosexuality. They confuse the freedom of the individual in a particular way with the action of crawling from one cesspool to another, and sometimes this comes down to the liberation of the penis and nothing more." This vision of homosexuality as the vice of hedonistic and asocial individuals, thereby becoming objective accomplices of despotic regimes, denotes a shift during the Soviet era to a conception of homosexuality linked to **Fascism**. Dramatist Anton Chekhov (who was also a physician) could not get beyond his scorn of lesbians, who were associated with prostitution. As for Vasily Rozanov (author of 1913's *People of Moonlight,* the first Russian book on homosexuality from a non-medical point of view), he opposed the ascetic and repressive Christianity of the church by advocating the cosmic sexuality of the Bible (for which he was the self-proclaimed "pornographic" minstrel), but to him, the homosexual appeared uniquely as an enemy of sex *per se* (a view that was perhaps based on the idea of it being the activity of the repressed). Whether lecherous or chaste, the homosexual was a deviant being, a corruptor, and an enemy of life and of society; he was also the object of contradictory fantasies and constituted a useful foil.

After the Russian Revolution in 1917, the Communist Party officially abolished all the old Tsarist laws, including the prohibition on homosexuality. Its **decriminalization**, however, was ambiguous. It stemmed from a psychopathological view that excused victims for their illness or **abnormality**, and ridiculed obscurant religious moralism. Inasmuch as it appeared to be second nature, the homosexuality of consenting adults seemed to bother no one, and its repression appeared cruel. But it was also believed that **treatment** would be eventually possible; for this, however, the cure must come from choice. In the 1930s, the Soviet Union praised itself for its progressive legislation in an article in the *Great Soviet Encyclopedia*.

However, in the name of an egalitarian morality and a totalitarian state, Stalinist virtue demanded a standardization of sexuality reduced to the reproductive function. The *a priori* suspect, pleasure, was only legitimized by the accomplishment of the social task. The Soviet citizen was enjoined to procreate and have children corresponding to state policy (which was entirely natalist after the Revolution) and "Soviet values": the **family** once again found its function as the primary "unit" of socialization. In this context, the reproductive role of sex became dogma, scientifically justified by the biological nature of the species, whereas the fundamentally social character of the "producers" (both economic and sexual)—which proved the entirety of Marx's theory—implied the responsibility of the Soviet public to the state (representative of the perfect society) in sexual matters. Homosexuality was, by contrast, a waste of energy and production. Moreover, growing anti-Nazi sentiment proved to be harmful to homosexuals as well, who were linked with the SS over the infamous Night of the Long Knives; in June 1934, Gorky published an article in *Pravda* entitled "Eradicate Homosexuality and Fascism Will Disappear." In 1933, Stalin introduced a new criminal code that made homosexuality a crime again, punishable by five years of hard labor (Article 154, then 121).

Repression of homosexuals in the Soviet Union began in earnest in 1933–34; Soviet justice was severe. In 1936, state prosecutor Nikolai Krylenko turned homosexuality into an anti-bourgeois and anti-Fascist issue. Homosexuals were accused of collusion with Fascism; they were the "dregs of society," "degraded rabble" from the former regime. Homosexuality was a sign of the moral decadence and irrational nihilism of a bourgeoisie in crisis, and it proved fatal during the purges. While the writer Kuzmin died of natural causes, his lover, Yuri Yurkun, was shot in 1938. An article on homosexuality in the 1952 edition of the *Great Soviet Encyclopedia* turned it into a Western phenomenon caused by alcoholism, sexual permissiveness, and capitalist social conditions. The existence of homosexuality in the Soviet Union was thus an insult and an impossibility; repression of the "enemies of the people" was ramped up by way of the **gulags**. But the

gulag helped to create a homosexuality of substitution through violence, where the presumed "passives," and those forced into passivity, became the "degraded" and scorned sexual objects, or the favorites of their protectors. Further, a section of the KGB was devoted to rounding up and arresting homosexuals, furnishing on average 1,000 new prisoners every year, that is to say between 50,000 and 60,000 until the fall of the regime. Homosexuality that resisted socialist conditions fell under the domain of **psychiatry** and "sexual perversions" (along with sadism and **pedophilia**); it was also noted that it was evident in certain psychopaths.

But a decree by President Boris Yeltsin abolished criminalization in 1993, one of many signs of democratization sent to the West. However, post-Soviet stigmatization of homosexuals has taken the form of irony; male homosexuals are considered "light blues" *(goluboy)*, while lesbians are designated as "pink girlies"). These condescending terms are strange avatars of the heterosexist system of gender marking from birth by use of colored ribbons on cribs and in children's parks, pale colors indicate infancy, so these terms for homosexuals suggest a blockage in male or female sexual development at an early stage: a form of vulgar Freudianism, which was popular in the Soviet Union. There is also the use of scornful and aggressive terms, such as *pedik* and *pidor*, abbreviations for pederast. Accusations of homosexuality are considered the ultimate insult among men. The questioning of one's virility—*Idi na khou* ("Go fuck yourself")—is not specifically aimed at *goluboys* and can be used in lieu of the popular *ieb tvoyou mat* ("Go fuck your mother"), which is just as humiliating. Meanwhile in politics, the eastern refinement of the frail Anastas Mikoyan, an Armenian who was a longtime Soviet statesman serving both Stalin and Khrushchev, was rumored to be a "**favorite**" of Stalin's team: how else could one explain his having survived the purges and his longevity in the higher circles of power? This rumor (or was it only a joke?) revealed a vulgar psychology which projected its logic onto those in power (who were both feared and reviled) and finding in this sexual reductionism a means to deprecate the tyrant (i.e. Stalin).

Many Russians, ambivalent toward "democracy" and skeptical of its success, associated the Soviet Union's breakup and the end of the social programs engendered by General Secretary of the Communist Party Leonid Brezhnev with the weakness of the new "feminine" regime; the decriminalization of homosexuality by Yeltsin was considered one more example. Viewed as the beneficiaries of Western liberalism, homosexuals are called "sexual democrats" by their critics, which reveals a popular Russian metaphor for the abuse of power (whereby the innocent population is "sodomized" by the freedom of the powerful) as well as a popular analogy (homosexuals are to sexuality what the corrupt are to democracy). To opponents, decriminalization was like an admission of complicity, and made out homosexuals to be the privileged ones in the new era of corruption. Gorky was thus not far off the mark: for Nationalists and those nostalgic for the Empire, the Orthodoxy, or the Stalinist egalitarian order, these perverted sensualists symbolized the moral perversion that is foreign to the Russian people, the result of the multifaceted penetration of the enemy into Holy Russia. The Orthodox Church ferociously rejected this opening up of the country, and demanded that the state protect minors and forbid perverts from having access to teaching or other positions of authority. In his 2002 book on the history of Russian boxing, Orthodox historian and patriot Andrei V. Grotovsky argues for the revival of nationalist, virile virtues and the teaching of boxing as a school of honor and socialization for young men. According to him, "the absence of tradition in the domain of sexual education produces the development of **inversion** (rejection of the sexual norm), which is linked to the appearance of sadism." Consequently, by applying Freud's theory and Orthodox spirituality, he sees **sports** as a remedy for moral decadence. In Russia (as well as Ukraine and Belarus), psychiatric interests have replaced criminalization, inviting the "abnormal" to undergo treatment, particularly in the case of victims of police harassment, accused of "hooliganism" for militant activities or meetings. This is a strange continuance of the association between political, moral, and sexual dissidence: with official state homophobia gone, homosexuals are persecuted by other means. The current in-between status of gays and lesbians is exemplified by the fact that 2008 will mark the third Pride parade in Moscow, provided it is not shut down by the police, which occurred with the first two.

—*Nicolas Plagne*

Engelstein, Laura. *The Keys to Happiness: Sex and the Search for Modernity in Fin-de-siècle Russia.* Ithaca, NY: Cornell Univ. Press, 1992.

Frémont, Benoît. "Out of the Blue: une histoire des homosexuels en Russie," *Regard sur l'Est,* nos. 26–27 (2001).

Karlinsky, Simon. "Russia's Gay Literature and Culture: The Impact of the October Revolution." In *Hidden From History: Reclaiming the Gay and Lesbian Past.* New York: Penguin, 1990.

Kon, Igor. *The Sexual Revolution in Russia from the Age of the Czars to Today.* New York: Free Press, 1995.

Kreise, Bernard. "Avant-propos." In *Les Derniers Instants de Pouchkine.* Toulouse, France: Bibliothèques Ombres, 2000.

Kuzmin, Mikhail. *Les Ailes.* Toulouse, France: Bibliothèques Ombres, 2000.

Levin, Eve. *Sex and Society in the World of the Orthodox Slavs 900-1700.* Ithaca, NY: Cornell Univ. Press, 1989.

Morozov, G., and V. Romassenko. *Neurologie et psychiatrie.* Moscow: Editions de la Paix (n.d.; some time after 1950).

Stern, Mikhaïl. *La Vie sexuelle en URSS.* Paris: Albin Michel, 1979.

Tuller, David. *Cracks in the Iron Closet: Travels in Gay and Lesbian Russia.* Chicago: Univ. of Chicago Press, 1996.

Vighnevski, Anatoli. *La Faucille et le rouble, la modernisation conservatrice en URSS.* Paris: Gallimard, 2000.

—*Balkans, the; Bible, the; Communism; Europe, Eastern & Central; Gulag; Heresy; Justinian I; Orthodoxy (Christian); Sodom and Gomorrah; Theology.*

S

SAPPHO

Sappho is the emblematic figure of female homosexuality; the term "Sapphics" is derived from her name, and the word "lesbian" from the island of Lesbos, where she lived. However, the meaning of these words was only established in nineteenth-century Europe; during Antiquity, lesbianism was described using very different terms which had nothing to do with Sappho. Over the centuries, based on Sappho's fragments that have reached us, a myth has been created around the poetess that is both shifting and paradoxical, making no distinction between the real "I" and the poetic "I"; further, the numerous "Fictions of Sappho" (literary responses to the poetess, as documented by scholar Joan Dejean in the book of the same name) have tended to obscure the original works' historical foundation. Sappho has become the temporally independent figure of lesbianism around which the different discourses on **lesbophobia** have crystallized.

Sappho lived on the Greek island of Lesbos at the end of the seventh century and beginning of the sixth century BCE. Among her poems (composed to be sung), the most famous describes a woman's physical demonstrations of love and desire for another woman (Fragment 31). By using a first-person voice, Sappho creates an atmosphere where natural landscape, music, aromas, and emotions are mixed. In her time, she incurred neither condemnation nor rejection for the homoeroticism expressed in her poetry. In Greece, she was praised for her talent and, if the comedy of the fifth and sixth centuries BCE depicted her as the lover of several men, it is most likely because she was a famous woman, and because in Athens, the female inhabitants of Lesbos had a bad reputation (the Greek verb *lesbiazein* generally means "to perform fellatio"); it was only at the end of the first century BCE in Rome that the question about Sappho's sexual orientation was first formulated (again, the distinction between the real "I" and the poetic "I" was never made). Thus, a double

discourse developed; the first one linked female homosexuality to sexual **debauchery** (Sappho becomes a woman with an unbalanced morality, a *tribade*), and the second spread the rumor of Sappho's suicide, who was said to have jumped from a rock on the island of Leucas (now Levkas) because of her unrequited love for the young boatman Phaon (Ovid, *Heroides,* XV).

Based on this discourse, Sappho, rediscovered in the sixteenth and seventeenth centuries CE, is constantly reinvented. The first fictions of Sappho were elaborated upon by philologists. In 1555, French poet Louise Labé (who is herself a historically disputed figure; according to one book, her poetry was the creation of a group of male poets) originated the concept of a heterosexual Sappho, which soon became predominant in France. Anne Le Fèvre, who edited a French translation of Sappho in 1660, clearly stated that Sappho liked women, without condemning or defending her; other scholars of the seventeenth century remained either undecided or in favor of Labé's concept. By the eighteenth century, Sappho's heterosexuality was undisputed, but during the course of the nineteenth century, German Hellenists started propagating the idea of a chaste Sappho; the first to do so was Friederich Gottlieb Welcker, in his pioneering philological study of Sappho in 1816, which explained that female homosexuality and poetic talent were not compatible. He was followed by Frenchmen like Paul-Pierre Rable in 1855, who translated only part of Fragment 31, and André Lebey in 1895, who chose to replace the female beloved with a masculine pronoun in "Ode to Aphrodite." Today, Edith Mora sees homophobic reactions in these interpretations of Sappho's work; K.J. Dover, while invoking the ambiguity of the texts themselves, demonstrates the weight of translators' prejudices who suppress "the only indication that the designated person is a woman"; Jack Winkler conjures up translations that retain the misogyny and homophobic anguish of philologists, and Holt N. Parker demonstrates that the "Sappho Schoolmistress" persona is a construction in service to a heterosexual masculine norm. Further, the fact that Welcker imagines a virtuous Sappho while justifying masculine homosexuality in Greek literature suggests that his response is a case of lesbophobia and a fear generated by the expression of female desire.

Between 1895 and 1910 in France, several authors proclaimed Sappho's homosexuality. The British-born lesbian poet Renée Vivien proposed a translation of Sappho's poems in 1903, enriched by new fragments found in Egypt. As Edith Mora has commented, Vivien made Sappho "more of a lesbian in the public opinion than she was in her own verses" by adding verses based on her own ideas. This new Sappho became the "mother lesbian, a guardian spirit, the embodiment of homosexual temptation," according to Sappho scholar Nicole Albert. In the 1875 edition of the Larousse dictionary, a "Sappho," by antonomasia, was a "woman whose genius or morality reminds us of the famous woman thus named." A shift from the chaste Sappho to the courtesan, then the sensual lesbian of the new fictions of Sappho, took place in French literature at the end of the nineteenth century. She was depicted as a courtesan by Emile Deschanel in 1847, and in 1884 Alphonse Daudet's *Sappho* is a prostitute with the experience of the entire "sexual spectrum … in all of Sappho's terrible glory." Baudelaire depicted her as the archetype of the "damned woman," while Verlaine made her into a wild persona who roams like a "female wolf" and "pulls her hair out by the handful."

The works of the first psychiatrists and sexologists at the end of the nineteenth century, such as Richard von Krafft-Ebing and Havelock Ellis, who defined homosexuality as sexual **inversion**, were affected by the lesbophobic content of the Sapphic novels. Sappho becomes the incarnate of the threat of lesbian **contagion** in Gabriel Fauré's *La Dernière journée de Sappho* (The last day of Sappho) (1900), in which she advocates a sexual revolution, teaching women how "to procure every voluptuous pleasure for themselves," and in *Les Désexués* (1924) by Charles Etienne and Odette Dulac, where the heroine becomes a lesbian after having kissed her music-hall partner who was playing the role of Sappho. The lesbian also becomes a clinical case: "a pathetic Sappho," "psychotic" in *Amants féminins* (Feminine lovers) by Adrienne St-Agen (1902). Even the name of the poet became an insult; in 1908, Jorau stigmatized Vivien as a "modern priestess of lesbian love," and "a Sappho," while "Billy," originator of the

Sapho 1900 [spelling correct] literary circle in 1951, qualified Vivien as a false Sappho. Thus, Sappho, homosexual once again, unleashed lesbophobic passions well into the twentieth century.

Today, as Joan Dejean writes, "Sappho remains a problem." Either the poet is construed as a lukewarm heterosexual as a consequence of lesbophobic prejudices, or her homosexuality is accepted and she is transformed into a sexually insatiable lesbian, which, in turn, feeds homophobic stereotypes. At the end of the twentieth century, homophobia is apparently expressed by not talking about it: little by little, Sappho, one of the greatest poets in history, has disappeared from collective culture and "Greek love" remains masculine.
—*Sandra Boehringer and Anne-Claire Rebreyend*

Albert, Nicole. "Saphisme et décadence dans l'art et la littérature en Europe à la fin du XIXe siècle." Thesis. Université Paris IV-Sorbonne, 1998.

Dejean, Joan. *Sapho, les fictions du désir. 1546–1937.* Paris: Hachette Supérieur, 1994. [Published in the US as *Fictions of Sapho, 1546-1937.* Chicago: Univ. of Chicago Press, 1989.]

Mora, Edith. *Sappho, histoire d'un poète et traduction intégrale de l'œuvre.* Paris: Flammarion, 1966.

Parker, Holt N. "Sappho Schoolmistress," *Transactions of the American Philological Association* no. 123 (1993).

—*Debauchery; Greece, Ancient; Heterosexism; History; Lesbophobia; Vice.*

SCANDAL

For centuries, the experience of scandal has pervaded gay and lesbian life. Homosexuality has long been associated with devilry and taboo, to the point that its mere possibility instilled terror (one can note that nineteenth-century **medicine**, under an apparent positivism, endorsed a rhetoric of horror and disgust). The discovery of a relative's homosexuality was often the result of intrusion, followed by a terse repudiation of the relative, either verbal or written. The reaction was always of shock, in the most physical sense of the word, which was manifested in the usual clinical signs of extreme emotion (fainting, crying, convulsions). The outbreak of the **AIDS** crisis exacerbated the scandalous shock, especially in terms of disclosing one's seropositivity at the same time, exemplified by the furor over the announcement of Rock Hudson's illness in 1985. During this period, many families were discovering that their relative was homosexual at the same time that they discovered that he was suffering from a mortal illness. This shock of revelation was generally followed by indignation: generations of homosexuals had to deal with being disowned by **family** and rejected by friends. Religious and social morality often played a role in this banishment and forced abandonment of a loved one.

The historical subjugation of women has made the situation of lesbians particularly fragile in case of a public scandal: it was common for families to intervene between women who formed a couple and to force them to separate, which is what happened to the writers Violet Trefusis and Vita Sackville-West in **England** in 1920. In short, millions of gays and lesbians have had to deal with the day when their secret life could or would be destroyed by the intrusion of others.

Many of these scandals had considerable repercussions outside the sphere of familial relations. We can cite some of the most famous, for example, the Marquis de **Custine**, who was assaulted by three soldiers in 1824; the Count de Germiny, who was arrested in a street urinal in Paris in 1876; Oscar **Wilde**, who was condemned to two years of hard labor in 1895; British Major-General Hector MacDonald, who was compelled to commit **suicide** in 1903; and the Prince of **Eulenburg** and Hertefeld of Germany, who was publicly accused of being Count von Moltke's lover. The list goes on: Alfred Redl, the Austrian colonel who was uncovered as not only a spy for the Russians in 1913 but also a homosexual, which led to his suicide; Ernst Röhm, chief of the SA, who was summarily executed during the Night of the Long Knives on July 1, 1934, by Nazi authorities who had pretended to have just discovered his homosexuality; Guy Burgess, the British double agent whose homosexuality was revealed to the press after he defected to the East in 1951; John Gielgud, the actor, arrested for cottaging (performing homosexual acts in a public toilet) in 1953; Lord Montagu, a British aristocrat prosecuted for gross indecency in 1953–54; British Member of Parliament Ian Harvey, forced to resign from the British cabinet after he was found with a horse-guard in St James' Park in 1958; Jeremy Thorpe, former leader of the British Liberal Party, who was forced to resign his seat in Parliament after he was accused of homosexuality and attempted murder in the 1970s; and Günter Kiessling,

the German general and a commander of NATO forces who in 1983 was regarded as a security risk after being accused of frequenting gay bars, leading to his early retirement.

All of these scandals have common characteristics. For one, they occur more frequently with men than women, given that lesbianism has tended to go unnoticed, was less often criminalized, and was considered less transgressive by the **media** to the extent that women were nearly totally excluded from the public sphere. For another, most of these scandals took place between 1876 and 1960; prior to this period, the taboo of homosexuality overrode any scandal. Details of the Custine affair did not appear in newspapers, but only circulated by word of mouth among the Parisian nobility. After the end of the 1960s, the forces that automatically condemned homosexuality began to falter; Rock Hudson gained more admirers than he lost when he revealed his homosexuality right before he died. For another, many of these scandals occurred in England: the devious tactics of tabloid newspapers, and the prolonged Victorianism prevalent in Great Britain through the "swinging sixties" and even beyond, created a favorable climate for scandal. Homosexual scandals were also frequently linked to very specific contexts: the advent of pious King Charles X in the Custine affair; the 1876 political fights between Republicans and Royalists, at the end of the moral Order, in the Germiny affair; the British Liberals' desire to hush up rumors about Prime Minister Lord Rosebery at the time of the Wilde affair; the stiffening of French-German relations after 1905 in the Eulenburg affair; the internal conflicts of the Nazi Party and the Hitlerian desire to stop the "German Revolution" and to embrace the values of the dominant classes of 1934; the Cold War and the fear of the "Homintern" at the basis of the British scandals of the 1950s; the ongoing tension of West-East relations at the time of the Kiessling affair in the early 1980s. The victims' social identity was also often a key element of the scandal; the most sensational ones were those which involved a person of privilege or authority whose fall from grace was unexpected: the Marquis de Custine, whose father and grandfather had been guillotined for being sympathizers with the French Revolution; the Count de Germiny, lawyer for the Jesuits; Oscar Wilde, best-selling author celebrated by all of London; the Prince of Eulenburg, friend of the Kaiser; Edward Montagu de Beaulieu, member of the House of Lords; MacDonald, Moltke, Redl, and Kiessling, all high-ranking officers; Röhm and Thorpe, political leaders; and Gielgud, one of the greatest actors of the twentieth century. Beginning at the end of the nineteenth century, these scandals were accompanied by a discourse led by the media, an absolutely necessary sounding board, whose denunciation was generally made in moral terms (e.g., as **vice** and decadence) and, increasingly, in medical and psychiatric terms (as **degeneration**, **contagion**, and depopulation). But they could also be denounced for political ends; the Germiny affair was used by the anticlericals against the right as well as the Jesuits; the Eulenburg affair was used against Kaiser Wilhelm II; and the Röhm affair was used by the Stalinists against the **Fascists**. Media coverage often took the form of degrading or heinous satire; in 1876–77, Parisian newspapers, in deriding the Count de Germiny, referred to street urinals as "*germinyères*," and pederast relations as "*germinyade*" or "*germinism.*"

The effects of homosexual scandal are considerable: it is why British politician Ian Harvey entitled his memoir *To Fall Like Lucifer*. Indeed, the ramifications of scandal resulted in a major break with one's previous life: personal and professional estrangement (it was dangerous to show solidarity with accused individuals because of the risk of guilt by association), followed by legal proceedings and **prison** (Germiny was sentenced to two months, Wilde two years, and Montagu one year). There was also social death: Custine remained a *persona non grata* until his death; letters of condolence were sent to Germiny's wife, as if he had died; Wilde became a social leper, insulted by the public, repudiated by some of his friends, and excluded by his own family; and Harvey, who, while he was officially only accused of breaking city parks laws for having public sex, was no longer acknowledged by his former colleagues of Parliament, and treated as a social pariah (he had to resign from all his clubs, was curtly scolded by his priest, made prejudiced potential employers flee, and rarely received social invitations): in 1971 he wrote, "I can count the number of invitations I received since 1958 on the fingers of both hands." Scandal also brought about political collapse: Harvey was forced to resign from his appointment at the Foreign Office and his seat in Harrow East, and Thorpe from the leadership of the British Liberal Party. Exile was another consequence: Custine moved about in Europe, Germiny settled down in Argentina, Wilde died in France, and

Harvey was advised to start a new life in Canada. Other ramifications include suicide (McDonald, Redl), murder (Röhm), and traumatized silence (Gielgud never spoke about his 1953 arrest, which he thought had cost him peerage in favor of his rival, Laurence Olivier). The families of victims were also profoundly affected by it: Germiny's family pathetically tried to bribe newspapers, while Wilde's wife and sons changed their surname to Holland. However, it was homosexuals as a whole who suffered the most from the consequences of scandal, whether it was the media's promulgation of homophobic sentiment, or the hardening of the stance taken by **police** on the issue. It could be seen in England during Wilde's trial (many homosexuals fled to France during this time) and that of Lord Montagu (several destroyed compromising documents). In Germany, the Night of the Long Knives, during which Röhm was murdered, was described by Goering and Goebbels to the public as a "purifying thunderstorm" to liberate Germany from "these morbid individuals"; it was followed by an increase of raids on cruising areas.

Such events weighed heavily on the lives of gays and lesbians ("their honor precarious, their liberty provisional," according to Proust in *Sodom and Gomorrah*), who for generations have been dominated by the fear of scandal: it is what explained the concern for the **closet** (W. Somerset Maugham lived his entire life in fear that his homosexuality would be publicly revealed), the need to live a double life (in 1946, young Alec Guinness saved his career by giving a false name to policemen who questioned him), the extreme caution during sexual encounters (Harvey wrote that he was very careful, during his encounters in the parks of London, to be neither recognizable nor "ransomable"), the forced acceptance of **insults**, injustice, and aggression, and the flight from blackmail (the 7th Earl Beauchamp exiled himself from England in 1931 after being denounced by his brother-in-law, the Duke of Westminster). It is certain that the suicide of many homosexuals, such as Viscount Harcourt's in 1922, was due to their unwillingness to face imminent scandal. However, one should not forget that the biggest homosexual scandals (Wilde, Eulenburg, Montagu) played a considerable role in the individual and collective awareness of homosexuals and thus in the history of the gay movement. Further, since the 1950s, public opinion became less scandalized by homosexuality than by the injustice of legal and police abuses resulting from it: when John Gielgud returned to the stage a few days after his arrest in 1953, he received a standing ovation (in Liverpool as well as in London) from audience members who clearly showed they were sympathetic.

A type of scandal particular to the twentieth century was the literary one. Major examples include Mikhail Kuzmin's *Wings* in 1906, Proust's *Sodom and Gomorrah* in 1921–22, André **Gide**'s *Corydon* in 1924 and *Si le grain ne meurt* (published in English as *If It Die*) in 1925, **Radclyffe Hall**'s *The Well Of Loneliness* in 1928, and Jean Genet's great works, *Notre-dame des fleurs* (*Our Lady of the Flowers*), *Miracle de la rose* (*Miracle of the Rose*), and *Le journal du voleur* (*The Thief's Journal*), between 1946 and 1949. This type of scandal, which occurred often in France because of publishers' relative freedom under the Second Republic, "often goes hand in hand with amused contempt" (Jean-Louis Bory), and enabled both reviewers and the most conservative moralists to denounce the "sulphurous" literature that would put teenagers at risk and to assert the necessity of **censorship**, which led to the French law of July 16, 1949 regarding publications intended for youth. It was not until the 1970s that homosexual scandals in literature diminished, at least in the West (E. M. Forster's *Maurice* was finally published without controversy in London in 1971, and Renaud Camus did not trigger any backlash with his explicit book *Tricks*, published in 1979). That said, in 1977, Great Britain, having maintained a law against blasphemy, prosecuted James Kirkup, the author and illustrator of a poem ("The Love That Dares To Speak Its Name") evoking the erotic attraction felt by a Roman centurion for Christ on the cross. In France, the novel *Prince et Léonardours* by Mathieu Lindon was threatened to be pulled from sale by the Ministry of the Interior in 1987, but, in the end, the scandal worked in the novel's favor and ensured its publicity.

Going against the grain, British tabloids have maintained the habit of both arousing and denouncing (the ambiguity between both notions is important here) homosexual scandals, no doubt because the British public remains fascinated by the sordid details about **private** lives of public figures and the revelations they produce. Recent victims include Conservative Member of Parliament Alan Amos, who was found with another man on Hampstead Heath in 1992, and forced out by his colleagues (three years later, he crossed sides and joined the rival Labour Party); Welsh Secretary of State Ron Davies, was who surprised in a cruising area in October 1998, and obliged to leave the Blair government; Peter Mandelson, an influential friend of Tony Blair and former Secretary of State for Northern Ireland, who resigned twice, in 1998 and 2001, though officially neither were due to homosexuality, which he never publicly admitted; and Conservative Member of Parliament Michael Portillo, who admitted in 1999 to having had homosexual relations during his years at Cambridge in order to avoid an impending **outing.** These scandals are never totally innocent: the tabloids underlined, with cruelty, that two of Portillo's previous lovers had died of AIDS complications, and in July 2001, a new fit of frenzy about his gay past contributed to the defeat of his candidacy (by only one vote) for the Conservative Party's leadership.

Finally, let's say that scandal helps us to define two types of homophobia. The homophobia that uses scandal is clearly supported by the media, which historically has believed in the "name and shame" strategy. Its message is directed at both homosexuals and the whole of society: that under no circumstances should homosexuality be acceptable; and homosexuals who do not want problems should remain invisible (this was, for example, implied by Egyptian authorities behind the spectacle of fifty-two homosexuals on trial in September 2001). One of the most common reasons for disclosing another person's homosexuality has been blackmail, particularly in Great Britain since the nineteenth century; jilted lovers and political rivals threatened to go to the newspapers with supporting letters and images. Homophobia without scandal avoids turning something into a media event, undoubtedly due to the belief that homosexuality is extremely **contagious**, the use of the word alone producing the effect. Communist **China** provides a lasting example, locking up people so accused and liquidating them without a word; but France also preferred discretion in these matters: until the eighteenth century, files on homosexuals were symbolically burned along with the condemned on the pyre; and silence was the norm in Great Britain before the reign of the tabloids. Silence was and is also a rule in countries or homophobic societies that pretend not to have any homosexuals in their ranks, notably the most conservative Muslim states, some countries in **Africa**, or the **Catholic** clergy. In the West, the age of scandal, in hindsight, appears as a type of final transition between the era of taboo and the era of indifference, between the period of the *crimen nefandum* ("unmentionable vice") and the period of human rights. It also corresponds to a specific moment in the history of journalism, when new media freedom enabled the introduction of new topics, although their conformist attitude prevents them from going beyond monotheistic prejudice.

Since the gay revolution in the 1970s, gays and lesbians in the West have worked to free homosexuality from scandal in every possible way: through geographical settings that allow people to be openly gay (Oxford and Cambridge; Greenwich Village and Chelsea in New York and Castro Street in San Francisco; Soho in London and the Marais in Paris; Mykonos in Greece and Sitges in Spain); in ending the need for discretion or having to live a double life (coming out is the best response to would-be blackmailers); and in the daily fight to convince media, the legal system, and society at large that homosexuality is commonplace. Today, when gays and lesbians "out" someone—which represents a reverse scandal, of sorts—it is not homosexuality they expose, but rather the lack of rectitude of the public figures who refuse to assume it.

—*Pierre Albertini*

Ahlstedt, Eva. *André Gide et le débat sur l'homosexuality: de L'Immoraliste (1902) à Si le grain ne meurt (1926).* Gothenburg, Sweden: Acta Universitatis Gothoburgensis, 1994.

David, Hugh. *On Queer Street: A Social History of British Homosexuality, 1895–1995.* London: Harper Collins, 1997.

Ellmann, Richard. *Oscar Wilde.* Paris: Gallimard, 1994.

Eribon, Dider. *Réflexions sur la question gay.* Paris: Fayard, 1999. [Published in the US as *Insult and the Making of the Gay Self.* Durham, NC: Duke University Press, 2004.]

Foldy, Michael S. *The Trials of Oscar Wilde: Deviance, Morality and Late Victorian Society.* New Haven, CT: Yale Univ. Press, 1997.

Gury, Christian. *L'Honneur perdu d'un politicien homosexuel [Germiny] en 1876.* Paris: Kimé, 1999.

Harvey, Ian. *To Fall Like Lucifer.* London: Sidgwick & Jackson, 1971.

Hull, Isabelle. *The Entourage of Kaiser Wilhelm II, 1888–1918.* Cambridge/London: Cambridge Univ. Press, 1982.

McLaren, Angus. *Sexual Blackmail: A Modern History.* Harvard: Harvard Univ. Press, 2002.

Morley, Sheridan. *John G: The Authorized Biography of John Gielgud.* London: Hodder & Stoughton, 2001.

Robinson, Christopher. *Scandal in the Ink: Male & Female Homosexuality in Twentieth-Century French Literature.* London: Cassell, 1995.

Tamagne, Florence. *Histoire de l'homosexualité en Europe.*

Berlin, Londres, Paris, 1919–1939.* Paris: Le Seuil, 2000. [Published in the US as *A History of Homosexuality in Europe: Berlin, London, Paris, 1919–1939.* New York: Algora, 2004.]

Thorpe, Jeremy. *In My Own Time: Reminiscences of a Liberal Leader.* London: Politico's Publishing, 1999.

Weeks, Jeffrey. *Coming Out: Homosexual Politics in Britain, from the Nineteenth Century to the Present Time.* London: Quartet Books, 1977.

—*Arenas, Reinaldo; Caricature; Closet, the; Custine, Astolphe de; Decadence; Gide, André; Literature; Media; Police; Radclyffe Hall, Marguerite; Rhetoric; School; Shame; Suicide; Treason; Turing, Alan; Viau, Théophile de; Vice; Violence; Wilde, Oscar.*

SCHOOL

School is often where gays and lesbians are first confronted by homophobia. It is here that **insults**, bullying, and violence create profound feelings of inferiority and **shame** in those who are targeted. School is also where some individuals display primitive, ultra-violent behavior prior to the discovery of their own homosexuality. The homophobic actions and words of children and adolescents, tolerated by adults even when they reach almost sadistic proportions, seem to serve as a sort of perverse collective education, as American writer Paul Monette points out in his autobiography *Becoming a Man* (1992). He recalls a scene from around 1955, when he witnesses a young eleven-year-old bully force a classmate that he accuses of being gay to swallow his spit. By doing so, the bully means to teach spectators, all children between the ages of ten and twelve, that to be moral, one must not only be not homosexual, but also one must hate them, as they represent the vilest of the vile. For those students who may already feel the pangs of same-sex attraction, this creates the need for absolute **discretion**: "Above all, don't show it."

The paradox of the institution of school is that it has played a central role in the history of homophobia in Western society, all the while providing a haven for those harboring homosexual feelings. In **France**, **police** reports from the eighteenth century mention that many sodomites first acquired "this taste" in high school (*collège*). From the Second French Empire (1852–70), one can find numerous reports from police inspectors and prosecutors similar to this one: "acts of pederasty are very common between the wretched children of this boarding house." In particular, boarding schools did not allow any input by students' families, and placed students in close contact with other students of various ages and stages of physical development; sometimes they even permitted some sexual activity so long as it was clandestine, such as touching and dormitory "visits." Yet, at the same time, homosexuality represented an enormous risk: any students caught red-handed were at risk of being shunned by their classmates and heavily punished by authorities. In France, homosexuality was considered the greatest shame in religious boarding schools as well as the public schools (*lycées*), as can be seen in the biography of writer Henri de Montherlant, who was kicked out of Ste-Croix de Neuilly school for this reason in 1913. In addition, until recently, French military boarding schools considered that any student "found in a bed other than one's own" was subject to punishment, usually grounding; this was also the case for preperatory students.

Things were not very different at the Ecole normale supérieure (the top university in Paris), despite the fact that students were older. At the beginning of the twentieth century, a *normalien* suspected of homosexuality was treated with violent hostility by his classmates, as revealed by the very homophobic geographer Raoul Blanchard in his memoir. Around 1930, in the same university, the personal habits of writer Robert Brasillach would be more shocking than his neo-fascist ideas (which eventually led to his execution for being a Nazi collaborator); further, it is well-known that Michel Foucault was depressed and suicidal while studying there from 1946 to 1951. But it is in the British public schools where the ambiguity reached its height: homosexuality was quite commonplace, because the supervision of boarding school residents was most often carried out by the oldest students, in an adolescent atmosphere of relative autonomy. Yet any discovery by authorities of a physical relationship between students was cause for expulsion; according to student slang, such expulsions were "for the usual thing." It should be noted here that the enduring development of homosexuality in the public schools of a country long considered homophobic is rather surprising: it is probable that many fathers, having gone through the experience themselves, knew what to expect when sending their own sons to boarding

school, and saw it only as a temporary affectation of little consequence (besides, beginning in the 1930s, the spread of Freudian discourse on the homosexual phase of adolescence would reassure even those who were most insecure about it). Boarding schools could also lead to homosexual abuse that was rather ambivalent, often associated with a wrongly assumed homosexuality. This is what Robert Musil recounted in 1906 in his novel *Die Verwirrungen des Zoglings Torless* (*The Confusions of Young Törless*), where the student Basini is used as a sexual slave by several of his classmates, who scorn him to the point of saying: "There is nothing between Basini and us, other than the pleasure that his groveling gives." It would also be incorrect to think that school attacks and rapes only occurred between students: Jean-Claude Caron showed that, in nineteenth-century France, a large number of ecclesiastical educators were denounced for **pedophilia** (most, it is true, were teachers in rather modest schools where the students, children of the common people, had no means to defend themselves).

Homophobia inspired many school reforms from the eighteenth to twentieth centuries. The concepts of physician Simon-Auguste Tissot (*Onanism: Or a Treatise Upon the Disorders Produced by Masturbation*, 1760), and later Ambroise Tardieu (*Etudes medico-légale sur les attentats aux mœurs* [Medical-legal studies of assaults against decency], 1857) long influenced school authorities in France. According to Tissot, any sexual act that does not lead to procreation causes physical weakness, while Tardieu believed that the true pederasts, who were few in number, corrupted the rest, who became "occasional" homosexuals. Acting on this, the heads of boarding schools (both public and private) increased the supervision of dormitories (in a way that never took place in England, where it was believed that character was built through self-policing) with the clear intention of preventing all sexual activity. Monseigneur Dupanloup once said that a dormitory supervisor had two obsessions, "special friendships and improper familiarities," and that he had to maintain at all times the rule of *numquam duo* (never in twos). In 1876, criminologist Cesare Lombroso echoed a similar affirmation in his *L'Uomo delinquente* (*Criminal Man*): "When you see two young men together, be wary, they are probably up to no good." For her part, author George Sand reminds us that this rule applied also to girls, around the beginning of the nineteenth century: "We were forbidden to go off together in twos, it had to be three. We were not allowed to embrace. They worried about our innocent communications." Near the end of the Second Empire era, school **sports** were often perceived as a means of channeling adolescent impulses, of increasing their aggressiveness; in short, of making students more masculine, and in doing so, diverting them from the homosexual **peril**.

Conversely, the bullying of boys who did not like or excel in sports or physical activity was without a doubt the most widespread form of homophobia in schools during the twentieth century. The opening scene of the 1996 British film *Beautiful Thing* combines the three homophobic elements common in this kind of situation: rejection (none of the soccer teams want Jamie), verbal abuse (Jamie is called "Hugh Janus," a rather obscene play on words), and the cowardice of witnesses (including the boy who would later become Jamie's lover).

It is often forgotten that the concept of coeducation was first put forward in France in 1872 by the chemist Henri Etienne Ste-Claire Deville in an attempt to stamp out **inversion**. To him, groupings of adolescents of the same sex could not help but lead to the "terrible **perversion** of instincts." In 1932's *Der Sexuelle Kampf der Jugend* (The sexual struggle of youth), psychoanalyst Wilhelm Reich suggested that the best way to fight against homosexuality (which, to him, was the result of an inhibition brought on by social conditioning) was by bringing both sexes together through coeducation. The environment in which coeducation was implemented in France in the 1960s can be aptly summed up by the homophobia apparent in the 1960 **Mirguet** amendment, which officially labeled homosexuality as a "social scourge" (across the Channel, some would make the same suggestion of coeducation in order to eradicate homosexuality from schools). A similar dialog took place during the 70s when Oxford and Cambridge Universities became coeducational, and in the 80s when the two Ecoles normales supérieures in Paris amalgamated; it had been implied that there were too many homosexuals in these institutions or that they produced too many "occasional" homosexuals, and that coeducation would put an end to this "unhealthy" situation.

Before long, sex education began to be taught in schools, with the clear goal of reinforcing heterosexual norms. Often conducted by **biology** teachers, it usually tied sexuality to reproduction and, as a result,

stigmatized homosexuality, evoking the old medical vocabulary to label it as a perversion. It is interesting to note that the last great vehicle for homophobia in the Soviet Union in the 80s was a sex education textbook written by Antonina Khripkova and Dimitri Kolesov.

Adolescent homosexuals react to homophobia at school in several different ways. Many lie low, necessary for survival in a hostile environment; by doing so, they maintain the appearance of accepting the law of the group and thus pass unnoticed. However, some begin a process of destabilization, which can border on self-destruction (one-third of adolescent **suicides** are said to be linked to homosexuality). In 1998, Darren Steele, a young student in Burton-upon-Trent, killed himself because his love of theater and cooking led his classmates to constantly call him a "poof." Another common response by adolescent homosexuals is to focus exclusively on the intellectual, a more discreet survival strategy and the means to begin constructing a gay identity (especially through reading), while waiting for personal emancipation later in life. Bullying is no doubt one explanation for the overrepresentation of homosexuals among higher-achieving students; journalist Alex Taylor often stated that it was because he was gay that he set himself the goal, during his adolescence in Cornwall, of getting into Oxford.

Obviously, such positive outcomes should neither justify nor excuse bullying. On this topic, the United States has made recent progress in the wake of the Jamie Nabozny case. In 1996, this Wisconsin high school student sued his former school district for not having protected him from several years of intense homophobic harassment in school. The Nabozny case established jurisprudence at the federal level, and it is now expected that administrative heads must provide protection for their gay and lesbian students. In addition, after a series of initiatives by Massachusetts Governor William Weld, school authorities in many areas have sanctioned the creation of gay and gay-friendly student clubs. A similar phenomenon occurred in Great Britain, despite the enactment of Clause 28 (a section of the Local Government Act) in 1988, which forbade schools from teaching that homosexual relationships were equal to heterosexual relationships (it was first repealed in Scotland in 2000 and then the rest of Britain in 2003). The struggle against homophobia in British schools was dependent on the courage of individual school administrations; this courage was sometimes significant: one school director defiantly maintained during the period that Clause 28 was in effect that "(w)e shall not treat homosexual relationships like a simulacrum of familial relationships, but as real family relationships, and we will always continue to do so." France is behind in this matter, in part because community support is less developed in schools, but also because the struggle against any form of harassment was initiated quite late. Nonetheless, universities and other higher education institutions in France are currently seeing an increase in the number of gay and lesbian student associations, such as Homonormalités, launched in 1997 by a group of students at the Ecole normale supérieure (including Louis-Georges Tin).

Another important aspect of school homophobia is the issue of how institutions treat gay and lesbian teachers. The Jesuit regents from Voltaire's day had a reputation for buggery—from time to time, authorities would intervene (in a letter of 1702, politician Pontchartrain reminded all "how important it is to be more stern with those regents and precepts who are corrupting schoolchildren"), but most often the only action taken was to make up **songs** about it; no one was overly concerned. Things changed radically in the nineteenth century, as school personnel could no longer count on the protection of ecclesiastical robes. From then on, the discovery of a teacher's homosexuality was an abominable **scandal**; a teacher who was a pederast was considered far more monstrous than a young female teacher who found herself pregnant. During 1807–08, Jean-Claude Alméry (headmaster of a school), was condemned to one year in **prison** for having tried to seduce his valet. In **England**, as in the United States, by the second half of the nineteenth century homosexuality was grounds for immediate and undisputable dismissal.

In France, the general inspectorate, sharing the common prejudices, were fiercely afraid of the "bad reputation" associated with homosexuality (until the period before World War II, matters of the "morality" of public servants were extremely important in the "reports to the minister") and the consequences for it were harsh. Prior to 1914, most female teachers discovered to be lesbian were either fired or forced to resign. And one can legitimately wonder that, if the excellent professor Jean Beaufret were not openly homosexual, would he have been demoted in the same way in 1950 in spite of the role he played as an officer of the Resistance (a claim that many of his colleagues could not make)? Behind this severity was the notion that homosexual

teachers were a disgrace to the educational profession as a whole; that they undermined the collective authority and posed a danger to students. Republican zeal no doubt reinforced the phenomenon: the **private** life of public school teachers had to be "spotless," because of their schools' competition with religious establishments. It was true, after all, that the **Catholic** right wing did not hesitate to lash out against the Ecole normale supérieure for enrolling young women after writer Gabrielle Reval made it the setting for lesbian love in her novel *Les Sévriennes*, published in 1900. The infinite cautiousness of gay writer Marcel Jouhandeau, who was a teacher at St-Jean de Passy and felt obliged to burn his manuscripts or publish them anonymously, clearly demonstrates how severely the Catholics dealt with non-conformists. But it is also interesting to see how laymen and anticlericals often displayed their own homophobia by subscribing to the concept of "**against nature**" and drawing connections between the clergy and pederasty. In France during the latter half of the Second Empire, governmental ministers often invoked morality to fight against the presence of the clergy in public education. On the other hand, although educators had a long tradition of sacerdotal celibacy, which was well regarded in the nineteenth century, the unmarried man began to appear to be a practicing pervert, or at least had the potential to become one. Homosexual teachers certainly could not count on the solidarity of their colleagues; up until the 1970s, a kind of Puritanism permeated the teaching profession, whether personal inclinations lay with the left wing (communists were often the most rigid) or the right. Teachers and administrators were usually part of the ambitious middle class, a group often inclined to uphold the concept of traditional families, and even the most liberal of teachers were not completely free of homophobic prejudice. One merely has be reminded of the outrageous personality that Jean-Paul Sartre (an instructor at Lycée Pasteur, and then Lycée Condorcet) assigned to his homosexual character Daniel Serrano in his trilogy of novels *Les Chemins de la liberté (The Roads to Freedom)*, who experiences an altogether physical ecstasy when the Germans arrive in Paris; or the sinister recurrence of the word *tapette* (queer) in the correspondence of Simone de Beauvoir (also a philosophy teacher) with her American lover Nelson Algren. Later, during the Fourth Republic, homosexuals teaching outside of metropolitan areas still found themselves victims of extreme solitude, such as the main character of Dominique Fernandez's novel *L'Etoile rose* (The pink star).

It is obvious that the confusion between homosexuality and pedophilia is the largest issue, an association that has caused considerable problems. The connection is particularly common in France, thanks to the highly inadequate name assigned to homosexuals by Auguste Ambroise Tardieu and the French medical community of the Second Empire (the word "pederast" refers both culturally to the Greek love of adolescents and etymologically to childhood). To public authorities, a homosexual teacher was not simply a bad example, but also a predator in a position of power. Given that this belief was grounded in what Tardieu and his popularizers had to say about homosexuality, it then led to the thought that students subjected to a "pederast" teacher risked becoming occasional homosexuals, which would then lead them to debasement and crime. In his 1998 book *Homosexualités et droit* (Homosexualities and the law), Daniel Borrillo demonstrated that the French laws protecting minors, assembled between 1850 and 1937, were based on the fear elicited by the "shameful passions" of teachers. As late as 1973, Jean-Luc Hennig, a young and brilliant professor of grammar, was suspended for having his students read a publication issued by the gay organization Front homosexuel d'action révolutionnaire (FHAR; Homosexual Revolutionary Action Front) entitled *Trois milliards de pervers* (Three billion perverts), as well as for providing a psychoanalytical interpretation of *Little Red Riding Hood*! The situation is even worse for homosexual teachers when a student becomes infatuated. In Austrian director Leontine Sagan's film *Mädchen in Uniform* (Girls in uniform) from 1931, although it is Manuela who falls in love with Miss von Bernburg, the teacher is the one forced to quit the school. In fact, it was to fight against the myth of the homosexual predator that Roger Peyrefitte wrote his novel *Les Amitiés particulières* (*Special Friendships*) in 1943, which demonstrates that homosexuality in boarding schools comes about less from the influence of adults, but rather the emotional evolution between the students themselves.

Things did not begin to change until the late 1960s. In the United States, again, it was a decision of the courts that sparked the change: in 1969, in its judgment on the case of *Morrison v. the State Board of Education*, the Supreme Court of California declared that a teacher sacked for "immorality in private life outside of the **workplace**" could be reinstated, which established an important precedent. That said, in 1978, the so-called Briggs Initiative proposed (in vain) to Californian voters that all homosexuals be banned from teaching. It is because the pedophiliac myth still persists that many American teachers today continue to hide their homosexuality from their students. In France, the situation began to relax in the 70s. Associate professor of literature Jean-Louis Bory contributed enormously to this with his writing and radio appearances which featured his devastating wit ("I'm not a danger to my students, I'm a danger to my students' fathers"). During the same period, Guy Hocquenghem and Dominique Fernandez became the first university professors to publicly announce their homosexuality on television. However, it should be pointed out that the ministry of education's first official recognition of homosexual teachers only occurred in 1999, with the inclusion of PaCS in its employer contracts. The situation in schools varies greatly depending on the institution: it is much easier to be openly homosexual for a university or preparatory school instructor, or those who work in privileged middle schools inside a major city. Otherwise, homosexual teachers still have a difficult time, especially those who work in elementary schools or daycare, where the connection between homosexuality and pedophilia is common, or worse, private schools, where teachers are subjected to harsh Catholic homophobia.

Homophobia has also been evident in school programs and practices, resulting at times in extraordinary symbolic **violence**. The Christianization of classical studies established long-standing taboos that are difficult to escape. Christian educators ("Homosexuality is a sin") and their positivist rivals ("Homosexuality is a disease") agreed at least that the matter should never be spoken of in front of students. This attitude seemed to set the expectation of "magical thinking"—that homosexuality was an aberration that was encouraged by its discussion and, thus, would disappear if never spoken of. Naturally, this did not lead to neutrality in terms of the content taught: the dream of a humanist return to the days of Antiquity butted up against the depiction of Virgilian shepherds and Attic pederasty; Plato's dialogues became mere catalogs of *horrenda* and *nefanda,* and all Greek literature needed to be carefully sanitized. In his 1851 essay *Le Ver rongeur des sociétés modernes ou le paganisme dans l'éducation* (The worm gnawing at modern society, or paganism in education), Jean-Joseph Gaume, a nineteenth-century clergyman, urged that the profane Greek authors, those masters of immorality, no longer be taught in schools. This taboo also extended to higher education: "Omit any reference to the unspeakable **vice** of the Greeks," a Cambridge tutor recommended to E.M. Forster in the 1900s; a Greek classics professor said to Georges Dumézil during World War I, "Now don't go imagining anything." Scholarly research has also long felt the influence of homophobia. In 1948, Henri-Irénée Marrou declared in *Histoire de l'éducation dans l'Antiquité* (*A History of Education in Antiquity*) that "studying the technicalities of inversion in Greek society is of little interest except to **psychiatry** and moral **theology**." And Robert Flacelière, with bourgeois prudishness, wrote in 1937 on the subject of pederasty in his *Vie quotidienne en Grèce au siècle de Périclès* (*Daily Life in Greece at the Time of Pericles*): "As unpleasant as the subject may be, it is impossible to simply ignore."

This discomfort is not limited simply to the classics of Antiquity. In England, Shakespeare's sonnets have for decades posed a very thorny problem; it would not be until the very end of the nineteenth century that universities began to recognize that the majority of his sonnets were addressed to a man, which in the Victorian context meant that the greatest English poet of all time was afflicted by the greatest vice imaginable. In France, when professors of literature were debating during the 1960s how to best integrate twentieth-century French **literature** into the high school curriculum (where it was not yet being taught), the debate kept getting hung up on the sexuality of André **Gide** and Marcel Proust. It is striking to note just how this discomfort (found in textbooks, like those of Lagarde and Michard, which are often inadvertently funny, such as when it introduces Proust's character of Charlus with the enigmatic title of "a strange character"), manifested in embarrassed phrasings and unquestioned prejudices, has passed from generation to generation almost right up to present day. Around 1980, teachers could still be found talking of the "Greek vice" in discussions about Emperor Hadrian or the "awful habits" of the revolutionary Jean-Jacques Régis de Cambacérès, or claiming during a philosophy course that "desire is born of the **difference** between the genders," at which their students would laugh. It is clear that even during that era, homosexuality was still not considered a legitimate subject by most professors at the Sorbonne, though centers of "gay studies" had been appearing in American colleges and universities since the early 70s (at the University of Nebraska, Yale University, the City University of New York, and the City College of San Francisco, to name a few). Even now, this sort of academic homophobia has not completely vanished: a 2002 issue of *Ravaillac* magazine, published by the students of the Lycée Henri IV, commented on one of the school's history teachers known for making remarks to his students that were as ridiculous as they were homophobic.

One of the great challenges of our time is to make the transition from the end of a taboo in society to the end of the same taboo in schools. It is clear that an objective discussion of homosexuality is needed in educational establishments from a very early age if we are to help the children of homosexuals to succeed, to help young gays and lesbians construct their identity without interference or pain, and to fight against the impact of homophobia outside of school. English-speaking countries have shown the way, but not without difficulty, because the growing need for cultural integration of sexual minorities encounters hostility from conservatives of all stripes (and often with strong Christian roots). In Great Britain, Clause 28 (now repealed) had its genesis in the uproar caused by the picture book *Jenny Lives with Eric and Martin,* a Danish book translated into English in 1983, in which little Jenny lives with her father and his male partner. The very homophobic Baroness Young (the British equivalent to France's Christine **Boutin**) then launched a crusade to save children and **families** (that is, Christian, heterosexual families) resulting in the approval of Clause 28 in 1988 and the subsequent restriction on purchasing gay and lesbian books for public libraries. In the US, resistance to teaching about homosexuality in the classroom or school library can be strong. In 1995, the school board in Merrimack, New Hampshire, banned any teaching of gay and lesbian issues "as a positive lifestyle alternative," taking its inspiration almost word for word from a proposed homophobic amendment by Senator Jesse Helms, which had been rejected by Congress the year before. This tougher stance nonetheless also elicited an adverse reaction: though gay and lesbian literature was excluded from most schools, one heterosexual New Hampshire teacher, Penny Culliton, had her rights upheld by the courts (1996–98) to use literary works containing homosexual characters in her classroom. Her case established jurisprudence and she became a national star.

The writing is on the wall: the fight is on over exactly what can be said about homosexuality to students in elementary, middle, and high schools. The exact question is this: should school be a place where heterosexist prejudice is challenged, or a place where a heterosexual symbolic order (that is, the specific prejudice of one sexuality as superior to the other) is imposed? The answer to this question will determine the extent of the fight against homophobia in schools (including the locker room and playing field). Bear in mind that, to conservatives, homophobic insults allow the heterosexual majority to "establish its identity" (and the sense of superiority that goes with it). Also worthy of debate is the place of homosexual issues in the educational curriculum. To the homophobic right wing, the simple act of talking about homosexuality without condemning it constitutes a sort of "homosexual **proselytism**." According to the British Christian Institute, teachers may bring up homosexuality in the classroom, but only on the condition that they first tell students that "most people disapprove of homosexuality." What the homophobes suspect is that the inclusion of the vast homosexual cultural heritage in the curriculum (from Plato's *Banquet* to Virginia Woolf's *To the Lighthouse*; from Proust's *In Search of Lost Time* to Thomas Mann's *Death in Venice*) could have the effect of demonstrating that homosexuality is a large part of human history (including some of the most beautiful things ever created), that it poses no danger to civilization, and that it is possible to be proud of being gay and lesbian. To anyone who fears the homosexual "**contagion**," this represents a terrible threat: if adolescent homosexuals no longer suffer for being what they are, if they no longer make any effort to try to be heterosexual, then homosexuality will sweep over all of society and carry away everything in its path. Almost everywhere, traditionalists are fighting to keep sex education classes strictly heterosexist; that is, that they equate sexuality with heterosexuality only, without regard for alternative forms of parenthood and procreation. With this in mind, pro-family groups in the United States have often successfully lobbied school boards not to bring up the question of sexual orientation at all in sex-education classes. In France, a circular from 1998 on "the education of sexuality" (as part of the fight against **AIDS**) at least sought to avoid biologism and **heterosexism**; at the same time, it should be pointed out that the same circular never once identified homosexuality as such and that, in these matters, a text is worth far less until it is practically applied. This only goes to show, in retrospect, how important it is that gay and lesbian issues and the interdiction of homophobia be explicitly included in school curricula—a fact of which authorities have finally become aware. It is only in this way that respect for the invisible coeducation of heterosexuals and homosexuals can be added to the respect for the visible coeducation of girls and boys.

In 2007, the slogan of the IDAHO Committee (International Day Against Homophobia) was "No to homophobia, yes to education." In that context, IDAHO President Louis-Georges Tin asked UNESCO to include the fight against homophobia in its international agenda, as education is one of its main objectives. Unfortunately, this request remains unaddressed.
—*Pierre Albertini* [Original essay updated by Arsenal Pulp Press]

Caron, Jean-Claude. *A l'école de la violence, châtiments et sévices dans l'institution scolaire au XIXe siècle*. Paris: Aubier, 1999.

Clauzard, Philippe. *Conversations sur l'homophobie, l'éducation comme rempart contre l'exclusion*. Paris: L'Harmattan, 2002.

Corlett, William. *Now and Then*. London: Abacus, 1995.

Eribon, Didier. *Réflexions sur la question gay*. Paris: Fayard, 1999. [Published in the US as *Insult and the Making of the Gay Self*. Durham, NC: Duke Univ. Press, 2004.]

———. *Michel Foucault*. Paris: Flammarion, 1989. [Published in the US as *Michel Foucault*. Cambridge, MA: Harvard Univ. Press, 1991.]

———, ed. *Les Etudes gay et lesbiennes*. Paris: Editions du Centre Pompidou, 1998.

Fernandez, Dominique. *L'Etoile rose*. Paris: Grasset, 1978.

Gathorne-Hardy, Jonathan. *The Public-School Phenomenon*. London: Hodder & Stoughton, 1977.

Harbeck, Karen, ed. *Coming out of the Classroom Closet: Gay and Lesbian Students, Teachers and Curricula*. New York: Haworth Press, 1992.

———. *Gay and Lesbian Educators: Personal Freedom, Public Constraints*. Malden: Amethyst Publications, 1997.

Harris, Simon. *Lesbian and Gay Issues in the English Classroom: The Importance of Being Honest*. Milton Keynes: Open Univ. Press, 1990.

Jennings, Kevin, ed. *One Teacher in Ten: Gay and Lesbian Educators Tell Their Stories*. Boston: Alyson Publications, 1994.

McNaron, Toni. *Poisoned Ivy: Lesbian and Gay Academics Confronting Homophobia*. Philadelphia: Temple Univ. Press, 1997.

Monette, Paul. *Becoming a Man: Half a Life Story*. London: Abacus, 1994.

Musil, Robert. *Les Désarrois de l'élève Törless*. Vienna: Wiener

Verlag, 1906. [Published in the US as *Confusions of the Young Törless*. New York: Penguin, 2001.]

Peyrefitte, Roger. *Les Amitiés particulières*. Marseille: J. Vigneau, 1943. [Published in the US as *Secret Friendships*. Clarence, NY: West-Art, 2000.]

Tamagne, Florence. *Histoire de l'homosexualité en Europe, Berlin, Londres, Paris, 1919–1939*. Paris: Le Seuil, 2000. [Published in the US as *A History of Homosexuality in Europe: Berlin, London, Paris, 1919–1939*. New York: Algora, 2004.]

Thierce, Agnès. *Histoire de l'adolescence (1850–1914)*. Paris: Belin, 1999.

—Censorship; Contagion; Heterosexism; History; Literature; Pedophilia; Sports; Suicide.

SELF-HATRED. *See* Shame

SEXUAL PERVERSIONS. *See* Perversions

SHAME

Like other stigmatized groups, gays and lesbians are, in many respects, "children of shame." Many of their personal stories are marked by periods of uneasiness and discomfort that show the difficulty of living in a heterosexual world consisting of repeated abasements, sometimes real, sometimes imagined; sometimes open, sometimes secret. Whether before they come out or long after, gays and lesbians face a relentless and cruel treatment by society, and the growing knowledge of belonging to a class of "unsuitable" people whom society does not want, which they are reminded of on a daily basis. Shame is a feeling of vulnerability that is universal, but not experienced equally across all categories of individuals. In theory, we are all equal in face of shame, but in the real social world, some are more "equal" than others. It is this inequality of fragility and vulnerability among social groups where a clearly political analysis of shame can be identified, as well as its strategic function in the heterosexist economy.

Shame is one of the most powerful mechanisms by which social order holds us in our presumed place in society, either by preventing "normal people" from straying from the "right path," or by provoking "abnormal people" to hide and remain out of sight by not publicly acknowledging their membership in a socially undesirable category. Even amongst the most happy and proud of being out, homosexual shame can exist in those afflicted for a long time, resurfacing at the most unexpected moments when one thought it had been long overcome (and staying with them until their death). As Didier Eribon writes: "There always is, at the turn of every sentence, a wound that can reopen; a new shame that can submerge me, or the old shame coming back to the surface." As the political result of the collective oppression, reproduced in a series of daily interactions, the shame suffered by gays and lesbians cannot be opposed except collectively in turn: it is a mechanism often too well anchored in our bodies, our subjectivities and in the objective structures of heterosexist society, to be simply revoked individually.

Shame: The Political Result of Oppression

As in any sentiment, even the most personal and intimate, shame does not drop out of the sky: it is part of a corporal economy which is a *political* economy. To "persist in its being," any economic and social order (whether capitalist, racist, sexist or homophobic) must make itself be recognized as legitimate, and to persist over time it must be internalized by those whom it subjugates. The heterosexist order exists according to this rule; it would have little impact if it were based purely on intellectual and rhetorical grounds. Through shame, the "objective" power of homophobia is in fact based on concrete reality: human beings are not pure spirits floating above society, but flesh and blood, socialized bodies composed of acquired reflexes and conscious dispositions, rendering them more or less controllable. It is this fundamental "corporality" that allows homophobia to function. In this way, in shame or in fear, in imposed or self-imposed **discretion**, or even the feeling of ridiculousness of inappropriateness, one's submission to the heterosexist order can take place against one's will, without having any power to change it. All of these social emotions can arise in us and take action against us seemingly against our will, exploiting the "subterranean complicities" (to use French sociologist Pierre Bourdieu's concept) that our conditioned bodies maintain with the consistencies and hierarchies of the dominant society. There is no need to imagine a homophobic conspiracy or a cynical orchestration of the oppression to understand how this phenomenon is possible. In fact, having been instructed in the inequality of the world, homosexuals are predisposed mentally and physically to recognize its social divisions and structures of authority, thereby (paradoxically) conferring upon homophobia part of the power that it exercises on them. In shame, the body in a sense "betrays" the soul by forcing the gay subject to perceive himself through the eyes of others (whether real or supposed) that is, in the end, through the heterosexist vision of the world. What is revealed by the durable power of shame in the lives of gays and lesbians is that their bodies often remain in the closet a lot longer than their will does. The human body, which allows us to open up to the world in order to understand it and act within it, is also the organ that at the same time makes us vulnerable to it: it is through this assumption that I give in to the prevailing social order ("It's stronger than me"), giving the structures and agents of homophobia the power to awaken my shame in the most ill-timed fashion, while at the same time I know so well that I "should not be ashamed" more than I "should not be ashamed anymore."

Shame feeds on a self-hatred that goes beyond its gay subjects because it is never completely individual nor completely conscious; it refers back to the incorporation of the original slights directed toward them by others. But this homophobia interiorized as "fear of the other within oneself" is not limited to fueling the shame in the social and psychological fire: it is often also projected into a "hate of oneself in the other," that is, a rejection of homosexuals other than oneself, in spite of common stigma (or rather because of it). Shame does not only "discipline" those who are dominated one by one, by isolating them from "sacred" society, it can also divide them *among themselves* by making their mutual identification, and thus their political mobilization, more difficult. Shame promotes isolation, which in turn promotes shame: without consciously meaning to do so, the heterosexist world is surprisingly efficient.

Michael Warner, in his book *The Trouble with Normal*, he distinguishes between shame (which concerned only acts) and stigma (which touched on the essential being of individuals, according to the definition of their social essence). To ignore this would blur the distinction between the voluntary transgression of the normal, universal individual who is satisfied with living within his social or sexual limit, and the abjection of the stigmatized individual beyond the very acts that he committed or was accused of committing and who accepts the infamous identity that is imposed on him,

sometimes for life. Stigma is a form of fundamental and permanent shame which taints acts before they even really exist; there is as much political distance between transgression and abjection as there is between free communication with the unchaste and the mere fact of being *identified* with the unchaste by society.

Such a distinction, however, must not dismiss the common (at least in Western society) metaphysical vision of the world which understands the acts of social subjects to be a revelation of their inner self. In reality, the impact of shame always exceeds that of the acts that may have caused it; the shameful act then becomes interchangeable with the essence (or image) of its author. Conversely, categories of stigmatized individuals such as gays and lesbians are conscious of their structural social fragility that renders them vulnerable to situations and interactions in which this insecurity can be activated and exploited. The shame experienced by homosexuals is then mutually reinforced by the stigma related to their social identity.

Shame: A Corporeal Emotion

Shame, as a typically corporeal emotion, is in fact a consequence of the contradictory hate found in all forms of racism, which involves people criticizing someone for his own nature (over which he has no control) so that he then blames himself for it while at the same time affirming that he himself is not responsible for it.

Homophobia as sexual racism has a sort of oxymoronic concept at its core: homosexuality as an immoral pathology whereby the homosexual is an incorrigible person to be corrected (confirmed by the reactionary response to **AIDS** as a shameful disease). We understand, as a consequence, that shame is weighed down by this paradoxical feeling of being at fault without having done anything, of feeling simply "out of place," discredited by one's own essence. This emotion, tragic in its signification, is that much more intense and cruel when, as is often the case, the awareness of betraying one's shame to the outside is added to it.

When shame erupts, whether through an intentional or unintentional act by oneself or by others, it is expressed in tangible manifestations of vulnerability and powerlessness, such as blushing, sweating, and shaking. These manifestations represent an urgent and irrepressible wish to disappear from the social scene, to run away and hide; and in a certain way, to suppress oneself: if not, not to be anymore, than at least, not to be there anymore. In other words, shame takes the homophobic stigma at its word: since for this society, a "wrong" sexual orientation makes one's entire being no longer pertinent, and hence that being looks for a way to revoke itself in a tragic attempt at regression. And since this being sticks to one's skin, the body tries to achieve this regression (to make itself small; to be discreet) for the sake of the mind. Symptoms of shame express the failure of one's being to achieve this regression. Everyone, at one time or another, can find themselves in this kind of situation that is so all-encompassing and so humiliating. But for many gays and lesbians, particularly those who do not live in large urban centers and their protective communities, this is real life. Before even being situational, gay shame is an existential shame.

Further, the shame experienced by gays and lesbians is something more specific than the humiliation incurred by other categories of those who are socially or economically dominated. It is not limited to the feeling of being irrelevant socially, or to representing a lack of taste or comfort in social and familial situations, but is also a painful recognition that even in one's *mode of jouissance*, one is abnormal; that is, in a position linked to the forfeiture and absence of control whereby the subject is at his most vulnerable in his humanity (and if it is a man, in his virility). That said, it is precisely this mode of *jouissance* that is supposed to define, according to the dominating "regime of truth" (as defined by Michel Foucault), a person's essence. Of course, this focus on *jouissance* has nothing that is "natural": on the contrary, it is a political construction that exploits the historical development of modesty (there is no shame without modesty) in "civilized" societies, to drive back the practices and persons that do not fit the dominant definition of normality.

Shame is thus total and reductive at the same time. Homophobic attitudes reduce gay identity to an orientation that is solely sexual and makes the sexual, thought of in terms of tendencies and of drives that are always more or less associated with animal acts, the origin of all actions and thoughts of gays and lesbians. Their entire being, then, becomes identified as a sort of "perverse drive." This is why homophobia does not only consider them as socially inadequate but also, and perhaps even, predominantly immodest. For heterosexist society, homosexuals are in a way "itinerant provocations": by the very fact that their sexuality is irregular, homophobic attitudes reduce them to nothing but their sexuality, and in doing so multiplies the inappropriateness of the abnormality by the indecency of **exhibitionism** (imposed by the enquiring and hypocritical look of domineering and moralistic people). By being so reduced through this scrutiny, homosexuals find themselves dispossessed of their **privacy**, their intimacy existing only to be ridiculed and symbolically exhibited as a negative example. No matter what gays and lesbians do to "desexualize" their identity, sometimes to the extreme, the end result is always the same: their very presence is an affront to decency and "good manners," subject to slurs, if not open **violence**.

In the context of someone who is "out of turn" with respect to the system of "normative" sexual development, while at the same time reduced to an animal and sexual drive, facing a society in which the "civilizating process" precisely tends to push the bodily sexual drives back into the sphere of intimacy and privacy (i.e. hidden), homosexual shame is then a privileged rapport with the feeling not only of being dirty, but also being dirty in public, that is, in an inappropriate and shocking situation. The homophobic world projects its own indecency and fascinated voyeurism onto this inverted being, who becomes the phantasmic spectacle of a dirty *jouissance*, and imposes on him the social humiliation of a symbolic nudity—nudity that is in reality both produced and evaded by the very look that undresses him, all the while accusing him of **scandal**. Shame is the result of gays' and lesbians' internalization of this dominant vision of themselves that reduces their being to a nude body which exhibits itself and its private organs, this body that possesses an animal drive, and a drive to dirtiness. It is the manifestation of a form of bodily allegiance to the idea that what is revealed about them (or threatened to be) returns them to something fundamental in the definition of their character, and that this "something" in his body or mind should or should have remained hidden. More radically, shame extorts the gay subject with the belief in the myth that there is really "something" to hide or reveal. Homophobia's strength is to create, at the same time and in the same move, shame of this "thing" and the thing we should be ashamed of.

Gays & Lesbians Between Shame & Pride
Through reductions, rejections, and threatening mechanisms, and their conscious and unconscious anticipations, shame directs gays and lesbians to become invisible by hiding themselves. Not in the sense

of privileged invisibility reserved for dominant forces of the universe, whose identities are a given, and who do not have to tell of themselves or admit themselves (never "Mommy, I am heterosexual"); this invisibility is that of the "good soldier," the one who sticks so much to the landscape that he ends up part of the social furniture. The invisibility stigma that gays incur is altogether different: it is the invisibility of oppressed, inhibited, inexpressible, unthinkable identities. The one who would prefer that none of that existed and had never existed. This way, if pride makes even more sense for gays and lesbians than for blacks (from whom they borrow the concept historically), it is that their invisibilization by shame has been one of the main means by which symbolic domination has been exerted upon them. The construction of gay identity, either personally or collectively, works precisely to resist this mechanism. Gay pride aims to regain gay identity by subverting the stigma of homosexuality, as much private as public, and by disarming its critics by reclaiming the identity originally assigned to it by homophobic society (the word "queer" is a good example). Pride is thus first and foremost a political strategy, and those who see it as simply misplaced narcissism demonstrate a refusal to face the facts and mechanisms of oppression. A mobilized gay and lesbian community serves not only as a means to political mobilization but also, more on a daily level, as protective shelter that allows gays to reconstruct their identities away from the domineering hierarchy whose beliefs, when internalized, produce shame and self-hatred.

Some, such as François Delor, however, insist on certain perverse effects of the pressure to feel pride, which can in turn be shameful; for gays and lesbians who cannot be proud, a shame arises from the fact of being ashamed. But how can one give shame its dignity back and not reduce it to a strictly negative side of identity without putting oneself on the side of oppressors by defending a reactionary discourse? If we really are children of shame, is there a way to remove ourselves from this matrix without at the same time being blinded by the slighting of our shameful origins? To help solve this dilemma and bring about a new perspective on gay shame, one should take note of the paradox at its heart: on one hand, it is another insidious form of the heterosexist order, with all its laws and hierarchies; on the other, it is a founding experience of gay and lesbian subjectivity, if not positive, then at least productive.

If it is shame that constitutes us, it is also shame that connects us: entering shame is at the same time acknowledging what we are, who we are, and to whom we are joined through the common experience of the homophobic social order. The just valorization of pride must not lead one to forget one's whole emotional life lived in shame or in the voids of oppression, of the perverse eroticization of its instruments and agents (which could be a way to disarm opponents and initiate a process toward pride, as Genet said) for the social and political awakening that this shame and the marginality that it imposes helps to produce and nourish. Just as pride always bears the mark of its shameful genealogy ("One is always a little ashamed of being proud of being gay," writes Guy Hocquenghem), shame, when fully assumed, when one ceases to be ashamed of being ashamed, contains a form of paradoxical pride which, explains Eribon, could constitute the starting point for self-reinvention toward something like our freedom.
—*Sébastien Chauvin*

Bourdieu, Pierre. *Méditations pascaliennes*. Paris: Le Seuil, 1997.

Delor, François. *Homosexualité, ordre symbolique, injure et discrimination: Impasses et destins des expériences érotiques minoritaires dans l'espace social et politique*. Brussels: Labor, 2003.

Douglas, Mary. *De la souillure*. Paris: La Découverte, 1992.

Elias, Norbert. *La Civilisation des mœurs*. Paris: Calmann-Lévy, 1973.

Eribon, Didier. *Une morale du minoritaire: Variations sur un thème de Jean Genet*. Paris: Fayard, 2001.

Goffman, Erving. *Stigmates*. Paris: Minuit, 1963. [Published in the US as *Stigma*. Englewood Cliffs, NJ: Prentice Hall, 1963.]

Hocquenghem, Guy. *Le Désir homosexuel* [1972]. Paris: Fayard, 2000. [Published in the US as *Homosexual Desire*. Durham, NC: Duke Univ. Press, 1993.]

Katz, Jack. *How Emotions Work*. Chicago: Univ. of Chicago Press, 1999.

Kaufman, Gershen, and Raphaël Lev. *Coming out of Shame: Transforming Gay and Lesbian Lives*. New York: Main Street Books, 1997.

Kosofsky Sedgwick, Eve. *Epistemology of the Closet*. Berkeley: Univ. of California Press, 1990.

Warner, Michael. *The Trouble with Normal: Sex, Politics, and the Ethics of Queer Life*. Boston: Harvard Univ. Press, 2000.

—*Abnormal; Closet, the; Exhibitionism; Heterophobia; Heterosexism; Privacy; Rhetoric; Suicide.*

SHEPARD, Matthew

Unfortunately, the tragic death of Matthew Shepard (1976-98) was, on the surface, nothing extraordinary. Homophobic murders are common in the United States (and in many other countries such as Mexico and Brazil, for instance), and numbers provided by the FBI seem to suggest that such murders are on the increase (even though this worrisome trend may partially be explained by the fact that figures are collected in a more systematic way and, moreover, victims and/or families are less ready than before to keep silent).

But what would have otherwise been just another news item became instead a major media event. It aroused reactions of sadness and compassion all over the country, and even internationally; at the same time, homophobic discourse became more violent and hateful, with certain groups claiming that Shepard would perish in the flames of Hell, as would any homosexual person. It became a political event as well: beyond LGBT organizations, many citizens felt personally connected to the case. President Bill Clinton himself said he was deeply shocked by this terrible act of violence, and the debate over homophobic hate crimes was discussed on a national level: specifically, should homophobic crimes be included in the category of hate crimes, and be subsequently condemned in the same way as racist and anti-Semitic crimes? Finally, it was a moral event, in which self-reflection led to a wake-up call of sorts; perhaps for the first time, the whole country was confronted with the idea that the real scandal was not homosexuality, but rather homophobia itself. In that sense, the murder of Matthew Shepard brought about a sort of symbolic rupture in America.

On Tuesday, October 6, 1998, twenty-one-year-old Matthew Shepard, a political science student at the University of Wyoming, was at the Fireside bar in Laramie. Two young men approached him claiming to be gay and suggested that he come with them in their car. Together, they drove outside the city limits to a remote rural area where both men violently attacked him, bound him to a gate, tortured him, cut his face, crushed his head, and left him for dead. Eighteen hours later, a cyclist came across Shepard's bound and brutalized body, at first mistaking him for a scarecrow. He was immediately brought to the hospital, but his condition was too fragile for doctors to attempt to operate. Shepard fell into a coma, and as he lay dying, a candlelight vigil was held by the people of Laramie.

Matthew Shepard passed away on Monday, October 12, 1998, at 12:53 a.m.

Reverend Fred Phelps, Minister of the Westboro Baptist Church Community, protesting during the funeral of Matthew Shepard.

Shepard's murder immediately mobilized gay and lesbian organizations into action. Three days after his death, another candlelight vigil was held on the stairs of the Capitol in Washington, DC; among those in attendance were Senator Ted Kennedy, Congressman Barney Frank, and actress Ellen DeGeneres, who only months earlier had come out publicly on her television series *Ellen*. The Human Rights Campaign, the largest LGBT lobby in the United States, launched a campaign inviting gays and lesbians around the world to dress in black in memory of Shepard. A private funeral took place on October 16 in Casper, Wyoming. However, anti-gay demonstrators attempted to disrupt the ceremony with cruel, hate-filled signs, such as "Matt in hell." Having organized more than a few demonstrations of this kind in the past, Reverend Fred Phelps of the fundamentalist Westboro Baptist Church subsequently unleashed heinous, hate-mongering rants against homosexuals including Shepard both on his website *godhatesfags.com* and in the **media**. Indeed, Phelps even petitioned the city of Casper in 2003 for a permit to build a monument praising Matthew's death as divine vindication.

On both sides of the issue, the mobilization continued. Vigils took place across the country as the murder became a national issue, emblematic of systemic homophobia in America. Both of Shepard's killers, Russel A. Henderson, twenty-one, and Aaron J. McKinney, twenty-two, were soon arrested. At their trial, the defense's strategy consisted of denying the homophobic character of the murder; it was claimed to be simply a robbery turned bad. Moreover, explained McKinney, "I do not hate gays; I even have a gay friend." Further, he also contended that he was completely unaware that Shepard was gay. That said, this theory completely contradicted both of the accused's first statements, their girlfriends' testimonies, and a letter written by McKinney himself, discovered afterward, in which he admitted: "Being a verry [sic] drunk homofobick [sic], I flipped out and began to pistol whip the fag with my gun." The defense subsequently tried a second tactic: the gay panic defense, which implicitly acknowledged the homophobic character of the murder. Frequently used in trials of this kind, this strategy allows the criminal to appear as the victim of the victim: McKinney indeed asserted that Shepard had made indecent advances, which, in a twisted sense of logic, would have "justified" his homophobic panic and, hence, murder. However, this brazen attempt to rationalize homophobic violence was overruled by the judge. In the end, both men were convicted and sentenced to two consecutive life terms in prison; they escaped the death penalty thanks to the intervention of Matthew's parents, Denis and Judy Shepard.

Since then, Matthew Shepard's murder has profoundly marked the American consciousness. Over thirty music artists have composed **songs** in his memory, including Melissa Etheridge, Tori Amos, and Elton John, and numerous plays, films, and works of literature have been produced. However, beyond the facts of the case, why did this particular tragedy resonate so deeply with the American public, both gay and straight? Indeed, there has never been a lack of homophobic murders every year, and until Shepard's, none had managed to gain the interest of the American people; not even Brandon Teena, the transgender who was raped and murdered and whose tragic story was depicted in the award-winning 1999 film *Boys Don't Cry.*

In the case of Matthew Shepard, several reasons can be identified. First of all, the circumstances of the crime had the feel of a full-scale American tragedy: a good-looking, nice young man set upon by two hateful criminals; the audacity of their attack; and the tragic martyr symbol of Shepard himself, bound and tortured, found in the middle of nowhere. But it was more than that; there was also his family. In past cases when gays or lesbians were murdered, it was not uncommon for their families to want to suppress the case to avoid disclosure of the deceased victim's sexuality. In Shepard's case, however, his parents wanted to make a lasting commitment to their son; they spoke out at rallies and to the media, and soon thereafter created the Matthew Shepard Foundation to fight against hate crimes, in memory of their son so his murder would not be in vain. The foundation's stated goal is "To replace hate with understanding, compassion and acceptance." Matthew's death also instigated the coordination of gay and lesbian networks, notably around the Human Rights Campaign, which played an instrumental role in helping to tell his story around the world. His murder crystallized the issue of homophobia for millions, making it personal and thus "real"; a revelatory moment which opened people's eyes to the reality of homophobic violence in the United States.

"But remember one thing," said Walter, a friend of Shepard's. "No matter what good comes out of this, the price paid will be too high."

The Matthew Shepard Act, a federal bill that proposes to amend the 1969 hate crime law to include crimes motivated by the victim's sexual orientation, currently awaits passage. Although the bill was approved by the United States Senate in September 2007, it is expected to be vetoed by President George W. Bush.

—*Louis-Georges Tin*

Berrill, Kevin, and Gregory Herek, eds. *Hate Crimes: Confronting Violence Against Lesbians and Gay Men.* London: Sage Publications, 1992.

Gibson, Scott, ed. *Blood and Tears: Poems for Matthew Shepard.* New York: Painted Leaf Press, 1999.

Human Rights Campaign. http://www.hrc.org (accessed April 24, 2008).

Kaufman, Moises. *The Laramie Project: A Play.* New York: Vintage, 2001.

Loffreda, Beth. *Losing Matt Shepard: Life and Politics in the Aftermath of an Antigay Murder.* New York: Columbia Univ. Press, 2000.

Mama, Robin, Mary Swigonski, and Kelly Ward, eds. *From Hate Crimes to Human Rights: A Tribute to Matthew Shepard.* Haworth Press, 2001.

—*North America; Protestantism; Violence.*

SIN. *See* Against Nature; Bible; Debauchery; Theology; Vice

SOCIAL CONSTRUCTIONISM. *See* Sociology

SOCIAL ORDER. *See* Symbolic Order

SOCIOLOGY

The very existence of the category of "homosexuality" is so well associated with the psycho-medical field that, at first glance, sociology would have no apparent link to the phenomenon of homophobia. In fact, for over a century, sociology's most common response to homosexuality has been silence. But this silence is not without significance: it is thus necessary to understand sociology "beyond sex." The last part of the twentieth century is the start of a new era; sexuality will break into the field of sociology under the simultaneous influences of internal evolutions and external events.

Sociology "Beyond Sex?"

Those who worked in the field that would eventually become sociology had no particular doctrine with regard to homosexuality, but rather opinions that had no direct relation to their theoretical work. Some expressed hatred (or disgust), or a form of tolerant comprehension, but, for the majority, we have no clue what their opinions were on the subject. The few elements that can be gleaned here or there stem only from chance or anecdote and for one simple reason: sociologically speaking, sexuality was not constituted as an object.

Rousseau, for one, made his disgust quite apparent, but this was based on his personal experience of having been the subject of three attempted seductions. The Moor who took care of him during his stay in Turin and who, after his initial caresses, expressed his desire to "go on to the most filthy liberties," had an impact on Rousseau that was so frightening that "the most hideous hag" was, in his eyes, transformed into an object of adoration by the memory of this encounter.

In a text that Gilles Deleuze qualified as "difficult and beautiful," Marx enigmatically noted the necessity of thinking of sexuality as a "relation between human sex and non-human sex," which opened the possibility of a non-heterosexist understanding of sexuality. But in *The Origin of the Family, Private Property and the State* (1884), Frederick Engels let loose a torrent of hate against what he called "filthy **vices against nature**"

by writing: "The debasement of women has had its revenge against men and has debased them to the point of making them fall into the repugnant practice of pederasty and to dishonor themselves by dishonoring their gods through the myth of Ganymede."

Expressed or not, this sharing of common prejudices would prove to be long lasting, and not only in Europe: in 1927, in a famous monograph in which he described the life of hobos, those itinerant and marginal workers of the great construction sites in turn-of-the-century America, Niels Anderson made moral judgments on the relatively common behavior of the group, notably the relations between men; moral judgments that did not seem to upset anyone. This type of "evidence" of ordinary homophobia was such that it even imposed itself on those who were in a position to analyze and fight it: it is difficult not to interpret the silence of the "invisible" homosexual Norbert Elias, a great theoretician of the process of the "civilization of morals," as the effect of powerful self-censorship. It is necessary to read between the lines in order to guess that he was quite conscious of the possibility of studying the field of multiple sexualities and their link to affection as a legitimate object, whose existence he briefly and discreetly suggested from time to time.

This absence of specific theorization is not in the least mysterious: sexuality was constructed as a scientific object in the fields of medicine and psychiatry, and it was in these same discourses that the term of homosexuality appeared. When Michel Foucault retraced the genealogy of a *scientia sexualis* contrasted with an *ars erotica,* in which he demonstrated the mechanisms of a new category, that of "perverts," he was not working in the realm of social science, but rather what would become the "humanities." And if we need to search for the emergence of counter-discourse, it may be found in **literature**: since the Romantic movement and throughout the entire twentieth century, there was a growing body of literature that was resistant to the dominant homophobia.

For all that, sociology was not absent from the scene: it was present in two methods that were both different yet invisible. The first was in the omnipresent form of "naïvely" **heteronormative** analyses, and the second was in the literary works that present fictional universes and characters, to which anti-homophobic sociological studies of the late twentieth century will confer a conceptual status.

To speak of heteronormativity is to name something

obvious that runs through the sociological tradition in its entirety: sexuality is reduced to its institutional forms; in other words, to the **family**. In this, French sociologist Emile Durkheim was exemplary. In 1892, on the subject of the conjugal family, which in his eyes represented the most complete family structure, he wrote: "Marriage is the foundation of the family and at the same time is derived from it. Thus, all sexual union that is not contracted in the matrimonial form is a perturbance of duty and the domestic bond, and, since the day that the State itself first intervened in family life, a disruption of public order." He further qualified the non-married couple as "immoral." In his other texts, notably *Le Suicide,* Durkheim analyzed celibacy as being dissolute, a chronic instability that disrupts the well-being of society, which requires the necessary integration of the individual among permanent and instituted groups.

Thus, Durkheim presented his argument. It is nonetheless interesting to question the conditions of a possible ordinary homophobia, that is to say "naïve" (there is no indication that Durkheim gave any thought to homosexuality). The reason is seemingly simple: sexual "**perversions**" belonging to the sphere of psychopathology—of individual psychology—were of no concern to "social facts" and did not enter into the field of sociology. A social pathology did exist, as an object of criminology, but it concerned crimes, not perversions. At the same time, there was a more profound motive than merely the divisions between clinical disciplines. Until very recently, one's **private** life, including sexual practices, was considered to be completely separate from public life. It was Herbert Marcuse, then Foucault, to whom we owe the establishment of an intrinsic link between power and sexuality. In this regard, Durkheim was neither worse nor better than other sociologists: the state's role in the institutionalization of "normal sexuality" seemed to him eminently positive for society's good functioning. Heteronormativity was simply the expression of a common view and expression. The heterosexist order was so evident, so visible, that it became totally invisible, even to the most enlightened minds.

Sociology in the Arena
Of the three sources from which anti-homophobic studies obtained their points of reference, the first was in the production of a sociology of deviance. In particular, it was the work of American sociologists who espoused a theoretical current that could be called "interactionist." Their powerful critique of the "normal vision" of the "abnormal" can be summarized in three points:

1. All transgressions of dominant standards are produced and constructed. No conduct, as strange or minor as it may be, is deviant unless it is designated as such. It is social *labeling* that makes it deviant. This complex operation results in a process of continuous collective interactions, in which the currents of opinion, the **media**—the "constructors of morality"—play a decisive role.

2. There exists, therefore, in varied forms, a general mechanism that produces "deviants": the symbolic humiliation, the constitution of certain groups or individuals into lesser members of society; thus it is legitimate that they be of little consideration, or even persecuted. This mechanism is *stigmatization,* or negative identification.

3. The effects of these mechanisms on their targets include self-loathing ("disidentification"); feelings of **shame**, isolation, and contempt for one's peers; grouping ("differential association"); collective struggles for rehabilitation (transforming the "stigma" into an "emblem"); and denunciation of repressive and discriminatory policies.

These studies (by Howard Becker and Erving Goffman, notably) did not directly deal with homosexuality (even if, in passing, homosexuals were included as one of many examples used to illustrate a particular analysis), but they gave rise to new ones, and their contribution was fundamental. They supplied a new theoretical framework where every deviance was denaturalized and susceptible to being considered from the point of view of an historical process, by which that which has been created can be undone. Homosexuals were de-characterized: they belonged to the vast category of those who, at any given time, found themselves among those who transgressed the norms; homophobia was linked to this grand gesture of social "labeling," subject to being analyzed and transformed. Homosexuals opened a breach in traditional sociological culture by enlarging the notion of deviance, equated until then with minor disruptions, such as juvenile delinquency, to include conduct that was "pointed out" and discriminated against. Larger still, homosexuals constrained sociologists to deal with the problem of the arbitrariness of standards by the virtue of their multiplicity, construction, and their ability to change.

It was from this theoretical arsenal that the first strictly sociological studies dedicated to gay lifestyles were conducted in the mid-1970s, including the mechanisms of deprecation and homophobic discrimination, and the individual or collective strategies of those responding to their own stigmatization. While sociology is transformed through itself and through the debates that are internal to the history of the discipline, its transformations are also obviously linked to social changes themselves and, as an adjunct to this, to activist movements.

The political developments linked to the experience of minorities in the United States, the appearance of strong and organized gay and feminist movements—in short, the explosion of militant protests in the political field—constituted the second source of inspiration for a sociological literature oriented against **heterosexism**. The growing interest in gay and lesbian studies in the US has no equivalent in **France**. It must be noted that gay and lesbian studies developed in an interdisciplinary way, at the crossroads of philosophy, history, and literature, while sociology remained largely foreign or resistant to this larger intellectual movement, in which sociologists still participate rather marginally.

The great issue for those working in gay and lesbian studies is "the politics of identity" and what we could call the "identity dilemma." Doesn't the fight against all forms of homophobia run the risk of confining homosexuals in the trap set by a heteronormative social order? Of imprisoning them in a homogenous category in which a person's complete identity is defined by his or her tastes, dispositions, and sexual practices? It is a dilemma that was brutally distilled by David Halperin, for whom the gay and lesbian identity is "both politically necessary and politically catastrophic," because it is "both a homophobic identity as it is totalizing and normalizing, and an identity of which all negation and all refusal are no less homophobic." The contemporary queer movement, dominated by the theoretical work of Eve Kosofsky Sedgwick, searches for a radical exit from this dilemma by deconstructing the very notion of gender, by tracing a path that is both non-separatist and non-assimilationist, and by "non-defining" the sexual (at the risk of dissolving it) as "the open matrix

of possibilities, divergences, convergences, dissonances, resonances, weaknesses, or excesses of meaning when the constitutive elements of someone's gender and sexuality are not constrained (or cannot be) to monolithic significations." Further, it would be necessary to acknowledge Foucault, who is not a sociologist, obviously, but whose work strongly inspires these debates.

However, be it a question of the sociology of deviance or of gay and lesbian studies, one thing is striking: the realities examined by these approaches—including the problems they uncover, and the concepts they construct—all existed previously in literary creation, as demonstrated by Didier Eribon's study on a "minority morality" based on Jean Genet's works. It is the reason that allows one speak of a "virtual sociology" with regard to the long period when sociology was either mute on the subject of homosexuality or passively collaborated with the ascendancy of a heteronormative power. Sociologists are in the habit of looking for their problems and their data in social "reality." They often forget that art (including literature) constitutes an inexhaustible and often premonitory reservoir of representations and theories which they would do well to seize: the fictions of artists anticipate and propose realities that may appear to have little legitimacy, or even seem outlandish, but that nonetheless constitute powerful devices of discursive resistance.

Regardless, gay and lesbian activism in France crystallized itself around two major events whose consequences for research have proven to be productive. Firstly, gay activism linked to **AIDS**; specifically, the idea that homosexuals were, first and foremost, individuals, albeit contaminated: not only did this help to shed homophobic stereotypes and reveal that homosexuals were as worthy and respectable as anyone else, but it also gave rise to institutionally supported research. There is no doubt that this research contributed to a better understanding of gay and lesbian experience as legitimate and not as the corrupt behavior of a few unhinged individuals.

The long battles that finally ended in the tumultuous adoption of the **PaCS** civil-union law for common-law couples (including gay and lesbian) revealed the depth of homophobic prejudice in its most vulgar form, including among eminent sociologists (such as Irène Théry). But they also permitted the emergence of positions on homosexuality from the heart of sociological study, that of family (notably the favorable and public positions taken by François de Singly), as well as the promotion of an entire series of studies on the sociological issues of the couple and parenthood.

In the end, ordinary heterosexism still pervades the field of sociology, especially in France. There is no laboratory or research network that has a program to study the issues directly linked to homosexuality and the social status of gays and lesbians. In this, the contrast with the US is staggering. However, even if dispersed or weak, the voices of sociologists is starting to be heard on the subject, and in an eminently positive sense, as demonstrated by the international meetings on gay and lesbian culture at the Centre Georges Pompidou in 1997, under the initiative of Eribon. There is the feeling that the years to come will strengthen this critical current, and that a new generation of sociologists will seize its discipline's vast theoretical inheritance in order to enrich the international debate on homosexuality.
—*Jean-Manuel de Queiroz*

Becker, Howard S. *Outsiders: Studies on Sociology of Deviance*. New York: The Free Press, 1963.

Bersani, Leo. *Homos*. Oxford: Oxford Univ. Press, 1996.

Borrillo, Daniel, Eric Fassin, and Marcela Iacub, eds. *Au-delà du PaCS, l'expertise familiale à l'épreuve de l'homosexualité*. Paris: Presses universitaires de France, 1999.

Butler, Judith. *Gender Trouble: Feminism and the Subversion of Identity*. New York: Routledge, 1990.

Duyvendak, Jan Willem. *Le Poids du politique, nouveaux mouvements sociaux en France*. Paris: L'Harmattan, 1994.

Dynes, Wayne R., and Stephen Donaldson, eds. *Ethnographic Studies of Homosexuality*. New York: Garland, 1992.

Eribon, Didier, ed. *Les Etudes gays et lesbiennes*. Paris: Editions "Supplémentaires," Centre Pompidou, 1998.

———. *Réflexions sur la question gay*. Paris: Fayard, "Histoire de la pensée", 1999. [Published in the US as *Insult and the Making of the Gay Self*. Durham, NC: Duke University Press, 2004.]

Goffman, Erving. *Stigma: Notes on the Management of Spoiled Identity*. Englewood Cliffs, NJ: Prentice Hall, 1963.

Herdt, Gilbert, and Andrew Boxer. *Children of Horizons: How Gays and Lesbians Teens are Leading a New Way out of the Closet*. New York: Beacon Press, 1993.

Kosofsky, Sedgwick Eve. *Epistemology of the Closet*. Berkeley: Univ. of California Press, 1990.

Plummer, Kenneth. *Sexual Stigma: An Interactionnist Account*. London: Routledge, 1975.

Pollak, Michael. *Les Homosexuels et le Sida. Sociologie d'une épidémie*: Paris: Métailié, 1988.

———, and Marie-Ange Schiltz. *Les Homo- et bisexuels masculins face au Sida. Six années d'enquête*. Paris: GSPM, 1991.

Seidman, Steven, ed. *Queer Theory/Sociology*. Cambridge/Oxford: Blackwell Publishers, 1996.

—*Abnormal; AIDS; Anthropology; Biology; Class; Essentialism/Constructionism; Heterosexism; History; Medicine; Psychoanalysis; Psychology; Suicide; Symbolic Order.*

SODOM AND GOMORRAH

The episode of Sodom and Gomorrah can be found in the book of Genesis (19:1–29). Visitors, who are either angels or men, appear at Lot's house in Sodom. Lot entertains them well, but since the other inhabitants

The biblical city, destroyed by divine wrath, inspired a literary and iconographical tradition, as indicated by French author Edmond Fazy's novel, published in 1903 (cover illustrated by Jossot). Fazy was one of many writers who used allusions to Sodom to depict homosexuals as tainted.

of the village want to "know" them (clearly, the verb has the sexual connotation), Lot must protect them; he even proposes his own daughters in exchange. The next day, God punishes the city as well as the city of Gomorrah by raining sulfur and fire upon them, a metaphor for Hell and divine punishment.

Today, this very well-known passage represents the most evident biblical taboo against homosexuality, but in reality, it has not always been like that. The traditional exegesis has sometimes interpreted the passage as an offense against the rules of hospitality towards Lot's visitors. Even better, the **Bible** itself (Epistle of Jude, verses 6-7) suggests a different form of transgression against God in this episode: the two visitors tried to establish undue relations between angelical and human orders; therefore, these angels disobeyed God by looking for an illicit business with men.

In other words, the privileged interpretation of Sodom and Gomorrah which condemns homosexual relations is not the only one in the Bible itself. Nevertheless, this condemnation appears as early as the second century BCE, when pious Jews violently criticized the influence of Greek morality and pederasty among their fellow citizens. Thereafter, this condemnation developed importantly among the first Christian thinkers (e.g., St Clement of Alexandria, John Chrysostom, and St Augustine), for whom homosexuality reflected a pagan way of life, before becoming a veritable common subject of religious rhetoric at the beginning of the thirteenth century.
—*Thierry Revol*

Ancien Testament [Old Testament]. Ecumenical translation of the Bible. Paris: Le Cerf/Les Bergers et les Mages, 1980.

Boswell, John. *Christianisme, tolérance sociale et homosexualité*. Paris: Gallimard, 1985. [Published in the US as *Christianity, Social Tolerance, and Homosexuality*. Chicago: Univ. of Chicago Press, 1980.]

Gilbert, Maurice. "La Bible et l'homosexualité," *Nouvelle Revue de théologie*, no. 109 (1987).

Hallam, Paul. *The Book of Sodom*. New York: Verso, 1993.

Jordan, Mark. *The Invention of Sodomy in Christian Theology*. Chicago: Univ. of Chicago Press, 1997.

McNeill, John. *L'Eglise et l'homosexuel, un plaidoyer*. Geneva: Labor et Fides, 1982. [Published in the US as *The Church and the Homosexual*. Kansas City: Sheed Andrews and McMeel, 1976.]

—*Against Nature; Bible, the; Catholic Church, the; Damien, Peter; Debauchery; Heresy: Islam; Judaism; Paul (of Tarsus); Theology; Vice.*

SODOMY. *See* Sodom and Gomorrah

SONGS (France)

The journals of Charles Collé, the famous French songwriter and dramatist from the eighteenth century, contained the "poetic projects and ... most secret thoughts" of a "poet of the open-air cabaret" (*poète de guinguette*); in it, he lamented: "I planned, long ago, to produce a satire about these gentlemen [i.e. homosexuals]. They are **against nature** reprobates, and their sin deserves an infernal treatment. But I do not know how to go about it, without offending modesty, by putting it to song. I am very disappointed that there is nothing that rhymes with buggerer [*bougre*]; with this little difficulty aside, I would be able to compose something proper by which to call them out." This joke reflects Collé's obsession with homosexuality which translated into an astonishing amount of epigrams, rhyming verses, and songs on the subject. The lack of a rhyme for "*bougre*" did not stop Collé (nor songwriters who either preceded or followed him) from mocking "these gentlemen," often with spirit, but sometimes too with spite. And when unable to compose something modest, these songwriters would turn with abandon to lewdness.

It is easy to find the origins of homophobic satire among the Latin poets Catullus, Martial, and Juvenal, as well as in the *Priapeia* and *Satyricon*. In **Italy** during the Renaissance, homophobic satire, chiefly playful in tone, was produced by neo-Latin poets such as Pacifico Massimi (*Hecatelegium*) and Antonio Beccadelli (*Hermaphroditus*), as well as popular authors such as Pietro Aretino (*Il Marescalco*), Boccaccio (*Decameron*), Antonio Vignale (*La Cazzaria*), and others. Homophobic works that were nastier in tone were rarer, such as those by Niccolò Franco (*Rime di contra Pietro Aretino*).

Despite the wealth of Italian satire, one of the earliest poems written to be sung is German in origin: the "Confutatio Proverbii Italici de Germanorum ebrietate In Pedicones Italos Carmen Impolitum phalenticum Conradi Leontorii Quinto Kalendas Decembris ex tempore Argentinae 1493" (Refutation of the Italian proverb on the drunkenness of Germans against the Italian pederasts, a Rude and phallic song by Conrad Leontorius, improvised the 27th of November 1493 at Regenburg). Undoubtedly composed during a drunken meeting of humanists, the purpose of this song was to take revenge upon the Italians, who traditionally insulted German national honor by mocking not only their fondness for liquor but also their general crudeness. Even at this early date, the song draws on the usual homophobic arsenal: demasculinization (through use of the word *cinaedus*, meaning "sodomite"), the invocation of the laws of the gods and Nature, and the idea that homosexuality is something foreign, in this case the "Italian **vice**."

In **France**, early satires that invoked homophobic sentiments were scathing, such as those by Etienne Jodelle, for example, whose final piece was a venomous diatribe ("Contre la Riere-Vénus" [Against the Riere-Vénus]), and Pierre de Ronsard, whose three homophobic sonnets are quoted in Pierre de L'Estoile's *Registre-journal* on the reign of **Henri III**. It is in this volume that the first true French songs can be found. In the absence of a melody, it is difficult to know for certain if a piece of verse (be it an epigram, a mocking ditty, or a vaudeville) was ever put to music, yet most of these verses are undoubtedly songs, even if only in the literary sense. They attack the King's royal **favorites** with extraordinary **violence**, calling down Heaven's wrath to punish them: "*Au grand diable soit telle engeance! / C'est de la graine de Florence, / Qui ruinera notre France, / Si Dieu, par son juste courroux, / Ne les abisme et perd trestous!*" (To the Devil with this crew! / It will be the seed of Florence / Who will ruin our France / Unless God in his just wrath / Ruins and scatters them all!); also, "*Dieu, par qui tout est rangé, / Fault-il que la France se perde, / Et que le peuple soit mangé, / Par ces beaux petits Fouille-merde!*" (God, by whom all is made right / Must France perish / And her people be consumed / By these pretty little shit-seekers!).

France's disorder during this tumultuous era is reflected in the songs about the disorder in the "Court of **Sodom**" where gender is nebulous ("*Que ce sont beaux compagnons / Que le Roy et tous ses mignons! / Ils ont le visage un peu palle, / Mais sont-ils femelle ou masle?*" [What good companions / Are the King and his minions! / Their faces are pale / But are they female or male?]) and the social order has been perverted ("*Un homme à l'autre se marie, / Et la femme à l'autre s'allie /*

Brouillans ensemble les ordures / De leurs deux semblables natures" [A man can marry another man / And woman with woman unite / Mixing together the offal / Of their common natures]). Lesbians are not spared from satire either, as demonstrated by a 1581 piece entitled *La Frigarelle*, which tells the story of a young woman confused by a "mannish" ("*hommace*") lesbian whom she takes to be a hermaphrodite, but who corrects her: "*Ha non, ha non … / Saché que je suis Femme, et que j'ai en moi / Rien qui ne soit différent des Femmes comme toi, / Mais j'ai entièrement tout le Désir d'un homme*" (Oh no, oh no … / Know that I am a Woman, and inside me / Is nothing different from Women like you / But I have in me all the Desire of a man"). L'Estoile does not hesitate to point out that these vile deeds are "certain signs of a great storm ready to break upon the State." The reign of Henri III is the only period in which songs make scapegoats of sodomites, blaming them for all the troubles of the kingdom. The difficult years of La Fronde (1648–1653), the French civil war over the policies of Cardinal (Jules) Mazarin, then the minister of France, resulted in various accusations of sodomy against the Cardinal by those who became known as the *mazarinades*, but these were made in a burlesque style, never invoking any sort of divine vengeance: "*Mazarin ce bougeron / Dit qu'il n'aime pas les cons / C'est un renégat, / Un bougre d'ingrat / De les avoir en hayne; / Il n'eust jamais esté qu'un fat / Sans celui de la Reyne/ Lon la / Sans celui de la Reyne*" (Mazarin, that bugger / Says he doesn't like cunts / He's a renegade / A bugger ingrate / To hate them so / He would be nothing more than a pig / Without that of the Queen / Loh la / Without that of the Queen). Or again, "*Suivez, empaleurs de garçons, / Jules, qui vos docteurs enseigne, / Il vous donnera des leçons. / … / Le bougre sçait en cent façons, / Pêcher un étron à la ligne.*" (Follow, you impalers of boys / Jules, who your doctors teach / He can give you lessons / … / The bugger knows a hundred ways / To catch a turd on a pole.).

Libertine Thought & Scandals

The dawn of libertine thinking in France at the beginning of the seventeenth century is surely responsible for a change of tone regarding the treatment of homosexuals. It should be said that the figureheads of this movement were almost all homosexual (or reputed to have been, at least); for instance, Théophile de **Viau**, Des Barreaux, Claude Le Petit, Dassoucy, St-Pavin (nicknamed the King of Sodom), Cyrano de Bergerac, and the Baron de Blot L'Eglise, Claude de Chouvigny, as well as many of their protectors, such as the Prince of Condé. With bravado, many libertines took up the defense of sodomites, or evoked their own personal takes on the subject in songs like the following (by the prolific Baron de Blot): "*Amy, le cul fut de tout temps / Le plaisir des honnestes gens / Et de Rome et de Grèce; / Tous nos docteurs l'ont déffendu, / Mais un auteur plus entendu / Dit qu'il est pour l'individu / Et le con pour l'espèce*" (My friend always, the ass / Is the honest man's pleasure / And of Rome and of Greece; / All our doctors have forbidden it, / But a more knowledgeable expert / Says it is good for the individual / While the cunt is just for the species), and "*Je ne demande au Seigneur / Pour bonheur, / Que d'estre buveur, fouleur, / Incrédule et sodomite, / Puis mourir, / Puis mourir, / Puis mourir d'une mort subite!*" (All I ask of the Lord / Is the pleasure / Of being a drinker, a winemaker, / An non-believer and a sodomite / Then die, / Then die, / Then die a swift death!). With the threat of being burned at the stake very real, these sodomites responded with songs themselves, such as this one improvised (in Latin) by the Prince of Condé and the Marquis de La Moussaye while facing the risk of drowning while sailing down the stormy Rhône: "*Le cher ami La Moussaye: / Bon Prince, quel temps! / Lanlanladerirette / Nous périrons sous cette pluie / Lanlanderiri. / Nos vies sont assurées / Car nous sommes sodomites / Lanlanladerirette / Et ne périrons que par le feu / Lanlanderiri*" (Our dear friend La Moussaye: / Good Prince, what weather! / *Lanlanladerirette* / We will perish out in such a rain / *Lanlanderiri*. / Our lives are safe / As we are sodomites / *Lanlanladerirette* / Our only death shall be by fire / *Lanlanderiri*).

This boldness was essentially a veiled form of self-derision, which could be likened to an early form of camp humor. But even though these songs mocked homophobia, it should be noted that the same libertines who composed them also penned some of the most homophobic missives of the *mazarinades*. For example, Cyrano de Bergerac, who once depicted an amiable homosexual culture in *L'Autre monde* (The other world), also wrote the ferocious *Ministre d'Etat flambé* (Minister of the burning state). As for the previously quoted Baron de Blot, he did not hesitate to sing cruelly about Cardinal Mazarin after the death of his nephew: "*L'oncle pleure comme une vache, / S'escriant: Hélas! quel malheur! / Il m'estoit neveu et bardache, / Et je l'avois mis en faveur*" (The uncle weeps like a cow, / Crying: Alas! What misfortune!/ He was both my

nephew and lover, / And I who favored him so). Not even homosexuality could escape the great French tradition in which "everything ends with a song." This recurring theme would swell into a crescendo that culminated during the French Revolution, as demonstrated by the hundreds of homophobic songs collected in the large (forty-two-volume) collection compiled by Pierre de Clairambault, which was reprinted and expanded by the Count de Maurepas. Most of these pieces detail the heterodox habits of figures well known to the public, revealing curious and compromising anecdotes about them.

In general, the songs were not more virulent than those which attacked the cuckolded, the impotent, and dissolute women. The homophobia expressed in them often highlighted the foreign origins of homosexuality. For example, one song insinuated that the questionable tastes of Philippe d'Orléans, the brother of King Louis XIV, was evidence that his real father was Cardinal Mazarin, an Italian: "*Philippe le petit cocu, / Quitte le con et prend le cu, / Lui-même est bien souvent foutu; / Il aime le derrière! / Et par là le vilain, / Fait bien voir que son père / Fut un Prélat romain*" (Philippe the little cuckold, / Quit the cunt and took the ass, / He himself is often screwed; / He loves the rear end! / And there the villain, / Does well, for his father, you see / Was a Roman prelate). In the same vein, the Italian origins of French composer Jean-Bapiste Lully were often referenced; for example, suggesting that while flattering a woman, he declared: "*Qui vous voit un moment est pour jamais charmé; / Moy qui suis Florentin, j'ay changé de côté*" (He who sees you but for a moment is charmed forever; / Even I, who is from Florence, have changed sides).

Many songs attacked monks, priests, and other clergy living in all-male enclaves, part of a long anti-clerical tradition at least as old as this 1566 song, in which a Cordelier monk declared: "*De filles n'avons nul besoin, / Car avons nous pas nos novices / Avecque lesquels prenons soins / De trouver toutes nos délices; / Et ce faisant n'avons point peur / D'en avoir aucun déshonneur*" (Of girls we have no need, / For have we not our novices / With which we take care / To find all our delights; / And doing so we have no fear / Of incurring any dishonor). The most common targets for attack were the Jesuits, for their educational tactics ("*On prétend qu'aux jeunes garçons, / Ils donnent d'étranges leçons*" [It's said that to the young boys / They give some strange lessons]); in the songs, "*jésuite*" was often paired with "*sodomite*" (but not always): "*Les jésuites, gens de goût fin / Et qui ne sont pas dupes, / Portent plus volontiers la main / Aux culottes qu'aux jupes / Et prouvent, par bonne raison / Et par fine doctrine, / Que le cul, plus étroit qu'un con, / Chatouille mieux la pine*" (The Jesuits, men of fine tastes / Who are not fools, / Are more inclined to place their hands / On pants than upon skirts / And prove, through good reasoning / And fine learning, / That the ass, narrower than the cunt, / Is better for tickling the rod).

By the seventeenth century, some songs started to convey the anxiety over the existence of homosexual networks. Not only did these songs mock close friendships that were suspect (such as that between Lully and the Duke of Vendôme, whose name caused no end of amusement when rhymed with Sodom), but they also targeted the list of the Court's homosexuals who had brought the Count of Vermandois, the young bastard son of Louis XIV, into their circle: "*On suit de bien près la piste / De tous les anticonistes / Pon, patapon, tarare pon pon. / Les dames, dans leur chagrin / Travaillent soir et matin / Pour en composer la liste*" (The trail is being closely followed / Of all those who disdain the cunt / *Pon, patapon, tarare pon pon.* / The ladies, in their chagrin / Work night and day / To put these names down in a list). The same kind of incriminations reared its head again fifty years later around the Freemasons and their secret rites, which were likened to homosexuality: "*De leur destin, / Si l'on faisait juges les dames, / De leur destin, / Ils auraient bientôt une triste fin. / Par elles, condamnés aux flames …*" (Of their fate / If women were made their judges / Of their fate, / Theirs would soon be a sad end. / For by these women, they would be condemned to burn at the stake …).

Shockingly, for decades afterwards, homophobic songwriters continued to target those homosexuals who were burned at the stake at the Place de Grève in Paris, including public figure Benjamin Deschaffours, executed in 1726, but most particularly Jacques Chausson, who was convicted of sodomy for the attempted rape of a young nobleman. Even though his execution took place in 1681, Chausson's name appeared in songs right up until the Revolution, some of which were extremely **violent**. Throughout the eighteenth century, songs continued to target well-known sodomites such as King Frederick the Great, whom Diderot once mocked: "*Et Sa Majesté prussienne, / Jamais à femme n'a touché / Sans même excepter la sienne.*" (And his Prussian majesty / Has never touched a woman / Not even his own wife.) Well-known lesbians, too, were now referred to in songs, including ac-

tress Françoise Raucourt and singer Sophie Arnould.

From the Specific to the General

During the course of the eighteenth century, songs generally stopped attacking certain individuals and religious and social groups and instead targeted categories of people defined purely by their sexual tastes, as shown in this song by Collé that seems sympathetic to these "gentlemen":

> Gentlemen, leave your lackeys behind, / And the sentinals; / And you, bright and fresh pages, / Return to the pretty women, / And come back to the threshold / Of our church of the cunt, / Sorry, infidels! / Though I do not mean to suggest / That you abandon Sodom, / I can permit, here and there, / That one must screw one's man! / But I say that it is brutal / To make one's fortune / As they do in Rome.

Many *sottisiers* of the eighteenth century (books which collected together saucy tales, epigrams, and bawdy songs), were made up in large part of pieces that were extremely positive toward homosexuality; the most well-known of these books were *Le Recueil du Cosmopolite* (1735) and *Les Muses en belle humeur* (1742). Some of the songs included in them were practically arguments in favor of sodomy, while others offered names of personalities known for indulging in it.

The eighteenth century ended with satires such as *Les Pantins des boulevards* (The buffoons of the boulevards), a stage play with songs that for the most part were favorable toward homosexuals; at the same time, another satire appeared featuring the kind of hostility not seen since *L'Anti-Rousseau*, in response to the increased visibility of homosexuals. Entitled *L'Ode aux bougres* (Ode to the buggers), it began: "*Monstres que la nature enfante parmi nous! / Bardaches bardachés, objet de mon courroux; / Exécrables pêcheurs d'excrémens à la ligne, / Dont je vois tous les jours croître la race indigne …*" (Monsters that nature spawns among us! / Foppish fops, object of my wrath; / Execrable fishers of excrement on the line, / Whom I see everyday adding to their indignant race …).

At the beginning of the nineteenth century, songs that ridiculed an entire class of people through a stereotype became more common, as shown by Pierre Jean de Béranger's "L'Hermaphrodite," about effeminate homosexuals: "*Admirez à la promenade / Ce petit être tant joli, / Qui près des jeunes gens est fade, / Près des* dames n'est que poli. / Son teint reluisant de pommade, / Par le carmin est embelli, / Joli petit fils, petit mignon, / Mâle ou femelle, je sais ton nom" (Admire on the promenade / This pretty little thing, / Who is so wan when next to young men, / And next to ladies is but polished. / His complexion shines with pomade, / And is embellished with crimson, / Pretty little boy, dainty dear, / Male or female, I know your name). Despite this tendency toward generalization here and there, songs could still be found that defended sodomy through humor, such as "Bougre" and "Panier aux ordures," which declared: "Non, le con de Vénus / Ne vaut pas un anus" (No, not even the cunt of Venus, / Is worth as much as an anus). Another phenomenon worth noting is that an increasing number of songs mentioned lesbianism, such as those found in Parnasse satirique du dix-neuvième siècle (1863) and its sequel, Le Nouveau Parnasse … (1866). These collections were a treasure trove of homophobic and lesbophobic songs depicting realistic scenes of lesbian romps and male prostitution.

By the middle of the nineteenth century, allusions to homosexuality started to appear in written pieces by authors such as Béranger, Gustave Nadaud, or Paul Emile Debraux. Usually hidden away inside comprehensive editions of their work, these pieces typically took a benign approach toward practices that were "out of the ordinary." The same attitude could be found in the anonymous songs of the carabins (medical students) in which any subject matter was permissible, unlike songs meant for the general public and thus subject to **censorship**, which was reintroduced to France by the Minister for Education and the Fine Arts in 1874. However, lyricists found ways of getting around it by incorporating saucy subtexts into their songs; the fact that homosexuality itself was not mentioned made them stand out all the more.

Cabaret shows were not affected by censorship until 1897, so songs in these shows occasionally dared to touch on the subject of homosexuality. In 1891, in Ailleurs, Maurice Donnay wrote a rather caustic monologue about turn-of-the-century habits. This theme was repeated by Yvette Guilbert, later set to music: "Elles ne sont point prolifiques / Mes unions évidemment / J'assiste aux amours saphiques / Des femmes qui n'ont point d'amant" (They are far from fruitful / My relations, obviously / I take part in Sapphic loves / With women who have no lovers). The following year, Léon Xanrof, another patron of the establishment, presented a sketch of elegant, effeminate boys living dissolute lives: Les P'tits crevés.

Gender Ambiguity

At the beginning of the twentieth century, Félix Mayol was the most famous star of the café-concert (cafés that also served as performance spaces) scene in France. He helped to crystallize the image of the folle (effeminate male), wearing a wig, a corsage on his lapel, and carrying a handkerchief; he performed with his back arched and made effeminate gestures. The folle became a main target of songwriters and (often crude) impressionists, to the great enjoyment of the general public.

The **Eulenberg affair**, the scandal in **Germany** over accusations of homosexual conduct among prominent members of Kaiser Wilhelm II's cabinet and entourage between 1907 and 1909, was apparently the subject of only one satirical song in Berlin, written by Otto Reuter ("Der Hirschfeld kommt," [Hirschfeld comes], recorded in 1908). In Paris, however, the scandal had a much bigger impact on French songwriters, who could not let this opportunity to satirize Germans pass by. Jean Péheu marked the occasion with a song entitled "Scandale teuton" (Teutonic scandal); another musician named Soubeyran recorded "Les Petits Soldats de Guillaume" (Guillaume's little soldiers). As well, the Folies-Bergères revue of December 1907 included a satirical piece on the subject; the highly anti-German lyrics illustrated France's highly vengeful attitude toward Germany since 1870.

The theme of the effeminate male continued to appear in songs and music-hall shows. Singer Charlotte Gaudet, a specialist in saucy verses, recorded "Le P'tit Jeune Homme" (The l'il young man) in 1909, whose lyrics contained a number of not-so-subtle plays on words: "Il a des petits mouchoirs brodés / et tout son linge est marqué P. D." (He has little embroidered hankies / And all his shirts are labelled F.A.G.) and "Il achète pour sa santé / de la vas'line de première qualité" (For his health he buys / Only the finest quality Vaseline). Meanwhile, Mayol, after announcing to the press his faux engagement to a woman, became a popular target for songwriters; no less than five songs were composed, such as "Les Fiançailles de Miss Tapette" (The engagement of Miss Fairy) and "Mayol reste jeune fille" (Mayol remains a young lady). Tired of being made the butt of jokes, Mayol devoted several indignant passages on the subject in his 1928 memoir: "Can a single entity truly be malignant enough to claim that it can govern the **private** lives of others? An artist should only be accountable to his clientele for his public performances, which are strictly limited to the role of the artist.…

I do not believe I need to justify myself to anyone; I owe them nothing, nothing at all, when it comes to my private life."

After World War I, it was the *garçonnes* (modern women with hair cut short) who became the subject of satire regarding sexual ambiguity. In 1923, Georgel published *La Garçonne* (modelled somewhat after La Régia, a female entertainer who often wore a smoking jacket when performing): "*La garçonne / se donne l'allure d'un garçon [...] / Elle croit, ça c'est certain / être du sexe masculin / La garçonne*" (La garçonne / dresses herself up like a boy [...] / She believes, it would seem / To be of the masculine sex / La garçonne). Some songs, inspired by the latest clothing styles, went much further than simply describing appearance, evoking the subject of androgyny. In 1925, the comedian Dréan exclaimed, "Is it a man, or is it a woman?" Two years later, Gaston Gabaroche (himself a married man, yet openly homosexual) sang "Les filles c'est de garçons" (Girls can be boys), which highlighted the feminist aspect of the *garçonnes*, which posed a threat to heterosexual men. Sexism and homophobia, hand in hand.

The 1920s marked the beginning of a period in France in which male homosexuality was affirmed (especially in Paris). Events such as the Carnaval Interlope (a gay masquerade ball in Paris that started in 1922), the publication of *Sodom and Gomorrah,* a fourth volume of *Remembrance of Things Past* by Marcel Proust, followed by *Corydon* by André **Gide**; and the short-lived gay publication *Inversions* all provoked reactionary responses from songwriters, a phenomenon similar to that in Harlem, in that the development of a minority subculture resulted in a homophobic response from the majority. In 1923, comedian Gaston Ouvrard composed a song entitled "Titi … toto … et Patata!" (Titi, Toto, and Patata!) about three flamboyant young men in underground Paris: "*Titi, Toto et Patata / Font des p'tit's manières et marchent toujours comme ça. / Ils poussent des ouh! Ils font des ah! / Des chichis des esbroufes et des tas de fla-flas*" (Titi, Toto, and Patata / Carry themselves in a special way and always walk like this / They exclaim, Ooh! / They cry out, Ah! / Fussy, pretentious, and making everything a big deal). Sandrey, a specialist in bawdy humor, recorded a song entitled "La Java des étourdis" (Scatterbrain java) in 1928, a caricature of homosexuals who frequented the *bals musette* (cafés where one could dance). That same year, Maurice Chevalier created "Si j'étais demoiselle" (If I were a girl), with lyrics by Albert Willemetz.

In 1929, the operetta *Louis XIV* debuted at La Scala, composed by Philippe Parès and Georges Van Parys, with lyrics by Serge Veber. In it, historical references to King Henri III were derisive: "*Pourquoi n'aimes-tu pas les femmes? Henri! Henri! Henri, c'est pas gentil …*" (Why can you not like women? Henri! Henri! Henri, it's just not nice …).

In the tradition of the *café-concert*, most songs with refrains were constructed according to extremely rigid formulas: e.g., the comic verse, the patriotic verse, and the bawdy verse. But the pervading culture engendered the development of a new style, the effeminate verse. A few notable titles were "Je n'suis pas celle que vous croyez" (I'm not the girl you think I am), 1925; "Quand on n'en a pas" (When you don't have any), 1925; "Le Bilboquet" (The cup-and-ball), 1930; "Emilienne," 1931; "La Tapette en bois" (The wooden beater), 1933; "Quand un vicomte" (When a viscount), 1935; and "Ca vaut mieux que d'attraper la scarlatine" (It's not as bad as catching scarlet fever), 1936. This form of ridicule was believed to have amused even the *folles* themselves, given the acceptance of homophobia in French society through its tradition of **humor**, in much the same way as racism or anti-Semitism (both of which were also frequent subjects of satirical songs) were accepted.

The duettists Gilles and Julien, part of the avant-garde music scene of the 1930s, were more sanctimonious. Their lively hits such as "Dollar" and "Le Jeu de massacre" (Knock 'em down game), as well as the homophobic "En serez-vous?" (Will you be one?) depicted the era's **decadence**; in one verse, homosexuality is equated to something fashionable, like the yo-yo, which was all the rage that year in the capital: "*Car en être ou ne pas en être / C'est la question qui s'pose à tous. / N'en étant pas, demain peut-être / En serez-vous? / Si vous en êtes, faut reconnaître / Qu'à notre époque, ça mène à tout. / Pour réussir, il faut en être/ Un p'tit effort, Zou! En serez-vous?*" (To be one, or not to be one / Is the question everyone asks. / If not one today, then tomorrow perhaps / Will you be one? / If you are one, you must admit / That today, it goes a long way. / To succeed, you must be one / Just try a little, hey! Will you be one?). Gilles and Julien were not "ones," but during this period, militant left-wingers considered homosexuality to be a bourgeois vice, a symptom of class (and, in a larger sense, society's) **degeneracy**. This trend of male duettists blossomed in the 1930s often for reasons that were more intimate than artistic (Charles and Johnny, for example).

The entertainer Georgius got into the swing of things with "Imprudentes!" (How imprudent!), a song recorded in 1933, describing the nightlife in the Bois de Boulogne, complete with an encounter with an effeminate boy ("a bouquet of pea flowers") and with a "big bearded giant." This appears to be the only song of the era which explicitly made reference to homosexual encounters, not to mention fashionable transvestites and high society gays. The author of more than 1,500 songs, Georgius was unique when it came to acerbic songs. No subject was safe from him, and homosexuals were among his favorite targets. Many of his songs contained allusions to the subject, such as "Si ça lui plaît" (If it pleases him), 1926; "Qu'est-ce qu'il faut faire pour gagner son bifteck!" (What does a man have to do to bring home the steak!), 1927; "Tais-toi!" (Shut up!) 1927; "Le Genre de la maison" (The way things work"), 1928; "La Pi-pipe en terre" (Little clay pipe"), 1932; "Les Frères siamois" (The Siamese brothers), 1938; and "Dans la cave de ma maison" (Down in my cellar), 1939. He rarely if ever targeted lesbians; indeed, the subject was remarkably absent from song lyrics in the 1930s, with the exceptions of such standard-bearers as Suzy Solidor, who sensually approached the topic in "Ouvre" (Open up) in 1933.

The Millstone Around the Neck

The unbridled spirit that flourished during the 1920s and 1930s did not survive the outbreak of World War II. Despite the threat of repression, homosexuality was tolerated in France during the German occupation (provided it was out of sight), although the young "swing kids" of the *zazou* movement, associated with the fashionable swing music of the period, were subjected to homophobic treatment. Suggestions of this can be found in some little-known songs, such as Georges Milton's "Zazou et zouza," which advocated the internment of gay *zazous*.

During the repressive climate in France inherited from the Vichy administration after liberation (for example, the discriminatory Vichy law of 1942 that forbade homosexual relations with a minor under the age of twenty-one was reaffirmed in 1945), allusions to homosexuality in song became quite rare. A popular waltz by Ouvrard in 1946, entitled "Julot ... prout ... prout," (Julot, fart, fart) told the story of a bad boy sentenced to hard labor who returns completely homosexual. Two years later, Lily Fayol recorded a song

(written by André Hornez) entitled "Entre ses bras" (In his arms), whose second verse is without equal:

> When he took me in his arms / I asked myself: What is it about him? / He puts on airs / And makes pouty faces / When he moves there's a little too much tra-la-la! / He would sigh and say: "Be careful / You're messing my perm!" / How his habits / Exasperate me / So I dropped him right then and there!

(Across the Atlantic, Broadway stage productions occasionally featured characters who were gay or effeminate: caricatures, more or less, or at least masculine actors in drag. The more significant examples can be found in shows such as 1938's *Hellzapoppin*, 1941's *Lady in the Dark*, 1944's *Mexican Hayride*, 1948's *As the Girls Go*, and 1948's *Where's Charley?*)

In Paris in 1950, the Empire revue featured a sketch entitled *Les Scandales parallèles* (Parallel scandals), full of less-than-charitable allusions to the habits of gay French cabaret singer Charles Trenet (which resulted in a few encounters with the law). In 1953, singer Robert Rocca performed "Ils en sont tous" (They're all like that) at the Caveau de la Huchette, a surrealistic song which vividly described an imaginary village where everyone was homosexual. In 1957, Guy Béart took a moralistic approach with his song "Qu'on est bien" (We'll be all right): "*Certains jouent quand même / les atouts de même couleur / Libre à eux, moi j'aime / Les valets pour les dam's / les trèfles pour les cœurs*" (Some people like to play / Trumps of all the same suit / Unlike them, I prefer / Jacks to go with queens / And clubs to go with hearts). However, these are only a few isolated examples; for the most part, homophobia among French songwriters in the 1950s took the form of self-censorship. This attitude corresponded with the intent of the gay magazine *Arcadie*, started by André Baudry in 1954, which advocated homosexuality provided it was discreet and respectful.

However, despite Hélène Martin's courageous musical adaptation of Jean Genet's *Condamné à mort* (Sentenced to death), the music of the early 1960s echoed the style of the early 1930s, denouncing the "fashion" of homosexuality. In 1962, the very macho Georges Brassens included a couplet on the subject in his song "Les Trompettes de la renommée" (The trumpets of fame): "*Sonneraient-elles plus fort ces divines trompettes / si, comme tout un chacun, j'étais un peu tapette?*

/ *Si je me déhanchais comme une demoiselle / et prenais tout à coup des allures de gazelle*" (Would those divine trumpets sound even louder / If, like each of them, I was just a little bit gay? / If I swayed my hips like a lady / Or looked doe-eyed at the drop of a hat?). The following year, Guy Béart riffed on the subject of sexual ambiguity with "Le Monsieur et le jeune homme" (The gentleman and the young man). Then in 1965, Henri Tachan launched a salvo against "Les PD" (Fags) on his first album, with rather caustic lyrics: "*Moi qui suis, Dieu soit loué, fierté congénitale / Le chevalier servant des amours dites normales / Du haut de mon donjon, je rêve de chasser / Jusqu'au dernier impie cette secte infernale*" (I am, God be praised, congenitally proud / A knight in the service of the normal kind of love / From the walls of my castle, I dream of vanquishing / To the very last sinner, this infernal sect). In 1967, Jacques Brel took his turn at cultivating homophobia with a rewritten version of his hit "Les Bonbons," in which the hero intends to give candy to his girlfriend but, after being seduced by her younger brother, he offers them to him instead. The subject would be simply amusing if not for the fact that Brel was using it to quash accusations of being effeminate.

Around the same time, Fernandel was amusing audiences with "Il en est" (He's one), which was full of suggestive innuendo and poor taste: "*Ta ta ta ta ta ta … Prout! Prout!*" (La la la la la la … Fart! Fart!"). The lyrics were written by Michel Rivgauche in 1966; when recently asked about the material, he declared that he never intended to be spiteful. He did admit that the song would never be considered acceptable today; as far as he was concerned, back then homosexuality was simply one of many subjects for jokes. Thus, the "popular" tendency of music of the period remained close to the spirit of the 1930s, when "aunties" were mocked and lesbians were ignored. Playing on the audience's assumed homophobia, dramatist Jean Poiret explored this tendency in 1972 with his play *La Cage aux folles*, which went on to become a hit French film in 1978.

Figureheads

Following the events of May 1968 in France, which included the involvement of a newly radical homosexual movement, French society became more openminded. Over-the-counter sales of the birth control pill (legal since December 19, 1967) and a new sexual freedom largely championed by young people were accompanied by an increased **tolerance** toward homosexuals. Singer-songwriter Michel Polnareff, sensitive to the subject of masculinity, played on this ambiguity in "Je suis un homme" (I am a man), written in 1970 in reaction to the homophobia of which he found himself victim: "*Les gens qui me voient / Passer dans la rue / Me traitent de pédé / Mais les femmes qui le croient / N'ont qu'à m'essayer*" (People who see me / Pass by on the street / Treat me like a queer / But the women who think so / Need but to give me a try). Following Frédéric Botton's sly take on the subject of homosexuality with the metaphorical "Les Pingouins" (The penguins), composed for Juliette Gréco in 1970, Charles Aznavour decided to tackle the subject in 1972 with "Comme ils disent" (Like they say). Its quietly familiar references, such as "J'habite seul avec Maman …" (I live alone with Mother), contrasted sharply with the militant image of the Front homosexuel d'action révolutionnaire (Homosexual Front for Revolutionary Action) in the streets of Paris around the same time. Thus, popular song's treatment of homosexuality changed from simple mockery to a sort of pathos, in keeping with the more sympathetic image of homosexuality as presented in the **media**. Nevertheless, thanks to its good intentions, the impact of Aznavour's song was like a tidal wave, coming as it did from such a famous singer. Aznavour himself said the song was meant to advocate tolerance: "It's a love song, like any other … except maybe even more important." In the few gays bars and nightclubs of the era (such as Le Nuage in St-Germain-des-Prés or Le Sept on rue Ste-Anne), "Comme ils disent" was undeniably the most successful song in France in 1972. The same maudlin quality appeared later in a song by the singer known as Dalida: "*Pour ne pas vivre seul / des filles aiment des filles / et l'on voit des garçons / épouser des garçons*" (So as not to live alone / Girls will love girls / And boys can be seen / Marrying boys). Here, homosexuality was presented as a solution of substitution.

The last singer of this period who dared to attack homosexuality aggressively was Michel Sardou, who in 1970 lashed out against homosexuals in the **army** ("*Le rire du sergent / La folle du régiment / La préférée du capitaine des dragons / Le rire du sergent / Un matin de printemps / M'a fait comprendre comment gagner du gallon*" [The sergeant's laughter / The regiment's dandy / The dragon captain's favorite girl / The sergeant's laughter / One spring morning / Taught me how one can earn ones stripes]), then touched on the subject of pedophilia at boarding school in "Le Surveillant général"

(The dean of boys). He added a sort of coda to his homophobic repertoire in 1976 with "J'accuse" (I blame), written by Pierre Delanoë: "*J'accuse les hommes de croire des hypocrites / Moitié pédés, moitié hermaphrodites / Qui jouent les durs pour enfoncer du beurre / Et s'agenouillent aussitôt qu'ils ont peur*" (I blame people for believing those hypocrites / Half queer, half hermaphrodite / Who pretend to be hard just to cut through the butter / Yet drop to their knees as soon as they're scared). But this would be the last of this genre, although in 1978, Serge Gainsbourg wrote a rather enigmatic song for the singer known as Régine, which included the lyrics "*Les femmes, ça fait pédé / C'est très efféminé / tellement efféminé / qu'ça fait pédé*" (Women, they look like fags / It's so effeminate / So very effeminate / That they look like fags), while Serge Lama attempted an awkwardly compassionate song: "Les amitiés particulières, c'est quand les filles nous font peur" (Special relationships, because we're scared of girls).

Reversing the Trend

With homosexuality more visible in the 1970s, the 1976 French rock opera *Starmania,* written by Michel Berger and Luc Plamondon, featured an androgynous character named Ziggy (a reference to the androgynous character of Ziggy Stardust, created a few years earlier by David Bowie); an English-language version of the show, entitled *Tycoon,* appeared in 1992, with new lyrics by Tim Rice. Throughout the show, Ziggy is accompanied by Marie-Jeanne, a typical "fag hag"; together, they sing "La Chanson de Ziggy" ("Ziggy's Song") and "Un garçon pas comme les autres" (A boy unlike all the others; renamed "Ziggy" in *Tycoon*); the latter song became the hymn of the new gay generation in France: "*Oui, je sais, il aime les garçons / Je devrais me faire une raison*" (Yes, I know, he likes boys / I should find myself a reason). This extremely positive depiction of homosexuality, the first large-scale popular work to do so, was due to the efforts of lyricist Plamondon, a Quebecer, who adopted an American-style openness on the subject. The authors of Broadway musicals, many of whom were gay themselves, were now regularly casting homosexuality in a favorable light, and took every opportunity to denounce homophobia in their work. Examples included *A Funny Thing Happened on the Way to the Forum* (1962), *Coco* (1969), *Applause* (1970), *Sugar* (a 1972 adaptation of the film *Some Like It Hot*), and later, an English-language adaptation of *La Cage aux Folles* (1983).

The production of *Starmania* at the Palais des Congrès in April 1979 coincided with the success of Alain Marcel's play *Essayez donc nos pédalos* (Take our pedalos for a ride), one of the first stage productions in France to depict homosexuals as neither caricatures nor objects of pity. These shows set the stage for Francis Lalanne's shocking 1980 song "La plus belle fois qu'on m'a dit je t'aime, c'est un mec qui me l'a dit" ("The Most beautiful time I heard I love you was when a guy said it to me). It was one of the first songs to attempt to erase the lines between straight and gay attraction: "*A chacun son amour / C'est pas l'mien voilà tout / Aimer les filles ou les garçons / C'est aimer de toute façon*" (To each their own love / It's just not mine, that's all / Loving girls or loving boys / Is loving, no matter what). Even more shocking were songs recorded by Jean Guidoni, all written by Pierre Philippe, which went along the same lines: "Je marche dans les villes" (I walk the city), "Viril" (Virile), and "Sirocco (Est-ce que c'est bon l'amour avec les militaires?)" (Sirocco [Is it good to love a soldier?]). From that point on, it became increasingly unacceptable in France to write a song that was blatantly homophobic. This evolution in thinking was taken to the legislative level in 1982 when the **discriminatory** law regarding sexual consent was abolished. Meanwhile, the French songs of the 1980s often handled the subject of homosexuality with ambiguity; these included Dalida's "Depuis qu'il vient chez nous" (Since he came home), Taxi Girl's "Cherchez le garçon" (Finding the boy), Indochine's "Le Troisième sexe" (The third sex), Barbara's "Qui est qui?" (Who is who?), and Mylène Farmer's "Maman a tort" (Mama was wrong) and "Sans contrefaçon" (No imitation).

In 1990, Pierre Grosz adapted the Spanish group Mecano's hit song into French, "Une femme avec une femme" (A woman with a woman), containing a hitherto unheard-of tone: "*Deux femmes qui se tiennent la main / Ça n'a rien qui peut gêner la morale / Là où le doute s'installe / C'est que ce geste se fasse sous la table*" (Two women holding hands / Is nothing to be ashamed of / But what is hard to understand / Is when it has to happen under the table). Michel Sardou, too, has a radical change of heart in 1991 with "Le Privilège," inviting more understanding and tolerance: "*Ça va faire drôle à la maison / Un garçon qui aime un garçon*" (It'll be kind of funny having at home / A boy who loves a boy).

The **AIDS** crisis marked a turning point in the history of gay culture, and it is within this context that a new trend in songwriting emerged. Like many of the AIDS prevention campaigns at the time, songs written on the subject avoided mentioning homosexuals, despite the fact that they were the group most affected by it. Only around 1995, more than ten years after the introduction of AIDS, did French songs start to lament its gay victims; these included Zaniboni's "Sid'habitude," Julos Beaucarne's "Carnet d'adresse" (Address book), and Jean Guidoni's "N'oublie jamais qui tu es" (Never forget who you are). Over the years, the visibility of homosexuals (especially men) was heightened as a result of the AIDS crisis; in particular, this visibility was marked by an impassioned activism. Meanwhile, a new homophile undercurrent in French pop music started around the mid-1990s; Juliette, Mouron, Etienne Daho, Lara Fabian, Zazie, and Renaud all released songs that were perfectly in sync with the advent of the PaCS (Pacte civil de solidarité; Civil solidarity pact: French legislation advocating domestic partnerships, including homosexual unions) debates.

Rap & Reggae as Reactionary Movements?

As a result of more progressive attitudes toward homosexuality, homophobic songs were relegated to the genres of American country music and, most of all, rap. Originating in the United States around 1979, the hip-hop movement spread to France in the early 1990s. Particularly aggressive examples of rap recorded around the end of the 1990s underscored the abyss between homosexuals and the young purveyors of the ultra-macho hip-hop scene. The subject of homosexuality was taboo in rap music unless it explicitly rejected it, typical of the attitude and style of French rappers such as Ménélik. MC Solaar, whose rap style was more melodic and poetic, always took a "gay-friendly" stance, once declaring, "J'ai invité le pape à la Gay Pride" (I invited the Pope to Gay Pride) in his 1988 song "La vie n'est qu'un moment" (Life is but a moment).

Of course, the precedent for French rap's homophobic tendencies lies in its American counterpart, which includes numerous examples of rappers performing hateful songs and making public anti-gay declarations. Among the most well-known of these is Eminem who, since the release of his first albums in the mid-1990s, has included several inflammatory references to homosexuals in his lyrics. His 2000 album *The Marshall Mathers LP* contained many aggressive tracks, including references to forcing fellow rappers to suck his dick and to holding "faggots" at knifepoint because

they keep "eggin' [him] on." On the track "Criminal," which incurred the wrath of gay, lesbian, and women's groups, he rapped: "My words are like a dagger with a jagged edge that'll stab you in the head whether you're a fag or a lez…. Hate fags? The answer is yes!" Feuds between rappers are also marked by homophobia; DMX once bragged of having proof that Ja Rule was homosexual during their bitter feud.

Meanwhile, examples of homophobia in French rap abound. In a song by Rohff entitled "On fait les choses" (We get stuff done), he declares: *"Mon stuff mérite de faire la une du journal télévisé / Mais on m'a dit que c'était des pédés qui produisaient / Donc en tant qu'anti-pédé, ton colon je viens briser. / Inutile, c'est pas la peine de sympathiser / Ce n'est pas de mon pedigree"* (My stuff is good enough for the news on TV / But they tell me that it just makes queers / For my anti-queer effort, then, I'll bust up your ass / Useless it's not worth sympathizing / It's not part of my pedigree). Rohff's 2001 track "Le Rap des barbares" (Barbarian rap) took another raw take on the subject matter: *"A c'qu'on dit, la plupart des rappers s'prennent pour les mauvais garçons / En c'qui m'concerne mélange pas les strings et les cal'çons / C'est pas du rap de merde, j'suis pas un pédé / J'rappe pour ceux qui s'démerdent, j'encule les condés"* (From what they say, most rappers think they're pretty bad boys / In my case, don't mix up g-strings with boxers / I don't do shitty rap, I'm no fag / I rap for those who can handle themselves; screw the cops).

The main purpose of this violent language (targeting only male homosexuals) appears to build up the virile image of the rebellious rapper. Under the guise of rebellion and provocation, the values touted by rappers are often reactionary: chauvinism, misogyny, violence, homophobia, and a general rejection of those who are perceived to be weak. While Eminem (whose lyrics appear to encourage rape, pedophilia, and homophobia) is one of the most striking examples of this, he is not alone; and rather than be taken to task for it, these rappers are touted by labels and radio stations, resulting in huge record sales and sold-out concerts.

The same goes for *ragga* (a derivative of reggae), whose rap influence includes lyrics that are also violent, chauvinistic, and homophobic. Reggae and ragga, it must be noted, stem from Jamaican culture, which has a long history of chauvinism and homophobic persecution. In this sense, Jamaican rap stars were even more radical in their homophobia. In 1992, Buju Banton caused a stir with his track "Boom Boom Bye Bye," which encouraged violence against the "batty boys" (homo-sexuals), including murder. A similar stance was taken by fellow Jamaican Shabba Ranks, to the detriment of his career, as gay rights organizations in both New York and Jamaica protested against him, calling into question the homophobic attitude of the rasta movement itself. At the request of his record label, Banton insisted that due to his religion he wasn't trying to incite anti-gay violence, though he never recanted his statements. He has since made amends, but the problem is far from resolved, as a new wave of homophobic rap artists and tracks have appeared in France in recent years, such as Elephant Man's "We Nuh Like Gay" and "Log On," T. O. K.'s "Chi Chi Man" (Jamaican slang for homosexuals), which called for gays to be burned alive; Capleton's "Bun Out Di Chi Chi," and lastly Beenie Man's "Damn," which declared "I'm dreaming of a New Jamaica, come to execute all the gays."

Thankfully, in rap, things have begun to evolve for the better. Eminem himself has tried to rehabilitate his image; at the 2001 Grammy Awards, he invited the openly gay Elton John to perform his song "Stan" with him. Even French rappers have curbed their homophobic tendencies, arguably due to a new period of maturity in the hip-hop movement. In April 2001, the French gay magazine *Têtu* even published a cover photo of rapper Doc Gyneco applying lipstick. Could this be a sign that, in some countries at least, homosexuality and popular song are finally on common ground?

—*Louis Godbout and Martin Pénet*

[Original essay updated by Arsenal Pulp Press.]

Chansonnier historique du XVIIIe siècle I–X. With an introduction, commentary, notes and index by Emile Raunié. Paris: A. Quantin, 1882.

Les Gaietés de Béranger à l'Eleutheropolis. A l'enseigne de Cupidon (n.p., n.d.).

Les Muses en belle humeur ou chansons et autres poésies joyeuses. Ville Franche, France: 1742.

Le Panier aux ordures, suivi de quelques chansons ejusdem farinae. By W. Field Canton and Tching-kong (n.p., n.d.).

Le Parnasse satyrique du dix-neuvième siècle. Recueil de pièces facétieuses, scatologiques, piquantes, pantagruéliques, gaillardes et satyriques des meilleurs auteurs contemporains, poètes, romanciers, journalistes etc., suivi du Nouveau Parnasse satyrique... (1863–1868). Brussels: 1881.

Recueil de pièces choisies rassemblées par les soins du Cosmopolite. Anconne, Uriel Brandant, 1735 (reprinted by a bibliophile society at 163 ex., Leyde, 1865, in fact Gay, Brussels).

Recueil dit de Maurepas, pièces libres, chansons, épigrammes et autres vers satiriques sur divers personnages des siècles de Louis XIV et Louis XV, accompagnés de remarques curieuses du temps; publiés pour la première fois d'après les manuscrits conservés à la Bibliothèque impériale, à Paris, avec des notices, des tables, etc., I–VI. Leyde, Netherlands: 1865.

Barbier, Pierre, and France Vernillat. *Histoire de France par les chansons.* Vol. 1–6. Paris: Gallimard, 1956–58.

Bazin, Hugues. *La Culture hip-hop.* Paris: Desclée de Brouwer, 1995.

Bordman, Gerald. *American Musical Theatre: A Chronicle.* Oxford/New York: Oxford Univ. Press, 1977.

Boucher, Manuel. *Le Rap, expression des lascars, Significations et enjeu du rap dans la société française.* Paris: L'Harmattan, 1999.

Brunschwig, Chantal, Louis-Jean Calvet, and Jean-Claude Klein. *Cent Ans de chanson française (1880-1980).* Paris: Le Seuil "Points," 1981.

Bruyas, Florian. *Histoire de l'opérette en France (1855-1965).* Lyon, France: Emmanuel Vitte, 1974.

Chauvreau, Philippe, and André Sallée. *Music-hall et café-concert.* Paris: Bordas, 1985.

Clum, John M. *Something for the Boys: Musical Theater and Gay Culture.* New York: St Martin's Press, 2001.

Collé, Charles. *Chansons badines de Collé.* New edition. Utrecht, Netherlands: J. Plecht, (c. 1881).

Condemi, Concetta. *Les Cafés-concerts, histoire d'un divertissement (1849–1914).* Paris: Quai Voltaire, 1992.

Hadleigh, Boze. *Sing Out! Gays and Lesbians in the Music World.* London: Barricade Books, 1997.

Herbert, Michel. *La Chanson à Montmartre.* Paris: La Table Ronde, 1967.

Jacques-Charles. *Cent Ans de music-hall: histoire générale du music-hall de ses origines à nos jours, en Grande-Bretagne, en France et aux États-Unis.* Geneva/Paris: Jeheber, 1956.

Mockus, Martha. "Queer Thoughts on Country Music and k.d. Lang." In *Queering in Pitch: The New Gay and Lesbian Musicology.* Edited by Philip Brett, Gary Thomas, and Elizabeth Wood. London/New York: Routledge, 1994.

"Le Rose et le rap," *Têtu* (2001).

Rowland, Ingrid D. "Revenge of the Regensburg Humanists, 1493," *The Sixteenth Century Journal* 25, no. 2. Kirksville, MO (1994).

Seifert, Lewis C. "Masculinity and Satires of 'Sodomites' in France, 1600-1715." In *Homosexuality in French History and Culture.* Edited by Jeffrey Merrick and Michael

Sibalis. New York: Harrington Park Press, 2001.

—Art; Comic Books; Bryant, Anita; Caricature; Censorship;
Dance; Eulenburg Affair, the; Heterosexism; Humor;
Literature; Music; Rhetoric; Scandal; Violence.

SOS HOMOPHOBIE

In the West, the fight against homophobia has become
a social and political issue whose complete history remains to be written. Since the beginning of the twentieth century, and especially since the 1970s, several
associations have made homophobia their principal
topic of concern; among these groups, the French association SOS homophobie constitutes a very interesting example.

The association's name was chosen to evoke the
name of another French anti-discrimination group,
SOS Racisme. Most of the association's founders
were former activists from the leftist organization
FAR (Fraction armée rouge; Red Army Fraction);
they held their first meeting in the fall of 1993. The
group quickly established itself in Paris by setting up
an anonymous helpline for victims of homophobic
violence in April 1994. Since then, it has expanded
to include a permanent telephone service to respond
specifically to problems of **violence** and **discrimination** encountered by gays and lesbians throughout
France. The organization's chief goals are: "to help
victims of homophobic abuse; to run homophobia
prevention activities; to achieve equality in rights between homosexual and heterosexual couples, and between homosexual and heterosexual individuals."

When the helpline was first established, the first
team was mobilized to organize and ensure the functioning of the helpline and to promote the number to
call. However, those involved quickly became divided
on the question of priorities and the more politicized
among them, familiar with the history of the battle for
gay rights, quit. From this point onward, two opposing strategies were at work: those who were adamant
that the helpline needed to be professional, above all
else, set against those believed in absolute action and
prevention, akin to the ACT UP approach. Despite this
divergence, however, the association survived.

The team that remained worked on redefining the
group's objectives and methods, and, little by little, SOS
homophobie became more credible as an organization.

Among its priorities was the development of an annual report on homophobia in France, which would
be made available to public authorities, the **media**,
and the public. This report gave SOS homophobie its
distinctiveness: that its helpline was not an end unto
itself, but rather a tool in the fight against homophobia. The annual report was premised on the idea that
mapping the spread of homophobia allowed for a better understanding of it, and thus underscore the need
for social tools to address it and ultimately prevent it.
The group's first annual report on homophobia was
released in June 1998.

SOS homophobie's conception of itself as an observatoire de l'homophobie (observatory of homophobia)
took shape with the helpline and the annual report. In
order to be more efficient, the willingness and ability
to anticipate, prevent, and educate people in order to
contain and condemn homophobia began to be asserted. Work began on convincing public authorities
to start prevention campaigns and adopt anti-homophobic policies.

Since then, the association has maintained its momentum: the structure works efficiently, the helpline
volunteers undergo intense training, and the frames
of reference are regularly updated and enhanced. The
annual report, which is elaborate and documented, is
now widely used by French media. Anti-homophobia sensitivity-training manuals are widely distributed
to labor unions, administrative offices, and the police.
Writers of the legislation against the incitement of
homophobic hatred and other legal material are inspired by the contributions from the association.

Will the association be forced to change in the future? The profile of homophobia in France has changed:
there are fewer cases of physical violence against gays
and lesbians, but at the same time it remains insidious,
manifested mostly in **insults** or in casual discrimination in daily life, in the **workplace**, neighborhood,
or **school**. Therefore, anti-homophobic mobilization
remains vital, especially since gays and lesbians have
yet to obtain equality with heterosexuals in social or
legal rights. SOS homophobie will continue to work
for these rights by collaborating more frequently with
politicians and governing bodies.

—Christine Le Doaré

Adam, Barry D., Jan Willem Duyvendak, and André
    Krouwel, eds. The Global Emergence of Gay and Lesbian
    Politics: National Imprints of a Worldwide Movement.

Philadelphia: Temple Univ. Press, 1999.

Duyvendak, Jan Willem. *Le Poids du politique, nouveaux mouvements sociaux en France.* Paris: L'Harmattan, 1994. [Published in the US as *The Power of Politics: New Social Movements in France.* Boulder, CO: Westview Press, 1995.]

Front homosexuel d'action révoluttionnaire (FHAR). *Rapport contre la* normalité. Paris: Éditions champ libre, 1971.

SOS homophobie. *Rapport sur l'homophobie.* Paris, 1997, 1998, 1999, 2000, 2001, 2002.

Thompson, Mark, ed. *The Long Road to Freedom: The Advocate History of the Gay and Lesbian Movement.* New York: St Martin's, 1994.

Working for Lesbian and Gay Members. Brussels: Public Services International and Education International, 1999.

—*Associations; Discrimination; France; Politics; Violence.*

SOUTHEAST ASIA

Southeast Asia is a complex region of very diverse cultures, spanning eleven countries, each with their own highly varied traditions and ethnic groups. This region has for centuries been a cultural crossroads for a varied range of influences: Chinese, Indian, Muslim, Animist, Hindu, Buddhist, and more recently, Western and Christian. These influences were added on top of previous cultural traditions, though often without any real mixing, to the point where within even a single country the various social groups can have very different cultures.

Given that each country in this region was influenced differently by the influx of cultures, the degree and type of homophobia varies from country to country. **Islam**, for instance, is very strong in Indonesia, Malaysia, and Brunei, but not in other countries where the Muslim community is far smaller. Thailand has never been colonized by Europeans, and this is undoubtedly why it has managed to escape a strong Puritanical influence. On the other hand, the Philippines spent almost 500 years under Spanish dominion, then American, and the majority of the population is Christian, at least officially. Yet in that country, there is no specific law against homosexuality. However, Singapore, Malaysia, and Myanmar (all countries colonized by the British) have laws explicitly targeting homosexuality, based on the Indian and Imperial British penal codes. The existence of these laws has contributed to the justification of state-approved homophobia, most notably in Singapore.

Insofar as homophobia is a cultural phenomenon, it is difficult to generalize about it in Southeast Asia, given that the region is not culturally homogenous. However, it is possible to examine the various cultures and the types of homophobia that each is susceptible to producing.

Indigenous Cultures

In the region there are many indigenous cultures; so again, it would be unfair to simply generalize. Nonetheless, certain common points can be seen in these cultures, especially when compared with the construction of homosexuality (and homophobia) in the Western world.

None of the principal languages of the region has a specific word for the terms "homosexual," "gay," and "lesbian," which shows that homosexual orientation is not objectified like it is in the Western world. This is not to say that homosexual behavior is unknown in these cultures, but that they do not designate sexual orientation as a specific gender aspect, or as the basis of an identity. However, there are often social ramifications for homosexual behavior in these cultures, especially when it seems as though these actions are subverting masculine and feminine social norms.

In Thai culture, for example, it is very important that an individual fulfill his or her social role, and in doing so give him or herself a positive image. To the indigenous cultures, homosexual behavior is not bad in and of itself (contrary to Western cultures where it is often seen as sinful or **against nature**), but it is considered an inappropriate tendency, and of little benefit to a person's social role.

Marriage is an important part of this social role. Through their agrarian traditions, these cultures see children as an essential crutch for their old age. The Buddhist belief that every action has a consequence pushes people very strongly to conform to the norms, because they fear the ill effects of their own desires. Thai culture draws a large distinction between public image and private reality. Also inspired by **Buddhism**, Thai society tolerates private deviations from the public norms, and while indulgence may find a way to express itself, this does not indicate social acceptance. Despite the fact that there are few legal or institutional sanctions against homosexuality, in a culture that is ideally non-confrontational, the very fact of acting against the social expectations of others is enough to provoke harsh reactions. Those whose homosexual behavior was revealed would often experience a deep sense of **shame** and dishonor.

Though the languages of Southeast Asia have no indigenous word to designate homosexuality, they do have a rather large vocabulary to identify transgender people: *kathoey* in Thailand, *acault* in Myanmar, *bakla* in the Philippines, *bapok* and *pondan* in Malaysia, and *waria* and *banci* in Indonesia. Transgenders are completely visible, openly subverting social norms, yet they are seen in general as an implacable phenomenon and most of the indigenous cultures have grudgingly conceded their place in society. Albeit, a limited place: transgender people are marginalized, considered as inferiors, and assigned to very specific social roles. In the Philippines, for instance, *baklas* usually are found working in beauty salons, as maids, or vendors in the open-air markets. They are also found in the entertainment industry, as part of the sex trade, offering their services to heterosexual men. Interestingly, they are also given a specific place in the processionals of the **Catholic Church**. In Thailand, aside from these religious functions, the social niche occupied by the *kathoeys* is more or less the same. They appear from time to time on television, but not due to any social acceptance, but simply because of an occasional theatrical or comic interest.

Within these niches they are tolerated; however, **tolerance** should not be confused with acceptance. Any time people of the so-called "third sex" attempt to leave the confines of their traditional niches, they encounter serious resistance. In 1996, for example, despite winning the Thailand championship, a volleyball team with six *kathoey* players (which called itself "the Iron Ladies") encountered a large amount of hostility when it was suggested they be recruited for the national Olympic team.

Chinese Communities

The waves of migration from **China** toward Southeast Asia have gone on for roughly the last 1,000 years, but have increased within the past century. In certain countries, especially Thailand, the Philippines, and Vietnam, these immigrants have been assimilated into the local population, adopting their languages and customs. The transition was made easier by religion: Buddhism in Thailand, Vietnam, Cambodia, and Myanmar, and **Christianity**, to which the Chinese in the Philippines soon converted. In traditionally Muslim countries,

such as Malaysia and Indonesia, the Chinese communities were a little more segregated. Whatever the case, whether more or less assimilated into the local populations, the Chinese still constitute distinct communities and make up a specific cultural group in Southeast Asia.

Chinese culture places a great importance on an individual's duties and familial responsibilities. This is further reinforced by the hierarchical structure of the extended family, which leaves little room for personal decisions regarding lifestyle. Undoubtedly, the society's patriarchal character makes matters of gender particularly strict. Nonetheless, the masculine ideal is not presented as some sort of swaggering machismo, but rather as an expression of wisdom, self-control, and sacrifice for family and social values. And the feminine ideal is based on respect for men and on the observation of familial virtues in the role of mother, grandmother, or wife.

Like many of the indigenous Southeast Asian cultures, the Chinese communities did not make sexual orientation a basis for identity. Originally, Chinese culture more or less tolerated homo-affective and homo-erotic relationships, so long as marriage and progeny were assured. Marriages were traditionally arranged by the respective families; no one married for love, and no one expected men to stay monogamous. Those who had the means often had multiple lovers, and it did not matter whether one had an extramarital affair with a man or with a woman.

However, the region's Chinese communities have since assimilated a few of the West's sexophobic and homophobic attitudes. In fact, the era in which these migrations took place is not without importance. Many Chinese came to Southeast Asia during the Qing dynasty and the beginning of the Republic, bringing with them the habits of the time. Humiliated, Chinese society felt as though it was in decline, compared to Western technological and military might. The Chinese questioned and rejected a good number of traditional Confucian values, including the old tolerance of different sexualities, which were now considered to be a waste of spirit and energy. In lieu of this, the Chinese adopted more Puritan principles (which were more in line with contemporary Western views), and those who immigrated to Southeast Asia only saw these opinions reinforced by the influence of the European colonial regimes. Along with the Puritanism came a strong homophobic sentiment, rooted in Judeo-Christian traditions, though none of these communities (except for the Philippines) would couch it in biblical terms. Instead of calling homosexuality a **sin**, a **perversion**, or an illness, it is considered a failure to live up to one's responsibilities. This kind of homophobia reprises the traditional themes of obedience to one's **family**, the necessity of marriage and male descendants, and gender roles. But contrary to the old indifference, **heterosexism** and monogamy are now strict requirements.

Nonetheless, the first signs of a gay and lesbian awareness opposing this social homophobia have started to appear in the Chinese world, especially in Hong Kong and Taiwan. In China proper, many films exploring alternate sexualities have been produced. Little by little, these films and magazines are trickling into Southeast Asia, but their impact is undoubtedly limited to Singapore and Malaysia (where the Chinese language is still spoken currently). Having adopted the local languages in other regions, other Chinese communities are less likely to be aware of these evolutions.

Colonialism & Christianity

Thailand aside, most of Southeast Asia was under European or American control during the first half of the twentieth century, and some regions had been colonized long before. Even Thailand, though officially independent, sought to shape itself according to the Western mold. Even today, the cultural impact of this influence is apparent. The elite in Southeast Asia are generally more westernized than the rest of the population; though when it comes to sexuality, their culture is often made up of the habits and conceptions of a much older westernization. Those who, during the colonial era, had parents rich enough to send them to schools run by Christian missionaries, were usually steeped in the Western morals of the day. These ideas were then assimilated by the cultural elite and transmitted to the next generation.

Under these conditions, the sexual morals of the Southeast Asian elite often appear outdated, lingering over debates and values that had their day in the Western world thirty to fifty years ago. Contrary to how it was perceived in the indigenous and Chinese traditions, homosexuality is now objectified—though because of the lack of a visible gay culture, it is often confused with the phenomenon of transgenderism. Homo-affective and homoerotic behaviors are considered illegitimate and often seen through the medical lens of psychopathology. From the Western world,

these elite have also inherited an aversion to physical contact between people of the same sex. The men of this class are notorious for refusing to shake hands with another man or lean on a man's shoulder—habits that are quite common in the indigenous cultures, to whom they represent nothing more than friendship.

In Singapore, where the anti-sodomy laws promulgated by the British were kept after independence, the opinion of the elite makes itself clearly known by way of state-sponsored homophobia. The **media** and the **cinema**, in particular, are under close surveillance for the depiction of images that dare to portray homosexuality in a positive light. **Censorship** is far less severe for heteroerotic depictions than for homoerotic imagery, which risks being labeled as pornographic. In 1997, the administration rejected, without giving any reasons, a request to create a gay and lesbian association. In 2000, it rejected again a request for a public forum on homosexual issues. This time, the refusal included a justification: given that homosexual acts were forbidden by law, the forum could not be authorized. Also, sex education taught in Singapore presents homosexuality in a very negative way, thus perpetuating ignorance and homophobia.

In Malaysia, struggles between factions within the ruling party made for liberal use of these anti-sodomy laws. Anwar Ibrahim, once deputy prime minister, who was seen as a rival by Prime Minister Mahathir, was convicted of sodomy, then sent to **prison**. Many Malaysians saw this less as a sign of the reinforcement of state-sponsored homophobia, but more as a purely political maneuver—though it certainly did not improve the public perception of homosexuality. In Thailand in 1996-97, the Rajabhat Institutes Council (an institution managing thirty-six training establishments for teachers) wanted to exclude students "of deviant sex or gender." Following public protests, the proposed law was finally abandoned. But the attempt itself clearly reveals the homophobia among the university elite, who are obviously far less understanding than the general population.

While Christianity was an import that accompanied European imperialism, it remains a religious minority, rarely making up more than 5% of the population with some exceptions: in Singapore, the number of Christians is closer to 15% of the total population, and ninety percent in the Philippines. In fact, Christianity is so deeply rooted in the Philippines that it has almost become an indigenous culture of its own, with its own specific rituals where the *baklas* have their role along with everyone else. Yet even in the Philippines, as in the rest of Southeast Asia, the more recent growth of Christianity is mostly linked to **Protestant** churches, many of whom practice a very conservative and literal form of the religion.

In Singapore, any public debate concerning homosexuality always stirs up violent objections from those following the Christian tradition. Arguments invoking sin, the concept of it being against nature, and biblical references are inevitably brandished. Choices, an **ex-gay** association (based on the American organization Exodus), has been operating in the area since 1990. It is a charismatic organization that boasts of its conversion therapy and uses all sorts of pressure to accomplish its ends. The organization is very media-savvy, and has access to numerous missionary-run schools, using these to instill guilt and **self-hatred**.

To demonstrate the role Christian culture plays in the debates surrounding homosexuality, it is sufficient to recall what took place in Hong Kong in the 1980s (though Hong Kong is today part of China, and not part of Southeast Asia proper). During that decade, after a series of **scandals** and blackmail implicating high-ranking **police** and government officials, the British colonial government ran a public poll regarding the **decriminalization** of homosexuality. In response, the churches and Christian associations immediately launched their own corresponding crusade against homosexuality.

Socialism

Socialism is another Western influence that is felt in Southeast Asia, though it mostly applies to Vietnam and, to a lesser degree, Laos and Myanmar. Vietnamese culture is strongly influenced by China, so much so that the same attitudes found in China are shared by Vietnam. In short, despite there being no legal repression as such, homosexual behavior is widely condemned and often leads to ostracism. There is a strong social pressure for a person to marry and have children.

As socialism began to take hold in the region, it added another layer of social control and conservatism. Even though homosexuals in Vietnam were not specifically targeted, the government did single out "individualists." It was this policy that led to the Vietnamese police arming patrols with scissors to cut the flares off of bell-bottom pants, seen as a manifestation of Western **decadence** and capitalism. In this climate of social intimidation, homosexuals and marginalized people of all types simply felt it would be too dangerous to express themselves.

Nonetheless, thanks to Confucianism, socialism in Vietnam is only a moderate cultural power. It is an open secret among the literati of Hanoi, for example, that the country's two official poets, Huy Can and Xuan Dieu, lived together for a very long time. Huy Can was even an appointed minister with the socialist regime and played an important role within the political establishment. Obviously, this Confucian and socialist regime is capable of looking the other way, when necessary.

In one village in the 1990s (80% of Vietnam is rural), a lesbian marriage was to take place and both families organized a large party to celebrate the occasion. However, as the news made its way around the world, the authorities decided to intervene, no doubt concerned about their public image. In general, though, things are usually more liberal.

Islam

Ninety percent of the Indonesian population and 60% of Malaysians are Muslim. The practice of Islam in this part of the world is relatively moderate and quite accommodating of pre-Islamic customs. Because of this, the cultural practices of these people often seem closer to those of their indigenous roots than that of Muslim fundamentalists.

Nonetheless, it is clear that Islam does not approve of homosexual behavior. Given the local culture of silence on these subjects, Muslims with homosexual tendencies are obliged to keep it secret, sharing only with their closest friends. Visibility can lead to ostracism from one's family, mockery from friends, and pressure from the mosques and from elders. Once discovered, lesbian relationships usually result in forced marriages, arranged to maintain a normal appearance. Under these conditions, homosexual relationships and affairs are usually conducted furtively and secretly.

For a few years now in Indonesia and Malaysia, many groups have called for a stricter form of Islam, such as Wahabbism. In general, their goal is to enforce *sharia*, Islamic religious law, to "cleanse" certain social and meeting places that (as far as they are concerned) only serve to promote the **vice**. In regards to sexuality, they strongly extol sexual abstinence prior to marriage, and the segregation of the sexes.

In Kaliurang (close to Yogyakarta) on November 11, 2000, the militia of one of these groups, armed with clubs, knives, and machetes, attacked an **AIDS** center which was essentially made up of *waria* and homosexual men. In their published declaration after the fact, members of the group used the presence of gays and *waria* there to justify their attack, proving that their action was not motivated by AIDS, but by homophobia, pure and simple. And this has not been an isolated incident. Frequently, men wearing Arab garb harass gays, *warias*, and their businesses. It remains to be seen if the number of these militant fundamentalist Muslims will increase, and if their homophobic activities will multiply with them.

The Sex Trade

The sex trade in Southeast Asia is worth mentioning because its negative connotations affect general attitudes toward homosexuals. Homosexual prostitution is present in almost every country in Southeast Asia (even in socialist Vietnam), but it is in Thailand that the phenomenon has taken on an unprecedented scale. Previously, the sex trade was geared toward locals; today, in certain areas, the clientele is foreign, to the point where sexual tourism is now virtually considered an economy unto itself. As well, recent information suggests that many pedophiles come to Thailand, Cambodia, and the Philippines specifically looking for young boys.

Those countries with a rampant sex trade have started to deal with the situation, either out of pride or simply for the public good. In 2001, Thailand's then Minister of the Interior Purachai launched a campaign to limit the excesses of the sex trade and the entertainment industry, a move that was well received by the general population. To date, the campaign has been carried out with moderation, respecting both homosexual and heterosexual meeting places, though from time to time the police, citing a need for stricter measures, have used this argument to harass homosexuals. For several months in 2001, the gay baths in Bangkok were regular targets for police raids, and television networks aired several reports on the "indecent" performances found in gay bars.

If the number of homosexual tourists continues to increase, involving a growing number of men in these countries, it is possible that a return to stricter rules will simply reinforce general homophobic attitudes. As well, if pedophilic tourism also continues to grow, one can only imagine the furious comparisons that will be drawn between **pedophilia** and homosexuality. Therein lies the danger that should be recognized.

Western Liberalism & a Gay & Lesbian Awareness

Few countries have not been touched by the ideas and values of contemporary Western liberalism, and Southeast Asia is no exception. The young elite class, especially those educated abroad, are the most susceptible to applying these ideas in their home countries.

Among these young elite, some have adopted Western styles, including the concept of sexual identity and of coming out, and the vocabulary of human rights. Those who are heterosexual often become more sympathetic to non-discrimination, diversity, and the recognition of non-traditional sexual orientations. Nonetheless, given that these youths are few in number and concentrated in the capital cities, the social changes this generation can bring about are somewhat restricted. Still, the gay scene is becoming increasingly visible in Manila, Singapore, Kuala Lumpur, Ho Chi Minh City, and Bangkok, if the growing number of homosexual bars and nightclubs is any indication. Even in heterosexual entertainment venues, an ambiguous sexual orientation can be quite fashionable.

Many Singaporean playwrights are introducing homosexual themes and content in their plays, and cinematographers in Thailand and the Philippines are integrating homosexual elements into their films—as demonstrated by *Satree lek* (*The Iron Ladies*), a lighthearted Thai film and box office hit which told the true story of the aforementioned volleyball players.

This gay and lesbian visibility has created a certain tension, if not an outright change in social attitudes. In Singapore's online community, despite the restrictions imposed by official censorship, the liberal viewpoint is being expressed more and more freely. Instead, it is the proponents of homophobia who have to defend their point of view, where previously their prejudices were considered so self-explanatory that there was no need to defend them. Inasmuch as homophobia is obliged to justify itself, this situation then paves the way for debate and change in public opinion.

For the past few years, government ministers in Singapore have had to declare their official policy on the subject. According to them, the laws against sodomy that currently exist are never enforced against consenting adults. Similarly, the liberal elite have started pushing for the relaxation of censorship. Things are improving, albeit slowly.

Under these conditions, it would be a mistake to believe that homophobia will progressively disappear altogether. Of course, Western liberalism is growing, but so are Christian conservatism and Muslim fundamentalism. As well, given that homosexuality is a new concept in the cultures of certain regions where it did not previously exist, concurrent with an increase in the valorization of free expression, homophobia is just as likely to grow in strength. In fact, there is growing evidence that gay bashing, previously unknown in Southeast Asia, is now sadly on the rise in the region.
—*Au Waipang*

Baba, Ismail. "Gay and Lesbian Couples in Malaysia," *Journal of Homosexuality* 40, no. 3 (2001).

Donaldson, Stephen, and Wayne Dynes. *Asian Homosexuality*. New York: Garland, 1992.

Jackson, Peter A. "Pre-Gay, Post-Queer: Thai Perspectives on Proliferating Gender/Sex Diversity in Asia," *Journal of Homosexuality* 40, no. 3 (2001).

———, and Gerard Sullivan, eds. "Lady Boys, Tom Boys, Rent Boys: Male and Female Homosexualities in Contemporary Thailand," *Journal of Gay and Lesbian Social Service* 9, no. 2 (1999).

———. "A Panoply of Roles: Sexual and Gender Diversity in Contemporary Thailand," *Journal of Gay and Lesbian Social Service* 9, no. 2 (1999).

Murray, Alison. "Let Them Take Ecstasy: Class and Jakarta Lesbians," *Journal of Homosexuality* 40, no. 3 (2001).

Sinnott, Megan. "Masculinity and Tom Identity in Thailand," *Journal of Homosexuality* 40, no. 3 (2001).

Storer, Graeme. "Rehearsing Gender and Sexuality in Modern Thailand: Masculinity and Male-Male Sex Behaviors," *Journal of Homosexuality* 40, no. 3 (2001).

Oetomo, Dede. "Gay Men in the Reformasi Era: Homophobic Violence Could Be a By-Product of the New Openness." http://www.insideindonesia.org/edit66/dedel.htm (site now discontinued).

Tan, L. Michael. "Survival through Pluralism: Emerging Gay Communities in the Philippines," *Journal of Homosexuality* 40, no. 3 (2001).

Wah-Shan, Chou. *Tongzhi: Politics of Same-Sex Eroticism in Chinese Societies*. Binghamton, NY: Harrington Park Press, 2000.

—*Buddhism; China; Communism; Hinduism; India, Pakistan, Bangladesh; Islam; Japan; Korea; Oceania; Protestantism.*

SPAIN

Spain has always occupied a peculiar place in the Western world. The establishment of enduring populations of Romans, Visigoths, and later Arabs in the Iberian Peninsula has fashioned a land of many faces. In this country of three principal religions—**Islam**, **Judaism**, and **Catholicism**—each community adopted its own model of male dominance, organizing and positioning the virility of its male population in opposition both to the feminine and to homosexuality. However, the presence of Islam as of the eighth century, including its persistence in Aragon (and in El Levante until the early seventeenth century) contributed to the Spanish attitude and mentality being undeniably tolerant.

Anxious to regulate the dissolute mores of the clergy which called to instruct the people and to lead by example, Christians of the Middle Ages based their repressive model on the sparse homophobic material of the Old and New Testaments (particularly from Leviticus, certain passages from St **Paul**, or from the writings of St Augustine and the Patristic tradition). The Penitentials (from the seventh to eleventh centuries), which were intended to guide the practice of confessors, made reference to homosexual practices, but nowhere did they declare that this **sin** was worse than any of the other erotic practices incriminated. However, in the thirteenth century, Thomas Aquinas established a hierarchy of hedonistic sins, whereby any erotic practice outside of **marriage** was considered a sin. Homosexuality was assigned to the gravest category of sins "**against nature**," alongside masturbation and bestiality. This homophobic concept would have a crucial influence on Christian morality and western culture from the end of the Middle Ages until today.

Under the rule of the Spanish Visigoth kings of the sixth and seventh centuries, the punishment reserved for homosexuals in the *Lex Visigothorum* (642–49 CE) was castration, shaving of the head, excommunication, banishment for life, and a hundred lashes of the whip. The arrival of the Arabs in 711 had the effect of instilling a climate of tolerance towards homosexuality. Nonetheless, the northern territories remained Christian, and those that the *Reconquista* returned to the Castilians, over time, adopted a Castilian version of the *Lex* and all of its homophobic articles under the name of *Fuero Juzgo*. In 1265, Alfonso X the Learned set out to unify the municipal legislative texts, and composed the *Fuero Real* (1255) and *Las Partidas* (1265). Both of these texts insisted on the horror of the sin of sodomy and recommended the death penalty by castration and hanging by the feet, a tendency that would be echoed even more cruelly in the *pragmática* of the Catholic Monarchs of Medina del Campo of 1497. Under the title of "How to Chastise the Abominable Sin Against Nature," it suggested burning at the stake or an alternative, the garrote, as well as the confiscation by the royal treasury of the entirety of the guilty party's possessions.

Beginning in the sixteenth century, the spread of homophobia in the peninsula was closely connected to the Tridentine ritual sanctifying Christian marriage, which replaced the old-fashioned virtues of celibacy with its exemplary nature. With the heterosexual model established, the stage was set for the repression of all deviances. The new development began a little earlier, in fact, with a decree by Pope Clement VII (on February 24, 1524) assigning the suppression of all sodomy within the peninsular kingdom of Aragon to the sole jurisdiction of the **Inquisition**. The decree explicitly described the homosexual habits of the Moorish minority, and the danger of "putrid contamination from these few black sheep to the healthy faithful." The repression of the homosexual men and women of Aragonese Spain began later, under the reign of Philip II (starting in 1560) and would continue unabated until the end of the seventeenth century. The distinction was made between "perfect" sodomy (where it involved two males), and "imperfect" sodomy (when it took place within a heterosexual relationship).

As late as 1630, the Inquisition hit hard and fast, overseeing the investigations in four-fifths of all trials. The people targeted were most often clergy (a direct effect of the Counter Reformation) and peasants. Very specific groups were also singled out: sailors, slaves, students, shepherds, all of whom shared in common a sense of social instability and few local roots. The number of foreigners indicted was flagrant: Italian sailors from the coastal ports, French travelers in Catalonia, Portuguese, and Turks. Homophobic repression and xenophobia were closely linked; this association ensured that the tribunal would have the people's collaboration, by way of denunciations. After a trial that would run for six and a half months, the guilty party incurred a punishment of 200 lashes of the whip and would be sentenced to the slave galleys for three to seven years, followed by an equivalent amount of time banished from the district. The sentence would be

communicated to them during an *auto da fé* (a lavish public ceremony, well-attended, which was intended to illustrate the example not to follow). Even worse, those homosexuals convicted of repeated practices would be sentenced to death; these cases made up a quarter of the accused. Capital punishment, known as *relaxe* (because the tribunal relaxed the punishment to the secular arm, the only group permitted to mete out a sentence of death), would follow about twenty-four hours after the *auto da fé*. Victims would be burned at the stake, which generally took place outside the walls of the city where the tribunal was based (Barcelona, Valencia, or Saragossa). But the energy of this machine of repression dwindled with the state's bankruptcies and devaluations. The priorities of Philip IV and his **favorite**, the Count-Duke of Olivares, seemed to be quite different from those of the inquisitors and their repression of everyday sodomy. No more accused were sentenced to death after 1633. As somber as this description may seem, the situation should be qualified further. Compared to other European countries, Spain stopped punishing homosexual acts very early. As well, however terrible the juridical practices of the Inquisition may have seemed, they did at least offer the accused the guarantee of a trial with due process; the same could not be said of the expeditious methods of the Castilian civil tribunals and the inflexibility of their verdicts. In Catalonia, for example, the position of chancellor of the *audiencia* (the civil court) was awarded to an ecclesiastic who, when he served beside his inquisitorial colleagues, refused to assign the death sentence—the inquisitorial tribunal of Barcelona only burned four homosexuals at the stake between 1560 and 1700. Records of trials and testimonies still exist today thanks to the Supreme Inquisition's system of secret archives. Queen Maria Cristina put an end to the tribunal's activities by royal decree on July 1, 1835.

The penal code of 1822, inspired by the French penal code, abandoned the **criminalization** of sodomy. It decriminalized private homosexual practices between adults, a measure conserved in the later penal codes of 1848, 1850, and 1870. By the second half of the nineteenth century, as in the rest of Europe, homosexuality progressively became construed as a mental illness, part of the psychiatric domain.

Nonetheless, the **army**'s military code (1884) and that of the navy (1888) preserved the crime of homosexuality, until the Military Justice Code of 1945, which unified the army, navy, and air force. Article 69 of the 1928 penal code, adopted under the dictatorship of General Primo de Rivera, reconnected with the past by imposing a punishment of two to twelve years in prison for anyone convicted of indecent offenses with a person of the same sex. Article 616 also stipulated that "whosoever engages habitually or scandalously in indecent acts with a person of the same sex, will be fined 1,000 to 10,000 pesetas and will be declared unfit for public service for a period of six to twelve years."

In 1932, the Second Spanish Republic (1931–39) removed these two items from the penal code. General Franco's dictatorship would leave matters as they were until July 15, 1954, when Articles 2 and 6 of the law on vagrancy were modified to include homosexuals in the same category as procurers, professional beggars, and the mentally ill. Homosexuals found in violation of the law were interned in specialized institutions, and later prohibited from living in certain predetermined areas.

On August 4, 1970, this law was replaced by one in which homosexuals as such were no longer targeted, but rather those guilty of repeated homosexual acts. The punishments remained unchanged. And while specialists of the law have noted a homophobic sensibility in both the Supreme Court and the spirit of the laws covering homosexual matters, accounts of the end of the Franco era describe a state of relative tolerance. As well, the first gay liberation group was created in response to the new law, which would not have the mention of "homosexual acts" removed until a decree on January 11, 1979.

The 1978 Constitution, in Article 14, stipulated that all Spaniards were equal before the law, and may not be discriminated against on account of birth, race, sex, or opinion; homosexuality was not specifically named. Fortunately, the interpretation of discrimination in this regard was extended to "any other personal or social condition or circumstance," leaving the door open to other applications.

A survey carried out by the Center for Sociological Research in 1988 on the tolerance of homosexuality in society revealed that 50% of respondents believed that homosexuality was reprehensible, 28% were indifferent, and the remaining were tolerant of it. Around the same time, sociologist Jesus Ibanez set out to prove that most Spanish are unconsciously homophobic by asking the question: "Would you approve if all pharmacists and all homosexuals were killed?" The answer most often took the form of a new question: "Why pharmacists?"

Spain's admittance into the European Union on January 1, 1986 permitted the country to benefit from the various European resolutions concerning gay and lesbian rights, including the one on February 8, 1994 which charged the European Commission with establishing a recommendation for all countries of the Union to abolish homophobic **discrimination**. Certain innovations, such as those granting the right of **marriage** or an equivalent legal union to gay and lesbian couples, led certain Spanish autonomous communities to adopt new laws on the status of common-law unions, including homosexual couples. The communities involved included Catalonia (1998), Aragon (1999), Navarre (2000), and the Valencian Community (2001). While the People's Party (PP) has called for the Spanish government to adopt the steps taken by the various autonomous communities, the Socialist Workers' Party (PSOE), for its part, announced that as of April 2001, it would adopt laws on homosexual unions in any autonomous community it leads. According to Pedro Zerolo, former president of the National Federation of Lesbians, Gays, Transsexuals, and Bisexuals (FELGTB), discussion on the status of couples is not longer pertinent, as the Socialist government passed legislation unconditionally authorizing gay and lesbian marriage and the right to **adoption**.

Coming out of the **closet** is becoming more common: dancer Nacho Duato, writer Terenci Moix, and even the Catalan socialist deputy Roberto Labandera, to name a few. In September of 2000, Lieutenant Colonel José Maria Sanchez-Silva appeared on the cover of the gay magazine, *Zero*; in an accompanying article, he declared that he wanted to "exercise his right to proclaim his homosexuality and to force laws to adapt to the social reality." But writer Francisco Umbral, who considered coming out of the closet to be akin to **exhibitionism**, wrote: "The one thing that pregnant women, infatuated fiancées, and homosexuals all have in common is the need to tell everything. Like those who claim to have seen the Virgin at Lourdes or Claudia Schiffer naked." As well, highly visual language stigmatizing homosexuals abounds: to "release one's feathers" and to "lose one's oil" (*soltar o tener pluma, perder aceite*) for men; "trucker-girl" and to "make scissors" (*camionera, hacer tijeras*) for women.

For the first time in 2001, Spain included an accounting of gay and lesbian common-law unions. The survey determined that there were 10,474 same-sex couples (3,619 female and 6,855 male), representing

just over one-tenth of 1% of Spain's 9.5 million households. The FELGTB responded that the results were misleading given the strong stigma still attached to homosexuality and the need for many gays and lesbians to remain "in the closet." But the fact that homosexuals were included in the census at all was a major step.
—*André Fernandez*

Aliaga, Juan Vicente, et al. *Identidad y diferencia, sobre cultura gay en España.* Barcelona/Madrid: Egales, 2000.

Bergman, Emilie, and Paul Julian Smith. *¡Entiendes!* Durham, NC: Duke Univ. Press, 1996. [Published in the US as *Entiendes?: Queer Readings, Hispanic Writings.* Durham, NC: Duke Univ. Press, 1995.]

Borrillo, Daniel, and Pierre Lascoumes, eds. *L'Homophobie: comment la définir, comment la combattre.* Paris: Ed. Prochoix, 1999.

Boswell, John. *Christianisme, tolérance sociale et homosexualité.* Paris: Gallimard, 1985. [Published in the US as *Christianity, Social Tolerance, and Homosexuality: Gay People in Western Europe from the Beginning of the Christian Era to the Fourteenth Century.* Chicago: Univ. of Chicago Press, 1980.]

Carrasco, Raphaël. *Inquisición y Represión sexual en Valencia.* Barcelona: Ed. Laertes, 1986.

Fernandez, André: *Au nom du sexe.* Paris: L'Harmattan, 2001.

García, Cárcel Ricardo, and Martinez Doris Moreno. *Inquisición, Historia Crítica.* Madrid: Temas de Hoy, "Historia", 2000.

Graullera Sanz, Vicente. "Delito de sodomía en la Valencia del siglo XVI." In *Torrens, Estudis i investigacions de Torrent i comarca.* Torrent, Spain: Publicació de l'Arxiu, Biblioteca i Museu de l'Ajuntament de Torrent, 1991–93.

Llamas, Ricardo. *Teoría torcida, prejuicios y discursos en torno a "la homosexualidad."* Madrid: Siglo Veintiuno de España Editores, 1998.

Mirabet y Mullol, Antoni. *Homosexualidad hoy.* Barcelona: Editorial Herder, 1985.

Nogueira, Charo. "El Nuevo Censo contabilizará las parejas de hecho y las uniones homosexuales," *El País* (August 15, 2001).

Pérez Canovas, Nicolas. *Homosexualidad, homosexuales y uniones homosexuales en el Derecho español.* Granada, Spain: Editorial Comares, 1996.

Perry, Mary Elizabeth. "The 'Nefarious Sin' in Early Modern Seville." In *The Pursuit of Sodomy: Male Homosexuality in Renaissance and Enlightment Europe.* Edited by Gérard Kent et al. New York: Harrington Park Press, 1989.

Villena, Miguel Ángel: "Un teniente coronel se declara 'gay' y pide respeto para los homosexuales," *El País* (September 3, 2000).

—Against Nature; Criminalization; Decriminalization (France); Fascism; Inquisition; Latin America; Theology.

SPORTS

The world of sports, with its hyper-masculine tendencies, has proven over time to be resolutely sexist and homophobic. Theoretical approaches and empirical studies, conducted in **North America** and Europe with male and female athletes of all levels, revealed evidence not only of homophobic behavior, but also an entrenched homophobic culture. These findings are not solely concerned with the practice of sports, but also its social representations. Sports foster an environment that is particularly conducive to stigmatization, apprehension, or outright rejection of those who do not adhere to the heterosexual norm. The characteristics specific to sports authorize the social function of homophobia in the establishment of a sexual **symbolic order**.

The modern concept of organized team sports was invented in **England** in the second half of the nineteenth century. Born out of an industrial, liberal, capitalist, and colonial society, it was immediately considered a means of virile training for the young men of Britain's elite, then consequently for all male members of the elite in the West. Reserved for men, sports corresponded both to a new type of physical leisure and a conditioning pedagogy aimed at producing physically strong men with equally strong characters.

After 150 years of development, sports remain a male prerogative, for the most part: practiced and watched mainly by men, it is also men who occupy the vast majority of management, training, and coaching positions, as well as **media**. Sports also reveal our cultural attitudes toward physical differences. These are categorized and organized into a hierarchy, from which they can then be evaluated. Differences are generally divided according to age, gender, physical size and weight, and skill level. Except for some mixed sports, organized competitions are usually premised on a strict separation of the sexes. All of these differentiations are descended from the reference point of the virile male athlete, who represents the ideal physical standard, and to whom all other performances are compared. The historic classification of bodies resulting from this depicts the model of the male conqueror as the ideal that one must strive to match, indicative of sports' close-minded, virile legacy that continues to this day.

The world of sports is thus—to evoke French anthropologist Maurice Godelier's formula—a contemporary "house of men," within which ideals and attitudes of manliness are learned and then propagated, in the same way as social connections between the sexes. Within this device, homophobia plays a particular role. It appears as a means, even a reference, for this learning. Indeed, homophobia in sports varies in its degree of visibility and level of **violence**. From uncomfortable silence to verbal **insults**, from denial to bashing, the entire palette of homophobic behavior is expressed in the world of sports. Perhaps the most visible and common forms of homophobic demonstrations are the songs and slogans of football (soccer) fans, whereby the assertion of the collective identity is built on belittling others. In this **rhetoric** of confrontation, the assertion of ascendancy, in particular, shifts to questioning the heterosexuality of opponents (not only players and fans, but also referees). The insults borrow widely from general homophobic verbal abuse, which associates homosexuality with passivity. To this effect, such badgering underscores the model of physical (and, by association, sexual) righteousness by asserting the will of virility and heterosexuality.

It would nevertheless be insufficient for the analysis to stop at the most visible demonstrations of homophobic culture observed in fans expressing their supportive passion. Also, restricting the dialogue to, for example, physical violence towards gays by players, or the exclusion from a team of an athlete following disclosure of his or her homosexuality, does not allow us to fully grasp how homophobia functions within the institution of sports. These cases exist but are rare. Nevertheless, they serve to instill fear in gay and lesbian athletes: the fear of being discovered, then subsequently manhandled or excluded. And although this form of homophobia in sports works in a less visible way, it is just as effective.

American sociologist Eric Anderson states that open homophobia is not very common within sports teams themselves, but this does not mean that homophobia is absent in the everyday life of teams and players. On the contrary, homophobia in sports is more insidious and sometimes imperceptible, creating a double culture of silence, in which gay and lesbian athletes hide their sexual identity in order to continue to be accepted by the group, while their family and friends pretend that their homosexuality is not possible, given that their loved one is an athlete.

In this way, homophobic speech is characterized by an absence of words, which contributes to invisibility. The fact that the question of homosexuality cannot be discussed constitutes an effective weapon in the assertion of heterosexual hegemony. Silence helps to impose the sexual symbolic order, especially since sexuality is not excluded from the discussions between team members, for example. Further, such comments deal with relations between men and women, which also strengthen the social order.

The role of silence on homosexuality in sports differs depending on whether the athlete is male or female. In women's sports, particularly teams, the athlete's silence quickly gives way to rumor and suspicion, and then to the emergence of homosexuality as "the problem." Negative connotations of lesbian athletes result from the idea that women are intruding in a man's world. They are especially strong as women involve themselves in sports that are socially understood as male. Breaking these behavioral rules, such women become "suspects" of homosexuality. At times, the concept is so pervasive that in North America some parents refuse to enroll their daughters in sports at all, for fear of gossip. Also, some athletes choose to quit altogether when they attain the senior level, fearing that they may become "corrupted" by their homosexual elders.

The rumors concerning the homosexuality of female athletes result from the traditional alignment of certain sports practices with the values of virility where, consequently, only tomboys, mannish women, or lesbians are the only possible result. The weight of imagination helps to create a different vision of the world of sports. It would appear "self-evident" that homosexual women are more numerous in team sports, simply because these sports are perceived as more virile.

Moreover, female team coaches and trainers often switch from silence to allusion when quizzed on homosexuality in their midst, which is essentially formulated as a problem, even a plague that should be eradicated. The presence of lesbian players, or simply the suggestion of their presence, is perceived as a difficulty, as is the question of trying to resolve it without speaking about it. Their presence questions the sexual symbolic order, which is inevitably heterosexual. The presentation of this as a problem conveys the fear of disorder as much as the fear of strangers. As well, apprehension is exacerbated by the fear that homosexuality can spread or be **contagious**.

Coaches and trainers react negatively to homosexual players as guarantors of this heterosexual symbolic order. It is out of the question to accept the difference, it is necessary to fight it and expel it. The rejection of lesbianism in sports, in particular, is further informed by a stiff perception of the social order and of sexuality that is either "normal" or corrupted and decadent. As for men, the traditional concept of the male order is inculcated throughout the socialization of young boys via sports; by learning a sport, they also learn to become men. They also learn specific gestures; not only those related to technique necessary for optimum performance, but also those of virile assertion: fists tightened, jaws clenched, eyes steely, as marks of determination.

The weight of words in the apprenticeship of masculinity is well-known. Insults learned in **school** take on a particular meaning in the world of sports where imposing one's dominion is a sign of virility. Thus, shy and frightened young boys are exhorted not to behave like girls; they also learn to assert, when confronted, that they are not fags, and to humiliate opponents by calling them sissies. These various responses, learned and repeated by children, help to construct the vision of a homophobic world, sometimes even before they understand what they really mean. Even if these terms do not yet possess any sexual connotations, boys who evoke them actively foster a form of masculinity that opposes both the female gender and those boys who do not behave "as men."

The frequency of homophobic comments in the world of male sports is such that gay athletes admit that they become immune to their negative connotations, even if they participate in the preservation of the gay identity as an inferior type of manliness. The acceptance and use of homophobic language perpetuates, within the sports world, male dominion and the hegemony of the heterosexual identity, especially since the logic of sports practice consists in searching for and asserting a physical superiority, which is inevitably accompanied by the symbolism of domination. In the end, the world of sports succeeds in stigmatizing both men who deviate from traditional virility and women who approach it, associating in a single act sexism and homophobia.

In reaction to this environment, a gay sports movement has gradually formed, originating first among gay and lesbian communities in the US and Canada, then in Europe. Sports teams and clubs made up exclusively of gays and lesbians are sprouting up, providing opportunities not only for homosexuals to participate in sports, but also another means for social interaction. In 1980, Tom Waddell, who participated in the 1968 Summer Olympics as a decathlete, led a group of San Francisco residents in conceiving a sporting event for gays and lesbians modeled on the Olympics that is now known internationally as the Gay Games. Such events, and the associations that participate in them, contribute to the identity and visibility of gay and lesbian communities. Their social reach exceeds the traditional world of sports and is translated by a wider social dynamic.

However, beyond the action that ensures the visibility of these stigmatized communities, it is important to underline the role of homophobia in the structuring of this sports movement as well. Indeed, the mobilization of gays and lesbians to engage in sports on their own terms is grounded by the symbolic violence exercised by the sports world generally, which is expressed through **insult**, deprecation, and mockery towards a sexual preference it rejects. The result is a feeling of exclusion, which in turn catalyzes gays and lesbians to create their own sports institutions, **associations**, and events, allowing them to escape the heteronormative effects of the institution of sports.

Nevertheless, the question of gender and sexuality always remains problematic in sports, as demonstrated by the story of the Lampang volleyball team in Thailand in 1996. When Mon and Jung, two transgendered homosexuals, were selected for the team, most of the other players resigned, and were subsequently replaced by a group of gays, transsexuals, and transvestites. Contrary to all expectations, they won the national championship in Thailand, although talk of their being considered for the national Olympic team started a wave of unprecedented homophobia. Their extraordinary story was the subject of a highly successful Thai film entitled *Satree lek* (*The Iron Ladies*). Said the team's then twenty-four-year-old founder, Danupol Nuengchang, "We can't make this statement as individuals, but maybe we can as an international team."

—*Philippe Liotard*

Alric, Tristan. *Le Sexe et le sport*. Paris: Chiron Editeur, 2002.
Baillette, Frédéric, and Philippe Liotard. *Sport et virilisme*. Montpellier: Ed. Quasimodo & Fils, 1999.

EGSLF, GISAH. *Building Bridges Between Regular and Gay/ Lesbian Sport*. The Hague, 1999.

Ferez, Sylvain, Yves Le Pogam, Philippe Liotard, Jean-Bernard Marie Moles, and Guillemette Pouliquen. "Homophobie et structuration des jeux sportifs homo-sexuels," *Corps et culture*, no. 6–7, "Métissages", 2003.

Griffin, Pat. *Strong Women, Deep Closet: Lesbians and Homophobia in Sport*. Champaign: Human Kinetics, 1998.

Hekma, Gert. "Gay Men and Lesbians in Organized Sports in the Netherlands," *Journal of Homosexuality* 35, no. 1 (1998).

Lenskyj, Helen. *Out of Bounds: Women, Sports, and Sexuality*. Toronto: The Women's Press, 1986.

Lefèvre, Nathalie. "Les Euro Games V: un analyseur du réseau sportif gai et lesbian," *Corps et Culture, Sport et lien social* 3 (1998).

Messner, Michael A., and Donald F. Sabo. *Sex, Violence and Power in Sports: Rethinking Masculinity*. Boston: Beacon Press, 1994.

Pouliquen, Guillemette. *L'Homophobie dans le sport*. Thesis. Université Paul-Valéry, Montpellier III, 2002.

Pronger, Brian. *The Arena of Masculinity: Sports, Homo-sexuality, and the Meaning of Sex*. Toronto: Univ. of Toronto Press, 1990.

Rotella, Robert J., and Mimi Murray. "Homophobia, the World of Sports, and Sport Psychology Consulting," *The Sport Psychologist* 5 (1991).

Saouter, Anne. *Etre rugby, jeux du masculin et du féminin*. Paris: Maison des Sciences de l'Homme, 2000.

Thong-Konthun, Yongiooth. *Sa Tree Lex (The Iron Ladies)*. Film. Distribution Orient-Pacific, 2000.

—*Armed Forces; Dance; Heterosexism; Insult; Rhetoric; School; Symbolic Order; Violence; Vocabulary.*

STERILITY

The supposed sterility of homosexuals is one of the regular topics of homophobic **rhetoric**, and of hetero-sexism, to justify the inequality between the sexualities with regard to couples and **families**. The conservative French politician Christine **Boutin**, for example, as-serted during **PaCS** civil union debates in 1999 that "[b]arren by nature, homosexuality does not corre-spond to demographic and educative criteria on which the duty of the State is based." However, when we try to pinpoint the specific definition of sterility in this con-text, it tends to disappear. The paradox becomes clear when we stop perceiving the rhetoric of homophobes as they themselves want to be perceived and, instead, grasp the profound nature of sterility. Far from being reduced to the various realizations of sterility through history (e.g., biological, moral, sexual, or psychologi-cal) the "sterility of homosexuals" refers to a symbolic mental structure of homophobia's unconscious, which, in fact, transcends all findings of "objective" allegation. In reality, in heterosexist discourse, sterility is above all *metaphysical* and, *ipso facto*, indisputable, at least for those who refer to it. This "metaphysical" nature generates two important consequences: on one hand, the gen-eral concept of sterility dominates over any specific content and cannot be "refuted" by scientific reason-ing; on the other, being beyond reality, it can impose itself upon this reality by trying, for example, to modify nature or to forbid certain possibilities in the name of the normative idea of nature as propagated by self-pro-claimed spokesmen.

The Archeology of "Sterility"

The modern version of the topic of sterility stems from two older traditions. The first one, of Greek ori-gin, evolves around the notion of *para phusin*, translated by the expression "against nature," or by the adjective "antiphysical," which was common enough in the eighteenth century. For the Greeks, *phusis* is nature's dynamic process of begetting. Therefore, in the begin-ning, the notion does not possess any real moral con-notation. It is under the late influence of the Stoic phi-losophers that the concept of nature acquired a much clearer *ethical* value. With this in mind, the heterosexual couple assumes a predominant importance that tends to disqualify homosexual relations, which were more valued in the ancient archaic and classical traditions. Influenced by the Stoics, the Christians' view strength-ens the moral valence of the notion of *para phusin*, nature being henceforth considered as God's work. Therefore, not only will *para phusin* be against nature in the dynamic sense, but also against morality, and against God Himself.

The other tradition is the Jewish tradition. In the Hebrew Bible, when Abraham was very old and his wife Sarah was infertile, Yahweh promised him un-countable progeny, "as numerous as grains of sand and stars in the sky." Thus the "promise to Abraham" be-came a leitmotif throughout the Bible. Sarah became pregnant, and indeed presented him with a progeny. The Jewish people were slowly establishing themselves.

And it is Abraham's nephew, Lot, who arrived at **Sodom and Gomorrah**. These two **perverse** and **sinful** cities were destroyed by divine punishment: fire and brimstone. In Judaism, fire is both a symbol of purification and sterility. But that is not all: when Lot's wife turned around to look at the disaster in spite of the divine ban, she was transformed into a pillar of salt; as a result, salt is also a symbol of sterility. We can see that the mythical coherence that associates sodomy, sexual abnormality, divine punishment, and symbolic sterility is deeply rooted in the past.

Cover of the satirical magazine *Le Rire* (1932), devoted to the *dames seules* (single women). "Silver Anniversary—And to say that we could have a son of twenty-five today."

It is in the Middle Ages that both traditions merge, notably through Thomas Aquinas, the Italian Catholic priest who is regarded by the church as the ideal teacher for those studying for the priesthood. But in those days, sterility was a notion whose axiological valence remains very ambiguous. Certainly, infertility remains associated with everything negative, a curse from God; but at the same time, the refusal to procreate can be interpreted as some kind of asceticism, or purity, as demonstrated by the rules of celibacy, abstinence, and chastity the clergy imposes on itself. Incidentally, the Knights Templar and other heretics of the Middle Ages, such as the Cathars, considered this purity, and

this refusal to reproduce, so important that they were accused of favoring relations between men. From then on, if infertility is a curse, the refusal of fertilization is nevertheless of potential value, although always suspected of a complacency that is **against nature**.

Under the Ancien Régime, this ambiguity of the notion of sterility continues. In the thinking attributed to the libertine, sodomy remains unnatural, certainly, but it is often introduced as an advantage, notably for women, because it does not result in any inconvenient pregnancy that would reveal infidelities and subsequently immobilize the would-be mother for the duration of her term. As Mirabeau said, "**debauchery** does not produce children." Pleasure between men or between women seems all the more free and attractive as it appears to be free from the constraints of reproduction. However, the idea of sexually ecstatic freedom is at the same time frightening and, in Christian rhetoric, the sterility of sodomitic relations often appears as the paradoxical opposite of an excessive prodigality or a wasteful spending of bodily fluids. Nineteenth-century French slang even gave gays the feminine label of *gâcheuses* (wasteful ones).

In the nineteenth and twentieth centuries, the notion underwent a series of mutations and was increasingly associated with the theory of **degeneration** and the diverse by-products of medical and scientific rhetoric. It is during this period that the idea spread that masturbation and **inversion** made an individual sterile: it was no longer the practice that was "sterile," but the person in general who became sterile. It is when the homosexual becomes a separate character in the medical and psychiatric discourse that sterility is no longer part of the practice, but becomes an integral part of the topic, thus defining its real "essence." Homosexuality is no longer part of a question of sin, but rather pathology: the "abnormality of the inverted" is related to a "nervous degeneration" that results in biological sterility. And even if the individual is not himself sterile (doctors are well obliged to recognize that he is not sterile, because homosexuals in those days were frequently married and had children), his children will be. And if his children are not sterile, the "scientific" curse will befall his grandchildren. This idea can still be found today in certain arguments stemming directly from the nineteenth century, such as that by psychoanalyst Jean-Pierre Winter, who described the supposed "symbolic wound" suffered by the child raised by same-sex parents in terms that would be laughable had they not been given serious consideration by a newspaper such as *Le Monde des débats* (March 2000): "It is likely that it is translated in the first, second, or even in the third generation, by a halt in the transmission of life: by madness, death, or sterility." The theory of degeneration thus adds the dimension of a morbid heredity to the agenda. In this perspective, the homosexual often appears as a sterile runt, someone who represents the "end of the race," the last stage of a sterility accumulated over the course of generations.

Thus, the rhetoric of the period propagated the fantasy of a collective sterility that could spread and destroy an entire state; this fear spread in a context that was increasingly marked by the expansion of nationalist movements in Europe. More than ever, a nation's power was defined by the number of its inhabitants and available soldiers: the management of populations evoked by Michel Foucault, which he called "biopower." The womb was thus the object of an official politic that required that women be reduced to their reproductive function; in the same way, the fear of a decrease in the birth rate, especially after World War I, justified the persecution of homosexuals: once again, sexism and homophobia were hand in hand. This paranoia, which was propagated all over Europe, peaked in Nazi **Germany** and Communist Soviet Union, regimes whose policies of the instrumentalization of the body made homosexuals sterile objects "by nature," useless to the state and dangerous to society: it was thus necessary to cure them—or get rid of them.

This vision of gay sterility as a threat to the state's power remains widely present in today's consciousness. In 1998, during a conference for the Concerned Women for America, Wilma Leftwich evoked the existence of a world plot "to reduce the American population thanks to the availability of abortion, the sterilization of mothers with many children, and the promotion of homosexuality." Moreover, beyond national concerns, homosexuality threatens humanity's very survival, which is often expressed as the ultimatum of the homophobic argument: "Yes, but if everybody was gay, there would be no one left," as if the human race would disappear from the face of the Earth if **discrimination** and homophobic persecution were to cease; an apocalyptic fantasy all the more absurd when those who propagate it are afraid of global overpopulation. Nevertheless, this argument remains common in various discourses; French novelist Marguerite **Duras**, for example, was not afraid to warn against the universal advent of homosexuality in 1987's *La Vie matérielle* (published in English as *Practicalities*): "It will be the greatest disaster of all times. Slowly at first. We'll observe a slight depopulation.... It is possible that we witness the final depopulation together. We would sleep all the time. The death of the last man would go unnoticed."

However, it is necessary to insist on the extremely particular character of this association between homosexuality and sterility. Indeed, even today, in numerous cultures in the Arab world, Africa, and Asia, homosexual practices are not at all incompatible with (heterosexual) **marriage** and procreation. In addition, in certain ethnic minorities of the Western world, within which the collective progeny has a greater fundamental value than the simple institution of marriage, many men try hard to conceive children before making a commitment to gay life. In fact, in these sectors of society, at least for men, the commandment of the "procreative order" would be as follows: "Whatever your sexuality is, if you have children, race is perennial and honor is upheld." While, in the Western framework, the simple fact of reminding people that homosexuals are not sterile often constitutes an incredible paradox, in several other societies, sterility does not constitute irrefutable symbolic evidence that could be used to oppose gay relations.

From Mythical Sterility to Forced Sterilization
The homophobic myth of sterility is inseparable from the paradox of "reproduction of the sterile." Guy Hocquenghem reminds us that "the transmission of homosexuality [retains] this slightly mysterious character of the advancements of desirous production; in *Lundis en prison* [Mondays in prison], Gustave Macé quoted a chief of police who defined gays as 'These people who, while not procreating, tend to multiply.'" Thus, the very idea of the sterility of gay relations must be deconstructed, even if it is necessary to untangle ourselves from the categories of social thinking, which in truth requires a certain effort. In reality, the notion of sterility only makes sense with regard to a reproductive end, which it fails to achieve. No one would think that kissing is a sterile practice, although, objectively, kissing does not produce a child; but since procreation is not the aim of a kiss, it is never thought as such. In addition, there is no reason for considering that other sexual practices (e.g., fellatio, cunnilingus, sodomy, or even simple caresses) are sterile, except if you believe

that the ultimate goal of any sexuality has to be pro-creation, which indeed is often the presupposition of traditional morality. From then on, as far as individuals do not expect pregnancy to result from kissing or from sodomy, it is technically inaccurate to speak of the sterility of these practices. Although it allegedly provides a form of social evidence that is difficult to shake, this idea of homosexual sterility is related to a historically dated device, the obstinacy of which betrays a lack of conceptual elaboration in the rhetoric of those who take advantage of it.

Under these conditions, the idea of "sterility" finally turns out to be neither true nor false, but simply *performative*: it tends to produce its own foundations by trying to impose itself upon social or biological reality, sometimes in a truly criminal logic. The reasoning is simple: gays are "sterile," and if they are not, they must be sterilized. Gays "cannot" have children, and if they have any, they must be taken away.

Conservative French politician Pierre Lellouche was undoubtedly aware of what he said when, from his seat in the National Assembly during the debates on PaCS, he shouted, "Sterilize them!"—which, sadly, became famous. Actually, since the beginning of the twentieth century concurrent with the first developments in **genetics**, medicine has often tried "to cure" homosexuals or, in the case of "failure," to sterilize them. A collective, forced sterilization was recommended as early as 1904 by Austrian psychiatrist Ernst Rudin, who, in 1933, joined a committee of experts on heredity overseen by Heinrich **Himmler**. As a result, the Nazis implemented this measure, but it was not carried out in a massive way because Himmler still "hoped to cure them."

More recently, the debates in **France** on the recognition of same-sex couples and their right to **adoption** created the perverse logic of a similar device, although obviously less violent. Indeed, until then, gays had often been accused of refusing to assume the "responsibilities" of family and parental "functions." Now, when gay couples wished to adopt, they were told that they had to get over their desire for a child. Currently, French law permits only the adoption of a same-sex partner's existing children; in effect, the symbolic sterility of homosexuals justifies, in return, the "social sterilization" carried out by the law.

The question of access to medically assisted conception that arose in the 1990s also brought to light a performative logic by which the supposed sterility of homosexuals is invoked as a pretense to refuse them the right to fertility. Therefore, the "bioethics" laws limited medically assisted conception only to single women and heterosexual couples. The paralogical functioning is always the same: such techniques aim to "repair" nature by giving sterile heterosexual couples an "artificial" access to reproduction. This capacity to be able to "repair nature" could give way to an awareness that this "nature" does not impose itself upon human choices, and that there is nothing that should prevent alternative conception techniques from being available to all. The tendency, however, has usually been carried out in the opposite direction: instead of accepting the idea that there is no transcendence of "nature," the powers-that-be choose to "mimic" nature instead, in an effort "to keep up appearances." It is this understanding of nature (denied *in practice* by the movement that purports to "repair" it) which is, in a strangely paradoxical gesture, opposite to the demands of gays and lesbians. Here, as elsewhere, free humanity alienates itself (and oppresses its homosexual members) by subjecting itself to the idols which it created.

French legal scholar Daniel Borrillo showed how the heterosexist argument linking heterosexual coitus to the survival of humanity has become increasingly ridiculous, considering modern reproduction techniques which, by means of a circular reasoning, are denied to gays and lesbians. However, ideas that perceive homosexuality as "pure desire" in comparison to heterosexuality (which is inevitably reproductive) do not lack for contradictions. Indeed, we do not force heterosexual bachelors to get married, or the bridegrooms to father children (or adopt them if they are biologically sterile). To define sexuality according to its reproductive value would, finally, mean forbidding contraceptive pills and abortion, which explains why the groups most violently opposed to contraception and the voluntary termination of pregnancy are also generally the most violently homophobic. As Borrillo says, not without humor: "One must wonder if the reproduction argument does not hide a certain anti-gay hostility." In the end, if, as Boutin said, homosexuality is a "sterile and short-lived project," this "sterility" can first be found in the mind of homophobes. This is exactly why it is dangerous for gays and lesbians.

—*Sébastien Chauvin and Louis-Georges Tin*

Borrillo, Daniel, *L'Homophobie*. Paris: Presses universitaires de France, "Que sais-je?" 2000.

Daniel, F. E. "Should Insane Criminals and Sexual Perverts

Be Permitted to Procreate?" *Medico-Legal Journal* (1893).

Ford, Norman. "Access to Infertility Clinics for Single Women and Lesbians?" *Chrisholm Health Ethics Bulletin* (Spring 2000).

Foucault, Michel. *Histoire de la sexualité.* Vol. 3. Paris: Gallimard, 1976–84. [Published in the US as *The History of Sexuality.* New York: Vintage Books, 1985.]

Gilbert, Maurice. "La Bible et l'homosexualité," *Nouvelle Revue de théologie,* no. 109 (1987).

Héritier, Françoise. *Masculin/Féminin, la pensée de la différence.* Paris: Ed. Odile Jacob, 1996.

Hocquenghem, Guy. *Le Désir homosexuel* (1972). Paris: Fayard, 2000. [Published in the US as *Homosexual Desire.* Durham, NC: Duke Univ. Press, 1993.]

Iacub, Marcela. *Le Crime était presque sexuel.* Paris: EPEL, 2001.

Jordan, Mark. *The Invention of Sodomy in Christian Theology.* Chicago: Univ. of Chicago Press, 1997.

Nadaud, Stéphane. *L'Homoparentalité, une chance pour la famille?* Paris: Fayard, 2002.

Patterson, Charlotte. "Children of Lesbian and Gay Parents: Summary of Research Findings." In *Lesbian and Gay Parents: A Resource for Psychologists.* American Psychological Association, 1995.

Rihal, Hervé. "L'Intérêt de l'enfant et la jurisprudence du Conseil d'Etat concernant les agréments en matière d'adoption," *RD sanit. Soc* 33, no. 3 (1997).

Théry, Irène. "Différence des sexes et différence des générations," *Esprit* (December 1996).

Winter, Jean-Pierre. "Gare aux enfants symboliquement modifiés," *Le Monde des débats* (March 2000).

—Adoption; Against Nature; Biology; Degeneracy; Marriage; Medicine; Parenting; Proselytism; Rhetoric; Theology.

STONEWALL

When eight officers from the New York Police Department's Public Morals Section raided the Stonewall Inn, a gay bar in Greenwich Village, on June 28, 1969, they thought they were performing a "routine" **police** operation. However, this raid, performed under the pretense of hunting for illegally sold alcohol, would constitute the symbolic beginning of the era of gay and lesbian "liberation."

Since the end of the nineteenth century, the practice of raiding social places of business constituted one of the most common modes of control over homo-sexuals by police forces, both in **North America** and Europe. This activity was made easier because of the general secrecy surrounding homosexual gatherings, which were restricted to specific locations and often related to prostitution or the illegal sale of alcohol. After World War II, the appearance of bars entirely devoted to the gay lifestyle did not change these police practices, which intensified in the United States during the era of **McCarthyism** and continued throughout the 1960s (and more sporadically during the 1970s). Most of the time, police would launch a raid under the pretext of checking for business or health violations; frequently, however, they checked patrons' identities, arresting those who had no identification, were transvestites, or were caught having sex on the premises. Admittedly, the legal consequences were not that severe, but the goal of these crackdowns was to compile a "homosexual" file, including the identification of those who worked for the government or a related agency. The regularity of these "crackdowns" put constant pressure on individuals who frequented gay establishments, a form of harassment aimed at breaking any semblance of community. As an example, in the weeks prior to Stonewall, five other gay bars in the Village were raided.

In 1969, the Stonewall Inn was a rather atypical bar on the New York scene. Owned by the mob, it was an establishment of dubious hygiene where middle-class gays mingled alongside drag queens and male prostitutes. It had become one of the most popular bars in the Village; it offered shows by go-go dancers and was reputed to be the only bar in New York where men could dance together. The Stonewall Inn was perceived by its clientele as a kind of haven, which perhaps explains why its owner fiercely protected it from police intrusions—at least until June 1969.

For the police, the actual raid of June 28 began as an oft-repeated scenario, which was supposed to be by the book: account for the absence of an alcohol license, ascertain the customers' identities, and gather up the offenders, who would include employees, drag queens, and those without identification. The officers detained them in the bar as they waited for the police van that would drive them to the station. It was the norm for those who were let go by the police to disappear quietly into the night. However, on this particular occasion, the customers remained outside the bar, and as every new person was "let go," he or she was welcomed by whistling, applause, and campy comments. When the police van arrived, officers led those who were being arrested to it, but as they were doing so the attitude of this curiously joyful throng outside, who had been joined by other gays and lesbians in the neighborhood, suddenly turned violent: the riot had begun. The crowd was finally sick of the endless police harassment. Under a rain of bricks and bottles, police officers were forced to take refuge in the bar, waiting for reinforcements who would eventually disperse the crowd. The night ended with thirteen arrests, while four police officers and an unknown number of protesters were injured. The next day, the protagonists from the previous night once again met face to face for a second night of rioting. This time it was less violent, however, the crowd was no less determined, and skirmishes between rioters and the police continued until four in the morning. There was yet another riot five days after the initial raid; on this occasion, over 1,000 people gathered at the bar, and caused extensive property damage during their protests. Throughout the week, as the protesters gained momentum, graffiti and political slogans appeared. Gay Power was born.

It has been suggested that the Stonewall riots were exacerbated by the fact that Judy Garland, the American actress and gay icon, had died five days earlier on June 22, and had been buried the day before the first confrontation. Her premature death at the age of forty-seven had had a profound impact on the gay community, and in fact many gay bars in the Village were draped in black as a sign of respect. But whatever the cause, in the annals of gay history, Stonewall marked a significant break with the past. Barely two weeks after the riots, the head of the New York branch of the homophile **association**, Mattachine Society, was giving a speech; when he reminded the audience of his movement's "integrationist" options, he was booed. Far from being concerned with the respectability of homophile associations, which were becoming obsolete, many gays joined the Black Panthers, the hippies, the opponents of the Vietnam War, and the radical feminists in the fight against state oppression and the "American" way of thinking. Within a few years, similar movements were born in Europe, Australia, and even South America. Everyone would recall that the first moment of true gay liberation started with a revolt by customers in a Mafia-owned bar who had simply had enough.

—*Pierre-Olivier de Busscher*

Altman, Dennis. *Homosexual Oppression and Liberation*. New York: Avon Books, 1973.

Chauncey, George. "Après Stonewall, le déplacement de la frontière entre le 'soi' public et le 'soi' privé," *Revue européenne d'histoire sociale*, no. 3 (2002).

Duberman, Martin. *Stonewall*. New York: Dutton, 1993.

—*Associations; Communitarianism; Closet, the; Hoover, J. Edgar; McCarthy, Joseph; North America; Police.*

SUICIDE

Psychological & Social Factors

How can an eminently individual act like suicide be linked to the morals of a society and standards concerning sexual behavior? Does not the decision to end one's life relate to the freedom of each person to choose his or her path, which may include the possibility to refuse it? In his youth, Werther, the central character of Goethe's *Die Leiden des jungen Werther* (*The Sorrows of Young Werther*), noted: "The question is not whether one is weak or strong, but if one can bear the weight of suffering, be it spiritual or physical." Moreover, self-destruction can stem from psychopathological factors; that is, mental illnesses rather than social illnesses, ranging from deep depression to delusions of persecution.

Yet since the publication of French sociologist Emile Durkheim's *Suicide* in 1897, the study of this phenomenon has revealed variations in suicide rates according to certain social characteristics and, notably, the degree of integration of individuals in their milieu. Still today, over a century after this trail-blazing work, the relationship between suicide and issues such as gender, age, marital status, and social standing is considered essential in any study of the phenomenon. Thus, suicide is an indicator of one's social disquiet or ill being.

Various studies have underlined the dangerous effects of family and environmental factors that result in suffering, both physical (e.g., deprivation) and spiritual (e.g., shame). Thus, the **discrimination**, denigration, ostracism, and harassment suffered by those whose sexual orientation is not conventional (i.e. lesbian, gay, bisexual, transgender) affects their well-being, as do the internal conflicts (cognitive dissonance) that they experience between, on one hand, social expectations, the imperatives of self-fulfillment, cultural dictates, and the assignment of sexual roles and, on the other, their personal aspirations that do not correspond to social and sexual norms in society, as expressed by Michel Foucault.

Homophobia as a Factor of Suffering

Our still homophobic society allows the proliferation of negative and aggressive attitudes towards LGBT people which can drive them toward feelings of desperation, depression, and suicide.

While the situation in **France** has evolved since the early 1990s, as revealed in the studies of Marie-Ange Schiltz, social shame still weighs heavily on the homosexual condition. The call to arms declared by André **Gide**'s *Corydon* (part of which was written prior to World War I) remains topical to this day: "To fight the repression of law and moral disapproval of pederasty [in order to] not doom … homosexuals to suicide." Thus today, the early schoolyard **insults** such as "fag," "queer," and "cocksucker" are considered to be the most derogatory and harmful to young homosexuals. It is telling of the amount of suffering experienced at an early age by young people who are just discovering their homo- or bisexual identity or are perceived (sometimes in error) as doing so.

Thus, young gays and lesbians can feel devastated by their failure to integrate socially with their peers, by reason of exclusion, rejection, contempt, and stigmatization within the private (**family**, friends) and public (**workplace**, **school**, **sports**) spheres, and by the distress of having to shed the heterosexual identity for which their childhood had prepared them (abandoning then the idea of fulfilling family expectations, or even having children). Michel Dorais demonstrated, based on interviews with young homosexuals in Quebec, that these painful feelings and experiences can lead to a loss of self-esteem and a loss of confidence in the future. In such cases, many factors that play an important role in the etiology of suicide and suicidal behavior are at play: e.g., depression, consumption of alcohol and drugs, family conflicts, and social isolation. Thus, it is not a single factor, but rather the combination of factors that is important: it has been suggested that the risk of suicide is multiplied sevenfold in cases when just three factors are present.

For adults, the difficulty in accepting a long-suppressed homosexuality can greatly shake one's psyche and lead to feelings of despair. Such feelings are intensified depending on the situation, such as if one is already in a heterosexual relationship, is rejected by his employer, lives in a rural community far from gay gathering places, has just learned his positive HIV status (as per the Swiss study Cochand and Bovet), or is at an advanced age.

Dealing with Discrimination

While studying this suffering, a question is often posed: might it be that homosexuality, rather than homophobia, is the source of mental pathology? The approaches that pathologize homosexuality and gender non-conformity are still very present in the minds of both the general public and some medical professionals.

Recent studies shed light on certain phenomena, such as the buffer effect of the family in cases of homophobic assault, the influence of public-service campaigns on homosexuality and **AIDS** that can reduce the frequency of suicidal thoughts, the fact that certain "at risk" behaviors vary according to gender, and the similarity in the effects of different forms of discrimination, such as racism and homophobia (as per an American study by Fergusson and Beautrais). All of these elements tend to support the hypothesis that homosexuality *per se* does not encourage suicidal thoughts and behavior in an individual, nor mental pathologies.

By considering these observations, it is possible to suggest that the uneasiness that may be present in those with homosexual tendencies is relative to the negative social perception of homosexuality. It is true that, in France, this perception has evolved over the last two decades (with the AIDS epidemic and the adoption of **PaCS**, notably), but this "**tolerance**" remains limited. According to Michel Bozon, "When, in a given culture, cultural scenarios specifically define authorized or desirable sexual acts, all different sexual practices are perceived and defined as transgressions." Homosexuality remains a discrediting trait for the person who has it, but this "shameful difference" is also an obstacle for the types of solidarity or defense that could be expressed, because of an effect of "**contagion**" which affects those who express that solidarity, as they are themselves accused of being homosexual because they showed support for a gay man or a lesbian.

Empirical Data

To measure the scale and importance of the phenomenon, it is necessary to study the sources of the statistics. In France, the mortality rate from suicide more than doubled among young men aged between 15 and 24 years in the period between 1950 and 1996 (increasing from 6.5 per 100,000 people to 14.5) and doubled among men aged between 25 and 44 for the same period (increasing from 19.4 to 37.1), thus almost equaling the rate for those aged between 45 and 74 (which has decreased from 49.7 to 39.7). Among women, these rates are lower (on average three times lower, settling at 4.3 per 100,000 in 1996 for those aged between 15 and 24 years, 10.7 for those aged between 25 and 44, and 16.3 for those aged between 45 and 74), but attempted suicides are more numerous among women than men, the rate reaching 2.6 for the younger age category (Badeyran and Parayre). In annual numbers, suicides are lower among the younger category than the older, but given the low death rate due to illness for this age group, suicide represents the primary cause of death among those aged 25 to 34 years. Alfred Nizard noted that "among industrialized Western societies with high suicide rates, France ranks below Finland, Denmark, and Austria, at a comparable level to that of Switzerland, Belgium, and the province of Quebec."

Statistics on the causes of death suffer from underreporting and a lack of information regarding the motives for suicide, which is an obstacle to understanding the link between homosexuality and these desperate individuals; it is thus interesting to study the risks of suicide by way of survey results. Of course, this work poses the problem that the extrapolation of these results cannot include the data from the people who have already committed suicide. American researchers Alan Bell and Martin Weinberg were among the first to demonstrate the higher risk of suicide among homosexual or bisexual individuals. In their now classic work, they demonstrated that the gay men in their sample population were significantly more anxious than heterosexual men, and that they had a greater tendency to report feelings of depression and thoughts of suicide. In half of the cases of suicide attempts by gay men, the respondents reported that the attempt "was related to the fact that they were gay."

Corroborating Results

Since the publishing of these landmark reports, many North American studies using representative samplings have delved deeper into the question. The reluctance (notably by medical professionals) to consider the gay population as being particularly "at risk" has certainly contributed to the improvement of the scientific quality of these studies, which were required to be irreproachable. Their results converged and highlighted the significantly higher risk of suicide for homosexuals or those with such tendencies. For example, an American study by Susan Cochran and Vickie Mays using a national sampling of 17- to 39-year-olds demonstrated that gay

men had an attempted suicide rate of 20% compared to 4% for exclusively heterosexual men. In a Minnesota study by Gary Remafedi and associates, using a sample of 12- to 19-year-olds, the attempted suicide rate of lesbians was 21% versus 15% for exclusively heterosexual girls. By analyzing these studies, we can see that the risk of lesbians attempting suicide is 40–90% greater than that of heterosexual girls; as for homosexual men, their risk was, according to the Cochran-Mays study, four to seven times greater than that for heterosexual men. These are important distinctions that leave no doubt as to the reality of the phenomenon; the variations between the estimates stem mostly from differences in definition (identity and/or sexual behavior) and scope (age, geographical area).

This does not mean that every LGBT person is living in a tragic situation, however. Happily in the present day, homosexuality tends to be not only one of the many possible options within the spectrum of human sexuality, but also a sexuality in which one can attain complete personal fulfillment. However, the bitter reality of homophobia—traditionally present in our society—and **heterosexism**—which considers that heterosexuality is the necessary sexual norm of every individual—is at the origin of much of the suffering and distress experienced by homosexuals from early childhood onward, and for which society as a whole must assume the human, moral, and financial weight and cost.

—*Jean-Marie Firdion*

Badeyan, Gérard, and Claudine Parayre. "Suicides et tentatives de suicide en France, une tentative de cadrage statistique," *Etudes et résultats*, no. 109 (2001).

Baudelot, Christian, and Roger Establet. *Durkheim et le suicide*. Paris: Presses universitaires de France, "Philosophies" collection, 1990.

Bell, Alan, and Martin Weinberg. *Homosexualités, un rapport officiel sur les comportements homosexuels masculins et féminins*. Paris: Albin Michel, 1978. [Published in the US as *Homosexualities: A Study of Diversity Among Men and Women*. New York: Simon and Schuster, 1979.]

Blum, Robert, Simone French, Gary Remafedi, Michael Resnick, and Mary Story. "The Relationship between Suicide Risk and Sexual Orientation: Results of a Population-Based Study," *American Journal of Public Health* 88, no. 1 (1998).

Bozon, Michel. "Les Significations sociales des actes sexuels," *Actes de la Recherche en sciences sociales*, no. 128 (1999).

Caroli, François, and Marie-Jeanne Guedj. *Le Suicide*. Paris: Flammarion, "Dominos" collection, 1999.

Cochand, Pierre, and Pierre Bovet. "HIV Infection and Suicide Risk: An Epidemiological Inquiry Among Male Homosexuals in Switzerland," *Social Psychiatry and Psychiatry Epidemiology* 33, no. 5 (1998).

Cochran, Susan, and Vickie Mays. "Lifetime Prevalence of Suicide Symptoms and Affective Disorders Among Men Reporting Same-Sex Sexual Partners," *American Journal of Public Health* 90, no. 4 (2000).

Debout, Michel. *La France du suicide*. Paris: Stock, 2002.

Dorais, Michel. *Mort ou Fif, la face cachée du suicide chez les garçons*. Montreal: VLB Editeur, 2001. [Published in Canada as *Dead Boys Can't Dance: Sexual Orientation, Masculinity, and Suicide*. Montreal: McGill-Queen's University Press, 2004.]

Fergusson, David, John Horwood, and Annette Beautrais. "Is Sexual Orientation Related to Mental-Health Problems and Suicidality in Young People?" *Arch. Gen. Psychiatry* 56 (1999).

Firdion, Jean-Marie, and Eric Verdier. *Homosexualités et suicide, etudes, témoignages et analyses*. Montblanc: H & O Editions, 2003.

Foucault, Michel. *Histoire de la sexualité*. Vol. I : "La volonté de savoir." Paris: Gallimard, 1976. [Published in the US as *The History of Sexuality*. New York: Pantheon Books, 1978.]

Goffman, Erving. *Stigmate, les usages sociaux des handicaps*. Paris: Minuit, 1975. [Published in the US as *Stigma*. Englewood Cliffs, NJ: Prentice-Hall, 1963.]

Hawton, Keith, Ella Arensman, Danuta Wasserman, et al. "Relation Between Attempted Suicide and Suicide Rates among Young People in Europe," *Journal of Epidemiology Community Health* 52, no. 3 (1998).

Nizard, Alfred. "Suicide et mal-être social," *Population & Sociétés*, no. 334 (1998).

Remafedi, Gary, ed. *Death by Denial: Studies of Suicide in Gay and Lesbian Teenagers*. Boston: Alyson Publications, 1994.

Rofes, Eric. "I Thought People like That Killed Themselves." In *Lesbians, Gay Men and Suicide*. San Francisco: Grey Fox Press, 1983.

Schiltz, Marie-Ange. "Parcours des jeunes homosexuels dans le contexte du VIH: la conquête de modes de vie," *Population* 52, no. 6 (1997).

—Arenas, Reinaldo; Discrimination; Family; Heterosexism; Insult; Psychology; Scandal; School; Shame; Sociology; Symbolic Order; Violence

SWITZERLAND

Since its formation in 1291, Switzerland has only recognized one form of conjugal union: **marriage** between a man and a woman. As elsewhere in Europe during the medieval era, it was the Christian church and the ancient patriarchal system that governed Swiss society. Relations between persons of the same sex were considered illegal, as demonstrated by the case of a knight named von Hohenberg and his page, who were burned at the stake in front of the gates of the city of Zurich in 1482 for the crime of sodomy. With the advent of the **Protestant** Reformation during the sixteenth and seventeenth centuries, acts "**against nature**" were still severely punished; between 1555 and 1670 in Calvinist Geneva, many men and women were executed for this reason, by decapitation, hanging, or drowning.

The French Revolution and the subsequent occupation of eastern and southern Switzerland by Napoleon's troops would, thanks to the application of the Napoleonic Code, lead to the decriminalization of same-sex relations in the regions of Geneva, Vaud, and Valais, as well as Ticino, whereas most of the German-speaking cantons continued to punish these acts with four to five years in **prison**. It would be necessary to wait for the promulgation of the new federal penal code in 1942 for same-sex relations to be decriminalized on a national scale, although this did not mean that political and religious institutions would cease spreading homophobia throughout every level of Swiss society.

Heinrich Hössli (1784–1864) was at the origin of the Swiss gay liberation movement. In 1836, Hössli, a respected milliner in the world of women's fashion, published the first volume of *Eros, die Männerliebe der Griechen* (Eros: the male love of the Greeks) (volume two was published in 1838). *Eros* retraced the history of love and sexual relationships between men in the areas of education, **literature**, and law from the time of **Ancient Greece** to the early nineteenth century. Hössli's book was the first modern work to explicitly defend love between men, including historical aspects that had been consciously forgotten or falsified; by doing so, the book was a condemnation of homophobia. It also had an enormous impact on the other precursor to the European gay liberation movement, Karl Heinrich Ulrichs of **Germany**.

At the dawning of the twentieth century, the first

sociopolitical gay liberation movements made their appearance in Germany, and by 1922, German-speaking Switzerland was the site of a good number of initiatives aiming to organize homosexuals and fight against homophobia. After several setbacks, the Schweizerische Freundschafts-Bewegung (Swiss Friendship Movement) was formed in Basel and Zurich in 1931. What is interesting is that the organization was headed by a woman, Anna Vock (1885–1962), known under the pseudonym of "Mammina," and that its membership included a great number of lesbians. This was doubtlessly due to the fact that most Swiss cantons, contrary to other European states, punished sexual relations between women as well. The group joined forces with two others, Damenclub Amicitia and Excentric-club in Zurich, and together they launched the first gay magazine in Switzerland, *Freundschafts-Banner* (Friendship banner), which appeared on January 2, 1932.

In 1934, actor Karl Meier, a.k.a. Rolf (1897–1974), discovered the magazine's existence and quickly became involved, writing a good many articles. Over the years, the lesbians began to withdraw from the organization, and Meier eventually became its president, turning the Swiss Friendship Movement into an entirely male group. In 1937, the magazine was re-baptized *Menschenrecht* (Human rights), before assuming its final name in 1942, *Der Kreis* (The circle). Meier ensured the magazine's uninterrupted publication through World War II; its readership was made up of a small, select group spread throughout many countries. A French edition appeared in 1943, followed by an English one in 1952. *Der Kreis* was the most influential gay magazine in the world until it ceased publication in 1967.

Persecuted by the Nazis, German homosexuals took refuge in Zurich during the 1930s. As a place of self-imposed exile for Magnus **Hirschfeld** from 1932 to 1933, as well as many others, Switzerland was the last bastion of (relative) freedom for gays during World War II and became the *de facto* European center of the gay liberation movement, though the movement was still nascent and somewhat clandestine.

Despite a democratic system renowned for its respect for and integration of minorities, Switzerland maintained many traditional—and even archaic—positions. For example, it was not until 1971 that women were given the right to vote, which says a lot about the deep roots of Switzerland's patriarchal values and the social roles handed down to men and women. Sexism

and its insidious progeny, homophobia, were thus rampant in the history of Switzerland.

As the gay liberation movements created before World War II died with their founders, it would be necessary to wait until the 1970s for the appearance of the next wave, the GHOG (Geneva Homosexual Group) and the GHL (Lausanne Homosexual Group), both adjuncts of France's FHAR (Homosexual Front for Revolutionary Action), which helped to launch the new era of gay visibility. The publications and media actions by this handful of visionaries marked an important turning point in the campaign to raise public awareness of its political and social aspirations. Not only did these activists face homophobia in their daily lives, but also attacks from other homosexuals who advocated **discretion** and non-action, such as those from the Lausanne group Symétrie (counterpart to André Baudry's French organization Arcadie). These French-speaking groups would quickly associate themselves with the German-speaking associations in Basel, Bern, Lucerne, St Gallen, and Zurich, giving birth to CHOSE (the Coordination of Swiss Homosexuals).

The first national Gay Liberation Day in Switzerland took place in Bern on June 23, 1979. Three hundred people gathered to commemorate the tenth anniversary of the **Stonewall** riots in New York and to demand an equal age of consent for all, the destruction of **police** files on homosexuals, and the legal recognition of gay and lesbian couples. In 1982, the Geneva association Dialogai was founded, whose aim was to create a space for dialogue and help for gays and lesbians as well as fight against homophobia; this was followed by OSEEH (Swiss Organization of Gay Teachers and Educators) in 1983, ASS (Swiss Aid Against AIDS) in 1985, OSL (Swiss Organization of Lesbians) in 1989, and in 1993, the Pink Cross, a national umbrella association whose key issue was the legal recognition of same-sex couples. In 1992, Article 194 of the penal code, which had set the age of consent at eighteen years for homosexual relations and sixteen years for heterosexual relations, was abrogated by popular vote, establishing equality in the age of consent.

Around the mid-90s, national petitions were launched requesting the legal recognition of same-sex couples. In 1998, an initiative by Swiss Liberal Party member Jean-Michel Gros from Geneva advocated the adoption of registered partnerships on the national scale. At the same time, the latest Swiss Federal Constitution, which took effect January 1, 2000, forbids

all **discrimination** based on lifestyle, without specifically mentioning homosexuality or homophobia. In
2001, the Canton of Geneva adopted a partnership
law, a mostly symbolic recognition as it was limited
to cantonal law. On June 5, 2005, a government-pro-
posed partnership law was approved by referendum by
the Swiss; the Eingetragene Partnerschaft, which literally means "registered partnership," allows same-sex
couples many of the same basic rights as those held by
married heterosexuals. The partnership law took effect
in early 2007.

Following the lead of Zurich, which for many years
celebrated its own Christopher Street Day, in 1997
numerous cities in French-speaking Switzerland began holding their own Lesbian and Gay Pride marches,
uniting tens of thousands of participants and spectators.
Then, a world first occurred in June 2001, when Swiss
President Moritz Leuenberger spoke before thousands
of people during Zurich's Christopher Street Day, the
first time a head of state had ever participated in a Pride
event. At the same time, a scandal erupted that sent waves
of indignation throughout the country: the publication
of a violently homophobic full-page article in a regional
newspaper by a minuscule, **far right** religious group
following the announcement of a Gay Pride parade in
the very Catholic canton of Valais. The parade ended
up being a great success, receiving widespread media
coverage, and resulted in the near-total banishment of
the religious homophobes. This event is indicative of
the point of view of a majority of the Swiss population
when it comes to same-sex love in the twenty-first
century: even though there remain some hard-core
bastions of homophobia, which are difficult to rehabilitate given centuries of **heterosexist** conditioning,
Switzerland has generally demonstrated a progressive
acceptance of the gay, lesbian, and bisexual realities.

—*Stéphane Riethauser*

Baier, Lionel. *La Parade (Notre Histoire)*. Film documentary
    about the Sion Gay Pride of 2001, in the Canton of
    Valais. Lausanne: Cinémanufacture, 2001.
Hogan, Steve, and Lee Hudson. *Completely Queer: The Gay
    and Lesbian Encyclopedia*. New York: Henry Holt, 1998.
Hössli, Heinrich. *Eros, Die Männerliebe der Griechen*. Vol 1.
    Glarus, Switzerland: 1836; Vol. 2. St Gallen, Switzerland:
    1838. Reprint, Berlin: Bilbliothek Rosa Winkel, 1996.
Manfred, Herzer, ed. *Goodbye to Berlin? 100 Jahre
    Schwulenbewegung*. Exhibition catalog. Berlin: Rosa
    Winkel, 1997.

Monter, William. "Sodomy and Heresy in Early Modern
    Switzerland," *Journal of Homosexuality* 6, nos. 1–2 (Fall/
    Winter, 1980–81).
Puff, Helmutt. *Sodomy in Reformation Germany and
    Switzerland, 1400–1600*. Chicago: Chicago Series on
    Sexuality and Society, 2003.
Schüle, Hannes. *Homosexualität im Schweizer Strafrecht*. Bern:
    1984.
Riethauser, Stéphane. *A visage découvert, des jeunes Suisses
    romands parlent de leur homosexualité*. Geneva: Ed. Slatkine,
    2000.

—*Associations; Discrimination; Germany; Heterosexism;
Protestantism.*

SYMBOLIC ORDER

Symbolic order, as defined by Jacques Lacan but originated by Claude Lévi-Strauss in 1949 (translated as
"Elementary Structures of Kinship"), is essentially the
order of signs, representations, significations, and images
whereby an individual is formed as a subject. It is one
of three orders that constitute the subject in Lacanian
psychoanalysis, the other two being the Imaginary and
the Real. The symbolic is made possible through acceptance of the laws and restrictions that control both
one's desire and communication; it is through the symbolic that one can enter a community of others.

The term "symbolic order" was used in **France**
by opponents of two issues that were passed into
law: gender parity in French politics (resulting in the
Parity Law of 2000) and civil unions between couples,
whether gay or straight (**PaCS** [Pacte civil de solidarité; or the Civil solidarity pact], passed into law in
1999). While one could have expected that supporters
of these laws might use the occasion to denounce the
sexist and homophobic patriarchy, there was none. All
the same, "symbolic order" was evoked as a type of
magic formula by opponents of one or the other of
the two laws, articulating the associations of gender
and homosexuality with representations of the **family**,
parenting, and their connections to power.

What then is this "symbolic order," which seemed to
be the formula that would block all discussion, for the
unique reason that the juxtaposition of the two words
was used by representatives of social sciences who set
themselves up as absolute experts? In any case, let's postulate that this "order" by no means stops all thought,

but rather designates injunctions that are cultural and thus relative, susceptible of being deconstructed, anchored in a location and in historicity.

But in France during debates on these issues, it was essentially three people—sociologist Irène Théry, philosopher Sylviane Agacinsky, and in the background, lawyer and psychoanalyst Pierre Legendre—who, through the **media** and their own publications, defined a limit that should not to be overtaken, beyond which society would not be able to legislate. For them, this limit refers back to the symbolic order, which boils down to the idea of inevitable and vital **gender difference**, the basis of a well-functioning society. For the sociologist, the philosopher, and the lawyer-psychoanalyst, it is a matter of not promoting any law susceptible of adversely affecting this gender difference conceived as an absolute. This accord did not, however, lead them to identical positions: Théry opposed the PaCS proposal while Agacinsky supported it. On the other hand, worried about the possible future impact of PaCS and in advance of any new proposition, these three came together on the issue of gay parenting to brandish the specter of symbolic order.

In effect, if the general motivation behind PaCS was to legally confirm the existence of couples (whether straight or gay) resistant to **marriage**, it was not supposed to create anything other than a couple, and, specifically, that for homosexual women and men. Yet alongside which structures is the couple considered a pillar, at least in Western societies? Family, children, and the succession of generations. In waving the flag of symbolic order—that is, an irreducible and necessary difference between the sexes—intellectuals who were using the formula could at least admit that same-sex couples could have the benefits of a contract to warrant their union; they could not, however accept that these couples might be acceptable parents: in their view, children must necessarily be the biological, artificial, or social products of a man and a woman. Thus, if lesbians and gay men have the right to a family, it must be composed solely of their ascendants; i.e. their own parents, etc. To simplify, where symbolic order dictates the rules, gay and lesbian couples would be subject to both biological and cultural sterilization. At a time when it is clear that the health, education, and well-being of children is in no way guaranteed by having two biological, heterosexual parents, and where heterosexual intercourse is no longer the only means of procreation (e.g., in vitro fertilization), it is amazing to

realize that certain technological and social amenities remain accessible to some and not to others.

How could those who argued for the acknowledgment of single mothers—those raising their children without the presence of a man, without this apparently essential plurality of genders—then refuse the right for same-sex couples to have children? The majority of parents throughout history may indeed be heterosexual, but this is beside the point: the law not only takes into consideration historical precedent; it also aims (depending on the country) to respect the rights of minorities, and/or to permit equality of people among themselves. Further, it is not a question of the inability to rein in this change (which is often suggested by arguments presented in terms of factual versus potential situations). Because then the argument of symbolic order will return not to forbid it, but to establish hierarchies among accepted familial concepts: e.g., good couples, good parents, bad couples, bad parents, all of them legal; but ultimately, in order to distinguish the best, one can always look to the so-called irreducible difference between sexes without gender.

So the problem with symbolic order is what it suggests should be the limit, and the way those who used this terminology in the past instrumentalized it: the expression is noble-sounding and sounds serious, and those who used it did not hesitate to mention their prestigious positions and university titles, even though their arguments were no longer the product of a scientific approach. Thus, symbolic order is nothing more than a misuse of authority, a construction; an empty threat of the intellectual elite to silence those who do not hide behind chaste expertise but simply offer their opinion as citizens. This is not a case where one must accuse those who think that family cannot be conceived in any way other than the heterosexual, childbearing couple: they have the right to believe it, so long as they do not use it as an authoritarian argument trimmed with the decorations of science, and if they do not abusively use the texts of Lévi-Strauss to impose what is, basically, a personal opinion.

We will not return to the numerous examples which, depending on the era and place, damage the idea that not only there would be everywhere and always a difference between the sexes, but moreover that this difference would be the only impassable difference. Developed by philosopher Geneviève Fraisse and historian Michèle Perrot, among others, these examples have often been popularized. We have to note that symbolic order, a popular phrase in recent years, collapses if we are vigilant in observing the subjectivity of the speaker's position, the strategies that he or she uses, and the ideologies defended. The focus on gay parenting has been a way to avoid asking general questions on parenting and the family, regardless of who they address. It has been a way to pass onto others questions which can likely be asked of all and, thus, likely hurt the heterosexual parenting model. The method is common: to avoid pointing fingers at many, nothing works like focusing attention on only a few.

—*Catherine Deschamps*

Borrillo, Daniel, Eric Fassin, and Marcela Iacub, eds. *Au-delà du PaCS. L'expertise familiale à l'épreuve de l'homosexualité.* Paris: Presses universitaires de France, 1999.

Delor, François. *Homosexualité, ordre symbolique, injure et discrimination: Impasses et destins des expériences érotiques minoritaires dans l'espace social et politique.* Brussels: Labor, 2003.

Favret-Saada, Jeanne. "La-Pensée-Levi-Strauss," *Journal des Anthropologues: Anthropologie des sexualités*, nos. 82–83. (2000).

Fraisse, Geneviève. "La Parité n'est pas l'égalité sociale," *Libération* (December 29, 1998).

Perrot, Michèle. "Oui, tenter cette expérience nouvelle," *Le Monde* (February 25, 1999).

—Adoption; Anthropology; Discrimination; Family; Gender Differences; Heterosexism; Marriage; Otherness; Parenting; Philosophy; Psychoanalysis; Rhetoric; Sociology; Sterility; Universalism/Differentialism.

T

THEODOSIUS I

The law of 390 CE decreed under Theodosius I that established burning as the most appropriate punishment for homosexual acts has been the subject of many debates. There is the question of whether Theodosius's true intentions were to target passive homosexuality in general, or male prostitution in particular. Theodosius was not the first Christian emperor to outlaw homosexuality; forty-eight years prior, in December 342 CE, Constantine I, the Emperor of the Western Roman Empire, decreed a similar law condemning passive homosexuality.

Theodosius was a devout Christian emperor, convinced that victory, especially during a battle against a conspirator, was dependent upon divine favor. In accordance with this belief, the respect of Christian morality represented for Theodosius an important politico-religious issue. Thus, his legislation was both part of a political trend to criminalize homosexuality in the Roman Empire of late Antiquity and a response to his own politico-religious preoccupations. However, beyond these political and personal agendas, Theodosius's law of 390 CE finds its roots in the arrest of a certain homosexual, an arrest which would infamously mark Theodosius's reign. This story is told, particularly, by Byzantine Church historians, such as Sozomen, who wrote in the fifth century.

In 390 CE, a famous charioteer was arrested and imprisoned for engaging in a homosexual act by Butheric, a Goth commander of Illyrian troupes in Thessalonica. At the time, chariot races at the hippodrome were a great passion for citizens of the Roman Empire, particularly in Rome and Constantinople. The victorious charioteers were true celebrities, their names, acclamations, and their victories immortalized in honorary statues and engraved epigrams. Thus, given

that prestigious races were soon to be held at the hippodrome in Thessalonica, Thessalonicans demanded that Porphyruis be released, demonstrating that, at the time, they did not consider a charioteer's homosexuality a serious enough motive to forbid a charioteer from participating in competition, and subsequently lowering the level of a sport that constituted one of the most popular attractions in the Roman Empire. When authorities refused, an insurrection ensued during which Butheric was killed. News of the incident angered Theodosius, who responded by subjecting the city to violent repression, resulting in the massacre of thousands. The Bishop Ambrose of Milan forbade Theodosius to enter the church and ordered him to perform penance.

This incident marked a turning point in the history of homosexuality, announcing a new era in which homosexuality would enter an epoch of shame and **criminalization**. However, it was not until the reign of Justinian I, in the sixth century, that a veritable state homophobia took place.

—*Georges Sidéris*

Cantarella, Eva. *Selon la nature, l'usage et la loi, la bisexualité dans le monde antique.* Paris: La Découverte, 1991. [Published in the US as *Bisexuality in the Ancient World.* New Haven, CT: Yale University Press, 2002.]

Cameron, Alan. *Porphyrius the Charioteer.* Oxford: Oxford Univ. Press, 1973.

Williams, Stephen and Gerard Friell. *Theodosius: The Empire at Bay.* London: B.T. Batsford, 1994.

—*Against Nature; Bible, the; Criminalization; Heresy; Justinian I; Paul (of Tarsus); Sodom and Gomorrah; Theology; Violence.*

THEOLOGY

Antiquity & Medieval Periods

During the early centuries of Christianity's existence, bishops, church hierarchy, and those who have been called the "church fathers," sought to formulate Christian doctrine. This theological task was accomplished by referencing the **Bible**, and in particular the New Testament; it also took into consideration the traditions and beliefs of the different churches. Certain local assemblies or ecumenical councils sometimes specified the wording of dogmatic principles or defined moral positions. These declarations were formulated in Greek or Latin, the two universal languages of Antiquity. Even though they adopted Christianity, the authors of these doctrines had received the usual elite education and had been immersed in the culture and **philosophy** of Antiquity, and were obviously influenced by them. The influence of the **vocabulary** of **rhetoric** (in the formulation of the truths of faith) and of the moral strictness of Stoic philosophy remained highly perceptible during the Church's first centuries, at a time when the Roman Empire was still powerful. This double influence was already evident in the writings of St **Paul**—himself a Roman citizen who wrote in Greek—which bear the mark of concepts used in Greek philosophy. It is thus that the expression "**against nature**" (unnatural) (Rom 1:26), frequently used (even today) to condemn homosexual acts, is not specific to Christianity, but belongs mostly to pagan philosophy. In reality, Christian morality at the beginning situated itself on the straight line of a certain popular stoicism which can be summarized by "living according to nature," i.e. conforming to the biological and procreative inevitability of the body and avoiding the disturbances engendered by passion or even pleasure.

Church fathers appropriated this interpretation of sexuality, in which it is always considered unsavory and shameful. As author John McNeil states: "Saint Augustine went so far as to categorize all attraction and all pleasure as sin," because the purely rational goal of sexuality was procreation within **marriage**. Therefore, homosexual relations were condemned. In reality, long before the ascension of state Christianity (**Theodosius**'s decree of 389 CE), Roman law had already taken into consideration the moral demands of Stoic philosophy, even though the application of such laws was not very strict: in 17 BCE, the *Lex Julia de*

adulteris was aimed at those who practiced **debauchery** with other men; in 342 CE, Christianity being already in place, Constantine and Constance proclaimed an edict against men who practiced passive homosexuality and threatened them with "cruel" punishment; in 390 CE, Valentine, Theodosius, and Arcadias threatened homosexuals with "vengeful fire" (the Biblical punishment of purifying fire); in 536 and 544 CE, **Justinian** rewrote the *Lex Julia de adulteris* in his *Novellae*, which was aimed at all those who engaged in homosexual acts, both active and passive, and explicitly incorporated Biblical text and punishment.

The decrees that civil authorities of the Empire imposed also appear in the church's conciliar decrees. The first ecumenical councils were mostly fixated on doctrine and the rejection of **heresies**; however, some local ecumenical assemblies legislated on questions of morality. Thus, in 314 CE in Ankara (Asia Minor), Canon 17 fulminated against "those who have committed the stain of sin with male animals or men." Here, the link between homosexuality and bestiality was obviously homophobic, but it was more often the case that homosexual acts were condemned under the guise of adultery; in other words, it was more the idea of extramarital relations that was targeted than homosexuality itself.

Starting in the thirteenth century, the Middle Ages saw a considerable increase in the amount and degree of homophobic thought and condemnation. Theologians of the time took homosexuality quite seriously and wanted to prove, intellectually, its harmfulness, whereas the councils, in the form of civil justice, passed severe condemnations. Thomas Aquinas (d. 1274), a Catholic priest of the Dominican order, was a great figure of philosophy who left a lasting mark on thirteenth-century theology. He was also one of the few to have reflected upon, with the rational weapons of scholasticism, relations between persons of the same gender (in the eleventh century, church reformer Peter **Damien** had denounced sin against nature with such vehemence that Pope Leo IX was forced to urge him to be more moderate). Starting with Aquinas, homosexuals, already condemned to the fires of Hell (as well as to actual pyres) for Biblical reasons, were also condemned for theological ones. Aquinas studied at the University of Paris under another Dominican, Albertus Magnus, who had declared that homosexuality was the most detestable of **vices** for a variety of reasons: it originated out of infernal passions; it had a repugnant odor, and those who practiced it were unable to purify themselves; and it was contagious, as are all diseases. The arguments were quite irrational, and demonstrated a homophobic sensibility founded on ideas from the Old Testament (Hell composed of fire and brimstone), on the dialectic of the pure and the impure borrowed from St Paul (by way of the metaphor of the contagious and incurable disease), and on irrational fear (i.e. subjective adjectives such as "detestable" and "repugnant").

Thomas Aquinas countered this fear with his cold intelligence, only to come to the same conclusions. He situated his reflection in the larger context of an argument on sexuality and femininity by taking up the previously used arguments of Stoic thought from Antiquity. His ideas specifically relating to homosexual relations appeared briefly in his *Summa theologica* (Comprehensive survey of theology) and, in a more developed manner, in *Quaestiones disputate* (Disputed issues). In the section pertaining to "The Virtues," temperance provided Aquinas with a platform to discuss same-sex relations, which he understood as debauchery in opposition to reason and the order ordained by God. With the essential finality of the sexual act being procreation, all that remained—i.e. sexual pleasure for its own sake—was nothing but vice. Thus, those who engaged in "egotistical" pleasure, as well as all sexual acts (including heterosexual) that did not express a shared love, were condemned as being "against nature" and consigned to the worst vices of lust (masturbation and bestiality, for example). It is important to note here a form of homophobia that persists to this day among those who claim to adhere to the **Catholic Church**: the denial that homosexuals can ever be loving. In fact, starting with Aquinas, the Church almost never considered homosexuality as *being*, but rather as *practice*, which allowed it to condemn homosexual acts and "compassionately" accept those who performed them.

During the Middle Ages, church councils and assemblies debated widely about homosexual relationships (mostly male). Leaving the theologians to prove the nuisance of these types of relationships, the Church contented itself with pronouncing the necessary condemnations and devising adequate punishments. Those who were accused of practicing homosexuality were often considered heretics and treated as such, as shown by the fourteenth-century arrest and trial of the Knights Templar on charges of heresy and immorality. Thus, in the penitential, the book of laws for confessor priests, penance is determined in conjunction with the sin and its severity. For homosexual acts, the penance proposed is always extremely harsh; at the end of the thirteenth century, sodomy became a special sin that fell within the province of bishops or the pope. With regard to morals, the most ambitious ecumenical council was the Fourth Lateran Council, summoned in 1215 by Pope Innocent III in order to "eradicate vice and favor virtue, correct abuses and reform morals, eliminate heresies and strengthen the faith." Because sodomy was not explicitly mentioned among the vices to eradicate, the ecumenical council left the responsibility of legislation and necessary action to the local assemblies. Thus, by 1120, the Council of Nabulus, in the eastern Latin states (now the Middle East), had already produced four canons against homosexual acts and had condemned the guilty to the pyre.

Despite the **violence** of conciliar texts, the Church called for homosexuals to repent, but left the matter to lay courts, which were often harsh. The tribunals of the **Inquisition**, during which heretics were hunted down, also functioned in the same manner: once guilt was established, it was the "secular arm" which took charge of enforcing the sentence. Civilian justice often treated heretics and sodomites the same by punishing them both with death by fire. Women convicted of the same crimes suffered identical sentences; they were often grouped in the same category as witches, and were also burned at the stake.

During the Middle Ages, as the Church became firmly established in the West, it acted as if it were seized by a siege mentality, ruthlessly pursuing anything that appeared to threaten it; theologians were put into service, and ecclesiastic assemblies established laws that were enforced by lay courts. The result was a more resolute persecution of homosexuals, although it is difficult to comprehend just how seriously they could have threatened religious life. In any case, as much from a theological point of view as a factual one, the period was obviously a homophobic one, and even more so toward the end of the Middle Ages.

However, it would appear that the imposing legal system put into place to deal with homosexuals, and the violently repressive discourse that went along with it, had rather limited effects. French historian Maurice Lever notes that between 1317 and 1789, "in the seventy-three trials for sodomy listed by Claude Courouve in France, only thirty-eight led to executions," not counting other punishments, such as torture, banishment, and prison. These thirty-eight executions seem very few, especially in light of the fact that some of the accused were also accused of rape, abduction, or murder. Despite the loss of archival documents (trial materials were burned along with the condemned), and other gaps in information available, a majority of accused "sodomites" might not have been (overly) worried about what civil or religious authorities might do to them. Nevertheless, the threat of death was quite real, and homophobic social pressure might have had a great effect on homosexuals during the period, especially because of its legitimization by the Church.

A look at the **literature** of the time confirms the ambiguity of the medieval point of view on homosexuality. Writings that deal with the subject are interesting because they do not describe "actual" examples of homosexuality, but rather imaginary representations. While the idea of love between a man and a woman appears in lyric poetry and fiction of the period, almost every medieval literary genre also values the friendship or companionship between characters of the same sex. We therefore find inseparable companions in literature (such as *The Song of Roland*'s Olivier and Roland) and unfailing friendships in novels (Lancelot and Gawain); additionally, historian John Boswell, among others, uncovered numerous examples of love poems that are clearly written with same-sex desire in mind. However, the majority of literary texts emphasize moral conformity and vigorously condemn same-sex relations: there is no obvious representation of homosexual characters. On the other hand, it is quite common, especially through female characters whose romantic intentions are unrequited, to insult a knight by calling him effeminate or insinuating his propensity for young men or boys (for example, in *Le Roman d'Enéas*, v. 8619–8675). Even in literary works, then, homosexual relationships are used as a foil in a society ruled by very homophobic moral and religious laws.

Modern & Contemporary Periods
The principles of Church dogma, or those truths that must be accepted as articles of faith, were not yet finalized during the first centuries of Christianity; they came into gradual existence through divine word, the Bible, and Church tradition: knowledge of the truth (of God, Christ, the Church) was not revealed all at once, but was the ongoing subject of theological research. This is why we can describe theology in terms of diachronic development. During the sixteenth century,

the **Protestant** Reformation put the Catholic Church into question (challenging its dogma, unity, clergy, etc.) and forced it to more clearly formulate certain truths and moral questions. The rational speculations of medieval scholasticism were not forgotten, but theologians, searching for a more scientific approach to biblical text, proposed a hierarchical organization of dogmatic principles while placing more emphasis on them. They finally presented moral recommendations for the actions and rituals that all true Christians must observe. In reality, the Counter-Reformation (sixteenth century), as it became known, was not revolutionary; it merely reaffirmed truths that had been made murky by abuse. The Church's view on homosexuality never swayed, however: the Church continued to firmly condemn it, even though popes who ruled during the Renaissance seemed to enjoy great freedom with regard to morals (but not greater than that enjoyed by twelfth-century popes, whose very licentious habits had also led to disciplinary reforms).

Since the Counter-Reformation, the Catholic community's position has remained rather fixed. It was as a result of the Second Vatican Council (Vatican II) (1962–65), however, that there was some innovation with regard to religious rites and ceremonies. The Council's agenda was extensive, and topics discussed included modern communications, relations between Christians and Jews, religious freedom, the role of laity in the church, liturgical worship, contacts with other Christians and with non-Christians, and the role and education of priests and bishops. Nevertheless, the Catholic Church remained steadfast when it came to its essential beliefs: the moral teachings of the Church never changed. As far as this assembly of bishops was concerned, marriage and sexuality were not only instituted for reasons of procreation and the education of children, but also so that "the mutual love between spouses … may progress and grow." Nevertheless, the pastoral approach to the faithful has had to evolve, for the bishops insisted on condemning the sin rather than the sinner; in other words, homosexual acts must be rejected, but not homosexuals themselves. This distinction, perhaps overly subtle, has not always been fully understood, given that homophobic remarks on the part of zealous pastors and the faithful alike, aimed at gay men and lesbians, remain frequent. The Church also maintains a separation between *being* and *acting* (one can be forgiven for being homosexual so long as he or she doesn't act on it), which can lead to a sort of schizophrenia among the gay faithful: destined for hell for what they do, but not for what they are.

At the beginning of the 1970s, confronted by a multitude of new proposals by very liberal pastors, church hierarchy and bishops attempted to settle on clear positions regarding homosexuality once and for all. The American Episcopal Conference was the first group to accomplish this, with a fifteen-page document entitled *Guiding Principles for Confessors Regarding Homosexuality*. The paper states that homosexuality is contrary to the procreative objective of human sexuality (which was Thomas Aquinas's argument during the Middle Ages) as well as contrary to marriage, which it defined as being "the expression of reciprocal love between husband and wife" (a more recent argument, as it can be found in Second Vatican Council texts). The views remain traditional and reveal nothing new. Yet there is another element that can be construed as positive: the document "encourages homosexual friendships," but on the condition that they remain "sexually non-active." In other words, permanent continence remains the only proposed solution for the homosexual problem. Continence is a form of abstinence that is regularly imposed by the Church; it is either temporary (at certain periods of the year, in the case of married couples) or permanent, but always chosen (such as by monks and priests). This type of sacrifice is also one of the most certain ways for the faithful to be free of sin and attain Heaven. Just as Christ, the faithful must suffer in order to pay for their sins. According to the Church, homosexuals are only offered a life of suffering, a permanent continence, which will lead to their ultimate salvation. (Other Episcopal Conferences only served to confirm the proposals put forward by the American Conference.)

In fact, if homosexual followers wish to follow the teachings of the Catholic Church to the letter, they have two possibilities from which to choose: conversion to heterosexuality, or permanent continence. In recent years, certain American sects have attempted to medically prove the possibility of "becoming heterosexual," but the Catholic Church, being perhaps more realistic, recognizes the definitive homosexual orientation of certain individuals. The second option, permanent continence, is perfectly compatible with traditional Christian ideology, which teaches that the body is loathsome, and that suffering leads to redemption. According to theologian John McNeill, the adoption of these ideas by gay individuals can only lead

to **self-hatred**: of one's body, desires, and identity. He concludes that "no other single group of human beings has ever been the object of injustice, persecution and suffering" as have homosexuals, and that "even if it is not responsible, the Church carries its share of responsibility for this situation."

The *Dictionnaire critique de théologie* (*Encyclopedia of Christian Theology*) offers a contemporary look at theological issues which at times only serves to confirm that certain things have not changed. Contributor Michael Banner, in his essay "Sexual (Ethic)," concludes by asking those who defend homosexuality, whether based on **anthropology** or a particular idea of creation, why they do not take sexual differentiation or the necessary split between the sexes, into account, and how their position relates to the teachings of the Bible. Thus, the initial question is more of an accusation: though homosexuals have suffered from centuries of social and religious persecution—persecution that was often initiated by the Church—they are still challenged to explain and defend themselves. The reference to anthropology tends to deny them any right to conceive of humanity in any way other than our relation to God, a relation that is defined solely by the Church itself. Finally, the terms "creation," "sexual **differences**," and "Bible" refer both to the condemnations in Scripture and the idea of the "unnatural."

From this we can see that there has been little evolution in analysis, and that the same homophobic views are reaffirmed. The whole of these arguments rests on two prejudicial principles. On one hand, each time the Catholic Church refers to homosexuals, the remarks are, to the letter, homophobic, as shown in biblical and theological declarations, condemnations, or writings. The second principle, which is more general, holds to the Church's hegemonic position, which proposes a system of totalitarian thought: its oppression of homosexuals is based on the belief that it is necessary in order to maintain not only the stability of the **family**, but social equilibrium itself. These, like all stereotypes, are false. It is unbelievable that homosexuals exercise such a strong influence on humanity, or even that the Church and the "traditional family" are so weak as to be destabilized by such a small minority. Furthermore, such ideas contradict the superiority complex that stems from the belief in Divine selection (Christians being confident that they are the bearers of truth).

A final form of Church homophobia can be identified in the oft-mentioned sentiment of compassion and **tolerance**. Both result from the same superiority complex; compassion implies that the other, i.e. the homosexual, is suffering in his state, which remains to be proven. One is not necessarily unhappy being homosexual per se, but can be as a result of this negative attitude. Compassion also implies a position of superiority in the view that the homosexual is unhappy, so one must understand him in his suffering; not only is the other (the homosexual) judged as being burdened, but that he needs to be consoled by someone stronger. The same psychological mechanism also comes into play with regard to the question of tolerance. By tolerating someone, one is judging him to be out of place; further, that he has not adapted to the world around him, but, despite everything, one allows him to live in it. The 1975 *Persona humana* declaration by the Vatican Congregation for the Doctrine of Faith speaks of "social maladjustment." In this, tolerance tends to diminish the other, looking down at him from an overbearing and superior point of view.

In fact, the Church has always tended to define homosexuals as incomplete individuals. *Persona humana* describes them as being blocked "by a sort of innate instinct or pathological constitution that is judged to be incurable," incapable of having sincere relationships and experiencing true love. Homosexual relationships are irremediably condemned to failure because they inherently "lack the integral sense of mutual giving and the context of true love." In this, we can recognize theories stemming from Freudian **psychoanalysis** which postulate that the ultimate form of human sexuality is heterosexual, homosexuality being a transitional state to be outgrown if one is to know complete psychological development.

In short, the present-day Catholic Church has continued its homophobic discourse, notably to justify its refusal to support **decriminalization** of homosexuality (for example, in Eastern Europe during the 1990s) or to recognize gay marriage or **parenting**. In addition to the traditional referencing of biblical texts and theologians from Antiquity and the Middle Ages, the Church bases its views on **psychological**, psychoanalytical, anthropological, or **sociological** studies. Likewise, its superiority complex, borne of its vocation to save families and all of humanity, helps it to arrive at determinations that are inevitably homophobic. Their moral intolerance is all the more dangerous in that it is now not only based on religious reasons but also on sciences that were *a priori* unknown and which

it interprets unilaterally. Thus, it adds a pseudo-scientific aspect to a homophobia that has historically been founded on moral and religious principles.

—*Thierry Revol*

Alberigo, Giuseppe, ed. *Conciles œcuméniques*. Vol. II-2: "Les décrets." Paris: Le Cerf, 1994.

Baile, Derrick Sherwin. *Homosexuality and the Western Christian Tradition*. London: Longmans, Green & Co., 1955.

Boswell, John. *Christianisme, tolérance sociale et homosexualité*. Paris: Gallimard, 1985. [Published in the US as *Homosexuality, Intolerance, and Christianity*. New York: Scholarship Committee, Gay Academic Union, 1981.]

"La Condition homosexuelle," *Lumière et Vie,* no. 47 (1980).

Congrégation pour la doctrine de la foi. "Au sujet des propositions de loi sur la non-discrimination des personnes homosexuelles." In *La Documentation catholique,* 1992. [Published in English as "Some Considerations Concerning the Response to Legislative Proposals on Non-Discrimination of Homosexual Persons." By The Congregation for the Doctrine of the Faith, The Roman Curia (July 23, 1992).]

———. *Lettre aux évêques de l'Église catholique sur l'attention pastorale à apporter aux personnes homosexuelles*. Paris: Téqui, 1986. [Published in English as "Letter to the Bishops of the Catholic Church on the Pastoral Care of Homosexual Persons." By The Congregation for the Doctrine of the Faith, The Roman Curia (October 1, 1986).]

———. "*Persona humana*. Déclaration sur quelques questions d'éthique sexuelle". In *La Documentation catholique,* 1976. [Published in English as "*Persona Humana*: Declaration on Certain Questions Concerning Sexual Ethics." By The Congregation for the Doctrine of the Faith, The Roman Curia (1975).]

Demur, Christian, and Denis Müller. *L'Homosexualité, un dialogue théologique*. Geneva: Labor et Fides, 1992.

Furey, Pat, and Jeanine Grammick, eds. *The Vatican and Homosexuality*. New York: Crossroad, 1988.

Gilbert, Maurice. "La Bible et l'homosexualité," *Nouvelle Revue de théologie,* no. 109 (1987).

Grammick, Jeanine, ed. *Homosexuality in the Priesthood and the Religious Life*. New York: Crossroad, 1989.

Hasbany, Richard, ed. *Homosexuality and Religion*. New York: Harrington Park Press, 1989.

Jordan, Mark. *The Invention of Sodomy in Christian Theology*. Chicago: Univ. of Chicago Press, 1997.

Lacoste, Jean-Yves, ed. *Dictionnaire critique de théologie*. Paris: Presses universitaires de France, 1998. [Published in the US as *Encyclopedia of Christian Theology*. New York: Routledge, 2005.]

Lever, Maurice. *Les Bûchers de Sodome*. Paris: Fayard, 1985.

"La Marée rose," *Permanences,* no. 340 (1997).

McNeill, John. *L'Eglise et l'homosexuel, un plaidoyer*. Geneva: Labor et Fides, 1982.

———. *Taking a Chance on God: Liberating Theology for Gays, Lesbians and Their Lovers, Families, and Friends*. Boston: Beacon Press, 1988.

Melton, Gordon. *The Churches Speak on Homosexuality*. Detroit: Gale Research, 1991.

Mott, Luiz. *Escravidào, homossexualidade e Demonologia*. Sao Paolo: Editora Icône, 1988.

Oraison, Marc. *La Question homosexuelle*. Paris: Le Seuil, 1975. [Published in the US as *The Homosexual Question*. New York: Harper & Row, 1977.]

Seow, Choon-Leong, ed. *Homosexuality and the Christian Community*. Louisville: Westminster Hohn Know Press, 1996.

Spong, John Selby. *Living in Sin? A Bishop Rethinks Human Sexuality*. San Francisco: Harper & Row, 1988.

Thévenot Xavier. *Homosexualités masculines et morale chrétienne*. Paris: Le Cerf, 1985.

Tigert, Lean McCall. *Coming Out While Staying In: Struggles and Celebrations of Lesbians, Gays, Bisexuals in the Church*. Cleveland: United Church Press, 1996.

Wolf, James. *Gay Priests*. New York: Harper & Row, 1989.

—Abnormal; Against Nature; Bible, the; Catholic Church, the; Damien, Peter; Debauchery; Ex-Gay; Family; Heresy; Inquisition; Judaism; Marriage; Orthodoxy (Christian); Paul (of Tarsus); Philosophy; Protestantism; Rhetoric; Sterility; Tolerance; Vice.

TOLERANCE

The worst thing about Christine **Boutin**, the French politician who became famous in 1998 for opposing the PaCS (Pacte civil de solidarité; Civil solidarity pact) domestic partnership plan in her country, was that she was sincere when she told gays and lesbians, "I love you." It has been common, particularly from Christian perspectives, for the love of another to appear as the basis for complete intolerance. And cries of "Burn the fags!" heard during the **anti-PaCS** demonstrations were doubtlessly the consequences of such love. Beware of those who love you.

This love/hate intolerance developed, at least in the Catholic West, under the **Inquisition** and became more refined during the Reformation, and today, it informs religious conservative attitudes toward sexual freedom as much as it did toward religious freedom in the past. Moreover, this system is summarized in two syllogisms by seventeenth-century French bishop Jacques-Benigne Bossnet: in the first, truth is one, and tolerance supposes plurality. Tolerance, therefore, undermines the foundations of truth. In the second, charity requires concern for the salvation of others who are damned through sin; therefore, tolerating the sins of others shows a severe lack of charity. In other words, tolerance of sin is worse than sin itself because sin is not only accepted, but also to a certain extent, legitimized and encouraged. To this degree, Nietzsche's words regarding "free-thinkers" still hold true for gays and lesbians today: "It is not their charity, but rather the impotence of their charity that has stopped modern-day Christians from burning us."

From this perspective, it is certain that gay liberation has followed, like a shadow, the historical and geographical growth of tolerance and the decline of the political power of the religions preaching salvation. Thus, that the defense of tolerance is not just a rearguard fight, at least in our liberal societies, which have at least succeeded in preventing the actions of religious intolerance.

At least three notable historical events have served to reveal the problematics underlying even the most sincere statements regarding tolerance. The first is **Stonewall** and its affirmation of gay pride, and a certain inalienable truth about one's sexual identity: it is difficult to reconcile such an affirmation with the inherent skepticism that accompanies the tolerance of the Enlightenment, as summarized by Voltaire: "We are all filled with weaknesses and mistakes; let us forgive each other our stupidities, it is Nature's first law." In light of this view, gay pride is dependent on the notion that gays or lesbians display no "weakness," "error," or "stupidity." The fight for identity, for the right to be openly gay or lesbian or simply to sweetly touch each other in public, is a fight for truth. It is not a question of being tolerated by mainstream society, but rather recognized, which in many regards constitutes a radically opposite demand. But one interpretation of this idea, disguised as tolerance, has an obvious homophobic **rhetoric** that is even internalized by some gays and lesbians: "We would like to accept homosexuals, but on the condition that they not be too obvious, that they be as discreet as possible, that they act one way, but not another." This conditional acceptance was clearly summarized by France's National Front leader Jean-Marie Le Pen when he asserted that, "The National Front includes homosexuals, *but* not queens," or Christine Boutin, when she declared that, "The right to homosexuality … does not automatically legitimize gay proselytism." In this way, homophobic tolerance follows a "yes, but" reasoning.

The second historical event is the appearance of **AIDS** in the early 1980s, which forced gays and lesbians to move from fighting for tolerance to the fighting against the *intolerable*. Certainly, this idea of intolerable had been in vogue since the 1970s. But at the dawn of the AIDS crisis, tolerance, understood then as *indifference*, became intolerable as gay activist groups such as ACT UP adopted slogans like "Silence = Death" and "We die, you do nothing." The issue had been completely turned around. It was no longer a question of fighting repression, but rather mainstream society's "laissez-faire" attitude toward the AIDS crisis. It was no longer a fight against an active, overt homophobia, but rather a passive one in which "eyes were wide shut." In short, the pandemic transformed gay and lesbian activism from a fight for difference into a fight against indifference. Here, it is important to remember the gay community's shifting status in the early 1980s, when the arrival of the "gay cancer" provided a new rationale for the stigmatization of and **discrimination** against gays and lesbians. The AIDS crisis, and its impact on society's tolerance of gays and lesbians, revealed a fundamental contradiction of all policies of tolerance: How can one be fundamentally tolerant without running the risk of tolerating the intolerable?

The third historical event that ruffled the standard of tolerance is the adoption of the civil solidarity reforms PaCS itself. In a sense, the adoption of PaCS stands as a marker of progressively tolerant liberal policies toward not only homosexuality but private consensual relationships in general. However, at the same time, it raises a legal conundrum. If homosexuality is solely a private and contractual matter, then legalized gay marriage is not possible, since marriage supposes arbitration by a third party, i.e. the state. In this way, the **adoption** rights of gays and lesbians cannot be considered either (children being not only of the private sphere but also partially of the public). In other words, with the adoption of PaCS, tolerance of homosexuality has become incompatible with true legal equality.

Tolerance is always conditional or limited: it is only possible under certain conditions and to a certain extent. More precisely, we could say that there are two types of limitations on tolerance. The negative limitation, of French origin, uses the Declaration of the Rights of Man and of the Citizen as its foundation: freedom appears as a purely negative notion; one is free to do anything that does not harm others nor disrupt law and order, as defined by the state. The positive limitation, of Anglo-Saxon origin, is based on John Locke's "A Letter Concerning Toleration": tolerance is extended to a limited faction of society, and is positively represented and defended by the state. (Locke specifically limits tolerance to all religious beliefs except atheism.) Whatever the case, advocating tolerance in regard to homosexuality undoubtedly conflicts with both of these negative and positive limitations.

Equality between heterosexuals and homosexuals will be achieved when tolerance is no longer limited or qualified or even an issue—just as no one talks about tolerance with regard to heterosexuality. However, it is important to understand the implications of such a proposal. First of all, according Michel Foucault's proposition in "La Volonté de Savoir" ("The Will to Know"), and virtually every American queer association thereafter, we should refuse to define our individual truth by and through sexuality. Furthermore, renouncing the politics of sexual identity, while allowing for the abandonment of repressive sexual hypotheses, could potentially undermine some of the very foundations of the sexual revolution. Moreover, such a strategic reversal would give credence to the homophobia of indifference: How can one fight AIDS if one refuses to name its first victims? How does one counter the odious likening of homosexuality to **pedophilia** if one refuses to assign a positive and specific definition to all sexual orientations? And how can one defend a progressive liberal policy toward homosexuality if one does not define homosexuality first?

In any case, it is essential to recognize that a criticism of tolerance, which oscillates between affirmation and negation of the definition of homosexuality, is just as fundamentally contradictory as a policy of tolerance, which oscillates between the acceptance and rejection of homosexuality. Thus, it is not possible to support a consistent notion of tolerance in the fight against homophobia as it is constantly altered by context and circumstance. However, it is also likely that the notion of tolerance will continue not only in societies presumed to be intolerant of gays and lesbians but in allegedly tolerant ones as well. All one needs to do is listen to Pope John Paul II, more than four centuries after the Saint Bartholomew's Day Massacre, declare that Catholicism is the only true religion. *Mutatis mutandis.* One can only conclude that the majority of effectively tolerant homophobes will remain tolerant only for as long as they are forced to.

—*Pierre Zaoui*

Aquinas, Thomas. *Summa theologiae [1266–1272].* Paris: Le Cerf, 1984. [Published in English as *Summa Theologica.*]

Bossuet, Jacques-Bénigne. "Avertissements aux protestants" (notably numbers 3 and 6). In *Œuvres complètes.* Paris: F. Lachat, 1962. First published in 1689–91.

Boswell, John. *Christianisme, tolérance sociale et homosexualité.* Paris: Gallimard, 1980. [Published in the US as *Christianity, Social tolerance, and Homosexuality.* Chicago: Univ. of Chicago Press, 1980.]

Diderot, D'Alembert. "Tolérance." In *L'Encyclopédie.* Paris: Flammarion, 1986.

Foucault, Michel. *La Volonté de savoir.* Paris: Gallimard, 1976.

Halperin, David. *Saint Foucault.* Paris: EPEL, 2000.

Legler, Joseph. *Histoire de la tolérance au siècle de la Réforme.* Paris: Aubier-Montaigne, 1955.

Locke, John. *Lettre sur la tolerance.* Paris: Presses universitaires de France, 1965. [Published in the US as *John Locke, A Letter Concerning Toleration.* Edited by John Horton and Susan Mendus. New York : Routledge, 1991.]

Thierry, Patrick. *La Tolérance: société démocratique, opinions, vices et vertus.* Paris: Presses universitaires de France, 1997.

Voltaire. "Tolérance." In *Dictionnaire philosophique.* Paris: Garnier-Flammarion, 1964. [Published in the US as *Philosophical Dictionary.* New York: Basic Books, 1962.]

—*Abnormal; Heterosexism; Philosophy; Rhetoric; Symbolic Order; Utilitarianism; Violence.*

TRANSPHOBIA

In the same way that gay men and lesbians are the targets of homophobia, transsexuals, transgenders, transvestites, drag queens, and drag kings are also the targets of discriminatory treatment. These groups do not primarily identify themselves through a specific sexuality that departs from the heterosexual model. Nonetheless, since the relation between sex, gender, and physical appearance upon which these identities are built continues to undermine the heterocentric establishment, transphobia expresses the hostility and the systematic aversion, be it more or less conscious, to individuals whose identity blurs the lines of sociosexual roles and transgresses the limits between sex and gender.

At the end of the nineteenth century, and in the wake of the studies by Magnus **Hirschfeld**, Richard von Krafft-Ebing, and Albert Moll in **Germany**, as well as Havelock Ellis and Henry Maudsley in **England**, psychiatrists focused on the entirety of recorded sexual pathologies: homosexuality, transvestism, fetishism, bestiality, **exhibitionism**, **pedophilia**, etc. Beginning with the first scientific observations and the description of these "**perversions**," categories are established, which lead to the distinctions between the various identities. Transsexuality is then assimilated to newly defined sexual pathologies in the same way as homosexuality and transvestism. In 1949, the American sexologist D.O. Cauldwell, who published a paper entitled "Psychopathia Transexualis" involving the case of a woman who sought a sex change operation, introduced the term "transsexualism."

Considered ill, individuals who presented gender identity troubles were submitted to medical authorities, who were charged with recommending therapies that would regulate their behavior and identity. From the moment transsexualism or transvestism were officially considered distinct from other deviant behavior, they could be assigned to specific institutional repression. Thereafter, but outside the parameters of the medical establishment, new identity categories began to develop, such as transgender, drag queen, and, most recently, drag king.

However, widely accepted ideas continue to assimilate transgenderism or transsexuality to homosexuality. Understood as "sicknesses," "depravities," and "questionable tendencies," they are in the same way regarded by social norms as strange, eccentric, and perverse. Thus, transphobia and homophobia are frequently confused. Moreover, it is possible to identify an entire repertoire of insults that are aimed simultaneously and interchangeably at homosexuals, transsexuals, and transvestites: "queer," "poof," "fag," "drag queen," "dyke," "cocksucker," et cetera. This assimilation reinforces the idea of belonging to the same community, a "community of insults" some might say, in which particular forms of socialization are developed that are subsequently exposed to the same forms of repression;

the 1969 **Stonewall** riots being the most famous example. These social groups also share a certain number of demands that are often expressed during Gay Pride (which has become LGBT Pride in many countries), a celebration and visible demonstration of the different facets of the community.

In fact, the expression of transphobia has certain characteristics that are very similar to homophobia, but it also contains elements that correspond to specific characteristics of the group being targeted. Its most brutal and obvious interpretation is, without a doubt, physical **violence** and intimidation; one need only think of the "bashings" and other assaults aimed at transgenders. Certain transsexuals describe the frequently brutal reactions of men who realize that the woman in his arms is not biologically female. The murder of transsexuals is still a common event in some countries, and many live in constant fear of being attacked or killed. In the late 1990s, many of Algeria's transsexuals (or "creatures," as they called themselves) fled the country, often at the behest of their families, in the wake of the Algerian Civil War and the persecution of groups that had been previously tolerated.

However, transphobia takes on many other forms, at first sight less overt than physical attacks, verbal assaults or irrational expressions of disgust or revulsion, but which are more insidious, akin to what French sociologist Pierre Bourdieu describes as symbolic violence. For many transsexuals, derision, contempt, repression, and institutionalized discriminatory treatment are manifestations of transphobia experienced on a daily basis.

The situation particular to transsexuals, whose gender identity does not correspond to their birth gender, is a rather explicit example of the institutionalization of transphobia. Moreover, the social relationships that transsexuals must sever in order to affirm their identity and their physical transformation—be it **family**, **school**, **work**, or, in some cases, country—are just so many circumstances in which the cultural aspects of transphobia are expressed. They constitute a social and political mechanism for **discrimination**. In fact, activities such as getting a passport or a new social insurance number, requests for political asylum in cases of expulsion or deportation, court appearances, and lodging complaints in cases of assault, are, for transsexuals, simply more opportunities to experience transphobia.

From a legal standpoint, the courts have tended to latently support the social ostracism of transsexuals, or

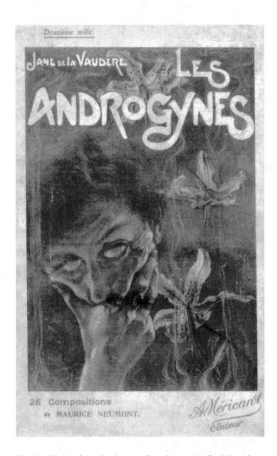

Plato's "Myth of the Androgyne" and new medical theories on the third sex blend in order to construct a particularly anguishing image. The catalog featuring this novel explains quite clearly the breadth of this work, published in 1902. "It was necessary to condemn these sexual dead-ends, not in a book of unrealistic morality, but in an attractive, captivating novel, by opposing shameful vice with triumphant love, love both frantic and passionate, which is the great savior of our race and the purifier of all carnal hideousness. This novel contains somber paintings, images of murder and of nightmare, but also pages flowered with delicate and burning passion."

created the conditions for its expression. As the French legal establishment is silent on the transsexual question (as well as the question of sex change), and French law does not define sex or gender, it is **jurisprudence** that, above all, establishes the basis of consideration and makes decisions regarding transsexuals. Thus, in **France**, until recently, transsexuals could only acquire non-gender-specific names such as Pat or Chris. Furthermore, a requested change in one's civil status—a determining issue for transsexuals, since it presides over the identification of every official document and, consequently, the determination of rights, notably with regard to family law—remains particularly difficult to obtain if one does not undergo a hormonal-surgical sex change. It is currently evident that the state and society push those who have gender identity issues toward surgery, which is particularly extensive; some transsexuals admit having undergone surgery in order to obtain official identification that reflected their gender identity and appearance.

At the end of the 1940s and through the 50s, transsexuals began to become more visible as a result of the publicity surrounding the surgical transformation of George Jorgensen into Christine Jorgensen. In 1952, endocrinologist Christian Hamburger, with the assistance of doctors Georg Sturup and E. Dahl-Iversen, operated on Jorgensen, an ex-US Army GI hero turned photographer, in what was the world's first sex-reassignment surgery. This case provided, on an international scale, new data on transsexuality and gender identity troubles, which, from that point on, were listed in the Diagnostic and Statistical Manual of Mental Disorders (DSM). Harry Benjamin, a German medical psychiatrist, advocated the use of the term "transsexual," which for him designated individuals who believed they belonged to the opposite sex, rather than their biological sex. The Harry Benjamin International Gender Dysphoria Association (now the World Professional Association for Transgender Health), devoted to the understanding and treatment of gender identity disorders, established a case management model that included a psychiatrist, a psychologist, an endocrinologist, and a surgeon.

However, when transsexuals enter the "official" network, it is without a doubt in their relations with experts—who are supposed to be the guarantors of their integration, and who hold the power to "reassign" their identity and gender—where transsexuals are confronted by the strongest expressions of transphobia: the comments of some doctors on the subject of transsexuals are not exempt from violence. For French psychiatrist Colette Chiland, for example, "the transsexual patient puts everything on the physical table, but places nothing on the psychological table." Agnes Oppenheimer speaks of a "refusal of mentalization"; according to her:

> Despite the differences (between transsexual individuals), certain common traits can be found, in particular the logic of their trite, preconceived and stereotypical discourses that is deprived of all metaphoric dimension. The narrative they propose is a negation of any history. The dialogue invokes the medical or social other, who he hopes to convince. Suffering, related to the unique discord between sex and gender, is emptied of all absolute belief, inseparable from the evolution of the syndrome to which the 'progresses' of science grant a status. The interlocutor is confronted by a logic that denies, affirms and demands.

The pressure takes on different forms during the journey that transsexuals must follow: constant criticism regarding their appearance ("Your hands aren't very feminine!"), the obligation to accept long-term psychiatric follow-up, tersely inappropriate diagnoses ("You're crazy"), and doctors who refuse to prescribe hormonal treatments for those who wish to avoid surgery. The list of potential harassments goes on.

Paradoxically, for many transsexuals, leading a "normal life" means having to live a double life in order to avoid rejection; having to "wear shirts and ties," i.e. hiding one's identity part of the time. Further, transsexuality's visibility provokes exclusion from the working world: many are forced to quit their jobs, or find it impossible to gain employment because the name or photo on official identification does not correspond to his or her physical appearance. In this context, turning to prostitution remains a way out for a number of transsexuals who decide to live as a woman, which reinforces the widespread belief that transsexuality is synonymous with prostitution. It is easy to understand how a system of exclusion feeds on itself.

Thus, the vagueness of terminologies and what they correspond to—who are the transsexuals, the transgenders, the drag queens?—contributes both to the power and the weakness of the term transphobia. Transphobia refers to attacks against those who, beyond sexual practices, have crossed the boundary that exists between the genders. Its power is to shed light on the virulent and institutionalized reaction against what it perceives as a threat to the traditional concepts of sex and gender, or relations between the two. Its weakness is to delineate a discrimination against individuals whose specific characteristics are confused, and who are almost as invisible as the term is uncommon. In effect, if the term "homophobia" only appeared belatedly around 1971—nearly 100 years after the word "homosexual"—"transphobia" is so recent that it is rarely listed in any dictionary. This lapse in English-language references is symptomatic of society's **heterosexist** denial of groups it finds disturbing. It testifies to a willingness to deny the existence of transsexuals, and consequently, their rights.

—*Gaëlle Krikorian*

Bourcier, Marie-Hélène. *Queer zones, politiques des identités sexuelles, des représentations et des savoirs*, Paris: Balland, 2001.

Bourdieu, Pierre. *La Domination masculine*. Paris: Le Seuil, 1998. [Published in the US as *Masculine Domination*. Stanford: Stanford Univ. Press, 2001.]

Cauldwell, David. "Psychopathia transexualis," *Sexology* 16 (1949).

Chiland, Colette. "Les Impasses du traitement du transsexualisme," *Perspectives Psy*. 36, no. 4 (1997).

Czermak, Marcel, and Henry Frignet. *Sur l'identité sexuelle. A propos du transsexualisme*. Vol. 2. Paris: Ed. de l'Association freudienne internationale, 1996.

Dual, Sandra. *Rencontre du troisième sexe*. Toulon: Ed. Gérard Blanc, 1999.

Graille, Patrick. *Les Hermaphrodites aux XVIIe et XVIIIe siècles*. Paris: Les Belles Lettres, 2001.

Krafft-Ebing, Richard von. *Psychopathia sexualis*. Paris: G. Carré, 1895. [Published in English as *Psychopathia Sexualis*.]

Oppenheimer, Agnès. "La Psychanalyse à l'épreuve du transsexualisme," *Perspectives Psy* 36, no. 4 (1997).

Pirani, Denise. "Quand les lumières de ta ville s'éteignent: minorités et clandestinité à Paris." Doctoral thesis. (n. p.) 1997.

Prochoix. *Transsexuel(les): le 3' genre?* no. 23 (2002).

Steinberg, Sylvie. *La Confusion des sexes, le travestissement de la Renaissance à la Révolution*. Paris: Fayard, 2001.

Le Transsexualisme en Europe. Strasbourg, France: Ed. du Conseil de l'Europe, 2000.

—*Biphobia; Gayphobia; Heterosexism; Lesbophobia; Symbolic Order; Violence.*

TREASON

The likening of homosexuals to traitors is a recurring theme in homophobic rhetoric. Since the end of the nineteenth century, this accusation, based on irrational arguments, has been the result of numerous political and military **scandals** implicating homosexuals.

In the collective imagination, the homosexual is often seen as "the other." He is a stranger, and one who voluntarily places himself on the fringe of society, be it familial or national. His conduct, analyzed in terms of immediate pleasure, is considered egotistical and narcissistic: by privileging a form of non-reproductive sexuality, the homosexual represents a threat that places civilization itself in **peril**. As such, he represents a threat to the social order. In fact, detractors also believe that the homosexual does not hesitate to breach class and social barriers in order to find new partners, thus endangering society's recognized hierarchies. Finally, seen as effeminate, the gay male is often accused of being ambivalent, weak, and gossipy, stereotypical traits of the female gender. Consequently, in times of crisis, homosexuals are, alongside other stigmatized minorities, the designated scapegoats for public condemnation.

The image of the homosexual as traitor also persists given that homosexuality is, in any given country or region, often considered a foreign import. In the eleventh century, it was considered an "Arab taste"; in the thirteenth century, it became a "French **vice**," then the "Italian vice" from the fourteenth to the sixteenth century, and finally the "English vice" from the eighteenth to the nineteenth century. In the East, homosexuality was generally viewed as a "Western vice"; and in places such as Africa, it was known as the "White vice." The controversial **Eulenburg affair** (1907–09), surrounding a series of court-martials and trials regarding accusations of homosexual conduct among prominent members of German Kaiser Wilhelm II's cabinet, resulted in homosexuality being referred to as a "German vice" in England and France. During World War I, however, the accusation of homosexuality took on a particularly threatening aspect. In *Le Temps retrouvé* (the last volume of *Remembrance of Things Past*, also known as *In Search of Lost Time*), Marcel Proust underlines this change in perspective: "Since the war, the tone had changed. The **inversion** of the baron was not the only thing denounced, but also his alleged German citizenship: 'Frau Bosch,' 'Frau van den Bosch,' were the usual nicknames given to Mr. de Charlus." In **England**, Member of Parliament Noel Pemberton Billing orchestrated a veritable witch-hunt against homosexuals; in 1918, he published an article in his journal *Imperialist* entitled "The First 47,000," which claimed that 47,000 Britons were being blackmailed by the German Secret Service for being homosexual. For his part, the journalist Arnold White declared that

German homosexuals were "systematically seducing" young British soldiers.

In the years between the wars, suspicions of treason were most often political in nature. The flourishing of a gay subculture in European capitals such as Berlin, London, and Paris was regarded with suspicion by a public haunted by fears of homosexual **contagion**; the development of militant gay groups further fed conspiracy rumors. During the same period, a group of British intellectuals, which included poets and writers such as W. H. Auden and Stephen Spender, was dubbed Homintern (short for "Homosexual Comintern") as a means of publicly declaring their communist sympathies and their association to a homosexual network. In **France**, meanwhile, the menace of a possible allegiance between communists and homosexuals was taken seriously: in certain military ports such as Toulon and Brest, where prostitution of sailors was a common occurrence, surveillance files were established in order to draw up a list of "public establishments frequented by gay sailors," so that "communist and gay propaganda" could be thoroughly recorded. After World War II, such homophobic **rhetoric** surfaced in the United States: Senator Joseph **McCarthy**'s witch-hunt against "the Reds" during the 1950s also included a campaign against homosexuals, orchestrated by Nebraska Senator Kenneth Wherry, who claimed notably that during the war, the State Department had been dominated by a homosexual elite that was prone to blackmail and that nearly "6,000 perverts" had infiltrated every level of government. Ironically, many of McCarthy's close friends and associates, such as his advisor Roy M. Cohn and FBI chief J. Edgar **Hoover**, were themselves "shameful" homosexuals. This homophobic crusade, which resulted in the firing of thousands of civil servants, had repercussions elsewhere in the world, notably in Great Britain, where the "Spies of Cambridge," Guy Burgess, Anthony Blunt, and Donald Maclean (who had defected to the East), represented the apogee of anti-gay paranoia in a context that once again connected homosexuality to **communism** and treason, portraying it as an offence against national security.

However, if during the 1920s, communist parties (especially the German KPD) had demonstrated a certain support for gay demands, their attitude toward homosexuals remained ambiguous. Starting in 1934, at a time when the USSR was establishing homophobic legislation, the Soviet party line thereafter likened ho-

mosexuality to a "fascist **perversion**." As for the Nazis in **Germany**, if it is true that certain Nazi groups, such as the SA, played on a homoerotic esthetic and valued virile relations, homosexuals themselves were, however, quickly eliminated. The accusation of treason took on a new visage: Nazi ideology regarded the homosexual as a degenerate, a traitor to the race who endangered the expansion of the Germanic state and therefore must be eliminated. However, despite the persecutions inflicted upon gays and lesbians under the Third Reich, the link suggested between homosexuality and **fascism** did not disappear quickly.

At times, the accusation of treason, along with many other homophobic stereotypes, was internalized by homosexuals. In 1942, French writer Maurice Sachs, who was both Jewish and gay, immigrated to Germany, where he worked most notably (and seemingly inexplicably) for the Wehrmacht secret service; imprisoned a year later in 1943, one story of his death is that he was lynched by his cellmates. Others, after the fashion of Jean Genet, succeeded in transforming disloyalty into glory and a way of life. In a society that viewed the homosexual as a **criminal**, those homosexuals who approved of being linked to treason saw in it a confirmation of their existence on the fringe of society; in a way, a proclamation of support for the enemy. Genet himself, whether he was working alongside the Black Panthers or Palestinian fighters, or whether he supported groups like the Red Army Faction, was always on the side of the excluded. In this way, homophobic prejudice is replaced by a new definition of fidelity and loyalty which flouts traditional patriotism.

—*Florence Tamagne*

Bérubé, Allan. *Coming Out Under Fire: Lesbian and Gay Americans and the Military During World War II*. New York: The Free Press, 1989
———. "Marching to a Different Drummer: Lesbian and Gay GI's in World War II." In *Hidden from History: Reclaiming the Gay and Lesbian Past*. Edited by George Chauncey, Martin Duberman, and Martha Vicinus. New York: New American Library, 1989.
Corber, Robert J. *Homosexuality in Cold War America: Resistance and the Crisis of Masculinity*. Durham, NC: Duke Univ. Press, 1997.
Davenport-Hines, Richard. *Sex, Death and Punishment: Attitudes to Sex and Sexuality in Britain since the Renaissance*. London: Fontana Press, 1990.
Gury, Christian. *L'Honneur perdu d'un capitaine homosexuel en*

1880. Paris: Kimé, 1999.

Raczymow, Henri. *Maurice Sachs ou les travaux forcés de la frivolité.* Paris, Gallimard, 1988.

Tamagne, Florence. *Histoire de l'homosexualité en Europe: Berlin, Londres, Paris, 1919–1939.* Paris: Le Seuil, 2000. [Published in the US as *A History of Homosexuality in Europe: Berlin, London, Paris, 1919–1939.* New York: Algora, 2004.]

White, Edmund. *Jean Genet.* Paris: Gallimard, 1993. [Published in the US as *Genet: A Biography.* New York: Knopf, 1993.]

—Armed Forces; Contagion; Eulenburg Affair, the; Hoover, J. Edgar; McCarthy, Joseph; North America; Peril; Rhetoric; Turing, Alan.

TREATMENT

Historically, the world of **medicine** has had two objectives when dealing with the issue of homosexuality: one, the curing of "inflicted" individuals, and another, a general concern for preventative measures in the name of "public health." In this sense, the history of how homosexuality has been treated by the medical establishment is comparable to the history of the treatment of tuberculosis or alcoholism. In **France**, for example, homosexuality was classified as one of the "social scourges," as pronounced by the 1960 **Mirguet** amendment in which homosexuality was officially equated with alcoholism and prostitution. At the same time, the repeated failures of medical science to "cure" homosexuals encouraged a great deal of "originality" among proposed methods that also opened the door to charlatans. As such, gay men and lesbians were often guinea pigs for a number of "behavioral re-education" methods along with alcoholics, drug addicts, and "psychopaths." Paradoxically, the question of treatment was often advanced by professionals who had never any fundamental role in the medical theory of homosexuality. Magnus **Hirschfeld**, the German physician, sexologist, and gay rights activist, never felt treatment was an issue due to his own homosexuality; Richard von Krafft-Ebing, the Austro-German psychiatrist and sexologist, did not believe in curative possibilities (except possibly with bisexuals); and Sigmund Freud in no way believed that his method of analysis could be useful in treating homosexuals. Among such theorists, only endocrinologists, given the nature of their disci-pline, were in favor of treatment—in particular hormonal therapy, which, in the framework of research protocols, fortunately involved only a few individual subjects, mainly in the United States and, in a more sinister way, Nazi **Germany**.

More frequent among methods in the first half of the twentieth century to treat homosexuals were therapeutic ones employed by psychiatrists designed to cure their patients. Among the multitude of available psychotherapies, founded on a mechanistic reading of Freud's *Three Essays on the Theory of Sexuality*, the main attempts were based principally on aversion therapy, which employed tactics such as emetics or electro-shock treatments in order to incite "disgust" in the individual toward his objects of desire. However, after World War II, many cases of "social deviance" were treated through lobotomies, particularly in the United States and in the former USSR.

Today, many who consider homosexuals to be "incorrigibles" who need to be corrected still believe that they can and should be cured. Many **Middle Eastern** countries use forced internment. Moreover, in the United States, groups of "**ex-gays**" (those who have renounced their homosexuality, often as a result of a religious awakening) suggest reparative therapies, a singular mix of prayer and psychotherapy, techniques which are increasingly supported by the religious right, which orchestrates sophisticated campaigns to promote the "rehabilitation" of homosexuals. Obviously, the success of this tactic is rather limited, as one can imagine, but the rise of such groups, notably in **Latin America** and **Southeast Asia,** supports the notion that the medical treatment of homosexuality is not only desirable, but also is possible. Further, recent **genetic** research in the United States that suggests that homosexual desire is natural and preordained ironically leaves the door open to the idea of "retroactive" therapy, in which eugenics (through prenatal diagnosis and modification of the incriminating gene) is used to "finally" eradicate homosexuality at the source. Finally, however, if all the proposed treatments fail, there is always the "final solution" proposed by Dr Paul Cameron who, speaking at the 1985 Conservative Political Action Conference in the US, said, "Unless we get medically lucky, in three or four years, one of the options discussed will be the extermination of homosexuals."

—*Pierre-Olivier de Busscher*

Cameron, Paul. "What Causes Homosexual Desire and

Can It Be Changed?" Washington, DC: Family Research Institute, 1992.

Katz, Jonathan. *Gay American History: Lesbians and Gay Men in the U.S.A.* New York: Crowell Company, 1976.

Kristof, Nicholas D. "China Using Electrodes to 'Cure' Homosexuals." *The New York Times* (January 29, 1990).

Rosario, Vernon (ed.). *Science and Homosexualities.* New York/London: Routledge, 1997.

—Biology; Degeneracy; Endocrinology; Ex-Gay; Fascism; Genetics; Hirschfeld, Magnus; Inversion; Medicine; Medicine, Legal; Mirguet, Paul; Perversions; Psychiatry; Psychoanalysis; Turing, Alan; Violence.

TURING, Alan

British mathematician Alan Turing (1912–54), often considered to be the father of modern computer science, remains one of the most famous victims of homophobia brought about by the hysteria caused by **McCarthyism** that found its way to Great Britain. The history of science will remember Turing for the major role he played during World War II as a code breaker, which allowed the Allies to decipher the German military code known as "Enigma." In 1952, however, the respected professor's life at the University of Manchester became a nightmare. After a brief relationship with a nineteen-year-old working-class youth named Arnold Murray, Turing discovered that his apartment had been robbed by one of Murray's friends. After filing a complaint, during the investigation, he admitted to having sexual relations with Murray. His testimony resulted in his and Murray's arrest for the crime of "gross indecency," punishable by two years' imprisonment. Both men pled guilty, but while Murray was released unconditionally, Turing was placed on probation and with compulsory medical **treatment**. At the same time, Turing was relieved of all duties relating to the encryption and decryption of code, as he was perceived as a security risk. He was also forced to take female hormones for a year in order to suppress his libido, and developed female traits as a result of the treatment, including breasts. Additionally, his every move was scrutinized as well as those of his associates (particularly his foreign friends), and he was physically separated from others at work, in a position specifically created for him at his university. Despondent, Turing eventually committed suicide in 1954 by eating a cyanide-laced apple.

Alan Turing's destiny was exactly that of an individual who was perceived as a "threat" or **"peril"** to national security because he was both a homosexual and a high-level scientist working in sensitive areas. His death made him a martyr in the homosexual cause; his story was the subject of the play *Breaking the Code* written by Hugh Whitemore, as well the opera *The Turing Test* written by Julian Wagstaff.
—*Pierre-Olivier de Busscher*

Hodges, Andrew. *Alan Turing: The Enigma.* New York: Simon & Schuster, 1983.

—Eulenburg Affair, the; Hoover, J. Edgar; McCarthy, Joseph; Medicine; North America; Scandal; Suicide; Treason; Violence.

U

UNITED STATES. *See* North America

UNIVERSALISM/DIFFERENTIALISM

The concepts of universalism and differentialism form an opposing binary that regularly serve as the basis for many intellectual debates in France. While this divide exists in many other countries, it has taken on remarkable significance in France, a remarkable importance, *a priori* defining positions, arguments, and theories. It has been—and still is—of crucial importance in dialogue concerning racism and sexism notably. Likewise on the question of homosexuality, as the debates regarding **PaCS** (Pacte civil de solidarité; Civil solidarity pact) have shown, these two poles have often been successful. Explicitly or not, the idea according to which the universal must transcend differences and impose itself upon them is present in many arguments, opposing themselves to differentialism, according to which identity builds itself first as a primary and unwavering difference. Truth be told, within the intellectual arena in France, universalism is clearly the dominant position, and as for the rest, no one claims to be explicitly on the side of differentialism, which appears mostly as an argumentative strategy that allows for the denouncing of political adversaries. But in reality, universalism can just as well serve as a strategic **rhetoric**, in that one philosophy or another may be used in a homophobic sense, sometimes by the same individuals, thus producing contradictory statements that nonetheless condemn homosexuality.

Normative Universalism
Conceived of in order to emancipate the individual from social, economic, and cultural determinism implicit in feudal society, political-judicial universalism is at the heart of the Enlightenment's rationalism. History, however, has demonstrated the ambiguity of such "liberation" when it serves, notably, to justify colonial paternalism. As a specific stance, universalism can become the strategy for a dominant group claiming to liberate another from the idiosyncratic "chains" to which it seems tied. This is evident in the heterosexist argument: In the name of the *de facto* heterosexual majority, homosexuality is dreaded as a specific deviance by **medicine**, **psychiatry**, or Christian morality; homosexuals thus being, according to Foucault's formula, "incorrigibles that need correcting." Human dignity and homosexuality are thus considered incompatible. In the universalist mirror, the homosexual difference appears to be an outgrowth, a defect, if not an outright crime. As physically and mentally healthy human beings, we cannot identify ourselves with this anomaly; the universalist idea of physical and mental hygiene seems to forbid it. In this scheme that all of humanity supposes fecundity and birth, heterosexual universalism is simply the expression of nature being conscious of itself and its pervasive laws. Thus, the homosexual is considered a moral or genetic monstrosity, situated somewhere between the thoughtless fool, the perverted libertine, and the unfortunate trisomic. In turn, as an object of curiosity, hate, compassion, and therapeutic trials, the homosexual is the incarnation of unacceptable, even aberrant, difference; it was as if citizenship were granted to the plague or cholera. From this perspective, to a certain extent, the homosexual is not a human being in the sense that humankind is a political animal, as his morals by definition contradict the laws of universalism required to form a society. He can have no rights, other than the right to change and to fall into line. His difference creates irrevocable controversy.

The Tribunal of Universal Reason

In recent years, universalist arguments have been especially put to use by an intellectualized homophobic rhetoric. (Notably in France during the debate over PaCS.) It is no longer homosexuals as individuals who are attacked, blamed, and pathologized, but homosexuality in general; a form of flawed logic. Going well beyond nature and biology, current heterosexist universalism bases itself, among other things, on a universal ontology, a "fact of reason," **gender differences**, and their complementary relationship to one another. Homosexuality is thus no longer only criticized for being "**unnatural**," spurning biological laws that impose the male/female relations in order to perpetuate the species and escape **sterility**. If homosexuality, reduced to a simple "desire of sameness," cannot be recognized by the state at the same level as heterosexuality, it is because homosexuality is ignorant of **symbolic order**, fundamental **otherness**, the "ultimate end of thought" (Françoise Héritier), the "hard core of reason," and the "universal principle of non-contradiction" (Pierre Legendre). Mixing logic and biology, these enigmatic assertions surprisingly recall cryptic and intimidating pre-Socratic fragments, during a time when the lack of empirical knowledge allowed the most audacious ideas to flower. In this case, intelligence, according in the Fragments of Anaxagoras, which causes motion and coming into being, is nothing more than a particular type of attraction between opposites, i.e. that of the *opposite sex*. Thus, it is ironic that this universalistic and heterosexist logic seem rather dismissive of ancient Greek thought, which, largely developed in a social context of homoerotic desire!

The Differentialist Symptom & Heterosexist Differentialism

Confronted with these banishments of correct law and good logic, homosexuality attempts to compose itself as a viable difference, both in human and social terms. In this historical process of progressive legitimization, the **decriminalization** of homosexuality, and the growing acknowledgement that it is not a mental illness, constitute a fundamental step. Today, officially, at least in Western societies, the homosexual is no longer considered a **criminal**, nor a sick person identified with a shameful or pathological difference, as had been the case in the Soviet Union under Stalinism, which saw gays and lesbians sent to **gulags** under Article 121 of the penal code. The affirmation of homosexual culture, sensibility, and humanity, from university conferences to Lesbian and Gay Pride celebrations, attempts to present an image of homosexuality as a worthy and possible difference, and that the attraction to people of the same gender is an *anthropological universal*, an omnipresent virtuality in all societies. Espoused by a good number of intellectuals, the homosexual cause becomes a just and universal one, in the refusal to make sexual orientation a criterion of **discrimination**: the idea that "they have a right to be different."

However, the differentialist argument, necessary for the affirmation of a healthy and happy identity, arouses perverse reactions: on one hand, the universalist, normative, and heterosexist argument classically interprets it as a *symptom*, claiming that the obsession with difference would lead to narcissism, the refusal of otherness, and immaturity. On the other hand, it is overtaken by a heterosexist argument that is progressive, liberal, **tolerant**, and happy with a festive sexual plurality. However, this sympathetic position has its limits as soon as one leaves the private sphere: for the same person, the father quickly overshadows the close friend. There is a sense that, if at night, a plurality of sexual practices can exist, come morning, there can only be one symbolic, heterosexual, order. The homosexual is required to behave differently in specific environments or situations; any open expression of homosexuality in public is likened to **exhibitionism**, even **proselytism**.

The differentialist argument thus tends to lock homosexuality away as a passionate research subject in the intellectual sphere, or in the private sphere of an extremely exotic universe; and each time this occurs, the heterosexist presupposition of public space and law remains unchanged.

Segregationist Differentialism or Obligation to be Different

The terrain of difference is, therefore, extremely slippery: the (theoretical) right to be different quickly becomes the difference between (actual) rights. According to heterosexist and differentialist logic, at best, the homosexual deserves his or her own specific space. Respect becomes social estrangement. Social recognition of a difference in sexual orientation is not trivial; it is in part the foundation of another distinct society. A tacit social contract is broken, and scission becomes inevitable. Segregationalism appears to be an unfortunate compromise, born from a blockage, between the guardians of heterosexist order and radical gay militants. The former keep the threat of gender confusion at a safe distance, preserving the universality of the model, while the latter are finally free to live their lives completely by their sexual orientation: to each his own, in his own **ghetto**, whether homosexual or heterosexual, each defined by his sexual practice and reduced to it, from an **essentialist** perspective. Homosexuals and heterosexuals remain linked by the smallest common denominator: the idea of giving sexual orientation a determined value. This retreat results in the exclusion from common law and by the eventual granting of special rights, such as PaCS, allowing for the preservation of the universalist illusion (since it applies to everyone, gay or straight) all the while confirming the differentialist reality, which objectively underscores the **discrimination** that forbids **marriage** for gays and lesbians.

Accepted in the private sphere, between *consenting* adults (as practices that most resemble crimes and misdemeanors), homosexuality once again becomes problematic when it aspires to universal heterosexual tasks, starting with the ability to become parents. Having children is the clearest symbol of a heterosexual prerogative in the sphere of perpetuating the human race, to the point of justifying beforehand marriage as a privileged, universal form of union for the purpose of conception. According to this view, heterosexual couples, being the only ones who are capable of biologically conceiving, would be the most *appropriate* choice for raising them. **Psychoanalysis** offers the arguments of the universality of the Oedipus complex in the make-up of the personality. The child who is raised and educated by homosexuals would be condemned to psychological stagnation or deviation; he would literally be denied access to a collective unconsciousness, to universal gender and generational differences, to the symbolic. The refusal of otherness is dangerously transmitted from social parent to child. In this view, homosexuality should remain what it is, a sexual and affective particularity: it should not acquire a following, neither publicly nor privately. It cannot aspire to institutionalization; it must remain shapeless, dispersed. It is the difference that individuals encounter by chance, on the fringe of the socially, logically, and biologically necessary universal.

What do we say then to gays and lesbians who, nonetheless, desire equal rights, or even a visibility equal to that of heterosexuals? Universalists would argue that by defining themselves thusly, they are renouncing themselves, committing a sort of crime against social

biodiversity, initiating a standardization of their difference, a regrettable decline of their folklore (no doubt linked to the sulfurous perfume of the forbidden). In short, that they acknowledge the acceptance of a heterosexual order: *an assault on their own difference.* On the other hand, they are accused of wanting their cake and eating it too; of wanting to profit from heterosexual rights without rising to responsibility of universality. *An attack on the universal.* They are thus commanded to be like everyone else when they appear different, and of being different when they attempt to be like everyone else.

Without a doubt, it would be progressive to do away with all need to classify the "homosexual species," a need that necessitates, beforehand, a universal gender. Thus, two blends are put into practice: on one hand, heterosexuality, general, becomes universal. On the other hand, homosexuality, different, becomes **abnormal**. By ceasing to criminalize homosexual practices, the Revolutionary penal code in France initiated the general rule of legal indifference with regards to each person's sexual life. The road toward a social indifference with respect to sexual orientation remains to be discovered.

—*Dalibor Frioux*

Agacinski, Sylviane. *Politique des sexes*. Paris: Le Seuil, 2001.

Delphy, Christine. "L'Humanitarisme républicain contre les mouvements homos," *Politique: La revue*, no. 5 (1997).

D'Emilio, John. *Sexual Politics, Sexual Communities: The Making of a Homosexual Minority in the United States, 1940–1970*. Chicago: Univ. of Chicago Press, 1983.

Elacheff, Caroline, Antoine Garapon, Nathalie Heinigh, Françoise Héritier, Aldo Naouri, Paul Veyne, and Heinz Wismann. "Ne laissons pas la critique du PaCS à la droite!" *Le Monde* (January 27, 1999).

Fassin, Eric. "L'Epouvantail américain: penser la discrimination française," *Vacarme*, no. 4/5 (1997).

Favret-Saada, Jeanne. "La-Pensée-Levi-Strauss." *Journal des anthropologues*, no. 82–83. (n.d.)

Fraïsse, Geneviève. *Muse de la raison*. Paris: Folio, 1995.

Lehendre, Pierre. "Nous assistons à une escalade de l'obscurantisme," *Le Monde* (October 23, 2001.)

Macé-Scaron, Joseph. *La Tentation communautaire*. Paris: Pion, 2001.

Pollak, Michael. "L'Homosexualité masculine, ou: le bonheur dans le ghetto?" *Communications*, no. 35 (1982). Revised edition in *Sexualités occidentals*. Edited by Philippe Ariès and André Béjin. Paris: Le Seuil, 1984.

Théry, Irène. "Différence des sexes et différence des generations," *Esprit* (December 1996).

Further Reading:

Spektorowski, Alberto. "The French New Right: Differentialism and the Idea of Ethnophilian Exclusionism." *Polity* 33, no. 2 (Winter 2000).

—Abnormal; Against Nature; Anti-PaCS; Communitarianism; Decriminalization (France); Essentialism/Constructionism; Exhibitionism; Gender Differences; Ghetto; Heterosexism; Marriage; Medicine; Otherness; Philosophy; Psychiatry; Psychoanalysis; Rhetoric; Sterility; Symbolic Order; Tolerance.

UNNATURAL. *See* Against Nature

UTILITARIANISM

Utilitarianism is a philosophical doctrine formulated by Jeremy Bentham and John Stuart Mill that establishes a mathematical rapport between the individual and the collective. Its main implications lay within moral, political, and economic spheres, as well as the sphere of criminal law.

In Chapter One of *An Introduction to the Principles of Morals and Legislation*, Jeremy Bentham states the following: "Nature has placed mankind under the governance of two sovereign masters, *pain* and *pleasure*." Bentham imagines utilitarianism as being founded on the principle of utility, which he synthesizes into a basic formula: it is the "principle of the greatest happiness for the largest number of individuals." Happiness is likened to pleasure and can be quantified in terms of probability and duration, according to an "arithmetics of pleasures." Thus, utilitarianism proposes reforms allowing for the best possible functioning of society that encourages human beings to search for happiness (maximum pleasure and minimum sorrow) in the most natural way possible.

Throughout his life, Jeremy Bentham (1748–1832) wrote hundreds of manuscript pages on the subject of homosexuality, but none were published during his lifetime. Even to this day, few of these texts are available. One exception is "Essay on Paederasty," 1785, in which Bentham formulates a strong utilitarianist criticism of penal measures directed against the crime of homosexuality by analyzing the foundation of hostility.

In it, he attempts to determine what exactly the crime is and questions whether it is a crime at all.

None of the arguments opposed to private homosexual relations between consenting adults stand up to utilitarian analysis, as homosexual relations do not produce any primary harm, only pleasure. While, like many progressive authors of his day, Bentham expresses a certain disapproval of homosexual practices, he concludes that it is impossible to determine a logical basis for the severity with which such practices are punished. Thus, Bentham questions the legal notion of a "crime **against nature**," which is neither a crime against peace nor law and order. Moreover, he argues that homosexuality does not harm women, since **marriage** remains the most common bond, nor does it harm population growth, for if an increase in population were a social priority, it would be logically necessary to forbid celibacy among priests and monks. Furthermore, homosexual relations between men are sources of pleasure that do not lead to unwanted pregnancy; they represent more of a social benefit than a social problem. Louis Crompton states that, in his final manuscripts on the subject, Bentham goes even further, abandoning the conventional language of disapproval and considering sexuality without the objective of procreation.

In 1814 and 1815, Bentham wrote many long critiques on traditional homophobia, which he regards as an irrational prejudice leading to cruelty and intolerance. When Bentham explores the basis of hostility towards homosexuality, he discovers its reasoning in (1) the propensity to confuse physical impurity with moral impurity, (2) a philosophical prejudice against pleasure, and (3) religion. Utilitarians use, notably, the notion of a third party against whom the crime is committed, which allows for the development of a new concept for qualifying behavior that was merely opposed to the official morality as criminal. The reference to the third party makes the existence of a precisely identifiable harm necessary, and leads to the condemnation of an action committed against an individual or an institution only, rather than the classical moral repression of the individual acting against him or herself.

The **philosophy** was very influential during the debates surrounding the **decriminalization** of homosexuality in English-speaking countries. The utilitarian notion of happiness is linked to other fundamental notions of English philosophy: namely individual liberty and the protection of **privacy**, which leads to the principles of minimal interference of the state, and the protection of the individual against the state's meddling in moral, political, and sexual matters of choice.

During the debate on decriminalization in Great Britain that began with the Wolfenden Commission's report in 1957—recommending the decriminalization of homosexual acts between consenting adults based on classical liberalism—H. L. H. Hart expressed utilitarian arguments *(Law, Liberty and Morality),* unlike Patrick **Devlin**, who formulated a series of classical arguments for partisans of **criminalization**.

Hart asserted that the law cannot prohibit homosexuality under the pretense that certain persons will feel morally assaulted at the thought of relations of which they disapprove occurring in the private sphere. "Punishing people because they cause this type of affliction would be equivalent to punishing them simply because others object to what they are doing; and the only liberty that could coexist with this extension of utilitarian principles is the liberty to do things against which no one can seriously object. Such liberty would be absolutely in vain and useless."

Hart also exposed that penal law inflicts suffering by requiring individuals to repress supposedly antisocial impulses. However, there is a radical difference between the homosexual act and "ordinary crime," and this difference must be taken into account in any legislation regarding homosexuality. The treatment of relations between persons of the same sex as criminal leads to a personal repression of the most fundamental impulses. When a state imposes a sexual morality, it leads to repercussions on society and on individuals that go much further than laws simply destined to limit underworld criminality.

Beyond its historical role in homosexual decriminalization, utilitarianism, with regards to reflection on homosexuality and gay **parenting**, allows for the application of the following principles: the individual can be dissociated from the collective; the happiness of the individual does not necessarily supersede the need for universal application of a society's morals.

Thus, the preponderance of utilitarianism, in association with humanism and **Protestantism** in Northern European countries—in which each individual is given the most likely chance of happiness in a society—brought about the first civil dispositions favorable to gays and lesbians. The first legal unions of same-sex couples without consequence on gay parenthood were adopted by Denmark (1989), Norway (1993), Sweden (1994), and the Netherlands (1997). Icelandic law (1996) on cohabitation or common-law marriage, and the Dutch proposition regarding changes to family law (1998) are also relatively favorable to gay parenting.

—*Flora Leroy-Forgeot*

Bentham, Jeremy. *Essay on Paederasty*. Lille, France: GayKitschCamp, 2003.

Crompton, Louis. "Jeremy Bentham's Essay on 'Paederasty': An Introduction." *Journal of Homosexuality* no. 3–4 and 4–1 (1978). (Fragments in Crompton, Louis. *Byron and Greek Love*. Berkeley: Univ. of California Press, 1985.)

Hart, H. L. A. *Law, Liberty and Morality*. Oxford: Oxford Univ. Press (The Harry Camp Lectures): 1963.

Leroy-Forgeot, Flora. *Histoire juridique de l'homosexualité en Europe*. Paris: Presses universitaires de France, 1997.

———, and Caroline Mécary. *Le Couple homosexuel et le droit*. Paris: Odile Jacob, 2001.

—*Criminalization; Decriminalization (France); Devlin, Patrick; England; Philosophy; Tolerance.*

V

VATICAN. *See* Catholic Church

VIAU, Théophile de

Théophile de Viau (1590–1626), a French baroque poet and dramatist, was born in Clairac to a **Protestant** family of minor nobility. His life was that of a poet-adventurer; he accompanied wandering comedians at the end of his adolescence, and became involved in different intrigues in the company of great lords of his time. He showed them how to live a life of elegant libertinage, something at which he happily excelled. After a sojourn in the United Provinces (now the Netherlands) and **England**, he returned to **France**, but in 1619 was driven out again due to his "rhymes unworthy of a Christian as much in faith as in dirt." In 1622, he renounced his Protestant faith, but this concession would not disarm the querulous zeal of Jesuits Garasse and Voisin, who denounced him in 1623 and attacked his works and his contributions to the *Parnasse satyrique* (an anonymous manuscript of licentious verses believed to be his). Judged in absentia, the poet was condemned to be burned at the stake. While he was out of the country, the sentence was carried out in effigy, but the poet was eventually caught as he was heading toward England and imprisoned in Paris for almost two years. In the meantime, scholars and writers actively debated Théophile's fate, resulting in numerous published pamphlets that were both for and against him. His lover, the young poet Jacques Vallée des Barreaux, and a few other friends pleaded the court on his behalf. In the end, he was banished again. However, the horrible conditions of an unjust detention from 1623 to 1625 would be the end of him: he died the following year.

During this affair, the various spies and witnesses, in concert with Jesuit determination and highly placed pressure, all contributed to what was at stake: by condemning Théophile the poet, authorities were condemning libertinage in France. Théophile was clearly an ideal target: because of his unapologetic behavior and beliefs, this "prince of poets" constituted, at least for his adversaries, a figure who was both eminently symbolic and relatively vulnerable. Attacks against Théophile were concentrated on two fronts, irreligiousness and sodomy, and the idea that both were irrevocably and naturally linked. From the start, Father Garasse, one of Théophile's principal opponents, was determined to bring down both of these sins. In an enormous *in quarto* (booklet) of more than 1,000 pages supporting the indictment, entitled *La Doctrine curieuse des beaux esprits de ce temps, ou prétendus tels* (The curious doctrine of beautiful minds of the present times, or pretended as such), he affirmed:

> I call Impious and Atheists, those who are more advanced in malice, who have the impudence of proffering horrible blasphemies against God; who commit abominable brutalities, who publish in sonnets their execrable infamies, who make Paris a Gomorrah, who get the *Parnasse satyrique* printed, who have this unfortunate advantage that they are so unnatural in their way of living, that one would not dare to refute them point by point for fear of teaching their **vices** and making the whiteness of the paper blush.

This declaration by the Jesuit reveals the tension between his wish of anathema and the necessity of silence. This is a constant of moralist rhetoric: on these abominable questions, rather than eloquent diatribe, a cold silence is often best, which prevents those who would not have had thought of it to want suddenly to try it. Nevertheless—and this is the paradox stressed by Father Garasse—those who commit these deeds "have this unfortunate advantage" of being able to practice them without being explicitly blamed or condemned. In short, the silence, which was supposed to contain licentiousness, was at great risk of favoring it. Given this, was it not better to denounce it very loudly?

Such was the case for Father Garasse, who freely vented his ire in an inflamed monologue:

> In times past, when there was still a bit of feeling
> and piety in the souls of good Frenchmen, on hear-
> ing the sole word of Sodomy, there would be talk
> of burning alive he who would only be suspected,
> and today, we see a book that is sold publicly in
> the palace's galleries and which has on the front an
> execrable sonnet.... Alas! Flames of **Sodom**, where
> are you? Whereas men are closing their eyes! Why
> do you not devour this abomination! Why do you
> not avenge the quarrels of God your Master, whose
> name is being profaned? Why do you not reduce
> to ashes these books which are more shameless
> than the houses and walls of Seboim, of Adama, of
> Sodom and Gomorrah ever were?

But at the same time, Garasse feared that divine anger would not distinguish between the innocent and the guilty in the same fire: "God's will that the same punishment happen and fall on the city of Paris, to purge the Sodomies and the brutalities of a hundred villains, who are able to bring down on us the fires of Heaven and engulf in their just punishment the innocence of 100,000 good souls. *Obsecro ne irascatur juror tuus Domine.*" The city thus had to be purged before God did it himself.

The trial of Théophile de Viau confirmed for many the link between sodomy and libertinage. This link was not evident at the beginning of the seventeenth century; the image of a sodomite certainly evoked sin, but in the wake of Théophile, the sodomite was more directly linked to the culture of **debauchery**, an image which subsists still in today's representations.

Finally, Théophile's case shows the paradoxical usage of silence in social discourse. Even if it was at the origin of his crime, the question of sodomy was often dodged and constituted a blind spot of the trial. With the exception of Garasse and a few others, attacks against Théophile subtly used detours and circumlocutions: was it best to remain silent, or to denounce publicly? Even today, on these questions, literary critics maintain an embarrassing silence. They admire the work of the poet, but prefer to forget certain personal aspects of the man, which in their eyes bring his reputation into disrepute, as if one could, especially with Théophile, separate the man from the poet. In this sense, they ex-

tend the opinion of the famous critic Antoine Adam, who, in 1935, was enthusiastic about Théophile, finding dramatic qualities of style, heart, and spirit, but to which he added: "Let us not talk about the infamous vice of which he was reproached, and in which it is not doubtful that he participated."

Just as well no one ever talks about it—or nearly.
—*Louis-Georges Tin*

Adam, Antoine. *Théophile de Viau et la libre pensée française en 1620.* Paris: Droz, 1935; Geneva: Slatkine Reprints, 1965.

Godard, Didier. *Le Goût de Monsieur, l'homosexualité masculine au XVIIe siècle.* Montblanc: H & O Editions, 2002.

Lachèvre, Frédéric. *Le Libertinage devant le Parlement de Paris, le procès du poète Théophile de Viau.* Paris: Champion, 1909.

Lever, Maurice. *Les Bûchers de Sodome.* Paris: Fayard, 1985.

Saba, Guido. *Fortunes et infortunes de Théophile de Viau, histoire de la critique suivie d'une bibliographie.* Paris: Klincksieck, 1997.

Viau, Théophile de. *Œuvres complètes.* Edited by Guido Saba. Paris: Nizet, 1978–87.

—*Abnormal; Against Nature; Bible, the; Censorship; Debauchery; Literature; Scandal; Sodom and Gomorrah; Theology; Vice; Wilde, Oscar.*

VICE

Moral harm and vice are not the same thing. Vice is an elaborate and precise notion which does not encompass all possible forms of reprobation. Technically, vice is the opposite of virtue: it is an acquired disposition to commit harmful acts on others or oneself. For homosexuality to be considered a vice, one would first have to show that it is acquired, i.e. a question of will, and second, that it is harmful to others or oneself. We can note that contemporary everyday language most often defines vice according to the first of these characteristics, which means that one is a slave to desires that are unhealthy, while classic thought appears to give more weight to the second characteristic.

Demonstrating the harmful character of homosexuality has not been easy historically. In his book *Christianity, Social Tolerance, and Homosexuality,* historian John Boswell traces the slow evolution of this idea, in particular the central role given to "Nature." Homosexuality only became a specific vice when the idea was introduced that it bears harm to Nature itself, and thus God's plan, of which it is the manifestation.

The publication of theologian Alain de Lille's *De Planctu naturae* (*The Complaint of Nature*) in the twelfth century is considered as an essential moment in the emergence of this notion of a sovereign nature. Nature is no longer the factual whole of spontaneously present beings in the world, but a legislator whose laws must be respected. Those who break these laws must be morally and severely condemned, as they adversely affect the order of the world.

In this perspective, the laws of nature can be discovered by observing animals, which are reputed to respect those laws. Curiously, an author such as Thomas Aquinas from the Middle Ages, who otherwise admitted the superiority and distinctiveness of humanity in relation to the rest of the animal kingdom, considered that in the matter of morals, animal behavior is the rule of human behavior. With bad faith that is surprising in such a rigorous author, Aquinas proposed the idea that given that homosexuality was not present in animals, it was morally wrong (this despite the fact the during the Middle Ages there was evidence put forward of homosexual behavior in certain animals, such as rabbits and weasels). But this argument applied to other human vices in addition to homosexuality, such as greed or drunkenness. As such, it is not sufficient evidence to make homosexuality the "supreme sin," as Aquinas referred to it in his *Summa Theologica*.

To distinguish homosexuality as the preeminent vice **against nature**, Aquinas had to introduce the idea that it was not only harmful to nature in general, but also that it was contrary to the very nature of the subject. Homosexuality was thus not only harmful to others (including Nature and God), but also to oneself.

We find a more elaborate version of this idea in Kant and his notion of "duty toward oneself." The central problem of Kantian sexual morality is the instrumentalization of bodies and the objectivization of persons. Kant perceived that erotic drive generally transforms the other into an object and does not respect it as a subject. This transformation into object obviously violates the moral imperative that postulates that one must never treat the other solely as a means, as he explained in *Foundations of the Metaphysics of Morals*. Moreover, Kant believed that the agent himself, in the sexual relation, agrees to become a simple means and not an end, and in this, he breaches the fundamental moral imperative: "The natural utilization that one sex makes of the sexual organs of the other is a sensual delight for which one of the parties gives him or herself to the other. In

this act, a man makes himself a thing, which contradicts the right of humanity in his individual self."

The Kantian solution to this moral problem is **marriage**: through marriage, the two future sexual partners publicly pledge to always respect each other, and to never consider the other solely as a means, but also as an end. Therefore, there can be no morally acceptable sexual relations outside marriage. However, this idea does not necessarily prove the heterosexual character of marriage: one can well imagine a contracted pledge of respect between two persons of the same sex, which would then open the possibility for them to have morally acceptable homosexual relations.

As for those who considered homosexuality a particularly serious vice, Kant then developed a new argument, more or less *ad hoc:* the idea of procreation as a normal end of human sexuality, which homosexuality evidently contravenes. One can also see in this argument a simple reformulation of the classic belief of vice that harms Nature itself.

As we understand it, classic thinking neglects, or maybe suggests, the question—nonetheless morally central—of the voluntary character of homosexuality. It was only in the nineteenth century with the introduction of psychiatric categories that this idea became significant. Under the general classification of "sexual **inversion**," French **medicine** distinguished the Uranian, who was the congenitally inverted, ill person who did not fall under moral judgment, from the pervert, who was voluntarily inverted. From a rhetorical point of view, it is only with this complete characterization that we can effectively speak of "vice." But it is also at this level of precision that the notion became more fragile and contestable. The concept of homosexuality as a vice defined as an acquired (and assumed) disposition to harm others (Nature) or self (as moral subject), proved to be short-lived. The voluntary nature of the homosexual tendency was questioned and criticized. In the postwar years, the most progressive psychologists and moralists stressed the involuntary character of the homosexual drive and, thus, rejected its assimilation to a form of vice.

At the end of the twentieth century, it became more difficult to rigorously conceive homosexuality as a vice, in that it is no longer thought of as an object of will. Condemnation of homosexuality is no longer commonly based on upholding moral order, but on anthropological, sociological, or psychoanalytical criteria. Popular morality will doubtlessly continue for a long time to name as "vice" what it instinctively wishes to censor, but it will no longer have theoretical foundations that will allow it to rigorously justify this aversion. In the history of the notion of homosexuality as a vice, we see the deployment of an idea, constructed and refined over seven centuries, but which finally lost all momentum due to its own vacuity.

—*Philippe Colomb*

Alain de Lille. *De Planctu naturae* (1176). Toronto: Pontifical Institute of Medieval Studies, 1980. [Published in English as *The Complaint of Nature*.]

Boswell, John. *Christianisme, tolérance sociale et homosexualité*. Paris: Gallimard, 1985. [Published in the US as *Christianity, Social Tolerance, and Homosexuality: Gay People in Western Europe from the Beginning of the Christian Era to the Fourteenth Century*. Chicago: Univ. of Chicago Press, 1980.]

Clifford, Allen, and Charles Berg. *Les Problèmes de l'homosexualité*. (Followed by *Ce que pense la population française de l'homosexualité*.) Paris: Les Yeux ouverts, 1962.

Foot, Philippa. *Virtues and Vices*. Berkeley: Univ. of California Press, 1978.

Kant, Immanuel. *Métaphysique des mœurs* (1796–97). In *Œuvres philosophiques, III. Les Derniers écrits*. Paris: Gallimard, 1986. [Published in English as *Foundations of the Metaphysics of Morals*.]

Thierry, Patrick. *La Tolérance: société démocratique, opinions, vices et vertus*. Paris: Presses universitaires de France, 1997.

Servez, Pierre. *Le Mal du siècle*. Givors, France: André Martel, 1955.

Thomas of Aquinas. *Summa theologiae* (1266–72). Paris: Le Cerf, 1984.

—*Against Nature; Bible, the; Damien, Peter; Debauchery; Heresy; Medicine; Paul (of Tarsus); Perversions; Philosophy; Theology.*

VILLON, François

François Villon (1431–63) was a great French poet at the end of the Middle Ages and also a criminal who served time in prison for robbery. The image that remains of him today is blurred. Villon presented himself as an *escolier,* a student who became *maistre es arts.* But this diploma, which should have paved the way for a beneficial administrative career, did not give him any advantage. He was the author of ballads and long poems, including "Le Lais" (The legacy) and "Le Testament," which were autobiographical and narrative, with philosophical and meditative qualities: they evoked the poet's highly pessimistic attitude towards life, death, illness, torture, and **prison.** Villon depicted himself as an erratic man who was chased from wherever he went, like an amorous martyr fleeing from the love of women (young girls, prostitutes, and proper ladies).

What we really know of Villon is only what he consented to write about himself in his poems, which is difficult to penetrate given his predilection for masks, alternative voices, and even aliases. It is difficult trying to reconstruct the details of his life, his years spent in exile and prison, and even the exact date of his death: he disappeared at the beginning of 1463, without his death ever being confirmed. The image that he proposed of his sexuality is no clearer. In his poems, he took liberties with the portrayals and first names of feminine characters. However, there are numerous hints that lead us to believe that the poet loved boys. In his *Ballades en jargon,* he seemed to employ a Parisian street slang which was derived partially from the gay jargon of the thirteenth century, *jobelin* (well represented in theater); but the sole use of this slang makes the ballads difficult to comprehend at first try. One must also mention his frequent contact with impoverished students and unemployed scholars, some of whom would also be condemned for theft and other crimes. Villon's own condemnation is still a source of confusion. It is almost certain that he was sent to prison, tortured, condemned to death, granted pardon, and finally exiled (the judiciary archives are among the only documents related to Villon that are left), but the different reasons for these condemnations, which included theft and murder, remain vague, and without doubt the poet's homosexuality must have played in his disfavor. In fact, as indicated by Thierry Martin, while "homosexuality in the fifteenth century enjoyed a relative **tolerance,**" death sentences could be pronounced in aggravating circumstances; and Villon had been implicated several times, alongside his other criminal charges.

All of these uncertain facts suggest an interference behind which lurks the shadow of homophobia: born of a hidden and disturbing truth and expressed in several ways. The truth is based on certain indisputable facts: Villon enjoyed the complicity of certain well-known homosexuals who had been arrested and condemned on numerous occasions; he wrote poems with clearly homosexual themes, in a language that also belonged to this milieu. It is beyond these findings, that no one questions anymore, that homophobia begins.

If one follows an inverse diachrony, one must note, even to this day, the refusal of a large part of the biographies and research on Villon to face the facts of his sexuality. Most of them do not take them into account or, worse, deliberately hide them. Homophobia thus is present, expressed in the negation of a truth almost established: the uneasiness of researchers is evident. This appears to have contributed to the interference in the image of the poet, and in particular, led to misinterpretations of his poetry, as evidenced in the work of Thierry Martin and Christine Martineau-Génieys. One can still read exhaustive critiques of Villon which make no mention of his homosexual penchants or even allusions to it. Certain (braver) researchers have, however, proposed translations of his homosexual ballads, such as Pierre Guiraud, as early as 1968, or more global interpretations of his work, such as Gert Pinkernell since 1975. Nonetheless, it is clear that Villon remains a victim of homophobia long after his death.

One must also take into account the homophobia that occurred in Villon's time, specifically that of the church, tribunals, and medieval society in general. This problem largely exceeds the poet or his work and thus is not further developed here, other than in its consequences for Villon's own personality. Villon's work, and the manner in which he expressed himself, prove that he frequented places where male homosexuality was practiced, and we can hardly believe that he himself had remained a stranger to those practices. However, the poet expressed himself in veiled terms. The *Ballades en jargon* are in particular ambiguous: the use of jargon make them difficult to access. Their interpretation in gay terms is not apparent at first glance and it seems as if the poet were trying to hide a part of their true meaning. In fact, on this same model, the entire work of Villon hides a reflexive homophobia: the author is often the mouthpiece of Nature and life; his poetic work seems to be opposed to the general perversion of society, as well as its **vice** and **sterility**. This is evidenced, for example, in Villon's violent criticisms against Bishop Thibault d'Aussigny, who had Villon arrested, and whom the poet accused of sodomy and practices **against nature**. After all, in poetry that was clearly more accessible than his *Ballades*, Villon integrated and assumed the homophobia of his era.

—*Thierry Revol*

Guiraud, Pierre. *Le Jargon de Villon ou le gai savoir de la co-quille*. Paris: Gallimard, 1968.

Martin, Thierry. *Villon: Ballades en argot homosexuel*. Paris: Mille et une nuits, 1998.

Martineau-Génieys, Christine. "L'Homosexualité dans *Le Lais* et *Le Testament* de François Villon," *Conformité et déviances au Moyen Age, Les Cahiers du CRISIMA*, no. 2 (1995).

Villon, François. *Poésies complètes*. Paris: Le Livre de Poche, 1991.

Villon hier et aujourd'hui, actes du colloque pour le 35e anniversaire de l'impression du Testament de Villon. Bibliothèque de la Ville de Paris (December 15–17, 1989). Paris, 1993.

—*Against Nature; Censorship; Damien, Peter; Literature; Theology.*

VIOLENCE

The notion of "gratuitous" violence is a fallacy. There is a reason for every human action, and homophobic violence does not break this rule. But a serious reflection on homophobia (as on all forms of racism) cannot be confined to vague and impoverished notions of prejudice, representation, or even ideology. In refusing to reduce violence to simple irrational impulses, these notions try to wrest them from arbitrary madness and succeed in part to make them less absurd and less unintelligible. But if we try to identify the causes of physical or verbal aggression in a psychological coherence, we will fail to see their social and practical ground, and, more widely, their sociological "necessity."

To avoid repeating the errors and proceedings of idealists and the politically correct—which believed they could change reality and make social violence disappear by simply changing the words through which it is expressed—homophobic violence (both verbal and physical) must be understood within a general economy of heterosexist domination. Certainly, this system of oppression translates into language and ideas, but it also materializes in the functioning of institutions (e.g., **school**, **army**, **marriage**, family, the state, and the legal system); it objectivizes itself in the structures of physical space (particularly urban), and is inscribed even in bodies, crystallized in most everyday practices which put into play social dispositions that are durably interiorized by individuals and groups. The understandable interest for linguistic subtleties and the violence of micro-interactions must then be inserted in a global and historical understanding of the phenomena. One can understand, particularly, how social order and its agents abuse homosexuals and regularly collide with their "nature," their identity, only if one understands at the same time that this identity (gay, lesbian, etc.) is constructed by oppression and in response to heterosexist domination. Homophobic violence is not absurd: it is the violence that a society reserves for its other, that part of itself which negatively defines it. To be gay or lesbian today is to be a child of that violence.

From Plural to Singular

Violence is defined as any number of abusive acts: physical, verbal, or symbolic; those that we feel, that we hear, and that we experience, ranging from the verbal **insults** of daily life to the mortal brutality of a baseball bat, through harassment, blackmail, and public demonstrations. As French sociologist Daniel Welzer-Lang contends, these homophobic acts of violence are perhaps more aptly described as **transphobic**: they are aimed less at same-sex love *per se* than "masculine" traits in women and "feminine" traits in men (i.e. therefore aim at persons who possess these traits without being homosexual). Often instigated by men, homophobic violence is usually motivated by sexuality and the reduction to the sexual, as is the case in the extreme example of the punitive rape of gays or lesbians. When the target is a lesbian, or perceived as such, the assault can be a punishment for the sexual unavailability of the victim toward not only the particular aggressors (there is often more than one), but also men in general, with whom the aggressors feel solidarity. When the rape victim is a gay man, it is, conversely (but not solely), his refusal or incapacity to "hold his rank" that is targeted.

Revealingly, while rapists do not always perceive the imposed and punitive sexual relation with a male homosexual as posing an explicit threat to their own heterosexuality (particularly because they do not think of the act itself as sexual relation, but as an action), they often take certain virile precautions intended to prevent the act from becoming **contagion**. These small yet significant rites are seen as necessary reparations for breaching the socio-sexual order.

However, the social efficacy of this physical violence—which, even in its most brutal forms, is never solely physical—and this verbal violence—which, even in its most euphemized forms, is always more than simply words—is not completely in the gesture or words which actualize it. Verbal and physical abuse hurts, but

it hurts that much more if it means "This is what you are, a second-class citizen, an abnormal and inferior being." By this interpolation, the attacker has the power to name without being named himself, to classify without being classified himself; to push his victim back into his social place by reminding him with each blow the superiority of "objective" norms and hierarchies. If these assaults can act inextricably on minds and bodies, it is because they are based on a **symbolic order** that they recite and reinforce. Such being the case, this order does not identify with a simple intellectual or political context that would be purely exterior to social actors, and would be exercised on them only in the mode of influence. Much more radically, the symbolic order penetrates to the most intimate of subjectivities, which it tends to produce in its image by creating individuals who spontaneously function according to its laws. Through "open" violence (which sometimes presents itself as only a threat), it literally summons the homosexual (or virtually homosexual) subject. Sometimes, it even paralyzes and renders him mute—as very often one does not have the words to describe oppression.

Thus, the violence of verbal or physical assaults draws its vexational efficacy from a continuous social conditioning that precedes it, in part, and which results in thinking habits, practical reflexes, and schemes of perception. The assault acts somewhat like a trigger which, activating our acquired psychological mechanisms and our conditioned reactions, liberates and mobilizes in an instant all social violence and energy accumulated by the history of an individual and his collective oppression. In other words, if physical and verbal aggressions sometimes have apparently disproportionate consequences in relation to their tangible and material reality (a "simple" word, a "slight" look, a "minor" hazing), it is because they are only recalling what is under everyone's nose, what is known and felt to the deepest of socialized consciences and bodies: they are that much more cruel and effective because what they say goes without saying.

The consequence of this systemic violence, reproduced in ordinary interactions, is often that it causes the repeated "enchanted submission" of victims, and this brought certain homosexuals to think of themselves in the language that is "**against nature**." It is this "symbolic violence"—to recall sociologist Pierre Bourdieu's concept—which is exercised, whenever oppression is felt as legitimate or "normal," and each time that a position dominated in the social relationships of gender or sexual identity come to be lived in the mode of "natural" evidence.

Symbolic Order & Social Order

As a matter of logic, this established symbolic order, which increases the effects of physical and verbal violence, also allows the injunctions of the sexual norm to exercise their most material effects without even having to be set out as explicit orders. One has to take seriously, for example, the concordant testimonies of those who committed homophobic crimes, who affirmed that they sincerely believed they were doing something good on behalf of the "homeland" or "morality," and did not understand what was wrong with their actions. If they continued to affirm it, it is because they correctly perceived that behind the guilty ambiguities of official declarations and the entanglement of signals which the society broadcasts, there exists a form of social suppression, and even encouragement, for their acts of hate.

How can one not see, in particular, that violence of individuals is rooted in the violence of law or, more indirectly, in normative anthropological theories and in certain psychoanalytical readings which ratify the inequality of rights? The violence of the state, which can be judicial, symbolic, or itself physical (through incarceration, torture, execution), survives in democratic societies in the form of discriminatory legal dispositions which continue to curb political struggles against homophobic violence. To cite only one example, it remains rather difficult, if not contradictory, to demand public action against everyday homophobia from a state that continues to approve an inequality of rights between heterosexuals and homosexuals. Could we imagine an "Anti-Semitism Act" whereby the state prohibits Jewish couples to marry or adopt children?

Open violence is, in some way, the "application decrees" of symbolic and judicial laws. It can often function as informal disciplinary actions or a call to order because this order is already present and observable on a daily basis, not only in consciousness but also in structures of the heterosexist world, which imposes them and imposes itself on homosexual persons ("No one is supposed to ignore symbolic order"). Even if they manage to partially free themselves from it subjectively, it would suffice to raise our eyes without hiding our faces in order to observe the denial of the facts. Thus, to contest these social rules or laws brings about the immediate accusation of denying them like

we deny brutal reality and, at best, being described as a politically correct hypocrite who runs away from the evidence and pretends to not recognize natural hierarchies or, at worst, as a mentally ill individual deserting the "real" world and substituting it with the delirium of one's illusory escapes.

In other words, symbolic order could not "naturalize," with as much success, the sexual divisions and hierarchies instituted by history if it were not based on an "objective" social world made of real **discriminations** and real inequities. For the homophobic vision of the world (which, as all dominating visions, tends to magically reverse the logic of its own effects), the subordinate position of gays and lesbians in the "order of things," of detectable visibilities and identities (a position that remains unknown as a product of domination), functions as an "objective" confirmation of their "just" downgrading in the order of senses, symbols, and dignities ("Homosexuals hide, so they must be ashamed of something!"). Further, the combined orchestration of homophobic reactions feeds the well-founded illusion ("well-founded" in the sense that it helps produce what it declares) of the transcendence and universality of social judgments that they contain and which, when they are not disarmed by counter-discourses and counter-practices, can function as real verdicts. Thus the most visible and scandalous forms of homophobic violence are nothing but the singular visible part of the heterosexist iceberg.

But this invisible violence of the sexual norm is also suffered, in one sense, by the same ones who are its main agents: aggression against homosexuals, "queens," and "abnormals" is a means to emphasize the distance (physical and symbolic) from the other by forgetting and detracting from the distance from oneself ("Be a man"). Thus by assaulting his victim, the violent homophobe is unloading the weight of the continuous struggle against failures of masculinity. In this way, homophobic violence is inscribed within a socio-psychic economy of sexist and heterosexist domination, and one cannot separate it from its incomprehensible character unless one understands that those who exact it feel not only authorized to commit it, but also viscerally attacked by their victim in return, whose very existence threatens to reveal their own vulnerability— the aggressors became the dominants dominated by their own domination. Hence, those who commit homophobic crimes are not simple puppets of the socio-sexual order: rather, they are the interested interpreters of its hierarchies.

Finally, there is without a doubt something such as a "law of conservation" of accumulated violence: there always remains the risk that the homosexual victim will turn the violence he experiences against his peers, even against himself, in self-destructive behaviors which can go as far as **suicide**. However, the political counter-violence of individual and collective resistance movements is often interpreted as "aggressive" or "hysterical" by the condescending dominant group (here, heterosexuals) which feels ill at ease in its own "normality."

It is thus an entire social and symbolic machinery which confers its strength to the varied forms of homophobic violence, from the most flagrant and odious brutalities to subtler forms, which deny their own violence, oppose all attempts at contestation through the rhetoric of common sense and nature, and are backed by social order and its main, so-called evidence. This leads to a fear among some gays and lesbians that attempts to contain homophobic violence are focused on the effects without attacking the causes. But if it is true, as mentioned by Didier Eribon, that it is always difficult to "criminalize common sense," one must not forget that, in spite of its unremitting logic, each time it was decided to attack its real roots, "common sense" never proved itself to be completely unchanged, nor absolutely invincible.

—*Sébastien Chauvin*

Amnesty International. *Identité sexuelle et persécutions*. EFAI, 2001.

Berrill, Kevin, and Gregory Herek, eds. *Hate Crimes: Confronting Violence Against Lesbians and Gay Men*. London: Sage, 1992.

Bourdieu, Pierre. *Méditations pascaliennes*. Paris: Le Seuil, 1997. [Published in the US as *Pascalian Meditations*. Stanford: Stanford Univ. Press, 2000.]

Cecco, John de, ed. *Bashers, Baiters and Bigots: Homophobia in American Society*. Binghamton, NY: Harrington Park Press, 1985.

Comstock, Gary David. *Violence against Lesbians and Gay Men*. New York: Columbia Univ. Press, 1991.

Delor, François. *Homosexualité, ordre symbolique, injure et discrimination: Impasses et destins des expériences érotiques minoritaires dans l'espace social et politique*. Brussels: Labor, 2003.

Eribon, Didier. "Ce que l'injure me dit. Quelques remarques sur le racisme et la discrimination." In *Papiers d'identité, interventions sur la question gay*. Paris: Fayard, 2000.

Herek, Gregory. "Psychological Heterosexism and Anti-Gay Violence: The Social Psychology of Bigotry and Bashing." In *Hate Crimes: Confronting Violence against Lesbians and*

Gay Men. London: Sage, 1992.

Kantor, Martin. *Homophobia: Description, Development and Dynamics of Gay Bashing*. Westport, CT: Praeger, 1998.

Mason, Gail, and Stephen Tomsen, eds. *Homophobic Violence*. Sydney: Hawkins Press, 1997.

SOS homophobie. *Rapport 2002 sur l'homophobie* [2002 report on homophobia].

—*Biphobia; Criminalization; Deportation; Gayphobia; Gulag; Heterosexism; Insult; Lesbophobia; Police; Rhetoric; Shame; Shepard, Matthew; Suicide; Symbolic Order; Transphobia; Vocabulary.*

VOCABULARY

Examining the words of homophobia requires a linguistic understanding of the gay phenomenon. Do the words used to express the homosexual reality stem from a logic that is representative of the world, or of rejection? The term "homosexual" echoes a simplistic behavioral dimension of the individual; some have preferred "homosensual," which they believed was more positive and less limited to the sexual dimension. Of the latter, enough cannot be said, since despite the sexual revolution of the 1970s, homosexuality remains largely taboo at the level of language—that is, outside of intimate or schoolyard conversations. The rhetoric and debate on the integration of the sexual dimension in democratic society are still particularly lacking. Thus, homosexuality is reduced to the congruent portion of the language of representation, that is to say, to silence. One will note that the terms "heterosexual" and "heterosexuality" only appear after, and as foils to, the terms "homosexual" and "homosexuality." The consideration *a priori* of the evidence might not impose denomination. Everyone is straight, aren't they? Why then the need to talk about it?

When examined closely, language has for centuries been expressing a standard that could be qualified as **heterosexist**. The world continues to be seen through the prism of the "normal" man, who is heterosexual, and who perpetuates his social dominance by language. For many, the words of homosexuality are then the words of homophobia. This is the risk that affects, in the social dynamic, all designations of human groups, which proceed by classification on the basis of normative criteria, the source of all prejudice and **discrimination**. As Didier Eribon explained, the homosexual is born from **insult**; it is by insult that he integrates this part of his socio-psychological identity. These insults, like many expressions of aggressiveness, doubtlessly results from anguish; specifically, feelings of a man who is afraid of failing in his social role as a man because he may be experiencing homosexual libido. Heteromale society denounces the incurred risk, the homosexual, as well as his role and behavior that are so contemptible in its heteronormal environment. The male must be powerful and dominating, and in order to achieve this he must stigmatize the passive and effeminate homosexual, who is weak and dominated. It is thus, first and foremost, this image of the homosexual that language will reflect.

We must note that lesbianism, while it does not escape rejection or insult, does not have the same place in the lexical field of homophobia. As women generally have little control over their own lexical creation, it is male power that invented the homophobic vocabulary. As a result, lesbians are poorly represented: *gouine, goudou, gousse, lesbiche,* and *camionneuse,* in French and "butch" or "dyke" in English. The insult toward lesbians aims to stigmatize those who, by their abnormal practices, refuse male sexual domination.

Homophobia is not only manifested in words but also by language attitudes that go from silence to the hijacking of words in order to subvert their meanings. It is based on these attitudes that we will classify terms that denigrate, which express hatred of the "other" while simultaneously denouncing heterosexist ignorance and stupidity.

Negation

The first manifestation of homophobia in language is marked by the absence of words, by silence, all underlined by the taboo of homosexuality. The world is, by default, heterosexual. The absence of positive or even neutral discourse, of identification models, in relation to a heterosexual majority that states its exploits, leads young gays and lesbians to isolation, even depression; add to this the plethora of insults thrown at random ("fag," "lezzie," "queer") in schoolyards. The **suicide** rate among gay youth is much higher than among heterosexual youth. This silence kills. The role that discourse can play in order to diffuse this trend has not been rigorously investigated. Despite public debates on equal rights, despite talk shows, or films and television series with openly gay or lesbian characters, homosexuality remains stigmatized, even if the evolution is resolutely positive, at least in the West.

Words to Express It

There are several ways to express homophobia, each one common to the general process of insult: the numerous adjectives based on stereotypically constructed traits: "passive," "effeminate," "soft," (poof, queen, queer), "mannish" (truck driver); the metaphoric-metonymic process which reduces everything to a unidimensional character (e.g., feminization, behavior); the use of turns of phrase which take the form of *kind of + name* (which creates a belittling subcategory) or "dirty"/"little"/ "big" + *name,* which are always insulting; the string that lists a series of denominations ("queer son of an X"); or rhetorical qualifications ("I have a very good gay friend, but …") that attempt to be gay-friendly when in fact they are a defensive mechanism to protect against the presumption of homophobia.

Neutral terms for homosexuality such as "gay" and "lesbian" (in English), *schwuler, homosexueller* (in German, where "homo" is deprecating), are not always sheltered from being used as insults, depending on expressions that preceded them or their corresponding terms in foreign languages. In what follows, we will try to classify vocabulary as a function of the attitude or trait stressed in the denomination. What appears each time is the attempt to decategorize, to declassify the homosexual from his identity and dignity, in order to re-categorize him based on traits considered negative and subsequently reject him because of his otherness.

One of the first attitudes of rejection, even unconsciously, consists in misrepresenting the object of the insult by neutralizing him, depersonalizing him, describing him as "that": "He or she is like that, but it doesn't bother me; better that than a broken leg." The insult is certainly not voluntary, but the term reveals the unease in view of what some call the "third sex."

The most flagrant misrepresentation in terms of homophobia is the feminization of the gay male to the point that, for many, it is the image of the effeminate passive that comes to mind when one thinks of a gay man. The homosexual male, all categories included, is reduced to "queen," "queer," and "aunt" (metaphors used to imply a form of kinship; in the time of Balzac, for example, the French equivalent of "brats," "cousins," and "aunts" was used depending on age) and its variants "aunty," "fairy," "sissy," and "faggot" (the latter term, a seal of infamy by which criminals or people of little virtue were marked as a faggot, in reference to the pyre). The French *pédale* stems from pederast, with a possible play on the position of the cyclist on his seat. This always-deprecating feminization refers to the homosexual in passive terms. No gay couple is safe from the question: "Which one plays the woman?" These feminizing characterizations are not unique to English; they are common in French as well as German (*tunte* or *schwuchtel*, roughly "aunt" and "aunty") and Spanish (*maricón* or *marica* for "fag" or "fairy"; *marica* means primarily "magpie," which could refer to nightgown; we also find this trait in the slender, effeminate gay *mariposa*, which initially means "butterfly").

One would expect an equivalent process of masculinization for lesbians. They would be real "blokes." So what do we find? In French, the only masculine term used—and rarely at that—is *Julius*. Except for this term, even when it is to stress the supposed virile trait of the lesbian, feminine forms of words are used: *camionneuse* (meaning "female truck driver," a reference to the largely masculine profession and the physical appearance to which she seems to be linked), and *hommase* ("man-girl") for a lesbian of masculine appearance. In this way, women will never even attain "masculine dignity"; the feminine appears to be a deliberate characteristic of the insult.

What then are the privileged traits in lesbian insults? There is geographical origin (Lesbos, the island where Sappho lived), which is not negative in itself. However, one must note that, historically, "lesbian" was first a masculine noun to designate a dainty, the male lover of a man. It is only later that the term was used to designate homosexual women. The French terms *gouine, gougne,* and *gougnotte* come from an old Norman noun meaning "slut." These words referred to prostitutes before being applied to lesbians, just as the verb *gougnotter* means "to have sexual relations with a woman." As for the term *gousse*, it came from the Old French word *gouce* meaning "bitch," then "debauched woman," or from the verb *gausser,* "to eat like a dog, in a gross manner." Even if synchronically these meanings are not present, it is nonetheless true that in the constitution of the vocabulary of homophobia, the lesbian is reduced to the rank of bitch or slut, that is to say, she is unworthy of being human or is less than human. The only thing, in heterosexist language, that could then save the lesbian is to submit to the norm, i.e. male domination.

Homosexuals are also designated by their activity or behavior, especially sexual practices. This is why gays hear themselves being called "sodomites," "buggers," "sods," and "cocksuckers" (in German *arschficker*, "ass-fucker"); lesbians are called "grazers" and "carpet munchers." One will note here the almost exclusive predominance of the passive character for denominations concerning gays.

Along the same line, when an injunction is invoked, it is usually akin to "fuck you" or "go get" + *passive verb*, not active (e.g., "screwed" or "buggered"; similarly, "Go screw yourself" or "Bugger off") (in Spanish, *¡vete a tomar por culo!, ¡que te den por culo!*).

The rarer "active" denomination for homosexuals refers to he who sexually penetrates, such as "bugger"; these terms tend to be used in **prisons**, and to designate sexual predators, including pedophiles. In this sense, the term *pederast,* "elder of the Greek gay couple" "who liked young boys," was used in the nineteenth century to wrongly describe all homosexuals. Through the erroneous use of this word, the confusion between homosexuality and **pedophilia** was integrated into the vocabulary.

The homophobe often calls on science to justify rejection and disparagement. Until the early 90s, the World Health Organization considered homosexuality to be an illness, and for a long time, **psychoanalysis** considered—and still does, according to certain schools—homosexuality to be a deviant behavior. Given this, use of the derogatory terms "pervert" and "invert" are often based on scientific attitudes.

The association with illness or harm increased as a result of the **AIDS** epidemic. Gays are considered an "at-risk population." There is a preference to stigmatize identifiable groups rather than risky behavior, which would also imply heterosexual men. The link between gays and AIDS persists; we find it today on Red Cross blood donor forms, which exclude gay males (a group) rather than individuals who have had multiple sexual partners (behavior). The confusion inherited from the history of vocabulary—pedophilia/ pederasty—continues, and in recent cases involving pedophilia, homosexuals as a group are once again accused of being pedophiles. The search for the origins of homosexuality has made its way to genetics: a "defective" gene could be identified as the cause of this "deviance." One can see the specter of eugenics rearing its ugly head in the event that an operation is possible to "fix" one's homosexuality.

Finally, homosexuality appears as an aggravating circumstance in certain legal matters where sexual orientation has no relevance. Thus, we have seen certain newspaper articles about hold-ups at automatic teller machines featuring such headlines as "The Assailant Was Gay" (when have we ever seen a title along the lines of "The Assailant Was Heterosexual"?). Such statements contribute to the association of homosexuality with an illness or offence and contribute, be it unconsciously, to the general homophobic climate.

The Wear & Tear of Words

The meanings of words that we use are sometimes eroded or modified. Today, "fuck" refers more often to a form of verbal punctuation that gives rhythm to a sentence, rather than to a sexual practice. It is the same for certain insults, which sometimes lose their basic semantic content and come to mean only the insult itself. When you call someone a "fag," it does not always refer to his sexual practices; sometimes it is only the will to reject him. In the same way, "We are not gay" does not necessarily refer to homosexuality, but sometimes only to weakness or fear. "Gay" then becomes the quintessential insult, a sad privilege.

This being said, history gives us examples that are more positive: in the old language, *bougre* ("bugger") meant homosexual, a negative term that in the Middle Ages was used to designate the Bulgarian heresy. Today, in French, a *bon bougre* ("good bugger") simply means "a good guy": the stigmatization has disappeared.

Internalization & Rehabilitation

The insult depends in great part on the context. Who speaks to whom, in what circumstances, and in whose presence? One cannot, in fact, neglect the importance of whether or not the insult is witnessed, which implies that a third person can take sides. If we speak mostly of the homophobic designation outside of the group (hetero-designation), we must still consider the way homosexuals designate themselves and each other (auto-designation).

There are two distinct mechanisms at work: internalization and rehabilitation. Internalized homophobia reproduces within the group, consciously or not, the rhetoric imposed from the exterior, particularly the rhetoric of the sin that one confesses (i.e. his or her homosexuality) and the **shame** that follows. However, it also consists of the recreation of sub-classes, among which some are rejected for the same reason homosexuals are rejected by heterosexuals: we can make distinctions between "queens," "femmes," "butch dykes," "leather men," "gym bunnies," and "the straight-acting." **Tolerance** is not an assumed way of life among gays themselves. Bisexuals are, for their part, sometimes reduced to the rank of the "repressed." That is, the same words can be used or perceived as being either laudatory or insulting, depending on the participants and the circumstances.

Finally, during the successive struggles for the right to both difference and indifference, gays and lesbians have rehabilitated and reinvested pejoratively used terms and transformed them into standards of protest. Insults become passports to pride. One is gay or lesbian, and proud to be as such. Nothing is confessed anymore: one comes out of the closet (without being outed). The most positively invested term is certainly the word "gay," which certainly refers to carefree, but is also quite resistant to insult: one has difficulty saying "damned gay" (compared to "damned fag").

Beyond the acknowledgment of gay and lesbian rights, particularly through their effect on language, it is the entire diversity of sexual behaviors that should be acknowledged and respected, and not only homo and hetero. This is partly the sense of the "queer" movement ("bizarre," "sick," "perverted"), which refuses the slightly normative conformism that is prevalent in the gay and lesbian community, sitting somewhere behind the affirmation of its identity.

—*Dan Van Raemdonck*

Delor, François. *Homosexualité, ordre symbolique, injure et discrimination.* Brussels: Labor, 2003.

Rey, Alain, ed. *Dictionnaire historique de la langue française.* Paris: Ed. Robert, 1998.

Eribon, Didier. *Réflexions sur la question gay.* Paris: Fayard, "Histoire de la pensée," 1999. [Published in the US as *Insult and the Making of the Gay Self.* Durham, NC: Duke University Press, 2004.]

Grahn, Judy. *Another Mother Tongue: Gay Words, Gay Worlds.* Boston: Beacon Press, 1990.

Larguèche, Evelyne. *L'Injure à fleur de peau.* Paris: L'Harmattan, 1993.

———. *Injure et sexualité.* Paris: Presses universitaires de France, 1997.

Peterkin, A. D. *Outbursts! A Queer Erotic Thesaurus.* Vancouver: Arsenal Pulp Press, 2003.

Rodgers, Bruce. *Gay Talk: A (Sometimes Outrageous) Dictionary of Gay Slang.* Formerly titled *The Queens Vernacular.* New York: Paragon Books, 1979.

Rosier, Laurence, and Philippe Ernotte. *Le Lexique clandestin, Français et Société 12.* Louvain-la-Neuve, Belgium: Duculot, 2000.

—*Abnormal; Caricature; Heterosexism; Humor; Insult; Literature; Media; Rhetoric.*

WILDE, Oscar

The 1895 trials and subsequent imprisonment of Oscar Wilde for the crime of gross indecency represented the height of Victorian-era homophobia, and a crucial turning point in the history of homosexuality in Western society. When his first trial began, Oscar Wilde was never more popular: his play, *The Importance of Being Earnest,* was a triumphant success, and as a brilliant conversationalist with a scathing wit, he was as much a celebrity by virtue of his outrageousness and flamboyant lifestyle as he was for his literary output (which included plays, novels, and poems). As a high priest of estheticism, Wilde's eccentric style made him a preferred target of caricaturists, who delighted in his fey mannerisms. But the world was at Oscar Wilde's feet: from London to Paris (by way of New York), aristocratic and high-society types alike fought over his droll presence at dinner parties and events. But sadly, in a few short months, the name Oscar Wilde became the most loathed and despised name in all of **England**.

Over the previous twenty years, Great Britain had known many **scandals** involving so-called "crimes **against nature.**" The trial for conspiracy to commit sodomy of two transvestites, Ernest Boulton and Frederick Park, in 1871; the Dublin Castle Affair in 1884; and finally the Cleveland Street scandal of 1889–90, which despite government efforts to cover it up, compromised a number of prominent aristocrats, all patrons of a male brothel with a penchant for telegraph messenger boys. According to the British gross indecency amendment of 1885, championed by Member of Parliament Henry Labouchère, "all acts of gross indecency" committed between men were punishable by two years' imprisonment, which may include hard labor. The sentence may have seemed relatively moderate in comparison to previous legislation (which called for a minimum of ten years' imprisonment), but the number of convictions climbed steeply. In effect, the deliberately vague wording of the amendment widened the law's application, which until then had only been applied to the "crime of sodomy"; and Oscar Wilde would become one of its most famous victims.

Wilde's first meaningful relationship with a man occurred in 1885 (a year after his marriage to Constance Lloyd), when he met a young Canadian by the name of Robert Baldwin Ross. Ross would become Wilde's lifelong friend, and, eventually, his literary executor. Before meeting Ross, however, it is believed that Wilde had his first homosexual encounters while attending Magdalen College at Oxford, where he arrived in 1874. There, he became a student of English essayist and literary critic Walter Pater who, in his collection of essays, *Studies in the History of the Renaissance* (1873), celebrated, *sotto voce,* the esthetics of German art historian Johann Joachim Winckelmann, and called for the rediscovery of classical (Greek) morality.

Wilde's marriage to Constance Lloyd in 1884 silenced (for a time) rumors of his homosexuality, which resurfaced in 1891 when he published his novel, *The Picture of Dorian Gray.* The ambiguous figure of the novel's young dandy, his double life, and his troubled relationship with his friend and portraitist Basil Hallward allowed for many levels of interpretation (whereas repeated allusions to Michelangelo, Montaigne, and Shakespeare were codes for the initiated reader). The year 1891 was also when Wilde became intimate with Lord Alfred Douglas (who went by the name of "Bosie"), son of John Sholto Douglas, the ninth Marquess of Queensberry. Although their relationship was short-lived, their attachment to one another endured: Bosie apparently introduced Wilde to London's homosexual underground of male brothels, procurers, and prostitutes, and to the pleasure of, in Wilde's words, "feasting with panthers."

As a result, Wilde's sexual recklessness put him at the mercy of potential blackmailers. Having a taste for provocation, he did not hesitate to receive, in hotels or at the Café Royal, young working-class boys whom he treated with generosity. And he and his friends wore green carnations on the opening night of his play, *Lady Windermere's Fan* (1892), which some interpreted as a homosexual code. Wilde's general insouciance, encouraged by Douglas, would reveal itself to be ultimately fatal: Victorian society only tolerated homosexuality if it were kept secret. By openly defying the unwritten rules of bourgeois conformity, Wilde became the target of rumors and accusations that became more and more overt: for one, Bosie's father, the Marquess of Queensberry, left a calling card for him at one of Wilde's hangouts, the Albermarle Club; on the back of the card, he wrote, "For Oscar Wilde, posing *Somdomite*" (sic). Supported by Douglas, who loathed his father, but against the advice of most of his friends, Wilde chose to put an end to these incidents and sued the Marquess for criminal libel.

At the libel trial, which opened on April 3, 1895, it quickly became apparent that the Marquess, the defendant, assumed the role of accuser: his lawyers had successfully gathered the testimonies of several young male prostitutes who revealed their sexual activities with Wilde. Despite Wilde's various witticisms spoken during the trial, it ended with a dismissal of the charges against the Marquess. Worse, it launched the start of two other trials, on April 26 and May 22, in which Wilde was now the defendant, accused of "committing acts of gross indecency with other male persons." Despite repeated pressure from friends who encouraged him to flee the country, Wilde refused to leave, choosing instead to face his accusers. During the first trial, when interrogated about his "crimes," he responded with a moving speech on the nature of "the love that dares not speak its name," resulting in a round of thunderous applause from those in attendance. The trial ended with the jury unable to reach a verdict, resulting in a second, and final, trial, presided over by Chief Justice Sir Alfred Wills, who declared, "This is the worst trial I have ever been given to judge." The trial lasted three days; on May 25, 1895, Wilde, the "High Priest of Decadents," according to the *National Observer*, was convicted of gross indecency and sentenced to two years of hard labor in prison. News of Wilde's conviction was received

with enthusiasm by both the public and the media, and he fell out of favor, both personally and professionally. As soon as his trials began, production of his plays was closed down, and an American tour of *A Woman of No Importance* was cancelled. Following Wilde's conviction, many renowned British homosexuals fled to **France**, where homosexuality was not a crime, while back at home, the majority of Wilde's friends quickly renounced him.

During his imprisonment, Wilde wrote one of his master works, *De Profundis,* a moving essay on spirituality and faith written as a letter to Lord Alfred Douglas, in which he confessed to his mistakes, but refuted any feelings of guilt. He was released from prison in 1897, a broken man. In self-imposed exile in France under the pseudonym of Sebastian Melmoth, and supported by some loyal friends who included Robert Ross, Wilde wrote the famous poem "The Ballad of Reading Gaol" in 1898. Wilde died in Paris two years later, in 1900, at the age of forty-six.

Oscar Wilde's conviction and imprisonment is without a doubt one of the most famous examples of the manifestations of society-wide homophobia in Western culture. The scandal of the trials and their subsequent repercussions served to introduce certain new homophobic stereotypes: at a moment when, under the combined influence of **law** and **medicine**, new ideas and understandings of homosexuality were emerging, the figure of Oscar Wilde—fey and effeminate—became, in the public eye, a symbol of **vice** and **decadence**. The homosexual, as "corruptor of youth," was perceived as a threat to the integrity of society, and as such, had to be unmasked. At the same time, in order to protect family morals and prevent all "imitation of the crime" (in the words of British Prime Minister Robert Gascoyne-Cecil, the Marquess of Salisbury), these "**perversions**" had to remain secret. In 1896, the Publication of Indecent Evidence bill was introduced in the British parliament, forbidding the publication of minutes from trials relating to homosexuality.

Paradoxically, Oscar Wilde's trials also played a determining role in the identification of a separate homosexual culture. By revealing the existence of an already well-organized gay subculture, at least in the larger cities, and by initiating discussions about (male) homosexuality in the media, a number of homosexual men all of a sudden became conscious that they were part of a group. Oscar Wilde, gay martyr, became the ultimate homosexual reference: his name was even used as code (the hero of E. M. Forster's 1914 novel, *Maurice*, defines himself as an "unnamable in the likes of Oscar Wilde"). *A contrario*, the reading of Wilde's works, even years after his death, could be considered scandalous: twenty years after Wilde's trials, future author Beverley Nichols, caught reading *The Picture of Dorian Gray*, was struck and insulted by his father, who spat on the book's cover before tearing it to bits. Oscar Wilde's disposition, the disgrace cast upon his name, and the infamy of his conviction and sentence were meant to be a warning to all young men on the dangers of homosexuality for many years to come.

—*Florence Tamagne*

Ellmann, Richard. *Oscar Wilde*. Paris: Gallimard, 1994. [Published in the US as *Oscar Wilde*. New York: Knopf, 1987.]

Jullian, Philippe. *Oscar Wilde*. Paris: Christian de Bartillat, 2000.

Merle, Robert. *Oscar Wilde ou la destinée de l'homosexuel*. Paris: Gallimard, 1985.

Sinfield, Alan. *The Wilde Century: Effeminacy, Oscar Wilde and the Queer Moment*. London: Cassel, 1994.

Vallet, Odon. *L'Affaire Oscar Wilde*. Paris: Gallimard, "Folio," 1997.

—*Decadence; England; Ireland; Literature; Police; Radclyffe Hall, Marguerite; Scandal; Vice.*

WORK. *See* Workplace

WORKPLACE

In 1914, German sexologist Magnus **Hirschfeld** revealed that, of the 10,000 cases of homosexuality that he had surveyed, 75% had contemplated **suicide**, and of that 25% had attempted it, due to the specific pressure under which they were forced to exist. The most common cause of suicide among homosexuals at the time was the fear of legal persecution and its consequences; in particular, the loss of employment.

Today, the difficulties encountered by gays and lesbians in the workplace appear in two distinct forms: individual **discrimination** on the one hand, and the relationship between professional activities (such as law) and gay or lesbian couples on the other. At the basis of individual discrimination is the hypothesis which

states that being active in the workforce contributes to the well-being of society; therefore, work has a positive connotation. From this, the potential for two discriminatory, homophobic positions clearly emerges: the refusal to recognize this contribution, and the denial of the right to contribute in the first place.

The refusal to recognize the contribution is the refusal to consider that gays and lesbians, or people associated with homosexuality, can contribute to the well-being of society. Thus, for example, philosophers of the Enlightenment such as Diderot or Voltaire generally contested the morality of the Ancien Régime and, notably, of the homosexuality they believed ran rampant among members of the church. To reinforce their political design, and their criticism of those in power, they associated the practice of sodomy in closed religious groups with the political **sterility** of these same groups. They explained that such groups did not serve the interest of society, but rather their own: a group whose alleged sexual practices caused it to close in upon itself was necessarily corrupt, because the rule of society was the exchange between groups. The philosophers condemned homosexual relations as a "caste" behavior which had nothing to do with them; it was a means to condemn political sterility by associating it with sexual sterility. The goal of these arguments was the political elimination of the targeted group and, at the same time, helped to perpetuate the stigmatization of homosexual practices.

For its part, the denial of the right to contribute consists of refusing to allow homosexuals to participate in the collective dynamic of the workplace. This attitude is notably illustrated in the 1993 film *Philadelphia*, in which the protagonist, whose homosexuality is revealed when he is afflicted with **AIDS**, is rejected by his employer and excluded from the virile fraternity of his coworkers.

In opposition to this old and strongly ingrained discriminatory logic, a dynamic of anti-discriminatory provisions has been asserted over the past few decades, especially in the wake of European companies working in collaboration with gay and lesbian **associations**. A recommendation by the 1981 Parliamentary Assembly of the European Council aimed to eliminate the discrimination faced by gays and lesbians, given that they should "enjoy the right to sexual self-determination." The assembly recommended, notably, that homosexuals benefit from equal treatment in the areas of employment, salary, and job security. As for the European

Union, in 1994 the European Parliament adopted a report that asked member states to end their respective discriminatory policies and practices founded on sexual orientation (known as the Roth Report). A few years later, Article 13 of the Amsterdam Treaty (an amendment of the 1992 treaty of the European Union), signed in 1997, and which took effect in 1999, stipulated that "Without prejudice to the other provisions of this Treaty and within the limits of the powers conferred by it upon the Community, the Council, acting unanimously on a proposal from the Commission and after consulting the European Parliament, may take appropriate action to combat discrimination occurred based on sex, racial or ethnic origin, religion or belief, disability, age or sexual orientation." The European Commission also produced provisions on discrimination on December 12, 1999, in advance to the development of a directive regarding employment which addressed discrimination based on sex, racial or ethnic origin, religion or belief, disability, age or sexual orientation. More recently, the European Union's Charter of Fundamental Rights, adopted on December 7, 2000, expressly stipulated that any and all discrimination based on sexual orientation (chapter 3, Article 21) was forbidden. These various texts had the positive effect of inscribing the question of sexual orientation and equal rights in the social and legal order, even if their application was in reality more difficult given their non-compulsory character and the hesitance of certain countries.

With regard to individual nations in Europe, a certain number of them had already instituted anti-discriminatory policies or legislation to protect gays and lesbians in the workplace. For example, in France, the penal code stipulates that it is illegal to discriminate based on "morals" in respect to employment. In Sweden, a national mediator exists who is charged with resolving conflicts between employers and employees. Nonetheless, anti-discrimination provisions, where they exist and are applied, often come up against the burden of proof and the insidious character of the offence, so much so that few gays and lesbians attempt to file a complaint.

Apart from individual cases of discrimination, it is significant that the right to work also appears to be a privileged area where social differences between homosexual and heterosexual couples are highlighted. It should be noted that in the European transportation sector, specifically rail and air, employees and their

unions lobbied employers, governments, and other authorities to modify their policies and definitions of spouses and couples with regard to same-sex benefits.

As for European authorities, there is a disparity between their progressive stance on dealing with individual cases of discrimination against gay and lesbian employees and their stagnant attitude toward same-sex rights in the workplace, such as benefits. On February 17, 1998, in a case involving a lesbian employee suing a British railway company for refusing to provide same-sex benefits, the European Court of Justice ruled against the employee, stating that different countries had different views on same-sex relationships and that it was up to individual governments to enforce rules. Beset once again, community jurisdictions and, more particularly, county courts adopted the same position in a January 28, 1999 judgment in a case where the plaintiff was in a registered partnership recognized by Swedish law. In both instances, the courts ruled that community law did not operate hand in hand between same-sex couples and cohabitation, in the first case, or marriage in the second. While judicial bodies of the European Union generally maintained an unfavorable stance on the issue, there were, however, some favorable ones which aimed to recognize the same-sex rights of employees of these same authorities. For example, the Roth Report of 1994 regarding the equal treatment of gays and lesbians had an immediate impact on the employees of the European Parliament.

In **France**, the legal definitions of spouse and couple, in general terms and in their relation to the country's labor law, have remained limited to the heteronormal standard. It was in 1989 that, for the first time, the French Court of Cassation (the court of last resort) made a pronouncement on the issue of gay cohabitation (i.e. common-law marriage) in two cases; in both, the court refused to recognize this arrangement and, by consequence, that it was subject to legal benefits. The first case involved an Air France flight attendant who had been refused a free ticket for his partner, even though the employee agreement stipulates that such tickets be granted to employees and "their legally married spouses or common-law partners." The second case involved a woman on social assistance and her partner, who had requested recognition under a 1978 law that "a person cohabitating, as though married, with the socially assisted individual" was entitled to legal benefits.

Legislation in some other European countries

regarding same-sex partnerships has also had broad effects on labor laws (e.g., the 1989 Danish law on "registered partnerships," the 1993 Norwegian law on "registered partnerships for homosexual couples," the 1994 Swedish law on "registered partnerships," the 1996 Icelandic law on "legalized common-law marriages," and the 1998 Dutch law on "registered partnerships"), while in other countries, legislation has had more limited effects, without consequence for the professional sector (e.g., the 1998 Belgian law on "legal cohabitation"). However, in 2003 Belgium became the second country to legalize same-sex marriage and laws against discrimination based on sexual orientation in areas like employment and housing came into effect.

At the same time, outside of Europe, the 90s was marked by a significant evolution in the rights of couples, specifically the partners of employees. In Israel in 1994, the supreme court ruled against El Al Airlines for refusing to give an employee's same-sex partner a free ticket that was offered to the spouses of married employees during religious holidays. Since 1995, the Knesset has extended the definition of "spouse" to same-sex partners regarding social insurance, as well as the military. In Canada in 1999, the government adopted a plan in which same-sex partners of public and military employees became entitled to a survivor's pension. In the same year, Quebec's National Assembly extended to the same rights as heterosexual common-law couples to gay couples in the areas of income tax, automobile insurance, social assistance, retirement and survivor's pension. On the other side of the continent, in San Francisco, the city issued domestic partner certificates to same-sex couples where at least one partner was a civic employee, though this certificate's value was only symbolic.

The evolution of private companies on the subject of gay and lesbian employees has revealed itself to be much more progressive than public ones, and many offer full benefits to the partners of their gay and lesbian employees. This is notably the case for Apple, Hewlett-Packard, Walt Disney, Time Warner, and IBM, among others.

—*Flora Leroy-Forgeot*

DeCrescenzo, Teresa, ed. *Gay and Lesbian Professionals in the Closet*. Binghamton, NY: Harrington Park Press, 1997.

Ellis, Alan, and Bob Powers. *A Manager's Guide to Sexual Orientation in the Workplace*. New York: Routledge, 1995.

Ellis, Alan, and Ellen Riggle. *Sexual Identity on the Job*. New York: Haworth Press, 1996.

Friskopp, Annette, and Sharon Silverstein. *Straight Jobs, Gay Lives: Gay and Lesbian Professionals*. Boston: Harvard Business School, 1996.

Leroy-Forgeot, Flora. *Histoire juridique de l'homosexualité en Europe*. Paris: Presses universitaires de France, 1997.

———, and Caroline Mécary. *Le Pacs*. Paris: Presses universitaires de France, "Que sais-je ?" 2000.

———. *Le Couple homosexuel et le droit*. Paris: Odile Jacob, 2001.

Lugas, Jay. *The Corporate Closet: The Professionals Lives of Gay Men in America*. New York: Free Press, 1993.

McNaught, Brian. *Gay Issues in the Workplace*. New York: St Martin's Press, 1994.

Mécary, Caroline. *Droit et homosexualité*. Paris: Dalloz, 2000.

Rasi, Richard, ed. *Out in the Workplace*. Boston: Alyson, 1995.

Simon, George, and Amy Zuckerman. *Sexual Orientation in the Workplace*. London: Sage, 1996.

SOS homophobie. *Rapports annuels* [Annual reports].

Spielman, Susan, and Liz Winfeld. *Straight Talk about Gays in the Workplace*. New York: Haworth Press, 2000.

—*Armed Forces; Associations; Discrimination; European Law; Marriage.*

PHOTO CREDITS

AIDS: Associated Press.

Caricature, Eulenburg Affair, Inversion, Police, Sterility: Patrick Cardon and GayKitschCamp.

Dance, Henri III: Bibliothèque nationale de France.

England: British Library.

Literature, Perversions, Politics, Sodom and Gomorrah, Transphobia: Louis Godbout and the Archives gaies du Québec.

Middle East: Agence France-Presse.

Publicity: Commercial Closet Association.

ACKNOWLEDGMENTS

Many people have contributed to the iconography of this work: I wish to thank Biffi, Gérard Koskovitch, Samira Ouardi, Laurent Avezou, and I would like to especially thank Patrick Cardon and Louis Godbout who, in great friendship, placed at our disposal the wealth of their precious documents.

—*Louis-Georges Tin*